FROMMER'S

COMPREHENSIVE TRAVEL GUIDE

SCANDINAVIA
'93-'94

by Darwin Porter
Assisted by Danforth Prince

PRENTICE HALL TRAVEL

NEW YORK • LONDON • TORONTO • SYDNEY • TOKYO • SINGAPORE

FROMMER BOOKS

Published by Prentice Hall General Reference
A division of Simon & Schuster Inc.
15 Columbus Circle
New York, NY 10023

ISBN: 0-671-84700-7
ISSN: 0278-1069

Design by Robert Bull Design
Maps by Geografix Inc.

Frommer's Editorial Staff

Editorial Director: Marilyn Wood
Editorial Manager/Senior Editor: Alice Fellows
Senior Editor: Lisa Renaud
Editors: Charlotte Allstrom, Thomas F. Hirsch, Peter Katucki, Sara Hinsey Raveret, Theodore Stavrou
Assistant Editors: Margaret Bowen, Lee Gray, Christopher Hollander, Ian Wilker
Editorial Assistants: Gretchen Henderson, Bethany Jewett
Managing Editor: Leanne Coupe

Special Sales

Bulk purchases of Frommer's Travel Guides are available at special discounts. The publishers are happy to custom-make publications for corporate clients who wish to use them as premiums or sales promotions. We can excerpt the contents, provide covers with corporate imprints, or create books to meet specific needs. For more information write to Special Sales, Prentice Hall Travel, Paramount Communications Building, 15 Columbus Circle, New York, NY 10023.

Manufactured in the United States of America

CONTENTS

PART TWO—NORWAY

PART THREE—SWEDEN

LIST OF MAPS

INVITATION TO THE READERS

In researching this book, I have come across many remarkable establishments, the best of which I have included here. I am sure that many of you will also come across appealing hotels, inns, restaurants, guesthouses, shops, and attractions. Please don't keep them to yourself. Share your experiences, especially if you want to comment on places that have been included in this edition that have changed for the worse. You can address your letters to:

Darwin Porter
Frommer's Scandinavia '93–'94
c/o Prentice Hall Travel
15 Columbus Circle
New York, NY 10023

A DISCLAIMER

Readers are advised that prices fluctuate in the course of time and travel information changes under the impact of the varied and volatile factors that affect the travel industry. Neither the author nor the publisher can be held responsible for the experiences of readers while traveling. Readers are invited to write to the publisher with ideas, comments, and suggestions for future editions.

SAFETY ADVISORY

Whenever you're traveling in an unfamiliar city or country, stay alert. Be aware of your immediate surroundings. Wear a moneybelt and keep a close eye on your possessions. Be particularly careful with cameras, purses, and wallets, all favorite targets of thieves and pickpockets.

CHAPTER 1

PLANNING A TRIP TO SCANDINAVIA

Although Scandinavia, as defined by this book, covers four distinct countries—Denmark, Norway, Sweden, and Finland—there are certain common cultural denominators and practical travel facts that apply to traveling in the region. That is what this chapter is about.

1. INFORMATION, DOCUMENTS & MONEY

SOURCES OF INFORMATION

Contact the following **tourist boards** at least 3 months in advance for maps, sightseeing information, ferry schedules, etc. In the **United States,** the Danish, Norwegian, and Swedish Tourist Boards can be reached at the following addresses: 655 Third Ave., New York, NY 10017 (tel. 212/949-2333); 8929 Wilshire Blvd., Beverly Hills, CA 90211 (tel. 213/854-1549); 150 N. Michigan Ave., Suite 2110, Chicago, IL 60601 (tel. 312/726-1120). The Finnish Tourist Board can be reached also at 655 Third Ave., New York, NY 10017 (tel. 212/949-2333) and at 1900 Ave. of Stars, Los Angeles, CA 90067 (tel. 818/277-5226).

In **Canada** contact the Danish Tourist Board at P.O. Box 115, Station N, Toronto, ON M8V 3S4 (tel. 416/823-9620). For the other three countries call or write the U.S. offices.

In **London** contact the Danish Tourist Board, Sceptre House, 169-173 Regent St., London W1R 8PY (tel. 071/734-2637); the Norwegian Tourist Board, Charles House, 5-11 Lower Regent St., London SW1Y 4LR (tel. 071/839-6255); Swedish Tourist Board, 29-31 Oxford St., London W1R 1RE (tel. 071/437-5816) and Finnish Tourist Board, 66-68 Haymarket, London SW1Y 4RS (tel. 071/839-4048).

For general information always check newspapers and magazines. To find the latest articles published about Scandinavia go to your library and ask for the *Reader's Guide to Periodical Literature,* and look up the city or country of interest.

You may also contact the State Department for background information. Write to the Superintendent of Documents, U.S. Government Printing Office, Washington, DC 20402 (tel. 202/783-3238).

You can also contact a **travel agent,** but make sure that the agent is a member of the American Society of Travel Agents (ASTA), so that you can complain to the Consumer Affairs Department of the Society at P.O. Box 23922, Washington, DC 20006 if you receive poor service.

DOCUMENTS

A valid **passport** is all an American, British, Canadian, Australian, or New Zealand citizen needs to enter Denmark, Norway, Sweden, or Finland. You only need to apply for a visa if you wish to stay more than 3 months.

Your current domestic **driver's license** is acceptable in Denmark, Norway, Sweden, and Finland—an international drivers' license is not required.

MONEY

Before leaving home it is advisable to secure traveler's checks and a small amount of foreign currency to cover costs on arrival overseas. Also take along about $200 in cash.

TRAVELER'S CHECKS Traveler's checks are the safest way to carry cash while traveling. Most banks will give you a better rate on traveler's checks than for cash. Checks denominated in U.S. dollars are accepted virtually anywhere, but in some cases (perhaps for ease of conversion into local currencies), you might want checks denominated in other currencies. It's best to purchase dollar checks in denominations of $20, $50, and $100.

Each of the agencies listed below will refund checks if lost or stolen, provided you produce documentation. When purchasing checks, ask about refund hotlines. American Express probably has the most offices around the world.

American Express (tel. toll free 800/221-7282 in the U.S. and Canada) charges a 1% commission. Checks are free to members of the American Automobile Association. The company issues checks denominated in U.S. dollars, Canadian dollars, British pounds sterling, Swiss francs, French francs, German marks, Saudi riyals, and Japanese yen, although the vast majority of checks sold in North America are denominated in U.S. dollars.

Citicorp (tel. toll free 800/645-6556 in the U.S., or 813/623-1709, collect, in Canada) issues checks in U.S. dollars, British pounds, German marks, and Japanese yen.

MasterCard International/Thomas Cook International (tel. toll free 800/223-9920 in the U.S. or collect at 609/987-7300 at the headquarters in Princeton, N.J., from other parts of the world) issues checks denominated in U.S. dollars, French francs, German marks, Dutch guilders, Spanish pesetas, Australian dollars, Japanese yen, Swiss francs, and Hong Kong dollars.

Barclays Bank/Bank of America (tel. toll free 800/221-2426 in the U.S. and Canada). Through Barclay's subsidiary, Interpayment Services, VISA traveler's checks are sold, which are denominated in U.S. dollars, British pounds, Swiss francs, French francs, German marks, and Japanese yen.

Foreign banks may ask up to 5% to convert your checks into Scandinavian currencies. Remember, also, that you get a better rate if you cash traveler's checks at the bank issuing them: VISA at Barclays, American Express at American Express, and so forth.

CREDIT CARDS These are useful throughout Scandinavia. American Express, Diners Club, and VISA are widely recognized. If you see a Eurocard or Access sign, it means that the establishment accepts MasterCard. With an American Express or VISA card you can also withdraw currency from cash machines at various locations. Always check with your credit-card company about this before leaving home.

2. PACKING TIPS

Pack as light as possible, taking only what you can carry (porters and carts are sometimes hard to find at transit terminals). Also airlines have recently become much stricter about luggage allowances. Checked luggage should not be more than 62 inches (width, plus length, plus height) and should not weigh more than 70 pounds. Carry-on luggage shouldn't be more than 45 inches and must fit under your seat or in the bins above.

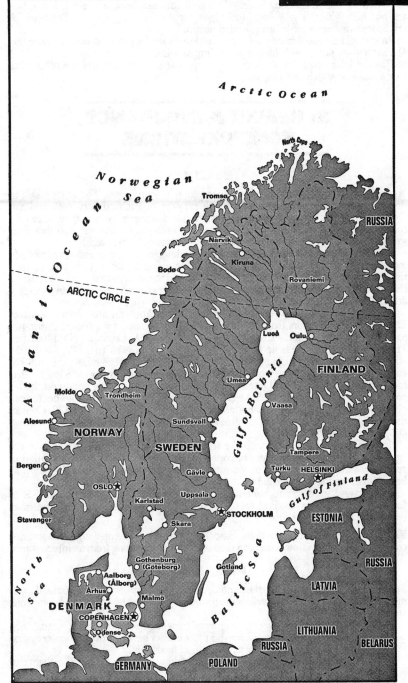

SCANDINAVIA

Arctic Ocean

Norwegian Sea

North Cape

Atlantic Ocean

Tromso

RUSSIA

Narvik

Kiruna

Bode

Rovaniemi

ARCTIC CIRCLE

Lueå

Oulu

Umea

FINLAND

Molde

Trondheim

Vaasa

Alesund

NORWAY

Sundsvall

Gulf of Bothnia

SWEDEN

Tampere

Bergen

Gävle

Turku

HELSINKI

OSLO ★

Uppsala

Gulf of Finland

Karlstad

★ STOCKHOLM

Stavanger

Skara

ESTONIA

North Sea

Gothenburg (Göteborg)

Gotland

RUSSIA

Aalborg (Ålborg)

LATVIA

Arhus

Malmö

Baltic Sea

DENMARK

LITHUANIA

COPENHAGEN ★

Odense

RUSSIA

BELARUS

GERMANY

POLAND

Wherever you're traveling in Scandinavia in summer, bring a sweater. Most days are not hot, which is why few hotels have air conditioning, even in Denmark. A raincoat with a removable lining is also useful.

In spring, fall, and winter bring a coat and in winter an extra sweater for those few places that are not as well heated as you might wish.

Take at least two pairs of shoes—if one gets soaked you can use the other. One pair should be sturdy walking shoes.

3. HEALTH & INSURANCE CONSIDERATIONS

HEALTH

You will encounter few health problems traveling in Scandinavia. The water is safe to drink, the milk is pasteurized, and health services of each country are excellent. Occasionally the change in diet may cause minor diarrhea so you may want to take some antidiarrhea medicine along. In summer, arrive at buffets early so that your smørrebrød open-face sandwiches made with mayonnaise are fresh.

Carry all your vital medicine in your carry-on luggage and bring enough prescribed medicines to sustain you during your stay. Bring along copies of your prescriptions that are written in the generic form. In Norway and Sweden, note that pharmacists by law cannot honor a prescription written outside the country; you will have to see a doctor and have one written if you need more or lose your medicines.

If you need a doctor, your hotel will find one. You can also obtain a list of English-speaking doctors from the International Association for Medical Assistance to Travelers (IAMAT) in the United States at 417 Center St., Lewiston, NY 14092 (tel. 716/754-4883); in Canada at 40 Regal Rd., Guelph, ON N1K (tel. 519/836-0102).

If you suffer from chronic illness, talk to your doctor before taking the trip. For conditions such as heart trouble, epilepsy, or diabetes, wear a Medic Alert Identification Tag, which will immediately alert any doctor to your condition. It also provides the number of Medic's Alert's 24-hour hotline so that a foreign doctor can obtain medical records for you. For a lifetime membership, the cost is $30. Contact the Medic Alert Foundation, P.O. Box 1009, Turlock, CA 95381-1009 (tel. toll free 800/432-5378).

In Denmark foreign visitors can be treated free in cases of sudden illness or the aggravation of a chronic disease, provided they did not come with the intention of getting treatment and provided they cannot be moved and return home. The transport home is the visitors' responsibility.

In Norway, Sweden, and Finland the national health plans do not cover U.S. or Canadian visitors. Any medical fees incurred must be paid in cash. (Fees are more reasonable than in most other western nations.)

VACCINATIONS There are no inoculations needed to enter any Scandinavian country, except for yellow fever, and then only if you're coming from an infected area.

INSURANCE

Before purchasing any additional insurance check your homeowner's, automobile, and medical insurance policies as well as the insurance provided by credit-card companies and auto and travel clubs.

Remember, Medicare covers U.S. citizens traveling in Mexico and Canada only.

Also note that to submit any claim you must always have thorough documentation including all receipts, police reports, medical records, etc.

If you are prepaying for your vacation or are taking a charter or any other flight that has severe cancellation penalties look into cancellation insurance.

The following companies provide further information:

Travel Guard International, 1145 Clark St., Stevens Point, WI 54481 (tel.

715/345-0505, or toll free 800/826-1300), which offers a comprehensive 7-day policy, including emergency assistance, accidental death, trip cancellation and interruption, medical coverage abroad, and lost luggage. It costs $52.

Travel Insurance Pak, Travelers Insurance Co., 1 Tower Sq. 10 NB, Hartford, CT 06183-5040 (tel. 203/277-2318, or toll free 800/243-3174), offers illness and accident coverage, costing from $10 for 6 to 10 days. For lost or damaged luggage, $500 worth of coverage costs $20 for 6 to 10 days. You can also get trip-cancellation insurance for $5.50.

Mutual of Omaha (Tele-Trip Company, Inc.), 3201 Farnam St., Omaha, NE 68131 (tel. toll free 800/228-9792), charges $13 and up for travel insurance packages that feature travel assistance services, trip cancellations, trip interruption, flight and baggage delays, accident, medical, sickness, accidental death and dismemberment, and medical evacuation coverages. Application for insurance can be taken over the phone for major credit-card holders.

HealthCare Abroad (MEDEX), Wallach & Co., 107 W. Federal St., P.O. Box 480, Middleburg, VA 22117-0480 (tel. 703/687-3166, or toll free 800/237-6615), offers a policy, good for 10 to 120 days, costing $3 a day, including accident and sickness coverage to the tune of $100,000. Medical evacuation is also included, along with a $25,000 accidental death and dismemberment compensation. Trip cancellation and lost or stolen luggage can also be written into this policy at a nominal cost.

WorldCare Travel Assistance Association, 1150 S. Olive St., Suite T2233, Los Angeles, CA 90015 (tel. 213/745-5550, or toll free 800/253-1877), features a 9- to 15-day policy, costing $105, including trip cancellation, lost or stolen luggage, legal assistance, and medical coverage and evacuation.

Access America, 6600 W. Broad St., Richmond, VA 23230 (tel. 804/285-3300, or toll free 800/424-3391), has a 24-hour hotline in case of an emergency and offers medical coverage for 9 to 15 days costing $49 for $10,000 of coverage. If you want medical plus trip cancellation, the charge is $89 for 9 to 15 days. A comprehensive package for $111 grants 9- to 15-day blanket coverage, including $50,000 worth of death benefits.

4. TIPS FOR THE DISABLED, SENIORS, SINGLES, STUDENTS & FAMILIES

FOR THE DISABLED

In the United States disabled travelers should start by contacting **Travel Information Service,** Moss Rehabilitation Hospital, 1200 W. Tabor Rd., Philadelphia, PA 19141-3099 (tel. 215/456-9603). It charges a nominal fee per package, which contains names and addresses of accessible hotels, restaurants, and attractions, often based on firsthand reports of travelers.

You can also obtain a free copy of **"Air Transportation of Handicapped Persons,"** published by the U.S. Department of Transportation. Write for Free Advisory Circular No. AC12032, Distribution Unit, U.S. Department of Transportation, Publications Division, M-4332, Washington, DC 20590.

You may also want to consider joining a tour for disabled visitors. Names and addresses of such tour operators can be obtained by writing to the **Society for the Advancement of Travel for the Handicapped,** 347 Fifth Ave., New York, NY 10016 (tel. 212/447-7284). Annual membership dues are $45, or $25 for senior citizens and students. Send a stamped, self-addressed envelope.

The **Federation of the Handicapped,** 211 W. 14th St., New York, NY 10011 (tel. 212/747-4268), also operates summer tours for members, who pay a yearly rate of $4.

For the blind, the best information source is the **American Foundation for the Blind,** 15 W. 16th St., New York, NY 10011 (tel. 212/620-2000, or toll free 800/232-5463).

Many Scandinavian countries, such as Denmark and Sweden, have been in the vanguard of providing services for the disabled. In general, trains, airlines, and ferries and department stores and malls are accessible. For information about wheelchair access, ferry and air travel, parking, and other information your best bet is to contact the tourist boards listed above.

In **Denmark** also write to DHF Dansk Handicap Forbund (Danish Handicapped Association), Kollektivhuset, Hans Knudsens Plads 1A, DK-2100 København O (tel. 31-29-35-55).

In **Norway** for further information write to the Norwegian Association of the Disabled, Box 9217, Vaterland, N-0134 Oslo 1 (tel. 22-17-02-55).

In **Sweden** about 2 million people have some disability and the country is very conscious of their needs. Contact the Swedish Tourist Board for their publication.

In **Finland** information about facilities can be obtained from Rullaten ry, Vartickylantie 9, SF-00950 Helsinki (tel. 90/322-069) which assists the disabled in travel planning. Further information is also available from Invalidilitto ry (Association of the Disabled), Kumpulantie 1A, SF-00520 Helsinki (tel. 90/718-466). Area Travel Agency, Kaisaniemenkatu 13A, SF-00100 Helsinki (tel. 90/018-551) specializes in travel for the disabled.

FOR SENIORS

There are a number of organizations that seniors can contact before setting out.

For your initial source of information, write for **"Travel Tips for Senior Citizens"** (publication no. 8970), distributed for $1 by the Superintendent of Documents, U.S. Government Printing Office, Washington, DC 20402 (tel. 202/783-5238). A booklet that is free is called **"101 Tips for the Mature Traveler."** Write or phone Grand Circle Travel, 347 Congress St., Suite 3A, Boston, MA 02210 (tel. 617/350-7500, or toll free 800/221-2610).

A dynamic travel organization for seniors is **Elderhostel,** 75 Federal St., Boston, MA 02110-1941 (tel. 617/426-7788). Established in 1975, it operates a number of good-value programs throughout Europe. Most courses last around 3 weeks, and include airfare, accommodations in student dormitories or modern inns, all meals, and tuition. They're not luxury vacations, but they are fun and fulfilling.

SAGA International Holidays is also well known for its all-inclusive tours for seniors. They prefer that you be at least 60 years old. Insurance is included in the net price of all their tours, which encompass dozens of locations in Europe and usually last for an average of 17 nights. Contact SAGA International Holidays, 120 Boylston St., Boston, MA 02116 (tel. 617/451-6808, or toll free 800/343-0273).

In the United States, the best organization to belong to is the **American Association of Retired Persons,** 601 E St. NW, Washington, DC 20049 (tel. 202/434-2277). Members are offered discounts on car rentals, hotels, and airfares. The association's group travel is provided by the AARP Travel Experience from American Express. Tours may be purchased through any American Express office or travel agent or by calling toll free 800/927-0111. Cruises may be purchased only by telephone (tel. toll free 800/745-4567). Flights to the various destinations are handled by either of these toll-free numbers as part of land arrangements or cruise bookings.

Information is also available from the **National Council of Senior Citizens,** 1331 F St. NW, Washington, DC 20004 (tel. 202/347-8800), which charges $12 per person or per couple, for which you receive a monthly newsletter, part of which is devoted to travel tips. Reduced discounts on hotel and auto rentals are available.

In **Denmark,** Seniors are granted discounts on rail travel and the ferries to Sweden and often for certain attractions and performances, including those at the Royal Theater. You may have to be a member of an organization to receive certain discounts.

In **Norway** seniors over 67 are entitled to 50% off the price of first- or second-class train fares. Ask for the discount at the ticket office.

In **Sweden** on Swedish State Railways visitors over 65 are granted 30% off first- and second-class train travel except on Friday and Sunday. In Stockholm discounts on transportation and concert, theater, and opera tickets are available.

In **Finland,** on Finnair flights, passengers aged 65 or over are entitled to a 50% reduction. Any generally accepted document of identification will suffice for this purpose. The passenger's date of birth has to be inserted in the "Fare Basis" column. The domestic route system is divided into blue, black, and red flights; the blue flights are those in the most demand, but reductions for seniors are not granted on the blue flights.

On Finnish national rails, visitors over 65 may buy a special card for 50 markkaa ($11) at any railway station in Finland, which entitles the holder a 50% reduction on rail travel.

FOR SINGLE TRAVELERS

Several organizations help singles save money by finding travel companions. **Jens Jurgen, Travel Companion** has made heroic efforts to match single travelers with like-minded companions. It's now the largest and best-listed company in the United States. Jens Jurgen, the German-born founder, charges $36 to $66 for a 6-month listing in his well-publicized records. New applicants interested in a travel companion fill out a form stating their preferences and needs. They then receive a minilisting of the kinds of potential partners who might be suitable for travel. Companions of the same or opposite sex can be requested. Listings are extensive. For an application and more information, write to Jens Jurgen, Travel Companion, P.O. Box P-833, Amityville, NY 11701. (tel. 516/454-0880; fax 516/454-0170).

Singleworld, 401 Theodore Fremd Ave., Rye, NY 10580 (tel. 914/967-3334, or toll free 800/223-6490), is a travel agency that operates tours geared to solo travel. Two basic types of tours are available: either a youth-oriented tour for people under 35 or jaunts for any age. Annual dues are $25.

Another agency to check is **Grand Circle Travel,** 347 Congress St., Boston, MA 02210 (tel. 617/350-7500, or toll free 800/221-2610), which offers escorted tours and cruises for retired people, including singles.

FOR STUDENTS

Bonafide students can avail themselves of a number of discounts in travel. The most wide-ranging travel service for students is **CIEE (Council on International Educational Exchange),** 205 E. 42nd St., New York, NY 10017 (tel. 212/661-1414). This outfit provides details about budget travel, studying abroad, working permits, insurance, but, most important, an International Student Identity Card (ISIC). It also sells a number of helpful publications, offers the free *Student Travel Catalogue,* and issues to bona fide students for $14 an International Student Identity Card. Call toll free 800/GET-ANID to find out where the closest office is to you.

To keep costs low, membership in the **IYHF (International Youth Hostel Federation)** is recommended. Many countries have branch offices, including **AYH (American Youth Hostels),** P.O. Box 37613, Washington, DC 20013-7613 (tel. 202/783-6161). Membership costs $25 annually unless you're under 18 (then only $15).

In **Norway** an ISIC gets you a 35% discount on domestic rail travel. Univers Reisen, Problemveien 2, Oslo (tel. 22-45-32-00), sells discounted air and rail tickets to people under 26. It's open Monday through Friday from 9am to 3:30pm (Metro: Blindern).

Students headed for **Finland** can take advantage of low-cost flights to and from Finland arranged by Travela Ltd., Mannerheimintie 5, SF-00100 Helsinki (tel. 90/624-101). Youth/student discounts are also granted on Finnish domestic routes.

FOR FAMILIES

Advance planning is the key to a successful overseas family vacation. If you have very small children you should discuss your vacation plans with your family doctor and take along such standard supplies as children's aspirin, a thermometer, Band-Aids, and the like.

On airlines, a special menu for children must be requested at least 24 hours in advance, but if baby food is required, bring your own and ask a flight attendant to warm it to the right temperature. Take along a "security blanket" for your child—a pacifier, a favorite toy or book, or, for older children, something to make them feel at home in different surroundings—a baseball cap, a favorite T-shirt, or some good-luck charm.

Make advance arrangements for cribs, bottle warmers, and car seats if you're driving anywhere.

Ask the hotel if it stocks baby food, and, if not, take some with you and plan to buy the rest in local supermarkets.

Draw up guidelines on bedtime, eating, keeping tidy, being in the sun, even shopping and spending—they'll make the vacation more enjoyable.

Family Travel Times is a newsletter about traveling with children. For $35 you get 10 issues. Subscribers can also call in with travel questions, but only from 10am to 1pm eastern standard time, Wednesday only. Contact TWYCH, which stands for Travel With Your Children, 80 Eighth Ave., New York, NY 10011 (tel. 212/206-0688).

On Finnair flights, the head of the family pays the full applicable one-way or round-trip adult fare, the spouse pays 75% of the fare, and children 12 to 23 pay 50%. Children 2 to 11 pay 25% of the fare. One infant child under 2 may be carried free.

On the Finnish national rail system, a maximum of two children under 6 travel free with one adult. A 50% reduction is granted for children ages 6 to 16.

Babysitters can be found at most hotels, but you should always insist, if possible, that the sitter speak English to avoid traumatic experiences for young children. Nearly all Scandinavian young people speak English, but many of the foreign workers in hotels don't.

5. ALTERNATIVE/ADVENTURE TRAVEL

HOMESTAYS, HOSPITALITY & HOME EXCHANGES

HOMESTAYS Servas, 11 John St., New York, NY 10038 (tel. 212/267-0252), is a nonprofit, nongovernmental, international, interfaith network of travelers and hosts whose goal is to help build world peace, goodwill, and understanding. They do this by providing opportunities for deeper, more personal contacts among people of diverse cultural and political backgrounds. Servas travelers are invited to share living space in a privately owned home with a community feeling, normally staying without charge for visits lasting a maximum of 2 days. Visitors pay a $55 annual fee, fill out an application, and are interviewed for suitability by one of more than 200 Servas interviewers throughout the country. They then receive a Servas directory listing the names and addresses of Servas hosts who will allow (and encourage) visitors in their homes.

PEOPLE TO PEOPLE Operating since 1971, **Friends Overseas** places American visitors to Scandinavia in touch with Scandinavians interested in meeting those with similar interests and backgrounds. Names and addresses are given to each applicant, and letters must be written before visitors depart; Scandinavians may not meet visitors unless they have ample time to plan. For more information, write to Friends Overseas, 68-04 Dartmouth St., Forest Hills, NY 11375. Send a self-addressed, stamped business-size envelope, including your age, occupation or occupational goals, approximate dates of your visit, and who you will be traveling with. Those writing from overseas must include the equivalent of $1.50 (U.S.) in return postage.

For $5, **International Visitors Information Service,** 733 15th St. NW, Suite

300, Washington, DC 20005 (tel. 202/783-6540), will mail anyone a booklet listing opportunities for contact with local residents in foreign countries. For example, if you want to find lodgings with a Swedish family whose members earn their living from the sea, this booklet will tell you how. Checks should be made out to Meridian/IVIS.

HOME EXCHANGES For home exchange that can be fun and save money, contact the following:

International Home Exchange Service, P.O. Box 190070, San Francisco, CA 94119 (tel. 415/435-3497), charges $35 for three directories annually. The fee includes a listing in one of them. Seniors get 20% off.

Vacation Exchange Club, P.O. Box 820, Haleiwa, HI 96712 (tel. 808/638-8747, or toll free 800/638-3841), although it has fewer listings, offers the same service. For $50, you get four directories a year and you're listed in one.

The Invented City, 41 Sutter St., Suite 1090, San Francisco, CA 94104 (tel. 415/673-0347), is another international home-exchange agency. Home-exchange listings are published three times a year: February, May, and November. A membership fee of $50 allows you to list your home, and you can also give your preferred time to travel, your occupation, and your hobbies.

EDUCATIONAL/STUDY TRIPS

WORKCAMPS Those between the ages of 18 and 30 can participate in a workcamp in Europe, joining a brigade of international volunteers. People pay their airfare to a country, but once there are given free room and board in exchange for socially significant work. Work time is limited to 5 days or 40 hours a week. Programs take place from June to September.

For information, contact the **Council on International Educational Exchange (CIEE),** 205 E. 42nd St., New York, NY 10017 (tel. 212/661-1414), which offers workcamp programs. A booklet about workcamps is distributed free, although there is a $125 placement fee.

IN DENMARK

The **International People's College** (Den Internationale Hojskole), Montebello Allé 1, DK-300, Helsingør (tel. 49-21-33-61), established in 1921 on a 13-acre campus 1 mile south of Helsingør Castle, fosters an environment of global learning. All courses are in English, and cover Danish culture and history, global politics, and world events. Sample courses might include intercultural studies, music, journalism, and weaving. The average student is 23, but many are in their 50s and 60s. Summer courses last between 2 and 3 weeks. The rest of the year 8-week courses and 16-week courses are available. The cost for summer courses is 2,000 kroner ($346) per week, including tuition, room and board, based on double occupancy, with a 200 kroner ($34.60) supplement for single occupancy. The total cost for 8 weeks and 16 weeks is 1,250 kroner ($216.30) per week based on double occupancy, with a 100 kroner ($17.30) supplement for single occupancy.

The **Danish Cultural Institute** (Det Danske Kultur ainstitute), Kultorvet 2, DK-1175 København K, Denmark (tel. 33-13-54-48), offers summer seminars in English, including Meeting Denmark, Care of the Elderly in Denmark, and Education for Adults. Credit programs are available, but many courses are geared toward professional groups from abroad. An especially interesting course for those with some knowledge of Danish is Danmark, Danskerne, Dansk, which includes language instruction.

Among Danish agents specializing in special-interest travel and professional study tours are: **Benns Rejser,** Nørregade 51, DK-7500 Holstebro (tel. 97-42-68-00).

IN NORWAY

TRACING YOUR NORWEGIAN ROOTS If you are of Norwegian ancestry, information on how to trace your family can be obtained from the Norwegian consulate nearest you. In Norway, contact the **Norwegian Emigration Center,** Bergjelandsgata 30, N-4012 Stavanger (tel. 51-50-12-67), for a catalog of information about Norwegian families who relocated in the United States.

In the United States, the **Family History Library of the Church of Jesus Christ of Latter Day Saints,** 35 N. West Temple, Salt Lake City, UT 84150 (tel. 801/240-2331), has extensive records of Norwegian families who emigrated to the United States and Canada. The library is open to the public without charge for genealogical research.

ADVENTURE/WILDERNESS TRIPS
IN NORWAY

BIRDWATCHING   Europe's largest bird sanctuaries are located in the Lofoten Islands of northern Norway. All kinds of seabirds can be found, including puffins, cormorants, razor-billed aulks, guillemots, gulls, and eider ducks. The outer islands of Vaerøy and Røst are famous for their giant bird colonies. Other bird sanctuaries are found at Runde Island, 2½ hours from Ålesund, and Fokstumyra, a national park near Dombås.

For more information, contact the following: **Lofoten Tourist Board,** Box 210, N-8301 Svolvaer (tel. 76-07-10-53); or **Christineborg Touristcenter,** N-6096 Runde (tel. 70-08-59-50).

In the United States, information and bookings of such trips are possible by contacting **Borton Overseas** (tel. toll free 800/843-0602); in Canada, **Quest Nature Tours** (tel. toll free 800/387-1483).

WHALE WATCHING   In Norway, you can get a glimpse of the 65-foot-long, 88,000-pound heavy sperm whales, the largest toothed whales in the world. You may also come across killer whales, harbor porpoises, mink whales, and white-beaked dolphins. Six-hour whale-watching tours are conducted in the Arctic Ocean where a guiding whale researcher will tell you about the life of the whales.

Information and bookings for whale watching can be made through **Passage Tours of Scandinavia,** 3100 Windamar St., Fort Lauderdale, FL 33304 (tel. toll free 800/548-5960). Whale watching in the Lofoten Islands is arranged by **Borton Overseas,** 5516 Lyndale Ave. South, Minneapolis, MN 55419 (tel. toll free 800/843-0602).

IN SWEDEN

The Swedish Tourist Board (see "Sources of Information," above) can provide information about wilderness trips and other activities. Or contact **Sweden Tours West,** Box 244, S-651 06, Karlstad, Sweden (tel. 054/10-21-70).

ADVENTURE TRIPS   Sarek, in the far north of Sweden, is Europe's last real wilderness, and here the Swede goes to wander in the mountains, pick mushrooms, gather berries, and fish. Along the mountain chain marking the Swedish-Norwegian border, Swedes have set up some 20 white-water-rafting stations on the Åre River, famous for its Tann Rapids.

Hiking is the most popular pastime. **Svenska Turistföreningen,** Drottninggatan 31-33, Box 25, S-101 20 Stockholm (tel. 08/790-31-00), operates mountain huts with anywhere from 10 to 30 beds, providing temporary accommodations in the area. The outfit knows the north of Sweden very well, and will advise about marked tracks, rowboats, the best excursions, the problems you are likely to encounter, communications, and transportation. They also sell trail and mountain maps.

HORSEBACK RIDING THROUGH THE WILDERNESS   There are numerous opportunities for overnight pack trips on horses in such regions as the forests of Värmland or Norrbotten, where reindeer, musk oxen, and other creatures roam. The most popular of the overnight horseback trips starts just north of the city of Karlstad in Värmland. Covered-wagon trips with overnight stopovers are also offered. A typical trip by horse begins in the lakeside village of Torsby and follows a forested trail that ascends a mountain. An average of 4 hours a day is spent on the horse, with meals cooked over an open fire.

In northern Sweden, the two popular starting points are Funäsdalen, close to the Norwegian border, and Ammarnäs, not far from the Arctic Circle and the Midnight Sun. These trips begin in June. Local tourist offices will provide information.

IN FINLAND

OFFBEAT TOURS A Gold Holiday in Tankavaara, beginning in the eastern Lapland village of Sodankylä, is offered every summer, costing 750 markkaa ($165) for two persons. The package includes 3 nights' accommodation in the holiday village of Tankavaara Gold Village, breakfast, a 2-day gold panning permit, a visit to the Gold Museum there and the Urho Kekkonen National Park. Further information is available from Lapland Travel, Maakuntakatu 10, SF-96100 Rovaniemi (tel. 960/346-052).

A White Nights Ride is a 6-day package including accommodation in holiday cabins, full board, insurance, and daily hikes through the Lappish forest and fell wilderness with campfire meals, culminating with a Midsummer Sun Ride on Midsummer Eve. The trip is offered only in the Midsummer week in June, costing 1,920 markkaa ($422.40) per person. Information is available from Lapland Travel, Maakuntakatu 10, SF-96100 Rovaniemi (tel. 960/346-052).

A canoeist can choose from many different kinds of water landscape in Finland; the coastal waters are dotted with thousands of islands, rivers flowing down to the sea, and rivers in the wilds of eastern and northern Finland. Probably the best canoeing waters are in the lake regions, especially among the lakes of the Great Saimaa. Shooting the rapids is a sport enjoyed in a number of rivers. Further information about this form of rugged tourism is available from the **Finnish Canoe Association,** Radiokatu 20, SF-00240 Helsinki (tel. 90/158-2363).

6. GETTING THERE

BY PLANE FROM THE U.S.

Before moving on to the specifics of each country, to secure the best-priced ticket you should know about fare structures, seasons, and other general rules of air travel.

First, always shop around by calling all the airlines that fly to your destination.

The cheapest fares prevail in the off-season and midweek. Scandinavia's off-season is winter (from about November 1 to March 21). Summer (about June through September) is peak season and the most expensive, while shoulder season (spring and fall) is in-between. In any season, midweek fares (Monday through Thursday) are the lowest.

REGULAR & APEX FARES

Regular fares include, in order of increasing expense, economy, business class, and first class. These tickets cost, but they carry no restrictions. In economy you pay for drinks and the seats are not spacious; in business the drinks are free, and the seats are wider; in first-class amenities and services are the best.

Currently the most popular discount fare is the **APEX** (advance-purchase excursion) which usually carries restrictions—advance-purchase requirements, minimum and/or maximum stays abroad—and cancellation or change of date penalties.

In addition, airlines often introduce special promotional discounted fares. Always check the travel sections of your local newspapers for advertisements about these.

BUCKET SHOPS, CHARTERS & OTHER OPTIONS

BUCKET SHOPS More politely referred to as consolidators these purchase large blocks of unsold seats from the airlines and sell them to the public at often dramatic discounts (from 20% to 35% off regular fares). Terms of payment may vary from the last minute to 45 days in advance. Check your local newspaper's travel section for their ads. Here are some recommendations to get you started:

Access International, 101 W. 31st St., Suite 1104, New York, NY 10001 (tel. 212/333-7280, or toll free 800/825-3633), may be the country's biggest consolidator. It specializes in discounted tickets to European capitals on regularly scheduled U.S. airlines.

Out west, you can try **Sunline Express Holidays, Inc.,** 607 Market St., San Francisco, CA 94105 (tel. 415/541-7800, or toll free 800/SUNLINE), or **Euro-Asia, Inc.,** 4203 E. Indian School Rd., Suite 210, Phoenix, AZ 85018 (tel. 602/955-2742, or toll free 800/525-3876).

Travel Avenue, 180 N. Des Plaines, Chicago, IL 60661 (tel. 312/876-1116, or toll free 800/333-3335), is a national agency whose headquarters are in Chicago. Its tickets are often cheaper than most shops, and it charges the customer only a $25 fee on international tickets, rather than taking the usual 10% commission from an airline. Travel Avenue rebates most of that back to the customer—hence, the lower fares.

CHARTER FLIGHTS Strictly speaking, a charter is a one-time-only flight between two predetermined points, for which the aircraft is reserved months in advance. Before paying for a charter, check the restrictions on your ticket or contract. You may be asked to purchase a tour package and pay far in advance, and you'll pay a stiff penalty (or forfeit the ticket entirely) if you cancel. Some charter ticket sellers offer an insurance policy for a legitimate cancellation (like hospitalization or a death in the family). Be aware that a charter might be canceled if the plane is not full.

Some charter companies have proved unreliable in the past. Among charter flight operations is a name possibly remembered from one's younger days, the **Council on International Educational Exchange Council Charters,** 205 E. 42nd St., New York, NY 10017 (tel. 212/661-1414). This outfit can arrange "charter seats on regularly scheduled aircraft" to such major European capitals, as Brussels, Paris, or Amsterdam where you can then take a train to Copenhagen.

Cne of the biggest New York charter operators is **Travac,** 989 Sixth Ave., New York, NY 10018 (tel. 212/563-3303, or toll free 800/TRAV-800), which operates charters from New York to European destinations.

REBATORS To confuse the situation even more, rebators also compete in the low-cost airfare market. A rebator can also be a bucket shop. These outfits pass along to the passenger part of their commission, although many of them assess a fee for their services. Most rebators offer discounts that range from 10% to 25% (but this could vary from place to place), plus a $20 handling charge. They are not the same as travel agents, although they sometimes offer similar services, including discounted land arrangements and car rentals.

Rebators include **Travel Avenue,** 180 N. Des Plaines, Chicago, IL 60661 (tel. 312/876-1116, or toll free 800/333-3335), and **The Smart Traveller,** 3111 SW 27th Ave., Miami, FL 33133 (tel. 305/448-3338, or toll free 800/448-3338).

STANDBY If you're a spontaneous traveler with no schedule demands and you don't mind hanging around the airport, then a standby fare may be for you. Your departure will depend on whether a seat opens up at the last minute. Not all airlines offer standby seats. Call around to see if any such ticket is offered at the last minute.

GOING AS A COURIER Couriers are hired by overnight air-freight firms hoping to skirt the often-tedious Customs delays that regular cargo faces on the other end. For the service, the courier pays the firm a fee much lower than the cost of the ticket, and sometimes may fly free. Don't worry, the service is legal—you won't be asked to haul in illegal drugs. Also, you don't actually handle the merchandise you're "transporting"; you just carry a document (a shipping invoice) to present to Customs when you arrive.

This cost-cutting technique is not for everyone—there are lots of restrictions and courier opportunities are hard to come by. You're allowed only one piece of carry-on luggage; your checked-baggage allowance is used by the courier firm to transport its cargo. Also, you fly alone; family or friends must make other arrangements.

Check with **Halbart Express,** 147-05 176th St., Jamaica, NY 11434 (tel. 718/656-8189 daily from 10am to 3pm). Also try **Now Voyager,** 74 Varick St., Suite 307, New York, NY 10013 (tel. 212/431-1616 daily from 11:30am to 6pm). An automatic telephone-answering system announces last-minute specials and the firm's fees for the round-trip. Courier services are also listed in the yellow pages or in advertisements in newspaper travel sections.

The **International Association of Air Travel Couriers,** P.O. Box 1349, Lake Worth, FL 33460 (tel. 407/582-8320), for an annual membership of $35, will send you six issues of its newsletter, *Shoestring Traveler,* and about half a dozen issues of *Air Courier Bulletin,* a directory of air-courier bargains around the world.

PACKAGE TOURS/CRUISES

For those travelers who feel more secure if everything is prearranged—hotels, transportation, sightseeing excursions, luggage handling, tips, taxes, and even meals, a package tour is the obvious choice, and it may even help save money.

One of the best tour operators to Scandinavia is **Bennett Tours,** 270 Madison Ave., New York, NY 10016 (tel. 212/532-5060, or toll free 800/221-2420). It offers land packages, with experienced guides and a wide range of prices.

Other reliable tour operators include **Holiday Tours of America,** 425 Madison Ave., Suite 1602, New York, NY 10017 (tel. 212/832-8989, or toll free 800/677-6454), or **Scantours, Inc.,** 1535 Sixth St., Suite 205, Santa Monica, CA 90401 (tel. 213/451-0911, or toll free 800/223-SCAN).

NORWAY The most popular cruises are of the fjords. **Scandinavian Seaways** (tel. toll free 800/533-3755) offers both a Norwegian fjord cruise (of the most famous and scenic fjords in the Bergen area), and also a North Cape cruise. Prices begin at $1,255 per person.

In summer, cruise-ship passengers always want to visit the North Cape to see the Midnight Sun. One of the best tours to take is by **Ocean Cruise Lines,** 1510 SE 17th St., Fort Lauderdale, FL 33316 (tel. 305/764-5566, or toll free 800/556-8850). It runs 7- to 14-day deluxe cruise tours of Scandinavia and Russia, including the Norwegian fjords and the North Cape, with prices from $2,495 per person.

Norwegian Arctic Trips, P.O. Box 700, Route 4, Enfield, NH 03748 (tel. 603/632-7654), specializes in adventure trips in the Norwegian Arctic and Lapland for small groups. For example, it offers a 12-day guided canoe-fishing trip for about $1,150 per person. It also features river adventures for the physically handicapped. It also offers ski touring and snowmobiling in Lapland and Spitsbergen (Svalbard).

SWEDEN Once in Sweden, the most popular tour is the ○ **Göta Canal cruise** from Gothenberg to Stockholm (or vice versa), dubbed the "Sweden in a nutshell" tour because it offers a wide overview of the country's geography in one trip. The tour (including all meals) costs from $889 (U.S.), takes 4 days, and operates from April to September. You can book through many travel agents, including the Bergen Line, 505 Fifth Ave., New York, NY 10017-4989 (tel. 212/986-2711, or toll free 800/323-7436).

FINLAND For the best of the North Country's tours (the most unusual of which occur in winter), the vast and beautiful wilderness regions of Finland can provide some of the most memorable expeditions in Europe. Among the many tour options are a **ski-trekking** venture into some of Lapland's wildest country with an experienced guide, or cross-country ski weekends in the country around Kuusamo, where Finland's Olympic teams have trained for years and where the trails are said to be among the best in Europe.

The best tours of Finland are offered by **Finnair** (tel. toll free 800/950-5000), including its most popular, the **Midnight Sun Flight** (Helsinki-Rovaniemi-Helsinki). This tour is offered June 1 to July 15 daily. Any Finnair office around the world can provide information about the tour possibilities for exploring Finland.

Finnair also offers a **reindeer safari,** where teams of sleds (one person and one reindeer per sled) make expeditions into Lapp communities far north of the Arctic Circle. Finally, for travelers who want to sail the Baltic, there's a **summer sailing**

safari, where each member sails his or her own boat among a flotilla of other vessels and then meets each evening for communal meals and activities at the islets scattered along the south of Finland.

If you'd like to see as much as possible of the highlights of Finland in the shortest possible time, consider the **Finland Grand Tour,** lasting 10 days and 9 nights. It is offered on certain days June through August. This tour is operated by the **Finland Travel Bureau,** Kaivokatu 10A, PB 319, SF-00101 Helsinki (tel. 90/18-261). Bookings can be made through any travel agent.

AIRLINES & FARES

Although there are no regularly scheduled passenger ship services between North America and Scandinavia, **cruise ships** sometimes call at Scandinavian ports. However, you'll almost certainly make your initial arrival in Scandinavia by air.

FLYING TO DENMARK Only two airlines offer nonstop flights from the U.S. to Copenhagen. **SAS** (Scandinavian Airlines Systems, tel. toll free 800/221-2350) has more nonstop flights to Scandinavia from more North American cities than any other airline, and more flights to and from Denmark and within Scandinavia than any other airline in the world. SAS offers nonstop flights to Copenhagen daily in midsummer, and almost every day in winter, from Los Angeles, Seattle, and Chicago, and daily flights regardless of the season from Newark, N.J.

SAS's routes to Copenhagen are contested only by **TWA** (Trans World Airlines; tel. toll free 800/221-2000), which flies to Copenhagen daily from New York's JFK.

At presstime, SAS offered one of the lowest prices in years for round-trip passage to Copenhagen from New York. With restrictions, and flying during specific off-peak seasons, tickets cost as little as $425 round-trip for passengers who paid for their tickets within 7 days after booking, who stayed abroad between 7 and 30 days, and who understood in advance that refunds and changes in flight dates were not permitted. A similar ticket from Chicago to Copenhagen cost $448 round-trip. Both tickets were increased by $50 for travel on a Friday, Saturday, or Sunday. These prices can and almost certainly will change during the lifetime of this edition, so it's best to confirm these prices before booking your ticket.

The options for reaching Copenhagen by air are amplified for passengers who decide to spend a few days in another European capital before journeying to the land of the Vikings. **British Airways** (tel. toll free 800/247-9297) offers convenient connections through London or Manchester to Copenhagen, with a price structure that sometimes makes a stopover in Britain less expensive than you might have

---

 FROMMER'S SMART TRAVELER:
SCANDINAVIAN AIRFARES

1. Shop all airlines that fly to your destination.
2. Always ask for the lowest fare—not just a discount fare.
3. Keep calling the airline—availability of cheap seats changes daily.
4. Fares to other Scandinavian cities are sometimes included in a transatlantic ticket at no extra charge. This must be specified when ticket is written.
5. For domestic flights in Scandinavia, ask about special passes and family discounts.
6. Try to fly in winter, spring, or fall—fares are lower at this time. Check out SAS's midwinter mini-fares.
7. Ask about the cost-conscious APEX (advance-purchase excursion) fare.
8. Find out if it's cheaper to fly on a weekday.
9. Read the section on bucket shops, charter flights, flying standby and going as a courier.

thought. Other European airlines with connections through their home countries to Copenhagen include **Icelandair** (tel. toll free 800/223-5500), **KLM** (tel. toll free 800/777-5553), and **Lufthansa** (tel. toll free 800/645-3880). Be warned, however, that unless you make all flight arrangements from within North America before you go, you might find some of these capital-hopping flights prohibitively expensive.

Nonstop flights to Copenhagen from the New York area take approximately 7½ hours; from Chicago, around 8½ hours; from Seattle, 9½ hours, and from Los Angeles, 11 hours.

FLYING TO NORWAY   All transatlantic flights from North America land in Oslo at either the relatively remote Gardemoen Airport or more conveniently at Fornebu Airport. **SAS** (tel. toll free 800/221-2350) flies nonstop from Newark to Oslo in about 7½ hours. Most other SAS flights from other North American cities are routed through Copenhagen to Oslo with flying times of 9¼ hours from Chicago, 10½ hours from Seattle, and 11½ hours from Los Angeles, not including the layover in Copenhagen.

Service on SAS is supplemented by recently inaugurated routes into Oslo on **Delta** (tel. toll free 800/221-1212). Delta flies three times a week in winter—and more frequently in summertime—between New York's JFK and Oslo's Fornebu. Connections from within Delta's vast North American network are usually efficient and convenient.

The prices mentioned above in "Flying to Denmark" are for the most part similar to within a few dollars of fares for flights to Oslo or Bergen. (In many cases, especially during special promotions, transatlantic passengers on SAS can transfer onto a Norwegian domestic flight from Oslo to Bergen for no additional charge.) Delta and SAS maintain roughly similar rates for transatlantic passage, but it's best to compare fares offered by both companies for last-minute price changes before your departure.

If you opt to fly to Norway on any other airline, you'll be routed through their respective gateway cities in Europe, sometimes with a continuation on a different airline. **British Airways** (tel. toll free 800/247-9297), for example, has dozens of daily flights from many North American cities to London, from which you can fly on with frequent air links to Oslo. **Icelandair** (tel. toll free 800/223-5500) is often an excellent choice for connections through its home port of Reykjavik. Likewise, **Lufthansa** (tel. toll free 800/645-3880), **Air France** (tel. toll free 800/237-2747), or **KLM** (tel. toll free 800/777-5553) will route you to Oslo through Frankfurt, Paris, or Amsterdam, respectively.

FLYING TO SWEDEN   East Coast passengers usually opt for **SAS** (tel. toll free 800/221-2350), or **TWA** (tel. toll free 800/221-2000), both of which fly every day from the New York area to Stockholm. Their major competitor is **American Airlines** (tel. toll free 800/443-7300), which offers daily flights to Stockholm from Chicago, and excellent connections through Chicago to American's vast North American network. At presstime, for departures between November and March (excluding the Christmas holidays) American offered fares as low as $448 round-trip for weekday departures from Chicago. Travel on a Friday, Saturday, or Sunday carried a supplemental charge of $50. This fare, matched for the most part by SAS, required a stay abroad of between 7 and 30 days, as well as several other restrictions. Although these fares would probably not be in effect by the time you finalized your vacation plans, something closely approximating those prices would probably be substituted. Clients originating in Los Angeles or Seattle usually flew SAS to Copenhagen, then connected onto one of the airline's frequent shuttle flights into Stockholm.

Other airlines fly to gateway European cities, and then connect onto other flights into Stockholm. **British Airways** (tel. toll free 800/247-9297), for example, flies from almost 20 North American cities into London, and then connects with around eight onward flights to Stockholm. **Delta** (tel. toll free 800/241-4141), **Northwest** (tel. toll free 800/225-2525), and **TWA** (tel. toll free 800/221-2000) also fly at frequent intervals to London, from which ongoing flights to Stockholm are available either on SAS or British Airways. Finally, **Icelandair** (tel. toll free 800/223-5500) has proven an excellent choice for travel to Stockholm thanks to connections through its home port of Reykjavik.

FLYING TO FINLAND Finnair (tel. toll free 800/950-5000), which flies to Helsinki from more parts of the world than any other airline, is the only airline that flies from anywhere in North America to Finland. From New York, Finnair flies nonstop on the 8-hour trip to Helsinki every day throughout the year.

At presstime, midsummer prices from New York to Helsinki cost between $998 and $1,028 round-trip, for passengers who booked 7 days in advance, and who agreed to remain abroad between 7 and 90 days. These prices were substantially lowered during Finnair's frequent promotional sales, when, if certain conditions were met, round-trip fares were reduced to between $548 and $598, depending on flight dates.

Several other airlines fly to gateway European cities and then connect to Helsinki. **British Airways** (tel. toll free 800/221-2350) flies from almost 20 U.S. cities to London's Heathrow airport, connecting to the 15 flights per week that then depart on Finnair for Helsinki. **SAS** (tel. toll free 800/221-2350) will fly you via Copenhagen from where there are three daily nonstop flights to Helsinki, taking about 1½ hours each.

BY TRAIN

TO DENMARK If you're in Europe, it's easy to get to Denmark by rail. Copenhagen is the main rail hub between Scandinavia and the rest of Europe. For example, the London-Copenhagen train via Ostende or Hoek van Holland leaves four times daily (22 hours). About 10 daily express trains run from Hamburg to Copenhagen (5½ hours). There are also intercity trains on the Merkur route from Karlsruhe (Germany) to Cologne to Hamburg to Copenhagen. The Berlin-Ostbahnhof–Copenhagen train (8½ hours) connects with East European trains. Two daily express trains make this run.

TO NORWAY/SWEDEN There are three daily trains from Copenhagen to Oslo, seven from Copenhagen to Stockholm and six from Copenhagen to Gothenburg. All connect to the Danish ferries operating either to Norway via Helsingør or Hirtshals or to Sweden via Helsingør or Frederikshavn.

TO FINLAND There is a rail and ferryboat link between London and Helsinki which goes via Ostende (Belgium), Cologne, Hamburg, and Stockholm. If you've taken the ferry from Stockholm and are arriving at Turku, on the west coast of Finland, you can catch one of the seven daily trains that will take you across southern Finland to Helsinki. The trip takes 2¼ hours. Rail connections are also possible from London to Den Hoek (The Netherlands), Bremen, Hamburg, and Stockholm. However, each of these itineraries takes about 50 hours, plus a 2-hour stopover in Stockholm. It's possible to reserve sleepers and couchettes, but do so as far in advance as possible. Helsinki is also linked by rail to the major cities of Finland (see individual city listings for details).

BY BUS

TO FINLAND There are international bus links to Finland, but this is the least convenient mode of transportation. One of the most popular would be a bus connection from Stockholm with a sea crossing to Turku, with continuing service by land to Helsinki.

It's also possible to take coaches from Gothenburg going cross country to Stockholm and to the ferry dock beyond, with land travel resuming after Turku on the same coach all the way to Helsinki.

For information about international bus connections and reservations, contact **Oy Matkahuolto Ab**, Lauttasaarentie 8, SF-00100 Helsinki (tel. 90/692-2088).

BY SHIP/FERRY

TO DENMARK It's also easy to travel by water from several ports to Denmark. Liners carrying both cars and passengers operate between England, Germany, Poland, Norway, and Sweden to Denmark. Check with your travel agent about these Denmark cruises.

From England   Scandinavia Seaways (tel. toll free 800/533-3755) runs vessels year-round between Harwich, England, and Esbjerg in West Jutland. Crossing takes between 16 and 20 hours. The same line also sails from Newcastle upon Tyne to Esbjerg, but only in summertime, as part of a passage requiring 22 hours. Overnight cabins and space for cars are available on both routes.

From Norway/Sweden   The **Bergen Line** (tel. 212/986-2711, or toll free 800/323-7436) operates vessels from Oslo to Hirtshals in North Jutland, part of Denmark.

Stena Line runs popular sea links from Oslo to Frederikshavn, North Jutland (11½ hours), and from Gothenburg, Sweden, to Frederikshavn (3 hours). For information, schedules, and fares, contact: Norstar Travel, 154 North Ave., Webster, NY 14580 (tel. 716/871-2600).

From Germany   GT-Link, Faergegärden, DK-4874 Gedser (tel. 53-87-92-33), runs car-ferries from Travemünde (the point closest to Denmark), to Gedser, southern Denmark (3½ hours).

TO NORWAY   From Denmark   Three major ferries operate from Denmark. The first, from Hirtshals to Kristiansand takes 5 hours on the Stena Line and can be booked in the United States through Norstar Travel, 154 North Ave., Webster, NY 14580 (tel. 716/872-2600); the second from Frederikshavn to Oslo takes 11 hours and can be reserved through the Larvik Line, Box 265, Skøyen, N-0212 Oslo 2 (tel. 22-52-15-40). It departs twice daily year-round, and includes a night crossing. The third, Scandinavian Seaways operates daily year-round from Copenhagen to Oslo overnight taking 16 hours. For reservations contact Scandinavian Seaways, Cypress Creek Business Park, 6555 NW 9th Ave., Fort Lauderdale, FL 33309-2049 (tel. 305/491-7909, or toll free 800/533-3755).

From Sweden   From Strømstad, Sweden, there is a daily crossing in summer to Sandefjord, Norway, taking 2½ hours. Bookings on this Scandi Line operation can be made through **Scandi Line,** Tollbugata 5, N-3200 Sandefjord (tel. 011/33-40-08-00).

From England   The **Bergen Line,** 505 Fifth Ave., New York, NY 10017 (tel. 212/986-2711, or toll free 800/323-7436), operates from Newcastle, England, and Stavanger and Bergen on the west coast of Norway.

TO SWEDEN   From Denmark   From Copenhagen, you can go to Malmö, Sweden, by hydrofoil. (This is identified locally as the *Flyvebadene*.) For information in Copenhagen, call 33-12-80-88. A first-class round-trip ticket from Copenhagen to Malmö costs 276 kroner ($47.20), and a second-class round-trip is 180 kroner ($31.10). Although the hydrofoil doesn't transport cars, this is the the easiest and fastest (and the most expensive) way for pedestrians to travel to Sweden. Travel time is 45 minutes. Hydrofoils depart from the corner of Havnegade and Nyhavn from a terminal directly on the seafront. Departures are daily every hour on the hour from 6am to 1am. In midsummer, make reservations.

Sweden can also be reached by a conventional ferryboat that transports cars. Ferries depart from Dragør, south of Copenhagen, and arrive at Limhamn, 3 miles south of Malmö. There are about 19 to 25 crossings daily which operate between 5:30am and 10pm. The cost for a round-trip, 1-day ticket, a car, driver, and up to five passengers is 395 kroner ($68.30) providing you return the same day. It's 490 kroner ($84.80) for a car and five passengers if you plan to spend a night or more. Walk-on pedestrians pay 32 kroner ($5.50) each way, and children under 16 go for half price. For more information, call 32-53-15-85 in Copenhagen.

Another possibility for motorists is to leave Copenhagen and drive north to Helsingør, where you can take a conventional ferryboat to Helsingborg, Sweden, departing three times an hour. This route is popular with Swedes and Danes because it costs less money and requires only 25 minutes for the crossing. The round-trip fare for a car and up to five passengers is 405 kroner ($70.10). Pedestrians pay 32 kroner ($5.50) round-trip. For information, call 49-21-12-55.

One final option appeals to Denmark-based drivers who want to take as broad a swing as possible through a historic and colorful part of southern Sweden. To accomplish this, drive to Dragør, south of Copenhagen, and take the ferry to

Limhamn, Sweden, 3 miles south of Malmö. Once there, visit Malmö and Helsingborg. Return to Denmark on the car-ferry to Helsingør (site of "Hamlet's Castle") and drive south back to Copenhagen. Round-trip cost for a car, a driver, and up to four passengers is 390 kroner ($67.50), providing the entire itinerary is completed within a single day.

From England Two English ports, Harwich and Newcastle upon Tyne, offer ferryboat service into Sweden. Harwich to Gothenberg, a passage of between 23 and 25 hours, is available year-round. Newcastle to Gothenberg, a crossing of 27 hours, is available only in summertime. Ferryboats on both routes offer overnight accommodations and the possibility of transporting cars. Prices tend to be less expensive for passengers booking their passage in advance through the company's U.S. agent. For details, call Scandinavian Seaways, Cypress Creek Business Park, 6555 NW 9th Ave., Suite 207, Fort Lauderdale, FL 33309 (tel. toll free 800/533-3755).

TO FINLAND From Sweden Frequent ferries run between Sweden and Finland, especially between Stockholm and Helsinki. Service is on either the Viking or Silja line. Each company also operates a twice-daily service from Stockholm to Turku on Finland's west coast.

From Germany The Silja Line also maintains regular passenger service between Travemünde (Germany) and Helsinki. Information about the Silja Line is obtained at Eteläesplanadi 14, SF-00131 Helsinki (tel. 90/18041). Information on the Viking Line is available at Mastokatu 1, SF-00160 Helsinki (tel. 90/12-351).

BY CAR

TO DENMARK You can easily drive to Denmark from Germany. Many drive to Jutland from such cities as Hamburg, Bremerhaven, or Lübeck. Jutland is linked to the central island of Funen by bridge. But from Funen you must take a car-ferry from Nyborg to the island of Zealand, site of Copenhagen. Once in West Zealand you will still have to drive east across the island to Copenhagen.

Car-ferry service to Denmark from the United Kingdom generally leaves passengers at Esbjerg, where they then have to cross from Jutland to Copenhagen. From Germany, it's possible to take a car-ferry from Travemünde, northeast of Lübeck, which deposits you at Gedser in Denmark. From there, connect with the E55, an express highway north to Copenhagen.

TO NORWAY If you're driving from the Continent you have to go via Sweden. From Copenhagen take the E47/55 express highway north from Copenhagen to Helsingør, catching the car-ferry to the Swedish city of Helsingborg. From there, E6 will take you into Oslo.

From Stockholm you can drive across Sweden along the E18 to Oslo.

TO SWEDEN The ferry routes from England to Denmark and from Denmark to Sweden are the most traveled, but there are better choices from the continent.

From Germany You can drive to the northern German port of Travemünde and catch the 7½-hour ferry to the Swedish port of Trelleborg, a short drive south of Malmö. This route saves many hours by avoiding transit through Denmark. If you want to visit Denmark before Sweden, you can take the 3-hour car-ferry from Travemünde to Gedser in southern Denmark. From Gedser the E64 and the E4 express highway head north to Copenhagen. After a visit there, you can take a car-ferry from Copenhagen to Malmö.

From Norway From Oslo, the E18 goes east via Karlstad all the way to Stockholm. This is a long but scenic drive. If you're in Denmark, car-ferries run frequently from Copenhagen to the southern Swedish city of Malmö and from Helsingør in North Zealand to Helsingborg on Sweden's west coast. To reach Stockholm from Malmö, take the E6 north along the coast in the direction of Helsingborg. In the Helsingborg area, turn northeast at the junction with the E4 and continue all across southern Sweden until you reach Stockholm. Part of this highway is an express motorway and part only a national highway.

TO FINLAND From anywhere in western Scandinavia the quickest route to Finland

is the E3 to Stockholm and the year-round 14- to 16-hour ferry
Helsinki.

From Germany From Travemünde year-round, there's a high-sp
that takes 22 hours to reach Helsinki.

From Denmark Take the car-ferry from Helsingør to Helsingborg in Swe
and then drive to Stockholm and catch the car-ferry to Helsinki or Turku.

7. GETTING AROUND SCANDINAVIA

AIR & RAIL PASSES [SCANDINAVIA & EUROPE]

The best way to get around the whole of Scandinavia is to take advantage of the **air and rail passes** that apply to the whole region, or, if you're traveling extensively in Europe, to use the special European passes. For additional country-specific information see the planning chapters for each country—Chapters 3, 12, 23, and 32.

If you plan to travel heavily on the European and/or British railroads, you will do well to secure the latest copy of the *Thomas Cook European Timetable of Railroads*. It is available exclusively in North America from **Forsyth Travel Library,** P.O. Box 2975, Shawnee Mission, KS 66201 (tel. toll free 800/FORSYTH), at a cost of $23.95 plus postage.

SAS'S VISIT SCANDINAVIA FARE This is a six-coupon ticket that's valid for travel on all SAS flights within and between Denmark, Norway, and Sweden, from July 1 to August 14. To get these slashed fares, passengers must have flown transatlantic on SAS. Each coupon costs $80.

THE SCANDINAVIAN RAIL PASS This allows you to travel the rail systems in Denmark, Norway, Sweden, and Finland (except for Stockholm's local train system).

It also allows a 50% discount on the following ferry routes: Copenhagen-Malmö; Copenhagen-Rønne; Rønne-Ystad; and Stockholm-Helsinki. It also gives you 50% off on express boats between Bergen, Flåm, and Årdalstangen; and Bergen, Slora, and Måløy, plus round-trip fares on the Larvik Line.

You pay $179 for the first class, $145 for second class for 4 days of travel within a 15-day period; $299 for first class, $239 for second class for 9 days of travel within a 21-day period; and $459 for first class, $349 for second class for 14 days of travel within a 1-month period. Reservations and information are available through **Rail Europe,** 226 Westchester Ave., White Plains, NY 10604 (tel. toll free 800/TGV-RAIL). Children between 4 and 11 travel for half price. Fares are subject to change, of course.

EURAILPASS If you're touring extensively in Europe, this might be a good bet. It's good for limited first-class rail travel in 17 European countries. With one ticket, you travel on special trains, whenever and wherever you please; more than 100,000 rail miles are at your disposal. The cost for 15 days is $430; for 21 days, $550; for 1 month, $680; for 2 months $920; and for 3 months, $1,150. Children under 12 pay half price, and children under 4 travel free. Fourteen-day or 1-month voyagers have to estimate rail distance before determining if such a pass is to their benefit. To obtain full advantage of the tickets for 15 days or 1 month, you'd have to spend a great deal of time on the train. Eurailpass holders are entitled to considerable reductions on certain buses and ferries. Travel agents in all towns, and railway agents in such major cities as New York, Montréal, or Los Angeles, sell all these tickets. A Eurailpass is available at the North American offices of CIT Travel Service, the French National Railroads, the German Federal Railroads, and the Swiss Federal Railways.

Eurail Saverpass is a money-saving ticket that offers discounted 15-day travel but only if groups of three people travel constantly and continuously together

ween April and September, or if two people travel constantly and continuously
_gether between October and March. The price of a Saverpass, valid all over Europe,
good for first-class only, is $340 for the 15 days.

Eurail Flexipass allows passengers to visit Europe with more flexibility. It is
valid in first class and offers the same privileges as the Eurailpass. However, it provides
a number of individual travel days which can be used over a much longer period of
consecutive days. That means it is possible to stay in one city and yet not lose a single
day of travel. There are three passes: 5 days within 15 days for $280, 9 days within 21
days for $450, and 14 days within 1 month for $610.

With many of the same qualifications and restrictions as the previously described
Flexipass is **Youth Flexipass.** Sold only to travelers under age 26, it allows 15 days
of second-class travel within 2 months for $420.

NORDTURIST PASS   If you're traveling primarily in Scandinavia, the Nordturist
Pass may be better and cheaper for you than the Eurailpass. This pass allows 21 days
unlimited travel by train throughout Norway, Sweden, Denmark, and Finland. It is
also valid on ferries between Oslo and Copenhagen and between Stockholm and
Helsinki. The pass gives you a 50% discount on the bus ticket: Bodø/Fauske-Kirkenes
in North Norway. The pass is sold at any rail station in Scandinavia. In the U.S. call
ScanAm toll free at 800/545-2204. Adults pay $348 first class, $261 second class;
youths 12 to 25 pay $261 first class, $194 second class; and children 4 to 11 pay $174
first class, $131 second class.

8. WHERE TO STAY

SPECIAL SCANDINAVIAN PASSES & DISCOUNTS

THE SCANDINAVIAN BONUS PASS   Tourists who purchase the Scandinavian
Bonus Pass get up to 50% discount off the rates at more than 80 first-class hotels in
Sweden, Denmark, and Norway. The pass is valid for an unlimited number of
overnight stays from May 15 to September 1 and on weekends from September 2 to
May 14. It costs $23. One pass is valid for two adults and their accompanying
children. Reservations are made free from participating hotel to hotel. Upon arrival at
a hotel, a guest presents the pass and gets the reduced rate. These rates in Denmark are
$41; in Norway, $39; and in Sweden, $45—each per person in a double room,
including breakfast, service charge, and VAT. Children up to 15 years of age stay free
in their parents room. The pass is available at many travel agents, including Holiday
Tours of America, 425 Madison Ave., New York, NY 10017 (tel. 212/832-8989 or
toll free 800/677-6454), and Scantours Inc., 1535 Sixth St., Suite 205, Santa Monica,
CA 90401 (tel. 310/452-0911, or toll free 800/223-SCAN).

THE SCANDIC SUMMER CHEQUE   This pass is an inexpensive product
designed for individual travelers. Reservations can be made in advance, and the checks
are valid at more than 120 hotels in Sweden, Denmark, Norway, and Finland, and
even at some hotels in Britain and on the Continent (Germany, Holland, Belgium, and
Austria). The check is valid from June 1 to August 31, costing $44 per person,
including breakfast. There is a supplement of $20 for single rooms. Children 12 and
under stay free in their parents' room. Many agencies sell this pass, including Holiday
Tours of America, 425 Madison Ave., New York, NY 10017 (tel. 212/832-8989, or
toll free 800/677-6454), and Scantours, 1535 Sixth St., Suite 205, Santa Monica, CA
90401 (tel. 310/451-0911, or toll free 800/223-SCAN).

BEST WESTERN HOTEL CHEQUE SCANDINAVIA   From May 15 to September 15, this program offers reduced rates for twin rooms including breakfast at some
140 hotels in Scandinavia. Single-room supplements are payable directly to the hotel.
Checks are about $41 each depending on the country and there is a minimum
purchase of five per person. The hotels are divided into categories. Basic checks are

accepted at "B" hotels; "A" and "S" hotel categories carry a supplement. Among the many agencies offering these are Scantours Inc. (tel. toll free 800/233-SCAN) and Holiday Tours of America (tel. toll free 800/677-6454).

IN DENMARK

Danish Inn Cheques are valid at 67 Danish inns for rooms with private bath and toilet. For $35 to $60 per person, a guest is entitled to an overnight stay in a double room, including breakfast. Children under 6 stay free in a parents' bed.

Checks are sold by **Scandinavian American World Tours, Inc.,** 933 Hwy. 23, Pompton Plains, NJ 07444 (tel. 201/835-3030, or toll free 800/835-3030).

IN NORWAY

You can obtain large reductions at 300 hotels, pensions (boardinghouses), and mountain lodges all over Norway—Oslo to the fjord district to the North Cape—by purchasing the **Norway Fjord Pass.** The pass is valid for standard-room accommodations (not for deluxe rooms or suites) and costs about $9 (U.S.). Holders of the pass are charged 200 to 410 kroner ($34.60 to $70.90) per night for a room, with breakfast included. You can reserve your room in advance at least 3 days before you plan to arrive, or just drop in at one of the hotels or pensions offering Fjord Pass accommodation. If that one is full, the staff will help you call another one nearby. At hotels offering such accommodation, the pass is valid from May 1 to September 30. You'll pay 120 kroner ($20.80) for single-room supplement. Children 3 to 15 years of age get 50% reductions. In the United States, the pass is sold at various agencies, including Borton Overseas, 5516 Lyndale Ave. S., Minneapolis, MN 55419 (tel. 612/824-4415, or toll free 800/843-0602).

IN SWEDEN

With a **Pro Skandinavia Voucher** you get reduced rates at more than 400 first-class or luxury hotels not only in Sweden, but in Finland, Norway, and Denmark

---

 FROMMER'S SMART TRAVELER: HOTELS

1. Always ask about midsummer reductions from late June to mid-August.
2. Ask also about weekend discounts, which may include Sunday as well as Friday and Saturday.
3. Remember the price you pay in reasonably priced hotels depends on the plumbing. Rooms with showers are cheaper than rooms with bath; rooms containing a sink with bath down the hall are cheapest.
4. Take advantage of special discounts, like the Scandinavian Bonus Pass, Finncheques, Danish Inn Cheques (see this chapter) etc.
5. At smaller, cheaper hotels that take credit cards, ask if cash will secure a reduction.
6. If you're going to spend a week at the hotel, ask about long-term discounts.
7. Parents should ask if children can stay free in the same room.

QUESTIONS TO ASK IF YOU'RE ON A BUDGET

1. Is there a garage? What's the charge for parking?
2. Is there a surcharge on either local or long-distance telephone calls? (There usually is and it could be as much as 40%. Make your calls from a phone box or from the post office.)
3. Is service included? If it's not, add 15% to the rates.
4. Are all taxes included?

as well. Vouchers are in effect from June 1 through September 1 and during weekends (Friday and Saturday) from September 1 to June 1. The price for a double room is two vouchers, including breakfast, tax, and services. No charge is made for children under 12, unless an extra bed is required (that charge represents one voucher). The price of each voucher is $47. Bookings must be made no more than 24 hours before arrival. More information is available from Haman Scandinavia U.S., Inc., 10866 Wilshire Blvd., Suite 1270, Westwood, Los Angeles, CA 90024 (tel. 301/475-7038, or toll free 800/476-1687).

IN FINLAND

Hotel-discount vouchers called **Finncheques** cut down considerably on costs at some hotels. Costing 175 markkaa ($38.50) each for 1 night's accommodation, Finncheques are valid from June 1 to August 31. Participating in the program are 252 hotels in 111 localities. Only the first night can be reserved in advance, and reservations at the next hotel are handled free. Finncheques can be used by one person each, but there is no lower limit to the number that can be bought. The single-room supplement is 75 markkaa ($16.50) at first-class hotels. Children aged 4 to 14 can have an extra bed placed in their parents' room for 75 markkaa ($16.50) per night. All supplements and charges for children are paid at the hotel.

Finncheques represent substantial savings, which might be 30% or more off the regular rates, but that varies from hotel to hotel. Finncheques are available from accredited Finncheque agents. In the U.S., agents are Fenno Tours, 12 S. Dixie Hwy., Lake Worth, FL 33460 (tel. 407/547-9538, or toll free 800/535-6714); Holiday Tours of America, 425 Madison Ave., New York, NY 10017 (tel. 212/832-8989, or toll free 800/677-6454), and Scantours, Inc., 1535 Sixth St., Suite 205, Santa Monica, CA 90401 (tel. 213/451-0911, or toll free 800/223-SCAN). For further information, contact the agents listed above or **Vesama Tours Ltd.,** Fredrikinkatu 48A, SF-0100 Helsinki (tel. 90/694-8877).

YOUTH HOSTELS

These are found throughout Scandinavia. The accommodations vary considerably from a renovated old manor farm in Denmark's Odense to a boat in Stockholm harbor.

Most hostels have small bedrooms sleeping four, and, occasionally, private rooms for families. They usually close between 1 and 4 pm and impose a curfew and lights-out after 11 pm. Other rules such as no smoking in the bedrooms may also be imposed.

Mandatory membership costs $25 for adults 18 to 54; $10 for under 18s; $15 for seniors; $35 for families; and $250 for life. In Canada costs are $25 for ages 18 and over ($35 for 2 years); $12 for those under 18; $40 for groups; and $175 for life membership. For information contact American Youth Hostels, P.O. Box 37613, Washington, DC 20013-7613 (tel. 202/783-6161), and in Canada, Canadian Hostelling Association, 1600 James Naismith Dr., Suite 608, Gloucester ON K1B 5N4, Canada (tel. 613/748-5638).

You can also become a member at any youth hostel or at the following headquarters in Scandinavia: Landsforeningen Danmarks Vandrerhjem, Vesterbrogade 39, DK-1620 København V, Denmark (tel. 33-31-36-12); Norske Vandrerhjem, Dronningensgate 26, N-0154, Oslo 1, Norway (tel. 22-42-14-10); Svenska Turistföreningen, Drottninggatan 31-38, P.O. Box 25, Stockholm, Sweden (tel. 08/790-31-00); or Finnish Youth Hostel Association, Yrjönkatu 38B, SF-00100 Helsinki, Finland (tel. 90/694-0377).

IN DENMARK   There are 101 youth hostels, and guests of all ages are welcomed. The hostels charge about 65 kroner ($11.20) per night, although nonmembers pay a 22 kroner ($3.80) supplement. Children under 2 are free. Breakfast is available for around 40 kroner ($6.90) at most places, and sleeping bags tend to be prohibited.

Accommodation is most often in a four-bedded room with private facilities, but some establishments offer only dormitory accommodations. Most hostels sell beer and wine and are open all night.

IN NORWAY There are about 900 modern well-maintained youth hostels and prices range from 60 to 130 kroner ($10.40 to 22.50) a night for a bed. Sheet sleeping sacks may be rented. Reasonably priced meals are served in most of them. Many maintain do-it-yourself kitchen facilities. Membership cards are accepted without formality at all hostels in Norway.

IN SWEDEN There are about 280 youth hostels, called Vandrarhem. Prices are usually 60 to 93 kronor ($11.30 to $17.50) for members; nonmembers pay an extra 36 kronor ($6.80). The hostels in Sweden are usually closed between 10am and 5pm daily.

IN FINLAND There are about 160 youth hostels, about 50 of which open all year, the rest in summer only. The rates depend on the hostel category and number of beds in a room and range from the least expensive, costing 30 markkaa ($6.60) a night, to the top rating, costing from 150 markkaa ($33).

FARMHOUSES/APARTMENTS

IN DENMARK The best way to see the heart of Denmark and meet the Danes is to spend a week on one of their farms. Take a pin and stick it anywhere on a map of Denmark away from the cities and seacoast, and you'll find a thatched and timbered farm, or perhaps a more modernized homestead. All are good bases—any point on the island can easily be reached on a day trip.

Select the part of Denmark you'd like to explore, then write the local tourist office in that area, stating your requirements, the number in your party, the length of your stay, the ages of your children (if any), and whether you want full or half board. A minimum stay of 7 days or more is desirable, but not always mandatory.

Even better is to write to **Bondegårdsferie/ferie på Landet** (National Association of Farm Tourism), Låsbyvej 20, 8660 Skanderborg, Denmark (tel. 86-52-41-50). If you'll send this outfit an international money order for $6 you'll get a catalog listing more than 150 farm holiday homes. Farms set their own prices, but in general you'll pay from 140 kroner ($24.20) per person for bed and breakfast or 210 kroner ($36.30) for half board. Children are granted reductions.

If you want greater independence, you can inquire about booking an apartment in the countryside of Denmark at the rate of 1,800 to 2,000 kroner ($311.40 to $346) per week for four to six people.

IN NORWAY Many farms in Norway have accommodations for visitors. You may participate in some of the farming activities or just relax. There are opportunities for hiking, fishing, or horseback riding. Most farms impose a 3-night minimum, with prices starting at $49 per person daily. Call Borton Overseas toll free in the U.S. at 800/843-0602 for more information or a booking.

IN FINLAND More than 70 English-speaking Finnish farm families have opened their homes for farm holidays. The farms, including some in Lapland, have one thing in common: an opportunity to meet with Finnish people at home and join in their farming activities, or just relax. You can reach your holiday destination most easily in your own car, but if you travel by train or bus, you can arrange to be met. The prices depend on the category in which a house has been placed. A minimum of 6 days is usually required for a farm holiday.

Bookings can be arranged through **Suomen 4H-liitto,** Abrahaminkatu 7, SF-00180 Helsinki (tel. 90/642-233). Prices range from 1,317 to 1,863 markkaa ($289.75 to $409.85) per person weekly, including full board.

CAMPING

IN DENMARK There are a number of pleasant, well-equipped campgrounds near Copenhagen and elsewhere. For information about campsites and facilities, contact the **Dansk Camping Union,** Gammel Kongevej 74D, DK-1850 København V (tel. 31-21-06-00). The cost of the official campgrounds is about 35 kroner ($6.10) per person. The Camping Union will sell you a campground handbook for 65 kroner ($11.20). A mandatory camping pass is available at all campgrounds for 25 kroner ($4.30) or you can purchase a family pass for 50 kroner ($8.60).

IN NORWAY   There are more than 970 authorized campsites in Norway, classified, according to standards and amenities, as one-, two-, and three-star camps. Charges vary according to the number of stars, but the charge for pitching a tent is from $4 to $12 (U.S.) per night. Cabins rent for $40 to $90 per night. Most campers prefer to live in the tents and prepare their own meals—without a doubt the cheapest way to go.

Norwegian campsites are comfortable and maintain high standards. Most have rental cabins/chalets, which are becoming increasingly popular. If you want to stay in one of these, make your reservation by telephone early in the afternoon. Camping chalets are usually fitted with four bunk beds with mattresses, chairs, and tables, and are electrically heated, with a hotplate for cooking. Other necessary equipment, such as pillows and blankets, must be provided by the camper. If you need more detailed information on camping, contact the Norwegian Automobile Club, **NAF Turistavdelingen,** Storgata 2, N-0155 Oslo 1 (tel. 22-34-15-00), for its manual.

IN SWEDEN   Some 780 sites are available, all approved and classified by the Swedish Tourist Board, which has high standards for such facilities. The best time for a camping holiday is from mid-May to September, but some sites remain open in winter as well.

Pitching a tent costs 50 to 80 kronor ($9.40 to $15.10) per night. A comprehensive book, *Camping Sverige,* is available at most Swedish bookstores.

IN FINLAND   There are about 360 campsites with some 6,300 camp cabins and holiday cottages. Most have cooking facilities, kiosks, and canteens where food, cigarettes, and candy are sold. Camping outside the campsite is forbidden. Camp cabins cost 150 to 300 markkaa ($33 to $66) per day. The price of an overnight stay at a campsite for a car, tent, or trailer, and two adults with or without children, is 27 to 75 markkaa ($5.95 to $16.50). This includes basic facilities, such as cooking and washing up. Campers with an international camping card (FICC) don't need a national camping card. Information about campsites is available at regional tourist offices. Information is also available from the **Finnish Travel Association,** Camping Department, Mikonkatu 25, PB 776, SF-00101 Helsinki (tel. 90/170-868).

SPECIAL ACCOMMODATIONS

IN NORWAY   Norway offers one of the least expensive vacation bargains in Europe: Ideal for outdoors-loving families or groups, **log-cabin chalets** are available throughout the country, on the side of a mountain or by the sea, in a protected valley or woodland, or by a freshwater lake. Some lie in chalet or cabin colonies; others are set on remote and lofty peaks. At night, by paraffin lamplight or the glow of a log fire, you can enjoy aquavit or an early supper, as many Norwegians do. Some cabins are fully equipped with hot and cold running water, showers, and electricity; others are more primitive. Naturally, the rental price varies according to the amenities, as well as the size (some have as many as three bedrooms, most with tiered bunks). The price range is usually $200 to $480 (U.S.) weekly, the latter price for completely modern accommodations. There are chalets in most parts of the country—in the mountains, near lakes, along the coast, and in the fjord country. For information or a booking, call Borton Overseas toll free at 800/843-0602.

Originally built to accommodate fishermen along the coastal waters, many **fishermen's huts** or *rorbuer* are rented to visitors. Most of these shanties lie in the Lofoten Islands, but they are also located in other parts of Norway. At water's edge, sea fishing is available, and rowboats are usually available for rent. Rental prices for the huts range from 150 to 700 kroner ($26 to $121.10) per night, depending on the quality of the cabin and the number of people it sleeps. Beds in most cabins are possible through Borton Overseas by calling toll free 800/843-0602.

Norway with its fresh air and great outdoors is the perfect place for a vacation at a spa. You can begin a new lifestyle and get pampered at several places, notably **Ullensvang Body Invest,** Hotel Ullensvang, N-5774 Lofthus i Hardanger (tel. 53-66-11-00), which offers spa vacations.

IN SWEDEN Many campsites also offer **cabins,** complete with bunk beds and kitchen. For families this might be a more preferred method of touring Sweden than pitching a tent. Most cabins with four beds cost 150 to 250 kronor ($28.30 to $47.15) per night, depending on the area. The Swedish Tourist Board will furnish details.

Svenska Turistföreningen, Drottninggatan 31-38, Stockholm (tel. 08/790-31-00), also operates **mountain huts** along hiking trails and in national parks, usually in the north. These huts rent for around 115 kronor ($20.05) per person nightly. Membership details are available from the STF office above.

IN FINLAND There are more than 200 **holiday villages** in Finland, many in the luxury class. These villages consist of self-contained bungalows by lakes and offer varied leisure activities, such as fishing, rowing, hiking, and swimming. Several are open all year. Some villages have hotel and restaurants for those who don't want to do their own cooking. Prices range from 1,100 to 2,700 markkaa ($242 to $594) per week in the best villages. The cottages contain two or five beds each.

There are also privately owned **holiday cottages** ranging from fishing huts on the coast to villas on the inland lakes, all fully furnished. Prices range from 600 to 3,500 markkaa ($132 to $770) per week, depending on location, size, and equipment.

For information and reservations, get in touch with regional tourist offices.

PART ONE

DENMARK

CHAPTER 2
GETTING TO KNOW DENMARK

The Danes may live in a small country, but they come on with a big welcome. Americans, Canadians, and their old friends, the British, are enthusiastically greeted—and in English too. Denmark should be an important stopover on even the most superficial whirlwind tour of Europe.

This country, made up mostly of islands, is a heavily industrialized nation, known for its products and arts and crafts. However, it does boast a quarter of a million farmers (and eight million pigs).

The late British novelist Evelyn Waugh (*Brideshead Revisited*) called the Danes "the most exhilarating people of Europe." Few Danes would dispute this. And neither would I.

1. GEOGRAPHY, HISTORY & POLITICS

GEOGRAPHY

In spite of its small size, Denmark has more than 4,500 miles of irregular coastline. It is a low-lying country, yet the Danes, with their characteristic good humor, will often tell visitors about their "mountains" (the highest hill on Jutland is around 550 feet).

THE REGIONS Mainland **Jutland** is the largest land area of Denmark, connected with the continent of Europe (Germany). Jutland (in Danish Jylland) is filled with sand dunes and moors along the west coast. Most of the rest of the land is devoted to agriculture and forestry. Fjords run miles inland on the eastern side of Jutland, the part facing Funen. Aalborg, in North Jutland, is one of the oldest cities of Denmark. Its history as a trading post goes back to the 11th century. Århus, also in Jutland, is the second-largest city of Denmark. It was a bishop's see as early as the 12th century.

The largest island of **Funen** (Fyn) has an area of 1,150 square miles. Called the garden of Denmark, it is best known to visitors because its major city, Odense, was the birthplace of Hans Christian Andersen. It has many farms, orchards, and much rolling countryside. Romantic old castles and manor houses pepper the southern part of the island. Funen has a number of important ports, including Nyborg in the east. Svendborg is a major port at the southern end of the island.

The island of **Zealand** (Sjaelland) in the east is the most visited, because it is the home of Copenhagen, the capital of Denmark. Zealand is the largest, the wealthiest, and the most densely populated of the Danish islands. Three islands to the south of Zealand are devoted mainly to agriculture: **Falster, Lolland,** and **Moen** (Møn). Roskilde is one of the major cities of Zealand, an old royal city lying some 20 miles west of Copenhagen. Many of the kings of Denmark are buried at its ancient cathedral. Visitors are even more fond of going to Helsingør (Elsinore in English), lying 25 miles north of Copenhagen. The attraction here is what is popularly called "Hamlet's Castle."

DATELINE

- **810** The reign of the first Danish king ends.
- **940–985** Harald Bluetooth brings Christianity to Denmark.
- **1013–42** The crowns of Denmark and England are united.
- **1397** Union of Kalmar unites Denmark, Norway, and Sweden.
- **1471** Sweden bows out. Denmark and Norway are ruled by Christian I (1426–81).
- **1530** Lutheran preachers bring the Reformation to Denmark.
- **1577–1648** Long reign of Christian IV brings prosperity, but ends in losing war with Sweden.
- **1814** Denmark cedes Norway to Sweden.
- **1866** Denmark loses Schleswig-Holstein to Prussia.
- **1915** New constitution gives Denmark universal suffrage.
- **1933** Denmark gains all of Greenland.
- **1940–45** Denmark is invaded

(continues)

HISTORY

The best archeological evidence indicates settlements in what is now Denmark before 10,000 B.C., as nomadic hunters gave way to Stone Age farmers. Agriculture developed further during the Bronze Age (1,600–400 B.C.); these early settlers practiced a pagan religion.

The first recorded Danish king was Godfred, who died in 810. However, he is known to have halted the Frankish conquests of the Holy Roman Emperor Charlemagne. Godfred's successor, Hemming, made a treaty marking the Eider River as the southern border of Denmark. This border held until 1864.

Two famous kings emerged in the 10th century: Gorm (883–940) and his son, Harald Bluetooth (940–985) who both united Denmark establishing its center at Jelling. Harald also established Christianity.

Harald conquered Norway and attempted to conquer England. Harald's son, Sweyn I, succeeded in conquering England in 1013. Under Sweyn's son, Canute II (994–1035), England, Denmark, and part of Sweden were ruled under one crown. After Canute's death, however, the Danish kingdom was reduced to only Denmark. Canute's nephew, Sweyn II, ruled the Danish kingdom, and upon his death his five sons governed Denmark successively.

The Holy Roman Empire was the "overlord" of Denmark until the Danes formed their own independent leadership under Archbishop Eskil (1100–82) and King Waldemar I (1131–82). A strong monarchy was established. During a celebration at Ringsted in 1190, the church and state were united. Archbishop Absalon (1128–1201), a soldier and statesman, is chiefly credited with restoring Danish political and ecclesiastical independence from German influences.

Waldemar II (1170–1241) helped to strengthen the Danish government. His son, Eric IV (1216–50), followed him as king, but argued with his brothers and the church. Eric's brother, Duke Abel of Schleswig, proclaimed himself king and assassinated Eric in 1250. Civil wars ensued, and three of the four successive kings were killed in battle. Eric VI (1274–1319) also carried on wars with Norway and Sweden. This led to decay in Denmark. Between 1332 and 1340 Denmark had no king and was ruled by nobles. Waldemar IV Atterdag (1320–75) became king by signing the peace treaty of Stralsund in 1370.

UNITED SCANDINAVIA The dynasty was left without a male heir after Waldemar IV died in 1375. King Olaf, his grandson, became king. Olaf brought about a union of the crowns of Denmark and Norway, and he was also heir to the throne of Sweden. The union of Denmark with Norway came about because Olaf was the son of Margaret (1353–1412), daughter of Waldemar and wife of Haakon VI Magnusson (1339–80), king of Norway. Margaret actually ruled the country as regent. When both Haakon and Olaf died, she was acknowledged as queen of Norway and Denmark. An ambitious woman, she wanted to rule over Norway, Sweden, and Denmark.

The Union of Kalmar came about in 1397. Margaret had her nephew, Eric of Pomerania (1382–1459), crowned king of all three countries as Eric VII. Margaret, however, continued to rule the country until her death.

Eric VII had no heirs, and he tried to pass the kingdom on to one of his family members in Pomerania. That didn't go over too well with the nobility, and he was dethroned in 1439 (he went to Gotland and became a pirate). The Danish Privy Council elected Christopher of Bavaria (Eric's nephew) in 1418, making him King Christopher III.

Upon Christopher's death, the Swedes wanted autonomy. Sweden elected King Charles VIII in 1471, and Denmark and Norway took a joint king, Christian I (1426–81).

DATELINE

- and occupied by Nazi Germany.
- **1949** Over some protests, Denmark joins NATO.
- **1953** New constitution provides for a single-chamber parliament.
- **1972** Denmark joins the European Economic Community; Margrethe, daughter of Frederik IX, becomes queen of Denmark.

THE 16TH CENTURY Christian II (1481–1559) came to the throne in 1513, but he was not liked. He didn't believe in democracy and he was loathed for letting the mother of his mistress control the finances of the kingdom. He recaptured Sweden in 1520, but was defeated a year later by Gustavus Vasa. Christian was deposed in 1523, and he fled to the Netherlands.

His successor, Frederik I (1471–1533), signed a charter granting many privileges to the nobility. Lutheranism became the national religion. The Reformation took hold in Denmark upon Frederik's death. Conflicts between Lutherans and Catholics erupted in a civil war, which ended in 1536 with the surrender of Copenhagen. The Danish Lutheran church was founded in 1536. This occurred during the reign of Christian III (1534–59), who tried to make the crown hereditary, but failed. Frederik II, Christian's son, was elected in 1559. Frederik launched a war against Eric XIV of Sweden, during a territorial dispute over provinces in the Baltic. This became the Seven Years' War of the North (1563–70), which the Danes failed to win.

WARS WITH SWEDEN Hostilities continued with Sweden, but the reign of Christian IV (1577–1648) was one of relative prosperity. Christiania (now Oslo) was named after him. However, in the closing years of his reign, Sweden invaded Jutland, defeating the Danes. By the Treaty of Christianopel, Denmark was forced to cede many of its former possessions to Sweden.

Frederik III (1609–70) tried to regain lost territories when Sweden went to war with Poland, but he was defeated by Charles X. Frederik ended up giving Sweden more territories than Denmark had had before the war. Charles X tried to attack Denmark so as to take over the whole country, but this time the Danes won, regaining lost territories. Sweden ended the war upon the death of Charles X in 1660.

The Skaane War (1675–79) was started by Christian V (1646–99), as the Danes attempted to gain more territories, but they lost. Frederik IV (1671–1730), his successor, resumed the war with Sweden in 1699. Named the Great Northern War, it raged from 1699 to 1730.

The 18th century brought much reform to Denmark, and the country took over colonies in the West Indies (now the U.S. Virgin Islands) and Greenland. Agriculture and trade prospered.

THE 19TH CENTURY At the start of the Napoleonic Wars, Denmark was neutral. In 1801 England destroyed the Danish fleet in Copenhagen, forcing Denmark to choose Napoléon's side. It was a disaster for Denmark. Napoléon lost the war in 1814, and peace was made at Kiel. Denmark was forced to yield Norway to Sweden and Heligoland to England. The Danes sank into poverty.

The rulers following the Napoleonic Wars, Frederik VI and Christian VIII, formed very conservative governments. In 1848 the people demanded a more liberal constitution. Absolute rule was abolished, and a government based on representation was set up by Frederik VII. The Danish constitution was signed on June 5, 1849.

In March 1848 the Schleswig-Holstein revolution began, lasting 2 years. The Danes initially triumphed over Prussia. But in the Treaty of Prague in 1866, Denmark again lost Schleswig-Holstein to Prussia.

A new constitution was drawn up on July 28, 1866, which was more conservative than the 1849 constitution. The conservatives quickly gained power, making reforms and improving the economy.

THE 20TH CENTURY When World War I broke out, Denmark remained neutral. However, the Danes mined their waters for Germany. The Danes joined the rest of Scandinavia in November of 1914 and adopted a uniform trade policy. Unemployment and increased taxes marked the war years. A new constitution was signed on June 5, 1915; the parliament consisted of two chambers, and equal voting rights for both men and women were acknowledged.

Because Germany was defeated in World War I, many people felt that all of Schleswig should be returned to Denmark, but in the end, the country retained only North Schleswig.

A new treaty was made between Iceland and Denmark in 1918. The countries were united under one king, although declared separate sovereign states. Danish armed forces represented Iceland.

Denmark helped to form the League of Nations and officially joined it in 1920. A crisis arose in 1931 over Greenland. As of 1921, Norway had claimed this territory. On April 5, 1933, in the Permanent Court of International Justice, Denmark gained all of Greenland.

In May 1939, Hitler asked Denmark to sign a nonaggression pact. Denmark accepted it; Norway and Sweden did not. The pact promised that Denmark and Germany would not go to war with each other for 10 years. When war broke out in 1939, Denmark declared its neutrality. Ties with Iceland were severed, and Greenland and the Faroe Islands were occupied by the United States and Great Britain, respectively.

In spite of their pact, Nazi forces invaded and occupied Denmark in 1940. In 1943, Hitler sent Gen. Hermann von Hanneken to control the Danes by martial law. Heroic Danish resistance continued against the German occupying forces. When Germany surrendered in 1945, British troops occupied Denmark. Denmark joined the United Nations.

After the war, the Liberal party under Knud Kristensen took over the government. In 1947 Kristensen resigned. The leader of the Social Democratic party under Hans Hedtoft ran the new government under King Frederik IX. The economy was sluggish until 1948.

In 1949 Denmark joined NATO. In 1953 the Scandinavian Council was formed, including Denmark, Norway, Sweden, and Iceland; the council lasted until 1961. Also

in 1953, Denmark adopted a new constitution, providing for a single-chamber parliament.

In 1972 Denmark became the sole Nordic member of the EEC. That same year, Queen Margrethe, born in 1940 (the year of the Nazi invasion), became queen of Denmark upon the death of her father, Frederik IX.

POLITICS

Denmark is a constitutional monarchy. The king or queen exercises power through the State Council and the Folketing (parliament). Prime ministers and other ministers are appointed by the king or queen, but approved by the parliament. There are dozens of Lower Courts of Justice, two Higher Courts, and a Supreme Court. An *ombudsman,* an independent official, supervises the constitution and investigates complaints made by citizens against government authorities.

2. FAMOUS DANES

H. C. Andersen   (1805–75) Famous writer of fairy tales, novels, dramas, and travel books. *The Little Mermaid* is probably the best known.

Jorn Asger   (b. 1914) Artist and famous member of the COBRA group (an acronym for Copenhagen, Brussels, Amsterdam) formed after WWII. He studied with Léger in Paris and was later influenced by Edvard Munch.

Tycho Brahe   (1546–1601) The astronomer who discovered the constellation Cassopeia was born in Scania, Denmark. He was also the astrologer and almanac maker for the royal family of King Frederik II. A planetarium named after him opened in Copenhagen in 1989.

Niels Bohr   (1885–1932) This famous Danish scientist formulated his theory of the structure of the atom, which became the basis of quantum physics. After winning the Nobel Prize in 1922, he established a center for atomic and nuclear research. In the closing years of World War II, he worked with the physicists at Los Alamos to develop the first atomic bomb.

Benjamin Christensen   (1879–1959) An early Scandinavian film director whose best loved film is *Haxan* (Witchcraft through the Ages—1922) with Christensen playing the Devil.

King Christian IV   (1577–1648) The country's most popular king was also a great builder, bringing the Renaissance to Denmark. As a king, he was less successful. Under his reign the Danish Army suffered dreadful losses in the Thirty Years' War. "Lucky in love, unlucky in war," he died in his bedroom at Rosenborg Castle in Copenhagen.

Isak Dinesen   (1885–1962) The pen name of Baroness Karen Blixen, famous for her autobiographical novel *Out of Africa* and her Gothic tales.

Carl Dreyer   (1889–1968) Genius of the Danish cinema. His masterpiece is *La Passion de Jeanne d'Arc,* a film consisting almost entirely of closeups. He took the trial of Joan of Arc which lasted 1½ years and condensed it to 2 hours on screen.

Jens Peter Jacobsen   (1847–85) Born in Thirsted, Jutland, Jacobsen was an independent and original writer—often cited for being "self-conscious and self-critical." Also a lyrical poet, he is mainly known for *Digte of Udkast,* written near the time of his death from tuberculosis.

Søren Kierkegaard   (1813–55) Philosopher and theological writer, a founding father of existentialism. His most important work was *Enten-Eller* (Either-Or).

Carl Nielsen   (1865–1931) One of Denmark's great composers.

Adam G. Oehlenschlager   (1779–1850) Leader of the Romantic movement in Danish theater. His best-known work is *Aladdin* (1805), based on the *Arabian Nights.*

Bertel Thorvaldsen   (1768–1844) Perhaps the greatest name in Danish sculpture. Often compared to Italy's Antoni Canova.

3. FOOD & DRINK

FOOD Danish food is the best in Scandinavia—in fact, it's among the best in Europe.

Breakfast Breakfast, to begin with, is usually big and hearty, fitting for a day of sightseeing. It usually consists of homemade breads, Danish cheeses, and often a boiled egg or salami. In most establishments, you may order bacon and eggs, two items with which this country is well stocked. You may prefer, however, simply the continental breakfast of Danish **wienerbrød** (pastry) and coffee. The "danish" is moist, airy, and rich.

Lunch At lunch, the national institution, the ubiquitous **smørrebrød,** open-face sandwiches, is introduced. Literally, this means "bread and butter," but the Danes stack this sandwich as if it were the Leaning Tower of Pisa—then they throw in a slice of curled cucumber and bits of parsley or perhaps sliced peaches or a mushroom for added color.

Two of these sandwiches can make a more-than-filling lunch. They are seen in the grandest dining salons all the way down to the lowliest pushcart. Many restaurants offer a wide selection; guests inspect a checklist and then mark the ones they want. Some are made with sliced pork (perhaps a prune on top), roast beef with béarnaise sauce and crispy fried bits of onion, or liver paste adorned with an olive or cucumber slice and a gelatin made from strong beef stock.

Smørrebrød is often served as an hors d'oeuvre. The most popular, most tempting, and usually most expensive of these delicacies is prepared with a mound of tiny Danish shrimp, on which a lemon slice and caviar often perch, sometimes fresh dill. The "ugly duckling" of the smørrebrød family: anything with a cold sunny-side-up egg on top of it.

Dinner The Danes keep farmers' hours for dinner: 6:30pm is common, although restaurants remain open much later. Many main-course dishes are commonly known to North Americans, but they are prepared with a distinct flourish in Denmark—dishes such as **lever med løg** (liver and fried onion), **bøf** (beef in a thousand different ways), **lammesteg** (roast lamb), or that old reliable, **flaeskesteg med rødkål** (roast pork with red cabbage).

The country's cooks are really noted for their fresh **fish** dishes. The tiny Danish shrimp (**rejer**) are splendid. Herring and kippers meet with much enthusiasm. Really

---

FROMMER'S SMART TRAVELER:
RESTAURANTS

1. Look for the *dagens ret* (daily special), which is usually reasonable in price and prepared fresh that day.
2. The best bargain meal in Denmark is the *Danmenu* (Danish lunch or dinner): two courses offered at a fixed price.
3. Ask for the *daglig kort* (daily card), which features less expensive dishes than those on the *spisekort* (menu).
4. Look for the lunch-only, cellar restaurants where you get good value with old-world charm.
5. Do as the Danes do and make your own *smørrebrød* (open-face sandwiches).
6. Save restaurants in the Tivoli for dessert and dine outside the amusement park. Tivoli restaurants charge about 30% more.
7. Drink beer with your meal. Wine is very expensive in Denmark.
8. Patronize ethnic restaurants, especially Chinese, as they are usually cheaper.

top-notch fish dishes include plaice (rodspaette), salmon (laks), mackerel (makrel), and boiled cod (kogt torsk).

Danish **cheese** is consumed at any of the three meals a day, then eaten on a premidnight smørrebrød at the Tivoli. Danish bleu is too familiar to need definition. For something softer and milder, try Havarti.

Among Danish specialties most worth sampling: **frikadeller,** the Danish meatballs or rissoles, prepared in numerous different ways. Also try a Danish omelet with a rasher of bacon covered with chopped chives and served in a skillet. A familiar dish is Danish hamburger patties topped with fried onions and coated with a rich brown gravy.

Choice **desserts:** Danish apple Charlotte, best when decorated with whipped cream, dried breadcrumbs, and chopped almonds. Another treat is *rødgrød med fløde*—prepared in numerous ways, but basically a jellied fruit-studded juice, over which the diner pours thick cream.

DRINK　As for your drink, **Carlsberg** or **Tuborg beer** is the national beverage of Denmark. A bottle of pilsner costs about half the price of the stronger, more decoratively labeled export beer. To keep from flattening his bank account, a Dane relies on the low-priced **fadøl** (draft beer). Foreigners on skimpy budgets are advised to do the same.

You may gravitate more to **aquavit** (schnapps to the English), which comes from the city of Aalborg in northern Jutland. The Danes, who usually drink it at mealtime, follow it with a beer chaser. Made from a distilling process using potatoes, aquavit should only be served icy cold.

For those with a daintier taste, the world-famous Danish liqueur, **Cherry Heering,** is a delightful drink, made from cherries as the name implies, and it's for consumption at any time other than during meals.

4. RECOMMENDED BOOKS, FILMS & RECORDINGS

BOOKS

HISTORY & PHILOSOPHY　*A Kierkegaard Anthology,* edited by Robert Bretall (Princeton University Press), explores the work of the Copenhagen-born philosopher who developed an almost-pathological sense of involvement in theology. A representative selection of some of his more significant works are included.

Copenhagen, A Historical Guide, by Torben Ejlersen (published by Høst & Søn in Denmark, and available at most bookstores there), an 88-page guide, takes you on a brief tour of the city that began as a ferry landing and became one of the most important capitals of Europe.

Of Danish Ways, written by two Danish-Americans, Ingeborg S. MacHiffic and Margaret A. Nielsen (Harper & Row, 1984), a delightful account of a land and its people, has a little bit of everything: history, social consciousness, customs, food, handcrafts, art, music, and theater.

BIOGRAPHY & LITERATURE　*Andersen's Fairy Tales,* by H. C. Andersen (New American Library), and *The Complete Hans Christian Andersen Fairy Tales* (Crown). These anthologies include all his most important works such as *The Little Mermaid, The Tinderbox, The Princess and the Pea.*

Danish Literature: A Short Critical Guide, by Paul Borum (Nordic Books), is a well-written review that explores Danish literature from the Middle Ages to the 1970s.

Out of Africa (Modern Library), *Letters from Africa* (University of Chicago Press), and *Seven Gothic Tales* (Random House) are all by Karen Blixen (Isak Dinesen), who gained renewed fame with the release of the 1985 film *Out of Africa,* with Meryl Streep and Robert Redford. One of the major authors of the 20th century, twice nominated for the Nobel Prize, Blixen's world lives on in these almost-flawless stories. *Seven Gothic Tales* is her masterpiece. Another title by Blixen is *Winter's Tales* (Penguin).

Isak Dinesen, by Judith Thurman (St. Martin's Press), is the definitive biography of the Danish writer who has been called "witch, sybil, lion hunter, coffee planter, aristocrat, and despot, a paradox in herself and a creator of paradoxes." The story chronicles an amazing life from an unhappy childhood in Denmark to marriage to Baron Blixen to immigration to Kenya to her passionate love affair with Denys Finch Hatton.

FILMS

Pelle the Conqueror, Katinka, and *Babette's Feast* have been the best-received Danish films in recent times. They played to acclaim at both festivals and art houses in Europe and America. *Pelle the Conqueror* won the Oscar as best foreign film in Hollywood.

Heaven and Hell (Himmel og Helvede) was directed by Morten Arnfred. Karina Skands plays Maria, a '60s child who wants to be a violinist but whose parents try to stifle her artistic ambitions.

Baby Doll brings a sinister tone, the story of a young mother on maternity leave at a broken-down farm. It's a bit of a psychological thriller and is very well done, bringing a self-inflicted nightmare to the quiet, tranquil countryside.

Arhus by Night, directed by Nils Malmros, disappointed many critics but won some fans. It is a virtual tribute to Truffaut's *Day for Night.* It tells the story of the making of a film in an otherwise drab and provincial town.

The Danes continue to excel in films for children, as exemplified in *Shower of Gold* (Guldregn) directed by Søren Kragh-Jacobsen. Four children in a suburb of Copenhagen discover a box stuffed with banknotes.

RECORDINGS

CLASSICAL In Denmark, the 125th anniversary of the birth of its greatest musical genius, **Carl Nielsen** (1865–1931) was commemorated in 1990. The occasion was marked with a fresh release of all his important works. These include his operas *Saul og David* (Saul and David; 1903) and *Maskerade* (1906), along with his symphonies, concertos, and choral and chamber music. Other important works in release include *Fynsk Forar* (The Spring of Funen) and *Taken Letter.*

FOLK Paul Dissing has a gravellike, unresonant voice, but is one of the most popular recording stars in Danish history. Danes say his humor cannot be translated. Some, but not all, of his music has been accompanied by Benny Andersen. Dissing's most popular album to date is *Ten Songs of Paul Dissing and Benny Andersen.*

Singing alone, playing a guitar, and occasionally backed up by one other guitarist, **Erik Grib** sings modern interpretations of 19th-century Danish folk songs. His 19th-century patriotic and nostalgic odes to Denmark profoundly touch his listeners. His most popular album to date is *To Sonia.*

Lars Lilholt sings nostalgic and richly poetic interpretations of Danish folk songs. His most famous album is *Near Contact.*

Kurt Ravn is better known as a mature actor in stage and cinema, but each of his recording efforts meets with critical approval. Recorded in Danish, his music is whimsical and poetic. His most popular album to date is *The Four Seasons.*

POP/ROCK Hanne Boel has been called Denmark's answer to Tina Turner. Moderately electronic with highly danceable music, her work is about life. Sometimes her music is accompanied by backup singers from West Africa. Her most famous album is *Dark Passion.*

D.A.D. (Disneyland after Dark). This group's music is comic, deliberately rude, and punkish. Their videos are a scream, and their most popular album to date is *No Fuel Left for the Pilgrims*.

Hotel Hunger is considered one of the best groups in Denmark. Oddly, their first success came in America. Their electronic music meets with wide approval, as did their best-known album, *This Is Where the Fun Starts*.

TV-2 (Stephan Brandt) is a Danish singer whose most famous slogan translates as "Real Men Don't Want to Hear Nonsense Anymore" (that is, from their ex-wives, present wives, alienated girlfriends, rueful parents, and frustrated bosses). This slogan became one of the most copied in the Danish advertising industry. The lyrics of TV-2 are far more important than the tunes.

CHAPTER 3
PLANNING A TRIP TO DENMARK

This chapter is devoted to the nitty-gritty of planning a trip to Denmark—costs, events, itineraries, and detailed practicalities like taxes, tipping, and emergencies. It should be read in conjunction with Chapter 1.

1. CURRENCY & COSTS

CASH/CURRENCY For currency, the Danes use the **krone** (crown), **kroner** in the plural, which breaks down into 100 **øre.** At press time, 1 krone equals approximately 17.3¢ U.S., or 5.78 kroner to the U.S. dollar. Of course, rates are subject to change, and you should check current rates before you go.

Banknotes in circulation include 50, 100, 500, and 1,000 kroner. Still in circulation (but being phased out) are 20-krone banknotes. Coins minted are 25 øre, 50 øre, 1 krone, and 5, 10, and 20 kroner. Still in circulation (but being phased out) are 5- and 10-øre coins.

When converting your currency into Danish kroner, beware of varying exchange rates. In general, banks offer the best rate, but even banks charge a commission for the service, often $2 or $3, depending on the transaction. Your hotel will offer the worst exchange rate.

WHAT THINGS COST IN COPENHAGEN	U.S. $
Taxi from the airport to the city center	21.60
Taxi from Central Station to Amalienborg Castle	10.00
Subway from Central Station to Amalienborg Castle	4.00
Local telephone call	.10
Double room at the Hotel d'Angleterre (deluxe)	346.00
Double room, with bath, at the Absalon Hotel (inexpensive)	129.80
Double room, without bath, at the Hotel Viking (inexpensive)	102.10

THE KRONE & THE DOLLAR

The dollar prices given in the Denmark section of this book, and in the table below, are based on an exchange rate of 1 krone = 17.3¢ U.S. Since world currencies fluctuate in value from time to time, these dollar values are given only as a guideline and may not be accurate at the time of your visit.

Kroner	U.S.	Kroner	U.S.
0.50	.08	50	8.65
1	.17	80	13.85
5	.85	100	17.30
10	1.75	125	21.60
15	2.60	175	30.30
25	4.35	200	34.60
30	5.20	300	51.90

	U.S.$
Buffet breakfast for one in a hotel	12.00–15.00
Lunch for one at the Els (moderate)	30.45
Lunch for one at Axelborg Bodega (budget)	15.00
Dinner for one, without wine, at Kommandaten (deluxe)	60.00
Dinner for one, without wine, at Prag (moderate)	40.00
Dinner for one, without wine, at Puk's Restaurant (inexpensive)	18.70
Pint of beer (draft pilsner)	3.80
Coca-Cola	2.50
Cup of coffee	2.50
Roll of Kodacolor film, 36 exposures	11.10
Admission to the Tivoli	4.00
Movie ticket	10.50
Theater ticket (at the Royal Theater)	8.70–43.30

WHAT THINGS COST IN ODENSE

	U.S. $
Average taxi ride within city limits	7.00
Local telephone call	.10
Double room at the Hotel H. C. Andersen (deluxe)	199.00
Double room, with bath, at the Windsor Hotel (inexpensive)	121.10
Double room, with bath, at Missionhotellet Ansgar (inexpensive)	96.90
Buffet breakfast for one in a hotel	10.00
Lunch for one at Den Gamle Kro (moderate)	18.20
Dinner for one, without wine, at Under Lindetraeet (deluxe)	73.50
Dinner for one, without wine, at Den Gamle Kro (moderate)	25.60
Dinner for one, without wine, at Sortebro Kro (moderate)	23.40
Pint of beer (draft pilsner)	3.20
Coca-Cola	1.90
Cup of coffee	2.25
Roll of Kodacolor film, 36 exposures	10.50

	U.S.$
Sightseeing Tour	10.40
Admission to Funen village	2.60
Movie ticket	9.00

2. WHEN TO GO — CLIMATE, HOLIDAYS & EVENTS

CLIMATE   Denmark is mild for a Scandinavian country—New England farmers experience harsher winters. Summer temperatures average between 61° and 77° Fahrenheit. Winter temperatures seldom go below 30° Fahrenheit, thanks to the warming waters of the Gulf Stream. Mid-April to November is a good time to visit.

Denmark's Average Daytime Temperatures & Rainfall

	Jan	Feb	Mar	Apr	May	June	July	Aug	Sept	Oct	Nov	Dec
Temp. (°F)	32	32	35	44	53	60	64	63	57	49	42	37
Rainfall "	1.9	1.5	1.2	1.5	1.7	1.8	2.8	2.6	2.4	2.3	1.9	1.9

HOLIDAYS   There may be a slight variation in some of these dates, so check with a local tourist office. Danish public holidays (and dates of those that do not vary) are: January 1 (New Year's Day), Maundy Thursday, Good Friday, Easter Sunday, Easter Monday, May 1 (Labor Day), Common Prayers Day, Ascension Day, Whitsunday, Whitmonday, June 5 (Constitution Day), December 25 (Christmas Day), and December 26 (Boxing Day).

DENMARK CALENDAR OF EVENTS

JULY

☐ **July 4,** Rebild, near Aalborg. One of the few places outside the United States to honor American Independence Day. For more information, contact the Aalborg Tourist Office, Osterågade 8, DK-9000 Aalborg (tel. 12-60-22).

☐ **Sønderborg Tilting Festival.** Dating back to the Middle Ages, the "tilting at the ring" tradition has only survived in the old town of Sønderborg on the island of Als in southern Jutland. While riding at a gallop, the horseman must use his lance to see how many times out of 24 he can take the ring. Parades, music, and entertainment are included. July 7–10. For more information, contact the Turistbureau, Rådhustorvet 7, DK-6400 Sønderborg (tel. 74-42-35-55).

AUGUST

☐ **Fire Festival Regatta,** Silkeborg. Denmark's oldest and biggest festival, its main features are nightly cruises on the lakes with thousands of candles illuminating the shores. On the last night, there is a fireworks display, the largest and most spectacular in northern Europe. Entertainment is provided by popular Danish artists at a large fun fair. For more information, contact the Turistbureau, Torvet 9, DK-8600 Silkeborg (tel. 86-82-19-11). August 2–4.

SEPTEMBER

☐ **Århus Festival Week.** A wide range of cultural activities, including opera, jazz, classical music, folk music, ballet, and theater are presented. Sporting activities and street parties abound as well. It is the largest cultural festival in Scandinavia. For more information, contact the Århus Tourist Office, Rådhuset, Århus C, DK-8000 Århus (tel. 86-12-16-00). Early September.

COPENHAGEN CALENDAR OF EVENTS

MAY

☐ **Ballet and Opera Festival.** Classical and modern dance and two operatic masterpieces are presented at the Old Stage of the Royal Theater in Copenhagen. For tickets, contact Royal Theater, Box 2185, DK-1017 København K, Denmark. Mid-May to June.

JUNE

☐ **Carnival in Copenhagen.** A great citywide event. There's also a children's carnival. June 2–4.

JULY

☐ **Copenhagen Jazz Festival.** Features international jazz musicians in the streets, squares, and theaters. Pick up a copy of *Copenhagen This Week* to find the venues of various performances. July 6–13.

AUGUST

☐ **Fall Ballet Festival.** The Royal Danish Ballet, acclaimed internationally, returns to its home to perform at the Old Stage of the Royal Theater, just before the tourist season ends. For tickets, contact the Royal Theater, Box 2185, DK-1017 København K, Denmark. Mid-August to September 1.

3. GETTING AROUND

BY PLANE

For those in a hurry, **SAS** (tel. 33-15-52-66 in Copenhagen) operates daily service between Copenhagen and points on Jutland's mainland. It's about 40 minutes to fly from Copenhagen to Aalborg, 35 minutes from Copenhagen to Århus, and 30 minutes from Copenhagen to Odense's Beldringe Airport.

Fares to other Danish cities are sometimes included in a transatlantic ticket at no extra charge, providing the extra cities are specified when the ticket is written.

For air travel in Denmark, **Danair** connects with Maersk Air, SAS, and Cimber Air. (Danair is not to be confused with a British Airline, Dan Air.) Between these local carriers, all parts of Denmark are accessible. An English-speaking sales representative will answer the phone if you call the sales office in Billund, Jutland (tel. 75-33-22-44).

In addition to flights within Denmark, Danair flies to Britain, the Netherlands, Norway, and Sweden, and offers competitive fares when compared to larger airlines.

BY TRAIN

Each city or town in Denmark is linked to Copenhagen by rail. Lyntog (tel. 33-14-17-01) express trains are fast and efficient.

On any train within Denmark, an adult accompanying a child between 4 and 11 will pay only 50% of the fare.

Senior citizens receive a 33% discount on one-way or round-trip tickets at any time of the day or year. No identification is needed at the time of purchase, although the conductor who checks your ticket might request proof of age if there is any doubt.

For regular passengers, regardless of age, there are reductions for travel to any point in Denmark on Tuesday, Wednesday, Thursday, and Saturday. You can also receive a discount if you plan to return to your point of departure on the same day.

If you're planning to do much rail travel within Denmark, then later visit the other Scandinavian countries, consider purchasing a **Nordturist Pass.** For information, refer to "Air and Rail Passes" in Chapter 1.

BY BUS

Unless you rent a private car, a bus is sometimes your only link to certain villages. In rural Denmark, buses connect with railway terminals.

Round-trip bus tickets are offered at one-way prices for seniors. These reductions are not available, however, on Saturday, Sunday, and during Christmas and Easter. All trips must be more than 20 miles for this reduction to be granted.

BY CAR

RENTALS Avis, Budget, and Hertz all offer well-serviced, well-maintained fleets of cars in Denmark. Depending on the company, you'll need to reserve a car 2 weeks in advance to guarantee the lowest rates. All three of them propose slightly higher rates to clients who reserve at least 48 hours in advance, but who don't fulfill the 2-week advance-rental requirement. Most expensive of all are the rates for walk-in clients who arrange their rentals on location in Denmark without any prior overseas reservation.

Each of the companies builds a certain amount of insurance into its rates that is adequate for most drivers and most accidents. If you have a mishap, however, and didn't purchase additional insurance (known within the car-rental industry as a collision damage waiver), you'll be responsible for between $1,000 and $2,000 worth of collision damage to your car. At Budget, which offered some of the most favorable insurance arrangements, clients who have a mishap and didn't pay for the additional insurance were responsible for the first 5,700 kroner ($986.10) of damage on small and medium-sized cars, and even more on the expensive cars. Renters can waive all financial responsibility by buying an optional insurance policy costing from around 85 kroner ($14.70) per day.

Advance payment with certain types of credit cards sometimes avoids the need for the additional insurance, although these provisions are dependent on the credit-card issuer, not on the car-rental company. Although some readers often use this technique to avoid payment for extra insurance, the legal fine print must be verified individually with the issuers of the credit card.

Budget (tel. toll free 800/527-0700 in the U.S.) has only 14 rental locations within Denmark, compared to 31 at Avis and 26 at Hertz, but at presstime, their prices were a bit lower. With a 14-day advance booking, the company's cheapest car—a two-door Fiat Uno with manual transmission—rented for around $218 per week. As at all the companies, the 25% government tax was extra. Budget's three Copenhagen locations include two branches at the city's airport (tel. 32-52-39-00), and in the center of Copenhagen at Nyropsgade 6 (tel. 33-13-39-00).

Avis maintains two offices in Copenhagen, one in the arrivals hall of the Copenhagen airport and another at Kampmannsgade 1 (tel. 33-15-22-99). Rates for its smallest car, a Ford Fiesta, were very similar to those at Budget.

Hertz (tel. toll free 800/654-3001 in the U.S.) offers a wide selection of cars. With the required advance booking of 14 days, Hertz charged the most expensive rate—1,400 kroner ($242.20), plus 25% tax—of the "big three" for rentals of its least expensive car, an Opel Corsa or Renault Clio. Membership in certain travel clubs or organizations might bring this price down a bit. Hertz's office in central Copenhagen is at Ved Vesterport 3 (tel. 33-12-77-00). Another office is at the Copenhagen airport (tel. 31-50-93-00).

When phoning around for your Danish rental car, don't overlook the services of a small company based in Harrison, N.Y., **Kemwell** (tel. toll free 800/678-0678 in the U.S.). Acting as the North American representative for two Danish-based car companies, Van Wijk and Pitzner, Kemwell usually offers attractive rental deals to North Americans who pay in full at least 10 days prior to departure.

DRIVING RULES To drive in Denmark, you must have a valid driver's license from your home country. You need car registration papers, a Green Card indicating insurance coverage, a national identity sticker for your car, and a red warning triangle in case of breakdown. If you're renting a car, the firm will supply these items.

Follow road signs (the markings are of the international variety) and drive on the right, passing on the left. Always stop for pedestrian crossings. Both driver and passengers are required by law to wear seat belts. Left dipping headlights are illegal in Denmark. For the most part, Danes are careful, considerate drivers. For information on good map sources, see "Fast Facts," at the end of this chapter.

BREAKDOWNS/ASSISTANCE In case of a car breakdown, emergency help and towing in Zealand is provided by **Falck** (tel. 33-14-22-22) in Copenhagen. Use the orange emergency phones along the motorways.

BY FERRY

Ferries connect much of Denmark, providing a vital link between major points like Funen and Zealand. During the summer, it's important to book ahead, particularly if you want to take your car aboard. Bookings on any of the state-owned ferries can be made at the **Central Railroad Station** in Copenhagen or through any of the local offices.

Reservations are not necessary for short crossings: Tickets are purchased on board and service is frequent.

For a day trip from Copenhagen to Sweden, drive to Dragør, south of Copenhagen, and take the ferry to Limhamn, Sweden, 3 miles south of Malmö. Once there, visit Malmö and Helsingborg. Return to Denmark on the car-ferry to Helsingør (site of "Hamlet's Castle") and drive south back to Copenhagen. Round-trip cost for a car, a driver, and up to five passengers is 395 kroner ($68.15) if you return within 1 day.

For additional information on ferries and getting to Sweden, see Chapter 1.

BY BICYCLE

Almost all Danish towns have bicycle rentals—check with the local tourist offices. Youth hostels are close enough to each other (about 12 miles apart) to make a biking trip possible. For those worried about their endurance, you can rent bicycles with auxiliary motors.

DVL Travel in Copenhagen runs 6 to 10 "ready-made" holiday bicycle excursions. Prices depend on whether you stay at youth hostels or at low-cost inns or hotels. All age groups are accepted (the oldest participant so far has been 78). Tours run from 3 to 9 days, and many offer a choice of full or half board. For information, you can contact the **Danish Tourist Board,** 655 Third Ave., New York, NY 10017 (tel. 212/949-2333).

Bicycles can be rented cheaply at train stations in North Zealand and returned at another station. For information on the **Take-the-Train, Rent-a-Bike** route, contact the tourist information office or the train station. The cost is 50 kroner ($8.70) a day.

SUGGESTED ITINERARIES

IF YOU HAVE 1 WEEK

Days 1-3: Spend your first 3 days in Copenhagen. After spending the first day recovering from the flight, have dinner at the Tivoli (in summer) or at Nyhaun (in winter). Spend the morning of the second day taking one of our walking tours (see Chapter 7); then (if it's summer) spend the afternoon wandering through Tivoli Gardens, listening to the free music. Devote Day 3 to more serious sightseeing, including visits to Christiansborg Palace and the Ny Carlsberg Glyptotek.

Day 4: Leave Copenhagen and head north, stopping over at the modern art museum, Louisiana, before heading to Helsingør, site of Kronborg Castle of Hamlet fame. Either spend the night in Helsingør or return to Copenhagen.

Day 5: Journey to Odense on the island of Funen, birthplace of Hans Christian Andersen. Spend the rest of the day and evening exploring its many attractions. What you didn't get done on Day 5 you can see the next morning.

Day 6: Stop in Roskilde, to see its cathedral and Viking Ship Museum. Return to Copenhagen and spend the night.

Day 7: Try another walking tour, and schedule interior visits to Rosenborg Castle and, if you have time, the National Museum. Return to the Tivoli for a farewell drink.

IF YOU HAVE 2 WEEKS

Day 1: Recover from jet lag and have dinner at the Tivoli (in summer) or at Scala (a restaurant complex across from Tivoli) if it's off-season.

Day 2: In the morning, take our first walking tour (see Chapter 7). Spend the afternoon wandering around Tivoli Gardens (in summer).

Day 3: Take another walking tour and visit Christiansborg Palace and Ny Carlsberg Glyptotek.

Day 4: Head north from Copenhagen, visit the modern art museum, Louisiana, and have lunch at Helsingør, site of Kronborg Castle of Hamlet fame. Spend the night in Helsingør.

Day 5: Explore North Zealand, with visits to the royal palace at Fredensborg and the 17th-century Frederiksborg Castle at Hillerød. Spend the night in Helsingør.

Day 6: Return to Copenhagen and take another walking tour. Visit Rosenborg Castle and the National Museum.

Day 7: Still in Copenhagen, explore the other attractions of Zealand, journeying outside the capital to the open-air museum, Frilandsmuseet. Head to Roskilde for lunch, visiting the cathedral, the Viking Ship Museum, and the Iron Age Village at Lejre.

Day 8: Head south from Copenhagen to explore South Zealand. Visit the old market town of Køge, Vallø Castle, and Selso Slot. Spend the night in a typical inn on Zealand.

Day 9: Head west, crossing mid-Zealand. At Korsør, take a ferry to Nyborg. Visit Nyborg Castle before driving to Odense to explore the city of Hans Christian Andersen. Stop overnight in Odense.

Day 10: Spend time exploring more of Odense. Then visit the Viking ship at Ladby and Egeskov Castle outside Odense.

Day 11: Drive south from Odense to Svendborg. Visit the nearby islands of Thurø and Tåsinge.

Day 12: From Svendborg, board a ferry (make a reservation) and head for the island of Aerø. Spend the night in the capital, Aerøskøbing, or at an island inn.

Day 13: Leave Aerø and return to Svendborg by ferry. Drive north toward Odense along Route 9 until you connect with the E20 west, the highway that will take you into Jutland. In Jutland, take Route 32 at the junction with the E20 to Ribe. Spend the night in Ribe.

Day 14: Leave Ribe in the morning and head for Silkeborg to visit Sky Mountain. Take a ride on a paddle steamer on Silkeborg Lakes. Visit the Silkeborg Museum. From Silkeborg, drive to Århus where you can explore the Old Town. Visit also Århus's Tivoli amusement park. Spend the night.

IF YOU HAVE 3 WEEKS

Days 1–12: Follow the first 12 days of the above itinerary.

Day 13: Leave Aerø in the morning and return by ferry to Svendborg. From Svendborg, take Route 44 west to Fåborg to explore the largely bucolic southwestern corner of the island.

Day 14: From Fåborg, take Route 43 north to Odense and connect with the express highway, E20, heading west to Jutland. Drive to Jelling, the seat of the 10th-century kings of Denmark. Accommodations are limited in Jelling, so stay overnight in Vejle, a short drive southeast of Jelling.

Day 15: From Jelling, take Routes E45 and 32 cross country to Ribe, of stork's-nest fame. Explore its attractions, including the cathedral and the smallest house in Denmark. Spend the night.

Day 16: Drive northwest from Ribe to Esbjerg. Take the 20-minute ferry ride to Fanø, an island of heather-covered moors and windswept sand dunes. Overnight at one of the *kros* (inns) on the island.

Day 17: From Fanø, take the return ferry to Esbjerg and head north along various routes to Silkeborg. Visit Sky Mountain and take a ride on a paddleboat steamer on Silkeborg Lakes. Also visit the Silkeborg Museum. Overnight in Silkeborg.

Day 18: From Silkeborg, drive east to Århus. Explore its many attractions, including Den Gamle By (the Old Town). Overnight in Århus.

Day 19: Leave Århus and drive to Ebeltoft, 32 miles northeast. Continue on to Randers for the night, or for more atmosphere, spend the night at Hvidsten Kro, on the outskirts of Hvidsten, lying between Randers and Mariager.

Day 20: Head north to Aalborg, where you can visit Lindholm Hoje, the largest Scandinavian burial site of the Viking period, the Aalborg Zoo, and yet another Tivoli.

Day 21: After Aalborg, spend the rest of the day exploring North Jutland, heading to either Frederikshavn, Hirtshals, or Skagen for an overnight stop. Skagen is the far northern tip of Jutland. At Frederikshavn you can take a car-ferry to Oslo to begin exploring Norway, or a car-ferry to Gothenburg if you're ready for Sweden.

 FAST **DENMARK**

American Express Offices in Copenhagen are at Amagertorv 18 (tel.

33-12-23-01), open Monday through Friday from 9am to 5pm (April to October, also on Saturday from 9am to noon).

Business Hours Most **banks** in Denmark are open Monday through Friday from 9:30am to 4pm (on Thursday to 6pm), but outside Copenhagen banking hours vary. **Stores** are generally open Monday through Thursday from 9am to 5:30pm, on Friday from 9am to 7 or 8pm, and on Saturday from noon to 2pm; most are closed Sunday.

Camera and Film Film is so expensive that I suggest you bring what you'll need. Film processing is also expensive, so wait until you're home. There are no special restrictions on taking photographs, except in certain museums (signs are generally posted). When in doubt, ask.

Customs Nearly all items that can safely be viewed as "personal" are allowed in duty-free. Tobacco is limited: you can bring in either 400 cigarettes or 100 cigars. You can also bring in 1½ liters (a standard bottle) of spirits or 2 liters of strong wine, depending on whether you are coming into Denmark from an EC or non-EC country. There are no restrictions on the import of currency into Denmark. Residents of Denmark can take out of the country only 5,000 kroner, but nonresidents can take a higher amount if they prove that the Danish kroner were brought in with them or obtained by conversion of foreign currency they imported.

Upon leaving Denmark, U.S. citizens who have been outside their home country for 48 hours or more are allowed to take home $400 worth of merchandise duty free—if they have claimed no similar exemption within the past 30 days. If you make purchases in Denmark, keep your receipts.

Dentists For a dentist in Copenhagen, see "Fast Facts" in Chapter 4. If you need emergency dental service outside Copenhagen, ask your hotel or host to phone **Falck** (tel. 33-14-22-22) for information about service in your area.

Doctors Most areas have doctors on duty 24 hours a day on Saturday, Sunday, and holidays; weekday emergency hours are 4pm to 7:30am. Every doctor speaks English.

Driving Rules See "Getting Around," above, in this chapter.

Drug Laws There are severe penalties in Denmark for possession, use, purchase, sale, or manufacturing of drugs. The quantity of the controlled substance is more important than the actual type of substance someone might possess. Danish police are particularly strict with any cases involving sales of drugs to children.

Drugstores They're known as *apoteker* in Danish, and are open Monday through Thursday from 9am to 5:30pm, on Friday from 9am to 7pm, and on Saturday from 9am to 1pm.

Electricity Voltage is generally 220 volts AC, 50 to 60 cycles, but in many camping sites 110-volt power plugs are also available. Adapters and transformers may be purchased in Denmark. It's always best to check at your hotel desk before using any electrical outlet.

Embassies In Copenhagen, the **U.S. Embassy** is at Dag Hammarsjölds Allé 24, DK-2100 København Ø (tel. 31-42-31-44); the **British Embassy,** at Kastelsvej 36-40, DK-2100 København Ø (tel. 31-26-46-00); the **Canadian Embassy,** at Kristen Berniskowsgade I, DK-1105 København K (tel. 33-12-22-99); and the **Australian Embassy,** at Kristianiagade 21, DK-2100 København (tel. 31-26-22-44).

Emergencies Dial **112** for the **fire department,** the **police,** an **ambulance,** or to report a **sea or air accident.** Emergency calls from public telephone kiosks are free (no coins).

Etiquette *God dag* (good day) is said to everyone. *Tak* means "thanks." You should bring flowers (never white ones) if invited to a private home for dinner. Shaking hands is virtually a ritual when you meet someone and take leave. Both men and women shake hands.

Holidays See "When to Go," above, in this chapter.

Language Danish is the national tongue. English is commonly spoken, especially among young people. You should have few, if any, language barriers. For the best phrase book, purchase a copy of *Danish for Travellers* published by Berlitz.

Laundry For listings of laundries, see the individual city chapters.

Liquor Laws   To consume alcohol in Danish bars, restaurants, or cafés, a client must be 18 or older. However, there are no age limits imposed upon children under 18 for either drinking at home or drinking, for example, from a bottle in a public park. Danish police tend to be lenient unless drinkers become raucous or uncontrollable. This policy changes abruptly as soon as the driver of a vehicle is apprehended while intoxicated. It is strictly illegal to drive with a blood/alcohol ratio of 0.8 or more. This could be produced by two drinks. If the ratio is 1.5, motorists will pay a serious fine. If the blood/alcohol ratio is more than 1.5, drivers can lose their license. If the ratio is 2.0 or more, a prison term of at least 14 days might follow. Such a ratio is usually produced by six to seven drinks.

Mail   In general **post offices** are open Monday through Friday from 9 or 10am to 5 or 6pm and on Saturday from 9am to noon; closed Sunday. It costs 4.75 kroner (90¢) to send a regular letter by air or surface mail to the United States or Canada and takes from 5 to 8 days to arrive. The rate for an ordinary postcard by air or surface is 3.75 kroner (60¢). The purchasing of **stamps** depends on the town, the circumstances, and the nearness of the post office. You might find stamps for sale at local gas stations or a butcher shop. All **mailboxes** are painted red and contain an embossed crown and trumpet of the Danish Postal Society. To mail a parcel, you must go to the post office.

Maps   The best map for touring Denmark is part of the series published by Hallwag. It can be purchased at all major bookstores in Copenhagen, including the most centrally located one, **Boghallen,** Rådhuspladsen 37 (tel. 33-11-85-11), in the Town Hall Square.

Newspapers and Magazines   English-language newspapers are sold at all major news kiosks in Copenhagen, but are much harder to come by in the provinces. London papers are flown in for early-morning deliveries, but you may find the *International Herald Tribune* more interesting. Pick up a copy of the booklet *Copenhagen This Week,* printed in English, which contains useful information.

Pets   A dog arriving from a rabies-free country is generally admitted if nothing is found wrong with it. Special permits are required to bring in animals other than dogs or cats. Many Danish hotels allow visitors to bring in their dogs, providing the dog is quiet and safe to be around. Fines can be issued if your dog fouls the pavement. Take the animal to one of the special "dog toilets" found in city parks.

Police   Dial **112** for police assistance.

Radio and TV   There are no English-language radio or TV stations broadcasting from Denmark. Only radios and TVs with satellite reception can receive a cornucopia of signals from countries such as Britain. News programs in English are broadcast Monday through Saturday at 8:30am on Radio Denmark, 93.85 MHz. Radio 1 (on 90.8 MHz VHF) features news and classical music. Channels 2 and 3 (96.5/93.9 MHz) include some entertainment, broadcast lighter news items, and offer light music. Most TV stations transmit from 7:30 to 11:30pm. Most films (many American ones) are shown in their original languages, with Danish subtitles.

Restrooms   All big plazas, such as Town Hall Square in Copenhagen, have public lavatories. In small towns and villages, head for the marketplace. Hygienic standards are usually adequate. Sometimes both men and women patronize the same toilets. Otherwise, men's rooms are marked HERRER or H, and women's rooms are marked DAMER or D.

Safety   Whenever you're traveling in an unfamiliar city or country, stay alert. Be aware of your immediate surroundings. Wear a moneybelt and don't sling your camera or purse over your shoulder; wear the strap diagonally across your body. This will minimize the possibility of your becoming a victim of crime. Every society has its criminals, but it's your responsibility to be alert.

Taxes   Denmark imposes a 25% VAT (value-added tax) on goods and services. In Denmark it is known as MOMS (pronounced "mumps"). Special tax-free exports are possible, and many stores will mail goods home to you, circumventing Moms. If you want to take your purchases with you, look for shops displaying DANISH TAX-FREE SHOPPING notices. Such shops offer tourists tax refunds for personal export. This refund applies to purchases of 600 kroner ($103.80) and up for U.S. and Canadian visitors. Your tax-free invoice must be stamped by Danish Customs when you leave the country. You can receive your refund at Copenhagen's Kastrup International Airport when you depart. If you depart by land or by sea, you can receive your refund by mail. Requests for refunds are to be sent by mail to Danish Tax-Free Shopping A/S, H.J. Holstvej 5A, DK-2605 Brøndby, Denmark. You will be reimbursed by check, cash, or credit-card credit in the currency you wish.

In order for the refund to apply, the 600 kroner must be spent in one store, but not necessarily at the same time. Some major department stores allow purchases to be made over several days or even weeks, at the end of which receipts will be tallied. Service and handling fees are deducted from the total, so actual refunds come to about 18%. Information on this program is available from the Danish Tourist Board (see "Information, Documents, and Money" in Chapter 1).

A 25% MOMS is included in your hotel and restaurant bills, service charges, and entrance fees, as well as on repair of foreign-registered cars. No refunds are possible on these items.

Telephone, Telex, and Fax Danish phones are fully automatic. Dial the eight-digit number. There are no city area codes. At public telephone booths, use two 50-øre coins or a 1-krone or 5-krone coin only. Don't insert coins until your party answers. You can make more than one call on the same payment if your time hasn't run out. Remember that it can be expensive to telephone from your hotel room. Emergency calls are free. The country code for Denmark is 45. This 2-digit number will precede any call which is intended for Denmark dialed from another country.

Most hotels in Denmark will send a fax or telex for you and put the charge on your bill.

In Copenhagen, to make phone calls or send faxes or telexes, go to the Telecommunications Center at the Central Railroad Station (tel. 33-14-20-00), open Monday through Friday from 8am to 10pm, on Saturday from 9am to 4pm, and on Sunday from 10am to 5pm.

Time Denmark operates on central European time—1 hour ahead of Greenwich mean time and 6 hours ahead of eastern standard time. Daylight saving time is observed from the end of March to the end of September.

Tipping Tips are expected on very few occasions, and even then you should give only 1 or 2 kroner. Porters charge according to fixed prices, and neither hairdressers/barbers nor movie ushers are usually tipped. Know that hotels, restaurants, and even taxis impose a 15% service charge in the rates they quote; service is "built into" the system. Not only that, but with the 25% MOMS, you'll end up paying an additional 37% for some services.

Only special services should be rewarded separately. Some Danes, in fact, are insulted if you offer them a tip.

Water Tap water is safe to drink throughout Denmark.

INTRODUCING COPENHAGEN

Copenhagen, the capital of Denmark, came from the word *københavn,* meaning "merchants' harbor." It grew in size and importance because of its position on the Øresund (The Sound), the body of water between Denmark and Sweden, guarding the entrance to the Baltic. From its humble beginnings, Copenhagen has become the largest city in Scandinavia, home to 1½ million people. It is the seat of the oldest kingdom in the world.

Over the centuries, Copenhagen suffered more than its share of disasters. In the 17th century the Swedes repeatedly besieged it and in the 18th century it fell to the plague and two devastating fires. The British attacked twice in the Napoleonic Wars in the early 1800s. Its last major disaster was in 1940 when the Nazis overpowered the little country and held it in its grip until 1945 when the British army moved in again, this time as liberators.

Copenhagen is a city with much charm, as reflected in its canals, narrow streets, and old houses. Its most famous resident was H. C. Andersen, whose memory still lives on in the city. Copenhagen's other world-renowned former citizen, Søren Kierkegaard, also used to take a morning constitutional in the city, plotting his next essay, all of which in time would make him the father of existentialism.

Copenhagen still retains some of the characteristics of a village. If you forget the suburbs, you can cover most of the central belt on foot, making it a great tourist spot. It's almost as if the city was designed for pedestrians, as reflected by its Strøget (strolling street), the longest and oldest walking street in Europe.

1. ORIENTATION

ARRIVING

BY PLANE   When you arrive at **Kastrup Airport** (tel. 31-50-93-33) outside Copenhagen, you can cut costs by taking an SAS coach into the city terminal. The SAS bus fare is 26 kroner ($4.50). A taxi to the city center will cost around 125 kroner ($21.60). Even cheaper is local bus no. 32, which leaves from the international arrivals terminal every 15 or 20 minutes for the Town Hall Square in central Copenhagen and costs only 12 kroner ($2.10). The same ticket will allow you to transfer to another city bus route, provided you do so within 1 hour after you purchased your initial ticket at the airport.

BY TRAIN   Trains arrive at the **Hoved banegård** (Central Railroad Station), in the very center of Copenhagen, near the Tivoli and the Rådhuspladsen. The station operates a room-service desk and a luggage-checking service. You can also exchange

WHAT'S SPECIAL ABOUT COPENHAGEN

Castles & Palaces

☐ Christiansborg Palace, center of political power in Denmark.

☐ Rosenborg Castle, Christian IV's Renaissance castle housing the treasures of the royal family.

☐ Amalienborg Palace, residence of the Danish royal family since 1794. Watch the changing of the guard.

Museums

☐ Open-air Museum (Frilandsmuseet), old houses on 86 acres that re-create Denmark's past.

☐ Ny Carlsberg Glyptotek, a great art museum of Scandinavia—modern works by the beer people.

☐ National Museum, storehouse of Danish treasures, one of the oldest and largest museums in the world.

☐ Thorvaldsen's Museum, housing Bertel Thorvaldsen's (1770–1884) collection, the biggest in neoclassical sculpture.

Parks/Gardens

☐ The Tivoli Gardens, 20 acres of fun and beauty in the heart of Copenhagen.

Buildings

☐ Round Tower, a 17th-century observatory with panoramic views.

☐ Rådhus (Town Hall), where you can climb up for an impressive view; also Jen Olsen's World Clock.

For the Kids

☐ Danish Toy Museum, toys from all over the world for all ages.

☐ Benneweis Circus, the last grand-style circus of Europe.

Special Events/Festivals

☐ Copenhagen Jazz Festival, the jazz mecca of northern Europe (July 6–13).

☐ Copenhagen Summer Festival, young Danish and foreign singers and musicians performing (July to mid-Aug).

money at the Bank Handelsbanken, which is open daily in summer from 7am to 10pm (closes at 9pm in winter). It even has a summer-only free shower at the Interrail Center, open daily from 6am to 11pm.

From the Central Railroad Station, you can connect with **S-tog,** the local subway system, with trains departing from platforms within the terminus itself. Ask at the information desk near Tracks 5 and 6 as to which train you should board to reach your destination.

For rail information, call 33-14-17-01.

BY BUS   Buses from Zealand or elsewhere in Denmark also pull into the Central Railroad Station (see above for services available there).

BY CAR   If you're driving from Germany, a car-ferry will take you from Travemünde to Gedser in southern Denmark. From Gedser, get on the E55 north, an express highway that will take you to the southern outskirts of Copenhagen. If you're coming from Sweden, and crossing at Helsingborg, you will land on the Danish side at Helsingør. From there take express highway E55 south to the northern outskirts of Copenhagen.

BY FERRY   Most ferryboats land at Havnegade at the end of the south side of Nyhavn, a short walk to the center of Copenhagen. Taxis also wait here for ferry arrivals. Most arrivals are from Malmö, Sweden; ferries from continental Europe usually land in South Zealand.

TOURIST INFORMATION

The **Copenhagen Tourist Information Center,** Bernstorffsgade 1 (tel. 33-11-13-25), across from the Tivoli's main entrance, dispenses information. In May it is open Monday through Friday from 9am to 5pm and on Saturday from 9am to 2pm. On Sunday and holidays, hours are 9am to 1pm. From June 1 to September 15, hours are daily from 9am to 6pm. From September 16 through April 30, hours are Monday through Friday from 9am to 5pm and on Saturday from 9am to noon.

CITY LAYOUT

MAIN ARTERIES & STREETS

The heart of Old Copenhagen is a maze of pedestrian streets, formed by Nørreport Station to the north, Town Hall Square (Rådhuspladsen) to the west, and Kongens Nytorv to the east. One continuous pedestrian route, **Strøget,** the world's longest pedestrian street, goes east from Town Hall Square to Kongens Nytorv, and is made up of five streets: Frederiksberggade, Nygade, Vimmelskaftet, Amagertorv, and Østergade. Strøget is lined with shops, bars, restaurants, and in summer sidewalk cafés. **Pistolstraede** is a maze of galleries, restaurants, and boutiques, all housed in restored 18th-century buildings.

    Fiolstraede (Violet Street), a dignified street with antiques shops and bookshops, cuts through the university (Latin Quarter). If you turn into Rosengaarden at the top of Fiolstraede, you will come to **Kultorvet** (Coal Square) just before you reach Nørreport Station. Here you join the third main pedestrian street, **Købmagergade** (Butcher Street), which winds around and finally meets Strøget on Amagertorv.

    At the end of Strøget you approach **Kongens Nytorv** (King's Square). This is the site of the Royal Theater and Magasin, the latter the largest department store in Copenhagen. This will put you at the beginning of **Nyhavn,** the former seamen's quarter that has been gentrified into an upmarket area of expensive restaurants, apartments, cafés, and boutiques.

    The government of Denmark is centered on the small island of **Slotsholmen,** which is connected to the center by eight different bridges. Several museums, notably Christiansborg Castle, are found here.

    The center of Copenhagen is **Rådhuspladsen** (Town Hall Square). From here it is a short walk to the Tivoli Gardens, the major attraction of Copenhagen, and the Central Railroad Station, the main railroad and subway terminus. The wide boulevard, **Vesterbrogade,** passes by Tivoli until it reaches the Central Railroad Station. Another major boulevard is named after Denmark's most famous writer, **H. C. Andersens Boulevard,** running along Rådhuspladsen and the Tivoli Gardens.

FINDING AN ADDRESS

All even numbers are on one side of the street, and on the opposite side are the alternating odd numbers. Buildings are listed in numerical order, but will often insert A, B, or C after the street number.

NEIGHBORHOODS IN BRIEF

    Tivoli Gardens In the heart of Copenhagen, on the south side of Rådhuspladsen, these amusement gardens were built on the site of former fortifications. A total of 160,000 flowers and 110,000 electric lightbulbs brighten the gardens. Built in 1843, Tivoli contains a collection of restaurants, dance halls, theaters, beer gardens, and lakes.

    Strøget This is the longest pedestrians-only street in Europe, beginning at Rådhuspladsen. The most interesting parts are Gammeltorv and Nytorv, "old" and "new" squares, lying on either side of Strøget. They are the site of fruit and vegetable markets, and stalls selling bric-a-brac and handmade jewelry. The word "Strøget" doesn't appear on any maps. Instead, Strøget encompasses five streets: Frederiksberggade, Nygade, Vimmelskaftet, Amagertorv, and Østergade.

Nyhavn   This is the harbor area, for years the haunt of sailors looking for tattoos and other diversions. Nowadays, it's one of the most elegant sections of the city, site of the deluxe Angleterre Hotel and many prestigious restaurants. The Royal Theater stands on Kongens Nytorv.

Indre By   This is the name given to the Old Town, heart of Copenhagen. Once filled with many monasteries, it is a maze of old streets, alleyways, and squares. If you cross Gammeltorv and Nørregade you will be in the university area, nicknamed the Latin Quarter, as in Paris. The Vor Frue Kirke (Cathedral of Copenhagen) is found here, as is Rudetårnet (Round Tower).

Slotsholmen   This island, site of Christiansborg Palace, was where Bishop Absalon built the first fortress in the city in 1167. Today it is the seat of the Danish parliament and the site of Thorvaldsen's Museum, among others. Slotsholmen is linked to Indre by bridges. You can also visit the Royal Library, the Theater Museum, and the Royal Stables. The 17th-century Børsen (stock exchange) is also here.

Christianshavn   This was the "new town" ordered by master builder Christian IV in the early 1500s. The town was originally constructed to house workers in the shipbuilding industry. Visitors come here today mainly to see the Danish Film Museum on Store Søndervoldstraede, and Vors Frelsers Kirke, on the corner of Prinsessegade and Skt. Annaegade. Visitors can climb the spire of this old church for a panoramic view.

Christiania   Within walking distance of Vor Frelsers Kirke at Christianshavn is this offbeat district, once a barracks for soldiers. Then many young and homeless people moved in without the city's permission proclaiming that Christiania was a "free city." It has been a controversial place ever since. Regrettably, this area, founded on idealism, also became a shelter for criminals. Craftshops and restaurants exist here; merchandise and food are fairly cheap, because the residents refuse to pay Denmark's crippling 25% tax.

Dragør   Except for the Tivoli, this seems to be everybody's favorite part of Copenhagen. It is especially recommended if you have time to see only Copenhagen and not the countryside. Dragør is a fishing village south of the city, with origins in the 16th century. Walk its cobblestone streets and enjoy its 65 old, red-roofed houses, designated national landmarks.

2. GETTING AROUND

Copenhagen is a walker's paradise, neat and compact. Many of the major sightseeing attractions are within a short distance of each other.

BY PUBLIC TRANSPORTATION

A joint zone fare system includes Copenhagen Transport buses and State Railway and S-tog trains in Copenhagen and North Zealand, plus some private railway routes in a

IMPRESSIONS

What strikes me now most as regards Denmark is the charm, beauty, and independence of the women.
—ARNOLD BENNETT, JOURNAL, 1913

The Danes that drench their cares in wine.
—BEN JONSON, ODE ALLEGORICAL, 1603

25-mile radius of the capital, enabling you to transfer from train to bus and vice versa with the same ticket.

A *grundbillet* (basic ticket) for both buses and trains costs 8 kroner ($1.40). You can buy 11 tickets for 80 kroner ($13.80), allowing nine separate journeys on buses or trains in three fare zones within 1 hour.

DISCOUNT PASSES The Copenhagen Card entitles you to free and unlimited travel by bus and rail throughout the metropolitan area (including North Zealand), 25% to 50% discounts on crossings to and from Sweden, and free admission to many sights and museums. The card is available for 1, 2, or 3 days and costs 105 kroner ($18.20), 170 kroner ($29.40), and 215 kroner ($37.20), respectively. Children ages 5 to 11 are given a 50% discount. For more information, contact the Copenhagen Tourist Information Center (see above).

Students who have an **International Student Identity Card** can get a number of travel breaks in Copenhagen including up to 35% discount on domestic rail travel. A card can be purchased in the United States at any Council Travel office. For the office nearest you, call toll free 800/GET-ANID.

For information about low-cost train, ferry, and plane trips, go to **Dis Rejser** (Students' International Committee), Skindergade 28 (tel. 33-11-00-44), in Copenhagen.

Discount tickets or cards are stamped and punched when they are placed face-up in automatic machines at the front of buses or in yellow machines on railway platforms.

Eurailpasses and Nordturist Pass tickets are accepted on local trains in Copenhagen.

BY BUS Copenhagen's well-maintained buses are the least expensive method of getting around. Most buses leave from Rådhuspladsen. A basic ticket allows 1 hour of travel and unlimited transfers within the zone where you started your trip. For information, call 31-95-17-01.

BY S-TOG [SUBWAY] The S-tog connects heartland Copenhagen with its suburbs. Tickets work under the same conditions as on the buses (see above). You can transfer from a bus line to an S-train on the same ticket. Eurailpass holders generally ride free. For more information, call 33-14-17-01 at any time.

BY TAXI

Watch for the FRI (free) sign or green light to hail a taxi. Be sure the taxis are metered. **TAXA** (tel. 31-35-35-35) operates the largest fleet of cabs. Tips are included in the meter price: 14 kroner ($2.40) at the drop of the flag and 7.20 kroner ($1.20) per kilometer thereafter, Monday through Friday from 6am to 6pm. From 6pm to 6am, and all day and night on Saturday and Sunday, the cost is 9.6 kroner ($1.70) per kilometer. Basic drop-of-the-flag costs remain the same, however. The average ride within the city limits costs 35 kroner to 70 kroner ($6.10 to $12.10). Drivers often speak English.

BY CAR

Copenhagen is a walking city. It is best to park your car in a city parking lot and pick it up when you're ready to explore the environs. Most car parks are open from 6 or 8am to 8pm (some until midnight). Many lots close Saturday afternoon and Sunday when stores shut down. The average rate is 15 kroner ($2.60) per hour or 45 to 75 kroner ($7.80 to $13) per 24 hours. Some centrally located car parks include **Dagmarhus Garager,** H. C. Andersens Blvd. 12 (tel. 33-13-90-06), and **Statoil,** Dronningens Tvaergade 4 (tel. 33-14-90-06).

For information on car rentals, see "Getting Around," in Chapter 3.

BY BICYCLE

To cut down on pollution caused by cars, Copenhagen operates a program called **Bycyklen** (City-Bike) which lets you borrow a bike by inserting a 20-kroner ($3.50) coin in one of hundreds of special bike racks installed all over the city. You can return the bike at any rack and your coin will be refunded! The bikes are painted a distinctive white to make them difficult to steal. If one rides one outside the city limits, police have little trouble spotting them as stolen. Repair people inspect the racks frequently to make sure the bikes are kept in good condition. More information about this program is available from Bycyklen Aps, 63E Nyhavn (tel. 33-13-28-37).

FAST
COPENHAGEN

Here's some helpful information pertaining only to Copenhagen and its suburbs. For general information about such matters, see "Fast Facts: Denmark" in Chapter 3.

American Express   Offices are at Amagertorv 18 (tel. 33-12-23-01), open Monday through Friday from 9am to 5pm (April to October, also on Saturday from 9am to noon).

Area Code   The country code for Denmark is 45. There are no city area codes. Each telephone number dialed within Denmark has 8 digits.

Babysitters   Try **Students** (tel. 31-22-96-96), open Monday through Thursday from 7 to 9am and 3 to 6pm, and on Saturday from 3 to 5pm. The cost is 25 kroner ($4.30) per hour, plus a 25 kroner booking fee.

Bookstores   One of the best and most centrally located is **Boghallen,** Rådhuspladsen 37 (tel. 33-11-85-11), in the Town Hall Square.

Business Hours   Most **banks** are open Monday through Friday from 9:30am to 4pm (on Thursday to 6pm). **Stores** are generally open Monday through Thursday from 9am to 5:30pm, on Friday from 9am to 7 or 8pm, and on Saturday from 9am to 2pm; most are closed Sunday. **Offices** are open Monday through Friday from 9 or 10am to 4 or 5pm.

Car Rentals   See "Getting Around" in Chapter 3.

Climate   See "When to Go" in Chapter 3.

Currency   See "Information, Documents, and Money" in Chapter 1.

Currency Exchange   Banks are generally your best bet. When banks are closed, you can exchange money at the Central Railroad Station kiosk, open daily from 7am to 10pm. The Bank of Tivoli is open May to mid-September, daily from noon to 11pm.

Dentist   During regular business hours, ask your hotel to call the nearest English-speaking dentist. For emergency dental treatment, go to **Tandlaegevagten,** Oslo Plads 14 (tel. 31-38-02-51), near Østerport Station and the U.S. Embassy. It's open Monday through Friday from 8 to 9:30pm and on Saturday, Sunday, and holidays from 10am to noon and 8 to 9:30pm. Be prepared to pay in cash.

Doctor   Dial 32-84-00-41 for house calls by physicians 24 hours a day. The doctor's fee is payable in cash. Virtually every doctor speaks English.

Drugstores   An *apoteker* (drugstore) open 24 hours a day in central Copenhagen is **Steno Apotek,** Vesterbrogade 6C (tel. 31-14-82-66).

Embassies and Consulates   See "Fast Facts: Denmark" in Chapter 3.

Emergencies   Dial **112** to report a fire or to call the police or an ambulance. State your phone number and address. Emergency calls from public telephones are free.

Eyeglasses   The largest and oldest optical chain in Denmark is **Synoptik,** Købmagergade 22 (tel. 33-15-05-38), with 80 other branches throughout Denmark. Most glasses can be replaced in 2 or 3 hours. Bifocals can take up to 3 days. They also specialize in soft and hard contact lenses, with hundreds of different types in stock.

Hairdresser   **Stuhr Coiffeur,** Scala, Axeltorv 2 (tel. 33-15-11-44), is located on the second floor of the shopping complex across from the Tivoli. Both men and women are received.

Holidays   See "When to Go" in Chapter 3.

Hospitals   The emergency room at **Kommunehospitalet,** Øster Farimagsgade 5 (tel. 31-15-85-00), is open 24 hours a day.

Information   See "Tourist Information," in "Orientation," in this chapter.

Laundry and Dry Cleaning Self-service laundries are all over Copenhagen—ask at your hotel for the one nearest you. A centrally located one is **Vask-Møntvask,** Holbergsgade 9, near the Royal Palace, open daily from 6am to 10pm. Another is **Møntvask,** Istegade 45, open daily from 7am to 9pm.

Your dry-cleaning needs can be taken care of at **Dry Cleaning,** Vester Farimagsgade 3 (tel. 33-12-45-45), a block from the Central Railroad Station. It's open Monday through Saturday from 8am to 6pm.

Libraries The best-stocked one is the **University of Copenhagen Library,** Fiolstraede 1, (tel. 33-13-08-75), near Round Tower, which has a large inventory of English-language publications.

Liquor Laws See "Fast Facts: Denmark" in Chapter 3.

Lost Property The **Lost & Found Property Office** at Slotsherrensvej 113, 2720 Vanløse (tel. 31-74-88-22), is open Monday through Friday from 9am to 4pm (until 5pm on Thursday). For property lost on buses phone 36-45-45-45; on trains, 36-44-20-10. These numbers can be called Monday through Friday only from 10am to 5pm.

Luggage Storage and Lockers Luggage can be stored in rental lockers at the Central Railroad Station. Lockers are accessible from 5:30am to 1am daily. Depending on the locker's size, daily rental fees range from 10 to 20 kroner ($1.70 to $3.50).

Newspapers Foreign newspapers, particularly the *International Herald Tribune* and *USA Today,* are available at the Central Railroad Station in front of the Palladium movie theater on Vesterbrogade, in Strøget, and at newsstands of the big hotels.

Photographic Needs In the Scala shopping and restaurant complex, **Express Photo,** Axeltorv 2 (tel. 33-15-27-80), will develop film in about an hour. It's open on Monday from 10am to 7pm, Tuesday through Thursday from 10am to 6pm, on Friday from 10am to 8pm, and on Saturday from 10am to 2pm.

Police In an emergency, dial **112.** For other matters, go to the **police station** at Nyrosgade 20 (tel. 33-91-14-48).

Post Office For information about the Copenhagen post office, phone 33-33-89-00, ext. 6101; otherwise, one cannot phone post offices. The **main post office,** where your general delivery (poste restante) letters can be picked up, is at Tietgensgade 39, DK-1704 København V (tel. 33-33-89-00). The post office at the Central Railroad Station is open Monday through Friday from 8am to 10pm, on Saturday from 9am to 4pm, and on Sunday from 10am to 5pm.

Radio See "Fast Facts: Denmark" in Chapter 3.

Religious Services St. Ansgar's Roman Catholic Church, Bredgade 64 (tel. 33-13-37-62); the English Church of St. Alban's (Anglo-Episcopalian) on Langelinie (tel. 31-62-77-36); the American Church (Protestant and interdenominational) at the U.S. Embassy, Dag Hammarskjølds Allé 24 (tel. 31-42-31-44); and the synagogue at Krystalgade 12 (tel. 33-12-88-68). The International Church of Copenhagen (affiliated with the American Lutheran church) holds services at the Vartov Church, Farvergade 27 (tel. 31-62-47-85), across from the Town Hall.

Restrooms Some public toilets can be found at the Rådhuspladsen (Town Hall'Square), the Central Railroad Station, and at all terminals. Look for the markings TOILETTER, WC, DAMER (women), or HERRER (men). There is no charge.

Safety Stay alert. Be aware of your immediate surroundings. Wear a moneybelt and don't sling your camera or purse across your shoulder; wear the strap diagonally across your body.

Shoe Repair Go to **Magasin,** Kongens Nytorv 13 (tel. 33-11-44-33), a leading Denmark department store, which has a great shoe-repair franchise in its basement, **Mister Minit.**

Taxes Throughout Denmark, you'll come across MOMS on your bills, a government-imposed value-added tax of 25%. It's included in hotel and restaurant bills, service charges, entrance fees, and in repair of foreign-registered cars. No refunds are given on these items. For more information, see "Savvy Shopping" in Chapter 7.

Taxi See "Getting Around" in this chapter.

Telegrams and Telex   The **main telegraph office** is at Købmagergade 37 (tel. 33-32-12-12). To send a telegram by phone, dial 0022. There are telex booths at the telegraph office, Købmagergade 37.

Telephone   For information on making telephone calls in Copenhagen, see "Fast Facts: Denmark" in Chapter 3. Telephone kiosks with operator assistance can be found at the post office in the Central Railroad Station and at the main telegraph office.

Television   See "Fast Facts: Denmark" in Chapter 3.

Tourist Information   See "Orientation" in this chapter.

Transit Information   Day or night, phone 31-95-17-01 for bus information or 33-14-17-01 for S-tog (subway) information.

3. NETWORKS & RESOURCES

FOR STUDENTS   The Copenhagen **Youth Information Center** (known as **Use It!**), Rådhusstraede 13, DK-1466 København K (tel. 33-15-65-18), provides information on places to visit, things to do, cheap accommodations and restaurants, and more. It issues reports on bed availability, and will also store your luggage for free. From June 15 to September 15, it is open daily from 9am to 7pm; the rest of the year, daily from 10am to 4pm.

FOR GAY MEN & LESBIANS   The national organization for gay men and lesbians is **Landsforeningen for Bøsser og Lesbiske,** Knabrostraede 3 (tel. 33-13-19-48), with branches in several cities such as Århus, Aalborg, and Odense. It was founded in 1948. Its café is open on Monday and Tuesday from 1pm to 2am, on Wednesday, Thursday, and Sunday from 1pm to 3am, and on Friday and Saturday from 1pm to 5am.

For the latest news and events, call the **National Gay Switchboard** (tel. 33-13-01-12), Friday through Monday from 8pm to midnight.

FOR WOMEN   The **Women's House** (Kvindehuset), at Gothersgade 37 (tel. 33-14-28-04), is a kind of information center, with several publications about the feminist movement. The house also operates the Bog Café. The house is open Monday through Friday from noon to 6pm; the café is open Monday and Thursday from 6 to 10pm.

CHAPTER 5

COPENHAGEN ACCOMMODATIONS

1. **NEAR KONGENS NYTORV & NYHAVN**
2. **NEAR RÅDHUSPLADSEN & TIVOLI**
3. **ON HELGOLANDSGADE & COLBJØRNSENSGADE**
4. **NEAR NØRREPORT STATION**
- **FROMMER'S COOL FOR KIDS: HOTELS**

Since Denmark doesn't have one of its own, I have devised a hotel-grading system, based on tariffs charged. If any hotel did not belong in its assigned category, it was not included. For example, any hotel deemed expensive that really wasn't worth it was not recommended. Few hotels had to be cut for this reason as the marketplace has a way of keeping prices in check.

Hotels are labeled **Very Expensive** if charging between about $250 and $485 per night for a double room. **Expensive** hotels have doubles for about $195 to $250; **Moderate**, $155 to $195; and **Inexpensive**, $55 to $155. Peak season in Denmark is summer, from May to September. It practically coincides with the schedule at the Tivoli. Once the Tivoli closes for the winter, plenty of rooms become available. Make sure to ask about winter discounts.

Nearly all doubles contain a private bath. Find out, though, whether this means a shower or a tub bath. You can undercut these prices by requesting a room without bath in hotels in the "Moderate" or "Inexpensive" categories.

Ask if breakfast is included. It usually is in most places, except many first-class choices.

Any accommodation labeled "Budget" falls into a special category—youth hostel, private home, etc. Budget suggests that the place is not a regular hotel, and offers the lowest possible price for a place to stay. Private homes are the cheapest.

Found throughout Scandinavia, **Mission hotels** service tourists of all faiths who are seeking comfortable, clean rooms in well-run hotels for a fair price. Copenhagen has several, each catering to a middle-class family trade. Although originally founded by the old-fashioned temperance society, now about half of Denmark's mission hotels are fully licensed.

RESERVATIONS SERVICE

At the Central Railroad Station, the tourist office maintains the useful hotel accommodations booking service **Vaerelseanvisningen** (tel. 33-12-40-45). The charge for this service, whether you have booked a private home or a luxury hotel, is 13 kroner ($2.20) per person. There is no charge for booking a hostel. A deposit must be paid at the kiosk, which will later be deducted from the room rent. For the room, you will have to pay a deposit of between 5 and 25 kroner (90¢ to $4.30), depending on the category of hotel you request. You are also given a city map and bus directions.

The kiosk will not accept reservations in advance. This facility can secure private accommodations only when the hotels in the indicated price range are fully booked. For clients who prefer to book hotel rooms in advance, see the Hotel Booking Service staff at the same kiosk (tel. 33-12-28-80).

The kiosk is open May 1 to the end of August, daily from 9am to midnight; in September, daily from 9am to 10pm; in October, Monday through Saturday from 9am to 5pm; November to March, Monday through Friday from 9am to 5pm and on

Saturday from 9am to noon; and in April, Monday through Saturday from 9am to 5pm.

1. NEAR KONGENS NYTORV & NYHAVN

Once the home of sailor joints and tattoo parlors, Nyhavn is now a fast-rising chic section of Copenhagen. The central canal filled with 19th-century boats and the 18th-century facades of the buildings surrounding it give the area its special atmosphere.

VERY EXPENSIVE

HOTEL D'ANGLETERRE, Kongens Nytorv 34, DK-1050 København K. Tel. 33-12-00-95. Fax 33-12-11-18. 118 rms, 12 suites. A/C MINIBAR TV TEL **Bus:** 1, 6, 9.

$ **Rates:** 1,800–2,100 kroner ($311.40–$363.30) single; 2,000–2,800 kroner ($346–$484.40) double; 4,300–9,800 kroner ($743.90–$1,695.40) suite. Breakfast 115 kroner ($19.90) extra. AE, DC, MC, V. **Parking:** 150 kroner ($26).

At the top of Nyhavn, this Leading Hotels of the World member is the premier choice for Denmark. The hotel was built in 1755 and extensively renovated in the 1980s. Guests have included H. C. Andersen and about every celebrity who's ever visited Denmark. It's a medley of styles: Empire, Louis XVI, and modern. Bedrooms are beautifully furnished with art objects and occasional antiques. Light color schemes, subdued lighting, and modern amenities continue to make this a desirable address.

Dining/Entertainment: The evening begins at The Bar, where everyone from rock stars to CEOs meet for a drink. La Brasserie, the hotel's democratically priced restaurant, caters to the "young and beautiful," whereas "The Restaurant" is acclaimed for its French cuisine and vintage wines. Light lunches and snacks are also available.

Services: Valet parking, room service from 7am to midnight, laundry service.
Facilities: In-house video, banquet and meeting facilities.

PHOENIX COPENHAGEN, Bredgade 37, DK-1260 København K. Tel. 33-95-95-00. Fax 33-33-98-33. 209 rms (all with bath), 3 suites. MINIBAR TV TEL **Bus:** 6, 9, 10.

$ **Rates:** 900–1,450 kroner ($155.70–$250.90) single; 1,450–2,050 kroner ($250.90–$354.70) double; from 2,500 kroner ($432.50) suite. AE, DC, MC, V.

More than any other hotel in Copenhagen, this top-of-the-line newcomer poses a serious challenge to the discreet grandeur of the nearby Hotel d'Angleterre. Opened in 1991, after 3 years of intensive rebuilding, the Phoenix rose from the ruined neoclassicism of a royal guesthouse originally built in the 1700s to house aristocratic courtiers of Amalienborg Palace. During World War II, the building was the home of a battalion of Nazi officers, and between 1945 and 1988, in much reduced circumstances, it was the headquarters of the now-almost-defunct Danish Communist Party. Beginning in 1988, tons of white and colored marble were imported to create the Louis XVI decor that has so impressed newcomers ever since. Bedrooms are tastefully elegant and discreet interpretations of Louis XVI.

Dining/Entertainment: A harpist provides evening entertainment for the lobby bar. On the premises is a Danish/French restaurant, the Von Plessen, as well as an English-inspired pub, Murdoch's.

Services: 24-hour room service, concierge, massage, laundry.
Facilities: Indoor swimming pool and health club; hairdresser/barber/ beautician next door.

71 NYHAVN, Nyhavn 71, DK-1051 København K. Tel. 33-11-85-85. Fax 33-93-15-85. 76 rms, 6 suites. MINIBAR TV TEL **Bus:** 1, 6, 9.

Absalon Hotel **18**
Hotel d' Angleterre **6**
Ascot Hotel **25**
Hotel Carlton **22**
Copenhagen Admiral Hotel **4**
Copenhagen Star **20**
Hotel Cosmopole **19**
Grand Hotel **14**
Ibsens Hotel **27**
Hotel Jørgensen **29**
Komfort Hotel **10**
Kong Arthur **28**
Kong Frederik **9**
Missionshotellet Ansgar **16**
Misionhotellet Nebo **21**
Hotel Neptun **3**
Palace Hotel **11**
Park Hotel **26**
Phoenix Copenhagen **2**
The Plaza **13**
Saga Hotel **17**
SAS Royal Hotel **12**
SAS Scandanavia Hotel **8**
Hotel Seelandia **15**
71 Nyhavn **7**
Sheraton Copenhagen Hotel **24**
Sophie Amalie Hotel **5**
Hotel Viking **1**
Hotel West **23**

Hovedvej

Lille Triangel
Garnisons Kirkegård
Kristianiagade
Østbanegade

Sortedam Dossering
Sortedams Sø
Holmens Kirkegård
Dag Hammerskjölds Alle
Østerport Station
Folke Bernadottes Allé
Forbindelsesvej

Øster Søgade
Oslo Plads

Østre Anlæg
Grønningen

Øster Farimagsgade
Øster Voldgade
Solvgade
Esplanaden

Rigensgade
Suensonsgade
Store Kongensgade
Bredgade
Toldbodgade

Solvgade
Kerkegade
Adelgade
Gernersgade

Øster Farimagsgade
Kronprinsessegade
Borgergade
1

Nørre Voldgade
Abenrå
Gothersgade
Store Kongensgade
2
Bredgade
3 **4**
Skt. Annae Plads
5

Pilestræde
6

Krystalgade
Købmager Gade
Kongens Nytorv
Nyhavn
Nyhavn

lestræde
Østergade
Holbergsgade
7

Vestergade
Amagertory
Højbro Plads
Niels Juelsgade
Havnegade

Frederiksberggade
Gl. Strand
Holmens Kanal
CHRISTIANSHAVN

dhus lads
10
Strandgade
Overgaden oven Vandet
Prinsessegade

11
9
Kongens Tolhusgade
Knippelsbro
Torvegade
Skt. Annae Gade

Andersens Boulevard
Vester Voldgade
Christians Brygge
Prinsessegade

Mitchellsgade
Hambrosgade
Langebro
Langebrogade
Christmas Møllers Plads

Sydbavnen
Stadsgraven
Ved Stadsgraven
To Airport

Thorshavnsgade
Amager Boulevard
8
Amager Fælled Vej

Inderbavnen

$ Rates (including buffet breakfast): 1,250–1,650 kroner ($216.30–$285.50) single; 1,550–1,950 kroner ($268.20–$337.40) double; from 2,400 kroner ($415.20) suite. AE, DC, MC, V.

Lying along Nyhavn, this hotel incorporated a modern interior into a 200-year-old warehouse whose red-brick walls rise above the wooden hulls of ships anchored in the adjacent canal. One of the few buildings in the area that was spared an 1807 British bombardment, the warehouse lasted until it opened as a hotel in 1971. Leather couches, small arched windows, comfortable baths, and carpeting distinguish the bedrooms. Facilities include a small bar area and an elegant restaurant, Pakhuskaelderen, serving French and Danish specialties. Dinner costs 315 kroner ($54.50); buffet lunches go for 175 kroner ($30.30).

EXPENSIVE

HOTEL NEPTUN, Skt. Annae Plads 18-20, DK-1250 København K. Tel. 31-13-89-00, or toll free 800/528-1234 in the U.S. Fax 33-14-12-50. 119 rms, 10 suites. MINIBAR TV TEL **Bus:** 1, 6, 9, 28.

$ Rates (including buffet breakfast): 870–1,070 kroner ($150.50–$185.10) single; 1,110–1,440 kroner ($192–$249.10) double; from 3,300 kroner ($570.90) suite. AE, DC, MC, V. **Parking:** Free. **Closed:** Dec 22–Jan 2.

Modernized in 1990, the interior of this hotel, originally built in 1854, resembles an upper-class living room, with English-style furniture, warm colors, paneling, and even a chess table. Some rooms overlook a quiet, covered interior courtyard, where you can have a drink in the summer. Bedrooms are tastefully furnished in modern style and have radios, trouser presses, and hairdryers. The hotel is located a block from the Nyhavn Canal, near many city attractions.

Dining/Entertainment: The Neptun Café/Restaurant is in a 150-year-old building with a cozy, bright atmosphere. Here you can enjoy a version of new Danish cuisine. A leading Danish food critic recently awarded this restaurant five stars out of a possible five. Meals begin at 200 kroner ($34.60).

Services: Laundry, babysitting, and 24-hour room service.

Facilities: Business center.

MODERATE

COPENHAGEN ADMIRAL HOTEL, Toldbodgade 24-28, DK-1253 København K. Tel. 31-11-82-82. Fax 33-32-36-07. 313 rms, 52 suites. TV TEL **Bus:** 1, 9, 10, 28, 41.

$ Rates: 620–805 kroner ($107.30–$139.30) single; 890–1,040 kroner ($154–$179.90) double; from 1,620 kroner ($280.30) suite. Breakfast buffet 86 kroner ($14.90) extra. Winter discounts. AE, MC, V. **Parking:** Free.

Only 2 blocks from Nyhavn Canal, this hotel was originally built as a granary in 1787. Guests navigate between the thick timbers and stone arches of the hotel infrastructure, where modern partitions have created a series of well-furnished, first-class bedrooms. Some rooms have harbor views. A popular luncheon buffet is served in the hotel restaurant. At night, formal service and French cuisine greet guests. Services include laundry, room service, and babysitting, and facilities feature a sauna and a solarium.

SOPHIE AMALIE HOTEL, Skt. Annae Plads 21, DK-1250 København K. Tel. 33-13-34-00. Fax 33-11-77-07. 117 rms (all with bath) 17 suites. A/C TV TEL **Bus:** 1, 9, 10, 28, 41.

$ Rates: 620–865 kroner ($107.30–$149.60) single; 890–1,040 kroner ($154–$179.90) double; 1,180–1,620 kroner ($204.10–$280.30) suite. Buffet breakfast 86 kroner ($14.90) extra. Winter discounts. AE, MC, V. **Parking:** Free.

Sophie Amalie is a first-class hotel that should be better known. Within walking distance of Nyhavn, it is convenient for exploring the business and shopping districts of the capital. It is a neighbor of Amalienborg, the royal palace of Denmark. The hotel dates from 1948, and has been vastly improved and upgraded over the years. Its bedrooms are furnished with the best of Scandinavian modern design. In the sixth-floor suites, a curved staircase leads from the living room to the bedroom. In the Restaurant Pinafore, French cuisine is served. The hotel also has a sauna, and provides room service, laundry, and babysitting.

INEXPENSIVE

HOTEL VIKING, Bredgade 65, DK-1260 København K. Tel. 33-12-45-50.
Fax 33-12-46-18. 91 rms (26 with bath). TEL **Bus:** 1, 6, 9, 10.
$ Rates (including continental breakfast): 380 kroner ($65.70) single without bath, 480 kroner ($83) single with bath; 590 kroner ($102.10) double without bath, 720 kroner ($124.60) double with bath. Winter discounts. DC, MC, V. **Closed:** Dec 21–Jan 1.

Only 4 blocks from the Central Railroad Station, this modern hotel is reasonably priced. Bedrooms are comfortable and clean, but a bit worn. Only breakfast is served. Room service for drinks is available 24 hours.

2. NEAR RÅDHUSPLADSEN & TIVOLI

Some of the most expensive hotels in Copenhagen are located here. In the heart of the city, centered around the Rådhuspladsen (Town Hall Square), the Tivoli, and the Central Railroad Station, you'll be near all public transportation and many attractions.

VERY EXPENSIVE

KONG FREDERIK, Vester Voldgade 25, DK-1552 København V. Tel. 33-12-59-02. Fax 33-93-59-01. 107 rms, 3 suites. MINIBAR TV TEL **Bus:** 1, 6, 28.
$ Rates: 1,500–1,750 kroner ($259.50–$302.80) single; 1,800–2,050 kroner ($311.40–$354.70) double; 2,250–6,000 kroner ($389.30–$1,038) suite. Buffet breakfast 100 kroner ($17.30) extra. AE, DC, MC, V. **Parking:** 85 kroner ($14.70). **Closed:** Dec 21–Jan 2.

Considered the smallest of the ultra-chic hotels of Copenhagen, the Kong Frederik still has the feeling of an unpretentious but elegant private club because of its discreet service, dark paneling, and labyrinth of antique-filled lounges. Originally built as two separate hotels around 1850, and unified around a central courtyard about 1900, it has always appealed to glamorous representatives of show biz. The frequently renovated bedrooms have conservatively traditional furniture in a wide array of styles, and contain hairdryers, separate shower cabinets, and radios.

Dining/Entertainment: The Queen's Grill, an excellent Danish and international restaurant, has entertained many a king. Meals are also served in a verdant courtyard, protected from the elements by a glass canopy. Amid the mellow panels of the Queen's Pub, you can order both food and drink (see "Evening Entertainment" in Chapter 7).

Services: Valet parking, same-day dry cleaning, laundry, 24-hour room service.

PALACE HOTEL, Rådhuspladsen 57, DK-1550 København V. Tel. 33-14-40-50. Fax 33-14-52-78. 155 rms, 4 suites. MINIBAR TV TEL **Bus:** 2, 30, 32, 33, 34, 35.
$ Rates (including buffet breakfast): 1,390–1,590 kroner ($240.50–$275.10) single; 1,590–1,790 kroner ($275.10–$309.70) double; 2,040–2,500 kroner ($352.90–$432.50) suite. AE, DC, MC, V.

Opened in 1910 and declared an historical landmark in 1985, Palace Hotel has been visited by Bob Hope, Audrey Hepburn, and Duke Ellington. Modern rooms are attractively furnished in a traditional style, with many amenities, such as trouser presses and hairdryers. The concierge is particularly helpful in arranging for theater tickets, tours, and transportation.

Dining/Entertainment: The Butterfly Bar on the ground floor has a Hollywood atmosphere, and the restaurant, Brasserie on the Square, serves both Danish and international food.

Services: Laundry, concierge.

Facilities: Safe-deposit box in rooms, parking garage, executive meeting rooms.

THE PLAZA, Bernstorffsgade 4, DK-1577 København V. Tel. 33-14-92-62. Fax 33-93-93-62. 77 rms, 6 suites. A/C MINIBAR TV TEL **Bus:** 1, 6.

$ Rates (including buffet breakfast): 1,400–1,800 kroner ($242.20–$311.40) single; 1,600–2,700 kroner ($276.80–$467.10) double; 2,850–5,850 kroner ($493.10–$1,012.10) suite. AE, DC, MC, V. **Closed:** Dec 25–Jan 1.

Set close to the railroad station, and richly imbued with a sense of turn-of-the-century nostalgia, this sophisticated overhaul of an older hotel has pleased many clients thanks to its mahogany paneling, first-class comfort, and antique furnishings. Plaza bedrooms have a look similar to something you might find in an English country house—traditional, yet with all the modern amenities.

Dining/Entertainment: The Library Bar provides one of the most charming oases in Copenhagen for a drink (see "Evening Entertainment" in Chapter 7). The plaza also contains the premier Russian restaurant of Scandinavia, the Alexander Nevski (see Chapter 6).

SAS ROYAL HOTEL, Hammerichsgade 1, DK-1611 København V. Tel. 33-14-14-12. Fax 33-14-14-21. 263 rms, 2 suites. A/C MINIBAR TV TEL **Bus:** 14, 16.

$ Rates: 2,010 kroner ($347.70) single; 2,310 kroner ($399.60) double. Breakfast 115 kroner ($19.90) extra. Royal Club (including continental breakfast), 2,400 kroner ($415.20) single; 2,600 kroner ($449.80) double; from 5,800 kroner ($1,003.40) suite. AE, DC, MC, V. **Parking:** 110 kroner ($19).

Long favored by business travelers, this international deluxe hotel in the city center, near the Tivoli and Town Hall Square, is filled with facilities and conveniences. The hotel has sleek modern Danish styling throughout. Rooms have such extra amenities as hairdryers and trouser presses. At the Royal Club on the top floors, guests are pampered for extra money: electronic safes, lounge with complimentary refreshments, speedier check-ins, and free admission to the hotel's facilities such as the dance club and gym.

Dining/Entertainment: The hotel has several restaurants and bars, including its prestigious Summit on the top floor. Others include Café Royal, a lobby bar, the Garden Bar, and New Fellini's nightclub (see "Evening Entertainment" in Chapter 7).

Services: SAS airline check-in, 24-hour room service, 3-hour laundry service, massage, hairstylist, "Office-for-a-Day."

Facilities: Gymnasium, sauna, and solarium.

SAS SCANDINAVIA HOTEL, Amager Blvd. 70, DK-2300 København S. Tel. 33-11-23-23. Fax 31-57-01-93. 542 rms, 51 suites. A/C MINIBAR TV TEL **Bus:** 5, 11, 30, 34.

$ Rates: 1,500–1,670 kroner ($259.50–$288.90) single; 1,700–1,890 kroner ($294.10–$327) double; buffet breakfast 115 kroner ($19.90). June–Aug, 745 kroner ($128.90) single; 990 kroner ($171.30) double. Royal Club (including continental breakfast) 2,200 kroner ($380.60) single; 2,400 kroner ($415.20) double; from 5,500 kroner ($951.50) penthouse suite. AE, DC, MC, V. **Parking:** Free.

A 5-minute walk east of the Tivoli, this international deluxe hotel is rated as the finest and largest modern hotel in the Danish capital, catering primarily to businesspeople. First-class bedrooms are attractive and comfortable, with many amenities such as a VCR with international movies, trouser press, and hairdryer. Unlike most of the other hotels of Copenhagen, these standard rooms are discounted in summer. Greater comfort is found on the top floors at the Royal Club where guests are given extra privileges such as free admission to all hotel facilities.

Dining/Entertainment: The Top of the Town is the only sky restaurant in Copenhagen. You can stop in just for a drink at the Sky Bar—and get the view for free. Others include a Thai restaurant, Blue Elephant, and an Italian restaurant, Mama's. For the increasing number of Japanese clients, or other visitors, there is also a Japanese restaurant, Kyoto. Gamblers enjoy the Casino Copenhagen, or go downstairs to the hotel nightclub, After 8.

Services: 24-hour room service, concierge, massages, secretarial assistance, SAS airline check-in, express laundry.

Facilities: Health club with indoor swimming pool, Business Service Center, conference facilities, business club rooms, Danish designer shops.

SHERATON COPENHAGEN HOTEL, Vester Søgade 6 (Box 337), DK-1601 København V. Tel. 33-14-35-35, or toll free 800/325-3535 in the U.S. Fax 33-32-12-23. 469 rms, 2 suites. A/C MINIBAR TV TEL **Bus:** 29.

$ Rates (including continental breakfast): 1,200–2,200 kroner ($207.60–$380.60) single; 1,750–2,500 kroner ($302.80–$432.50) double; from 2,800 kroner ($484.40) suite. AE, DC, MC, V. **Parking:** 120 kroner ($20.80).

Two blocks from the Tivoli Gardens and the major shopping district, this chain hotel makes a good impression in the Danish capital. A business executive's favorite, the Sheraton Copenhagen has been massively renovated. The hotel was given a thorough overhaul in safety equipment such as fire alarms and smoke detectors, individual adjustable air conditioners were added, and the sixth floor was made for nonsmokers only. Rooms are bright and modern, and contain many amenities, such as eight international TV channels. The most expensive accommodations are on the top two executive floors.

Dining/Entertainment: The King's Court is the hotel's prestigious restaurant, although meals can also be had at the Felix. The Red Lion Pub is ideal for a drink or nighttime buffet. The King's Court Champagne and Piano Bar provides international entertainment.

Services: 24-hour room service, manicures and pedicures, massages, concierge, laundry service, secretarial services.

Facilities: Parking, health club, shopping arcade, car rental.

MODERATE

ASCOT HOTEL, Studiestraede 57, DK-1554 København V. Tel. 33-12-60-00. Fax 33-14-60-40. 102 rms (all with bath). 20 suites. TV TEL **Bus:** 14, 16.

$ Rates (including buffet breakfast): 670–815 kroner ($115.90–$141) single; 815–1,120 kroner ($141–$193.80) double; from 1,120 kroner ($193.80) suite. AE, DC, MC, V. **Parking:** Free.

On a small side street 5 minutes from Town Hall Square, the Ascot is a traditional 19th-century building. Cleverly modernized, it has turned into one of the best small hotels in Copenhagen. The atmosphere is inviting, and bedrooms are sleek and modern, each comfortable and well maintained. Free parking facilities, same-day laundry, and dry cleaning are available. There's also a bar.

GRAND HOTEL, Vesterbrogade 9A, DK-1620 København V. Tel. 31-31-36-00. Fax 31-31-33-50. 147 rms, 2 suites. MINIBAR TV TEL **Bus:** 1, 6, 16, 27, 28, 29.

$ Rates (including buffet breakfast): 780–990 kroner ($134.90–$171.30) single; 990–1,210 kroner ($171.30–$209.30) double; from 2,300 kroner ($397.90) suite. AE, DC, MC, V.

A 1988 renovation brought this landmark near the Central Railroad Station a new life. The charm of the old was preserved, but the bedrooms and baths are new, each tastefully furnished and well maintained. Modern amenities such as in-room movies were added. The Grand Bar overflows in summer onto a sidewalk café, and the Grand Restaurant serves freshly prepared Danish specialties. Laundry, room service, and babysitting are provided.

KOMFORT HOTEL, Løngangstraede 27, DK-1468 København K. Tel. 31-12-65-70. Fax 33-15-28-99. 201 rms (all with bath or shower) TV TEL **Bus:** 1, 5, 6.

$ Rates (including buffet breakfast): 740 kroner ($128) single; 1,130 kroner ($195.50) double. AE, DC, MC, V. **Parking:** 50 kroner ($8.70). **Closed:** Dec 23–Jan 1.

Close to the Town Hall, Komfort Hotel offers clean rooms, attractive modern decor, and good value. There's a parking garage on the premises, and laundry, babysitting, and room service are provided. The popular restaurant, Strikes, offers international meals from 185 kroner ($32). Specialties include spareribs, shish kebab, chicken Kiev, and surf-and-turf. There is also an English-inspired pub, John Bull, on the premises.

KONG ARTHUR, Nørre Søgade 11, DK-1370 København K. Tel. 33-11-12-12. Fax 33-32-61-30. 90 rms (all with bath), 7 suites. MINIBAR TV TEL **Bus:** 5, 7, 16.

$ Rates (including Danish breakfast): 845–915 kroner ($146.20–$158.30) single; 995–1,095 kroner ($172.10–$189.40) double; from 1,800 kroner ($311.40) suite. AE, DC, MC, V. **Parking:** Free.

Ⓢ Originally conceived as an orphanage when it was built in 1882, this good-value hotel sits behind a private courtyard next to the tree-lined Peblinge Lake in a residential part of town. It has been completely renovated into a contemporary hostelry, with a new wing with more spacious rooms added in 1990. Each of the comfortably furnished and carpeted bedrooms is freshly painted and has an in-home video, safe, and hairdryer. The hotel has a sauna and provides room service and babysitting. Breakfast is taken in a greenhouselike room that is large and sun-filled if the weather's right. The hotel also has a nice restaurant and cozy café, serving Danish specialties.

PARK HOTEL, Jarmers Plads 3, DK-1551 København V. Tel. 31-13-30-00. Fax 33-14-30-33. 64 rms (58 with bath). TV TEL **Bus:** 14, 16.

$ Rates: 598 kroner ($103.50) single without bath, 745 kroner ($128.90) single with bath; 875 kroner ($151.40) double without bath, 995 kroner ($172.10) double with bath. Breakfast 75 kroner ($13) extra. Winter discounts. AE, DC, MC, V.

The Park Hotel houses my favorite breakfast room in the city. One wall is adorned with the radiator covers from six vintage automobiles while other walls have an airplane propeller from 1916, a collection of antique auto headlights, and lots of machine-age posters and engravings. Bedrooms have tasteful furniture, marble-covered baths, thick carpeting, and lithographs. Babysitting and room service are available.

INEXPENSIVE

HOTEL CARLTON, Halmtorvet 14, DK-1260 København V. Tel. 31-21-25-51. 60 rms (12 with bath). TEL **Bus:** 10.

$ Rates (including buffet breakfast): 305–370 kroner ($52.80–$64) single without bath, 550 kroner ($95.20) single with bath; 550–730 kroner ($95.20–$126.30) double without bath, 920 kroner ($159.20) double with bath. AE, DC, MC, V.

Ⓢ This 19th-century hotel, located near Amalienborg Palace, the harbor, and *The Little Mermaid,* has elaborate detail and some grand antiques. Rooms have been modernized and filled with functional Nordic furniture. There are baths on every floor and an all-night bar.

HOTEL WEST, Dannebrogsgade 8, DK-1661 København V. Tel. 31-24-27-61. 24 rms (10 with bath). **Bus:** 6, 27, 28.

$ Rates: 190–210 kroner ($32.90–$36.30) single; 310–410 kroner ($53.60–$70.90) double. Extra bed 100 kroner ($17.30). Winter discounts; 10% discounts on stays of more than 3 nights. No credit cards.

Ⓢ Hotel West takes up two floors of a 1900 corner building about a 10-minute walk from the railway station. There's a public sitting room. Rooms are small, but clean and well maintained. Only a few singles are available; most are twin-bedded and can be used as three-, four-, or five-bedded units. No breakfast is served, but many eating places are nearby as well as a laundry and supermarket. Ten rooms have a small refrigerator (not a minibar).

MISSIONSHOTELLET NEBO, Istedgade 6, DK-1650 København V. Tel. 31-21-12-17. Fax 31-23-47-73. 150 rms (72 with bath). TV TEL **Bus:** 6, 16, 28, 41.

$ Rates (including breakfast): 350 kroner ($60.60) single without bath, 540 kroner ($93.40) single with bath; 570 kroner ($98.60) double without bath, 830 kroner ($143.60) double with bath. Extra bed 130 kroner ($22.50). AE, DC, MC, V. **Parking:** 20 kroner ($3.50).

This hotel near the railroad station is a quiet retreat, with clean, up-to-date rooms. The lobby is tiny, and a lounge opens onto a side courtyard. Rooms are small, furnished in a Nordic functional style. Bathrooms are on all floors.

---

3. ON HELGOLANDSGADE & COLBJØRNSENSGADE

Copenhagen's main sleeping street is near the Central Railroad Station, where Helgolandsgade runs parallel to Colbjørnsensgade. The many moderately priced accommodations here can be booked through a central office at Helgolandsgade 4 (tel. 31-31-43-44). Colbjørnsensgade, parallel to Helgolandsgade, is the second major sleeping street. From either street, you are within easy walking distance of Rådhuspladsen and the Tivoli.

Beginning in the early 1970s, this area behind the railroad station became one of the major porno districts of Europe, but hotel renovations, much-publicized civic efforts, and the gradual decline of the porno shops have led to a continuing gentrification.

Today, with the original 19th-century facades for the most part still intact and often gracefully restored, the district is safer than you might think, and often presents some of the best hotel values in Copenhagen.

MODERATE

COPENHAGEN STAR, Colbjørnsensgade 13, DK-1652 København V. Tel. 31-22-11-00. Fax 31-22-21-99. 131 rms (all with bath), 3 suites. TV TEL MINIBAR **Bus:** 6, 16, 28, 41.

$ Rates (including breakfast): 890 kroner ($154) single; 1,120 kroner ($193.80) double; 1,280 kroner ($221.40) suite. AE, DC, MC, V.

Located a short walk from the railroad station, this hotel was created in 1990 when a simple older hotel was connected to a neighboring building and upgraded into a comfortable and stylish whole. Its neoclassical facade, originally built around 1880, is painted a peach-toned beige. The outside is lit with neon, and the hotel design is definitely postmodern, as reflected by an interior design which uses leather chairs, teakwood tables, and an abundance of granite columns. On the premises is a bar, although the only meal served is breakfast.

HOTEL COSMOPOLE, Colbjørnsensgade 5-11, DK-1652 København V. Tel. 31-21-33-33. Fax 31-31-33-99. 208 rms (all with bath). TV TEL **Bus:** 6, 10, 16, 28, 41.

$ Rates (including breakfast): 750 kroner ($129.80) single; 910 kroner ($157.40) double. Winter discounts. AE, DC, MC, V.

Operated by a chain that manages several other Danish tourist hotels, large but unpretentious Hotel Cosmopole is composed of two connected 19th-century buildings identified as Cosmopole I and Cosmopole II. (Cosmopole II is known to many local residents as Hotel Union.) Rooms are simple, efficient, and modern, and include such amenities as clock radios and hairdryers. There's a bar on the premises, but the only meal served is breakfast. Laundry service and babysitting can be provided.

INEXPENSIVE

ABSALON HOTEL, Helgolandsgade 15, DK-1653 København V. Tel. 31-24-22-11. Fax 31-24-34-11. 253 rms (177 with bath), 2 suites. **Bus:** 6, 10, 16, 28, 41.

$ Rates (including all-you-can-eat buffet breakfast): 400 kroner ($69.20) single without bath, 735 kroner ($127.20) single with bath; 500 kroner ($86.50) double without bath, 750–900 kroner ($129.80–$155.70) double with bath; from 1,300 kroner ($224.90) suite. Winter discounts. AE, DC, MC, V. **Closed:** Dec 18–Jan 2.

The four thick-walled town houses that the Nedergaard family joined into one building began their existence as a hotel in 1938. Its origins are based on a love story that unfolded at the nearby railroad station. Shortly after the ancestor of the present owners began his first job as a door porter at a neighboring hotel, he was asked to go to the station to retrieve a new babysitter who had just arrived from Jutland. They met, fell in love, and bought the first of what would eventually become four interconnected buildings and one of the best-managed hotels in the neighborhood. Two of their children were born in Room 108 of the present hotel, including one of the brothers you'll probably meet behind the reception desk today.

Absalon Hotel was tastefully and efficiently renovated in 1985 to the best standards of this budget-conscious neighborhood. You'll find a spacious blue-and-white breakfast room, a reception area trimmed in hardwood paneling, and an attentive staff directed by Eric and Mogens Nedergaard. Bedrooms are simple and modern; those with private bathrooms also contain TVs, trouser presses, and hairdryers. There are also laundry facilities. The hotel's basement restaurant, Absalon's Kaelder, is one of the best and most reasonably priced in the neighborhood, with meals costing from 130 kroner ($22.50).

HOTEL SEELANDIA, Helgolandsgade 12, DK-1653 København V. Tel. 31-31-46-10. Fax 31-31-46-10. 86 rms (67 with bath). TV TEL **Bus:** 6, 10, 16, 28, 41.

$ Rates (including breakfast): 400 kroner ($69.20) single without bath, 660 kroner ($114.20) single with bath; 550 kroner ($95.20) double without bath, 860 kroner ($148.80) double with bath. AE, DC, MC, V. **Closed:** Dec 20–Jan 2.

Solidly built in 1928 behind the railroad station, Hotel Seelandia was renovated into a new, comfortably modern format in 1983. A longtime favorite of budget-conscious families, it is well maintained and well cleaned. Furnishings are simple, in a Scandinavian-modern style. Laundry facilities are available, and babysitting can be arranged.

MISSIONSHOTELLET ANSGAR, Colbjørnsensgade 29, DK-1652 København V. Tel. 31-21-21-96. Fax 31-21-61-91. 87 rms (64 with bath). TEL **Bus:** 6, 10, 16, 28, 41.

$ Rates (including breakfast): 380 kroner ($65.70) single without bath, 585 kroner ($101.20) single with bath; 560 kroner ($96.90) double without bath, 820 kroner ($141.90) double with bath. AE, DC, MC, V. **Parking:** Free.

Comfortable and cozy, Ansgar's rooms are decorated with modern Danish furniture. There are showers and baths on each floor (no charge for use). A dozen large rooms that can accommodate up to six are perfect for families, and are available at negotiable rates. There is often free 24-hour parking outside the hotel. Guests arriving at Kastrup Airport can take the SAS bus to the Air Terminal at the Central Railroad Station, walk through the station, and be inside the hotel in less than 4 minutes.

SAGA HOTEL, Colbjørnsensgade 18-20, DK-1652 København V. Tel. 31-24-99-67. Fax 31-24-60-33. 76 rms (15 with bath). **Bus:** 6, 10, 16, 28, 41.

$ Rates (including buffet breakfast): 320 kroner ($55.40) single without bath, 620 kroner ($107.30) single with bath; 440 kroner ($76.10) double without bath, 900 kroner ($155.70) double with bath. Extra bed 160–190 kroner ($27.70–$32.90). Winter discounts. AE, DC, MC, V.

This is a reasonably priced and solidly acceptable choice among the hotels on this sometimes-troublesome street. You walk up one flight to reach the reception area. The simple but comfortable bedrooms are on the upper floors of the nonelevator building, so if you don't mind the upward climb, Saga might be appropriate for you. About five rooms have a TV. Laundry facilities are available.

4. NEAR NØRREPORT STATION

INEXPENSIVE

IBSENS HOTEL, Vendersgade 23, DK-1363 København K. Tel. 33-13-19-13. Fax 33-13-19-16. 49 rms (6 with bath). TV TEL **Bus:** 5, 7E, 14, 16.

$ Rates (including buffet breakfast): 375 kroner ($64.90) single without bath; 500 kroner ($86.50) double without bath, 600–800 kroner ($103.80–$138.40) double with shower or bath. Extra bed 150 kroner ($26). No credit cards. **Parking:** 45 kroner ($7.80). **Closed:** Dec 22–Jan 2.

 Preferred by budget-conscious travelers and families, Ibsens Hotel, built in 1906, offers clean, comfortable, and well-maintained bedrooms traditionally furnished. Most rooms are doubles and triples, and each has hot and cold water. Showers and toilets are on every corridor. Only breakfast is served, but many restaurants and cafés are nearby. The hotel is near Nørreport Station and the Botanical Gardens.

A GAY HOTEL

HOTEL JØRGENSEN, Rømersgade 11, DK-1362 København K. Tel. 33-13-81-66. Fax 33-15-51-05. 12 double rms (all with shower), 12 dormitory rms. TV **Bus:** 14, 16.

$ Rates (including continental breakfast): 300–475 kroner ($51.90–$82.20) single; 400–575 kroner ($69.20–$99.50) double; 85 kroner ($14.70) per person in dormitory rooms. AE, DC, MC, V. **Parking:** 50 kroner ($8.70).

This white stucco hotel, lying on a busy boulevard in central Copenhagen, has an obvious allure for gay men and lesbians, but also welcomes straight people. The staff is most helpful. Prices are reasonable. Bedrooms are conventional and well organized. The dormitory rooms are segregated according to men and women—six each. The hotel also runs the popular Café Adagio in its basement.

ⓕ FROMMER'S COOL FOR KIDS: HOTELS

Kong Arthur   (see p. 64) Once a home for Danish orphans, this is a safe haven near tree-lined Peblinge Lake in a residential section.

Hotel Carlton   (see p. 64) One of the best bets for families on a budget. Plenty of extra beds for children and within walking distance to the *The Little Mermaid*.

Missionshotellet Nebo   (see p. 65) A longtime family favorite, this hotel rents rooms with extra beds for children. It's a clean, safe environment.

Missionshotellet Ansgar   (see p. 66) Children under 3 stay free, and extra beds are available for kids under 12. Twelve large rooms can accommodate up to six family members in each.

CHAPTER 6

COPENHAGEN DINING

It is estimated that there are more than 2,000 cafés, snack bars, and restaurants in Copenhagen. Most of these restaurants are either in the Tivoli or centered around the Rådhuspladsen (Town Hall Square), the Central Railroad Station, or in Nyhavn. Others lie in the center of the shopping district, in streets branching off from the Strøget.

You pay for the privilege of dining in the Tivoli; prices are always higher. Reservations are not usually important, but it's best to call in advance. Nearly everyone answering phones in restaurants speaks English.

In restaurants rated **Very Expensive,** you'll spend $50 and up per person for dinner, excluding drinks. Meals in restaurants judged **Expensive** cost about $35 to $50 for a dinner; **Moderate,** $25 to $35. In restaurants considered **Inexpensive,** figure about $20 to $25 for dinner. You can dine for less than $20 at **budget** restaurants.

1. NEAR KONGENS NYTORV & NYHAVN

VERY EXPENSIVE

KOMMANDANTEN, Ny Adelgade 7. Tel. 33-12-09-90.
   Cuisine: INTERNATIONAL. **Reservations:** Required. **Bus:** 1, 6.
$ **Prices:** Fixed-price menus 320–695 kroner ($55.40–$120.20); appetizers 95–135 kroner ($16.40–$23.40); main dishes 195–215 kroner ($33.70–$37.20). AE, DC, MC, V.
   Open: Lunch Mon–Fri noon–2:30pm; dinner Mon–Sat 5:30–10pm.

⭐ Built in 1698 and the former residence of the military commander of Copenhagen, Kommandanten is the epitome of Danish chic and charm. Have an apéritif in the charming bar before going upstairs to one of the beautiful rooms, painted in a cobalt blue.

The finest seasonal ingredients are used, and the menu changes every 2 weeks. You might be offered the grilled catch of the day, breast of duck with port wine sauce, grilled turbot with a spinach sauce, or a gratinée of shellfish. The service is perhaps the best in Copenhagen. Before leaving, look at the valuable Andy Warhol original of Queen Margrethe II in the downstairs dining room.

KONG HANS KAELDER, Vingårdsstraede 6. Tel. 33-11-68-68.

Cuisine: INTERNATIONAL. **Reservations:** Required. **Bus:** 1, 6, 9.

$ Prices: Fixed-price menus 295–695 kroner ($51–$120.20); appetizers 105–145 kroner ($18.20–$25.10); main courses 275–305 kroner ($47.60–$52.80). AE, DC, MC, V.

Open: Dinner only, Mon–Sat 6pm–midnight. **Closed:** July 15–Aug 15.

★ This vaulted Gothic cellar, once owned by King Hans (1455–1513), may be the best restaurant in Denmark. Located on "the oldest corner of Copenhagen," it has been carefully restored and is now a Relais Gourmands. H. C. Andersen lived above it and even wrote some of his finest stories here.

Alsace-born Daniel Letz, a leading chef of Scandinavia, creates dishes that one critic claimed "to have been prepared by Matisse or Picasso." The menu changes, but try the breast of duck with figs and lime, quails in a pot-au-feu, or tournedos in a foie gras sauce. Or order filet of lamb with coriander or filet of turbot in an eggplant-and-saffron sauce. For dessert, the plum ice cream with Armagnac is delectably smooth.

EXPENSIVE

LEONORE CHRISTINE, Nyhavn 9. Tel. 33-13-50-40.

Cuisine: DANISH/FRENCH. **Reservations:** Required. **Bus:** 1, 6, 9.

$ Prices: Appetizers 75–125 kroner ($13–$21.60); main dishes 195–215 ($33.70–$37.20); fixed-price lunch 225 kroner ($38.90); fixed-price dinner 358 kroner ($61.90). AE, DC, MC, V.

Open: Lunch Mon–Sat noon–3pm; dinner Mon–Sat 6–10pm.

This restaurant, on the sunny (south) side of the canal, probably is the best restaurant at Nyhavn. In a 1681 building, the decor is elegant. You can sample Danish veal filet with salsify, guinea fowl with wild cranberries, oven-baked fjord salmon with oysters, Danish lamb with rhubarb, and grilled redfish with squash. The wine list is extensive.

MODERATE

CAFE LUMSKEBUGTEN, Esplanaden 21. Tel. 33-15-60-29.

Cuisine: DANISH. **Reservations:** Recommended. **Bus:** 1, 6, 9.

$ Prices: Appetizers 48–180 kroner ($8.30–$31.10); main dishes 120–190 kroner ($20.80–$32.90); fixed-price lunch 190 kroner ($32.90); fixed-price dinner 390 kroner ($67.50). AE, DC, MC, V.

Open: Lunch daily 11am–4pm; dinner daily 6–10:30pm.

Established in 1854 by Karen Marguerita Krog, this restaurant at the end of the Esplanden was a haven for sailors, serving hash, homemade beer, and schnapps. As Krog's legend grew, aristocrats, artists, and members of the Danish royal family joined the diners. Even today the honorary beef hash is still served.

Two glistening white dining rooms are outfitted with antique ships' models, oil paintings, and pinewood floors. The food is excellent, as is the service. Try the tartare of salmon with herbs, fishcakes (more a flan than a cake), fried herring, baked codfish, or sugar-marinated salmon with mustard-cream sauce.

LA BRASSERIE, in the Hotel d'Angleterre, Kongens Nytorv 34. Tel. 33-12-00-95.

Cuisine: FRENCH. **Reservations:** Recommended. **Bus:** 1, 6, 9.

$ Prices: Appetizers 38–125 kroner ($6.60–$21.60); main dishes 125–175 kroner ($21.60–$30.30). AE, DC, MC, V.

Open: Mon–Sat 11am–10pm.

This is a terrace bar-café-restaurant, similar to those seen in Paris, where the famous and those who'd like to be often dine in an informal bustling atmosphere. It is especially popular among young Danish professional people. The food is market fresh, and the menu is changed frequently based on what's fresh, good, and available. Many enjoy smørrebrød selections at lunch, then return for dinner to begin with garlic-flavored escargots, sautéed duck liver, freshly crisp salads, or antipasto. You can also order full and substantial main dishes, ranging from fresh fish such as sole, pheasant, or beef tenderloin.

RESTAURANT ELS, Store Strandstraede 3. Tel. 33-14-13-41.

  Cuisine: DANISH/FRENCH. **Reservations:** Recommended. **Bus:** 1, 6, 10.
$ Prices: 3-course dinner 296 kroner ($51.20); 2-course lunch 176 kroner ($30.45);
appetizers 48–62 kroner ($8.30–$10.75); main dishes 138–162 kroner ($23.90–
$28). AE, DC, MC, V.
  Open: Lunch daily noon–3pm; dinner daily 5:30–10pm.

Just off Kongens Nytorv, Restaurant Els preserves its original 1853 decor. Several
19th-century murals thought to be the work of Danish classical artist Constantin
Hansen (1804–1880) are displayed. H. C. Andersen was a regular here.

  Meals are priced on a daily changing fixed-price basis, but a selection of Danish
open-face sandwiches are offered at lunch for those wanting a lighter meal. The
cuisine at night is French, accompanied by excellent wines. Food is based on what is
fresh at the market.

  A fish menu is featured nightly, including, for example, honey-smoked salmon,
lobster ragoût in puff pastry, filet of Dover sole with saffron sauce, followed by
black-currant sorbet with cassis. A la carte dishes are likely to include a truffle-baked
chicken liver parfait with red currants, fresh mussels steamed in white wine with
herbs, honey-fried guinea hen with ginger and peppers, or beef ribeye steak with
escargots.

RESTAURANT GILLELEJE, Nyhavn 10. Tel. 33-12-58-58.
  Cuisine: DANISH/INTERNATIONAL. **Reservations:** Required. **Bus:** 8, 9, 10.
$ Prices: Appetizers 48–72 kroner ($8.30–$12.50); main dishes 148–245 kroner
($25.60–$42.40); fixed-price lunch 124 kroner ($21.50); fixed-price dinner 198
kroner ($34.30). AE, DC, MC, V.
  Open: Lunch Mon–Sat 11am–3pm; dinner Mon–Sat 5–11pm. **Closed:** July.

The nautical decor is appealing but diners come for the elaborate *rijsttafel* (rice table),
offering flavored rice and an endless procession of meats, fish, spices, garnishes, and
sauces. However, to be served a rijsttafel, you must call in advance to order it. Other
specialties include whisky steak flambé with grilled tomatoes, fish soup, and Danish
herring platter. Desserts like papaya and passion-fruit sorbets are available.

VICTOR'S CAFE, Ny Østergade 8. Tel. 33-13-36-12.
  Cuisine: DANISH/FRENCH. **Reservations:** Recommended. **Bus:** 1, 6, 9.
$ Prices: Fixed-price meal 205–275 kroner ($35.50–$47.60) at dinner, 140 kroner
($24.20) at lunch; appetizers 65–85 kroner ($11.25–$14.70); main dishes 145–
170 kroner ($25.10–$29.40). AE, DC, MC, V.
  Open: Lunch daily 11:30am–3pm; dinner daily 6–11pm.

This is the Danish version of Paris's famous La Coupole. Decorated in a sophisticated
bistro style, it has a café at one end and a restaurant at the other. The art-oriented
crowd can sit at the curved, illuminated bar or at one of the tables. The popular Victor
Plate, costing 105 kroner ($18.20) at lunch, offers three food items. You can also
choose from a selection of open-face sandwiches in the 38 kroner to 65 kroner ($6.60
to $11.25) range. Look for the daily specials posted on the blackboard. Try breast of
wild duckling with plums and celery, ragoût of fish with red peppers, or baked salmon
with chervil sauce and artichoke heart. The fish menu changes daily.

INEXPENSIVE

RESTAURANT PARNAS, Lille Kongensgade 16. Tel. 33-11-49-10.
  Cuisine: DANISH. **Reservations:** Required. **Bus:** 1, 6, 9, 10, 29.
$ Prices: Appetizers 30–60 kroner ($5.20–$10.40); main dishes 69–155 kroner
($11.90–$26.80). AE, DC, MC, V.
  Open: Mon–Thurs 5pm–3am, Sat 6pm–5am.

Opposite the city's largest department store, Magasin, this is a late-night refuge
decorated like a warm, rustic, old-fashioned Danish *kro* (inn). Begin with three
different kinds of herring or marinated salmon, following with fried sliced pork with
parsley sauce, several different preparations of sole and salmon, or the house specialty,
a Parnas Gryde combining grilled sirloin with bacon, marrow, and mushrooms, with
béarnaise sauce on the side. This platter has been on the menu since the restaurant

opened in the 1930s. After midnight a limited menu is available. Live music begins at 8:30pm.

2. NEAR RÅDHUSPLADSEN & TIVOLI

EXPENSIVE

ALEXANDER NEVSKI, in the Plaza Hotel, Bernstorffsgade 4. Tel. 33-14-92-62.
   Cuisine: RUSSIAN. **Reservations:** Required. **Bus:** 1, 6.
$ **Prices:** Appetizers 45–150 kroner ($7.80–$26); main dishes 140–210 kroner ($24.20–$36.30). AE, DC, MC, V.
   Open: Lunch Mon–Sat 11:30am–3:30pm; dinner Mon–Sat 4:30–11:30pm.
The only Russian restaurant in Denmark, it's named after a prince of Novgorod, a Russian national hero of the 1200s. After a drink in the Library Bar (see "Evening Entertainment" in Chapter 7), proceed into the czarist-style restaurant. An impressive range of caviar and more than 20 different vodkas are available.

Some dishes are Russian classics; others are rediscovered recipes. Most food preparation is visible through an opening in the kitchen. Order steaks skewered on fencing swords, marinated in brandy, and then flambéed at your table. Try blinis with caviar, sautéed fresh fish with a pomegranate and pumpkin compote, or beef Stroganoff for two. The sauté of guinea fowl with Jerusalem artichokes is another specialty. Finish with tea from a samovar, after ordering the rum baba with cranberry icing and a vanilla sauce.

MODERATE

COPENHAGEN CORNER, H. C. Andersens Blvd. 18. Tel. 33-91-45-45.
   Cuisine: SCANDINAVIAN. **Reservations:** Recommended. **Bus:** 1, 6, 8.
$ **Prices:** 2-course meals 138–250 kroner ($23.90–$43.30); 3-course meals 340 kroner ($58.80); appetizers 55–135 kroner ($9.50–$23.40); main dishes 85–210 kroner ($14.70–$36.30). AE, DC, MC, V.
   Open: Daily 11am–midnight.
Opening onto Rådhuspladsen, around the corner from the Tivoli, Copenhagen Corner is decorated like a greenhouse. The decor is modern Scandinavian, with two large oil paintings by Danish masters P. S. Croyer and Michael Ancher. The menu is extensive, including several different preparations of Norwegian salmon. Meat dishes include Danish duckling in its own juice. Try also the roast filet of reindeer with cloudberries glazed in acacia honey.

HANA KYOTO, Vimmelskaftet 39, Strøgarkaden. Tel. 33-32-22-96.
   Cuisine: SUSHI. **Reservations:** Recommended. **Bus:** 1, 6, 28.
$ **Prices:** Fixed-price meals 160–220 kroner ($27.70–$38.10) at dinner, 65–100 kroner ($11.20–$17.30) at lunch; sushi 15–50 kroner ($2.60–$8.70) per piece of raw fish before it is cut. AE, DC, MC, V.
   Open: Lunch Mon–Fri noon–3pm; dinner Mon–Fri 5–10pm.
This is the only sushi bar in Copenhagen. Located on the Strøget, it's decorated in typical Japanese simplicity. It imports fresh fish and shellfish from Japan, Britain, Iceland, Greenland, Norway, and the Mediterranean. (The chef will cook the fish upon request.) Tuna, salmon, and eel are the most popular raw fish that Danes order. The chef does not serve typical Japanese dishes such as sukiyaki. A fixed-price dinner includes soup, appetizers, a main-course selection of raw fish, and tea.

RESTAURANT PRAG, Amagerbrogade 37. Tel. 31-54-44-44.
   Cuisine: DANISH. **Reservations:** Recommended. **Bus:** 2, 9.
$ **Prices:** Fixed-price menus 158–255 kroner ($27.30–$44.10); menu gastronomique 405 kroner ($70.10); appetizers 58–99 kroner ($10–$17.10); main dishes 138–208 kroner ($23.90–$36). AE, DC, MC, V.

DENMARK

Copenhagen

Lille Triangel
Gamisons Kirkegård
Hovedvej
Kristianiagade
Østbanegade
Dag Hammerskjörds Alle
Østerport Station
Forbindelsesvej
Holmens Kirkegård
Østerport Station
Folke Bernadottes Alle
Oslo Plads
Østre Anlæg
Stockholms Gade
Øster Farimagsgade
Øster Søgade
Sortedam Dossering
Sortedams Sø
Fredensbro
Vej

Øster Voldgade
Sølvgade
Øster Farimagsgade
Selvgade
Øster Farimagsgade
Rigensgade
Kronprinsessegade
Kerkegade
Adelgade
Borgergade
Gernersgade
Suensonsgade
Store Kongensgade
Grønningen
Esplanaden
Bredgade
Toldbodgade

thersgade
Nørre Voldgade
Abenrå
Pilestræde
Købmagergade
Gothersgade
Store Kongensgade
Bredgade

Skt. Annae Plads

Krystalgade
diestraede
Vestergade
Frederiksberggade
Gl. Strand
Amagertorv
Højbro Plads
Østergade
Kongens Nytorv
Nyhavn
Nyhavn
Holbergsgade
Niels Juels gade
Holmens Kanal
Haunegade
Inderhavnen

CHRISTIANSHAVN

àdhus Plads
H.C. Andersens Boulevard
Vester Voldgade
Kongens Tøjhusgade
Christians Brygge
Knippelsbro
Strandgade
Overgaden oven Vandet
Prinsessegade
Skt. Annae Gade

Mitchelsgade
Hambrosgade
Langebro
Langebrogade
Christians Brygge
Torvegade
Prinsessegade

Sydhavnen
Thorshavnsgade
Amager Boulevard
Stadsgraven
Ved Stadsgraven
Christmas Møllers Plads
Amager Fælled Vej
To Airport

Church ✝   Post Office ⊠   Information ⊙

Open: Lunch Mon–Fri 11:30am–3pm; dinner Mon–Sat 5–10pm.

Near the SAS Scandinavia Hotel, east of Tivoli, this famous Copenhagen restaurant has never been better. Established in 1910 as the Café Sonderborg, it has a new lease on life under talented chef Jan Michelsen. It fills the entire block, incorporating an English-style library, and is like a warmly accommodating Danish *kro* (inn), with dark-wood trim, white stucco walls, and impeccable service.

As much attention is paid to the way a dish looks as to the way it tastes. Try the warm leek terrine with a mushroom salad, sautéed fish of the day, lobster bisque with cognac, or filet of veal with a red wine sauce and stuffed onions. The wild duck with spinach is also excellent.

VIKING STEAK HOUSE, Scala, Axeltorv 2. Tel. 33-15-37-99.
> **Cuisine:** BEEF. **Reservations:** Not required. **Bus:** 1, 6, 8.
> **$ Prices:** Appetizers 52–108 kroner ($9–$18.70); main dishes 98–208 kroner ($17–$36); 3-course lunch 78 kroner ($13.50); children's lunch menu 38 kroner ($6.60). AE, DC, MC, V.
> **Open:** Daily 11am–midnight.

The most expensive dish is lobster from a live tank at the front, but most come to sample the Danish beef steak, priced according to weight. In this second-floor dining room in the Scala complex across from the Tivoli you check off the kind of steak you want on a card and return it to the waitress.

INEXPENSIVE

CHILI, Vandkunsten 1. Tel. 33-91-19-18.
> **Cuisine:** MEXICAN. **Reservations:** Recommended. **Bus:** 5, 14, 16, 28, 41.
> **$ Prices:** Appetizers 25–60 kroner ($4.30–$10.40); main dishes 41–90 kroner ($7.10–$15.60). No credit cards.
> **Open:** Mon–Wed 11am–11pm, Thurs–Sat 11am–midnight, Sun 1–9pm.

A short walk from Rådhuspladsen, Chili is the latest reincarnation of the famous old Tokanten, a landmark eating house. It's decorated in the colors of the American Southwest, warm reds, greens, and blues. Many kinds of hamburgers are available, plus a Tex-Mex salad and chili con carne. Service is fast.

CITY ROCK CAFE, Scala, Axeltorv 2. Tel. 33-15-45-40.
> **Cuisine:** AMERICAN. **Reservations:** Not required. **Bus:** 1, 6, 8.
> **$ Prices:** Appetizers 38–62 kroner ($6.60–$10.70); sandwiches 51–65 kroner ($8.80–$11.20). No credit cards.
> **Open:** Daily 11am–10pm.

This is one of the busiest café/bars at Scala. Rock 'n' roll music from the '60s to the '90s is played against a backdrop of banquettes made from the rear end of a 1959 Cadillac and an antique Harley-Davidson motorcycle spotlit and displayed as pop art. Kids feast on such fare as a Malibu salad with rice, ham, and olives, or Pacific sandwiches (tuna and cucumber), and, of course, hamburgers.

GREEN'S RESTAURANT, Grønnegade 12-14. Tel. 33-15-16-90.
> **Cuisine:** VEGETARIAN. **Reservations:** Recommended. **Bus:** 7, 17, 43.
> **$ Prices:** Salad bar 75 kroner ($13); appetizers 46–75 kroner ($8–$13); main dishes 78–139 kroner ($13.50–$24). MC, V.
> **Open:** Lunch Mon–Sat 11:30am–5pm; dinner Mon–Thurs 5:30–9pm.

This popular vegetarian restaurant lies in a commercial neighborhood, off Pistolstraede, at the edge of a pedestrians-only courtyard. It has a cobblestone-covered outdoor terrace for summer dining. You can order onion quiche, vegetarian pizzas, pita-bread sandwiches, a daily soup, fresh-squeezed juice, and a vegetarian dish of the day. Many make a meal just from the salad bar. At lunchtime it is buffet style and at night there's full service.

PUK'S RESTAURANT, Vandkunsten 8. Tel. 33-11-14-17.
> **Cuisine:** DANISH. **Reservations:** Required (summer and Dec only). **Bus:** 28, 29, 41.

$ Prices: Fixed-price menu 108 kroner ($18.70); appetizers 42–68 kroner ($7.30–$11.80); main dishes 36–175 kroner ($6.20–$30.30). AE, DC, MC, V.
Open: Daily 10:30am–5am (kitchen closes at 4am Mon–Sat, at 2am Sun).
Puk's lies in the basement of what was once a 1750 brewery. Take the outside stairs down; the street-level pub is different from Puk's. Smørrebrød is presented more as platters of food than as sandwiches. One of the best-liked is a platter containing six kinds of smoked fish. You can also order Danish meatballs and herring platters.

BUDGET

AXELBORG BODEGA, Axeltorv 1. Tel. 33-11-06-38.
Cuisine: DANISH. **Reservations:** Recommended. **Bus:** 1, 6.
$ Prices: Appetizers 28–55 kroner ($4.80–$9.50); main dishes 60–120 kroner ($10.40–$20.80); 2-course Danmenu at lunch 85 kroner ($14.70). AE, DC, MC, V.
Open: Daily 11:30am–9:30pm (bar open 10am–2am).
Across from the circus and near Scala and Tivoli, this well-established 1912 Danish café has outdoor tables. Order the *dagens ret* (daily special). Typical Danish dishes are featured, including *frikadeller* (meatballs) and pork chops. A wide selection of smørrebrød is also available, costing from 35 kroner ($6.10).

3. NEAR ROSENBORG SLOT

VERY EXPENSIVE

ST. GERTRUDS KLOSTER, Hauser Plads 32. Tel. 33-14-66-30.
Cuisine: INTERNATIONAL. **Reservations:** Required. **Bus:** 4E, 7E, 14, 16.
$ Prices: 3-course menus 366–445 kroner ($63.30–$77); 6-course menu dégustation 675 kroner ($116.80); appetizers 90–185 kroner ($15.60–$32); main dishes 198–260 kroner ($34.30–$45). AE, DC, MC, V.
Open: Dinner only, daily 5–11:15pm. **Closed:** Dec 25–Jan 1.
Near Nørreport Station and south of Rosenborg Castle, this is the most romantic restaurant in Copenhagen. There's no electricity in the labyrinth of 14th-century underground vaults, and the hundreds of flickering candles, open grill, iron sconces, and rough-hewn furniture create the most elegant medieval ambience. Have an apéritif in the darkly paneled library. Try the fresh homemade foie gras with black truffles, lobster served in a turbot bouillon, scallops sautéed with herbs in sauterne, venison (year-round) with green asparagus and truffle sauce, or a fish-and-shellfish terrine studded with chunks of lobster and salmon.

EXPENSIVE

LES ETOILES ET UNE ROSE, Dronningens Tvaergade 43. Tel. 33-15-05-54.
Cuisine: DANISH/FRENCH. **Reservations:** Required. **Bus:** 6, 8, 28, 41.
$ Prices: 6-course menu gourmet 445 kroner ($77); appetizers 75–125 kroner ($13–$21.60); main dishes 175–235 kroner ($30.30–$40.70). AE, DC, MC, V.
Open: Lunch Mon–Fri noon–2pm; dinner Mon–Sat 5:30–10pm. **Closed:** Jan 1–14.
Hidden by a 1950s apartment complex, near the Royal Theater, lies one of the top restaurants in Copenhagen. Inside, the Mandrup family operates an apéritif bar, a pale-green and white dining room, and an outdoor terrace for warm-weather meals. They earn their truly international reputation every night by serving such dishes as terrine of guinea fowl with truffles on a bed of spinach and honey-sautéed rhubarb ragoût of fresh seafood in puff pastry with root vegetables, and entrecôte of Danish lamb roasted with fresh herbs and covered in a mustard-cream sauce. The chef's "fish fantasy" combines seven different kinds of fish and shellfish.

4. AT GRÅBRØDRE TORV

MODERATE

BØF & OST, Gråbrødre Torv 13. Tel. 31-11-99-11.
  Cuisine: DANISH/FRENCH. **Reservations:** Required. **Bus:** 5.
  $ Prices: Fixed-price dinner 215 kroner ($37.20); fixed-price lunch 78 kroner ($13.50); appetizers 59–290 kroner ($10.20–$50.20); main dishes 115–159 kroner ($19.90–$27.50). DC, MC, V.
  Open: Lunch Mon–Sat 11:30am–4pm; dinner Mon–Sat 4–10:30pm. **Closed:** Dec 24–25 and Jan 1.

The "Beef & Cheese" is housed in a 1728 building, its cellars from a medieval monastery. In summer, there is a pleasant outdoor terrace, overlooking Gray Friars Square. Specialties include lobster soup, salmon savoie, Danish Heltling caviar, a cheese plate with six different selections, and some of the best grilled tenderloin in town.

PEDER OXE'S RESTAURANT/VINKAELDER WINE BAR, Gråbrødre Torv 11. Tel. 33-11-00-77.
  Cuisine: DANISH. **Reservations:** Recommended. **Bus:** 5.
  $ Prices: Appetizers 65–95 kroner ($11.20–$16.40); main dishes 85–149 kroner ($14.70–$25.80); fixed-price lunch 78 kroner ($13.50). DC, MC, V.
  Open: Daily 11:30am–1am.

In the Middle Ages this was the site of a monastery, but the present building dates from the 1700s. The restaurant and wine bar was established in the 1970s, and continues in popularity among the young. A salad bar is included in the price of the main course, but it is so tempting that many opt to have it alone, costing 65 kroner ($11.20) per person. Dishes include lobster soup, salmon tartare, oysters, open-face sandwiches, hamburgers, and fresh fish.

5. NEAR KULTORVET

INEXPENSIVE

RISTORANTE ITALIANO, Fiolstraede 2. Tel. 33-11-12-95.
  Cuisine: ITALIAN. **Reservations:** Recommended. **Bus:** 5.
  $ Prices: Pizzas and pastas 49–69 kroner ($8.50–$11.90). AE, DC, MC, V.
  Open: Daily 11am–2am (kitchen closes at 1am).

This fun restaurant is patronized mainly by students from nearby University of Copenhagen. Pizzas (Danish-Italian style) are featured, as well as lots of good pasta. Spaghetti Pavarotti is a specialty. Meat and fish courses are also available.

6. NEAR CHRISTIANSBORG

EXPENSIVE

KROGS FISKERESTAURANT, Gammel Strand 38. Tel. 33-15-89-15.
  Cuisine: SEAFOOD. **Reservations:** Required. **Bus:** 2, 10, 16.
  $ Prices: Fixed-price menu 375 kroner ($64.90) for 3 courses, 425 kroner ($73.50) for 4 courses; appetizers 98–175 kroner ($17–$30.30); main dishes 205–350 kroner ($35.50–$60.60). AE, DC, MC, V.
  Open: Lunch Mon–Sat noon–3pm; dinner Mon–Sat 5–10pm.

Situated near Christiansborg Castle, this 1789 building has been a restaurant since 1910, serving delectable seafood. Choices include lobster soup, bouillabaisse, natural oysters, mussels steamed in white wine, and poached salmon-trout. A limited selection of meat dishes is available.

NOUVELLE, Gammel Strand 34. Tel. 33-13-50-18.
Cuisine: DANISH. **Reservations:** Required. **Bus:** 28, 29, 41.
$ Prices: 4-course dinner 395 kroner ($68.30); 3-course lunch 235 kroner ($40.70); appetizers 75–125 kroner ($13–$21.60); main dishes 175–218 kroner ($30.30–$37.70). AE, DC, MC, V.
Open: Lunch Mon–Fri 11:30am–3pm; dinner Mon–Sat 7:30–9pm. **Closed:** Dec 22–Jan 6.

In an elegant dining-room setting, Nouvelle is one of the capital's special restaurants. It is on the first floor of a gray 1870 house beside a canal. The color scheme is dark and light tones of yellow, with gray and purple accents. The cuisine is modern Danish with such dishes as corn pie with beluga caviar and cold bouillon-marinated vegetables, and cream of turbot soup spiced with sauterne. Try the fricassée of sole with mussels and pear or haunch of venison with damson plum sauce and a timbale of marrow.

MODERATE

DEN GYLDNE FORTUN, Ved Stranden 18. Tel. 33-12-20-11.
Cuisine: DANISH/SEAFOOD. **Reservations:** Recommended. **Bus:** 1, 6, 10.
$ Prices: Fixed-price meals 295–335 kroner ($51–$58) at dinner, 155 kroner ($26.80) at lunch; appetizers 66–112 kroner ($11.40–$19.40); main dishes 155–305 kroner ($26.80–$52.80). AE, DC, MC.
Open: Lunch daily noon–3pm; dinner daily 6pm–midnight.

Popular at lunchtime, this restaurant opposite Christiansborg Castle is a real "golden fortune," as the name translates. Dating from 1796, it has been visited by H. C. Andersen, Jenny Lind, and Henry Wadsworth Longfellow. You climb green marble stairs to enter the formal restaurant resembling an English club. Amid crystal chandeliers and modern lithographs, you'll enjoy good-tasting fresh fish. Look for daily specials or sample the herring, poached sole, Baltic salmon, or a Danish beef dish. Try a Scandinavian bouillabaisse.

FISKEKAELDEREN, Ved Stranden 18. Tel. 33-12-20-11.
Cuisine: SEAFOOD. **Reservations:** Required. **Bus:** 1, 6, 10.
$ Prices: Appetizers 65–110 kroner ($11.20–$19); main dishes 155–275 kroner ($26.80–$47.60). AE, DC, MC, V.
Open: Mon–Fri noon–11:30pm, Sat–Sun 5–10:30pm.

Though the building dates from 1750, Fiskekaelderen was established in 1975, and is today considered the best seafood restaurant in Copenhagen. It prides itself on very fresh fish either imported from the Mediterranean or caught in the waters of the North Atlantic. Warmly nautical in decor, it has a bubbling lobster tank and an ice table displaying the fish of the day. Try the terrine of smoked fish with seaweed and deep-fried artichokes, Danish fish soup, stuffed sole poached in white wine and glazed with hollandaise sauce, or fricassée of three types of fish in a saffron-flavored bouillon with noodles. Some beef dishes, such as Charolais sirloin, are also served.

7. IN TIVOLI

Food prices inside Tivoli are about 30% higher than elsewhere. Try skipping dessert at a restaurant and picking up a less expensive treat at one of the many stands. Take bus 1, 6, 8, 16, 29, 30, 32, or 33 to reach the park and any of the following restaurants.
Note: These restaurants are open only from May to mid-September.

VERY EXPENSIVE

BELLE TERRASSE, Vesterbrogade 3, Tivoli. Tel. 33-12-11-36.

Cuisine: DANISH/FRENCH. **Reservations:** Required.

$ **Prices:** Fixed-price dinner 325–445 kroner ($56.20–$77); fixed-price lunch 285 kroner ($49.30); appetizers 85–175 kroner ($14.70–$30.30); main dishes 195–285 kroner ($33.70–$49.30). AE, DC, MC, V.

Open: Daily noon–11pm.

A seductive menu and a glamorous, flower-filled terrace lures diners to one of Tivoli's best restaurants. Guests such as Marlene Dietrich have enjoyed the Belle Epoque atmosphere in this octagonal greenhouselike dining room. The cuisine is refined and dignified, the service formal. Begin with the consommé of lobster soup with ravioli of chives, followed by salmon on a bed of leeks with saffron sauce or filet of veal with morels.

DIVAN II, Vesterbrogade 3, Tivoli. Tel. 33-12-51-51.

Cuisine: DANISH/FRENCH. **Reservations:** Required.

$ **Prices:** Appetizers 105–355 kroner ($18.20–$61.40); main dishes 205–335 kroner ($35.50–$58); fixed-price lunch 355 kroner ($61.40); fixed-price dinner 495 kroner ($85.60). DC, MC.

Open: Lunch daily noon–3pm; dinner daily 6–10:30pm.

This may be the most expensive restaurant in Denmark. It may also be the best. Service is impeccable in this exquisite gardenlike setting where the chef selects only the finest ingredients. Try the poached turbot with morels, Baltic salmon with glazed vegetables, or roast stuffed duckling with truffles.

EXPENSIVE

LA CREVETTE, Vesterbrogade 3, Tivoli. Tel. 33-14-68-47.

Cuisine: SEAFOOD. **Reservations:** Required.

$ **Prices:** Fixed-price meal 345 kroner ($59.70) at dinner, 210 kroner ($36.30) at lunch; appetizers 95–145 kroner ($16.40–$25.10); main dishes 155–255 kroner ($26.80–$44.10). AE, DC, MC, V.

Open: Daily noon–11pm.

The only seafood restaurant in the Tivoli, La Crevette has an outdoor terrace and an elegant modern dining room. The seafood is prepared in a French international style. Specialties include salmon marinated in cognac, fish terrine, a three-herring platter, oven-baked turbot with tiny shrimp, grilled lobster, and a handful of well-seasoned meat dishes such as vegetable-stuffed breast of guinea fowl with a mushroom-and-boletus sauce.

DIVAN I, Vesterbrogade 3, Tivoli. Tel. 33-11-42-42.

Cuisine: FRENCH. **Reservations:** Required.

$ **Prices:** Fixed-price meals 295–405 kroner ($51–$70.10) at dinner, 235 kroner ($40.70) at lunch; appetizers 85–195 kroner ($14.70–$33.70); main dishes 175–250 kroner ($30.30–$43.30). AE, DC, MC, V.

Open: Daily noon–11pm (drinks until midnight).

Opened the same year as the Tivoli, this popular gardenlike restaurant has been run by the same family since 1913. Be assured of a refined French cuisine and service, and a good view of the Tivoli Gardens. For appetizers, try smoked salmon and pickled salmon with dill, or perhaps the goose liver pâté en croûte with sauterne jelly. Among hot appetizers, the lobster bisque is always a favorite, as is the grilled scallops with mango cream and truffles. Among fish dishes, sample sole meunière, or in the poultry and meat category, Danish venison with a juniper sauce or braised breast of guinea fowl with marinated savoy cabbage and a tomato-thyme sauce.

LOUISE NIMB, Vesterbrogade 3, Tivoli. Tel. 33-14-60-03.

Cuisine: DANISH/FRENCH. **Reservations:** Required.

$ **Prices:** Fixed-price menu 325 kroner ($56.20); appetizers 49–165 kroner ($8.50–$28.50); main dishes 195–220 kroner ($33.70–$38.10). AE, DC, MC, V.

Open: Lunch daily noon–4pm; dinner daily 5–11pm.

Next door to its companion restaurant, La Crevette, this may be the most formal restaurant in Tivoli, styled like a Moorish pavilion. It is decorated with antique accessories, and looks out over the fountains and flowers of the Tivoli. Why the name

Louise Nimb? She was the establishment's long-departed female chef who ladled up soup from a then much smaller kitchen. Dinner might include grilled salmon with red-wine butter, rib roast of beef, and tournedos in a calvados-based sauce. There is live piano music during dinner.

MODERATE

FAERGEKROEN, Vesterbrogade 3, Tivoli. Tel. 33-12-94-12.
   Cuisine: DANISH. **Reservations:** Not required.
$ Prices: Appetizers 25–50 kroner ($4.30–$8.70); main dishes 70–147 kroner ($12.10–$25.40); fixed-price lunch 85 kroner ($14.70). AE, DC, MC, V.
   Open: Daily 10am–midnight (hot food 11am–9:45pm).

Nestled amid a cluster of trees at the edge of the lake, this restaurant resembles a pink half-timbered Danish cottage. In warm weather, try to sit on the outside dining terrace. The menu offers drinks, snacks, and full meals. The latter might include an array of omelets, beef with horseradish, fried plaice with melted butter, pork chops with red cabbage, curried chicken, and fried meatballs. A pianist provides sing-along music every evening starting at 8pm.

GRØFTEN, Vesterbrogade 3, Tivoli. Tel. 33-12-11-25.
   Cuisine: DANISH. **Reservations:** Not required.
$ Prices: Fixed-price 2-course menu 90 kroner ($15.60); appetizers 39–98 kroner ($6.70–$17); main dishes 75–150 kroner ($13–$26). DC, MC, V.
   Open: Daily 11am–11pm.

I think this is the best budget restaurant in Tivoli, offering a tourist menu that could be tomato soup with crisp French bread, followed by ground beef with gravy, grilled mushrooms, and tiny new potatoes. It's located next to the Pantomime Theater, and most diners eat outside.

8. ON THE OUTSKIRTS

EXPENSIVE

RESTAURANT SAISON, in the Hotel Skovshoved, Strandvejen 267, Charlottenlund. Tel. 31-64-00-28.
   Cuisine: DANISH/FRENCH. **Reservations:** Required. **Bus:** 6.
$ Prices: Fixed-price meals 325–495 kroner ($56.20–$85.60) at dinner, 235 kroner ($40.70) at lunch; appetizers 75–115 kroner ($13–$19.90); main dishes 155–205 kroner ($26.80–$35.50). AE, DC, MC, V.
   Open: Lunch Mon–Sat noon–2pm; dinner Mon–Sat 6–10pm. **Closed:** Dec 24–26 and Jan. 1.

One of Denmark's finest restaurants lies 5 miles north of Copenhagen in a 1900 red-brick hotel. From the ground-floor dining room you can look across the water to Sweden. Guests can dine in either the white room or the red room, the latter painted with pseudo-Egyptian murals by turn-of-the-century students in exchange for a free room. There is also a glassed-in terrace. One fixed-price menu is devoted to local fare such as a vegetable terrine with salted salmon or roast rabbit. Dishes change, but typical items include parsley-and-oyster soup, layered casserole of salmon and cabbage with a crab sauce, and sautéed halibut with forest mushrooms. Game, such as venison, is served in season.

SØLLERØD KRO, Sollerrødvej 35, Holte-Søllerød. Tel. 42-80-25-05.
   Cuisine: DANISH/INTERNATIONAL. **Reservations:** Required. **Directions:** Take highway E4 toward Holte and exit at Søllerød; or take the S-train to Holte and taxi the rest of the way.
$ Prices: Fixed-price dinner 600 kroner ($103.80); appetizers 130–165 kroner ($22.50–$28.50); main dishes 175–280 kroner ($30.30–$48.40). AE, DC, MC, V.
   Open: Daily 11:30am–10pm.

In a historic model village 11 miles north of Copenhagen, this traditional 1677 inn with a thatched roof and whitewashed walls is the top-rated restaurant of Zealand outside the capital. Located inside a flower-filled garden with outdoor courtyard dining, the setting is idyllic. Try such dishes as lobster bisque, filet of sole with Norwegian lobster and a lobster sauce, or loin of Danish lamb with herbs baked en croûte. From May to August, crevettes de fjord (shrimp from the fjord) is a feature.

MODERATE

RESTAURANT PAUSTIAN, Kalkbraenderiløbskaj 2. Tel. 31-18-55-01.
   Cuisine: DANISH. **Reservations:** Recommended.
$ **Prices:** Fixed-price lunch 185 kroner ($32); appetizers 65–105 kroner ($11.20–$18.20); main dishes 115–160 kroner ($19.90–$27.70). AE, DC, MC, V.
   Open: Lunch only, Mon–Fri noon–4pm, Sat noon–3pm.
Amid an industrial landscape 3 miles north of the city center along the North Harbor, this restaurant is part of the showroom for a large furniture outlet. In a futuristically modern building, it is worth the excursion. Combine lunch with a shopping trip to survey some of the finest Scandinavian furniture, including reproductions of the old masters such as Charles Eames and Alvar Aalto. The restaurant has cobalt-blue majolica tile, high-tech lighting, and big windows framing cranes and masts of ships in the harbor. The cuisine uses the best of Danish produce. Begin with fresh oysters or mussel soup with leeks and garlic. Then try smoked salmon with spinach or veal kidney with mustard sauce.

9. SPECIALTY DINING

LOCAL FAVORITES

The favorite lunch of Scandinavians, particularly Danes, is *smørrebrød* (an open-face sandwich). The purest form of smørrebrød is made with Danish dark rye bread, called *rugbrød,* although other types of bread are sometimes used. Most taverns and cafés offer smørrebrød, but there are also many places that just serve this on a take-out basis.

INEXPENSIVE

LILLE LAEKKERBISKEN, Gammel Strand 34. Tel. 33-32-04-00.
   Cuisine: DANISH. **Reservations:** Not accepted. **Bus:** 28, 29, 41.
$ **Prices:** Appetizers 32–45 kroner ($5.50–$7.80); main dishes 45–95 kroner ($7.80–$16.40); fixed-price lunch 125 kroner ($21.60). AE, DC, MC, V.
   Open: Lunch only, Mon–Sat 11:30am–4pm.
This lunch-only restaurant, in the same building as the elegant Nouvelle, has walls covered with 19th-century oil paintings and old tapestries. It offers a full array of

 FROMMER'S COOL FOR KIDS:
RESTAURANTS

City Rock Café (see p. 74) A busy café, rock 'n' roll music from the '60s to the '90s is played against a backdrop of banquettes made from a 1959 Cadillac and a Harley-Davidson motorcycle.

Copenhagen Corner (see p. 71) A special children's menu with such dishes as shrimp cocktail and grilled rump steak are offered.

smørrebrød along with such hot main dishes as fried plaice. Tables are placed outside as weather allows.

RESTAURANT OSTEHJØRNET, Store Kongensgade 56. Tel. 33-15-85-77.

Cuisine: DANISH. **Reservations:** Recommended. **Bus:** 1, 10.
$ **Prices:** Appetizers 55 kroner ($9.50); main dishes 80–95 kroner ($13.80–$16.40). DC, MC, V.
  Open: June and Aug–Sept. Mon–Fri 11:30am–6pm; Oct–May, Mon–Fri 11:30am–6pm, Sat 11:30am–3pm. **Closed:** July.

Since this restaurant is so popular at lunchtime that a dozen or so diners are turned away, the secret is to arrive early or late. There are a variety of Danish specialties, but I prefer the seafood salads made fresh daily. I recommend the herring salad, the mussel salad, quiche Lorraine, veal Cordon Bleu, smoked turkey, sweetbreads, and the ham and cheese omelets. A smart dessert choice might be a delectable fruit tart with a hint of chocolate. The restaurant lies one floor above street level in an 18th-century building.

BUDGET

SLØTSKAELDEREN, Fortunstraede 4. Tel. 33-11-15-37.

Cuisine: DANISH. **Reservations:** Recommended. **Bus:** 1, 6, 10.
$ **Prices:** Smørrebrød (open-face sandwiches) 25–75 kroner ($4.30–$13). DC, MC, V.
  Open: Tues–Sat 11am–3pm.

This is the star of the smørrebrød. This landmark opened in 1797, but since 1910 has been owned by the same family. Habitués call the place "Gitte Kik," the name of the owner and granddaughter of the founder. Everything—the Danish wood trim, the framed old photographs, and the gold walls—add up to *hygge,* a coziness that has attracted such notables as the prince of Denmark. Try the marinated salmon, fresh tiny shrimp, or hot frikadeller. The smoked-eel and scrambled-egg sandwich is said to be the best of its kind.

DINING COMPLEX

Scala, Axeltorv 2, was originally conceived in 1851 as the Danish National Amusement Center, a collection of shops, cafés, and amusement arcades for the wintertime. Close to the Tivoli, City Hall, and the Central Railroad Station, it thrived until 1958. In 1987 it was purchased and renovated, then reopened in 1989 as the most extensive range of bars, restaurants, cinemas, and nightlife possibilities in the Danish capital.

Restaurants in Scala are open daily from 11am to midnight or 1am. Reservations are almost never required. Establishments accept major credit cards (AE, DC, MC, V).

AFTERNOON TEA

LA GLACE, Skoubogade 3-5. Tel. 33-14-46-46.

Cuisine: PASTRIES. **Reservations:** Not accepted. **Bus:** 1, 6, 8.
$ **Prices:** Pastries 8–19 kroner ($1.40–$3.30); coffee, tea, hot chocolate 21 kroner ($3.60). No credit cards.
  Open: Mon–Sat 8am–5:30pm.

Open since 1879, this time-honored pastry shop offers a pot of coffee or chocolate for 21 kroner ($3.60), and a variety of cakes, pastries, and chocolates. Try a slice of *sportkage* (sportsman's cake), composed of whipped cream, crumbled nougat, macaroons, and profiteroles that have been glazed in caramel. If chocolate is your bag, you'll appreciate the *Othellokage* (macaroons, custard cream, and outrageous amounts of chocolate).

CAFES

CAFEEN NIKOLAJ, Nikolaj Plads 12. Tel. 33-11-63-13.

Cuisine: DANISH. **Reservations:** Not accepted. **Bus:** 2, 6, 10, 27, 28, 29.
$ Prices: Appetizers 32–55 kroner ($5.50–$9.50); main dishes 50–98 kroner ($8.70–$17). AE, DC.
Open: Mon–Sat noon–5pm.

This unusual café is located within the monument which, circa 1530, was the scene of the thundering sermons of Hans Tausen, a father of the Danish Reformation. It serves typically Danish lunches, including open-face sandwiches, soups, herring, and sliced ham and cheese.

SKINDBUKSEN, Lille Kongensgade 4, off Kongens Nytorv. Tel. 33-12-90-37.

Cuisine: DANISH. **Reservations:** Not accepted. **Bus:** 1, 6, 10, 27, 28, 29.
$ Prices: Appetizers 29–49 kroner ($5–$8.50); main dishes 39–98 kroner ($6.70–$17); fixed-price lunch 59 kroner ($10.20). AE, DC, MC, V.
Open: Daily 11am–1am (kitchen closes at 8:45pm).

This atmospheric landmark, well known among the beer drinkers, serves lobscouse—a meat-potato stew (mainly potatoes). It's so popular that it is frequently sold out by noon. Smørrebrød is also available. Other items include soups, pâtés, shrimp, and beef with béarnaise sauce.

STREET FOOD

Copenhagen has many hot-dog stands, chicken and fish grills, and smørrebrød counters, providing good, quick, and inexpensive meals.

Hot-dog stands, especially those around the Rådhuspladsen, offer *polser* (steamed or grilled hot dogs) with shredded onions on top and pommes frites (french fries) on the side.

The **bageri** or **konditori** (bakery) found on almost every block, sells fresh bread, rolls, and Danish pastries.

Viktualiehandler (small food shops), throughout the city, are the closest thing to a New York deli. You can buy roast beef with log (fried onions) included free. The best buy is smoked fish. Ask for a Bornholmer, a large, boneless sardine from the Danish island of Bornholm, or for røgost, a popular and inexpensive smoked cheese.

Yogurt fans will be delighted to know that the Danish variety is cheap and tasty. It's available in small containers—just peel off the cover and drink it right out of the cup as the Danes do. *Hytte ret* (cottage cheese) is also good and cheap, but it's sold only in Irma stores.

PICNIC FARE & WHERE TO EAT IT

You can picnic in any of the city parks in the town center. Try Kongsgarten near Kongens Nytorv, the Kastellet area near *The Little Mermaid* statue, Botanisk Have (site of the Botanical Gardens), the lakeside promenades in southeastern Copenhagen, and the old moat at Christianshavn. Remember not to litter.

Pick up some Danish smørrebrød to take out. The most central location for this is **Centrum Smørrebrød,** Vesterbrogade 6 (tel. 33-12-80-76), which is open 24 hours a day. The location is near the Tivoli and the Central Railroad Station. Sandwiches range from 16.50 to 35 kroner ($2.90 to $6.10).

Another branch is **City Smørrebrød,** Gothersgade 12 (tel. 33-15-75-42), open Monday to Friday only from 8am to 6pm. Only take-out smørrebrød is served, as there are no sit-down tables. Prices range from 21 kroner to 37 kroner ($3.60 to $6.40). One of the best-established take-out places of its kind, it has been doing a thriving business since World War II.

CHAPTER 7

WHAT TO SEE & DO IN COPENHAGEN

With all the emphasis on amusement parks, shopping expeditions, beer-drinking cellars and gardens, and bustling nighttime spots, some visitors to Copenhagen tend to overlook the galleries, museums, and castles that make the city so special. There are so many little hidden nooks of charm waiting to be explored that it's hard to decide what to do first.

SUGGESTED ITINERARIES

IF YOU HAVE 1 DAY

Day 1: Take Walking Tour 1 through the old city (see below in this chapter), which will give you time to recover from jet lag. Spend the late afternoon at Christiansborg Castle on Slotsholmen island where the queen of Denmark receives guests. Early in the evening head to the Tivoli.

IF YOU HAVE 2 DAYS

Day 1: See "If You Have 1 Day," above.

Day 2: Visit Amalienborg Palace, the queen's residence. Try to time your visit to witness the changing of the guard. Continue beyond the palace to *The Little Mermaid* statue. In the afternoon, see the art treasures of Ny Carlsberg Glyptotek. At night, visit Scala, the restaurant-and-shopping complex.

IF YOU HAVE 3 DAYS

Days 1–2: See "If You Have 2 Days," above.

Day 3: In the morning, visit the 17th-century Rosenborg Castle, summer palace of King Christian IV. Afterward, wander through the park and gardens. Have lunch at one of the restaurants lining the canal at Nyhavn, the traditional seamen's quarter of Copenhagen. In the afternoon, go to Rundetårn (Round Tower) for a panoramic view of the city, and if time remains, stop in at the National Museum and Denmark's Fight for Freedom Museum.

IF YOU HAVE 5 DAYS

Days 1-3: See "If You Have 3 Days," above.

Day 4: Head north from Copenhagen to Louisiana, the modern-art museum, and continue on to Helsingør to visit Kronborg Castle, famously associated with Shakespeare's Hamlet. Return by train to Copenhagen in time for a stroll along the Strøget, the longest walking street in Europe. For dinner, head to Dragør.

Day 5: Visit Frilandsmuseet, at Lyngby, a half-hour train ride from Copenhagen. Have lunch at the park. Return to Copenhagen and take the second of our walking tours (see below in this chapter). If time remains, tour a beer factory, either Carlsberg or Tuborg. Pay a final visit to the Tivoli to cap your adventure in the Danish capital.

1. THE TOP ATTRACTIONS

TIVOLI GARDENS, Vesterbrogade 3. Tel. 33-15-10-01.

Since it opened in 1843, this 20-acre garden and amusement park in the center of Copenhagen has been a resounding success, with its merry-go-round of tiny Viking ships, its games of chance and skill (pinball arcades, slot machines, shooting galleries), and its Ferris wheel of hot-air balloons and cabin seats. There's even a playground for children.

An Arabian-style fantasy palace, with towers and arches, houses more than two dozen restaurants in all price ranges, from a lakeside inn to a beer garden. Take a walk around the edge of the tiny lake with its ducks, swans, and boats.

A parade of the red-uniformed Tivoli Boys Guard takes place on weekends at 6:30 and 8:30pm, and their regimental band gives concerts on Saturday at 3:30pm on the open-air stage. The oldest building at Tivoli, the Chinese-style Pantomime Theater, with its peacock curtain, stages pantomimes in the evening.

For more specifics on all the nighttime happenings in Tivoli—fireworks, brass bands, orchestras, discos, variety acts—see "Evening Entertainment" in this chapter.

Admission: 23 kroner ($4) adults, 12 kroner ($2.10) children under 12 10am-1pm; 33 kroner ($5.70) adults, 17 kroner ($2.90) children 1pm-midnight. Each ride costs 8-16 kroner ($1.40-$2.80); 140 kroner ($24.20) per person for Tivoli-Tour-Pass and for all 25 amusements.

Open: Daily 10am-midnight. **Closed:** Mid-Sept to late Apr. **Bus:** 1, 16, 29.

STATENS MUSEUM FOR KUNST (Royal Museum of Fine Arts), Sølvgade 48-50. Tel. 33-91-21-26.

This well-stocked art museum houses foreign painting and sculpture from the 13th century to the present. There are Dutch golden age landscapes and marine paintings by Rubens and his school plus portraits by Frans Hals and Rembrandt. The Danish golden age is represented by Eckersberg, Købke, and Hansen. French 20th-century art includes 20 works by Matisse. In the Royal Print Room are 300,000 drawings, prints, lithographs, and other works by such artists as Dürer, Rembrandt, Matisse, and Picasso.

Admission: Free.

Open: Tues-Sun 10am-4:30pm. **Bus:** 10, 24, 43, 84.

DEN HIRSCHSPRUNGSKE SAMLING (The Hirschsprung Collection), Stockholmsgade 20. Tel. 31-42-03-36.

This collection of Danish art from the 19th and early 20th centuries lies in Ostre Anlaeg, a park in the city center. Heinrich Hirschsprung (1836-1908), a tobacco merchant, created the collection and it has been growing ever since. The emphasis is on the Danish golden age with such artists as Eckersberg, Købke, Lundbye, and Marstrand. Some furnishings from the artists' homes are exhibited.

IMPRESSIONS

There is nothing of Hamlet in their character.
—R. H. BRUCE LOCKHART, *MY EUROPE*, 1952

Copenhagen is the best-built city of the north.
—WILLIAM COXE, *TRAVELS*, 1792

Admission: 20 kroner ($3.50) adults; free for children under 16.
Open: Wed–Sat 1–4pm, Sun 11am–4pm. **Bus:** 40, 42, 43.

ROSENBORG CASTLE, Øster Voldgade 4A. Tel. 33-15-32-86.

⭐ Founded by Christian IV in the 17th century, this red-brick Renaissance-style castle houses everything from narwhal-tusked and ivory coronation chairs to Frederik VII's baby shoes–all from the Danish Royal family. Officially, its biggest draws are the dazzling crown jewels and regalia in the basement Treasury, where a lavishly decorated coronation saddle from 1596 is also shown. Try to see the Knights Hall (Room 21), with its coronation seat, three silver lions, and relics from the 1700s. Another important attraction is Room 3 used by founding father Christian IV (lucky in love, unlucky in war), who died in this bedroom decorated with Asian lacquer art and a stucco ceiling. The King's Garden (Have) surrounds the castle, and the Botanical Gardens are across the street.
Admission: 30 kroner ($5.20) adults, 5 kroner (90¢) children under 15.
Open: May–Aug, daily 10am–3pm; Sept–Oct, daily 11am–3pm; off-season, Tues–Sun 11am–3pm. Imperial jewels open Tues, Fri, and Sun 11am–2pm. **Bus:** 5, 10, 14. **S-tog:** Nørreport.

CHRISTIANSBORG PALACE, Christiansborg Slotsplads. Tel. 33-92-64-92.

⭐ This granite-and-copper palace, located on the Slotsholmen—a small island that has been the center of political power in Denmark for more than 800 years—houses the Danish parliament, the Supreme Court, the prime ministers's offices, and the Royal Reception Rooms. A guide will lead you through richly decorated rooms, including the Throne Room, banqueting hall, and Queen's Library. Before entering, you will be asked to put on soft overshoes to protect the floors.
On the grounds, visit the well-preserved ruins of the 1167 castle of Bishop Absalon, founder of Copenhagen.
Admission: Royal Reception Rooms, 25 kroner ($4.30) adults, 10 kroner ($1.70) children; parliament, free; castle ruins, 12 kroner ($2.10) adults, 5 kroner (90¢) children.
Open: Palace, May–Sept, English-language tours Tues–Sun at 11am, 1pm, and 3pm; Oct–Apr, English-language tours Tues–Fri and Sun at 11am and 1pm. Castle ruins, May–Sept, daily 9:30am–3:30pm; Oct–Apr, Mon–Fri and Sun 9:30am–

IN THEIR FOOTSTEPS

Søren Kierkegaard (1813–55) A founder of existentialism, Kierkegaard developed an almost-pathological sense of involvement in theology. His best-known work, *Either-Or*, written in 1843, shows his advocacy of a Christianity exclusively oriented to the Bible. "A melancholy Dane," he wrote many novels, including in 1849 *The Sickness Unto Death*.
• **Birthplace:** Born in Copenhagen, he was the seventh child of a prosperous wool merchant.
• **Residence:** A 19th-century house adjacent to the Court House building on Nytorv in Copenhagen.
• **Resting Place:** Assistens Kirkegård, Copenhagen.

DENMARK

Copenhagen

COPENHAGEN ATTRACTIONS

Church ■†

Post Office ⊠

Information ●

3:30pm. English-language tours of the parliament are given mid-June to late Sept, Sun–Fri 10am–4pm. **Bus:** 1, 2, 5, 8, 9.

NY CARLSBERG GLYPTOTEK, Dantes Plads 7. Tel. 33-91-10-65.

The Glyptotek, behind the Tivoli, is one of the most important art museums in Scandinavia. Founded by the 19th-century art collector Carl Jacobsen, Mr. Carlsberg Beer himself, the museum comprises two distinct departments, modern and antiquities. The modern section has both French and Danish art, mainly from the 19th century. Sculpture, including works by Rodin, is on the ground floor, and works of Impressionists and related artists, including van Gogh's *Landscape from St. Rémy,* are on the upper floors. Egyptian, Greek, and Roman art are on the main floor; and Etruscan, Greek, and Cypriot art are on the lower floor. A conservatory separates the two departments. The Egyptian collection is particularly outstanding. The most notable prize is a prehistoric rendering of a hippopotamus. Fine Greek originals (headless Apollo, Niobe's tragic children) and Roman copies of original Greek bronzes (4th-century Hercules) are also displayed, as are some of the noblest Roman busts—Pompey, Virgil, Augustus, Trajan. A favorite of mine is the Etruscan art display (sarcophagi, a winged lion, bronzes, pottery).

French masterpieces include works by Manet (*The Absinthe Drinker*), Monet, Degas, and Renoir. About 30 of Gauguin's works are here, as well as Cézanne's famous *Portrait of the Artist.* Also noteworthy is French sculpture, such as Rodin's *The Burghers of Calais* and a Degas bronze set.

Admission: 15 kroner ($2.60) adults, children free.

Open: May–Aug, Tues–Sun 10am–4pm; Sept–Apr, Tues–Sat noon–3pm, Sun 10am–4pm. **Bus:** 1, 2, 5, 8, 10, 13, 32.

NATIONALMUSEET (National Museum), Frederiksholms Kanal 12, opposite Christiansborg Palace. Tel. 33-13-44-11.

A gigantic repository of anthropological artifacts, this museum is divided primarily into four departments. The Danish collections date from the Stone Age to the present and include Viking stones, helmets, and fragments of battle gear. Don't miss the "lur" horn, a Bronze Age musical instrument, among the most ancient instruments in Europe, and the world-famous "Sun Chariot," an elegant Bronze Age piece of pagan art. The ecclesiastical art exhibit includes the 12th-century Lisbjerg Altar, a blending of pagan and Christian styles. Royal collections of medals and coins are also featured, as are the 3rd-century Gundestrup silver caldron, the Roman Hoby Cups depicting Homeric legends, and relics of the Eskimo culture and the people of Greenland.

Admission: 20 kroner ($3.50) adults; children free.

Open: June 16–Sept 15, Tues–Sun 10am–4pm; Sept 16–June 15, Tues–Fri 11am–3pm, Sat–Sun noon–4pm. Guided tours Sun at 2pm. **Bus:** 1, 2, 6, 9, 10.

THORVALDSEN'S MUSEUM, Porthusgade 2. Tel. 33-32-15-32.

Located on Slotsholmen next door to Christiansborg, this great collection of Bertel Thorvaldsen (1770–1844) neoclassical sculpture represents the romanticism of

---

IN THEIR FOOTSTEPS

H. C. Andersen (1805–75) His first children's stories were published in 1835. The writer's goal was "to become famous," and some 168 fairy tales later, including *The Ugly Duckling, The Steadfast Tin Soldier,* and *The Little Mermaid,* Andersen got his wish.

• **Birthplace:** Born in the slums of Odense, Andersen had a poor cobbler for a father and a superstitious washerwoman for a mother.

• **Residences:** He traveled Europe, but lived at such addresses in Copenhagen as Nyhavn 67, Nyhavn 18, Nyhavn 20, and Vingårdsstraede 6.

• **Resting Place:** Assistens Kirkegård, Copenhagen.

the 18th and 19th centuries. The sculptor is famous for his classically restrained works and mythological subjects—Cupid and Psyche, Adonis, Jason, Hercules, Ganymede, Mercury—all displayed at the museum. Thorvaldsen's personal collection of art is also shown, everything from Egyptian relics of Ptolemy to contemporary paintings. Thorvaldsen is buried in the courtyard of his museum.

Admission: 20 kroner ($3.50) adults; children free.
Open: Tues–Sun 10am–5pm. **Bus:** 1, 2, 6, 8, 10.

FRIHEDSMUSEET (Museum of Danish Resistance, 1940–45), Churchillparken. Tel. 33-13-77-14.

On display are relics of torture and concentration camps, the equipment used for the wireless and illegal films, British propaganda leaflets, satirical caricatures of Hitler, information about Danish Jews and conversely about Danish Nazis, and the paralyzing nationwide strikes. An armed car, used against Danish Nazi informers and collaborators, is on the grounds. All exhibition texts are in English.

Admission: Free.
Open: May to mid-Sept, Tues–Sat 10am–4pm, Sun 10am–5pm; Sept 16–Apr, Tues–Sat 11am–3pm, Sun 11am–4pm. Free guided tours given: May to mid-Sept, Sun at 2:30pm, Thurs at 2pm; June–Aug, Tues at 2pm. English-language tapes are also available. **Bus:** 1, 6, 9.

FRILANDSMUSEET (Open-Air Museum), Kongevejen 100. Tel. 42-85-02-92.

This reconstructed village in Lyngbøy, on the fringes of Copenhagen, recaptures Denmark's onetime rural character. The "museum" is nearly 90 acres, a 2-mile walk around the compound, and includes a dozen authentically re-created buildings—farmsteads, windmills, fishermen's cottages. Exhibits include a half-timbered 18th-century farmstead from one of the tiny windswept Danish islands, a primitive longhouse from the remote Faroe Islands, thatched fishermen's huts from Jutland, tower windmills, and a potter's workshop from the mid-19th century.

On summer afternoons, organized activities are staged. On a recent visit, folk dancers in native costume performed and there were demonstrations of lace making and loom weaving.

The park is about 9 miles from the Central Railroad Station. At the entryway to the museum is an old-style restaurant.

Admission: 20 kroner ($3.50) adults; children free.
Open: Mid-Apr to Sept, daily 10am–5pm; Oct 1–14, daily 10am–3pm; Oct 15–mid-Apr, Sun 10am–3pm. **S-tog:** From the Central Railroad Station to Sorgenfri (leaving every 20 minutes). **Bus:** 184, 194.

2. MORE ATTRACTIONS

AMALIENBORG PALACE, Slotsplads.

These four 18th-century French-style rococo mansions—opening onto one of the most attractive squares (Amalienborg) in Europe—have been the home of the Danish royal family since 1794 when Christiansborg burned. Visitors are not allowed inside, but many flock to witness the changing of the guard at noon when the royal family is in residence. A swallowtail flag at mast signifies that the queen is in Copenhagen—and not at her North Zealand summer home, Fredensborg Palace.

The Royal Life Guard in black bearskin busbies (like the hussars) leaves Rosenborg Castle at 11:30am and marches along Gothersgade, Nørrevold, Frederiksborggade, Købmagergade, Østergade, Kongens Nytorv, Bredgade, Sankt Annae Plads, and Amaliegade to Amalienborg. After the event, the guard, still accompanied by the band, returns to Rosenborg Castle via Frederiksgade, Store Kongensgade, and Gothersgade.

Bus: 1, 6, 9, 10.

TØJHUSMUSEET (Royal Arsenal Museum), Tøjhusgade 3. Tel. 33-11-60-37.

On the grounds of Christiansborg, this museum features a fantastic display of weapons used for hunting and warfare. On the main floor—the longest vaulted Renaissance hall in Europe—is Cannon Hall, stocked with mortars, tanks, 1909 airplanes suspended from the ceiling, howitzers, a 21-ton German armored car, and a Nazi V-1 rocket. Above Cannon Hall is the impressive Arms Chamber, with one of the world's finest collections of hand weapons. Many trophy banners hang above the wall cases of swords, and all Danish trophies since 1659 are kept in the museum. The museum building dates to 1598–1604.

Admission: Free.

Open: May–Sept, Tues–Sat 1–4pm, Sun 10am–4pm; Oct–Apr, Tues–Sat 1–3pm, Sun 11am–4pm. **Bus:** 1, 2, 5, 6, 8.

KUNSTINDUSTRIMUSEET (Museum of Decorative and Applied Art), Bredgade 68. Tel. 33-14-94-52.

Built between 1752 and 1757 under King Frederik V, this rococo building, houses European decorative and applied art from the Middle Ages to the present. Collections of furniture, tapestries, pottery, porcelain, glass, and silver are displayed, as are Chinese and Japanese art and handcrafts. The library contains around 63,000 books and periodicals dealing with arts and crafts, architecture, costumes, advertising, photography, and industrial design.

Admission: Museum, 20 kroner ($3.50) Sun, holidays, and daily July–Aug; free other times. Library free.

Open: Museum, Tues–Sun 1–4pm; library, Tues–Sat 10am–4pm. **Bus:** 1, 6, 9. **S-tog:** Østerport.

RUNDETÅRN (Round Tower), Kebmagergade 52A. Tel. 33-93-66-60.

This 17th-century public observatory, attached to a church, is visited by thousands

---

 FROMMER'S FAVORITE COPENHAGEN EXPERIENCES

Sitting at an Outdoor Café   Because of Copenhagen's long gray winters, sitting at an outdoor café in the summer and drinking beer or eating is always a favorite pastime. The best spot is at Nyhavn (New Harbor), beginning at Kongens Nytorv. Enjoy ice cream while admiring the tall rigged ships with bow sprits moored in the canal.

Going to the Tivoli   This is the quintessential summer adventure in Copenhagen, a tradition since 1843. It's an amusement park with a difference—even the merry-go-rounds are unusual, using a fleet of Viking ships instead of the usual horses.

Strolling the Strøget   In Danish, the word *strøget* means "to stroll"—and that's exactly what all born-to-shop addicts do along this nearly three-quarter-mile stretch, from the Rådhuspladsen to Kongens Nytorv.

Exploring Alternative Lifestyles   Not for everybody, but worth a look, is a trip to the Free City of Christiania, on the island of Christianshavn (take bus no. 8 from Rådhuspladsen). Since 1971, some 1,000 "squatters" have illegally declared themselves a free city, taking over 130 former army barracks spread across 20 acres. You can shop, dine, and talk to the natives about this experimental community with its own doctors, clubs, and stores. It even flies its own flag.

who climb the spiral ramp (no steps) for a panoramic view of Copenhagen. The tower is one of the crowning architectural achievements of the Christian IV era. Peter the Great, in Denmark for a state visit, galloped up the ramp on horseback, preceded by his carriage-drawn czarina. On the premises is a Bibliotekssalen (Library Hall), offering changing exhibitions devoted to art, culture, history, and science.

Admission: 12 kroner ($2.10) adults, 5 kroner (90¢) children.

Open: Apr–Oct, Mon–Sat 10am–5pm, Sun noon–4pm. **Bus:** 5, 7E, 14, 16, 42, 43.

RÅDHUS (Town Hall), Rådhuspladsen. Tel. 33-15-38-00.

Built in 1905, the Town Hall contains impressive statues of H. C. Andersen and Niels Bohr, the Noble Prize–winning physicist. Jens Olden's famous World Clock is open for viewing Monday through Friday from 10:30am to 12:30pm and on Saturday at noon. King Frederik IX set the clock on December 15, 1955. The clockwork is so exact that the aberration in 300 years is 0.4 seconds. Climb the tower for an impressive view.

Admission: Rådhus, 10 kroner ($1.70) for all; clock, 8 kroner ($1.40) adults, 5 kroner ($0.90) children.

Open: Rådhus, Mon–Wed and Fri 9:30am–3pm, Thurs 9:30am–4pm, Sat guided tour at 10am; tower, Mon–Fri at 11am and 2pm, Sat at 11am. **Bus:** 1, 6, 8.

VOR FRUE KIRKE (Copenhagen Cathedral), Nørregade. Tel. 33-14-41-28.

This Greek Renaissance-style church, built in the early 19th century near Copenhagen University, features Bertel Thorvaldsen's white marble neoclassical works including *Christ and the Apostles*. The funeral of H. C. Andersen took place here in 1875, and that of Søren Kierkegaard in 1855.

Admission: Free.

Open: Mon–Fri 9am–5pm. **Bus:** 5.

MARBLE CHURCH (or Frederik's Church), Frederiksgade 4. Tel. 33-15-37-63.

This 2-century-old church, with its green copper dome—one of the largest in the world—is a short walk from Amalienborg Palace. After an unsuccessful start during the neoclassical revival of the 1750s in Denmark, the church was finally completed in Roman baroque style in 1894. In many ways it is even more impressive than Copenhagen's cathedral.

Admission: Church, free; dome, 5 kroner (90¢).

Open: Church, Mon–Sat 11am–2pm; dome, Sat at 11am. **Bus:** 1, 6, 9, 10.

DEN LILLE HAVFRUE (The Little Mermaid), Langelinie.

The one statue *everybody* wants to see in Copenhagen is the life-size bronze of the *Den lille Havfrue,* inspired by H. C. Andersen's *The Little Mermaid,* one of the world's most famous fairy tales. The statue, unveiled in 1913, was sculpted by Edvard Eriksen. It rests on rocks right off the shore. The mermaid has been attacked more than once, losing an arm in one misadventure, decapitated in another.

Nearby is the **Gefion Fountain,** sculpted by Anders Bundgaard. Gefion, a Scandinavian mythological goddess, plowed Zealand away from Sweden by turning her sons into oxen. Also in the area is **Kastellet** at Langelinie (tel. 33-11-22-33). This ruined citadel was fortified in the 17th century, and can be explored daily from 6am to sunset. Admission is free.

In summer, a special "Mermaid Bus" leaves from Rådhuspladsen (Vester Voldgade) at 10:30am (thereafter at half-hour intervals until 5:30pm). On the "Langelinie" bus there's a 20-minute stopover at *The Little Mermaid.* If you want more time, take bus no. 1, 6, or 9.

DAVIDS SAMLING, Kronprinsessegade 30. Tel. 33-13-55-64.

Its status as a privately funded museum, plus the excellence of its collection, make this a most unusual museum. Established by a Danish attorney, C. L. David (1878–1960), shortly after World War II on the premises of his private house across from the park surrounding Rosenborg Castle, the collection features European art, decorative art, and the largest Islamic collection in the Nordic world.

David's other major bequest to Denmark was his summer villa in the northern suburbs of Copenhagen at Marienborg, which is for the use of the Danish prime minister.

Admission: Free.
Open: Tues–Sun 1–4pm. **Bus:** 10, 17, 43.

BOTANISK HAVE (Botanical Gardens), Gothersgade 128. Tel. 33-12-74-60.

Planted from 1871 to 1874, the Botanical Gardens are located at a lake that was once part of the city's defensive moat. Across from Rosenborg Castle, it contains hothouses growing both tropical and subtropical plants. Special features include a cactus house and a palm house, all of which appear even more exotic in the far northern country of Denmark. An alpine garden contains mountain plants from all over the world.

Admission: Free.
Open: Summer, daily 8:30am–6pm; winter, daily 8:30am–4pm.
Bus: 5, 7, 14, 16, 40, 42, 43. **S-tog:** Nørreport.

3. COOL FOR KIDS

Copenhagen is a wonderful place for children, and many so-called adult attractions also appeal to children. If you're traveling with children, don't miss the **Tivoli,** *The Little Mermaid* at Langelinie, and the changing of the Queen's Royal Life Guard at **Amalienborg Palace,** including the entire parade to and from that royal residence. Kids also enjoy **Frilandsmuseet,** the open-air museum. (For details on the above sights, see "The Top Attractions" and "More Attractions," above.)

Other attractions great for kids include the following:

LEGETØJMUSEET (Danish Toy Museum), Valkendorfsgade 13. Tel. 33-14-10-09.

Come see a fascinating collection of toys from all over the world for children of all ages. Toys range from antique dolls and dollhouses to mechanical devices to games and books to hobbyhorses.

Admission: 20 kroner ($3.50) adults, 10 kroner ($1.70) children.
Open: Sat–Thurs 9–4pm. **S-tog:** Nørreport. **Bus:** 6, 9, 10, 14, 16.

LOUIS TUSSAUD WAX MUSEUM, H. C. Andersens Blvd. 22. Tel. 33-14-29-22.

Now a part of Tivoli, the Louis Tussaud Wax Museum is a major commercial attraction in Copenhagen. It features more than 200 wax figures, everybody from Danish kings and queens to Leonardo da Vinci. Children can visit the Snow Queen's Castle, or watch Frankenstein and Dracula guard the monsters and vampires.

Admission: 42 kroner ($7.30) adults, 20 kroner ($3.50) children.
Open: Apr 29–Sept 13, daily 10am–11pm; Sept 14–Apr 28, daily 10am–4:30pm.
Closed: Jan 1–5. **Bus:** 1, 2, 16, 28, 29, 41.

CIRKUS BENNEWEIS, Jernbanegade 8. Tel. 33-14-44-43.

The Benneweis Circus, opposite Tivoli Gardens, is one of the last grand-style circuses left in Europe. Five generations of Benneweises have run the circus nonstop in spite of two world wars. Bareback riders, tumblers, clowns, aerialists, trained seals—this is the real thing. Tickets can be purchased at the ticket office in the circus building between noon and 8pm.

Admission: 50–140 kroner ($8.70–$24.20).

Open: May–Aug, Tues–Fri at 8pm, Sat at 4 and 8pm, Sun at 4pm. **S-tog:** Hovedbanegård. **Bus:** 1, 2, 6, 8, 14, 16.

BAKKEN AMUSEMENT PARK, Dyrehavevej 62, Klampenborg. Tel. 31-63-35-44.

On the northern edge of Copenhagen, about 7½ miles from the city center, this amusement park was created 35 years before the Pilgrims landed at Plymouth Rock. It's a local favorite, featuring roller coasters, dancing, the tunnel of love, and a merry-go-round. Open-air restaurants are plentiful, as are snack bars and ice-cream booths. Proceeds from the amusements support this unspoiled natural preserve. There are no cars, only bicycles and horse-drawn carriages. Bakken is about a 20-minute ride from the Central Railroad Station.

Admission: Free.

Open: Late Mar–late Aug, daily 1pm–midnight. **Closed:** Late Aug–late Mar. **S-tog:** "Klampenborg" from Central Railroad Station to Klampenborg Station; then walk through Deer Park or take a horse-drawn cab.

TYCHO BRAHE PLANETARIUM, Gammel Kongevej 10. Tel. 33-12-12-24.

The marvel of the night sky, with its planets, galaxies, star clusters, and comets is created by a star projector using the planetarium dome as a screen and space theater. Named after the famed Danish astronomer, Tycho Brahe (1546–1601), the planetarium also stages Omnimax film productions. There's an information center and a restaurant.

Admission: 10 kroner ($1.70) for exhibitions; 45–85 kroner ($7.80–$14.70), depending on show, for Omnimax films.

Open: Daily 10:30am–9:30pm. **Bus:** 1, 14.

ZOOLOGISK HAVE (Copenhagen Zoo), Roskildevej 32. Tel. 36-30-20-01.

With more than 2,000 animals from Greenland to Africa, this zoo boasts spacious new habitats for reindeer and musk oxen as well as an open roaming area for lions. Take a ride up the small wooden Eiffel Tower or walk across the street, and let your kids enjoy the petting zoo. The zoo is mobbed on Sunday.

Admission: 40 kroner ($6.90) adults, 20 kroner ($3.50) children.

Open: Daily 9am–6pm. **Bus:** 28, 29, 41.

DENMARK'S AQUARIUM, Strandvejen, Charlottenlund. Tel. 31-62-32-83.

Opened in 1939, this is one of the most extensive aquariums in Europe, lying north of Copenhagen along the Øresund coast. Its large tanks are famous for their decoration. Hundreds of salt and freshwater species are exhibited. One tank houses bloodthirsty piranha from South America. The aquarium is located in Charlottenlund Fort Park, north of Copenhagen.

Admission: 30 kroner ($5.20) adults, 15 kroner ($2.60) children.

Open: Mar–Oct, daily 10am–6pm; Nov–Feb, daily 10am–4pm. **S-tog:** Line C to Charlottenlund. **Bus:** 6.

EKSPERIMENTARIUM [Science Hall], Tuborg Brewery, Standvejen 54. Tel. 39-27-33-33.

Located in the old mineral-water bottling hall of Tuborg breweries (see "Special-Interest Sightseeing," below), this museum has a hands-on approach to science. Its director claims it is one of the most extensive and technologically advanced museums of its type in northern Europe. Visitors use not only their hands but all of their senses as they participate in some 250 exhibitions and demonstrations divided into three themes: "Man," "Nature," and "The Interaction Between Man and Nature." Visitors can, for example, play with ozone shadows, test a favorite suntan lotion, examine drinking water, or compare air pollution in two different cities. Families can work as a team to examine enzymes, make a camera from paper, or test perfume. Exhibitions change frequently.

Admission: 50 kroner ($8.70) adults, 35 kroner ($6.10) children 5–14.
Open: Mon, Wed, and Fri 9am–6pm; Tues–Thurs 11am–6pm. **S-tog:** Hellerup or Svanemøllen. **Bus:** 6 from center of Copenhagen.

4. SPECIAL-INTEREST SIGHTSEEING

FOR THE LITERARY ENTHUSIAST

Admirers of H. C. Andersen may want to seek out the various addresses at which he lived in Copenhagen. These include Nyhavn 18, Nyhavn 20, and Nyhavn 67. He also lived for a time at Vingårdsstraede 6.

KØBENHAVNS BYMUSEUM [Copenhagen City Museum], Vesterbrogade 59. Tel. 31-21-07-72.
The permanent exhibition here presents the history of Copenhagen in artifacts and pictures. Devoted to Søren Kierkegaard (1813–55), the father of existentialism, this museum in a smaller separate department exhibits his drawings, letters, books, photographs, and personal belongings.
Admission: Free.
Open: Oct–Apr, daily 1–5pm; May–Sept, daily 10am–4pm. **Bus:** 6, 16, 27, 28.

ASSISTENS KIRKEGÅRD [Assistens Cemetery], Nørrebrogade/Kapelvej.
The largest cemetery in Copenhagen, dating from 1711, it contains the tombs of Søren Kierkegaard, H. C. Andersen, and Martin Andersen Nexø, a famous novelist of the working class. The cemetery is now a public park.
Admission: Free.
Open: Daily sunrise–sunset. **Bus:** 5, 7, 16, 17, 18.

FOR THE ARCHITECTURE ENTHUSIAST

BØRSEN [Stock Exchange], Børsgade.
One of the most unusual buildings in Copenhagen, on Slotsholmen, it must be viewed from the outside, as its interior is not open to the public. Architects Hans and Lorenz Steenwinkel built the long, low Renaissance structure for Christian IV. The spire, 177 feet high, looks like a quartet of intertwined dragon tails. The Stock Exchange is no longer housed here; the building is now the headquarters of the Chamber of Commerce.
Bus: 1, 2, 5, 6, 8, 9.

GRUNDTVIGS KIRKE [Grundtvig Church], På Bjerget, Bispebjerg. Tel. 31-81-54-42.
Resembling a huge organ, this church, built from 1921 to 1940, was designed by Jensen Klint, who died before it was completed. It is estimated that six million yellow bricks went into its construction. The interior is 250 feet wide and 115 feet high. The church is a popular venue for concerts.
Admission: Free.
Open: May 15–Sept 15, Mon–Sat 9am–4:45pm, Sun noon–4pm; Sept 16–May 14, Sun noon–1pm. **Bus:** 19.

FOR BEER DRINKERS

CARLSBERG BREWERIES, Ny Carlsberg Vej 140. Tel. 31-21-12-21, ext. 1312.
A favorite is a visit to a world-famous Danish brewery, Carlsberg or Tuborg. The Carlsberg tour is more popular, lasting 90 minutes, including the beer party at the end where guests sample the products. The Carlsberg plant stands on 62 acres of grounds, including a grain elevator, the tallest building in Copenhagen. Visitors are escorted through the brew houses, and are shown yeast cellars and storage basements. The

for children. For information, contact the Copenhagen Tourist Information Center, Bernstorffsgade 1 (tel. 33-11-13-25).

6. SPECIAL/FREE EVENTS

Much of Copenhagen is a summer festival, especially at the **Tivoli Gardens.** Although there's an entrance fee, many of the concerts and other presentations are free once inside. A total of 150 performances per summer are presented at the Concert Hall. Of these, more than 100 are free. Pantomime performances at the Pantomime Theater are also free. Performances on the open-air stage are free every night (closed Monday). Likewise, the other amusement park, **Bakken,** has many free events—and you don't have to pay an admission to enter—only if you patronize the various attractions.

The **birthday of Queen Margrethe** on April 16 is a celebration with the queen and the royal family driving through the pedestrian street, Strøget, in a stagecoach escorted by hussars in gala.

A **Ballet and Opera Festival** (mid-May to June) takes place at the Royal Theater, offering classical and modern dance, and operatic masterpieces.

Carnival in Copenhagen (June 2–4) is a great event where dressed-up Copenhageners move about the city in samba rhythm. The event is climaxed by a children's carnival on June 4.

The **Copenhagen Jazz Festival** (July 6–13) features the best of international jazz musicians.

The highly acclaimed Royal Danish Ballet performs at the Royal Theater for the **Fall Ballet Festival** (mid-August to September 1).

7. SAVVY SHOPPING

THE SHOPPING SCENE

Copenhagen is in the vanguard of shopping in Europe and much of the action takes place on **Strøget,** a pedestrian street in the heart of the capital. The Strøget begins on Frederiksberggade, north of Rådhuspladsen, and winds to Østergade, which opens onto Kongens Nytorv. This jam-packed street is lined with stores selling everything from porcelain statues of *Youthful Boldness* to Greenland shrimp to Kay Bojesen's teak monkeys.

Between stops, have a drink at an outdoor café, or just sit on a bench and watch the crowds.

Two other walking areas are nearby—**Gråbødre Torv** and **Fiolstraede**— where you can browse through antiques shops and bookstores.

Bredgade, beginning at Kongens Nytorv, is the antiques district of Copenhagen. Prices tend to be very high. **Laederstraede** is another shopping street that competes with Bredgade for antiques.

BEST BUYS In a country famed for its designers and craftspeople, you'll find your best buys in stainless steel, porcelain, china, glassware, toys (Kay Bojesen's wooden animals in particular), functionally designed furniture, textiles (napkins to rugs), and jewelry (decorative, silver, and semiprecious stones).

STORE HOURS In general, shopping hours are Monday through Thursday from 9am to 5:30pm, until 7 or 8pm on Friday, and until 2pm on Saturday. Most shops are closed Sunday except the kiosks and supermarket at the Central Railroad Station. Here you can purchase food until 10pm or midnight. The Central Railroad Station's bakery is open until 9pm, and one of the kiosks at the Rådhuspladsen, selling papers, film, and souvenirs, is open 24 hours.

SHIPPING IT HOME & RECOVERING VAT   Denmark imposes a 25% tax on goods and services, a "value-added tax" known in Denmark as MOMS (pronounced "mumps"). However, special tax-free exports are possible. Many stores will mail goods to your home so as to avoid paying MOMS. If you want to take your purchases with you, look for shops displaying DANISH TAX-FREE SHOPPING notices. Such shops offer tourists tax refunds for personal export. This refund applies to purchases over 600 kroner ($103.80) for visitors from the United States and Canada. Your tax-free invoice must be stamped by Danish Customs when you leave the country. You can receive your refund at Copenhagen's Kastrup International Airport when you depart. If you depart by land or by sea, you can receive your refund by mail. Requests for refunds are to be sent by mail to Danish Tax-Free Shopping A/S, 5 H. J. Holstvej, DK-2605 Brøndby, Denmark. You will be reimbursed by check, cash, or credit-card credit in the currency you wish.

The 600 kroner must be spent in one store for the refund to apply, but some major department stores allow purchases to be made over several days or even weeks, at the end of which the receipts will be tallied. Service and handling fees are deducted from the total, so actual refunds come to about 18%. Information on this program is available from the Danish Tourist Board (see "Taxes" in "Fast Facts: Denmark" in Chapter 3).

SHOPPING A TO Z
ART GALLERIES & AUCTION HOUSES

ARNE BRUUN RASMUSSEN, Bredgade 33. Tel. 33-13-69-11.
   Established shortly after World War II, this is the leading auction house in Denmark. The new season begins in August with an auction of paintings and fine artworks. July is usually quiet, although the premises remain open for appraisals and purchases. Viewing time is allowed before auctions, which take place about once a month. Auctions are also devoted to modern art, wine, coins, books, manuscripts, and antique weapons. Bus: 1, 6, 9, 10.

BRANNERS BIBLIOPHILE ANTIKVARIAT, Bredgade 10. Tel. 33-15-91-87.
   If you're interested in engravings and woodcuts, this is the best place. It stands near Kongens Nytorv. Founded in 1946, this shop also sells maps, decorative prints, and rare books. Bus: 1, 6, 9, 10.

COURT GALLERY, Østergade 24. Tel. 33-11-20-50.
   Located on the Strøget, this shop showcases contemporary art, both European and American. Summer exhibitions of graphics, oils, acrylics, sculpture, gouache, watercolors, and drawings can be seen. Bus: 1, 6, 9.

GALERIE ASBAEK, Ny Adelgade 8-10. Tel. 33-15-40-04.
   This sophisticated art gallery is housed in a 1722 building that was Copenhagen's first theater. Galerie Asbaek has a five-floor permanent exhibition of the best local artists along with changing exhibitions of Scandinavian and foreign artists. There is a bookshop, a video room, and a café serving French-inspired Danish food. Graphics and posters are available for purchase. Bus: 1, 6, 9, 10, 28, 29, 41.

KUNSTHALLENS KUNSTAUKTIONER, Gothersgade 9. Tel. 33-32-52-00.
   Established in 1926, this is Europe's leading dealer in the pan-European school of painting known as COBRA (acronym for Copenhagen, Brussels, and Amsterdam, from where the artists originated). These works, produced from 1948 to 1951, were an important precursor of abstract expressionism. The gallery holds 12 auctions yearly, eight with modern art; the others concentrate on the 19th century. July is slow, although the premises are open for inspection and appraisals. Bus: 1, 6, 9, 10.

BOOKSTORES
BOGHALLEN, Rådhuspladsen 37. Tel. 33-11-85-11.

This big store carries many books in English, as well as a wide selection of travel-related literature, including maps. You can also purchase books (in English) on Danish themes, such as the collected works of H. C. Andersen. The shop is at Town Hall Square. Bus: 2, 8, 30.

DEPARTMENT STORES

ILLUM'S, Østergade 52. Tel. 33-14-40-02.
One of Denmark's top department stores, Illum's lies on the Strøget. Take time to browse through its vast world of Danish and Scandinavian design. There is a restaurant and a special export cash desk at street level. Bus: 1, 6, 9, 10.

MAGASIN, Kongens Nytorv 13. Tel. 33-11-44-33.
One of the most elegant department stores, Magasin is the biggest in Scandinavia. It offers a complete assortment of Danish designer fashion, a large selection of glass and porcelain, and plenty of souvenirs. Goods are shipped abroad tax-free. Bus: 1, 6, 9, 10.

FASHIONS

BRODRENE ANDERSEN, Østergade 7-9. Tel. 33-15-15-77.
A distinguished purveyor of "personal furnishings for gentlemen" (and increasingly for women), it has an atmosphere of quiet dignity. The clothes are mostly German and Italian and, to a lesser degree, French. Bus: 1, 6, 9, 10.

GERA STOFFER, Østergade 36-38. Tel. 33-15-33-62.
This treasure house is unmatched in Scandinavia for the quality and beauty of its haute-couture fabrics. It is the third-largest fabric dealer in Europe. Bus: 43.

SWEATER MARKET, Frederiksberggade 15. Tel. 33-15-27-73.
Take your pick from top-grade cardigans, pullovers, hats, scarves, and mittens, handknitted in Denmark of 100% wool. There's also a large selection of Icelandic wool jackets and coats. Catalog sent upon request. Bus: 2, 8, 30.

HOME FURNISHINGS

ILLUMS BOLIGHUS, Amagertorv 10, on Strøget. Tel. 33-14-19-41.
A sophisticated center of modern design, this is one of Europe's finest showcases for household furnishings and accessories. Browse through furniture, lamps, rugs, textiles, bedding, glassware, kitchenware, flatware, china, jewelry, and ceramics. The store also sells fashions and accessories for women and men. There's even a gift shop. Bus: 28, 29, or 41.

LYSBERG, HANSEN & THERP, Bredgade 3. Tel. 33-14-47-87.
This 80-year-old shop is a great interior-decorating center offering fabrics, carpets, and furniture. Admire the decorated apartments furnished in impeccable taste. The company manufactures its own furniture in traditional design and imports fabrics, usually from Germany or France. Try to visit their gift shop which has many hard-to-find creations. Bus: 1, 6, 9, 10.

PAUSTIAN, Kalkbraenderiløbskaj 2. Tel. 31-18-45-11.
The leading furniture showroom in Copenhagen, located in the somewhat distant industrial Nordhavn section, this display house will ship anywhere in the world. The finest of Scandinavian design is on display, along with reproductions of the classics. There's a well-recommended adjoining restaurant. S-tog: Nordhavn.

NEEDLEWORK

EVA ROSENSTAND A/S—CLARA WAEVER, Østergade 42. Tel. 33-13-29-40.
Danish-designed cross-stitch embroideries are sold here. The materials are usually linen in medium or coarser grades, but pure wool and cotton are also available. There

is also an admission-free needlework museum, the only one of its kind in Europe. Bus: 1, 6, 9, 10.

PEWTER & SILVER

GEORG JENSEN, Amagertorv 4. Tel. 33-11-40-80.

Legendary Georg Jensen is known for its fine silver. For the connoisseur, there is no better address, for they display the largest and best collection of Jensen hollowware in Europe. Gold and silver jewelry in traditional and modern Danish design are also featured. There's a department specializing in Georg Jensen seconds. Bus: 1, 6, 9, 10.

HANS HANSEN SØV, Amagertorv 16. Tel. 33-15-60-67.

Less expensive than Georg Jensen, this is also a great silver shop, run by the same family since 1906. A high standard of craftsmanship is reflected in the contemporary silver pieces on sale. Some items are made of rosewood and inlaid with sterling silver. Gold jewelry is also sold. Bus: 28, 29, 41.

PORCELAIN

HOLMEGAARDS GLASVAERKER, Østergade 15. Tel. 33-12-44-77.

This is the only major producer of glasswork in Denmark. Its Wellington pattern, for example, was created in 1859 and is available once again. The Holmegaard glasses and the Regiment Bar set reflect solid craftsmanship. Bus: 1, 6, 9, 10.

PETER KROG, Bredgade 4. Tel. 33-12-45-55.

Peter Krog features fine silver, jewelry, and objets d'art of outstanding quality and value, bought up in the sales of large estates and reconditioned if necessary. Occasionally, among Russian works of art, he has works by Carl Fabergé, and the establishment is known for Georg Jensen used silver. Bus: 1, 6, 9, 10.

ROYAL COPENHAGEN AND BING & GRØNDAHL PORCELAIN, Amagertorv 6. Tel. 33-13-71-81.

Royal Copenhagen's trademark, three blue wavy lines, has come to symbolize quality in porcelain throughout the world. Founded in 1775, the factory was a royal possession for a century before passing into private hands in 1868. Royal Copenhagen's Christmas plates are a collector's item. The factory has turned out a new plate each year since 1908, most of the motifs depicting the Danish countryside in winter. On the top floor is a *huge* selection of seconds, and unless you're an expert, you can't tell. Visitors can inspect the factory at Smallegade 45 (tel. 31-86-48-48), where tours are given on Tuesday and Thursday at 9:45am. You can't make purchases at the factory. Bus: 28, 29, 41.

SKANDINAVISK GLAS/A.B. SCHOU, Ny Østergade 4. Tel. 33-13-80-95.

Porcelain pieces from Royal Copenhagen, Waterford crystal, porcelain from the Porsgrund factory in Norway, Lalique from Paris, Orrefors from Sweden, Lladró from Spain, and Wedgwood from England are all offered here. If you like to comparison-shop among famous competitors, this is the place. The exhibition of collectors' plates is the largest in Scandinavia. Bus: 1, 6, 9, 10.

TIN-CENTRET/THE PEWTER CENTRE, Ny Østergade 2. Tel. 33-14-82-00.

Scandinavia's largest selection of beautiful handmade pewter is found here, the exclusive sales outlet in Denmark for several Scandinavian and EC producers of high-quality handmade pewter. Apart from that, the outlet also sells Danish Flora Danica jewelry and German beer steins with pewter lids. Bus: 1, 9, 10.

SHOPPING CENTERS

COPENHAGEN AIRPORT SHOPPING CENTER

For excellent buys in Scandinavian merchandise, as well as tax-free goods, I recommend the shopping center at the airport. Scandinavian products here cannot be sold at higher prices than those in downtown Copenhagen. A VAT-refund office is located nearby.

SCALA, Axeltorv 2. Tel. 33-15-12-15.
Across from the Tivoli Gardens, this is the densest collection of shops in Copenhagen. On five floors of stylish architecture it contains a full array of shops appealing to a wide variety of income levels. The complex is also loaded with restaurants and shops, offering both Danish and international food. A bevy of escalators carries shoppers up and down among the various floors. Bus: 6, 16, 28.

8. EVENING ENTERTAINMENT

Danes really know how to party. A good night means a late night, and on warm weekends, hundreds of rowdy revelers crowd Strøget until sunrise. Merrymaking in Copenhagen is not just for the younger crowd; jazz clubs, traditional beer houses, and wine cellars are routinely packed with people of all ages. Of course, the city has a more serious cultural side as well, exemplified by excellent theaters, operas, ballets, and a circus that shouldn't be missed.

THE ENTERTAINMENT SCENE

To find out what's happening at the time of your visit, pick up a free copy of **Copenhagen This Week** at the tourist information center. Ignore the "Copenhagen by Night" section, which is usually devoted to women advertising themselves as companions to visiting males. Turn instead to the section marked "Events Calendar," which has a week-by-week roundup of the most interesting entertainment and sightseeing events taking place in the Danish capital at the time of your visit.

For discounted seats (sometimes as much as 50% off the regular ticket price) go in person to a ticket kiosk across from the Nørreport train station, lying at the corner of Fiolstraede and Norre Voldgade. Discount tickets are sold only on the day of performance. Tickets are sold Monday through Friday from noon to 7pm and on Saturday from noon to 3pm.

THE PERFORMING ARTS

MERMAID THEATER, Sankt Peders Straede 27. Tel. 33-11-43-03.
Established in 1970, this is one of the three or four permanent English-language theaters in Europe outside the United Kingdom. It is committed to presenting exclusively English-language theatrical productions. Some of its plays are translated from other languages, including Chekhov's *The Harmfulness of Tobacco* and Hans Christian Andersen's *A Night in Roskilde*. Other presentations are American or British works. The box office is open Monday through Saturday from noon to 4pm. S-tog: Nørreport.
Tickets: 60–125 kroner ($10.40–$21.60). **Closed:** Dec 22–Jan 8.

ROYAL THEATER, Kongens Nytorv. Tel. 33-14-10-02.
A great winter bargain in Copenhagen is a performance by the world-renowned **Royal Danish Ballet** or **Royal Danish Opera,** dating from 1748. Because the arts are state subsidized in Denmark, ticket prices are comparatively low, and some seats are often available at the box office the day before a performance. The season runs from September to May. Bus: 1, 6, 9, 10.
Tickets: 50–250 kroner ($8.70–$43.30); half price for seniors 67 and up and young people under 26.

A CULTURAL CENTER

BOLTEN'S, Kongens Nytorv. Tel. 33-14-88-78.
The city's newest cultural center is housed in an 18th-century once-private

residence. You get 19 hours of activities here daily, but it closes at 3am for a general cleanup. Anything is likely to be happening here at any given time. Call the number above for information or tickets to various events, or, better yet, stroll by to see what's happening.

The repertoire is likely to include everything from theater productions to musical concerts, certainly art gallery showings and international exhibitions. The structure's 11 original yellow-painted buildings provide a historical perspective to the modern architecture, creating a "city within a city."

The range of venues includes bazaars, an imported 19th-century French brasserie, six cafés, various restaurants, a ticket kiosk for selling tickets not only for Bolten's but for various events in Copenhagen (see phone number above), and a number of specialty shops, even offices and departments.

The main building is Industrien, named for Copenhagen's former House of Industry. Inspired by the cabarets of Berlin, the main floor houses a theater café featuring Diamanten, one of Denmark's most avant-garde indoor and outdoor stages. The windows of this diamond-shaped stage open to Bolten's main courtyard, and can be raised to produce an outdoor theater or lowered to enclose a café. Above the theater café are several exhibition rooms displaying international art collections.

Beneath Industrien is a theater called Undergruden (check at the kiosk to see what might be presented at the time of your visit). It stages everything from variety shows and musicals to special morning shows for children. Sometimes it offers late-night American stand-up comedians who are booked for performances for night owls.

THE CLUB & MUSIC SCENE
NIGHTCLUBS/CABARET

HAND I HANKE, Griffen Feldtsgade 20. Tel. 33-37-20-70.
This popular hangout for young people offers a pub upstairs and folk music, blues, and rock on Tuesday, Thursday, Friday, and Saturday downstairs. There's no music in June and July, but otherwise everything is open all year. The pub is open daily from 2pm to 1:30am; downstairs, August to May, daily from 9pm to 1am. Bus: 5, 7, 8, 16.

Admission: 30–45 kroner ($5.20–$7.80), depending on the show, including the first drink.

NEW FELLINI'S, in the SAS Royal Hotel, Hammerichsgade 1. Tel. 33-93-32-39.
Fellini's provides a sophisticated after-dark rendezvous, with excellent acoustics. Cavelike and intimate, it is dark with subtle lighting and strobes. It's frequented by mature business clients of upscale hotels. International variety shows are presented at midnight, and the club is open only on Thursday, Friday, and Saturday from 9pm to 5am. Shows are presented around midnight. Drinks cost 65 kroner ($11.20). Bus: 2, 8, 13, 14, 16.

Admission: 65 kroner ($11.20).

JAZZ & BLUES

DE TRE MUSKETERER (The Three Musketeers), Nikolaj Plads 25. Tel. 33-11-25-07.
Established in the 1970s, this is a leading jazz house. The establishment consists of a long and narrow room, with a gregarious bar. A different musical group is featured nightly. The venue is traditional jazz every night except Monday, when modern jazz is offered. A jazz band, such as the Red Hot Chili Peppers, plays nightly. Beer costs 23 to 26 kroner ($4 to $4.50); drinks, 40 kroner ($6.90). It's open Monday through Thursday from 8pm to 2am and on Friday and Saturday from 8pm to 3am. In winter there are also Sunday-afternoon jam sessions from 3 to 6pm. Bus: 2, 6, 28, 41.

Admission: 35–50 kroner ($6.10–$8.70), depending on the performance; Sun afternoon, free.

JAZZHUSET MONTMARTRE, Nørregade 41. Tel. 33-11-46-67.
Attracting music lovers of all ages, this is the center of modern jazz in Denmark, if

not Europe, luring the world's finest jazz musicians. During the week you can hear soul and funk as well. The club also houses the Café Monten, which provides piano concerts on Tuesday, Wednesday, and Thursday afternoons. The club is open Monday through Friday from 11pm to 5am and on Saturday and Sunday from 8pm to 5am. Beer costs 23 kroner to 25 kroner ($4 to $4.30); drinks 40 kroner ($6.90). Bus: 5, 7, 14, 16.

Admission: 50–250 kroner ($8.70–$43.30), depending on the performance.

RÅDHUSKROEN, Løngangsstraede 21. Tel. 33-11-64-53.

Rådhuskroen is a candlelit drinking spot that offers blues music, 90% of which is performed by Scandinavian groups. Some of the best jazz in the city is also played at this popular student hangout. It's open daily from 8pm to 4am; live music usually begins at 10pm. Bottled beer costs 20 kroner ($3.50). Bus: 2, 8, 30.

Admission: Free Sun–Thurs; 40 kroner ($6.90) Sat–Sun.

DANCE CLUBS

AXEL DISCO, Axeltorv 2, Scala. Tel. 33-13-03-78.

Located in the Scala complex, this basement dance club attracts well-dressed clients over 20. Inside there's a large and electronically hip dance floor (the longest in town), a tequila bar, a beer bar, and a cocktail bar. Beer costs 20 kroner to 45 kroner ($3.50 to $7.80), and drinks run 25 kroner ($4.30). The music is recorded. Men are encouraged to wear jackets. The place is open on Friday and Saturday from 11pm to 5am. Bus: 6, 16, 28.

Admission: 50 kroner ($8.70).

CLUB EXALON, Frederiksberggade 38. Tel. 33-11-08-66.

In the city center on the Strøget, Club Exalon is one of the best-established nightspots in Copenhagen, with a history under the Exalon name going back 30 years, and a reputation as a nightspot predating World War II. It operates on three different floors of bars and dance floors. In the cellar, live music begins in 45-minute sets and alternates with recorded music the rest of the night. The other floors have other ambiences with recorded music and commodious bar areas. The club is open from Sunday through Thursday from 11pm to 5am, Friday and Saturday from 10am to 5am. Beer averages 22 kroner ($3.80). Bus: 28, 29, 41.

Admission: Free Sun; 40–50 kroner ($6.90–$8.70) Mon–Sat, depending on music.

DEN RØDE PIMPERNEL, H. C. Andersens Blvd. 7. Tel. 33-12-20-32.

The lively, clublike atmosphere of the Scarlet Pimpernel, near Rådhuspladsen, makes it a good place for dancing. The club is on two levels: one for recorded music, the other for live music. People are admitted only after an inspection through a peephole. A live band plays a variety of dance music. It's open Tuesday through Thursday from 9pm to 3am and on Friday and Saturday from 9pm to 5am. A beer will set you back 27 kroner ($4.70) and mixed drinks run 48 kroner ($8.30). Bus: 2, 8, 30.

Admission: Free Tues–Thurs; 40 kroner ($6.90) Fri–Sat.

THE BAR SCENE

PUBS

DET LILLE APOTEK, Store Kannikestraede 15. Tel. 33-12-56-06.

This is a good spot for English-speaking foreign students to meet their Danish contemporaries. Platters of food—such as fish filet with asparagus and caviar, cold sliced salmon and caviar and chive sauce, seafood salad, and roast beef—are offered daily from 11am to 11pm, costing 60 kroner to 82 kroner ($10.40 to $14.20). Beer runs 24 kroner ($4.20). It's open Monday through Wednesday from 11am to midnight. Closed: December 24–25 and 31. Bus: 2, 5, 8, 30.

DROP INN, Kompagnistraede 34. Tel. 33-11-24-04.

This is not a disco, but it does offer live and iconoclastic bands who perform for young people in their late teens and 20s. There's no dress code. The room combines antique and modern oil paintings and a long bar. It's open daily from 11pm to 5am. Beer costs 17 kroner to 22 kroner ($2.90 to $3.80). Bus: 28, 29, 41.

LAURITS BETJENT, Ved Stranden 16. Tel. 33-12-03-01.

A popular nightspot has stood here since 1850. The ground floor is not all there is to this place. The upstairs attracts all ages who come to this barnlike place for the beer, which seems to be the favorite drink. While some dance to the recorded or live music, others chat near the long bar. Jazz, blues, country music, or rock groups are featured every Friday and Saturday. It's open Monday through Saturday from 10pm to 5am. Beer costs 20 kroner to 23 kroner ($3.50 to $4); drinks, 36 kroner ($6.20). Bus: 2, 6, 9, 43.

LIBRARY BAR, in the Hotel Plaza, Bernstorffsgade 4. Tel. 33-14-92-62.

Frequently visited by celebrities and royalty, the Library Bar was once rated by Malcolm Forbes as one of the top five bars in the world. In a setting of antique books and works of art, you can order everything from a cappuccino to a cocktail. The setting is the lobby level of the landmark Plaza, commissioned in 1913 by King Frederik VIII. The bar was originally designed and built as the hotel's ballroom. Oregon pine was used for the paneling. The oversize mural of George Washington and his men is from 1910. It's open Monday through Saturday from 2pm to 1am and on Sunday from 2pm to midnight. Beer costs 24 kroner ($4.20); drinks begin at 40 kroner ($7). Bus: 1, 6.

NYHAVN 17, Nyhavn 17. Tel. 33-12-54-19.

This is the last of the honky-tonks that used to make up the former sailors' quarter. This café is a short walk from the patrician Kongens Nytorv and the d'Angleterre luxury hotel. In summer you can sit outside. It's open daily from 9am to 1am. Beer costs 22 kroner ($3.80) and drinks run 35 kroner ($6.10). Bus: 1, 6, 9, 10.

THE QUEEN'S PUB, in the Kong Frederik Hotel, Vester Voldgade 25. Tel. 33-12-59-02.

A popular spot, the Queen's Pub is connected to one of the city's most prestigious hotels. Amid English walnut paneling and mirrors etched with elaborate Victorian patterns, you can settle back and enjoy. It's open daily from 11:30am to 1am. Beer costs 17 kroner to 35 kroner ($2.90 to $6.10), drinks from 50 kroner ($8.70). Bus: 1, 2, 6, 8, 28.

VIN & OLGOD, Skindergade 45. Tel. 33-13-26-25.

A dancing, drinking, singing, and snack complex, Vin & Olgod is complete with a tavern, a pub, a bodega, and a main beer hall. When the band plays on stage, everybody sings along. If you don't know the words, printed music sheets are provided. In any room, light beer and a variety of snacks are available. It's open Monday through Saturday from 8pm to 2am. A half liter of beer costs 38 kroner ($6.60) and drinks run 45 kroner ($7.80). Bus: 5, 7, 14.

Admission: 25 kroner ($4.30) Mon–Thurs; 50 kroner ($8.70) Fri–Sat.

WINE BARS

HVIIDS VINSTUE, Kongens Nytorv 19. Tel. 33-15-10-64.

Built in 1670, this old wine cellar is a dimly lit safe haven for an eclectic crowd. In December only, a combination of red wine and cognac is served. It's open Monday through Saturday from 10am to 1am; closed Sunday in July and August. Beer runs 17 kroner to 22 kroner ($2.90 to $3.80); wine costs 24 kroner ($4.20). Bus: 1, 6, 9, 10.

THE GAY SCENE

AN ACTIVITIES CENTER

PAN SOCIETY, Knabrostraede 3. Tel. 33-13-19-48.

This nationwide organization was established in 1948 for the protection and advancement of gay rights. Its headquarters is inside a 19th-century yellow building off the Strøget. A dance club occupies three of its floors, and a modern café is on the ground floor. Thursday night is for women only. Every night is gay night, although a lot of straight people patronize the place because the music is so good. The center is open Sunday through Tuesday 1pm to 3am; Wednesday and Thursday 1pm to 4am, Friday and Saturday 1pm to 5am. Beer costs 24 kroner ($4.20); drinks, 39 kroner ($6.70). Bus: 28, 29, 41.

Admission: Dance club, 30–55 kroner ($5.20–$9.50).

BAR & PUBS

ERIK DEN RØDE, Amagerbrogade 40. Tel. 31-57-40-80.

At the corner of Holmbladgade, this pub has the interior of a cozy Danish *kro* (inn). It's a popular venue for gay businessmen who drop by to enjoy the frikadeller, filet of plaice, or grilled or roast beef. Appetizers cost around 35 kroner ($6.10); main dishes, 50 kroner to 100 kroner ($8.70 to $17.30). A beer runs 20 kroner ($3.50). Bus: 2, 5, 9, 11, 13.

PINK CLUB, Farvergade 10. Tel. 33-11-26-07.

A new Copenhagen gay bar, it has a long bar with the atmosphere of a darkly upholstered private men's club. It's open Sunday through Thursday from 6pm to 4am and Saturday and Sunday from 6pm to 5am. Beer costs 16 kroner to 19 kroner ($2.80 to $3.30). Bus: 2, 8, 30.

THE MEN'S BAR, Teglgårdsstraede 3. Tel. 33-12-73-03.

This is the only leather bar in town, filled with an unusual collection of uniforms, leather, and levis. There's one bar and a decor outfitted in shades of gray, black, and stainless steel. Hours are daily from 3pm to 2am. A beer will set you back 16 to 19 kroner ($2.80 to $3.30). Bus: 2, 8, 30.

TIVOLI AT NIGHT

In the center of the gardens, the large **open-air stage** books vaudeville acts (tumbling clowns, acrobats, aerialists) who give two performances nightly, at 7 and 9pm (also at 5pm on the weekend). Spectators have to go through the turnstiles for seats, but there's an unobstructed view from the outside for standees. Special arrangements with jazz, beat, and folklore groups also take place during the season. Admission is free.

Near the Vesterbrogade 3 entrance, the 150-year-old outdoor **Pantomime Theater,** with a Chinese stage and peacock curtain, opens Monday through Saturday at 7:45pm, revealing a repertory of 16 different commedia dell'arte productions (the entertaining trio: Pierrot, Columbine, and Harlequin), authentic pantomimes that have been performed continuously in Copenhagen since 1801. Admission is free. Classic ballets, accompanied by the Tivoli Promenade Orchestra, are performed on the stage at 9:45pm.

The modern **Tivolis Koncertsal** (concert hall) is a great place to hear talented and famous artists, led by equally famous conductors. Inaugurated in 1956, the concert hall has a seating capacity of 2,000, and its season, lasting for more than 4 months beginning in May, has been called "the most extensive music festival in the world." Performances of everything from symphony to opera are held Monday through Saturday at 7:30pm. Good seats are available at prices ranging from 50 kroner to 90 kroner ($8.70 to $15.60) and up when major artists are performing—but most performances are free. Ballet usually costs 200 kroner ($34.60). Tickets are sold at the main booking office on Vesterbrogade 3 (tel. 33-15-10-12).

Tivoli Glassalen (tel. 33-11-86-75) is housed in an octagonal gazebolike building with a glass, gilt-capped canopy. Depending on its repertoire, the program might interest you. Performances here are often comedic/satirical performances by Danish comedians in Danish, and these are not usually of interest to non-Danish audiences. But there are also musical revues. Of all the theaters within Tivoli, this seems to be the least rigidly scheduled and the most open to the eccentricities of scheduling. Tickets range from 155 kroner to 195 kroner ($26.80 to $33.70).

Jazzhus Slukefter (tel. 33-11-11-13) offers some of the best jazz in Copenhagen, often attracting big names from the United States. The club is open Monday through Saturday from 8pm to 2am. When the gardens close, you can enter from the street, the Bernstorffsgade. Most concerts begin at 9:30pm, and the entrance fee is 40 kroner ($6.90). Beer costs 22 kroner to 28 kroner ($3.80 to $4.80).

GAMBLING

CASINO COPENHAGEN, in the SAS Scandinavia Hotel, Amager Blvd. 70. Tel. 33-11-23-24.

In this previously recommended first-class hotel, Danish authorities allowed the country's first fully licensed casino to open right after Christmas in 1990. Today gamblers play such popular games as roulette, baccarat, and blackjack. The whole operation is overseen by Casinos of Austria, the largest casino operator in Europe. Bus: 5, 11, 30, 34.

Open: Daily 4pm–4am.
Admission: 40 kroner ($6.90).

9. EASY EXCURSIONS

BEACHES

The nearest beach to Copenhagen is **Bellevue** (take the S-train to Klampenborg), but the water is not recommended for swimming. If you like to swim at a sandy beach, take a trip (by train or car) to the beaches at North Zealand—**Gilleleje, Hornbaek, Liseleje,** and **Tisvildeleje.** Although these are family beaches, minimum bathing attire is worn.

To reach any of these beaches, take the train to Helsingør and then continue by bus. Or you can make connections by train to Hillerød and switch to a local train. Check at the railroad station for details. If you drive, you may want to stay for the evening discos at the little beach resort towns dotting the north coast of Zealand.

DRAGØR

Visit the past in this old seafaring town on the island of Amager, 3 miles south of Copenhagen's Kastrup Airport. It is filled with well-preserved half-timbered, ocher and pink 18th-century cottages with steep red-tile or thatch roofs, many of which are under the protection of the National Trust.

Dragør (pronounced *Drah*-wer) was a busy port on the herring-rich Baltic Sea in the early Middle Ages, and when fishing fell off, it became just another sleepy little waterfront village. After 1520, Amager Island and its villages—Dragør and Store Magleby—were inhabited by the Dutch, who brought their own customs, Low-German language, and agricultural expertise to Amager, especially their love of bulb flowers. In Copenhagen, you still see wooden-shoed Amager selling their hyacinths, tulips, daffodils, and lilies in the streets.

Dragør is a 35-minute trip on bus no. 30, 33, or 73E from the Rådhuspladsen (Town Hall Square) in Copenhagen.

WHAT TO SEE & DO

DRAGØR MUSEUM, Havnepladsen 4. Tel. 32-53-41-06.

The exhibits at this harborfront museum show how the Amager Dutch lived from prehistoric times to the 20th century. Farming, goose breeding, seafaring, fishing, ship piloting, and ship salvage are delineated through pictures and artifacts.

Admission: 10 kroner ($1.70) adults, 5 kroner (90¢) children.
Open: May–Sept, Tues–Fri 2–5pm, Sat–Sun and holidays noon–6pm. **Bus:** 30, 33, 73E.

STUDIO OF CHRISTIAN MOLSTED, Blegerstraede 1. Tel. 32-53-41-06.

Next door to the Dragør Museum, visit the studio of noted Danish marine artist Christian Molsted (1862–1930), where many pictures and topographical drawings of Dragør are displayed.
Admission: 10 kroner ($1.70) adults, 5 kroner (90¢) children.
Open: May–Sept, Sat–Sun 2–5pm. **Bus:** 30, 33, 73E.

AMAGER MUSEUM, Hovedgaden 4-12, Store Magleby. Tel. 32-53-02-50.

A rich trove of historic treasures is found in this museum outside Dragør. Exhibits reveal the affluence achieved by the Amager Dutch, with rich textiles, fine embroidery, and such amenities as carved silver buckles and buttons. Room interiors of a Dutch house are especially interesting, showing how these people decorated their homes and lived in comfort.
Admission: 10 kroner ($1.70) adults, 5 kroner (90¢) children.
Open: June–Aug, Wed–Sun 11am–3pm; Sept–May, Wed and Sun 11am–3pm. **Bus:** 30, 33, 73E.

WHERE TO STAY
Inexpensive

HOTEL DRAGØR FAERGEGAARD, Drogdensvej 43, DK-2791 Dragør. Tel. 32-53-01-87. 23 rms (all with bath). TEL **Bus:** 30, 33, 73E.
$ Rates (including breakfast): 650–700 kroner ($112.50–$121.10) single; 660–730 kroner ($114.20–$126.30) double. AE, DC, MC.
Although most people visit this hotel for its food, it also offers comfortable old-fashioned bedrooms. You'll get a real feel for a country Danish inn, yet you're only 20 minutes from the Copenhagen Town Hall. You can also enjoy the hotel's excellent cuisine. There are six different preparations of herring, a Dragør Plate of mixed meats and pâtés, schnitzels, soups, and smørrebrød. Full meals begin at 190 kroner ($32.90). The dining room is open for lunch and dinner daily from 11am to 10pm.

WHERE TO DINE
Expensive

CAFE BEGHUSET, Strandgade 14. Tel. 32-53-01-36.
Cuisine: DANISH/FRENCH. **Reservations:** Not required. **Bus:** 30, 33, 73E.
$ Prices: Appetizers 45–66 kroner ($7.80–$11.40); main dishes 89–158 kroner ($15.40–$27.30); 3-course dinner 198 kroner ($34.30). DC, MC, V.
Open: Dinner daily 5:30–10pm.
This charming café and restaurant on a cobblestone street in the center of town looks like an idyllic country cottage. To reach the restaurant section, you'll walk through a likable café. The restaurant offers such dishes as fish soup, Swedish caviar, thinly sliced smoked lamb with a balsamic dressing on a bed of seasonal greens, and fresh oysters. Main courses include guinea fowl braised in red wine served with bacon of veal (their own invention) and herbs and Dragør plaice roasted in butter and served either with parsley sauce or a bacon-thyme sauce.

Moderate

STRANDHOTEL, Strandlinbyn 9, Havnen. Tel. 32-53-00-75.
Cuisine: DANISH. **Reservations:** Recommended. **Bus:** 30, 33, 73E.
$ Prices: Appetizers 40–46 kroner ($6.90–$8); main dishes 95–120 kroner ($16.40–$20.80); lunch smørrebrød 36 kroner ($6.20). AE, DC, MC, V.
Open: Daily 10:30am–10:30pm. **Closed:** Jan–Feb.
Stop in here where King Frederik III ate his favorite eel soup and where Søren Kierkegaard dined as well. You can enjoy full meals including filet of pork in paprika sauce, smoked eel, fried or poached plaice, and trout with almonds. At lunch, one of the best arrays of smørrebrød in town is served.

DRAGØR KRO, Kongvejen 23. Tel. 32-53-01-87.

Cuisine: DANISH/FRENCH. **Reservations:** Recommended. **Bus:** 30, 33, 73E.
$ Prices: Fixed-price dinner 110 kroner ($19) for 2 courses, 135–200 kroner ($23.40–$34.60) for 3 courses; appetizers 36–80 kroner ($6.20–$13.80); main dishes 72–160 kroner ($12.50–$27.70). AE, DC, MC, V.
Open: Daily noon–9:30pm (10:30pm in summer). **Closed:** Dec 22–Jan 15.

A series of half-paneled dining rooms are found in this 1721 building. There is a rose-filled courtyard for outdoor dining and drinking. You can select a filet of plaice with white wine sauce, or perhaps filet of veal in mustard sauce. "Falling star" is a house specialty (boiled or fried fish with caviar and shrimp).

CHAPTER 8

ZEALAND & NEARBY ISLANDS

Although Copenhagen is Zealand's largest city, the island is rich with other attractions.

Many prefer to explore the island on day-trips from the capital, since distances between attractions are short. The most popular day-trip is a tour of three royal castles in North Zealand: Kronborg Castle at Shakespeare's Elsinore, the royal family's summer palace at Fredensborg, and the 17th-century castle of Frederiksborg at Hillerød.

Along the way, a popular stop is the Louisiana Museum, on the so-called Danish Riviera. The building is as architecturally interesting as the ever-changing exhibits of stunning modern art housed inside.

Once you've explored Hamlet's Castle, you might take a geological field trip to the white chalky cliffs and glacial deposits on the island of Møn.

SEEING ZEALAND & NEARBY ISLANDS
GETTING AROUND

Zealand (Sjaelland in Danish) is best explored by car, although it has an excellent bus and train network. By either bus or train you can reach all the important destinations outside Copenhagen in the following time periods: Helsingør, 50 minutes; Hillerød, 40 minutes; Roskilde, 20 minutes; Køge, 1 hour.

Inquire about schedule information at the Central Railroad Station in Copenhagen. At the information desk of the Danish State Railways you can request a round-trip ticket that will also include admission charges to certain major attractions.

The **Copenhagen Card** is a cost-saving device allowing unlimited travel on buses and trains in Copenhagen, North Zealand, Roskilde, and Køge. Without this card, travel can be pricey because there's no discount on round-trip tickets.

Many roads in Zealand have cycle tracks if you'd like to explore by bicycle. Most cars use the expressway highways, so it's safer to take the older secondary roads.

If you prefer an organized tour, inquire about the possibilities at the Copenhagen tourist office. The most popular tour is called the Castle Tour of North Zealand, visiting Kronborg, Fredensborg, and Frederiksborg. It takes 7 hours.

A SUGGESTED ITINERARY

Zealand can be explored from Copenhagen, but you'll get more of a feel for it by spending 2 or 3 nights in a Zealand *kro* (inn) or local hotel.

Day 1: Drive up the Danish Riviera coastline stopping at the Louisiana Art Museum, then continuing to Helsingør for the night.

WHAT'S SPECIAL ABOUT ZEALAND

Beaches

☐ Denmark's Riviera is Strandvejen. Quiet, sandy beaches.

☐ The tranquil, sandy beaches of Møn, an island in the Baltic Sea.

Castles & Palaces

☐ Kronborg—"Hamlet's Castle"—the most visited place outside Copenhagen.

☐ Frederiksborg Castle, the premier castle of Scandinavia, called the Danish Versailles.

☐ Selsø Slot, the country's first Renaissance castle.

Great Cathedrals

☐ Roskilde Cathedral, resting place of 38 Danish kings and queens.

Ancient Ruins

☐ Five Viking vessels rescued from Roskilde Fjord on display near Roskilde.

Art Museums

☐ Louisiana Art Museum at Humlebaek, Denmark's most controversial modern-art museum.

Natural Attractions

☐ The white cliffs of Møn, created a million years ago by the sea.

Literary Pilgrimages

☐ Rungstedlund, home of Karen Blixen/Isak Dinesen, famed for *Out of Africa*.

Special Events

☐ Viking Pageant at Frederikssund, a 2-week festival (late June).

☐ Roskilde festival draws rock music lovers worldwide (early June).

Day 2: Explore Hamlet's Castle (Kronborg) and other attractions in the morning; then take a day-trip on the ferry to Helsingborg, Sweden. Return to Helsingør for the night.

Day 3: Stop off at the queen's summer home (outside visits only) at Fredensborg in the morning, then continue to Hillerød in the west to see Frederiksborg Castle. Drive to the Roskilde for the night.

Day 4: While in Roskilde, explore its attractions, including Roskilde Cathedral and the Viking Ship Museum. In the afternoon visit the Forsøgscenter, 5 miles west, site of a reconstructed Iron Age community.

Day 5: Drive to Køge, south of Copenhagen (take connecting Route 6). Have lunch, look around, and head for Stege, the capital of Møn, for the night. Explore the white cliffs, prehistoric burial sights, and medieval churches. Return to Copenhagen for the night.

1. RUNGSTEDLUND

15 miles N of Copenhagen

GETTING THERE   By Train   A Kystbanen train departs from Copenhagen's Central Railroad Station, taking 30 minutes.

By Bus   Buses for Rungstedlund leave from Copenhagen's Central Railroad Station.

By Car Head north from Copenhagen along the E4 to Helsingør until you reach the turnoff east marked RUNGSTED.

Since the 1985 release of *Out of Africa*, starring Robert Redford and Meryl Streep, thousands of literary and movie fans have been visiting the former home of Karen Blixen, who wrote under the pen name Isak Dinesen. Her home, **Rungstedlund,** Runsted Strandvej III, is midway between Copenhagen and Helsingør on the coastal road.

Her father, Wilhelm Dinesen, purchased the estate in 1879. Blixen left in 1914 for Kenya when she married Bror von Blixen Fenicke, but returned in 1931 and stayed until her death in 1962.

It was at Rungstedlund that Blixen wrote her first major success, *Seven Gothic Tales*, which many literary critics consider more memorable than *Out of Africa*. She also wrote collections of stories, *Winter's Tales* and *Last Tales,* here. Before Dinesen's father acquired the property, it was known as Rungsted Kro (inn), attracting travelers going north from Copenhagen to Helsingør.

Blixen wrote in Ewald's Room, named to honor the poet Johannes Ewald who stayed at the place when it was an inn. Four years before her death, Blixen established the Rungstedlund Foundation, which owns the property and its 40-acre garden and bird sanctuary. The gardens have long been open to the public, but in 1991 the foundation invited Queen Margrethe to open the museum.

In one part of the museum is a small gallery with exhibits in oil, pastel, and charcoal—all works by Blixen.

Visitors pay 30 kroner ($5.20) to enter, although children under 12 go free. Hours are May 1 through September daily from 1am to 5pm; off-season Wednesday to Friday from 1 to 4pm and Saturday and Sunday from 11am to 4pm.

Blixen is buried in the grove at the foot of Edwaldshøj.

WHERE TO DINE

EXPENSIVE

RESTAURANT NOKKEN, Rungsted Havn 44. Tel. 42-57-13-14.
   Cuisine: DANISH. **Reservations:** Recommended.
$ Prices: Appetizers 65–128 kroner ($11.20–$22.10); main dishes 100–200 kroner ($17.30–$34.60); fixed-price lunch 185 kroner ($32); fixed-price dinner 245–265 kroner ($42.40–$45.80). AE, DC, MC, V.
   Open: Lunch daily noon–4pm; dinner daily 6–10pm. Bar, summer, daily noon–1 or 2am; winter, Sun–Thurs noon–11pm, Fri–Sat noon–2am.
Amid light-grained paneling and whimsical nautical accessories, you can enjoy one of the best meals to be found along the Danish Riviera. A sweeping wall of windows

---

IN THEIR FOOTSTEPS

Karen Blixen/Isak Dinesen (1885–1962) Twice nominated for the Nobel Prize, Blixen, writing under the name Isak Dinesen, was a major 20th-century author. Her works included *Seven Gothic Tales* and her serene memoir, *Out of Africa,* about her life in Kenya.
   • **Birthplace:** Born in Rungstedlund, she was the daughter of an aristocrat, Wilhelm Dinesen, soldier, sportsman, and writer.
   • **Residences:** Her father's estate, Rungstedlund, in Zealand, and a Kenyan coffee plantation where she fell in love with Denys Finch Hatton.
   • **Resting Place:** In the grove at the foot of Edwaldshøj, near her father's estate.

encompasses the sea, the boats, and a view of the Swedish coast. Specialties include filet of prime beef with thyme and snails, double lamb chops with aromatic herbs, scampi orientale, oven-baked lemon sole, and heather-honey ice cream.

2. HUMLEBAEK & LOUISIANA

20 miles N of Copenhagen

GETTING THERE   By Train   Humlebaek, the nearest town to Louisiana, may be reached by train from Copenhagen (København-Helsingør). Two trains per hour leave from the main station in Copenhagen (trip time is 40 minutes). Once at Humlebaek, the museum is a 10-minute walk.

By Bus   Take the S-train, Line A or B, to Lyngby station. From there, take bus no. 388 along the coast road. There is a bus stop at the museum.

By Car   Take the Strandvej (coastal road no. 152) from Copenhagen. The scenic drive takes about 45 minutes.

Established in 1958, the ✪ **Louisiana Art Museum,** G. Strandvej 13 (tel. 42-19-07-19), is idyllically situated in a 19th-century mansion on the Danish Riviera surrounded by elegant gardens, opening directly onto the Øresund. The modern art displayed is paintings and sculptures by masters (Giacometti and Henry Moore, to name two) as well as the best and most controversial works of modern art. In particular, look for paintings by Carl-Henning Pedersen. Occasionally, there are Chinese or Egyptian art exhibits as well as concerts. The museum name came from the first owner of the estate, Alexander Brun, who had three wives, each named Louise. Admission is 40 kroner ($6.90) for adults, free for children under 16. It's open Thursday through Tuesday from 10am to 5pm and on Wednesday from 10am to 10pm. Closed: December 24–25 and 31.

WHERE TO DINE

EXPENSIVE

GAMLA HUMLEBAEK KRO, Ny Strandvej 2A. Tel. 42-19-05-69.
   Cuisine: DANISH. **Reservations:** Recommended.
$ Prices: Appetizers 60–75 kroner ($10.40–$13); main dishes 160–175 kroner ($27.70–$30.30); fixed-price menu 175 kroner ($30.30). AE, DC, MC, V.
   Open: Daily noon–9:30pm.
A perfect lunch spot for visitors to the Louisiana Museum, the inn was built in 1722. Selections might include médaillons of veal with morel sauce, stuffed filet of plaice, and herring with sherry. Lunchtime platters, meals unto themselves, cost from 80 kroner to 125 kroner ($13.80 to $21.60).

3. HELSINGØR (ELSINORE)

25 miles N of Copenhagen

GETTING THERE   By Train   There are frequent trains from Copenhagen taking 50 minutes.

By Bus   Some 30 buses daily leave Copenhagen for the 1-hour trip to Helsingør.

By Car   Take the E-4 north from Copenhagen.

ESSENTIALS The **Tourist Office,** at Havnepladsen (tel. 49-21-13-33), is open daily from 9am to 5pm.

Helsingør (Elsinore in English) is visited chiefly for "Hamlet's Castle." Aside from its literary associations, the town has a certain charm: a quiet market square, medieval lanes, old half-timbered and brick buildings, remains of its once prosperous shipping industry.

In 1429 King Erik of Pomerania ruled that ships passing Helsingør had to pay sound dues. The town quickly developed into the focal point for international shipping, bringing in a lot of revenue. King Erik also built the Castle of Krogen, later rebuilt by Christian IV as the Castle of Kronborg. For a while Helsingør prospered and grew so much it was the second-largest town in the country.

WHAT TO SEE & DO

Guided tours of the city, costing 25 kroner ($4.30) per person, are conducted every Monday in July at 7pm. Inquire at the Tourist Office.

KRONBORG SLOT, Kronborg. Tel. 49-21-30-78.

There is no evidence that Shakespeare ever saw this sandstone-and-copper Dutch Renaissance-style castle, full of intriguing secret passages and casemates, but he made it famous in *Hamlet.* According to 12th-century historian Saxo Grammaticus, though, if Hamlet had really existed, he would have been centuries before Kronborg was erected (1574–85). Over the years, some famous productions of the Shakespearian play have been staged here. One great performance was Derek Jacobi's interpretation in 1979. In 1954 the parts of Hamlet and Ophelia were played by Richard Burton and Claire Bloom.

The castle was restored in 1629 by Christian IV after it was gutted by fire. During its history, it has been looted, bombarded, occupied by Swedes, and used as a barracks from 1785 to 1922. Don't miss the starkly furnished Great Hall (the largest in northern Europe), the church with its original oak furnishings, and the royal chambers. Its bleak and austere atmosphere adds to its drama. Kronborg also contains a collection of wool and silk tapestries, great old oaken chests, and cupboards. In the basement sits Holger Danske, the mythological hero believed to aid Denmark when the country is threatened. The **Danish Maritime Museum** (tel. 49-21-06-85) is also on the premises, which explores the history of Danish shipping.

Guided tours are given every half hour October to April. In summer you can walk around on your own. The castle is half a mile from the rail station.

Admission: 20 kroner ($3.50) adults, 10 kroner ($1.70) children 6–14.

Open: May–Sept, daily 10:30am–5pm; Oct and Apr, Tues–Sun 11am–4pm; Nov–Mar, Tues–Sun 11am–3pm. **Closed:** Christmas Day.

KARMELITERKLOSTRET, Sct. Annagade 38. Tel. 49-21-17-74.

This well-preserved 15th-century former Carmelite monastery is the best of its kind in Scandinavia. It's located at the intersection of Havnegade and Kronborgvej.

Admission: 10 kroner ($1.75) adults, 5 kroner (85¢) children.

Open: Guided tours daily at 2pm (also at 11am from mid-Apr to mid-Oct). **Bus:** 801, 802, 803, 331.

SCT. MARIAE CHURCH, Sct. Annagade 38. Tel. 49-21-17-74.

A monastery complex with late 15th-century frescoes, St. Mary's also contains the organ played by baroque composer Dietrich Buxtehude from 1660 to 1668 (still in use). The church lies near the intersection of Havnegade and Kronborgvej.

Admission: Free.

Open: May 16–Sept 15, daily noon–3pm; off-season, daily noon–2pm.

ST. OLAI CHURCH, Sct. Annagade 12. Tel. 49-21-04-43.

Built between 1480 and 1559, this christening chapel is worth a visit. The interior of the church and the baptistry in particular are one-of-a-kind. The spired church is connected to the Carmelite cloisters. The church lies near the intersection of Havnegade and Kronborgvej.

Admission: Free.

Open: Mon–Sat 10am–4pm. **Bus:** 801, 802, 803, 331.

HELSINGØR BYMUSEUM, Sct. Annagade 36. Tel. 49-21-00-98.

Installed in part of the Carmelite monastery (see above), this museum houses the town's historic archives and various exhibits. In 1630 it was the local poorhouse, and for a long time a hospital, specializing in brain operations. Some tools used by these early surgeons are displayed, and are rather gruesome. The museum also has a fine scale model of the town in 1801.

Admission: 10 kroner ($1.70) adults, 5 kroner (90¢) children.

Open: Daily noon–4pm. **Bus:** 801, 802, 803, 331.

MARIENLYST SLOT, Marienlyst Allé 32. Tel. 49-21-00-98.

Another municipal museum, built in 1587 as a summer palace and rebuilt around 1760, Marienlyst Castle houses many of Helsingør's historic relics, with changing exhibits of arts and crafts.

Admission: 20 kroner ($3.50) adults, 10 kroner ($1.70) children.

Open: June–Aug, Thurs–Tues noon–5pm, Wed noon–5pm and 7–10pm; Sept–May, Sat–Sun 2–5pm. **Bus:** 340, 801, 802.

DANMARKS TEKNISKE MUSEUM (Technical Museum of Denmark), Nodre Strandvej 23. Tel. 42-22-26-11.

This museum contains technical, industrial, scientific, and transportation exhibits, including the oldest Danish airplanes and trains, the world's first typewriter, and the world's first electromagnetic sound recorder (tape recorder). There's also an 1888 Danish automobile, Hammelvognen.

Admission: 20 kroner ($3.50) adults, 10 kroner ($1.70) children.

Open: Daily 10am–5pm. **Bus:** 340.

WHERE TO STAY
EXPENSIVE

HOTEL MARIENLYST, Nordre Standvej 2, DK-3000 Helsingør. Tel. 49-20-35-30. Fax 49-26-26-26. 200 rms (all with bath), 9 suites. TV TEL **Bus:** 340.

$ Rates (including breakfast): 880 kroner ($152.20) single; 1,180 kroner ($204.10) double; from 1,765 kroner ($305.30) suite. AE, DC, MC, V. **Parking:** Free.

Located on the western outskirts of town beyond the castle, this hotel is about as close to Las Vegas as you'll get in Denmark. Today comprised of a compound of three buildings, its headquarters and oldest core was built around 1850, and with the largest of its annexes built in the mid-1970s. With a panoramic view over the gray sea toward Sweden, this hotel contains a glossy outbuilding with one of only six gambling casinos in Denmark. Facilities include a sauna and an indoor swimming pool.

MODERATE

HOTEL HAMLET, Bramstraede 5, DK-3000 Helsingør. Tel. 49-21-05-91. Fax 49-20-01-30. 36 rms (all with bath). TV TEL **Bus:** 801, 802.

$ Rates (including breakfast): 625–795 kroner ($108.10–$137.50) single; 855–1,060 kroner ($147.90–$183.40) double. AE, DC, MC, V.

Each bedroom is carpeted and half-paneled, and has antique pinewood doors and English club-style furniture. The hotel's restaurant, Ophelia, is also recommended (see "Where to Dine," below). The hotel is well situated, lying close to Kronborg Castle and the ferry to Sweden.

INEXPENSIVE

SKANDIA HOTEL, Bramstraede 1, DK-3000 Helsingør. Tel. 49-21-09-02. Fax 49-26-54-90. 44 rms (9 with bath). **Bus:** 801, 802.

$ Rates (including breakfast): 300 kroner ($51.90) single without bath, 400 kroner ($69.20) single with bath; 500 kroner ($86.50) double without bath; 640 kroner ($110.70) double with bath. AE, DC, MC, V. **Parking:** Free.

The budget choice in town, the Skandia has clean and spacious rooms filled with comfortable, albeit slightly dowdy, furniture. The hotel is set behind a red-brick facade along a street running parallel to the port. It's near the harbor and close to the ferry to Sweden.

WHERE TO DINE

Typical Danish hot meals, such as *hakkebof* (hamburger steak), *frikadeller* (Danish rissoles), rib roast with red cabbage, cooked or fried flounder or herring, and aeggekage (egg cake) with bacon, are served in the local restaurants. Some restaurants offer a Danmenu, a typical Danish meal. In Helsingør, you'll also find many fast-food places, and you won't want to miss the celebrated ice-cream wafers.

MODERATE

FAERGAARDEN, Stengade 81B. Tel. 49-21-39-46.
Cuisine: INTERNATIONAL. **Reservations:** Not required. **Bus:** 801, 802.
$ Prices: Appetizers 35–60 kroner ($6.10–$10.40); main dishes 65–129 kroner ($11.20–$22.30); fixed-price lunch 79 kroner ($13.70); fixed-price dinner 120 kroner ($20.80). AE, DC, MC, V.
Open: Daily noon–10pm. **Closed:** Mon in winter and Jan.

This restaurant, set in a former Customs house from 1770, virtually enjoys the dining monopoly in Helsingør. It consists of four restaurants in one, including Bøf & Grøn, a beef restaurant; Bamboo, a Chinese restaurant; Gringo's Cantina, a Mexican restaurant; and Overhuset, a night restaurant (midnight to 5am daily), serving light dishes, including cold platters of meat and fish and open-face sandwiches. All the restaurants are comparably priced.

OPHELIA RESTAURANT, in the Hotel Hamlet, Bramstraede 5. Tel. 49-21-28-02.
Cuisine: DANISH/FRENCH. **Reservations:** Not required. **Bus:** 801, 802.
$ Prices: Appetizers 35–90 kroner ($6.10–$15.60); main dishes 120–250 kroner ($20.80–$43.30); 2-course dinner 160 kroner ($27.70); fixed-price lunch 105 kroner ($18.20). AE, DC, MC, V.
Open: Daily 11:30am–10pm.

Ophelia is the most appealing restaurant in town. In the elegantly rustic dining room, photos of various world *Hamlet* productions line the brick walls. Specialties include butter-fried plaice with shrimp, pepper-pickled Baltic salmon, steak with bordelaise sauce, and richly caloric desserts. Lunches will probably only set you back half as much as dinner.

In the basement is a tavern-style disco, the Shakespeare Club, where an over-30 crowd drinks and dances Wednesday to Monday after 8pm. On weekends guests pay 25 kroner ($4.30) cover, and beer costs the same.

INEXPENSIVE

CAFETERIA SAN REMO, Stengade 53. Tel. 42-21-00-55.
Cuisine: DANISH. **Reservations:** Not required. **Bus:** 801, 802.
$ Prices: Appetizers 22–48 kroner ($3.80–$8.30); main dishes 28–85 kroner ($4.80–$14.70). No credit cards.
Open: June–July, daily 9am–9pm; Aug–May, daily 11am–6pm.

A down-to-earth self-service place with crystal chandeliers, the San Remo offers 35 different meals, including frikadeller (Ping-Pong meatballs) and potatoes. At the corner of Bjergegade, in a traffic-free shopping mall, the cafeteria lies half a block from the harbor. It dates from 1904 and is in a building with a Dutch architectural influence.

4. FREDENSBORG

6 miles W of Helsingør, 25 miles N of Copenhagen

GETTING THERE By Train From Copenhagen's Central Railroad Station, frequent trains run to Fredensborg.

By Bus Bus nos. 336 and 384 from Copenhagen's Central Railroad Station run to Fredensborg.

By Car From Copenhagen, head north on the E55 toward Helsingør, turning west on Route 6.

___

The splendid early 18th-century Italian-style **Fredensborg Palace** (tel. 42-28-00-25) is the summer home of the royal family. It was particularly celebrated during the reign of Christian IX, who assembled the greats of European royalty here in the days of Queen Victoria. Rooms open for public viewing are those actually used by the royal family. When the queen is in residence, visitors assemble at noon to watch the changing of the guard. On Thursday, except in July, the queen often appears to acknowledge a regimental band concert in her honor. Bus no. 336 stops nearby.

The palace can be visited only in July, daily from 1 to 5pm. Admission is 8 kroner ($1.40) for adults, 3 kroner (50¢) for children. The extensive grounds are open all summer.

WHERE TO STAY & DINE
MODERATE

HOTEL STORE KRO, Slotsgade 6, DK-3480 Fredensborg. Tel. 42-38-00-47. 49 rms (all with bath). TEL **Bus:** 336, 733E.
$ Rates (including breakfast): 600–750 kroner ($103.80–$129.80) single; 800–1,100 kroner ($138.40–$190.30) double. AE, DC, MC, V. **Parking:** Free.
A 10-minute walk from the train station and only 5 minutes from Esrum Lake, the hotel was commissioned in 1723 by King Frederik IV. Well-furnished rooms, rich in character, reflect its proximity to the royal residence. Facilities include a sauna and a billiard and dart room. If you're stopping in for lunch, count on spending from 250 kroner ($43.30). Lunch is served daily from noon to 3pm and dinner from 6 to 10pm. Dishes include such favorites as escalope of turkey fried in honey with mushrooms and parsley gravy.

___

5. HILLERØD

22 miles NW of Copenhagen

GETTING THERE By Train The S-train from Copenhagen's Central Railroad Station departs every 20 minutes and takes 35 minutes.

By Bus There are no buses from Copenhagen to Hillerød.

By Car Take Route 16 north from Copenhagen.

ESSENTIALS The **Tourist Office,** at Slotsgade 52 (tel. 42-26-28-52), is open daily 9am–5pm.

___

Hillerød offers some very interesting sights, including one of Scandinavia's most beautiful castles. It would be ideal to be in Hillerød at the time of the Viking festival in summer (see below).

WHAT TO SEE & DO

THE MUSEUM OF NATURAL HISTORY AT FREDERIKSBORG CASTLE, Fredensborgvej. Tel. 42-26-04-39.

★ This moated *slot* (castle), known as the Danish Versailles, is perhaps the major castle in all Scandinavia. Like Kronborg, it was built in Dutch Renaissance style (red brick, copper roof, sandstone facade). The oldest parts date from 1560 and the reign of Frederik II. However, the main part of the castle was erected by his son, Christian IV, from 1600 to 1620. In 1859 the castle was ravaged by fire, but it has been restored. Now it is a major national history museum.

Among its many sights are the sumptuously decorated and gilded chapel (be sure to see the king's pew and the wooden organ built by Esajas Compenius in 1610) where Danish kings were once crowned, and the Great Hall. In addition, Frederiksborg houses an extensive collection of portraits, historical paintings, and furnishings (ebony cabinets, four-poster beds, tapestries, enameled miniatures, coats-of-arms).

To reach the castle, it's a 15-minute walk from the train station or a short taxi ride.
Admission: 30 kroner ($5.20) adults, 5 kroner (90¢) children 6–14.
Open: May–Sept, daily 10am–5pm; Oct and Apr, daily 10am–4pm; Nov–Mar, daily 11am–3pm. **Bus:** 701, 702.

NORDSJAELLANDSK FOLKEMUSEUM (North Zealand Folk Museum), Helsingørsgade 65. Tel. 42-26-43-79.

Collections depict the rural history of North Zealand, with special emphasis on the preindustrialization era. Native textiles and costumes are also exhibited.

There are supplementary displays at **Sophienborg,** Sophienborgvej 38 (tel. 42-26-43-79), an estate on the western outskirts of Hillerød. Sophienborg is easily reached by bus no. 734 from the Hillerød station. From there, it's an 8-minute walk. By car, take either Frederiksvaerksgade or Herredsvejen, turn right at Tulstrupvej, and follow signs to Sophienborg. It keeps the same hours as the folk museum, and admission is on the same ticket.
Admission: 10 kroner ($1.75) adults; children free.
Open: Museum and supplementary collections, June 24–Aug 26, Tues–Sun 11am–4pm; Aug 27–June 23, Tues–Sun 11am–4pm.

AEBELHOLT ABBEY, Aebelholtsvang 4, Melkse. Tel. 42-11-03-51.

This religious complex, 3½ miles west of Hillerød and founded in 1175 by Abbot Wilhelm, was one of Denmark's largest medieval ecclesiastical communities. The buildings were destroyed after the Reformation, but excavations have made it possible to establish the original outline of the complex. Numerous skeletons collected from the cemetery attest to the advanced medical knowledge of the monks who nursed people prior to their death. The skeletons are on view in a museum near the ruins.
Admission: 12 kroner ($2.10) adults, 5 kroner (90¢) children.
Open: Apr, Sat–Sun 1–4pm; May–Aug, Tues–Sun 10am–4pm; Sept, Tues–Sun 1–4pm; Oct, Sat–Sun 1–4pm. **Bus:** 124 from Hillerød.

A NEARBY VIKING PAGEANT

Frederikssund is a little town 8 miles southwest of Hillerød and 30 miles northwest of Copenhagen. It stages a 2-week Viking festival each summer where Nordic sagas are sometimes revived—and the record is set straight about who "discovered" America five centuries before Christopher Columbus. *Hamlet* is rarely performed anymore. Instead, a revolving series of plays, medieval and modern, concerning the Vikings, are what it's all about.

The festival begins the last week in June. The traditional play is performed nightly at 8pm and a Viking banquet follows. Tickets for the festival are 55 kroner ($9.50) for adults, 12 kroner ($2.10) for children. The banquet costs 110 kroner ($19) for adults (children under 16 are not invited to the banquet). You can take a train from Copenhagen's Central Railroad Station at 6:15pm Monday through Friday or at

5:57pm on Saturday and Sunday. From the station at Frederikssund, it's a 20-minute walk to the site of the pageant. For details, contact the tourist information office in Copenhagen or phone 42-31-06-85, the Frederikssund Tourist Office.

WHERE TO DINE
INEXPENSIVE

SAN REMO, Helsingørsgade 30. Tel. 48-24-30-30.
 Cuisine: ITALIAN/GREEK. **Reservations:** Recommended.
$ **Prices:** Appetizers 48–52 kroner ($8.30–$9); main courses 54–152 kroner ($9.30–$26.30). DC, MC, V.
 Open: Tues–Sun 4pm–midnight.
In a commercial district of town, a 10-minute walk north of the railway station, this restaurant offers a whimsical array of Mediterranean food and a decor awash with memorabilia from Italy and Greece. Menu items include pastas, pizzas, Greek salads, grilled fish and grilled meats, moussaka, and a well-flavored version of stuffed vine leaves.

SLOTSHERRENS KRO, Frederiksborg Slot. Tel. 42-26-75-16.
 Cuisine: DANISH. **Reservations:** Not required. **Bus:** 701.
$ **Prices:** Main dishes 28–130 kroner ($4.80–$22.50); fixed-price menu 89 kroner ($15.40). No credit cards.
 Open: Apr–Oct, daily 10am–9pm.
On the grounds of Frederiksborg Castle, a 15-minute walk from the train station, is a well-established inn that serves good, reliable Danish food. Main dishes are more than generous.

AN EXCURSION TO SELSØ SLOT

Selsø Slot, Selsøvej 30 (tel. 42-32-01-71), is Denmark's first Renaissance castle, built in 1576 and renovated in the baroque style in 1733. Located at Hornsherred, east of Skibby, south of Skuldelev, and 35 miles west of Copenhagen, Selsø is one of the few private manor houses on Zealand that can be explored thoroughly.

The Great Hall and adjoining rooms are maintained as they were in 1733, with 14-foot-high marble panels, ornate plaster ceilings, and fine paintings. A children's room with hundreds of tin soldiers, the basement, vaults dating from around 1560, an old manor kitchen with open fireplace and a scullery, old tools, and a dungeon below the gatehouse are features worth seeing. Cultural events such as orchestra concerts are staged annually.

Admission is 25 kroner ($4.30) for adults, 10 kroner ($1.70) for children. The castle is open May and June on Saturday and Sunday from 1 to 4pm; July, Tuesday to Sunday from 11am to 4pm, and August to September, Saturday and Sunday from 1 to 4pm.

---

6. ROSKILDE
20 miles W of Copenhagen

GETTING THERE By Train Trains leave three times an hour from Copenhagen's Central Railroad Station on the 35-minute trip to Roskilde.

By Bus Buses depart for Roskilde several times daily from Copenhagen's Central Railroad Station.

By Car Take the express highway 21 west from Copenhagen.

ESSENTIALS The **Roskilde Turistbureau,** Fondens Bro, DK-4000 Roskilde (tel. 42-35-27-00), provides a pamphlet with a walking tour of Roskilde. The office is open April to June, Monday through Friday from 9am to 5pm and on Saturday from 10am to 1pm; July and August, Monday through Friday from 9am to 7pm, on

Saturday from 9am to 2pm, and on Sunday from 10am to 2pm; September and October, Monday through Friday from 9am to 5pm and on Saturday from 10am to 1pm; November to March, Monday through Thursday from 9am to 5pm and on Friday from 9am to 4pm.

SPECIAL EVENTS The **Roskilde Festival,** held outdoors on a large grassy field, draws rock music lovers to town. To get information on the festival—dates and performances—call 42-37-04-48 or write to the Roskilde Turistbureau (see above).

Roskilde, once a great ecclesiastical seat, was the country's leading city until the mid-15th century. Today its twin-spired cathedral is the major pilgrimage center of Denmark.

WHAT TO SEE & DO
LIFE-SEEING TOURS

The tourist office offers what they call "Life-Seeing Tours," matching foreign visitors with local people of similar interests and arranging trips to their homes, factories, and recreational places. These tours are for groups of around 10 or more only, and must be arranged well in advance with the tourist office.

THE TOP ATTRACTIONS

ROSKILDE DOMKIRKE, Domkirkestraede 10. Tel. 42-35-16-24.

Roskilde Cathedral is the resting place of 38 Danish kings and queens and countless noblemen and clergy. Their sarcophagi are placed in four chapels and behind the altar. In 1985 the burial site of King Frederik IX was added outside the cathedral, near the northwest tower. The present Gothic-Romanesque cathedral was constructed during the 12th century, and although damaged by a fire in 1968, it has since been restored, along with the magnificent altarpiece. In the cathedral, above the entrance door, clockwork toys, dating from around 1500, play a short tune.

Admission: 3 kroner (50¢) adults, 1 kroner (15¢) children.

Open: Apr, Mon–Sat 9am–5:45pm, Sun 12:30–3:45pm; May–Aug, Mon–Sat 9am–5:45pm, Sun 12:30–5:45pm; Sept, Mon–Sat 9am–5:45pm, Sun 12:30–3:45pm; Oct–Mar, Mon–Sat 10am–5:45pm, Sun 12:30–3:45pm. **Bus:** 602, 603, 604.

VIKING SHIP MUSEUM, Strandengen. Tel. 42-35-65-55.

Five vessels found in Roskilde Fjord, and painstakingly pieced together from hundreds of pieces of wreckage, are on display here. It is presumed that the craft (dating from 1000–50) were deliberately sunk about 12.5 miles north of Roskilde at the narrowest section of the fjord. The discovery was relatively unprotected and unpublicized until 1957 when the Danish National Museum carried out a series of underwater excavations.

Also displayed is a merchant cargo ship used by the Vikings, a small ferry or fishing boat, and a Danish Viking warship similar to the ones portrayed in the Bayeux Tapestry. Also discovered was a "longship," a Viking man-of-war that terrorized European coasts. Copies of Viking jewelry may be purchased in the museum gift shop, and there is a cafeteria.

Admission: 28 kroner ($4.80) adults, 18 kroner ($3.10) children.

Open: Apr–Oct, daily 9am–5pm; Nov–Mar, daily 10am–4pm. **Bus:** 358.

THE ROSKILDE MUSEUM, Sankt Ols Gade 18. Tel. 42-36-60-44.

Located 100 yards from the Town Square, this museum, set in a former merchant's house, contains a collection of the celebrated Hedebo embroidery, regional costumes, and antique toys. Exhibits also include a skeleton of an aurochs, a unique Viking tomb, and a large number of medieval finds from the town. The museum also has a grocer's courtyard, with the shop in operation.

Admission: 5 kroner (90¢) adults; children free.

Open: June–Aug, daily 11am–5pm; Sept–May, Mon–Sat 2–4pm, Sun 2–5pm. **Closed:** Dec 24–25 and Dec 31–Jan 1. **Bus:** 601, 602, 603, 605.

MORE ATTRACTIONS

The **St. Jørgensbjerg quarter** was originally a small fishing village, and a number of old, half-timbered houses, some with thatched roofs, remain. The houses cluster around St. Jørgensbjerg Church, Kirkegade, which dates from 1080. The church is open to visitors for part of June, all of July, and part of August, Monday through Saturday from 10am to 2pm.

Roskilde has a number of old springs, some once considered holy and thought to have healing powers. For a short period in the 1800s, the biggest spring, **Maglekilde,** was the center of a hydropathic establishment.

Roskilde Park offers a great view of the fjord, and during the summer contemporary music concerts are held here every Tuesday night. Also during the summer, the steamship *Skjelskor* takes passengers on tours of the fjord on Saturday and Sunday at 2 and 3:30pm.

Throughout the year, a **vegetable, flower, and flea market** is held at the Town Hall Square, Staendertorvet, Wednesday and Saturday morning.

NEARBY ATTRACTIONS

THE TRAMWAY MUSEUM, Skjoldenaesholm, Skjoldenaesvej 107. Tel. 31-59-80-22.
Some 10 miles southwest of Roskilde, in a pleasant woodland area close to Glydenveshj, the Tramway Museum with its collection of antique trams is situated on the highest point on Zealand, 416 feet above sea level. To reach the museum, board an old tram at the entrance and travel the 1,000 feet to the main building.
Admission: 25 kroner ($4.30) adults, 10 kroner ($1.70) children.
Open: May–June and Aug 10–Oct 25, Sat 1–5pm, Sun 10am–5pm; June 23–Aug 9, Sat 1–5pm, Tues–Thurs and Sun 10am–5pm. **Closed:** Oct 26–Apr. **Bus:** 248.

HISTORISK ARKAEOLOGISK FORSØGSCENTER, Slangeallen 2, DK-4320 Lejre. Tel. 42-38-02-45.
Five miles west of Roskilde, this archeological research center, Lejre Forsøgscenter, is the site of a reconstructed Iron Age community on 25 acres of woodland. The main feature is clay-wall and thatch houses built with tools just as they were some 2,000 years ago. Staffers re-create the physical working conditions as they thatch Iron Age huts, plow with "ards," harvest grain with flint sickles, weave, and make pottery by an open fire. They also sail in dugout canoes, grind corn with a stone, and bake in direct fire. Visitors can take part in these activities. Jutland black pottery is produced here, and at the gift shop handcrafts are for sale. There are picnic tables and an old-style cafeteria offering light meals.
Admission: 40 kroner ($6.90) adults, 20 kroner ($3.50) children.
Open: May–Sept, daily 10am–5pm. **Closed:** Oct–Apr. **Transportation:** Take the train from Copenhagen to Lejre, then bus 233 to the center.

LEDREBORG PARK OG SLOT, Allé 2, DK-4320 Lejre. Tel. 46-48-00-38.
A baroque manor house and French/English-style park 4½ miles southwest of Roskilde and 27 miles west of Copenhagen, Ledreborg is one of the best-preserved monuments in Denmark. Near the manor is a passage grave dating from the late Stone Age, approximately 3000 B.C.
Admission: 40 kroner ($6.90) adults, 20 kroner ($3.50) children 6–16.
Open: July, daily 11am–4pm; June and Aug, Sun 11am–4pm. **Transportation:** From Copenhagen's Central Railroad Station, take the direct train to Lejre, leaving hourly and taking 35 minutes. From Lejre station, take the 3-minute bus ride to the castle and park.

WHERE TO STAY
MODERATE

HOTEL PRINSDEN, Algade 13, DK-4000 Roskilde. Tel. 42-35-80-10. Fax 42-35-81-10. 52 rms (all with bath). MINIBAR TV TEL **Bus:** 602, 603.

$ Rates (including breakfast): 665 kroner ($115) single; 890 kroner ($154) double. AE, DC, MC, V.

This century-old hotel is a good bet. A cozy, comfortable family hotel in the town center, a 5-minute walk from the cathedral, it's attractive and smartly furnished. Children under 12 stay free in their parents' room. At the ground-floor restaurant, you can enjoy a wide selection of Danish dishes and international specialties.

SCANDIC HOTEL ROSKILDE, Søndre Ringvej 33. Tel. 46-32-46-32. Fax 46-32-02-32. 98 rms (all with bath), 8 suites. MINIBAR TV TEL

$ Rates (including breakfast): 495–795 kroner ($85.60–$137.50) single; 895 kroner ($154.80) double; from 1,350 kroner ($233.60) suite. AE, DC, MC, V. **Parking:** Free.

Considered the best in Roskilde, this chain hotel offers a sleek modern decor and excellent facilities, including a spa pool, sauna, and solarium. The bedrooms are handsomely furnished and well equipped. The hotel also has a good restaurant, serving both Danish and international dishes, and a cocktail bar. Parking is free in front of the three-story hotel. It's located on the ring road directly south of the green belt, Roskilde Ring, on the southern outskirts of the city.

INEXPENSIVE

ROSKILDE MOTOR HOTEL, Montelvej 28, DK-4000 Roskilde. Tel. 42-35-43-85. Fax 46-32-19-85. 54 rms (14 with bath).

$ Rates (including breakfast): 315 kroner ($54.50) single without bath, 485 kroner ($83.90) single with bath; 435 kroner ($75.30) double without bath, 640 kroner ($110.70) double with bath. DC, MC, V. **Parking:** Free.

A 5-minute drive from the town center along Route 21, this popular motel has a dining room with excellent grilled chicken and meats. The motel basically offers no frills, but each of the modern rooms is comfortable and clean. The motel also has its own garage.

SR HOTEL & KURSUSCENTER, Maglegårdsvej 10, DK-4000 Roskilde. Tel. 42-35-66-88. Fax 42-35-85-86. 70 rms (all with bath). TV TEL **Bus:** 212, 232, 605.

$ Rates (including breakfast): 445–495 kroner ($77–$85.60) single; 545–595 kroner ($94.30–$102.90) double. AE, DC, MC, V. **Parking:** Free.

Not far from the A1 motorway, this Danish-modern hostelry offers clean, comfortable bedrooms, all done with Scandinavian modern design. The restaurant, Octavia, is designed as an octagonal room, with a Danish buffet in the center. Part of the hotel is devoted to conference facilities for Danske Slagsterier (The Federation of Danish Pig Producers and Slaughterhouses).

SVOGERSLEV KRO, Hovedgaden 45, Svogerslev, DK-4000 Roskilde. Tel. 46-38-30-05. 18 rms (all with bath). TV TEL **Bus:** Hourly connections from the town center (602).

$ Rates (including breakfast): 425 kroner ($73.50) single; 525 kroner ($90.80) double. DC, MC, V. **Parking:** Free.

This charmingly cozy inn is in an old fishing hamlet about 2½ miles from the town center. Rooms are handsomely furnished in a modern style and well kept. The kitchen serves Danish open-face sandwiches and an array of international dishes.

WHERE TO DINE

INEXPENSIVE

CLUB 42/RESTAURANT DEN HVIDE FUGL, Skomagergade 42. Tel. 42-35-17-64.
   Cuisine: DANISH/INTERNATIONAL. **Reservations:** Recommended.

$ Prices: 2-course fixed-price menu 85 kroner ($14.70); appetizers 26–43 kroner ($4.50–$7.40); main dishes 85–150 kroner ($14.70–$26). DC, MC, V.
   Open: Lunch Mon–Sat 11am–3pm; dinner Mon–Sat 5–10pm.

In the center of town, 200 yards from the bus and train station, this establishment has a large and impressive menu. Its best bargain is its two-course Danmenu at lunch. Lunch includes a selection of cold dishes and open-face sandwiches. Dinner is a big affair, with fresh fish or charcoal-grilled items including pepper steak. A children's menu is also offered. There is a large parking lot behind the restaurant.

RESTAURANT TOPPEN, Bymarken 37. Tel. 42-36-04-12.
   Cuisine: DANISH. **Reservations:** Recommended. **Bus:** 603.
$ Prices: Appetizers 30–75 kroner ($5.20–$13); main dishes 75–130 kroner ($13–$22.50). DC, MC, V.
   Open: Sat–Sun noon–10pm; dinner Tues–Fri 4:30pm–10pm.
At the top of a water tower 274 feet above sea level, Restaurant Toppen offers a splendid view of the whole town, the surrounding country, and Roskilde Fjord—all from the dining room. Begin with a shrimp cocktail served with dill and lemon, which is accompanied by salad, bread, and butter. Main dishes are likely to include sirloin of pork à la Toppen with mushrooms and a béarnaise sauce, accompanied by a baked potato and salad. For dessert, try the chef's nut cake with fruit sauce and sour cream. The restaurant lies 1 mile west of the town center between Vindingevej and Københavnsvej. The water tower which contains it does not revolve electronically, but some clients, in the words of the management "Get the feeling that it's turning only if they drink enough." There's a free elevator to the top.

---

7. KØGE

25 miles S of Copenhagen

GETTING THERE   By Train   Take the S-railway extension from Copenhagen. Service is every 20 minutes throughout the day. The trip takes 35 minutes.

By Bus   Bus no. 21 departs frequently from Copenhagen's Central Railroad Station.

By Car   From Copenhagen, head south along the express highway E20/E55.

ESSENTIALS   Guided tours of Køge are arranged through the **Tourist Office,** Vestergade 1 (tel. 53-65-58-00); open Mon–Fri 9am–5pm, Sat 9am–2pm. English is spoken.

Køge in the Middle Ages developed a controversial reputation as a witch-burning center. This old market town still retains a medieval aura, with its brick and half-timbered buildings. It's a convenient first stop if you're heading south from Copenhagen to the island of Møn.

WHAT TO SEE & DO

Walk down **Kirkestraede,** lined with graceful old houses. A small building, no 20, near the church, is reputed to be "the oldest dated half-timbered house in Denmark," from 1527. In front of the house at Smedegarden 13, near an ancient tree, are a couple of porchstones from the Middle Ages, said to be the only pair in Denmark in their original position. Nearby is the attractive **St. Nicolai Church,** Kirkestraede 29 (tel. 53-65-13-59), open daily Sunday through Friday from 10am to noon (mid-June to early September, 10am to 4pm). Admission is free. Look for the carved angels on the pews, all without noses thanks to Swedish troops who came this way. Guided tours of the tower are given at 11am, noon, and 1pm Monday through Friday from June to September for 5 kroner (90¢).

THE KØGE MUSEUM, Nørregade 4. Tel. 53-65-02-62.
   This fine museum surrounded by a beautiful garden near the town square is devoted to the history of culture in South Zealand. It consists of six well-furnished rooms and a kitchen with implements used between 1640 and 1899. Displays of

costumes, textiles, carriages, farm equipment, crafts from artisan's guilds, and other historical artifacts of the area are featured. Curiously, there is a windowpane where H. C. Andersen scratched the words (translated, of course): "Oh, God, oh, God in Køge." There's a collection of 322 coins from all over Scandinavia and Europe—the oldest coin is a Palatinate taler from 1548. The oldest house in Køge, from the early 16th century, was moved to this site from the main square.

Admission: 10 kroner ($1.70) adults, 5 kroner (90¢) children.

Open: June–Aug, daily 10am–5pm; Sept–May, Mon–Fri 2–5pm, Sat–Sun 1–5pm.

KUNSTMUSEET KØGE SKITSESAMLING (Museum of Art), Nørregade 29. Tel. 53-66-24-14.

Mainly featuring 20th-century works, this museum near the train station also contains a collection of sketches and models showing the process of actualizing a work of art, from idea to final creation. In addition to the permanent collection, the museum arranges special exhibitions, films, and lectures.

Admission: 10 kroner ($1.75) adults; free for children.

Open: Tues–Sun 11am–5pm.

HEGNETSLUND KERAMIK, Teglvaerksvej 11. Tel. 53-67-45-71.

Founded in 1892, Hegnetslund Keramik features Danish arts and crafts. Stoneware, ceramics, terra-cotta pieces, and other products are for sale in the display room. The workshop can also be visited.

Admission: Free.

Open: Mon–Fri 10am–5pm. **Directions:** Head along Svansbjergvej over the viaduct (the second road to the left is Tegvaerksvej). The factory is opposite an Esso station on Vordingborgvej.

A NEARBY ATTRACTION

VALLØ CASTLE, Vallø.

This castle with French-style gardens was built between the 16th and the 18th century, and has been converted today into modern housing for old-age pensioners. Explore the sweeping gardens, with their lakes, moats, rare trees, and rose and dahlia flowerbeds. The castle is located 4 miles south of Køge between Herfølge and the east coast.

Admission: Free.

Open: Apr–Oct, daily 10am–sunset. **Closed:** Nov–Mar.

WHERE TO STAY
MODERATE

HOTEL HVIDE HUS, Strandvejen 111, DK-4600 Køge. Tel. 53-65-35-90.

Fax 53-66-33-14. 118 rms (all with bath). MINIBAR TV TEL

$ Rates (including breakfast): 750 kroner ($129.80) single; 950 kroner ($164.40) double. AE, DC, MC, V. **Parking:** Free.

A great bet for an overnight stay or lunch visit, this attractive modern hotel has well-furnished bedrooms decorated in a Nordic style, many with balconies. The restaurant offers a view of Køge Bay, and there is also a bar and lounge. Other facilities include a sauna and solarium. The hotel lies east of the center along the water.

A NEARBY ACCOMMODATION
Inexpensive

SØNDERGAARD, Krogen 15, DK-4632 Bjaeverskov. Tel. 53-67-00-15.

Fax 53-67-11-12. 30 rms (16 with bath). TV **Bus:** 246, 250.

$ Rates (including breakfast): 360 kroner ($62.30) single without bath, 500 kroner ($86.50) single with bath; 525 kroner ($90.80) double without bath, 600 kroner ($103.80) double with bath. DC, MC, V. **Parking:** Free.

About 25 miles from Copenhagen, between Køge and Ringsted, Søndergaard is a modern bed-and-breakfast family-style hotel with a heated swimming pool and sauna. The rooms are bright and simply furnished, and 20 have minibars and 9 contain phones. If you have a car, it's about 10-minute drive to the beach.

8. MØN

80 miles S of Copenhagen

GETTING THERE   By Train   From Copenhagen's Central Railroad Station, take a train to Vordingborg in South Zealand. From there, take a bus to Stege, Møn's capital.

By Bus   Take bus no. 64 from Vordingborg in South Zealand to Stege. On the island, bus service is scarce. You'll need a car to explore.

By Car   Cross over from Zealand on the Dronning Alexandrines Bridge; then proceed through the old country town of Stege.

ESSENTIALS   The local tourist office, **Møns Turistforening**, Storegade 5, DK-4780 Stege (tel. 55-81-44-11), is open Mon–Fri 9am–5pm, Sat 9am–2pm.

In the southeast corner of Denmark, off Zealand, this little island's big attraction is 400-foot ✪ **Møns Klint**, 4 miles of white chalky cliffs that rise dramatically from the Baltic Sea. Møns Klint is cut by the Baltic Sea in a large pile of ice-transported chalk masses and glacial deposits. The chalk was formed from calcareous ooze 75 million years ago. The ooze that precipitated from the sea water enclosed shells of marine animals that are now fossils. The glacial deposits date from the last million years. They originated partly as boulder clay deposited by inland ice and partly as bedded clay and sand containing marine mussels. The boulders on the beach have dropped from the cliff and have been rounded by wave erosion.

WHAT TO SEE & DO

Møns Klint can be viewed from the east of the island if you have a car. Leave Stege, passing through Elmelunde. Once at Elmelunde, continue for another 6 miles east to the coast for the best view of the cliffs.

   Stege, the capital of Møn, with a 16th-century Mill Gate, received its charter in 1268. During its turbulent history, it was often invaded, sometimes by Swedish mercenaries. Known for its primitive frescoes, **Stege Church** is one of the largest in the country, with a massive tower striped in brick and chalk. It is one of many whitewashed churches found on Møn that contain 14th-century frescoes depicting rural life.

   Møn is known for the **prehistoric remains** that are scattered about the island. For detailed information, the Stege tourist office (see above) publishes a booklet called *Prehistoric Monuments of Møn*. Several Neolithic chambered tombs known as "giants' graves" were discovered. As the legend goes, the western part of the island was ruled by a "jolly green giant" called Green Huntsman and the eastern part of the island was the domain of another giant, Upsal.

   After a visit to the cliffs, I suggest a short detour north to **Liselund,** a small thatched, palatial summer home from 1795 surrounded by lovely park grounds in the northeastern part of the little island. H. C. Andersen wrote *The Tinder Box* while staying in the Swiss cottage. The park is called a "folly" of the 18th century, when it was constructed by Bosc de la Calmette, a royal chamberlain who was inspired by Marie Antoinette's Le Hameau at Versailles. You can buy refreshments at a small Swiss-style chalet filled with antlers and antiques. The admission-free park is open daily until sunset all year.

   The inveterate island collector may also want to explore two isolated communities, the islands of **Bogø** and **Nyord,** which are connected to Møn by bridge and causeway. Bogø has only one village, an old town that had shipping connections with Iceland in the 19th century. The other island, Nyord, off the northwest coast of Møn, has for 3 centuries been divided among just 20 farms. Cars are not allowed on Nyord.

WHERE TO STAY & DINE
INEXPENSIVE

HOTEL STEGE BUGT, Langelinie 48, DK-4780 Stege. Tel. 55-81-54-54.
Fax 55-81-58-90. 22 rms (all with bath), 5 suites. MINIBAR TV TEL
$ Rates (including breakfast): 400–550 kroner ($69.20–$95.20) single; 525–750 kroner ($90.80–$129.80) double; from 850 kroner ($147.10) suite. AE, DC, MC, V. **Parking:** Free.

One of the best hotels on the island, Stege Bugt is also the most central. Many of its modern and well-furnished bedrooms open onto balconies overlooking the sea. Bedrooms have many thoughtful amenities. The hotel's restaurant specializes in fresh fish and grill specialties. It serves meals daily until 10pm. A large park and mound are nearby.

CHAPTER 9

FUNEN

- **WHAT'S SPECIAL ABOUT FUNEN**
1. **NYBORG**
2. **ODENSE**
3. **SVENDBORG**
4. **FAABORG**
5. **ÆRØ**

Funen, the second-largest Danish island, separates Zealand from the mainland peninsula, Jutland. Known as Fyn in Danish, it offers unique attractions, from a Viking ship to runic stones.

H. C. Andersen was born in Funen in the town of Odense. A visit to the storyteller's native island is a journey into a land of hop gardens and orchards along the roadsides, busy harbors, market towns, castles, and stately manor houses.

Funen has some 700 miles of coastline, with wide sandy beaches in some parts, while woods and grass grow all the way to the water's edge in others. Steep cliffs provide sweeping views of the Baltic or the Kattegat.

SEEING FUNEN

GETTING THERE

Funen is reached by the Little Belt bridges at Middelfart (Jutland), which is the road crossing from continental Europe, or by Nyborg-Korsør ferry from the island of Zealand. An L-train from Copenhagen to Odense takes about 3 hours.

Once on the island, a private rented car is ideal, but the major towns, such as Svendborg and Faaborg, provide frequent bus service from the capital of Odense. Bus tickets can be bought on the bus; train tickets should be bought in advance at the train stations. Round-trip discounts are not granted, but 1-day tourist tickets are sold at the rail station in Odense.

To reach the island of Ærø, you'll need to take a ferry from Svendborg.

Because Funen is small and relatively flat, you might consider a bicycle itinerary provided by the local tourist office. Bicycles can be rented at train stations.

A SUGGESTED ITINERARY

After touring Zealand and Copenhagen, take the car-ferry from Korsør (on Zealand), landing at Nyborg on Funen in the west.

Day 1: Spend the morning exploring Nyborg Castle. Have lunch, and then travel west on the E20 (an express highway) to Odense.

Day 2: Explore Odense and its nearby attractions, including the Viking ship at Ladby and Egeskov Castle. Spend the night.

Day 3: Explore the port city of Svendborg, south of Odense, and its neighboring islands of Tåsigne and Thurø in the South Funen archipelago. Return to Odense and spend the night.

Day 4: Head west to Faaborg and walk around its Old Town. Ask at the tourist office about boat tours and maps outlining afternoon trips in the environs.

WHAT'S SPECIAL ABOUT FUNEN

Beaches
☐ The most popular for swimming are at Kerteminde, Hasmark, Flyvesandet, Ristinge, Marstal, and Spodsbjerg.

Great Towns/Villages
☐ Odense, the capital, offering lots of attractions in the hometown of Hans Christian Andersen.

☐ Faaborg, an old seaport, idyllically set, one of Denmark's best-preserved market towns.

☐ Ærøskøbing, capital of the island of Ærø—a lilliputian souvenir of the past.

Ancient Castles
☐ Egeskov Castle, the best-preserved Renaissance castle of its type in Europe.

☐ Valdemar's Slot on the island of Troense, built by King Christian IV in 1639.

☐ Nyborg Castle, its ramparts still intact, the oldest royal seat in Scandinavia.

Literary Pilgrimages
☐ H. C. Andersen's House at Odense, filled with memorabilia, like a walking stick and a top hat of the fairy-tale writer.

Idyllic Islands
☐ Ærø, the pearl of the South Funen archipelago, a sleepy memory of a maritime past.

☐ Tåsinge, the largest island in the South Funen archipelago, with its memories of Elvira Madigan, a doomed woman in love.

Special Events/Festivals
☐ Hans Christian Andersen's plays at the open-air theater in Funen Village, outside Odense (mid-July to mid-August).

☐ Annual July festival at Faaborg, with entertainment, dances, and an amusement park.

1. NYBORG

81 miles W of Copenhagen

GETTING THERE   By Train   Trains depart Copenhagen for Odense hourly with a stopover in Nyborg, where you take a ferry from Zealand to Funen.

By Bus   Buses run from Copenhagen to Odense, with a transfer through Nyborg via ferry.

By Car   Take the E-20 expressway west from Copenhagen to Korsør in West Zealand. From there take a car-ferry (see below).

By Ferry   Three lines run from Nyborg to Korsør on Zealand, with about 21 crossings a day, taking 50 minutes. The DSB car-ferries depart every 40 minutes (for information and reservations, call 65-31-40-54). Another car-ferry, Vognamnsruten (tel. 53-57-02-04), makes the run every hour on the half hour. Finally, DSB also runs a ferry for trains and foot passengers, hourly between Korsør and Nyborg (call 65-31-11-91 for information).

ESSENTIALS   The **Nyborg Tourist Office,** located at Torvet 9 (tel. 65-31-02-80), is open Mon–Fri 9am–5pm, Sat 9am–2pm.

If you take a ferry linking Zealand and Funen, you'll dock at this old seaport and market town, a perfect place to explore before heading to Odense or Copenhagen.

Founded some 700 years ago, with a population today of 18,500, Nyborg is considered one of the oldest towns in Denmark. Its location in the middle of the trade route between Zealand in the east and Jutland in the west has helped boost its importance. In medieval times, from about 1200 to 1413, Nyborg was the capital of Denmark. Medieval buildings and well-preserved ramparts are testaments to that era. The town square of Nyborg, the **Torvet,** was formed in 1540, when a block of houses was demolished to make room for the royal tournaments of Christian III.

In 1988 one of the world's largest combined bridge-and-tunnel projects began. By 1993 trains will be able to cross **Store Baelt** (Great Belt), which separates Funen and Zealand. In 1996 it is anticipated that cars and trucks will also be able to cross. When this is completed, for the first time Copenhagen will be linked to continental Europe by road.

In summer, Denmark's oldest open-air theater, **Nyborg Voldspil,** performs an annual musical or operetta under the light beeches on the old castle ramparts. Throughout the summer the castle's Great Hall is the setting for concerts of classical music with international soloists. Inquire at the tourist office (see above) for more details.

WHAT TO SEE & DO

NYBORG CASTLE, Slotspladsen. Tel. 65-31-02-07.

Founded in 1170, Nyborg Castle, with its ramparts still intact, is the oldest royal seat in Scandinavia. Denmark's first constitution was signed in this moated castle by King Erik Glipping in 1282, and Nyborg Castle was the seat of the Danish parliament, the Danehof, until 1413. The present furnishings date primarily from the 17th century, when Nyborg was a resplendent Renaissance palace. It's located directly north of the Torvet in the town center.

Admission: 15 kroner ($2.60) adults, 8 kroner ($1.40) children.

Open: Mar–May and Sept–Oct, Tues–Sun 10am–3pm; June–Aug, daily 10am–5pm. **Closed:** Nov–Feb. **Bus:** 1, 2, 3.

VOR FRUE KIRKE, Adelgade. Tel. 65-31-16-08.

Dating from the late 14th and the early 15th century, the Church of Our Lady has a fine Gothic spire, three aisles, wood carvings, old epitaphs, candelabra, and model ships. Nightly at 9:45, the Watchman's Bell from 1523 is rung—a tradition with origins far back in the town's history. Opposite the church is the 12th-century chapter house of the Order of St. John (Korsbrødregård), with a fine vaulted cellar now converted into a gift shop. The church is located at the end of the Kongegade in the town center.

Admission: Free.

Open: Summer, daily 9am–6pm; winter, daily 9am–4pm.

MADS LERCHES GÅRD (Nyborg og Omegns Museet), Slotsgade 11. Tel. 65-31-02-07.

Mads Lerches Gård is housed in a well-preserved half-timbered merchant's house built in 1601. You'll see interesting artifacts of the region from prehistoric to modern times.

Admission: 15 kroner ($2.60) adults, 8 kroner ($1.40) children.

Open: Mar–May and Sept–Oct, Tues–Sun 10am–3pm; June–Aug, daily 10am–4pm. **Closed:** Nov–Feb. **Bus:** 1, 3, 4.

WHERE TO STAY & DINE

INEXPENSIVE

HOTEL HESSELET, Christianslundsvej 119, DK-5800 Nyborg. Tel. 65-31-30-29, or toll free 800/528-1234 in the U.S. Fax 65-31-29-58. 46 rms (all with bath), 3 suites. MINIBAR TV TEL **Bus:** 3.

$ **Rates:** Winter, 710 kroner ($122.80) single; 990 kroner ($171.30) double. Summer, 400 kroner ($69.20) single; 800 kroner ($138.40) double. Year-round, from 1,300 kroner ($224.90) suites. Breakfast 95 kroner ($16.40) extra. AE, DC, MC, V. **Parking:** Free. **Closed:** Dec 18–Jan 7.

⭐ This is an excellent choice, classified as a Best Western member and the most stylish hotel in the region. Spacious bedrooms, oriental carpets, leather couches, fireplaces, and sunken living rooms create a glamorous look. An indoor swimming pool is ringed with semitropical plants. Six tennis courts and an 18-hole golf course lie within close reach. The hotel is known for its conference facilities. Its restaurant specializes in French cuisine, and is among the finest in Eastern Funen. The hotel is about 2 miles northwest of the Knundshoved ferry terminal, a mile east of the rail station.

HOTEL NYBORG STRAND, Østerøvej 2, DK-5800 Nyborg. Tel. 65-31-31-31. Fax 65-31-37-01. 245 rms (all with bath). TV TEL **Bus:** 3.

$ **Rates** (including breakfast): Winter, 350–550 kroner ($60.60–$95.20) single; 650–795 kroner ($112.50–$137.50) double; from 1,320 kroner ($228.40) suite. Summer 295–440 kroner ($51–$76.10) single; 520–595 kroner ($90–$102.90) double; from 1,050 kroner ($181.70) suite. AE, DC, MC, V. **Parking:** Free. **Closed:** Dec 19–Jan 3.

Dating from 1899, Hotel Nyborg Strand is probably the largest and most popular conference hotel in Funen. On the premises are a pair of saunas, a bistro, a café, a private sand-and-pebble beach, and an indoor swimming pool. Two restaurants serve Danish and international cuisine. The hotel is located a mile east of the rail station, near the beach.

---

2. ODENSE

97 miles W of Copenhagen

GETTING THERE By Train   Some 32 trains daily leave Copenhagen's Central Railroad Station, taking 3 hours.

By Bus   Buses arrive frequently from Copenhagen, going by car-ferry from Korsør to Nyborg.

By Car   Take the E20 expressway west from Copenhagen to Korsør. There, board a car-ferry to Nyborg. Once on Funen, continue west on the E20.

ESSENTIALS   The **Odense Tourist Association,** Rådhuset (tel. 66-12-75-20), is open mid-June through August Mon–Sat 9am–7pm, Sun 11am–7pm; off-season Mon–Fri 9am–5pm, Sat 10am–1pm. It will help arrange excursions and also sells an **Odense Adventure Pass,** giving you access to 13 museums, the Odense Zoo, the Funen Tivoli, six indoor swimming pools, and the H. C. Andersen plays. You can also take a river cruise with the pass and travel free on the city buses and DBS trains within the municipality. The pass is valid for 2 days and costs 70 kroner ($12.10) for adults and 35 kroner ($6.10) for children under 14.

This ancient town, the third largest in Denmark, has changed greatly since its famous citizen, H. C. Andersen, walked its streets. But it's still possible to discover a few unspoiled spots from yesteryear.

The capital is a smart base for exploring the rest of the island—trips north to the Viking ship at Ladby, or south to the château country and the archipelago.

WHAT TO SEE & DO

At the Odense Tourist Association, you can purchase tickets and receive information on a **2-hour sightseeing tour,** held Monday to Saturday from June 24 to August 31. The charge is 60 kroner ($10.40) for adults, 30 kroner ($5.20) for children. Also at the tourist office, you can find out about the **Hans Christian Andersen plays** in the open-air theater in the Funen Village, presented from mid-July to mid-August. Tickets cost 35 kroner ($6.10) for adults, 20 kroner ($3.50) for children. During this time, Odense is overrun with fans of the storyteller. If no accommodations are available, the tourist office will book guests into private homes.

H. C. ANDERSENS HUS, Hans Jensensstraede 37-45. Tel. 66-13-13-72.

⭐ The object of most Funen pilgrimages is the "hus" and museum of H. C. Andersen, popular with both adults and children. Much H.C.A. memorabilia is here: his famous walking stick, top hat, battered portmanteau, plus letters to his dear friend Miss Jenny Lind and fellow writer Charles Dickens. In addition, hundreds of documents, manuscripts, and reprints of his books in dozens of languages are displayed.

Admission: 15 kroner ($2.60) adults, 3 kroner (50¢) children.
Open: Apr–May, daily 10am–5pm; June–Aug, daily 9am–6pm; Sept, daily 10am–5pm; Oct–Mar, daily 10am–3pm. **Bus:** 2.

H. C. ANDERSENS BARNDOMSHJEM (Andersen's Childhood Home), Munkemøllestraede 3. Tel. 66-13-13-72.

Visit Andersen's humble childhood home, where the fairy-tale writer lived between the ages of 2 and 14. From what is known of Andersen's childhood, his mother was a drunken, superstitious washerwoman, and Andersen was a gawky boy, lumbering and graceless, the victim of his fellow urchins' cruel jabs. However, all is serene at the cottage today; in fact, the little house has a certain unpretentious charm, and the "garden still blooms," as in *The Snow Queen*.

Admission: 3 kroner (50¢) adults, 2 kroner (30¢) children.
Open: Apr–Sept, daily 10am–5pm; Oct–Mar, daily noon–3pm. **Bus:** 2.

ST. CANUTE'S CATHEDRAL, Klosterbakken 2. Tel. 66-12-03-92.

Despite its unimpressive facade, this is perhaps the most important Gothic-style building in Denmark. A popular feature of this 13th-century brick building is the elegant triptych gold altar screen, carved by Calus Berg in 1526 at the request of Queen Christine. King Canute, the patron of the church, was killed by angry Jutland taxpayers in 1086 and then canonized 15 years later. The church stands opposite the Town Hall. All city buses meet at Klingenberg, just by the cathedral.

Admission: Free.
Open: Mid-May to mid-Sept, Mon–Sat 10am–5pm, Sun and holidays 11:30am–3:30pm; mid-Sept to mid-May, Mon–Fri 10am–4pm, Sat 10am–noon. **Bus:** 2.

FUNEN VILLAGE/DEN FYNSKE LANDSBY, Sejerskovvej 20. Tel. 66-13-13-72.

A big open-air regional culture museum, this is an archive of 18th- and 19th-century Funen life. Located in the Hunderup Woods, old buildings—a toll house, weaver's shop, windmill, farming homestead, jail, vicarage, village school, even a brickworks—were reassembled and authentically furnished. Plays and folk dances are staged at the Greek theater. In addition, you can visit workshops, see a coppersmith at work, as well as a basket maker, spoon cutter, blacksmith, and weaver.

Admission: Apr–May and Sept–Oct, 15 kroner ($2.60) adults, 5 kroner (90¢) children; June–Aug, 20 kroner ($3.50) adults, 10 kroner ($1.70) children.
Open: Apr–May and Sept–Oct, daily 9am–4pm; June–Aug, daily 9am–7:30pm. **Bus:** 2 from Flakhaven to museum, 1½ miles from the town center.

DANISH RAILWAY MUSEUM, Dannebrogsgade 24. Tel. 66-12-01-48.

Displayed are original locomotives and carriages from the past century depicting Denmark's railway history, including the first railroad acquired in 1847. One of the oldest locomotives in the collection, an "A-Machine," dates from 1888. Also on display are two royal coaches, a double-decker carriage, and a model railway. The museum is adjacent to the train station.

Admission: 15 kroner ($2.60) adults, 9 kroner ($1.60) children.
Open: May–Sept, daily 10am–4pm; Oct–Apr, Sun 10am–4pm, Mon–Sat 10am–1pm. **Bus:** 2.

CARL NIELSEN MUSEET, Claus Bergsgade 11. Tel. 66-13-13-72.

Adjoining the Odense Concert Hall, this museum documents the life and work of composer Carl Nielsen and his wife, sculptor Anne Marie Nielsen. Visitors hear excerpts of Nielsen's music while they look at the exhibits and biographical slide show. Parking is available outside the concert hall. Elevator service available.

Admission: 10 kroner ($1.75) adults, 2 kroner (35¢) children.
Open: June–Sept, daily 10am–4pm. **Closed:** Oct–May. **Bus:** 2.

NEARBY ATTRACTIONS

LADBYSKIBET, Vikingevej 123, Ladby. Tel. 65-32-16-67.

Ladby, 12 miles northeast of Odense, is the site of a 72-foot-long 10th-century Viking ship, discovered in 1935. Remains of the ship are displayed along with replicas from the excavation (the genuine articles are in the National Museum in Copenhagen). A skeleton of the pagan chieftain buried in this looted ship was never found, just the bones of his nearly dozen horses and dogs.
Admission: 15 kroner ($2.60) adults; free for children under 16.
Open: May–Sept, Tues–Sun 10am–6pm; Oct–Apr, Tues–Sun 10am–3pm. **Bus:** 482 from Kerteminde, reached by bus from Odense.

EGESKOV CASTLE, Egeskovgade 18, Kvaerndrup. Tel. 62-27-10-16.

⭐ This 1554 Renaissance water castle with magnificent gardens, northeast of Faaborg at Kvaerndrup, is the most romantic and splendid of Denmark's fortified manors. The castle was built on oak pillars in the middle of a moat or small lake. International experts consider it the best-preserved Renaissance castle of its type in Europe.

Every year, some 200,000 visitors roam the 30-acre park and castle located on the main road between Svendborg and Odense. There's an automobile, horse carriage, and airplane museum on the grounds as well. Chamber-music concerts are held in the magnificent Great Hall of the castle on 10 summer Sundays beginning in late June, starting at 5pm.

The most dramatic story in the castle's history is about an unfortunate maiden, Rigborg, who was seduced by a young nobleman and bore him a child out of wedlock. Banished to the castle, she was imprisoned by her father in a tower from 1599 to 1604.
Admission: Castle, park, and museum, 60 kroner ($10.40) adults, 30 kroner ($5.20) children under 12; park and museum only, 40 kroner ($6.90) adults, 20 kroner ($3.50) children.
Open: Park, June–Aug, daily 9am–6pm; May and Sept, daily 10am–5pm. Castle, May–Aug daily 10am–5pm. **Closed:** Oct–May. **Bus:** 920 from Nyborg to Egeskov.

FRYDENLUND, Skovvej 50, Naarup, DK-5690 Tommerup. Tel. 64-76-13-22.

This bird sanctuary and park is 12¼ miles southwest from Odense (signposted near the village of Tommerup). Some 200 different species of pheasants, ducks, geese, storks, ostriches, parrots, and owls, among others, from all parts of the world, live here. There are more than 120 aviaries and some 20 parkland areas in an old farm setting, with many flowers, bushes, and trees. You can enjoy coffee and homemade pastries in the café or bring your own lunch.
Admission: 25 kroner ($4.30) adults, 10 kroner ($1.70) children.
Open: Easter–May and Sept–Oct, daily 10am–4pm; June–Aug, daily 10am–6pm. **Closed:** Nov–Easter.

FUNEN AQUARIUM ROLD (Aquatic World), Roldvej 53, Rold, DK-5492 Vissenbjerg. Tel. 64-83-14-12.

The largest in Europe, this attraction consists of 30 aquariums. Some 3,000 specimens include 300 species of such fish as sharks, electric eels, piranhas, and dragon fish. There are also 20 large outdoor aviaries.
Admission: 30 kroner ($5.20) adults, 15 kroner ($2.60) children.
Open: Apr–Oct, daily 10am–7pm; Nov–Mar, daily 10am–6pm. **Directions:** Take the E20 express highway 10 miles west from Odense, until the turnoff to Vissenbjerg. **Bus:** 831 from Odense.

CARL NIELSEN'S BARNDOMSHJEM, Odensevej 2A, near Lyndelse. Tel. 66-13-13-72.

Eight miles from Odense, the childhood house of the famous composer is now a museum and archive of his life. Nielsen lived here during the last 5 years of his childhood until his confirmation in 1879. Two studies have been made into commemorative rooms, where the collections illustrate the composer's life.

Admission: 3 kroner (50¢) adults, 2 kroner (30¢) children.
Open: May–Aug, 11am–3pm. **Closed:** Sept–Apr. **Bus:** 960, 962.

WHERE TO STAY

The easy-to-find hotels in Odense are clustered around the railway station.

EXPENSIVE

HOTEL H. C. ANDERSEN, Claus Bergsgade 7, DK-Odense C. Tel. 66-14-78-00. Fax 66-14-78-00. 148 rms (all with bath). MINIBAR TV TEL **Bus:** 4, 5.
$ **Rates** (including breakfast): 860 kroner ($148.80) single; 1,150 kroner ($199) double. AE, DC, MC, V. **Parking:** Free.

The H. C. Andersen is a first-class hostelry, with attractively furnished bedrooms. You can dine in the Hans Christian Restaurant, have your drinks at the Fairy-Tale bar, and be entertained in the Nattergalen (Nightingale) nightclub, which has live music. The island's only casino, in a modern glass atrium, offers blackjack, roulette, and baccarat. The hotel has an exercise room, billiard tables, table tennis, a sauna, and a solarium.

MODERATE

ODENSE PLAZA HOTEL, Østre Stationsvej 24, DK-5000 Odense. Tel. 66-11-77-45. Fax 66-14-41-45. 70 rms (all with bath), 8 suites. MINIBAR TV TEL **Bus:** 31, 33, 35, 36.
$ **Rates** (including breakfast): 660–760 kroner ($114.20–$131.50) single; 900–1,100 kroner ($155.70–$190.30) double; from 1,300 kroner ($224.90) suite. AE, DC, MC, V.

Completely renovated in 1985, this hotel is one of the most alluring hostelries in town. Each tastefully conservative bedroom contains, among other amenities, a color TV with English-language video, and a hairdryer. Facilities include a sauna, solarium, and health club. Both laundry and room service are available.

There's a French-inspired restaurant with a modern cuisine and impeccable service.

INEXPENSIVE

MISSIONSHOTELLET ANSGAR, Østre Stationsvej 32, DK-5000 Odense. Tel. 66-11-96-93. Fax 66-11-96-75. 44 rms (all with bath). TV TEL **Bus:** 22.
$ **Rates** (including breakfast): 365–450 kroner ($63.10–$77.90) single; 560–620 kroner ($96.90–$107.30) double. AE, DC, MC, V.

Ⓢ This hotel is conveniently located behind a stone-and-brick facade. A ground-floor restaurant serves well-prepared and reasonably priced meals.

MOTEL ODENSE, Hunderupgade 2, DK-5000 Odense. Tel. 66-11-42-13. Fax 65-91-15-13. 62 rms (all with bath). TV TEL
$ **Rates** (including breakfast): 595–725 kroner ($102.90–$125.40) single; 745–950 kroner ($128.90–$164.40) double. AE, DC, MC, V. **Parking:** Free.

On Route A1 at the A9 junction, 1 mile from the town center, this 82-bed motel in a half-timbered renovated farmhouse offers compact and well-furnished bedrooms; 17 rooms have a minibar. A well-appointed first-class restaurant is on the premises, serving French and Danish cuisine.

SARA GRAND HOTEL, Jernbanegade 18, DK-5000 Odense. Tel. 66-11-71-71. Fax 66-14-11-71. 139 rms (all with bath). MINIBAR TV TEL

$ Rates (including breakfast): Summer, 535 kroner ($92.60) single; 700 kroner ($121.10) double; from 1,100 kroner ($190.30) suite. Winter, 685–970 kroner ($118.50–$167.80) single; 970–1,120 kroner ($167.80–$193.80) double; 1,150–2,300 kroner ($199–$397.90) suite. AE, DC, MC, V. **Parking:** Free.

This hotel's four-story 19th-century brick facade rises in a gabled Neo-Romanesque style from a street corner close to the center of town. The interior contains many traditional trappings, but public rooms are modernized. The plushly conservative bedrooms include a radio and color TV with video. Other facilities include a sauna, solarium, and high-ceilinged bar. There's a pleasant restaurant, Grand Terrasse, which opens onto an outdoor terrace in summer. Other dining facilities include the winter-only Hot News Café and the Grand Gourmet Restaurant. There is occasional weekend dance music.

WINDSOR HOTEL, Vindegade 45, DK-5000 Odense. Tel. 66-12-06-52.
Fax 65-91-00-23. 62 rms (all with bath). TV TEL **Bus:** 4.
$ Rates (including breakfast): 500–850 kroner ($86.50–$147.10) single; 700–1,040 kroner ($121.10–$179.90) double. DC, MC, V.

Built in 1898, this cozy, well-furnished red-brick hotel occupies a quiet street corner close to the center of town near the rail station. High-ceilinged bedrooms are clean and comfortable. They're furnished with well-crafted copies of 18th-century furniture. There's an elegant and stylish restaurant, a popular pub with exposed brick. Room and laundry service are provided.

WHERE TO DINE

EXPENSIVE

UNDER LINDETRAEET, Ramsherred 2. Tel. 66-12-92-86.
Cuisine: DANISH/INTERNATIONAL. **Reservations:** Required. **Bus:** 2.
$ Prices: Fixed-price dinner 425 kroner ($73.50); appetizers 58–162 kroner ($10–$28); main dishes 132–225 kroner ($22.80–$38.90). DC, MC, V.
Open: Daily 9am–midnight. **Closed:** July 4–24.

This inn, 2½ centuries old, is located across the street from H. C. Andersen's house. For a quarter of a century, this has been a landmark restaurant in Odense, providing a menu based on fresh and high-quality ingredients. Many fish and meat dishes are Cordon Bleu–inspired. The atmosphere is old world, and in summer, meals and light refreshments are served outside under linden trees. Artists often sit here to sketch Andersen's house.

MODERATE

DEN GAMBLE KRO, Overgade 23. Tel. 66-12-14-33.
Cuisine: DANISH/FRENCH. **Reservations:** Recommended. **Bus:** 4.
$ Prices: Fixed-price dinner 148 kroner ($25.60) for 2 courses, 200 kroner ($34.60) for 3 courses, 238 kroner ($41.20) for 4 courses; fixed-price lunches 105–165 kroner ($18.20–$28.50); appetizers 49–89 kroner ($8.50–$15.40); main dishes 115–235 kroner ($19.90–$40.70). DC, MC, V.
Open: Mon–Sat 11am–11pm, Sun 10am–9:30pm.

A well-preserved 1683 inn in the town center, its two dining rooms are cozy and furnished with antiques. Cozier still is the brick-vaulted cellar, with its oak tables and antique chairs. For a main course, try tournedos chasseur, pepper steak flambé, or salmon gratinée. In season, game dishes are a specialty. Dinners are accompanied by a covered loaf of hot French bread, cutting board provided. Luncheon-platter specials include marinated salmon with mustard dressing. The house's dessert special is crêpes Suzette.

RODE 7, Østre Stationsvej 34. Tel. 66-12-30-99.

Cuisine: DANISH. **Reservations:** Recommended.

$ **Prices:** 3-course fixed-price menu (summer) 190 kroner ($32.90); appetizers 45–65 kroner ($7.80–$11.20); main dishes 130–170 kroner ($22.50–$29.40). No credit cards.

Open: Dinner only, Mon–Fri 5–11pm.

Installed in a century-old house with a lot of character, this restaurant is owned by culinary artist Anker Daugger. Specialties include steak au poivre, English beef, mixed grill, and herb-flavored lamb. It's near the harbor, the railway station, and the Royal Theater.

SORTEBRO KRO, Sejerskovvej 20. Tel. 66-13-28-26.

Cuisine: DANISH. **Reservations:** Not required. **Bus:** 25, 26 from Flakhaven.

$ **Prices:** Danish cold board 135 kroner ($23.40); appetizers 40–80 kroner ($6.90–$13.80); main dishes 75–160 kroner ($13–$27.70). AE, DC, MC, V.

Open: Mon–Sat 10am–11pm, Sun 10am–4pm.

Outside the entrance to Funen Village, the open-air culture museum, Sortebro Kro is a coaching inn that dates from 1807. The interior is an attraction in its own right: long refectory tables, sagging ceilings with overhead beams, three-legged chairs, florid handmade chests, and crockery cupboards. Country meals are served featuring popular all-you-can-eat Danish cold board.

EVENING ENTERTAINMENT

NATTERGALEN, in the Hotel H. C. Andersen, Claus Bergsgade 7. Tel. 66-14-78-00.

This is the place to dance to live music. The crowd tends to be over 30. Beer costs 28 kroner ($4.80). It's open Monday through Wednesday from 10pm to 3am and Thursday through Saturday from 10pm to 4am. **Bus:** 4, 5.

Admission: Free.

3. SVENDBORG

27 miles S of Odense, 91 miles W of Copenhagen

GETTING THERE **By Train** Twenty trains a day leave from Odense's rail station, taking 1 hour to Svendborg.

By Bus Daily, 18 buses leave from Odense's bus station, taking 1 hour 30 minutes.

By Car Drive south from Odense along Route 9.

ESSENTIALS The **Svendborg Tourist Office** is at Centrumpladsen (tel. 62-21-09-80). Hours are January 2 to June 13 and September 1 to December 22, Monday through Friday, from 9am to 5pm and Saturday from 9am to noon. From mid-June through August, hours are daily Monday through Friday from 9am to 5pm and on Saturday from 9am to 5pm.

This old port on Svendborg Sound has long been a popular boating center where you can see yachts, ketches, and kayaks in the harbor. The town still retains some of its medieval heritage, but most of it has been torn down in the name of progress. Most visitors find that Svendborg makes a good base for touring the Danish château country and the South Funen archipelago as well.

Svendborg is a market town. On Saturday morning check out the cobblestone central plaza where flowers and fish are sold. Wander through the many winding streets where brick and half-timbered buildings still stand. On **Ragergade** you'll see the old homes of early seafarers. **Møllergade,** a pedestrian street, is one of the oldest streets in town, with about 100 different shops.

For the literary buff, the German writer Bertolt Brecht lived at Skovsbo Strand west of Svendborg from 1933 to 1939, leaving at the outbreak of World War II. It was during this period that he wrote *Mother Courage and Her Children.*

WHAT TO SEE & DO

VIEBAELTEGÅRD, Grubbemøllevej 13. Tel. 62-21-02-61.

The headquarters for Svendborg County Museum's four branches, Viebaeltegård is housed in a former poorhouse/workhouse constructed in 1872, the only one of its kind still existing in a Danish town. These social-welfare buildings, including the garden, are now a historical monument. Inside, see displays from ancient times and the Middle Ages, including excavation finds from old Svendborg and South Funen. Crafts and other workshops are offered, including goldsmithing, pottery making, and printing. There is a big museum shop. You can picnic in the garden. The museum is located in the town center near the intersection with Dronningemaen.

Admission: 15 kroner ($2.60) adults; children free when accompanied by an adult.

Open: Jan–Feb, Mon–Fri 1–4pm; Mar–Apr, daily 1–4pm; May–June 15, daily 10am–4pm; June 16–Oct 25, daily 10am–5pm; Oct 26–Dec, daily 1–4pm.

ANNE HVIDES GÅRD, Fruerstraede 3. Tel. 62-21-02-61.

The oldest secular house in Svendborg, another branch of the County Museum, it was built around 1558. It is a beautiful half-timbered structure with 18th- and 19th-century interiors, and collections of Svendborg silver, glass, copper, brass, and faïence. It is located in the direct center of Torvet.

Admission: 15 kroner ($2.60) adults; children free when accompanied by an adult.

Open: May–Sept, Tues–Sun 10am–4pm; Oct–Apr, by arrangement with the main office.

SVENDBORG ZOOLOGISKE MUSEUM, Dronningemaen 30. Tel. 62-21-06-50.

Danish zoological specimens and large dioramas showing animal immigration and habitat are displayed. Many exhibits have sound effects. Make sure to stop in at the whale house where the skeleton of a 56-foot sei whale that beached itself on Tåsinge island in 1955 can be seen.

Admission: 15 kroner ($2.60) adults, 10 kroner ($1.70) children.

Open: Apr–Sept, daily 9am–5pm; Oct–Mar, Mon–Fri 9am–4pm, Sat–Sun 10am–4pm. **Bus:** 205, 206, 208.

ST. NICOLAJ CHURCH, Sct. Nicolajgade 2B. Tel. 62-21-12-96.

On one of the city's oldest shopping streets stands Svendborg's oldest house of worship. Built before 1200 in the Romanesque style and last restored in 1892, its red-brick walls and white vaulting complement the fine altarpiece and stained-glass windows. The church is in a cluster of old houses off Kyseborgstraede, in the vicinity of Gerrits Plads. Enter through the south door.

Admission: Free.

Open: July–Aug, daily 8am–4pm; Sept–June, daily 8am–noon.

VOR FRUE SOGN, Frue Kirkestraede 4. Tel. 62-21-11-61.

On the hill where the old Castle Swineburg stood, this Romanesque-Gothic church, dating from 1253, has a carillon of 27 bells, played four times a day. Since 1660 the bells have rung at noon. From the tourist office at Torvet, walk up the steps leading to the rise on which the church stands, overlooking the Old Town and the harbor.

Admission: Free.

Open: Summer, daily 8am–5pm. **Closed:** Rest of year.

ST. JØRGEN'S CHURCH, Strandvej 97. Tel. 62-21-14-73.

St. George's Church, located below the Svendborgsund Bridge, is the medieval Sct. Jørgensgård, the leprosy hospital built outside the town. The core of the church is a Gothic longhouse with a three-sided chancel, probably from the late 13th century. During restoration of the church in 1961, an archeological dig of the floor disclosed traces of a wooden building believed to be a predecessor of the present house of worship. Note the lovely glass mosaics in the building.

Admission: Free.

Open: Summer, daily 8am–5pm. **Closed:** Rest of year.

NEARBY ATTRACTIONS

On Thurø

This horseshoe-shaped island, connected to Funen by a causeway, is filled with orchards and well-cared-for gardens, giving it the title "The Garden of Denmark." The island was once the property of the manor house, Bjornemose, but the Thurineans wanted liberty, so they joined together to buy back Thurø in 1810, an event commemorated by a stone proclaiming freedom from manorial domination.

There's a beautiful old church on Thurø, and good beaches can be found at Smørmosen, Thurø Rev, and Grasten.

On Tåsinge

The largest island in the South Funen archipelago, Tåsinge has been connected to Funen by the Svendborg Sound Bridge since 1966. **Troense,** the "skipper town" of Tåsinge, is one of the best-preserved villages in Denmark where many half-timbered houses still stand on Badstuen and Grønnegade, the latter declared Denmark's prettiest street.

The island was the setting for a famous tragic love story depicted in the film *Elvira Madigan*. After checking out of a hotel in Svendborg, Danish artist Elvira Madigan and her lover Sixten Sparre, a Swedish lieutenant, crossed by ferry to Tåsinge, where together they committed suicide. The "Romeo and Juliet" of Denmark were buried in the Landet churchyard in the middle of Tåsinge, where many brides, even today, throw their wedding bouquets on their graves. The centenary of these two lovers was widely observed in 1989 throughout Scandinavia and their death on a July day gave rise to many ballads.

The island is best explored by car—drive over the causeway (follow Route 9). Local bus 200 also goes there. However, the most important attraction, Valdemar's Slot, can be seen by taking the vintage steamer, MS *Helge*, which departs several times daily from the harbor at Svendborg. Tickets are sold on board or at Svendborg Tourist Office, Centrumpladsen (tel. 62-21-09-80).

MARITIME MUSEUM, Strandgade 1, Troense. Tel. 62-22-52-32.

The Maritime Museum, the final branch of the County Museum, is housed in a 1790 school, and traces maritime history from the early 19th century to the present. Pictures of ships, panoramas, yachting models, and memorabilia of the trade routes to China and East India including Staffordshire figures, Liverpool ware, Sunderland china, ropework art, and ships in bottles are displayed.

Admission: 10 kroner ($1.70) adults, children 1–14, free.

Open: Jan 2–Apr, Mon–Fri 9am–5pm, Sat 9:30am–noon; May–Oct daily 9am–5pm; Nov–Dec 30 Mon–Fri 9am–5pm; Sat 9am–noon. **Directions:** Cross the causeway to Tåsigne, turn left and then left again, heading down Bregningevej toward the water. Turn right at Troensevej and follow signs to the old port of Troense and to the old village school (now the museum) on Strandgade.

VALDEMAR'S SLOT, Slotsallen 100, Troense. Tel. 62-22-61-06.

Valdemar's Slot was built between 1639 and 1644 by orders of King Christian IV for his son, Valdemar Christian. In 1678 it was given to naval hero Niels Juel for his third victory over the Swedes in a Køge Bay battle. The Juel family still owns the *slot,* which is in considerably better condition than when the admiral arrived. He found that the enemy Swedes had occupied the estate, sending the copper roof home to make bullets and stabling horses in the church. The castle is now a museum.

Valdemar's Castle Church, in the south wing, was cleaned up by Admiral Juel, consecrated in 1687, and has been used for worship ever since. Two stories high, it's overarched by three star vaults and illuminated by Gothic windows.

Admission: 30 kroner ($5.20) adults, 10 kroner ($1.70) children.

Open: May–Sept, daily 10am–5pm; Easter–Apr and Oct, Sat–Sun and holidays 10am–5pm. **Closed:** Nov–Easter. **Directions:** Take the MS *Helge* from Svendborg harbor. By car, from Troense follow Slotsallen to the castle.

TÅSINGE SKIPPERHJEM & FOLKEMINDESAMLING, Kirkebakken 1, Bregninge. Tel. 62-22-71-44.

Set in an 1826 school building, this private historical collection contains model and bottled ships, a coin collection, and revealing archives of Tåsinge history. A small collection of memorabilia is associated with the tragic love drama of Elvira and Sixten. In another building, you can see what a typical sea captain's house looked like some 100 years ago.

Admission: 10 kroner ($1.70) adults, 5 kroner (90¢) children.

Open: Mid-May to Aug, daily 10am–4pm. **Closed:** Sept–mid-May. **Bus:** 980 from Svendborg. **Directions:** From Valdemar's Slot, turn right by two thatched cottages and left again at the next junction. Follow the signs to Bregninge.

BREGNINGE KIRKEBAKKE, Kirkebakken 1, Bregninge.

If the weather is clear, be sure to climb the Bregninge church tower for panoramic views of the island and the Funen archipelago. To the south are the Bregninge Hills, whose wooded slopes are popular for outings. Originally Romanesque, the church's porch dates from the 16th century and its north wing from the 18th century. Inside, you'll see a Romanesque granite font, a head of Christ on the north wall dating from about 1250, and a 1621 pulpit with rich ornamentation. In the porch is a tombstone with arcade decoration, the image of a vicar, and runic letters.

Admission: Free.

Open: Summer, Mon–Fri 8am–8pm; winter, Mon–Fri 8–11am and 1–4pm. **Bus:** 980 from Svendborg.

WHERE TO STAY

MODERATE

HOTEL SVENDBORG, Centrumpladsen, DK-5700 Svendborg. Tel. 62-21-17-00. Fax 62-21-90-12. 87 rms (all with bath). A/C MINIBAR TV TEL **Bus:** 200, 208.

$ Rates (including breakfast): 600–750 kroner ($103.80–$129.80) single; 785–980 kroner ($135.80–$169.50) double. Summer discounts. AE, DC, MC, V. **Closed:** Dec 24–30.

This clean and stylish hotel offers the best accommodations in Svendborg. Bedrooms are comfortable, and room service is provided. Adjacent to the lobby is a café-bar with its own glassed-in front terrace and a modern high-ceilinged restaurant serving fresh food prepared from seasonal ingredients.

INEXPENSIVE

HOTEL ROYAL, Toldbodvej 5, DK-5700 Svendborg. Tel. 62-21-21-13. 24 rms (4 with bath). **Bus:** 200, 208, 980.

$ Rates: 235–298 kroner ($40.70–$51.60) single without bath, 450 kroner ($77.90) single with bath; 420–440 kroner ($72.70–$76.10) double without bath, 550 kroner ($95.20) double with bath. Breakfast 50 kroner ($8.70) extra. AE, DC, MC, V.

⑤ A 1930s hotel of modest comforts, this is for those who prefer a central location opposite the bus and rail stations. Rooms are simply furnished, each equipped with hot and cold running water. Adequate bathrooms are on each floor. Only breakfast is served, although a bar and café are on the premises.

HOTEL TRE ROSER, Fåborgvej 90, DK-5700 Svendborg. Tel. 62-21-64-26. Fax 62-21-15-26. 12 rms, 58 apartments (all with bath). TEL

$ Rates (including breakfast): 450 kroner ($77.90) single; 650 kroner ($112.50) double; 4,000 kroner ($692) weekly apartment. DC, MC, V. **Parking:** Free.

Tre Roser offers attractively furnished apartments suitable for one to five people, with well-equipped kitchens. Most guests stay by the week, but apartments can be rented on a daily basis if available. The dozen bedrooms are short on frills but clean and comfortable. In the main building is a reputable restaurant, TV room, sauna, billiard room, and table tennis. Outside is a big swimming pool, a paddling pool and playground for children, and patio. The hotel is located about 3 miles from the nearest bathing beaches. A 5-minute drive will bring you to the Svendborg Golf Course, where Tre Roser guests play free.

MISSIONSHOTELLET STELLA MARIS, Kogtvedvaenget 3, DK-5700 Svendborg. Tel. 62-21-38-91. Fax 62-22-41-74. 25 rms (13 with bath). **Directions:** From Svendborg, head west along Kogtvedvej. **Bus:** 202.

$ Rates (including breakfast): 235 kroner ($40.70) single without bath, 310 kroner ($53.60) single with bath; 435 kroner ($75.30) double without bath, 580 kroner ($100.30) double with bath. MC, V.

Missionshotellet Stella Maris is an old-fashioned place, the former dormer house of a large estate. The bedroom furniture may be dated, but all is comfortable, and the patina of time has given the hotel a certain dignity. Seaview units opening onto Svendborg Sound are more expensive. A private park leads directly to the sound. The restaurant serves typical regional dishes.

NEARBY ACCOMMODATIONS
At Oure: Inexpensive

MAJORGÅRDEN, Landevejen 155, DK-5883 Oure. Tel. 62-28-18-19. 4 rms (none with bath). **Bus:** 910 running between Svendborg and Nyborg.

$ Rates (including breakfast): 235 kroner ($40.70) single; 345 kroner ($59.70) double. DC, MC, V. **Parking:** Free.

On the coast road, 7 miles from Svendborg and 20 miles from Nyborg, this 1761 white-brick inn has been cherished by such illustrious Danes as tenor Lauritz Melchior. Outside, a bower of roses grows against the walls, low white tables are on the lawn for coffee, and a little pond at the rear is filled with ducks. An old horse stable has been turned into a bar, complete with bowling lanes. The rooms sit cozily above the restaurant under the roofline. Two have old-fashioned fixtures and furnishings, and the others are much more modern.

If you're just driving by, stop in for a "plate of the inn"—two kinds of herring, plaice, meatballs, meat sausages, liver paste, and cheese for 98 kroner ($17). A large selection of fish and meat dishes is also available, costing 190 kroner ($32.90) and up.

At Stenstrup: Inexpensive

STENSTRUP KRO, Jernbanevej 2, DK-5771 Strenstrup. Tel. 62-26-15-14. Fax 62-26-33-92. 20 rms (12 with bath).

$ Rates: 210 kroner ($36.30) single without bath, 302 kroner ($52.20) single with bath; 350 kroner ($60.60) double without bath, 450 kroner ($77.90) double with bath. Breakfast costs 45 kroner ($7.80) extra. MC, V. **Parking:** Free.

Located at the end of a side street at the edge of town, this is well known as a hotel and a popular restaurant. The building dates from the turn of the century. A motel wing, built in 1971, contains respectably conservative accommodations. The country-style restaurant serves lunch, drinks, snacks, and dinner every day of the year from noon to 9pm. Typical dishes include beef casserole, pork flavored with herbs, and the chef's special steak. Dinners cost from 175 kroner ($30.30). However, a special menu of luncheon platters ranges in price from 32 kroner to 75 kroner ($5.50 to $13).

On Thurø: Inexpensive

HOTEL & PENSION RØGERIET, Måroddevej 22 Thurø, DK-5700 Svendborg. Tel. 62-20-50-84. 16 rms (14 with bath). **Bus:** 201.

$ **Rates** (including breakfast): 260 kroner ($45) single without bath, 360 kroner ($62.30) single with bath; 510 kroner ($88.20) double without bath, 560 kroner ($96.90) double with bath. MC, V. **Parking:** Free. **Closed:** Dec–Jan.

Three miles from Svendborg, on its own private beach, is this lovely old Danish compound, "The Smokehouse" in English, furnished in a homelike, personalized style. Comfortable chairs are set on the terraces so you may soak in the sound and the Isle of Tåsinge. Rooms are well furnished with antiques, and most have balconies. Home-style Danish cooking is served in the cozy dining room. Paintings by the Funen artist Niels Hansen decorate the walls.

On Tåsinge: Inexpensive

HOTEL TROENSE, Strandgade 5-7, Troense, DK-5700 Svendborg. Tel. 62-22-54-12. Fax 62-22-78-12. 31 rms (27 with bath). TV **Bus:** 200.

$ **Rates** (including breakfast): 430 kroner ($74.40) single; 650 kroner ($112.50) double. DC, MC, V. **Parking:** Free.

Since 1905 this establishment has been well known as both hotel and restaurant. Most rooms are in the main white-walled building, and a few are in comfortable annexes nearby. A fixed-price meal in the nautically designed dining room runs 175 kroner ($30.30) for two courses, 200 kroner ($34.60) for three courses. Specialties include filet of lemon sole; plaice stuffed with shrimp, asparagus, and mushrooms; and médaillons of pork with cream-and-curry sauce. The restaurant is open for lunch and dinner every day.

WHERE TO DINE
INEXPENSIVE

BORGEN, Faergevej 34. Tel. 62-21-29-76.
Cuisine: DANISH. **Reservations:** Recommended.
$ **Prices:** Appetizers 36–72 kroner ($6.20–$12.50); main dishes 55–175 kroner ($9.50–$30.30). DC, MC, V.
Open: Tues–Sun 11am–9:30pm. **Closed:** Mon in winter.

A four-story harborfront building, this restaurant has an outdoor terrace with views of the water and a separate bar. Built as a private house in 1916, it was sold to a Dane just before World War II. He was later accused of collaborating with the Nazis and quickly sold it to a private men's club, which has maintained a restaurant on the premises since 1946. The restaurant serves *lobscous* (Danish hash), steamed *borgen* (house) steak with elaborate garnishes, potato boats, and a herb sauce. The promotional meal of the chef offers a choice of six different kinds of steak for only 79 kroner ($13.70).

SUNDET, Havnpladsen 5A. Tel. 62-21-07-19.
Cuisine: DANISH/FRENCH. **Reservations:** Recommended.
$ **Prices:** Appetizers 35–55 kroner ($6.10–$9.50); main dishes 55–110 kroner ($9.50–$19); lunch smørrebrød from 28 kroner ($4.80) each. No credit cards.
Open: Daily 11am–midnight.

A 5-minute walk south of the commercial center, this waterfront restaurant is the oldest in town, built some 160 years ago in a stone house painted white. From its windows or summer terrace, you can see the harbor with its ferryboats, trawlers, and pleasure yachts. The chef specializes in fresh fish and meat, including a French-inspired bouillabaisse. The house flounder is the best in town—grilled with fennel and served with a butter sauce. The separate bar is popular with the locals.

NEARBY DINING
In Bregninge: Moderate

BREGNINGE KRO, Sundbrovej 54. Tel. 62-22-54-75.
Cuisine: DANISH/INTERNATIONAL. **Reservations:** Recommended. **Bus:** 980 from Svendborg.

$ Prices: Appetizers 45–65 kroner ($7.80–$11.20); main dishes 110–165 kroner ($19–$28.50). DC, MC, V.
Open: Lunch Tues–Sun 11am–3pm; dinner Tues–Sun 5–9pm. **Closed:** Mon in winter.

Three miles south of Svendborg on the main road in the heart of the village is an old-fashioned country inn that has been serving abundant farm-style meals since 1900. A large variety of Danish and international cuisine and wines are served. Dishes may include English-style curry soup, tournedos (perfectly prepared), or a local fish called "red tongue" in English, which is served as a filet with a mushroom-and-sherry sauce.

In Vester Skerninge: Inexpensive

VESTER SKERNINGE KRO, Krovej 9. Tel. 62-24-10-04.
Cuisine: DANISH. **Reservations:** Recommended.
$ Prices: Appetizers 35–65 kroner ($6.10–$11.20); main dishes 65–155 kroner ($11.20–$26.80). No credit cards.
Open: Wed–Mon 11am–9pm.

In the hamlet of Vester Skerninge, 7 miles west of Svendborg along Route 44, this *kro* (inn) was established in 1772, and has been dispensing generous portions of simple Danish food ever since. Behind a half-timbered facade, guests can order such dishes as clear or cream-based soups, English or French beefsteak, and wienerschnitzel.

---

4. FAABORG

17 miles W of Svendborg, 112 miles W of Copenhagen

GETTING THERE By Train Frequent trains connect Faaborg with both Odense and Svendborg. Connections can be made to Copenhagen.

By Bus Thirty buses a day run between Odense and Faaborg, taking 1 hour.

By Car From Svendborg, head west on Route 44; from Odense, go south on Route 43.

ESSENTIALS The **Faaborg and District Tourist Association,** Havnegade 2 (tel. 62-61-07-07), is open Mon–Fri 9am–5pm, Sat 9am–2pm. It provides information on sightseeing and the annual July festival, beginning on the 4th, with entertainment, dances, an amusement park, and much more.

Faaborg (also written Fåborg), a small seaside town of red-roofed buildings, is a good base for exploring southwestern Funen. Crowned by an old belfry, Faaborg has a number of well-preserved buildings, among them the medieval **Vesterport,** all that's left of Faaborg's walled fortifications.

You'll find here one of the best collections of Funen paintings and sculpture, particularly the work of Kai Nielsen, an important modern Danish sculptor. One controversial sculpture by Nielsen that has been denounced as obscene by some and praised by others is **Ymerbrond** (Ymer Wall), displayed in the market square (a copy is in the Museum of Faaborg). The sculpture depicts a man drinking from the udder of a bony cow while the cow licks a baby.

WHAT TO SEE & DO

FAABORG MUSEUM, Grønnegade 75. Tel. 62-61-06-45.
Located near the bus station, this museum has a rich collection of work by Kai Nielsen. Aside from his works, the museum displays paintings by such outstanding local artists as Peter Hansen, Johannes Larsen, and Fritz Syberg. In the octagonal rotunda of the museum is a huge statue commissioned by Mads Rasmussen, a wealthy

art patron who bore the nickname "Mads Tomato." The museum has a café, open from June to September, serving lunch and coffee.

Admission: 15 kroner ($2.60) adults; free for children.

Open: Apr–Oct, daily 10am–4pm; Nov–Mar, Sat–Sun and holidays 11am–3pm.

DEN GAMLE GAARD [The Old Merchant's House], Holkegade 1. Tel. 62-61-33-38.

This 1725 house was established as a municipal museum in 1932 and displays Faaborg life in the 18th and 19th centuries. Various furnishings (some of which were the property of Riborg Voight, an early love of H. C. Andersen's), glass, china, and faïence indicating Faaborg's past importance as a trade and shipping center are also on view. Exhibits from Lyk, including beautiful textiles and embroidery, are in the back.

The museum lies in the town center near the marketplace and harbor.

Admission: 15 kroner ($2.60) adults, free for children.

Open: May 15–Sept 15, daily 10:30am–4:30pm. **Closed:** Sept 16–May 14.

KLOKKETÅRNET, Tarnstraede.

This old belfry is the landmark of Faaborg—it's all that's left of the 13th-century Church of Sct. Nicolai, the first church in town, which was demolished around 1600. The town's old fire sledge is also here. The carillon bells play hymns four times a day. The belfry is directly in the town center near the marketplace.

Admission: 2 kroner (30¢) adults, 1 kroner (20¢) children.

Open: Mid-June to mid-Sept, Mon–Fri 10am–noon and 2–4pm; Sat 10am–noon. **Closed:** Mid-Sept to mid-June.

WHERE TO STAY

INEXPENSIVE

HOTEL FAABORG FJORD, Svendborgvej 175, DK-5600 Faaborg. Tel. 62-61-10-10. Fax 62-61-10-17. 131 rms (127 with bath). TV TEL

$ Rates (including breakfast): 455 kroner ($78.70) single without bath, 530 kroner ($91.70) single with bath; 640 kroner ($110.70) double without bath, 780 kroner ($134.90) double with bath. AE, DC, MC, V. **Parking:** Free.

Set on its own park at the eastern edge of town, this modern year-round hotel has comfortable rooms, each with a balcony/terrace. An indoor swimming pool and sauna are among the amenities. The restaurant offers a magnificent sea view, good food, and an excellent wine cellar. Live music is played for dancing on Saturday night.

HOTEL-PENSION MOSEGÅRD, Nabgyden 31, DK-5600 Faaborg. Tel. 62-61-56-91. 22 rms (8 with bath). TV

$ Rates (including breakfast): 290 kroner ($50.20) single without bath, 400 kroner ($69.20) single with bath; 470 kroner ($81.30) double without bath, 580 kroner ($100.30) double with bath. DC, MC, V. **Parking:** Free.

This is an oasis of charm and Danish comfort located near the beach 3 miles east of Faaborg. Many stay here on a weekly basis and full-board terms are available, but most guests prefer to tour during the day. Rooms are furnished in an old-fashioned country style—snug and comfortable.

NEARBY ACCOMMODATIONS

Expensive

FALSLED KRO, Assensvej 513, Falsled, DK-5642 Millinge. Tel. 62-68-11-11. Fax 62-68-11-62. 14 rms (all with bath), 3 suites. TEL **Bus:** 930.

$ Rates: 700 kroner ($121.10) single; 800–1,570 kroner ($138.40–$271.60) double; 1,875–2,200 kroner ($324.40–$380.60) suite. Breakfast 120 kroner ($20.80) extra. AE, DC, MC, V. **Parking:** Free. **Closed:** Jan–Feb.

The epitome of a Danish roadside inn, a former 15th-century smugglers' inn Falsled Kro has been converted into a premier hotel, the finest in Funen. A Relais & Châteaux, it offers tradition and quality in its colony of thatched buildings clustered around a cobbled courtyard with a fountain. Each accommodation is elegantly furnished and comfortable—some in converted outbuildings, others in cottages across the road. Eleven rooms have a TV and seven are fitted with minibars. A garden leads to the water and a yacht harbor. It's located west of Faaborg on Route 329.

Dining/Entertainment: Many critics rate the hotel restaurant the best in Denmark. Growing many of its own vegetables, the *kro* uses only fresh, seasonal produce. Inspired by France, cooking is in the modern style. The owners breed quail that are cooked and served with a port wine sauce. Sea trout and turbot are caught locally. The chef's seafood platter is perhaps the most outstanding in the country. Try salmon grilled or flamed over fennel. Game dishes predominate in autumn. The kitchen also bakes its own bread and cakes. The wine list is well chosen.

Services: Laundry, babysitting, room service, luggage service, translations and guide service.

Facilities: Tennis courts 500 yards away, horseback riding 3 miles away, fishing and bathing areas, helipad, parking area.

Moderate

STEENSGAARD HERREGÅRDSPENSION, Steensgaard, DK-5642 Millinge. Tel. 62-61-94-90. Fax 62-61-78-61. 20 rms (17 with bath). MINIBAR TEL **Bus:** 920, 930.

$ Rates (including breakfast): 350 kroner ($60.60) single without bath, 600 kroner ($103.80) single with bath; 780 kroner ($134.90) double without bath, 980 kroner ($169.50) double with bath. AE, DC, MC, V. **Parking:** Free.

⑤ Few places in Denmark are as evocative of bygone manorial life as this 12th-century brick-and-timber house. About 4 miles northwest of Faaborg, the oldest section of this hotel dates from 1310, possibly earlier. Bedrooms are comfortably furnished, often stylishly so with antiques.

You can eat here even if you are not a guest if you make reservations far enough in advance. Dinner is served at 7pm sharp. Fixed-price lunches go for 150 kroner ($25.95); dinners, 250 kroner ($43.30). Your meal might include champagne soup, roe deer with juniper berries, or salmon en papillote with local herbs.

Inexpensive

KORINTH KRO, Reventlowsvej 10, DK-5600 Faaborg. Tel. 62-65-10-23. 32 rms (10 with bath). TV

$ Rates (including breakfast): 220 kroner ($38.10) single without bath, 325 kroner ($56.20) single with bath; 325 kroner ($56.20) double without bath, 425 kroner ($73.50) double with bath. Breakfast 45 kroner ($7.80) extra. AE, DC, MC, V. **Parking:** Free.

Five miles northeast of Faaborg along Route 8, this hotel features comfortably old-fashioned bedrooms, a sauna, solarium, children's playground, and rear garden. The building was originally intended as a school where local farm girls could learn weaving, but became an inn in 1801. Today it's shielded from the main road by a screen of architectural gingerbread, a red-tile roof, and scores of climbing vines. If you wish, you can just drop in for lunch or dinner. Main courses in the restaurant cost from 65 kroner to 148 kroner ($11.20 to $25.60).

WHERE TO DINE

INEXPENSIVE

RESTAURANT KLINTEN, Klintallée 1. Tel. 62-61-32-00.
   Cuisine: DANISH. **Reservations:** Recommended.
$ Prices: Appetizers 40–50 kroner ($6.90–$8.70); main dishes 80–195 kroner ($13.80–$33.70). DC, MC, V.
   Open: Coffee and apéritifs daily 5–9pm; dinner daily 5–9pm.
This attractive restaurant, overlooking the water a quarter mile north of the commercial center, is a great place to eat in Faaborg. The building was erected in 1977, and the restaurant is known for its big windows and panoramic view of a verdant offshore island. The kitchen is open until 9pm, but guests often stay much

longer. Appetizers include smoked salmon with mustard sauce, avocado soup, perhaps marinated mushrooms, and such main dishes as chicken breast en papillote.

---

5. ÆRØ

18 miles across the water S of Svendborg, 110 miles W of Copenhagen

GETTING THERE   By Car & Ferry   If you're traveling by car from Copenhagen, make a reservation on the car-ferry. The trip to Ærø takes about an hour. From Svendborg, take a ferry to Æroskøbing through the South Funen archipelago. The ferry makes six daily round-trips, carrying 700 passengers and 70 cars. There is a café on board. For a schedule, ask at the tourist office or at the ferry office at the harbor in Svendborg. Bookings are made through **A/S Dampskibsselskabet Ærø** in Æroskøbing (tel. 62-52-10-18).

Getting Around   If possible, take a car on the ferry since there is very limited bus service on Ærø. Bus no. 990 runs every hour on the hour in the afternoon between Æroskøbing, Marstal, and Søby. Morning service is greatly curtailed. Tourist offices (see below) provide bus schedules, which change seasonally. Tickets can be bought on the bus. For bus information in Æroskøbing, call 62-52-11-03.

If you're interested in a **bus tour** of the island, call Mads "Bus" Jensen (tel. 62-58-13-13).

ESSENTIALS   The **Marstal Tourist Office** is at Kirkestraede 29 (tel. 62-53-19-60), and the **Æroskøbing Tourist Office** is at Torvet (tel. 62-52-13-00). They are open Mon–Sat 9am–5pm.

An interesting Denmark excursion is to the Baltic Sea island of Ærø, 22 miles long and 6 miles wide. The island has little seaside and country hamlets linked by winding, sometimes single-lane roads, with thatch-roofed farmhouses in pastures and cultivated fields. Ærø has both sand and pebble beaches.

There are many good places on Ærø to eat and sleep—cozy inns in the country and comfortable little hotels in town. Try some of the local rye bread; it's said to be the best in Denmark. With your aquavit (schnapps), ask for a dash of Riga balsam bitters, a tradition that started when Ærø men sailed to Riga, found these bitters, and used them ever since in their aquavit.

WHAT TO SEE & DO

ÆROSKØBING

The neat little village of ✪ Æroskøbing is a 13th-century market town, which came to be known as a skippers' town in the 17th century. Called "a lilliputian souvenir of the past," with its small gingerbread houses, intricately carved wooden doors, and cast-iron lamps, few Scandinavian towns have retained their heritage as much as Æroskøbing. In the heyday of the windjammer, nearly 100 commercial sailing ships made Æroskøbing their home port.

SØBY

The ferry from Faaborg docks at Søby, in the northwestern sector of the island. Before rushing to Æroskøbing, visit a mellow manorial property, **Søbygård.** Now in ruins, this manor house is complete with moat and dank dungeons.

Photographers are fond of the local **church** with its octagonal steeple that dates to about 1200, with many later additions and alterations over the centuries. See, in particular, Claus Berg's triptych, a primitive rendition of the Crucifixion.

FLASKESKIBSSAMLINGEN, Smedegade 22. Tel. 62-52-29-51.
The seafaring life is documented in this museum of Peter Jacobsen's ships in bottles, which represents his life's work. Upon his death in 1960 at the age of 84, this

former cook had crafted more than 1,600 bottled ships and some 150 model sailing vessels built to scale, earning him the reputation in Ærøskøbing of "the ancient mariner." The museum also has Ærø clocks, furniture, china, and carved works by sculptor H. C. Petersen.

Admission: 10 kroner ($1.70) adults, 5 kroner (90¢) children.
Open: May–Sept, daily 9am–5pm; Oct–Apr, daily 10am–4pm.

HAMMERICHS HUS, Brogade 3-5. Tel. 62-52-29-50.
This house is filled with 18th-century antiques and porcelain.
Admission: 5 kroner (90¢).
Open: Daily 10am–noon and 2–4pm.

MARSTAL

This thriving little port on the east coast of Ærø has had a reputation in sailors' circles since the days of the tall ships. The harbor, protected by a granite jetty, is still busy, with a shipyard producing steel and wooden vessels, an engine factory, a ferry terminal, and one of Denmark's biggest yacht basins. The street names of Marstal attest to its seafaring background: Skonnertvej, Barkvej, and Galeasevej (Schooner, Bark, and Ketch Road); Danish naval heroes; and seven Ferry Lanes.

Visit the **seamen's church** with a spire and illuminated clock in the town center. Inside are ship models and an altarpiece that depicts Christ stilling the tempest at sea.

Twice a day a mail boat takes a limited number of passengers on a 45-minute trip to tiny **Birkholm Island,** for swimming and exploration. There are no cars on Birkholm. Reservations on the mail boat can be made at the Marstal Tourist Office.

JENS HANSEN'S MARITIME MUSEUM, Prinsensgade 1. Tel. 62-53-23-31.
This museum contains collections of ship models, old maritime equipment, and objets d'art brought home by sailors from foreign shores.
Admission: 20 kroner ($3.50) adults, 8 kroner ($1.40) children.
Open: Oct–Apr, Mon–Fri 10am–4pm; May and Sept, daily 10am–4pm; June and Aug, daily 9am–5pm; July, daily 9am–10pm.

MAREN MINORS MINDE, Teglgade 9.
This old skipper's house has been converted into a museum of local nautical artifacts.
Admission: 5 kroner (90¢) adults, 2 kroner (30¢) children.
Open: Mid-Aug to late Oct, daily 9am–5pm. **Closed:** Late Oct to mid-Aug.

WHERE TO STAY

IN ÆRØSKØBING

Inexpensive

DET LILLE HOTEL, Smedegate 33, DK-5970 Ærøskøbing. Tel. 62-52-23-00. 6 rms (none with bath).
$ **Rates** (including breakfast): 250 kroner ($43.30) single; 390 kroner ($67.50) double. No credit cards. **Parking:** Free on street. **Closed:** Mid-Oct to mid-Apr.

Det Lille Hotel has simple but cozy bedrooms. Meals at the terrace restaurant cost 120 kroner ($20.80) each and include pork chops with vegetables, ham cutlets with mushrooms and paprika-flavored potatoes, beef steaks, fried chicken, and hash. Food is served from 11:30am to 2pm and 5:30 to 9pm. The hotel is 100 yards from the ferry and harbor.

HOTEL ÆRØHUS, Vestergade 38, DK-5970 Ærøskøbing. Tel. 62-52-10-03. Fax 62-52-21-23. 70 rms (40 with bath). MINIBAR TV TEL
$ **Rates** (including breakfast): 225 kroner ($38.90) single without bath, 405 kroner ($70.10) single with bath; 390 kroner ($67.50) double without bath, 610 kroner ($105.50) double with bath. AE, DC, MC, V. **Parking:** Free. **Closed:** Dec 24–Feb 1.
Painted a salmon pink, this typical Danish inn has tile roofs and black half-timbers.

Dormer windows peer like eyes from its steeply pitched roof. Inside it's charming, with many traditional features, such as copper kettles hanging from the ceiling and warm lamps glowing. Bedrooms are modernized but traditional. You can also enjoy good Danish meals here. In summer, there's dining in the large garden. The hotel is a 3-minute walk from the harbor. Live music is played on summer weekends.

OUTSIDE ÆRØSKØBING

Inexpensive

VINDEBAL KRO, Vindeballe Gade 1, DK-5970 Ærøskøbing. Tel. 62-52-16-13. 4 rms (none with bath).

$ Rates (including breakfast): 200 kroner ($34.60) single; 350 kroner ($60.60) double. MC, V. **Parking:** Free.

This charming country inn, built in 1888, is located on the road between Søby and Marstal, 3 miles from the old town of Ærøskøbing and is close to the sea. Rooms are without frills, and guests share the lounge with TV. The inn also has a simple restaurant where platters of food cost from 90 kroner ($15.60) each. Nonresidents can drop in for a well-prepared meal daily from 11am to 9:30pm.

IN MARSTAL

Inexpensive

ÆRØ KONGRESHOTEL, Egehovedvej 4, DK-5960 Marstal. Tel. 62-53-33-20. Fax 62-53-31-50. 80 rms (all with bath), 20 suites. MINIBAR TV TEL **Bus:** 990 to Marstal.

$ Rates (including breakfast): 400 kroner ($69.20) single; 700 kroner ($121.10) double; from 920 kroner ($159.20) suite. DC, MC, V. **Parking:** Free. **Closed:** Dec 15–Feb 1.

A 5-minute walk south of the center of Marstal and a quarter mile from the beach, this hotel, opened in 1989, is the largest and most up-to-date on the island. Set in a windswept landscape of seagrass and sweeping vistas, rooms are first class, decorated in pastel colors, with all the amenities such as private baths. Suites are twice the size of regular rooms. There is an excellent restaurant, Østersøen, and one bar.

HOTEL MARSTAL, Droningstraede 1A, DK-5960 Marstal. Tel. 62-53-13-52. 7 rms (none with bath).

$ Rates: 205 kroner ($35.50) single; 330 kroner ($57.10) double. No credit cards. **Parking:** Free.

This old-fashioned hotel offers clean accommodations in a regional atmosphere. Most rooms have large windows and dark paneling. Full meals, served daily in the restaurant at lunch and dinner, cost 150 kroner ($26) and might include crab cocktail, salmon filet with French bread, pepper steak, or veal Cordon Bleu. Fixed-price two-course meals cost 95 kroner ($16.40), and special platters for children are available. The hotel is in the town center, 2 minutes from the harbor.

OUTSIDE MARSTAL

Inexpensive

DUNKAER KRO, Dunkaervej 1, Dunkaer, DK-5970 Ærøskøbing. Tel. 62-52-16-14. 8 rms (none with bath).

$ Rates: 185 kroner ($32) single; 295 kroner ($51) double. Breakfast 45 kroner ($7.80) extra. AE, MC, V. **Parking:** Free.

Located in the middle of the island, 5 miles outside Marstal on the road to Søby, this family-owned 1802 inn is a rambling, twin-gabled structure, with enough charm to suit the most ardent traditionalist. Quaintness prevails, from the thatched roof to the old grandfather clock standing in the dining room. Rooms are cozy and clean. In summer, food is served in an attractive old garden. You can order an old-fashioned Danish breakfast at an extra charge, or a hearty, filling dish of the day for 78 kroner ($13.50), complete with all the trimmings.

WHERE TO DINE
IN ÆRØSKØBING
Inexpensive

RESTAURANT MUMM, Søndergade 12, Ærøskøbing. Tel. 62-52-12-12.
Cuisine: AMERICAN/INTERNATIONAL. **Reservations:** Not required.
$ Prices: Appetizers 35–65 kroner ($6.10–$11.20); main dishes 45–85 kroner ($7.80–$14.70); fixed-price lunch 85 kroner ($14.70). AE, DC, MC, V.
Open: July–Aug, daily 11am–11pm; Apr 15–June and Sept, Tues–Sun noon–10pm. **Closed:** Oct–Apr 14.

Restaurant Mumm, in the town center near the Torv, enjoys a reputation for well-prepared recipes that sometimes carry a North American flavor thanks to the long-ago sojourn of the chef, Grethe Mumm-Christensen, in Salinas, Calif. Specialties include American filet steak, a salad buffet, mussel soup, lobster cocktail, and grilled scampi.

CHAPTER 10

JUTLAND

Dramatically different from the rest of Denmark, Jutland (Jylland in Danish) is a peninsula of heather-covered moors, fjords, farmland, lakes, and sand dunes. Besides its three major tourist centers—Ribe in the south, and Århus and Aalborg (Ålborg) in the north—there are countless old inns and off-the-beaten-path hamlets.

The mainland of Jutland lies between the North Sea, Skagerrak, and the Kattegat. It is 250 miles from the northern tip of Jutland, Skagen, to the German border in the south. The North Sea washes up on miles of sandy beaches, making this a favorite holiday place for Danes.

The meadows of Jutland are filled with rich birdlife and winding rivers; nature walks are an excellent way to spend time. The heart of Jutland is mainly beech forest and lakeland, sprinkled with some towns of modest size and light industry. Steep hills surround the deep fjords of the east coast. Gabled houses in the marshlands of South Jutland add to the charm of the peninsula. Two of the most popular vacation islands are Rømø and Fanø, off the southwest coast. Here, many traditional homes of fishermen and ship captains have been preserved.

Those who are heading to Germany after Denmark might want to make the northern swing first (Århus and Aalborg), stopping at Ribe on their way south. On the other hand, those heading north to Norway or Sweden should cross the mainland of Jutland into Ribe in the southeast, then steer north for the major sight at the top of the peninsula.

The Little Belt Bridge at Middelfart connects the island of Funen with the mainland, leading to Fredericia, where our tour begins.

SEEING JUTLAND

GETTING THERE

Flying into Jutland airports, primarily Århus, Billund, and Aalborg, is the fastest.

From Copenhagen, ferry links to North Jutland are possible from Kalundborg to Århus, Hundested to Grenå, Sjaellands Odde to Ebeltoft, and others. All these ferries transport cars.

Trains labeled "IC" or "L" offer the fastest service from Copenhagen to Jutland, taking 5 to 6 hours. Likewise, trains from the continent pass through northern Germany en route to Jutland.

Jutland is crisscrossed by a network of buses, most of which are operated by the Danish State Railways (DSB). No reductions are granted for round-trip tickets.

By car, take express highway E20 which runs across Funen. Motorists have to take a ferry from Korsør (Zealand), but can then drive all the way across the bridge into

WHAT'S SPECIAL ABOUT JUTLAND

Beaches
- ☐ Fanø island's 11-mile sandy beach—something special.
- ☐ Rømø island's western shore, one of the North Sea's premier sandy beaches; nude bathing.

Great Towns/Villages
- ☐ Ribe, of stork's nest fame—once a Viking port, now the prettiest town in Denmark.
- ☐ Jelling, "the birthplace of Denmark," and Harald Bluetooth's favorite.
- ☐ Ebeltoft, Denmark's classic market town of cobbled streets and half-timbered houses.

Castles & Palaces
- ☐ Rosenholm, near Århus, a moated Renaissance manor set in 35 acres of parkland.
- ☐ Clausholm, near Århus, an early baroque palace, place of banishment for Queen Anna Sophie

Churches & Abbeys
- ☐ The Rhineland-inspired Cathedral of Ribe, dating from 1150.
- ☐ The Black Friars St. Catherine's Church and Monastery, at Ribe, a well-preserved abbey.

Ace Attractions
- ☐ The 2,200-year-old Tollund Man at the Silkeborg Museum, prehistory's "most unspoiled face."
- ☐ Den Gamble By, a re-created Danish village in an open-air museum.

Special Events/Festivals
- ☐ Århus Festival, Scandinavia's biggest cultural event (early September).
- ☐ Ildfestregatta, Denmark's largest and oldest folk festival at Silkeborg, taking place on an excursion boat (early August).

East Jutland. Since Jutland is relatively flat, you may consider renting a bicycle. Railroad stations often rent them, or will direct you to the nearest place that does.

A SUGGESTED ITINERARY

If pressed for time, consider the following route:

Day 1: Cross the bridge from Funen at Middelfart and head west across Jutland on Route 32 to the old town of Ribe. Spend the night.

Day 2: Drive north to Esbjerg and take the 20-minute ferry crossing to Fanø. Spend the night in Fanø at an old inn.

Day 3: Cross Jutland again, heading east for a night in Silkeborg.

Day 4: Explore Århus's attractions and old manors. Spend the night.

Day 5: Drive to Ebeltoft, northeast of Århus, for a night in this ideal market town.

Day 6: Head north, stopping for lunch in Randers. Plan an overnight stay in Aalborg, Jutland's largest city.

Day 7: Return to Copenhagen or spend another night in Jutland, heading to its "Land's End," Skagen, in the northeastern corner. At Frederikshavn, northeast of Aalborg, catch a car-ferry to Norway.

1. JELLING

7 miles W of Vejle, 90 miles W of Copenhagen

GETTING THERE By Train Jelling is a 20-minutes train ride from Vejle on the run to Struer and Herning. Trains depart about once an hour Monday through Friday, less frequently on weekends.

By Bus   Connections are possible from Vejle's bus station. Take bus no. 214.

By Car   From Vejle, take Route A18 north.

This sleepy little village is historically important as the 10th-century seat of Danish kings Gorm the Old and Harald Bluetooth, Gorm's son.

WHAT TO SEE & DO

In front of Jelling's village church stand two ✪ **runic stones** that practically mark the beginning of recorded Danish history. (Don't expect Stonehenge.) One stone commemorates Queen Thyre, Gorm's wife and "Denmark's ornament." The other, a bigger, triangular hunk of granite, was ordered sculpted by Bluetooth to honor his father, although in fact it is a testimonial to his own conquests and the conversion of the Danes to Christianity.

The ancient tumuli (burial mounds) near the church are called **Gorm's Hill** and **Thyre's Hill.** A recent excavation revealed another burial chamber, under the site of the first **Jelling Church,** built around A.D. 960. It contained skeletons and large quantities of gold thread; Viking artifacts included silver figurines—all of which lead archeologists to believe that this burial chamber once housed royalty, perhaps even the earthly remains of Gorm and Thyre.

WHERE TO STAY
INEXPENSIVE

JELLING KRO, Gormsgade 16, DK-7300 Jelling. Tel. 75-87-10-06. Fax 75-87-25-75. 10 rms (5 with bath). **Bus:** 214.

$ Rates (including breakfast): 300 kroner ($51.90) single without bath, 350 kroner ($60.60) single with bath; 400 kroner ($69.20) double without bath, 540 kroner ($93.40) double with bath. AE, DC, MC, V. **Parking:** Free.

In the center of the village, this 200-year-old *kro* (inn) is across the street from the famous burial hill where Denmark "began." Behind a yellow-ocher facade, the main building contains five bathless rooms, charming but without many amenities. A recently constructed annex across the street offers modern accommodations with full baths, kitchenettes, and TVs. The hotel restaurant is open daily except Wednesday in winter. Food is served from 8am to 9:30pm, a three-course dinner costing 250 kroner ($43.25). Main dishes are likely to include sautéed breast of turkey, Danish beefsteak, and veal steak.

TØSBY KRO, Bredsten Landevej 12, DK-7300 Jelling. Tel. 75-88-11-23. 7 rms (none with bath). **Bus:** 214, 907 from Vejle.

$ Rates: 170 kroner ($29.40) single; 260 kroner ($45) double. Breakfast 45 kroner ($7.80) extra. MC, V. **Parking:** Free.

Only a few miles from the well-known Legoland i Billund and from the Lions Park in Givskud, 4 miles west of Jelling, this little 1882 inn is actually a boardinghouse where most guests are Norwegian or Danish. Rooms are pleasantly furnished. The Danish food is well prepared. A generous lunch or dinner costs 95 kroner ($16.40).

---

2. RIBE

20 miles S of Esbjerg, 186 miles W of Copenhagen

GETTING THERE   By Train   Ribe is connected by hourly trains from Copenhagen via Bramming. Frequent connections are possible between Tønder (near the German border) and Esbjerg, a major part of the West Jutland coast.

By Bus   There are frequent bus connections into Ribe from the following towns:

Esbjerg, Åbenraa, Bramming, Gram, and Jels. Exact routings and times of departure are available at the tourist offices, and tickets can be bought on the bus.

By Car   If you're crossing from East Jutland, take Route 32 cross country. If you're coming from mainland Europe, take Route 11 north from Tønder. Esbjerg is connected to Ribe by Route 24, which feeds into Route 11 south.

ESSENTIALS   The **Ribe Tourist Office,** at Torvet 3-5 (tel. 75-42-15-00), is open Mon–Fri 9am–5pm, Sat 9am–2pm. It is one of the more helpful in Denmark.

Ribe, a town of narrow cobblestone lanes, half-timbered and crooked houses, became legendary because of the graceful storks that build their nests on top of the town's red-roofed medieval houses. Every year citizens in the oldest town of Denmark face the same question: Will the storks fly back in April?

This port was an important trading center during the Viking era in the 9th century and became an episcopal seat in 948, when one of the first Christian churches in Denmark was established here. It was also the royal residence of the ruling Valdemars around 1200.

In medieval days Ribe was linked by sea-trade routes to England, Germany, Friesland, the Mediterranean, and other ports, but then its waters receded. Today it is surrounded by marshes, much like a landlocked Moby-Dick. The town watchman still makes his rounds—armed with his lantern and trusty staff—since the ancient custom was revived in 1936.

At **Skibbroen,** you can see a full-size replica of an evert, a ship that used to carry much of Ribe's seafaring goods. Skibbroen is the harbor, used today only by pleasure craft and the excursion boat *Riberhus,* which operates from May to September, taking passengers through the marshlands around Ribe to the Kammerslusen (sluice) and the tidal flats.

WHAT TO SEE & DO

CATHEDRAL OF RIBE, Torvet. Tel. 75-42-06-19.

⭐ This stone-and-brick cathedral, the crowning achievement of this little town, was under construction from 1150 to 1175. Inspired by Rhineland architecture, it's a good example of the Romanesque influence on Danish architecture, despite its Gothic arches. A century later a tower was added: Climb it if you want to see how the storks view Ribe—and if you have the stamina. Try to see the legendary "Cat's Head Door," once the principal entranceway to the church, and the granite tympanum—*Removal of the Cross*—the most significant piece of medieval sculpture left in Denmark. Mosaics, stained glass, and frescoes done in the eastern apse are by artist Carl-Henning Pedersen. The church is located in the town center off Sønderportsgade.

Admission: 5 kroner (90¢) adults, 1 krone (20¢) children.

Open: Oct–Apr, Mon–Sat 11am–3pm, Sun 1–3pm; May and Sept, daily 10am–5pm; July–Aug, daily 10am–6pm.

ST. CATHERINE'S CHURCH AND MONASTERY, Sct. Catherine's Plads. Tel. 75-42-05-34.

⭐ The Black Friars (Dominicans) came to Ribe in 1228 and began constructing a church and chapter house (the east wing of a monastery), and parts of the original edifice can still be seen, especially the southern wall. The present church, near Dagmarsgade, with nave and aisles, dates from the first half of the 15th century, and the tower is from 1617. Extensive restorations have made this one of the best-preserved abbeys in Scandinavia. Only the monks' stalls and the Romanesque font remain from the Middle Ages. The handsome pulpit dates from 1591 and the altarpiece from 1650.

You can walk through the cloisters and see ship models and religious paintings hanging in the southern aisle. Tombstones of Ribe citizens from the Reformation and later are along the outer walls of the church.

Across the street is the smallest house in Ribe, a brick-and-timber structure, a private home not open to the public. For information, phone the tourist office (tel. 75-42-15-00).

Admission: Church, free; cloisters, 3 kroner (50¢) adults, 1 krone (20¢) children.
Open: May–Sept, daily 10am–noon and 2–5pm; Oct–Apr, daily 2–4pm. **Bus:** 19.

HANS TAUSENS HUS, Torvet. Tel. 75-42-00-55.

The history of the Ribe area from the Stone Age (some 10,000 years ago) to today is exhibited along with finds from the Viking Age dating back to the earliest days of Ribe, between 700 and 800. Hans Tausens Hus faces the cathedral.

Admission: 10 kroner ($1.70) adults, 3 kroner (50¢) children.
Open: Summer, daily 10am–5pm; autumn and spring, Tues–Sun 11am–3pm; winter, Tues–Sun 11am–1pm. **Closed:** Mon Sept–May.

RIBE RÅDHUSSAMLING (Town Hall Museum), Stenbogade. Tel. 75-42-00-55.

The oldest existing town hall in Denmark, originally built in 1496, the medieval Town Hall Museum houses the town's artifacts and archives. Included are a 16th-century executioner's sword, ceremonial swords, the town's money chest, antique tradesmen's signs, and a depiction of the "iron hand," still a symbol of police authority. Enter from Støckens Plads.

Admission: 5 kroner (90¢) adults, 3 kroner (50¢) children.
Open: May–Sept, Mon–Fri 1–3pm. **Closed:** Oct–Apr.

RIBE KUNSTMUSEUM, Sct. Nicolaigade 10. Tel. 75-42-03-62.

An extensive collection of Danish art is displayed at the Ribe Kunstmuseum including works of acclaimed Danish artists like Eckersberg, Kobke, C. A. Jensen, Hammershøj, and Juel. Housed in a stately mid-19th-century villa in a garden on the Ribe River, many paintings are from the Golden Age of Danish art. Occasionally the museum changes exhibitions.

Admission: 10 kroner ($1.75) adults, free for children.
Open: June 15–Sept 14, daily 11am–4pm; Sept 15–June 14, Tues–Sun 1–4pm.

WHERE TO STAY

MODERATE

HOTEL DAGMAR, Torvet 1, DK-6760 Ribe. Tel. 75-42-00-33, or toll free 800/528-1234 in the U.S. Fax 75-42-36-52. 50 rms (all with bath). MINIBAR TV TEL

$ Rates (including breakfast): 550–850 kroner ($95.20–$147.10) single; 750–1,050 kroner ($129.80–$181.70) double. AE, DC, MC, V.

A Denmark legend, this historic 1581 hotel claims the most glamorous address in the region. Converted from a private home in 1850, it's named after a medieval Danish queen. Bedrooms are well furnished and comfortable. Every Friday and Saturday night except in summer there is music and dancing. The hotel's restaurant is recommended below.

INEXPENSIVE

KALVSLUND KRO, Koldingvej 105 at Kalvslund, DK-6760 Ribe. Tel. 75-43-70-12. 6 rms (none with bath). **Bus:** 57, 921 from Ribe.

$ Rates (including breakfast): 200 kroner ($34.60) single; 400 kroner ($69.20) double. No credit cards. **Parking:** Free.

An 1865 Danish inn 5½ miles north of Ribe on Route 11, the Kalvslund Kro offers comfortable rooms but few frills. The furniture, according to the management, "is old but not antique." Breakfast is served, but costs extra. The restaurant serves home-style cooking. The food I've sampled was well prepared and well presented. Full meals cost 75 kroner to 110 kroner ($13 to $19), including such dishes as asparagus soup, Danish beef with sautéed onions, and pork cutlets. It's open daily in summer, 8am to 10pm, but only on Friday, Saturday, and Sunday in winter.

SØNDER HOTEL JYLLAND, 22 Sønderportsgade, DK-6760 Ribe. Tel. 75-42-04-66. 8 rms (none with bath).

$ Rates (including breakfast): 210 kroner ($36.30) single; 420 kroner ($72.70) double. AE, MC, V.

Located behind a century-old red-brick facade, 100 yards south of the cathedral, this hotel is respectable and clean. None of the simple rooms has a private bath, but because of the lack of hotels in Ribe, it's often fully booked. The spacious dining room serves well-prepared and generous portions of Danish specialties every day at lunch and dinner.

WHERE TO DINE

EXPENSIVE

RESTAURANT DAGMAR, in the Hotel Dagmar, Torvet 1. Tel. 75-42-00-33.

Cuisine: DANISH/INTERNATIONAL. **Reservations:** Required.

$ Prices: Fixed-price meals 325 kroner ($56.20) at dinner, 146 kroner ($25.30) at lunch; appetizers 75–115 kroner ($13–$19.90); main dishes 176–225 kroner ($30.40–$38.90). AE, DC, MC, V.

Open: Daily noon–10pm.

Opposite the cathedral near the train station, the Hotel Dagmar's four dining rooms are a 19th-century dream of ornate furnishings and accessories. The international cuisine is the best in town, and it's impeccably served and complemented by a sophisticated wine list. Generally two different fresh fish dishes of the day are offered. Among meat and poultry selections, you might sample partridge in cabbage with mushroom fricassée and a chive sauce or filet of Danish lamb with celeriac and tomato fondue. There are also two cozy cellar restaurants.

INEXPENSIVE

VAERTSHUSET SAELHUNDEN, Skibbroen 13. Tel. 75-42-09-46.

Cuisine: DANISH. **Reservations:** Not required.

$ Prices: Appetizers 22–32 kroner ($3.80–$5.50); main dishes 62–125 kroner ($10.70–$21.60). DC, MC, V.

Open: Daily noon–8:45pm.

This charming little restaurant stands amid stately trees near the edge of the town's narrow canal just north of the cathedral. The low-slung brick building dates from the 1600s, although in the 18th and 19th centuries it was the town's shoe factory. The dining room, the Seals Room, is decorated with many pictures and seal skins. Regional dishes include *skipperlavskovs* (beef, potatoes, and onions concocted into a hash) served with brown bread and a beetroot salad. Also featured are ox tenderloin, clear bouillon with meatballs, and fried filet of plaice. In summer, you can sit in the cozy yard.

WEIS' STUE, Torvet 2, DK-6760 Ribe. Tel. 75-42-07-00.

Cuisine: DANISH. **Reservations:** Recommended.

$ Prices: Appetizers 40–55 kroner ($6.90–$9.50); main dishes 60–125 kroner ($10.40–$21.60). No credit cards.

Open: Daily 11am–9pm.

This 200-year-old brick-and-timber Lilliput inn, on the market square across from the cathedral, serves scrumptious food. My most recent dinner here consisted of marinated herring with raw onions, shrimp with mayonnaise and lemon, smoked Greenland halibut with scrambled eggs, liver paste with mushrooms, sliced ham and Italian salad, filet with onions, and two sorts of cheese with bread and butter.

The inn also rents four bathless rooms, charging 200 kroner ($34.60) for the one very cramped single and 450 kroner ($77.90) for the other three doubles. Rates include breakfast.

EASY EXCURSIONS FROM RIBE

Off the west coast of Jutland, **Rømø,** a North Frisian island, is the largest Danish island in the North Sea. It is about 5½ miles long and 4 miles wide. The western shore opens onto the North Sea, whereas the east coast facing the mainland is bounded by tidal shallows. The northwest corner of the island is a restricted military zone.

The island, which is separated from the German island of Sylt by the Lister Deep, has a wild, windswept appearance and is particularly known for its nude sunbathing, as is the German island of Sylt. In summer, Rømø is filled with tourists, especially Germans, but off-season it's one of the sleepiest places in Europe.

To reach Rømø, take the 6-mile stone causeway from mainland Jutland. You can take a bus south from Ribe to Skaerbaek and then bus no. 29 across the tidal flats to Rømø.

If you'd like to continue your trip to Sylt from Rømø, take a car-ferry from the Danish fishing village of Havneby to the far northern German town of List.

---

3. ESBJERG

58 miles W of Vejle, 105 miles SW of Århus, 173 miles W of Copenhagen

GETTING THERE By Plane   Flights arrive at Esbjerg from Aberdeen and Dundee in Scotland and also from Humberside in England. Flights also arrive from London at Billund Airport. There is also air service several times a day from Copenhagen.

By Train   Connections are possible almost hourly from Copenhagen and Frederikshavn via Fredericia.

By Bus   About three buses daily depart for Esbjerg from Frederikshavn, Aalborg, Viborg, and Herning.

By Car   From all corners of Denmark, highways lead to Esbjerg. From the German border in the south, take Route 11 north, heading left at the junction with Route 24. From Funen in the east, take the E20 express highway west across Jutland.

By Ferry   Esbjerg has three weekly ferry departures heading for Harwich in England all year. Summer ferries connect Esbjerg with Newcastle.

ESSENTIALS   The **Esbjerg Tourist Office,** Skolegade 33 (tel. 75-12-55-89), is open Mon–Fri 9am–5pm, Sat 9am–noon.

Esbjerg's harbor, with its easy accessibility to the North Sea, is a perfect shipping point for large agricultural exports to Great Britain, making it Denmark's largest fishing port. In recent years the oil and natural gas deposits in the North Sea have made Esbjerg the country's oil city. Many ships here are used as supply vessels for the Danish oil rigs.

Esbjerg is laid out with straight, wide streets, square town sections, and a large town square. There is a long pedestrian street, plus many specialty shops and large shopping centers.

Buses service the town, and you can make connections to other parts of the country. From the harbor, you can take a ferry year-round to Harwich, England, and to Newcastle, England, and the Faroe Islands in summer. For information, contact **DFDS,** Englands-terminalen (tel. 75-12-48-00). You can also connect by ferry with

Fanø (see below), a 20-minute crossing made every 30 minutes in summer, hourly in winter. Information is available from **Fanø-overfarten** (tel. 75-12-00-00).

WHAT TO SEE & DO

BOGTRYKMUSEET, Borgergade 6. Tel. 75-13-53-63.

The largest working presswork museum in Denmark, it's built and furnished like a medium-size Danish printing office. Exhibits of printed work and presses trace the craft of printing through 500 years. You can see the process as it developed from handset type and printing on cumbersome man-powered presses to the fast, accurate production with modern state-of-the-art equipment.

Admission: 15 kroner ($2.60) adults; free for children under 14.
Open: May–Sept, Mon–Fri 2–5pm. **Closed:** Oct–Apr. **Bus:** 1, 5, 6, 8, 9.

ESBJERG MUSEUM, Nørregade 25. Tel. 75-12-78-11.

This museum gives an all-around impression of the background of the town, its development, and special characteristics. Old houses, streets, squares, and the harbor are depicted in various exhibitions. A special prehistoric section opened in 1992. From the bus and train stations, follow signs for a quarter mile; the museum lies off Torvetgade.

Admission: 10 kroner ($1.75) adults; free for children under 14.
Open: Tues–Sun 10am–4pm. **Closed:** Dec 24–25, Jan 1, June 5. **Bus:** 1, 5, 6, 8, 9.

FISKERI-OG-SØFARTSMUSEET, SALT-VANDSAKVARIET, AND SAELA-RIUM, Tarphagvej 2. Tel. 75-15-06-66.

In this huge open-air tank the animals are fed daily at 11am and 2:30pm. Down below, you can watch the antics of the seals underwater through glass.

Admission: 30 kroner ($5.20) adults, 15 kroner ($2.60) children.
Open: June–Aug, daily 10am–6pm; off-season, daily 10am–4pm. **Bus:** 22, 23, 30.

WHERE TO STAY

INEXPENSIVE

ANSGAR HOTEL, Skolegade 36, DK-6700 Esbjerg. Tel. 75-12-82-44. Fax 75-13-95-40. 65 rms (all with bath). MINIBAR TV TEL **Bus:** 1, 5, 6, 9, 21.

$ Rates (including breakfast): 385–435 kroner ($66.60–$75.30) single; 575–610 kroner ($99.50–$105.50) double. AE, DC, MC, V. **Parking:** Free.

This well-established three-story hotel, in the center of town overlooking the square, is near the shopping street. Rooms are modern and comfortable. The hotel's restaurant serves international as well as Danish fare, and there is also a lounge.

HOTEL BRITANNIA, Torvet, DK-6701 Esbjerg. Tel. 75-13-01-11. Fax 75-45-20-85. 79 rms (all with bath). MINIBAR TV TEL **Bus:** 22.

$ Rates (including breakfast): 475–575 kroner ($82.20–$99.50) single; 620–700 kroner ($107.30–$121.10) double. AE, DC, MC, V.

Considered one of the best hotels in town, rooms here are comfortably furnished. On the premises are a tastefully decorated modern restaurant and pub, serving Danish and international specialties.

SCANDIC HOTEL OLYMPIC, Strandbygade 3, DK-6700 Esbjerg. Tel. 75-18-11-88. Fax 75-18-11-08. 87 rms (all with bath). MINIBAR TV TEL **Bus:** 1, 11, 12.

$ Rates (including breakfast): 695 kroner ($120.20) single or double. AE, DC, MC, V. **Parking:** Free.

On a tree-lined street in the center of town, this impressively bulky hotel is a member of a Scandinavian chain. You don't get surprises in decor or amenities, but you get dependable comfort in its well-furnished bedrooms. Each has comfortable modern furniture and a number of amenities. Facilities include a sauna, solarium, ample parking, and some shops and kiosks.

WHERE TO DINE
EXPENSIVE

RESTAURANT PAKHUSET, Dokvej 3. Tel. 75-12-74-55.
Cuisine: DANISH. **Reservations:** Recommended. **Bus:** 5.
$ Prices: 5-course fixed-price dinner 310 kroner ($53.60); appetizers 65–98 kroner ($11.20–$17); main dishes 140–205 kroner ($24.20–$35.50). DC, MC, V.
Open: Lunch Mon–Fri noon–3pm; dinner Mon–Fri 5–10pm.

The red-brick building was built in 1902 as an auction hall for the tons of fish hauled from nearby waterways. Set a few paces from the ferryboats that depart for Fanø, the building (whose name translates as "warehouse") now functions as a restaurant and art gallery. Within a heavily trussed and beamed interior similar to that of a high-ceilinged chapel, oil paintings by Danish artists are displayed and often purchased by diners. Food items are modernized versions of traditional Danish favorites, with light-textured preparations of fresh fish and vegetables.

4. FANØ

Sønderho: 10 miles W of Esbjerg,
Nordby: 1 mile W of Esbjerg, 176 miles W of Copenhagen

GETTING THERE   By Car   At Esbjerg you can board a ferry (see below) for the trip to Fanø, which has one main road, stretching from Nordby in the north to Sønderho in the south.

By Ferry   Ferries depart from the harbor of Esbjerg in West Jutland for the island in winter. The price of a one-way ticket is 18 kroner ($3.10) for adults and 10 kroner ($1.70) for children. For more information, call DSB at 75-12-00-00.

A 20-minute ferry ride from Esbjerg will take you to **Nordby,** a logical starting point for an exploration of Fanø, where you'll find heather-covered moors, windswept sand dunes, fir trees, wild deer, and bird sanctuaries. From Ribe, Fanø makes for a great day's excursion (or longer if there's time).

Fanø is a popular summer resort among the Danes, Germans, and English. **Sønderho,** on the southern tip, with its memorial to sailors drowned at sea, is my favorite spot—somewhat desolate, but that's its charm.

WHAT TO SEE & DO

A summer highlight on Fanø is the **Fannikerdagene** festival, the first weekend in July, which offers traditional dancing, costumes, and events connected with the days when sailing ships played a major part in community life.

If you miss the festival, try to be on Fanø the third Sunday in July for **Sønderho Day.** High point of the festive day is a wedding procession that passes through the town to the square by the old mill. Traditional costumes and bridal dances are some of the attractions.

WHERE TO STAY & DINE
INEXPENSIVE

FANØ KROGAARD, Langelinie 11, Nordby, DK-6720 Fanø. Tel. 75-16-20-52. Fax 75-16-23-00. 12 rms (8 with bath). TV
$ Rates (including breakfast): 300 kroner ($51.90) single without bath, 450 kroner ($77.90) single with bath; 450 kroner ($77.90) double without bath, 600 kroner ($103.80) double with bath. DC, MC, V. **Parking:** Free.

S This old-fashioned inn, originally constructed in 1624, has been welcoming wayfarers ever since. Located 100 yards from the ferry dock, rooms are simple but cozy, comfortable, and nautical. Rooms without bath lie in a century-old annex a short walk from the main building. The owner, Jorn Fischer, is also a fisherman, and specialties vary according to the catch of the day. Meals begin at 200 kroner ($34.60). In July and August service is daily from noon to 9:30pm. During the rest of the year, service is Sunday through Thursday from noon to 8:30pm and on Friday and Saturday from noon to 9:30pm. There is also a popular bar, open daily from 8am to midnight, and an outdoor terrace used in summer.

SØNDERHO KRO, Kropladsen 11, Sønderho, DK-6720 Fanø. Tel. 75-16-40-09. Fax 75-16-43-85. 8 rms (all with bath). TEL

$ Rates: 425–600 kroner ($73.50–$103.80) single; 540–890 kroner ($93.40–$154) double. Breakfast 60 kroner ($10.40) extra; half board 600 kroner ($103.80) per person. AE, DC, MC, V. **Parking:** Free.

A 1722 thatch-roofed, ivy-covered inn, this National Trust House nestled behind the sand dunes is an unbeatable choice. Each room has a distinctive character, yet all fit into the traditional atmosphere of the inn. Antiques add a touch. The first-floor lounge has views of the tidal flats, and the dining room is atmospheric as well. The cuisine is superb and plentiful, with meals beginning at 250 kroner ($43.30). Sønderho Kro is 8 miles south of the Nordby ferry dock; a bus connects with ferry arrivals.

5. ÅRHUS

43 miles S of Aalborg; 109 miles W of Copenhagen

GETTING THERE By Plane Both SAS and Danair fly from Copenhagen to Århus. Flights arrive daily from London, Oslo, and Malmö, Sweden. An airport bus runs directly from the airport to the Central Station in Århus.

By Train About 5 or 6 trains a day make the 5-hour trip from Århus to Copenhagen. Some 20 trains a day connect Aalborg with Århus, taking 1 hour 40 minutes. From Frederikshavn, the North Jutland port and ferry-arrival point from Norway, some 20 trains a day run to Århus, taking 3 hours.

By Bus Two buses daily make the 4-hour run to Århus from Copenhagen.

By Car From the east, cross Funen on the E20 express highway, heading north at the junction with E45. From the north German border, drive all the way along E45. From Frederikshavn and Aalborg in the north, head south along E45.

ESSENTIALS The tourist office, **Århus Turistforening,** is located in the Rådhuset, DK-8000 Århus C (tel. 86-12-16-00).

GETTING AROUND A **Tourist Ticket,** costing 35 kroner ($6.10), can be purchased at the Tourist Office or from a vending machine on the rear platform of the Central Bus Station (tel. 86-12-86-22)—bus drivers do not sell this ticket. The ticket, valid for 2 hours, is for an unlimited number of rides on all bus routes in Zones 1 to 4. The ticket is also good for a 2½–hour guided tour of Århus. Two children under 12 can travel on one Tourist Ticket.

Jutland's capital, the second-largest city in Denmark, Århus is a cultural center, a university town combined with a lively port. Aside from enjoying the city's many restaurants, hotels, and nighttime amusements, you can use Århus as a good base for excursions to Silkeborg, Ebeltoft, and the moated manors and castles to the north.

WHAT TO SEE & DO

For the best introduction to Århus, head for the town hall's tourist office, where a 2½-hour **sightseeing tour** leaves daily at 10am from June 25 to September 8, costing 25 kroner ($4.30) per person.

DEN GAMLE BY, Vesterbrogade. Tel. 86-12-31-88.

⭐ The top sight in Århus, Den Gamle By displays more than 70 buildings representing Danish urban life from the 16th to the mid-19th century, re-created in a botanical garden. This open-air museum is different from similar museums near Copenhagen and Odense, where the emphasis is on rural life. Visitors walk through the authentic-looking workshops of bookbinders, carpenters, hatters, and more. A popular attraction is the Burgomaster's House, a wealthy merchant's antique-stuffed, half-timbered home, built at the end of the 16th century. Make sure to see the Textile Collection and the Old Elsinore Theater, erected in the early 19th century. Inquire at the ticket office. Summer music programs are staged, and there's a restaurant and beer cellar.

Admission: 35 kroner ($6.10) adults; free for children under 16.
Open: May to mid-Oct, daily 9am–5pm; spring and fall, daily 11am–3pm; winter, daily 11am–1pm. **Bus:** 3, 5, 10, 14, 15, 16, 17.

CATHEDRAL OF ST. CLEMENS, Bispetorvet. Tel. 86-123-845.

This late Gothic red-brick, copper-roofed cathedral, crowned by a 315-foot spire, begun at the beginning of the 13th century and completed in the 15th, is the longest cathedral in Denmark, practically as deep as its spire is tall. Of chief interest here is the Renaissance pulpit, 15th-century triptych, and 18th-century pipe organ. (After the cathedral, I suggest a visit to the nearby medievalesque arcade at Vestergade 3, with half-timbered buildings, rock garden, aviary, and antique interiors.)

Admission: Free.
Open: May–Sept, Mon–Fri (if no ceremonies are being held) 9:30am–4pm; Oct–Apr, Mon–Fri 10am–3pm. **Bus:** 3, 11, 54, 56.

VIKINGEMUSEET, St. Clemens Torv 6. Tel. 86-27-24-33.

Down the steps to the left of the cathedral is a Viking Museum where the remains of the town's old Viking walls have been found. After seeing the museum, visitors are invited to enter the bank. There is always an admission-free exhibition of Danish artists in the basement next to the storage room.

Admission: Free.
Open: Mon–Wed and Fri 9:30am–4pm, Thurs 9:30am–6pm. **Bus:** 3, 11, 54, 56.

RÅDHUSET, Park Allé. Tel. 86-13-20-00.

A crowning architectural achievement in the center of Århus, the Rådhuset, or Town Hall, was built between 1936 and 1941 to commemorate the 500th anniversary of the Århus charter. Arne Jacobsen was one of the designers—and it's been the subject of controversy ever since. The modern marble-plated structure with lots of airy space and plenty of glass can be seen on a free guided tour. There's an elevator (or 346 steps) to the top of the 197-foot tower, where a carillon occasionally rings.

Admission: Free.
Open: June 20–Sept, Mon–Fri at noon and 2pm. **Bus:** 3, 4, 5, 14.

FORHISTORISK MUSEUM—MOESGÅRD, Moesgård Manor. Tel. 86-27-24-33.

The former Århus Museum is now an archeological and ethnographic museum in a country setting about 5 miles from town, at Moesgård Manor. It owns the incredibly well-preserved 2,000-year-old Grauballe man, who had lain since the Iron Age in a bog in central Jutland. Outside in the park and woods is an open-air museum that displays prehistoric reconstructions and a prehistoric "trackway."

Admission: 25 kroner ($4.30) adults, free for children under 15.
Open: Apr–Sept, daily 10am–5pm; Oct–Mar, Tues–Sun 10am–4pm. **Bus:** 6 from the railway station.

VOR FRUE KIRKE, Frue Kirkeplads. Tel. 86-12-12-43.

A 13th-century church, this was the former abbey church of the Dominican brothers (1240). Worth inspection is St. Nicholas Church under the chancel, the oldest stone church in Scandinavia, dating back to Viking days (1060). On Sunday there are services at 9 and 10am.

Admission: Free.
Open: May–Oct, Mon–Sat 9:30am–4pm; Nov–Apr, Mon–Sat 10am–3pm.
Bus: 7, 10, 17.

NEARBY ATTRACTIONS

LEGOLAND, Nordmarksvej, 7190 Billund. Tel. 75-33-13-33.
At this family amusement park, the main attraction is Miniland, a landscape built of approximately 33 million Lego bricks showing the world's famous landscapes and buildings in miniature. There is also a real Wild West town where you can see a copy of the rock-hewn portraits at Mount Rushmore, and a 45-foot monument of Sitting Bull. Visit the world-famous antique doll and dollhouse collection, mechanical toys, various educational exhibitions, and of course all the adult and kiddie rides. Other attractions include Titania's Palace, the largest and most expensive miniature palace in the world, and an antique collection of gadgets. To reach Legoland, head south from Århus along Route E45 toward Vejle. At Billund center, travel along Åstvej.
Admission: 45 kroner ($7.80) adults, 25 kroner ($4.30) children.
Open: May–Sept 15, daily 10am–8pm. **Closed:** Sept 16–Apr. **Bus:** 912.

JYSK AUTOMOBILMUSEUM (Jutland Car Museum), DK-8883 Gjern. Tel. 86-87-50-50.
Near Silkeborg at Gjern, this is the only automobile museum in Jutland, featuring 135 vintage automobiles dating from 1900 to 1948. Sixty-five different makes are represented, among them the V12-cylinder Auburn, V12-cylinder Cadillac, 1947 Crosley, the famous Renault Taxis de la Marne, Kissel, Hotchkiss, Jordan, Vivinus, Rolls-Royce, and Maserati. A number of motorcycles are also displayed.
Admission: 35 kroner ($6.10) adults, 15 kroner ($2.60) children.
Open: Apr, Sat–Sun 10am–5pm; May–Sept 15, daily 10am–6pm; Sept 16–Nov 1, Sat–Sun 10am–5pm. **Closed:** Nov 2–Mar. **Bus:** Silkeborg-Gjern.

ØM KLOSTER MUSEUM, Munnkevej 8, Emborg near Gamle Ry, DK-8660 Skanderborg. Tel. 86-89-81-94.
At Emborg, on the north bank of a lake, are the ruins of a Cistercian monastery dating from 1172. Skeletons from the monastery hospital are displayed for those inclined to view them. Besides the church site and monks' graves there is a medicinal herb garden.
Admission: 20 kroner ($3.50) adults, 8 kroner ($1.40) children.
Open: May–Aug, Tues–Sun 9am–6pm; Apr and Sept, Tues–Sun 9am–5pm; Oct 1–21, Tues–Sun 9am–4pm. **Closed:** Late Oct–Mar. **Bus:** 15, 59, 94, 95.

WHERE TO STAY

Low-cost accommodations in this lively university city are limited. Those on strict budgets should go to the tourist office in the Århus Town Hall (tel. 86-12-16-00) for bookings in **private homes.** Office hours, mid-June to mid-August, are daily from 9am to 8pm; mid-August to mid-September daily from 9am to 7pm; from mid-September to mid-June, Monday through Friday from 9:30am to 4:30pm and on Saturday from 10am to 1pm.

EXPENSIVE

ATLANTIC HOTEL, Europaplads 12-14, DK-8000 Århus C. Tel. 86-13-11-11. Fax 86-13-23-43. 107 rms (all with bath). MINIBAR TV TEL **Bus:** 6.
$ Rates (including breakfast): 790–890 kroner ($136.70–$154) single; 1,035–1,190 kroner ($179.10–$205.90) double. AE, DC, MC, V.
A favorite of commercial travelers, the Atlantic has comfortably streamlined bedrooms, each with a balcony. There is also an attractively decorated restaurant, plus a Scottish-style pub. Danish and international dishes are served.

HOTEL ROYAL, Stove Torv 4, DK-8000 Århus C. Tel. 86-12-00-11. Fax 86-76-04-04. 106 rms (all with bath), 7 suites. MINIBAR TV TEL **Bus:** 56, 58.
$ Rates (including breakfast): Winter, 850–1,250 kroner ($147.10–$216.30) sin-

gle; 1,050–1,600 kroner ($181.70–$276.80) double; from 1,800 kroner ($311.40) suite. Summer, 550–950 kroner ($95.20–$164.40) single; 700–1,200 kroner ($121.10–$207.60) double; from 1,400 kroner ($242.20) suite. AE, DC, MC, V. **Parking:** 10 kroner ($1.70) per hour.

⭐ This is the most glamorous place to stay in town. The date established in gilt letters on its neobaroque facade commemorates the hotel's establishment in 1838. There have been numerous additions and upgradings since. The Royal stands close to the city's symbol, its cathedral. After you've registered, a vintage elevator will take you to one of the bedrooms, many quite spacious. You can enjoy Danish meals in the mezzanine-level greenhouse restaurant, the Queen's Garden.

INEXPENSIVE

ERIKSEN'S HOTEL, Banegårdsgade 6-8, DK-8000 Århus C. Tel. 86-13-62-96. Fax 86-13-76-76. 18 rms (none with bath). **Bus:** 16, 17.

$ **Rates:** 230–235 kroner ($39.80–$40.70) single; 400–410 kroner ($69.20–$70.90) double. Breakfast 30 kroner ($5.20) extra. MC, V.

Ⓢ This hotel is the best bargain in the vicinity of the rail station. More rooming house than hotel, Eriksen's is utilitarian, clean, and recently modernized. Showers are just outside the rooms. In addition to breakfast, the hotel also serves a quick lunch and is licensed for beer.

MISSIONSHOTELLET ANSGAR, Banegårdsplads 14, DK-8100 Århus C. Tel. 86-12-41-22. Fax 86-20-29-04. 169 rms (153 with bath). TEL **Bus:** 3, 17, 56, 58.

$ **Rates** (including breakfast): Old wing, 275 kroner ($47.60) single without bath; 515 kroner ($89.10) double without bath. New wing, 500 kroner ($86.50) single with bath; 750 kroner ($129.80) double with bath. DC, MC, V.

A dignified and traditional hotel, convenient to the Town Hall, it offers a full range of rooms in different price ranges. Bedrooms are all tastefully decorated, many with modern furnishings. There's plenty of lounging room, and the food and service in the dining room are fine.

PARK HOTEL, Sonder Allé 3, DK-8000 Århus C. Tel. 86-12-32-31. 14 rms (none with bath). **Bus:** 3, 4, 5, 14.

$ **Rates:** 225–235 kroner ($38.90–$40.70) single; 330–375 kroner ($57.10–$64.90) double. Breakfast 40 kroner ($6.90) extra. DC, MC, V. **Parking:** free.

On two floors of a 1930s apartment building, the Park has an upper-story reception area located in a sunny pair of comfortably old-fashioned rooms with a corner bar. Rooms are clean and bright, with built-in light-grained furniture and big windows. The hotel, open all year, is near a busy commercial street on a corner at Town Hall Square.

WHERE TO DINE

VERY EXPENSIVE

GAMMEL ÅBYHOJ, Bakkeallé 1, Åbyhoj. Tel. 86-15-77-33.
   Cuisine: FRENCH. **Reservations:** Required. **Bus:** 5, 10, 16, 94, 17.

$ **Prices:** Fixed-price meals 425 kroner ($73.50) at dinner, 300 kroner ($51.90) at lunch; appetizers 95–210 kroner ($16.40–$36.30); main dishes 175–280 kroner ($30.30–$48.40). AE, DC, MC, V.
   Open: Mon–Sat 11:30am–midnight.

⭐ One of the few Relais & Châteaux in Denmark, the ritzy Gammel Åbyhoj lies in an affluent suburb about a mile west of the town center. The building dates from 1909 when it was a private residence for a city railway tycoon. Since 1989 it has been run by the French-born chef, Michel Michaud. First enjoy a drink in the lounge, where the built-in furniture carries a hint of art deco styling. Cold-weather fires illuminate the hardwood and French chairs in the twin dining rooms. There's even a walnut-shaded courtyard and arbor-covered solarium for warm-weather dining.

The limited menu is based on fresh ingredients. Typical dishes might include veal filet with braised endive, terrine of foie gras, and a succulent version of tournedos, along with such rich desserts as a chocolate marquise with a kiwi-cream sauce.

RESTAURANT DE 4 ARSTIDER (The Four Seasons), Aboulevarden 47. Tel. 86-19-96-96.
Cuisine: FRENCH. **Reservations:** Required. **Bus:** 1, 2, 3, 6, 9, 16.
$ Prices: Fixed-price meals 225 kroner ($38.90) for a 4-course vegetarian meal, 350 kroner ($60.60) for a 4-course dinner, 425 kroner ($73.50) for a 6-course "surprise" meal; appetizers 78–98 kroner ($13.50–$17); main dishes 188–198 kroner ($32.50–$34.30). AE, DC, MC, V.
Open: Lunch Mon–Sat noon–2:30pm; dinner Mon–Sat 6–10:30pm. **Closed:** July.

⭐ Easily the most charming restaurant in the city center, lying beside the Århus Canal, the property is co-owned by maître d' and artist Ulrik Witt, whose whimsical abstract paintings line paneled walls. His co-owner, Jonna Hald, is probably the best-known female chef in Denmark. Some of the carefully presented specialties include fresh asparagus with foie gras and butter sauce, filet of red snapper with pink peppercorns, lobster with tomato sauce, and succulent preparations of lamb and veal. In the autumn, you can enjoy game dishes. You can order an apéritif in the lounge amid 19th-century antique chests and comfortable settees.

EXPENSIVE

RESTAURANT MAHLER, Vestergade 39. Tel. 86-19-06-96.
Cuisine: DANISH/FRENCH. **Reservations:** Required. **Bus:** 7, 10, 17.
$ Prices: 3-course fixed-price dinner 250 kroner ($43.30); appetizers 65–110 kroner ($11.20–$19); main dishes 165–195 kroner ($28.50–$33.70). DC, MC, V.
Open: Dinner Tues–Sat 6pm–midnight. **Closed:** 3 weeks in July.
This pleasant restaurant in the center of town offers a different menu every 2 weeks. You might find sweetbreads, filet mignon, filet of veal with tomato sauce, quenelles of pike perch in saffron sauce, or partridge with cranberries and stuffed cabbage. On Friday and Saturday nights the chef turns to a particular region of Europe, usually France, and prepares the specialties of that area, perhaps Alsace or the Loire Valley.

INEXPENSIVE

DEN GREMME AELLENG (The Ugly Duckling), Østergade 12. Tel. 86-13-99-63.
Cuisine: DANISH BUFFETS. **Reservations:** Not required. **Bus:** 2, 6, 17.
$ Prices: All-you-can-eat lunch or evening buffet 100 kroner ($17.30). AE, DC, MC, V.
Open: Lunch daily noon–2:30pm; dinner daily 5:30–10:30pm.
This cost-conscious member of a chain whose restaurants are scattered throughout Denmark offers a self-service Danish buffet. At lunchtime, dishes include at least 10 different preparations of herring, Nordic meatballs, and an amply varied salad bar. In the late afternoon, a different array is laid out. These usually include such hot dishes as casseroles, meats, and vegetables, plus Danish cheeses and a salad bar.

GULDHORNET, Banegårdsplads 10. Tel. 86-12-02-62.
Cuisine: DANISH/FRENCH. **Reservations:** Recommended. **Bus:** 3, 17, 56, 58.
$ Prices: 3-course fixed-price lunch or dinner 110–150 kroner ($19–$26); appetizers 35–60 kroner ($6.05–$10.40); main dishes 78–158 kroner ($13.50–$27.30). DC, MC, V.
Open: Daily 10am–11pm.

🆂 Immediately opposite as you exit the Århus Railroad Station stands Guldhornet, warm and cozy, with hanging lamps and brightly colored tables. The restaurant, whose name translates as "The Golden Horn," has been feeding hungry locals since 1937, and is today filled with a warm, modern decor, with lots of plants and paintings. The fixed-price meal is a good value, including marinated salmon, beefsteak, salad bar, and ice cream. A Danish specialty worth trying is Gulhornet Sorte Grude, a stew bowl filled with succulent chunks of pork and turkey with onions and mushrooms and usually served with rice.

TEATER BODEGA, Skolegade 7. Tel. 86-12-19-17.
 Cuisine: DANISH. **Reservations:** Recommended. **Bus:** 6.
$ **Prices:** Appetizers 30–55 kroner ($5.20–$9.50); main dishes 68–155 kroner ($11.80–$26.80); lunchtime smørrebrød 25–60 kroner ($4.30–$10.40). DC, MC, V.
 Open: Mon–Sat 11am–11:30pm.

Originally established at a different address in 1907, Teater Bodega in 1951 moved across the street from both the Århus Dramatic Theater and the Århus Cathedral. It tries to provide an amusing dining ambience for theater and art lovers. The walls are covered with illustrations of theatrical costumes along with other thespian memorabilia. The food is solid and flavorful in the Danish country style. Various kinds of Danish hash, including biksemad, are served along with regular or large portions of Danish roast beef. There's also English and French beef, fried plaice, and flounder.

BUDGET

MUNKESTUEN, Klostertorvet 5. Tel. 86-12-95-67.
 Cuisine: DANISH/INTERNATIONAL. **Reservations:** Not accepted. **Bus:** 1, 2, 6, 9.
$ **Prices:** Appetizers 24 kroner ($4.20); main dishes 40–95 kroner ($6.90–$16.40). No credit cards.
 Open: Daily 11am–midnight.

You almost invariably stumble upon this charming old place if you're out sightseeing. This small and cozy inn with a courtyard is in the old Klostertorv across from Frue Kloster Abbey. Dishes depend on seasonal fresh produce. The owner, Lise Poulsen, says she gets inspiration from the culinary traditions of the world, but still cooks everything "the Danish way."

EVENING ENTERTAINMENT

MUSIKHUSET ÅRHUS, Thomas Jensens Allé. Tel. 86-13-43-44.
 Opened in 1982, this concert hall is the home of the Århus Symphony Orchestra, the Danish National Opera, and the Århus Festival. Events range from ballets to musicals to symphony concerts. Programs are presented on the great stage, the small stage, and the cabaret stage, as well as in the amphitheater and on the foyer stages where free performances are held year-round. The foyer, open daily from 9am to 11pm, is where the booking office, information desk, café/restaurant, and record and souvenir shops are located. For information, and to purchase tickets, ask in the foyer or at the tourist bureau. Bus: 16, 17.
 Admission: Foyer, free; performances, tickets 50–300 kroner ($8.70–$51.90).

TIVOLI-FRIHEDEN, Skovbrynet. Tel. 86-14-73-00.
 Århus's version of Copenhagen's Tivoli, Tivoli-Friheden has its own particular character. Located in a forest, it is bright and modern, almost like a nighttime fairyland. Entertainment includes an open-air theater, art shows, concerts, and clowns. It's open late April to mid-August, daily from 10am to 11pm. Bus: 4.
 Admission: 25 kroner ($4.30) adults, 15 kroner ($2.60) children.

6. SILKEBORG

27 miles W of Århus, 174 miles W of Copenhagen

GETTING THERE By Train Trains run frequently throughout the day between Århus and Silkeborg and between Copenhagen (via Fredericia) and Silkeborg.

By Bus Frequent buses run daily connecting Silkeborg with Århus.

By Car   From Århus, head west along Route 15.

ESSENTIALS   The tourist office, **Silkeborg Turistbureau,** located at Torvet 9, DK-8600 Silkeborg (tel. 86-82-19-11), is open Mon–Fri 9am–5pm, Sat 9am–noon.

The center of the Danish Lake District, it's definitely worth a 1-day jaunt west from Århus to visit the riverside town of Silkeborg. Lying in the midst of some of Denmark's most beautiful scenery, it's a great spot to explore **Himmelbjerget** (Sky Mountain), the highest peak in low-lying Denmark. But be warned: The "mountain" is less than 500 feet high and won't dazzle those who've just come from Norway.

WHAT TO SEE & DO

The most intriguing way to see Sky Mountain and the surrounding countryside is aboard the paddle steamer *Hjejle,* operating since 1861, and sailing frequently in summer. For schedules and information, call **Hjejle Co. Ltd.** (tel. 86-82-07-66).

SILKEBORG CULTURAL MUSEUM, Hovegardsvej 7. Tel. 86-82-14-99.
   This 18th-century manor by the Guden River, directly east of Torvet, houses the 2,200-year-old **Tollund Man,** discovered in a peat bog in 1950. His face is considered the most unspoiled of all man's early ancestors. The body was so well preserved, in fact, that scientists were able to determine the contents of his last supper: flax, barley, and oats. His head capped by fur, the Tollund Man was strangled by a plaited leather string—probably the victim of a ritual sacrifice. An equally well preserved body, known as the Elling Girl, was found near the same spot. Scientists estimate she was about 25 years old when she died in 210 B.C.
   The museum also has a special exhibition of old Danish glass, a clogmaker's workshop, a collection of stone implements, antique jewelry, and artifacts from the ruins of Silkeborg Castle.
   Admission: 20 kroner ($3.50) adults, 5 kroner (90¢) children.
   Open: Apr to mid-Oct, daily 10am–5pm; Oct to mid-Apr, Wed and Sat, Sun noon–4pm. **Bus:** 10.

SILKEBORG KUNSTMUSEUM, Gudenavej 7-9. Tel. 86-82-53-88.
   This museum offers unique exhibitions, including Asger Jorn's paintings and ceramics. The museum also displays paintings by members of the COBRA School (Copenhagen, Brussels, and Amsterdam, from where the artists originated). Much of their work was produced between 1948 and 1951. Special exhibitions are also staged.
   Admission: 20 kroner ($3.50) adults, free for children under 16.
   Open: Apr–Oct, Tues–Sun 10am–5pm; Nov–Mar, Tues–Fri noon–4pm, Sat–Sun 10am–4pm. **Bus:** 10.

NEARBY ATTRACTIONS

The **triangle tour** of three of East Jutland's most attractive manor houses is one of the greatest treasures on the Danish peninsula.

ROSENHOLM SLOT, DK-8543 Hornslet. Tel. 86-99-40-10.
   ★ On an islet 13 miles north of Århus and half a mile north of Hornslet, this moated Renaissance manor has been the home of the Rosenkrantzes for 4 centuries. The four-winged castle, encircled by about 35 acres of parkland, houses a Great Hall (its most important room), as well as a large collection of Flemish woven and gilded leather tapestries, old paintings, Spanish furniture, a vaulted gallery walk, and pigskin-bound folios.
   Admission: 40 kroner ($6.90) adults, 10 kroner ($1.70) children.
   Open: June 20–Aug 5, Mon–Fri 10am–5pm. **Closed:** Aug 6–June 19. **Bus:** 119, 121 from Århus's Central Bus Station.

CLAUSHOLM, Voldum, DK-8370 Hadsten. Tel. 86-49-10-40.
   Eight miles southeast of Randers and 19 miles north of Århus, 17th-century Clausholm is a splendid baroque palace—one of the earliest in Denmark. It was

commissioned by King Frederik IV's chancellor, whose teenage daughter, Anna Sophie, married the king. When Frederik died, his son by his first marriage banished the queen to Clausholm, where she lived with her own court until her death in 1743.

The rooms of the castle are basically unaltered since Anna Sophie's day, but few of the original furnishings remain. The salons and ballroom feature elaborate stucco ceilings and decorated panels, and there is an excellent collection of Danish rococo and Empire furnishings that have replaced the original pieces. The Queen's Chapel, where Anna Sophie and her court worshiped, is unchanged and contains the oldest organ in Denmark. In 1976 the Italian baroque gardens were reopened, complete with a symmetrically designed fountain system.

With sufficient notice, arrangement can be made for a special tour of the castle conducted by one of the owners.

Admission (including guided tour): 25 kroner ($4.30) adults, 5 kroner (90¢) children.

Open: June–Aug 15, daily 11am–5pm; May and Aug 16–31, 2–5pm, Sun 11am–5pm. **Bus:** 221 from Randers.

GAMMEL ESTRUP, Jyllands Herregårdsmuseum, Randersvej 2-4, DK-8983 Auning.

This Renaissance manor was owned by two families for six centuries, but today it houses the **Jutland Manor House Museum** (tel. 86-48-30-01) in the main building and the **Danish Agricultural Museum** (tel. 86-48-34-44) in the earlier out buildings. Built on medieval fortified grounds, the origins of Gammel Estrup go back to the 14th century, with major rebuilding of the present structure in the early 1600s. The Manor House Museum, with Great Hall, chapel, and many other rooms, is richly decorated with stucco ceilings, tapestries, and paintings from the 17th and 18th centuries. The Agricultural Museum has tools and machines used over several centuries and a special exhibition showing "the year of the farmer."

Admission: For each museum, 20 kroner ($3.50) adults, 5 kroner (90¢) children.

Open: Jutland Manor House, Apr–Sept, daily 10am–5pm; Oct–Mar, Tues–Sun 11am–3pm; Agricultural Museum, daily 10am–5pm. **Directions:** From Silkeborg, take Route 46 northeast to Randers; from there, Route 16 east to Auning. **Bus:** 214.

WHERE TO STAY

The **Silkeborg Turistbureau,** at Torvet 9 (tel. 86-82-19-11), can book you into nearby **private homes.**

MODERATE

HOTEL IMPALA, Vestre Ringvej 53, DK-8600 Silkeborg. Tel. 86-82-03-00. Fax 86-81-40-66. 60 rms (all with bath). MINIBAR TV TEL

$ Rates: 610–650 kroner ($105.50–$112.50) single; 910–970 kroner ($157.40–$167.80) double. AE, DC, MC, V.

One of the best hotels in the area, the Impala has streamlined rooms with angular Danish-modern furniture and private balconies. Outside, gardens slope past an artificial pond to the highway. Its rustic core was built as a farmhouse in 1890, and several modern chalet extensions were added in 1975 when it became a hotel. It's located west of Langsø Lake.

Lunch and dinner are served daily in the upstairs dining room to drop-ins as well as to hotel guests. Specialties include braised halibut with spinach and saffron, lemon sole and freshwater crayfish à la nage, and breast of duck with cherry sauce. A full list of European wines is available. Full meals cost from 250 kroner ($43.30).

INEXPENSIVE

HOTEL DANIA, Torvet 5, DK-8600 Silkeborg. Tel. 86-82-01-11. Fax 86-80-20-04. 47 rms (all with bath). TV TEL **Bus:** 3.

$ Rates (including breakfast): 560–600 kroner ($96.90–$103.80) single; 695–750 kroner ($120.20–$129.80) double. AE, DC, MC, V. **Parking:** Free.

Right on the marketplace and 5 minutes from the railroad station, the Dania has been a tradition since 1848. While antiques fill the corridors and reception lounge, the rooms have been completely renovated in a functional, modern style. Outdoor dining on the square is popular in summer, and the hotel has the longest outdoor restaurant in Denmark, serving typical Danish food along with Scandinavian and French dishes. On Thursday, Friday, and Saturday nights, a bar with disco dancing is popular, and there is live entertainment on Friday and Saturday.

SCANDIC HOTEL SILKEBORG, Udgårdsvej 2, DK-8600 Silkeborg. Tel. 86-80-35-33. Fax 86-80-35-06. 17 rms (all with bath), 3 suites. A/C MINIBAR TV TEL **Bus:** 3 from the railroad station.

$ **Rates** (including breakfast): 495–745 kroner ($85.60–$128.90) single or double; from 1,400 kroner ($242.20) suite. AE, DC, MC, V. **Closed:** Dec 21–Jan 5.

This is the newest (1990) and largest hotel in Silkeborg, 1½ miles from the town center in a residential neighborhood surrounded by fields and forests. Each room is well furnished and decorated in strong violets, reds, and blues. On the premises are two restaurants, an indoor pool, a sauna, health club, and solarium. The most glamorous restaurant, Guldenanden (Golden Duck), is open for lunch and dinner daily, with full meals costing 190 kroner to 275 kroner ($32.90 to $47.60).

SVOSTRUP KRO, Svostrupvej 60, Svostrup, DK-8600 Silkeborg. Tel. 86-87-70-04. 14 rms (4 with bath). **Bus:** 313 from Silkeborg.

$ **Rates:** 260 kroner ($45) single without bath, 480 kroner ($83) single with bath; 380 kroner ($65.70) double without bath, 540 kroner ($93.40) double with bath. Breakfast 40 kroner ($6.90) extra. DC, MC, V. **Parking:** Free.

In the center of Svostrup, 6 miles north of Silkeborg, this stylish hotel is a former bargeman's inn built in 1832. Situated on farmland between the Gruden River and the Gjern Hills, rooms are comfortable. The inn also has a good restaurant, open daily from 7am to midnight, with meals beginning at 160 kroner ($27.70). The kitchen specializes in fish, including many different preparations of salmon, and also prepares excellent steaks and chateaubriand.

NEARBY ACCOMMODATIONS

RY

Inexpensive

GAMMEL RYE KRO, Ryesgade 8, Gammel Ry, DK-8680 Ry. Tel. 86-89-80-42. Fax 86-89-85-46. 15 rms (all with bath). TV **Bus:** 311 from Århus.

$ **Rates** (including breakfast): 425 kroner ($73.50) single; 680 kroner ($117.60) double. DC, MC, V. **Parking:** Free.

This historic inn near the main square of Old (Gammel) Ry is typical of the dozens of unpretentious, simply furnished, but modernized inns of the Jutland countryside. The place looks like a large white farmhouse, set 200 yards north of the village church and the town market square. Its history goes back 400 years to other inns set on the same spot, although Gammel Rye Kro is about 150 years old.

The restaurant offers two-course fixed-price lunches or dinners for 90 kroner ($15.60). Food is served daily from 7am to 11pm. Dishes include such typical Danish specialties as fish filet with béarnaise sauce, local beef with onion, fried eel, and an old-fashioned hash, biksemad.

ANS

Inexpensive

KONGENSBRO KRO, Gamle Kongevej 70, DK-8643 Ans. Tel. 86-87-92-17. 15 rms (all with bath), 2 suites. TEL

$ **Rates** (including breakfast): 550–695 kroner ($95.20–$120.20) single or double; from 750 kroner ($129.80) suite. AE, DC, MC, V. **Closed:** Dec 23–24 and Dec 31–Jan 5. **Parking:** Free.

This charming place lies between Ans and Århus, about a 10-mile drive north of Silkeborg. Accommodations are pleasantly cozy, and some rooms have TVs. Since

1949 it has been the property of the Andersens, a family of well-known chefs (matriarch Else is the author of five cookbooks). Meals are served daily from noon to 3pm and 6 to 9pm. A midday two-course meal begins at 95 kroner ($16.40). Specialties include frikadeller with red cabbage, quail with a port wine sauce, and locally caught trout in puff pastry with dill sauce.

7. EBELTOFT

33 miles NE of Århus, 209 miles W of Copenhagen

GETTING THERE   By Train   Go as far as Århus by train, connecting to Copenhagen via Fredericia. At Århus Central Station, board bus no. 123 for Ebeltoft.

By Bus   Bus no. 123 runs from Århus to Ebeltoft and Randers.

By Car   Take Route 15 northeast from Århus, cutting south onto Route 21.

ESSENTIALS   The **Ebeltoft Turistbureau,** at Torvet 9-11 (tel. 86-34-14-00), is open Mon–Fri 9am–5pm, Sat 10am–1pm.

A well-preserved town of half-timbered buildings, Ebeltoft ("apple orchard" in English) is the capital of the Mols hill country. This is a village of cobblestone streets, hidden-away lanes, old inns, and ruddy-faced fishermen who still carry on the profession of their ancestors.

WHAT TO SEE & DO

FRIGATE *JYLLAND*, Strandvejen 4. Tel. 86-34-10-99.
   The *Jylland,* dating from 1860, is the oldest man-of-war in Denmark and the world's longest wooden ship. The frigate is moored in the harbor.
   Admission: 20 kroner ($3.50) adults, 5 kroner (90¢) children.
   Open: Apr–Sept, daily 10am–5pm. **Closed:** Oct–Mar.

DET GAMLE RÅDHUS, Torvet. Tel. 86-34-13-82.
   The Town Hall looks as if it had been erected just for kindergarten children to play in—don't miss this 1789 building, a museum housing an ethnographical collection from Thailand and an old post office. It's located in the town center north of Strandvejen.
   Admission: 10 kroner ($1.70) adults, 5 kroner (90¢) children.
   Open: June–Aug, Tues–Sun 10am–5pm; Sept–May, Tues–Sun 11am–3pm.

FARVERGÅRDEN, Adelgade 13-15. Tel. 86-34-13-82.
   Dating from 1772, the oldest part of this dyeworks is from 1683. Exhibits include the living quarters with original furniture, the dye facilities with a pressing room, a dye room with boilers, a printing room, and a stable wing with a coach house dating from the early 18th century. It's located directly west of Torvet in the town center.
   Admission: 10 kroner ($1.70) adults, 5 kroner (90¢) children.
   Open: Mid-May to late May and the first 2 weeks in Sept, daily 11am–3pm; June and Aug, daily 10am–4pm; July, daily 10am–5pm; off-season, by special arrangement only.

WHERE TO STAY & DINE

MODERATE

HOTEL EBELTOFFT STRAND, Nordre Strandvej 3, DK-8400 Ebeltoft.
   Tel. 86-34-33-00. Fax 86-34-46-36. 68 rms (all with bath). MINIBAR TV TEL
   Bus: 123 from Århus.

$ Rates (including breakfast): 600–800 kroner ($103.80–$138.40) single; 890–1,190 kroner ($154–$205.90) double. AE, DC, MC, V. **Parking:** free.

Centrally located, this comfortable late-1970s hostelry has rooms overlooking Ebeltoft Bay. All rooms have balconies or terraces. Facilities include tennis courts, horseback riding, an indoor swimming pool, and a sauna. The hotel also has a restaurant, bar, open fireplace, and playground. The location is a 5-minute drive to the ferry and 15 minutes to Tirstrup Airport.

INEXPENSIVE

EBELTOFT PARKHOTEL, Vibaek Strandvej 4, DK-8400 Ebeltoft. Tel. 86-34-32-22. Fax 86-34-49-41. 70 rms (all with bath). TEL **Bus:** 123 from Århus.

$ Rates (including breakfast): 500–600 kroner ($86.50–$103.80) single; 700–800 kroner ($121.10–$138.40) double. AE, DC, MC, V. **Parking:** Free.

The Ebeltoft, a hotel built in the 1960s and modernized since then, is about 1,000 feet from a fine, sandy beach, and a brisk 20-minute walk from the Old Town. All rooms have radios and most have TVs. For recreation, use the sauna, swimming pool, and bicycle trainers, or play table tennis and billiards. The hotel has both a bar and a restaurant. As you enter Ebeltoft, the hotel is on the left side at the town entrance.

HOTEL HVIDE HUS, Strandgårdshøj 1, DK-8400 Ebeltoft. Tel. 86-34-14-66. Fax 86-34-49-69. 100 rms (all with bath), 4 junior suites. MINIBAR TV TEL **Bus:** 123 from Århus.

$ Rates (including breakfast): 640 kroner ($110.70) single; 840 kroner ($145.30) double; from 1,050 kroner ($181.70) suite. AE, DC, MC, V. **Parking:** 50 kroner ($8.70). **Closed:** Dec 25–Jan 1.

An elegant establishment built in 1963, the Hvide Hus provides comfortable and well-furnished rooms with terraces, radios, and refrigerators. Recreational facilities include an exercise room, sauna, solarium, swimming pool, and golf course. A nightclub, Molbostuen, is on the premises, as is a restaurant open until midnight.

MOLS KROEN, Hovegaden 16, Femmoller Strand, DK-8400 Ebeltoft. Tel. 86-36-22-00. Fax 86-36-23-00. 25 rms (17 with bath). **Bus:** 123 from Århus.

$ Rates (including breakfast): 260 kroner ($45) single without bath, 390 kroner ($67.50) single with bath; 385 kroner ($66.60) double without bath, 720 kroner ($124.60) double with bath. AE, DC, MC, V. **Parking:** Free. **Closed:** Dec 24–Jan 8.

Combining 1920s nostalgia with modernity, the attractive rooms here have half-canopied beds and some open onto terraces that overlook the Mols Hills. A fine white beach is just 350 feet away.

The hotel restaurant ranks as one of the finest in the area. The staff takes time to present the food with some flourish, and the quality is first class. On a special weekend arrangement, you get 5 o'clock tea, a three-course dinner, a dance, a bed for the night, and a brunch the following morning—all for 450 kroner ($77.90) per person.

---

8. RANDERS

23 miles N of Århus, 200 miles W of Copenhagen

GETTING THERE   By Train   Trains run hourly between Copenhagen and Randers. There are rail links with Aalborg and Århus.

By Bus   There is frequent bus service (no. 118) between Århus and Randers. It takes only 50 minutes to reach Randers from Århus. Bus tickets can be purchased once you board.

By Car   Head north from Århus along the E45.

ESSENTIALS   The **Randers Tourist Office** (Helligåndshuset), at Erik Menveds

Plads 1 (tel. 86-42-44-77), is open Mon–Fri 9am–5pm, Sat 9am–1pm.

The sixth-largest town in Denmark, with 60,000 inhabitants, Randers was founded at the point where Denmark's longest river, the Gudenå, becomes a natural fjord for the traffic between the northern and southern parts of Denmark.

WHAT TO SEE & DO

As you stroll through the medieval streets and lanes of Randers, you'll see several beautiful, well-preserved half-timbered houses from the 16th and 17th centuries that were originally built by prosperous merchants.

The tourist office, on Erik Menveds Plads, lies in one of the town's most famous buildings, **Helligåndshuset,** or the House of the Holy Ghost. Constructed around 1500 by monks, it was a home for the aged until the Reformation in 1536.

Armed with a map from the tourist office, walk from here along Denmark's first pedestrian street, **Houmeden,** inaugurated in 1963. The half-timbered houses on the north side of the street date from around 1560. You come out at **Town Hall Square,** center of Randers. On the western side of the square is the oldest stone house in Randers, dating from 1468. Town Hall, on the east side of the square, was built in 1778.

Heading east behind Town Hall, continue down Rosengade and Nygade. On the corner is **Fideikommishuset,** constructed in 1833 by Joseph Carl Wulff, a prominent Jew. This was a large Jewish quarter until the 19th century. Nygade 4 is the oldest half-timbered house in Randers, from 1550.

Turn right onto Østervold, which more or less follows the line of the old moat that used to exist in Randers running along the ramparts. At the northern end, Nørrestraede climbs to the town's courthouse and prison. On the corner of Nørrestraede and Østervold is one of the oldest school buildings in Randers, from 1861.

For a final look, visit **St. Mortens Church,** along Kirkegade. Built as the church for the Holy Ghost monastery around 1500, it is considered one of Denmark's most attractive town churches. Note the beautifully carved doors to the main entrance.

If time allows, visit the city's numerous green areas and parks for peaceful walks or jogging. In particular, the **Gudenå Valley** is idyllic.

WHERE TO STAY

INEXPENSIVE

HOTEL RANDERS, Torvegade 11, DK-8900 Randers. Tel. 86-42-34-22.
Fax 86-40-15-86. 60 rms (all with bath), 6 suites. TV TEL **Bus:** 2, 10, 11.
$ Rates (including breakfast): 385–650 kroner ($66.60–$112.50) single; 650–850 kroner ($112.50–$147.10) double; from 1,150 kroner ($199) suite. AE, DC, MC, V. **Parking:** 15 kroner ($2.60). **Closed:** Dec 23–Jan 2.

Popular with American tourists, this beautiful, historic 1856 hotel has kept its original charm, combining elegant style and old Danish tradition. The rooms are tastefully furnished. There are two restaurants and a grill room, serving Danish and international food. The Maritim Bar is a charming rendezvous spot. Services include laundry and dry-cleaning and babysitting.

MISSIONHOTEL, Østervold 42, DK-8900 Randers. Tel. 86-43-77-88.
Fax 86-41-31-11. 20 rms (all with bath). TV TEL **Bus:** 2, 10, 11.
$ Rates (including breakfast): 300–345 kroner ($51.90–$59.70) single; 475–600 kroner ($82.20–$103.80) double. DC, MC, V. **Parking:** Free.
In the center of town, a 2-minute walk from the bus station, the shopping district, and the restaurants and sights of Randers, this completely renovated hotel offers bright, well-furnished bedrooms with private baths and views of the harbor. There is a cozy lounge.

WHERE TO DINE

INEXPENSIVE

HVIDSTEN KRO, Mariagevej 450, Hvidsten, DK-8981 Spentrup. Tel. 86-47-70-22.
   Cuisine: DANISH. **Reservations:** Required in summer. **Bus:** 235 from Randers.

$ Prices: Fixed-price menu 85–150 kroner ($14.70–$26); appetizers 40–60 kroner ($6.90–$10.40); main dishes 45–150 kroner ($7.80–$26). DC, MC, V.
   Open: Daily 11:30am–7:30pm. **Closed:** Mon Sept–May.

(S) A thatched farmhouse between Randers and Mariager, this establishment has doubled as a country inn since 1634, making it one of the oldest in Denmark.
   The furnishings at the five-room main inn, used only for dining, are memorable: copper, brass, ceramics, samovars, deeply recessed windows, old sea chests, and walls painted with primitive murals. Waitresses wear floor-length, cotton checked kitchen aprons.
   For a stopover or for a home-cooked, farm-style meal, Hvidsten Kro is unbeatable. One of the reasons for its fame is its five-course "Gudruns Recipe" meal, which costs only 160 kroner ($27.70). It's possible, too, to order only a half recipe—herring, bacon omelet, and the Dansk koldt bord—for 88 kroner ($15.20), a huge meal in itself.
   The bedrooms in the guesthouse out back are bright and clean, but small, containing hot and cold running water. Singles go for 130 kroner ($22.50); doubles are 230 kroner ($39.80).

---

9. MARIAGER

36 miles N of Århus, 213 miles W of Copenhagen

GETTING THERE   By Train   There is no direct train to Mariager. Trains run from Aalborg to Hobro, east of Mariager, every 30 minutes, and trains from Århus to Hobro run hourly. Take the bus from Hobro.

By Bus   Buses to Mariager run hourly from Hadsun, Hobro, or Randers. The ride from all three takes about half an hour.

By Car   Take the E45 north from Randers and head east at the junction of Route 555.

ESSENTIALS   The **Mariager Tourist Association,** located at Torvet 4, DK-9550 Mariager (tel. 98-54-13-77), is open Mon–Fri 9am–5pm, Sat 10am–2pm.

Aalborg-bound motorists with time should stop over at Mariager, "the city of the roses." In a charming setting overlooking Mariager Fjord, the town has quaint cobblestone streets and half-timbered, red-roofed buildings.

WHAT TO SEE & DO

Eight miles east of Hobro, at the western end of the Mariager Fjord, Mariager (Maria's Field) is the tiniest town in Denmark. It was only a little fishing hamlet with ferry service on the way between Randers and Aalborg before the founding of the Brigettine Abbey around 1410, after which it became an active commercial and trading center. Many buildings have been preserved from this era, among them the **abbey church,** which may be seen as you walk around the paved streets of the town.

An **18th-century merchant's house,** considered one of the most beautiful buildings in Mariager, houses a museum, art gallery, and parish community center. In the courtyard, there's a well-preserved long gallery.

WHERE TO STAY

If you can't find a hotel room, the Mariager Tourist Association will help book you in a private home or boardinghouse.

INEXPENSIVE

HOTEL POSTGÅRDEN, Torvet 6A, DK-9550 Mariager. Tel. 98-54-10-12.
   Fax 98-54-24-64. 14 rms (all with bath). TV TEL **Bus:** "Mariager" bus from Randers or Århus.
$ Rates (including breakfast): 395 kroner ($68.30) single; 580 kroner ($100.30) double. AE, DC, MC, V. **Parking:** Free.
If you're passing through Mariager, the road will take you right past the Hotel Postgården, which looks out onto the marketplace and the small Town Hall. Dating from 1710, this hotel was restored in 1982 and rents out lovely rooms. Locals meet for drinks at the popular hotel pub.

MOTEL LANDGANGEN, Oxendalen 1, DK-9550 Mariager. Tel. 98-54-11-22. 11 rms (7 with bath).
$ Rates (including breakfast): 250 kroner ($43.30) single without bath, 300 kroner ($51.90) single with bath; 360 kroner ($62.30) double without bath, 435 kroner ($75.30) double with bath. AE, DC, MC, V. **Parking:** Free.
Set beside the river a 5-minute walk north of the abbey church, the white exterior and simple architecture of this building dates from the late 1960s. Rooms are clean and neat, although relatively simple. The ones with private bath also have telephone and TV; the bathless ones do not. The place is even better known as a restaurant, which is open in summer, daily from noon to 9pm, and in winter, Wednesday through Monday from noon to 8pm. Its dining room features Danish specialties and cozy furniture with a view of the water. Full meals range from 160 kroner to 230 kroner ($27.70 to $39.80).

---

10. AALBORG (ÅLBORG)

69 miles N of Århus, 238 miles W of Copenhagen

GETTING THERE   By Plane   Aalborg airport, 3 miles from the city center, has many daily connections to Copenhagen.

By Train   Twenty trains a day connect Aalborg and Århus, taking 40 minutes. Some 25 connecting daily trains at Århus go to Copenhagen via Fredericia.

By Bus   Frequent buses run between Århus and Aalborg. The bus station in Aalborg is the transport center for all of northern Jutland, with buses fanning out in all directions. For all bus information in the area, call **Nordjyllands Trafikselskab** (tel. 98-12-96-12).

ESSENTIALS   The **Aalborg Tourist Bureau,** located at Østerågade 8, DK-9000 Aalborg (tel. 98-12-60-22), is open Mon–Fri 9am–5pm, Sat 9am–2pm.

The largest city of northern Jutland, Aalborg (Ålborg) has a worldwide reputation as a producer of aquavit. Although essentially a shipping town and commercial center, it makes a good base for sightseers, with its many hotels, attractions (a blend of old and new), its more than 200 restaurants, and its nightlife.

History is a living reality in Aalborg. The city was founded 1,000 years ago when the Viking fleets assembled in these parts before sailing on their predatory expeditions. The original atmosphere of Aalborg is preserved in its old streets and alleys. Near the Church of Our Lady are many beautifully restored and reconstructed houses, some of which date from the 16th century.

Denmark's largest forest, **Rold,** where robber-bandits once roamed as they did in Sherwood, is right outside town. Also, **Rebild National Park** is the site of the yearly American Fourth of July celebration.

Not far from Aalborg, on the west coast of northern Jutland, are some of the finest beaches in northern Europe, stretching from Slettestrand to Skagen. The beach-resort towns of **Blokhus** and **Løkken** are especially popular with Danes, Germans, and Swedes. Blokhus is about 18 miles from Aalborg.

WHAT TO SEE & DO

JENS BANG'S STONEHOUSE, Østerågade 9.

This six-floor mansion, built in 1624 in a glittering Renaissance style, once belonged to a wealthy merchant. The historic wine cellar, Duus Vinkjaelder (see "Where to Dine," below), is the meeting place of the Guild of Christian IV. On the ground floor is an old apothecary shop. The mansion itself is still privately owned and is not open to the public.
Bus: 3, 5, 10, 11.

BUDOLFI KIRKE, Algade. Tel. 98-13-49-28.

This elaborately decorated cathedral is dedicated to St. Botolph, patron saint of sailors. Inside the church, which dates from 1500, are unusual pews, paintings from the 16th to the 18th century, Renaissance pulpits, and a baroque font. The spire was built in the 1700s. A carillon sounds daily, every hour from 9am to 10pm.
Admission: Free.
Open: Mon–Fri 9am–3pm, Sat 9am–noon. **Bus:** 3, 5, 10, 11.

NORDJYLLANDS KUNSTMUSEUM (North Jutland Museum of Modern and Contemporary Art), Kong Christians Allé 50. Tel. 98-13-80-88.

The museum building is a prime example of modern Scandinavian architecture. Built from 1968 to 1972, it was designed by Elissa and Alvar Aalto and Jean-Jacques Baruel as a showplace for 20th-century Danish and international art, with changing exhibitions. There are galleries, sculpture gardens, two auditoriums, a children's museum, an outdoor amphitheater, and a restaurant, the Museumscafeen.
Admission: 20 kroner ($3.50) adults; free for students and children.
Open: Mid-May to mid-Sept, daily 10am–5pm; mid-Sept to mid-May, Tues–Sun 10am–5pm. **Bus:** 1, 4, 8, 10, 11.

AALBORG TOWER, Søndre Skovvej, at Skovbakken. Tel. 98-12-01-02.

From this tower rising 325 feet above sea level, there's a perfect view of the city and the fjord.
Admission: 10 kroner ($1.70) adults, 5 kroner (90¢) children.
Open: Apr 12–June 15 and Aug 16–Sept 1, daily 10am–5pm; June 16–Aug 15, daily 10am–7pm. **Closed:** Sept 2–Apr 11. **Bus:** 1, 4, 8.

AALBORG ZOOLOGISKE HAVE, Mølleparkvej 63. Tel. 98-13-07-33.

Mølleparken is a large park with a lookout where you can see most of Aalborg and the Isle of Egholm (look for Roda Reilinger's sculpture *Noah's Ark*). In the park is the second-largest zoo in Scandinavia, where animal specimens from all over the world wander freely in surroundings designed to duplicate an open African range. Apes and beasts of prey are kept under minimal restrictions. There is a good restaurant inside the zoo, and snack bars here and there.
Admission: 45 kroner ($7.80) adults, 15 kroner ($2.60) children 4–12.
Open: Mar–Nov, daily 9am–5pm. **Closed:** Dec–Feb. **Bus:** 1.

MONASTERY OF THE HOLY GHOST, C. W. Obels Plads.

This vine-covered monastery is the oldest social-welfare institution in Denmark, as well as the oldest building in Aalborg, dating back to 1431. The step-gabled monastery, in the heart of the shopping malls, is well preserved. See the refectory, the vaulted storage cellars and "prison," the whitewashed cloisters, and the chapter house with its 16th-century frescoes.

Admission: Guided tour, 20 kroner ($3.50) adults, 10 kroner ($1.70) children.
Open: Late June–mid-Aug, guided tour Mon–Fri 2pm; other dates see Aalborg Tourist Bureau.

A WATER-SPORTS PARK

WATERLAND, Vandmanden 5. Tel. 98-18-92-00.

Aalborg's 6,600-square-yard indoor water-sports park offers a 650-foot water chute, wave and bubble pools, grottoes, and waterfalls to swim under, plus tideways, fountains, sauna, sunlamps, and an exercise room. An open-air swimming pool heated in winter is connected by channels to an indoor pool, so you can swim outdoors year-round. There is also a cafeteria.

Admission: 60 kroner ($10.40) adults, 30 kroner ($5.20) children 4–12.
Open: Mon–Fri 10am–8pm, Sat–Sun 10am–7pm. **Bus:** 8, 10, 11.

AALBORG TOURS

From late June to mid-August you can take an English-language bus tour to see the sights of Greater Aalborg. The 2½-hour tour costs 20 kroner ($3.50) for adults and 10 kroner ($1.70) for children. Information and tickets are available at the Aalborg Tourist Bureau, Østerågade 8 (tel. 98-12-60-22).

Another possibility is an English-speaking taxi driver who will take you past the city highlights. The maximum number of passengers is four, and the tour lasts 1½ hours. The price for four people starts at 400 kroner ($69.20). For details, ask at the Aalborg Tourist Bureau.

NEARBY ATTRACTIONS

The remains of a Viking hamlet and the largest burial site from the Germanic Iron Age and Viking Age (more than 700 cremation graves, including about 150 ship settings) have been excavated at **Lindholm Høje,** near Nørresundby, north of Aalborg. Set in park surroundings, the excavations are open to the public year-round. Finds from the site are on view at the **Lindholm Høje Museet,** Vendilavej 11 (tel. 98-17-55-22). The museum is open daily June through August from 10am to 7pm. Admission is 20 kroner ($3.50) for adults, 10 kroner ($1.70) for children. Take a 10-minute bus ride (bus no. 6, which leaves every 10 minutes during the day) from the Aalborg town center; then it's a 10-minute walk.

A magnificent Renaissance castle dating from 1588, **Voergård Slot,** Flauenskjold (tel. 98-86-71-08), is filled with sculpture, Louis XVI furnishings, a banqueting hall, grand salon, and works by Goya and Rubens. Admission is 30 kroner ($5.20) for adults, 15 kroner ($2.60) for children. Take the E45 north from Aalborg, cutting east on Route 559 to Dronningland. Follow signs from there. It's open June to August, Monday through Saturday from 2 to 5pm and on Sunday and holidays from 10am to 5pm; Easter holidays, 10am to 5pm (Easter eve, 2 to 5pm).

Americans who are in Jutland on the Fourth of July should make a beeline to the **Rebild National Park,** 18 miles south of Aalborg. On these heather dunes, Danes, Danish-Americans, and Americans celebrate American Independence Day. The program often features opera singers, folk dancers, choirs, and glee clubs, together with well-known speakers. In the park is the **Lincoln Memorial Log Cabin and Immigrant Museum,** devoted to mementos of Danish immigration to the United States.

A 1-hour bus ride takes you to the resort town of **Blokhus** and the broad white beaches of the North Sea coast. Not far from here is a 124-acre amusement park, **Fårup Sommerland and Waterpark,** Pirupvejen, DK-9493 Saltum (tel. 98-88-16-00), which offers many possibilities of fun and relaxation for both children and adults.

The water park, largest of its kind in Denmark, has wild rivers, a speed slide, a surf hill, and water slides. Admission is 70 kroner ($12.10) for adults or children (children under 4, free). It's open mid-May to August, daily from 10am to 7pm. **Bus:** 200 from Aalborg.

WHERE TO STAY

EXPENSIVE

HOTEL HVIDE HUS, Vesterbro, DK-9000 Aalborg. Tel. 98-13-84-00. Fax 98-13-51-22. 200 rms (all with bath). TV TEL **Bus:** 1, 4, 8, 10, 11.

$ Prices (including breakfast): 910 kroner ($157.40) single; 1,130–1,300 kroner ($195.50–$224.90) double. AE, DC, MC, V. **Parking:** 50 kroner ($8.70).

This is a first-rate hotel that many international businesspeople are now using instead of the traditional Hotel Phoenix. Bedrooms are well furnished in a fresh Scandinavian-modern style. Many have private balconies with a view of Aalborg. On the 15th floor is a restaurant offering Danish and international specialties. Meals are attractively served and presented. Room service, laundry, and babysitting can be arranged, and the hotel also provides a sauna and a swimming pool.

MODERATE

LIMSFORDSHOTELLET, Ved Stranden 14-16, DK-9000 Aalborg. Tel. 98-16-43-33. Fax 98-16-17-47. 180 rms (all with bath), 5 suites. MINIBAR TV TEL **Bus:** 1, 4, 40, 46.

$ Rates (including breakfast): 715 kroner ($123.70) single; 900 kroner ($155.70) double; from 925 kroner ($160) suite. AE, DC, MC, V. **Parking:** Free. **Closed:** Dec 23–25.

With its daring design, this is the most avant-garde hotel in town. It's located near Jomfru Anegade, a street packed with bars and restaurants. In the center of town, within a 3-minute walk east of the cathedral, the hotel opens onto the famous Limsjorden Canal. The public rooms are sparsely furnished with modern, streamlined furniture. The hotel has a handful of bars and restaurants and a sauna. Many of the comfortable bedrooms overlook the harbor. In the basement is a piano bar, an autumnal fantasy of warm shades of brown, open from 5pm to 1 or 2am. There is also a casino.

SLOTSHOTELLET, Rendsburggade 5, DK-9100 Aalborg. Tel. 98-10-14-00. Fax 98-11-65-70. 144 rms (all with bath), 8 suites. TV TEL **Bus:** 1, 3, 5, 7.

$ Rates (including breakfast): 700 kroner ($121.10) single; 975 kroner ($168.70) double. AE, DC, MC, V. **Parking:** Free.

Stylish and comfortable, this tasteful and well-designed hotel opened in 1986, and it is located a few blocks from the town center within view of the harbor. The hotel lies adjacent to the most important waterway in Aalborg, the Limsjorden Canal, and it is about a 2-minute walk east from the cathedral. There is a café and bar, and the bedrooms are modern. A large breakfast is served daily. Facilities include a solarium, fitness room, sauna, and table tennis. Handicap facilities are provided.

INEXPENSIVE

AALBORG SØMANDSHJEM, Østerborg 27, DK-9000 Aalborg. Tel. 98-12-19-00. Fax 98-11-76-97. 56 rms (47 with bath). TV **Bus:** 38.

$ Rates (including breakfast): 300 kroner ($51.90) single without bath, 400 kroner ($69.20) single with bath; 460 kroner ($79.60) double without shower, 580 kroner ($100.30) double with shower and toilet. AE, DC, MC, V. **Parking:** Free.

The 1956 exterior is functional and businesslike, but the public rooms are simple and welcoming. Rooms are light and airy, but not stylishly decorated, and the bathrooms are small. The hotel was completely renovated in 1988, and some rooms were equipped with phones. The rooms without bath or shower are small singles. The hotel restaurant does not serve alcohol, but offers a daily two-course lunch or dinner for 65 kroner ($11.20). The hotel is a 20-minute walk east of the railway on the eastern outskirts of town, close to the Tivoliland amusement park.

HOTEL ANSGAR, Prinsensgade 14-16, DK-9000 Aalborg. Tel. 98-13-37-33. Fax 98-16-52-82. 40 rms (28 with bath). MINIBAR TV TEL **Bus:** 2, 12, 54.
$ Rates (including breakfast): 400 kroner ($69.20) single without bath, 500 kroner ($86.50) single with bath; 500 kroner ($86.50) double without bath, 785 kroner ($135.80) double with bath. AE, DC, MC, V. **Closed:** Dec 23–Jan 6.
Opposite the railroad station, this 1906 landmark hotel offers rooms that have recently been redecorated in a light, modern style. The hotel has a garden patio, exercise room, sauna, solarium, Jacuzzi, and table tennis. Other than a breakfast room, there is no restaurant, although the hotel has a bar.

PARK HOTEL, Boulevarden 41, DK-9000 Aalborg. Tel. 98-12-31-33. Fax 89-13-31-66. 81 rms (all with bath). TV TEL **Bus:** 2, 10, 11, 13.
$ Rates (including breakfast): 500–750 kroner ($86.50–$129.80) single; 550–850 kroner ($95.20–$147.10) double; from 800 kroner ($138.40) suite. AE, DC, MC, V. **Parking:** Free.
The original 18th-century atmosphere has been preserved but the hotel has been carefully modernized throughout the years. Rooms are clean, comfortable, and modern. The hotel also has a restaurant serving both Scandinavian and international food, but the major restaurant street of Aalborg is just a 5-minute walk from the Park. Room service is provided, as is babysitting. Facilities include a health club.

NEARBY ACCOMMODATIONS
Inexpensive

HOTEL SCHEELSMINDE, Scheelsmindevej 35, DK-9100 Aalborg. Tel. 98-18-32-33. Fax 98-18-33-34. 70 rms (all with bath). TV TEL **Bus:** 4, 6, 41, 42.
$ Rates (including breakfast): 620 kroner ($107.30) single; 850 kroner ($147.10) double. AE, DC, MC, V. **Parking:** Free.
This is one of my favorite hotels in the city, and it should appeal to motorists in particular. In classic surroundings, you can escape the noise of Aalborg and wander at leisure through the hotel's large private grounds. Each room is decorated in pastel colors with a light modern decor. Reservations are strongly advised during peak season, because of the hotel's popularity.
You might also like to dine here, since the hotel chef is equally at home with Danish and international specialties. The restaurant was designed with large windows overlooking the park. It is open daily from 11am to 10pm, offering fixed-price meals at 108 kroner ($18.70) for two courses and 145 kroner ($25.10) for three courses. Facilities include an indoor swimming pool, Jacuzzi, and sauna.

WHERE TO DINE

As previously mentioned, a number of restaurants throughout Denmark, including some in Aalborg, serve a **Danmenu,** a two-course lunch or dinner of traditional Danish food with local specialties, going for around 95 kroner ($16.40). These restaurants are easy to find, identifiable by the special Danmenu sign. **Jomfru Anegade** is perhaps the most famous restaurant street in Denmark. The cooking, I've found, is some of the best in Jutland.

MODERATE

FYRTØJET, Jomfru Anegade 17. Tel. 98-13-73-77.
Cuisine: DANISH/INTERNATIONAL. **Reservations:** Recommended. **Bus:** 1, 3, 5, 15.
$ Prices: Appetizers 30–50 kroner ($5.20–$8.70); main dishes 70–140 kroner ($12.10–$24.20); fixed-price lunch 50 kroner ($8.70). DC, MC, V.
Open: Mon–Sat 11:30am–midnight, Sun 5–11pm.

S A cozy, small restaurant in the center of town, Fyrtøjet serves at outdoor tables in summer. I suggest the almueplatte, a Danish specialty, a so-called peasant's plate, with marinated herring, curry salad, two warm rissoles, cold potato salad and chives, and deep-fried Camembert cheese with black-currant jam. Other main dishes include stuffed plaice with shrimp, pepper steak, and breast of duck.

LAYALINA, Ved Stranden 7-9. Tel. 98-11-60-56.
   Cuisine: LEBANESE/INTERNATIONAL. **Reservations:** Not required. **Bus:** 1, 3, 5.
$ **Prices:** Fixed-price dinner 84 kroner ($14.50); appetizers 29–69 kroner ($5–$11.90); main dishes 69–189 kroner ($11.90–$32.70). AE, DC, MC, V.
   Open: Daily 5–11pm.

Layalina means "our pleasant nights" in Arabic. Its owners are Lebanese, and they have decorated the restaurant warmly, with Middle Eastern handmade artifacts. Exotic dishes such as shish kebab and hummus are served in an atmosphere of genuine Middle Eastern hospitality. The house special is three brochettes with lamb, meatballs, and spicy sausage.

REGENSEN, Jomfru Anegade 16. Tel. 98-12-59-77.
   Cuisine: DANISH. **Reservations:** Not required. **Bus:** 1, 3, 5.
$ **Prices:** Appetizers 40–64 kroner ($6.90–$11.10); main dishes 98–254 kroner ($17–$43.90). AE, DC, MC, V.
   Open: Daily 11am–1am.

A family-type restaurant a 5-minute walk east of Nytorv, this is a good bet for reasonably priced meals. The cavernous brick dining room is usually lively with a crowd of locals and tourists. The restaurant is housed on the ground level of one of the street's oldest buildings dating from around the turn of the century. You are likely to be offered typical Danish fare, including herring, pepper steak flambé, cold roast beef, and the fresh fish of the day.

RESTAURANT CAFEEN AND DUFY, Jomfru Anegade 8. Tel. 98-16-34-44.
   Cuisine: DANISH. **Reservations:** Required. **Bus:** 1, 3, 5.
$ **Prices:** Fixed-price meals 59 kroner ($10.20) at lunch, 89 kroner ($15.40) at dinner; appetizers 35–70 kroner ($6.10–$12.10); main dishes 119–150 kroner ($20.60–$26). DC, MC, V.
   Open: Lunch daily 11:30am–4pm; dinner daily 4–11:30pm.

The sophisticated decor, attentive service, and superb cuisine make this glistening pair of restaurants the very best on a street crammed with places to eat. The same kitchen prepares the tempting specialties served in the downstairs bistro and in the more formal upstairs restaurant. The menu and prices are the same in both restaurants. Choices might include the best chunky lobster soup in the region, served with sour cream, followed by sautéed Skagen shrimp, fish pâté, roast breast of duck with madeira sauce, or Dijon-style beef. There's dining on the outdoor terrace in summer.

BUDGET

HOLLES VINSTUE, Algade 57. Tel. 98-13-84-88.
   Cuisine: DANISH. **Reservations:** Not required. **Bus:** 1, 3, 5.
$ **Prices:** Appetizers 22–32 kroner ($3.80–$5.50); main dishes 42–65 kroner ($7.30–$11.20); smørrebrød 20 kroner ($3.50). No credit cards.
   Open: Mon–Fri 10am–midnight, Sat 10am–4pm.

S A 4-minute walk west of Nytorv, this is a popular wine bar and restaurant with an inviting atmosphere. The owners sell wine by the bottle or glass. You can order hefty smørrebrød (open-face sandwiches) or you can ask for more substantial meals, including a wienerschnitzel, various omelets, some Danish stews or hashes, and fish filets.

FOR LIGHT MEALS & SNACKS

DUUS VINKJAELDER, Østerågade 9. Tel. 98-12-50-56.

Cuisine: DANISH. **Reservations:** Not required. **Bus:** 1, 3, 5.
$ Prices: Snacks 16–39 kroner ($2.80–$6.70); wine by the glass 20 kroner ($3.50). MC, V.
Open: Mon–Fri 11–1am, Sat 10am–2am.

This old-world 1624 cellar lies beneath one of the most famous private Renaissance mansions (Jens Bang's Stonehouse), a 2-minute walk east of the cathedral. It features a selection of beer and wine (ever had Rainwater Madeira?), but it's a bit skimpy on the food. It's more of a snack restaurant and a wine bar than a full-fledged restaurant. However, you can order a plate of Danish hash (biksemad), or a burger, perhaps some pâté.

EVENING ENTERTAINMENT

TIVOLILAND, Karolinelundsvej. Tel. 98-12-33-15.
Tivoliland, an amusement park for the family, has lots of snap and sparkle, even though it is a copy of the more famous garden of Copenhagen. A "China Town" theme park, an open-air stage, good restaurants, a pizzeria, dancing, sing-alongs, Scandinavia's only boomerang roller coaster (with screws and loops both forward and backward), a roundabout vertical ride, and a cinema with a 180° screen are some of the 80 attractions. It's open April to September, daily from 10am to 10pm. Bus: 1, 8, 13, 19.
Admission: 30 kroner ($5.20) adults, 20 kroner ($3.50) children.

AMBASSADOR, Vesterbro 76. Tel. 98-12-62-22.
Originally built in the late 1950s as a private house, this establishment was later expanded into the largest and most popular nightlife complex in the region. Its street level contains the Dancing Palace, where conservative and traditional dance music is performed by live bands for crowds who enjoy dancing cheek to cheek. Conceived as a supper club, it serves Danish food as part of full meals priced from 150 kroner to 200 kroner ($26 to $34.60) each. Upstairs, electronic music is broadcast to a hyperactive and much younger crowd in Annabell's Disco. Tucked away in a quieter corner near the disco is the Algiers Bar, suitable for quiet dialogues in a setting inspired by the Casbah. The cost of admission allows anyone to wander at will among all three venues. Beer and liquor cost 26 kroner to 32 kroner ($4.50 to $5.50) each. It's open Tuesday to Thursday 9pm to 5am, Friday and Saturday 7pm to 5am.
Admission: Tues–Thurs 20 kroner ($3.50); Fri–Sat 50 kroner ($8.70); admission is refunded to anyone who orders dinner.

11. FREDERIKSHAVN

40 miles NE of Aalborg, 238 miles W of Copenhagen

GETTING THERE By Train From Århus, 20 daily trains run north to Frederikshavn, the trip taking 3 hours.

By Bus Frequent buses run between Aalborg and Frederikshavn.

By Car Head north from Aalborg along the E45 to Frederikshavn.

ESSENTIALS The **Frederikshavn Turistbureau,** Brotorvet 1, DK-9900 Frederikshavn (tel. 98-42-32-66), near the ferry dock, is open daily during the summer season 8:30am–8:30pm (Sun 8:30–11am, 4–8:30pm); the rest of the year, Mon–Sat 9am–4pm.

For many, this eastern coastal town is a final stopover in Denmark. Ferry connections with Sweden (Gothenburg) or Norway (Oslo, Moss, and Larvik) make it the gateway city to these other Scandinavian countries. The **Swedish Stena Line** (tel. 98-42-43-66) maintains luxury ferry service with sailings from Frederikshavn to Gothenburg and Oslo.

WHAT TO SEE & DO

BANGSBO MUSEUM, Dronning Margrethsvej 6. Tel. 98-43-31-11.
    In a wooded area beside the Deer Park at the edge of town, 18th-century buildings were constructed on the site of a 1364 manor house. The old barn, from 1580, one of the oldest in Denmark, houses antique farm equipment and implements. The main house has a collection of handcrafts made from human hair, a large display of relics from World War II, and a nautical section including ship models, figureheads, and other mementos. An early medieval ship similar to the vessels used by the Vikings is in one of the stable buildings.
    Admission: 20 kroner ($3.50) adults, 5 kroner (90¢) children.
    Open: Apr–Oct, daily 10am–5pm; Nov–Mar, Tues–Sun 10am–5pm. **Bus:** 1, 2.

CLOOSTÅRNET, Brønderslevvej 61. Tel. 98-48-60-69.
    Out in the country, lying about 3 miles west of the center, stands this tower. It rises nearly 200 feet, offering extensive views of the area. In fair weather, you can see most of the surrounding district, Vendyssel. An elevator takes you to the top.
    Admission: 10 kroner ($1.70) adults, 2 kroner (30¢) children.
    Open: May to mid-June, Mon–Fri 1–6pm, Sat–Sun 10am–6pm; mid-June to mid-Aug, daily 10am–6pm; mid-Aug to Aug 31, daily 1–6pm. **Closed:** Sept–Apr. **Bus:** 210, 225.

WHERE TO STAY

In case you miss the boat and need a room, the **Frederikshavn Turistbureau** (tel. 98-42-32-66) will book you into a private home, from 170 kroner ($29.40) for a double.

EXPENSIVE

FREDERIKSHAVN SØMANDSHJEM, Tordenskjoldsgade 14, DK-9910
    Frederikshavn. Tel. 98-42-09-77. Fax 98-43-18-99. 192 rms (all with bath), 23 suites. MINIBAR TV TEL **Bus:** 1, 2.
$ Rates (including breakfast): 850 kroner ($147.10) single; 1,150 kroner ($199) double; from 1,750 kroner ($302.80) suite. AE, DC, MC, V.
In the center of town, near the shopping area and not far from the harbor, this 1987 hotel has a heated pool, Jacuzzis, saunas, fitness facilities, and a solarium. It is one of the largest hotels in Denmark outside Copenhagen. Some units can be converted into three- and four-bed accommodations, suitable for families, and a number of rooms are equipped for handicapped persons. Good food is served in the gourmet restaurant, the luncheon room, and the pool coffee shop. There is also a nightclub.

HOTEL JUTLANDIA, Havnepladsen 1, DK-9900 Frederikshavn. Tel. 98-42-42-00. Fax 98-42-38-72. 104 rms (all with bath). MINIBAR TV TEL **Bus:** 1, 2.
$ Rates (including breakfast): 695–950 kroner ($120.20–$164.40) single; 880–2,000 kroner ($152.20–$346) double. AE, DC, MC, V. **Parking:** 50 kroner ($8.70).
Opposite the harbor, the Jutlandia has a splendid view. The hotel is well managed and maintained. Comfortable bedrooms are furnished in contemporary styling. Jutlandia also has a good restaurant, serving Danish and international food.

PARK HOTEL, Jernbanegade 7, DK-9900 Frederikshavn. Tel. 98-42-22-55. Fax 98-42-20-36. 30 rms (all with bath). TEL **Bus:** 1, 2.
$ Rates (including breakfast): 350 kroner ($60.60) single without bath, 600 kroner ($103.80) single with bath; 875 kroner ($151.40) double without bath, 1,450 kroner ($250.90) double with bath. AE, DC, MC, V.
An atmospheric choice with a certain charm, this is a member of the Romantic Hotels & Restaurants of Europe built in 1880 in an old French and English style. Many of the handsomely furnished traditional bedrooms have marble bathrooms and a private terrace. Some rooms contain a minibar and TV. The Park is especially noted for its

gourmet restaurant, Gastronomen, which serves an international cuisine. Laundry and room service are provided. A swimming pool and health club are next door.

INEXPENSIVE

HOFFMAN'S HOTEL, Tordenskjoldsgade 1, DK-9900 Frederikshavn. Tel. 98-42-21-66. 73 rms (37 with bath). TV TEL **Bus:** 1, 2.

$ **Rates** (including breakfast): 375 kroner ($64.90) single without bath, 420 kroner ($72.70) single with bath; 550 kroner ($95.20) double without bath, 640 kroner ($110.70) double with bath. AE, DC, MC, V. **Parking:** 20 kroner ($3.50).

In the center of Frederikshavn (the car park at the rear is convenient for ferry departures), rooms here are comfortable and attractively furnished. You can have lunch or dinner in the hotel's cafeteria, open May to September, daily from 8am to 6pm.

HOTEL MARIEHØNEN, Danmarksgade 40, DK-9900 Frederikshavn. Tel. 98-42-01-22. Fax 98-43-40-99. 32 rms (10 with bath). TEL **Bus:** 1, 2.

$ **Rates** (including breakfast): 250 kroner ($43.30) single without bath, 340 kroner ($58.80) single with bath; 350 kroner ($60.60) double without bath, 570 kroner ($98.60) double with bath. AE, DC, MC, V.

Right in the heart of Frederikshavn, this is an old but pleasant hostelry. It receives passengers mainly going to either Oslo or Gothenburg. Rooms are not stylish, but are clean and comfortable. The hotel also operates a good restaurant.

WHERE TO DINE

INEXPENSIVE

RESTAURANT VINKAELDEREN, Havnegade 8. Tel. 98-42-02-70.
Cuisine: DANISH. **Reservations:** Not required. **Bus:** 1, 2.

$ **Prices:** 3-course fixed-price meal 120 kroner ($20.80); appetizers 32–70 kroner ($5.50–$12.10); main dishes 70–170 kroner ($12.10–$29.40). AE, DC, MC, V.
Open: Daily 11am–midnight.

Lying midway between the harbor and the center of town, this restaurant is recognized by its red-brick facade, bull's-eye glass windows, and multiple carriage lamps. Originally established after World War II, it has a warmly rustic coziness enhanced by the racks of European wines on the walls. House wines cost 23 kroner ($4) per glass. Fresh fish and Danish beef dishes are a specialty. The fixed-price menu is served day and night.

BUDGET

FLADSTRAND, Rimmensgade 2. Tel. 98-42-24-27.
Cuisine: DANISH. **Reservations:** Not required. **Bus:** 1, 2.

$ **Prices:** Appetizers 22–38 kroner ($3.80–$6.60); main dishes 42–100 kroner ($7.30–$17.30). No credit cards.
Open: Sun–Thurs 8am–10pm, Fri–Sat 8am–midnight.

Named after the historic center of town, this popular and unpretentious restaurant was established more than 70 years ago. It's a charming and old-fashioned place. The kitchen serves generous portions of hearty fare, including a herring plate, wienerschnitzel, fresh fish, and Danish beef dishes. It feeds a sizable number of city residents at breakfast at 8 each morning, offering bacon and eggs for 45 kroner ($7.80).

12. SKAGEN

25 miles N of Frederikshavn, 303 miles W of Copenhagen

GETTING THERE By Train Twelve trains a day depart from Frederikshavn for Skagen, taking 40 minutes.

By Bus   Eleven buses a day leave from Frederikshavn for Skagen, taking 1 hour.

By Car   Head north from Frederikshavn along the E45.

ESSENTIALS   The **Tourist Office,** at Skt. Laurentii Vej 18 (tel. 98-44-13-77), is open Mon–Sat 9am–5pm.

Skagen is the "Land's End" of Denmark—the far northern stretches of mainland Jutland on its eastern coast. It has been compared to a "bony finger" pointing into the North Sea. Pronounced "skane," Skagen is the second-biggest fishing port in Denmark. In recent years it has attracted a thriving little artists' colony that has done much to enliven the town.

WHAT TO SEE & DO

If you walk to a point of land called **Grenener,** you will be at the top of the continent of mainland Europe and can tip your toes into the Skagerrak and Kattegat seas. Another charming oasis to seek out is **Gammel Skagen,** a little seaside resort set against a backdrop of dunes and sea grass.

SKAGEN MUSEUM, Brøndumsvej 4. Tel. 98-44-64-44.

The most important attraction of the town, this museum displays the works of local artists, many from the 1930s when Skagen was a thriving art colony. You'll see many paintings by P. S. Krøyer (1851–1909) and Michael Ancher (1849–1909) and Anna Ancher (1859–1935).

Admission: 25 kroner ($4.30) adults; free for children.

Open: Apr and Oct, daily 11am–3pm; May and Sept, daily 10am–5pm; June–Aug, daily 10am–6pm; Nov–Mar, Wed–Fri 1–3pm, Sat–Sun 11am–3pm.

HOME OF MICHAEL AND ANNA ANCHER, Markvej 2. Tel. 98-44-30-09.

You can visit the home of these artists whose work is on display in the Skagen Museum.

Admission: 20 kroner ($3.50) adults, 10 kroner ($1.70) children.

Open: Apr and Oct, daily 11am–3pm; May–June 20 and Aug 16–Sept, daily 10am–5pm; June 21–Aug 15, daily 10am–6pm; Nov–Mar, Sat–Sun 11am–3pm.

WHERE TO STAY
MODERATE

HOTEL SKAGEN, Gammel Landevej 39, DK-9990 Skagen. Tel. 98-44-22-33. Fax 98-44-21-34. 81 rms (all with bath), 24 suites. TV TEL

$ Rates (including breakfast): 590 kroner ($102.10) single; 885 kroner ($153.10) double; from 995 kroner ($172.10) suite. AE, DC, MC, V. **Closed:** Dec 23–Apr 1.
Parking: Free.

One of the best hotels in the area, it was completely rebuilt after a fire in 1986. Today, better than ever, bedrooms are modern, attractive, and functionally furnished. The hotel is located beside the main road to the south, a 10-minute walk from the city center. Its La Mer Restaurant is one of the biggest at Skagen. It is open between noon and 10pm, serving continuously throughout the afternoon. The modern dining room has big windows providing a view of the pleasant garden outside. Main courses cost from 80 kroner to 150 kroner ($13.80 to $26).

WHERE TO DINE
EXPENSIVE

SKAGEN FISKE RESTAURANT, Fiskehuskaj 13. Tel. 98-44-68-54.

Cuisine: DANISH. **Reservations:** Recommended.

$ Prices: Appetizers 45–110 kroner ($7.80–$19); main dishes 110–195 kroner ($19–$33.70); fixed-price lunch 165 kroner ($28.50); fixed-price dinner 295 kroner ($51). No credit cards.

Open: Lunch daily noon–4:30pm; dinner daily 6–10pm. **Closed:** Sept to mid-May.

Considered the best in town, this restaurant stands in a row of little, peak-roofed fishermen's cottages at the fish harbor. Here the yachting crowd from Skagen harbor often crowds into the downstairs tavern with its sand-covered floor. Large plates of shrimp are served at bare tables, or you can eat outside in fair weather at picnic tables. Many patrons show up here at happy hour to watch the sunset. At the more formal restaurant upstairs, you can enjoy such dishes as salmon tartare or sea salmon cooked in red wine. In summer, folksingers often entertain.

In the bar, which stays open until 2am, you can enjoy the chef's famous fiskefrikadeller daily from 11am to 5pm, for 40 kroner ($6.90). In the evenings, beginning at 11:15pm, management often presents a cabaret or other entertainment, upstairs, costing from 50 kroner to 60 kroner ($8.70 to $10.40) for admission.

MODERATE

BODILLAS KRO, Østerstrandweg 11. Tel. 98-44-33-00.
   Cuisine: DANISH. **Reservations:** Not required.
$ Prices: Appetizers 50–95 kroner ($8.70–$16.40); main dishes 100–158 kroner ($17.30–$27.30); smørrebrød 35 kroner ($6.10) each. DC, MC, V.
   Open: Daily 11:30am–10pm.

Warm, cozy, and modern, this centrally located street-level restaurant is filled with old-fashioned landscape paintings and a big-windowed view over the boats bobbing at anchor in Skagen's harbor. Food is plentiful, well flavored, and unpretentious, and includes the house specialty of fried filet of plaice plus Danish meatballs and a selection of stews and hash.

PART TWO

NORWAY

CHAPTER 11

GETTING TO KNOW NORWAY

Land of the midnight sun and glacier-born fjords, Norway is a special experience.

The name Norway (in Norwegian, Norge or Noreg) is derived from *Norvegr,* meaning "the way of the north." The term was used by the Vikings more than 1,000 years ago for the shipping route along the Norwegian west coast. For the 4 million Norwegians—seafarers since the dawn of history—it seems natural to give the country a nautical name.

To the ancients, Norway was a mythical land. A journey to it was laden with unspeakable perils. Writers called the mythical land Ultima Thule, and feared that it was inhabited by strange, barbaric, even fabulous creatures. In the 4th century B.C. the Greek writer Pytheas thought the laws of nature did not apply there, claiming that everything—water, earth—floated in midair. Herodotus claimed that in Norway feathers were constantly being blown into one's face and that feathers covered everything—an early attempt perhaps to describe a snowstorm.

Norway is a land of tradition, as exemplified by its rustic stave churches and folk dances stepped to the airs of a fiddler. But Norway is also modern. It is a technologically advanced nation, rich in petroleum and hydroelectric energy. Norwegians also enjoy a well-developed public system of social insurance, comprising old-age pensions, health insurance, unemployment insurance, and rehabilitation assistance. The system is financed by contributions from the insured, which makes Norway one of the most heavily taxed nations on earth.

One of the last great natural frontiers of the world, Norway invites exploration, with its steep and jagged fjords, salmon-teeming rivers, glaciers, mountains, and meadows. In winter the shimmering aurora borealis is the lure, giving way to the midnight sun of summer.

1. GEOGRAPHY, HISTORY & POLITICS

GEOGRAPHY

Norway measures some 1,100 miles in length, and it is an extremely narrow mountainous country: 70% of the land is covered by mountains, glaciers, lakes, and wasteland, and less than 4% of the territory is arable. In the Jotunheimen range in

? DID YOU KNOW . . . ?

- Norwegians have one of the highest per capita incomes in the world.
- While medieval alchemists were trying to make gold, they instead discovered *akevitt* (aquavit, or schnapps), the national "firewater" of Norway.
- Norway has the world's largest foreign trade per capita.
- The average population density of Norway is only 13 inhabitants per square kilometer, compared to 96 for Europe as a whole.
- Norway, sharing a short land border with Russia, disputes with the Russians control of a sea area the size of Belgium, Switzerland, and Austria combined.
- Hammerfest in northern Norway is the northernmost town in the world.
- More people of Norwegian descent (five million) live in the United States than in Norway itself.

south-central Norway are the highest mountain peaks in Europe north of the Alps. The country has some 1,700 glaciers. Along the coast a string of about 50,000 islands shelter the mainland against the worst effects of Atlantic storms. The largest tracts of agricultural land are found in south-central Norway: north and south of Oslo, south of the city of Stavanger on the west coast, around the Trondheim fjord in central Norway, and also in the country of Troms in the far north.

WESTERN NORWAY   Western Norway is fabled for its fjords. A fjord is a saltwater arm of the sea, stretching inland, and many date from the end of the Ice Age. Some fjords cut their way into mountain ranges as high as 3,300 feet. The longest fjord in western Norway is the **Sognefjord,** north of Bergen, winding its way 110 miles inland. Other major fjords in the district are Nordfjord, Geirangerfjord, and Hardangerfjord. The capital of the fjord district is **Bergen,** the second-largest city in Norway but the largest on the west coast. It is the best starting point for trips through the fjord district.

CENTRAL NORWAY   Fjords are also common in central Norway, the largest being **Trondheimsfjord** and **Narnsfjord.** It's not unusual for roads to pass waterfalls that cascade straight down into the fjords. Central Norway is filled with many thick forests and snowcapped peaks. **Trondheim** is its largest city and the most interesting in Norway to visit after Oslo and Bergen. **Ålesund** is also a tourist center with its own charm, as is **Molde.** Both are good centers for exploring the district.

EASTERN NORWAY   Eastern Norway, bordering Sweden, has gentler land than the west. It is characterized by its clear blue lakes, rolling hills, and green valleys. In some ways it's the most traditional part of the country. It contains many fertile valleys, and, because of that, was one of the first to be populated. Some of the biggest valleys are Valdres, Østerdal, Hallingdal, Numedal, and Gudbrandsdalen. Campers and hikers in summer frequent the great forests of the Hedmark region, site of Norway's longest river, the Glomma (Glåma), flowing for some 360 miles. Many ski resorts are found in the area, none more notable than **Geilo** and **Lillehammer,** the latter the scheduled site of the 1994 Olympics. Of course, the greatest attraction of Norway— and its most visited destination—is the capital, **Oslo,** rising from the shores of Oslofjord. But much, much more about that later.

SOUTHERN NORWAY   Southern Norway is sometimes called the Riviera of Norway, because of its unspoiled and uncrowded beaches. It's also a favorite port of call for the yachting crowd. **Stavanger** is the largest city of southern Norway, and

---

IMPRESSIONS

I would not enter Norway again for all the firs in Scandinavia. The blight of temperance has settled on the place.
—ARCHER GRANT OF STROUD, GLOUCESTERSHIRE, 1912

November always seemed to me the Norway of the year.
—EMILY DICKINSON, 1864

also the most visited. But there is much more to explore in this Telemark region, which is filled with lakes and canals used for canoeing and boating in summer. In **Skien**, lake steamers are boarded for trips on an inland series of canals. The southern part of **Kristiansand** is a link between Norway and continental Europe. Ferries from abroad dock here. In the area is **Hamresanden Beach**, stretching for 6 miles, one of the longest stretches of uninterrupted beachfront in Europe. Along the western half of the district are found more fjords, notably Lysefjord, Sandefjord, and Vindefjord.

NORTHERN NORWAY Northern Norway, the "Land of the Midnight Sun," lies near the top of the earth. It's a region of craggy cliffs that soar down into the sea and of deep fertile valleys along with deserted moors. It has islands with sparse, if any, population where life has remained unchanged for generations. The capital of the Nordland region is **Bodø,** a base for Arctic fishing trips and visits to the wild Glomfjord whose glacier water is chilled year-round. Norway's second-largest glacier, Svartisen, is also in this region, as is the city of **Narvik,** a major Arctic port and the gateway to the Lofoten Islands, which are filled with fishing villages.

TROMS The main city in the region of Troms is **Tromsø,** from which polar explorations are launched. Troms contains one of Norway's most impressive mountain ranges, the **Lyngs Alps,** drawing winter skiers and summer hikers.

FINNMARK At the very top of Norway is the Finnmark region, home of the Samis or Lapps. Centers here include the Lapp town of **Kautokeino** and **Hammerfest,** the northernmost city of the world. Most tourists visit Finnmark to see the **North Cape,** Europe's northernmost point and an ideal viewing spot for the Midnight Sun.

DATELINE

- **800–1050** The age of the Vikings, when Norsemen terrorized European coastlines.
- **872** Harald Fairhair conquers many small provinces and reigns as first king.
- **1001** Leif Eriksson discovers America (or so the sagas claim).
- **1030** Christianity is firmly established; Olaf II is declared a saint.
- **1066** The Viking age ends with the defeat of Harald III in England.
- **1350** The Black Death wipes out

(continues)

HISTORY

Norway has been inhabited since around 14,000 B.C., the first people appearing as the ice sheets melted over Scandinavia. The early settlers hunted reindeer and other game in these northern lands. Some 5,000 to 6,000 years ago, settlers turned to agriculture, especially around the Oslofjord. In the Roman era, there were links to the countries of the south, as unearthed artifacts have disclosed.

THE AGE OF THE VIKINGS Prehistory came to an end during the Viking era, roughly A.D. 800 to 1050. Much of what is known about this era wasn't written down, but has been revealed through sagas passed by word of mouth or by archeological digs. Some scholars date the looting of the Lindisfarne monastery in northern England in 793 as the beginning of the "age of the Vikings."

"The Vikings are coming!" became a dreadful cry along the coastlines of Europe. The victims expected fire and sword. Scandinavian historians are usually kinder to the Vikings, citing the fact they often came to trade and colonize. From Norway, the Vikings branched out to settle in the Orkney and Shetland Islands (now part of Scotland). They also settled in the Scottish Hebrides and on the Isle of Man. Settlements were made on Greenland and Iceland, which the Vikings found uninhabited. Norse communities on Greenland eventually died out. The sagas claim that Leif

Eriksson discovered "wineland of the good" in 1001, a reference to the American continent. Many scholars, however, claimed that Vikings in their seaworthy long ships navigated to America long before Leif Eriksson.

The road to unifying Norway was rough. In 872 Harald Fairhair, winning a battle near Stavanger, conquered many of the provinces of Norway, but other battles for unification would take decades. Harald was followed by his son, Eric I, or "Bloody Axe" as his enemies called him. Eric began his reign by assassinating two of his eight brothers. He later killed five other brothers, leaving only one, before he himself died in Cumberland (England) in 954. Eric was followed by his brother, Haakon, who became king. Haakon tried to convert Norwegians to Christianity but did not succeed. Eric's sons schemed to capture Haakon so that one of them could become king. The rulers of Denmark aided the heirs and Haakon died in 960 in the Battle of Fitjar. Harald II Graafell, one of Eric's sons, became king of Norway. Cruel and oppressive, he died in a battle in 970.

Haakon, son of Sigurd of Lade, next became king of Norway. He resisted Danish attacks and ruled for around 25 years, dying in a peasant riot in 995. He was followed by Olaf I Trygvasson, who continued the spread of Christianity throughout Norway, trying to convert Greenland and Iceland as well. At war with Denmark, he died in the battle of Swold in 1000, and Norway was divided between Denmark and the Jarl of Lade.

Olaf II Haraldsson was a Viking until 1015, when he became king of all Norway. Although oppressive and often cruel, he continued the spread of Christianity. Canute of Denmark invaded Norway in 1028, sending Olaf fleeing to England. Upon his return in 1030, he died in the Battle of Stirklestad. Canute's son, Sweyn, ruled Norway from 1028 to 1035. Sweyn was forced out when Olaf II was proclaimed a saint and his son, Magnus I, was made king. Magnus was also king of Denmark, a position he lost when Canute's nephew led a revolt against him and was killed. With the sainthood of Olaf, Christianity was firmly established in Norway.

Harald Sigurdsson ruled Norway from 1046, known as Harald III. He was king of Norway and Denmark, and died in 1066, when he lost the Battle of Stamford Bridge in England. His death is taken to end the Viking age.

THE MIDDLE AGES Kings came and went, winning and losing battles, dying on the field. Wars with Denmark continued, and civil wars raged from 1130 to 1227. But through it all, towns and the church continued to grow. Under King Haakon V in the 13th century, Oslo became the capital of Norway. The Black Death reached Norway in 1350 and wiped out much of the population.

From 1319 to 1343 Norway and Sweden had a joint monarch, Haakon VI (1340–80), son of the Swedish king, Magnus Eriksson. Haakon was the lawful heir to the throne of Norway. He married Margaret, daughter

DATELINE

much of the population.

- **1397** Margaret becomes Queen of Norway, Denmark, and Sweden at the Union of Kalmar.

- **1439** Danish rule is imposed on Norway.

- **1814** Norway breaks from Denmark and adopts a constitution, but comes under Swedish rule.

- **1905** The Norwegian parliament breaks from Sweden and declares independence.

- **1914** Norway declares its neutrality in World War I.

- **1920** Norway joins the League of Nations, ending isolation.

- **1940** Nazi troops invade Norway; the king and government flee.

- **1945** Norway regains independence and executes its Nazi puppet ruler Quisling.

- **1960s** Oil boom hits Norway.

- **1986** Labor party votes first woman prime minister, G. H. Brundtland.

- **1989** Center-right coalition regains power.

- **1990** Brundtland becomes prime minister again.

of Danish king Valdemar Atterdag. Their son, Olaf, was chosen to be the Danish king upon the death of Valdemar in 1375. He inherited the throne of Norway after his father died in 1380, thus bringing Norway into a union with Denmark. This union was to last until 1814.

UNION WITH DENMARK Olaf died at the age of 17, and Margaret ruled as regent of Norway, Denmark, and Sweden. She ruled through her nephew, Eric of Pomerania, who had become king of Norway in 1389. He was recognized as a joint ruler at Kalmar. Margaret, however, actually ruled the country until her death in 1412.

Eric of Pomerania tried to continue to rule the three countries, but Sweden and Norway rebelled. Eric fled in 1439 and Christopher III of Bavaria became the ruler, imposing Danish rule over Norway.

Norway slowly disintegrated under Danish rule. Denmark led Norway into the Seven Years' War in 1563, and took unfair advantage of its position in trade, in the military, even in surrendering Norwegian land to Sweden. In the Napoleonic Wars, from 1807 to 1814, Denmark and Norway were allied with France, although this brought them much economic hardship. Famine was widespread.

By 1813 Sweden wanted to take Norway, having lost Finland to the Russian czar in the east. In 1814 Frederik VI surrendered to the allies against Napoléon and handed Norway over to his Swedish opponents. That officially ended 434 years of Danish rule.

SECESSION FROM DENMARK On May 17, 1814, at a meeting at Eidsvoll, an assembly adopted a constitution and chose Christian Frederik as the Norwegian king. May 17, to this day, is celebrated as the Norwegian national day. The Swedes objected and launched a military campaign, eventually subduing the Norwegians. The Swedes accepted the Norwegian constitution, but only within a union of the two kingdoms. Christian Frederik fled.

In the immediate years to come, Norway suffered through one of its greatest depressions. Norway's parliamentary assembly, the Storting (Stortinget), engaged in repeated conflicts with Swedish monarchs. Bernadotte ruled over both Norway and Sweden as King Charles XIV in 1818.

By the 1830s the economy of Norway had improved. The first railway line was laid in 1854. Its merchant fleet drastically increased between 1850 and 1880.

From the 1880s on, the Liberals in the Norwegian Storting brought much-needed reform to the country. But by the end of the century the conflict with Sweden was growing, as more and more Norwegians demanded independence.

In August 1905 the Storting decided to dissolve the union with Sweden. Sweden agreed to let Norway rule itself. In October 1905 an election took place in Norway and the son of Denmark's king was proclaimed king of Norway. He chose the name Haakon VII.

AN INDEPENDENT NORWAY Free at last, Norway enjoyed peace and prosperity until the beginning of World War I. Even though the economy was progressing, thousands of Norwegians emigrated to the United States around the turn of the century. In 1914 Norway joined with Sweden and Denmark in declaring a policy of neutrality. Despite this declaration, around 2,000 Norwegian seamen lost their lives in World War I because of submarine attacks and underwater mines.

In 1920 Norway became a member of the League of Nations, ending its policy of isolation. At the outbreak of World War II, Norway again declared its neutrality. Nonetheless, Allied forces mined Norway's waters in 1940, and the Nazis attacked on April 9, 1940. Great Britain and France provided some military assistance, but

---

IMPRESSIONS

Norway is a hard country: hard to know, hard to shoot over, and hard—very hard—to fall down on: but hard to forsake and harder to forget.
—J. A. LEES, PEAKS AND PINES, ANOTHER NORWAY BOOK, 1899

Norway fell after a 2-month struggle. The government and the royal family fled into exile in England. With them they brought 1,000 ships of the Norwegian merchant fleet. In spite of the resistance movement, Norway was occupied until the end of the war in 1945, with Vidkun Quisling, the Norwegian minister of defense in the 1930s, serving the Nazis as leader of the puppet government.

Quisling was executed following the Nazi retreat from Norway. On June 7 of that year the government in exile returned from Britain. The retreating Germans had followed a scorched-earth policy in Finnmark, destroying almost everything of value. In the late 1940s Norway began to rebuild its shattered economy.

After an abortive attempt to form a Nordic defense alliance, Norway, along with Denmark, joined NATO in 1949. The Communist party tried to gain influence in Norway, but failed.

By the 1960s oil prospecting in the North Sea had yielded rich finds; this resulted in a profound restructuring of Norwegian trade and industry. In 1972 Norway voted not to enter the Common Market, following a bitter political dispute.

Norway had a nonsocialist government from 1981 to 1986. In 1986 Labor party leader Gro Harlem Brundtland headed a minority government as Norway's first female prime minister, and introduced seven women into her 18-member cabinet. Soon, however, tumbling oil prices and the subsequent unemployment that it brought led to a recession. The Labor government lost the 1989 elections. A center-right coalition took over the government, composed of the Center party, Conservatives, and the Christian Democrats. In November 1990, Brundtland returned to office as prime minister, this time with nine women in her 19-member cabinet. In 1991, Olav V died and was succeeded by his son Harald V.

Today the government of Norway faces problems familiar in many parts of the world: violent crime, drugs, immigration control, unemployment, and acid rain and pollution, much of it coming from Great Britain. Concern about acid rain and pollution from Britain was so severe that a 1987 visit from Margaret Thatcher brought out the riot police.

New elections are slated for 1993, but, for many, the big event for Norway will take place in 1994, when Lillehammer hosts the Winter Olympics.

POLITICS

Norway is a constitutional monarchy, with the 150-member National Assembly (Storting) exercising legislative power. But the country is in the vanguard of the advanced socialized nations, with compulsory national insurance, old-age pensions, unemployment insurance, family allowances, and holidays with pay for all workers.

2. FAMOUS NORWEGIANS

Bjørnstjerne Bjørnson (1832–1910) A great Norwegian writer, he wrote many folk tales that inspired Henrik Ibsen. In 1857, he took over Ibsen's job as director of the Bergen Theater. His historical plays brought him world acclaim, and he became radically involved in Norwegian nationalism, campaigning for an independent country. One of his poems became the national anthem of Norway, *Ja, vi elsker dette landet* (Yes, I Love This Land). He won the Nobel Prize in 1903.

Kirsten Flagstad (1895–1962) This great Wagnerian singer in the history of opera was born in Hamar, Norway. Her 1933 performance at the Wagner Festival in

IMPRESSIONS

I know the Norwegians from Illinois, and I know that no immigrants have
advanced America more than they.
—ABRAHAM LINCOLN

Bayreuth, Germany, brought her world acclaim. She made her debut at the Metropolitan Opera House in New York City in 1935 as Sieglinde in *Die Walküre*.

Edvard Grieg (1843–1907) "The Chopin of the North." Norway's national composer who adapted themes from folk music in *Peer Gynt Suite* for example. Born in Bergen to an English father and Norwegian mother.

Knut Hamsun (1859–1952) At age 19, in 1888, a Danish magazine published a portion of his novel, *Hunger*. This novel, along with *Growth of the Soil* and *The Women at the Well*, earned him international fame. In 1920 he won the Nobel Prize for literature.

Thor Heyerdahl (1914–   ) This ethnologist began in 1937 the first expedition in the Pacific. In 1947, he led the celebrated *Kon-Tiki* expedition from Peru to Polynesia, and in 1951 won an Academy Award for his documentary (see the *Kon-Tiki* Museum in Chapter 15). In 1969 and 1970, he led two *Ra* expeditions. Many of his books have become best-sellers, including *Aku Aku*, a study of Easter Island translated into 32 languages.

Sigurd Hoel (1890–1960) Writer whose best known work is *One Day in October* (1931).

Henrik Ibsen (1828–1906) Great modernist-realist playwright. Author of *A Doll's House, Hedda Gabler, The Master Builder,* and *Peer Gynt*.

Trygve Lie (1896–1968) A leading labor party lawyer and politician, in 1940 Lie was named foreign minister of a Norwegian government in exile during the Nazi occupation. In 1946, he was elected Secretary-General of the United Nations for five years. In 1950 he undertook a "great peace mission," and also supported the United Nations effort to send troops to Korea. In 1951, his term was extended as Secretary-General, but he resigned because of continuous Soviet refusal to recognize him.

Edvard Munch (1863–1944) The greatest Scandinavian painter. His famous works include the gut-wrenching *The Scream* (1893) and *The Bridge* (1901). See his murals at Oslo University.

Fridtjof Nansen (1861–1930) A great world explorer, he dreamed of crossing the ice caps of Greenland, a remarkable feat that brought him glory in 1889. He led the Norwegian delegation to the first assembly of the League of Nations in 1920, and in 1922 was awarded the Nobel Peace Prize for his work repatriating prisoners of war.

Liv Ullmann (1938–   ) The famous Norwegian actress made her stage debut in 1957, and became known in the 1960s for her work with the National Theater. World acclaim came through roles in films of Ingmar Bergman, her lover at the time. These included *Cries and Whispers, Scenes from a Marriage,* and *Persona*. She's appeared on Broadway and has written two volumes of memoirs.

Sigrid Undset (1882–1949) Writer. *Kristen Lavransdatter* is considered her masterpiece.

Adolf Gustav Vigeland (1869–1943) Sculptor whose monumental works are one of Oslo's major sights. A controversial artist—some claim a genius, others a madman. See the obelisk in Frognerpark.

3. SPORTS & RECREATION

BICYCLING   Bikes can be rented virtually anywhere in Norway. Inquire at your hotel or the local tourist office. The Norwegian Mountain Touring Association (see "Hiking," below, for address) provides inexpensive lodging for people taking overnight bike trips. For suggestions of tours, maps, and brochures, contact **Den Rustne Eike,** Enga 2, N-0458 Oslo, (tel. 22-83-72-31). This is the only large bike-rental firm in Oslo. In addition to renting bikes, it arranges guided tours in the Oslo area and to other parts of Norway. Tours last from 3 hours to 14 days.

IMPRESSIONS

People shall be made to understand the greatness of my art; when facing it, they shall learn to remove their hats, as if in a cathedral.
—EDVARD MUNCH

DIVING   Excellent diving centers provide diving trips and instruction. Divers into harpooning often catch their own dinner, with many kinds of fish from which to make a selection. Conditions for submarine photography are generally good, with an underwater visibility of 30 to 100 feet. Many shipwrecks are found along Norway's extensive coastline and fjords. Diving vacation packages are provided by **Barmanns Dykkesenter,** Langveien 72B, N-6500 Kristiansund N (tel. 71-64-65-11).

FISHING   Norway is long famous for its grand salmon and trout fishing. The main season for salmon fishing lasts from June to August, though June and July are the best months. Sea trout fishing takes place from June to September, but is best in August. The season for brown trout fishing varies with altitude.

People 16 years of age or older must purchase a fishing license for 60 kroner ($10.40). National fishing licenses can be purchased at local post offices; fishing in the ocean is free.

Some companies even arrange fishing tours in Norway, including **Passage Tours of Scandinavia** (tel. toll free 800/548-5960 in the U.S. for more information).

GOLF   Many golf clubs in Norway open their greens to foreign guests. Unlike some countries, greens fees in Norway tend to be moderate. Clubs include the **Oslo Golf Klubb** (18 holes), at Bogstad, Oslo (tel. 22-50-44-02), and the **Bergen Golf Club** (9 holes), Aastvedt, Ovre Ervik, at Bergen (tel. 55-18-20-77).

HIKING   Much of Norway is made up of mountains and wilderness, so hiking is a favorite pastime, enjoyed by the Norwegians themselves as much as visitors. The Norwegian Mountain Touring Association provides guided hikes lasting from 1 to 2 weeks. Of course, hikes are for people in at least average physical condition. The cost for a 1-week hiking tour, including meals and overnight stays, ranges from 2,400 to 3,000 kroner ($415.20 to $519). More information is available from the **Norwegian Mountain Touring Association,** Box 1963, Vika, N-0125 Oslo 1 (tel. 22-83-25-50).

HORSEBACK RIDING   Many companies offer tours of Norway's wilderness, taking in some of its more spectacular natural scenes. These can range from a few hours to a full week, and they're available all over Norway. Luggage is transported by car. Some of the candidates that offer such tours are **Bolton Overseas** (tel. toll free 800/843-0602 in the U.S.).

SAILING   In summer, the long coast of Norway can be a yachting person's challenge. The most tranquil havens are along the southern coast. For information on yacht and sailboat rentals, contact local tourist offices or **Norges Seilforbund,** Hauger Skolevei 1, N-1351 Rud (tel. 67-56-88-00).

IMPRESSIONS

I have saved the world from a mediocre painter and given the world a literary genius.
—HENRIK IBSEN'S WIFE SUSANNA

Only when you see the provincialism of Oslo do you appreciate the wonderfulness of Ibsen.
—ARNOLD BENNETT, JOURNAL, 1929

SKIING Norway's skiing terrain is among the best in the world. The optimum times for skiing are in February and March (the first 2 weeks in April are usually good also). Two of the principal resorts, **Geilo** and **Voss,** lie on the Oslo-Bergen rail line. The most famous and easily accessible resort is **Lillehammer,** north of Oslo. In and around the Norwegian capital skiing is common; the deservingly famed ski jump, **Holmenkollen,** with its companion ski museum, is minutes from the heart of Oslo. The yearly ski championship here in March draws ace skiers from all over Europe and North America.

Norwegian ski resorts are known for their informality, evident both in the ski schools and in the atmosphere. Simple folklore and hearty good fun replace the sophisticated après-ski life often found in alpine resorts. Incidentally, "ski" is an Old Norse word, as is "slalom."

A great part of the Norwegian skiing is cross country, perfect for the amateur. But there is plentiful terrain for the more skilled. Curling, sleigh rides, and skating also are popular winter sports. All major centers have ski lifts, and equipment in Norway is much cheaper to rent than it is in luxury resorts like St. Moritz.

Skiing is not only a winter sport in Norway. Summer skiing, both downhill and cross country, normally takes place at summer ski centers near glaciers. Several establishments provide information about this type of skiing. They include **Galdhopiggen,** Sommerskisenter, N-2687 Bøverdalen (tel. 06-21-21-42), and **Folgefonn Sommarskisenter,** N-5627 Jondal (tel. 94-76-56-35).

4. FOOD & DRINK

FOOD

MEALS & DINING CUSTOMS Most working Norwegians seldom eat lunch, grabbing a quick open-face sandwich, or smørbrød, at their offices. But in major towns and cities, lunch is generally served from 1 to 3pm. The *middag,* the main meal of the day, is generally eaten between 4:30 and 6pm. Many restaurants serve this popular middag from 1 to 8pm. In late-closing restaurants it's possible to dine much later, until around midnight in Oslo. Long after middag time a Norwegian family will have *aftens,* a smørbrød supper that will see them through the night.

THE CUISINE The chief criticism leveled against Norwegian cooking is that it's too bland. The food is always abundant (the Norwegians are known for their second helpings), substantial, and well prepared—but no threat to the French for a Cordon Bleu prize.

Norwegians are proud—and rightly so—of many of their tempting specialties, ranging from **boiled cod** (considered a delicacy) to reindeer steak smothered in brown gravy and accompanied by tart little **lingonberries,** which resemble wild cranberries.

Norway relies on fish, both freshwater and saltwater, for much of its food supply. Prepared in countless ways, fish is usually well cooked—and always fresh, a good bet indeed. Try, in particular, the aforementioned boiled cod; it's always—but always— served with boiled potatoes.

In early summer, **kokt laks** (boiled salmon) is a highly rated delicacy. **Kreps** (crayfish) is another big production as it is in Finland, and **ørret** (mountain trout), preferably broiled and served with fresh lemon, is a guaranteed treat. A recommendation for top-notch fare: **fiske-gratin** (fish soufflé), delicately seasoned.

Norwegians love their fatty smoked eel (**røket al**), although many foreigners have a tendency to whip by this one on the smörgåsbord table. The national appetizer is brine-cured herring with raw onions.

You may want to try **reindeer steak** or **faar-i-kaal,** the national dish, a heavily peppered cabbage-and-mutton stew served with boiled potatoes. A fisher's or a farmer's favorite is **lapskus** (hash, to us), prepared with whatever's left over in the kitchen. The North American palate seems to take kindly to **kjøttkaker,** the Norwegian hamburger—often pork patties—served with sautéed onions, brown gravy, and boiled potatoes.

The **boiled potato** is ubiquitous. Incidentally, the Norwegian prefers it without butter—just a bit of parsley. Nowadays fresh vegetables and crisp salads are a regular feature of the Norwegian diet as well.

Rømmergrøt is a sour-cream porridge covered with melted butter, brown sugar, and cinnamon. If they're in season, try the good-tasting, amber-colored **muiter** (cloudberries). An additional treat, well made in Norway, is a pancake accompanied by lingonberries.

Frokost (breakfast) is often a whopping **koldtbord,** the famous cold board consisting of herring and goat's milk cheese, and often such fare as salmon and soft-boiled eggs, plus **wienerbrød** (Danish pastry). At this time, most tourists encounter the ever-popular **flatbrød,** paper-thin crisp rye bread. Many visitors may not want to spend the extra kroner for this big spread, but those going on glacier expeditions need this early-morning fortification.

Incidentally, **smörgåsbord** and smørrebrød (**smørbrød** in Norway) are very popular in Norway, although they seem to be served here without the elaborate ritual typical of Denmark and Sweden. Customarily, smörgåsbord in Norway is only a prelude to the main meal.

DRINK

Norway has strict laws regarding the sale of alcohol. Beer and wine may be served in hotels and restaurants 7 days a week, but hard liquor can be sold only between 3 and 11:45pm—and never on Sunday. Visitors can buy the precious stuff from the Vinmonopolet, the state liquor-and-wine monopoly (see below). The restriction on hard liquor may be a bonus for budgeteers, since Norwegian prices are sky-high, in line with all the Scandinavian countries. *Warning:* Unless visitors ask for a favorite brand of gin or scotch, they may be served a sour-tasting Norwegian home brew.

The Norwegians, like the Danes, are essentially beer drinkers. Low in alcohol content is **pils,** a light lager, but the **lagerøl** is so low in alcoholic content (less than 2.5%) that it's a substitute for water only. The stronger Norwegian beer is the Export, available at higher prices. Two other types of beer are Brigg and Zero.

FROMMER'S SMART TRAVELER: RESTAURANTS

VALUE-CONSCIOUS DINERS MAY WANT TO CONSIDER THE FOLLOWING:

1. Look for the *dagens menu* or daily special that is reasonable in price and was prepared fresh that day.
2. Order fixed-priced menus, especially at lunch. Often you can dine in some of the most expensive restaurants by patronizing them at lunch and ordering from the set menu.
3. Do as the Norwegians do: Prepare one or two *smørbrød* (open-faced sandwiches) for lunch.
4. Watch the booze—it can add greatly to the cost of any meal.
5. Go ethnic—there are some great inexpensive foreign dining spots. Norwegian restaurants tend to be expensive.
6. Best bet for a quick and inexpensive meal is a *konditori,* or bakery tearoom. Look for the cafeterias as well.
7. Fill up at the traditional Norwegian *koldtbord* (cold board) at breakfast buffets, so you'll need only a light lunch.

The other national drink is **akevitt** (sometimes written as aquavit or schnapps). Who would ever think that potatoes and caraway seeds could knock a person under the table? It's that potent, although it's misnamed the "water of life." Norwegians gulp down beer as a chaser. Aquavit (try Linie Akevitt) is sloshed around in oak vats all the way to Australia and back—for added flavor.

The stores of **Vinmonopolet,** the monopoly that sells wines and spirits, are open Monday through Wednesday from 10am to 5pm, on Thursday from 9am to 6pm, and on Friday from 9am to 5pm. The Vinmonopolet is closed on Saturday in all towns except Kirkenes, Bodø, Ålesund, Trondheim, Haugesund, and Arendal. Alcoholic beverages are not sold to anyone under 20 years of age.

5. RECOMMENDED BOOKS, FILMS & RECORDINGS

BOOKS

HISTORY & MYTHOLOGY *The Vikings,* by Johannes Brøndsted (Penguin), is one of the most enjoyable and best-written documents of the Age of the Vikings.

Quisling: A Study in Treason, by Oddvar K. Hoidal (Oxford University Press), studies the world's most famous traitor, Quisling, who was executed by the Norwegians for running the Nazi puppet government there.

The Vinland Sagas: The Norse Discovery of America, translated by Magnús Magnússon and Hermann Palsson (Penguin). Viking fans will not put down this incredible saga, detailing how Viking Norwegians sailed in their long ships to the eastern coast of "Vinland" (America) as early as the 10th century.

The Norwegians, by Arthur Spencer (David & Charles), is the best book on the market today for understanding the Norwegian people and their advanced society.

ADVENTURE *The Kon-Tiki Expedition,* by Thor Heyerdahl (Washington Square Press), made into a film, details the saga of a modern Norwegian "Viking," who set out on a raft with five comrades and sailed 4,300 miles in 1947—all the way from Peru to Polynesia. *Kon-Tiki Man: An Illustrated Biography of Thor Heyerdahl,* by Thor Heyerdahl with Christopher Ralling (Chronicle), highlights Heyerdahl's attempt to document his idea that Polynesia was settled by people migrating west by water from South America rather than from Asia.

LITERATURE & THEATER *The Governor's Daughter,* by Camilla Collett (several editions), published in 1854, is called the first modern Norwegian novel.

Ibsen Plays: One to Six, by Henrik Ibsen (Heinemann Educational), presents the works of Norway's greatest playwright, including *A Doll's House* and *Hedda Gabler.*

The Ferry Crossing, by Edvard Hoem (Garland), a success in 1989, depicts a tiny Norwegian coastal village in an unorthodox story form.

FILMS

Norwegian filmmakers have yet to equal the success of *Pathfinder* in the late 1980s, which was nominated for an Academy Award as best foreign film.

The most recent best film to come out of Norway (available on video) is *Karachi,* directed by Oddvar Einarson (his *X* won an award at the Venice Film Festival in 1987). *Karachi* deals with drug trafficking between Pakistan and Scandinavia.

RECORDINGS

CLASSICAL *Peer Gynt,* by Edvard Grieg, performed by the Oslo Philharmonic Orchestra, conducted by Esa-Pekka Salonen.

Violin Interpretations, by Terje Tønnesen. Along with Lars Anders Tomter (viola) and Reidun Askeland (piano), this Norwegian violinist plays interpretations of Grieg's Violin Sonata, interpretations of Norwegian composer Johan Halvorsen's adaptations of Handel's violin works, and interpretations of Bjarne Brustad's compositions for solo violin.

MODERN OPERA *Which Witch,* a rock opera, is performed by the musical group Dollie de Luxe. Most of it was composed by Norwegian singer/composer Benedicte Adrian. Accompanying her on keyboard is Ingrid Bjornow.

FOLK *Norwegian Peasant Dances* (Opus 72), by Edvard Grieg, with original fiddle tunes from Telemark, is a musical oddity, even in Norway. This recording alternates Grieg's peasant dances between violin renditions by Norwegian Knut Buen and piano interpretations of the same melody by Norwegian Einar Steen-Nøkleberg.

Rosensfole, Agnes Buen. Known as a "natural" singer, Ms. Buen is accompanied by Norway's best saxophonist, Jan Garbarek, who is better known for his jazz interpretations. He adds texture and greater depth to Ms. Buen's renditions of Norwegian folk melodies.

JAZZ *Norske Rytmekonger,* by Norske Rytmekonger ("Norwegian Rhythm Kings"), is the popular band featured on this enormously successful recording. They are considered Norway's finest interpreters of New Orleans–style jazz.

Cherokee, by Egil Kapstad. Kapstad interprets jazz on his piano, including bee-bop, and is considered among Norway's top jazz musicians.

PLANNING A TRIP TO NORWAY

This chapter is devoted to the nitty-gritty of planning a trip to Norway—costs, events, itineraries, and detailed practicalities like taxes, tipping, and emergencies. It should be read in conjunction with Chapter 1.

1. CURRENCY & COSTS

CURRENCY The Norwegians use the **kroner** and **øre**—simple for those who have mastered the Danish currency system. Bank notes are issued in 10, 50, 100, 500, and 1,000 kroner. Nickel coins are issued in 10 and 50 øre, 1 krone, and 5 and 10 kroner.

Warning: The Norwegian krone (sometimes abbreviated NOK) differs in value from the krone used in Denmark, Iceland, and Sweden. Currently, the Norwegian krone and the Danish krone are virtually on par, but that's not always been the case.

WHAT THINGS COST IN OSLO	U.S. $
Taxi from Fornebu Airport to the city center	18.00
Bus from Fornebu Airport to the city center	5.20
Local telephone call	.35
Double room at the Grand Hotel (deluxe)	320.10
Double room at the Stefan Hotel (moderate)	203.30
Double room at the Munch Hotel (inexpensive)	118.50
Continental breakfast	7.50
Lunch for one at Bristol Grill (moderate)	27.70
Lunch for one at Mamma Rosa (budget)	21.00
Dinner for one, without wine, at Etoile (expensive)	50.00
Dinner for one, without wine, at D. S. Louise (expensive)	44.50
Dinner for one, without wine, at Gamla Rådhus (inexpensive)	25.00
Pint of beer (draft pilsner)	7.50
Coca-Cola (in a restaurant)	3.20
Cup of coffee	2.20
Roll of Kodacolor film, 24 exposures	10.50
Admission to Viking Ship Museum	2.60

	US$
Movie ticket	8.00
Theater ticket (at National Theater)	18.20

WHAT THINGS COST IN BERGEN — U.S. $

	U.S. $
Taxi from Bergen Airport to the city center	31.10
Bus from Bergen Airport to the city center	6.20
Local telephone call	.35
Double room at the Hotel Norge (deluxe)	159.20
Double room at the Augustin (moderate)	136.70
Double room at the Fagerheim Pensjion (budget)	51.90
Continental breakfast	6.50
Smörgåsbord lunch for one at Ole Bull Restaurant	28.50
Lunch for one at Kaffistova (budget)	8.00
Dinner for one, without wine, at Bellevue (deluxe)	60.00
Dinner for one, without wine, at Holberg-Stuen (moderate)	30.00
Dinner for one, without wine, at Wessel-Stuen (moderate)	15.00
Pint of beer (draft pilsner)	7.10
Coca-Cola (in a restaurant)	5.20

THE KRONE & THE DOLLAR

At this writing $1 = 6 Norwegian kroner (or 1 Norwegian krone = 17¢), and this was the rate of exchange used to calculate the dollar values given in the Norway chapters (rounded to the nearest nickel). This rate fluctuates from time to time and may not be the same when you travel to Norway. Therefore the following table should be used only as a guide:

Kroner	U.S. $	Kroner	U.S. $
0.25	.04	125	21.60
0.50	.09	150	25.95
1	.17	175	30.30
5	.90	200	34.60
10	1.75	225	38.90
15	2.60	250	43.25
20	3.50	300	51.90
25	4.30	350	60.55
30	5.20	400	69.20
40	6.90	450	77.85
50	8.65	500	86.50
60	10.40	600	103.80
70	12.10	700	121.10
80	13.80	800	138.40
90	15.60	900	155.70
100	17.30	1,000	173.00

	US$
Cup of coffee	2.25
Roll of Kodacolor film, 24 exposures	8.50
Admission to Det Hanseatiske Museum	2.60
Movie ticket	8.65
Theater ticket (at Den Nationale Scene)	13.00–34.60

2. WHEN TO GO — CLIMATE, HOLIDAYS & EVENTS

CLIMATE

In summer the average temperature in Oslo ranges from 57°F to 65°F. In January it hovers around 27°F—ideal for winter sports.

The western coast of Norway is warmed by the Gulf Stream, and winters tend to be temperate. Rainfall, however, is heavy.

Above the Arctic Circle, the sun shines night and day from mid-May until late July. In contrast, the North Cape plunges into darkness for about 2 months in winter.

Norway's Average Daytime Temperatures [°F]

	Jan	Feb	Mar	Apr	May	June	July	Aug	Sept	Oct	Nov	Dec
Oslo	25	26	32	41	51	60	64	61	53	42	33	27
Bergen/ Stavanger	35	35	38	41	40	55	59	58	54	47	42	38
Trondheim	27	27	31	38	47	53	58	57	50	42	35	31

MIDNIGHT SUN Norway is the land of the Midnight Sun. In summer the sun never fully sets in the northern part of the nation and even in the south there is daylight as late as 11pm and the sun rises around 3am.

The best vantage points and dates in Norway on which to see the spectacle of the Midnight Sun are as follows: **North Cape,** May 12 to August 1; **Hammerfest,** May 14 to July 30; **Tromsø,** May 19 to July 26; **Lofoten Islands,** May 23 to July 17; **Harstad,** May 23 to July 22. All locations can be reached by public transportation.

Keep in mind that although the sun may be shining at midnight, it's not as strong as at midday. Bring along a warm jacket or sweater.

HOLIDAYS

Norway celebrates the following public holidays: January 1 (New Year's Day), Maundy Thursday, Good Friday, Easter, May 1 (Labor Day), Ascension Day, May 17 (Independence Day), Whitmonday, December 25 (Christmas), and December 26 (Boxing Day).

NORWAY
CALENDAR OF EVENTS

Dates given may not be exact; they only give a general indication of time. Check with the tourist office before planning to attend an actual event.

JANUARY

☐ **Northern Lights Festival,** Tromsø. Classical and contemporary music performances by musicians from Norway and abroad. January 18–21.

FEBRUARY

☐ **Kristiansund Opera Festival.** Featuring Kristiansund Opera's own productions of opera and ballet, including art exhibitions, concerts, and other types of information. February 2–11.

MARCH

☐ **Birkebeiner Race.** This historic and international ski race crosses the mountains between Rena and Lillehammer, site of the 1994 Olympics, in a 33-mile cross-country trek. March 18.
☐ **Narvik Winter Festival,** Narvik. Sports events, carnivals, concerts, and opera performances highlight this festival dedicated to the people who built the railway across northern Norway and Sweden. March 24–April 1.
☐ **Nordic Film Festival,** Kristiansand. The public is invited to screenings of Nordic films. March 28–April 1.

APRIL

☐ **Voss Jazz Festival,** Voss. Three days of jazz and folk-music performances are presented by European and American artists. April 6–8.

MAY

☐ **The Viking Run.** An international half-marathon is staged in the Sognefjord with marathon queen Grete Waitz. Some participants stay over for summer skiing, glacier climbing, biking, boating, and mountain climbing. May 26.

✪ *BERGEN INTERNATIONAL FESTIVAL A world-class music event that features artists from Norway and around the world. This is one of the largest annual musical events in Scandinavia.*
Where: Various venues at Bergen. When: May 20–31. How: Details about the events and where and how to attend them are supplied by the Bergen International Festival, Box 183, N-5001 Bergen (tel. 55-21-61-00).

JUNE

☐ **Emigration Festival,** Stavanger. Commemoration of Norwegian immigration to North America. Exhibitions, concerts, theater, folklore. June 7–21.
☐ **Folk Music Festival,** Nesbyen. Traditional Norwegian folk music is performed. June 8–10.
☐ **North Cape March.** This trek from Honningsvåg to the North Cape is one of the world's toughest. Round-trip march is 42 miles. June 16.

- ☐ **Midsummer Night.** Celebrations and bonfires all over Norway. June 23.
- ☐ **Emigration Festival,** Kvinesdal. Commemorates the Norwegian immigration to the United States. June 26–July 1.
- ☐ **International Choir Festival,** Leirvik. Choirs from Europe and the United States participate in this festival. June 28–July 1.

JULY

- ☐ **Kongsberg Jazz Festival.** International artists participate in one of the most important jazz festivals in Scandinavia, with open-air concerts. July 4–8.
- ☐ **Midnight Sun Marathon.** The marathon takes place in Tromsø in northern Norway and starts at midnight. July 7.

✪ *MOLDE INTERNATIONAL JAZZ FESTIVAL The "City of Roses" is the site of Norway's oldest jazz festival, annually attracting international stars from both sides of the Atlantic.*
    Where: Venues in Molde. When: July 13–18. How: For details about the events and how to attend them, contact the Molde Jazz Festival, Box 271, N-6401 Molde (tel. 71-21-60-00).

AUGUST

- ☐ **The Peer Gynt Festival,** Vinstra. Art exhibitions, evenings of music and song, parades in national costumes, and other events honor the fictional character Peer Gynt, from the Ibsen play of the same name. August 3–12.
- ☐ **Telemark Festival.** International festival of folk music and folk dance taking place in Bø where many famous fiddlers, dancers, and singers live. August 9–12.

SEPTEMBER

- ☐ **International Salmon Fishing Festival,** Suldalslagen. Takes place outside Stavanger in western Norway; participants come from Norway and abroad.

OSLO
CALENDAR OF EVENTS

MARCH

✪ *HOLMENKOLLEN SKI FESTIVAL One of Europe's largest ski festivals, with World Cup Nordic skiing and biathlons, international ski-jumping competitions, and Norway's largest cross-country race for amateurs.*
    Where: Holmenkollen Ski Jump on the outskirts of Oslo. When: March 12–15. How: Contact Skiforeningen, Kongeveien 5, Holmenkollen, N-0390 Oslo 3 (tel. 22-14-16-90), for details about participating or attending.

MAY

- ☐ **The Grete Waitz Run.** A run for women only through the streets of Oslo, with participation by marathon great Grete Waitz. May 12.

JUNE

- ☐ **The Faerder Sailing Race.** Some 1,000 sailing boats participate in this race, ending in Borre, by the Oslofjord. June 9.

JULY

- ☐ **Mobil Bislett Games.** International athletic competitions in Oslo are staged, with professional participants from all over the world. July 14.
- ☐ **Norway Cup International Youth Soccer Tournament.** The world's largest youth soccer tournament draws 1,000 teams from around the world to Oslo. July 28–August 4.

AUGUST

- ☐ **Chamber Music Festival.** Oslo is host to chamber music concerts by both Norwegian and foreign musicians in Akershus Castle and Fortress, which dates from A.D. 1300. August 3–12.
- ☐ **The Oslo Jazz Festival.** Annual jazz festival in Oslo featuring music from the earliest years of jazz, the 1920 to 1925 era, with classical concerts, opera, and ballet. August 8–12.
- ☐ **World Cup Summer Ski Jumping.** Takes place in Marikollen, Raelingen, just outside the center of Oslo. August 19.

SEPTEMBER

- ☐ **Oslo Marathon.** An annual event drawing some of Norway's best long-distance runners. September 8.

DECEMBER

- ✪ **NOBEL PEACE PRIZE CEREMONY** *A major event on the Oslo calendar, drawing the most world interest.*
  Where: *Oslo City Hall.* ***When:*** *December 10.* ***How:*** *Attendance by invitation only. Information available at Nobel Institute, Drammensveien 19, N-0255 Oslo 2 (tel. 22-44-36-80).*

3. GETTING AROUND

BY PLANE

Norway has excellent air service. In addition to SAS, two independent airways, Braathens SAFE and Wideroe Flyveselskap, provide a quick and convenient means of getting around a large country with many hard-to-reach areas. All three airlines offer mini-fares, reduced rates available when booked outside Norway.

BRAATHENS SAFE A top-notch independent airline, the Norwegian flag carrier Braathens SAFE (tel. 67-59-70-00 in Oslo; 56-23-23-25 in Bergen), carries more passengers on domestic routes than any other airline in Norway. It operates charter flights throughout Europe and North Africa and has regularly scheduled routings inside Norway, linking major cities as well as more remote places not covered by other airlines. Its air routes directly link Oslo to all major cities in the country along with frequent flights along the coast from Oslo to Tromsø and farther north to Longyearbyen on the island of Spitsbergen.

You might also inquire about the **Visit Norway Pass** offered by Braathens SAFE, which grants reductions and is valid for 1 month between May 1 and September 30. There are two sets of fares: one for so-called short journeys and one for long journeys. Flights between airports in North Norway count as short journeys, while flights from South Norway to North Norway or vice versa count as long journeys. A one-way fare for a short journey is $57, whereas a one-way fare for a long journey is $114. The Visit Norway Pass also entitles you to a free Scandinavian Bonus Pass valid from June 1 to September 1 and worth 150 kroner ($26). It offers substantial discounts at 43 Inter Nor Hotels in Norway. The pass is sold by airlines that have agreements with Braathens SAFE. It is also sold at STS Tour Consultants, 6033 W. Century Blvd., Suite 850, Los Angeles, CA 90045 (tel. 213/410-9533).

SAS SAS crisscrosses Norway with a number of regularly scheduled domestic flights, connecting Bergen, Oslo, Trondheim, and Bodø. It's also possible to fly to the Arctic gateway of Tromsø; to Alta in Finnmark, the heart of Lapland; and to Kirkenes, near the Russian border. Call SAS in Oslo at 22-17-00-20, or toll free 800/221-2350 in the U.S.

SAS offers a 1-6 coupon ticket within Scandinavia, including Norway, its price based on the number of coupons purchased. The fare is valid for 3 months from the date of arrival in Scandinavia. Tickets can only be purchased in North America. Contact SAS or your travel agent. For more information, see "Air and Rail Passes" in Chapter 1.

OTHER AIRLINES Some minor carriers within Norway—notably **Widero** (tel. 22-73-65-00 in Oslo) and **Norsk Air** (tel. 56-99-82-21 in Bergen)—offer summer discounts on tickets purchased from June 25 through August 15. These airlines fly to a total of 41 destinations within Norway. For tickets, contact the airlines directly at airport offices or local travel agents within Norway.

BY TRAIN

Norway is crisscrossed by a network of electric and diesel-electric trains that run as far as Bodø, 62 miles beyond the Arctic Circle. (After that, visitors have to take a coastal steamer, plane, or bus along the run to Tromsø and the North Cape.)

The most popular run is between Oslo and Bergen, a distance of 300 miles. Often visitors with limited time choose this train route for its fabled mountains, gorges, white-water rivers, and fjords. Conductors often stop for major scenic views.

Second-class travel on Norwegian trains is recommended. In fact, second class in Norway is as good as or better than second-class travel anywhere else in Europe, with reclining seats and lots of unexpected comforts. The one-way second-class fare to Bergen from Oslo is $66, and $99 in first class. Another popular run, from Oslo to the railway's northern terminus at Bodø, some 800 rail miles, costs $120 one-way in second class or $180 in first class.

One of the country's logical scenic trips—from Bergen to Bodø—is not possible because of the terrain, so trains to Bodø leave from Oslo, not Bergen. The express trains are called *Hurtigtog/Ekspress,* while regular trains are called *Persontog* (usually second-class seats only).

On express and other main trains you have to reserve seats at the train's starting station. Sleepers and seats are priced per person and evaluated by the number of berths in each compartment. Children 4 to 15 years of age and senior citizens pay 50% off the regular adult fare. Group and midweek tickets are also available.

There are special compartments for the physically handicapped on most medium- and long-distance trains. These may be used by persons in wheelchairs and others with physical handicaps as well as their companions.

Travelers over age 67 are entitled to a 50% discount, called an **Honnorrabatt**, on Norwegian train journeys of over 31 miles. During special periods, reductions are also offered on the popular coastal steamers. The spouse of someone over 67 can also receive the 50% discount.

With a **Mini-Price Ticket** you can travel as far as you like one-way second class for about $66. There is no mileage limitation. No stopovers are allowed except for a change of trains. These discount tickets are valid only on long distance trains Monday through Thursday. Mini-Price Tickets can be purchased at any railway station in Norway.

If you're planning to include Norway in an overall European itinerary, you might consider the **Eurailpass.** If you're planning extensive rail travel only in the Scandinavian countries, then a **Nordturist Pass** might be for you. For more information, refer to "Air and Rail Passes" in Chapter 1.

BY BUS

Where the train or coastal steamer stops, a scenic bus is usually waiting to take passengers the rest of the way. Norway's bus system is excellent, linking remote, off-the-beaten-path villages along the fjords. Numerous all-inclusive motorcoach tours—often combined with steamer travel—are offered from Bergen or Oslo in summer. The train ends its northward run in Bodø, but it's possible to take the Polar Express bus, 39 miles east of Bodø in Fauske. This fascinating bus trip spans the distance along the Arctic Highway through Finnmark (Lapland) to Kirkenes near the Russian border and back. The Kirkenes run operates from June to October, but the service is year-round from Fauske to Alta in Finnmark. Passengers are guaranteed hotel accommodations along the way.

Buses are equipped with air conditioning, toilets, adjustable seats, reading lights, and telephone. Reservations are not accepted on most buses, and payment is made to the driver on board. Fares depend on the distance traveled. Children under 4 travel free, and children 4 to 16 and senior citizens pay half price. For the Oslo-Sweden-Hammerfest "Express 2000," a 30-hour trip, reservations must be made in advance.

For more data about bus travel in Norway, contact **Nor-Way Bussterminal,** Havnegata, Oslo Sentralstasjon (tel. 22-33-01-91) in Oslo, or call **Passage Tours of Scandinavia** toll free in the U.S. at 800/548-5960.

BY CAR & FERRY

Dazzling scenery awaits you at nearly every turn. Some of the roads are less than perfect (often dirt or gravel) but passable. Most mountain roads are open by May 1; the so-called motoring season lasts from mid-May to the end of September. In western Norway hairpin curves are common, but if you're willing to settle for doing less than 150 miles a day you needn't worry. The easiest and most convenient touring territory is in and around Oslo and the trek southward, from the capital to Stavanger. You can drive to the North Cape by car.

Bringing a car into Norway is not a problem. Drivers must have their national driver's license, car registration book, "warning triangle," and an insurance "Green Card" (obtainable from Customs upon entering Norway).

Mostly privately run, car-ferries in the western fjord country and in the north are essential to transportation. Motorists should ask the tourist bureau for a free map, "Norway By Car," and a timetable outlining car-ferry services. Some ferries will accept advance reservations. Since the ferries are vital to the transportation system—and are mostly used by Norwegians—the cost for passengers or for car transport is low.

RENTALS **Hertz, Avis,** and **Budget** offer well-serviced, well-maintained fleets of rental cars within Norway. Prices and rental terms tend to be about the same at all three of the companies, although each tries to schedule promotional deals throughout the calendar year, making one of the other suddenly more attractive. Also offering strong competition is a small but reliable company called **Kemwell** (tel. toll free 800/678-0678) based in Harrison, N.Y. More than any of the big-three outfits mentioned above, Kemwell works in close association with such airlines as Delta and SAS, offering deeply discounted car rentals to anyone buying certain categories of tickets to Scandinavia on either of those airlines.

Of the remaining companies mentioned above, the cheapest, Avis (tel. toll free 800/331-2112), charged around $286 per week for a cramped but peppy Fiat Uno for cars reserved 14 days prior to departure from the U.S. Close on its heels was Budget, charging $320 per week for their cheapest vehicle, a Ford Fiesta with unlimited mileage. Hertz proposed substantially more: $398 per week for their cheapest car, a Fiat Uno. At all companies, the 20% government tax cost extra. The companies maintain offices at one or both of Oslo's airports, as well as offices in downtown Oslo, and at airports and city centers throughout Norway. These prices can and will change during the lifetime of this edition, with (as mentioned earlier) last-minute price promotions substantially altering the relative values represented by each of the contenders.

Insurance All the companies built a nominal insurance coverage into their rates, but it's probably not sufficient for most drivers and most accidents. If you have a mishap and didn't purchase additional insurance, you'll be responsible for around 15,000 kroner ($2,595) worth of damage (and sometimes much more), depending on the company you rent from. To avoid this responsibility, you can opt to accept an additional insurance policy (known as a collision damage waiver) priced at between $17 and $20 per day, depending on the company. (These insurance prices are sometimes built into a total package price, making mathematical comparisons of the insurance clauses offered by the competing companies somewhat more confusing.) I usually find that buying the additional insurance is well worth the added expense, considering the unfamiliar driving conditions you're likely to encounter abroad.

Note that when certain types of credit cards are used to pay for a car rental, no additional insurance purchases are necessary. Although many readers have availed themselves of this cost-saving device, the fine print of these insurance options must be individually verified directly with the issuer of any particular credit card.

Regardless of the insurance you opt for, remember that driving after having consumed even a small amount of alcohol is punishable by heavy fines and/or imprisonment.

GASOLINE In and around Oslo you'll find plenty of gasoline stations. However, if you're planning long drives on offbeat roads, always ask where the next station is. Gasoline prices are always changing in Norway based on market conditions, and gas is much more expensive in the remote north than in the south.

DRIVING RULES Don't drink and drive. All Scandinavian countries are fanatically strict about drunken drivers.

It is mandatory for all cars and trucks in Norway to have their headlights on—day and night—as a safety measure.

Cars are driven on the right-hand side of the road.

ROAD MAPS Ask for road maps at local tourist offices, bookstores, or the **Norwegian Automobile Club,** Storgata 2, N-0155 Oslo 1 (tel. 22-34-14-00). The best commercial road maps on Norway are published by Hallweg.

BREAKDOWNS/ASSISTANCE If your car breaks down in Norway, call the rental company first. Otherwise, contact one of the following:

In Oslo: Falken Rescue Service (tel. 22-23-20-85, 24 hours daily), NAF Alarm (tel. 22-42-94-00, 24 hours daily), or Viking Rescue Reserve (tel. 22-60-60-90, 24 hours daily).

In Bergen: Falken Rescue Service (tel. 56-32-62-00) or Viking Rescue Service (tel. 56-29-22-22).

In Stavanger: Falken Rescue Service (tel. 51-58-60-20, 24 hours daily) or Viking Rescue Service (tel. 51-58-29-00, 24 hours daily).

BY RV By law, trailers rented in Norway cannot be wider than 7½ feet and the combined length of car and trailer cannot be longer than 59 feet. Some roads are not suitable for such recreational vehicles. Inquire at the rental agency about the route you plan to take.

For more information in the U.S., call **Tumlare Travel Organization Inc.** toll free at 800/223-4664.

BY STEAMER

Some visitors have agreed that the fjords of western Norway are among the most beautiful sights in Europe. For a seagoing view of them, nothing beats the indomitable steamer ships which ply the offshore waters of Norway carrying mail, supplies, and passengers. Those with the time and a taste for offbeat adventures can book a 12-day, all-inclusive round-trip steamer trip from Bergen to Kirkenes (one of Norway's most northerly ports), encompassing some 2,500 miles of jagged and scenic coastline.

Because of the long distances, steamers are equipped with cabins similar to those on a transatlantic liner. Depending on the accommodations and the time of year, cabins cost between $935 and $2,400 per person, double occupancy, for the 12-day round-trip excursion. Single cabins cost from $1,015 to $2,700. Because July and August are the most expensive sailings, many visitors opt for spring or autumn sailings as cost-saving devices. All meals are included in the price. Children under 12 receive a 25% discount on round-trip voyages. Steamers make scheduled stops in hamlets and cities along the way, which range from a half hour to a half day, depending on the size of the port. Passengers who prefer to spend more time in selected cities usually opt for port-to-port tickets, on which children under 12 receive a 50% discount. Be warned in advance, however, that booking cabins on a port-to-port basis during July and August is often extremely difficult because of the popularity of these fjord cruises.

For reservations and information, contact the **Bergen Line,** 505 Fifth Ave., New York, NY 10017 (tel. 212/986-2711, or toll free 800/323-7436). If you only want to receive brochures, call toll free 800/666-2374.

SUGGESTED ITINERARIES

IF YOU HAVE 1 WEEK

Day 1: Fly to Oslo, check into a hotel, and relax. Few can fight the jetlag on their first day in the Norwegian capital.

Day 2: After breakfast in Oslo, take the ferry to the Bygdøy peninsula for a look in the *Kon-Tiki* Museum, the polar ship *Fram,* the Viking ships, and the Norwegian Folk Museum, breaking for lunch when ready.

Day 3: While still in Oslo, visit the 75-acre Frogner Park to see the Vigeland sculptures and view the collection of paintings by Edvard Munch. You should have enough time to see the Henie-Onstad Foundation art center 7 miles from Oslo. Return in time to go to the Lookout Tower and ski jump at Holmenkollen where you can dine, enjoying a superb view of Oslo.

Day 4: Head south on a fascinating day trip from Oslo to some of the major towns along the Oslofjord. In the morning, drive to Fredrikstad on the Glomma River, taking in its Old Town and visiting Norway Silver Designs, its handcraft center. Drive back to Moss and take a ferry across the fjord. From Horten on the west bank, drive south to Tønsberg, Norway's oldest town (visit the Vestfold Folk Museum), and then on to Sandefjord, the former whaling capital with a whaling museum. Drive back to Oslo for dinner.

Day 5: Leaving Oslo by train, head west for Bergen on a 300-mile "day-trip"—one of the highlights of European travel. You literally go across the rooftop of Norway, past the ski resorts of Geilo and Voss. After this dramatic trip, you'll arrive in Bergen.

Day 6: Explore Bergen's many attractions, such as Trolls' Hill (the summer villa of composer Edvard Grieg).

Day 7: For 1 day and night, go to Ulvik on the Hardangerfjord in the western fjord district, reached by public transport from Bergen. This beautiful town is typical of the fjord towns in the entire district.

IF YOU HAVE 2 WEEKS

Days 1–7: Spend the first week as described above.

Day 8: While still based in Ulvik (see "Day 7," above), continue to explore the fjord district.

Day 9: Return to Bergen, then fly to Trondheim, also a major sightseeing attraction.

Day 10: If it's summer, take a 13-hour train ride from Trondheim to Bodø on the Midnight Sun Special. Spend the night in Bodø, north of the Arctic Circle.

Day 11: From Bodø, fly to Tromsø, 250 miles north of the Arctic Circle (it does not have rail service). Stay overnight in Tromsø and see its limited, but interesting, attractions.

Day 12: Rent a car in Tromsø and head north for the last leg of the trip: a 280-mile run over the Arctic Highway. I suggest that you spend the night in Alta. The road is slow-going, as it wraps itself around inlets and fjords.

Day 13: Continue driving north to Hammerfest, the most northerly town in the world of any major size. Stay overnight.

Day 14: From Hammerfest, take an excursion boat directly to the North Cape. Those with more time can drive to Honningsvåg, the world's northernmost village, the gateway to the North Cape. Buses leave from its marketplace daily, heading for the cape, a 22-mile run.

Return to Tromsø where air connections can be made to Oslo and your return flight to North America or to another Scandinavian capital.

IF YOU HAVE 3 WEEKS

Days 1–4: Spend the first 4 days as described in "If You Have 1 Week," above.

Day 5: Explore Oslo in greater depth, visiting Akershus Castle, with its Norwegian Resistance Museum, and the National Gallery. Take one of the walking tours mapped out for Oslo—two if you have the time and the stamina (see Chapter 15).

Day 6: Drive north from Oslo along the E6 to the ski resort of Lillehammer, site of the 1994 Winter Olympics. Stop for lunch at Gjøvik, "the white town on Lake Mjøsa," arriving in Lillehammer in time to view the Sandvig Collections. Either overnight in Lillehammer or return to Oslo.

Day 7: Leave either Oslo or Lillehammer by train, depending on where you spent the night, heading west for Bergen across the rooftop of Europe.

Day 8: Spend the day sightseeing Bergen, visiting Trolls' Hill (the summer villa of composer Edvard Grieg).

Day 9: Take a trip to the Hardangerfjord and the Folgefonn glacier. Bus trips depart from Bergen for this full-day tour.

Day 10: Board an express steamer from Bergen to Gudvangen to see the Sognefjord, the longest fjord in Norway. From Gudvangen, go by bus to Voss, a famous ski resort.

Day 11: Spend another day in Voss taking excursions and exploring the area.

Day 12: Return to Bergen for an overnight stay. Relax.

Day 13: From Bergen, go to Ålesund at the top of the fjord country and explore the town.

Day 14: While still in Ålesund, take a sightseeing tour for the day to Geiranger, one of the most famous resorts in the fjord country. Waterfalls are in and around the area. Return to Ålesund for the night.

Day 15: From Ålesund, make air connections to Trondheim, the third-largest city of Norway and a historic capital. Explore some of its attractions.

Day 16: Explore Trondheim fully and spend the night.

Day 17–21: Follow the schedule outlined for Days 10 to 14 listed in "If You Have 2 Weeks," above.

FAST
NORWAY

Business Hours Most **banks** are open Monday through Friday from 8:15am to 3:30pm (on Thursday to 5pm); closed Saturday and Sunday. The

Fellesbanken's Exchange at the Oslo Central Railway Station (tel. 22-41-26-11) is open Monday through Friday from 8am to midnight, on Saturday from 8am to 7pm, and on Sunday from 8am to noon. There's a bank at Fornebu Airport, open daily from 7am to 10:30pm. There is also a bank at Gardermoen Airport. Most **businesses** are open Monday through Friday from 9am to 4pm. **Stores** are generally open Monday through Friday from 9am to 5pm (many stay open late on Thursday until 6pm or 7pm) and on Saturday from 9am to 1 or 2pm. Sunday closings are observed.

Cigarettes   Tobacco kiosks carry Norwegian brands of American-blended cigarettes that are cheaper than the British and American brands on sale.

Currency   See "Currency and Costs," above.

Customs   With certain food exceptions, personal effects, intended for your own use, can be brought into Norway. If you take them with you when you leave, you can bring in cameras, binoculars, radios, portable TV sets, and the like, as well as fishing and camping equipment. Americans or Canadians can bring in 400 cigarettes, or 500 grams of tobacco and 200 sheets of cigarette paper, or 50 cigars; and 1 liter of spirits or 1 liter of wine. Britons can bring in 200 cigarettes, or 250 grams of tobacco and 200 sheets of cigarette paper; 1 liter of spirits; and 1 liter of wine.

Upon leaving, you can hold up to 5,000 kroner ($865) in Norwegian cash.

Dentists   For emergency dental services, ask your hotel or host for the nearest dentist. Most Norwegian dentists speak English.

Doctors   If you become ill or injured while in Norway, hotel staffs can refer you to a local doctor, nearly all of whom speak English. If not at a hotel, call the nearest 24-hour emergency medical phone number: 22-20-10-90 in Oslo, 56-32-11-20 in Bergen, 72-59-88-00 in Trondheim, 51-53-33-33 in Stavanger, and 77-38-30-00 in Tromsø.

Driving Rules   See "Getting Around," above.

Drug Laws   There are severe penalties in Norway for any activities related to the possession, use, purchase, sale, or manufacturing of drugs. Penalties are often based on quantity, but that can vary. Possession of what is deemed a small amount of drugs, either hard or soft, can lead to a heavy fine and deportation. Possession of a "large" amount of drugs can elicit a prison term ranging anywhere from 3 months to 15 years, depending on the circumstances. Norwegian police are particularly strict with any cases involving sales of drugs to children, and the courts tend to impose maximum prison terms in such cases.

Drugstores   Drugstores, called *Apotek,* are open during normal business hours.

Electricity   Norway has 220 volts, 50–30 cycles, A.C., and standard continental two-pin plugs are used. Transformers and adapters will be needed with Canadian and American equipment. Always inquire at your hotel before plugging in any electrical equipment.

Embassies and Consulates   In case you lose your passport or have some other emergency, contact your embassy in Oslo. The **U.S. Embassy** is at Drammensveien 18, N-0255 Oslo 2 (tel. 22-44-85-50); the **British Embassy,** at Thomas Heftyes Gate 8, N-0264 Oslo 2 (tel. 22-55-24-00); and the **Canadian Embassy,** at Oscarsgate 20, N-0352 Oslo 3 (tel. 22-46-69-55). Travelers from Australia, Ireland, and New Zealand should contact the British Embassy. The British consulate is at Strandgaten 18 in Bergen (tel. 56-32-07-11).

Emergencies   In Norway, dial **000** for the police nationwide; to report a fire, dial **001,** and to request an ambulance, call **003.**

Etiquette   Norwegians, for the most part, are well mannered, and expect you to be too. "Good day" is said to everyone, and "Thank you" is said even for a simple service or favor. You should always bring flowers or candy if invited to a private home for dinner. Shaking hands is a ritual when you meet someone or take leave. Both women and men shake hands.

Gasoline   See "Getting Around," above.

Hitchhiking   Look clean and you'll find it an acceptable custom. If you're heading from Oslo to Bergen and the western fjord district, board the local train to Skøyen and then try to hitch a ride from Drammensveien. From Trondheim and points north, catch the T-bane train to Carl Berners Plads and position yourself along the Trondheimsveien.

Language A nationwide controversy: Danish-Norwegian (*riksmaal*) is commonly spoken, but a rise of patriotic spirit has caused Norwegians to turn to New Norwegian (*landsmaal*). But English is spoken almost universally in Norway, certainly by most people engaged in the tourist business.

Laundry and Dry Cleaning Laundry and dry-cleaning services are provided at most hotels. There are coin-operated laundries and dry-cleaners in most Norwegian cities.

Liquor Laws Most restaurants, pubs, and bars in Norway are licensed to serve liquor, wine, and beer. The drinking age in Norway is 18 for beer and wine and 20 for liquor.

Mail Airmail letters or postcards to the U.S. and Canada cost 5.20 kroner (90¢) for up to 20 grams (7/10 oz.). It takes an airmail letter 7 to 10 days to reach Norway from the U.S. or vice versa. The biggest post office in Norway is Oslo Central Post Office, Dronningensgate 15, Oslo 1 (tel. 22-40-78-23). Mailboxes are a vibrant red, embossed with the trumpet symbol of the Norwegian postal service. They are found on walls, at chest level, in various places throughout cities and towns. Stamps can be bought at magazine kiosks or from town merchants.

Only the post office can weigh, evaluate, and tell you the different options for time or the various regulations that apply to parcels. Shipments to places outside Norway require a declaration on a preprinted form, stating the contents and value of the package.

Maps Many tourist offices supply free maps of their district. You can also contact the **Norwegian Automobile Club**, Storgata 2, N-0155 Oslo 1 (tel. 22-34-14-00). Bookstores throughout Norway always sell detailed maps of the country for those planning extensive touring. The most reliable ones are published by Hallweg.

Pets Leave your pet at home. Fearing the risk of rabies, Norway does not allow dogs, cats, and other domestic animals into the country without a permit from the Ministry of Agriculture. The quarantine period for dogs and cats is 4 months.

Police Dial **000** nationwide for police assistance.

Radio and TV Radio and television broadcasts are in Norwegian. However, Norwegian National Radio (NRK) has news summaries in English several times weekly.

Restrooms All terminals, big city squares, and the like have public lavatories. In small towns and villages, head for the marketplace. Hygienic standards are usually adequate. If you patronize the toilets in a privately run establishment, such as a café, it is considered polite to buy a small pastry or coffee.

Safety Whenever you're traveling in an unfamiliar city or country, stay alert. Be aware of your immediate surroundings. Wear a moneybelt and don't sling your camera or purse over your shoulder; wear the strap diagonally across your body. This will minimize the possibility of your becoming a victim of crime. Every society has its criminals. It's your responsibility to be aware and alert even in the most heavily touristed areas.

Taxes Norway is not a member of the European Community, but imposes a 20% value-added tax on most goods and services, which is figured into your final bill. However, if you make your purchases in any store bearing the TAX-FREE sign, you will be entitled to a 10% to 15% refund in cash for purchases over 300 kroner ($51.90). Just ask the shop assistant for a tax-free shopping check, showing your passport to indicate that you're from the United States or Canada. You may not use the articles purchased before leaving Norway, and they must be taken out of the country within 4 weeks of purchase. Complete the information required on the back of the check you are given at the store, and then report at your point of departure at an area marked by the TAX-FREE sign, not at Customs. Your refund check will be exchanged there in kroner for the amount due you. Norway's tax-free checks can also be repaid in Sweden, Finland, and Denmark. Refunds are available at all points of departure—airports, ferry and cruise-ship terminals, borders, and train stations.

Telephone and Telegrams Direct-dial long-distance calls can be made to the United States and Canada from most phones in Norway by dialing 095, then the country code (1 for the U.S. and Canada), and the area code and phone number you wish to reach. Check at the hotel front desk before placing a call. Norwegian coins of 1 krone (20¢) and 5 kroner (90¢) are used in pay phones in Norway.

Telegrams can be sent from private or public phones by dialing 0138.

Time   At noon, eastern standard time (EST) in New York City, it's 6pm in Norway. Norway goes on summer time around March 28 (the date varies every year), until around September 26.

Tipping   Hotels, depending on their classification, add 10% to 15% to your bill, which handles most matters, unless someone on staff has done some special service for you. Most bellhops get at least 5 kroner (90¢) to 10 kroner ($1.70) per suitcase. Nearly all restaurants add a service charge of up to 15% to your bill. Barbers and hairdressers aren't usually tipped, but toilet attendants and hatcheck people expect at least 2 kroner (30¢). Don't tip theater ushers. Taxi drivers do not expect tips unless they handle heavy luggage.

Water   Water is generally safe to drink throughout Norway.

Yellow Pages   It's often difficult to find a listing, especially if you don't know the Norwegian name for the service you are seeking. Hotel desks tend to be helpful.

INTRODUCING OSLO

Oslo was founded in the mid-11th century by a Viking king and became the capital around 1300 under King Haakon V. In the course of its history the city burned down several times, and was completely destroyed by fire in 1824. However, the master builder, Christian IV, King of Denmark and Norway, ordered the town rebuilt near the Akershus Castle. He named the new town Christiania, after himself, and that was its official name until 1924, when the city celebrated its 300-year jubilee and reverted to the old name of Oslo.

In 1814 Norway was separated from Denmark and united with Sweden, a union that lasted until 1905. During that period, the Royal Palace, the House of Parliament, the old university, the National Theater, and the National Gallery were built.

After World War II, Oslo grew to 175 square miles. It's one of the 10 largest capitals in the world in sheer area. The city is one of the most heavily forested on earth—in all this land area fewer than half a million Norwegians live and work.

One of the oldest Scandinavian capital cities, Oslo has never been a mainstream European tourist site. Many have the impression that it's lean on attractions. In fact, it is a culturally rich capital with many diversions, enough to fill at least 3 or 4 busy days. It is also the center for many easy excursions along the Oslofjord or to towns and villages in its environs, both north and south.

In recent years Oslo has surprisingly grown from what even the Scandinavians viewed as a Nordic backwater to one of the most happening cities of Europe. Restaurants, nightclubs, cafés, shopping complexes, and other venues have opened as never before. A kind of Nordic joie de vivre permeates the city. The only problem is that it's expensive, one of the most expensive cities of Europe. Proceed with caution if you're on a strict budget.

One final point: Every inhabitant of Oslo is a nature lover. Locals spend much time devoted to pursuits in the forest or on the fjord. It takes only half an hour by tram into the hills from Parliament or the Royal Palace to the 154-foot Tryvann Observation Tower where you have a view over the lushest part of the capital—Oslo Marka, the giant forest. It was here in the Krogskogen forests that many Norwegian folktales took place—tales of princesses, kings, penniless heroes, and the inevitable forest "trolls." And from the same tower in summer you can look down on hundreds of sailboats, motorboats, and windsurfers enjoying the numerous islands of the Oslo archipelago.

1. ORIENTATION

ARRIVING

BY PLANE The domestic airport, **Fornebu** (tel. 67-59-36-13) at Snaroya, is 5½ miles from Oslo. The international airport, **Gardermoen** (tel. 63-97-80-20), 1 hour

WHAT'S SPECIAL ABOUT OSLO

Beaches
☐ Oslo's archipelago of islands in the inner fjord is a summer playground. Take a ferry to the beach.

Monuments/Buildings
☐ Akershus Castle and Fortress, dating from 1300 but rebuilt in the 17th century. Walk its ramparts.

☐ City Hall (Rådhus), inaugurated in 1950 and decorated by the country's leading painters and sculptors, honors Oslo's 900th anniversary.

Museums
☐ Folk Museum, 170 buildings from all over Norway, including a 1200 stave church, were moved here. Life in the 18th century goes on.

☐ Munch Museum, showcasing Edvard Munch, Scandinavia's greatest painter.

☐ Viking Ship Museum, housing the *Oseberg, Gokstad,* and *Tune* ships from A.D. 800–900.

Parks/Gardens
☐ Vigeland Sculpture Park, where the often-bizarre world of sculptor Gustav Vigeland is depicted.

For the Kids
☐ *Kon-Tiki* Museum, displaying the balsa raft that Thor Heyerdahl used to make a dangerous voyage across the Pacific.

Offbeat Oddities
☐ Ski Museum, the world's oldest, containing everything from a 2,500-year-old ski to a polar ski.

Scenic Vistas
☐ The Tryvann Observation Tower, the highest point in Oslo, offering some 30,000 square miles of fjord country spread before you.

Special Events/Festivals
☐ Holmenkollen Ski Festival, attracting the world's best cross-country skiers and jumpers (March).

---

from the city center, receives mostly TWA and charter flights. If you have a choice, it's far better—and less expensive—to arrive at Fornebu, because of its more convenient location. Fornebu services both domestic and international flights of SAS and other intra-European airlines, including British Airways and Icelandair.

SAS operates a bus service from both terminals to the Central Station and other points in Oslo every 15 minutes. The fare is 65 kroner ($11.20) to and from Gardermoen and 30 kroner ($5.20) to and from Fornebu.

BY TRAIN Trains from the Continent and from Sweden or Copenhagen pull into **Oslo Sentralstasjon,** Jernbanetorget 1 at the beginning of Karl Johans Gate, in the center of the city. The station is open daily from 7am to 11pm. From the Central Station, you can catch trains heading for Bergen, Trondheim, "end-of-the-line" Bodø, and all other rail links in Norway. You can also take trams to all major parts of Oslo. Lockers and a luggage office are available at the station, and you can also exchange money here. For train information, call 22-36-68-00.

BY CAR If you're driving from mainland Europe, the fastest way to reach Oslo is to take the car-ferry from Frederikshavn (Denmark). You can also take a car-ferry from Copenhagen, or drive from Copenhagen by crossing over to Helsingborg (Sweden) from Helsingør (Denmark). Once at Helsingborg, take the E6 north all the way to Stockholm. If you're driving from Stockholm to Oslo, take the E18 west all the way. Once you near the outskirts of Oslo from any direction, follow the signs into the Sentrum.

BY FERRY Ferries from Europe arrive at the Oslo port, a 15-minute walk (or a short taxi ride) from the center. From Denmark, Scandinavia's link with the Continent, ferries depart for Oslo from Copenhagen, Hirtshals, and Frederikshavn.

From Strømstad (Sweden), there is a daily crossing in summer to Sandefjord (Norway), taking 2½ hours; from Sandefjord, it's an easy drive or train ride north to Oslo.

TOURIST INFORMATION

Assistance and information for visitors is available at the **Tourist Information Office** at Rådhuset (City Hall), Rådhusgaten 19, N-0037 Oslo 1 (tel. 22-83-00-50). Entrance is on the harborside. Free maps, brochures, sightseeing tickets, and guide services are available. The office is open mid-May to mid-September, Monday through Saturday from 8:30am to 4pm and on Sunday from 9am to 5pm; late September to early May, Monday through Friday from 8:30am to 4pm and on Saturday from 8:30am to 2:30pm.

There is also an information office at the **Oslo Sentralstasjon** (Central Station), Jernbanetorget 1, at the beginning of Karl Johans Gate (tel. 22-17-11-24), open daily from 8am to 11pm.

CITY LAYOUT

MAIN ARTERIES & STREETS

Oslo is at the mouth of the 60-mile-long Oslofjord. Opening onto the harbor is **Rådhusplassen,** dominated by the modern **City Hall,** a major attraction. Guided bus tours leave from this point, and the launches that cruise the fjords depart from the pier facing the municipal building (it's possible to catch Bygdøy-bound ferries from the quay at Rådhusplassen).

Out on a promontory to the east is **Akershus Castle.** At **Bygdøy,** the much larger peninsula which juts out to the west, four of Oslo's major attractions can be found: the Viking ships, the *Fram* Museum, *Kon-Tiki* raft, and the Folk Museum.

Karl Johans Gate, Oslo's main street, mainly for shopping and strolling, is north of City Hall Square. This boulevard begins at Østbanestasjonen (East Station) and stretches all the way to the 19th-century **Royal Palace** at the western end.

A short walk from the palace is the famed **Students' Grove** (the University of Oslo is nearby), where everybody gathers on a summer day to socialize. Dominating this center is the **National Theater,** guarded by statues of Ibsen and Bjørnson, the two greatest names in Norwegian theater. South of the theater and near the harbor is **Stortingsgate,** another shop-filled street.

The main city square is **Stortorvet,** although it is no longer the center of city life, having lost that position to Karl Johans Gate.

At a subway stop near the National Theater, it's possible to head out for **Tryvannstårnet,** the loftiest lookout town in Scandinavia, and to the **Holmenkollen Ski Jump.**

FINDING AN ADDRESS

Street numbers begin on the south side of streets running on a north-south axis, and on the eastern end of streets running on an east-west axis. All odd numbers lie on one side of the street, and all even numbers are on the opposite side of the street. In some cases, a large building contains several establishments, and different addresses are designated as 3A, 3B, and 3C.

NEIGHBORHOODS IN BRIEF

Oslo is made for walking—in fact, you can walk from the Central Station all the way to the Royal Palace (Slottet) in a straight line. Except for excursions to museum-loaded Bygdøy peninsula and the Holmenkollen Ski Jump, most attractions can be covered on foot.

Oslo does not break up into separate neighborhoods or districts like London and Paris. It consists mainly of **central Oslo,** with the Central Station on the eastern side of the city center and the Royal Palace on the west. Karl Johans Gate, the main street, connects these two points. There are almost 50 museums and galleries in Central Oslo, enough to fill many a rainy day. The most interesting include Akershus Castle, the Norwegian Resistance Museum, and the National Gallery.

The streets Drammensveien and Frognerveien lead northwest to **Frognerpark** (whose main entrance is on Kirkeveien). Site of the Vigeland Sculpture Park, which brings together some masterpieces of Gustav Vigeland (1869–1943), this is a delightful area.

Old Town or Gamlebyen lies south of the Parliament Building (the Storting) and Karl Johans Gate. This section contains some of the most old-fashioned restaurants of Oslo, along with the Norwegian Resistance Museum and the Old Town Hall.

Aker Brygge, the newest neighborhood of Oslo, sprouted up in the old wharf area down by the mouth of the Oslofjord, land formerly reserved for shipbuilding yards. Fueled by oil wealth, steel-and-glass buildings rise from what was a relatively dilapidated section. Now some of the best shops, theaters, restaurants, and cultural attractions are here, along with apartments for such well-heeled owners as Diana Ross.

In **eastern Oslo** the neighborhood centers around the Botanisk Hage (Botanic Garden), the Zoological Museum, and the Munch Museum in Tøyen.

To the west of Oslo, 4 miles by car but better reached by car-ferry, is the **Bygdøy peninsula,** containing important city attractions like the Norwegian Folk Museum, the Viking ships, the *Fram* Museum, and *Kon-Tiki.*

Many neighborhoods of Oslo lie along the **Oslofjord,** which stretches for more than 60 miles northward from the Skagerrak to Oslo, filled with basins which are dotted with islands. (There are 40 islands alone in the immediate Oslo archipelago.)

Nearly all visitors to Oslo head for **Holmenkollen,** a wooded range of hills northwest of the town rising to about 1,740 feet. It can be reached by electric train from the National Theater in the center of Oslo in 35 minutes.

Marka, Oslo's forest, is a great recreation area, offering hiking, bicycle riding, skiing, fishing, wild berry picking, jogging trails, and more. It contains 343 lakes, 310 miles of ski trails, 387 miles of trails and roads, 11 sports chalets, and 24 ski jumps and alpine slopes.

STREET MAPS

Maps of Oslo are distributed free at the tourist office (see above). For extensive exploring, especially of some of the back streets of Oslo, you may need a more detailed map. The best and most comprehensive is *Falk Plan,* a pocket-size map with a street index that can be opened and folded like a wallet. It is sold at most newsstands in central Oslo. If you don't find it, go to the city's most central bookstore, **Tanum Libris,** Karl Johans Gate 43 (tel. 22-41-11-00).

2. GETTING AROUND

BY PUBLIC TRANSPORTATION

Oslo has an efficient citywide network of buses, trams (streetcars), and subways. Buses and electric trains take passengers to the suburbs; ferry departures to Bygdøy from May to October are from the harbor in front of Oslo Rådhuset (City Hall).

DISCOUNT PASSES

The **Oslo Card (Oslo-Kortet)** is offered to help you become acquainted with the city at a fraction of normal costs. It allows free travel on public transport, free admission to famous museums and other top sights, favorable rates on sightseeing buses and boats, a rebate on your car rental, special treats in restaurants, and reduced rates in any of 23 hotels in the Oslo area, including some of the finest. You may purchase the card in hotels and fine stores, from travel agents, at tourist information offices, and in the branches of Sparebanken Oslo Akershus. It costs 90 kroner ($15.60) for adults for 1 day, 130 kroner ($22.50) for 2 days, and 160 kroner ($27.70) for 3 days. Children pay 40 kroner ($6.90), 60 kroner ($10.40), and 75 kroner ($13), respectively.

Convenient for visitors who do not purchase the Oslo Card is the 24-hour **Tourist Ticket (Turistkort),** which lets you travel anywhere in Oslo whenever you wish, by bus, tram, subway, local railway, or boat, including the Bygdøy ferries in summer. The Tourist Ticket costs 45 kroner ($7.80) for adults, half fare for children under 16 (children under 4 travel free). The ticket will be stamped when it's used for the first time and will then be good for the next 24 hours.

BY BUS, TRAM & SUBWAY

Jernbanetorget is the major bus and tram terminal stop in Oslo. Most buses and trams passing through the heart of town stop at Wessels Plass, next to the Parliament, or at Stortorget, the main marketplace. Many also stop at the National Theater or University Square on Karl Johans Gate as well as Oslo's suburbs.

By subway, the T-banen has four branch lines east and the Western Suburban route (including Holmenkollen) has four lines to the residential sections and recreation grounds west and north of the city. Subways and trains to Oslo's environs leave from near the National Theater on Karl Johans Gate.

For information about timetables and fares, call **Trafikanten** at 22-17-17-36.

Automated machines cancel prebought tickets. Single-journey tickets are also sold by the drivers for 13 kroner ($2.20). Children travel for half fare. A 12-coupon "Maxi" card costs 140 kroner ($24.20), and a four-coupon "Mini" card goes for 60 kroner ($10.40); both are half price for children. Maxi and Mini cards can be used for unlimited transfers within 1 hour of the time the ticket is stamped.

BY TAXI

If you need to order a taxi in advance, call 22-38-80-70, 24 hours a day. Reserve at least 1 hour in advance.

The approximate fare from Gardermoen to Oslo is 530 kroner ($91.70), and from Fornebu, 90 kroner to 130 kroner ($15.60 to $22.50). (The fare for Gardermoen can be greatly reduced if you order the taxi in advance.)

All taxis are equipped with an official taxi meter, and Norwegian cab drivers are honest. When a car is available, a roof light goes on. Taxis can be hailed on the street, providing they are more than 100 yards from a rank. The worst time to hail a taxi is Monday through Saturday from 8:30 to 10am and Monday through Friday from 3 to 5pm.

BY CAR

This is not a practical means of getting around Oslo because parking is limited. Besides, an efficient network of public transportation makes use of a private car unnecessary. You can even reach the most isolated sights in the environs by public transportation.

Cars are towed away if found illegally parked. There are multistory parking lots in the city center including **Vika Park og Service,** Munkedamsveien 27 (tel. 22-83-26-19), and **Vestre Vika Bilpark,** Dronning Mauds Gate (tel. 22-83-35-35). For car problems, call the **NAF Alarm Center** (tel. 22-42-94-00), open 24 hours a day.

For more information see "Getting Around" in Chapter 12.

BY FERRY

In summer, beginning in mid-April, ferries depart for Bygdøy from Pier 3 in front of the Oslo Rådhuset. For schedule information, call **Båtservice** (tel. 22-20-07-15). It's recommended that you use a ferry or bus to Bygdøy since parking conditions there are crowded. Other ferries leave for various parts of the Oslofjord. Inquire at the **Tourist Information Office** at Rådhuset (tel. 22-83-00-50).

BY BICYCLE

Den Rustne Eike, Enga 2 (tel. 22-83-72-31), behind the tourist office, rents bikes at moderate rates, complete with free maps of interesting routes in Oslo and its environs. The cost is 95 kroner ($16.40) per day or 300 kroner ($51.90) per week, with a 500 kroner ($86.50) deposit required. It's open daily 10am to 6:30pm, May to October.

FAST OSLO

American Express The representative is **Winge Reisebyrå,** Karl Johans Gate 33 (tel. 22-42-76-50), open Monday through Friday from 8:30am to 5pm.

Area Code The former area code for Oslo, 02, is now part of the eight-digit number. As in Denmark, no area codes are necessary.

Babysitters Oslovian hotels are often helpful in enlisting the help of a chambermaid for "child-minding." Give at least a day's notice, two if you can. You can also contact the tourist office (see above) where a list of available sitters is kept on file and updated frequently. The cost varies, but it's often 70 kroner ($12.10) per hour.

Bookstores Oslo has a number of bookstores throughout the city. The most central (also one of the best stocked) is **Tanum Libris,** Karl Johans Gate 43 (tel. 22-41-11-00).

Currency Exchange **Banks** will exchange most foreign currencies or cash traveler's checks (bring your passport). If banks are closed, try the **Currency Exchange Office** at the Oslo Sentralstasjon, Jernbanetorget 1 (tel. 22-17-14-00), open June to September, daily from 7am to 11pm; October to May, Monday through Friday from 8am to noon and 1:30 to 8:30pm, on Saturday from 8am to 7pm, and on Sunday from 8am to noon.

Dentist In an emergency contact **Tøyen Senter,** Kolstadgate 18 (tel. 22-67-48-46), open Monday through Friday from 8 to 11pm and on Saturday, Sunday, and holidays from 11am to 2pm. Private dentists may also be called if you can wait (in volume 1B of the telephone directory, look under *Tannleger);* there's rarely a language barrier.

Doctors There are two emergency clinics. The 24-hour **Oslo Municipal Casualty Clinic** is at Storgata 40 (tel. 22-20-10-90); equipped with ambulances, it handles mainly accident cases. For more routine medical assistance you can contact the biggest hospital in Oslo, **Ullaval,** Kirkeveien 166 (tel. 22-11-80-80). To consult a private doctor, nearly all of whom speak English, see the telephone directory (look in volume 1B under *Leger)* or ask at your hotel for a doctor recommendation. Some larger hotels have arrangements with doctors in case a guest becomes ill.

Drugstores An all-night pharmacy is **Jernbanetorvets Apotek,** Jernbanetorget 4A (tel. 22-41-24-82).

Embassies and Consulates See "Fast Facts: Norway" in Chapter 12.

Emergencies Dial the Oslo police at **002;** report a fire at **001;** call an ambulance at **003.**

Eyeglasses **Optiker,** Karl Johans Gate 20 (tel. 22-42-85-14), is a big supplier, and very centrally located. Most contact lenses are immediately in stock. It takes about 2 days for unusual prescriptions.

Gasoline The Esso station, **Abelhaugen,** Haakon VII Gate 9 (tel. 22-11-23-26), is open 24 hours.

Hairdressers and Barbers Your best bet is **Jazz Frisor,** Bygdøy Allé 19 (tel. 22-55-98-00), which is open Monday to Saturday from 10am to 7pm. Men and women both should call for an appointment. A woman's haircut costs 290 kroner ($50.20); a man's haircut 200 kroner ($34.60).

Information See "Tourist Information" in "Orientation," in this chapter.

Laundry and Dry Cleaning A self-service laundry is **Majorstua Mynstvaskeri,** Vibes Gate 15 (tel. 22-69-43-17), open Monday through Friday from 8am to 8pm and on Saturday from 8am to 5pm. Sunday hours are noon to 5pm. Washing and drying are usually finished in 1 hour. You must have your coins ready to put in the machines. Be careful with trying to get dry cleaning done in the city. It's extremely expensive, and many establishments take more than a week to return the clothing. Try **Oslo American Rens** Griniveien (tel. 22-50-57-41), which promises 24-hour service.

Libraries   The Oslo municipal library, **Diechmann Library,** Henrik Ibsens Gate 1 (tel. 22-20-43-63), is the largest in Norway, containing many English-language volumes, a children's department, and a music department. It's open Monday through Friday from 8:15am to 8pm (to 6pm in summer) and on Saturday from 8:15am to 3pm.

Lost Property   The Lost and Found Office, **Hittegodskontoret,** at Grønlandsleiret 44 (tel. 22-66-98-65), is open May 15 to September 15, Monday through Friday from 8:15am to 2:15pm; September 16 to May 14, Monday through Friday from 8:15am to 3:15pm.

Luggage Storage and Lockers   Facilities for luggage storage are available at the **Oslo Sentralstasjon,** Jernbanetorget 1, at the beginning of Karl Johans Gate (tel. 22-17-14-00), open daily from 7am to 11pm. Lockers cost 20 kroner to 30 kroner ($3.50 to $5.20), depending on size.

Newspapers and Magazines   English-language newspapers and magazines are sold (at least in the summer months) at newsstands (kiosks) throughout Oslo. International editions, including the *International Herald Tribune,* and *USA Today* are always available.

Photographic Needs   Try **Foto Service,** at Karl Johans Gate 33 (tel. 22-42-98-04), for supplies, including black-and-white and color film. Film can be developed in 1 hour. It's open Monday through Friday from 9am to 5pm and on Saturday from 10am to 2pm.

Police   Dial 002.

Post Office   The **Oslo General Post Office** is at Dronningensgate 15, with its entrance at the corner of Prinsensgate (tel. 22-40-78-23). It's open Monday through Friday from 8am to 8pm and on Saturday from 9am to 3pm; closed Sunday and public holidays. If you've sent your mail general delivery (mark it "Poste Restante"), you can collect it here, providing you have your passport.

Radio and TV   The most important broadcaster is the Norwegian government, which owns and controls emissions on the NRK station. Oslo receives many signals from other countries, including BBC broadcasts from London. Radio Norway International broadcasts on MHz frequency.

Religious Services   Evangelical Lutheran is the official state religion, but there is complete religious freedom for all. The **American Lutheran Church** is at Frinznersgate 15 (tel. 22-44-35-84). Other churches (with services in Norwegian) include **St. Olav's Church,** which has mass for Roman Catholics, at Akersveien 5 (tel. 22-20-72-26). There's a Baptist church, **Baptistmenighet,** at Hausmannsgate 22 (tel. 22-20-76-49), and a Methodist church, **Centralkirken,** St. Olavsgate 28 (tel. 22-20-03-01). **Det Mosaiske Trossamfund Synagogue** is at Bergstien 13-15 (tel. 22-69-29-66).

Restrooms   Clean public toilets can be found throughout the city center, as well as in parks, and all bus, rail, and air terminals. For a detailed list, contact the Tourist Information Office.

Safety   Whenever you're traveling in an unfamiliar city or country, stay alert. Be aware of your immediate surroundings. Wear a moneybelt and don't sling your camera or purse over your shoulder; wear the strap diagonally across your body. This will minimize the possibility of your becoming a victim of crime. Every society has its criminals. It's your responsibility to be aware and alert even in the most heavily touristed areas.

Shoe Repairs   The best service is in the basement of **Steen & Strøm,** 23 Kongensgate (tel. 22-41-68-00), the city's leading department store. Unless there's a rush, routine service can often be rendered on the spot.

Taxes   Oslo has no special city taxes. You pay the same "value-added tax" throughout the country (see "Fast Facts: Norway" in Chapter 12).

Taxis   See "Getting Around" in this chapter.

Telephone, Telegrams, and Telex   Phone calls can be made and telegrams and telexes can be sent at the **Telecommunications Office,** Kongensgate 21 (tel. 22-40-55-09). Hours are Monday through Friday from 8:30am to 9pm and on Saturday and Sunday from 10am to 5pm. The entrance is from Prinsensgate. For operator assistance in English, dial 093. To send telegrams, dial 013. Try not to make long-distance calls from your hotel, where the charges are often doubled or tripled. For instance in dialing abroad, call 0115, or ask the hotel operator for help.

   Transit Information   For information about tram and bus travel, call **Trafikanten** (tel. 22-17-17-36), located in front of the Central Station. For information about train travel, go to the Central Station or call 22-36-68-00.

   Weather   See the temperature chart in Chapter 12.

3. NETWORKS & RESOURCES

FOR STUDENTS   Oslo's **Ungdomsinformasjonen** (Oslo Municipal Youth Information Office), at Akersgaten 57 (tel. 22-11-04-09), is helpful if you're planning to hitchhike through Norway because it can often match riders and drivers. The center will also dispense information about youth-oriented activities, cheap accommodations, low-cost restaurants, and more.

   The **University of Oslo** sponsors a 6-week International Summer School from June 27 to August 7. It is open to qualified participants from all over the world. Courses are offered in humanities, social sciences, and environmental protection. The fee of $2,190 covers field trips, registration, and room and board at Blindern Student Home. You can receive a detailed catalog and application from: Oslo International Summer School, North American Admissions Office, c/o Saint Olaf College, 1520 Saint Olaf Ave., Northfield MN 55057-1098 (tel. 507/646-3269).

FOR GAY MEN & LESBIANS   Call the **Gay Switchboard** (tel. 22-11-36-60) anytime daily between 8 and 11pm. An English-speaking representative will provide you with the latest details about gay and lesbian life in Oslo as well as what clubs are currently in vogue.

   Tromsø Bokhandel, Kristian Augustsgate 19 (tel. 22-20-25-09), sells a wide range of gay and lesbian books. This is the largest bookstore of its kind in Norway, specializing in gay-related literature in five languages.

FOR WOMEN   Violent crimes against women, including rape, are extremely rare in Norway. However, the usual precautions and discretion smart women exercise anywhere should be followed in Norway. Norway has a rape crisis center called **Krisesenter** (tel. 22-37-47-00), operating 24 hours a day.

CHAPTER 14

OSLO ACCOMMODATIONS & DINING

I n recent years, many of Oslo's major hotels and restaurants have been completely restored or rebuilt, and now the city offers some of the finest in European accommodations and dining. This is not to mention the many establishments that have opened for the first time in Oslo, bringing to the city a more modern and international flair.

1. OSLO ACCOMMODATIONS

By the standards of many cities in the United States or Canada, hotels in Oslo are very expensive indeed, even the so-called moderate ones. Therefore, the category of "Moderate" means it's moderate for Oslo. In your hometown, the moderate price might buy you luxury.

Hotels labeled **Very Expensive** charge $290 to $340 a night for a double in winter; **Expensive,** $225 to $290; **Moderate,** $140 to $225; and **Inexpensive,** $100 to $140. Breakfast is almost always included in these prices, and it's usually a generous Norwegian buffet.

Before these high prices make you cancel your trip, read on. Oslovian hotels lose most of their business travelers—the main source of their revenue—during the peak tourist visiting months of midsummer. Even though the town is filled with visitors at this time, many hoteliers slash their prices. July is always a month for discounts. Some hotels extend their discounts from June 21 to mid-August. Regular pricing usually begins in mid-August. For exact dates of these discounts, check with the hotel.

Likewise, hoteliers slash prices on weekends. A weekend is most often defined as Friday and Saturday, maybe Sunday. Sometimes regular prices are charged on Sunday night. Again, hotels often change their policies, so it's best to check what the price scale is going to be when making reservations. Don't always count on a discount; a sudden conference in the city could result in increased prices.

The most economy-minded tourists will cut prices even more by booking into one of the more old-fashioned hotels that still offer a number of rooms without private bath. Sometimes a shower is included in a room, but no toilet. In most cases, corridor toilets and bathrooms are in adequate supply. Even the bathless rooms will usually offer a sink with hot and cold running water.

HOTEL RESERVATIONS The worst months for finding a place to stay in Oslo are May, June, September, and October, since many business conferences are held at this time. July and August are better, even though that's the peak time of the summer tourist invasion.

The **Innkvartering** kiosk at the Central Station, Jernbanetorget 1 (tel. 22-83-00-50), will help visitors who need a room in a hurry upon arrival. If they can't find a hotel in the price range you specify, they'll book you into a private home or apartment. That will cost from 400 kroner ($69.20) for a bathless double, from 300 kroner ($51.90) for a single. The service charge for on-the-spot booking is 17 kroner ($2.90), plus a small deposit. Minimum stay is 2 days.

The accommodation center is open May to the end of September, daily from 7am to 11pm, and October to the end of April, daily from 8am to 11pm. It is closed on some holidays.

Oslo Promotion, Vestbaneplassen 1, can assist visitors with overnight accommodation in hotels and boardinghouses. Advance booking must be requested in a written application to Oslo Promotion, Vestbaneplassen 1, N-0205, Oslo 2, 21 days before your arrival date and must contain the following: name and address, dates of arrival and departure, required standard and price class, and a bank draft for 100 kroner or $17.30 per person. This payment includes a booking fee of 30 kroner ($5.20) and a deposit to the establishment in which your rooms are reserved. The deposit will be deducted from your bill upon departure. Cancellations must be made in writing at least 8 days before the date of arrival and sent directly to the accommodation address. A full refund cannot be guaranteed. Visitors will receive a written confirmation of their reservations with a receipt for the advance payment. Hotel rates are given in the group's price list. Private home accommodations cannot be booked in advance, but are handled upon your arrival at the accommodation office at the Central Station (see above).

The office is open May 1 to the end of September, daily from 7am to 11pm; October to April, daily from 8am to 11pm.

Note: Tariffs quoted below for hotels include service charge and tax.

IN THE CENTER

VERY EXPENSIVE

GRAND HOTEL, Karl Johans Gate 31, N-0159 Oslo 1. Tel. 22-42-93-90, or toll free 800/223-5652 in the U.S. Fax 22-42-12-25. 290 rms (all with bath), 50 suites. MINIBAR TV TEL **Metro:** Stortinget.

$ Rates (including buffet breakfast): Summer, 630–675 kroner ($109–$116.80) single; 910–1,000 kroner ($157.40–$173) double. Winter, 1,450–1,900 kroner ($250.90–$328.70) single; 1,850–2,850 kroner ($320.10–$493.10) double. Year-round, from 3,050 kroner ($527.70) suite. AE, DC, MC, V. **Parking:** 85 kroner ($14.70).

Norway's leading hotel, located on the wide boulevard that leads to the Royal Palace, this stone-walled hotel with its mansard gables and copper tower has been an integral part of Oslo life since it was built in 1874. Famous guests include Arctic explorer Roald Amundsen, Edvard Munch, Gen. Dwight Eisenhower, Charlie Chaplin, Henry Ford, and Henrik Ibsen, who was especially fond of the place. More recent guests have included Helmut Kohl, Michael Jackson, and Elton John.

Bedrooms are either in the 19th-century core or in one of the tasteful new additions. The modern rooms contain plush facilities and electronic amenities, and the older ones have been completely modernized as well to offer luxurious comfort. Some accommodations have air conditioning.

Dining/Entertainment: The hotel has several restaurants, serving both international and Scandinavian food. Two, the Palmen and the Grand Café, offer live entertainment. The Grand Café is the most famous in Oslo, but you can also partake of the French-inspired cuisine at Etoile or enjoy the British clublike atmosphere of the Grand Grill. The lobby-level Limelight Bar is connected to the Oslo Nye Teater next door, and the Etoile Bar is an informal meeting place next to the swimming pool.

Services: Laundry and room service, guide services, message desk, express checkout, safety-deposit boxes, and a sophisticated concierge.

Facilities: Indoor swimming pool, sauna, solarium, boutiques, car-rental desk.

HOTEL CONTINENTAL, Stortingsgaten 24-26, N-0117 Oslo 1. Tel. 22-41-90-60. Fax 22-42-96-89. 169 rms (all with bath), 12 suites. A/C MINIBAR TV TEL **Metro:** Stortinget.

$ **Rates** (including breakfast): Winter, 1,450–1,650 kroner ($250.90–$285.50) single; 1,850 kroner ($320.10) double. Summer, 775 kroner ($134.10) single; 1,090 kroner ($188.60) double. Year-round, from 2,800 kroner ($484.40) suite. AE, DC, MC, V. **Parking:** 85 kroner ($14.70).

⭐ One of the leading hotels of Europe, right in the city center midway between the Royal Palace and the City Hall, the Continental is rich in tradition and quality. Built in 1900, it has been owned by the same family for four generations. Personal service is a hallmark of the hotel. Bedrooms have style and grace and are furnished in light Nordic tones with many amenities.

Dining/Entertainment: Annen Etage is a gourmet restaurant, one of the finest in Norway. The Lipp is more moderately priced with an excellent grill menu, and the Theatercafeen is northern Europe's only surviving Viennese café. The Continental Bar contains Norway's largest privately owned collection of Edvard Munch paintings, and the Loftet is the hotel's disco, built like an attic. Breakfast is served at Carolines.

Services: Babysitter upon request, laundry, room service.

Facilities: Private underground garage, newsstand, perfumery, men's hairdresser.

SAS SCANDINAVIA, Holbergsgate 30, N-0166 Oslo 1. Tel. 22-11-30-00. Fax 22-11-30-17. 487 rms (all with bath), 4 suites. A/C MINIBAR TV TEL **Bus:** 17, 76.

$ **Rates** (including breakfast): Standard rooms, Mon–Thurs 1,535 kroner ($265.60) single, 1,760 kroner ($304.50) double; Fri–Sun 775 kroner ($134.10) single, 930 kroner ($160.90) double. Children under 15 free. Royal Club, Mon–Thurs 1,785 kroner ($308.80) single, 2,020 kroner ($399.50) double; Fri–Sun 1,380 kroner ($238.70) single, 1,520 kroner ($263) double. From 3,000 kroner ($519) suite. AE, DC, MC, V. **Parking:** 120 kroner ($20.80).

Near the Royal Palace, this is one of two hotels in the Oslo area operated by Scandinavian Airlines (the other is at the airport). From many of its nicely decorated and well-furnished bedrooms, there are views of the fjord. The best rooms are in the Royal Club, spread across three separate floors with their own breakfast lounge, electronic safe, and such extra touches as bathrobes, slippers, and fruit baskets.

Dining/Entertainment: The hotel operates five restaurants, including the Holberg, one of Oslo's best restaurants. Less expensive, the Brasseriet serves from an excellent menu amid an art deco–inspired chic. You can drink and eat at Charly's and the Galaxy. The Summit 21 is spectacular, a "sky bar" on the 21st floor with views over the city.

Services: Room service, babysitting, express laundry service, complete business services, express SAS airline check-ins.

Facilities: Health club, exercise room, swimming pool, sauna.

EXPENSIVE

BRISTOL, Kristian IV's Gate 7, N-0164 Oslo 1. Tel. 22-41-58-40. Fax 22-42-85-51. 141 rms (all with bath), 4 suites. A/C MINIBAR TV TEL **Metro:** Stortinget.

$ **Rates** (including breakfast): Sept–June, Mon–Thurs 1,170 kroner ($202.40) single; 1,490 kroner ($257.80) double. July–Aug, Mon–Thurs 670 kroner ($115.90) single; 810 kroner ($140.10) double. Year-round, Fri–Sat 485 kroner ($83.90) single; 770 kroner ($133.20) double. Year-round 2,500 kroner ($432.50) suite. AE, DC, MC, V.

⭐ In the heart of the city, on a side street north of Karl Johans Gate, this 1920s-era hotel is warm, inviting, and luxurious. The Moorish-inspired lobby, with its Winter Garden and Library Bar, sets the elegant tone. Bedrooms have special character, most often furnished in light Nordic pastels, homelike and comfortable. Many thoughtful amenities are installed.

Dining/Entertainment. The Bristol has several drinking and dining possibilities, including the intimate Bristol Grill, featuring meats grilled over charcoal and seafood. Bristol Night Spot is a dine-and-dance restaurant, with live bands and a welcoming bar. You can also enjoy a drink at the Bristol Lounge.

Services: Room service, laundry and dry-cleaning service, babysitting.

Facilities: Studio Bristol for hair and skin care.

MODERATE

BONDEHEIMEN, Rosenkrantzgate 8, N-0159 Oslo 1. Tel. 22-42-95-30. Fax 22-41-94-37. 76 rms (all with bath). MINIBAR TV TEL **Tram:** 7, 11.

$ Rates (including breakfast): Summer and Fri–Sat year-round, 540 kroner ($93.40) single; 690 kroner ($119.40) double. Winter, Mon–Thurs 780–940 kroner ($134.90–$162.60) single; 1,040–1,090 kroner ($179.90–$188.60) double. AE, DC, MC, V.

In the city center, only a short block from the Students' Grove at Karl Johans Gate, the Bondeheimen was built in 1913 by a cooperative of farmers and students to provide inexpensive, clean, and safe accommodations when they visited Oslo from the countryside. Each bedroom is outfitted with modern Norwegian furniture. The minibar has drinks but no alcohol. At street level is a self-service Kaffistova (cafeteria), dispensing good Norwegian food.

HOTEL IMI, Staffeldts Gate 4, N-0166 Oslo 1. Tel. 22-20-53-30. Fax 22-11-17-49. 66 rms (all with bath). MINIBAR TV TEL **Tram:** 11.

$ Rates (including breakfast): 750–850 kroner ($129.80–$147.10) single; 1,000 kroner ($173) double. Children under 18 stay free. AE, DC, MC, V.

A popular alcohol-free Mission hotel, the IMI is a half block from the Royal Palace grounds near the airport bus terminal, a taxi stand, and a tram stop. Its restaurant serves three meals a day, including a Norwegian cold table buffet from noon to 4pm; and à la carte dishes are featured from 4 to 9pm. You can order a packed lunch. The hotel was built in 1935, and all but a few of the comfortable bedrooms were renovated in 1990. Many bedrooms have big windows.

RICA TRIANGEL HOTEL, Holbergs Plass 1, N-0166 Oslo 1. Tel. 22-20-88-55. Fax 22-20-78-25. 144 rms (all with bath). MINIBAR TV TEL **Bus:** 72. **Tram:** 7, 8, 11.

$ Rates (including breakfast): 945 kroner ($163.50) single; 1,050 kroner ($181.70) double. Fri–Sun and summer, 600 kroner ($103.80) single; 750 kroner ($129.80) double. AE, DC, MC, V.

Near the Royal Palace and the main street of Oslo (Karl Johans Gate), this hotel is an excellent bed-and-breakfast establishment built in 1915 and renewed in 1989. Bedrooms are furnished in light Nordic pastels, with a number of amenities. For longer stays, ask about the studios, large and bright and furnished with a pantry and dining table. Around the corner, the apartment annex was built in 1985. One of the studios, for example, begins at 650 kroner ($112.50) per night based on a weekly rental. The air terminal bus is only 50 yards away.

STEFAN HOTEL, Rosenkrantzgate 1, N-0159 Oslo 1. Tel. 22-42-92-50. Fax 22-33-70-22. 130 rms (all with bath). A/C MINIBAR TV TEL **Tram:** 7, 11.

$ Rates (including breakfast): Summer, 550 kroner ($95.20) single; 800 kroner ($138.40) double. Winter, 1,075 kroner ($186) single; 1,175 kroner ($203.30) double. AE, DC, MC, V. **Parking:** 80 kroner ($13.80).

In an excellent location in the center of the city, this hotel is clean, comfortable, and unpretentious. Built in 1952, it has been modernized and much improved since then, with a health club added in 1992. Bedrooms are well furnished and maintained. Facilities for the handicapped are available in two bedrooms. In the evening guests can enjoy selections from a Norwegian cold-table buffet.

0 ▭▭▭▭ 400 m
        440 y

Frogner-
parken

Major-
stuveien 18

Bogstad 17
veien

Pilestredet

Uranienborgveien

Kirkeveien

Gyldenløvesgate

Oscars gata

Hegde haugsveien

Wergelandsveien

15

Briskebyveien

President Harbitz gata

Camilla Colletts vei

16

14

Nordraaks
plass

Halvdan
Svartesgata

Frognerveien

Eckersbergs-
gata

Løvenskiolds gata

Gyldenløvesgate

13

Riddervolds
gata

Slottsparken

Slottet

Thomas-Heftyes-Gate

Meltzers gata

Dronningparken

Elisenbergs-
gerveien

Oscarsgata

Inkognitogata

Drammensveien

Bygdøy Allé

Frederik-Stangs-Gate

Frognerveien

Løkke-
veien

Dr. Mauds
Gate

Nobelsgata

Thomas-Heftyes-Gate

12

Bygdøy Allé

Drammensveien

Cort-Adelers-Gate

Parkveien

Ruseløkkveien

Munkedamsveien

Mogen Thorsensgate

Observatoriegata

Drammensveien

Thomas-Heftyes-Gate

Gabelsgate

Niels-Juels-Gate

9

10

Drammensveien

Munkedamsveien

11

Frognerstranda

Fjellinjen

Filipstadveien

Frognerkilen

↓ To Bygdøy Peninsula

NORWAY

Oslo ★

Hotel Ambassadeur 16
Bondeheimen 3
Bristol 2
Hotel Continental 11
Fønix 8
Gabelshus 9
Grand Hotel 4

Gyldenløve 17
Holmenkollen Park
  Hotel Rica 18
Hotel IMI 15
Nørrona 5
Norum Hotel 12
Oslo Plaza Hotel 7

OSLO ACCOMMODATIONS

Metro Stop ⓜ

Church ✝

Post Office ⊠

Information ⓘ

Rica Triangel Hotel **14**
Ritz Hotel **10**
Royal Christiania **6**
SAS Park Royal Hotel **11**
SAS Scandinavia **14**
Stefan Hotel **1**
White House **13**

INEXPENSIVE

MUNCH, Munchsgaten 5, N-0130 Oslo 1. Tel. 22-42-42-75. Fax 22-20-64-69. 180 rms (all with bath). MINIBAR TV TEL **Metro:** Stortinget. **Tram:** 7, 11. **Bus:** 37.

$ Rates (including breakfast): Summer, 355 kroner ($61.40) single; 480 kroner ($83) double. Winter, 585 kroner ($101.20) single; 685 kroner ($118.50) double. AE, DC, MC, V. **Parking:** 100 kroner ($17.30).

⑤ Five minutes north of Karl Johans Gate is this good one-star hotel—really like a bed-and-breakfast. Built in 1983, it offers comfortably furnished, well-maintained, and functional bedrooms, decorated with reproductions of Edvard Munch paintings. There is no bar or restaurant, but the surrounding neighborhood is well supplied.

NORRØNA, Grensen 19, N-0159 Oslo 1. Tel. 22-42-64-00. Fax 22-33-25-65. 50 rms (all with bath). TV TEL **Bus:** 17. **Tram:** 1, 7. **Metro:** Stortinget.

$ Rates (including breakfast): Sun–Thurs in winter, 685 kroner ($118.50) single; 795 kroner ($137.50) double. Summer and Fri–Sat year-round, 550 kroner ($95.20) single; 795 kroner ($137.50) double. AE, DC, MC, V. **Parking:** 65 kroner ($11.20) for 12 hours.

In the heart of Oslo's old section, occupying the upper floors of a modernized building, this hotel is ideal for families. It's a safe, clean haven, with a reasonably priced cafeteria. Convenient to both sightseeing and shopping, it offers well-equipped rooms furnished in Scandinavian modern, a few with private balconies. Many rooms are large enough that families of three and four can be accommodated. The lounge is homelike and informal.

IN THE WEST END

EXPENSIVE

HOTEL AMBASSADEUR, Camilla Colletts Vei 15, N-0258 Oslo 2. Tel. 22-44-18-35. Fax 22-44-47-91. 42 rms (all with bath), 8 suites. MINIBAR TV TEL **Bus:** 21.

$ Rates (including breakfast): Summer, 500–600 kroner ($86.50–$103.80) single; 700 kroner ($121.10) double; from 900 kroner ($155.70) suite. Winter, 950–1,200 kroner ($164.40–$207.60) single; 1,400 kroner ($242.20) double; from 1,600 kroner ($276.80) suite. AE, DC, MC, V.

Located in the west end in the vicinity of the Royal Palace, this hotel is considered intimate by Oslo standards. Sometimes attracting diplomats, it is a first-class executive hotel with personalized service. Each room is decorated in a different style, evoking such places as classical Rome or colonial Shanghai. Particularly attractive is the hotel's basement bar, with an English club atmosphere. The sophisticated restaurant, Sabroso, offers full meals, such as marinated salmon and smoked filet of partridge, priced from 350 kroner ($60.60). It is one of Oslo's best restaurants, decorated with paintings and an elegant decor. A swimming pool and sauna are on the lower ground floor.

MODERATE

FØNIX, Dronningensgate 19, N-0154 Oslo 1. Tel. 22-42-59-57. Fax 22-33-12-10. 66 rms (17 with bath). TEL **Metro:** Jernbanetorget.

$ Rates (including breakfast): 400 kroner ($69.20) single without bath, 460 kroner ($79.60) single with bath; 500–600 kroner ($86.50–$103.80) double without bath, 850 kroner ($147.10) double with bath. Extra bed 200 kroner ($34.60). AE, MC, DC, V.

A 3-minute walk from the Central Station, the Hotel Fønix offers great value. Though constructed in 1924, the hotel has been frequently redecorated. For the single traveler on a budget, the hotel is a good bet, as it offers 38 single rooms without bath. Breakfast is served in its restaurant, Kristine, furnished with turn-of-the-century oak dining suites. The hotel is fully licensed and serves an international cuisine.

GABELSHUS, Gabels Gate 16, N-0205 Oslo 2. Tel. 22-55-22-60. Fax 22-44-27-30. 45 rms (all with bath). TV TEL **Bus:** 9.
$ Rates (including breakfast): Mon–Thurs 800 kroner ($138.40) single; 1,000 kroner ($173) double. Fri–Sun 550 kroner ($95.20) single; 800 kroner ($138.40) double. AE, DC, MC, V. **Parking:** Free.
Lying on a quiet, tree-lined street in the west end, this hotel building dates from 1912 and it has been a small hotel since 1945. Discreetly conservative, the look is that of an English manor house, laced with climbing ivy. Public rooms are filled with antiques, art, burnished copper, and working fireplaces. Each of the bedrooms is decorated with tasteful colors and textiles, some with terraces. The elegant restaurant serves meals costing from 160 kroner ($27.70). It's a brisk 15-minute walk from the town center.

GYLDENLØVE (The Golden Lion), Bogstadveien 20, N-0355 Oslo 3. Tel. 22-60-10-90. Fax 22-60-33-90. 169 rms (all with bath). MINIBAR TV TEL **Tram:** 1, 11.
$ Rates (including breakfast): Summer and Fri–Sun year-round, 390 kroner ($67.50) single; 590 kroner ($102.10) double. Winter, Mon–Thurs 690 kroner ($119.40) single; 890 kroner ($154) double. AE, DC, MC, V.
Originally conceived in an angular eight-story format in 1937, this once-dowdy *hospits* was radically upgraded to four-star status in 1992 and incorporated into a well-recommended chain of Norwegian hotels (the Rainbow chain). Located within a 10-minute walk of the Royal Palace, on a tree-lined street known for its small and exclusive boutiques, it contains bedrooms with Scandinavian-modern styling and fresh colors. Management plans to add both a bar and a restaurant.

NORUM HOTEL, Bygdøy Allé 53, N-0265 Oslo 2. Tel. 22-44-79-90. Fax 22-44-92-39. 59 rms (all with bath). MINIBAR TV TEL **Bus:** 30, 31.
$ Rates (including breakfast): Sun–Thurs 980 kroner ($169.50) single; 1,150 kroner ($199) double. Fri–Sat 550 kroner ($95.20) single; 650 kroner ($112.50) double. AE, DC, MC, V.
Located in a residential neighborhood, a brisk walk from Vigeland Park, this hotel looks like a turreted castle. It was built in 1912 with baroque copper-covered towers, a steep roofline, arched and embellished windows, and walls of yellow brick. The entrance lies through a triangular rose garden. There is a bar and adjoining restaurant.

RITZ HOTEL, Frederick Stangs Gate 3, N-0272 Oslo 2. Tel. 22-44-39-60. Fax 22-44-67-13. 52 rms (all with bath). TV TEL **Tram:** 9.
$ Rates (including breakfast): Mon–Thurs 800 kroner ($138.40) single; 1,000 kroner ($173) double. Fri–Sun 550 kroner ($95.20) single; 650 kroner ($112.50) double. AE, DC, MC, V. **Parking:** Free.
On the western outskirts of Oslo, a 2-minute walk from the British Embassy, this well-run 1915 hotel is owned by the slightly more upscale Gabelshus (see above). In an area of expensive private villas, it offers good value for the neighborhood. Rooms are well maintained and comfortable. Drinks are served in the rooms at all hours. The hotel's restaurant serves meals for 260 kroner ($45).

WHITE HOUSE, President Harbitz Gate 18, N-0259 Oslo 2. Tel. 22-44-19-60. Fax 22-55-04-30. 21 rms (all with bath). MINIBAR TV TEL **Tram:** 1.
$ Rates (including breakfast): Sun–Thurs in winter, 650 kroner ($112.50) single; 800 kroner ($138.40) double. Summer and Fri–Sat year-round, 450 kroner ($77.90) single; 600 kroner ($103.80) double. AE, DC, MC, V.
Only 15 minutes by foot from the city center, the White House is in Breskeby, a

residential section in back of the Royal Palace. It was built around 1900 as a private house, but has been greatly modernized since. Rooms are simply furnished but comfortable. There's a fondue restaurant, Den Lille Fondue, where you can dine inside or on an outdoor wooden platform overlooking the street in summer. It is open daily from 5 to 11pm.

NEAR THE CENTRAL STATION

VERY EXPENSIVE

OSLO PLAZA HOTEL, Sonja Henies Plass 3, N-0107 Oslo 1. Tel. 22-17-10-00. Fax 22-17-73-00. 650 rms (all with bath), 19 suites. A/C MINIBAR TV TEL **Bus:** 14, 24, 71.

$ Rates (including breakfast): Standard rooms, Sun–Thurs (except midsummer), 1,145 kroner ($198.10) single, 1,445 kroner ($250) double; midsummer and Fri–Sat year-round, 695 kroner ($120.20) single, 950 kroner ($164.40) double. Plaza Tower, winter, Sun–Thurs 1,595 kroner ($275.90) single, 1,895 kroner ($327.80) double; midsummer and Fri–Sat 1,100 kroner ($190.30) single; 1,350 kroner ($233.60) double. AE, DC, MC, V. **Parking:** 50 kroner ($8.70).

Opened by the late King Olav V in 1990, this 37-floor "skyscraper" stands in the Vaterland district, near the railway station. It is the largest hotel in northern Europe, with its public Skywalk on the top floor, the highest viewing point. Guests flock to Scandinavia's tallest building for rooms, dining, and entertainment. Plaza Tower is a hotel within a hotel, with greater service, comfort, and quality in the bedrooms. All rooms are tastefully furnished in modern colors, with a number of amenities. Much of the hotel is decorated with original art, including paintings by prominent Norwegian artists.

Dining/Entertainment: Brasserie Abelone is a popular French brasserie and Ristorante Lakata is a classical Italian restaurant serving dinner only. The Jens Jap Bar is decorated like an English library, and Lilletorvet in the lobby lounge serves homemade pastries. Skybar is the highest supper club in Scandinavia.

Services: Babysitting, room service, laundry and dry cleaning, business services.

Facilities: Health center, sauna, solarium, indoor swimming pool, largest convention center in northern Europe, Sonja Henie Ballroom (named after the famous Norwegian skating champion and film star).

EXPENSIVE

ROYAL CHRISTIANIA, Biskop Gunnerus Gate 3, N-0106 Oslo 1. Tel. 22-42-94-10. Fax 22-42-46-22. 383 rms (all with bath), 73 suites. A/C MINIBAR TV TEL **Bus:** 30, 31, 41. **Tram:** 2.

$ Rates (including breakfast): Winter, 1,095–1,450 kroner ($189.40–$250.90) single; 1,595 kroner ($275.90) double; from 1,795 kroner ($310.50) suite. Summer, 550–770 kroner ($95.20–$133.20) single; 795–1,495 kroner ($137.50–$258.60) double; from 1,270 kroner ($219.70) suite. AE, DC, MC, V. **Parking:** Free.

Fifty yards from the rail station, this is a five-star luxury hotel that opened in 1990 in the Vaterland district following a total rebuilding. The hotel was originally constructed for the 1952 Oslo Winter Olympics. Rooms are quiet, comfortable, and tastefully designed.

Dining/Entertainment: The Christiania has three restaurants and five bars, serving international, American, Italian, and Scandinavian food. The Atrium opens onto a view of a "forest" of greenery with a waterfall, La Trattoria serves excellent pasta and meat dishes, and Christian IV is the classic choice with top-notch service. Guests in winter can enjoy a drink in front of the fireplace in the Library, or patronize the Frederik Piano Bar. Vintage wine is served at Baccus, the pub is called Off-Side, and Clockworks is the late-night café and disco.

Services: 24-hour room service, babysitting, massage, business services, laundry.

Facilities: Circular pool with wave machine, solarium, Finnish sauna, Turkish bath, boutiques, basement parking.

NEAR THE HOLMENKOLLEN SKI JUMP

EXPENSIVE

HOLMENKOLLEN PARK HOTEL RICA, Kongeveien 26, N-0390 Oslo 3.
Tel. 22-14-60-90, or toll free 800/223-5652 in the U.S. Fax 22-14-61-92. 191 rms (all with bath), 8 suites. A/C MINIBAR TV TEL **Bus:** Holmenkollen, from the center.

$ Rates (including breakfast): Mon–Thurs in winter, 1,145–1,345 kroner ($198.10–$232.70) single; 1,245–1,445 kroner ($215.40–$250) double. Summer and Fri–Sun year-round, 695–825 kroner ($120.20–$142.70) single; 795–895 kroner ($137.50–$154.80) double. Year-round, from 1,995 kroner ($345.10) suite. AE, DC, MC, V. **Parking:** Free.

Holmenkollen Park Hotel Rica lies on Holmenkollen hill near the famous ski jump, only 15 minutes from the city center. Opened in 1982 as an enlargement of an original timber building, the hotel has Viking carvings and characteristic turrets dating back to 1894. Holm Munthe, the architect, was a modern pioneer in the "dragon motif" and the hotel itself is a work of art, with paintings and decorations by famous Norwegian artists. The hotel's panoramic views open onto the greater Oslo area, with its fjords. Most bedrooms are in new wings that have been added to the original structure.

Dining/Entertainment: In the old part, the gourmet restaurant is De Fem Stuer (The Five Rooms), which is beautifully decorated in the old Norwegian style with lots of paneling and elegant accessories. Meals are also served in the Bakeriet (The Bakery), with grill specialties and a copious salad bar. Drinks are offered in the Atrium, with green plants and forest views. There is also a lobby bar and nightclub.

Services: Babysitting, room service.

Facilities: Swimming pool, saunas, whirlpool, illuminated ski tracks outside the door.

FORNEBU AIRPORT

MODERATE

SAS PARK ROYAL HOTEL, Fornebuparken, N-1324 Lysaker-Oslo. Tel.

Ⓕ FROMMER'S COOL FOR KIDS: HOTELS

Bristol (see p. 222) One of the most elegant and comfortable hotels of Oslo welcomes children and lets those under 15 stay free in their parents' room. The chef will even put a "junior steak" on the grill.

Holmenkollen Park Hotel Rica (see p. 229) A kid-pleaser if there ever was one in both summer and winter. It's near the famous ski jump and has its own swimming pool and sports facilities. Children under 4 stay free; those 4 to 16 get a 50% discount in three- or four-bedded rooms.

Norrøna (see p. 226) A reliable choice, attracting the economy-minded family trade. An extra bed in a parent's room costs 125 kroner ($21.60), and there's a moderately priced café on the premises.

Royal Christiania (see p. 228) Kids delight in the circular pool with a wave machine. Fruit juices and snacks are served in the afternoon. Babysitting can be arranged.

67-12-02-20. Fax 67-12-00-11. 254 rms (all with bath), 10 junior suites. A/C MINIBAR TV TEL **Bus:** 31.

$ Rates (including breakfast): Standard rooms 990 kroner ($171.30) single, 1,190 kroner ($205.90) double; Royal Club, 1,350 kroner ($233.60) single, 1,550 kroner ($268.20) double, from 1,875 kroner ($324.40) suite. AE, DC, MC, V. **Parking:** Free.

In Fornebu Park close to the Oslofjord and 2 minutes by car from the airport, this hotel opened in 1971 as a member of SAS International Hotels. Aimed primarily at business clients, it also welcomes sightseers, especially those who want to be near the airport for convenient departures. Bedrooms have attractive styling and furnishings, often in autumnal tones. The Royal Club, a hotel within the hotel, has upgraded services and facilities.

Dining/Entertainment: The hotel has one restaurant, Fornebu Park, known for its international kitchen and Scandinavian specialties. There is also the Symphony Bar, offering sandwiches and a light lunch menu.

Services: Laundry service, SAS Euroclass check-in, SAS Service Center (hotel reservations, air tickets, car rental, and the like), room service.

Facilities: Health club, sauna, whirlpool, lobby shop with newsstand, tennis court, solarium.

2. OSLO DINING

In the past few years Oslo has had an explosion of restaurants unprecedented in Scandinavia. You can now "dine around the world" without leaving Oslo. The biggest concentration of restaurants is at Aker Brygge, a former shipbuilding yard on the harborfront—now turned into the smartest dining and shopping complex in Norway.

Not all restaurants in Oslo are new. Some have long associations with artists and writers, like the Grand Café, former stamping ground of Henrik Ibsen and Edvard Munch, and the Theatercafeen and Blom.

The influx of foreigners in recent years has led to the growth of international restaurants, represented by Mexico, Turkey, Morocco, China, Greece, and others. Among the European cuisines, French and Italian are the most popular; many restaurants offer American-style food as well.

At nearly all restaurants recommended below, a 15% service charge is included, as is the 20% value-added tax. No further tipping is required, although it is customary to leave some small change if service has been good. Of course, that added 35% means that many restaurant tabs appear unreasonably high.

The **Very Expensive** category indicates meals that generally cost $60 or more per person; **Expensive,** $40 to $60; **Moderate,** $25 to $40; and **Inexpensive,** under $25. Wine and beer can be lethal to your final bill, so be careful.

IN THE CENTER

VERY EXPENSIVE

D'ARTAGNAN, Øvre Slottsgate 16. Tel. 22-41-50-62.
Cuisine: FRENCH. **Reservations:** Required. **Bus:** 27, 29, 30, 41, 61.
$ Prices: Fixed-price menu 575 kroner ($99.50); appetizers 110–165 kroner ($19–$28.50); main dishes 230–275 kroner ($39.80–$47.60). AE, DC, MC, V.
Open: Dinner only, Mon–Fri (also Sat Oct–Christmas) 4:30pm–midnight.
Closed: July 4–Aug 4 and Dec 20–Jan 8.

Named after one of the dashing three musketeers, the owner's childhood hero, this is a temple of gastronomy. Freddie Neilsen uses some of the best Norwegian ingredients for his menu, which changes four or five times a year, as the seasons do. There's no sign in front, giving the restaurant the allure of a private club, but a discreet brass plaque announces the place, and you ring a bell to enter. One flight up is a bar with Chesterfield sofas where you can order an apéritif and peruse the menu.

The dining room is up another flight of stairs, with pink marble tables, a royal-blue color scheme, and lots of silver accents. Selections include sole baked in shellfish in spiced butter, reindeer with white sherry sauce, quail in phyllo pastry with duck-liver sauce, and an appetizer of Norwegian bouillabaisse, cooled and refrigerated until it congeals into a terrine. It's served with a garlicky rouille and a saffron-flavored vinaigrette.

HOLBERG, in the SAS Scandinavia Hotel, Holbergsgate 30. Tel. 22-11-30-00.

Cuisine: FRENCH. **Reservations:** Required. **Bus:** 17, 76.
$ **Prices:** Fixed-price menu 395 kroner ($68.30) for 3 courses; appetizers 98–185 kroner ($17–$32); main dishes 198–285 kroner ($34.30–$49.30). AE, DC, MC, V.

Open: Dinner only, Tues–Sat 5–11pm. **Closed:** July.

Generally acclaimed as one of the finest restaurants in Oslo—if not the finest—this restaurant is on the ground floor of the SAS Scandinavia Hotel (see "Oslo Accommodations" in this chapter). Enjoy an apéritif in the Klims Bar, then head to the intensely formal dining room ringed with costumes draped on mannequins honoring characters in various plays by Holberg, for whom the restaurant is named. Service is formal and the trappings are elegant.

The menu changes based on seasonal ingredients, but you are likely to be offered such appetizers as fricassée of mushrooms with smoked mussels or a tureen of eel with horseradish sauce and herbs. For a main dish, try fricassée of anglerfish and crab with fine vegetables and saffron, or breast of duck. Desserts are elegant, including apples gratinée with raisins in a cinnamon-flavored ice cream.

EXPENSIVE

ANNEN ETAGE, in the Hotel Continental, Stortingsgaten 24. Tel. 22-41-90-60.

Cuisine: FRENCH. **Reservations:** Required. **Metro:** Stortinget.
$ **Prices:** Appetizers 80–200 kroner ($13.80–$34.60); main dishes 170–260 kroner ($29.40–$45). AE, DC, MC, V.

Open: Mon–Fri 4–10:40pm, Sun 3–7pm.

In one of the grandest Norwegian hotels, the name of this restaurant—"second floor" in English—hardly prepares you for the refined service, elegant decor, and quality food. The restaurant still retains its Belle Epoque ambience of gilded Corinthian columns and pink, red, and white floral patterns.

The menu is seasonally adjusted, but you are likely to be offered game pâté, followed by rack of reindeer with chanterelles, breast of black grouse with red wine sauce, grilled salmon, or rack of lamb with parsley and artichokes.

BLOM, Karl Johans Gate 41B. Tel. 22-42-73-00.

Cuisine: NORWEGIAN/INTERNATIONAL. **Reservations:** Required. **Metro:** Stortinget.
$ **Prices:** Fixed-price dinner 375 kroner ($64.90); fixed-price lunch 195 kroner ($33.70); appetizers 59–145 kroner ($10.20–$25.10); main dishes 195–255 kroner ($33.70–$44.10). AE, DC, MC, V.

Open: Lunch Mon–Sat 11:30am–3pm; dinner Mon–Sat 3pm–midnight.

Considered a cultural and architectural landmark, this restaurant was painstakingly re-created to its original glory as the symbol of bohemian life in the early 20th century. Cultural giants dined here, including Charles Chaplin, Edvard Grieg, Henrik Ibsen, Edvard Munch, and Gustav Vigeland—and they are commemorated by heraldic plaques, each depicting important symbols of their careers.

Food is tasty and well prepared. At dinner, full meals might include marinated filet of reindeer with a morel-cream sauce, lamb cutlet with lamb médaillons in a Dijon mustard and rosemary sauce, beef tenderloin with red wine and onions, and a host of fresh fish dishes. The wine list is one of the most complete in Oslo. A smörgåsbord is priced on a per-portion basis, unless you select from an array of open-face sandwiches.

BRASSERIET, in the SAS Scandinavia Hotel, Holbersgate 30. Tel. 22-11-30-00.
   Cuisine: FRENCH. **Reservations:** Not required. **Bus:** 17, 76.
$ Prices: Appetizers 50–100 kroner ($8.70–$17.30); main dishes 120–190 kroner ($20.80–$32.90). AE, DC, MC, V.
   Open: Lunch daily noon–3pm; dinner daily 6–11pm.
Many prefer this simpler and more reasonably priced fare to that of the more elegant Holberg, also in the SAS Scandinavia. After passing through the modern bar, Le Bar, a fantasy of neon and minimalist lines, you enter this large French-style brasserie, with potted palms and art deco accents. The salad bar is extremely fresh. Behind a visible grill, a battalion of uniformed chefs produce your dinner, turning out such selections as Norwegian salmon with mustard sauce, jumbo shrimp with Pernod (prepared at your table), and spinach pasta with smoked salmon.

D. S. LOUISE, Stranden 3, Aker Brygge. Tel. 22-83-00-60.
   Cuisine: NORWEGIAN. **Reservations:** Recommended. **Bus:** 27.
$ Prices: Fixed-price menus 257–359 kroner ($44.50–$62.15); appetizers 64–88 kroner ($11.10–$15.20); main dishes 150–218 kroner ($26–$37.70). AE, DC, MC, V.
   Open: Mon–Sat 11:30am–11pm, Sun 11:30am–10:30pm.
By most standards, this is judged to be the best restaurant in the harborfront shopping-and-dining complex, Aker Brygge. On street level and outfitted in a warmly textured sheathing of hardwood, with lots of nautical accents, it takes its name from a 19th-century Norwegian steamboat. The chef prepares such specialties as braised hare with brussels sprouts and stewed mushrooms and cranberries, and a "cold symphony" of shrimp, salmon, hare, roast beef, potato salad, and cheese. It's a meal unto itself. A house specialty, also a meal unto itself, is the Brygge Tallerken, fried horsemeat with stewed mushrooms.

ETOILE, in the Grand Hotel, Karl Johans Gate 31. Tel. 22-42-93-90.
   Cuisine: FRENCH. **Reservations:** Required. **Metro:** Stortinget.
$ Prices: Appetizers 90–200 kroner ($15.60–$34.60); main dishes 175–260 kroner ($30.30–$45). AE, DC, MC, V.
   Open: Dinner only, Mon–Sat 4–11:15pm.
On the sixth floor of the new wing of Oslo's Grand Hotel, this restaurant is distinctively modern and serves a fine cuisine. To reach it, take a special elevator to the right of the hotel entrance. Sloping walls of glass open onto views of Oslo's historic district, and the place is illuminated in the evening by candlelight.
   In the evening, you can enjoy such à la carte dishes as tartare of both smoked and fresh salmon with chopped onion and sour cream, filet of wild boar with pommes dauphinoise, and médaillons of venison in Pernod. The headchef is Ms. Aud Hansen, the most famous female member of the Norwegian culinary Olympic team. She specializes in a French cuisine, using mainly Norwegian ingredients.

MODERATE

BAROCK, Universitetsgaten 26. Tel. 22-42-44-20.
   Cuisine: NORWEGIAN. **Reservations:** Required on weekends. **Metro:** Stortinget.
$ Prices: Appetizers 68–95 kroner ($11.80–$16.40); main dishes 168–210 kroner ($29.10–$36.30). AE, DC, MC, V.
   Open: Dinner only, Tues–Sat 6pm–12:30am, Sun–Mon 8pm–12:30am.
A glamorous café/restaurant, Barock is decorated in a neo-Edwardian style with palms, faux marble columns, and crystal chandeliers. You can enjoy smoked breast of

duckling with vinaigrette sauce and mango, and baked halibut with lemon-cream sauce and garlic. After dinner, you will be admitted free to the adjacent nightclub, Humla (see "Evening Entertainment," in Chapter 15).

BRASSERIE COSTA, Klingenberg 4. Tel. 22-42-41-30.
   Cuisine: ITALIAN. **Reservations:** Recommended. **Bus:** 27, 29. **Tram:** 1, 2, 9.
$ Prices: Antipasti 39–87 kroner ($6.70–$15.10); pastas 78–88 kroner ($13.50–$15.20); main dishes 128–195 kroner ($22.10–$33.70). AE, DC, MC, V.
   Open: Restaurant, summer, daily 4–11:30pm; winter, daily 3–11:30pm. Café/bar, summer, daily 4pm–1:30am; winter, daily 3pm–1:30am.
Owned by Italian-born Constantino Lemme, who has made a lifetime endeavor of establishing Italian restaurants in Norway, including Mamma Rosa (see below), this fashionable place serves the finest Italian food in Oslo. The trappings are elegant, and the service excellent. Guests enter through a bar and café where they can either order drinks or select from the full menu at prices 10% to 15% lower than in the main and more formal restaurant. Try such dishes as tenderloin of beef with forest mushrooms in a brandy-cream sauce, filet of hare with rosemary, or pâté of pheasant. The antipasti are always a temptation, as is the array of pasta and fresh fish dishes.

BRISTOL GRILL, in the Bristol Hotel, Kristian IV's Gate 7. Tel. 22-41-58-40.
   Cuisine: FRENCH. **Reservations:** Required. **Metro:** Stortinget.
$ Prices: Appetizers 55–100 kroner ($9.50–$17.30); main dishes 98–230 kroner ($17–$39.80). AE, DC, MC, V.
   Open: Lunch daily 11:30am–2pm; dinner daily 2–11:30pm.
Set in this 1920s hotel (see "Oslo Accommodations" in this chapter), this street-level restaurant has a rich decor with great charm and paneled walls. Try an appetizer like mousse of pheasant Périgord and follow with marinated halibut in a mustard sauce, bouillabaisse provençale, fried sea devil with white wine, or a charcoal-grill specialty.

GRAND CAFE, in the Grand Hotel, Karl Johans Gate 31. Tel. 22-33-48-70.
   Cuisine: NORWEGIAN. **Reservations:** Recommended. **Metro:** Stortinget.
$ Prices: Appetizers 35–80 kroner ($6.10–$13.80); main dishes 86–135 kroner ($14.90–$23.40). AE, DC, MC, V.
   Open: Mon–Sat 11am–11:30pm, Sun noon–11:30pm.
This is the grand old café of Oslo, steeped in legend and tradition. Ibsen, who used to patronize the Grand Café, enjoying whale steaks, is depicted, along with Edvard Munch and many others, in a large mural on one wall. A postcard sold at the reception desk will identify them in the mural.
   Food can include everything from a napoleon with coffee to a full meal. Dishes include fried stingray, standard veal and beef dishes, reindeer steaks, and elk stew. Sandwiches are also available, costing 42 to 75 kroner ($7.25 to $13). Sunday jazz buffets with live music cost 185 kroner ($32) per person and are performed from January to May and September to Christmas.

PALMEN, in the Grand Hotel, Karl Johans Gate 31. Tel. 22-42-93-90.
   Cuisine: NORWEGIAN/FRENCH. **Reservations:** Recommended. **Metro:** Stortinget.
$ Prices: Appetizers 50–75 kroner ($8.70–$13); main dishes 115–145 kroner ($19.90–$25.10); open-faced sandwiches and pastries 60–115 kroner ($10.40–$19.90); pot of tea 25 kroner ($4.30) per person. AE, DC, MC, V.
   Open: Daily 11:30am–7:30pm.
Originally conceived during the Edwardian era as a plant-filled oasis in the heart of Norway's most prestigious hotel, Palmen has enjoyed a renaissance as politicians, media personalities, and Norwegian artists have chosen it as the preferred daytime venue. Amid tiled walls and clusters of potted palms, guests sit in upholstered armchairs reminiscent of the grandest moments of the Gilded Age. Lunch and early-dinner menus of salads, open-faced sandwiches, and elegant platters are served

0 |=====| 400 m
440 y

N

Frogner-
parken

Frognerparken

Major-
stuveien

Bogstad veien

Pilestredet

Kerkeveien

Uranienborgveien

Oscars gata

Hegde haugsveien

Gyldenløvesgate

Wergelandsveien

Briskebyveien

President Harbitz gata

Camilla Colletts vei

Parkveien

Nordraaks
plas

Halvdan
Svartesgata

Frognerveien

Eckersbergs-
gata

Løvenskiolds gate

Gyldenløvesgate

Ridervolds
gata

Slottsparken

Slottet

Thomas-Heftyes-Gate

Meltzers gata

Inkognitogata

Dronningparken

Elisenber-
gerveien

Oscarsgata

Frognerveien

Drammensveien

Bygdøy Allé

Frederik-Stangs-Gate

Bygdøy Allé

Løkke-
veien

Nobelsgata

Thomas-Heftyes-Gate

Mogen Thorsensgate

Cort-Adelers-Gate

Dr. Mauds
Gate

Niels-Juels-Gate

Drammensveien

Parkveien

Observatoriegata

Ruseløkkveien

Munkedamsveien

Thomas-Heftyes-Gate

Gabelsgate

Drammensveien

Munkedamsveien

Drammensveien

Frognerstranda

Fjellinjen

Filipstadveien

↓ To Bygdøy Peninsula

Frognerkilen

NORWAY

Oslo ★

3 Brødre ⑫	Bristol Grill ④
Aker Brygge ㉑	Brasserie Costa ⑲
Annen Etage ⑩	D'Artagnan ⑧
Bagatelle ㉒	Dionysos ①
Barock ②	D. S. Louise ㉑
Blom ⑤	Engebret Café ⑰
Brasseriet ⑱	Étoile ⑥

Metro Stop Ⓜ

Church ⸶

Post Office ⊠

Information ⓘ

Frisksport Vegeta Vertshus ⓴

Frognerseteren Hoved-
Restaurant ㉕

Fru Blom ❺

Gamla Rådhus ⓰

Grand Café ❻

Handverkeran ❸

Holberg ⓲

Kastangen ㉓

Lipp ❿

Mamma Rosa ⓭

Najaden ㉔

New Orleans ⓫

Norrona Café ❼

Palmen ❽

Samson ⓯

Steen & Strøm ⓮

Theatercafeen ❿

Tostrupkjelleren ❾

simultaneously with steaming pots of tea and trolleys that are wheeled around by pleasant waitresses in long red skirts.

NEW ORLEANS, Universitetsgata 26. Tel. 22-42-96-35.
   Cuisine: LOUISIANA CREOLE. **Reservations:** Recommended. **Metro:** Stortinget.
$ **Prices:** Appetizers 32–45 kroner ($5.50–$7.80); main dishes 123–172 kroner ($21.30–$29.80). AE, DC, MC, V.
   Open: Daily 5pm–midnight.
Nothing in Scandinavia evokes with such pith the aura of turn-of-the-century New Orleans. Set within a cellar whose decor includes splashes of scarlet and a reassuring glimmer of gilding, New Orleans bathes its diners in recorded Dixieland music and the culinary flavors of the Mississippi Delta. Menu items include hickory-smoked spareribs, blackened fish with Créole seasoning, jambalaya, chicken breast with crawfish, and blackened prime rib with "bullfighter" garlic butter.

THEATERCAFEEN, in the Hotel Continental, Stortingsgate 24. Tel. 22-41-90-60.
   Cuisine: NORWEGIAN. **Reservations:** Recommended. **Metro:** Stortinget.
$ **Prices:** Fixed-price meals 190 kroner ($32.90) at dinner, 155 kroner ($26.80) at lunch; appetizers 35–110 kroner ($6.10–$19); main dishes 95–250 kroner ($16.40–$43.30). AE, DC, MC, V.
   Open: Mon–Sat 11am–10:45pm, Sun noon–9:45pm.
The last of the grand Viennese cafés, Theatercafeen competes with the Grand Café for theatergoers, present-day *boulevardiers,* and businesspeople. With soft lighting, antique bronze, cut-glass lighting fixtures, and art nouveau mirrors, this large and sophisticated restaurant is beautiful. A bar area plus a musicians' gallery complete the ambience. Music is usually performed from 4 to 6pm and 8 to 11pm. Daily specials are served only from 3 to 7pm. You can enjoy Norwegian fjord salmon, reindeer with mushrooms, mussels with white wine in sour cream, and a "fish and sea fruit" pot.

3 BRØDRE, Øvre Slottsgate 14. Tel. 22-42-39-00.
   Cuisine: NORWEGIAN. **Reservations:** Not required. **Bus:** 27, 29, 30.
$ **Prices:** Appetizers 50–80 kroner ($8.70–$13.80); main dishes 125–190 kroner ($21.60–$32.90). AE, DC, MC, V.
   Open: Kaelleren, daily 3–11:30pm. Street-level bar, Sun–Tues 11am–12:30am, Wed–Sat 11am–2:30am. Piano bar, Sun–Tues 3pm–12:30am, Wed–Sat 3pm–2:30am.
"Three Brothers" is named after the glove manufacturers who once occupied the

---

IN THEIR FOOTSTEPS

Edvard Munch (1863–1944) The "world's greatest expressionist" and "the handsomest man in Norway" wrote, "Illness, madness, and death were the black angels who stood guard over my cot, and they have followed me throughout my life." A one-man show in 1889 at the age of 25 launched his career. His influence on the development of modern expressionism was considered as great as that of van Gogh. He became Scandinavia's greatest painter, and his series of paintings, entitled *From Modern Spiritual Life*, established his genius.
   • **Birthplace:** December 12, 1863, at Loten, Norway.
   • **Favorite Haunts:** Grand Café in Oslo where he joined a group "of radical bohemians"; provincial towns along the Oslofjord.
   • **Resting Place:** Ground of Honor, Vår Frelsers Gravlund, Oslo, where he was buried in an unadorned tomb, his sister refusing a request from the German command for a state funeral.

building. The street level is devoted to a bustling bar. The Kaelleren, downstairs, serves soup as an appetizer, followed by cheese and meat fondues. Or you might begin with Norwegian salmon tartare or snails, and follow with an almond-and-garlic gratinée. The most popular appetizer is a selection of fresh mussels poached with leek, parsley, garlic, and cream. For a main course, try the fried catfish with prawns, mussels, red peppers, and capers, or beefsteak with béarnaise sauce. The upstairs has been turned into a piano bar. A large beer costs 36 kroner ($6.20).

INEXPENSIVE

DIONYSOS, Calmeyersgate 11. Tel. 22-60-78-64.
  Cuisine: GREEK. **Reservations:** Recommended. **Tram:** 1, 2, 11.
$ **Prices:** Appetizers 38–62 kroner ($6.60–$10.70); main dishes 85–135 kroner ($14.70–$23.40). AE, MC, V.
  Open: Daily 3–11pm.
The decor is similar to a family-oriented tavern in Athens. Specialties include dishes from Cyprus, Crete, Thessalonika, and the Pelopponese. An exuberant group of Greek-born waiters serve such dishes as Gastra Manis (from northern Greece, made with oxmeat and eggplant, pepperoni, vegetable, and potatoes), moussaka, souvlaki, and a wide selection of kebabs. Recorded bouzouki music is played from 7pm to midnight, and the bar stays open until 2:30am on Monday and Saturday.

GAMLA RÅDHUS (Old Town Hall), Nedre Slottsgate 1. Tel. 22-42-01-07.
  Cuisine: NORWEGIAN. **Reservations:** Recommended. **Bus:** 27, 29, 30, 41, 61.
$ **Prices:** Appetizers 40–70 kroner ($6.90–$12.10); main dishes 100–200 kroner ($17.30–$34.60); lunch open-face sandwiches 45–55 kroner ($7.80–$9.50). AE, DC, MC, V.
  Open: Mon–Fri 11am–11pm, Sat 5–11pm. Kroen Bar, Mon–Fri 3pm–midnight, Sat 6pm–midnight.
The oldest restaurant in Oslo, Gamla Rådhus is located in what in 1641 was Oslo's Town Hall. In the spacious dining room, a full array of open-face sandwiches is served at noon. A la carte dinner selections can be made from a varied menu including fresh fish, game, and Norwegian specialties. If you're watching your budget, enjoy your plate of food with a glass of beer or mineral water at the wood-paneled Kroen Bar.

MAMMA ROSA, Øvre Slottsgate 12. Tel. 22-42-01-30.
  Cuisine: ITALIAN. **Reservations:** Not required. **Metro:** Stortinget.
$ **Prices:** Appetizers 50–70 kroner ($8.70–$12.10); main dishes 65–150 kroner ($11.20–$26). AE, DC, MC, V.
  Open: Mon–Sat noon–11:30pm, Sun 1–10:30pm.
The popularity of this Italian-style trattoria is a good indication of Norwegians'

IN THEIR FOOTSTEPS

Henrik Ibsen (1828–1906) Ibsen attained towering stature as a world dramatist. *Brand* (1866) and *Peer Gynt* (1867) are recognized as two of the finest plays of the 19th century. *A Doll's House* (1879) was his word on the hollowness of the marriage morality of his day. Other masterpieces include *Ghosts* (1881), *Hedda Gabler* (1890), and *The Master Builder* (1892).
  • **Birthplace:** Born March 20, 1828, at Skien, Norway.
  • **Favorite Haunts:** The Bergen Theater (1851–57); Dresden, Germany (1868–91); Oslo (1891–1906), where he patronized the Grand Café twice a day.
  • **Resting Place:** The Ground of Honor, Vår Frelsers Gravlund, in Oslo.

changing tastes. The dining room's decor is a "reproduction rococo," and it lies one floor above street level. You can order 10 kinds of pizzas, fried scampi and squid, rigatoni of the house, pasta Mamma Rosa (three kinds of pasta with three sauces), grilled steaks, and gelato.

IN THE WEST END

VERY EXPENSIVE

BAGATELLE, Bygdøy Allé 3. Tel. 22-44-63-97.
   Cuisine: FRENCH. **Reservations:** Required. **Bus:** 30, 31, 41, 72, 73.
$ **Prices:** Fixed-price meals 650 kroner ($112.50) at dinner, 350 kroner ($60.60) at lunch; appetizers 120–175 kroner ($20.80–$30.30); main dishes 220–275 kroner ($38.10–$47.60). AE, DC, MC, V.
   Open: Lunch Mon–Fri 11:30am–2pm; dinner Tues–Sat 6–10pm. **Closed:** July.
⭐ This contemporary, informal French restaurant in the west end is widely regarded as the premier dining choice in Oslo. For most of this century there has been a French restaurant on this spot, but in 1982 it introduced a light, modern cuisine, based on market-fresh ingredients. Fish and seafood are featured, but the menu changes daily, depending on the market and the whim of its owner and chef, Eyvind Hellstrøm. You are likely to sample such superb dishes as a Norwegian lobster salad, paupiettes of sole with chives, or calf's head with tarragon butter.

MODERATE

KASTANJEN, Bygdøy Allé 18. Tel. 22-43-44-67.
   Cuisine: NORWEGIAN. **Reservations:** Required on weekends. **Tram:** 30.
$ **Prices:** Appetizers 60–75 kroner ($10.40–$13); main dishes 110–210 kroner ($19–$36.30). AE, DC, MC, V.
   Open: Mon–Sat 4–10pm. **Closed:** July.
Named for the chestnut trees that line the street on which it sits, this restaurant lies in the western residential section of Oslo, near several embassies. The decor is modern, warm, and unpretentious. The menu, illuminated by candlelight, changes monthly, and is based on seasonal ingredients. Six or seven dishes every night could, depending on their size, be ordered as either appetizers or main courses, including salmon with crayfish. There are one or two luxurious items among the main-dish selections, but most courses are priced at 110 kroner ($19). Monkfish is sautéed and served with a crayfish sauce, or you might order reindeer, which is first sautéed, then baked, and finally served with reindeer gravy and red currants.

NEAR THE HOLMENKOLLEN SKI JUMP

EXPENSIVE

FROGNERSETEREN HOVED-RESTAURANT, Holmenkollveien 200. Tel. 22-14-37-36.
   Cuisine: NORWEGIAN. **Reservations:** Recommended. **Tram:** Frognerseterbanen.
$ **Prices:** Fixed-price menus 190–280 kroner ($32.90–$48.40); appetizers 75–140 kroner ($13–$24.20); main dishes 165–240 kroner ($28.50–$41.50). AE, DC, MC, V.
   Open: Cafeteria, daily 10am–11pm. Restaurant, daily 11am–11pm.
On a mountain ledge, this log Norse lodge, furnished like a grand chalet, offers a spectacular view of Oslo and the fjord. This restaurant is a historic monument, originally built by entrepreneur Thomas Heftey in 1890, a few steps uphill from his family estate, which is still standing. In addition to the dining room, there is a café with prices about 15% lower, as well as a breezy outdoor terrace for snacks and beer. The chef specializes in game, including pheasant pâté with Cumberland sauce,

médaillons of reindeer, and filet of elk fried in honey and nuts. You can also order Norwegian salmon—poached, marinated, or smoked.

The restaurant is a 40-minute ride to the terminal stop some 1,600 feet above sea level. Be warned: It is 1,000 feet downhill to the restaurant from the Holmenkollen railway stop.

AT BYGDØY
MODERATE

NAJADEN, Bygdøynesveien 37. Tel. 22-43-81-80.
 Cuisine: NORWEGIAN. **Reservations:** Recommended. **Bus:** 30. **Ferry:** Bygdøy.
$ **Prices:** Appetizers 65–70 kroner ($11.20–$12.10); main dishes 155–210 kroner ($26.80–$36.30); dinner fish buffet 200 kroner ($34.60); summer lunch buffet 175 kroner ($30.30). AE, DC, MC, V.
 Open: Summer, Mon–Sat 11am–10pm, Sun noon–5pm; spring and autumn, Mon–Sat 11am–8pm, Sun noon–5pm; winter, Mon–Sat 11am–8pm, Sun noon–5pm.

In the Norwegian Maritime Museum, this restaurant overlooks an exhibition room of sculptures removed from 19th-century clipper ships. The popular summer luncheon buffet offers an elaborate array of fish and meat dishes, open from 11am to 3pm; the rest of the year, à la carte lunch service is featured. Children under 16 pay half price. In the evening, a more expensive—and more elaborate—fish table is laid out containing more than 40 different preparations of seafood. A Sunday buffet is available year-round.

SPECIALTY DINING
SELF-SERVICE CAFETERIAS
Inexpensive

NØRRONA CAFÉ, Grensen 19. Tel. 22-42-64-00.
 Cuisine: NORWEGIAN. **Reservations:** Not required. **Tram:** 7, 11.
$ **Prices:** Smørbrød 28–42 kroner ($4.80–$7.30); salads and soups 25–35 kroner ($4.30–$6.10); main dishes 39–80 kroner ($6.70–$13.80); fixed-price lunch 60 kroner ($10.40). No credit cards.
 Open: Mon 10:30am–6pm, Tues–Fri 8am–6:30pm, Sat 9am–4pm, Sun noon–5pm.

⑤ In high-priced Oslo it is no wonder that this cost-conscious cafeteria survives here, one floor above street level in the commercial center of town. Many shoppers prefer to drop in here for a smørbrød (open-face sandwich). Full hot meals are also served, including Norwegian fish soup and pork cutlets, as well as salads. You might finish off with one of the freshly made desserts.

SAMSON, Øvre Slottsgate 21. Tel. 22-42-55-62.
 Cuisine: NORWEGIAN. **Reservations:** Not required. **Bus:** 27.
$ **Prices:** Appetizers 28–55 kroner ($4.80–$9.50); main dishes 60–120 kroner ($10.40–$20.80). No credit cards.
 Open: Mon–Fri 8am–8pm, Sat 8am–5pm.

At the corner of Karl Johans Gate in an 1894 building, this modern big-windowed cafeteria overlooks a pedestrian street. Its familiar dishes include filet mignon, pepper steak, wienerschnitzel, and beef Stroganoff. You pay for your meal at a counter, and the waitress carries it to your table. Samson earned its good reputation from the dozen or so bakeries and pastry shops it operates throughout Oslo, so you can always be sure the pastries are fresh.

DEPARTMENT STORE DINING
Inexpensive

STEEN & STRØM, Kongensgate 23. Tel. 22-41-68-00.

Cuisine: NORWEGIAN. **Reservations:** Not required. **Bus:** 27, 29, 30, 31, 41.

$ Prices: Cafeteria, hot platters 57–90 kroner ($9.90–$15.60); sandwiches 28–45 kroner ($4.80–$7.80). Gamlestua, appetizers 38–48 kroner ($6.60–$8.30); main dishes 89–145 kroner ($15.40–$25.10). AE, DC, MC, V.

Open: Mon–Wed 10am–6pm, Thurs–Fri 10am–7pm, Sat 9am–5pm.

On the top of Norway's largest department store is a self-service cafeteria and an Old Norse dining room, the Gamlestua, both keeping the same hours. The cafeteria has a wide selection of open-face sandwiches and cakes. I recently had a roast beef delight with rémoulade sauce. The elegant and more formal Gamlestua specializes in Norwegian recipes, and meals can include lamb chops, fried liver, and fresh fish, topped off with either Norwegian sour-cream pudding or almond cake.

LOCAL FAVORITES

Moderate

ENGEBRET CAFE, Bankplassen 1. Tel. 22-33-66-94.

Cuisine: NORWEGIAN. **Reservations:** Recommended. **Bus:** 27, 29, 30.

$ Prices: Appetizers 58–78 kroner ($10–$13.50); main dishes 119–219 kroner ($20.60–$37.90); lunch smørbrød 32–90 kroner ($5.50–$15.60); *dagens menu* 85 kroner ($14.70). AE, DC, MC, V.

Open: Mon–Fri 11am–midnight, Sat noon–midnight. **Closed:** July.

 An enduring Oslovian favorite since it was established in 1857, this restaurant is housed in two landmark buildings joined together and lying directly north of Akershus Castle. It has an old-fashioned atmosphere and good food. From noon to 6pm, a *dagens menu* (daily menu) is good value. You get one course, perhaps Norwegian shark in a butter sauce, plus coffee. During lunch, a tempting selection of open-face sandwiches is available. The menu grows more elaborate in the evening when you might begin with a terrine of game with blackberry port wine sauce or Engebret's fish soup. You can go on to order such dishes as red wild boar with whortleberry sauce or Engebret's big fishpot. For dessert, try the cloudberry parfait.

TOSTRUPKJELLEREN, Karl Johans Gate 25. Tel. 22-42-14-17.

Cuisine: STEAKS. **Reservations:** Recommended. **Metro:** Stortinget.

$ Prices: Appetizers 45–88 kroner ($7.80–$15.20); main dishes 85–240 kroner ($14.70–$41.50). AE, DC, MC, V.

Open: Mon–Thurs 2pm–midnight; Fri–Sat 2pm–4pm.

Set only a few paces from the Norwegian Parliament building, this restaurant is considered the best of Oslo's cellar restaurants. At least most members of the Norwegian Parliament seem to agree, as many of them eat here weekdays. Journalists also frequent the place, perhaps hoping to pick up a story. The antique restaurant dates from 1897, and it is accessible via a narrow outside staircase. It has sturdy furniture and a venerable decor like a Teutonic beer hall.

This restaurant serves grilled steaks and imbues its ambience with Iberian flair from a mostly Spanish staff. Adjacent to the modern dining room lies a piano bar,

---

Ⓕ FROMMER'S COOL FOR KIDS: RESTAURANTS

Mamma Rosa (see p. 237) The best place to fill up on 10 kinds of pizzas or one of the pasta dishes, each a meal in itself.

Najaden (see p. 239) As if being housed in the Norwegian Maritime Museum weren't attraction enough for kids, they can also enjoy an elaborate summer buffet at half price. But they must be under 16.

open Monday to Saturday, from 9am until closing, where whisky with soda costs from 36 kroner to 55 kroner ($6.20 to $9.50), depending on the brand.

HANDVERKERAN, Rosenkrantzgate 7. Tel. 22-42-07-50.
   Cuisine: NORWEGIAN. **Reservations:** Recommended. **Tram:** 7, 11.
$ **Prices:** Appetizers 55–80 kroner ($9.50–$13.80); main dishes 100–170 kroner ($17.30–$29.40); lunch platters 50–100 kroner ($8.70–$17.30); sandwiches 50–62 kroner ($8.70–$10.70). AE, DC, MC, V.
   Open: Mon–Sat 11am–11pm.

Lying right off Karl Johans Gate, the Carpenter's Restaurant (its English name) attracts many journalists and politicians. Except for an occasional "brightening up," the place is much as it was when it was first established in 1900. Sandwiches and hot food are served until 2pm; after that, the à la carte menu becomes available. Dishes include both cured and smoked salmon, reindeer steak with cream sauce and potatoes, and leg of lamb. Specialties are "sea devil" and beefsteaks. Sea devil is North Atlantic shark, which is served grilled with garlic and fresh vegetables.

VEGETARIAN
Moderate

LIPP, in the Hotel Continental, Roald Amundsens Gate at Stortings-gaten. Tel. 22-41-90-60.
   Cuisine: INTERNATIONAL. **Reservations:** Recommended. **Metro:** Stortinget.
$ **Prices:** Appetizers 68–98 kroner ($11.80–$17); main dishes 98–200 kroner ($17–$34.60). AE, DC, MC, V.
   Open: Mon–Sat 11am–11pm, Sun 3–11pm.

Stylish, sophisticated, and lighthearted, this recently restored art deco brasserie evokes Paris in the 1920s. Painted a clear yellow, with an alert staff traditionally dressed, bistro-style, in black vests, it serves such specialties as salmon with wolffish in a white wine sauce and filet of reindeer in a mushroom sauce. Lighter fare includes a sophisticated array of salads and pastas.

Inexpensive

FRISKPORT VEGETA VERTSHUS, Munkedamsveien 3B. Tel. 22-83-42-32.
   Cuisine: VEGETARIAN. **Reservations:** Not required. **Bus:** 27.
$ **Prices:** Soups and salads 25 kroner ($4.30); unlimited buffet 98 kroner ($17). AE, DC, MC, V.
   Open: Daily 10am–11pm.

Since 1938 this basement cafeteria near the Rådhus, a stronghold of social activism and news of countercultural activities, is the only major vegetarian restaurant in town. At street level is a café where you help yourself to a buffet of 30 salad dishes and a large number of hot dishes, along with bread, butter, cheese, and coffee. The kitchen is also proud of its pizza. You can order juices, mineral water, soft drinks, or nonalcoholic wine. If someone wants to go only once to the buffet, a small plate costs 61 kroner ($10.60), a large plate 69 kroner ($11.90).

A WINE BAR
Inexpensive

FRU BLOM, Karl Johans Gate 41B. Tel. 22-42-73-00.
   Cuisine: NORWEGIAN. **Reservations:** Recommended. **Metro:** Stortinget.
$ **Prices:** Soups 35 kroner ($6.10); main dishes 68–135 kroner ($11.80–$23.40). AE, DC, MC, V.
   Open: Mon–Sat 11am–11pm.

Set in a commercial shopping arcade midway between the Royal Castle and Parliament, this informal wine bar has a prominent stand-up bar and a cluster of dining tables set out front beneath a glassed-in roof. It is run by the owners of one of the most famous restaurants of Oslo, Blom (see above), although prices here are much lower. It was established in 1985 next to its century-old parent. The food is prepared by the excellent Blom cooks, and the wine bar is one of the best buys in Oslo, concerning price and the quality of the cuisine.

You might begin with *dagens suppe* (soup of the day), followed by such dishes as chef's salad, with bacon, cheese, and egg. The day's specials are often fresh seafood. The cheesecake is delectable. All this is washed down with some French or Italian wines, even American. The wine bar inside is like a bodega, with decanters, old wine auction notices, and large barrels. Vintage wine is served by the glass. You can also order a cappuccino or sample a cognac.

DINING CLUSTERS

One of the Oslovian's favorite pastimes is to visit **Aker Brygge,** a waterfront plot of land which, until developers restored it, was a dilapidated shipbuilding yard, lying directly west of the Rådhus. The design is postmodern and futuristic, combining more shopping, entertainment, and dining diversions into one area than anywhere else in Norway. Many people, some of them *en famille,* come here to sample the various restaurants and cafés, watch the people, and listen to the array of music playing in the bars. Part of the fun is strolling through the complex and picking the restaurant of your choice. Norwegian food is served along with a representative selection of foreign food offerings, including American. Especially recommendable is **D. S. Louise.** In summer, both foreigners and locals fill the outdoor tables overlooking the active harbor life. Many nightlife possibilities exist here (see "Evening Entertainment," in Chapter 15). To reach it, take bus no. 27 or walk down from the center.

PICNIC FARE & WHERE TO EAT IT

Oslo is filled with picture-perfect vistas that call for a bottle of wine and a picnic. Delicatessens are scattered throughout the city. One of the best is **Køltzow,** Verkstedhallen, Stranden 3, in Aker Brygge (tel. 22-83-00-70). Here you can order a platter of fresh oysters to take out or a paper bag loaded with ready-to-eat portions of shrimp and a container of salt. Buy a loaf of bread, select some bite-sized portions of butter, pick up plastic utensils, and head for the Bygdøy peninsula. You can also order fancy fare as well, including salmon pâté, shellfish pâté, or a vegetable pâté studded with crabmeat. There is also an array of sandwiches priced from 55 kroner to 70 kroner ($9.50 to $12.10) each. It's open Monday through Friday from 10am to 8pm, on Saturday from 10am to 6pm. Sunday from 1 to 6pm. Ferries for Bygdøy depart just a short walk from this deli. Take bus no. 21 or 27.

In the area, right in front of Rådhuset, you can join Oslovians for a special picnic treat. From 7 to 8pm, shrimp fishermen pull their fishing boats into harbor having just caught and cooked a fresh batch of shrimp after a night at sea. You can order shrimp in bags, coming in two sizes, priced from 30 kroner to 45 kroner ($5.20 to $7.80). Seafood fanciers take their shrimp to the dock's edge, remove the shells, and feast away. The fishermen usually stick around all day until they've sold the last batch—saving just enough for their own families.

CHAPTER 15

WHAT TO SEE & DO IN OSLO

Some would be happy to come to Oslo just for the views of the harborfront city and Oslofjord. Panoramas are a major attraction, especially that from Tryvannstårnet, a 390-foot observation tower atop 1,900-foot-high Tryvann Hill in the environs (see below). But there are many man-made attractions worthy of your time and exploration. The beautiful surroundings make these sights even more appealing.

SUGGESTED ITINERARIES

IF YOU HAVE 1 DAY

Arm yourself with a bag of freshly cooked shrimp—purchased right off the shrimp boats at the harbor in front of the Rådhus—and take a ferry over to the Bygdøy peninsula. Explore some of Oslo's major attractions—they're within walking distance of each other. Explore the Viking ships, the polar ship *Fram,* the *Kon-Tiki* Museum, the Norwegian Maritime Museum, and the Norwegian Folk Museum. In the late afternoon, go to Frogner Park to admire the Vigeland sculptures.

IF YOU HAVE 2 DAYS

Day 1: See "If You Have 1 Day," above.

Day 2: Take a Frommer walking tour (see below), have lunch in a Norwegian restaurant, and explore the Edvard Munch Museum in the afternoon. In summer, visit Studenter Lunden, the students' grove near the National Theater for some beer and fresh air.

IF YOU HAVE 3 DAYS

Days 1 & 2: See "If You Have 2 Days," above.

Day 3: Take another Frommer walking tour (see below), eating lunch along the way. Explore Akershus Castle and the adjoining Norwegian Resistance Museum in the afternoon. By late afternoon, visit the lofty lookout tower at Tryvannstårnet and see the Skimuseet at Holmenkollen, taking in a view of Oslo's environs. Have dinner at Holmenkollen.

IF YOU HAVE 5 DAYS

Days 1–3: See "If You Have 3 Days," above.

Day 4: Head south from Oslo for a 1-day excursion to the Oslofjord country, with stopovers at the Old Town at Fredrikstad; Tønsberg, Norway's oldest town; and Sandefjord, an old whaling town. Head back to Oslo for the night.

Day 5: See the rest of Oslo's major sights, like the National Gallery, the Historical Museum, and the Henie-Onstad Art Center 7 miles from Oslo—a stunning museum of modern art.

1. THE TOP ATTRACTIONS

VIKINGSKIPHUSET (Viking Ship Museum), Huk Aveny 35, Bygdøy. Tel. 22-43-83-79.

Displayed here are three Viking burial vessels, excavated on the shores of the Oslofjord and preserved in clay. The most spectacular find is the 9th-century *Oseberg*, discovered near Norway's oldest town. This 64-foot dragon ship features a wealth of ornaments and is believed to have been the burial chamber of Harald Fairhair's grandmother and her slave.

The *Gokstad* find is a great example of Viking vessels because it's so well preserved. The smaller *Tune* ship was never restored. Look for the *Oseberg* animal-head post, the elegantly carved sleigh used by Viking royalty, and the *Oseberg* four-wheeled cart.

Admission: 15 kroner ($2.60) adults, 7 kroner ($1.20) children.

Open: May–Aug, daily 10am–6pm; Sept, daily 11am–5pm; Apr and Oct, daily 11am–4pm; Nov–Mar, daily 11am–3pm. **Ferry:** In summer, leaves from Pier 3 facing Rådhuset. **Bus:** 30 from the National Theater to polar ship *Fram* and *Kon-Tiki* Museum (see below).

POLAR SHIP *FRAM*, Bygdøynes. Tel. 22-43-83-70.

A long walk from the Viking ships, the Frammuseet contains the sturdy polar exploration ship *Fram*, which Fridtjof Nansen sailed across the Arctic (1893–96). The vessel was later used by the famed Norwegian explorer Roald Amundsen, the first man to reach the South Pole (1911).

Admission: 15 kroner ($2.60) adults, 8 kroner ($1.40) children.

Open: May–Aug, daily 10am–5:45pm; Sept, daily 1–4:45pm; Oct, daily noon–2:45pm; Mar 23–Apr, daily 11am–2:45pm. **Closed:** Nov–Mar 22. **Ferry:** In summer, leaves from Pier 3 facing Rådhuset. **Bus:** 30 from the National Theater.

KON-TIKI MUSEUM, Bygdøynesveien 36. Tel. 22-43-80-50.

Kon-Tiki is the world-famed balsa-log raft that the young Norwegian scientist Thor Heyerdahl and his five comrades sailed in for 4,300 miles in 1947—all the way from Callao, Peru, to Raroia, Polynesia.

Besides the raft, there are other exhibits from Heyerdahl's subsequent visit to Easter Island: casts of stone giants and small originals, a facsimile of the whale shark, and an Easter Island family cave, with a collection of sacred lava figurines hoarded in secret underground passages by inhabitants of that island. The museum also houses the original papyrus *Ra II* in which Heyerdahl crossed the Atlantic in 1970.

Admission: 15 kroner ($2.60) adults, 8 kroner ($1.40) children.

Open: Mid-May to Aug, daily 10am–6pm; Sept and Apr to mid-May, daily

10:30am–5pm; Oct–Mar, daily 10:30am–4pm. **Ferry:** In summer from Pier 3 facing Rådhuset. **Bus:** 30 from the National Theater.

NORSK SJØFARTSMUSEUM (Norwegian Maritime Museum), Bygdøynesveien 37. Tel. 22-43-82-40.

This museum chronicles the maritime history and culture of Norway, complete with a ship's deck with helm and chart house. There is also a three-deck-high section of the passenger steamer *Sandnaes.*

The Boat Hall features a fine collection of original small craft, including the fully restored polar vessel *Gjoa,* used by Roald Amundsen in his search for America's Northwest Passage. The three-masted schooner *Svanen* (Swan) is moored at the museum. Built in Svendborg, Denmark, in 1916 and later sailing under both Norwegian and Swedish flags, the ship now belongs to the museum and is used as a training vessel and school ship for young people.

Admission: Museum and boat hall, 15 kroner ($2.60) adults, 8 kroner ($1.40) children.

Open: May–Sept, daily 10am–8pm; Oct–Apr, Mon–Sat 10:30am–4pm, Sun 10:30am–5pm. **Ferry:** In summer, leaves from Pier 3 facing Rådhuset. **Bus:** 30 from the National Theater.

NORWEGIAN FOLK MUSEUM, Museumsveien 10. Tel. 22-43-70-20.

From all over Norway, 140 original buildings have been transported and reassembled on 35 acres on the Bygdøy peninsula. This open-air folk museum, the oldest of its kind in the country, includes a number of medieval buildings, such as the Raulandstua, one of the oldest wooden dwellings still standing in Norway, and a stave church from about 1200. The rural buildings are grouped together by region of origin, while the urban houses have been laid out in the form of an old town.

Inside, the museum has 225,000 exhibits, capturing every imaginable facet of Norwegian life, past and present. Furniture, household utensils, clothing, woven fabrics, and tapestries are displayed, along with fine examples of rose painting and wood carving. Farming implements and logging gear pay tribute to the development of agriculture and forestry in Norway. One of the most celebrated displays is Henrik Ibsen's completely reassembled study, transported from his home at Arbiensgate 1 in Oslo, where he lived until his death in 1906. Also look for the outstanding exhibition on Norway's Lapp population.

The museum also contains a fascinating musical and ecclesiastical section. Recitals are frequently held here using the historic instruments from the museum collection.

Admission: 35 kroner ($6.10) adults, 10 kroner ($1.70) children.

Open: May 15–June 14, daily 11am–4pm; June 15–Sept 15, daily 10am–6pm; Sept 16–30 daily noon–4pm; Oct–Mar, Tues–Sun noon–4pm; Apr–May 14, daily noon–4pm. **Ferry:** From Pier 3, near Rådhuset. **Bus:** 30.

VIGELAND SCULPTURE PARK, Frogner Park, Nobelsgata 32. Tel. 22-44-23-06.

The lifetime work of Gustav Vigeland, Norway's greatest sculptor, is displayed in the 75-acre Frogner Park in western Oslo. Nearly 211 sculptures in granite, bronze, and iron can be admired. See in particular his four granite columns, symbolizing the fight between humanity and evil (a dragon, the embodiment of evil, embraces a woman). The angry boy is perhaps the most photographed statue in the park, but the really celebrated work is the 52-foot-high monolith, composed of 121 figures of colossal size—all carved into one piece of stone.

Nearby, the **Vigeland Museum,** at Nobelsgate 32 (tel. 22-44-23-06), is the sculptor's former studio, containing more of his works, sketches, and woodcuts.

Admission: Park, free; Museum, 20 kroner ($3.50) adults, 10 kroner ($1.70) children.

Open: Park, daily 24 hours. Museum, May–Sept, Tues–Sat 10am–6pm, Sun noon–7pm; Oct–Apr, Tues–Sat noon–4pm, Sun noon–6pm. **Metro:** Majorstua. **Bus:** 30. **Tram:** 2.

EDVARD MUNCH MUSEUM, Tøyengate 53. Tel. 22-67-37-74.

BYGDØY PENINSULA

Bestukilen

Lysakerfjorden

Frognerkilen

Killingen

Hengsengveien

Dronning-Blancas-Vei

Wergelsveien

Christian Fr. V.

Oscarshall-veien

19

Museums-veien

Christian-Frederiks-Veien

Strømsborgveien

20

Hukenvn

Langvikbukta

Langviks-veien

21

22

23

Frederiksborgveien

Bygdøyveien

Paradisbukta

Lille Herbern

Store Herbern

Bekkebukta

Majorstuveien

Bogstadveien

Pilestredet

Hegdehaugsveien

Wergelandsveien

Parkveien

Nordraak plas

Slottsparken

16

Slottet

15

Dronningparken

Drammensvei

18

Frogner-parken

17

Kierkeveien

Gyldenløvesgate

Halvdan Svartesgata

Frognerveien

Eckersbergsgata

Thomas-Heftyes-Gate

Elisenbergveien

Bygdøy Allé

Nobelsgata

Thomas-Heftyes-Gate

Frederik-Stangs-Gate

Mogen Thorsensgate

Thomas-Heftyes-Gate

Gabelsgate

Niels-Juels-Gate

Bygdøy Allé

Frognerveien

Drammensveien

Løkkeveien

Cort-Adelers-Gate

Dr. Mauds Gate

Parkveien

Ruseløkkveien

Observatoriegata

Munkedamsveien

Drammensveien

Munkedamsveien

Frognerstranda

Frognerkilen

Fjellinjen

Filipstadveien

↓ To Bygdøy Peninsula

NORWAY

Oslo

Akershus Castle **14**	Historisk Museum **6**
Botanisk Hage og Museum **1**	Konserthuset **12**
Christiania Bymodell **14**	Kunstindustrimuseet **2**
Edvard Munch Museum **1**	Museet for Samtidskunst **15**
Forsvarsmuseet **14**	Nasjonalgalleriet **5**
Frogner Park **17**	Nationaltheatret **8**
Gamle Aker Kirke **3**	Norges Hjemmefront-museum **13**

Metro Stop **M**

Church **✝**

Post Office ⊠

Information **ⓘ**

Oslo Bymuseum **17**
Rådhuset **11**
Royal Palace (Slottet) **15**
Stortinget (Parliament) **10**
Slottsparken **16**
Trefoldighetskirken **4**
Vigeland Sculpture
   Garten **18**

BYGDØY PENNINSULA
Kon-Tiki Museum **21**
Norsk Sjøfartsmuseum **23**
Norwegian Folk Museum **19**
Polar Ship *Fram* **22**
Vikingskiphuset **20**

✪ Devoted exclusively to the works of Edvard Munch (1863–1944), considered the leading painter of Scandinavia, the exhibit, his gift to the city, traces his work from early realism to his latter-day expressionism. The collection comprises 1,100 paintings, some 4,500 drawings, around 18,000 prints, numerous graphic plates, six sculptures, and important documentary material. The pictures are changed periodically.

Admission: 40 kroner ($6.90) adults, 15 kroner ($2.60) children.
Open: June–Sept 15, Mon–Sat 10am–8pm, Sun noon–8pm; Sept 16–May, Tues–Sat 10am–4pm, Sun noon–8pm. **Metro:** Tøyen. **Bus:** 29 from Rådhusplassen.

RÅDHUSET (City Hall), Rådhusplassen. Tel. 22-41-00-90.

Called everything from "aggressively ugly" to the "pride of Norway," the modern city hall, inaugurated in 1950, must be seen to be judged. Its simple brick exterior with double towers houses, among other things, the stunning troll-size (85 by 43 feet) wall painted by Henrik Sørensen and the mural *Life* by Edvard Munch. The rest of the city hall contains tapestries, frescoes, sculpture, and wood carvings by Dagfin Werenskiold. Guided tours in English are available. In the courtyard, you can see the astronomical clock and Dyre Vaa's swan fountain.

Admission: Free.
Open: Apr–Sept, Mon–Sat 10am–3pm, Sun noon–3pm; Oct–Mar, Mon–Sat 11am–2pm, Sun noon–3pm. **Bus:** 27.

AKERSHUS CASTLE, Festnings-Plassen. Tel. 22-41-25-21.

One of the oldest historical monuments in Oslo, Akershus Castle was built in 1300 by King Haakon V Magnusson. It was a fortress and a royal residence for several centuries. A fire in 1527 devastated the northern wing, and the castle was rebuilt and transformed into a royal Renaissance palace under the Danish-Norwegian king, Christian IV. Now it's used by the Norwegian government for state occasions. Guided tours are offered Monday–Saturday at 11am, 1pm, and 3pm (on Sunday at 1 and 3pm).

Admission: 10 kroner ($1.70) adults, 5 kroner (90¢) children.
Open: Apr 14–30, Sun 12:30–4pm; May–Sept 15, Mon–Sat 10am–4pm, Sun 12:30–4pm; Sept 16–Oct, Sun 12:30–4pm. **Closed:** Nov–Apr 13. **Tram:** 1, 2, 9.

NORGES HJEMMEFRONTMUSEUM (Norway's Resistance Museum), Akershus Fortress. Tel. 22-40-31-38.

From underground printing presses to radio transmitters, beginning with the German attack in 1940 until the liberation in 1945, this museum documents World War II resistance activities. Outside is a monument dedicated to Norwegian patriots, many of whom were executed at this spot by the Nazis during the war.

Admission: 15 kroner ($2.60) adults, 5 kroner (90¢) children.
Open: Mid-Apr to Sept, daily 10am–4pm; Oct–Apr, Mon–Sat 10am–3pm, Sun 11am–4pm. **Tram:** 1, 2, 9.

FORSVARSMUSEET (Armed Forces Museum), Akershus Fortress. Tel. 22-40-35-82.

While in the area of Akershus Fortress, you can also explore this museum documenting Norwegian military history from the dawn of the 16th century to 1950. Guns, tanks, bombs, and planes are all here, from a fighter plane left over from the "Great War" to a Spitfire from World War II. All these weapons and modern artillery are housed in a former military arsenal. The museum has its own cafeteria.

Admission: Free.
Open: June–Aug, Mon–Fri 10am–6pm, Sat–Sun 11am–4pm; Sept–May, Mon–Fri 10am–3pm, Sat–Sun 11am–4pm. **Tram:** 1, 2, 9.

TRYVANNSTÅRNET (Lookout Tower), Voksenkollen. Tel. 22-14-67-11.

The loftiest lookout tower in Scandinavia—the gallery is approximately 1,900 feet above sea level—offers a view of the Oslofjord with Sweden to the east.

A walk down the hill takes us back to Frognerseteren (see "Oslo Dining" in Chapter 14). You can take another 20-minute walk down the hill to the Holmenkollen ski jump, the site of the 1952 Olympic competitions. It's also the site of Norway's highlight of winter sports, the **Holmenkollen Ski Festival** where elite skiers of the world gather for competitions in downhill, slalom, giant slalom, cross-country ski races, and jumping.

Admission: 25 kroner ($4.30) adults, 15 kroner ($2.60) children.

Open: Oct–Apr, Mon–Fri 10am–3pm, Sat–Sun 11am–4pm; May and Sept, daily 10am–7pm; June, daily 10am–7pm; July, daily 9am–10pm; Aug, daily 9am–8pm.

Subway: Holmenkollen SST Line 15 from near the National Theater to Voksenkollen, a 30-minute ride; then an uphill 15-minute walk.

SKIMUSEET (Ski Museum), Kongeveien 5, Holmenkollen. Tel. 22-92-32-00.

At Holmenkollen, an elevator takes visitors up another tower for a view of Oslo and the fjord. At the base of the ski jump is the Ski Museum (Skimuseet), displaying a wide range of exhibits, including a 4,000-year-old pictograph from Rødøy in Nordland, which documents skiing's thousand-year-old history. The oldest ski in the museum dates from around A.D. 600. The museum has exhibits of Nansen's and Amundsen's polar expeditions, plus skis and historical items from various parts of Norway, including the first "modern" skis dating from around 1870.

Admission: Museum and ski jump, 25 kroner ($4.30) adults, 15 kroner ($2.60) children.

Open: May and Sept, daily 10am–5pm; June, daily 10am–7pm; July, daily 9am–10pm; Aug, daily 9am–8pm; Oct–Apr, Mon–Fri 10am–3pm, Sat–Sun 11am–4pm. **Transportation:** See the Lookout Tower and Ski Museum, above.

2. MORE ATTRACTIONS

NASJONALGALLERIET (National Gallery), Universitetsgaten 13. Tel. 22-20-04-04.

 ## FROMMER'S FAVORITE OSLO EXPERIENCES

Enjoying Fresh Shrimp off the Boats Head for the harbor in front of Rådhuset and buy a bag of freshly caught and cooked shrimp from a shrimp fisherman. Get a beer at an Aker Brygge Café and shell and eat your shrimp along the harbor.

Experiencing Life of the Fjords In summer, head for the harbor where boats wait to take you sightseeing, fishing, or to the beaches.

Hanging Out in Students' Grove Summer is short in Oslo, and it's savored. Late-night drinkers sit in open-air beer gardens, enjoying the pale nights that have no end.

Listening to the Street Musicians By the hundreds, musicians flock to Oslo in summer. You can enjoy their music along Karl Johans Gate and at the Marketplace.

Taking the Ferry to Bygdøy Bygdøy peninsula is a treasure trove of Viking ships, Thor Heyerdahl's *Kon-Tiki*, seafood buffets, a sailboat harbor, bathing beaches, and a folk museum with old farmsteads, houses, and often folk dancing.

This state museum, a short walk from Students' Grove, has a good collection of works by world-famous artists, including Cézanne and Matisse, but it is recommended chiefly for its paintings by Norwegians—particularly the leading Romantic landscape painter, Johan Christian Dahl, who flourished in the early 19th century. Three other outstanding Norwegian artists were highly valued for their realistic works: Harriet Backer (a leading painter in the 1880s famous for interior portraits of Norwegian life), Christian Krohg (subjects from seafarers to prostitutes), and Erik Werenskiold (see his *Peasant Funeral*). On the main staircase is a display of Norwegian sculpture from 1910 to 1945. See particularly the works of Gustav Vigeland and the two rooms devoted to Edvard Munch (see his much-reproduced *The Scream,* painted in 1893).
Admission: Free.
Open: Mon–Wed and Fri–Sat 10am–4pm, Thurs 10am–8pm, Sun 11am–3pm.
Tram: 7, 11.

OSLO DOMKIRKHE (Oslo Cathedral), Stortovet 1. Tel. 22-41-27-93.

Oslo's 17th-century cathedral at Stortovet (the Marketplace) was restored in 1950, when its modern tempera ceiling decorations were completed by Hugo Lous Mohr. The cathedral contains works by 20th-century Norwegian artists, including bronze doors by Dagfin Werenskiold. Don't miss the pulpit and altar dating from the cathedral's earliest days, its stained-glass windows by Emanuel Vigeland (not to be confused with the sculptor, Gustav) in the choir and Borgar Hauglid in the transepts, and its five-story-tall organ. A bilingual service (Norwegian and English) is conducted on Wednesday at noon, church concerts on Wednesday at 7:30pm, and an organ recital on Saturday at noon (summer only).
Admission: Free.
Open: Mon–Fri 10am–3pm. **Bus:** 17. **Metro:** Stortinget.

HISTORISK MUSEUM (Historical Museum), Frederiksgate 2. Tel. 22-41-63-00.

Devoted to enthnography, antiquities, and numismatics, this museum near Karl Johans Gate houses an interesting collection of prehistoric objects and antiquities on the ground floor, with Viking artifacts, and a display of gold and silver from the 5th through the 13th century in the Treasure House. The collection also contains gold objects from about A.D. 600 to 800. Don't miss the reddish Ringerike Alstad Stone in the medieval hall, which was carved in relief; and the Dynna Stone, an 11th-century runic stone honoring the fairest maiden in Hadeland. There is also a rich collection of ecclesiastical art in a series of portals from stave churches. The museum is operated by the University of Oslo Universitetets Oldsaksamling.
Admission: Free.
Open: May 15–Sept 14, Tues–Sun 11am–3pm; Sept 16–May 14, Tues–Sun noon–3pm. **Tram:** 7, 11.

HENIE-ONSTAD KUNSTSENTER (Henie-Onstad Art Center), N-1311 Hkvikodden, Baerum. Tel. 67-54-30-50.

On a handsome site beside Oslofjord, 7 miles from Oslo, ex-movie star and skating champion Sonja Henie and her husband Niels Onstad, the shipping tycoon, opened a museum to combine and display their art collection. An especially good 20th-century collection, there are some 1,800 works by Munch, Picasso, Matisse, Léger, Bonnard, and Miró. Miss Henie's contributions can be seen in her Trophy Room (three Olympic gold medals—she was the star at the 1936 competition—and 10 world skating championships). In all, she garnered 600 trophies and medals.
Besides the permanent collection, there are plays, concerts, films, and special exhibitions. An open-air theater-in-the-round is used in summer for folklore programs, jazz concerts, and song recitals. On the premises is a top-notch, partly self-service, grill restaurant, the **Piruetten,** for the budget traveler.
Admission: 20 kroner ($3.50) adults, 10 kroner ($1.70) children.
Open: Jan–May and Sept–Dec, Mon 11am–5pm, Tue–Fri 9am–9pm, Sat–Sun

11am–5pm; June–Aug, Mon 11am–5pm, Tues–Fri 9am–9pm, Sat–Sun 11am–7pm. **Bus:** 151, 153, 161, 162, 251, 261 to Høvikodden.

KUNSTINDUSTRIMUSEET (Museum of Applied Art), St. Olavs Gate 1. Tel. 22-20-35-78.

Founded in 1876, this is one of the oldest museums in Norway and among the oldest applied arts museums in Europe. Extensive collections of handcrafts and industrial designs from both Norway and abroad range from the 7th century to today, including exhibitions of furniture, glass, metal, ceramic ware, textiles, and fashion, the latter displayed in the Royal Norwegian Costume Gallery. The collections include some 35,000 objects covering a period of 2,500 years. The first floor is devoted to temporary exhibitions of modern crafts and design. The museum gives lectures and guided tours, and also holds concerts in its Norwegian gallery. Café Solliløkken and the museum shop on the ground floor are installed in rooms from the 1830s, originally belonging to a small country house.

   Admission: 15 kroner ($2.60) adults, 10 kroner ($1.70) children.
   Open: Tues–Fri 11am–3pm, Sat–Sun noon–4pm. **Metro:** Stortinget. **Bus:** 37.

MUSEET FOR SAMTIDSKUNST (Museum of Contemporary Art), Bankplassen 4. Tel. 22-33-58-20.

One of Oslo's newest museums, this collection acquired by the state in postwar years, opened in 1990 presenting an array of international and Norwegian contemporary art. Once grouped together in the National Gallery, it now has more room to "breathe" in its new home.

   Admission: Free.
   Open: Tues–Fri 11am–7pm, Sat–Sun 11am–4pm. **Tram:** 1, 2, 9. **Bus:** 1, 2, 9, 10.

STORTINGET (Parliament), Karl Johans Gate 22. Tel. 22-31-30-50.

Constructed in 1861 to 1866, the Norwegian Parliament in the center of town was richly decorated by contemporary Norwegian artists. The style is neo-Romanesque. Guided tours are obligatory.

   Admission: Free.
   Open: Guided tours, July–Aug, Mon–Fri at 11am, noon, and 1pm. **Closed:** Sept–June. **Metro:** Stortinget.

PARKS & GARDENS

Marka, the thick forest that surrounds Oslo, might be considered a giant pleasure park, but there are others.

BOTANISK HAGE OG MUSEUM (Botanical Gardens), Sarsgate 1. Tel. 22-68-69-60.

At Tøyen, near the Munch Museum, this is an oasis in the heart of Oslo. In this far northern clime, many exotic plants grow, including cacti, orchids, and palms. More than 1,000 different mountain plants can be viewed in the rock garden, with its waterfalls. There is also a museum in the park, with a botanical art exhibition.

   Admission: Free.
   Open: Apr 15–Sept 15, Mon–Fri 7am–8pm, Sat–Sun 10am–8pm; Sept 16–Apr 14, Mon–Fri 7am–5pm, Sat–Sun 10am–5pm. **Bus:** 20.

SLOTTSPARKEN, Drammensveien 1.

Unlike Buckingham Palace, the park surrounding the Royal Palace (*Slottet*) is open to the public year-round. The changing of the guard takes place daily at 1:30pm. When the king is in residence, the Royal Guard band plays Monday through Friday.

   The palace was constructed from 1825 to 1848. Some first-time visitors are surprised at how open and relatively unguarded the palace is, standing without walls or rails. You can walk through the grounds, but can't go inside unless you have an invitation from the king. The statue at the front of the castle, at the end of Karl Johans Gate, is of Karl XIV Johan himself, who ruled over both Norway and Sweden. He ordered the palace constructed, but died before it was finished.

Admission: Free.
Open: Daily dawn–dusk. **Metro:** Stortinget.

3. COOL FOR KIDS

Oslo rivals Copenhagen when it comes to attractions suitable for both children and grownups. The top thrill of a trip in the fjord is, I am sure, seeing the Viking burial ships that have been excavated on the Bygdøy peninsula, and the Norwegian Maritime Museum and Boat Hall.

Other sights, already discussed, that are of special interest to children include: the polar exploration ship *Fram,* which bore both Nansen and Amundsen on their ventures to the North and South Poles; the balsa-log raft *Kon-Tiki,* in which Thor Heyerdahl made his historic journey across the Pacific; the lookout tower, ski jump, and Ski Museum at Holmenkollen; the folk museum, depicting life in Norway since the Middle Ages; and the ancient fortress on the Oslofjord, Akershus Castle.

NORGESPARKEN TUSENFRYD, Vinterbro by the E6/E18/Mosseveien. Tel. 64-94-63-63.
It's not the Tivoli Gardens of Copenhagen, but this family amusement park, 12 miles from the Central Station, is lots of fun, nevertheless. It offers more than 20 attractions, including a roller coaster with a loop and corkscrew, a log run, an amphitheater with all-day entertainment, and many games of skill or chance.

Admission: 120 kroner ($20.80) adults, 95 kroner ($16.40) children.
Open: June 4–Aug 14, daily 11am–8:30pm; Aug 15–Sept 9, Sat–Sun 11am–8:30pm. **Closed:** Sept 10–June 3. **Bus:** 541.

BARNEKUNST MUSEUM (International Children's Art Museum), Lille Frøersveien 4. Tel. 22-46-85-73.
From more than 130 countries, the collection in this unique museum is children's art—drawings, paintings, ceramics, sculpture, tapestries, and handcrafts. Some I inspected would have pleased Picasso, I'm certain. There is also a children's workshop devoted to paintings, drawings, music, and dancing.

Admission: 25 kroner ($4.30) adults, 15 kroner ($2.60) children.
Open: June 5–Aug 8, Mon–Fri 11am–5pm; during the school year, Tues–Thurs 9:30am–2pm. **Bus:** 72.

4. SPECIAL-INTEREST SIGHTSEEING

FOR THE ART LOVER

AULA (Great Hall), University of Oslo, Karl Johans Gate 47. Tel. 22-42-90-10, ext. 756.
Devotees of the work of Edvard Munch will not only want to see the Munch Museum but the Great Hall of the university where Scandinavia's greatest artist painted murals on the walls. Regrettably, it is open only in July.

Admission: Free.
Open: July only, Mon–Fri noon–2pm. **Metro:** Stortinget.

FOR THE LITERARY ENTHUSIAST

Consider "Walking Tour 2," below, which follows in the footsteps of Ibsen.

EDVARD MUNCH MUSEUM, Tøyengate 53. Tel. 22-67-37-74.
This repository of much of the life's work of Edvard Munch, has already been previewed. But a special exhibition focuses on Munch's stage designs for the plays of Henrik Ibsen, including two of his most popular works, *Hedda Gabler* and *Ghosts*. Woodcuts are preserved that were based on *The Pretenders* and there is also a series of drawings related to *Peer Gynt* and the production of *When We Dead Awaken*. Look, also, for Munch's painting of Ibsen at his favorite table at the Grand Café.
Admission: 40 kroner ($6.90) adults, 15 kroner ($2.60) children.
Open: May–Sept, Mon–Sat 10am–8pm, Sun noon–8pm; Oct–Apr, Tues–Sat 10am–4pm, Sun noon–8pm. **Metro:** Tøyen. **Bus:** 29 from Rådhusplassen.

OSLO BYMUSEUM (City Museum), Frognerveien 67. Tel. 22-43-06-45.
Housed in the 1790 Frogner Manor at Frogner Park, site of the Vigeland sculptures, this museum surveys the history of Oslo, of interest in itself. But it also contains mementos of Henrik Ibsen, like the chair and marble-top table where he sat at the Grand Café. Four glasses from which he drank are engraved with his name.
Admission: 15 kroner ($2.60) adults, 5 kroner (90¢) children.
Open: June–Aug, Mon–Fri 10am–6pm, Sat–Sun 10am–5pm; Sept–May, Mon–Fri 10am–4pm, Sat–Sun 11am–4pm. **Metro:** Majorstua.

FOR THE ARCHITECTURE LOVER

Those interested in modern architecture should head to **Vaterland,** in East Oslo. One of Oslo's major development sites, launched in the 1980s, this "city within a city" includes a 9,000-seat hall for musical and sporting events, an art gallery, a train station, and large conference facilities.

Those interested in recycling old districts will also want to explore **Aker Brygge,** west of City Hall. Located along the harbor, "the Fisherman's Wharf of Oslo" opened in 1986 in what had been former shipbuilding yards. Today it is a modern complex of shops, nightspots, restaurants, delis, wine bars, and ice-cream parlors.

ARKITEKTURMUSEUM (Architecture Museum), Josefinesgate 32 –34. Tel. 22-60-22-90.
Located in Homans byen, a residential area from the 19th century, this museum has alternating architectural exhibits and a library.
Admission: Free.
Open: Sept–May 15, Mon–Fri 9am–3pm, Thurs 9am–8pm; May 16–Aug, Mon–Fri 9am–3pm. **Tram:** 1, 11.

CHRISTIANIA BYMODELL, Høymagasinet, Akershus Festning. Tel. 22-33-31-47.
Norway's capital was first called Oslo, then Christiania, then Oslo again. Today an area in the historic district, this architectural model of the city of Christiania in the year 1838 is part of a multimedia program shown on screen tracing the city's history from its foundation in 1624 until 1840.
Admission: 20 kroner ($3.50) adults; 10 kroner ($1.70) children.
Open: June–Sept 15, Tues–Sun 11am–5pm. **Closed:** Sept 16–May. **Tram:** 1, 2, 9.

GAMLE AKER KIRKE (Old Aker Church), Geitmyrsveien 7D. Tel. 22-46-11-68.
Originally constructed in 1100, this is the oldest stone church in Scandinavia still in use as a parish church. Guided tours are conducted year-round.
Admission: Free.

Open: Mon–Thurs noon–2pm; guided tours, Sat at 11am and Sun at 6pm.
Metro: Stortinget.

WALKING TOUR 1 — HISTORIC OSLO

Start: Aker Brygge.
Finish: Royal Palace.
Time: 2½ hours.
Best Time: Any day it's not raining.

Start at the:

1. **Harbor of Aker Brygge,** to the west of Rådhuset, with its fine view of Akershus Castle. This steel-and-glass complex is a rebuilt district of shops and restaurants that was developed from the old shipbuilding grounds of Oslo. From Aker Brygge, head east along Rådhusplassen, looking at:
2. **Rådhuset,** on your left. The city hall of Oslo, built in 1950 with double towers, is decorated with artwork by Norwegian artists. Climb the steps at the east end of the square to see the:
3. **Statue of Franklin D. Roosevelt** (you have to climb a slight hill). Eleanor Roosevelt flew to Oslo to dedicate the statue.

   As you traverse this area, you will be in the heart of the Renaissance city from the 1600s. Take Rådhusgata east to:
4. **Christiania Torv,** a traffic hub. The yellow house on your left is the Young Artists Association, but once it was the home of the dreaded executioner. His fee depended on the type of execution performed.

REFUELING STOP   To the right of the Young Artists Association is the **Kafé Celsius,** Rådhusgaten 19 (tel. 22-42-45-39), Oslo's oldest residential house. Today it is a charming arts-oriented café serving tasty food, with sandwiches costing from 38 kroner ($6.60). You can also order pasta salads and such dishes as ratatouille or tortellini. On cold days, a fireplace burns. Hours are Tuesday to Sunday from 11:30am to 1am.

Continue along Rådhusgata, turning right onto Nedre Slottsgate. Walk to the end of the street. At Myntgata, turn right and pass through a gate. You are now on the greater grounds of Akershus Castle. The first building on the right is the:
5. **Norwegian Resistance Museum,** which has displays of events related to the Nazi occupation of Norway from 1940 to 1945. Also at the site is:
6. **Akershus Castle and Fortress,** dating from 1300 but rebuilt in the 17th century. Take a guided tour of the fortress and walk its ramparts. Pause on the grounds to look at the:
7. **Execution Site** in front of the Norwegian Resistance Museum. Nazis took prisoners here, often Norwegian freedom fighters, and shot them. There's a memorial to the resistance movement, and you'll have a good view of the harbor in the distance.

   Cross the drawbridge to the east and continue through the castle grounds to the:
8. **National Monument to the German Occupation** commemorating the suffering the country endured at the hands of the Nazis. After seeing the monument, turn north into:
9. **Grev Wedels Plass,** the site of Den Gamle Logen (freemason's lodge) where in 1850 Ibsen wrote poems. Head north along Kirkegata until you reach:
10. **Bankplassen,** site of the old Bank of Norway. Today the old bank is now the Museum of Contemporary Art, Bankplassen 4, with the state collection of international and Norwegian modern art gathered since World War II. This

WALKING TOUR — HISTORIC OSLO

finish here ⑯

① start here

① Harbor of Aker Brygge
② Rådhuset
③ Statue of Franklin D. Roosevelt
④ Christiania Torv
⑤ Norwegian Resistance Museum
⑥ Akershus Castle and Fortress
⑦ Execution Site
⑧ National Monument to the German Occupation
⑨ Grev Wedels Plass
⑩ Bankplassen
⑪ Oslo Sentralstasjon
⑫ Karl Johans Gate
⑬ Basarhallene
⑭ Oslo Domkirke
⑮ Norwegian Parliament (Stortinget)
⑯ Royal Palace (Slottet)

OSLO

Historic Oslo Area

square was once the social center of Oslo, and Ibsen staged his first play here in 1851 at a theater that later burned down in 1877.

From Bankplassen, turn right onto Revierstredet and left again onto Dronningens Gate. At one time the waterfront came up to this point. Go right at Tollbugata at the Central Post Office. At the intersection with Fred Olsens Gate, turn left and walk to the:

11. **Oslo Sentralstasjon,** Oslo's rail hub, where trains arrive from the Continent and also depart from all points linked by train in Norway. Turn left onto:

12. **Karl Johans Gate,** the main pedestrian-free street that stretches from the Central Station in the east and to the Royal Palace in the west end. On your right, you pass:

13. **Basarhallene,** a huge complex filled with boutiques and various shops.
Turn right at Kirkegata heading for:

14. **Oslo Domkirke,** Stortovet, the 17th-century cathedral at Oslo's old market-place. Like the city hall, the cathedral is decorated with outstanding works by Norwegian artists.

From Stortovet, walk west along Grensen until you reach the following stopover.

REFUELING STOP The atmosphere of old Oslo lives on at the **Stortovets Gjaestgiveri,** Grensen 1 (tel. 22-42-88-63), located on a busy commercial street. This drinking and dining emporium, dating from the 1600s, is often filled with spirited beer drinkers. Hours are daily from noon to 11pm.

Continue west on Grensen until you reach Lille Grensen. Cut left onto this street, returning to Karl Johans Gate. On your left will be the:

15. **Norwegian Parliament (Stortinget),** Karl Johans Gate 22. Constructed in 1861 to 1866, it is richly decorated by contemporary Norwegian artists.

Continue west along Karl Johans Gate, passing many of the monuments covered on "Walking Tour 2" (see below). Eventually you reach the:

16. **Royal Palace (Slottet),** Drammensveien 1, residence of the king of Norway. Public access is possible only to the park.

WALKING TOUR 2 —— IN THE FOOTSTEPS OF IBSEN & MUNCH

Start: National Theater.
Finish: National Gallery.
Time: 2 hours.
Best Time: Any day it's not raining.

The tour begins at:

1. **Nationaltheatret,** Stortingsgaten 15, lying off Karl Johans Gate near Studenter Lunden (Students' Grove) in Oslo's center. Study your map in front of the Henrik Ibsen statue at the theater where many of his plays were first performed and are still being presented. The Norwegian National Theater (tel. 22-41-16-40), inaugurated in 1899 with a rococo salon in gold and red, is considered one of the most beautiful in Europe. Guided tours are possible year-round on Monday at 6pm. From June 15 to July 8, daily tours are given at 5pm. Tours cost 30 kroner ($5.20) for adults and 15 kroner ($2.60) for children. Phone for information.

Facing the statue of Ibsen, continue up the Stortingsgaten in the direction of the Royal Palace (Slottet). Cut left at the intersection and walk along Ruselokkveien. The Vika Shopping Terraces, an unattractive row of modern storefronts tacked onto an elegant 1880 Victorian terrace, used to be among

Oslo's grandest apartments. In World War II it was the Nazi headquarters. Continue along this complex to the end, turning right onto Dronnings Mauds Gate, which quickly becomes Lokkeveien.

At the first building on the right, you come to the:

2. Private apartment of Ibsen. Look for the blue plaque marking the building. The playwright lived here from 1891 to 1899, moving when his wife complained she didn't like the address, even though it was one of Oslo's most elegant. Ibsen wrote two plays while living here.

Turn right onto Arbinsgate and walk to the end of the street until you reach Drammensveien:

3. Ibsen's last address. At the first building on the left, at the corner of Arbinsgate and Drammensveien, you will see an Omega store, but look for the blue plaque on the building. Ibsen lived here from 1895 until his death. He often sat in the window, a light casting a glow over his white hair. People lined up in the street below to get a look at him. The great Italian actress, Eleanora Duse, came this way to bid him a final *adieu*, but he was too ill to see her. She stood outside in the snow and blew him kisses.

The king of Norway used to give Ibsen a key to enter the private gardens surrounding the Royal Palace (everybody has that privilege today).

Turn right on Drammensveien and continue back to the National Theater. Take Karl Johans Gate, on the left side of the theater, and walk east. On your left, you'll pass the:

4. University of Oslo, Karl Johans Gate 47 (tel. 22-42-90-91), where Aula, the great hall of the university, was decorated with murals by Edvard Munch. The hall is open to the public only in July.

Twice a day Ibsen walked along this same sidewalk to the Grand Café. Admirers often threw rose petals in his path, but he pretended not to see them. He was called "the Sphinx," because he wouldn't talk to anybody.

REFUELING STOP The **Grand Café,** Karl Johans Gate 31, was the center of social life for the literati and the artistic elite, including Munch. It was—and is—the most fashionable café in Oslo (see Chapter 14). At the far wall of the café, you can see Per Krogh's famous mural painted in 1928. Ibsen, the man in the top hat and the gray beard, is at the far left, and Munch—called the handsomest man in Norway—is seated at the second window from the right at the far right of the window. The poet and playwright, Bjørnstjerne Bjørnson, can be spotted on the street outside (second window from the left, wearing a top hat)—he wouldn't deign to come into the café. At the café you can order food and drink, a big meal or a snack.

Returning to the street outside, note the National Parliament Building (Stortinget) on your left.

Proceed left and turn left onto Lillegrensen. Cross the major boulevard, Grensen, and walk straight to:

5. Akersgata, the street of the funeral cortège of Ibsen. Services were conducted at the Holy Trinity Church on June 1, 1906. Veer left to see the:

6. Birthplace of Ibsen's son. On your left, at the corner of Teatergata and Akersgata, is the site of the famous Strømberg Theater, which burned down in 1835. It was also a residence: Ibsen's son was born here in 1859.

Also on Akersgata is:

7. Trefoldighetskirken (Holy Trinity Church), site of Ibsen's funeral. A little farther along Akersgata is St. Olav's Church. Turn on the right side of this imposing house of worship onto Akersveien and go to:

8. Damplassen, a small square—one of the most charming in Oslo—that doesn't appear on most maps. Norway's greatest poet, Henrik Wergeland, lived in the pink house on this square from 1839 to 1841.

Take a right at the square and head down:

9. Damstredet, a typical old Oslo street, with antique wooden houses mainly occupied by artists.

Damstredet winds downhill to Fredensborgveien, where a left turn and a short walk will take you to Maridalsveien, a busy but dull thoroughfare. As you walk north along this street, on the west side, look for a large, unmarked gateway, inside of which are wide stone steps. Climb to the top, follow a little pathway, and go past gardens and flower beds. Pass a set of brick apartment buildings on the left, and proceed instead to a little street:

10. Telthusbakken, where you'll see a whole row of early Oslo wooden houses. Look right in the far distance at the green building where Munch used to live. Telthusbakken leads to Akersveien and on your left you can see:

11. Gamle Aker Kirke (Old Aker Church) (tel. 22-46-11-68). Enter at Akersbakken, where Akersveien and Akersbakken intersect. Built in 1100, this is the oldest stone parish church in Scandinavia still in use. It stands on a green hill with an old graveyard around it, inside a stone wall.

A short block from the church along Akersbakken (veer left outside the front of the church and go around a corner), you come to the north entrance of:

12. Vår Frelsers Gravlund (Our Savior's Cemetery), the city's expansive burial ground. In a section designated the Ground of Honor, famous Norwegians are buried, including Munch, Ibsen, and Bjørnson. Signs do not point the way, but it's easy to see a tall obelisk. This is the:

13. Tomb of Ibsen. His wife, Susanna, whom he called "the cat," is buried to the playwright's immediate left. She died in 1914. The hammer on the obelisk is symbolic of his work *The Miner,* indicating how he "dug deep" into the soul of Norway.

To the right of Ibsen's tomb is the:

14. Tomb of Bjørnson (1832–1910), who once raised money to send Ibsen to Italy. Before the birth of their children, Ibsen and Bjørnson agreed that one would have a son and the other a daughter, and they would both grow up to get married. Miraculously, Ibsen had a son, Bjørnson a daughter, and they did grow up to get married. Bjørnson wrote the national anthem of Norway, and his tomb is draped in a stone representation of a Norwegian flag.

To the far right of Bjørnson's tomb is the:

15. Tomb of Edvard Munch. Scandinavia's greatest painter (born 1863) has a completely unadorned tomb. If you're visiting on a snowy day, it will be completely buried, as its marker lies close to the earth. Munch died in 1944 during the darkest days of the Nazi occupation of Norway. His sister turned down a request from the German command to give Munch a state funeral, feeling that it would be inappropriate. The grave has remained unadorned since 1944.

On the west side of the cemetery, you'll come to Ullevålsveien. Turn left on this busy street and go back south toward the center of Oslo. You'll soon see St. Olav's Church, this time on your left. But stay on the west side of the street where Ullevålsveien intersects with St. Olavs Gate.

16. Kunstindustrimuseet, St. Olavs Gate 1, is the museum of applied art (see "More Attractions," above). Even if you don't have time to visit the museum, you may want to go inside to patronize its café.

After visiting the museum, continue along St. Olavs to:

17. Pilestredet. Look to your immediate right. A wall plaque on a decaying building commemorates the fact that Munch lived here from 1868 to 1875. When demolition teams started to raze the building, counter-culture groups illegally took it over and have been occupying the building ever since. On its brick wall side, the Munch masterpiece, *The Scream,* has been re-created in spray paint. Munch came to this building when he was 5, and many of his "memory paintings" were of the interior.

At Pilestredet, turn left. One block later, turn right onto Universitetsgate, heading south toward Karl Johans Gate. You'll pass a number of architecturally interesting buildings, and will eventually arrive at the:

18. National Gallery, Universitetsgata 13, where the state has deposited the largest collection of Norwegian and foreign art. Two separate rooms are devoted solely to masterpieces by Munch.

5. ORGANIZED TOURS

CRUISES AROUND THE FJORD   Departing from Pier 3 in front of Oslo Rådhuset (City Hall), **Båtservice Sightseeing,** Rådhusbrygge 3, Rådhusplassen (tel. 22-20-02-17), offers a 50-minute mini-cruise boat tour, with a view of the harbor and the city, including the ancient fortress of Akershus and the islands in the inner part of Oslofjord. Cruises depart mid-May to late August, daily on the hour from 10am to 8pm (limited sailing at the beginning and end of the season). Adults pay 50 kroner ($8.70); children, 25 kroner ($4.30).

If you have more time, take the 2-hour fjord cruise through the maze of islands and narrow sounds in the fjord. Departures are May 1 to mid-September, daily at 10:30am and 1, 3:30, and 5:45pm; the cost is 100 kroner ($17.30) for adults, 50 kroner ($8.70) for children. Refreshments are available on board. There are variants of this cruise, such as the fjord cruise with lunch, also 2 hours, leaving May 1 to mid-September, daily at 10:30am, and costing 250 kroner ($43.30) for adults, 200 kroner ($34.60) for children. After the 2-hour fjord cruise, the boat anchors so passengers can go ashore for lunch at Najaden restaurant.

An evening fjord cruise (2½ hours), including a maritime buffet, also at the Najaden, leaves from late June to the end of August, Monday to Saturday at 5:45pm. Prices are 295 kroner ($51) for adults, 245 kroner ($42.40) for children.

CITY TOURS   **HMK** tours has been showing visitors around Oslo for more than a century. From May 1 to September 30, they have a 3-hour morning sightseeing jaunt that costs 150 kroner ($26) for adults and 75 kroner ($13) for children. The bus visits Akershus, Frogner Park and the Vigeland sculptures, and then the Holmenkollen Ski Jump for a view of Oslo and its fjord, before going on to the Munch Museum.

You might also want to take the 3-hour afternoon tour, costing 170 kroner ($29.40) for adults, 85 kroner ($14.70) for children. Leaving at 2:30pm, it concentrates on the museums of Bygdøy, including the Norwegian Folk Museum and the Viking ships, as well as *Fram* and *Kon-Tiki.*

Starting point is the harbor side of Rådhuset, and passengers should arrive 15 minutes before departure. Authorized guides speak English. The tours are operated by **H. M. Kristiansens Automobilbyrå,** Hegdehaugsveien 4 (tel. 22-20-82-06).

6. SPECIAL/FREE EVENTS

Always check at the **tourist office** for a list of events likely to be planned during the week of your visit. Many are free, including summer jazz concerts at the National Theater. In front of the theater, along Students' Grove, you'll see much street entertainment, including singers, clowns, musicians, and jugglers.

Concerts are presented in the chapel of **Akershus Castle and Fortress,** Akershus Command, on Sunday at 2pm. During the summer, promenade music, parades, drill marches, exhibitions, and various theatrical performances are also presented on the castle grounds.

The March **Holmenkollen Ski Festival** is one of the most exciting times to visit the Norwegian capital. On the last day, the world's most thrilling ski jumps are presented.

In June, the **Færder sailing race** attracts some 1,000 sailboats that compete on the Oslofjord.

Constitution Day, July 4, brings out a parade of colorfully costumed children marching through Oslo.

In August, the **Chamber Music Festival** at Akershus Castle and Fortress presents concerts by both Norwegian and foreign musicians.

The **Oslo Jazz Festival,** also in August, includes not only old-time jazz, but classical concerts, opera, and ballet performances as well.

7. SPORTS/RECREATION

From spring to fall, the Oslofjord is a mecca for swimming, sailing, windsurfing, and angling. Daily excursions are arranged by motor launch at the harbor. Surburban forest areas await hikers, bicyclists, and anglers in summer. In winter, the area is ideal terrain for cross-country skiing on marked trails illuminated at night, as well as downhill or slalom, tobogganning, skating, and more. Safaris by Land Rover are arranged year-round.

BEACHES   Avoid the inner-harbor area because of pollution. The nearest and most popular beach is at **Hovedøya,** which is also the site of the 12th-century Cistercian monastery erected by English monks. Swimming is from a rocky shore. Also try **Drøbak,** 24 miles south of Oslo (take bus no. 541).

Øslovian beach devotees cite **Gressholmen** and **Langøyene,** a 15-minute ride from Vippetangen, as having the finest beaches in the Oslo environs. Nudism is practiced at beaches on the southern side of Langøyene.

The closest safe beaches are those on the west of Bygdøy peninsula, the museum island reached by bus no. 30 from the National Theater. These include **Huk** and **Paradisbukta.** There's nude bathing at Huk. Beaches are also at **Langåra,** lying 10 miles west of Oslo. Take the local train to Sandvika and make ferry connections from there.

On the east side of the fjord, an array of beaches is reached by taking bus no. 75B from Jernbanetorget in East Oslo. Departures are about every hour on weekends. The closest beach, a 12-minute ride, is **Ulvøya,** which is one of the best and considered the safest for children. Nudists journey on to **Standskogen.**

FISHING   The fishing is just great in Oslofjord and the forest lakes of Marka. However, you need a fishing permit, which can be purchased in most shops at a cost of 90 kroner ($15.60). A state fee of 60 kroner ($10.40) must also be paid at any local post office.

GOLF   Members of recognized golf clubs are allowed to play at **Oslo Golfklubb,** Bogstad (tel. 22-50-44-02). In addition to charging greens fees ranging from 100 kroner to 120 kroner ($17.30 to $20.80), the club will also rent clubs and equipment.

GYMS   One of the best is **Harald' Gym,** Hausmannsgate 6 (tel. 22-20-34-96), which accepts nonmembers, charging 40 kroner ($6.90) entrance, plus another 40 kroner ($6.90) for use of the solarium. It is open Monday through Friday from 9am to 9pm and on Saturday and Sunday from 10am to 5pm.

HORSE RACING   The **Øvrevoll Racecourse,** Vollsveien 132 (tel. 67-95-62-00), is open from mid-April to mid-November, with races on Monday and Thursday at 6pm. It is the only racetrack in Norway. Take bus no. 132 to Eiksmarka.

SKIING   A 15-minute tram or bus ride from central Oslo will take you to Oslo's winter wonderland, a 1,612-mile ski-track network, estimated to be the distance between Oslo and Tunis in North Africa. Many ski schools and instructors operate in winter. You can even go on a sleigh ride wrapped in sheepskin. Other activities include dogsled rides, snowshoe trekking, and Marka forest safaris. There is a total of 14 slalom slopes to select from, along with ski jumps in all shapes and sizes, including the most famous one at Holmenkollen. The tourist authorities at Oslo Promotion will provide specific details about changing venues from many of these activities.

SWIMMING POOLS & BATHS   The most centrally located municipal bath is **Vestkantbadet,** Sommerrogate 1 (tel. 22-44-07-26), offering Finnish sauna or

Roman baths Monday to Saturday from 7:30am to 7:30pm. It costs 65 kroner ($11.20) to enter but only 30 kroner ($5.20) for persons over 67. The pool is reserved for men on Monday, Friday, and Saturday from 1 to 5pm, for women on Tuesday, Wednesday, Thursday, and Saturday from 7am to noon. It's located near the American Embassy, about a mile north of Oslo's center. The baths are closed during most of July and part of August.

For outdoor swimming, **Frognerbadet,** Middelthunsgate 28 (tel. 22-44-07-26), in Frogner Park, has an open-air pool near the Vigeland sculptures (take tram no. 2 from the National Theater). The entrance fee is 30 kroner ($5.20) for adults, 22 kroner ($3.80) for children. It's open mid-May to mid-September, Monday through Friday from 7am to 8pm.

TENNIS   The municipal courts at **Frogner Park** are usually fully booked for the season by the locals, but apply at the kiosk about a vacancy that might become available.

One of your best bets is **Njårdhallen,** Sorkedalsveien 106 (tel. 22-14-15-93), which is open Monday through Friday from 7am to 10pm providing both indoor and outdoor courts.

WINDSURFING   You can rent windsurfing equipment at **Sport Windsurfing Center,** Bygdøy Allé 60A (tel. 22-44-79-28). They will also inform you on the best places to windsurf and other such details.

8. SAVVY SHOPPING

THE SHOPPING SCENE   The best buys include sportswear, silver and enamelware, traditional handcrafts, pewter, glass by Hadeland Glassverk (founded in 1762), teak furniture, and stainless steel.

Oslo has many **traffic-free streets** for strollers and shoppers. The heart of this district is the **Strøget,** where more than two dozen shops sell everything from Norwegian handcrafts to enameled silver jewelry. At the marketplace on Strøget, you can, in fair weather, stop for a glass of beer at an open-air restaurant. Many stores are clustered along **Karl Johans Gate** and the streets branching off from it.

Hours: Shops are generally open Monday through Friday from 9am to 5pm (in summer until 4pm). On Saturday most close by 1pm (2 or 3pm at some larger stores), and they are closed on Sunday.

Shipping It Home and Recovering VAT: Norway imposes a 20% value-added tax (called VAT) on goods purchased. But there are ways of avoiding paying this tax. See "Taxes" in "Fast Facts: Norway" in Chapter 12.

Special tax-free exports are possible, with many stores mailing goods home to you, which makes the payment of tax and its recovery unnecessary.

SHOPPING A TO Z
ARTS & CRAFTS

NORWAY DESIGNS, Stortingsgaten 28. Tel. 22-83-11-00.
   This is the country's headquarters for high-quality Norwegian and Scandinavian arts and crafts. An ideal shopping center for ceramics, glassware, pottery, textiles (there's a fashion shop), rugs, souvenirs, and silverware. Norway Designs has all the crafts that have given Norwegians an international reputation as outstanding designers. Metro: Stortinget.

DEN NORSKE HUSFLIDSFORENING, Møllergata 4. Tel. 22-42-10-75.
   Near the Marketplace and the cathedral, Husfliden, as it's called, is the display and retail center for the Norwegian Association of Home Arts and Crafts, founded in 1891. Today it is almost eight times larger than any of its competitors, offering an unparalleled opportunity to see assembled over two floors the very finest of Norwegian design in ceramics, glassware, furniture, and woodworking. You can also

purchase souvenirs, gifts, textiles, rugs, knotted Rya rugs, embroidery, wrought iron, and fabrics by the yard. Goods are shipped all over the world. Metro: Stortinget.

BOOKS

DAMMS ANTIKVARIAT, Tollbodgaten 25-27. Tel. 22-41-04-02.
A bookshop since 1843 specializes in old and rare books, atlases and maps, and nautical prints. Metro: Stortinget.

TANUM KARL JOHAN, Karl Johans Gate 38. Tel. 22-42-93-10.
A fine Oslo bookstore, lying in the center of town, it offers a staggering selection, including many English titles. Metro: Stortinget.

TANUM LIBRIS, Karl Johans Gate 43. Tel. 22-41-11-00.
A leading Oslo bookstore, well stocked in English titles, both fiction and nonfiction. It is particularly known for its selection of travel guides, including maps of Oslo and Norway. Metro: Stortinget.

CHILDREN'S WEAR

KID COOL, Stranden 3, Aker Brygge. Tel. 22-83-17-84.
This is a well-stocked branch of a leading children's clothing manufacturer in Oslo, part of a Europe-wide chain based in Belgium. Set in the shopping and restaurant complex west of Rådhuset, it has an impressive array of merchandise. Bus: 27.

DEPARTMENT STORES

GLASMAGASINET, Stortovet 9. Tel. 22-42-53-05.
Claiming that smaller boutiques tend to charge more, locals usually head for this big department store, specializing in unusual accessories for the home and kitchen. It might qualify as the biggest outlet of the Hadelands Glassverk (Glassworks) in all of Norway. It also contains a ground-floor coffee shop and restaurants on both the second and third floors. Metro: Stortinget. Bus: 7, 8, 11, 37, 92.

STEEN & STRØM, Kongensgate 23. Tel. 22-41-68-00.
The largest department store in Norway, Steen & Strøm is a treasure house of hundreds of Nordic items—from the ground-floor souvenir shop to the sales departments on the top floors. Look for hand-knitted sweaters, hand-painted wooden dishes reflecting traditional Norwegian art, hand-knitted caps, and pewter dinner plates made from old molds. Metro: Stortinget.

FOLK COSTUMES

HEIMEN, Rosenkrantzgate 8. Tel. 22-11-11-25.
A leading purveyor of both modern and traditional Norwegian handcrafts and costumes, Heimen carries folk costumes, antiques and reproductions, along with a choice of more than three dozen different *bunads* (styles) for the family to select from, including different regions of Norway, both north and south. Clothing is sold for women, men, and children. Hand-knitted sweaters in traditional Norwegian patterns are a special item, as are pewter and brass items. It's about a block from Karl Johans Gate. Metro: Stortinget. Tram: 7, 8, 11.

GLASS

HADELAND GLASSVERK, N-3520 Jevnaker. Tel. 61-31-05-55.
The most famous name in Norwegian glass, dating from 1762, can easily be reached by public transportation. You can see glass being blown and shaped, and visit a glass museum and a gallery with changing exhibitions. You can also purchase Hadeland's complete collection, and "seconds" are sold at reduced prices. There's a restaurant on the premises. The complex is also open on Sunday from noon to 6pm. Bus: Take the Hønefoss/Jevnaker bus from Vaterland, leaving hourly; phone 61-19-92-38 for the bus schedule.

JEWELRY, ENAMELWARE & SILVER

DAVID-ANDERSEN, Karl Johans Gate 20. Tel. 22-41-69-55.
This outstanding Norway jeweler, established more than a century ago, distributes enameled demitasse spoons and sterling-silver bracelets with enamel, available in many stunning colors such as turquoise and dark blue. The multicolored butterfly pins are also popular in sterling silver (gold-plated) with enamel. David-Andersen's collection of Saga silver is inspired by traditional features in Norwegian folklore and from Viking designs, combined with the pristine beauty of today's design. The store now offers an exquisite collection of pewter items. Metro: Stortinget.

MUSIC

NORSK MUSIKFORLAG, Karl Johans Gate 39. Tel. 22-42-53-67.
Set in the town center on the main street, this store's selection isn't the largest but is carefully chosen. Metro: Stortinget.

PEWTER

TINNBODEN, Tordenskioldsgate 7. Tel. 22-42-24-61.
Some of the best pewter dinnerware available in Oslo is offered here, near Rådhuset close to the harbor. The shop also sells gift articles and souvenirs. It has no annual closing. Tram: 1, 2, 9.

HEYERDAHL, Fridtjof Nansens Plass 6. Tel. 22-41-59-18.
Next to the Rådhusplassen, this store offers one of the city's most imaginative collections of pewter. You can buy a menagerie of Arctic animals fashioned from walrus tusk, stone and brass vessels, and ashtrays made of a glistening copper ore mined in northern Norway. There's also gold and silver jewelry. Metro: Stortinget.

SHOPPING MALLS

Oslo has three large shopping arcades, including Aker Brygge at the west side of the harbor, a short walk from Rådhuset; and Oslo City and Galleri Oslo, both near the Central Station.

Oslo City, Stenersgate 1, opposite the Central Station, has become the biggest shopping center in Norway, with an array of shops selling all types of merchandise. You can also dine here in a number of restaurants.

Also near the Central Station, **Galleri Oslo,** at Vaterland, has been called Europe's longest indoor shopping street. You can find everything in the same complex. Activity goes on day and evening until midnight, including Sunday. A walkway connects Galleri Oslo to the Central Station.

Aker Brygge is a unique shopping venue by the Oslofjord. It is virtually a city within a city, with a wide array of merchandise. The complex also includes restaurants, theaters, cinemas, and cafés.

SWEATERS

OSLO SWEATER SHOP, in the SAS Scandinavia Hotel, Holbergsgate 30. Tel. 22-11-29-22.
Some 5,000 handcrafted sweaters are stocked here close to the Royal Palace. Try them on before you buy. Metro: Stortinget.

SOUVENIRS & GIFTS

WILLIAM SCHMIDT, Karl Johans Gate 41. Tel. 22-42-02-88.
Established in 1853, William Schmidt is a leading purveyor of unique souvenirs, including pewter items (everything from Viking ships to beer goblets), Norwegian dolls in national costumes, wood carvings (the troll collection is the most outstanding in Oslo), and sealskin items such as moccasins and handbags. The shop specializes in

hand-knitted cardigans, pullovers, gloves, and caps. Sweaters are made from moth-proofed 100% Norwegian wool. Metro: Stortinget.

9. EVENING ENTERTAINMENT

Oslo is fast emerging as a bustling nightlife city. Midnight is no longer a hint for everybody to call it a night. Today, Oslo boasts 100 night cafés, clubs, and restaurants—and 34 of these stay open until 4 in the morning.

The autumn and winter seasons are for cabarets, theater, and concerts. There are four cabaret stages and nine theater stages, all offering productions except in summer. Oslo is also a favorite destination of international performing artists in classical music, pop, rock, and jazz.

For movie lovers, Oslo has a lot to offer. The city is considered to have one of the best and most extensive selections of movies in Europe, with 30 screens and five large film complexes. All films are shown in their original languages, with subtitles.

THE ENTERTAINMENT SCENE

The best way to find out what's happening at the time of your visit is to pick up a copy of *What's On in Oslo,* detailing concerts and theaters and other useful information.

Oslo doesn't offer any agents specializing in discounted tickets, as they do in such cities as London. However, to compensate, it offers an exceptional number of free events. These are documented in the monthly "diary" of *What's On in Oslo.* The guide also lists the latest exhibitions at art galleries, which might be a delightful way to spend the early part of an evening.

You don't always have to go to the theater to purchase tickets. Tickets to the theater, ballet, and opera are sold at **Billettsentralen,** Karl Johans Gate 35 (tel. 22-44-76-77).

The **Oslo Philharmonic,** now world famous, plays regularly under the leadership of Mariss Janson. Regrettably, you cannot hear them from June 20 until the first of September.

If you visit Oslo sometime other than summer, you also have a chance to see its thriving opera and ballet company, **Den Norske Opera.** Unfortunately for those who don't speak Norwegian, performances at the **Nationaltheatret,** which is always presenting Ibsen, are in Norwegian. However some devotees who know Ibsen plays well in their own language have attended performances just to hear what Ibsen sounded like in the original version.

THE PERFORMING ARTS
CLASSICAL MUSIC

KONSERTHUS, Munkedamsveien 15. Tel. 22-83-32-00.

THE MAJOR CONCERT/PERFORMING HALLS

Konserthus, Munkedamsveien 15 (tel. 22-83-32-00). Home of the Oslo Philharmonic.

Nationaltheatret (National Theater), Stortingsgaten 15 (tel. 22-41-16-40). Ibsen and Bjørnson in the original.

Den Norske Opera (Norwegian National Opera), Storgaten 23C (tel. 22-42-94-75 for information, 22-42-77-24 to order tickets). Norwegian opera and ballet.

Two blocks from the National Theater, this is the home of the widely acclaimed Oslo Philharmonic. Performances are given autumn to spring, on Thursday and Friday. Guest companies from around the world often appear on other nights. The hall is closed from June 20 until the middle of August, except for occasional folkloric groups whose appearances are announced in *What's On in Oslo*. Metro: Stortinget.
Tickets: 90–135 kroner ($15.60–$23.40).
Open: Box office, Mon–Fri noon–8pm, Sat 10am–1pm.

THEATER

NATIONALTHEATRET (National Theater), Stortingsgaten 15. Tel. 22-41-16-40.

At the upper end of the Students' Grove, this theater opens in August, so it may be of interest to off-season theater lovers who want to hear Ibsen and Bjørnson in the original. Avant-garde productions get a fair trial at the **Amfiscenen** in the same building. There are no performances in July and August. Guest companies often perform plays in English. Metro: Stortinget.
Tickets: 105–155 kroner ($18.20–$26.80).
Open: Box office, Mon–Fri 8:30am–7:30pm, Sat 11am–6pm.

OPERA & DANCE

DEN NORSKE OPERA (Norwegian National Opera), Storgaten 23C. Tel. 22-42-94-75.

The 1931 building, originally a movie theater, was adapted for better acoustics and dedicated in 1959 to the Norwegian National Opera. Besides opera, it is also the leading venue for ballet. The Norwegian opera and ballet troupes combined to form Den Norske Opera. The company performs some 20 different operas and operettas every year. Ballet performances alternate with opera presentations. There are no performances from mid-June to August. Unlike some European opera companies, tickets are generally available to nonsubscribers. Bus: 56, 62, 66.
Tickets: 60–200 kroner ($10.40–$34.60), except for galas. Seats can be reserved in advance and paid for with credit cards.
Open: Box office, Mon–Sat 10am–6pm. On performance night box office remains open until 7:30pm.

SUMMER CULTURAL ENTERTAINMENT

The **Bondeungdomslaget** (Folk Dance Group of the Young Farmers' Union) performs in July and August at the Oslo Konserthus, Munkedamsveien 15 (tel. 22-83-32-00). The 1-hour performances are given on Monday and Thursday at 9pm. Tickets cost 75 kroner ($13) for adults and 40 kroner ($6.90) for children. Metro: Stortinget.

The **Norwegian Folk Museum** on Bygdøy presents folk-dance performances by its own ensemble in summer at the museum's open-air theater (see *What's On in Oslo* for details). Tickets are 80 kroner ($13.80) for adults and 50 kroner ($8.70) for children. Take the ferry from Pier 3 near Rådhuset.

THE CLUB & MUSIC SCENE
NIGHTCLUBS/CABARET

GLEDES HUSET LUDVIK (Ludvik's Fun House), Torggata 16. Tel. 22-42-88-80.

One of Oslo's most unusual clubs is set within the high-ceilinged premises of what was the city's busiest 19th-century public bathhouse. The difficult-to-find entrance is on Henrik Ibsens Gate, around the corner from the official address. You traverse a trompe-l'oeil footbridge and enter a zany world of scantily clad plastic mannequins, antique sleighs, rocking chairs, brass horns, and old-time memorabilia attached to the ceiling. The place is a full-fledged restaurant, serving such dishes as pepper steak, cured salmon with mustard sauce, and cured elkmeat steak. The last food orders go in at 11pm, but the singing and drinking continue until 2am. The club often features cabaret but the schedule varies, especially in the slower summer months. On most nights they host Karaoke parties. This is a Japanese nightlife craze where members of the audience, microphone in hand, sing to an orchestral track while reading the lyrics from a TV monitor above the stage. Ludvik's is open daily from 5pm to 2am. Meals cost 150 kroner ($26); beer, 39 kroner ($6.70). Tram: 1, 2, 7, 11.

Admission: 50–100 kroner ($8.70–$17.30) on cabaret nights, free other nights.

HUMLA, Universitetsgaten 26. Tel. 22-42-44-20.

A labyrinth of hallways, dance areas, and bars, Humla contains one of the best restaurants in Oslo, the Barock (see Chapter 14). The interior is strikingly stylish. You can dine at café tables on a carpeted balcony overlooking a theater where acts are interspersed with disco music. At the **Dizzie Theater and the Humla Restaurant,** the stage features cabaret acts which usually last for 90 minutes including drag, pop-rock nostalgic revues, and Norwegian comedy. The program changes monthly. Tables are cleared away and disco music plays until 3:30am. You can also dine on the mezzanine.

John's Bar, thanks to its murals, pays tribute to a 19th-century folk legend about a Norwegian and two Swedes who set off together to see the world. The **Exit Disco,** which is open very late, lies four floors above the street. The joke in Oslo is, if you're drunk by the time you start up, you will have sobered by the time you reach the top, as there is no elevator. The decor includes potted cactus, Oriental carpets, and a DJ playing from the chassis of an old American car.

The Dizzie Theater and Humla Restaurant are open Tuesday through Saturday from 8pm to 3:30am; John's Bar, Wednesday through Monday from 6pm to 12:30am; the Exit Disco, on Wednesday from midnight to 3:30am, on Friday and Saturday from 11pm to 3:30am, and on Sunday from 12:30 to 3:30am. A beer in John's Bar will cost 32 kroner ($5.50); in the Exit disco, 39 kroner ($6.70). Metro: Stortinget.

Admission: Dizzie Theater, 225–275 kroner ($38.90–$47.60) for dinner and show; Exit Disco, 50 kroner ($8.70) cover charge Fri–Sat.

DANCE CLUBS/DISCOS

LOFTET, in the Hotel Continental, Stortingsgaten 26 (entrance on Roald Amundsens Gate). Tel. 22-41-90-60.

This disco has a unique setting: five small rooms built as a loft, each having a different decor. You have to be 22 years of age to get in, and on weekends you should arrive by 8pm or else be prepared to wait in line. Open Tuesday through Thursday from 8pm to 2am, on Friday and Saturday from 8pm to 4am. A half liter of *pils* will cost 39 kroner ($6.70). Metro: Stortinget.

Admission: 30–50 kroner ($5.20–$8.70) cover charge.

ROX CLUB, in the SAS Scandinavia Hotel, Holbergsgate 30. Tel. 22-11-30-00.

This glistening dance club is designed for the conservatively affluent clientele who stay at this upscale hotel. The place caters to an over-30 crowd. It's open Monday through Saturday from 10pm to 3:30am. Drinks cost from 45 kroner ($7.80). Metro: Stortinget.

Admission: 50 kroner ($8.70); free for hotel guests.

JAZZ/ROCK

ROCKEFELLER MUSIC HALL, Torggata 16. Tel. 22-20-32-32.

With a capacity for 1,000 patrons, this is one of the largest establishments of its kind in Oslo, calling itself both a concert hall and a club. It lies one floor above street level in a 1910 building, originally a public bath. Four nights a week (call for dates) live concerts are presented. Musical forms include everything from reggae to rock to jazz. On nights when no concert is given, films are shown on a wide screen. Small dishes of food, such as pastas and sandwiches, are available in the café section. Most of the crowd seems in the 18 to 37 age bracket. It's open Sunday through Thursday from 8pm to 1am and on Friday and Saturday from 9pm to 4am. Show time is about 1 hour after the door's open. A beer costs 29 kroner to 36 kroner ($5 to $6.20); snacks, 20 kroner to 60 kroner ($3.50 to $10.40). Metro: Stortinget.

Admission: 40–200 kroner ($6.90–$34.60) cover charge, depending on the entertainment.

THE BAR SCENE
PUBS/BARS

LIMELIGHT, in the Grand Hotel, Karl Johans Gate 31. Tel. 22-42-93-90.
Steeped in the atmosphere of the theater, this fashionable Oslo bar has a connecting passage to the theater next door (Oslo Nye Teater). It's a favorite rendezvous for drinks before or after a show. Open daily from 3pm to midnight. A beer or mixed drink costs 40 kroner ($6.90). Metro: Stortinget.

LIBRARY BAR, in the Hotel Bristol, Kristian IV's Gate 7. Tel. 22-41-58-40.
This may be the best spot in the Bristol for people-watching, in a lobby reminiscent of the Edwardian era. You'll be sheltered behind racks and racks of leather-bound books, which you can actually remove and read. The total effect is like being inside a well-furnished private club, with potted palms. Live piano music is presented at lunchtime when you can order from a selection of open-faced sandwiches for 39 kroner to 66 kroner ($6.80 to $11.45). Specialty cocktails have such demure names as "Take Me Home," "Norwegian Kiss," and "Prince of Norway." It's open daily from 10am to 2:30am; alcohol is served from 1pm to midnight. A beer will cost you 39 kroner ($6.70); mixed drinks, 45 kroner ($7.80). Metro: Stortinget.

SKY BAR, in the Oslo Plaza Hotel, Sonja Henies Plads 3. Tel. 22-17-10-00.
The loftiest bar in Norway, this aptly named place crowns the 37-floor deluxe Oslo Plaza Hotel. To reach it, you take a glassed-in elevator from a separate entrance outside the hotel. Upstairs, the view is spectacular, and the decor has lots of black granite and russet-colored marble, a bar very much of the 1990s. It has both bustling standup areas and sitdown couches, with a piano perched amid the hubbub. On weekends, the line is long at the elevator. The bartender's special is the "Oslo Plaza," made with vodka, amaretto, and Coca-Cola, topped off with cream. It's open daily from 5pm to 3:30am. Beer costs 39 kroner ($6.70); mixed drinks, 45 kroner ($7.80). Bus: 14, 24, 71.

Admission: 50 kroner ($8.70) cover charge Fri–Sat after 9pm.

ETOILE BAR, in the Grand Hotel, Karl Johans Gate 31. Tel. 22-42-93-90.
Drawing members of parliament across the street, this is a grand bar attached to an equally grand restaurant in a new wing of Norway's greatest hotel, the Grand. It is encased with windows opening onto views of historic Oslo and close to the hotel's swimming pool and sauna. The appearances and interests of the clients change visibly throughout the day, from businesspeople during the day to a more spirited crowd at night. To reach it, you take a special elevator that departs from the right of the hotel entrance. Drinks include brandy sours, several Caribbean-inspired rum drinks, and the house special, a "Yellow Sweater." You'll pay 35 kroner ($6.10) for a beer, 48 kroner to 65 kroner ($8.30 to $11.20) for a more potent libation. This Star is open Monday through Saturday from 3pm to 12:30am. Metro: Stortinget.

KLIMS BAR/HOLBERG RESTAURANT BAR, in the SAS Scandinavia Hotel, Holbergsgate 30. Tel. 22-11-30-00.
On the ground level of this first-class hotel, Klims was designed as an apéritif bar for what many consider Oslo's best restaurant, the Holberg. But the fact that it contains some exceptional murals has turned it into a bit of a drinking haven in its own right. The murals were painted by the Danish-born artist, Bjørd Viinblad in 1975, showing an allegorical and fantastical menagerie of dragons, flying leopards, and talking flowers. The characters portray the childhood legend of Nils Klims, a story originally written by Holberg that is dear to the hearts of every Scandinavian child. Enjoy a drink at the marble-top bar: beer is 38 kroner ($6.60) a mixed drink, 45

kroner ($7.80). Klims is open Tuesday through Saturday from 5pm to midnight. Bus: 17, 76.

CONTINENTAL BAR, in the Hotel Continental, Stortingsgaten 24–26. Tel. 22-41-90-60.

On the street level of the Hotel Continental (see Chapter 14) near the National Theater, this is an oval room with a bronze statue of a musician in the center. It's a chic and sophisticated place. The walls are hung with the largest collection of Munch paintings in the world outside museums. Many were purchased in 1934. For fear of theft (several paintings were stolen, and later recovered), two or three of the works are now judicious copies. The bar is open Monday through Saturday from 3 to 11:30pm. Sandwiches are available for 56 kroner to 75 kroner ($9.70 to $13); drinks begin at 45 kroner ($7.80). Metro: Stortinget.

SUPPER CLUBS

BRISTOL NIGHT SPOT, in the Hotel Bristol, Kristian IV's Gate 7. Tel. 22-41-58-40.

The entrance to this nightclub is clearly visible from the sidewalk near the main entrance to the hotel. A popular bar with an intimately lit restaurant, a dance floor, and a vague Iberian decor, this has become one of the most popular places in Oslo. Conservative dress is suggested. A dance band provides the music from 8pm. Main dishes include poached salmon with butter-cream sauce, chateaubriand with béarnaise sauce, filet of veal Oscar with asparagus, and a mixed grill. Cocktails include tequila sunrises, margaritas, and a Norwegian high-powered bomb, *Fjellbekk* (mountain stream), made with aquavit, vodka, lime juice, and Sprite. Meals cost around 250 kroner ($43.30) drinks, 45 kroner ($7.80). It's open Tuesday through Thursday from 8pm to 2am and on Friday and Saturday from 8pm to 4:30am. Reservations are recommended. Metro: Stortinget.

NIGHT CAFES

CRUISE CAFE, Stranden 3, Aker Brygge. Tel. 22-83-64-30.

The most popular bar in this dining-and-shopping complex west of Rådhuset is packed with a devoted clientele who like the woodsy decor, the music (often live), and the conviviality. Sometimes there's a live concert, at which time a cover charge is imposed. The culinary venue is burgers and beer—a Cruiseburger costs 50 kroner ($8.70)—with a handful of Norwegian dishes thrown in. It's open on Monday and Tuesday from noon to 1am, on Wednesday and Thursday from noon to 1:30am, on Friday and Saturday from 1pm to 1am. Bus: 27.

Admission: 80–240 kroner ($13.80–$41.50) cover charge, when there's live music, depending on the band.

BROKER CAFE, Bogstadveien 27. Tel. 22-69-36-47.

By day this is a somewhat demure café serving morning coffee and light meals. Its greatest panache, however, occurs later in the evening when a rock-conscious, hip crowd convenes for drink, conversation, and food. The decor dates from around the turn of the century, including lots of mirrors and Belle Epoque trappings. The food includes lasagne, sandwiches, and salads for 55 kroner to 80 kroner ($9.50 to $13.80); a beer costs from 35 kroner ($6.10). The café is open Monday through Thursday from 11am to 1am, on Friday and Saturday from 11am to 2:30am, and on Sunday from noon to 12:30am. Tram: 9 or 11.

CAFE LORRY, Parkveien 12. Tel. 22-69-69-04.

This café prides itself on stocking more kinds of beer—81 in all—than any other nightclub in Norway. Most are made in Norway, and many are so esoteric that they're known only to the most dedicated. Ask a member of the staff for a recommendation. Lots of clients sing at the piano, deciding to perform spontaneously and sudsily. The serious drinking begins after 5pm, and the decor is rustic. Beer costs 24.50 kroner to 41 kroner ($4.20 to $7.10). The place can be fun. It's open Monday through Saturday from 8am to 2:30am and on Sunday from 11am to 2am. Tram: 11.

AFTER-HOUR DRINKING & DINING

TRAPPE BIERSTUBE, Møllergata 23. Tel. 22-11-05-06.
This establishment shares a building (but not necessarily the clientele) with the premier gay bar of Oslo, Enke. Hours are geared to coincide with the hunger pangs of late-night Oslovian society, who might yearn for hamburgers and snacks at impossibly late hours. Hamburgers cost 52 kroner ($9) and beer goes for 37 kroner ($6.40). Don't expect a conservative clientele. The largest wall sports a life-size mural of a guitar-toting Julie Andrews skipping over an Austrian Alp. In fact, this place used to be called Maria von Trapp, but the estate of that famous Austrian woman whose family was depicted in *The Sound of Music,* sued and forced a name change. The stube opens daily from 11pm to 4am. Metro: Stortinget.

GAY & LESBIAN DRINKING & DINING

ENKE (Widow), Møllergata 23. Tel. 22-11-05-60.
This is the premier gay bar of Norway. Its street-level cocktail and beer bar is a major gathering place for young people. Lesbians are welcome, but the clientele is mostly male. Downstairs is a disco, and a few steps away, a dungeonlike leather bar consciously decorated like an S&M parlor. Beer costs 37 kroner ($6.40). It's open daily from 6pm to 4am. There is no disco on Monday and Tuesday. There's a drag show every Wednesday and Sunday. Metro: Stortinget.
Admission: Free for the bar; 50 kroner ($8.70) Fri–Sat night at the disco.

WHY NOT? Teatergata 3. Tel. 22-36-36-36.
This up-and-coming gay nightclub, popular with both men and women, maintains a bar on its street level and a disco in its basement. Beer costs 37 kroner ($6.40). The bar is open daily from 6pm to 4am; the disco, Wednesday to Sunday from 8:30pm. Metro: Stortinget.
Admission: Free Sun–Thurs, 50 kroner ($8.70) entrance Fri–Sat.

LONDON PUB, Rosenkrantzgatan 10. Tel. 22-41-41-26.
Containing a street-level pub, and a quieter and somewhat calmer cocktail bar upstairs, this is a popular gay bar, attracting both men and women. It is not a disco and no food is served. Depending on the time of day, beer costs from 23 kroner ($4) to 34 kroner ($5.90). It's open daily from 3pm to 4am. Metro: Stortinget.
Admission: Free.

MOVIES

American or British import films are shown in English, with Norwegian subtitles. Patrons line up at the cinemas for tickets in the same way that Americans might frequent Broadway shows. Tickets are sold for specific performances only. Many theaters have three showings nightly, at 5, 7, and 9pm, but the big road-show specials usually are shown only once in an evening, generally at 7:30pm. One of the most centrally located cinemas, showing first-run features, is the **Colosseum,** Fridtjof Nansensvei 8 (tel. 22-46-39-60). Tram: 1, 2, 11.

CHAPTER 16

EASY EXCURSIONS FROM OSLO

1. FREDRIKSTAD
- **WHAT'S SPECIAL ABOUT THE ENVIRONS OF OSLO**

2. TØNSBERG

3. SANDEFJORD

4. LILLEHAMMER

5. THE PEER GYNT ROAD

The environs of Oslo offer an array of 1-day excursions available to visitors either by boat, car, or bus.

The chief center is Fredrikstad, in Østfold on the east bank of Oslofjord. A trip here can be combined—all in 1 day—with visits to the ports of Tønsberg and Sandefjord, on the west bank, by crossing over on the ferry from Moss to Horten, then heading south.

The major center in the north is the summer resort and ski center of Lillehammer, site of the 1994 Olympics. Those who overnight in the area can also take the famous Peer Gynt Road the following day, a route Ibsen traveled while researching his masterpiece, *Peer Gynt*.

SEEING OSLO'S ENVIRONS

GETTING THERE Both sides of the Oslofjord south of Oslo are serviced by frequent trains from the capital. Trains go down the eastern side to Moss, Fredrikstad, and Halden, and trains traverse the western side to Drammen, Tønsberg, Sandefjord, and Larvik.

If you want to cross the fjord, on either side, go to Moss or Horten. A 40-minute car-and-passenger ferry plies the fjord connecting both banks. In summer it's also possible to cross from Strømstad, Sweden, to Sandefjord. Frequent trains also run north from Oslo to Lillehammer, which is the best center for touring the many attractions north of Oslo, including the Peer Gynt Road.

A SUGGESTED ITINERARY Go south from Oslo for 2 nights, taking your time exploring the old towns of Fredrikstad, Tønsberg, and Sandefjord. On the third day, drive north to Lillehammer where you can easily spend 3 days, exploring not only the attractions of this summer-and-winter resort, but using it as a base for driving around Peer Gynt country and other sights, including museum-filled Hamar.

---

1. FREDRIKSTAD

60 miles S of Oslo

GETTING THERE **By Train** Trains from Oslo's Central Station depart for Fredrikstad in the south about every 2 hours.

By Bus There is frequent bus service daily from Oslo to Fredrikstad.

By Car Take Highway E6 south from Oslo heading toward Moss. Continue past Moss until you reach the junction at Route 110, which is signposted south to Fredrikstad.

ESSENTIALS For information, the **Fredrikstad Turistkontor,** on Turistsenteret in Gamle Fredrikstad (tel. 69-32-03-30), is open Mon–Fri 8am–7pm and Sat 10am–7pm (June–Sept) and Mon–Fri 8am–4pm (Oct–May).

WHAT'S SPECIAL ABOUT THE ENVIRONS OF OSLO

Great Towns/Villages

☐ Tønsberg, the oldest town in Norway, with historic districts and a folk museum.

☐ Fredrikstad, a well-preserved fortress town with an artisan quarter.

☐ Lillehammer, a premier European ski resort, site of the 1994 Winter Olympics.

Scenic Drives

☐ The Peer Gynt Road, northwest of Lillehammer—immortalized by Henrik Ibsen.

☐ Oldtidsveien, the highway of the ancients, near Fredrikstad—the most concentrated collection of archeological monuments in Norway.

For the Kids

☐ Hunderfossen Family Park, near Lillehammer—50 activities for both children and adults.

Museums

☐ The Sandvig Collections at Lillehammer—150 old buildings recreate the Norway of yesterday.

☐ Vestfold Folk Museum at Tønsberg, with many Viking and whaling treasures.

☐ Commander Christensen's Whaling Museum at Sandefjord, with memorabilia of the great whaling days.

In recent years Fredrikstad has become a major tourist center, thanks to its Old Town and 17th-century fortress. Across the river on the west is a modern industrial section, and although a bridge links the two sections, the best way to reach the Old Town is by ferry, costing 2 kroner (30¢). The departure point is about 4 blocks from the Fredrikstad railroad—simply follow the crowd out the main door of the station and make an obvious left turn and continue down to the shore of the river.

WHAT TO SEE & DO

Fredrikstad was founded in 1567 as a market town on the Glomma River. **Fredrikstad Fortress,** in use until 1903 and boasting some 200 cannons at its peak, is still used by Norway's military forces. The main guardroom and old convict prison are now the **Fredrikstad Museum,** Gamleslaveri (tel. 69-39-43-82), open May through September, Monday through Friday from 10am to 5pm and on Saturday and Sunday from noon to 5pm. During the rest of the year it's closed. Admission is 10 kroner ($1.70) for adults, free for children.

Outside the gates of the Old Town is **Kongsten Fort,** on what was first called Gallows Hill, an execution site. When Fredrikstad Fortress was built, it was provisionally fortified in 1677, becoming known as Svenskeskremme (Swede Scarer). Today's Kongsten Fort was subsequently built there, with 20 cannons, underground chambers, passages, and countermines.

You can take guided tours in the Old Town to visit the church, the museum, and the glass-blowing and silver-design operations belonging to **Norway Silver Designs,** a society of artists and artisans. Its headquarters are in one of the old houses in the Old Town at Kirkegaten 28A (tel. 69-32-06-78), open Monday through Friday from 9am to 4pm and on Saturday from 9am to 1pm. You can visit its showrooms anytime during these hours, but to see the actual products being made and the place where classes are given, you must take a 1-hour guided tour for 18 kroner ($3.10). Tours are given Monday through Friday at 9:30am, 11am, 12:30pm, and 2pm.

After leaving Fredrikstad, take a drive along the ✪ **Oldtidsveien,** or the "highway of the ancients," the most concentrated collection of archeological monuments in Norway. It lies along Highway 110 between Fredrikstad and Skjeberg. The ancient monuments include 3,000-year-old rock carvings at Begby, Hornes, and Solberg, and 2,000-year-old burial grounds at Hunn with stone circles.

Other attractions include **Tomta** (tel. 69-34-50-33), the 1872 birthplace of explorer Roald Amundsen, at Borge, N-1650 Sellebakk, where a museum and monument are now dedicated to him. They are located between Fredrikstad and Sarpsborg, off the E6, and the house is open Tuesday and Friday from 10am to 3pm and on Sunday from noon to 4pm. Admission is 10 kroner ($1.70) adults, 5 kroner (90¢) children.

WHERE TO STAY
INEXPENSIVE

HOTEL CITY, Nygård 44-46, N-1600 Fredrikstad. Tel. 69-31-77-50. Fax 69-31-30-90. 102 rms (all with bath). MINIBAR TV TEL **Bus:** 31.

$ Rates (including breakfast): Winter, Mon-Fri 975 kroner ($168.70) single; 1,175 kroner ($203.30) double. Winter Sat-Sun and June 23-Aug 10, 600 kroner ($103.80) single; 800 kroner ($138.40) double. AE, DC, MC, V. **Parking:** 50 kroner ($8.70).

Located in the town center, about 500 yards from the rail station, this is a stylish hotel, in spite of an exterior that looks like an office building. The interior has a quasi-high-tech decor, and each comfortable bedroom is furnished in good taste. On the premises are a basement restaurant with a nightclub and dance music, three bars, and a winter-garden café with marble sheathing.

NYE VICTORIA HOTEL, Turngaten 3, N-1600 Fredrikstad. Tel. 69-31-11-65. Fax 69-31-87-55. 55 rms (all with bath). TV TEL **Bus:** 31.

$ Rates (including breakfast): Winter, 730-975 kroner ($126.30-$168.70) single; 1,175 kroner ($203.30) double. Summer, 520 kroner ($90) single; 685 kroner ($118.50) double. AE, DC, MC, V.

The oldest hotel in town, originally established in 1883, the Victoria was completely renovated in 1989. It overlooks the most idyllic park in town. Bedrooms are comfortable, and a restaurant and bar are on the premises. An international cuisine is served. It's near the train station.

WHERE TO DINE
MODERATE

RESTAURANT TAMBUREN, Faergeportgate 78. Tel. 69-32-03-13.
Cuisine: NORWEGIAN. **Reservations:** Recommended. **Bus:** Marked "Gamlebyen" from the center.
$ Prices: Appetizers 48-68 kroner ($8.30-$11.80); main dishes 90-180 kroner ($15.60-$31.10). AE, DC, MC, V.
Open: Pub, daily 6pm-midnight; dining room, daily noon-midnight.

For tradition and atmosphere, this restaurant has no competition within the Old Town. Originally built in the 19th century as the home of a village priest, the rebuilt Gothic-inspired structure has a popular courtyard for warm-weather outdoor dining. The basement pub has an open fireplace. Served in the dining room are well-prepared meals that include two kinds of entrecôte, beef, and pork, along with mixed grills, fish, and five kinds of open-face sandwiches. On summer weekends there's live music nightly after 9pm.

2. TØNSBERG

64 miles S of Oslo

GETTING THERE   By Plane   The nearest air service is at Torp Airport, lying halfway between Sandefjord and Tønsberg. It has connections to Bergen, Stavanger, and Copenhagen.

By Train Tønsberg is about 1½ hours by train from Oslo, and 16 trains arrive daily from Oslo. The train station is in the city center.

By Bus Frequent buses arrive from Oslo, and the Tønsberg district has good connections to Sandefjord (see below). Buses usually leave Tønsberg hourly, traversing the district, including stops at Horten.

By Car Take Highway 18 south from Oslo via Drammen.

By Boat From mid-June until the last week in August, Tønsberg has a hydrofoil connection with Oslo, twice daily.

ESSENTIALS For information, **Tourist Information,** Storgaten 55 (tel. 33-31-02-20), is open Mon–Sat 10am–5pm (June, Aug), daily 10am–8pm (July), and Mon–Fri 9am–4pm (Sept–May).

Bordering the western bank of the Oslofjord, Tønsberg is Norway's oldest town. It is divided into a historic area, filled with old clapboard-sided houses, and the commercial center, where the marketplace is located. The 40-square-mile town has some 31,000 inhabitants.

Tønsberg was founded a year before King Harald Fairhair united parts of the country in 872, and this Viking town became a royal coronation site. Svend Foyn, the man who invented modern whaling and seal hunting, was born here.

WHAT TO SEE & DO

Slottsfjellet, a huge hill fortress directly ahead of the train station, is touted as "the Acropolis of Norway." But it has only some meager ruins, and people mostly come here for the view from the lookout tower. Built in 1888, **Slottsfjelltårnet** (tel. 33-31-80-00) is open May 18 to June 23, Monday through Friday from 10am to 3pm; June 24 to August 25, Monday through Friday from 11am to 6pm and on Sunday from 1 to 6pm. Admission is 7 kroner ($1.20) for adults and 2 kroner (30¢) for children.

Nordbyen is the old and scenic part of town, with well-preserved houses. **Haugar** cemetery at Møllebakken, is right in the center of town, with the Viking graves of King Harald's sons, Olav and Sigrød.

Sem Church, Hageveien 32 (tel. 33-36-93-99), the oldest in Vestfold, was built of stone in the Romanesque style around 1100. It is open Tuesday through Friday from 9am to 2pm; inquire at the vestry. Admission is free.

You should also see **Fjerdingen,** a street of charming restored houses near the mountain farmstead. Tønsberg was also a Hanseatic town during the Middle Ages, and some houses have been redone in typical Hanseatic style.

In the **Vestfold Folk Museum,** Frammannsveien 30 (tel. 33-31-29-19), there are many Viking and whaling treasures. One of the chief sights is the skeleton of a blue whale, the largest animal the world has ever known (sometimes weighing 150 tons). There is also a real Viking ship displayed, the *Klastad* from Tjolling, built about A.D. 800.

In the rural section of the museum, visit the **Vestfold Farm,** which includes a 1600 Hynne house, a timbered barn from Bøen, a storehouse from Fadum (with the characteristic apron), the Heierstadloft (oldest preserved timbered building in Vestfold, ca. 1350), a smithy with a charcoal shed, a grain-drying house, and a mountain farmstead.

Still at the museum, have lunch at a real mountain farmstead—a typical meal, with rømmergrøt (porridge made with sour cream) and other farm foods. The area is perfect for a picnic.

Admission is 15 kroner ($2.60) for adults, free for children. From mid-May to mid-September, it is open Monday through Saturday from 10am to 5pm and on

Sunday and holidays from 1 to 5pm; from mid-September to mid-May, Monday through Friday from 10am to 2pm and on Sunday from noon to 5pm.

WHERE TO STAY
MODERATE

GRAND HOTEL, Øvre Langgate 65-67, N-3100 Tønsberg. Tel. 33-31-22-03. Fax 33-31-28-92. 63 rms (all with bath), 3 suites. MINIBAR TV TEL

$ Rates (including breakfast): Summer and weekends year-round, 600 kroner ($103.80) single; 750 kroner ($129.80) double; from 960 kroner ($166.10) suite. Winter, 840–940 kroner ($145.30–$162.60) single; 990–1,090 kroner ($171.30–$188.60) double; from 1,260 kroner ($218) suite. AE, DC, MC, V. **Parking:** Free.

The Grand Hotel's elaborate exterior is a reminder of this hotel's pretensions when it was built in 1931. The interior has been modernized and the rooms are comfortably contemporary. On the premises are two restaurants and a nightclub. The hotel has a health studio and a sauna. It's located in the town center directly south of Hauger.

HOTEL KLUBBEN, Nedre Langgate 49, N-3100 Tønsberg. Tel. 33-31-15-11. Fax 33-31-31-99. 94 rms (all with bath). MINIBAR TV TEL

$ Rates (including breakfast): Mon–Thurs 995 kroner ($172.10) single; 1,125 kroner ($194.60) double; Fri–Sun 670 kroner ($115.90) single; 790 kroner ($136.70) double. AE, DC, MC, V. **Parking:** Free.

Part of a well-known Norwegian chain, this balconied 1968 hotel, east of Storgaten, has a glassed-in restaurant-terrace overlooking the water. The bedrooms are comfortable and well furnished. There are a handful of bars and restaurants, and a small art gallery. You'll also have access to the town's modern theater.

INEXPENSIVE

HOTEL MARITIM, Storgaten 17, N-3100 Tønsberg. Tel. 33-31-71-00. 35 rms (all with bath). TV TEL **Directions:** See below.

$ Rates (including breakfast): Winter, 550–650 kroner ($95.20–$112.50) single; 700–750 kroner ($121.10–$129.80) double. Summer, 450–550 kroner ($77.90–$95.20) single; 580–650 kroner ($100.30–$112.50) double. AE, DC, MC, V.

This 1955 hotel is owned and operated by one of Norway's seamen's associations. Located on a square sloping down to the harbor, it occupies a four-story building, with the reception area on the third floor. Each room is well furnished and has a color scheme of either pink or white. Some rooms overlook the harbor, and all of them have carpeting and a comfortably modernized decor. It's a 10-minute walk east of the rail station on the main pedestrian street.

WHERE TO DINE
MODERATE

FREGATTEN, Storgaten 17. Tel. 33-31-47-76.
   Cuisine: INTERNATIONAL. **Reservations:** Not required. **Directions:** See below.
$ Prices: Appetizers 45–90 kroner ($7.80–$15.60); main dishes 150–200 kroner ($26–$34.60). AE, DC, MC, V.
   Open: Mon–Sat noon–10pm.

In the town center, in the Hotel Maritim building, Fregatten is one of the best restaurants in Tønsberg. In a pleasant, nautical dining room main courses like filet of reindeer with mushroom sauce and filet of tenderloin with paprika sauce and fresh vegetables are served. You'll also find fresh fish, often served with shrimp-and-lobster sauce. It's a 10-minute walk east of the rail station.

INEXPENSIVE

HÅNDVERKEREN, Møllergate 6. Tel. 33-31-23-88.
   Cuisine: NORWEGIAN. **Reservations:** Not required.

$ Prices: Appetizers 45–70 kroner ($7.80–$12.10); main dishes 50–150 kroner ($8.70–$26); Sun fixed-price menu 115–140 kroner ($19.90–$24.20). AE, DC, MC, V.
Open: Mon–Sat 9:30am–11pm, Sun 1–11pm.

In an 1890 clapboard-sided house, this establishment has a tastefully decorated dining room and a summer café. A preferred dining room is richly paneled and carpeted. A three-course meal could include shrimp cocktail, fresh fish of the day, T-bone steak with béarnaise sauce, beef with onions, entrecôte with salad, and foaming mugs of Norwegian beer. Filet of reindeer is a specialty. One part of the restaurant has been transformed into a popular pub, keeping the same hours and charging 39 kroner ($6.70) for a half-liter of beer.

3. SANDEFJORD

68 miles S of Oslo, 15 miles S of Tønsberg, 9 miles N of Larvik

GETTING THERE   By Train   There are five daily express trains from Oslo, reaching Sandefjord in about 2 hours.

By Bus   Frequent buses run between Oslo and Sandefjord daily. There are also good bus connections between Tønsberg and Sandefjord.

By Car   Take the E18 south from Oslo all the way to Sandefjord.

By Ferry   There is a daily ferry connection to Strømstad, Sweden, taking 2½ hours. For information, call **Scandi Line,** Tollbugata 5 (tel. 33-46-08-00).

ESSENTIALS   For information, **Sandefjord Reiselivsforening,** Skippergaten 7 (tel. 33-46-05-90), is open Mon–Sat 10am–5pm (June, Aug), daily 10am–8pm (July), and Mon–Fri 9am–4pm (Sept–May).

A summer resort, Sandefjord takes its name from a 6-mile fjord. Once a major whaling town, Sandefjord has built up the third-largest merchant fleet in Norway.

WHAT TO SEE & DO

At the southern end of Jernbanealléen, near a marina for pleasure craft, stands the great **Whaling Monument,** dedicated to the industry on which modern Sandefjord was founded.

Lying off Storgata, **Commander Christensen's Whaling Museum,** Museumsgaten 39 (tel. 33-46-32-51), has a replica of the mighty blue whale (its tongue weighs 3½ tons). Visiting hours are May to September daily from 11am to 4pm; in winter, on Sunday only, from noon to 4pm. Admission is 10 kroner ($1.70) for adults, free for children.

WHERE TO STAY

EXPENSIVE

RICA PARK HOTEL, Strand Promenaden 9, N-3200 Sandefjord. Tel. 33-46-55-50. Fax 33-46-79-00. 160 rms (all with bath). MINIBAR TV TEL
$ Rates (including breakfast): 900–1,100 kroner ($155.70–$190.30) single; 1,140–1,440 kroner ($197.20–$249.10) double. AE, DC, MC, V. **Parking:** Free.
By far the most stylish, comfortable, and prestigious hotel in the region, the Rica Park overlooks the harbor and a city meadow. Each bedroom is unusually opulent, filled with rich fabrics, carpeting, and furniture. The sophisticated public rooms include a library-style bar, an elegant restaurant, and a handful of formal salons. On the premises is a disco and a saltwater swimming pool. It's located off Hystadveien.

MODERATE

ATLANTIC HOME HOTEL, Jernbanealléen 33, N-3200 Sandefjord. Tel. 33-46-80-00. Fax 33-46-80-20. 74 rms (all with bath), 5 suites. MINIBAR TV TEL

$ Rates (including breakfast and light dinner): Winter, Sun–Thurs 850 kroner ($147.10) single; 950 kroner ($164.40) double; from 1,290 kroner ($223.20) suite for two. Winter, Fri–Sat 590 kroner ($102.10) single; 690 kroner ($119.40) double; from 1,090 kroner ($188.60) suite for two. June 23–Aug 28, 490 kroner ($84.80) single; 550 kroner ($95.20) double; from 1,090 kroner ($188.60) suite for two. AE, DC, MC, V. **Parking:** Free.

Built on the site of an older structure, this hotel respected its 1914 origins in its new design. The tasteful interior takes the whaling theme as its motif. Bedrooms have sleek modern styling and a number of amenities. Suites have their own fireplaces and Jacuzzi's, and three rooms are equipped for the handicapped. Children under 4 stay free, and children 4 to 16 are charged half price, in their parents' room. The hotel's Bistro La Coquille is furnished in a French provincial style, offering excellent food and service. The restaurant is not on the hotel grounds, but lies a 5-minute walk away toward the town center. The hotel is off Storgata.

INEXPENSIVE

HOTEL KONG CARL, Torvgaten 9, N-3200 Sandefjord. Tel. 33-46-31-17. Fax 33-46-31-19. 29 rms (all with bath). TV TEL

$ Rates (including breakfast): 380–550 kroner ($65.70–$95.20) single; 560–650 kroner ($96.90–$112.50) double. DC, MC, V. **Parking:** Free.

Near the town center and marketplace, the country Victorian white clapboard-sided house dates from 1690. The hotel's cathedral-ceilinged annex is used extensively as a conference center. Bedrooms are simply furnished, but comfortable and inviting. Four contain a minibar. Lunch and dinner in the unpretentious Norwegian-style restaurant cost from 150 kroner ($26) each, served daily except Sunday. You can have a beer on the terrace in the summer.

WHERE TO DINE

MODERATE

EDGAR LUDI'S GOURMET, Rådhusgaten 7. Tel. 33-36-27-41.
Cuisine: NORWEGIAN. **Reservations:** Recommended.
$ Prices: Appetizers 55–85 kroner ($9.50–$14.70); main dishes 120–200 kroner ($20.80–$34.60). AE, DC, MC, V.
Open: Daily noon–11pm.

This pleasant, sunny restaurant, in a new building in the center of the Old Town off Torggata, is one of the best dining spots around. Amid carefully focused lighting, mirrors, and palms, you can enjoy lamb filet with spinach and lemon sauce, burgundy snails in puff pastry, and warm salmon soufflé.

---

4. LILLEHAMMER

105 miles N of Oslo, 226 miles S of Trondheim

GETTING THERE By Plane Visitors fly to either Fornebu or Gardermoen airport in the Oslo area, then go by bus or train to Lillehammer.

By Train Express trains from Oslo take about 2 hours and 20 minutes, and local trains take around 3 hours. Depending on the time of year, five to eight trains per day leave Oslo for Lillehammer.

By Bus Frequent buses run between Oslo and Lillehammer.

By Car Head north from Oslo along the E6.

ESSENTIALS The **Lillehammer Tourist Office,** at Jernbanegaten 2 (tel. 61-25-92-99), is open Mon–Fri 9am–8:30pm, Sat 9am–6pm, and Sun 11am–6pm (mid-June–late Aug) and Mon–Fri 9am–4pm and Sat 10am–1pm (Sept–early June).

SPECIAL EVENTS The 17th **Olympic Winter Games** is scheduled to begin in Lillehammer on February 12, 1994. It will represent the largest sports event Norway has ever organized. For 16 days, world attention will focus on Lillehammer, which is the smallest town ever to be asked to host the Olympics. Details can be obtained by contacting the **Lillehammer Olympic Organizing Committee,** Elvegata 19 (P.O. Box 106), N-2601 Lillehammer, Norway (tel. 61-27-19-94).

Surrounded by mountains, Lillehammer, a favorite resort for Europeans, is at the head of Lake Mjøsa. Host to the 1994 Winter Olympics, the town is already busy preparing.

The Hafjell Alpine Center, the main venue for alpine competitions in 1994, is situated about 9 miles away from the center of Lillehammer, with seven lifts and 12 miles of alpine slopes. Lillehammer is also the starting point for 250 miles of prepared tracks, 3 miles of which are illuminated. The ski center has three lifts and 2 miles of alpine slopes.

Lillehammer gears up for its winter sports season in December. In addition to its ski center, Lillehammer has an important admission-free skating rink (open in winter Monday through Friday from 11am to 9pm and on Sunday from 11am to 5pm). All this activity is supplemented in winter by festivals, folklore nights, and ski races.

WHAT TO SEE & DO

During the peak summer season, usually June 20 to August 20, the tourist bureau schedules several excursions, including one to the **Maihaugen Open-Air Museum (The Sandvig Collections)** and one on **Lake Mjøsa** on board the *White Swan of Lake Mjøsa,* a 135-year-old paddle steamer. Ask the tourist bureau (see above) for a list of activities.

MAIHAUGEN OPEN-AIR MUSEUM (The Sandvig Collections), Maihaugveien 1. Tel. 61-25-01-35.

✪ This museum of provincial culture has assembled 150 buildings (more than 40,000 exhibits), ranging from manor farms to the cottage of the poorest yeoman worker. The houses reassembled here and furnished in 17th- to 18th-century style, came from all over the Gudbrandsdal (Gudbrands Valley). See, in particular, the Garmo Stave Church from 1200. A collection of 37 old workshops range from gunsmithing to wood engraving. A large exhibition covers Norwegian history from 10,000 B.C. to the present. The city's concert hall is also located at the museum. The museum has three different cafeterias that present Norwegian food. The site is southeast of Lillehammer, about half a mile from the town center. (It is only a 10-minute walk from the main street in Lillehammer up to the entrance.)

Admission: 40 kroner ($6.90) adults, 15 kroner ($2.60) children.

Open: May and Sept, daily 10am–4pm; June–Aug, old workshops and indoor museum only, daily 11am–2pm. **Bus:** Route 007.

LILLEHAMMER BYS MALERISAMLING (Lillehammer Town Art Museum), Kirkegata 69. Tel. 61-25-19-44.

Founded in 1921, Norway's third-largest gallery has more than 800 works of Norwegian art dating from the early 19th century through the present. From September to April, lectures and various music performances are given. It lies on the north side of the main square, Stortorget.

Admission: 20 kroner ($3.50) adults, free for children under 12.

Open: June–Aug, Tues–Fri 11am–4pm, Sat 10am–2pm, Sun noon–4pm.

LILLEPUTTHAMMER, Øyergjestegård, Øyer. Tel. 61-27-73-35-15.

Adjoining the Øyer Inn is a miniature town depicting Lillehammer around the turn of the century. Some houses are populated with mechanical dolls in old-fashioned costumes; there's a small moving-picture theater in another. In another house, real children can play, paint, and draw. A minitrain goes through a park that has play areas and ponies for children to ride. There is a cafeteria and gift shop. It's located 10½ miles north of Lillehammer.

Admission: 30 kroner ($5.20) adults, 15 kroner ($2.60) children.

Open: June 16–Aug 12, daily 10am–7pm. **Closed:** Aug 13–June 15.

HUNDERFOSSEN FAMILY PARK, N-2638 Fåberg. Tel. 61-27-72-22.

Here you will find an interesting presentation of the most popular Norwegian fairy tales, as well as more than 50 activities for both children and adults, and lots of space just to roam around. There is a cafeteria and swimming pool. A 40-foot troll at the gate welcomes visitors. The park is 7½ miles north of Lillehammer on the E6.

Admission: 100 kroner ($17.30) adults, 90 kroner ($15.60) children.

Open: May 30–June 19, daily 10am–5pm; June 20–Aug 17, daily 10am–8pm.

Bus: Marked "Hunderfossen" from Lillehammer.

MUSEUM OF NORWEGIAN VEHICLE HISTORY, Lilletorget 7. Tel. 61-25-61-65.

Norway's only vehicle museum shows the development of transportation from the first sledges and wagons to the car of today. It's east of the town center; from the bus stop, head out Elvegata.

Admission: 25 kroner ($4.30) adults, 12 kroner ($2.10) children.

Open: Mid-June to Aug, daily 10am–6pm; Sept, Mon–Fri 11am–3pm, Sat–Sun 11am–4pm.

SPORTS/RECREATION IN LILLEHAMMER

SKIING Ideal for both professional and neophyte skiers, Lillehammer has a 307-foot slope for the show-offs, and a smaller jump suitable for amateurs. Ski lifts take skiers 1,500 feet above sea level up the slalom slope, and more than 250 miles of marked skiing trails are packed by machines. Daily skiing classes are offered at the Lillehammer Ski School, and several cross-country tours are held weekly. Ask at the tourist office (see above) for details.

SPORTS FACILITIES The first hall erected for the 1994 Olympics, **Kristins Hall,** Stampesletta (tel. 61-25-49-50), has an ice rink, a sports hall, a curling rink, and an athletic track. It is open Monday through Friday 7am to midnight; Saturday 8am to 8pm; Sunday 8am to 11pm. Bus: 003 or 005.

The hall stands at the **Stampesletta Central Sports Stadium,** an extensive sports grounds behind the town center. The stadium has three grass playing fields, one gravel field, two handball courts, an athletic track, and a show-jumping ring. It will be the central stadium for the Olympics.

The **Kringsjå Indoor Tennis Courts** are at Hammersengveien. Call the Lillehammer Tennis Club (tel. 61-26-00-65) for details about how to play.

NEARBY ATTRACTIONS
In Follebu

AULESTAD, N-2620 Follebu. Tel. 61-22-03-26.

Only 12 miles northwest of Lillehammer, Aulestad is the home of Norway's Nobel Prize–winning poet Bjørnstjerne Bjørnson (1832–1910). He purchased the farm in 1875 and was living here when he learned of his Nobel laurels in 1903. The home is now a national museum.

Admission: 20 kroner ($3.50) adults, 10 kroner ($1.70) children.

Open: Mid-May to May 31 and the first 2 weeks of Sept, daily 11am–2:30pm; June and Aug, daily 10am–4pm; July, daily 10am–5:30pm. **Closed:** Mid-Sept to mid-May.

In Hamar

Some 36 miles from Lillehammer, in the heart of rich farmland, is Hamar, Norway's largest inland town, and the home of Kirsten Flagstad, the famous operatic soprano, born here in 1885. In addition to the following attractions, Hamar also has the remains of a medieval cathedral, from around 1150, and a bishop's palace.

KIRSTEN FLAGSTAD MUSEUM, Kirkegate 11. Tel. 62-51-03-64.

Lying 50 yards from the marketplace and 10 minutes from the railroad station, this museum contains Flagstad's memorial collection. The Metropolitan Opera in New York City contributed items, including some of the gowns she wore in her famous operatic roles. Flagstad recordings can be heard in a special room of the museum.

Admission: 15 kroner ($2.60) adults, 5 kroner (90¢) children.

Open: June 20–Aug 16, daily 10am–4pm. **Closed:** Aug 17–June 19.

NSB JERNBANEMUSEET, Strandveien 132. Tel. 62-51-31-60.

This museum collects and displays bits of Norwegian rail history since its beginning in the 1840s. Vehicles include models from 1861 to 1950, among them three royal coaches and several steam locomotives weighing up to 150 tons. There is a museum park with several station buildings, railway tracks, and other exhibits, as well as a "dining car" serving snacks and refreshments. A small train travels along the grounds of the amusement park; trips cost 10 kroner ($1.70) for adults and 5 kroner (90¢) for children.

Admission: 20 kroner ($3.50) adults, 10 kroner ($1.70) children.

Open: May 24–Sept 13, daily 10am–4pm; July, daily 10am–6pm. **Closed:** Sept 14–May 23. **Directions:** Bus 1 from railroad station or a 30-minute walk from the town center heading north along the shore of Lake Mjøsa.

INTERFERENS HOLOGRAFI, Strandveien 100, Domkirkeodden. Tel. 62-52-50-50.

At Domkirkeodden, Hamar's museum and recreation area, about a mile from the town center and rail station, Mr. and Mrs. Olav Skipnes have assembled Norway's first and largest exhibition of holography. The projected holographic images are created by a special laser technique and give the observer an illusion of seeing objects in their natural three dimensions. They sometimes seem to penetrate out of the image plane and float in the air. The exhibition comprises some 100 holograms.

Admission: 25 kroner ($4.30) adults, 15 kroner ($2.60) children.

Open: Mid-May to mid-June, Tues–Sun 11am–4pm; mid-June to Aug, Tues–Sun 11am–6pm; Sept to mid-May, Sat–Sun 11am–4pm. **Directions:** You can reach the exhibition by taxi, on foot, or by renting a bicycle at the rail or bus station. From the center, starting at the quay of the old paddlewheel steamer *Skibladner,* a promenade path along the shore of Lake Mjøsa leads to the area.

HEDMARK KUNSTNERSENTER (Hedmark Artists' Center), Strandveien 98. Tel. 62-53-07-77.

This center offers changing exhibitions of local artworks. It's beautifully situated by Lake Mjøsa west of town, which makes for a pleasant walk along the lake.

Admission: 10 kroner ($1.70) adults; children free.

Open: Mon–Fri 9am–3pm.

WHERE TO STAY

EXPENSIVE

RICA VICTORIA HOTEL, Storgate 84B, N-2600 Lillehammer. Tel. 61-25-00-49. Fax 61-25-24-74. 118 rms (all with bath). MINIBAR TV TEL

$ Rates (including breakfast): Winter, Sun–Thurs 925 kroner ($160) single; 1,225 kroner ($211.90) double. Winter, Fri–Sat 525 kroner ($90.80) single; 850 kroner ($147.10) double. Summer, Sun–Thurs 560 kroner ($96.90) single; 850 kroner ($147.10) double. Summer, Fri–Sat 495 kroner ($85.60) single; 750 kroner ($129.80) double. AE, DC, MC, V.

Rica Victoria was established in 1872, and new wings filled with modern comfort were extended in 1963 and 1976. Each of the well-furnished bedrooms contains comfortably upholstered chairs and sofas. Known for its conference facilities, the hotel also has a bar, blazing fireplaces, and several restaurants, including the Victorianhjørnet, seating 100 guests, and the regular dining room seating 180 guests.

Guests also enjoy dancing in the Rica Plaza Dancing Club. The hotel is 300 yards from the rail station.

MODERATE

DØLAHEIMEN HOTELL & KAFETERIA, Jernbanegaten 3, N-2600 Lillehammer. Tel. 61-25-88-66. 90 rms (all with bath). TV TEL
$ Rates: 400–1,250 kroner ($69.20–$216.30) single; 600–1,500 kroner ($103.80–$259.50) double. AE, DC, MC, V. **Parking:** Free.

A modern hotel and cafeteria in the center of Lillehammer at the rail and bus stations, the Dølaheimen is usually heavily booked in July and early August, so reservations are important. An informal atmosphere prevails; children are welcome. Rooms are sleek, functional, and comfortable. The hotel was greatly extended in 1992. The newer rooms are more expensive. There's a large air-conditioned cafeteria with a separate room for nonsmokers, a sitting room, and an upstairs TV lounge. Parking is available for the handicapped. Facilities includes a sauna and a solarium.

LILLEHAMMER HOTEL, Turisthotellveien 27B, N-2600 Lillehammer. Tel. 61-25-48-00. Fax 61-25-73-33. 196 rms (all with bath). MINIBAR TV TEL
$ Rates (including breakfast): 895–995 kroner ($154.80–$172.10) single; 1,045–1,150 kroner ($180.80–$199) double. AE, DC, MC, V. **Parking:** Free.

A luxurious and sports-oriented hotel, this establishment is located in a forested 8-acre park near the Lillehammer ski center and the Maihaugen Open-Air Museum. Bedrooms are tastefully modern, some equipped for the handicapped. The hotel has three restaurants featuring both evening dance music and buffets. On the premises are conference facilities, and outdoor and indoor pools, with saunas and a solarium. The wood and marble-trimmed public areas are among the most glamorous in the region.

About a mile away across Lake Mjøsa, the hotel maintains its own sports center with a terrace, where you can rent sailboats and canoes, waterski, or sit on the flower-strewn terrace to enjoy the view. To reach the hotel, take a taxi from the rail station.

OPPLAND HOTEL, Hamarveien 2, N-2600 Lillehammer. Tel. 61-25-85-00. Fax 61-25-53-25. 75 rms (all with bath). MINIBAR TV TEL
$ Rates (including breakfast): Winter, 875–950 kroner ($151.40–$164.40) single; 980–1,050 kroner ($169.50–$181.70) double. Summer, 575–675 kroner ($99.50–$116.80) single; 750–850 kroner ($129.80–$147.10) double. AE, DC, MC, V. **Parking:** 40 kroner ($6.90).

Constructed in 1951, this hotel was later extended in two different decades and was completely modernized again in 1990. Half a mile south of the rail station, it is near the ski center and is a good starting point for cross-country skiing. It offers modern, comfortable, and well-furnished bedrooms. The hotel also makes a good drinking and dining center (see Baccus Bar and Halvdans Stue, below).

INEXPENSIVE

GJESTEHUSET ERSGAARD, Nordseterveien 201, N-2600 Lillehammer. Tel. 61-25-06-84. Fax 61-25-31-09. 30 rms (16 with bath). **Directions:** See below.
$ Rates (including breakfast): 300 kroner ($51.90) single without bath; 430 kroner ($74.40) single with bath; 500 kroner ($86.50) double without bath, 580 kroner ($100.30) double with bath. DC, MC, V. **Closed:** Dec 23–28. **Parking:** Free.

A pleasant family hotel created from a 1570 farm on the outskirts of town, Ersgaard sits atop a mountain overlooking the resort and Lake Mjøsa. If you have a car, this makes for a pleasant stay. Bedrooms are modest but adequately furnished. The Norwegian buffet breakfast features assorted jams, cheese (even goat), Norwegian herring, cold cuts, fresh bread, boiled eggs, a choice of cereal, and coffee, tea, milk, or juice. A complete lunch or dinner will cost from 135 kroner ($23.40). Bus service from Lillehammer is available twice a day. The hotel is 1 mile from the town center in the center of the Olympic Park; follow signs to Nordseter.

NEARBY PLACES TO STAY
Inexpensive

RUSTAD HOTELL AND FJELLSTUE, N-2612 Sjusjøen. Tel. 62-56-34-08.
Fax 62-56-35-74. 52 rms (26 with bath). **Bus:** Sjusjøen from Lillehammer.

$ **Rates** (including breakfast): Winter, 270 kroner ($46.70) single without bath, 720 kroner ($124.60) single with bath; 450 kroner ($77.90) double without bath, 750 kroner ($129.80) double with bath. Summer, 215 kroner ($37.20) single without bath, 340 kroner ($58.80) single with bath; 430 kroner ($74.40) double without bath, 680 kroner ($117.60) double with bath. No credit cards. **Parking:** Free.

Some visitors might want to settle in the wilderness at this favorite spot, about 14 miles north of Lillehammer. This log-and-timber chalet is on the edge of a lake (there's a dock for swimming and boats) and surrounded by private grounds. The well-furnished bedrooms have views of the lake or mountains, and country-style meals are served. In winter, people enjoy one of the best ski terrains in Norway, and there's horseback riding in summer. The public rooms are furnished in antiques.

WHERE TO DINE
MODERATE

HALVDANS STUE, in the Oppland Hotel, Hamarveien 2. Tel. 61-25-85-00.
Cuisine: NORWEGIAN. **Reservations:** Not required.
$ **Prices:** Appetizers 52–85 kroner ($9–$14.70); main dishes 155–210 kroner ($26.80–$36.30). AE, DC, MC, V.
Open: Daily 7am–10:30pm.

Located in the Oppland Hotel (see "Where to Stay," above), a half mile south of the rail station, this restaurant is popular with visitors and locals. The decor is warmly traditional, with a color scheme of pink and brown. The food is good, the service helpful, and the portions generous. Try such dishes as filet of codfish with beetroot and leek sauce or roast duckling with orange sauce. It's possible to order a one-course supper for only 58 kroner ($10).

QUEEN RESTAURANT, in the Rica Victoria Hotel, Storgate 84B. Tel. 61-25-00-49.
Cuisine: NORWEGIAN/INTERNATIONAL. **Reservations:** Recommended.
$ **Prices:** Appetizers 39–45 kroner ($6.70–$7.80); main dishes 79–225 kroner ($13.70–$38.90); 2-course lunch with coffee 145 kroner ($25.10); dinner with coffee 185 kroner ($32). AE, DC, MC, V.
Open: Lunch daily 11am–3pm; dinner daily 3pm–11pm.

Considered one of the best restaurants in town, the Queen occupies lobby-level premises at the Rica Victoria Hotel (see "Where to Stay" above). Its windows overlook the city center. The decor is modern, with a color scheme of pastel blues and greens, with touches of pale pink. Specialties include mountain trout fried in sour cream and boiled catfish with butter sauce and cucumber salad. Main dishes range from *frikadeller* (meatballs), the cheapest item on the menu, to chateaubriand, the most expensive. The set menus are good value. A cold buffet is served for the same cost as the fixed-price lunch, and a warm buffet is offered at night for the same price as the set dinner. It's a 3-minute walk north of the rail station.

VICTORIANHJØRNET (Victorian Corner), in the Rica Victoria Hotel, Storgate 84B. Tel. 61-25-00-49.
Cuisine: STEAKS/PIZZA. **Reservations:** Not required.
$ **Prices:** Pizzas 68–145 kroner ($11.80–$25.10); main dishes 128–150 kroner ($22.10–$26); deli specials, served until 7pm, 68 kroner ($11.80) per platter. AE, DC, MC, V.
Open: Sun–Fri noon–midnight, Sat 11am–midnight.

One floor above lobby level in the Rica Victoria Hotel (see "Where to Stay," above) is a bistro, pizzeria, and steak house serving good and reasonably priced meals. The decor is red and white with an old-fashioned woodsy ambience. The place doubles as a pub, but is better known as a steak house. Both pizzas and steaks come in different sizes and are priced accordingly. It's a 3-minute walk north of the rail station.

INEXPENSIVE

BRYGGERIKJELLERN, Elvagata 19. Tel. 61-25-23-30.
  Cuisine: NORWEGIAN. **Reservations:** Not required.
$ Prices: Salad 50 kroner ($8.70); main dishes 65–140 kroner ($11.20–$24.20). AE, DC, MC, V.
  Open: Mon 6–11pm, Tues–Fri 6pm–1am, Sat 1pm–1am, Sun 3pm–1am.
In 1969 this 1814 brewery, a 7-minute walk east of the rail station, was transformed into a pub/restaurant serving beer, steaks, and main dishes, and it has done a roaring business ever since. It's especially popular in winter with skiers. Salads are the only appetizers. Many people come here just to drink, paying 35.50 kroner ($6.15) for a half-liter of beer. The Disco Brenneriet (The Distillery) is connected to the restaurant, charging from 40 kroner to 60 kroner ($6.90 to $10.40) for entrance, depending on the night of the week. It is open Wednesday through Saturday from 9pm to 2am.

NEARBY PLACES TO DINE
Inexpensive

KIRKESTUEN CAFETERIA, Maihaugveien 1. Tel. 61-25-39-59.
  Cuisine: NORWEGIAN. **Reservations:** Not required. **Bus:** 007 (Nybu) for half a mile southeast of the town center.
$ Prices: Appetizers 35–45 kroner ($6.10–$7.80); main dishes 50–100 kroner ($8.70–$17.30). AE, MC, V.
  Open: June 18–Aug 16, daily 11am–5:30pm. **Closed:** Aug 17–June 17.
This cafeteria is located in an old hillside country inn, among the ancient buildings of a folk museum. Traditional Norwegian dishes and a wide selection of open-face sandwiches are featured. You can order such typical dishes as *rømmergrøt* (sour-cream porridge), followed by fried trout with salad and potatoes.

EVENING ENTERTAINMENT

In addition to the disco at the Bryggerikjellern (see "Where to Dine," above), you might try the following establishments.

BACCUS BAR, in the Oppland Hotel, Hamarveien 2. Tel. 61-25-85-00.
  This is one of the town's leading discos, with a DJ who plays recorded music. It lies in the cellar beneath the Oppland Hotel, a half mile south of the rail station. Beer costs 38 kroner ($6.60). It's open Monday through Saturday from 6pm to 1am; music begins at 8:30pm.
  Admission: 40–50 kroner ($6.90–$8.70).

RICA PLAZA DANCING, in the Rica Victoria Hotel, Storgate 84B. Tel. 61-25-00-49.
  The minimum age at this hotel dancing club is 21. It's accessible through the hotel lobby or by a separate entrance. Inside, the decor is rustic and couples—mostly in their 20s and 30s—dance to recorded music. It's open Monday through Saturday from 8pm to 1am. A beer costs 32 kroner ($5.50).
  Admission: 50 kroner ($8.70); free for hotel residents.

5. THE PEER GYNT ROAD

✪ The road between Lillehammer and the town of Vinstra, 38 miles long (not counting detours), takes you right into the heart of Peer Gynt country. Henrik Ibsen came this way when he was researching his masterpiece *Peer Gynt,* published in 1867 and later set to music by Edvard Grieg. Ibsen based his tale in part on the exploits of one Per (spelled with only one *e*) Gynt Haga, a real-life Norwegian folk hero noted for such exploits as riding on the backs of reindeer at breakneck speed.

As you drive through the Gudbrandsdal (Gudbrands Valley), you can travel the same route that bewitched the original hero, and outside Vinstra you can visit the monument to Per Gynt Haga, the Peer Gynt prototype, in the cemetery adjoining the Sødorp Church, 1 mile south of town.

The Peer Gynt country is a magnificent unspoiled mountain region with altitudes varying from 2,526 to 4,920 feet. This is one of Norway's oldest and best-known sports districts. The skiing center at Fefor was opened as early as 1904, and it was here that the adventurous Capt. Robert Falcon Scott tested the equipment for his expedition to the South Pole.

Here a respect for tradition is combined with modern skiing facilities. The area features 248 miles of prepared double track for cross-country skiing and 10 ski-lift and downhill facilities. It's suitable for those who'd like to combine cross-country and alpine skiing.

The region is also a lure to summer travelers, as the Peer Gynt Road passes mountains, farmsteads, fish-filled lakes, wild game, and alpine flowers.

The best source of information about touring in the area, **Vinstra Turist og Messekontor,** Nedre Gate 5A (tel. 61-29-01-66), is open Mon–Fri 10am–5pm (June–Aug) and Mon–Fri 10am–4pm (Sept–May).

WHERE TO STAY IN PEER GYNT COUNTRY

Most people travel the Peer Gynt Road as an excursion from Lillehammer. But if you'd like to stay around for a few days, here are several recommended accommodations.

EXPENSIVE

DALSETER HØYFJELLSHOTELL, Gudbrandsdalen, N-2628 Espedalen. Tel. 61-29-99-10. Fax 61-29-99-41. 90 rms (all with bath). TEL **Bus:** Espedalen bus from Lillehammer.

$ Rates: Winter (including full board; minimum stay of 3 days), 730–845 kroner ($126.30–$146.20) single; 1,280–1,510 kroner ($221.40–$261.20) double. Summer (including breakfast), 365 kroner ($63.10) single; 550 kroner ($95.20) double. **Parking:** Free. **Closed:** Oct 1–Dec 26 and May.

This 1963 hotel set on a hillside overlooking forests and mountains caters to families, and it was overhauled and upgraded in 1990. The views are stunning. Bedrooms are outfitted in a cozy, comfortable Norwegian style, with lots of heat in winter. Meals in the warm, contemporary dining room are well prepared. Evening dance music contributes to the ambience. There's a dining room, an indoor swimming pool, a gymnasium, an intricate network or well-marked hiking or skiing trails, and fishing facilities.

FEFOR HIFJELLSHOTELL, Fefor, N-2640 Vinstra. Tel. 61-29-00-99. Fax 61-29-17-60. 120 rms (all with bath). TEL

$ Rates (including half board): Winter, 820 kroner ($141.90) single, 1,460 kroner ($252.60) double; summer, 690 kroner ($119.40) single, 1,140 kroner ($197.20) double. AE, DC, MC, V. **Parking:** Free. **Closed:** May.

This hotel's interesting exterior features red Nordic dragons on the roof of its older wing, dating from 1891. The modern addition has the best rooms, but there are magnificent views in each section. The public rooms feature fireplaces, heavy iron chandeliers, and lots of comfortable nooks and cubbyholes. There's an indoor and an outdoor swimming pool, ski runs, boating facilities, organized children's activities, and an ice-skating rink. It's located on the shores of Lake Fefor. In October and November, it is open only on Friday, Saturday, and Sunday nights.

GAUSDAL HIFJELLSHOTELL, Gausdal, N-26220 Svingvoll. Tel. 61-22-85-00. Fax 61-22-85-20. 125 rms (all with bath). TEL

$ Rates: Winter (including full board), 680 kroner ($117.60) single; 1,280 kroner ($221.40) double. Summer (breakfast included), 400 kroner ($69.20) single; 720 kroner ($124.60) double. AE, DC, MC, V. **Parking:** Free.

The hotel sits in the center of the small but popular mountain resort of Gausdal, 10 miles west of Tretten, the nearest rail station, and the owners will send a car to pick you up there. Originally built in 1876, it was set afire by the Nazis in 1944. In 1956, it rose again as a hotel, with attractively furnished and modernized bedrooms, many opening onto views of the mountains. There are facilities for tennis, swimming, a sauna, and a pool. Miles of hiking or ski trails surround the hotel, and provisions are made for downhill and cross-country skiing, horseback riding, and hill climbing. The hotel is especially popular as a ski center in winter.

If you're just passing through Gausdal, you can patronize a lunchtime smörgåsbord for 150 kroner ($26) per person or a fixed-price dinner for 195 kroner ($33.70).

MODERATE

SKEIKAMPEN HØIFJELLSHOTELL, N-2622 Skeikampen. Tel. 61-22-85-05. Fax 61-22-75-20. 83 rms (all with bath). TV TEL **Train:** Dovrebanen railway from Lillehammer to the Tretten station.

$ Rates: Winter (including full board), 630 kroner ($109) single; 1,100 kroner ($190.30) double. Summer (including breakfast), 380 kroner ($65.70) single; 600 kroner ($103.80) double. AE, DC, MC, V. **Parking:** Free.

⑤ In many ways, this is the best hotel in the region, with attractive public rooms filled with antique and modern Scandinavian furniture and acres of woodland grounds. The snug and cozy bedrooms, decorated in "Nordic light" pastels, are distributed in such a way that most of them open onto scenic views. Sports lovers will find an indoor pool, a sauna, a ski lift adjacent to a smaller rope tow for beginners, and a ski school with child-care facilities. As the hotel is right at the timber line, both forested and rocky paths are well marked for climbers.

On the premises is a Spanish-influenced bodega, with the best wine stock in the region. Wine-tasting parties and semiformal dinners are held here at least three times a week. A lunch buffet costs 175 kroner ($30.30). The hotel lies 11 miles from the Tretten railway station. Arrangements can be made in advance for a hotel car or a taxi to pick you up.

WADAHL HIFJELLSHOTELL, N-2645 Harpefoss. Tel. 61-29-83-00. Fax 61-29-83-60. 100 rms (all with bath), 3 junior suites. MINIBAR TV TEL

$ Rates (including breakfast): Winter, 510–715 kroner ($88.20–$123.70) single; 780–990 kroner ($134.90–$171.30) double; from 1,090 kroner ($188.60) suite. Summer, 510–610 kroner ($88.20–$105.50) single; 780–880 kroner ($134.90–$152.20) double; from 920 kroner ($159.20) suite. MC, V. **Parking:** 50 kroner ($8.70). **Closed:** Oct 30–Nov 15 and Apr 30–May 20.

Originally established in 1900 as a survival station for the high mountains around it, it became a hotel in 1930 and has been enlarged several times since. Rooms are comfortably furnished and modernized. Winter is high season, and because of the hotel's isolation, guests usually plan to eat here. Patrons enjoy the tasty dinners and evening dance music here. Facilities include a large outdoor pool, an indoor pool, tennis courts, horseback-riding facilities, saunas, and a year-round sun terrace. The hotel is 11 miles southwest of Vinstra, the nearest rail station, and 9 miles northwest of Harpefoss, which has no rail link. There is no public transport to the hotel, but arrangements can be made to have you picked up at the rail station.

CHAPTER 17

KRISTIANSAND S, STAVANGER & SOUTHERN NORWAY

The coastal lands of southern Norway, shaped geographically like a half moon, are often called Norway's Riviera because of their beaches, bays, and sailing opportunities. Within this area, the Telemark region is known for its lakes and canals which are used for summer boating and canoeing. From Skien visitors can explore this water network. Arendal is a charming old town with a harbor near some of the best beaches. Kristiansand S is a link between Norway and the rest of Europe. The Christiansholm Fortress has stood here since 1674, and the town is near a 6-mile-long beach, Haresanden. In the western part of the region, the Lysefjord, Sandefjord, and the Vindefjord are easily accessible from Stavanger, the largest city in southern Norway.

The southern part of Norway is called Sørlandet, a land of hills, valleys, mountains, rivers, and lakes. The area gets more sunshine than any other place in Norway and northern Europe. Gulf Stream temperatures make bathing possible in summer. This section is the major domestic vacation choice for Norwegians.

Rogaland is the southwestern part of the country, and it has been called "Norway in a nutshell" because of its great variety of nature. Fjords, mountains, green valleys, beaches, old towns and villages, a mild climate, and countless fishing possibilities make this a vacation land.

The district lives today in the technological future, thanks to its oil industry, but it also harks back to the country's oldest inhabitants. Here, the Viking king Harald Fairhair gathered most of Norway into one kingdom in A.D. 872. The locals say that it was from here that the Vikings sailed to discover America.

Rogaland also consists of the hilly Dalane in the south, the flat Jaeren (farmland), the beautiful Ryfylke, and in the north, Karmøy and Haugesund.

SEEING SOUTHERN NORWAY

GETTING THERE

If you're flying or taking the train, Stavanger in the southwest or Kristiansand S in the center of the southern coast make the best gateways to the area and also have the most frequent connections. Fred Olsen Lines sails between Denmark and Kristiansand S daily all year if you're in Denmark and want to begin your exploration of Norway in its southern tier.

If you're driving from Oslo, you can travel all the way to Stavanger on a good

WHAT'S SPECIAL ABOUT
SOUTHERN NORWAY

Great Towns/Villages

☐ Skien, Henrik Ibsen's hometown, the best center for touring the old and historic county of Telemark.

☐ Stavanger, a historic, well-preserved old town, an oil boom center, and an excursion base for fjord tours.

☐ Kristiansand S, founded by Christian IV, the best center for exploring the "Norwegian Riviera."

Museums

☐ Aust-Agder Museet, at Arendal, one of the country's oldest, showcasing the folklore of the Norwegian south.

☐ Vest Agder Fylkes, at Kristiansand S, one of Norway's largest open-air museums.

Ancient Monuments

☐ The Heddal Stave Church, at Heddal, dating from 1147, one of Norway's best preserved.

Scenic Wonders

☐ The Telemark Canal, a scenic journey through lock and lake deep in the heart of folkloric region.

☐ Pulpit Rock, outside Stavanger, towering 1,800 feet above the Lysefjord.

Cool for Kids

☐ Kristiansand S Zoo, set on 100 acres, with many exotic animals and many from the Nordic climes.

Literary Pilgrimages

☐ Venstøp Farm, near Skien, the childhood home of Henrik Ibsen, filled with family memorabilia.

Special Events/Festivals

☐ The North Sea Festival, a sea-fishing festival at Haugesund in June.

---

express highway, the E18. It or its subsidiary routes connect most of the places recommended in this chapter.

If you're in the west of Norway at Bergen, it's best either to fly to Stavanger or to take the hydrofoil or car-ferry.

A SUGGESTED ITINERARY

Day 1: From Oslo, go south to Ibsen's hometown of Skien for a 2-night stopover. See the sights of Skien.

Day 2: Take the 10-hour trip up the Telemark Canal.

Day 3: Returning to the E18, continue southwest for a third night in the Arendal area which has many interesting sights.

Day 4: Explore Kristiansand S and spend the night.

Day 5 & 6: Drive or board the train to Stavanger, taking fjord cruises and exploring its Old Town.

---

1. SKIEN

86 miles S of Oslo, 19 miles W of
the Larvik-Frederikshavn (Denmark) ferry connection

GETTING THERE   By Plane   Daily flights arrive from Oslo at Skien Airport, 2 miles from the town center.

By Train   From Oslo's Central Station, the Vestfold express train goes first to

Larvik and then to Skien. Skien is also the beginning of another rail link to Oslo via Kongsberg and Drammen. Trip time to Oslo is 3 hours.

By Bus Daily buses arrive from the Central Station in Oslo. Skien is also the center for buses branching out to the Telemark district. If you plan to tour Telemark by bus, call Ruteopplysningen (tel. 35-52-79-74) for schedules.

By Car Take the E18 south from Oslo.

ESSENTIALS Skien Turistkontor, at Kongensgate 31 (tel. 35-52-82-27), is open Mon–Sat 10am–5pm (June, Aug), daily 10am–8pm (July), and 9am–4pm (Sept–May).

Skien is a bustling industrial town and the administrative capital of Telemark county. Long proud of its association with playwright Henrik Ibsen (1828–1906), a native of Skien, it is visited not only for its Ibsen associations, but because it is the principal gateway to Telemark.

Skien is an old town, dating from 1100, although it wasn't until 1358 that it received its royal charter. It has been ravished by fire and floods over the centuries, several of which destroyed the town. The last disastrous fire occurred in 1886, and a new town had to be created out of the debris. Skien covers an area of 489 square miles, with nearly 50,000 inhabitants.

WHAT TO SEE & DO

Ibsen left Skien in 1843 when he was 15 years old, returning only briefly as part of an unsuccessful attempt to borrow some money to enter prep school in Oslo. He lived at several addresses in Skien, including a small house in an old neighborhood, Snipetorp 27, near the town center. The house on Snipetorp is one of several in the neighborhood that have been proclaimed protected monuments. Ibsen's former home is now a cultural center and an art gallery.

VENSTØP FARM, Venstøp. Tel. 35-52-35-94.

Ibsen's childhood home, Venstøp Farm is furnished with objects actually used by the Ibsen family as well as period pieces. The building dates from the early 1800s. Two paintings are by Ibsen—he had originally wanted to become an artist, but his wife ("the cat") insisted that he be a playwright, thus (in her words) giving the world a great dramatic talent but sparing it a mediocre artist. The farm is 3 miles north of the town center.

Admission: 15 kroner ($2.60) adults, 7 kroner ($1.20) children.
Open: June–Sept 1, Mon–Sat noon–5pm, Sun noon–6pm.

HISTORICAL MUSEUM OF TELEMARK, Brekkepark. Tel. 35-52-35-94.

This museum displays some 20 old buildings from different districts of Telemark. The museum collections feature folk and national costumes, textiles, handcrafts, and wood carving. Some buildings are furnished with authentic pieces, ranging from the Renaissance to Victorian days. A special section is centered on Henrik Ibsen. A restaurant and open-air theater are found in the park.

Admission: 10 kroner ($1.70) adults, 5 kroner (90¢) children.
Open: May 12–June 23, Tues–Sat 10am–2pm, Sun noon–6pm; June 24–Sept 1, Tues–Sat noon–4pm, Sun noon–6pm. **Closed:** Sept 2–May 11.

WHERE TO STAY

MODERATE

HØYERS HOTELL, Kongensgate 6, N-3701 Skien. Tel. 35-52-05-40. Fax 35-52-26-08. 70 rms (all with bath). MINIBAR TV TEL
$ Rates (including breakfast): Mon–Thurs (except midsummer), 650 kroner ($112.50) single; 840 kroner ($145.30) double. Midsummer and Fri–Sun year-round, 450 kroner ($77.90) single; 550 kroner ($95.20) double. AE, DC, MC, V.
Parking: Free.

Long a traditional favorite, the hotel was originally built in 1900, and it stands today in the center of gardens stretching to the water. A 3-minute taxi ride from the rail station, it offers some of the best bedrooms in town, each comfortably and attractively furnished. Five are reserved for nonsmokers. Facilities include a dance restaurant (see "Where to Dine," below), a fully licensed bar, and a solarium.

RICA IBSEN HOTEL, Kongensgate 33, N-3700 Skien. Tel. 35-52-49-00.
Fax 35-52-61-86. 199 rms (all with bath). TV TEL
$ Rates (including breakfast): Winter, Sun–Thurs 900 kroner ($155.70) single, 1,050 kroner ($181.70) double; Fri–Sat 525 kroner ($90.80) single, 700 kroner ($121.10) double. Late June to mid-Aug, 440 kroner ($76.10) single; 630 kroner ($109) double. AE, DC, MC, V. **Parking:** 50 kroner ($8.70).

This well-rated hotel stands near Brekkepark where Ibsen is said to have received much of his early inspiration. A stylish hotel, considered the best in town, it was designed and built in 1979 of red brick and panes of insulated glass. It boasts a high-ceilinged interior jammed with many trees, whose combined effect is to create the impression of a vast greenhouse burgeoning with seasonal flowers and plants. Each room is well furnished and maintained and decorated with contemporary styling. Twelve rooms are reserved for nonsmokers and there is also a no-smoking area in the breakfast room. It's located in the center of Skien, a quarter mile from the rail station.

Dining/Entertainment: The hotel restaurant is Susannah's (see "Where to Dine," below), and there's also a dance bar (Susi), a bar lounge, and a nightclub.
Services: Room service.
Facilities: Indoor swimming pool, sauna, solarium, private garage.

WHERE TO DINE
EXPENSIVE

BODEN SPISERI, Langbryggene 5. Tel. 35-52-61-70.
Cuisine: NORWEGIAN. **Reservations:** Required.
$ Prices: Appetizers 60–90 kroner ($10.40–$15.60); main dishes 150–200 kroner ($26–$34.60). AE, DC, MC, V.
Open: Dinner only, Mon–Fri 3:30pm–midnight, Sat 6pm–midnight, Sun 3–9pm.

Although it was established as recently as 1987, this quickly became known as the town's most charmingly old-fashioned restaurant. A 10-minute walk south of the station, it's in a clapboard-sided building originally erected as a harborfront warehouse more than a century ago. The staff speaks English. For their specialties, try cured filet of venison in thin slices as an appetizer, followed perhaps by filet of reindeer with juniper berries, and a medley of fresh vegetables: broccoli, cauliflower, and grilled tomatoes. The preferred dish of many clients is a three-fish casserole studded with mussels and shrimp and served in a wine-based cream sauce.

MODERATE

SUSANNAH'S RESTAURANT, in the Rica Ibsen Hotel, Kongensgate 33. Tel. 35-52-49-90.
Cuisine: NORWEGIAN. **Reservations:** Recommended.
$ Prices: Appetizers 50–90 kroner ($8.70–$15.60); main dishes 120–230 kroner ($20.80–$39.80). AE, DC, MC, V.
Open: Daily 11am–11pm.

This restaurant is filled with the same bounty of trees and flowers that adorn the "greenhouse lobby." It is a big-windowed restaurant that later in the evening becomes a dance place where older, conservative couples come to have a good time. Fresh fish, lamb, and Norwegian beef are featured. It's on the ground floor of the Rica Ibsen Hotel (see "Where to Stay," above), in the center of Skien a quarter mile from the train station.

RESTAURANT COUENAR, in the Høyers Hotell, Kongensgate 6. Tel. 35-52-05-40.
Cuisine: NORWEGIAN. **Reservations:** Recommended.

$ Prices: Appetizers 50–60 kroner ($8.70–$10.40); main dishes 82–130 kroner ($14.20–$22.50); smørbrød 22–75 kroner ($3.80–$13). AE, DC, MC, V.
Open: Daily 11am–11pm.

This is a good choice for moderately priced food served at the oldest and most traditional hotel in town half a mile south of the rail station. During the day many locals drop in for smørbrød. But the kitchen also prepares substantial meals, including excellent Norwegian fish dishes, such as river salmon and fjord shrimp. Reindeer and game are also featured. After 10pm, the restaurant becomes a nightclub. Hotel guests are admitted free, but others pay a 75 kroner ($13) cover charge.

EASY EXCURSIONS IN TELEMARK

From Skien you can take a famous boat tour up the *Telemark Canal. Both the MS *Victoria* and MS *Ringnes* run the stretch between Skien and Dalen, deep in Telemark, a 10-hour trip on this inland waterway, at a cost of 200 kroner ($34.60) or half price for children. You go through lock and lake. Departures from Skien are at 8:30am. When the boat stops to negotiate the locks, you are allowed to get off and stroll the canal banks. Bookings are possible in Skien through **Telemarksreiser,** Nedre Hjellegate 18 (tel. 35-53-03-00).

Once at Dalen, Route 37 leads north to **Rjukan,** the center of southern Norway. This sleepy town once played a major role in world history, as depicted in the Kirk Douglas film *The Heroes of Telemark*. In 1943 the valley was heavily guarded by Nazi troops, as the Germans were working here on the first atomic bomb experiments to develop "heavy water." Norwegian saboteurs, in the face of incredible odds, managed to climb down the steep, icy gulch to blow up the Vemork Plant of Norsk Hydro. The towering peak of Mount Gausta at 6,000 feet prevents the sun from shining on Rjukan for 5 months every year.

Alternatively, near Dalen, you can join the E76 leading east back to Oslo. But stop at the ✪ **Heddal Stave Church,** in Heddal, 4 miles west of Notodden (tel. 33-62-02-50 for information). This is the largest of the preserved Norwegian stave churches. Erected in 1147 and dedicated to the Virgin Mary, it has fine carved portals with traditional dragon-and-tendril ornamentations and fantastic human figures. The structure is 85 feet high and 65 feet long, and contains a dozen columns inside. It is considered the architectural wonder of southern Norway. The bishop's chair inside is from the pre-Christian era, probably 900 to 1,000 years old. It is open May 15 to June 20, daily from 10am to 5pm; June 21 to August 20 daily from 9am to 7pm; and August 21 to September 15, daily from 10am to 5pm (closed September 16 to May 14). Admission is 15 kroner ($2.60) for adults; free for children.

2. ARENDAL

149 miles SW of Oslo, 43 miles E of Kristiansand S

GETTING THERE   By Train   Four trains a day arrive from Oslo, requiring a change of trains at Nelaug. Trip time, including the transfer, is 4½ hours.

By Bus   There is direct bus service daily from Oslo, with two or three stops along the way; trip time is 4 hours. The name of the bus leaving from Oslo is Sorlandsekpressen, destination Oslo/Arendal/Kristiansand S.

By Hydrofoil   From June 15 to August 15, hydrofoils link Arendal and Oslo. Departures are at 9am from in front of the Rådhuset in Oslo and take 5 hours. The cost is 230 kroner ($39.80) each way. The scenery is breathtaking.

By Car   Take the E18 west from Oslo.

ESSENTIALS   Arendal Tourist Office, in the heart of the Old Town at Nedre Tyholmsveien 7B (tel. 37-12-21-93), is open Mon–Sat 10am–5pm (June, Aug), daily 10am–8pm (July), and Mon–Fri 9am–4pm (Sept–May).

The administrative center of the Aust-Agder district, this southern port city was once known as "the Venice of Scandinavia," because of its canals. But following a disastrous fire, they were turned into wide streets. Its sheltered harbor is one of the most colorful along the coast.

For the best look at old Arendal, go to **Tyholmen** in the center, with its handsomely preserved wooden houses of the 18th century. In summer, the harbor, **Pollen**, is filled with boats and people, as this is one of the most popular centers for domestic tourism in Norway. Many Norwegians come here to take boat trips among the neighboring skerries, and they also traverse the delta of the Nid River.

WHAT TO SEE & DO

ARENDAL RÅDHUS, Rådhusgata 19. Tel. 37-12-29-80.

The Rådhus, or Town Hall, in the center of town, still houses the administrative offices of the city. It's better known as the second-largest timber building in Norway and the country's single tallest timber structure. Built in 1815, the building has some 300 antique portraits, most of them painted in the 19th century, the largest such collection in Norway.

Admission: Free. English-language guided tours cost 15 kroner ($2.50).
Open: Mon–Fri 9am–3pm.

AUST-AGDER MUSEET, Parkveien 16. Tel. 37-12-24-22.

This museum, established in 1832, is one of the largest and most important in the area. Showcasing the folklore of the region, it is filled with memorabilia of the history of the town, mainly artifacts relating to its seafaring heyday. The museum is 1 mile north of the town center; to reach it, follow the signs in the direction of Oslo.

Admission: 10 kroner ($1.70) adults, 5 kroner (90¢) children.
Open: Mon–Fri 9am–3pm, Sat 9am–1pm, Sun noon–3pm.

WHERE TO STAY

MODERATE

TYHOLMEN HOTEL, Teaterplassen 2, N-4800 Arendal. Tel. 37-12-68-00. Fax 37-12-68-01. 54 rms (all with bath). TV TEL

$ Rates (including breakfast): Sept–May, Sun–Thurs, 1,040 kroner ($179.90) single; 1,200 kroner ($207.60) double. June–Aug and Fri–Sat year-round, 580 kroner ($100.30) single; 830 kroner ($143.60) double. AE, DC, MC, V. **Parking:** Free.

Enjoying dramatic views of one of Norway's loveliest harbors, this hotel is the most interesting in town. Architecturally, it was inspired by the 1800s, the heyday of the sailing vessels that put Arendal on the map. It offers handsomely furnished bedrooms—try for a harbor view. The hotel has an outdoor restaurant, Bryggekanten, which is a summer favorite, and a lounge bar, Åtte Glass. There is also a coffee shop, Spiseriet. Its glamorous restaurant, Tre Seil, and its steak house, Ruffan, are recommended separately (see "Where to Dine," below). It's a 2-minute walk south of the bus station.

WHERE TO DINE

EXPENSIVE

RUFFAN, in the Tyholmen Hotel, Teaterplassen 2. Tel. 35-12-68-00.

Cuisine: STEAKS. **Reservations:** Recommended.
$ Prices: Appetizers 72–129 kroner ($12.50–$22.30); main dishes 180–260 kroner ($31.10–$45). AE, DC, MC, V.
Open: Dinner only, daily 6–11pm.

For people with hearty appetites, this is one of the favored dining spots, a 2-minute walk south of the bus station. It is a cozy cellar kind of place located in the Tyholmen Hotel (see "Where to Stay," above). Its decor is strongly nautical. Appetizers might include a West Indian–inspired dish of minced shrimp with chili peppers toasted with grilled avocado and served with soy sauce. The chef makes excellent stuffed baked potatoes and such standards as lamb chops and chicken. But most guests visit for the specialty, grilled steak.

TRE SEIL, in the Tyholmen Hotel, Teaterplassen 2. Tel. 35-12-68-00.
   Cuisine: NORWEGIAN. **Reservations:** Recommended.
$ **Prices:** Appetizers 62–119 kroner ($10.70–$20.60); main dishes 160–175 kroner ($27.70–$30.30). AE, DC, MC, V.
   Open: Dinner only, Mon–Sat 6–11pm, Sun 1–6pm.

"Three Sails" is the most prestigious restaurant in town, a 2-minute walk south of the bus station. Its decor is nautical, and big windows look out over the moored yachts and boats in the harbor. You can enjoy excellent cuisine and formal service. Try, for example, salmon with sour-cream sauce and Norwegian crabs; large prawns gratinée with garlic, herbs, and butter; or an unusual dish from north-central Norway—grilled filet of reindeer saddle served next to grilled filet of salmon and accompanied by sautéed mushrooms and vegetables.

MODERATE

BOTANICA, in the Phønix Hotel, Fiergangen 1. Tel. 35-12-51-60.
   Cuisine: NORWEGIAN/FRENCH. **Reservations:** Not required.
$ **Prices:** Appetizers 62–75 kroner ($10.70–$13); main dishes 85–195 kroner ($14.70–$33.70); smørbrød 25–85 kroner ($4.30–$14.70). DC, MC, V.
   Open: Mon–Sat 10am–midnight, Sun 1pm–midnight.

The decor, as befits the restaurant's name, has plants and a red-and-green color scheme. Lunch here is unpretentious and simple. Many prefer to take one of the selections of smørbrød. There is also an impressive salad bar priced at 55 kroner ($9.50) if you'd like to make a meal of it. Dinner is more elaborate, including such dishes as prawn cocktail or escargots bourguignons to get you going, followed by such tasty dishes as deep-fried scrod or pepper steak. The place is a quarter mile from the train station.

EASY EXCURSIONS

In the bay of Arendal, **Merdøy Island** is like getting caught in a time capsule. It is virtually intact architecturally from its prosperous 19th-century seafaring days. Today its clapboard-sided houses still have their allure.

There are no restaurants, only a small café, and a lovely bathing beach.

The **Merdøgård Museum** (tel. 35-12-24-22) on the island is run by the Aust-Agder Museum (see "What to See and Do," above). This museum is a perfectly preserved early 19th-century house, with the furnishings intact, of a long-departed sea captain. A guardian lives on the premises to show you around. It's open from June 24 through August 15, Monday through Friday 9am to 3pm; Saturday 9am to 1pm, and Sunday noon to 3pm. Admission is 10 kroner ($1.70) for adults and 5 kroner (90¢) for children.

To reach the island, take a ferry departing for Pollen at Arendal's harborfront. Departures are three or four times daily, and the boat makes stops at two or three other islands before reaching Merdøy. The ferry costs 15 kroner ($2.60) each way, and the trip takes 20 minutes. The tourist office (see above) will supply you with exact departure times, which change frequently.

Twelve miles west of the center of Arendal is Grimstad, site of the **Grimstad Bymuseum-Ibsenhuset,** Henrik Ibsen Gate 14 (tel. 35-14-46-53), in the center of town. Henrik Ibsen worked in this town at a pharmacy, while pressing his suit for the pharmacist's daughter. Ibsen wrote his first play, *Catalina*, here. The Grimstad museum includes the old pharmacy and Ibsen's house. It's open May to September, daily from 11am to 5pm. Admission 15 kroner ($2.60) for adults, 5 kroner (90¢) for children.

Farther afield, **Northhølm,** Route 7, (N-4890 Grimstad), 4 miles west of Grimstad, is open June to August, Monday through Friday, from 9am to 3pm, charging 10 kroner ($1.70) admission for all. The former home of Knut Hamsun is today privately owned, so hours are subject to change. Winning the Nobel Prize in 1918, this writer, called the "Balzac of Norway," purchased this residence, which he turned into a model farm. His novels gave a vivid portrait of 19th-century Norwegian values. Much memorabilia of Hamsun remains in the house. His works are still very popular in Germany, almost more so than they are in Norway.

3. KRISTIANSAND S

327 miles SE of Bergen, 213 miles SW of Oslo

GETTING THERE By Plane Kristiansand Municipal Airport is located at Kjevik, 10 miles out of town. Both Braathens SAFE and SAS airlines service the town.

By Train Five trains a day connect Kristiansand S with Oslo, taking 4 to 5 hours, depending on the train.

By Bus Kristiansand S is connected by bus to Oslo, with one departure daily, taking 7½ hours.

By Ferry International ferries link Kristiansand S to Hirtshals, in the northern part of Jutland in Denmark. Ferries cross once or twice daily, depending on the time of year, taking 4 hours.

By Car Take the E18 west from Oslo or the E18 east from Stavanger.

ESSENTIALS Go to **Turist information,** Henrik Wergelandsgata 17 (tel. 38-29-53-69).

People heading to Bergen and the fjord country often arrive in Norway at Kristiansand S (not to be confused with Kristiansund N in the north). The biggest city and an important port of Sørtlandet (the south coast), Kristiansand S has been called "the pearl of the Norwegian Riviera."

Founded by King Christian in 1641, Kristiansand S is a busy port and industrial center, yet it has many charming old streets and antique houses clustered cozily together. Water surrounds the city.

Kristiansand S is the largest town in the south and Norway's largest ferry port. **Kvadraturen,** "the quadrant," is known for its right-angled street plan that was influenced by the Renaissance period's strict adherence to form. **Markens** is the town's pedestrian precinct and meeting place.

WHAT TO SEE & DO

It's worth a visit to **Christiansholm Fort,** at Østre Havn, dating back to 1674 and often the center of local handcraft exhibitions; the **Fish Quay,** with its troughs and tanks full of live fish; and **Kristiansand Cathedral,** Kirkegaten (tel. 38-22-13-11), one of the largest churches in Norway. Built in the neo-Gothic style, it was dedicated in 1885. It is open May 1 to September 1, daily from 10am to 4pm.

One of the oldest and most beautiful parish churches in the area is **Oddernes Klokkerkontor,** Jegersbergeveien 6, a mile from the town center, reached by bus no. 22. The midnave and choir were built around 1040. May to early September, the church is open Monday through Friday from 9am to 2pm; to visit it at other times, call 38-29-01-87 at least a day in advance.

VEST AGDER FYLKES-MUSEUM, Hongsgård, Vigeveien 22B. Tel. 38-29-02-28.

One of the largest open-air museums in Norway, it contains nearly 30 farm and city buildings moved to the site. Some are equipped with provincial furnishings, glass, and stoneware. It's a short distance from the town center.

Admission: 20 kroner ($3.50) adults, 10 kroner ($1.70) children.

Open: June 20–Aug 20, Mon–Sat 10am–6pm, May 21–June 19 and Aug 21–Sept 14, Sun noon–6pm. **Closed:** Sept 15–May 20.

KRISTIANSAND NATURAL HISTORY MUSEUM AND GIMLE BOTANICAL GARDENS, Gimleveien 23. Tel. 35-29-23-88.

The present exhibitions, which opened in 1990, show part of the natural history of south Norway. Colorful minerals are on display, and the museum includes a botanical garden with Norway's largest collection of cacti. From the center of town, motorists can take the E18 east, crossing a bridge, then following the signs. Bus no. 22 also runs there.

Admission: 20 kroner ($3.50) adults, 5 kroner (90¢) children.
Open: June 20–Aug 20, Tues–Fri 10am–6pm, Sat–Mon noon–6pm; Aug 21–Dec 20 and Jan 2–June 19, Tues–Fri 10am–3pm, Sun noon–5pm (closed Sat and Mon).

KRISTIANSAND ZOO, along E18. Tel. 35-24-62-00.

This 100-acre **zoo** contains many exotic specimens, including some Nordic species. Animals roam in large open enclosures. Norway's biggest **amusement park** is on the same grounds, containing "Troll Valley," a playland, a bobsled track, a water slide, an amphitheater, and a goldmining town. It's located 7 miles east of Kristiansand S on the E18.

Admission: 120 kroner ($20.80) adults, 100 kroner ($17.30) children.
Open: Zoo and park, summer, daily 10am–7pm; winter, daily 10am–4pm.

NEARBY ATTRACTIONS

The **Setesdalsbanen,** Grovane, N-4700 Vennesla (tel. 38-25-64-82), runs a steam train along 3 miles of narrow-gauge track. The locomotive, dating from 1901, starts its run at Grovane, 12½ miles from Kristiansand, leaving at 11:30am, 1pm, and 2:30pm on Sunday from mid-June to the end of August. Fares are 40 kroner ($6.90) for adults and 20 kroner ($3.50) for children along the Grovane-Beihklen run. Take bus 30 or 31.

The countryside surrounding Kristiansand consists of rolling meadows, birch-clad hills, deep valleys, and mountain moors; you'll see the nicest scenery along the E18 either going east or west.

West of **Mandal** stands Norway's southernmost point, with a lighthouse dating from 1655. The Dutch town of **Flekkefjord** on the Grise Fjord, with its low wooden buildings, narrow twisting streets, and warehouses, is particularly worth seeing.

A drive along Route 9 toward the **Setesdal and Sirdal moors** offers a variety of scenery and the chance to view traditional Norwegian life.

Kristiansand's sightseeing boat, **MB Maarten,** tours the idyllic offshore islands leaving mid-June to mid-August, weekdays from the fish quay at 10am. In July there are also departures at 1 and 3pm.

WHERE TO STAY

Some hotels in Kristiansand offer up to a 40% discount from mid-June to mid-August. The prices include rooms with bath or shower, toilet, and breakfast—sometimes even the luncheon buffet. Always inquire if any midsummer discounts are offered.

EXPENSIVE

CALEDONIAN, Vestre Strandgate 7, N-4601 Kristiansand S. Tel. 38-22-91-00. Fax 38-22-59-90. 205 rms (all with bath). MINIBAR TV TEL

$ Rates (including breakfast): Winter, Sun–Thurs 1,040 kroner ($179.90) single; 1,395 kroner ($241.30) double. Fri–Sat year-round and midsummer, 625 kroner ($108.10) single; 750 kroner ($129.80) double. AE, DC, MC, V. **Parking:** 50 kroner ($8.70).

This prestigious place is considered the largest full-service hotel in the southern part of Norway, and it's within walking distance of the rail station, bus station, and ferry terminal. Theater, cinema, and shopping areas are nearby. The hotel was built in 1968, near the fish market in the center of town. Bedrooms are modern and stylish.

Dining/Entertainment: The Hotel's Café Jens is a popular all-day rendezvous for light meals and drinks. Other nighttime venues include the DaCapo Piano Bar, the

CD Discothèque, and Telford's Pub. The most preferred restaurant is an upmarket steak and fish dining room, Camilla's, serving dinner only nightly from 6 to 11:30pm. Full meals here cost from 280 kroner ($48.40) each.

Services: Room service, laundry, babysitting.

Facilities: Garage, wheelchair access.

MODERATE

ERNST PARK HOTEL, Rådhusgaten 2, N-4601 Kristiansand S. Tel. 38-22-14-00. Fax 38-22-03-07. 113 rms (all with bath), 4 suites. MINIBAR TV TEL

$ Rates (including breakfast): Winter, 995–1,045 kroner ($172.10–$180.80) single; 1,045–1,150 kroner ($180.80–$199) double. Summer, 510–995 kroner ($88.20–$172.10) single; 710–1,150 kroner ($122.80–$199) double. Year-round, 1,200–1,400 kroner ($207.60–$242.20) suite. AE, DC, MC, V. **Parking:** 40 kroner ($6.90).

⭐ Since this hotel opened more than 130 years ago, it has been the traditional favorite for a southern stopover. The building was completely renovated in 1988, but care was taken to preserve its classic look. The hotel is beautifully run and managed, and the bedrooms have contemporary styling. It's 200 yards from the central bus terminal, rail station, and ferry dock.

Dining/Entertainment: The Restaurant Børsen, the main restaurant of the hotel, has an English atmosphere, whereas the Brasserie Børsen is an informal indoor/outdoor restaurant with a conservatory. The lobby bar, near the conservatory, is called the Børsen Bar, and the hotel's nightclub is Night Ca. On the ground floor is a pub, Øl & Vinstuen.

Services: Laundry/dry cleaning, secretarial services, room service; helpful reception desk.

Facilities: Basement parking (request when booking room), *biblioteket* (library).

RICA FREGATTEN HOTEL, Dronningensgata 66–68, N-4601 Kristiansand S. Tel. 35-22-15-00. Fax 35-22-01-19. 47 rms (all with bath). TV TEL
$ Rates: 520 kroner ($90) single; 680 kroner ($117.60) double. AE, DC, MC, V.
Its proximity to the water makes the Rica Fregatten a good choice for boaters. The bedrooms have modern furnishings. The establishment's social center is a pub with brass embellishments. It's in the town center, a half mile from the rail station.

INEXPENSIVE

HOTEL BONDEHEIMEN, Kirkegaten 15, N-4611 Kristiansand S. Tel. 35-22-44-40. 36 rms (all with bath). TEL
$ Rates (including breakfast): 360–480 kroner ($62.30–$83) single; 550–650 kroner ($95.20–$112.50) double. AE, MC, V.

🅢 In the town center near the bus terminal, the Bondeheimen has comfortable and adequately furnished rooms. It has lounges and a cafeteria offering Norwegian food until 5pm.

WHERE TO DINE

MODERATE

BAKGÅRDEN, Tollbødgate 5. Tel. 35-22-79-55.
Cuisine: NORWEGIAN/INTERNATIONAL. **Reservations:** Required. **Bus:** 1, 10.
$ Prices: Appetizers 54–87 kroner ($9.30–$15.10); main dishes 147–198 kroner ($25.40–$34.30). AE, DC, MC, V.
Open: Dinner only, Mon–Sat 6–11pm.
This is a well-established and good restaurant lying in a turn-of-the-century building whose interior is accented with bare wooden tables, wooden chairs, and a collection of oil-burning lamps. The food is an unending festival celebrating southern Europe,

with additional flair added by borrowing recipes from around the world, although dishes are tailored to local palates. Appetizers might include a Mexican ceviche, or snails in garlic butter followed by grilled filet of pheasant with grapes or tenderloin steak with mussels. The food is the most imaginative in town.

SJØHUSET (Sea House), Østre Strandgate 12A. Tel. 35-22-62-60.
   Cuisine: NORWEGIAN/FRENCH. **Reservations:** Required in midsummer.
   Bus: 1, 10.
$ **Prices:** Appetizers 48–78 kroner ($8.30–$13.50); main dishes 136–180 kroner ($23.50–$31.10). AE, DC, MC, V.
   Open: June–July, daily 11:30am–midnight; Aug–May, Mon–Sat 3pm–midnight.
Set directly on the harborfront in the center of town, this restaurant is in a century-old former salt warehouse whose oxblood-red clapboard-sided walls are still distinctive. Inside, you see the massive structural beams of its original construction and a blazing stone-sided fireplace. In summer, guests prefer the waterfront terrace instead. Specialties include an assorted platter of fish, including anglerfish, salmon, and a third type determined by the day's catch. The fish is poached in white wine and served with a Noilly Prat sauce along with shrimp, asparagus, and rice. The meat specialty is chateaubriand with a béarnaise sauce.

---

4. STAVANGER

100 miles S of Bergen, 376 miles W of Oslo

GETTING THERE   By Plane   Flights land at **Stavanger International Airport** at Sola from Copenhagen, Esbjerg/Århus, Gothenburg, London, Newcastle, Glasgow, Aberdeen, Amsterdam, and Paris, with good connections from Bergen and Oslo. An SAS bus will take you to the town center for 35 kroner ($6.10).

By Train   Three trains a day cross Norway from Oslo to Stavanger, taking 9 hours.

By Bus   Stavanger has bus links with Kristiansand S, running once or twice a day, taking 5 hours.

By Ferry   In Bergen, it's better to take a car-ferry, the *Kystveien* to Stavanger, as driving there will take you on a 93-mile detour that includes three ferry crossings. In Bergen tickets are issued on board, but vehicles must be booked in advance (tel. 56-14-11-00 between 8am and 3:30pm, June through August). The fare is 170 kroner ($29.40) for adults, 100 kroner ($17.30) for children. The ferry lands on Randaberg, north of Stavanger. Route 14 takes you the rest of the way there.

By Car   From Kristiansand S, continue west until you reach the end of the E18 in Stavanger.

By Hydrofoil   From Bergen, connections take 4½ hours. There are two or three daily departures. The cost is 410 kroner ($70.90) per person. You get a 50% discount with a Nordturist Pass.

ESSENTIALS   Stavanger Tourist Board, Jernbaneveien 3 (tel. 51-53-51-00), next to the railroad station, is open Mon–Sat 9am–4pm and Sun 10am–4pm (June–Aug) and Mon–Fri 9am–4pm and Sat 9am–1pm (Sept–May).
   A **Stavanger Card,** free to visitors staying in Stavanger hotels, offers a 50% reduction on Flaggrutens high-speed boats between Stavanger and Bergen, the same discount on all scheduled buses in Stavanger, and a 25% discount on Westamaran services. The card, obtainable only in Stavanger (ask at your hotel) also grants discounts at cinemas, theaters, museums, car-rental agencies, city and fjord sightseeing trips, and the Kongeparken amusement park.

Stavanger, Norway's fourth-largest town, on the Ryfylkefjord, has always been a bustling seaport with a thriving fish-canning industry. Today it's also the oil capital of Norway—although this has made it more cosmopolitan, it remains a charming seaport amid beautiful surroundings. The old marketplace, where fish and vegetables have been sold since the 9th century, is set against the cathedral, dating from 1125.

WHAT TO SEE & DO

Gamle Stavanger, in the heart of town, is filled with some 150 wooden houses, cobblestone streets, climbing steep hills, fascinating quays, and well-preserved old homes, some with picket fences. It is considered northern Europe's best-preserved wooden-house settlement. It was built at the end of the 17th and 18th centuries with money brought home by seafarers.

The **Stavanger Domkirke,** Haakon VII's Gate 7 (tel. 51-52-42-61), which faces the marketplace, is one of Norway's most outstanding medieval monuments, dedicated around 1125. After a fire in 1272, the Gothic-style chancel was added. The magnificent 1125 Norman-style nave remains. See the fine memorial tablets and the enormous pulpit, outstanding examples of baroque art in Norway.

It's open mid-May to mid-September, Monday through Saturday from 9am to 6pm and on Sunday from 1 to 6pm; in other months, daily from 9am to 2pm. Sunday service is at 11am.

There are many opportunities to see goldsmiths, silversmiths, and enamel workers at their crafts in and around Stavanger. For details, call the tourist office (see above).

The **Stavanger Museum** consists of three parts. Archeology, zoology, cultural history, and local crafts exhibits can be seen at **Musegate 16.** The **Maritime Museum,** Nedre Strandgaten 17-19, contains exhibits on local shipbuilding, the Stavanger harbor, the herring room (1808–70), a general store, and a ship/store owner's dwelling. The **Canning Museum,** Øvre Strandgaten 88, is a restored canning factory with production facilities intact. For information about the museums phone 51-52-60-35. All are open mid-June to mid-August, Tuesday through Sunday from 11am to 3pm; the remainder of the year, Sunday only from 11am to 3pm. Admission is 10 kroner ($1.70) for adults, free for children.

The **Ullandhaug Tower,** 3 miles from the center, offers a gorgeous view. Take bus no. 10, departing from St. Olavsgården and heading for Gosen. The one-way fare is 10 kroner ($1.70) for adults, 5 kroner (90¢) for children.

The **Norwegian Emigration Center,** Bergjelandsgata 30 (tel. 51-50-12-67), is headquarters for tracing ancestors who went from Norway to America. Its archives are based on sources from throughout Norway. It's open Monday through Friday from 9am to 3pm.

The **Ledaal Mansion,** Eiganesveien 45 (tel. 51-52-60-35), built in 1800, is now the local royal residence, belonging to the Stavanger Museum. The mansion can be reached by walking a quarter of a mile from the railroad station. It is open June 15 to August 15, Tuesday through Saturday from 11am to 5pm and on Sunday from 11am to 4pm. Admission is 10 kroner ($1.70) for adults, 5 kroner (90¢) for children.

Breidablikk, Eiganesveien 40A (tel. 51-52-60-35), built in 1880, is another mansion run by the Stavanger Museum. It keeps the same hours and charges the same admission as Ledaal (see above).

TOURS

For a 2-hour tour of the **sights of Stavanger,** including the Ryfylkefjord, a guided motorcoach tour leaves June 1 to August 31, Monday through Saturday at 1pm from in front of the cathedral (visited at the end of the tour). Cost is 105 kroner ($18.20) for adults, 75 kroner ($13) for children.

For an economy tour, take bus no. 10, 12, 17, 40, or 50 from St. Olavsgården for a circular ride around Stavanger. The 1-hour ride costs 12 kroner ($2.10).

Pulpit Rock (Prejestolen) is a landmark towering 1,800 feet above Lysefjord; it can be visited on either a boat or a bus trip, or by a car-ferry trip and short drive, taking about 45 minutes from Stavanger. If you want to climb the rock, you can take a boat-bus-hiking jaunt; a pathway leads to the top. The boat trip, lasting 2½ to 3 hours, leaves Skagen Quai in June, July, and August, on Monday, Tuesday, Thursday, Friday, and Saturday at 10am. From July 1 to August 20, there is also an afternoon departure on Monday, Tuesday, Thursday, Friday, and Saturday at 3pm, plus a sailing on Wednesday and Sunday at 5pm. The trip costs 175 kroner ($30.30) for adults, 85 kroner ($14.70) for children.

For the same prices, a longer trip is offered from July 1 to August 20, leaving on Monday and Saturday at 10:30am from Skagenkaien, and lasting about 8 hours. The tour starts by boat to Meling and continues by bus to Prekestolhytten (the Pulpit Cabin), from which a 4-hour hike up and down Pulpit Rock allows you to see the impressive Lysefjord. There is no tour leader.

Finally, you can take any number of independent fjord excursions on one of the ships of the White Fleet that traverse the Ryfylkefjord. For tickets and help with itineraries, go to the **Clipperkontoret,** Skagenkaien 18 (tel. 51-52-02-67).

WHERE TO STAY

A branch of the **Stavanger Tourist Board** (see above) is in the Kulturhuset, Sølveberggata 2 (tel. 51-53-51-00). This office will book you in a private home for 150 kroner ($26) per person and up.

EXPENSIVE

ATLANTIC HOTEL, Olav V's Gate 3, N-4001 Stavanger. Tel. 51-52-75-20. Fax 51-56-10-75. 345 rms (all with bath), 5 suites. MINIBAR TV TEL **Bus:** 5, 15.

$ **Rates** (including breakfast): Winter, Sun–Thurs 995–1,195 kroner ($172.10–$206.70) single; 1,395 kroner ($241.30) double; from 3,200 kroner ($553.60) suite. Winter, Fri–Sat 690 kroner ($119.40) single; 750 kroner ($129.80) double; from 2,200 kroner ($380.60) suite. Late June to mid-Aug, 625 kroner ($108.10) single; 750 kroner ($129.80) double; from 2,200 kroner ($380.60) suite. AE, DC, MC, V. **Parking:** Free.

The Atlantic Hotel has long been the leading choice of Stavanger hotels. A member of Reso Hotels, a Norwegian chain, it stands right in the heart of town a 2-minute walk from the Old Town, with views of Lake Breiavatnet. The hotel offers spacious and well-furnished bedrooms and a wide array of nightlife and dining facilities. Some of its restaurants are recommended below (see "Where to Dine"), including its Antique Restaurant for gourmet dining. It also has two English-style pubs and bars, including King Oscar and Alexander, plus the Café Ajax.

VICTORIA HOTEL, Skansegate 1, N-4001 Stavanger. Tel. 51-52-05-26. Fax 51-52-71-48. 107 rms (all with bath). A/C MINIBAR TV TEL **Bus:** 5, 15.

$ **Rates** (including breakfast): Winter, Sun–Thurs 1,050 kroner ($181.70) single; 1,300 kroner ($224.90) double. Winter, Fri–Sat 550 kroner ($95.20) single; 800 kroner ($138.40) double. Midsummer, 420 kroner ($72.70) single; 530 kroner ($91.70) double. AE, DC, MC, V. **Parking:** Free.

Dating from 1900, this hotel was built with a brick facade and an ornate portico in the city center. In spite of modernizations, much original ornamentation has remained, and it is still the preferred choice for the traditionalist. It is a first-class hotel with views over the harbor. Bedrooms are well furnished and attractively styled, and extra amenities include trouser press and hairdryer. Furnishings, color schemes, and room sizes vary in different parts of the hotel. The Prinsen Steakhouse offers the finest beef in town, and you can arrive early for an apéritif in the English-style Queen Victoria Bar. Parking is available near the hotel, and services include laundry facilities and room service. It's directly east of Stavanger Cathedral.

MODERATE

RESO KNA HOTELLET, Lagårdsveien 61, N-4001 Stavanger. Tel. 51-52-85-00. Fax 51-53-59-97. 200 rms (all with bath). TV TEL **Bus:** 5, 15.

$ **Rates:** Winter Sun–Thurs (including half board), 895 kroner ($154.80) single; 1,145 kroner ($198.10) double. Winter Fri–Sat (including breakfast), 550 kroner ($95.20) single; 590 kroner ($102.10) double. Summer (including breakfast), 650 kroner ($112.50) single; 750 kroner ($129.80) double. AE, DC, MC, V. **Parking:** Free.

Centrally located 900 yards from the marketplace, this Reso Hotels chain member was built in 1959 and completely modernized in the 1980s, with a new wing added with 120 extra rooms. Bedrooms are comfortably and attractively furnished with many amenities. Two floors are reserved for nonsmokers. The hotel is known for its food, which is served in the Grillen, the Havestuen, and the Stavangerstuen. Guests meet for drinks in the Bar Ocean. The hotel also has a garage for 130 cars.

SAS ROYAL HOTEL, Lokkeveien 26, N-4001 Stavanger. Tel. 51-56-70-00, or toll free 800/221-2350 in the U.S. Fax 51-56-74-60. 204 rms (all with bath), 8 suites. A/C MINIBAR TV TEL **Bus:** 5, 15.

$ Rates (including breakfast): Summer and Fri–Sat year-round, 720 kroner ($124.60) single; 800–900 kroner ($138.40–$155.70) double. Winter, 1,250 kroner ($216.30) single; 1,400–1,500 kroner ($242.20–$259.50) double. Year-round, 1,650–3,350 kroner ($285.50–$579.60) suite. AE, DC, MC, V. **Parking:** 60 kroner ($10.40).

⭐ Erected in 1987, this distinctively stylish hotel is a 4-minute walk from the town center. Its bedrooms, which rise in balconied tiers above an atrium core, are designed with either an Italian, Japanese, American, or Scandinavian flair. The American rooms are clean, conservatively elegant, and comfortable; Italian units appear to have emerged straight from a Milanese design showcase; and the Japanese rooms are complete with lacquer screens and lots of light-grained pieces (even rice-paper window blinds). Rooms contain hairdryers and trouser presses.

Dining/Entertainment: The Harlequin Lobby Restaurant, serving three meals a day, has a seven-story-high ceiling. The Chicago Bar & Grill is recommended separately (see "Where to Dine," below).

Services: SAS airline check-in in the hotel lobby, "office-for-a-day" center, 24-hour room service, 3-hour express laundry.

Facilities: Swimming pool, sauna, solarium, whirlpool.

INEXPENSIVE

BERGELAND GJESTGIVERI, Vikedalsgate 1A, N-4012 Stavanger. Tel. 51-53-41-10. Fax 51-53-35-99. 29 rms (20 with shower, no toilet). **Bus:** 5, 15.

$ Rates (including breakfast): 320 kroner ($55.40) single without shower, 390 kroner ($67.50) single with shower; 420 kroner ($72.70) double without shower, 490 kroner ($84.80) double with shower. AE, DC, MC, V.

Ⓢ This is a modest, comfortable, boardinghouse in a quiet residential area 450 yards from the rail station. Not all rooms have showers, and those that do contain no private toilets. However, shared hallway bathrooms are adequate. Throughout the day you can order simple platters of food, perhaps bacon and eggs, though there is no restaurant. Breakfast, however, is served. The place is simple and basic, but clean and comfortable—and definitely considered a bargain for Stavanger.

ROGALANDSHEIMEN GJESTGIVERI, Musegatan 18, N-4010 Stavanger. Tel. 51-52-01-88. 15 rms (none with bath). **Bus:** 78.

$ Rates (including breakfast): Winter, 340–390 kroner ($58.80–$67.50) single; 400–490 kroner ($69.20–$84.80) double; from 600 kroner ($103.80) family room. Summer, 240–290 kroner ($41.50–$50.20) single; 350–390 kroner ($60.60–$67.50) double; from 400 kroner ($69.20) family room. No credit cards. **Parking:** Free.

Ⓢ This 1890 Norwegian guesthouse has old-fashioned, comfortable rooms, three of which are rented as family rooms. Although only breakfast is available, the guesthouse is only a few minutes walk to the center of Stavanger and 10 minutes from the rail station.

WHERE TO DINE

EXPENSIVE

ANTIQUE, in the Atlantic Hotel, Olav V's Gate 3. Tel. 51-52-75-20.
  Cuisine: FRENCH/NORWEGIAN. **Reservations:** Required.

$ Prices: Appetizers 50–90 kroner ($8.70–$15.60); main dishes 75–200 kroner ($13–$34.60); fixed-price lunch platters 70–85 kroner ($12.10–$14.70). AE, DC, MC, V.

Open: Mon–Fri noon–midnight, Sat 5pm–midnight, Sun noon–11pm.

Next to the city park with views of the small lake, Breiavatnet, this is one of the finest dining rooms in Stavanger. In spite of the name, Antique, the decor of the restaurant is modern. Every night the restaurant offers four different types of freshly caught fish. The chef is also known for his lamb dishes. Mostly the cookery is French inspired, but also includes some Norwegian specialties. The restaurant has a cellar filled with exotic wines. Clients are sometimes invited downstairs for a look at the vintages and a taste of "this or that." Try the pepper steak Armagnac flambé, finishing with crêpes Suzette.

CHICAGO BAR & GRILL, in the SAS Royal Hotel, Lokkeveien 26. Tel. 51-56-70-00.

Cuisine: AMERICAN. **Reservations:** Not required. **Bus:** 5, 15.

$ Prices: Appetizers 58–92 kroner ($10–$15.90); main dishes 157–245 kroner ($27.20–$42.40). AE, DC, MC, V.

Open: Dinner only, Mon–Sat 6–11:30pm.

On the lobby level of the SAS Royal Hotel (see "Where to Stay," above), this sophisticated dining spot is a 4-minute walk from the old town center. The decor is inspired by the U.S. gangster era of Chicago in the 1930s. The kitchen imports the biggest volume of U.S.-bred beef in the region, including prime tenderloin, sirloin steaks, and filet steaks—the full range of American beef grilled to your request and served on a sizzling hot platter. For appetizers, try either the Manhattan clam chowder or seafood Charleston. Some patrons come just to drink at the adjoining bar where a half-liter of beer costs 39 kroner ($6.70).

JANS MATS & VINHUS, Breitorget. Tel. 51-52-45-02.

Cuisine: NORWEGIAN/FRENCH. **Reservations:** Required. **Bus:** 2, 5, 12.

$ Prices: Fixed-price menu 375 kroner ($64.90); appetizers 70–85 kroner ($12.10–$14.70); main dishes 210–255 kroner ($36.30–$44.10). AE, DC, MC, V.

Open: Dinner only, Mon–Sat 6–10:30pm.

★ This establishment, considered by some as the best restaurant in Stavanger, occupies a well-accessorized underground cellar whose stone walls were originally laid in 1850. The color scheme includes candlelight, and the wine list is extensive. The daily menu changes frequently but is likely to include such dishes as salmon à la nage, pan-fried filet of monkfish on a bed of fresh spinach with a saffron-cream sauce, and tenderloin of beef with a fresh mushroom sauce and fresh vegetables. For dessert, choose from an assiette of homemade ice creams and sherbets with fresh seasonal berries. You can reach it by walking north of the rail station. It's in a small shopping complex in the city center.

STRAEN, Nedre Strandgate 15. Tel. 51-52-61-00.

Cuisine: SEAFOOD. **Reservations:** Recommended. **Bus:** 5, 15.

$ Prices: Fixed-price menu 295 kroner ($51); appetizers 80–105 kroner ($13.80–$18.20); main dishes 175–225 kroner ($30.30–$38.90). AE, DC, MC, V.

Open: Dinner only, Mon–Sat 5–11pm.

Straen is a leading seafood restaurant in Stavanger, its windows opening onto a view of the harbor. In a complex that includes a café, outdoor restaurant, small bar, and nightspot, it is reached by crossing a cobblestone courtyard. You can order homemade cream of fish soup, fresh mussels in white wine, steamed or fried halibut, or baked filet of codfish, all delectable. A famous specialty is the "fish symphony." Straen is located in the town center on the west side of the main quay.

MODERATE

SJØHUSET SKAGEN, Skagenkaien 16. Tel. 51-52-61-90.

Cuisine: INTERNATIONAL. **Reservations:** Recommended.

$ Prices: Fixed-price menu 150 kroner ($26); appetizers 35–75 kroner ($6.10–$13); main dishes 80–167 kroner ($13.80–$28.90). AE, DC, MC, V.
Open: Daily 11:30am–11:30pm.

This first-class 300-year-old restaurant at the harbor, packed with antiques, is in an old timbered boathouse. The decor is nautical, ranging from models of sailing ships to fishing equipment. Naturally, the kitchen specializes in fresh fish dishes. Begin with the French fish soup. Try the grilled Norwegian salmon or sautéed filets of monkfish. You can also order meat dishes, including grilled filet of reindeer and steak chasseur.

INEXPENSIVE

LA GONDOLA, Nytorget 8. Tel. 51-53-42-35.
   Cuisine: ITALIAN. **Reservations:** Recommended. **Bus:** 5, 15.
$ Prices: Appetizers 35–55 kroner ($6.10–$9.50); main dishes 75–130 kroner ($13–$22.50); pizzas from 55 kroner ($9.50). AE, DC, MC, V.
   Open: Mon–Sat 11:30am–11pm, Sun 1–11pm.
La Gondola is a steak house and pizzeria connected to the more formal Mongolian Grill and Chinese Restaurant. Its best value is its Sunday buffet from 1 to 7pm, costing 98 kroner ($17) for adults and 54 kroner ($9.30) for children. The pizza oven is fired for lunch as well as dinner, and you can also order pizzas to take out. If you'd like more formal food, order one of the grills, including a T-bone steak Floretine style. Other Italian dishes are offered, including scaloppine alla boscaiola (filets of pork with tomato sauce and mushrooms) and veal with shrimp, asparagus, and béarnaise sauce. It's in the town center across from the police station.

EVENING ENTERTAINMENT

COBRA CLUB, in the Atlantic Hotel, Olav V's Gate 3. Tel. 51-52-75-20.
   A leading nighttime rendezvous, the Cobra Club bills itself as an "adult disco and sets a minimum age of 24." You can dance to the latest music or drink in a black and mirrored setting. Technically, this is a members-only club, but visitors to Stavanger are often allowed in. It's in the cellar of the Atlantic Hotel (see "Where to Stay," above), a 2-minute walk from the Old Town. The club is open Tuesday through Saturday from 10pm to 4am, and no jeans are allowed. Beer costs 39 kroner ($6.70), and mixed drinks go for 45 kroner ($7.80).
   Admission: 50 kroner ($8.70) to nonhotel residents; 40 kroner ($6.90) to residents.

AMADEUS DANCING, in the Atlantic Hotel, Olav's V's Gate 3. Tel. 51-52-75-20.
   A "grown-up" dance bar for people over 25 years old, Amadeus Dancing is adjacent to the Antique Restaurant (see "Where to Dine," above). Part of a supper club, it's open for disco dancing only 4 nights a week: Tuesday, Wednesday, Friday, and Saturday from 9pm to 2am. The minimum age is 24, and no jeans are allowed. A beer will set you back 40 kroner ($6.90); mixed drinks, 45 kroner ($7.80).
   Admission: 50 kroner ($8.70); free for diners at the Antique Restaurant.

5. HAUGESUND

35 miles N of Stavanger, 65 miles S of Bergen, 295 miles W of Oslo

GETTING THERE   By Plane   Flights arrive at Haugesund Airport in Karmøy. There are seven daily flights from Oslo, and two flights each from Bergen and Stavanger.

By Train   There is no train service. The nearest rail depot is at Stavanger, from which you can reach Haugesund by express boat (see below).

By Bus   There is bus service daily from Oslo to Haugesund, taking 9 hours.

By Car   The E76 Haukeli Highway, known as "the road of the conquerors," runs from Oslo in the east across Norway, ending at Haugesund. You go through varied and dramatic scenery from the fields of eastern Norway, through the valleys of Telemark, over the mountain plateau of Haukeli at a height of 3,300 feet, finally reaching the fjords of western Norway. Allow about 10 hours for this drive, one of the most famous in Europe.

By Boat   Three express boats make the 1½-hour run daily from Stavanger to Haugesund. Express boats from Bergen also make the trip, taking 3 hours.

ESSENTIALS   For information, **Reisetrafikkforeningen for Haugesund og Distriktene,** Smedesundet 90 (tel. 52-72-52-55), is open daily 9am–7pm (June–Aug) and Mon–Fri 9am–4pm and Sat 9am–1pm (Sept–May).

Haugesund is a shipping port with century-old herring fisheries. Hardangerfjord lies to the north and Ryfylke to the south.

Haugesund is also a center of the offshore oil industry which has brought prosperity to the region. In many ways it's a typical urban center of western Norway, lying in the region between the Hardangerfjord and Boknafjord. There's always something interesting to watch in the Haugesund harbor, plus opportunities for fishing trips and excursions into the nearby fjord district.

WHAT TO SEE & DO

The most interesting sight is the raspberry-pink **Town Hall,** with its flower-filled square and cobbled marketplace. The gift of a local shipping magnate, the Haugesund Town Hall continues a Norwegian tradition of having local artists decorate municipal buildings.

About a mile north of the town is a 55-foot granite obelisk, **Haraldhaugen,** erected in 1872 in honor of Norway's unification under Harald Fairhair (his burial mound is believed to be on the spot). Each county (*fylke*) contributed a stone pillar.

For information about any number of day tours from Haugesund, go to the **tourist bureau** (see above). A popular round-trip excursion is to Norway's most populous island, **Karmøy,** south of Haugesund. This island was strategic in Viking times, and is linked to the mainland today by Karmsund Bridge, one of the largest in the country.

WHERE TO STAY
MODERATE

AMANDA HOME HOTEL, Smedasundet 93, N-5500 Haugesund. Tel. 51-71-74-00. Fax 51-72-86-21. 77 rms (all with bath), 3 suites. A/C MINIBAR TV TEL

$ Rates (including breakfast): July and Fri–Sat year-round, 550 kroner ($95.20) single; 700 kroner ($121.10) double. Sun–Thurs Aug–June, 885 kroner ($153.10) single, 1,090 kroner ($188.60) double. Year-round, 1,450 kroner ($250.90) suites. AE, DC, MC, V. **Parking:** Free.

This imposingly old-fashioned building, constructed in the early 20th century, was once an office building. In 1989 its owners converted it to a hotel and added an extension with details similar to the old structure. It has as a central theme the history of motion pictures and the Amanda statuette, Norway's equivalent of Hollywood's Oscar. Each bedroom has an individual decor based on stills and movie posters. Most of the comfortable and attractively furnished rooms open onto the waterfront. Breakfast is the only meal served. The Amanda is in the town center on the waterfront.

RICA MARITIM HOTELL, Asbygata 3, N-5500 Haugesund. Tel. 52-71-11-00. Fax 51-71-64-77. 247 rms (all with bath), 2 suites. MINIBAR TV TEL

$ Rates (including breakfast): Weekdays (except midsummer), 850 kroner ($147.10) single; 1,220 kroner ($211.10) double. Midsummer and weekends year-round, 480 kroner ($83) single; 720 kroner ($124.60) double. Year-round, 1,320 kroner ($12.50) suites. AE, DC, MC, V. **Parking:** Free.

The most distinctively modern building along the harbor, this is the biggest hotel in Haugesund. In August it's especially crowded with people connected with the Norwegian film industry—the Amanda (the Norwegian equivalent of the Oscar) is presented here at the hotel. The most palatial quarters at the hotel are named for Norwegian actress Liv Ullmann. Bedrooms are plush and modern with many amenities. A bar to the left of the lobby has a pianist playing till midnight. The hotel has a dining room seating 200 and a nightclub.

INEXPENSIVE

HOTEL NEPTUN, Haraldsgate 207, N-5500 Haugesund. Tel. 51-71-44-55. Fax 51-71-44-55. 58 rms (all with bath). TV

$ Rates (including breakfast): Sat–Sun 450 kroner ($77.90) single; 650 kroner ($112.50) double. Summer discounts available with Norway Fjord Pass: 360 kroner ($62.30) single; 540 kroner ($93.40) double. AE, DC, MC, V. **Parking:** Free.

Located 5 minutes from the express boat terminal for Stavanger and Bergen in the commercial center of town at the end of the main street, this hotel does not have a bar or formal restaurant, but does offer an unlicensed cafeteria serving good-tasting Norwegian dishes. On the top floor is a terrace with a view of the harbor. Bedrooms are simply but comfortably furnished, and everything is well maintained.

WHERE TO DINE
EXPENSIVE

CAPTAIN'S SALOON/CAPTAIN'S CABIN, Skjoldavn 1. Tel. 51-72-14-40.

Cuisine: NORWEGIAN. **Reservations:** Required on weekends.

$ Prices: Appetizers 68–88 kroner ($11.80–$15.20); main dishes 155–189 kroner ($26.80–$32.70). AE, DC, MC, V.

Open: Restaurant, Mon–Sat 6pm–midnight, Sun 2–11pm; pub, Mon–Sat noon–1am, Sun 1pm–1am.

The stone-sided building containing the best restaurant in Haugesund is owned by the Norwegian Seamen's Association. Its cellar, the Captain's Saloon, has an array of maritime artifacts salvaged from old ships. It offers a savory fish-inspired menu. You can sample freshly caught Norwegian fish prepared in many different ways. The bill of fare is likely to feature scampi, anglerfish, catfish, or shark. At street level is the pub, the Captain's Cabin, where a half-liter of beer costs 35 kroner ($6.10). You can visit for lunch, ordering smørbrød, costing 28 kroner to 75 kroner ($4.80 to $13), or a hot platter of food. It's located at the top of a flight of steps leading down to the harbor, a 1-minute walk from the town center.

LOTHE'S MAT & VINHUS, Skippergate 4. Tel. 51-71-22-01.

Cuisine: NORWEGIAN/FRENCH. **Reservations:** Required.

$ Prices: Appetizers 50–85 kroner ($8.70–$14.70); main dishes 170–200 kroner ($29.40–$34.60); fixed-price lunch 138 kroner ($23.90); fixed-price dinner 348 kroner ($60.20). AE, DC, MC, V.

Open: Restaurant, daily noon–midnight; pub, daily 6pm–1:30am.

This two-floor restaurant a 2-minute walk from the harbor is housed in a white clapboard-sided building constructed as a private home 150 years ago. The restaurant is on one side and a pub is on the other. To travel between the two sections, you need to go outside, "five steps down and five steps up." The decor of both places is old-fashioned and illuminated with a combination of oil lamps and candles. Service is polite and efficient in the restaurant, where you can order such specialties as lobster salad, poached filet of sole with butter sauce, and pepper steak. In the pub, a glass of wine costs from 28 kroner ($4.80).

BERGEN

In western Norway the landscape takes on an awesome beauty, with iridescent glaciers, deep fjords that slash into rugged, snowcapped mountains, roaring waterfalls, and secluded valleys that lie at the end of corkscrew-twisting roads. From Bergen the most beautiful fjords to visit are: Hardanger (best at blossom time, May and early June) to the south; Sogne, Norway's longest fjord, immediately to the north; and the Nordfjord north of that. A popular excursion on the Nordfjord takes visitors from Loen to Olden along rivers and lakes to the Brixdal Glacier.

If you have time, on Hardangerfjord you can stop over at one of the fjord resorts like Ulvik or Lofthus. From many vantage points it's possible to see the Folgefonn Glacier, Norway's second-largest ice field, which spans more than 100 square miles. Other stopover suggestions include the summer resorts (winter ski centers) of Voss and Geilo. For resorts in the fjord district, refer to Chapter 19.

Bergen, with its many sightseeing attractions, good hotels, boardinghouses, and restaurants, and its excellent boat, rail, and coach connections, makes the best center in the fjord district.

It's an ancient city that looms large in Viking sagas. Until the 14th century it was the seat of the medieval kingdom of Norway. The Hanseatic merchants established a major trading post here, holding sway until the 18th century.

Bergen has survived many disasters, including several fires and the explosion of a Nazi ship during World War II. It's a town with important traditions in shipping, banking, and insurance, and its modern industries are expanding rapidly.

1. ORIENTATION

ARRIVING

BY PLANE **Bergen Airport** (tel. 55-99-82-50), at Flesland, is 12 miles south of the city. It offers intercontinental routes to and from New York, Los Angeles, Seattle, Chicago, and Montréal.

Frequent **airport bus** service makes a circuit from the airport to the SAS Royal Hotel, Braathens SAFE's office at the Hotel Norge, and the city bus station. For

WHAT'S SPECIAL ABOUT BERGEN

Historic Districts
- [ ] Bryggen, where warehouses and commercial buildings of the Hanseatic trading days are re-created along the harborfront.

Museums
- [ ] Bryggens Museum, a cultural-history museum based on extensive excavations of Bergen of the Middle Ages.
- [ ] Gamle Bergen, an open-air museum with around 35 wooden houses—a living example of Bergen architecture during the 18th and 19th centuries.

Ancient Buildings
- [ ] Rosenkrantz Tower, erected as a fortified official residence by a feudal lord in the 1560s.

Musical Shrines
- [ ] Troldhaugen, home of the great composer Edvard Grieg for 22 years, where some of his best-known works were composed.

Scenic Tours
- [ ] "Norway in a Nutshell," a do-it-yourself tour that encapsulates the best of Norway in 12 hours.
- [ ] An express steamer to Gudvangen to view Norway's longest fjord, Sognefjord.

Special Events/Festivals
- [ ] Bergen International Festival, a cavalcade of music, drama, opera, ballet, and folklore, including performances of Grieg's works (late May to early June).
- [ ] Fana Folklore, a tradition-laden country festival staged throughout the summer.

---

departure times, inquire at the airlines or at the Tourist Information Center. One-way fare on the airport bus is 36 kroner ($6.20).

BY TRAIN Day and night trains arrive from Oslo and stations en route. For information, phone 55-31-93-05. Trip time is 8½ hours from Oslo to Bergen.

BY BUS Express buses travel to Bergen from Oslo, Trondheim, Ålesund, and the Nordfjord area. Trip time from Oslo is 11 hours.

BY CAR A toll is charged on all vehicles driven into the city center Monday through Friday from 6am to 10pm. A single ticket costs 5 kroner (90¢); a book of 20 tickets, 90 kroner ($15.60).

To cross from Oslo to Bergen is a mountain drive filled with dramatic scenery. Since the country is split by mountains, there is no direct road. You can take the southern route, the E76, going through mountain passes until the junction with Route 47; then head north to the ferry crossing at Kinsarvik that goes across the fjords to the E16 leading west to Bergen. The northern route is via Highway 7, going through the resort of Geilo, to the junction with Route 47; then head south to Kinsarvik. After crossing on the ferry, you arrive at the E16. Head west to reach Bergen.

Passengers with lots of time often spend 2 or 3 days driving from Bergen to Oslo, enjoying the fjords and snowcapped peaks along the way, stopping off to photograph waterfalls, fjord villages, perhaps ancient stave churches.

To cut down on this driving time, motorists in a greater rush can cut through a new tunnel—almost 7 miles long, the longest in northern Europe—going between Flåm (see Chapter 19) and Gudvangen. From Gudvangen, motorists can follow E16 southwest to Bergen.

TOURIST INFORMATION

For information, maps, and brochures about Bergen and its environs, the **Tourist Information Center,** Torgalmenningen 12 (tel. 55-32-14-80), is open Mon–Sat 8:30am–9pm and Sun 10am–7pm (May–Sept) and Mon–Sat 10am–4pm (Oct–Apr).

The Tourist Information Center will also help you find accommodations (see below), exchange foreign currency, and cash traveler's checks when banks are closed.

CITY LAYOUT

Bergen is squeezed between mountain ranges and bounded by water. The center of the city lies between the harbor, **Bryggen** (see below), the railway station, and the main square, called **Torgalmenningen.**

Like Rome, Bergen is said to have grown up around seven hills. For the best overall view, take the funicular to **Fløien** (see "More Attractions," below). The northern-most section of the city is **Sandviken,** filled with old warehouses. The area south of central Bergen has recently developed at an incredible rate.

In the center of Bergen, you will be caught up in the charm of cobblestone streets as you explore the quayside with its medieval houses, the open-air fish market, the city center with its colonnaded shops and cafés, and **Gamle Bergen,** where you can step back to the early 19th century.

2. GETTING AROUND

BY BUS

The **Central Bus Station** (Bystasjonen), Strømgaten 8 (tel. 55-32-67-80), is the terminal for all buses serving the environs of Bergen and the Hardanger area, as well as the airport bus. The station has luggage storage, shops, and a restaurant. City buses are all marked with their destination and route number.

Special 48-hour **tourist tickets** for unlimited travel are available at the Tourist Information Center at Torgalmenningen 12. The pass allows unlimited transit on the yellow-sided city buses, which traverse a 3-mile radius of the city center. The cost of the pass is 60 kroner ($10.40), and it's in effect from May through September.

BY TAXI

Taxis are readily available at the airport, or phone 55-99-09-90. A ride from the Bergen Airport to the center costs 180 kroner ($31.10). Sightseeing by taxi costs 250 kroner ($43.30) per hour.

BY CAR

For convenient indoor parking, try the **Bygarasjen Busstation** (tel. 55-32-53-60), a large indoor garage near the bus and train stations, about a 5-minute walk from the city center. It's open 24 hours a day and charges 8 kroner ($1.40) per hour from 7am to 5pm. From 5pm to 7am, the charge is only 5 kroner (90¢) per hour. You can park 24 hours a day for 80 kroner ($13.80).

RENTAL CARS   **Hertz** in Bergen is at the airport (tel. 55-32-79-20, or toll free 800/654-3001 in North America) and downtown at Nygårdsgate 89 (same phone). For a 2-day rental, the smallest car is a Ford Fiesta or Peugeot 205, costing 475 kroner ($82.20) per day, plus 5 kroner (90¢) per kilometer, plus 20% tax.

Avis is at the Bergen Airport (tel. 55-22-76-18) and downtown at Lars Hillesgate

20 (tel. 55-32-01-03, or toll free 800/331-2112 in North America). For a 2-day rental, their smallest car is a Ford Fiesta or a Renault 5, costing 500 kroner ($86.50) per day, plus 5.25 kroner ($0.90) per kilometer, plus 20% tax.

Budget is at the Bergen Airport (tel. 55-22-75-27) or downtown at Tide Auto, A/S Nordnes (tel. 55-31-14-13, or toll free 800/472-3323 in North America). Budget is the least expensive of the three companies, with a Ford Fiesta costing from 400 kroner ($69.20) per day, plus 4 kroner (70¢) per kilometer, plus 20% tax, plus an optional collision-damage waiver.

BY FERRY

You can take a ferry across the harbor Monday through Friday from 6:45am to 4:15pm, but they don't run on Saturday and Sunday. One-way fares are 10 kroner ($1.70) for adults, 5 kroner (90¢) for children.

COASTAL STEAMERS

Express boats leave from Munkebryggen (tel. 55-23-87-00 for departure information), heading for Hardangerfjord and Sunnhordland. Steamers leave from Möhlenspriskaien (tel. 55-32-40-15) heading for Sognefjord, Nordfjord, and Sunnfjord. Local steamers serving the island and fjords immediately north of Bergen dock at the inner harbor on the left-hand side of the fish market at Strandkaiterminalen.

FAST FACTS   BERGEN

American Express   In Bergen, it's represented by **Winge Travel Bureau,** Christian Michelsens Gate 1–3 (tel. 55-90-12-90), open Monday through Friday from 8:30am to 4pm and on Saturday from 8:30am to 1pm.

Area Code   In 1993, Bergen, along with the rest of Norway, switched from an area code system to new 8-digit dialing.

Banking   Banking transactions can be handled at **Fokus Bank,** Rådstuplass 2–3 (tel. 55-21-86-00), with branches at Bystasjonen (Central Bus Station) Strømgate 8, and Strandgaten 77.

Bookstores   One of the best, with a wide range of books in English, is **F. Beyer Bok-og Papirhandel,** Strandgaten 4 (tel. 55-32-11-80).

Business Hours   **Banks** are usually open Monday through Friday from 8:15am to 3:30pm, and on Thursday until 6pm. Most **businesses** are open Monday through Friday from 9am to 4pm. **Shops** are generally open on Monday through Friday from 9am to 4:30pm, and on Thursday until 7pm (sometimes also on Friday until 7pm); Saturday hours are 9am to 2pm.

Car Rentals   See "Getting Around" in this chapter.

Currency Exchange   There is a currency exchange at the Bergen Airport. In town, you can exchange money at any one of several banks. When banks are closed, you can exchange money at the tourist office (see above).

Dentists   Emergency care is available at Lars Hillesgate 30 (tel. 55-32-11-20), daily from 10 to 11am and 7 to 9pm.

Doctors   For medical assistance, call **Accident Clinic,** Lars Hillesgate 30 (tel. 55-32-11-00), which is open 24 hours. Your hotel will also set up an appointment with an English-speaking doctor if it is not an emergency.

Drugstores   A 24-hour pharmacy is **Apoteket Nordstjernen,** at the Central Bus Station (tel. 55-31-68-84).

Embassies and Consulates   Most foreign nationals will have to contact their embassies in Oslo if they have a problem; only Great Britain maintains a consulate in Bergen, at Strandgaten 18 (tel. 55-32-07-11).

Emergencies   For the police, dial **002;** to report a fire, call **001;** for an ambulance, dial **003.**

Eyeglasses A good optician is **Optiker Svabø,** Strandgaten 18 (tel. 55-31-69-51).

Hairdressers and Barbers One of the best in town is **Kappers Frisørsalong,** Neumannsgata 18 (tel. 55-23-01-25).

Hospitals A medical center, **Accident Clinic,** open day and night, is located at Lars Hillesgate 30 (tel. 55-32-11-00). There is a general hospital, but you can't go directly there. You must either go through the Accident Clinic or call Skyebesøkformidling (Sick Call Help) at 55-32-33-20.

Laundry and Dry Cleaning Try **Jarlens Vaskoteque,** Lille Øvregate 17 (tel. 55-32-55-04), near Hotel Victoria in a little alley about 50 yards northeast of the 17th-century church, Korskirken, off Kong Oscars Gate.

Libraries The **Bergen Public Library,** Strømgaten (tel. 55-31-97-50), is open in July and August on Tuesday, Wednesday, and Friday from 9am to 3pm, on Monday and Thursday from 9am to 7pm, and on Saturday from 9am to 1pm; the rest of the year, Monday through Friday from 9am to 8pm and on Saturday from 9am to 2pm.

Lost Property This problem is handled by **Hittegodskontoret,** Nygaten 1 (tel. 55-21-66-00), open Monday through Saturday from 9am to 2pm.

Luggage Storage and Lockers Both locker rental and luggage storage are available at **Jernbanestasjonen** (railway station), Strømgaten 1 (tel. 55-31-96-40), open daily from 6:45am to 11pm.

Photographic Needs Go to **Foto Knutsen,** Galleriet, Torgalmenningen 8 (tel. 55-31-16-78), next to the Tourist Information Center.

Police Call 002.

Post Office The main post office, Byparken (by the City Park; tel. 55-31-81-00), is open Monday through Friday from 8am to 5pm (to 7pm on Thursday) and on Saturday from 9am to 1pm.

Religious Services Lutheran services are held in English in the **Domkirken,** the Norwegian state church's cathedral, Kong Oscars Gate (tel. 55-31-04-70), at 9:30am on Sunday in June, and August. **St. Paul's Roman Catholic Church,** Christiesgate 16 (tel. 55-32-54-10), celebrates masses in English on Sunday at 10am.

Shoe Repairs Try **Mr. Minit Sko & Nøkkelservice,** Galleriet, Torgalmenningen (tel. 55-96-06-40), open Monday through Saturday from 9am to 8pm.

Taxes Bergen imposes no city taxes other than the value-added tax on all goods and services in Norway.

Taxis See "Getting Around" in this chapter.

Telegram Dial 0138 to send a telegram. The **Telegraph Building,** Byparken (by the City Park), is open Monday through Saturday from 8am to 8pm and on Sunday from 2 to 7pm.

Telephone Public telephones take 1-kroner (20¢) coins. Local calls cost 2 kroner (30¢). To call abroad, dial 0115.

3. ACCOMMODATIONS

Easily found at Torgalmenningen 12, the **Tourist Information Center** (see above) not only books guests into hotels but secures accommodations in private homes. More than 30 families take in guests during the summer months.

The booking service costs 15 kroner to 30 kroner ($2.60 to $5.20), but prospective guests also pay a deposit that is deducted from the final bill. Rooms in private homes are usually priced at 145 to 170 kroner ($25.10 to $29.10) single, 235 to 295 kroner

($40.65 to $51) double, with no service charge. Breakfast costs 40 kroner ($6.90) extra.

Rates quoted for the hotels below include service and tax. Many deluxe and first-class places lower their tariffs considerably on weekends and at midsummer. Reductions, when available, are cited under rates.

EXPENSIVE

HOTEL ADMIRAL, C. Sundtsgata 9, N-5001 Bergen. Tel. 55-32-47-30.
Fax 55-23-30-92. 107 rms (all with bath). MINIBAR TV TEL **Bus:** 2, 3, 4.

$ Rates (including breakfast): Summer, 615 kroner ($106.40) single; 780 kroner ($134.90) double. Winter, 950–1,100 kroner ($164.40–$190.30) single; 1,290–1,390 kroner ($223.20–$240.50) double. AE, DC, MC, V.

This is one of the town's most unusual hotels, originally built in 1906 but renovated in 1987. The bedrooms are comfortable, well furnished, and also well maintained. There is an attractive piano bar off the lobby, as well as a first-class restaurant, Emily, known for its seafood.

HOTEL NORGE, Ole Bulls Plass 2–4, N-5001 Bergen. Tel. 55-21-01-00,
or toll free 800/223-5652 in North America. Fax 55-21-02-99. 347 rms (all with bath), 12 suites. MINIBAR TV TEL **Bus:** 2, 3, 4.

$ Rates (including breakfast): Weekdays 1,225–1,490 kroner ($211.90–$257.80) single; 1,490–1,640 kroner ($257.80–$283.70) double. Weekends 670–910 kroner ($115.90–$157.40) single; 920–1,050 kroner ($159.20–$181.70) double. From 3,100 kroner ($536.30) suite. Children under 12 stay free in their parents' room. DC, MC, V.

In the city center, near Torgalmenningen, the Norge has been a Bergen tradition since 1885. In World War II the Gestapo made it their headquarters, but it reopened as a hotel after the war. Because of structural flaws, it was torn down and rebuilt in 1962. It is a favorite with visiting celebrities. Each accommodation has TV with in-house videos and some have oversize bathtubs big enough for two. Some units open onto private balconies overlooking the begonia-ringed borders of a nearby park. The hotel is a member of the Steingenberger Reservations System.

Dining/Entertainment: The hotel offers the widest array of drinking and dining establishments in Bergen, including its gourmet restaurant, Grillen, and Ole Bull, an informal place for lunch and light meals. Homemade pastries are served in the morning at Bakdakinen, and à la carte meals are available there at lunch and dinner. The Café 003 is a night café. Drinking places include the Balcony Bar, Koggen Piano Bar, and Bull's Eye, the last an English pub on the corner. The Pandora Night Club is a leading nightlife venue.

Services: 24-hour room service, laundry, babysitting.

Facilities: Swimming pool, solarium, sauna, Jacuzzi, gym, garage.

NEPTUN, Walckendorffsgate 8, N-5001 Bergen. Tel. 55-90-10-00. Fax
55-23-32-02. 121 rms (all with bath), 6 suites. MINIBAR TV TEL **Bus:** 1, 5, 9.

$ Rates (including breakfast): 1,055–1,225 kroner ($182.50–$211.90) single; 1,295–1,495 kroner ($224–$258.60) double; from 1,650 kroner ($285.50) suite. AE, DC, MC, V. **Parking:** 50 kroner ($8.70). **Closed:** Dec 25–Jan 2.

Close to the harbor and fish market, this is a modern and handsomely decorated hotel in the city center, known for its collection of Norwegian modern art. The owner, Hans Inge Bruarøy, is head of the Bergen Arts Society and collecting paintings is his passion. The hotel was recently expanded, a new floor of upgraded accommodations added. Many prefer its comfortable and spacious accommodations to all others in Bergen. Each room is attractively styled and well maintained.

Dining and drinking facilities include the Restaurant Lucullus, the Ludvig Bar, and the Bistro Pascal. There is a 20-car basement garage.

SAS ROYAL HOTEL, Byrggen, N-5000 Bergen. Tel. 55-31-80-00, or toll
free 800/221-2350 in the U.S. Fax 55-32-48-08. 267 rms (all with bath), 8 suites. A/C MINIBAR TV TEL **Bus:** 1, 5, 9.

$ Rates (including breakfast): 1,195–1,445 kroner ($206.70–$250) single; 1,260–

1,600 kroner ($218–$276.80) double; from 2,100 kroner ($363.30) suite. AE, DC, MC, V. **Parking:** 85 kroner ($14.70).

Opened in 1982, this hotel stands on ancient ground, having been built on the fire-ravaged site of old warehouses that stood here since 1170. Houses along Bryggen (The Quay) were reconstructed in the old style and SAS maintained the spirit of the architecture in creating this excellent hotel. During construction, many Hanseatic artifacts were unearthed and are on display.

The hotel is completely modernized with what is considered almost the finest services and amenities in Bergen. Bedrooms are beautifully maintained, each with lithographs and comfortably upholstered furniture. Sixty rooms are reserved for nonsmokers. The hotel attracts mainly commercial clients in winter.

Dining/Entertainment: Guests can dine in the hotel's Gourmet Restaurant, after enjoying drinks in the cocktail lounge. There is also a Café Royal. The hotel has a nightclub, Engelen, and a pub, Madam Felle.

Services: Business service center, secretarial service, 24-hour room service, laundry, babysitting, SAS Euroclass check-in.

Facilities: Indoor swimming pool, sauna, health club, private basement garage, car-rental desk.

MODERATE

AUGUSTIN HOTEL, C. Sundtsgate 24, N-5004 Bergen. Tel. 55-23-00-25. Fax 55-23-31-30. 38 rms (all with bath). MINIBAR TV TEL **Bus:** 1, 5, 9.
$ **Rates** (including breakfast): Summer and Fri–Sat year-round, 475–600 kroner ($82.20–$103.80) single; 650–800 kroner ($112.50–$138.40) double. Winter Sun–Thurs, 595–680 kroner ($102.90–$117.60) single; 790–880 kroner ($136.70–$152.20) double. AE, DC, MC, V. **Parking:** 30 kroner ($5.20).

The Augustin Hotel, a 5-minute walk west of the harborfront, has been a family favorite since 1917. The rooms were remodeled in the mid-1980s, and are pleasantly furnished. A good Norwegian breakfast is served in the residents' breakfast room. The hotel also has a traditional pâtisserie, Augusta, serving hot and cold dishes, and an attractive bistro for light lunches, hot meals, salads, and sandwiches. It serves only beer and wine.

GRAND HOTEL TERMINUS, Kong Oscars Gate 71, N-5018 Bergen. Tel. 55-31-16-55. Fax 55-31-85-76. 130 rms (all with bath). TV TEL **Bus:** 2, 4.
$ **Rates** (including breakfast): 900 kroner ($155.70) single; 1,050–1,250 kroner ($181.70–$216.30) double. AE, DC, MC, V.

A Bergen landmark since 1928, this hotel, located between the bus and rail stations, offers quality and tradition. Bedrooms are modernized and furnished attractively in light Nordic pastels, containing such extra amenities as radios and hairdryers. The hotel offers an excellent restaurant and often presents Norwegian buffets. Guests gather in the lounge after dinner for coffee.

HOTELL HORDAHEIMEN, C. Sundtsgate 18, N-5004 Bergen. Tel. 55-23-23-20. Fax 55-23-49-50. 69 rms (60 with bath). TV TEL **Bus:** 1, 5, 9.
$ **Rates** (including breakfast): 575 kroner ($99.50) single without shower, 690 kroner ($119.40) single with shower; 860 kroner ($148.80) double with shower. AE, DC, MC, V.

Operated by the Bondeungdomslaget i Bergen, an association that sponsors cultural and folklore programs, the hotel has become a Bergen base for many young people from nearby districts. The lounge and dining rooms have been tastefully designed and coordinated, and the bedrooms—simple and utilitarian—are immaculate. A room without bath has a hot- and cold-water basin. Reasonably priced meals are served in the restaurant one flight up. No alcohol is served.

ROSENKRANTZ, Rosenkrantzgate 7, N-5003 Bergen. Tel. 55-31-50-00. Fax 55-31-14-76. 129 rms (all with bath). MINIBAR TV TEL **Bus:** 1, 5, 9.
$ **Rates** (including breakfast): 820 kroner ($141.90) single; 1,000 kroner ($173) double. AE, DC, MC, V. **Parking:** 85 kroner ($14.75).

This 1921 hotel stands near Bryggen in the city center. The lobby, sheathed in white marble, leads to a comfortable dining room and bar. Rooms are pleasantly furnished, all updated and equipped with modern amenities including hairdryers. Twenty rooms are reserved for nonsmokers. Facilities include a TV lounge, a piano bar, a restaurant, Harmoni, and a nightclub, Rubinen, with live music. Next door to the hotel is a covered parking garage.

SUITELL EDVARD GRIEG, Sandsliåsen 50, N-5049 Sandsli. Tel. 55-22-99-01. Fax 55-22-99-85. 148 rms (all with bath). **Bus:** From Platform 16 at the Bergen bus station, take any bus marked "Milde/Hjellstad (Øvre Nestun)."

$ **Rates** (including breakfast): Midsummer and Fri–Sat year-round, 1,140 kroner ($197.20) single or double. The rest of the year, Sun–Thurs, 1,220 kroner ($211.10) single or double occupancy. AE, DC, MC, V. **Parking:** Free.

Norway's first all-suite hotel lies 12 miles south of Bergen and 3 miles from the Bergen airport. Opened in 1987, it has a modern design, with walls of glass illuminating the lobby. Each suite has a bedroom, bathroom, and lounge, and each is luxuriously furnished. Three suites are equipped for wheelchair guests. Monday through Friday guests can dine in the intimate and expensive Mozart Restaurant, or can enjoy Norwegian and international food in the H. C. Andersen restaurant. The lobby bar, Nordraak, is a cozy rendezvous, and patrons can also dance at the Liszt nightclub. Free airport transfers are arranged for arriving and departing guests.

VICTORIA HOTEL, Kong Oscars Gate 29, N-5017 Bergen. Tel. 55-31-50-30. Fax 55-32-81-78. 43 rms (all with bath). MINIBAR TV TEL **Bus:** 2, 4.

$ **Rates** (including breakfast): 620–950 kroner ($107.30–$164.40) single; 890–1,050 kroner ($154–$181.70) double. AE, DC, MC, V. **Parking:** 65 kroner ($11.20).

Midway between the harbor and the railway station, this hotel, constructed around 1912 but completely rebuilt in 1985, is a longtime favorite, for both its comfort and its tradition. Each of the well-furnished bedrooms has a distinct color theme of red, yellow, orange, blue, or green. Five rooms are for nonsmokers. The hotels' restaurant is the only Japanese restaurant in Bergen. There is also a breakfast room and a lounge with an open fireplace. The Victoria is licensed to sell beer and wine.

INEXPENSIVE

ROMANTIK HOTEL PARK, Harald Hårfagresgaten 35 and Parkveien 22, N-5007 Bergen. Tel. 55-32-09-60. Fax 55-31-03-34. 40 rms (all with bath). TV TEL **Bus:** 1, 3, 4.

$ **Rates** (including breakfast): 430–540 kroner ($74.40–$93.40) single; 560–630 kroner ($96.90–$109) double. AE, V. **Parking:** Free.

Located in an attractive university area, this is a converted 1890 town house. Rooms are traditionally furnished, and 15 contain a minibar. In summer, reserve well in advance. The Park is a 10-minute walk from the train and bus stations.

BUDGET

FAGERHEIM PENSJON, Kalvedalsveien 49A, N-5018 Bergen. Tel. 55-31-01-72. 20 rms (none with bath). **Bus:** 2, 4, 7, 11 from the post office.

$ **Rates:** 190–230 kroner ($32.90–$39.80) single; 300–340 kroner ($51.90–$58.80) double. Extra bed 80 kroner ($13.80). Breakfast 35 kroner ($6.10) extra. No credit cards. **Parking:** Free.

This attractively old-fashioned 1900 hillside house lies about 6 minutes from the town center. A few of the homelike bedrooms have small kitchens. Most accommodations have a view of the water and city. A garden surrounds the house.

MYKLEBUST PENSION, Rosenbergsgate 19, N-5015 Bergen. Tel. 55-90-16-70. 6 rms (2 with bath). TV TEL **Bus:** 2, 3, 4.

$ **Rates:** 320 kroner ($55.40) single without bath (available only May–Sept); 370

kroner ($64) double without bath, 400 kroner ($69.20) double with bath. Breakfast 45 kroner ($7.80) extra. No credit cards.

A 15-minute walk from the rail station, rooms in this boardinghouse are furnished in contemporary Norwegian style, and all have hot and cold running water, with shower and toilet close by. Breakfast, brought to your room at the time you request, costs extra and consists of ham, cheese, egg, bread, rolls, marmalade, butter, jam, coffee, milk, and juice. In a central hallway, guests may use a stove, refrigerator, washing machine, and dishes and utensils.

SORTLAND PENSJON, Vestre Torggate 20B, N-5015 Bergen. Tel. 55-31-88-67. 10 rms (3 with shower). **Bus:** 11, 16, 17.

$ Rates: 180 kroner ($31.10) single or double without shower; 250 kroner ($43.30) single or double with shower. Breakfast 60 kroner ($10.40) extra. No credit cards.

This economy find lies right in the center of Bergen, a 2-minute walk west of Ole Bulls Plass and the landmark Hotel Norge, midway between the tourist information office and Johanneskirken. Originally built as a private family home in 1906, it has been converted to receive guests. Rooms are simply furnished, but clean and comfortable, and adequate showers are in the corridor. Mr. Sortland is your English-speaking host.

4. DINING

EXPENSIVE

BANCO ROTTO, Vågsalmenningen 14-22. Tel. 55-32-75-20.
Cuisine: NORWEGIAN. **Reservations:** Required. **Bus:** 1, 5, 9.
$ Prices: Appetizers 58-80 kroner ($10-$13.80); main dishes 140-230 kroner ($24.20-$39.80); fixed-price lunch platter 85 kroner ($14.70); fixed-price dinner platter 110 kroner ($19). AE, DC, MC, V.
Open: Daily 11am-11:15pm (bar, daily 6pm-12:30am). **Closed:** Sun in winter.
You'll pass between ornate iron lampposts to reach the interior of this restaurant, housed in a former 1875 bank. A 2-minute walk from the harborfront, this dignified restaurant serves specialties that include scampi with scallops in vermouth sauce, North Cape catfish, roast sirloin of beef, médaillons of reindeer, hot apple cake, and a wide selection of wines. A luxurious bar adjoins the restaurant, with drinks costing from 50 kroner ($8.70).

ENHJØRNINGEN (Unicorn), Enhjørningsgården Bryggen. Tel. 55-32-79-19.
Cuisine: SEAFOOD. **Reservations:** Required. **Bus:** 1, 5, 9.
$ Prices: Lunch seafood buffet 145 kroner ($25.10); appetizers 58-85 kroner ($10-$14.70); main dishes 162-210 kroner ($28-$36.30). AE, DC, MC, V.
Open: Lunch, May-Oct, daily noon-4pm. Dinner, May-Aug, daily 4-11pm; Sept-Apr, Mon-Sat 4-11pm.
Enhjørningen is one of Bergen's major seafood restaurants. Within its handful of dining rooms, you'll find a neo-Victorian decor, plants, and well-prepared seafood specialties. There's an all-you-can eat seafood luncheon buffet.

FISKEKROEN, Zacchariasbrygge 50. Tel. 55-31-75-66.
Cuisine: FISH/GAME. **Reservations:** Required. **Bus:** 1, 5, 9.
$ Prices: Appetizers 59-98 kroner ($10.20-$17); main dishes 179-225 kroner ($31-$38.90). AE, DC, MC, V.
Open: Sun-Fri 4-11pm, Sat noon-11pm.
Considered one of the smallest (36 seats) and most exclusive restaurants in Bergen, this fish and game restaurant occupies a rustically elegant premises one floor above street level in the historic (and rebuilt) Zacchariasbrygge harborfront complex. Interior decoration includes a bubbling aquarium, a panoramic view of the harbor, and a menagerie of artfully stuffed animals. Menu specialties

change with the seasons and might include a symphony of fish (salmon, wolffish, and anglerfish in a lobster sauce), fried filet of reindeer with game sauce, filet of moose with a mushroom cream sauce, and several different preparations of venison.

RESTAURANT BELLEVUE, Bellevuebakken 9. Tel. 55-31-02-40.
   Cuisine: NORWEGIAN. **Reservations:** Required. **Bus:** 11.
   $ **Prices:** Appetizers 85–145 kroner ($14.70–$25.10); main dishes 200–265 kroner ($34.60–$45.80). AE, DC, MC, V.
   Open: Dinner only, Mon–Fri 6–11pm. **Closed:** Sat–Sun and Jan–Mar.
A stylish panoramic restaurant high on a hill, the Bellevue was originally built as a midsummer retreat in 1796. Have predinner drinks in the bar and follow with a meal of warm fish mousse stuffed with shellfish-and-lobster sauce, a terrine of vegetables with herb sauce, tournedos garnished with lobster, or a "symphony" of fresh fish and shellfish. The homemade ice cream studded with seasonal berries makes for a refreshing dessert.

MODERATE

HOLBERG-STUEN, Torgalmenningen 6. Tel. 55-31-80-15.
   Cuisine: NORWEGIAN. **Reservations:** Not required. **Bus:** 1, 5, 9.
   $ **Prices:** Appetizers 55–68 kroner ($9.50–$11.80); main dishes 75–135 kroner ($13–$23.40). AE, DC, MC, V.
   Open: Mon–Sat 10am–12:30am, Sun 1pm–12:30am.
One floor above street level, this 1927 restaurant lies midway between the harborfront fish market and Ole Bulls Plass. It has a beer cellar atmosphere, with beamed ceilings, an open log fire, leaded-glass casement windows, high-back settles, and armchairs. Hearty diners devour fish filet in white wine sauce, accompanied by prawns, mushrooms, and asparagus. Good for late-night drinking.

OLE BULL RESTAURANT, in the Hotel Norge, Ole Bulls Plass 2–4 Tel. 55-21-01-00.
   Cuisine: NORWEGIAN. **Reservations:** Recommended. **Bus:** 2, 3, 4.
   $ **Prices:** Smörgåsbord 165 kroner ($28.50) per person; appetizers 58–88 kroner ($10–$15.20); main dishes 145–195 kroner ($25.10–$33.70). AE, DC, MC, V.
   Open: Daily noon–11pm.
This well-managed restaurant offers the best smörgåsbord in town, served daily from noon to 6pm. Time-tested Norwegian dishes are also served—platter after platter of freshly prepared meat and fish dishes. You can also dine à la carte in the evening. Try the fresh fish—it's always reliable.

WESSEL-STUEN, Engen 14. Tel. 55-90-08-20.
   Cuisine: NORWEGIAN. **Reservations:** Not required. **Bus:** 2, 3, 4.
   $ **Prices:** Appetizers 29–52 kroner ($5–$9); main dishes 98–142 kroner ($17–$24.60); 1-course *dagens* menu 60–90 kroner ($10.40–$15.60). AE, DC, MC, V.
   Open: Daily 11:30am–12:30am.
This bodega-style restaurant has all the trappings of an 18th-century wine cellar and was named for the humorist Johan Herman Wessel, who wrote such works as *Love Without Stockings*. The restaurant is decorated in old tavern style with beamed ceilings, and its adjoining pub is a famous meeting place for locals. Meals are likely to include such dishes as pan-fried cod tongues, black-pepper steak, sautéed salmon with shrimp, spaghetti Napoli, and barbecued spareribs. Every day the chef features a different steak special, one of the most popular dishes in town.

INEXPENSIVE

BRYGGELOFTET/BRUGGESTUEN, Bryggen 6. Tel. 55-31-06-30.
   Cuisine: NORWEGIAN. **Reservations:** Not required. **Bus:** 1, 5, 9.
   $ **Prices:** Appetizers 38–59 kroner ($6.60–$10.20); main dishes 68–175 kroner ($11.80–$30.30); lunchtime smørbrød 28–72 kroner ($4.80–$12.50). AE, DC, MC, V.

IMPRESSIONS

Reaching Bergen we fail to find it particularly attractive. Everything is fishy. You eat fish and drink fish and smell fish and breathe fish.
—LILIAM LELAND, *TRAVELLING ALONE, A WOMAN'S JOURNEY ROUND THE WORLD,*
1890

Open: Mon–Sat 10am–11:30pm, Sun 1–11:30pm.
Bryggeloftet/Bruggestuen is the best-established restaurant along the harborfront. At street level the Bruggestuen has low ceiling beams, carved banquettes, and 19th-century murals of old Bergen, along with dozens of clipper-ship models. For a more formal meal, head upstairs for the Bryggeloftet, with its high ceilings and wood paneling. A dinner in either section might include grilled porbeagle (a form of whitefish) served with shrimp, mussels, and a white wine sauce, roast reindeer with cream sauce, or pepper steak with a salad. Several different preparations of salmon and herring are featured, along with roast pork with Norwegian sour cabbage.

BUDGET

CAFETERIA KAFFISTOVA, Torget 1. Tel. 55-31-66-27.
   Cuisine: NORWEGIAN. **Reservations:** Not required. **Bus:** 1, 5, 9.
$ Prices: Cafeteria, smørbrød 26–48 kroner ($4.50–$8.30); main dishes 48–62 kroner ($8.30–$10.70). Restaurant, main dishes 55–98 kroner ($9.50–$17). No credit cards.
   Open: Summer, daily 8am–10pm; winter, Mon–Fri 8am–7pm, Sat 9am–4pm, Sun 11am–6pm.
A great all-around choice for economy dining in Bergen, this place has a modern self-service cafeteria on the lower floor and, one floor above street level, a full-fledged restaurant. There are no particular appetizers, since the price of your main course includes either soup or coffee, which makes this place a real bargain for Bergen. Many interesting smørbrød concoctions are served along with hot dishes. Among the à la carte offerings are rømmergrøt (sour-cream porridge), cured mutton, and trout.

5. ATTRACTIONS

SUGGESTED ITINERARIES

IF YOU HAVE 1 DAY

Take in all the top attractions of Bergen, including the old Hanseatic Bryggen, with its nearby museums; explore the shops and artisan workshops along the harbor; and, to cap your day, take the funicular to Fløien for a panoramic view.

IF YOU HAVE 2 DAYS

Day 1: See "If You Have 1 Day," above.

Day 2: Head for the environs of Bergen, which can be reached by public transportation. Visit Troldhaugen, Edvard Grieg's former home. In the afternoon, journey to Ole Bull's Villa, 16 miles south of Bergen.

IF YOU HAVE 3 DAYS

Days 1 & 2: See "If You Have 2 Days," above.

Day 3: Take the 12-hour "Norway in a Nutshell" tour (see "Easy Excursions," below).

IF YOU HAVE 5 DAYS

Days 1–3: See "If You Have 3 Days," above.

Day 4: Explore the Hardangerfjord and the Folgefonn Glacier by round-trip coach from Bergen (see "Easy Excursions," below).

Day 5: Explore Sognefjord by express steamer, going by bus via Voss, and returning by train to Bergen (see "Easy Excursions," below).

THE TOP ATTRACTIONS

In addition to the sights below, take a stroll around ✪ **Bryggen.** This row of Hanseatic timbered houses, rebuilt along the waterfront after the disastrous fire of 1702, is what remains of medieval Bergen. The northern half burned to the ground as late as 1955. Bryggen has been incorporated into UNESCO's World Heritage List as one of the world's most significant cultural and historical re-creations of a medieval settlement, skillfully incorporated in the surroundings of modern Bergen. It is a center for arts and crafts, where painters, weavers, and craftspeople have their workshops. As you stroll along, you'll see that some of these workshops are open to the public.

DET HANSEATISKE MUSEUM, Finnegårdsgaten 1A, Bryggen. Tel. 55-31-41-89.

✪ In one of the best-preserved wooden buildings at Bryggen, this museum illustrates Bergen's commercial life on the wharf centuries ago. German merchants, representatives of the Hanseatic League centered in Lübeck, lived in these medieval houses built in long rows up from the harbor. With dried cod, grain, and salt as articles of exchange, fishermen from northern Norway met German merchants during the busy summer season. The museum is furnished with authentic articles dating from 1704.

Admission: 15 kroner ($2.60) adults, 8 kroner ($1.40) children (free for children Oct–Apr).

Open: June–Aug, daily 9am–5pm; May and Sept, daily 11am–2pm; Oct–Apr, Sun–Mon, Wed, and Fri 11am–2pm. **Bus:** 1, 5, 9.

MARIAKIRKE [St. Mary's Church], Dreggen. Tel. 55-31-59-60.

The oldest building in Bergen (its exact date is unknown, but perhaps from the mid-12th century) is this Romanesque church, one of the most beautiful in Norway. Its altar is the oldest ornament in the church, and there's a baroque pulpit donated by Hanseatic merchants with carved figures depicting everything from Chastity to Naked Truth. Church music concerts are given from May until the end of August nearly every night.

Admission: 10 kroner ($1.70) adults; children free.

Open: May 15–Sept 15, Mon–Fri 11am–4pm; Sept 16–May 14, Tues–Fri noon–1:30pm. **Bus:** 1, 5, 9.

RASMUS MEYERS COLLECTIONS, Rasmus Meyers Allé 3–5. Tel. 55-97-80-00.

Within walking distance of the fish market, this museum houses an excellent display of Norwegian paintings. The star attractions are the egg-shaped figures of Edvard Munch, but two important 19th-century artists, Christian Krohg and Harriet Backer, are also represented.

Admission: May 15–Sept 15, 15 kroner ($2.60) adults, 8 kroner ($1.40) children. Free off-season.

Open: May 15–Sept 15, daily 11am–4pm; off-season, Wed–Mon noon–3pm. **Bus:** 1, 5, 9.

HÅKONSHALLEN [Håkon's Hall], Bradbenken. Tel. 55-31-60-67.

If you walk along the water from Bryggen, you come upon the Håkonshallen, built between 1247 and 1261, later restored following damage in a 1944 fire. This is the largest and most imposing building remaining on the site of the royal residence of Bergen, and was the political center of the 13th-century kingdom of Norway. Guided tours are conducted hourly.

Admission: 10 kroner ($1.70) adults, 5 kroner (90¢) children.

Open: Mid-May to mid-Sept, daily 10am–4pm; off-season, Fri–Wed noon–3pm, Thurs 3–6pm.

ROSENKRANTZ TOWER, Bradbenken. Tel. 55-31-43-80.

Originally a fortified royal residence in the 13th century, Rosenkrantz Tower was rebuilt and enlarged in the 1560s. It was constructed by the governor of Bergenhus (Bergen Castle), Erik Rosenkrantz, as a combined defense and residential tower. It has been restored. Two older structures were incorporated into the tower: King Magnus the Lawmender's keep from about 1260 and Jørgen Hanssøn's keep from about 1520. Guided tours of the tower and Håkonshallen (see above) leave about every hour.

Admission: 10 kroner ($1.70) adults, 5 kroner (90¢) children.

Open: May 15–Sept 14, daily 10am–4pm; Sept 15–May 14, Sun noon–3pm. **Bus:** 1, 5, 9.

MORE ATTRACTIONS

FUNICULAR TO FLØIEN

A short walk from the fish market is the station where the funicular heads up to Fløien, the most famous of Bergen's seven hills. At 1,050 feet, the view of city, the neighboring hills and the harbor is worth every ore.

Admission: Round-trip, 26 kroner ($4.50) adults, 12 kroner ($2.10) children.

Open: Daily 8am–11pm, with departures every 30 minutes. **Bus:** 6.

BRYGGENS MUSEUM, Bryggen. Tel. 55-31-67-10.

Displaying artifacts unearthed during extensive archeological excavations of Bryggen from 1955 to 1972, exhibits include remains of the oldest buildings in Bergen, dating from the 12th century, in their original settings. You can also see runic inscriptions and changing exhibitions. The museum illustrates the daily and cultural life of Bergen in the Middle Ages.

Admission: 10 kroner ($1.70) adults; free for children.

Open: May–Aug, daily 10am–5pm; Sept–Apr, Mon–Fri 11am–3pm, Sun noon–4pm. **Bus:** 1, 5, 9.

BERGEN AQUARIUM, Nordnesparken 2. Tel. 55-23-85-00.

A 15-minute walk from the city center, this aquarium is one of the largest and finest in Scandinavia. The marine life is exceptional, including seals, penguins, lobsters, and piranhas. In the outer hall you can dip your hand into the shallow pool and literally get the feel of the fish in unpolluted water pumped up from a depth of 400 feet in the fjord outside. As you step into the twilight of the main aquarium hall, you plunge into the sea in a giant diving bell. Nine glassed-in tanks, each containing about 62,500 gallons of water, ring the hall. Downstairs is a wide range of marine life in 42 small aquaria demonstrating many colorful forms of sea life and illustrating evolutionary development.

Admission: 30 kroner ($5.20) adults, 15 kroner ($2.60) children.

Open: May–Sept, daily 9am–8pm; Oct–Apr, daily 10am–6pm. **Bus:** 4 from the town center.

TROLDHAUGEN [Trolls' Hill], at Troldhaugen, Hop. Tel. 55-91-17-91.

⭐ This Victorian house, in beautiful rural surroundings at Hop, near Bergen, was the summer villa of composer Edvard Grieg. The house still contains Grieg's own furniture, paintings, and other mementos. His Steinway grand piano is frequently used at concerts given in the house during the annual Bergen festival, as well as at Troldhaugen's own summer concerts. Grieg and his wife, Nina, are buried in a cliff grotto on the estate. At his cottage by the sea, he composed many of his famous works.

Admission: 15 kroner ($2.60) adults, 8 kroner ($1.40) children.

Open: May 2–Oct 1, daily 10:30am–1:30pm and 2:30–5:30pm. **Closed:** Oct 2–May 1. **Bus:** Hop-bound buses leave from the bus station at Bergen (Platforms 18–20). Once the bus lets you off, turn right, walk about 200 yards, then turn left at Hopsvegen. From there just follow the signs to Troldhaugen, a 20- to 30-minute walk.

GAMLE BERGEN, Elsesro, Sandviken. Tel. 55-25-78-50.

At Elsesro and Sandviken is a collection of houses set in a park from the 18th and 19th centuries. The Old Town is complete with streets, an open square, and narrow alleyways. Some of the interiors are exceptional, including a merchant's living room in the typical style of the 1870s—with padded sofas, heavy curtains, potted plants—a perfect setting for Ibsen's *A Doll's House.*

Admission: 25 kroner ($4.30) adults, 15 kroner ($2.60) children.

Open: Houses, mid-May to mid-Sept, guided tours daily every hour noon–6pm. Park and restaurant, mid-May to mid-Sept, daily 11am–10pm. **Closed:** Late Sept–early May. **Bus:** 1 or 9 from the Bergen post office leaves every 10 minutes.

GAMLEHAUGEN, Fjøsanger. Tel. 55-91-19-50.

Gamlehaugen is the king's Bergen residence, and was the home of the prime minister, Christian Michelsen. The garden is always open to the public.

Admission: 10 kroner ($1.70) adults, 5 kroner (90¢) children.

Open: June–Sept, Mon–Fri 10am–noon. **Bus:** Fjøsanger-bound bus from Central Bus Station.

IN NEARBY LYSØEN

MUSEET LYSØEN/OLE BULL'S VILLA, Lysøen. Tel. 55-30-90-77.

On the island of Lysøen, 16 miles south of Bergen, stands the villa and concert hall built in 1872 to 1873 for the world-famous violin virtuoso and Norwegian national hero, Ole Bull. The building, now a national monument, is just as it was when the musician died in 1880. Eight miles of trails built by Bull meander around the island.

Admission: 25 kroner ($4.30) adults, 10 kroner ($1.70) children.

Open: Guided tours of villa, mid-May to Sept, Mon–Sat noon–4pm, Sun 11am–5pm. **Closed:** Oct–early May. **Directions:** Drive or take a bus (from Platform 20 at the Bergen bus station; marked "Fana-Os-Milde") to Sørestraumen on road 553; then take the Ole Bull ferry from Sørestraumen, Buena Kai. Round-trip ferryboat fare is 25 kroner ($4.30) adults, 10 kroner ($1.70) children. Visits to the museum and villa must be carefully calibrated to coincide with the lonely ferryboat plying back and forth across the channel. When the site is open, ferryboats are timed to coincide with museum visits, and they depart the mainland at hourly intervals, with the last boat leaving a few minutes after the museum closes.

ORGANIZED TOURS

A 1-hour tram tour uses the city tram lines and specially designed red-sided tramcars equipped with multilingual headsets. They depart every hour on the hour from a spot in front of the Bergen City Tourist Office. The cost is 60 kroner ($10.40) adults and 30 kroner ($5.20) for children for a 1-hour tram tour encompassing all the most obvious monuments of Bergen. It operates daily from May to September, from 10am to 7pm. The most popular and most highly recommended tour of Bergen is still the 2-hour city tour, which departs daily at 10am, and covers all major sightseeing attractions. These include the Hanseatic Museum and the 12th-century St. Mary's Church. Like the shorter tour described above, it operates from May to September, and costs 100 kroner ($17.30) for adults, 50 kroner ($8.70) for children. A final tour, offered during the same dates, requires 3 hours, includes everything in tour 2, and also includes visits to Grieg's home and either Old Bergen or the manor house of Damsgård, which is located about 2 miles west of the city center, across the estuary. The cost of the 3-hour tour is 150 kroner ($26); half price for children. Departures are daily at 3:30pm from May to September.

For information on any and all of these, contact the tourist office at Torgalmenningen 12 (tel. 55-32-14-80).

6. SPECIAL/FREE EVENTS

The jam-packed **Bergen International Festival,** scheduled for May 20 to 31, is famous for its talented performances in music, drama, opera, ballet, and folklore. The works of Edvard Grieg dominate the festivities. Concerts are held daily at his former home, Troldhaugen, and the modern concert hall bearing his name, featuring such international artists as André Previn and Murray Perahia. Concerts are also given in the 700-year-old Håkonshallen or in the 12th-century St. Mary's Church, and folklore performances round out the events. Den Nationale Scene performs Ibsen and contemporary plays. In the last few years, concerts have also been held at Lysøen, former home of the 19th-century Bergen-born violin virtuoso, Ole Bull. For festival information, contact Greig Hall, Lars Hillesgate 3A (Box 183), N-5001 Bergen (tel. 55-21-61-00).

From June 24 to August 1 recitals are held at **Troldhaugen,** Edvard Grieg's former home, every Wednesday and Sunday at 8pm. From early September to mid-October, there are also Sunday matinees at 1pm. Tickets are available from the Tourist Information Center (see above) or at the entrance.

Visitors are invited by **Fana Folklore** to a traditional Norwegian country festival that takes place in an 800-year-old Fana church where the organist plays a miniconcert of hymns. Then you'll be taken to a private home where you're treated like friends of the family with true Norwegian farm hospitality, to join in their festivals following old customs and accompanied by plenty of food, song, music, and lively dances.

Buses leave from Festplassen in Bergen June 5 to August 31 on Monday, Tuesday, Thursday, and Friday at 7pm (extra evenings in May and September). The price, which includes everything—and that means a full meal—is 170 kroner ($29.40). Tickets are sold at most hotel reception desks, at travel agents, and at the A. S. Kunst Souvenir Shop, Torgalmenningen 9.

7. SPORTS/RECREATION

FISHING   In the region of Bergen, anyone can fish in seawater without restrictions. If you plan to fish in fresh water (ponds, streams, and most of the best salmon and trout rivers), you'll need a fishing permit. These are sold at any post office in Norway. You'll also need the permission of whomever owns the land on either side of the stream.

GOLF   The **Åstveit Golf Course** (tel. 55-18-20-77) has nine holes and allows nonmembers, but call in advance. It's a 15-minute drive north of Bergen on Route 16. You can also take the Åsane bus from the central station in Bergen.

SWIMMING   Swim in the heated saltwater pool at the **Sentralbadet,** Teatersgaten 9 (tel. 55-23-10-34). For hours, check the tourist office. Adults pay 25 kroner ($4.30); children, 10 kroner ($1.70).

For open-air swimming, go to **Tømmersvågen,** 15 minutes from the center on the Eidsvåg bus no. 1.

TENNIS   **Tennis Paradis,** Highway R1, 5040 Paradis (tel. 55-91-01-13), lies 6 miles south of Bergen. The club contains five indoor courts, several outdoor courts, four squash courts, badminton courts, and a health club/gym. It's open daily from 7am to 11pm throughout the year.

WALKING   Only 10 minutes away from town by the funicular, several roads and footpaths lead to **Mount Fløien,** an unspoiled wood and mountain terrace with lakes and rivers.

The **Bergen Touring Club,** C. Sundtsgate 3 (tel. 55-32-22-30), arranges walking tours farther afield and supplies information on huts and mountain routes all over Norway. They also provide maps and advice on where to hike.

8. SAVVY SHOPPING

As mentioned, shoppers who live outside Scandinavia and spend more than 300 kroner ($51.90) in a tax-free tourist shop get between 10% and 15% of the purchase refunded when they leave Norway. You will receive your refund in cash even if you have used a credit card.

THE SHOPPING SCENE

Real bargain sleuths head to the **Marketplace (Torget),** where many local handcrafts from the western fjord district are displayed, including rugs and handmade tablecloths. This is one of the few places in Norway where bargaining is welcomed. The market keeps no set hours, but is best visited between 8am and noon. Take bus 1, 5, or 9.

Hours Stores are generally open Monday through Friday from 9am to 4:30pm (to 7pm on Thursday; some shops also on Friday) and on Saturday from 9am to 2pm (some to 1pm). Shopping centers outside the city are open Monday through Friday from 10am to 8pm and on Saturday from 9am to 4pm. Some food stores stay open until 8pm Monday through Friday, to 6pm on Saturday.

SHOPPING A TO Z
DEPARTMENT STORES

SUNDT & CO., Torgalmenningen. Tel. 55-38-80-20.
Bergen's leading department store stands near the tourist information booth. Excellent buys include linen tablecloths, purses for women, and Norwegian knitwear, plus a vast array of souvenirs.

FASHION

KLØVERHUSET, Strandkaien 10. Tel. 55-32-77-20.
Next to the fish market on the harbor, this four-story shopping center has been Bergen's largest fashion store since 1923. Besides the latest in modern design, it also offers good bargains, such as moderately priced and attractively designed knitted sweaters, gloves, and Lapp jackets. There's a special gift shop open only in summer.

HANDCRAFTS

Aside from the stores listed below, in and around Bryggen Brukskunst, the restored Old Town near the wharf, many craftspeople have taken over old houses to ply the ancient Norwegian trades. Crafts boutiques here often display Bergen souvenirs, many based on designs 300 to 1,500 years old. For example, I purchased a reproduction of a cruciform pilgrim's badge (Romanesque in style). Other tempting items are likely to include sheepskin-lined booties or exquisitely styled handwoven woolen dresses.

HUSFLIDEN I BERGEN, Vågsalmenningen 3. Tel. 55-31-78-70.
You'll find the widest selection of national handcrafts here—the finest handmade knitwear from the western district, along with woodwork, brass, and pewterware.

PRYDKUNST-HJERTHOLM, Olav Kyrres Gate 7. Tel. 55-31-70-27.
The leading outlet for glassware and ceramics, it purchases much of its merchandise directly from the studios of artisans who turn out quality goods not only in glass

and ceramics, but also in pewter, wood, and textiles. Gift articles and souvenirs are also sold. It's a 2-minute walk from the Tourist Information Center.

JEWELRY

DAVID-ANDERSEN, Torgalmenningen 10. Tel. 55-31-00-80.
This is the Bergen branch of the most famous jewelry store in Norway. Its better-stocked store was previewed under "Savvy Shopping" in Chapter 15. The collection of hand-painted enamel on sterling silver is exceptional, although they have far more expensive items as well.

SHOPPING MALLS

GALLERIET, Torgalmenningen 8. Tel. 55-32-45-50.
This is the most important shopping complex in the Bergen area, with 60 different stores offering tax-free shopping. Close to Bergen's fish market, it offers a wide array of various kinds of merchandise, and features summer sales and special exhibitions. It also has several fast-food places. Open Monday through Friday from 9am to 8pm and on Saturday from 9am to 4pm.

9. EVENING ENTERTAINMENT

THE PERFORMING ARTS

GRIEGHALLEN, Lars Hillesgate 3A. Tel. 55-31-31-04.
Opened in mid-1978, the modern Grieg Hall is Bergen's monumental showcase for music, drama, and a host of other cultural events. The stage is large enough to accommodate an entire grand opera production, and the main foyer will comfortably seat 1,500 guests for lunch or dinner. Snack bars provide drinks and light snacks throughout the performances. On the street level the building features an arcade of shops, and the upper floors house the offices of the Philharmonic Orchestra and the Bergen International Festival.

The Bergen Symphony Orchestra, founded in 1765, performs here from August to May, on Thursday at 7:30pm and often on Saturday at 12:30pm. Its repertoire consists of classical and contemporary music, as well as visiting productions of opera. International conductors and soloists perform. **Bus:** 2, 3, 4.
Tickets: 80–250 kroner ($13.80–$43.30).

DEN NATIONAL SCENE, Engen 1. Tel. 55-90-17-88.

IN THEIR FOOTSTEPS

Edvard Grieg (1843–1907) "The Chopin of the North," Grieg wrote his first composition at the age of 9, and in time he became a romantic musician under Mendelssohn and Schumann. Themes from folk music are successfully exploited in the *Peer Gynt Suite* (1888). He was Norway's first composer to become famous throughout Europe.
  • **Birthplace:** June 15, 1843, in Bergen.
  • **Favorite Haunts:** Rome where he met Franz Liszt; Christiania (now Oslo) where he became a member of the Royal Musical Academy of Sweden in 1872, and his beloved Troldhaugen (Trolls' Hill) outside Bergen.
  • **Resting Place:** He died on September 4, 1907, and was buried in a cliff grotto at Troldhaugen (open to the public).

September to June is the season for Norway's oldest theater, founded in the mid-19th century. Its repertoire consists of classical Norwegian and international drama, contemporary plays, frequent productions of music drama, as well as visiting productions of opera and ballet. **Bus:** 2, 3, 4.

Tickets: 75–200 kroner ($13–$34.60).

SUMMER CULTURAL ENTERTAINMENT

BERGEN FOLKLORE, Bryggens Museum, Bryggen. Tel. 55-24-89-29.

The Bjørgvin Regional folk-dancing troupe arranges a folklore program at this museum mid-June to mid-August, on Monday and Wednesday at 8:30pm. The program lasts about an hour, consisting of traditional folk dances and music from rural Norway. Tickets are on sale at the Tourist Information Center or at the door. **Bus:** 1, 5, 9.

Admission: 70 kroner ($12.10).

THE CLUB & MUSIC SCENE

RUBINEN, Rosenkrantzgate 7. Tel. 51-31-50-00.

Rubinen is one of Bergen's most popular nightclubs. It plays all kinds of danceable and drinkable music, including country western and rock 'n' roll. Drinks cost about 45 kroner ($7.80). It's open Tuesday through Sunday from 8pm to 3am, with live music nightly. Bus: 2, 3, 4.

Admission: 50 kroner ($8.70).

PANDORA NIGHT CLUB, in the Hotel Norge, Ole Bulls Plass 2–4. Tel. 51-21-01-00.

Close to Torgalmenningen, this disco and dance bar caters to an over-30 crowd in relatively plush comfort. If you want to hear the latest music from New York or London, this is the place. A scotch and soda costs 55 kroner ($9.50); a beer 50 kroner ($8.70). It's open Wednesday to Saturday from 9pm to 3am. Bus: 2, 3, 4.

Admission: 30–60 kroner ($5.20–$10.40).

ENGELEN, in the SAS Royal Hotel, Bryggen. Tel. 55-54-30-00.

This is one of Bergen's more affluent and elegant discos. Its music features the latest releases. Light meals are available, and drinks cost 56 kroner ($9.70) or 48 kroner ($8.30) for beer. It's open Tuesday through Saturday from 8pm to 2:30am. Bus: 1, 5, 9.

Admission: 50 kroner ($8.70).

VILLA AMORINI, Rasmus Meyers Allé. Tel. 55-31-00-39.

Especially popular with students from Bergen's collection of universities and technical schools, this is probably the most frequented club in Bergen for drinkers and dancers aged 30 and under. Drinks costs from 40 kroner ($6.90), and it is open Thursday through Saturday from 9pm to 3am. Bus: 2, 3, 4.

Admission: 50 kroner ($8.70).

MAXIME, Ole Bulls Plass 9. Tel. 55-90-07-70.

Its street level contains a popular bar where many of Bergen's student crowd come to meet and be met. In the cellar, a disco rocks to electronic music through the night. Drinks cost from 40 kroner ($6.90), and hours are Thursday through Saturday from 8:30pm to 3am. Bus: 2, 3, 4.

Admission: 50 kroner ($8.70).

THE BAR SCENE

KONTORET PUB, Ole Bulls Plass 8–10. Tel. 55-90-07-60.

Perhaps the most frequented pub in the town center, the Kontoret is located in the Hotel Norge next to the Dickens restaurant and pub. Drinkers can wander freely between the two places, as they are interconnected and are also accessible through exterior doors. In the Kontoret Pub you can order the same food served at Dickens, although most people seem to come here to drink. The local brew is called Hansa; a half liter of draft beer is 39 kroner ($6.70). The pub is open Sunday through Friday from 4pm to 12:30am and on Saturday from noon to 12:30am. Bus: 2, 3, 4.

ZACCHARIASBRYGGE PUB, Zacchariasbrygge 50. Tel. 55-31-03-60.
   Set on the harborfront of Old Bergen, in the same oxblood-colored former warehouse as the restaurant Fiskekroen (see "Dining," above), this place is one of Bergen's most popular, and sometimes noisiest, pubs. Mingling with copious quantities of flowing suds at 39 kroner ($6.70) for a half-pint of lager—and French and Italian wines for 38 kroner ($6.60) a glass—are the sounds of piano music and a live singer. There's additional seating on the upper floor. The pub is open daily from 11am to 1am. Bus: 1, 5, 9.

STUDIO 52, C. Sundtsgata 52. Tel. 55-23-32-25.
   Well known and widely noted for its role as Bergen's only gay bar, this bar and disco welcomes gay men and gay women (as well as their heterosexual friends) into an ambience where many of the patrons seem to know one another. Many gay newcomers consider it a useful device for sounding out the gay scene in Bergen shortly after their arrival. Beer costs 38 kroner ($6.60). Open Wednesday to Sunday 8:30pm to 1am. Bus: 2, 3, 4.
   Admission: 50 kroner ($8.70) Fri–Sat.

MOVIES

Bergen has a number of movie theaters, such as **Konsertpaleet,** Neumannsgate 3 (tel. 55-31-96-20), and **Forum,** in Danmarkplass (tel. 55-29-80-70), showing all films in the original versions. The earliest performance is at 11am; the latest at 11pm.

10. NETWORKS & RESOURCES

FOR STUDENTS   About a 12-minute walk from Torgalmenningen, **Kilroy Travel,** Studentsamskipnaden, Parkveien (tel. 55-32-64-00), sells discount tickets on both planes and boats. For example, you might get discounts on flights to either Stockholm or Copenhagen. You can also get discounts on steamers to Newcastle in northern England. Some of these discounts range as high as 25% off regular prices. To qualify for many of Kilroy's best money-saving deals, you should either be under age 26 or provide proof of your status as a full-time student.

FOR GAY MEN & WOMEN   The **Gay Switchboard** in Bergen (tel. 55-31-05-77) provides information daily from 7 to 11pm.
   You might call one of the gay liberation organizations for information about activities in Bergen. Try **DNF-48,** Kalfarveien 32A (tel. 55-31-05-77), open Monday through Friday from 10am to 4pm.
   Homofil Bevegelse i Bergen (HBB), Nygårdsgaten 2A (tel. 55-31-21-39), is a gay rights movement serving Bergen and western Norway. Call for information about its disco, operated on Saturday from 10pm to 2am. An open house is staged at its office and café on Thursday from 7 to 10pm and on Saturday from 2 to 5pm.

FOR WOMEN   The local branch of the International Women's Organization is **Zonta,** St. Hanshaugen 56, Fyllingsdalen (tel. 55-16-19-92). The contact in Bergen is Berit Wollan.

11. EASY EXCURSIONS

✪ Two of Norway's most famous fjords, the **Hardanger** and the **Sognefjord,** can easily be explored from Bergen. The least expensive way to see the Hardangerfjord and the **Folgefonn Glacier** is to take a round-trip coach from the Central Bus Station, Strømgaten 8, leaving from Platform 1 daily at 10:20am all year. The full-day self-guided tour includes a luncheon stopover at Utne or Lofthus and returns to Bergen around 9pm; round-trip fare is 260 kroner ($45), excluding lunch.

Norway's longest fjord, Sognefjord, can be crossed by express steamer to **Gudvangen.** From Gudvangen, passengers go to Flåm. From Flåm, a train runs back to Bergen. That is but one of several alternatives for visiting this world-famed fjord. You can go by train, bus, and then a boat for 485 kroner ($83.90) round-trip. Details of the various possibilities are available from the tourist office (see above).

NORWAY IN A NUTSHELL

✪ This 12-hour tour is the most exciting 1-day tour in the country, encompassing two arms of **Sognefjord,** and the train ride from **Myrdal** down to **Flåm** (a drop of 2,900 feet, past seemingly endless waterfalls). In June, July, and August, the tour leaves at 9:15am from the Bergen railroad station; guests have lunch at Flåm, then board a river steamer for Gudvangen, where they hop on a bus to Voss, then a train back to Bergen. The round-trip fare, excluding meals, is 375 kroner ($64.90) for adults, 190 kroner ($32.90) for children. Holders of Eurail or Scandinavian Rail Passes get a reduction.

CHAPTER 19

THE FJORD DISTRICT

Western Norway is the heart of fjord country. Norwegian fjords are narrow arms of the sea, snaking their way inland. It took three million years to form the furrows and fissures that give western Norway its distinctive look. At some points the fjords become so narrow that a boat can hardly wedge between the mountainsides.

Bergen is the best departure point for trips to the fjords: to the south lies the famous Hardangerfjord and to the north the Sognefjord, cutting 111 miles inland.

About 1½ hours from Bergen, Voss is a famous ski resort that is also well situated between both the Hardangerfjord and the Sognefjord.

We'll start in the towns around the Hardangerfjord—Lofthus, Kinsarvik, Eidfjord and Ulvik, make a detour to Voss, and then move north to the towns around the Sognefjord like Balestrand and Flåm.

SEEING THE FJORD DISTRICT
GETTING THERE

Bergen is the traditional gateway to the fjord country. From Bergen, you have a choice of several options for getting about the district; the most expensive is by private car. Most of the towns and villages have road connections, although you'll have to take several car-ferries to cross the fjords. Boat excursions, many of which leave from Bergen, are the traditional way to see the fjords. In summer, dozens of possibilities await you. Contact the Bergen Tourist Office for details.

Of the towns recommended in this chapter, Voss and Geilo, both winter ski centers and summer mountain resorts, have the best rail connections with Oslo and Bergen. But all the fjord towns and villages are connected by buses that make their way carefully through the mountains and along the fjords, with vistas in all directions. Of course, travel by bus from place to place is time-consuming and often there are only two to five departures a day, depending on business, so you have to plan your connections in advance. Details about bus routes in the fjord district are available at the Central Station in Bergen.

A SUGGESTED ITINERARY

Days 1 & 2: From Bergen, explore the Hardangerfjord first and plan a 2-night stopover in one of these fjord villages: Utne, Lofthus, Kinsarvik, or Ulvik. Many visitors think Ulvik is the prettiest place. Explore some folk museums in the region and take long walks along the fjords.

Day 3: Journey to Voss for the night.

Day 4: Take the electric tram to Flåm for an overnight stay.

WHAT'S SPECIAL ABOUT THE FJORD DISTRICT

Great Towns/Villages

☐ Lofthus, in the Hardanger fjord district, once the haunt of Edvard Grieg and other artists.

☐ Ulvik, on an arm of the Hardangerfjord, everybody's fantasy of a Norwegian fjord village.

Great Resorts

☐ Voss, a folkloric resort popular year round; winter sports enthusiasts join its "ski circus."

☐ Geilo, in the Hol mountain district, with 81 miles of marked tracks for cross-country skiing.

The Fjords

☐ Sognefjord, cutting 111 miles inland, the longest and most strident of Norway's fjords.

☐ Hardangerfjord, extending for 75 miles; its shores contain fruit plantations, and blossom time is when to go.

Scenic Wonders

☐ Hardangervidda National Park, on the largest high-mountain plateau in Europe, home to 20,000 wild reindeer.

☐ Jostedal Glacier, largest glacier in Europe and the second biggest in the world.

Museums

☐ Hardanger Folk Museum at Utne, where old timbered houses from fjord villages have been preserved.

☐ Voss Folk Museum at Mølster, a time capsule preserving the old ways of Norwegian farmlife.

Churches

☐ Kinsarvik Church, dating from the 12th century, one of Norway's oldest stone churches.

Day 5: Travel to Balestrand for the night.

Day 6: Still in Balestrand, take an excursion on the Sognefjord, Norway's longest fjord.

Day 7: Return to Voss from Balestrand and take the train east for a final stopover in Geilo, from which you can easily journey to Oslo and your next destination.

---

1. UTNE

81 miles E of Bergen, 28 miles N of Odda

GETTING THERE   By Ferry   In the west board the ferry at Kvanndal; in the east, at Kinsarvik. There are frequent departures.

By Train   Connections are possible from Voss 24 miles in the east, on the main Bergen-Oslo line.

By Bus   Connections are made via Odda in the south and from Bergen in the west.

By Car   Head east from Bergen along the E16. At Kvanndal, board the ferry for Utne.

Utne has a view of the entrances to three fjords: Indre Samla, Granvin, and Eid. Across Utnefjorden, the formidable bulk of Oksen (7,953 feet) rises from the headland separating the Granvin and the Eid fjords. A great ravine breaches the steep slope of Oksen. Utnefjorden is almost 2 miles wide opposite Utne and nearly 2,700 feet deep in places, making it deeper than any other part of the Hardangerfjord.

Utne is at the northern end of the Folgefonn peninsula, with mountains looming nearby. Two valleys converge on the town, Utnedalen to the east and Fossdalen to the west. The river through Fossdalen forms fine falls as it drops through the woods toward the end of its course, dividing into two branches as it reaches the fjord.

WHAT TO SEE & DO

The **Hardanger Folk Museum,** lying near the ferry quay at Utne (tel. 53-46-69-00), founded in 1911, exhibits old timber buildings, furnished according to their eras, from several parts of Inner Hardanger. By the fjord are old boathouses and a general store that once stood on the quayside. Twenty wooden houses are in the open-air portion of the museum. In the administrative building are local arts and crafts, national costumes, data on the fruit-growing industry, and a review of tourism in the 18th and 19th centuries.

The museum is open daily from 10am to 4pm, charging 20 kroner ($3.50) for adults, free for children. In July it is open daily from 10am to 7pm. There are two branch museums, one near Lofthus and one between Kinsarvik and Eidfjord (see below).

When fjords were the highways of western Norway, Utne was an important junction. The **Romantik Utne Hotel** (see below) opened in 1772.

About 10 miles away from Utne lies **Agatunet,** a small village of buildings preserved on their original sites. The oldest building is **Lagmannstova,** the 13th-century Judge's House. Agatunet is open mid-May to mid-September, daily from 10am to noon and 2 to 4pm. Admission is 10 kroner ($1.70) for adults, 5 kroner (90¢) for children.

WHERE TO STAY
INEXPENSIVE

ROMANTIK UTNE HOTEL, N-5797 Utne i Hardanger. Tel. 53-46-69-83.
Fax 53-46-99-50. 23 rms (19 with bath).
$ Rates (including breakfast): 380 kroner ($65.70) single without bath, 500 kroner ($86.50) single with bath; 600 kroner ($103.80) double without bath, 750 kroner ($129.80) double with bath. AE, DC, MC, V. **Parking:** Free.
The 1772 Utne Hotel is the oldest hotel in Norway still in operation—for five generations the proprietors have devotedly served their guests. They run a relaxed, cozy, homelike place. If you'd like to relax in a comfortable, antique-filled atmosphere of hospitality, this is the place, just a few minutes from the ferry quay. You can have lunch à la carte, and dinner for 180 kroner ($31.10) and up.

2. LOFTHUS

236 miles W of Oslo, 87 miles E of Bergen

GETTING THERE   By Ferry   Board the ferry at Kvanndal for Kinsarvik where you can make bus connections south to Lofthus.

By Train   Connections are possible from Voss, 31 miles to the east, on the main Bergen-Oslo line.

By Bus   Bus service takes 1 hour from Odda in the south, 15 minutes from Kinsarvik in the north. From Bergen you can go by express bus/boat in 2½ hours.

By Car   Take the E16 east from Bergen to Kvanndal, where you can board a car-ferry to Kinsarvik. At Kinsarvik, head south on Route 47 to Lofthus.

ESSENTIALS   See Kinsarvik, below.

A favorite spot in the Hardanger district is sleepy Lofthus, once the haunt of Edvard Grieg and other artists. On the fjord, the resort is enveloped by snowcapped mountains, farms, and orchards. Hovering in the background is the Folgefonn Glacier.

Lofthus is actually the collective name for several groups of farms—Helleland, Eidnes, Lofthus, Opedal, Århus, and Ullensvang—extending from north to south along the eastern coastal slopes of Sørfjorden, 4 to 5 miles south of Kinsarvik Bay.

The discovery of a runic stone at Pedal, the oldest and largest group of farms, established that the area has been peopled since about 600 A.D. Cistercian monks came to Opedal seven centuries later and pioneered a fruit-growing industry. Their footpaths are still used and many have benefitted from the 616 steps, the Monks' Staircase, that makes its way up the steep gradient to the Vidda.

The church and buildings of Ullensvang lie around the mouth of the Opo River. The Gothic stone church was probably built at the end of the 13th century, and the builders may have been Scottish masons. Ullensvang was the name of the ancient farm where the *prestegård* (church farm) stands facing the church. It is now the name of the church, the hamlet, the parish, and the *kommune*, and the site of the most famous hotel in the region (see below).

WHAT TO SEE & DO

Almost 4 miles from Kinsarvik on Route 47 to Odda, a minor road forks left providing an alternative route to Lofthus. A short distance from the fork is the **Skredhaugen Museum,** N-5774 Lofthus (tel. 53-66-61-86), a branch of the Hardanger Folk Museum at Utne. A collection of 10 timber houses gathered from the area and furnished according to their period can be seen. There's also an art gallery filled with artworks. The museum is open from June 10 to August 20 Monday through Saturday from 11am to 4pm and on Sunday from noon to 4pm. Admission is 20 kroner ($3.50) for adults, free for children.

WHERE TO STAY

MODERATE

HOTEL ULLENSVANG, N-5774 Lofthus i Hardanger. Tel. 53-66-11-00.
Fax 53-66-15-20. 130 rms (all with bath). TV TEL

$ **Rates** (including breakfast): 775 kroner ($134.10) standard single, 1,065 kroner ($184.20) deluxe single; 850 kroner ($147.10) standard double, 1,630 kroner ($282) deluxe twin. AE, DC, MC, V. **Parking:** Free. **Closed:** Dec 22–28.

✪ Once a romantic inn on the edge of the Hardangerfjord, a retreat of Edvard Grieg—his piano is still kept in a cottage on the grounds—it was greatly expanded in the 1970s and is now the best-known "health farm" in Norway. "Farm" is hardly the word for this place, however. It's a beautifully equipped modern structure with a garden opening onto the shoreline, with views of the Folgefonn Glacier. Run by the Utne family for four generations, it offers rooms ranging from standard to deluxe. All are handsomely furnished with a number of amenities. The modest beginning in 1846 as a guesthouse has given way to a modern resort hotel, but an old-fashioned tradition of hospitality remains. Scandinavian kings, Emperor Wilhelm II, and European nobility have patronized the hotel.

Dining/Entertainment: The dining room seats 500 people (see "Where to Dine," below). International bands are often brought in to entertain guests. The hotel has a modern cocktail bar.

Services: Hairdresser, room service, laundry.

Facilities: Rowboats for fjord cruises, sailboats, heated swimming pool, whirlpool, game room, solarium, sauna, gym, jet spa, tennis court, squash court.

BUDGET

ULLENSVANG GJESTEHEIM, N-5774 Loftus i Hardanger. Tel. 53-66-12-36. 17 rms (none with bath).
$ **Rates** (including breakfast): Summer, 250 kroner ($43.30) single; 400 kroner ($69.20) double. Winter, 200 kroner ($34.60) single; 300 kroner ($51.90) double. No credit cards. **Parking:** Free.

S Ullensvang Gjesteheim is a cozy, homelike guesthouse in the town center, furnished with a personal touch. Rooms are quiet and have hot and cold running water. Close to the rooms are shared baths. The dining room serves the Norwegian *koldbord* for breakfast, and Norwegian specialties at lunch and dinner. You will relish their home-cooked food—both lunch and dinner go for 130 kroner ($22.50). In the garden are two old houses of the 16th century, the Borvehouse and Bleiehouse, which guests may visit.

WHERE TO DINE
MODERATE

RESTAURANT ULLENSVANG, Lofthus i Hardanger. Tel. 53-66-11-00.
   Cuisine: NORWEGIAN. **Reservations:** Recommended.
$ Prices: Dinner buffet 245 kroner ($42.40); 3-course lunch 170 kroner ($29.40); appetizers 40–70 kroner ($6.90–$12.10); main dishes 160–220 kroner ($27.70–$38.10). AE, DC, MC, V.
   Open: Lunch daily 1–3pm; dinner daily 7–9:30pm. **Closed:** Dec 22–28.
A hearty three-course Norwegian lunch is offered here, but most guests come in for the buffet dinner spread of at least 65 dishes—everything from jellied salmon to homemade cakes. Occasionally folk dancing is staged, and guests are invited to join in. Six nights a week there's a live band for dancing. It's located in the town center on the edge of the Hardangerfjord.

---

3. KINSARVIK

74 miles E of Bergen, 24 miles S of Voss, 223 miles W of Oslo

GETTING THERE   By Train   The Bergen Railroad running between Bergen and Oslo will take you to the Voss station, the nearest terminal to Kinsarvik. There are 14 arrivals and departures a day. From Voss, you can journey to Kinsarvik by bus. Trip time from Oslo to Voss is 5½ hours.

By Bus   Bus service takes 1¼ hours from Odda, 15 minutes from Lofthus. The bus trip from Bergen takes 2½ hours, and 50 minutes from Voss, the nearest rail connection.

By Car   Take E16 east from Bergen to Kvanndal, and then board car ferry to Kinsarvik.

By Boat   Boats leaving from Kvanndal on the northern coast of the Hardangerfjord take about 45 minutes.

ESSENTIALS   The tourist office, **Ullensvang Reiselivslag,** N-5780 Kinsarvik (tel. 53-66-11-12), in the village center, is open daily 9am–8pm (June–Aug) and Mon–Fri 9am–4pm and Sat 9am–1pm (Sept–May).

The main village of Kinsarvik stands on a glacier-formed ridge at the mouth of the Kinso River, which flows into four magnificent waterfalls as it drops from the plateau to Husedalen on its way to the sea. From early times Kinsarvik was the marketplace for the region.

   Kinsarvik was the principal timber port of Hardanger in the 17th and early 18th century. When the export of timber was transferred to Bergen in 1750, Kinsarvik developed a shipbuilding industry that continued until 1870, when it became a center for wood carving. Today a pewter factory is one of its principal industries.

WHAT TO SEE & DO

The plot of grass that slopes to a stony beach near the Kinsarvik ferry terminal is **Skiperstod,** site of a boathouse for naval longships from about 900 until 1350.
   Borstova, the building on the fjord side of the green facing the church, was

constructed partly from the timbers of St. Olav's Guildhall, the meeting place of the local guild until 1680. It is now a council chamber and social center.

Kinsarvik Church, said to have been built by Scottish masterbuilders at the end of the 12th century, is one of the oldest stone churches in Norway. The interior was restored in 1961 to its pre-Reformation condition. It has a 17th-century pulpit painted by Peter Reimers, a painted and carved altarpiece, and medieval frescoes.

The stone column (*minnestein*) on the green commemorates the local men who fought in the wars that led to the end of the union with Denmark in 1814.

The **Hardanger Recreation Park (Tillegg i tekst),** in the middle of Kinsarvik, is open on Saturday and Sunday from May to the end of September, daily from mid-June to the end of August.

About 9 miles from Kinsarvik en route to Eidfjord, off Highway 7, the **Bu Museum,** N-5782 Ringøy (tel. 53-66-69-00), has three old houses containing furniture and domestic and craft equipment. The basement of an old farmhouse is filled with artifacts dating from the Stone Age to modern times. The museum also has a collection of national costumes from the Hardanger area. It is open June 1 to August 10 from 11am to 4pm. Admission is 20 kroner ($3.50) for adults; children free.

WHERE TO STAY

INEXPENSIVE

KINSARVIK FJORD HOTEL, N-5780 Kinsarvik. Tel. 53-66-31-00. Fax 53-66-34-71. 116 rms (62 with bath). TV TEL

$ Rates (including breakfast): 550 kroner ($95.20) single without bath, 570 kroner ($98.60) single with bath; 700 kroner ($121.10) double without bath, 740 kroner ($128) double with bath. AE, DC, MC, V. **Parking:** Free.

Modern and well equipped, this is a family-type place. Both the public rooms and guest bedrooms have attractive modern styling, many opening onto views. Rooms are well maintained and comfortably furnished, and children sharing a room with their parents get a 50% reduction on meals.

Even if you don't stay here, you might like to have lunch for 175 kroner ($30.30) or dinner for 200 kroner ($34.60) in the pleasant dining room. The hotel is known for its generous buffets.

HARDING MOTELL OG HYTTETUN, N-5780 Kinsarvik. Tel. 53-66-31-82. Fax 53-66-33-45. 27 chalets (all with bath). TV

$ Rates: 595–725 kroner ($102.90–$125.40) per chalet. AE, DC, MC, V. **Parking:** Free.

This cluster of holiday chalets lies along national highway 7. Chalets are fully equipped, and 10 of them contain private phones. Guests prepare their own breakfast in individual kitchens. One large chalet has eight beds.

4. EIDFJORD

93 miles E of Bergen, 209 miles W of Oslo

GETTING THERE **By Train** Take the train from Bergen to Voss, where a connecting bus will take you the rest of the way.

By Bus Buses for Eidfjord depart three or four times a day from Voss, taking 1¾ hours. Part of the route across the Eidfjord itself requires a 10-minute ferryboat ride. In summer the ferry departs every 10 minutes, and in winter every 40 minutes.

By Car From Odda in the south, take Route 47 north; from Geilo in the east, take Route 7 west. The drive takes an hour.

ESSENTIALS The **Tourist Office,** located in the town center (tel. 53-66-51-77), is open daily 9am–7pm (June–Aug). There are no street names.

At the northern tip of the Hardangerfjord lies the Eidfjord district. Approximately 1,000 people live here, supporting themselves with agriculture, tourism, and cottage industries. The area is a paradise for hikers and home to the continent's largest herd of wild reindeer. Mountain trout with sour cream is a regional food specialty.

WHAT TO SEE & DO

The county contains nearly one-quarter of **☯ Hardangervidda National Park,** which is on the largest high-mountain plateau in Europe, home to 20,000 wild reindeer. Well-marked hiking trails connect a series of 15 tourist huts.

Several canyons, including the renowned **Måbø Valley,** lead down from the plateau to the fjords. Here you'll see the famous 550-foot Voringfoss waterfall; the Valurefoss in Hjømo Valley has a free fall of almost 800 feet.

Part of the 1,000-year-old road across Norway, traversing the Måbø Valley, has been restored for hardy hikers.

In Sima Valley, about 3¾ miles from the center of Eidfjord, you can visit the **Sima Power Plant,** one of the largest hydroelectric plants in Europe. Guided tours are given, and one of the dams built for the plant, the enormous Sysendam, can be seen from the R7 road.

A small mountain farm, **Kjeaasen,** nearly 2,000 feet above sea level, can be reached by car. From Kjeaasen you have a splendid view. The footpath is recommended only to those in good physical condition.

The 14th-century stone **Eidfjord Old Church** can be visited with a guide—make arrangements at the tourist office.

Numerous lakes and rivers offer good trout fishing, and in two rivers, the Eio and the Bjoreio, as well as in the Eidfjord Lake, you can fish for salmon. The local tourist office has rowboats and bicycles for rent.

WHERE TO STAY
BUDGET

HOTELL VØRINGSFOSS, N-5783 Eidfjord. Tel. 53-66-55-00. Fax 53-66-55-05. 50 rms (all with bath).

$ Rates (including breakfast): 350 kroner ($60.60) single; 475 kroner ($82.20) double. AE, DC, MC, V. **Parking:** Free.

⑤ Hotell Vøringsfoss lies by the fjord in Nedre Eidfjord, 20 paces from the bus station. The hotel represents a pleasing combination of the old and the new, as it has been accommodating guests since the 1880s but was extended and modernized over the years. Six of the bedrooms are modern, while the others are more old-fashioned but with comfortable furniture. Many open onto views of Eidfjord, and 40 of the bedrooms have TV and phone. The hotel contains four restaurants, ranging from an unpretentious pub to a more upscale place.

---

5. ULVIK

93 miles E of Bergen, 64 miles W of Geilo, 25 miles W of Voss

GETTING THERE   By Train and Bus   From Bergen or Oslo, take the train to Voss where you can catch a bus for the 25-mile ride to Ulvik (45 minutes). There are five daily buses in summer from Voss and three daily buses in winter. Buses stop in front of the Ulvik church in the town center (there is no formal bus station).

By Car   From Voss, head east on the E16, continuing east at the junction with Route 572.

ESSENTIALS   Ulvik Tourist Office (tel. 56-52-63-60), in the town center, is open daily 9am–8pm (June–Aug). It will arrange any number of excursions—from trips on fjord steamers to bus tours to the Osa Mountains.

Ulvik is that rarity—an unspoiled resort—lying like a fist at the end of an arm of the Hardangerfjord surrounded in summer by misty peaks and fruit farms. The village's century-old church is attractively decorated in the style of the region.

WHERE TO STAY

MODERATE

BRAKANES HOTEL, N-5730 Ulvik. Tel. 56-52-61-05. Fax 56-52-64-10. 100 rms (all with bath). MINIBAR TV TEL

$ Rates (including breakfast): 895 kroner ($154.80) single; 1,100–1,300 kroner ($190.30–$224.90) double. AE, DC, MC, V. **Parking:** Free.

The view of the Hardangerfjord and the surrounding forest is famous from this well-recommended hotel near the town center at the edge of the fjord. Originally built 130 years ago, all that remains of the original building is one small dining room. The balconied and skylight-covered modern building you see today evolved from a series of reconstructions beginning in the 1960s. Bedrooms are beautifully maintained. Facilities include a sauna, pool room, and tennis courts. In summer plane rides can be arranged over the fjords. Windsurfing and boat rentals are available. The hotel also offers the area's best-known nightlife choice.

STRAND HOTEL OG MOTEL, N-5730 Ulvik. Tel. 56-52-63-05. Fax 56-52-64-10. 41 rms (all with bath).

$ Rates (including breakfast): 795 kroner ($137.50) single; 990–1,100 kroner ($171.30–$190.30) double. AE, DC, MC, V. **Parking:** Free. **Closed:** Mid-Oct to late Apr.

This hotel, fronting the fjord, is a bungalow-style building. All bedrooms are completely up-to-date and overlook the fjord. The owners have added a motel with a dozen rooms; seven of these newer units contain private balconies, and four have private terraces. It is licensed for beer and wine, and has a dining room where you can order meals for 95 kroner to 200 kroner ($16.40 to $34.60). Waterskiing, motorboat rides, and rowing are available. There's also a heated indoor swimming pool and sauna. It's a 5-minute walk from the town center.

INEXPENSIVE

ULVIK FJORD PENSJONAT, N-5730 Ulvik. Tel. 56-52-61-70. Fax 56-52-61-60. 20 rms (all with bath). TEL

$ Rates (including breakfast): 290 kroner ($50.20) single without bath, 400 kroner ($69.20) single with bath; 480 kroner ($83) double without bath, 580 kroner ($100.30) double with bath. No credit cards. **Parking:** Free. **Closed:** Oct–Apr.

(S) Ulvik Fjord Pensjonat, constructed in two stages, in 1946 and 1977, is one of the finest guesthouses along the Hardangerfjord. Rooms are spacious and pleasantly furnished in a regional Norwegian style. You are welcomed by the Hammer family, who won the Norwegian Hospitality Prize of 1989. They invite you to use their sauna and solarium and to partake in their good-tasting fjord cooking.

ULVIK HOTEL, N-5730 Ulvik. Tel. 56-52-62-00. Fax 56-52-66-41. 58 rms (all with bath). TEL

$ Rates (including breakfast): 525–560 kroner ($90.80–$96.90) single; 740–800 kroner ($128–$138.40) double. AE, DC, MC, V. **Parking:** Free.

The hotel was built in 1946, with a significant addition in 1972; the garden is separated from the fjord only by a road. Bedrooms are modern and comfortable, painted in light pastels. More than half of them overlook the fjord. A dining room is reserved for boarding guests, but the A La Carte Restaurant (that's its name) set on the hotel's street level is more stylish, serving excellent Norwegian food. Shrimp and salmon are the most popular items on the menu. Live music and a nightclub format are presented Wednesday through Sunday from 9pm to either midnight or 1am. It's located on the fjord in the town center.

6. VOSS

78 miles E of Bergen, 255 miles W of Oslo

GETTING THERE   By Train   Train service takes about 1½ hours from Bergen, 1½ hours from Myrdal, and 2¼ hours from Flåm. About 14 trains running between Bergen and Oslo stop daily at Voss. Trip time between Voss and Oslo is 8½ hours.

By Bus   One bus daily runs between Bergen and Voss, taking 2¼ hours; and between Voss and Oslo, taking 11 hours.

By Car   From Bergen, take the E16 east all the way to Voss.

ESSENTIALS   For information, the **Voss Turistkontor,** Vangsgate 81 (tel. 56-51-17-16), is open Mon–Sat 9am–7pm and Sun 2–6pm (June–Aug) and Mon–Fri 9am–4pm (Sept–May).

Between the Sogne and Hardanger fjords. Voss is a famous year-round resort, also known for its folklore. It was the birthplace of football hero Knut Rockne. Maybe the trolls don't strike fear into the hearts of farm children anymore, but they are still called out of hiding to give the visitors a little fun.

Voss is a natural base for exploring the two largest fjords in Norway, the Sognefjord to the north and the Hardangerfjord to the south. In and around Voss are glaciers, mountains, fjords, waterfalls, orchards, rivers, and lakes.

WHAT TO SEE & DO

In addition to the attractions below, don't miss seeing **St. Olav's Cross,** Skulegata, near the Voss Cinema. It's the oldest historic relic in Voss, believed to have been raised when the townspeople adopted Christianity in 1023.

A ride on the **Hangursbanen Cable Car** (tel. 56-51-18-17) will be a memorable part of your visit, offering beautiful views of Voss and the environs. Refreshments or meals are available at the mountaintop restaurant. The hardy take the cable up, then spend the rest of the afternoon strolling leisurely down the mountain. A round-trip ride costs 40 kroner ($6.90) for adults, 30 kroner ($5.20) for children. Entrance to the cable car is on a hillside after a 10-minute walk north of the center.

VANGSKYRKJE, Vangsgata 3. Tel. 56-51-22-78.

This 13th-century church with a timbered tower in the center of Voss contains a striking Renaissance pulpit, stone altar and triptych, fine wood carvings, and a painted ceiling. It's a 5-minute walk east of the rail station.

Admission: Free.

Open: June–Aug, daily 9am–7pm. **Closed:** Sept–May.

FINNESLOFTET, Finne. Tel. 56-51-11-00.

About a mile west of Voss in Finne, Finnesloftet is one of the oldest timbered

IN THEIR FOOTSTEPS

Ludwig Holberg (1684–1754) After various careers, Holberg achieved major success in Copenhagen, writing Danish comedies. His most famous, produced in 1724, was called *Henrik and Pernille*. The 32 comedies he produced are largely responsible for his reputation as "the father of Danish literature," although he was Norwegian born.

● **Birthplace:** December 3, 1684, in Bergen, where he was soon orphaned.

● **Residences:** Voss (Norway), Oxford (England), and Copenhagen where he was to know his greatest success.

● **Resting Place:** Dying in Copenhagen on January 27, 1754, at the age of 70, he was buried at Sorø in Zealand.

houses in Norway, dating from the mid-13th century. It's a 15-minute walk west of the rail station.

Admission: 15 kroner ($2.60).

Open: June 25–Aug 11, daily 10am–4pm. **Closed:** Aug 12–June 24.

VOSS FOLKEMUSEUM, Mølster. Tel. 56-51-15-11.

A collection of authentically furnished houses, this museum shows what early farm life was like. The new building also displays selected items from the museum's collection of home crafts. Take a taxi from the center.

Admission: 15 kroner ($2.60) adults; free for children.

Open: May 10–Sept 15, daily 10am–5pm; Sept 16–May 9, Mon–Fri 10am–3pm.

SKIING

Voss is continually adding to its facilities, and is definitely in the race to overtake Geilo and Lillehammer as Norway's most popular winter playground. Its chair lifts, ski lifts, and aerial cableway carry passengers up 2,625 feet.

The town offers what it calls a "ski circus": Beginners take the Hangursbanen cable car; one ski lift (3,000 feet long) goes from Traastolen to the top of Slettafjell (with a wide choice of downhill runs); the Bavallen lift is for the slalom slopes; and the downhill runs are at Lonehorgi.

Lessons at the **Ski School** (tel. 56-51-18-17), at the end of the cable-car run, are moderate in cost. The tourist office and hotels can arrange bookings.

Parents can park children ages 3 to 7 in a "snow nursery" while they spend the day skiing. Kids over 7 can ski. A special branch of the Ski School handles these youngsters. Ski equipment—everything from boots to touring skis—can be rented.

WHERE TO STAY

MODERATE

FLEISCHERS HOTEL, Evangerveiten 13, N-5700 Voss. Tel. 56-51-11-55. Fax 56-51-22-89. 71 rms (all with bath). MINIBAR TV TEL

$ Rates (including breakfast): 800 kroner ($138.40) single; 950 kroner ($164.40) double. AE, DC, MC, V. **Parking:** Free.

On the lakefront right beside the Voss Rail Station, Fleischers couldn't be more convenient: The Bergen-Oslo train stops out back. The gracious 1889 frame hotel added a modern wing that has 30 units, all with private showers, toilets, kitchenettes, and terraces overlooking the lake. In the old part of the hotel, rooms are old-fashioned. The hotel features a dining room, billiard room, sauna, solarium, library, and two bars.

HOTEL JARL, Voss Sentrum, N-5700 Voss. Tel. 56-51-19-33. Fax 56-51-37-69. 80 rms (all with bath), 6 suites. MINIBAR TV TEL

$ Rates (including breakfast): 520–740 kroner ($90–$128) single; 740–1,180 kroner ($128–$204.10) double; from 1,250 kroner ($216.30) suite. AE, DC, MC, V. **Parking:** Free.

In this centrally situated hotel are singles, doubles, and family rooms, each furnished with comfortably modern styling. Other facilities include attractive public rooms, an indoor swimming pool, a sauna bath, an English pub, game room, and a popular nightclub, Knight's Club. You can take your meals in the pleasant dining room, or relax in an intimate bistro and bar. The Hotel Jarl is in the town center by the bridges.

PARK HOTEL VOSSEVANGEN, Uttrågate, N-5701 Voss. Tel. 56-51-13-22. Fax 56-51-00-39. 63 rms (all with bath). MINIBAR TV TEL

$ Rates (including breakfast): 675–975 kroner ($116.80–$168.70) single; 975–1,250 kroner ($168.70–$216.30) double. AE, DC, MC, V. **Parking:** Free.

In 1990 this hotel merged itself architecturally with its neighbor, the Vossevangen Hotel. Shortly after their union, an architect joined the two sections with a covered passageway. The Park was built in 1961 and the Vossevangen in 1954. Bedrooms are attractively furnished. The hotel is family-owned and contains the best restaurant in town, the Elysée (see "Where to Dine," below). Facilities include the Café Stationen, the Pentagon Dance Bar, and the Pianissimo Bar. It's located in the center, about 100 yards from the rail station.

BUDGET

BAVALLSTOVA PENSJONAT, Bavallsvegen 272, N-5700 Voss. Tel. 56-51-18-73. 17 rms (14 with bath).

$ **Rates:** 300 kroner ($51.90) single without bath; 350 kroner ($60.60) single with bath; 350 kroner ($60.60) double without bath, 380 kroner ($65.70) double with bath. Half board 300 kroner ($51.90) per person extra. No credit cards. **Parking:** Free.

This is an immaculate and comfortable boardinghouse, about 3¼ miles from the center of Voss, near the Bavallen ski lift. Rebuilt in 1982, it has tasteful, restful bedrooms, all doubles, although single occupancy is possible. The bright cafeteria has a panoramic view of Voss, the lake below, and the mountains beyond. There is a large lounge with an open fireplace.

KRINGSJÅ PENSION, Strengjarhavgen 6, N-5700 Voss. Tel. 56-51-16-27. Fax 56-51-63-30. 18 rms (15 with bath).

$ **Rates** (including breakfast): 320 kroner ($55.40) single without bath, 350 kroner ($60.60) single with bath; 480 kroner ($83) double without bath, 520 kroner ($90) double with bath. AE, DC, MC, V. **Parking:** Free.

Kringsjå Pension is an inviting guesthouse. The public rooms are spacious and airy, and the bedrooms, all twins, are functionally furnished. You'll pay from 110 kroner ($19) for lunch or dinner.

NØRING PENSJONAT, Uttrågate 41, N-5700 Voss. Tel. 56-51-12-11. 21 rms (none with bath).

$ **Rates** (including breakfast): 350 kroner ($60.60) single; 540 kroner ($93.40) double. AE, DC, MC, V. **Parking:** Free.

S Nøring Pension is a first-class pension built near the river in 1949, about a 10-minute walk from the town center, providing clean, functional accommodations. Half the rooms face the mountains. Licensed for beer and wine, the boardinghouse serves good hearty breakfasts. The lounge opens onto a terrace.

WHERE TO DINE
MODERATE

ELYSEE, in the Park Hotel Vossevangen, Uttrågate. Tel. 56-51-13-22.
Cuisine: FRENCH/NORWEGIAN. **Reservations:** Recommended.
$ **Prices:** Appetizers 40–60 kroner ($6.90–$10.40); main dishes 145–215 kroner ($25.10–$37.20); lunch smörgåsbord 170 kroner ($29.40) per person. AE, DC, MC, V.
Open: Daily noon–11pm.
This is the prestige restaurant of town, with more than 10,000 bottles of wine in inventory, the finest list in the fjord district. The decor is neoclassical, modeled on Greek motifs, and the location is on the lobby level of the Park Hotel Vossevangen (see "Where to Stay," above). Fresh Norwegian salmon is poached in white wine and served with a herb sauce, or you can order such typical dishes as filet of lamb provençale or filet of roast venison with lingonberry sauce.

FLEISCHERS RESTAURANT, Evangerveiten 13. Tel. 56-51-11-55.
Cuisine: NORWEGIAN. **Reservations:** Recommended.
$ **Prices:** Appetizers 50–72 kroner ($8.70–$12.50); main dishes 165–182 kroner ($28.50–$31.50); lunch smörgåsbord 155 kroner ($26.80); 4-course fixed-price dinner 210 kroner ($36.30). AE, DC, MC, V.
Open: Mon–Sat 1–10:30pm, Sun 1–9:45pm.
The dining room of this landmark hotel, a few steps away from the Voss Rail Station, hasn't been altered since the hotel opened a century ago. The colors are dark reds and

dark greens, a medley of Victorian tradition. Long the leading restaurant in the Voss area, Fleischers remains the favorite of the traditionalist. Its lunchtime smörgåsbord is a lavish array of all-you-can-eat Norwegian delicacies. Specialties include smoked salmon, filet of beef, gratinated filet of lamb, and filets of pork and veal.

INEXPENSIVE

VANGEN CAFE, Vangen Super-Market, Vangsgate. Tel. 56-51-12-05.
   Cuisine: NORWEGIAN. **Reservations:** Not required.
$ Prices: Soup 20 kroner ($3.50); smørbrød 28–35 kroner ($4.80–$6.10); *dagens* menu 60–80 kroner ($10.40–$13.80). No credit cards.
   Open: Mon–Fri 9:30am–6pm, Sat 9:30am–3pm, Sun noon–6pm.
This is the least expensive cafeteria-style outlet in Voss, sitting one floor above street level over a small souvenir shop and food market in the center of town, a 5-minute walk south of the rail station. Soft drinks and fruit juices are sold, but no alcohol, not even beer or wine. The daily *dagens* menu is the best food value in town.

EVENING ENTERTAINMENT

FLEISCHERS TOP SPOT NIGHTCLUB, in Fleischers Hotel, Evanger-veiten 13. Tel. 56-51-11-55.
   In the cellar of Fleischers Hotel (see "Where to Stay," above), this is the best-established nightlife spot in Voss. Dance bands play nightly for an older crowd who believe in dressing up a bit. Many people come here just to drink—beer costs 39 kroner ($6.70)—but it's also possible to order full meals, for 160 kroner to 250 kroner ($27.70 to $43.30). Steak platters are a feature. It's open Monday through Thursday from 9pm to 1am and on Friday and Saturday from 9pm to 3am.
   Admission: 35–50 kroner ($6.10–$8.70).

AN EXCURSION TO THE SOGNEFJORD

Motorists with more time may want to visit the Sognefjord district, the largest of all Norwegian fjords. From Voss the northern route leads to **Vik.** The scenery is beautiful, and the road goes along for miles across a desolate tableland at 3,000 feet above sea level. The lakes on a summer day appear green, and on the distant slopes is snow.
   In Vik, try to see the stave church, one of the most attractive in Norway. Then take the road to **Vangsnes,** where you can make ferry connections across the Sognefjord to Balestrand or Dragsvik. Once across, take Route 5 north. The highway is steep, bringing you through pleasant countryside with waterfalls until you reach **Viksdalen,** about 40 miles from Dragsvik.

---

7. BALESTRAND

53 miles N of Flåm, 56 miles N of Voss, 130 miles NE of Bergen

GETTING THERE   By Train   From either Bergen or Oslo, trains run several times daily to Voss or Flåm, from which bus and ferry connections can be made north to Balestrand.

By Bus   Good bus connections cover the inner Sogn area, Voss, and Nordfjord.

By Car   From Voss, take Route 13 north of Vangsnes, and board a car-ferry there for the short crossing northwest to Balestrand.

By Boat   Two express boats operate daily from Bergen harbor taking 3½ hours.

ESSENTIALS For information, the **Tourist Office,** in the town center (tel. 57-69-12-55), is open Mon–Sat 8:30am–1:30pm and 3–6pm and Sun 11am–3pm (June–Aug).

Long known for its arts and crafts, Balestrand lies on the northern rim of Sognefjord, at the junction of the Vetlefjord, the Esefjord, and the Fjaerlandsfjord.

WHAT TO SEE & DO

The staff at the tourist office (see above) will help you organize your exploration and also put you in touch with local craftspeople. Pick up an excursion program and purchase tickets for any of the scheduled 1½-day tours—for example, a taxi plane across the **Jostedal Glacier** (see "Fjaerland," below).

Kaiser Wilhelm II, a frequent visitor to Balestrand, presented the district with two statues of old Norse heroes, King Bele and Fridtjof the Bold, standing in the center. Another sight in town is the English church of **St. Olav** in Balestrand, a tiny wooden building, dating from 1897.

You can explore by setting out in nearly every direction, on good country lanes with little traffic, or a wide choice of marked trails and upland farm tracks. A touring map may be purchased at the tourist office. There is good sea fishing, as well as lake and river trout fishing. Fishing tackle, rowboats, and bicycles can all be rented in the area.

WHERE TO STAY

MODERATE

KVIKNE'S HOTEL, Balholm, N-5850 Balestrand. Tel. 57-69-11-01. Fax 57-69-15-02. 19 rms (all with bath). TEL
$ Prices (including breakfast): 650 kroner ($112.50) single; 930 kroner ($160.90) double. AE, DC, MC, V. **Parking:** Free. **Closed:** Oct–Apr.
Originally built as a summer retreat for vacationing Europeans in 1913, this hotel was much enlarged in 1970. At its core it is an elaborately detailed building with balconies, opening onto the edge of the fjord. All but a few of the bedrooms have fjord views. The hotel has a large dining room, several lounges, and a dance club. Sports such as waterskiing, windsurfing, and fjord fishing can be arranged, as can helicopter flights to the Jostedal Glacier. Facilities include whirlpool, sauna, and solarium.

INEXPENSIVE

DRAGSVIK FJORD HOTEL, Dragsvik, N-5850 Balestrand. Tel. 57-69-12-93. Fax 57-69-13-83. 33 rms (15 with bath). TEL
$ Rates (including breakfast): 400 kroner ($69.20) single without bath, 490 kroner ($84.80) single with bath; 550 kroner ($95.20) double without bath, 650 kroner ($112.50) double with bath. AE, MC, V. **Parking:** Free.
Located about half a mile from Balestrand, and 300 yards from the ferry quay at Dragsvik, this hotel is moderately priced. Doubles in the new wing have the most up-to-date plumbing. The large dining room offers a spectacular view of the Fjaerlandsfjord. The hotel has a private swimming area. You can also rent bicycles and rowboats.

BUDGET

MIDTNES PENSJONAT, N-5850 Balestrand. Tel. 57-69-11-33. Fax 57-69-15-84. 34 rms (all with bath).
$ Rates: 330 kroner ($57.10) single without bath, 350 kroner ($60.60) single with bath; 410 kroner ($70.90) double without bath, 480 kroner ($83) double with bath. Breakfast 50 kroner ($8.70) extra. No credit cards. **Parking:** Free.

The well-run and reasonably priced boardinghouse, in the center of Balestrand, next to the English church, is family-owned and -managed. The rooms are pleasantly furnished, most of them opening onto Sognefjord which has a private pier with rowboats. The boardinghouse, which is fully licensed, also offers good food, a full luncheon for 110 kroner ($19) and dinner for 150 kroner ($26). Meals are served in a dining room opening onto a view of the fjord.

8. FJAERLAND

56 miles N of Voss, 111 miles NE of Bergen

GETTING THERE   By Train   The nearest railway station with a boat connection is in Flåm (see below).

By Boat   Express boats from Bergen take 4 hours; boats from Flåm take 2 hours. There is also service from Balestrand (see above).

By Car   From Skei in the west, take Route 625 east, going through a mountain tunnel. The distance is 12 miles, and no ferry crossings are necessary.

This fertile farming district at the top of the Fjaerlandsfjord is a starting point for tours of the Jostedal Glacier, along marked trails and upland farm tracks. For a description of the Jostedal Glacier, refer to "Easy Excursions" below. There is daily bus service from Fjaerland to the glacier, where there is good hiking on the glacier plateau.

The **Norsk Bremuseum** (Norwegian Glacier Museum; tel. 57-69-31-01), opened in 1991, lying about a mile north of the village center. The set designer for *Star Wars* supplied some of the special effects. A large screen shows a film about glacier ice trekking, and a fiberglass glacial maze is complete with "blue ice." Two arms of the Jostedal can be seen from the museum. Admission is 55 kroner ($9.50) for adults, 30 kroner ($5.20) for children. The museum is open May through September daily from 10am to 6pm. In October, hours are daily from 10:30am to 5pm. It is closed from November through April.

WHERE TO STAY

MODERATE

HOTEL MUNDAL, N-5855 Fjaerland. Tel. 57-69-31-01. Fax 57-69-31-79. 40 rms (all with bath). TEL
$ Rates (including breakfast): 695 kroner ($120.20) single; 730–1,300 kroner ($126.30–$224.90) double. V. **Parking:** Free. **Closed:** Nov 15–Apr 1.
No two bedrooms are alike in the Hotel Mundal, and the living rooms are spacious and attractively furnished, partly with antiques. Guests enjoy browsing in the hotel library. Lunches or dinners cost from 160 kroner ($27.70), and the food is excellent. The hotel, which dates from 1891, often presents folk dancing and live music.

INEXPENSIVE

FJAERLAND FJORDSTUE, N-5855 Fjaerland. Tel. 57-69-31-61. Fax 57-69-32-00. 18 rms (all with bath).
$ Rates (including breakfast): 450 kroner ($77.90) single without bath, 550 kroner ($95.20) single with bath; 600 kroner ($103.80) double without bath, 750 kroner ($129.80) double with bath. No credit cards. **Parking:** Free.
This hotel, whose English name means "fjord's living room," was originally built as a private house in 1936, but converted to a hotel in 1947. It lies a 2-minute walk north of the ferry terminal. People usually stay here between May 1 and mid-October. Each

bedroom is painted in light pastel colors, very Norwegian, with traditional furniture, and half of them overlook the fjord.

EASY EXCURSIONS

JOSTEDAL GLACIER

⭐ One of Norway's most outstanding sights is the Jostedal Glacier, the largest in Europe and second largest in the world. Between the Sognefjord and the Nordfjord, above a valley called Briksdal, the glacier is about a mile above sea level and almost 350 feet wide. Most of the icy giant can be circled by visitors, depending on the choice of route.

Most people are satisfied simply to go by excursion boat from Bergen and up the Nordfjord. Boats enter the fjord from the Norwegian Sea some 40 miles south of Ålesund.

For a more complete view, however, you can approach Jostedal by road, going about 65 miles north from the Sognefjord to reach the roads that go around the ice mass.

Medium-size cruise liners make their way up the Nordfjord to dock at the little town of Olden at the fjord's head. From Olden, a road leads to the Briksdal Valley and the **Briksdal Mountain Lodge,** about a 45-minute bus or car trip. From the lodge, you can walk to the base of the glacier or go in a two-wheel cart the lodge will supply. Up to five people can ride in the horse-drawn carts. If you're adventurous you may choose to go on foot, but the road is rough and muddy and should only be tackled by the hearty. Walk across the bridge, then follow a trail up to Jostedal Glacier. Wrap up in foul-weather gear, as it's cool and misty in the area.

The portion of the glacier visited from Olden is just one of the seven arms of the mighty ice giant, a remnant of the frigid coat that once covered all of Norway.

At Skei, at the base of Lake Jølster, 37 miles from Olden, a road goes under the glacier for more than 4 miles until it reaches Fjaerland. Until 1986, there was no road link to Fjaerland at all.

---

9. FLÅM

40 miles E of Voss, 217 miles W of Oslo

GETTING THERE   By Train   The best—and most exciting—approach to Flåm is aboard the ✪ **electric train from Myrdal,** which has good connections from both Bergen and Oslo. The electric train follows a 12-mile route overlooking a 2,844-foot drop, stopping occasionally for passengers to photograph spectacular waterfalls. Trip time is 50 minutes. In winter, about four or five trains a day make the run to Flåm. In summer, depending on business, they are much more frequent, beginning at 4am and running throughout the day.

By Bus   Monday through Saturday, one bus daily runs between Aurland and Flåm, taking 30 minutes.

By Ferry   May to September, two fjord ferries per day cross between Aurland and Flåm, taking 30 minutes. Flåm can also be reached by high-speed express boats from Bergen, Balestrand (see above), and Leikanger. Only passengers are carried aboard—no cars.

By Car   Road links are possible from Aurland in the north (take Route 601 south).

Essentials   The small **Tourist Office,** near the rail station, is open daily 8:15am–8:30pm (June–mid-Aug).

Flåm (pronounced Flawm) lies on the Aurlandsfjord, a tip of the more famous Sognefjord. In the village you can visit the old church dating from 1667, with painted walls done in typical Norwegian country style.

WHERE TO STAY
MODERATE

FRETHEIM HOTELL, N-5743 Flåm. **Tel. 57-63-22-00.** Fax 57-63-23-03. 75 rms (70 with bath). TV TEL

$ Rates (including breakfast): 550 kroner ($95.15) single without bath, 600 kroner ($103.80) single with bath; 740 kroner ($128) double without bath, 950 kroner ($164.35) double with bath. AE, MC, V. **Parking:** Free.

Dating from the 1860s, this is one of the oldest and most historic hotels in the region. Although its bedrooms have been modernized, its lounges, dining rooms, and public areas have retained the high ceilings, wood paneling, and old-fashioned details of the original construction. In addition to its restaurant (open to nonguests), the hotel also has a moderately priced cafeteria and a bar. It's located across the street from the rail station.

HEIMLY LODGE AND MARINA, N-5743 Flåm. **Tel. 57-63-23-00.** Fax 57-63-23-40. 40 rms (35 with bath).

$ Rates (including breakfast): 375 kroner ($64.90) single without bath, 650 kroner ($112.50) single with bath; 590 kroner ($102.10) double without bath, 850 kroner ($147.10) double with bath. MC, V. **Closed:** Nov–Feb. **Parking:** Free.

Near the end of the electric railway, this lodge was created by Dr. Otto Tokvam some 45 years ago as a ski school but later converted to a hotel containing many antiques and old-fashioned pieces. It is an A-frame chalet, close to the waterfront, the Sognefjorden, with views in many directions. Bedrooms are cozy. Tennis, badminton, swimming, waterskiing, salmon and trout fishing, and motorboating are all available. Facilities also include a cafeteria and a pub.

---

10. GEILO

149 miles W of Oslo, 149 miles E of Bergen

GETTING THERE By Air Degali Airport is 16 miles from Geilo. **Nørving Airlines** has scheduled flights daily from Oslo, taking 30 minutes, and from Bergen, taking 35 minutes.

By Train Train service takes 2¼ hours from Flåm, 1½ hours from Myrdal, and 4 hours from Oslo or Bergen. Four trains run from either Bergen or Oslo daily.

By Bus Bus connections are possible from Oslo's Central Station, but tourist officials recommend the train as Geilo is on the main rail link between Bergen and Oslo.

By Car From Oslo, head west on Route 7 all the way.

ESSENTIALS The **Turistkontoret** (tel. 32-09-52-06), in the town center, is open Mon–Sat 9am–7pm and Sun 2–6pm (June–Aug) and Mon–Fri 9am–4pm (Sept–May). The town doesn't use street addresses, but everything is easy to find.

One of Norway's best-known ski resorts, Geilo, some 2,600 feet above sea level in the Hol mountain district, is also an attractive summer resort. Although it is not in the fjord country, it is included in this chapter because it is a "gateway" to the fjord country on the route from Oslo to Bergen. Geilo lies halfway between Oslo and Bergen.

In the Geilo area, there are 81 miles of marked tracks for cross-country skiing in winter.

WHAT TO SEE & DO

The main ski season is January through March. The **Ski School** has more than two dozen instructors, known for their patience with amateurs. Other amusements include sleigh rides, curling, and skating at the **Geilo Stadium.**

From here you can visit the historical museum in **Hol,** 6 miles northeast of Geilo, to see 16th-century wood carvings, as well as a 12th-century stave church. Another destination is the ancient Viking burial ground at **Fekjo.** The tourist office will provide maps and help you plan day excursions.

Of course, the chair-lift ride is good for scenery—mountain plateau and fjord. The terminal for the lift is a short walk from the railway station.

WHERE TO STAY

VERY EXPENSIVE

DR. HOLMS HOTEL, N-3580 Geilo. Tel. 32-09-56-22. Fax 32-09-66-20. 124 rms (all with bath), 5 suites. MINIBAR TV TEL

$ Rates (including breakfast): Winter, 1,010–1,220 kroner ($174.70–$211.10) single; 1,620–1,820 kroner ($280.30–$314.90) double; from 2,040 kroner ($352.90) suite. Summer, 520–730 kroner ($90–$126.30) single; 650–1,060 kroner ($112.50–$183.40) double; from 1,440 kroner ($249.10) suite. AE, DC, MC, V. **Parking:** 30 kroner ($5.20).

⭐ One of the most famous resort hotels in Norway, Dr. Holms is the finest place to stay in the area. Located near the rail station, you get elegance, comfort, and traditional styling. Dr. J. C. Holm opened the hotel in 1909 but since then there has been a lot of changes, including the addition of two completely new wings and a swimming complex. The final facelift was in 1989. The original works of art decorating the hotel have been retained. Rooms are beautifully furnished with traditional styling and many amenities, such as trouser press, radio, and TV with satellite and video channels. Rates can go higher on special weekends in winter.

Dining/Entertainment: In days gone by, a world-famous violinist, Garaguli, performed *Ave Maria* in the main lounge. Artists still perform there, or you can enjoy drinks in the three bars, including the Skiers' Bar, the après-ski favorite. Guests can dine in the 400-seat dining room or book a table in the 40-seat Le Monarque, the hotel's specialty restaurant. Camus is the hotel's nightlife venue.

Services: 24-hour room service, babysitting, laundry.

Facilities: Swimming pool, gym, sauna, library, conservatory, conference center, tennis courts, heated ski stall.

MODERATE

BARDØLA HØYFJELLSHOTEL, N-3580 Geilo. Tel. 32-09-54-00. Fax 32-09-66-79. 57 rms (all with bath), 45 suites. MINIBAR TV TEL

$ Rates (including breakfast): 775–925 kroner ($134.10–$160) single; 975–1,125 kroner ($168.70–$194.60) double. Suite supplement 200 kroner ($34.60) per person. AE, DC, MC, V. **Parking:** Free.

In tranquil surroundings in the environs of Geilo, less than a mile from the Geilo rail station, this well-run hotel is inviting in both summer and winter. It has a high standard of comfort, and the largest number of suites of any hotel in the area. On certain winter weekends rates may rise sharply. Inside is a swimming pool, a Jacuzzi, massage parlor, sun studio, and a hairdressing salon. Outdoor facilities include a heated pool and tennis courts.

GEILO HOTEL, P.O. Box 113, N-3581 Geilo. Tel. 32-09-55-11. Fax 32-09-67-30. 72 rms (all with bath). MINIBAR TV TEL

$ Rates (including breakfast): Winter, 650 kroner ($112.50) single; 1,000 kroner ($173) double. Summer, 550 kroner ($95.20) single; 800 kroner ($138.40) double. AE, DC, MC, V. **Parking:** Free.

This was the first hotel to open in Geilo, and its oldest part dates from 1880. It was renovated in 1990 and now its accommodations are better than ever. Rooms are attractively furnished. The nearest ski lift is about 200 yards from the hotel. The hotel offers room service and babysitting, and has such facilities as a sauna, whirlpool, one restaurant serving Scandinavian food, and two bars. The hotel is 300 yards from the rail station.

HOTELL ALPIN, N-3580 Geilo. Tel. 32-09-55-44. Fax 32-09-53-90. 26 rms (all with bath).
$ Rates: Winter (with half board), 460–600 kroner ($79.60–$103.80) single; 820–2,200 kroner ($141.90–$380.60) double. Summer (including breakfast), 330 kroner ($57.10) single; 460–600 kroner ($79.60–$103.80) double. AE, DC, MC, V. **Parking:** Free.

In the center of the village, 500 yards east of the rail station, the Hotell Alpin has an intimate atmosphere with soft lighting and wood paneling in the halls and smaller lounges. The restaurant offers a good à la carte menu, and there's dancing during the evening in season. Views from the windows open to the mountains and rivers. Bedrooms contain modern Scandinavian furnishings.

VESTLIA HØYFJELLSHOTELL, N-3580 Geilo. Tel. 32-09-56-11. Fax 32-09-66-89. MINIBAR TV
$ Rates (including breakfast): Winter, 725–950 kroner ($125.40–$164.40) single; 940–1,640 kroner ($162.60–$283.70) double. Summer, 450–640 kroner ($77.90–$110.70) single; 580–1,020 kroner ($100.30–$176.50) double. AE, DC, MC, V. **Parking:** Free.

This is not a big fancy hotel, but guests keep coming back. The location is 200 yards from the ski lifts and cross-country slopes, 1 mile from the Geilo rail station. It is also a good summertime choice, as guests go hiking, boating, or even horseback riding. Regular bedrooms, all doubles, are furnished in an attractive ski-chalet style, with lots of wood. Some big family rooms with four beds are available, which cost the same as the regular double rooms. The hotel has a swimming pool, sauna, and solarium, plus two restaurants. Scandinavia buffets are served, and live dance music is provided.

WHERE TO DINE
EXPENSIVE

LE MONARQUE, in the Dr. Holms Hotel. Tel. 32-09-56-22.
Cuisine: FRENCH. **Reservations:** Required.
$ Prices: Appetizers 90–170 kroner ($15.60–$29.40); main dishes 200–325 kroner ($34.60–$56.20). AE, DC, MC, V.
Open: Dinner only, daily 7–11pm.

⭐ This is the premier restaurant of Geilo, near the rail station. It is the most exclusive dining spot at the resort, and the decor is richly warm and formal. It lies one floor above street level at Dr. Holms Hotel (see "Where to Stay," above). Main dishes change with the season, but filet of reindeer is a specialty. The finest European wines are served, including Château Dr. Holms, produced in France.

MODERATE

GRILL ALPIN, Geiloveien. Tel. 32-09-53-84.
Cuisine: STEAKS. **Reservations:** Not required.
$ Prices: Appetizers 30–60 kroner ($5.20–$10.40); main dishes 75–170 kroner ($13–$29.40). AE, DC, MC, V.
Open: Dinner only, Tues–Sat 4–10:30pm. **Closed:** Nov.

This is a cozy little grill, specializing in steak, located across from the rail station, on the premises of Café Alpin. Other selections include grilled elk steak and Norwegian-style mutton stew.

INEXPENSIVE

CAFE ALPIN, Geiloveien. Tel. 32-09-53-84.
Cuisine: NORWEGIAN. **Reservations:** Not required.

$ Prices: Appetizers 15–45 kroner ($2.60–$7.80); main dishes 55–80 kroner ($9.50–$13.80). AE, DC, MC, V.

Open: Mon–Sat 9am–7pm, Sun 11am–7pm.

On the second floor, above the bank and next to the tourist bureau, this café is the best economy dining choice in town. It's good for coffee, sandwiches, or a hot meal. The cafeteria serves hot meals from noon.

If it's on the menu, try the creamed fish soup. For main dishes, you may want to try such Norwegian specialties as chopped reindeer meatcakes with mixed vegetables or cured herring with sliced beets, raw onions, and boiled potatoes. For dessert, a tempting selection of Norwegian pastries is offered.

EVENING ENTERTAINMENT

NIGHTCLUB CAMUS, in the Dr. Holms Hotel. Tel. 32-09-56-22.

This is the chic dance club of the Dr. Holms Hotel (see "Where to Stay," above), near the rail station. No jeans are permitted, and it's best to dress up a bit. A beer will cost 39 kroner ($6.70). It's open October to April, Monday through Saturday from 9pm to 2am.

Admission: 50 kroner ($8.70); free for hotel residents.

CHAPTER 20

TRONDHEIM & MIDDLE NORWAY

Our exploration of middle Norway begins north of Bergen—often called the top of the fjord country. Ålesund, Geiranger, Åndalsnes, and Molde are four centers that make ideal headquarters, not only for their beauty and sights, but as starting points for excursions. The northward journey eventually continues to medieval Trondheim. Trondheim, the ancient capital of Norway, is the third most interesting city to visit in Norway, following Oslo and Bergen.

SEEING TRONDHEIM & MIDDLE NORWAY

GETTING THERE

Trondheim is in many ways the best gateway to middle Norway, because of its air connections with Bergen and Oslo and its rail link with Oslo. If you'd like to see the "top of the fjord country," consider flying to Ålesund from Bergen and using it as a base for exploring the area. A train from Oslo also runs to Åndalsnes, another good base for touring the northern sector of the western fjord district. If you're driving, plan to take a lot of car-ferries to get from one shore to another. Once you land at a gateway, frequent buses connect the major towns of interest.

A SUGGESTED ITINERARY

Days 1 & 2: From Oslo, take the E6 north to Trondheim. Spend the second day exploring the attractions in and around this historic city.

Day 3: Drive south or take public transport to Røros to explore this perfectly preserved copper-mining town.

Day 4: Head for the northern part of the western fjord country, flying from Trondheim to Ålesund for the night.

Day 5: Spend the morning seeing the sights of Ålesund, then take a bus to Åndalsnes for the night.

Day 6: Head south by bus to Geiranger to explore the most beautiful fjords.

Day 7: Return to Åndalsnes. Transfer by bus to Molde for the night.

WHAT'S SPECIAL ABOUT MIDDLE NORWAY

Great Towns/Villages

☐ Trondheim, ancient capital of Norway and its third-largest city, filled with monuments.

☐ Røros, a national treasure, an old mining town so well preserved it's on the World Heritage List.

☐ Ålesund, "top of the fjord country," spread over three islands against a backdrop of the Sunnmøre Alps.

Ancient Monuments

☐ Nidaros Cathedral, at Trondheim, from the 11th century, once the burial place of medieval Norwegian kings.

Museums

☐ Trøndelag Folk Museum, outside Trondheim, Norway's main folk museum—there's even a tiny stave church.

☐ Sunnmøre Museum, outside Ålesund, depicting rural life from the Middle Ages to around 1900.

Scenic Wonders

☐ Geirangerfjord, considered by many Norwegians their most majestic fjord.

☐ Seven Sisters Waterfall, one of the most spectacular in Norway, with masses of water plunging downhill over a sheer rock face.

☐ Trollstigveien (Troll's Path), the route to Åndalsnes, a zigzagging road with hairpin bends through the mountains.

Special Events/Festivals

☐ Molde Jazz Festival, in midsummer, drawing jazz artists from around the world.

1. ÅLESUND

79 miles W of Åndalsnes, 82 miles (and two ferry rides)
SW of Kristiansund N, 37 miles (and one ferry ride) SW of Molde

GETTING THERE **By Plane** The easiest way to reach Ålesund is to fly from Bergen, arriving at Ålesund/Vigra airport (tel. 70-18-32-45 for flight information; 70-18-37-00 for airport), a 15-minute taxi or airport-bus ride from the town center. There are also daily flights from Bodø, Haugesund, Kristiansand S, Oslo, Røros, Stavanger, Tromsø, and Trondheim. Flights are on Braathens SAFE, Skateflua (tel. 70-12-58-00) in Ålesund.

By Train Go to Åndalsnes and then take a bus from the railway station to Ålesund. A daily train arrives from Oslo.

By Bus Most tourist buses run June 15 to end of August. Good connections are possible from Åndalsnes, the nearest rail terminal. One bus a day also runs from Bergen, taking 11 hours. One or two buses a day arrive from Trondheim, taking 8½ hours.

By Coastal Steamer The coastal steamer departs Bergen daily at 10pm and arrives at Ålesund at noon the following day.

By Car Take the A69 west from Åndalsnes all the way to Ålesund. A car-ferry operates between Åndalsnes and Ålesund.

ESSENTIALS **Ålesund Reiselivslag,** Rådhuset (tel. 70-12-12-02), provides tourist information daily 9am–7pm (June–Aug) and Mon–Fri 10am–4pm (Sept–May).

Ålesund is at the top of the fjord country, spread over three islands in an archipelago, with the snowcapped Sunnmøre Alps in the background. The islanders once earned their living from fishing.

After a fire destroyed the town in 1904, Ålesund was rebuilt in the "in" style of the times, art nouveau. Towers, turrets, and medieval romantic facades are pure art nouveau, and the Ålesund version includes elements from Nordic mythology.

WHAT TO SEE & DO

There are many sights in Ålesund, most works of nature. The mountain guardian of the area is **Aksla** (600 feet), a scenic sanctuary with a terrace restaurant, offering a view of fjord landscape, ancient Viking islands, and the Sunnmøre mountains. In the harbor nestles the flat island of **Giske,** believed to have been the birthplace of Rollo, 10th-century founder of the duchy of Normandy and father of William the Conqueror. The island today is inhabited by farmers and people who earn their living from the sea.

Inquire at the tourist bureau about tours, as well as daily excursions to the fjords of **Romsdal, Geiranger,** and **Hjorund.** The most popular excursion is to **Fjellstua** (see my mountaintop dining recommendation in "Where to Dine," below).

Birdwatchers head for **Runde,** Norway's southernmost bird rock, where some 170,000 pairs of seabirds breed every year. It is Norway's third-largest bird cliff. Strict regulations protect the four bird sanctuaries—the western cliffs and the northern slopes of Runde, Kløfjellet and Hellestien, and the Grasøyane Islands. You can visit Runde by boat between June and August 1, with departures at 11am. The trip costs 225 kroner ($38.90) for adults and 60 kroner ($10.40) for children. Departures are daily abroad the *Lea Kristina,* sailing from Skansegata in Ålesund. For reservations, call 70-13-16-66.

Tunnels now connect Ålesund to the islands of **Ellingsøy, Valderøy, Vigra,** and **Giske.** On Giske, visit the 12th-century marble church. The island has white sandy beaches and a bird sanctuary at Makkevika. The toll for the tunnel-bridge system is 35 kroner ($6.10) per car and driver, 15 kroner ($2.60) for each passenger.

SUNNMØRE MUSEUM, Borgundgavlen. Tel. 70-13-40-24.

⊗ The Sunnmøre Museum, on the outskirts of Ålesund midway between Ålesund and Spjelkavik, 2 miles east of the town center, includes some 40 original houses in open-air displays that show rural life in the Sunnmøre district from the late Middle Ages to around 1900. Outbuildings include a sawmill, a boat-builder's shed, a fishermen's inn, and a small 1743 boarding school. One of Norway's most complete collections of fishing boats is in the boat halls. Near the museum are the remains of a medieval town.

Admission: 25 kroner ($4.30) adults, 10 kroner ($1.70) children.

Open: May 24–June 21, Mon–Fri 11am–3pm, Sat–Sun noon–3pm; June 22–Aug 30, Mon–Fri 11am–3pm, Sat–Sun noon–3pm. **Closed:** Aug 31–May 23. **Bus:** 13, 14, 18, 24, 24A.

ÅLESUND MUSEUM, Rasmus Rønnebergsgate 16. Tel. 70-12-31-70.

The development of hunting and fishing methods, shipbuilding, and life in Ålesund before and after the big fire of 1904 are the subjects of this museum off Korsegata near the harbor. Of special interest are a large-scale model of Ålesund and the boat *Uraed,* called *Brudeegget,* the prototype of today's covered rescue boats.

Admission: 10 kroner ($1.70) adults, 5 kroner (90¢) children.

Open: Daily noon–3pm.

MITTELALTER-MUSEUM (Medieval Museum), Katevågen 2, Borgund-kaupangen. Tel. 70-13-59-66.

Borgundkaupangen was the main center of Sunnmøre and the most important ecclesiastical center between Bergen and Trondheim from the end of the Viking period around 1000 to 1500. The Medieval Museum is built 2 miles east of Ålesund over the carefully excavated remnants of buildings from the 12th century. Artifacts from the excavations give an idea of the history of this small market town. Excavations uncovered the remains of dwelling houses, roads, jetties, and large warehouses. The finds reflect a versatile community, earning its living by fishing, hunting, trade, and different handcrafts.

Admission: 10 kroner ($1.75) adults, 5 kroner (90¢) children.

Open: Late May–Aug, Wed 5–7pm, Sat–Sun noon–3pm. **Closed:** Sept to mid-May. **Bus:** 14, 16, 18.

WHERE TO STAY

If you wish, at midsummer or on a weekend year-round, most hotels lower their prices.

EXPENSIVE

RICA PARKEN, Storgata 16, N-6002 Ålesund. Tel. 70-12-50-50. Fax 70-12-21-64. 132 rms (all with bath), 6 suites. A/C MINIBAR TV TEL

$ Rates (including breakfast): Sun–Thurs (except summer), 1,025 kroner ($177.30) single, 1,320 kroner ($228.40) double. Midsummer and Fri–Sat year-round, 550 kroner ($95.15) single, 750 kroner ($129.75) double. Year-round, from 1,500 kroner ($259.50) suite. AE, DC, MC, V. **Parking:** Free.

Built in 1981, this hotel has a tasteful modern design. The hotel's Brasserie Normandie is one of the city's best dining places. A dancing bar, Queen's Park, is a popular disco, and the Galleri Flora is both a café and an art gallery. A health club with a sauna is also on the premises. The Rica Parken is a 5-minute walk north of the bus station.

MODERATE

RICA SKANSEN HOTEL, Kongensgata 27, N-6002 Ålesund. Tel. 70-12-29-38. Fax 70-12-66-60. 89 rms (all with bath), 10 suites. MINIBAR TV TEL

$ Rates (including breakfast): Sun–Thurs except May–Aug 15, 730 kroner ($126.30) single; 995 kroner ($172.10) double; Fri–Sat and May–Aug 15, 475 kroner ($82.20) single; 650 kroner ($112.50) double. Year-round, from 2,000 kroner ($346) suite. AE, DC, MC, V. **Parking:** Free.

Originally built in 1954, most of what you see today is the result of a complete overhaul made in 1988 that turned this hotel into one of the most desirable in town. This conventional-looking hotel, at the edge of the historic center, near the bus station, has bedrooms with comfortable furniture. On the premises is an elegant restaurant, with dance floor. There is also an informal brasserie and an indoor swimming pool with a sauna.

SCANDINAVIE, Løvenvoldgata 8, N-6002 Ålesund. Tel. 70-12-31-31. Fax 70-12-94-88. 70 rms (all with bath), 4 suites. MINIBAR TV TEL

$ Rates (including breakfast): Winter, Sun–Thurs 895 kroner ($154.80) single; 1,080 kroner ($186.80) double. Winter Fri–Sat and midsummer, 495 kroner ($85.60) single; 670 kroner ($115.90) double. Year-round, 1,650 kroner ($285.50) suite. AE, DC, MC, V. **Parking:** Free.

Lying just north of the rail station, this hotel was originally built in 1905 following a great fire. It is one of the most authentic art nouveau buildings in Ålesund, with a much modernized interior that still evokes the art nouveau theme. The color schemes of the bedrooms are cool pastels. Set off the lobby, the main restaurant—known as Grandma's Kitchen—specializes in 19th-century Norwegian recipes. In the cellar is the Kjelleren Pizza pub.

INEXPENSIVE

ATLANTICA, Rasmus Rønnebergsgata 4, N-6002 Ålesund. Tel. 70-12-91-00. Fax 70-12-62-52. 52 rms (all with bath). A/C MINIBAR TV TEL

$ Rates (including breakfast): Sun–Thurs 620 kroner ($107.30) single; 650 kroner ($112.50) double. June 15–Aug 15 (discounts to holders of Norwegian Fjordpass),

420 kroner ($72.70) single; 600 kroner ($103.80) double. AE, DC, MC, V.
Parking: Free.

A modern hotel beside the City Council building in the heart of town, this hotel was partly reconstructed in 1990. Today it is one of the best moderately priced establishments in town. From most of its tasteful, well-furnished bedrooms, in contemporary styling, there is a view of the Borgundfjord and the mountains beyond. Top-floor bedrooms have their own balconies. Transportation is convenient as the bus terminal is only 50 yards away, and there is also a taxi stand beside the hotel. The Café Brosundet serves both traditional Norwegian food and an international menu.

BRYGGEN HOME HOTEL, Apotekergata 1-3, N-6021 Ålesund. Tel. 70-12-64-00. Fax 70-12-11-80. 82 rms (all with bath), 1 suite, 3 junior suites. A/C MINIBAR TV TEL **Bus:** Brunnholmen bus stops nearby.

$ Rates (including breakfast): Sun–Thurs 825 kroner ($142.70) single; 600 kroner ($103.80) double. Suite 1,050–1,250 kroner ($181.70–$216.30). AE, DC, MC, V.
Parking: Free.

The steeply gabled, six-story building containing this hotel, originally constructed in 1906, was a fish-processing factory. Today it is a tasteful, well-run hotel, among the most luxurious in the area. It contains a library with a working fireplace and a glassed-in display of the tools used by the workmen who constructed the original building. The interior decor incorporates the trunklike original structure beams into an otherwise very modern design. Bedrooms are contemporary and tastefully furnished. Many open onto views of the town's famous canal, Brosundet. Use of the sauna and solarium is free to guests, and on weekdays there's a buffet of waffles between 3 and 7pm.

WHERE TO DINE

EXPENSIVE

SJØBUA FISKERESTAURANT, Brunholmgata 1. Tel. 70-12-71-00.
Cuisine: SEAFOOD. **Reservations:** Recommended.
$ Prices: Appetizers 65–85 kroner ($11.20–$14.70); main dishes 190–230 kroner ($32.90–$39.80). AE, DC, MC, V.
Open: Mon–Sat 2–11pm.

The rustic walls of this 1907 warehouse were retained in this restaurant, with part of the foundation on piers sunk into the harbor. The interior trusses and timbers were restored, making this restaurant as memorable architecturally as it is gastronomically. You can select a lobster from a holding tank near the entrance or have a drink in the marine-style bar, which has a blazing fireplace in winter. If you arrive in summer, you may prefer Flottman's Bar, next door under the same management—a floating barge skillfully converted into a bar with sun parasols. Specialties include fresh fish from the Norwegian coast. You might try the three-fish platter fried in butter or whitefish with shrimp and mussels.

TOLDBØDEN, Tollbugaten 2. Tel. 70-53-53-10.
Cuisine: INTERNATIONAL. **Reservations:** Recommended.
$ Prices: Restaurant appetizers 55–70 kroner ($9.50–$12.10); restaurant main dishes 104–300 kroner ($18–$51.90); pub platters 60–100 kroner ($10.40–$17.30). AE, DC, MC, V.
Open: Restaurant, daily 4–11pm. Pub, Sun–Thurs 11am–1am, Fri–Sat 11am–3am.

Described as a sophisticated combination of an American steak house and a North European citadel of nouvelle cuisine, this restaurant was established in 1992 in one of the most beautiful art nouveau buildings in Ålesund. Set directly beside the harbor, it was originally built as the headquarters for the royal tollhouse, from which duties were collected from ships entering and leaving the harbor. Today, the premises is divided between an English/Irish pub and a more formal restaurant. In the pub, foaming half-liters of lager accompany steaming platters of whatever the chef decides to feature that day. In the more formal restaurant, dining tables on an outdoor terrace overlooking the harbor are in great demand during warm weather. Menu specialties in both sections include a wide array of steaks priced according to weight, including pampas steak and filet mignon in brandy sauce. Equally popular are the many fresh fish dishes, such as filet of monkfish with mango chutney and curry sauce.

MODERATE

RESTAURANT FJELLSTUA, Fjellstua. Tel. 70-12-65-82.
Cuisine: NORWEGIAN/CONTINENTAL. **Reservations:** Recommended.
$ **Prices:** Appetizers 30–50 kroner ($5.20–$8.70); main dishes 75–130 kroner ($13–$22.50). AE, DC, MC, V.
Open: Daily 10am–10pm. **Closed:** Jan–Feb.
You can drive to this restaurant's mountaintop location via a complicated system of roads, but some elect to climb the 418 rock-hewn steps from a park below. In warm weather you might sit on the outdoor terrace and order hamburgers, sandwiches, or beer from a charcoal grill. Full meals might include Ålesund fish soup, grilled lamb cutlets, pork schnitzels, or steak in a red wine sauce. You select your food from a cafeteria-style display case, pay for it at the cashier, and a waiter will bring it to your table.

RESTAURANT GULLIX, Rådstugata 5B. Tel. 70-12-05-48.
Cuisine: INTERNATIONAL. **Reservations:** Required.
$ **Prices:** Fixed-price platters 70–100 kroner ($12.10–$17.30); appetizers 54–65 kroner ($9.30–$11.20); main dishes 120–180 kroner ($20.80–$31.10). AE, DC, MC, V.
Open: Daily 2–11pm.
Filled with decorative objects, this place, near the Town Hall, has the ambience of a charming Iberian *tasca*. Full meals include beef filet marinated in a red wine sauce, pepper steak, Scandinavian catfish, roast leg of pork, and when the ingredients are fresh, a Spanish paella. The fixed-price platters mentioned above are really meals unto themselves.

EVENING ENTERTAINMENT

ENTERTAINMENT HOUSE, Keiser Wilhelmsgata 25. Tel. 70-12-70-14.
This is the major nightlife venue for Ålesund, consisting of a pub, disco, and piano bar. The **Musik Pub** serves Norwegian food, including smørbrød throughout the day, costing 32 kroner to 38 kroner ($5.50 to $6.60), or daily hot platters priced at 68 kroner ($11.80) each. These meals are served daily from 11am to 5pm. The pub then reopens at 10pm on Thursday, Friday, and Saturday nights for presentations of karaoke, the Japanese sing-along sensation.

The **Fregatten Bar** is a disco, open nightly at 8:30pm, with drinks costing from 40 kroner ($6.90) each. A **Piano Bar** on the third floor often has a live pianist and a more sedate ambience appreciated by conversationalists. The Entertainment House lies only a 2-minute walk south of the bus station. The complex, depending on business, usually stays open until 3am.

Admission: 50 kroner ($8.70) Fri–Sat; free Sun–Thurs.

---

2. GEIRANGER

307 miles NW of Oslo, 65 miles E of Ålesund, 50 miles S of Åndalsnes

GETTING THERE **By Plane** The nearest airport is Ålesund/Vigra airport (tel. 70-18-32-45 for flight information; 70-18-37-00 for airport). You go the rest of the way by bus.

By Train The nearest railway station with direct bus connections is in Åndalsnes. The rest of the journey is by bus.

By Bus Geiranger has bus connections with Åndalsnes, Ålesund, Otta, Stryn, and Nordfjordeid.

By Car   You have a choice of some of the most exciting roads and awe-inspiring scenery in Norway. Geiranger may be reached by Trollstigveien and Ørneveien from the north; by Geirangerveien, across the Grotli mountain moors, from the east; by the coast road from the south via Hellesylt, and then by ferry down the fjord; or from Ålesund via Linge.

By Boat   The *Bergen-Nordfjordeid* has express boat connections (with direct bus hookups). Call 70-26-30-99 at the Geiranger dock for schedule information.

ESSENTIALS   Geiranger og Stranda Reiselivslag, Rådhuset (tel. 70-25-00-44), supplies tourist information daily 9am–7pm (June–Aug).

Most Norwegians consider the Geiranger their most majestic fjord. The village at the top of this narrow fjord is one of the most famous resorts in the fjord country.

WHAT TO SEE & DO

Perched on rocky ledges, high above the fjord, are a number of small farmsteads. Waterfalls, such as the celebrated **Seven Sisters (Syr Søstre),** the **Wooer,** and the **Bridal Veil,** cascade down the rock face.

Most hotels will arrange excursions by bus, boat, and car, or fishing trips on the fjord. Rowboats and fishing tackle are also available for rent at many hotels.

You can take a 3-hour boat cruise. En route to Valldal, on this tour you'll pass the already-mentioned Seven Sisters, a waterfall plunging down over a sheer wall. Details, which change from season to season, are available from the tourist office (see above). Obviously, the most routes and the most tour options are available in the peak summer visiting season, usually July to mid-August.

From Valldal, also connected by car-ferry to the village of Geiranger, you can continue on a 2-hour bus trip on **Trollstigveien** (Troll's Path) over the mountains, zigzagging down to the village of Åndalsnes, our next stopover.

Or you can return to Geiranger by bus on the **Eagle's Road.** This route allows you to visit a waterfall, then takes you down 3,280 feet with 11 hairpin turns. At the top, a toll road, open around mid-July, allows you to climb to the summit of **Dalsnibba** (4,757 ft.) for a breathtaking panorama.

WHERE TO STAY & DINE
MODERATE

UNION TURISTHOTELL, N-6216 Geiranger. Tel. 70-25-30-00. Fax 70-25-31-61. 162 rms (all with bath). MINIBAR TV TEL
$ Rates (including breakfast): 740 kroner ($128) single; 1,100 kroner ($190.30) double. AE, DC, MC, V. **Parking:** Free.
An old family hotel going back to 1891, the Union has been updated. The public rooms, especially one done in the old style, are comfortable and pleasantly furnished. The Union is fully licensed, and in the peak season folk dancing is presented 2 or 3 nights a week. Dinners cost from 185 kroner ($32). The staff can arrange for you to go out in a rowboat with or without outboard motors, and cars, owned by the hotel, can be rented for excursions. Outside, the hotel has a large garden with a heated swimming pool, and inside is another swimming pool, plus saunas and a Turkish steam bath. The hotel is in the town center overlooking the fjord.

GEIRANGER HOTEL, N-6216 Geiranger. Tel. 70-25-30-05. Fax 70-25-31-70. 129 rms (32 with bath). TEL
$ Rates (including breakfast): 680 kroner ($117.60) single; 860 kroner ($148.80) double. AE, DC, MC, V. **Parking:** Free.
The Geiranger Hotel has been around in the middle of the village since 1973. The better units, facing the fjord, have balconies with great views. Each room is tastefully furnished in modern style. The hotel is licensed, with a cafeteria and a pizza bar, and is

known for its good food, with a meal costing from 185 kroner ($32). One public room has dancing and an open fireplace (nights can be chilly here, even in summer). Rowing boats are rented, and licenses can be easily obtained for fishing on the fjord. There are excursions to waterfalls, glaciers, and mountain farms.

3. ÅNDALSNES

79 miles E of Ålesund, 658 miles W of Oslo

GETTING THERE By Train Trains run daily from Oslo to Åndalsnes, taking 6 to 8 hours.

By Bus Åndalsnes is linked by daily buses to Geiranger (in June and July only), taking 3 to 4 hours. Three to four daily buses connect to Ålesund, taking 2 hours 20 minutes.

By Car Take the E6 northwest from Oslo toward Lillehammer. At Dombås, head west on the E69 to Åndalsnes.

ESSENTIALS You can arrange lodgings with private families or obtain information at the tourist office, **Turistkontoret,** N-6301 Åndalsnes (tel. 71-22-16-22), which is open daily 9am–7pm (June–Aug).

A summer resort at the foot of the mountains and at the head of the **Romsdalsfjord,** Åndalsnes attracts rock climbers and fishing enthusiasts (there are trout and salmon in the Rauma River).

One of the most exciting approaches to the village—and worth a day's excursion—is the zigzagging **Trollstigveien** (Troll's Path), with hairpin bends through the mountains. Excursions are arranged in July to the **Geiranger Fjord** (past the Seven Sisters waterfall), to **Romsdal Valley,** and to **Eikesdal,** as well as to **Mardal Foss,** the highest falling water in northern Europe, a drop of 1,000 feet.

WHERE TO STAY & DINE

MODERATE

GRAND HOTEL BELLEVUE, Åndalsgate 5, N-6300 Åndalsnes. Tel. 71-22-10-11. Fax 71-22-60-38. 46 rms (all with bath). MINIBAR TV TEL
$ Rates (including breakfast): 580 kroner ($100.30) single; 800–900 kroner ($138.40–$155.70) double. AE, DC, MC, V. **Parking:** Free.
Each bedroom in the Grand Hotel has a mountain view, and about half have views of the Romsdalsfjord as well. The better accommodations are on the recently renovated third floor. The hotel has a large dining room, the Fun Pub, and a disco. The Grand Hotel Bellevue is a quarter mile from the train station.

INEXPENSIVE

RAUMA PENSJONAT, Vollan 16, N-6300 Åndalsnes. Tel. 71-22-12-33. Fax 71-22-12-33. 16 rms (9 with bath). TV TEL
$ Rates (including breakfast): 295 kroner ($51) single without bath, 500 kroner ($86.50) single with bath; 400 kroner ($69.20) double without bath, 650 kroner ($112.50) double with bath. AE, DC, MC, V. **Parking:** Free.
S A short walk from the train station, the Rauma Pensjonat is perfect for those who want a moderately priced place. Reopened in 1989 after a total overhaul, the hotel offers functionally furnished and tasteful bedrooms in light Nordic pastels. There are views of the mountaintops from the bedroom windows. The hotel's café offers a varied menu.

NEARBY ACCOMMODATIONS
Budget

GJERSET PENSJONAT, Torvik, N-6320 Isfjorden. Tel. 71-22-59-66. 8 rms (5 with bath), 5 suites. **Directions:** From Åndalsnes, take the bus marked MOLDE and ask the driver to let you off at the pension.

$ Rates: 200 kroner ($34.60) single without bath, 250 kroner ($43.30) single with bath; 270 kroner ($46.70) double without bath, 350 kroner ($60.60) double with bath; from 500 kroner ($86.50) suite. V. **Parking:** Free.

This pension, at the head of the lake in this small Norwegian village, is a little guesthouse in idyllic surroundings. Rooms are pleasant, the food is good, and you can even catch your dinner in the lake, taking it back to the guesthouse to be prepared for you. Dinner costs from 100 kroner ($17.30), and Gjerset is licensed for beer and wine. The pension is on Route 64 between Åndalsnes and Molde, 12 miles outside Åndalsnes.

---

4. MOLDE

31 miles NW of Åndalsnes, 43 miles NE of Ålesund

GETTING THERE By Plane Åro Airport is a 10-minute drive from the town center, 2 miles to the east. There are daily flights to Oslo, Bergen, and Trondheim.

By Train You can go from Oslo as far as Åndalsnes by train. From there, you must take a connecting bus to Molde.

By Bus Buses run from Åndalsnes to Molde, taking 1½ hours. In the same time, you can also take daily buses to Ålesund or Kristiansund N.

By Car Driving should take about 1½ hours from Åndalsnes or Ålesund, 3 hours from Dombås, or 4 hours from Trondheim. From Trondheim, take the E6 south to Dombås and then connect with the E69 west. From Ålesund, take the E69 east. From Molde, board the ferry to Vikebukt and then go east on the E69.

By Ferry Coming from either Ålesund or Åndalsnes, board the frequent car-ferries at Vikebukt or at Vestnes for the crossing north to Molde.

By Coastal Steamer/Express Boat The coastal steamer *Hurtigruten* visits Molde on its way between Bergen and Hammerfest (both directions). There is also a daily express boat going between Molde and Ålesund.

ESSENTIALS The **Molde Travel Association,** Storgata 1, N-6401 Molde (tel. 71-25-71-33), will provide tourist information and assist in arranging excursions. It's open Mon–Sat 9am–6pm and Sun 10am–6pm (summer) and Mon–Sat 9am–1pm (off-season).

Norway's "city of jazz and roses" is famed for its view of 87 white-capped Romsdal Alps. When the Nazis attacked Norway during World War II, Molde briefly became, in effect, the country's capital, since the king and the gold reserves were here. King Haakon VII hid in a forest outside the town until he and his son, the future King Olav V, could board a boat for England. Three hundred houses were destroyed during the German bombings in 1940.

The name of Molde, from the Molde farm that occupied much of the area, has appeared in records since the Middle Ages. It was officially recognized as a trading place in 1614, and King Christian IV signed a royal decree declaring that Molde was a trading city in 1742. The city celebrated its 250th anniversary in 1992.

WHAT TO SEE & DO

In addition to the sights below, guides will point out **Moldegård,** which was the main house of the old Molde farm, built in 1710 by Hans Nobel. Henrik Ibsen lived here in 1885. Bjørnstjerne Bjørnson, who wrote Norway's national anthem, among other poems, also visited often, as late as 1907.

Don't miss the view of the 87 peaks of the Romsdal Alps. Best known are the Romsdalshorn (5,115 ft.) and the Troll Tinder (6,250 ft.). You can also see the island-studded fjord from the **Belvedere Varden,** 1,300 feet high. Visitors can take a taxi up and get the driver to wait for 20 minutes, or enjoy a 1-hour walk to the top.

MOLDE DOMKIRKE, Kirkebaken 2. Tel. 71-25-14-19.

In the heart of town, Molde Cathedral, the largest postwar cathedral in Norway, was erected in 1957—the third church built on this site. Its simplicity and purity of line are enhanced by white-brick walls, deeply recessed mullion windows, a blue-and-beige ceiling, and a rose window behind a pipe organ. It's located near Torget.

Admission: Free.

Open: Daily 10am–3:30pm.

RÅDHUSET (Town Hall), Rådhusplassen. Tel. 71-25-32-33.

The modern Town Hall, near Torget, is probably one of the best-conceived municipal buildings in the world. Its executive offices on the upper level open onto a winter garden with hanging baskets. Marble floors and stone walls blend harmoniously, and domes and skylights capture the northern lights. The roof terrace has a garden with 2,000 roses.

Admission: Free.

Open: Mon–Fri 9am–5pm.

ROMSDALMUSEET (Romsdal Museum), Romsdal Park. Tel. 71-25-25-34.

The Romsdal Museum, a 10-minute walk from the town center, comprises some 45 wooden houses that have been carefully reassembled on the outskirts of Molde. In summer, children in regional costumes perform folk dances here. The buildings range from a 15th-century *aarestue* (log cabin) to a medieval-style chapel. Coffee, cakes, ice cream, and soft drinks are available.

Admission: 20 kroner ($3.50).

Open: Mid-June to mid-Aug, daily 10am–6pm; mid-Aug to mid-June, daily 10am–2pm.

NEARBY ATTRACTIONS

In **Bjorset,** about 1½ miles from Molde, are three rock carvings dating from prehistoric times. Admission is free.

The so-called **Troll Church,** near Eide, is a natural wonder, with several underground caves and grottoes, many of them unexplored. There's also a 45-foot waterfall. To get there by car, take road no. 67 toward Eide, stopping at the TROLKYRKJA sign. From there, walk for 1½ hours over a steep path. You can catch a bus heading for Eide at the Molde terminal.

The **Vey Stone Church** on **Vey Island** dates from the 11th century. The little village of Kaupangen was the center of Romsdal until the 14th century. If you'd like to visit, make your request through the tourist office (see above), which will give a key to the church to a boatman who is hired on a chartered basis. Transit time is 30 minutes, and the cost is 60 kroner ($10.40) per person, providing four or five visitors agree to make the trip.

The **Fisheries Museum** (tel. 71-25-25-34) on the island of Hjertøya is part of the Romsdal Museum in Molde. Its collections consist of about 25 old buildings from the western coast of Romsdal, including dwellings, boathouses, a mechanics' workshop, and other maritime buildings. There are a number of authentic old fishing boats and fishing gear, and you can see how the Norwegian coastal fishermen, sealers, and whalers lived. The water taxi leaves from the marketplace, Torget, in the center of Molde during the museum's open hours, from mid-June to mid-August, Monday through Saturday from 10am to 3:30pm and on Sunday from noon to 3:30pm.

Round-trip boat fare is 15 kroner ($2.60) for adults, 10 kroner ($1.70) for children. Trip time is 10 minutes. The museum costs adults 30 kroner ($5.20), children 15 kroner ($2.60).

WHERE TO STAY

Many hotels offer summer reductions to holders of the Norway Fjordpass or the Scandinavian Bonus Pass (see Chapters 1 and 12). However, summer discounts do not apply during the jazz festival.

MODERATE

ALEXANDRA HOTEL, Storgata 1-7, N-4601 Molde. Tel. 71-25-11-33. Fax 71-21-66-35. 151 rms (all with bath), 11 suites. MINIBAR TV TEL

$ Rates (including breakfast): Winter, Sun–Thurs 930 kroner ($160.90) single; 1,140 kroner ($197.20) double. Winter, Fri–Sat 530 kroner ($91.70) single; 760 kroner ($131.50) double. Summer (to holders of Scandinavian Bonus Pass), 490 kroner ($84.80) single; 680 kroner ($117.60) double. Year-round, from 1,500 kroner ($259.50) suite. AE, DC, MC, V. **Parking:** Free.

This hotel on the main street of town overlooks the public garden and the nearby fjord. A streamlined, tasteful lobby leads to comfortable bedrooms, with leather-upholstered couches, carpeting, and large baths. On the premises are an indoor swimming pool, a sauna, several restaurants (one of which, Gamle Molde, is recommended separately; see "Where to Dine," below), and a popular bar.

HOTELL MOLDE, Storgata 19, N-6400 Molde. Tel. 71-21-58-88. Fax 71-21-58-90. 36 rms (all with bath). MINIBAR TV TEL

$ Rates (including breakfast): Sun–Thurs 690 kroner ($119.40) single; 930 kroner ($160.90) double. Fri–Sat and midsummer, 490 kroner ($84.80) single; 660 kroner ($114.20) double. AE, DC, MC, V. **Parking:** Free.

S This hotel is in the commercial center of town near Torget. The hotel dates from around 1910, although it was radically renovated in the 1980s. All the functional rooms have private showers and toilets. The hotel also has a reasonably priced restaurant, The Bank (see "Where to Dine," below).

INEXPENSIVE

HOTEL NOBEL, Amtmann Kroghsgaten 5, N-6400 Molde. Tel. 71-25-15-55. Fax 71-21-59-54. 42 rms (all with bath). MINIBAR TV TEL

$ Rates (including breakfast): Summer and Fri–Sat year-round, 450 kroner ($77.90) single; 650 kroner ($112.50) double. Sun–Thurs (except summer), 620 kroner ($107.30) single; 880 kroner ($152.20) double. AE, DC, MC, V. **Parking:** Free.

A few minutes' walk from the wharf, the main street, and the bus station, the Nobel is well decorated in light colors and rattan furniture. Owned by the nearby Alexandra, all the facilities of the larger hotel (see above) are available to guests at this bed-and-breakfast hotel. Rooms are simply but comfortably furnished.

NEARBY ACCOMMODATIONS

Inexpensive

KNAUSEN MOLDE, Hytter, N-6400 Molde. Tel. 71-25-15-77. Fax 71-21-52-87. 68 rms (all with bath). TV TEL

$ Rates (including breakfast): Summer and weekends year-round, 445 kroner ($77) single; 590 kroner ($102.10) double. Winter, weekdays 625 kroner ($108.10) single; 725 kroner ($125.40) double. AE, DC, MC, V. **Parking:** Free.

S Lying close to the local airport 2 miles east of the town center, this hotel, which commands views over the Romsdal mountains and the Fannefjord, caters to convention groups and nature lovers. About half the bedrooms have balconies overlooking the faraway fjord. Additional accommodations in 18 outlying cottages are known for their peace and quiet. A Missionhotel, it serves no alcohol, but well-prepared meals are offered in the dining room.

WHERE TO DINE
MODERATE

GAMLE MOLDE, in the Alexandra Hotel, Storgata 1. Tel. 71-25-11-33.
Cuisine: NORWEGIAN. **Reservations:** Recommended.
$ **Prices:** Appetizers 25–50 kroner ($4.30–$8.70); main dishes 160–175 kroner ($27.70–$30.30); daily platters (until 6pm) 75 kroner ($13). AE, DC, MC, V.
Open: Mon–Sat 11am–11pm, Sun 11am–11pm.

Large portions of well-prepared food at reasonable prices are offered in the Gamle Molde, which is decorated like a Norwegian tavern, with antiques and massive ceiling timbers. At lunch, there is a well-stocked salad bar, and dinner main dishes are likely to include three kinds of grilled steak, marinated house salmon, and fresh fish. Filet of reindeer and chateaubriand are specialties. It's a short walk from the Town Hall in the center.

NAUST-GRYTA, Havnegata 47. Tel. 71-25-10-30.
Cuisine: SEAFOOD. **Reservations:** Recommended.
$ **Prices:** Appetizers 35–50 kroner ($6.10–$8.70); main dishes 85–140 kroner ($14.70–$24.20). V.
Open: Mon–Thurs 10am–11pm, Fri–Sat 10am–3am, Sun noon–11pm.

Naust-Gryta is the best fish restaurant in town, with a large dining terrace in summer and a nautical decor—even the tables are shaped like fish. Menu selections include "sea wolf," scallops, and the chef's special fish soup. Meat eaters can choose pepper steak or spareribs. At night many young people come here to order pizza and beer. It's on the waterfront near the bus station.

TOSCANA, Romsdalsgate 20. Tel. 71-25-64-11.
Cuisine: ITALIAN. **Reservations:** Required.
$ **Prices:** Appetizers 48–75 kroner ($8.30–$13); main dishes 75–168 kroner ($13–$29.10). AE, DC, MC, V.
Open: Sun–Thurs 2pm–midnight, Fri–Sat 1pm–midnight.

In a building constructed in 1910 as a private home, a 5-minute walk north of the bus station, this is the best Italian restaurant in the area. Its staff includes a combination of Italian and Norwegian cooks. Specialties include beef with Gorgonzola, filet à la crème, pampas steak (with onions and spices, grilled), six kinds of pasta, and six preparations of fish. Naturally, the larder is filled with Italian wines.

THE BANK, in the Hotell Molde, Storgata 19. Tel. 71-12-58-88.
Cuisine: INTERNATIONAL. **Reservations:** Recommended in restaurant only.
$ **Prices:** Appetizers 50–65 kroner ($8.70–$11.20); main courses 90–145 kroner ($15.60–$25.10). AE, DC, MC, V.
Open: Restaurant, Sun–Thurs noon–10:30pm, Fri–Sat noon–midnight. Pub, Sun–Thurs 3pm–midnight, Fri–Sat 3pm–2am.

On the street level of the previously recommended hotel, this restaurant serves a medley of food that includes selections from Mexico, Spain, Italy, America, and Scandinavia. You might begin with gazpacho, followed by pastas, tacos, pepper steak, filet mignon, and a wide array of fish dishes, especially salmon. Many visitors precede a meal here with a drink in the adjacent pub, the Office. Both the Office and the Bank are whimsically decorated with a medley of cash registers, typewriters, and adding machines. A half-liter of beer in the pub costs 39 kroner ($6.70).

---

5. KRISTIANSUND N

42 miles N of Molde, 658 miles NW of Oslo, 405 miles N of Bergen

GETTING THERE By Plane Kvernberget Airport lies close to the town center. Three arrivals a day wing in from each of Norway's biggest cities: Trondheim,

Oslo, and Bergen. The bus trip from the airport to the center takes 15 minutes, and the bus will stop at individual hotels.

By Train   The nearest railway stations are in Oppdal and Åndalsnes, with bus connections meeting the trains.

By Bus   There are daily bus connections to Trondheim, Molde, Oppdal, and Åndalsnes.

By Car   From Molde in the south, drive north along Route 67 (two ferry crossings).

By Coastal Steamer   The coastal steamer **Hurtigruten** arrives at Kristiansund twice a day—once southbound, the other headed for the North Cape.

ESSENTIALS   The **Kristiansund Travel Association,** Kaptein Bødtkersgata, N-6501 Kristiansund N (tel. 71-67-72-11), offers tourist information and assistance Mon–Fri 8:30am–8pm, Sat 8:30am–6pm, and Sun 10am–6pm (June–late Aug) and Mon–Fri 9am–4pm and Sat 9am–1pm (late Aug–May).

SPECIAL EVENTS   Kristiansund has a special **Opera Week** in early February in the Festiviteten culture center. Ballets, concerts, and theater productions are staged, and sometimes jazz concerts.

Almost entirely destroyed in World War II, this coastal town spread over three islands has been rebuilt into a modern city. It is the main service base for oil activities on the mid-Norwegian continental shelf.

WHAT TO SEE & DO

With a fan-shaped ground plan and side walls that slope in toward the choir, the **Kirkelander Church** is a fine example of nontraditional ecclesiastical architecture.

At the **Nordmøre Museum,** Knudtzondalen (tel. 71-76-15-78), by the Atlanten Stadium, archeological exhibits show how people have lived in the Nordmøre district for 9,000 years, where codfish was perhaps the most sought-after product of the North Sea before the discovery of oil. In the museum you can see how fish were treated and dried on rocks to produce *klippfish,* a major export. All buses going to the center pass the museum; the bus stop is Idrettshall Svømmehall. It's open Tuesday through Friday from 10am to 2pm and on Sunday from noon to 3pm. Admission is 15 kroner ($2.60) for adults and 10 kroner ($1.70) for children.

In the **Wolbrygga** section of the museum, at the Vågen (harbor), you can see a complete barrel-making operation, rope-making equipment, and some old boats from the area. Woldbrygga can be reached by taking the ferry *Sundbåten* to Gomalandet and walking from there.

At the same harbor is another part of the museum, **Mellomvaerftet,** where you can park your car and walk along the seaside to watch the restoration of old boats in the shipyard *(vareftet).* The museum branch lies on the west side of the bay and is a short walk from the center.

NEARBY ATTRACTIONS

Often likened to Scotland's St. Kilda,   ✪ **Grip,** near Kristiansund, is one of the most fascinating of Norway's offshore islands and, until about 20 years ago, the only one permanently occupied. Today it has only summer residents, with regular boat service from Kristiansund, costing 100 kroner ($17.30) for adults and 55 kroner ($9.50) for children round-trip.

Of special interest on this flat, rocky piece of land is the 14th-century stave church. The walls of the choir were repainted and decorated in 1621 with motifs from the Old and New Testaments. The beautiful little altar chalice from 1520 is one of only two such cups in the country.

You can also visit the island of **Smøla** in summer by taking the ferry from Kristiansund to Straumen, the capital of Smøla. On the way, the ferry passes the island of Edøy, with a stone church from about 1250. A bus tour of Smøla is available from Straumen. The cost of the ferry is 104 kroner ($18) for adults and 58 kroner ($10) for children.

WHERE TO STAY
MODERATE

BARON HOTEL, Hauggata 16, N-6500 Kristiansund N. Tel. 71-67-40-11. Fax 71-67-76-50. 45 rms (all with bath), 5 mini-suites. MINIBAR TV TEL
$ Rates (including breakfast): Sun–Thurs 900 kroner ($155.70) single; 1,150 kroner ($199) double. Fri–Sat and summer, 450 kroner ($77.90) single; 600 kroner ($103.80) double. Year-round, 1,150 kroner ($199) suite. AE, DC, MC, V.

Originally built in the 1970s, this hotel was radically reconstructed in 1988 and is now one of the most alluring properties in the region. Bedrooms are modern and tastefully furnished. Mini-suites rent for the same prices as regular doubles and are distributed to favorite clients of the hotel. Each bedroom has individual character. The most elegant meeting place in town is the Piano Bar of this hotel. Everything is bright and inviting. The care and attention are exceptional. For example, special bed linen is provided for guests suffering from allergies. Its restaurant, Baron, is recommended separately (see "Where to Dine," below). The Baron is on the harborfront in the town center, a 2-minute walk west of the bus station.

GRAND HOTEL, Bernstorffstredet 1, N-6500 Kristiansund N. Tel. 71-67-30-11. Fax 71-67-23-70. 115 rms (all with bath), 2 suites. MINIBAR TV TEL
$ Rates: Winter, weekdays 975 kroner ($168.70) single; 1,100 kroner ($190.30) double. Summer and weekends year-round, 480 kroner ($83) single; 585 kroner ($101.20) double. Year-round, from 1,200 kroner ($207.60) suite. AE, DC, MC, V.
Parking: Free.

Originally built in the 1890s as the grandest hotel in the region, the Grand was remodeled and doubled in size during two renovations in the 1980s. Rooms are modern, well furnished, and accessorized. The hotel's Restaurant Consulen and its Grippsalen Night Club are recommended separately (see "Where to Dine" and "Evening Entertainment," below). It's a 5-minute walk south of the bus station.

WHERE TO DINE
EXPENSIVE

CONSULEN, in the Grand Hotel, Bernstorffstredet 1. Tel. 71-67-30-11.
Cuisine: NORWEGIAN/FRENCH. **Reservations:** Recommended.
$ Prices: Appetizers 72–80 kroner ($12.50–$13.80); main dishes 152–175 kroner ($26.30–$30.30); 1-plate lunch special 85 kroner ($14.70); 3-course menu 155 kroner ($26.80). AE, DC, MC, V.
Open: Daily 1–11pm.

One of the most popular restaurants in town, south of the bus station, the Consulen is housed on the lobby level of the Grand Hotel (see "Where to Stay," above). The decor includes comfortable banquettes and lots of wood trim. Its fixed-price menu at both lunch and dinner is the most favored item on the menu. It changes daily and is usually most satisfying. Menu items include a combination plate of both smoked and marinated salmon for an appetizer, and main courses like filet of blue halibut poached in red wine. A separate bar is attached where guests often arrive early for an apéritif.

MODERATE

BARON RESTAURANT, in the Baron Hotel, Hauggata 16. Tel. 71-67-40-11.
Cuisine: NORWEGIAN/FRENCH. **Reservations:** Recommended.
$ Prices: Fixed-price menu 155 kroner ($26.80); appetizers 40–60 kroner ($6.90–$10.40); main dishes 100–185 kroner ($17.30–$32). AE, DC, MC, V.
Open: Dinner only, Mon–Sat 5–11pm, Sun 2–9pm.

A formal Piano Bar, laden with dark colors and leather-upholstery sofas, lies adjacent to this sophisticated restaurant that many consider the best in town. In an elegant setting, you can often select such innovative dishes as catfish flambéed with cognac and served with a mango purée. A Norwegian seafood buffet is served nightly. It's on the harborfront in the town center, west of the bus station.

EVENING ENTERTAINMENT

GRIPPSALEN NIGHT CLUB, in the Grand Hotel, Bernstorffstredet 1. Tel. 71-67-30-11.
   The leading nightlife venue of town, the Grippsalen is a supper club where people come to drink and dance. You can also order full meals for 200 kroner to 225 kroner ($34.60 to $38.90). A conservative crowd of well-dressed local residents patronizes this establishment, enjoying the sounds of a dance band. It's open Monday through Saturday from 9pm to 3am, but is most popular on Friday and Saturday nights. Beer costs 39 kroner ($6.70). The place is a 5-minute walk south of the bus station.
   Admission: 50 kroner ($8.70).

---

6. TRONDHEIM

425 miles N of Bergen, 345 miles NW of Oslo

GETTING THERE   By Plane   Vaernes Airport is 20 miles from town. Bus service to the city center costs 40 kroner ($6.90) and takes about 30 minutes. Several flights arrive daily from Bergen and Oslo.

By Train   Two trains a day connect Stockholm and Trondheim taking 12 hours. Three trains arrive daily on the 7-hour trip from Oslo.

By Bus   Buses run between Trondheim and Bergen once a day, taking 15 hours. One or two buses also leave for Molde and Ålesund, taking 6 to 8 hours, respectively.

By Coastal Steamer   The coastal express steamer on the northbound route from Bergen to Kirkenes calls daily at Trondheim.

By Car   Take the E6 north of Oslo via Lillehammer all the way to Trondheim.

ESSENTIALS   The **Trondheim Tourist Office,** Munkegaten 19 (tel. 73-92-94-05), near the marketplace, will reserve hotel accommodations or provide rooms in private homes. For this service, the staff levies a fee of 15 kroner ($2.60) in a single or 20 kroner ($3.50) in shared rooms. The cost of rooms in private homes ranges from 160 kroner to 180 kroner ($27.70 to $31.10) in a single or from 280 kroner to 320 kroner ($48.40 to $55.40) in a double. The tourist office collects 30 kroner ($5.20) per room, which is then deducted from the overall cost at checkout time. Summer hours are Mon–Sat 9am–8pm and Sun 10am–6pm; off-season hours are Mon–Fri 9am–4pm and Sat 9am–1pm.

DEPARTURES   Buses leave from the bus terminal, Erling Skakkes Gate 40, 75 minutes before departures of SAS and Braathens SAFE flights, driving via the SAFE terminal at the Royal Garden Hotel, Kjøpmannsgate 73.

Founded by the Viking king Olaf I Tryggvason in the 10th century, Trondheim is Norway's third-largest city, scenic, pleasant, and an active university center. The city lies on the south bay of the Trondheim Fjord, and at the mouth of the Nidelven River.
   Noted for its timbered architecture, Trondheim retains much of its medieval past, most notably the Gothic-style Nidaros Cathedral. Until the early 1200s Trondheim was the medieval capital of Norway. Pilgrims came from all over Europe to worship at the shrine of Olav, who was canonized in 1031. But with the coming of the Reformation, the fortunes of the city declined.

GETTING AROUND

You can travel all over Trondheim and to outlying areas on Trondheim city buses, operated by **Trondheim Trafikkselskap** (TT), Dronningens Gate (tel. 73-54-71-00). Several types of tickets are available, according to how much you intend to travel. Tickets for single rides are sold on buses for exact change (if you don't have the right amount and have to pay too much, you'll get a credit slip from the driver, which can be redeemed at the TT office or on a later trip). Tickets for a single ride cost 12 kroner ($2.10) for adults, 6 kroner ($1) for children 4 to 16, and 20 kroner ($3.50) for a family. **Multijourney Cards,** good for 12 trips, cost 138 kroner ($23.90) for adults, 68 kroner ($11.80) for children, and are sold at the TT office, at the bus station, post offices, kiosks, and at some shops. **Day Cards,** allowing unlimited travel within 24 hours, sell for 35 kroner ($6.10) per person, 50 kroner ($8.70) for a family.

WHAT TO SEE & DO

NIDAROS CATHEDRAL, Bispegaten 5. Tel. 73-50-12-12.

Dating from the 11th century, this cathedral is one of the major ecclesiastical buildings in Scandinavia. Once the burial place of the medieval Norwegian kings, it was also the site of the coronation of King Haakon VII in 1906, an event that marked the beginning of modern Norway.

A classical European cathedral representing different architectural styles, including Gothic and Romanesque, it features a stunningly intricate rose window on the west front. Gustav Vigeland carved the gargoyles and grotesques for the head tower and northern transept. The 12th-century **Archbishop's Palace,** Erkebispegården, is behind the cathedral. It's located in the town center near the Rådhus.

Admission: Cathedral and palace, 10 kroner ($1.70) adults, 5 kroner (90¢) children.

Open: Cathedral, May 1–14 and Sept 1–14, Mon–Fri 10am–2:30pm, Sat 10am–2pm, Sun 1:30–3pm; May 15–June 14, Mon–Fri 9:30am–3pm, Sat 9:30am–2pm, Sun 1:30–4pm; June 15–Aug, Mon–Fri 9:30am–5:30pm, Sat 9:30am–2pm, Sun 1:30–4pm; Sept 15–Apr, Mon–Fri noon–2:30pm, Sat 11:30am–2pm, Sun 1:30–3pm. Palace, mid-June to mid-Aug, Mon–Fri 9am–3pm, Sat 9am–2pm, Sun noon–3pm. **Bus:** 2, 5, 6, 7, 9.

STIFTSGÅRDEN, Munkegaten 23. Tel. 73-52-24-73.

This buttercup-yellow royal palace near the marketplace was built as a private home by a rich merchant's widow in the 1770s, when Trondheim began to regain its prosperity. It is the largest wooden building in Scandinavia, perhaps in all of northern Europe. The furnishings are unpretentious, an amalgam of various design styles.

Admission: 10 kroner ($1.70) adults, 5 kroner (90¢) children.

Open: June–Aug, Mon–Sat 10am–2pm. **Closed:** Sept–May. **Bus:** 2, 5, 6, 7, 9.

MUSEUM OF MUSIC HISTORY, Lade Allé 60, 2 miles from the center of town at Ringve Manor. Tel. 73-92-24-11.

This museum can be viewed only on guided tours. At specified times musical presentations are performed on the carefully preserved antique instruments, including an impressive collection of spinets, harpsichords, clavichords, pianofortes, and string and wind instruments. Also on the premises is an old *kro* (inn), where visitors can have waffles, light refreshments, and coffee. The mansion was the birthplace of Admiral Tordenskiold, the Norwegian sea hero.

Admission: 40 kroner ($6.90) adults, 15 kroner ($2.60) children.

Open: Guided tours, May 20–June, daily at 11am, noon, 12:30pm, 2:30pm; July–Aug 10, daily at 11am and 12:30, 2:30, and 4:30pm; Aug 11–31, daily at 11am, 12:20pm, and 2:30pm; Sept, daily at noon and 2pm; Oct–May 19, Sun at 1:30pm. **Bus:** 3, 4 to Lade Church.

TYHOLTTÅRNET, Otto Nielsens Vei 4, Blussuvoll. Tel. 73-51-31-66.

This 400-feet-high concrete tower, built in 1985, is today the tallest structure in middle Norway. Its function is to relay radio signals along the coast. Lying 3 miles east of Trondheim, the tower offers a sweeping view over the entire area. Its restaurant is recommended separately (see "Where to Dine," below). However, you can visit the viewing gallery even if you don't patronize the restaurant.

Admission: 20 kroner ($3.50) adults, 10 kroner ($1.70) children.

Open: Viewing gallery, Mon–Sat 11:30am–11:30pm, Sun and holidays noon–7pm. **Bus:** 20, 60 (ask the driver to tell you when to get off).

TRØNDELAG FOLK MUSEUM, Sverresborg Allé. Tel. 73-53-14-90.

At Norway's main folk-culture museum, farmhouses, cottages, Samic huts, and city buildings depict scenes of everyday life and festivities for a 300-year period. There is even a tiny stave church. A special attraction is the ski museum with a lively introduction to this region's long skiing tradition. Every Sunday in July and August, demonstrations of old handcrafts are given. Tours are available in English.

Admission: 30 kroner ($5.20) adults, 10 kroner ($1.70) children.

Open: May 20–Aug, daily 11am–6pm. **Closed:** Sept–May 19. **Bus:** 8, 9 from Dronningsgate to Wullumsgaarden.

MUSEUM OF NATURAL HISTORY AND ARCHEOLOGY, University of Trondheim, Erling SkakkesGate 47. Tel. 73-59-21-45.

Located at the University of Trondheim, this museum features collections and exhibits covering natural history, archeology, and the social history of central Norway, spanning prehistoric times to the Middle Ages. Special features include a diorama display of birds, archeological displays, collections of church art, and a small ethnographic exhibition. One exhibition, opened in 1990, shows the most important habitats of central Norway and thus of central Scandinavia. The exhibition also shows how people have used and exploited nature through history.

Admission: 10 kroner ($1.70) adults, 5 kroner (90¢) children.

Open: Mon–Fri 10am–3pm, Sun noon–3pm. **Bus:** 63.

ORGANIZED TOURS

June through August, a bus tour departs daily at noon from the marketplace, lasting 1½ hours and costing 80 kroner ($13.80). Its main attraction is a guided tour through the cathedral (admission not included in the price). During the last 3 weeks of July, an additional tour leaves at 2:30pm.

There are also daily boat trips, leaving Ravnkloa for **Munkholmen Island** at 10am and every hour thereafter until 5pm. Monks Island (its English name) was used in ancient times as an execution site. In the 11th century, Benedictine monks constructed a monastery here, probably one of the first two monasteries in Scandinavia. In 1658 it was turned into a prison fort. You're given a guided tour of the island's historical fortress. Lunch, not included in the fare, is available at Munkholmen. The boat fare is 22 kroner ($3.80) for adults, 13 kroner ($2.20) for children. Bookings for the Munkholmen trip can be made at Nye Sentrum Hotell, Lilletorget (tel. 73-52-05-24).

WHERE TO STAY

Remember that many hotels offer special summer prices from the end of June to the end of August. The rest of the year, hotels offer 2-night weekend reductions.

EXPENSIVE

GRAND HOTEL OLAV, Kjøpmannsgate 48, N-7001 Trondheim. Tel. 73-53-53-10. Fax 73-53-57-20. 98 rms, 6 suites. A/C MINIBAR TV TEL **Bus:** 54.

$ Rates (including breakfast): Summer and weekends year-round, 620 kroner ($107.30) single, 850 kroner ($147.10) double. Winter, weekdays 1,045–1,470 kroner ($180.80–$254.30) single; 1,225–1,650 kroner ($211.90–$285.50) double. Year-round, 1,800–4,000 kroner ($311.40–$692) suite. AE, DC, MC, V. **Parking:** 70 kroner ($12.10).

This is the newest and probably the most stylish hotel in Trondheim. It was designed in 1989 by the same architect who constructed, several years previously, the Royal

Garden Hotel, which lies nearby and which is considered the Grand Olav's strongest competitor. The Grand Olav lies amid a cement-sided complex of buildings that includes a handful of elegant boutiques as well as Trondheim's largest concert hall. The six floors of its very modern interior are, all at the same time, plush, conservative, and imaginative, with each bedroom different in color scheme and decorative style from its hallmates.

Dining/Entertainment: The hotel contains a lobby-level bar (the Fiolinen), and an upscale and elegant modern restaurant, the Scenarion, where full meals cost from around 300 kroner ($51.90) each. In the Bierstube, pints of lager might accompany a platter of Danish hash. In the cellar, the Nightclub Classic opens nightly from 9pm to 3am, charging 45 kroner ($7.80) entrance to members of a conservative clientele.

Services: Laundry, room service, babysitting.

Facilities: On-premises hairdresser and massage facilities; boutiques in the adjacent shopping mall.

ROYAL GARDEN HOTEL, Kjøpmannsgate 73, N-7001 Trondheim. Tel. 73-52-11-00. Fax 73-53-17-66. 297 rms (all with bath), 9 suites. MINIBAR TV TEL **Bus:** 54.

$ Rates (including breakfast): Summer and weekends year-round, 590–795 kroner ($102.10–$137.50) single; 680–890 kroner ($117.60–$154) double. Winter, weekdays 1,040–1,290 kroner ($179.90–$223.20) single; 1,350 kroner ($233.60) double. Year-round, 1,900 kroner ($328.70) suite. AE, DC, MC, V. **Parking:** 70 kroner ($12.10).

This architecturally innovative hotel lies at the northwestern edge of the Old Town, southwest of the rail station. It opened in 1984, with a soaring lobby atrium and lavishly furnished and plant-filled public rooms. The comfortable bedrooms were each designed as a double.

Dining/Entertainment: On one of its indoor terraces, evening piano music is played at the bar. There are two elegant restaurants, Cicignon, with live dance music, and the more formal and expensive Prins Olav Grill, both with views of the harbor.

Services: Laundry, babysitting, room service.

Facilities: Sauna, health club, solarium, indoor swimming pool, boutiques.

MODERATE

BRITANNIA HOTEL, Dronningens Gate 5, N-7001 Trondheim. Tel. 73-53-00-40. Fax 73-51-29-00. 177 rms (all with bath), 3 suites. MINIBAR TV TEL **Bus:** 2, 5, 6, 7, 9.

$ Rates (including breakfast): Winter, Sun–Thurs 795 kroner ($137.50) single; 995 kroner ($172.10) double. Winter, Fri–Sat 520 kroner ($90) single; 750 kroner ($129.80) double. Summer, 495 kroner ($85.60) single; 720 kroner ($124.60) double. Year-round, from 1,850 kroner ($320.10) suite. AE, DC, MC, V. **Parking:** 70 kroner ($12.10).

Originally built at the turn of the century, this is Trondheim's traditional hotel, with many of its original details intact. The columned, marble lobby is imposing, and the ornate Palm Garden (Palmehave) with its art nouveau winter garden, fountain, and violinist captures the grand spirit of the place. Each bedroom has been renovated with soft carpets and pastel-colored upholsteries. There's also a stylish and intimate piano bar.

HOTEL AUGUSTIN, Kongensgate 26, N-7011 Trondheim. Tel. 73-52-83-48. Fax 73-51-55-01. 69 rms (all with bath), 6 suites. MINIBAR TV TEL **Bus:** 2, 5, 6, 7, 9.

$ Rates: Winter, Sun–Thurs 725 kroner ($125.40) single; 995 kroner ($172.10) double; 995 kroner ($172.10) suite. Winter, Fri–Sat 425 kroner ($73.50) single; 525 kroner ($90.80) double; 625 kroner ($108.10) suite. June 15–Aug 10, 460 kroner ($79.60) single; 560 kroner ($96.90) double; 660 kroner ($114.20) suite. AE, DC, MC, V.

In the center of Trondheim, only a short walk from the marketplace, the Augustin offers spacious rooms with wide beds, trouser presses, and hairdryers. Some rooms are reserved for nonsmokers. The hotel serves only breakfast, but sandwiches and hot drinks are available 24 hours a day. The hotel was an older building that was completely overhauled in the 1980s.

HOTEL RESIDENCE, Munkegaten 26, N-7011 Trondheim. Tel. 73-52-83-80. Fax 73-52-64-60. 66 rms (all with bath), 6 suites. MINIBAR TV TEL **Bus:** 2, 5, 6, 7, 9.

$ Rates (including breakfast): Winter, Sun–Thurs 820 kroner ($141.90) single; 920 kroner ($159.20) double or suite. Winter, Fri–Sat 490 kroner ($84.80) single; 590 kroner ($102.10) double or suite. Summer, 540 kroner ($93.40) single; 660 kroner ($114.20) double or suite. AE, DC, MC, V. **Parking:** 100 kroner ($17.30).

Located on the market square across the street from the Royal Palace, the Hotel Residence, built in 1915 in *Jugendstil (art nouveau)*, has recently been renovated and there are extra amenities. Suites cost the same as regular doubles. The American Bar is the popular watering hole in the evening; outside is the Wintergarden, a café where both refreshments and food are served. Next to the bar, you'll find an excellent dining room, known as "The Restaurant" with an exceptional wine cellar. A dinner here costs from 200 kroner ($34.60). The restaurant is open only from late May to late August.

INEXPENSIVE

GILDEVAGEN HOTELL, Söndre Gate 22B, N-7010 Trondheim. Tel. 73-51-01-00. Fax 73-52-38-98. 90 rms (all with bath). MINIBAR TV TEL **Bus:** 2, 5, 6, 7, 9.

$ Rates (including breakfast): Mid-June to mid-Aug and weekends year-round, 450 kroner ($77.90) single; 600 kroner ($103.80) double. Winter, weekdays 645–720 kroner ($111.60–$124.60) single; 745–795 kroner ($128.90–$137.50) double. AE, DC, MC, V. **Parking:** 30 kroner ($5.20).

⑤ Locals often cite this hotel as offering good value. It lies a short walk uphill from the harbor, near the Old Town's famous bridge and the train station. The best (most modern) rooms lie on the second and third floors, as they were the most recently renovated. The bedrooms, for the most part, are quite large, with phones, TVs, and videos. Meals, including the big Norwegian cold-table breakfast, are served in the old-fashioned dining room, but there is also a cheaper cafeteria.

TRONDHEIM HOTELL, Kongensgate 15, N-7013 Trondheim. Tel. 73-52-70-30. Fax 73-51-60-58. 140 rms (all with bath). A/C MINIBAR TV TEL **Bus:** 2, 5, 6, 7, 9.

$ Rates (including breakfast): Winter, Sun–Thurs 645 kroner ($111.60) single; 795 kroner ($137.50) double. Winter, Fri–Sat 400 kroner ($69.20) single; 550 kroner ($95.20) double. Summer, 500 kroner ($86.50) single; 600 kroner ($103.80) double. AE, DC, MC, V. **Parking:** 100 kroner ($17.30).

The Trondheim Hotell, near the market square, offers spacious bedrooms with upholstered furniture in pastel shades, many with an extra foldaway bed. Some rooms are suitable for the handicapped and others are reserved for nonsmokers. Constructed in 1913, it was renovated and expanded in 1990. Its Pub Adrian serves light international meals, and its Sola Bar is a popular rendezvous. Guests of the hotel have free entrance to the Monte Cristo Disco nearby. Parking facilities are available, as is a self-service laundry.

BUDGET

SINGSAKER STUDENTERHJEM, Rogertsgate 1, N-7016 Trondheim. Tel. 73-52-00-92. 106 rms (16 with bath). TEL **Bus:** 63.

$ Rates (including breakfast): 320 kroner ($55.40) single without bath, 360 kroner ($62.30) single with bath; 440 kroner ($76.10) double without bath, 550 kroner ($95.20) double with bath. AE, DC, MC, V. **Closed:** Aug 20–June 15.

⑤ This student residential hall is also a choice bargain hotel in summer. It's about a 10-minute walk from the center of Trondheim. Bedrooms are cozy—and all have water basins. The dining room serves good, wholesome breakfasts. In the evening, young people gather around the open fireplace or play billiards or other games. The hotel is licensed to sell beer and wine.

WHERE TO DINE

Try a local specialty **vafler med øst** (waffle and cheese), sold at most cafeterias and restaurants.

EXPENSIVE

BRYGGEN, Øvre Bakklandet 66. Tel. 73-52-02-30.
   Cuisine: NORWEGIAN/FRENCH. **Reservations:** Recommended.
$ **Prices:** 3-course fixed-price menu 335 kroner ($58); appetizers 60–85 kroner ($10.40–$14.70); main dishes 185–198 kroner ($32–$34.30). AE, DC, MC, V.
   Open: Mon–Sat 4–11pm. **Closed:** 2 weeks in mid-July.

★ One of the most atmospheric restaurants in Trondheim lies within what was originally built as a warehouse whose heavily trussed brick interior dates from 1849. Set on the verdant banks of the Nidelven River, a few steps from the town's oldest bridge (the Gamle Bybro), the restaurant lies within a 15-minute walk of the town center. Inside, tasteful accessories stress Norwegian design in blue and white. Menu items vary with the season and might include fish-and-shellfish soup, suprême of Norwegian duck, médaillons of reindeer in a juniper-berry cream sauce, or poached fresh fish of the day.

JONATHAN'S, in the Brittania Hotel, Dronningens Gate 5. Tel. 73-53-00-40.
   Cuisine: NORWEGIAN/FRENCH. **Reservations:** Required. **Bus:** 2, 5, 6, 7, 9.
$ **Prices:** Appetizers 50–105 kroner ($8.70–$18.20); main dishes 165–230 kroner ($28.50–$39.80). AE, DC, MC, V.
   Open: Lunch Mon–Sat 11am–3pm; dinner Mon–Sat 6–11pm.
Rich with atmosphere, Jonathan's is designed like a Mediterranean wine cellar, with antiques, a big open fireplace, and waiters colorfully dressed as troubadours. Dinner might include canapés of shrimp, smoked salmon, and local caviar, followed by grilled salmon garnished with shellfish and fresh vegetables or several kinds of grilled steaks, perhaps a veal schnitzel.

MONTE CRISTO, Prinsensgaten 38. Tel. 73-52-18-80.
   Cuisine: NORWEGIAN/INTERNATIONAL. **Reservations:** Recommended on weekends. **Bus:** 2, 5, 6, 7, 9.
$ **Prices:** Appetizers 40–60 kroner ($6.90–$10.40); main dishes 150–210 kroner ($26–$36.30). AE, DC, MC, V.
   Open: Restaurant, Mon–Sat 7–11:30pm. Disco, Mon–Sat 9pm–3am.
Considered the region's busiest and most popular supper club, the Monte Cristo lies within the thick walls of what was originally built as a private house in 1832. In addition to its simple but flavorful food, a meal within its rustic confines offers the added advantage of dancing to the music of some of the leading traditional dance bands in Norway and Sweden. Overhead hang an assortment of antique farm implements, which might be the envy of any provincial museum. Menu items include filet of monkfish in a sour cream sauce, barbecued spareribs in a spicy Cajun sauce, and filet of Norwegian lamb. Upstairs is a disco frequented by a younger clientele who appreciate the flashing lights. Entrance to the disco is free for diners, but priced at between 40 kroner and 60 kroner ($6.90 to $10.40) for others.

RESTAURANT TYHOLTTÅRNET [TÅRNRESTAURANTEN GALAKSEN],
   Otto Nielsens Vei 4, Blussuvoll. Tel. 73-51-31-66.
   Cuisine: NORWEGIAN/INTERNATIONAL. **Reservations:** Recommended on weekends. **Bus:** 20, 60.
$ **Prices:** Appetizers 55–75 kroner ($9.50–$13); main dishes 165–195 kroner ($28.50–$33.70), 2-course fixed-price lunch 145 kroner ($25.10). AE, DC, MC, V.
   Open: Mon–Sat 11:30am–midnight, Sun noon–7pm.
This restaurant lies 3 miles east of Trondheim's commercial center, near the summit

of the region's tallest building—a cement-sided tower built in 1985 to transmit radio signals along the Norwegian coastline. Throughout your meal, the restaurant's floor will revolve one full revolution per hour, enough to give you sweeping views over the entire spectrum of the surrounding mountains and coastline. Specialties include cold, thinly sliced, marinated salmon; filet of reindeer in a juniper-berry game sauce; and fresh filet of monkfish in a sauce composed of crème fraîche with soya.

Many local residents come here just for the view from the tower's observation gallery, which is described in "What to See and Do," above in this section, and which lies one floor below the restaurant. If you dine, the cost of your ride up in the elevator will be refunded.

MODERATE

HAVFRUEN FISKERESTAURANT, Kjøpmannsgate 7. Tel. 73-53-26-26.

Cuisine: SEAFOOD. **Reservations:** Required. **Bus:** 2, 5, 6, 7, 9.

$ Prices: Appetizers 40–100 kroner ($6.90–$17.30); main dishes 130–200 kroner ($22.50–$34.60). AE, DC, MC, V.

Open: Dinner Mon–Sat 4–10:30pm.

Known as Trondheim's "one and only fish restaurant," Havfruen (in English, "mermaid") is located in a 19th-century warehouse near the Nidelven River and decorated, naturally, in a nautical style. It lies opposite the bank of the river from the previously recommended Bryggen restaurant, a 15-minute walk west of the town center. Its premises is one of the oldest of several such warehouses in this historic district. The menu changes based on the availability of fresh fish. Specialties include peppered filet of salmon and poached halibut in a crabmeat sauce.

TAVERN PÅ SVERRESBORG, Sverresborg Allé. Tel. 73-52-09-32.

Cuisine: NORWEGIAN. **Reservations:** Required. **Bus:** 8, 9.

$ Prices: Appetizers 40–60 kroner ($6.90–$10.40); main dishes 100–160 kroner ($17.30–$27.70). MC, V.

Open: Mon–Fri 4pm–midnight, Sat 2pm–midnight, Sun noon–midnight.

The restaurant lies 3 miles south of Trondheim's commercial center, adjacent to the entrance of the previously recommended Trøndelag Folk Museum. Built as a private house in 1739, and later transformed into a clapboard-sided tavern, it is one of the very few wooden buildings of its age remaining within this part of Norway. Today, cramped, and cozy, it's the most vivid time-warp in town. Synchronized with its wide-plank flooring and antique rustic accessories is its emphasis on 18th- and 19th-century recipes which evoke the culinary skills of an earlier era. This wood-framed tavern, once a merchant's house, is now a national shrine. Try the blandet spekemat, served with flatbrød; it consists of thinly sliced smoked ham, diced meat, slices of salami, smoked mutton, and little garnishes of lettuce and tomato. Other comparably priced items include *rømmergrøt* (sour-cream porridge), *finnbiff* (reindeer meat), omelets, herring, and meatballs.

EVENING ENTERTAINMENT

For disco action, refer to Monte Cristo under "Where to Dine," above.

STUDIO HJORTEN, in the Royal Garden Hotel, Kjøpmannsgate 73. Tel. 73-52-11-00.

This hotel nightclub has a fun and relaxing ambience. You can dance into the wee hours of the morning to disco music, with live music on Sunday. Tuned to younger nightclubbers, it's open daily from 9pm to 3am. A beer will set you back 39 kroner ($6.70); a scotch and soda, 50 kroner ($8.70). **Bus:** 54.

Admission: 50 kroner ($8.70) Tues–Thurs, 70 kroner ($12.10) Fri–Sat.

SOMMER'N, in the Prinsen Hotel, Kongensgate 30. Tel. 73-53-06-50.

A place popular with locals during the summer, Sommer'n offers live music as well as disco, and is a good place to go if you want to get away from the mobs of teenagers at the nightspots. It's open Monday through Saturday from 8pm to 2am; closed September to May. Beer costs 39 kroner ($6.70).

Admission: 60 kroner ($10.40); free for hotel guests.

EASY EXCURSIONS

The islands of **Hitra** (Ansnes) and **Frøya** (Sistranda) can be reached by fast steamer operating from Trondheim Monday through Saturday. For more information, ask at the tourist information office in Trondheim.

Hitra is one of Norway's largest islands, with a weatherbeaten and varied scenery of forests, wooded hills, well-stocked lakes, weathered rocks, and small fjords. It is also known for the large herds of red deer that roam here. The **Dolm Church,** and **Dolmen town,** a miniature community designed and built by a Dolmoy crofter and fisherman, are other attractions. When you have reached Hitra, you should make the hop across to neighboring Frøya by ferry.

7. RØROS

99 miles SE of Trondheim, 248 miles N of Oslo

GETTING THERE   By Plane   The airport is near the town center. Flights wing in daily from Trondheim and Oslo.

By Train   Røros has rail links with Oslo and Trondheim. One or two daily trains arrive from Trondheim, taking 3 hours, and from Oslo, taking 5½ hours.

By Bus   One or two buses a day connect Trondheim with Røros, taking 3¼ hours.

By Car   From Trondheim, take the E6 south to the junction of Route 30, where you should head east for Røros.

ESSENTIALS   The tourist office, **Røros Reiselivslag,** Bergmannsplassen, N-7460 Røros (tel. 72-41-11-65), offers assistance in sightseeing and arranging accommodations. It's open daily 9am–8pm (June–Aug).

Røros is perhaps the most characteristic of Norway's mining towns. More than 300 years old, with some 80 preserved houses still in use, Røros was the home of Johan Falkberget, the author who lived at Ratvollen and died in 1967.

WHAT TO SEE & DO

The best way to see Røros in summer is to take a **guided walk through the Old Town,** starting at the Røros tourist office and ending with a guided tour of the Røros Church built in 1650. From June 1 to June 22, tours leave Monday through Saturday at 11am; June 23 to August 19, Monday through Saturday at noon and 3pm and on Sunday at 3pm; and August 20 to September 9, Monday through Friday at 11am. Adults pay 25 kroner ($4.30); children, 15 kroner ($2.60).

At the tourist office (see above) you can also arrange a guided tour of **Olav's Mine,** which consists of two mines, Nyberget and Kronprins Olavsgruva. All other copper mines in the area have been closed; only these have been kept open to show people what they are like. Daily guided tours are conducted throughout the summer. Olavsgruva, site of the mine, is 6 miles east of Røros and buses run daily from the town center. The tourist office will give you a timetable.

Guided tours are conducted from June 1 to June 22, Monday through Saturday at 1pm and 3pm and on Sunday at noon; June 23 to August 10, daily at 10:30am, noon, and 1:30, 3, 4:30, and 6pm; August 20 to September 9, Monday through Saturday at 1pm and 3pm and on Sunday at noon. Admission is 35 kroner ($6.10) for adults and 18 kroner ($3.10) for children. Bus fares to reach the site are 50 kroner ($8.70) for adults and 20 kroner ($3.50) for children.

You'll find easy mountain rambling, excursions and boat trips on Lake Femunden, visits to Funäsdalen in Sweden, fishing in rivers and lakes, and good shopping and walking in the town center.

WHERE TO STAY & DINE

MODERATE

BERGSTADENS TURISTHOTEL, Osloveien 2, N-7460 Røros. Tel. 72-41-11-11. Fax 72-41-01-55. 69 rms (all with bath), 2 suites. MINIBAR TV TEL

$ Rates (including breakfast): Sun–Thurs year-round, 820 kroner ($141.90) single; 915 kroner ($158.30) double; from 1,195 kroner ($206.70) suite. Summer, 680 kroner ($117.60) single; 825 kroner ($142.70) double; from 1,095 kroner ($189.40) suite. AE, DC, MC, V. **Parking:** Free.

In the center of the resort, near the rail station, this hotel was built before World War II. Each of the comfortably furnished bedrooms, many painted in pale pinks or blues, opens onto views of the mountains. Most of the rooms were recently restored. It also contains a pub, a dancing bar, a cafeteria, and two different restaurants.

INEXPENSIVE

HOTEL RØROS, An-Bagrittsvei, N-7460 Røros. Tel. 72-41-10-11. Fax 72-41-00-22. 115 rms (all with bath), 1 suite, 3 mini-suites. MINIBAR TV TEL

$ Rates (including breakfast): Summer, 640 kroner ($110.70) single; 710 kroner ($122.85) double. Off-season, 770–890 kroner ($133.20–$154) single; 1,000–1,120 kroner ($173–$193.80) double. Suite, from 1,240 kroner year round. AE, DC, MC, V. **Parking:** Free.

This hotel enjoys a good view from its high-altitude position over the town, north of the rail station. It was built in the mid-1950s but enlarged many times since. Bedrooms are decorated in light pastels such as yellow, pink, or blue, each opening onto either a view of the town below or the mountains. An orchestra plays for dancing 6 nights a week, and the hotel has a disco, nightclub, swimming pool, and sauna. For outdoor sports, there is a tennis court and mini-golf. A special feature of the hotel is its offering of a *mattorg* (a smørgåsbord to which barbecued foods have been added). A lunchtime visit to this table costs 150 kroner ($26), rising to 185 kroner ($32) in the evening.

CHAPTER 21

BODØ, TROMSØ & NORTHERN NORWAY

The great stretch along the coast—beyond the Arctic Circle to the North Cape and Norwegian Lapland (Finnmark)—is a memorable journey. The first county in the land of sunlit nights is Nordland, beyond the Arctic Circle, with Bodø as its capital. Nordland is the second-largest county of Norway, and together with Troms and Finnmark comprise what is geographically known as northern Norway.

Nordland stretches northward along the border of Sweden, a full 310 miles to the mountains of Troms where the Vesterålen archipelago blends with the long arm of the Lofoten Islands. Nordland links southern and northern Norway, tenuously at one point, since it is only 4 miles wide between the sea and the Swedish border.

Its natural phenomena have figured into world literature. Edgar Allan Poe's maelstrom in the book *Tales of the Grotesque and Arabesque* is based on the Moskenesstraumen of Nordland, and Jules Verne wrote about the same maelstrom in his book *20,000 Leagues Under the Sea.*

The region of northern Norway is steeped in history and legend. At the end of the last Ice Age, Norse people arrived to make a precarious living between the glaciers and the water's edge. Their presence is immortalized in rock carvings. The original inhabitants, however, were the Lapps, who roamed the heaths and mountains with their reindeer herds. Where the E6 highway crosses the Arctic Circle, in the Saltfjell mountains, the Lapps erected their sacrificial stones in pagan times.

The weather is always unpredictable in the region. July, every now and then, brings snow.

Troms and Finnmark are northern Norway's northernmost provinces, and Tromsø is often called the "capital of the north." Viking lords once operated a trading empire from Troms. Today it is estimated that some half of the local citizens live offshore.

In Finnmark, everything is virtually new. The land was devastated by the fleeing Nazi army in World War II, and with the advance of the Soviet army and their bombs, Hitler ordered a "scorched earth" policy for Finnmark.

Most foreign visitors come to the north of Norway to see the **Nordkapp** (North

WHAT'S SPECIAL ABOUT NORTHERN NORWAY

Great Towns/Villages
☐ Bodø, north of the Arctic Circle, the capital of Nordland, a county of scenic wonders.

☐ Tromsø, the capital of northern Norway, a bustling, thriving city of summer Midnight Suns and Arctic winters.

Scenic Wonders
☐ The Arctic Circle—crossing it is a major goal of world travelers.

☐ The Midnight Sun, north of the circle—sunny nights and bright days in midsummer.

☐ North Cape, the goal of the long trek north, a polar coastline, bleak and harsh—Europe's northernmost point.

☐ The aurora borealis, the flaming spectacle of the Arctic winter sky.

☐ Svartisen Glacier, an ice plateau covering 150 square miles of high mountains and narrow fjords.

Ace Attractions
☐ The Planetarium at Tromsø, the world's northernmost such site, best for viewing the mysterious Arctic sky.

Island Excursions
☐ The offshore polar islands of Lofoten-Vesterålen, a beautiful region, filled with bird life.

Special Events
☐ Two midsummer events—the North Norway Festival and the International Sea Fishing Festival at Harstad.

Cape) and the **Midnight Sun,** which is visible from the middle of May until the end of July (see below). Kirkenes is the last town before you face the Russian border.

THE NORTHERN LIGHTS

The **Arctic Circle** marks the bounds of the ○ **Midnight Sun** of the Arctic summer and the sunless winters of the north. Nevertheless, scientists have calculated that in spite of up to 2 months of twilight winter days in the north, the sunny nights and the bright days for the rest of the year, the moonlight, starlight, and northern lights together give more light in the course of a year than you can experience at the Equator.

Crossing the Arctic Circle is perhaps one of the primary reasons visitors choose to come to Scandinavia. To a tourist it is a major event in world exploration.

Then there are the northern lights, the ○ **aurora borealis,** the flaming spectacle of the Arctic winter sky, with its flickering and undulating movement in yellow-green, green, red, and violet. During the hours of the magnetic midnight, between 6 and 10pm, the light can be so strong that you can read a newspaper outdoors. So mysterious, powerful, and alarming is the aurora that when it was observed in the more southerly skies, people took it as an omen of impending disaster. The lights are actually caused by electrically charged particles entering the atmosphere and controlled by the active magnetic fields of the earth itself.

SEEING NORTHERN NORWAY
GETTING THERE

The easiest way to explore the region is to take a Bergen coastal steamer that stops off at the North Cape, the northernmost extension of Europe, lit by the Midnight Sun. Bodø is the best center for exploring Nordland, and it can be reached by plane from Oslo. The county of Troms is best explored with Tromsø as your gateway. It, too, has good plane connections with Oslo. Flying to Bodø and Tromsø is the fastest way of reaching this vast expanse of land.

The Nordland rail line ends in Bodø, but it's possible to travel from Stockholm to remote Narvik, north of Bodø, by train. There are airports at Alta, Lakselv, Vadsø, and Kirkenes, near the Russian border, for those wishing to see Finnmark, the northernmost province of Norway. If you're traveling independently, exploring Finnmark by bus, Honninsvåg is the best center for viewing the North Cape. If you are going by car, the E6 and other roads will take you to many places, and ferries and bridges link the northern locales.

In the far north there are no rail lines. Visitors who prefer not to fly or drive can take the bus, which goes from village to village even in the worst weather.

A SUGGESTED ITINERARY

If you have time, northern Norway is a rewarding target in Europe. The problem is, it takes time.

Day 1: Go to Bodø for the night.

Day 2 & 3: From Bodø, take an excursion to the Lofoten and Vesterålen Islands, reached by boat or plane.

Day 4: Return to Bodø and fly to Tromsø to see its attractions.

Day 5: Transfer to Alta for the night.

Day 6: From a base either in Honningsvåg or Hammerfest, journey by boat and bus to the North Cape.

1. BODØ

889 miles north of Bergen, 466 miles north of Trondheim,
811 miles north of Oslo

GETTING THERE By Plane Bodø is connected to Oslo by daily flights, taking 1½ hours, and to Trondheim, taking 1 hour.

By Train Bodø can be reached from Oslo by rail, as it lies at the termination of the Nordland train. Two trains a day leave Trondheim for Bodø, taking 10 hours 20 minutes.

By Bus Fauske is a terminus transport hub along the E6 highway to the north and Route 80 west to Bodø. It has bus links to Bodø at the rate of two daily, taking 1 hour 10 minutes. If you take the train from Stockholm to Narvik, north of Bodø, you can make bus connections to Fauske and Bodø, taking 5 hours.

MIDNIGHT SUN

The sun is visible 24 hours a day as follows:

Spitsbergen, Norway	April 20–August 21
Hammerfest, Norway	May 12–August 1
Tromsø, Norway	May 14–July 30
Harstad, Norway	May 23–July 22
Svolvaer (Lofoten), Norway	May 23–July 22
Bodø, Norway	June 1–July 13

By Coastal Steamer Bodø is a stopover on the coastal express steamer (*Hurtigrute*) from Bergen in the south to Kirkenes in the north.

By Car Take the E6 highway north from Trondheim until you reach Fauske at the junction of Route 80 west to Bodø.

ESSENTIALS The **Bodø Tourist Office,** Sjøgaten 21, N-8000 Bodø (tel. 75-52-60-00), in the town center, is open Mon–Fri 9am–4:30pm and Sat 9am–2pm.

This seaport, the terminus of the Nordland railway, lies just north of the Arctic Circle. Visitors flock to Bodø, the capital of Nordland, for a glimpse of the Midnight Sun, which shines brightly from June 1 to July 13. But don't always expect to have a clear view of it at this time, as many nights are rainy or hazy. Bodø citizens eventually pay for this extra daylight: The sun completely disappears from December 19 to January 9.

Excursions are possible in many directions—to both glaciers and bird islands, but most important, to the Lofoten Islands (see below).

WHAT TO SEE & DO

BODØ DOMKIRKE, Torv Gate 12. Tel. 75-52-17-50.

Completed in 1956, this is the most notable postwar building built since German bombers leveled Bodø on May 27, 1940. Inside are tufted rugs depicting ecclesiastial themes, wall hangings, and a stained-glass window that captures the northern lights. A memorial outside honors those killed in the war: "No one mentioned, no one forgotten." There's also an outstanding spire that stands separate from the main building.

Admission: Free.

Open: May–Sept, daily 10am–3pm. **Closed:** Oct–Apr.

BODIN KIRKE, Gamle Riks Vei 68. Tel. 75-56-36-70.

Dating from 1240, this church is 2 miles east of the town center. Inside, you can see a baroque altarpiece. This is the most famous church in the district, and one of the few in the north that remains from the Middle Ages. Local residents revere it, in spite of its simple ornamentation and lack of spatial pretensions.

Admission: Free.

Open: May–Sept, daily 10am–8pm. **Closed:** Oct–Apr. **Bus:** 12 from the station.

NORDLANDMUSEET (Nordland Museum), Prinsengate 116. Tel. 75-52-16-40.

Located in the city center, exhibits depict the history of the town and the lives of the Lapps. You can also see and appreciate the elegant lines of the Nordland boat.

Admission: 10 kroner ($1.70) adults, 2 kroner (35¢) children.

Open: Mon–Fri 9am–3pm, Sat 10am–3pm, Sun noon–3pm.

SPORTS/RECREATION

If you feel like riding horseback into the Midnight Sun, **Bodø Hestecenter,** Soloya Gård (tel. 75-51-41-48), a little more than 9 miles from Bodø, rents horses. Buses go there Monday through Friday morning and evening and Saturday morning. For more information, call the Bodø Tourist Office. The cost is from 110 kroner ($19) per hour.

Svømmehallen, Sivert Nielsens Gate 63 (tel. 75-53-54-80), is an indoor swimming pool open Monday through Friday from 8:30am to 8pm, on Saturday from 12:30 to 8pm, and on Sunday from noon to 4pm. Price per hour is 25 kroner ($4.30) for adults and 13 kroner ($2.20) for children.

WHERE TO STAY

The Bodø Tourist Office (see above) will help you arrange for a room in a private home or hotel.

EXPENSIVE

DIPLOMAT HOTEL, Sjorgata 23, N-8001 Bodø. Tel. 75-52-70-00. Fax 75-52-24-60. 104 rms (all with bath), 3 suites. MINIBAR TV TEL

$ **Rates** (including breakfast): Summer, 550 kroner ($95.20) single; 670 kroner ($115.90) double. Winter, weekdays 1,000 kroner ($173) single; 1,250 kroner ($216.30) double. Winter, weekends 600 kroner ($103.80) single; 750 kroner ($129.80) double. Year-round, 1,400 kroner ($242.20) suite. AE, DC, MC, V. **Parking:** 70 kroner ($12.10).

Opening onto a view of Vestfjorden, this is one of Bodø's best hotels, built in 1986 with an enlargement in 1990. All the well-furnished bedrooms have large writing desks. The hotel's popular restaurants are recommended separately (see "Where to Dine," below). The hotel is located at the harbor.

SAS ROYAL HOTEL, Storgaten 2, N-8000 Bodø. Tel. 75-52-41-00, or toll free 800/221-2350 in the U.S. Fax 75-52-74-93. 184 rms (all with bath), 6 suites. MINIBAR TV TEL

$ **Rates** (including breakfast): May–Aug and Fri–Sat in winter, 595 kroner ($102.90) single; 690 kroner ($119.40) double. Winter, Sun–Thurs 1,190 kroner ($205.90) single, 1,390 kroner ($240.50) double. Year-round, from 2,000 kroner ($346) suite. AE, DC, MC, V. **Parking:** Free.

By far the finest hotel in the area, this is a glistening modern hotel, with several bars and dining facilities. Bedrooms are furnished in sleek contemporary style. The Royal is on the main street directly on the harborfront.

Dining/Entertainment: Guests drink at the Marlene Bar or go dancing at Marlene Dancing, later enjoying a drink at the Top 13, a panoramic bar. Less formal facilities include the Pizzakjeller'n and the Baquette'n and Balustraden coffee shops.

Services: "Office-for-a-day," express laundry service, 16-hour room service, SAS airline check-in at lobby.

Facilities: Sauna, solarium.

MODERATE

BODØ HOTEL, Professor Schyttesgate 5, N-8001 Bodø. Tel. 75-52-69-00. Fax 75-52-57-78. 32 rms (all with bath), 1 suite. TV TEL

$ **Rates** (including breakfast): Winter weekends and summer, 450 kroner ($77.90) single; 600 kroner ($103.80) double. Winter, weekdays 710 kroner ($122.80) single; 870 kroner ($150.50) double. Year-round, from 900 kroner ($155.70) suite. AE, DC, MC, V. **Parking:** Free.

Opening in 1987, this hotel quickly became known for its good value. In the town center 2½ blocks from the harbor, it has a helpful staff and modern rooms, each with satellite TV. It also offers no-smoking rooms and is equipped for the handicapped. A different color scheme is found on each of the hotel's five floors. The hotel is fully licensed and operates the Café Gamle, open daily from 11am to 7pm, serving attractive lunchtime and early-dinner platters priced from 60 kroner to 75 kroner ($10.40 to $13).

INEXPENSIVE

CENTRUM HOTEL, Storgaten 39, N-8001 Bodø. Tel. 75-52-48-88. Fax 75-52-58-90. 18 rms (all with bath). TV TEL

$ **Rates** (including breakfast): Winter weekends and summer, 450 kroner ($77.90) single; 400 kroner ($69.20) double. Winter, weekdays 500 kroner ($86.50) single; 650 kroner ($112.50) double. AE, DC, MC, V. **Parking:** Free.

Rooms in this boardinghouse near the harbor are adequately furnished, clean, and respectable. The upstairs restaurant serves beer and wine. Parking is available. It is located near the railway, boat, and bus terminals and minutes by taxi from the airport.

BUDGET

NORRØNA, Storgaten 4, N-8000 Bodø. Tel. 75-52-41-18. Fax 75-52-33-88. 101 rms (58 with bath). TEL
$ Rates (including breakfast): Winter, 275 kroner ($47.60) single without bath, 375 kroner ($64.90) single with bath; 375 kroner ($64.90) double without bath, 450 kroner ($77.90) double with bath. Summer, 275 kroner ($47.60) single with or without bath; 375 kroner ($64.90) double with or without bath. AE, DC, **Parking:** Free.

The Norrøna is run by the SAS Royal Hotel, which uses it primarily as a bed-and-breakfast. A functional, modern building, it stands in the center of Bodø, offering comfortable, simply furnished bedrooms. Those with private bath also contain TV. In summer, all rooms are priced the same, regardless of plumbing. As a guest, you can enjoy the same privileges as patrons of the more expensive SAS Royal Hotel, which lies just down the harbor. The hotel operates a coffee shop as well as a British-style pub, Piccadilly.

WHERE TO DINE

EXPENSIVE

MARLENE, in the SAS Royal Hotel, Storgaten 2. Tel. 75-52-41-00.
    Cuisine: SEAFOOD/INTERNATIONAL/NORWEGIAN. **Reservations:** Recommended.
$ Prices: Summer seafood buffet 165 kroner ($28.50); appetizers 58–110 kroner ($10–$19); main dishes 156–210 kroner ($27–$36.30). AE, DC, MC, V.
    Open: Daily noon–11:30pm.

Marlene has the best summer seafood buffet in town. From late June to late August you can enjoy various local seafood dishes, including fried squid, smoked halibut, fresh shrimp, coalfish, and cod. You have a selection of sauces to go with the fish, as well as fish soup, prepared in the style of northern Norway, and finish with a selection of desserts. At any time of the year you can order cream of wild-mushroom soup, or a seafood appetizer that includes an entire fjord crab garnished with shrimp. Specialties are grilled filet of reindeer and grilled monkfish. It's located on the waterfront.

MODERATE

BLIX, in the Diplomat Hotel, Sjorgata 23. Tel. 75-52-70-00.
    Cuisine: NORWEGIAN. **Reservations:** Not required.
$ Prices: Appetizers 25–52 kroner ($4.30–$9); main dishes 74–142 kroner ($12.80–$24.60); daily lunch plate 80 kroner ($13.80). AE, DC, MC, V.
    Open: Mon–Sat 3pm–midnight, Sun 2pm–midnight.

Not as expensive as the Oasen (see below) in the same hotel, this restaurant is preferred by the working locals. The decor has an old-fashioned allure with a scattering of antiques. On the lobby level, the restaurant has a separate entrance opening directly onto the street. Try lasagne, steaks, filet of reindeer, or other wholesome and ribsticking—and flavorful—fare. It's located on the harbor.

OASEN, in the Diplomat Hotel, Sjorgata 23. Tel. 75-52-70-00.
    Cuisine: NORWEGIAN/INTERNATIONAL. **Reservations:** Required.
$ Prices: Appetizers 42–45 kroner ($7.30–$7.80); main dishes 75–185 kroner ($13–$32); daily lunch plate 80 kroner ($13.80). AE, DC, MC, V.
    Open: Mon–Sat noon–11:30pm.

This is the most upscale restaurant in the Diplomat Hotel and one of the best dining rooms in the area. It is very modern in decor, with a theme based on autumnal colors, opening onto a view of the harbor. Fish is the specialty, beginning with fish soup, and followed by anglerfish, salmon, or whatever the fishermen caught that day. The lunch plate referred to above is available only in summer from noon to 7pm.

INEXPENSIVE

CHINA PALACE, Havnegata 1. Tel. 75-52-23-39.

Cuisine: CHINESE/INTERNATIONAL. **Reservations:** Recommended.
$ Prices: Appetizers 30–65 kroner ($5.20–$11.20); main dishes 80–190 kroner ($13.80–$32.90). AE, DC, MC, V.
Open: Daily 2–11pm.

By anyone's estimate, this is the best and by far the most unusual Chinese restaurant in North Norway, with a carefully stylized decor. Set in the cellar of a log-sided modern building 3 blocks inland from the harbor, the restaurant contains an enormous aquarium, a botanist's dream of verdant plants, and a series of bamboo bridges that lead to isolated tables scattered across a simulated tropical lagoon. Drinks are as foamy, fruity, and colorful as you might expect, and menu choices include a wide array of Chinese and Polynesian-inspired beef, pork, and chicken dishes.

NORMANDIE, Havnegata 1. Tel. 75-52-18-32.
Cuisine: INTERNATIONAL. **Reservations:** Recommended.
$ Prices: Salads 50 kroner ($8.70); pizzas 60–170 kroner ($10.40–$29.40); main dishes 100–180 kroner ($17.30–$31.10); lunchtime all-you-can-eat cold buffet 49 kroner ($8.50) per person. AE, DC, MC, V.
Open: Mon–Thurs 11am–2am, Fri–Sat 11am–3am, Sun 3pm–midnight.

Located in a log-sided building that also contains China Palace (see above), on a main street 3 blocks inland from the harbor, Normandie prides itself on its authentic Viking decor. The restaurant contains panels, beams, and timbers carved into motifs similar to those carried to northern France (Normandy) long ago by Viking invaders. The restaurant serves wine by the glass and pizzas ranging in size from petite to humongous. No one minds if you just drop in for a drink or glass of wine, but if you want a full meal, menu choices include a "Black and White" platter composed of filets of beef and pork accompanied with béarnaise and pepper sauces, gratin of chicken covered with Gorgonzola sauce, cheese fondues and soufflés, steaks, and several different kinds of pasta.

EVENING ENTERTAINMENT

TOP 13, in the SAS Royal Hotel, Storgaten 2. Tel. 75-52-41-00.
For a grand view of Bodø and the harbor, go to this "hut" perched like a top hat on the roof of the SAS Royal Hotel. There is bar service Monday through Saturday from 11am to 2am. Beer costs 39 kroner ($6.70).

MARLENE DANCING, in the SAS Royal Hotel, Storgaten 2. Tel. 75-52-41-00.
At Marlene Dancing, the preferred spot for dancing in Bodø, the surroundings are elegant and the latest in recorded music is played. Even though it opens earlier, most people don't show up until 9:30pm. The Marlene Cabinett, with a fireplace, is a little offshoot restaurant serving late-night suppers and snacks for about the same price as those within the Marlene restaurant (see above). The place is open Monday through Thursday from 6pm to 2am and on Friday and Saturday from 6pm to 3am. Beer runs 39 kroner ($6.70).
Admission: 50 kroner ($8.70).

VANHULLET NIGHTCLUB, in the Diplomat Hotel, Sjorgata 23. Tel. 75-52-70-00.
This is probably the most elegant and exclusive nightclub in Bodø. The restaurant has a strict door policy—no "rowdies" allowed. Recorded music is played for dancing. It is open Monday through Thursday from 8pm to 1:20am, Friday and Saturday 8pm to 2:30am.
Admission: 40 kroner ($6.90); free to hotel residents.

EASY EXCURSIONS

THE MAELSTROM From Bodø, you can take a bus to the mighty maelstrom, the ✪ **Saltstraumen Eddy,** some 20 miles away. The variation between high- and low-tide levels pushes immense volumes of water through narrow fjords, creating huge whirlpools. When these whirling "kettles," as the eddies are called, and the surrounding vibrate, they produce an odd yelling sound. Saltstraumen is nearly 2 miles long and only about 500 feet wide, with billions of gallons of water pressed through at speeds of about 10 knots. The bus trip takes 40 minutes each way and leaves daily from the Bodø bus station five times a day, costing 40 kroner ($6.90) for adults, half price for children. It's best to go in the morning. A taxi excursion costs 300 kroner ($51.90).

A GLACIER EXCURSION One of Norway's major tourist attractions, **Svartisen** is second in size only to the Jostedal Glacier. This ice plateau 65 feet above sea level covers 150 square miles of high mountains and narrow fjords. About 100 miles from Bodø, the glacier can be reached by car, although a boat crossing over the Svartisenfjord is more exciting. Tours to the glacier on the Helgeland Express, a combination bus and ferryboat excursion, are offered from Bodø several times in summer on Saturday. The charge is 250 kroner ($43.30) for adults, 125 kroner ($21.60) for children under 16. The tours leave Bodø at 1pm and return at 8pm. You can go ashore to examine the Engaglacier and visit the inn there. Call **Nordtrafikk** (tel. 75-55-21-15), a local tour operator, for more details, or to book a ticket. The tourist office (see above) will also provide details about this excursion.

2. LOFOTEN & VESTERÅLEN ISLANDS

Svolvaer: 174 miles W of Narvik, 174 miles N of Bodø, 298 miles S of Tromsø

GETTING THERE By Plane Svolvaer is served by Widerøe Airline. Planes leave Bodø five times a day.

By Bus There are bus connections to Vesterålen and to Fauske/Bodø to coincide with train service. There are also connections to Narvik to link with the Swedish railway. You can take a bus to Ulvsvåg on the main E6, then catch a connecting bus to Skutvik, where you can board a ferry to Svolvaer.

By Car The quickest way to drive to the Lofoten Islands is to take the Skutvik-Svolvaer ferry, a 2-hour trip, with eight crossings daily in summer. There is also ferry service to the bird islands, Røst and Vaerky. For information and reservations, call **Ofotens og Vesterålens Dampskibsselskab A/S**, Box 57, N-8501 Narvik (tel. 76-94-72-52).

By Coastal Steamer Coastal steamers leaving from Bergen and other places along the coast call daily at Stamsund and Svolvaer. The steamer leaves Bodø at 3pm daily.

ESSENTIALS Tourist information is available from the **Lofoten Tourist Board**, Box 210, N-8301 Svolvaer (tel. 76-07-10-53). The **Vesterålen Travel Association**, Box 243, N-8401 Sortland (tel. 76-12-15-15), will help you figure out where to stay and what to do in the islands.

The island kingdom of Lofoten/Vesterålen, considered one of the most beautiful regions of Norway, lies 123 miles north of the Arctic Circle and has a population of 35,000 spread out among both the large and small islands. Many travelers come just to fish, but the area offers a rich bird life and abundant flora. The summer brings the Midnight Sun from mid-May to the end of July.

THE LOFOTEN ISLANDS

The Lofoten Islands start in the east at Vågan and stretch seaward toward the southwest to Røst and Skomvaer. The steep Lofoten mountain peaks—often called the Lofotwall—shelter a stretch of farmland and deep fjords, and offer natural protection from the elements resulting in stable weather.

The North Atlantic drift of the Gulf Stream contributes to the seasonal Lofoten fishing, Lofotfisket. Beyond Lofoten, and especially in the Vestfjord, are spawned the Arctic Sea codfish, with huge harvesting operations carried on between January and April.

The first inhabitants of the Lofoten were nomads who survived by hunting and fishing, but excavations show that agriculture was practiced here at least 4,000 years ago. Farming, fishing, and trading were Viking pursuits and examples of Viking housing sites can be seen on Vestbågøya, where more than 1,000 burial mounds from the period have been registered in the area.

Harsh treatment by the Nazis during World War II played a major part in the creation of the famous Norwegian resistance movement. Allied forces that landed here to harass the German iron-ore boats sailing from Narvik withdrew in June 1940. They took as many of the island civilians as they could with them to Scotland for the duration of the war.

Today the Lofotens and their neighbors to the north, the Vesterålen Islands (see below), have modern towns with shops, hotels, restaurants, and public transport.

WHAT TO SEE & DO

Outdoor activities range from mountain climbing to diving, canoeing, rambling through the countryside, birdwatching (see "Røst and Vaerøy," below), whale watching, sailing, riding, downhill and cross-country skiing, and ice fishing.

There are handcraft shops at Svolvaer, Leknes, Sørvågen, and Vaerøy.

Examples of a special old-fashioned method of knitting, needle binding, used as far back as Viking times, can also be found here. The **Glass Cabin** at Vikten, near Napp, is northern Norway's only such studio. Open to the public, it offers products of top-quality and original design. The craftsperson Hans Gjertsen, a smith at Sund, is known for his well-made cormorants cast in steel.

The Lofoten Islands are visited by many artists, and there are galleries at Svolvaer, Oersnes, Stamsund, and Leknes, with local and international artists represented. The North Norway Artists' Center is also in Svolvaer.

The fishing village of **Nusfjord** has been cited by UNESCO for its beautiful, well-preserved historic buildings, especially traditional *rorbuer* (see "Where to Stay," below), fishermen's cabins.

VESTVÅGØY MUSEUM, Fygleveien 109. Tel. 76-08-00-43.

At Fygle, near Leknes, this museum has exhibits depicting the lifestyle of the Lofoten fisherman-farmer. It's on the main road at Fygle, 1 mile from Leknes and 9 miles from Stamsund.

Admission: 10 kroner ($1.70) adults, 5 kroner (90¢) children.

Open: June–Aug, Mon–Fri 11am–4pm, Sat noon–3pm. **Closed:** Sept–May.

LOFOTEN MUSEUM, Kabelvåg. No phone.

The islands' regional museum, it depicts past life in the Lofoten Islands. Excavations are underway at the site of an old northern Norwegian trading post, Vagar, Europe's northernmost town in the Middle Ages. The museum is located on the outskirts of Kabelvåg, 3 miles from Svolvaer.

Admission: 10 kroner ($1.70) adults, 5 kroner (90¢) children.

Open: June–Aug, Mon–Fri 9am–3pm, Sat–Sun 11am–3pm. **Closed:** Sept–May.

Røst and Vaerøy

Mountains speckled with birds range from Andøy in the north all the way to the southern tip of Lofoten. Many different seabirds can be seen during nesting season, but the most famous nesting cliffs are at Røst and Vaerøy, remote Lofoten islands that can be reached by steamer, plane, or helicopter.

On the flat island of **Røstlandet,** the main attraction is the bird sanctuary, made up of approximately 1,000 little offshore islands comprising the mini-archipelago of

Røst. Here, the highly prized eider duck can be found. Locals provide small nesting shelters for the ducks and collect the eiderdown after the ducklings are hatched. Cormorants and seagulls nest on the steep cliffs. Puffins nest at the end of narrow tunnels in the grassy hills, while the auk and the sea eagle nest high up on ledges.

Vaerky's **Mount Mostadfjell** is the nesting place for more than 1½ million seabirds, including sea eagles, auks, puffins, guillemots, kittiwakes, cormorants, and others that breed from May through August.

The **North Vaerøy Church,** with its onion-shaped dome, was brought here from Vagån in 1799. The altarpiece, from around 1400, is a late-medieval English alabaster relief depicting the Annunciation, the Three Magi, the Resurrection, and the Ascension.

For information about these islands, get in touch with the Lofoten Tourist Board or the ferry company, **Ofotens og Vesterålens Dampskibsselskab A/S,** Box 57, N-8501 Narvik (tel. 76-94-72-52).

WHERE TO STAY & DINE

In addition to hotels, guesthouses, and campsites, the Lofoten and Vesterålen Islands offer temporary (holiday) lodging in old traditional fishermen's cottages known as *rorbuer,* and a larger, usually more modern, version (often two stories), a *sjøhus* (sea house). The traditional *rorbu* was built on the edge of the water, often on piles, with enough room for 10 bunks, a kitchen, and an entrance hall used as a work and storage room. Many *rorbu* today are still simple and unpretentious, but some have electricity, a wood stove, a kitchenette with a sink, and running water. Others have been equipped with such modern amenities as separate bedrooms, with private showers and toilets.

The Lofoten Tourist Board publishes an accommodations guide to the Lofoten Islands, and information about lodging on the Vesterålen Islands is available from their tourist board (see "Essentials," above).

In Stamsund: Inexpensive

STAMSUND LOFOTEN, N-8340 Stamsund. Tel. 76-08-93-00. Fax 76-08-96-55. 28 rms (all with bath). TEL

$ Rates (including breakfast): 375 kroner ($64.90) single; 600 kroner ($103.80) double. AE, DC, MC, V. **Parking:** Free.
This hotel is in the heart of town, with a view of the harbor. Bedrooms are simply furnished. Many have TVs. On the premises is a licensed bar and restaurant. The luncheon buffet costs 160 kroner ($27.70).

In Svolvaer: Inexpensive

NORTON HOTEL LOFOTEN, Sivert Nelsen Gate, N-8300 Svolvaer. Tel. 76-07-12-00. Fax 76-07-08-50. 48 rms (all with bath), 2 suites. MINIBAR TV TEL

$ Rates (including breakfast): Summer, 795 kroner ($137.50) single; 920 kroner ($159.20) double; from 1,100 kroner ($190.30) suite. Winter, 500 kroner ($86.50) single; 600 kroner ($103.80) double; from 800 kroner ($138.40) suite. AE, DC, MC, V. **Parking:** Free.
About half the well-furnished bedrooms at this 1978 hotel in the town center, near the express-steamer quay, overlook the sea. On the premises is a fully licensed bar and a lively disco. Meals range from 135 kroner to 200 kroner ($23.40 to $34.60) in the Restaurant Skarven, which specializes in fish and steak.

VESTFJORD HOTEL, Box 386, N-8301 Svolvaer. Tel. 76-07-08-70. Fax 76-07-08-54. 57 rms (all with bath), 1 suite. TV TEL

$ Rates (including breakfast): 525–725 kroner ($90.80–$125.40) single; 700–930 kroner ($121.10–$160.90) double; from 980 kroner ($169.50) suite. AE, DC, MC, V. **Parking:** Free.
This hotel, near the quay and bus station, is the first thing yachtsmen see when they enter the harbor. Bedrooms are functional; 20 contain a minibar, and many overlook

the sea. On the premises is a wood-paneled restaurant specializing in fresh fish, and a fully licensed bar. Facilities include a lobby bar, sauna, solarium, and winter garden.

THE VESTERÅLEN ISLANDS

Farther north, but with a gentler landscape and richer farmlands than the Lofotens, the Vesterålen Islands, known for their fishing, have a landscape ranging from marshlands to farms to craggy mountains and white beaches.

The islands are linked with the E6 by six bridges. In addition there are three ports of call for the coastal steamer *Hurtigruten,* as well as two airports. On these islands, you can see the Troll Fjord, fishing villages, bird rocks, museums, old trading centers, and in summer, the Andenes Sea Fishing Festival and an arts festival, Sommer-Melbu, are held.

Like Lofoten, Vesterålen offers accommodations in both the *rorbu* and the *sjøhus* categories.

The **Vesterålen Travel Association,** Box 243, N-8401 Sortland (tel. 76-12-15-55), will help you figure out where to stay and what to do in the islands.

WHERE TO STAY IN SORTLAND
Inexpensive

SORTLAND NORDIC HOTEL, 59 Vesterålsgaten, Langøy Island, N-8401 Sortland. Tel. 76-12-18-33. Fax 76-12-22-02. 81 rms (60 with bath). TV TEL
$ Rates (including breakfast): Summer (with Scandinavian Bonus Pass), 300–350 kroner ($51.90–$60.60) single without bath; 580 kroner ($100.30) double with bath. Winter, Sun–Thurs 385–585 kroner ($66.60–$101.20) single without bath; 950 kroner ($164.40) double with bath. Winter, Fri–Sat 250–300 kroner ($43.30–$51.90) single without bath; 500 kroner ($86.50) double with bath. AE, DC, MC, V.
Parking: Free.

The only hotel in town, this building near the water is divided into a cluster of structures, the oldest dating from 1968. Bedrooms are unpretentious, decorated in tones of blue or brown. Rooms without private facilities are all singles; many have partial baths—(shower but no toilet). The hotel has a restaurant, a licensed bar, and the island's most popular disco. The hotel also has its own activity room, a sauna, and a solarium. Boats can be rented and fishing trips arranged.

---

3. NARVIK
187 miles NE of Bodø, 919 miles N of Oslo

GETTING THERE By Train Two to three trains a day run from Stockholm, taking 21 to 24 hours.

By Bus Two buses a day go from Fauske/Bodø, taking 5 hours.

By Car The E6 highway that begins at Oslo continues north, passing through Narvik.

ESSENTIALS The **tourist office,** located at Kongensgate 66 (tel. 76-94-33-09), is open Mon–Sat 9am–9pm and Sun noon–9pm (mid-June–mid-Aug and Mon–Fri 9am–4pm (late Aug–early June).

This ice-free seaport on the Ofotfjord is in Nordland fylke (county), 250 miles north of the Arctic Circle. Narvik boasts Europe's most modern shipping harbor for iron ore, founded in 1903 when the Ofoten railway line was completed to transport iron ore around the world. It's a magnificent scenic route (the northernmost electrified railway line in the world) through precipitous mountain terrain, tunnels, ridges, and across tall stone embankments.

Only 6½ miles from Narvik, Straumsnes station is the last permanent habitation as you go east. The last Norwegian station, Bjørnfjell, is well above the timber line and about 3 hours from Kiruna, Sweden, some 87 miles north of the Arctic Circle. You can catch a train there to Stockholm. In 1984 a road was opened between Kiruna and Narvik.

WHAT TO SEE & DO

To get a good look at Narvik, take the cable car, **Gondolbanen,** in back of the bus station. The car operates from March to October, charging 80 kroner ($13.80) round-trip. In just 13 minutes it takes you to an altitude of 2,100 feet, at the top of Fagernesfjell where you can admire the impressive panorama of the town and its surroundings. The last cable car returns at midnight.

The **Midnight Sun** shines from May 27 to July 19, and August is noted for its "mysterious lighting."

In the gardens at the railway station, you can see what may be the only remaining train engine constructed in Trollhattan, Sweden, in 1882.

NORDLAND RØDE KORS KRIGSMINNEMUSEUM (Var Museum). Tel. 76-94-44-26.

Near Torghallene in the town center, this is one of the most important sights in town. Most of Narvik was destroyed by the Germans, who occupied it until the end of World War II. Following Hitler's attack on Denmark and Norway, a bitter battle raged for 2 months for Narvik and its iron ore. German forces fought troops from France, Poland, and Norway, and a considerable British flotilla at sea. The battle meant the destruction of the iron-ore-shipping installations and of the town. Depicted are events of that era as well as experiences of the civilian population and foreign POWs.

Admission: 20 kroner ($3.50) adults, 10 kroner ($1.70) children.
Open: Mon–Sat 10am–8pm, Sun 1–8pm.

LOFOTEN MUSEUM, Parkhallen. Tel. 76-94-47-32.

In the town center, this museum preserves the cultural history of the area.
Admission: 15 kroner ($2.60) adults, 5 kroner (90¢) children.
Open: June 25–Aug 8, daily 10am–4pm; Aug 9–June 24, Mon–Fri 11am–4pm.

WHERE TO STAY

Narvik's hotels tend to be expensive, so your best bet is to book a room in a private home through the tourist office (see above). The average cost is from 200 kroner ($34.60) double nightly.

INEXPENSIVE

GRAND ROYAL, Kongensgate 64, N-8500 Narvik. Tel. 76-94-15-00. Fax 76-94-55-31. 110 rms (all with bath), 5 suites. MINIBAR TV TEL **Bus:** 14, 15, 16, 17.
$ Rates (including breakfast): Summer, 550 kroner ($95.20) single; 790 kroner ($136.70) double. Winter, Sun–Thurs 965 kroner ($166.90) single; 1,075 kroner ($186) double. Winter, Fri–Sat 550 kroner ($95.20) single; 670 kroner ($115.90) double. Year-round, from 1,500 kroner ($259.50) suite. AE, DC, MC, V. **Parking:** Free.

In the town center, this hotel, the largest and best equipped in Narvik, opens onto the main street midway between the rail station and the harborfront. Originally built in the 1920s, it has seen many enlargements since. It is one of the few buildings in Narvik to escape destruction in World War II, and is called the Grand Royal because the late King Olav was a frequent visitor (his portraits adorn some of the public rooms). Bedrooms are traditionally furnished, among the most tasteful in the area. The finest restaurant in town is also here (see "Where to Dine," below).

NORDST JERNEN HOTEL, Kongensgate 26, N-8500 Narvik. Tel. 76-94-41-20. Fax 76-94-75-06. 30 rms (all with bath). TV TEL **Bus:** 14, 16.
$ Rates (including breakfast): Winter, Sun–Thurs 550 kroner ($95.20) single; 650

kroner ($112.50) double. Winter Fri–Sat and summer, 425 kroner ($73.50) single; 525 kroner ($90.80) double. DC, MC, V. **Parking:** Free.

⑤   In the town center, south of the bus station, this is one of Narvik's few buildings to escape the burnings of World War II. It has long been known as one of the best hotels for value in the area, offering bedrooms short on style but clean and respectable. Rooms vary in size. Facilities include a fully licensed restaurant and a lounge.

WHERE TO DINE

INEXPENSIVE

ROYAL BLUE, in the Grand Royal Hotel, Kongensgate 64. Tel. 76-94-15-00.

  Cuisine: NORWEGIAN. **Reservations:** Recommended. **Bus:** 14, 15, 16, 17.

$ **Prices:** Appetizers 30–70 kroner ($5.20–$12.10); main dishes 75–200 kroner ($13–$34.60); fixed-price lunch 125 kroner ($21.60); fixed-price dinner 143 kroner ($24.70). AE, DC, MC, V.

  Open: Daily noon–11:15pm.

The best restaurant in the region is decorated with appropriate colors of strong royal blues. It is the preferred choice of visiting dignitaries, including the king of Norway. Service is polite and the food delectable. Specialties include thinly sliced, sauna-smoked ham with asparagus, cured salmon with crème fraîche, reindeer curry with brussels sprouts and apricots, and large beefsteaks. It's located on the lobby level of the Grand Royal (see "Where to Stay," above).

---

4. TROMSØ

1,084 miles N of Oslo, 352 miles N of Bodø

GETTING THERE   **By Plane**   At Langnes Airport, there are eight daily flights from Oslo, nine from Bergen, five from Trondheim, and one from Svalbard. Flights from Oslo take 1 hour 40 minutes; flights from Bergen take 3 hours 10 minutes. You can easily fly here from Bodø.

By Train   No rail line runs to Tromsø. The nearest rail connection is through Narvik (see above). From there, you must go the rest of the way by bus.

By Bus   Two or three bus connections can be made from Narvik, taking 5½ hours.

By Car   Take the E6 from Oslo all the way north.

By Coastal Steamer   *Hurtigrute* steamer connections can be made from either Narvik or Bodø. There is also a daily year-round service of coastal express liners from Bergen to Tromsø. Northbound ships arrive at 2:15pm, and southbound ships leave at 11:45pm.

ESSENTIALS   The **Tromsø Tourist Office** is located at Storgata 61-63 (tel. 77-61-00-00). Local transportation in Tromsø is provided by a network of bus and fast ferry service.

Tromsø, the gateway to the Arctic, is a North Sea boomtown, a trade and financial center. The surrounding snow-topped mountain peaks reach 6,000 feet, and mountain plateaus have good fishing lakes and birch forests.

With 50,000 inhabitants, Tromsø is the administrative center of the county of Troms, a trade center, and the site of one of Norway's four universities. It serves as the capital of northern Norway, and it's the country's fourth-largest finance center.

Lying some 250 miles north of the Arctic Circle, Tromsø gets the Midnight Sun from May 19 to July 26—but not one ray comes through from November 25 to January 21. The climate has a heat record of 86° Fahrenheit and a low of −4°.

WHAT TO SEE & DO

In addition to the sights below, don't miss taking the **Tromsdalen funicular** (tel. 72-63-51-21), which leaves from Fjellheisen, the entry station to a cable car that takes passengers on a lofty ride to 1,400 feet above sea level, where you'll have an unparalleled view of Tromsø and its environs. A round-trip ticket is 45 kroner ($7.80) for adults and 20 kroner ($3.50) for children, and the funicular runs March to September, daily from 10am to 5pm. From June to August it also operates from 9pm to 12:30am if it's midnight sunny.

TROMSDALEN KIRKE (Arctic Church), along the E78. Tel. 77-63-76-11.
Across the longest (approximately 1,100 yards) suspension bridge in Scandinavia is the Arctic Church, a stunning example of modern architecture. It was built in the shape of an iceberg, with aluminum on the outside that glistens in the Midnight Sun. Organ recitals are given twice a week in summer.
Admission: 5 kroner (90¢).
Open: June to mid-Aug, Mon–Sat 10am–5pm, Sun 1–5pm. **Closed:** Mid-Aug to May. **Bus:** 30, 36.

TROMSØ CATHEDRAL, Kirkegata. Tel. 77-68-25-48.
One of Norway's largest wooden churches, the 1861 Tromsø cathedral is the world's northernmost Protestant cathedral. Sunday services are at 11am. It's 200 yards from the harbor.
Admission: Free.
Open: June 15–Aug 15, Tues–Fri 11am–4pm. **Closed:** Aug 16–June 14. **Bus:** 27, 37, 38.

TROMSØ MUSEUM, Folkeparken. Tel. 76-64-50-00.
A 20-minute walk from the town center, the Tromsø Museum traces the life—both animal and human—inhabiting the wilderness north of the Arctic Circle. Of special interest is an extensive exhibition on Lapp culture. In addition, a good assortment of medieval church art and furnishings is displayed, plus botanical, zoological (Arctic birds and mammals), and geological displays.
Admission: 10 kroner ($1.70) adults, 5 kroner (90¢) children.
Open: June–Aug, daily 9am–9pm; Sept–May, Mon–Fri 8:30am–3:30pm, Sat noon–3pm, Sun 11am–4pm. **Bus:** 21, 27.

POLARMUSEET, Søndre Tollbugate 11B. Tel. 77-68-43-73.
Founded in 1976 in an 1830s Customs warehouse, the Polar Museum contains exhibits depicting hunting and research activities in polar regions, especially in the Arctic. It stands opposite the Tromsø Museum, north of Stortorget.
Admission: 20 kroner ($3.50) adults, 5 kroner (90¢) children.
Open: May 15–Aug 31, daily 11am–6pm; Sept 1–May 14, daily 11am–3pm. **Bus:** 21.

NORDLYSPLANETARIET (Northern Lights Planetarium), Universitesområdet, Breivika. Tel. 77-67-60-00.
Here you can enjoy the northern lights, the Midnight Sun, and the starry sky in Norway's first planetarium open to the public, and the northernmost in the world. Experience the city in the film *Arctic Light* and the multimedia show *Tromsø, Tromsø,* or travel into space with the space-shuttle film. It is especially recommended to those who arrive in Tromsø too late to view some of the wonders of the northern sky.
Admission: 50 kroner ($8.70) adults, 25 kroner ($4.30) children.
Open: Variable schedule; call for information on show times. **Bus:** 25, 37.

WHERE TO STAY

You can arrange for a room in a private home through the Tromsø Tourist Office, Storgata 61-63 (tel. 77-61-00-00). Count on spending from 150 kroner to 250 kroner ($26 to $43.30) for a single, from 200 kroner to 350 kroner ($34.60 to $60.60) for a double, plus a booking fee.

EXPENSIVE

GRAND NORDIC HOTEL, Storgata 44, N-9001 Tromsø. Tel. 77-68-55-00. Fax 77-68-25-00. 103 rms (all with bath), 15 junior suites. MINIBAR TV TEL **Bus:** 21.
$ Rates (including breakfast): Winter weekends and summer, 525 kroner ($90.80) single; 700 kroner ($121.10) double. Winter weekdays, 1,015 kroner ($175.60) single; 1,225 kroner ($211.90) double. Year round, from 1,300 kroner ($224.90) suite. AE, DC, MC, V. **Parking:** 25 kroner ($4.30).
Located in the heart of the city's business and shopping area, the Grand Nordic is conveniently near public transportation and attractions. The hotel's bedrooms, including junior suites, have extra features like radios, trouser presses, and hairdryers. Twenty rooms are set aside for nonsmokers. The hotel has a restaurant, a rôtisserie, two bars, a nightclub, a pub, and a winter garden.

SAS ROYAL HOTEL, Sjøgata 7, N-9001 Tromsø. Tel. 77-65-60-00, or toll free 800/221-2350 in the U.S. Fax 77-65-61-10. 193 rms (all with bath), 5 suites. MINIBAR TV TEL **Bus:** 21.
$ Rates (including breakfast): 1,160–1,190 kroner ($200.70–$205.90) single; 1,350–1,390 kroner ($233.60–$240.50) double; from 1,750 kroner ($302.80) suite. AE, DC, MC, V. **Parking:** Free.
This handsome hotel, centrally located near the harbor, offers stunning views from the top floor. Built in the 1960s, the hotel is the most visible and prominent—and also the best—in Tromsø, with the most varied assortment of drinking, dining, and dancing facilities. Bedrooms are tastefully furnished and equipped with trouser presses and hairdryers. The Café Royal serves sandwiches, cakes, and coffee, as well as dinner. Charley's Bar & Grill, the Rorbua Pub, and Jonas, the pizza and beer emporium, are recommended separately (see "Where to Dine" and "Evening Entertainment," below).

MODERATE

SAGA HOTEL, Richard Withs Plass 2, N-9000 Tromsø. Tel. 77-68-11-80. Fax 77-68-23-80. 54 rms (all with bath). MINIBAR TV TEL **Bus:** 27, 37.
$ Rates (including breakfast): Winter weekends and midsummer, 550 kroner ($95.20) single; 650 kroner ($112.50) double. Winter weekdays, 850 kroner ($147.10) single; 1,000 kroner ($173) double. AE, DC, MC, V. **Parking:** 35 kroner ($6.10).
The accommodations at this 1970s hotel are cozy, and each has satellite TV, coffee percolator, hairdryer, trouser press, and alcohol-free minibar. The restaurant serves good Norwegian food.

WITH HOME HOTEL, Sjøgata 35-37, N-9000 Tromsø. Tel. 77-68-70-00. Fax 77-68-96-16. 76 rms (all with bath). MINIBAR TV TEL **Bus:** 28, 30, 36.
$ Rates (including breakfast): Midsummer and winter weekends, 600 kroner ($103.80) single; 730 kroner ($126.30) double. Winter weekdays, 975 kroner ($168.70) single; 1,085 kroner ($187.70) double. AE, DC, MC, V. **Parking:** Free.
Directly on the harborfront a 10-minute walk north of the bus station, this hotel opened in 1989 and immediately became known as one of the best in town. The original building burned in 1972, but has been rebuilt faithfully in the same style. It has memorabilia in the lobby of its original owners, the local steamship company,

Troms Fylkes dampskipsselskap. Each bedroom is decorated in a warm, earth-toned colored scheme. Most open onto views of the port. The hotel has a sauna and Jacuzzi.

INEXPENSIVE

TROMSDAL GJESTGIVERI, Tyttebaerveien 11, N-9020 Tromsdalen. Tel. 77-63-59-44. Fax 77-63-68-97. 25 rms (18 with bath). TEL **Bus:** 30, 36.

$ Rates (including breakfast): 320 kroner ($55.40) single without bath, 415 kroner ($71.80) single with bath; 465 kroner ($80.40) double without bath, 600 kroner ($103.80) double with bath. AE, DC, MC, V. **Parking:** Free. **Closed:** Dec 22–Jan 3.

(S) Lying half a mile north of the Tromsø cathedral in a residential neighborhood, this little guesthouse is painted yellow. Originally constructed in the 1950s but enlarged 20 years later, it is surrounded by nature. Bedrooms are functional and clean. The establishment's unpretentious restaurant is open daily, with main dishes costing 75 kroner to 130 kroner ($13 to $22.50).

WHERE TO DINE

EXPENSIVE

CHARLEY'S BAR & GRILL, in the SAS Royal Hotel, Sjøgata 7. Tel. 77-65-60-00.

Cuisine: INTERNATIONAL. **Reservations:** Required. **Bus:** 21.

$ Prices: Appetizers 72–85 kroner ($12.50–$14.70); main dishes 172–210 kroner ($29.80–$36.30). AE, DC, MC, V.

Open: Daily 11am–11:30pm.

One floor above street level in the SAS Royal Hotel (see "Where to Stay," above), this restaurant is elegant and formal, with a conservatively modern decor. The kitchen turns out a number of good-tasting specialties, including filet of reindeer, pan-fried, with blackcurrant sauce and mushrooms. A special entrecôte is served with corn on the cob and baked potatoes, or you may prefer a "symphony" of fish and shellfish. Adjacent to the restaurant is Charley's Bar (see below).

PEPPERMØLLEN MAT & VINHUS, Storgata 42. Tel. 77-68-62-60.

Cuisine: NORWEGIAN. **Reservations:** Not required. **Bus:** 28, 30.

$ Prices: Fixed-price menus 270–310 kroner ($46.70–$53.60); appetizers 54–82 kroner ($9.30–$14.20); main dishes 166–220 kroner ($28.70–$38.10). AE, DC, MC, V.

Open: Mon–Thurs 4–11pm, Fri–Sat 3–11:30pm.

(★) A 5-minute walk south of the bus station, the oldest restaurant in town, originally built as a private home for a pharmacist, was a favorite stopover for famed explorer Roald Amundsen on his way to and from the Arctic Circle. The dining room, one flight up, has a sort of Gay '90s atmosphere and is decorated with photos of famous explorers. Dishes include smoked trout (cured), reindeer tongue in a white wine sauce, Peppermill steak, and a skewer of fish, as well as vegetarian dishes. Besides beverages, the low-key Apoteke Bar offers snacks and light meals. The bar is open Monday through Saturday from 3pm to midnight, charging 36 kroner ($6.20) for a bottle of beer.

MODERATE

BRANKOS MAT-OG VINHUS, Storgata 57. Tel. 77-68-26-73.

Cuisine: YUGOSLAVIAN. **Reservations:** Recommended. **Bus:** 28, 30.

$ Prices: Appetizers 38–85 kroner ($6.60–$14.70); main dishes 95–225 kroner ($16.40–$38.90). AE, DC, MC, V.

Open: Daily 4pm–midnight.

This genuine Yugoslav restaurant has an intimate, cozy atmosphere and attentive service. Specialties include two types of goulash, a gypsy sword (shish kebab flambé), Serbian bean soup, rack of lamb, snails with garlic butter, and frogs' legs. Many Yugoslav wines are stocked. It's right across the street from the Grand Nordic Hotel.

VERTSHUSET SKARVEN, Strandtorget 1. Tel. 77-68-20-20.
   Cuisine: NORWEGIAN. **Reservations:** Recommended. **Bus:** 28, 30.
$ Prices: Appetizers 42–68 kroner ($7.30–$11.80); main dishes 80–195 kroner ($13.80–$33.70). AE, DC, MC, V.
   Open: Pub, Mon–Thurs noon–3am, Fri–Sat noon–1:20am, Sun 3pm–12:30am. Restaurant, daily 4pm–midnight.

Originally built as a butter factory, this building in the center of Tromsø now houses the Strandtorgets Verthus pub on the ground level, where a half-pint of beer is 39 kroner ($6.70), and snacks or meals are available. One floor above street level is Restaurant Arctandria, serving Arctic cuisine—dishes like reindeer casserole, Arctic catfish, porbeagle shark, and seaweed-and-shellfish soup.

NEARBY DINING
Inexpensive

FAGERNES RESTAURANT, in the Fagernes Hotell, Ramfjordbotn. Tel. 77-69-21-00.
   Cuisine: NORWEGIAN. **Reservations:** Recommended. **Bus:** 14.
$ Prices: Fixed-price menu 85 kroner ($14.70); appetizers 25–42 kroner ($4.30–$7.30); main dishes 75–115 kroner ($13–$19.90). AE, DC, MC, V.
   Open: Daily 7:30am–9pm.

Popular with motorists and sports people, this is a good Norwegian restaurant that grew from humble beginnings as a roadside diner. It offers simple and wholesome food served by a helpful staff. Sunday is the busiest day, when many families drive down from Tromsø to dine here. Try salted lamb served with "swedes" (that's rutabagas), or rock cod from the nearby fjord. It is either stewed in a cream sauce or fried and served with coleslaw. There is also an array of steaks, and roast pork is invariably featured. It's 14 miles south of Tromsø, beside the main road leading south.

EVENING ENTERTAINMENT

CHARLEY'S BAR, in the SAS Royal Hotel, Sjøgata 7. Tel. 77-65-60-00.
   This bar sits one floor above street level adjacent to Charley's Bar & Grill (see "Where to Dine," above). There is no dress code, and the minimum age is 25. The music is disco, and the atmosphere is elegant and sophisticated. It's open Monday through Thursday from 6pm to 1:30am and on Friday and Saturday from 6pm to 3:30am. Beer costs 39 kroner ($6.70). Bus: 21.

JONAS, in the SAS Royal Hotel, Sjøgata 7. Tel. 77-65-60-00.
   This place sells only pizza and beer, and has a "color shock" decor with amusingly garish shades of yellows and reds. Pizzas come in small, medium, large, and the really humongous "maxi pizza"—the biggest in northern Norway—and cost 70 kroner to 120 kroner ($12.10 to $20.80). Beer runs 39 kroner ($6.70). It's open Sunday through Thursday from noon to 1:30am and on Friday and Saturday from noon to 3:30am. Bus: 21.

RORBUA PUB, in the SAS Royal Hotel, Sjøgata 7. Tel. 77-65-60-00.
   Beamed and rustic, and not very large, this is nevertheless the most famous pub in Tromsø. It's usually very crowded throughout the day, and sometimes live music is played on Friday and Saturday nights. Large mugs of beer are served—at 39 kroner ($6.70)—but the only food offered is a bowl of steamy and rich beef-and-potato soup, enough to stave off starvation; it costs 38 kroner ($6.60). Many people show up early in the day and order it as lunch. The pub is open daily from noon to midnight, and there's never a cover charge. Bus: 21.

COMPANIET, Storgaten 12. Tel. 77-68-12-50.
   One of the most popular of Tromsø's independently operated discos, this busy place also contains a restaurant. Most clients, however, head here for dancing, mingling with a well-dressed clientele in their 30s and 40s. It is open Monday through Thursday from 7pm to 1:30am and on Friday and Saturday from 7pm to 2:30am. Bus: 21.

Admission: 34–35 kroner ($5.90–$6.10), depending on the night of the week.

---

5. ALTA

503 miles N of Bodø, 205 miles N of Tromsø, 1,236 miles N of Oslo

GETTING THERE By Plane   Daily flights leave Oslo for Alta, taking 3 hours.

By Bus   There are two daily buses from Fauske to Nordkjosbota, with one daily bus continuing to Alta for an overnight stopover; total trip time is 11 hours. One bus leaves Tromsø daily, taking 7 hours.

ESSENTIALS   The **Alta Tourist Office** (tel. 78-43-50-41) is open Mon–Fri 9am–7pm, Sat 9am–4pm, and Sun noon–7pm (summer).

Alta is famous for attracting millionaire fishers to the Altafjord, said to have the best salmon waters in the world. But most visitors come to Alta because it is a major traffic hub for those going on to the North Cape; public transport stops in Alta for the night so travelers can take the connecting bus to Honningsvåg the following morning. Buses also depart from Alta along the great northern highway, the E6, heading south to Kautokeino or north to the final stop at Kirkenes.

For years, Alta belonged to Finland and was inhabited almost solely by Lapps, who until the end of World War II held a famous fair here. Because of fires and wars, everything in Alta is relatively new.

Alta is the administrative capital of Finnmark county. It is also home of the Alta Bataljon, which covered the retreat of the French and British forces from the Nazis at Narvik in the infamous battle of World War II.

WHAT TO SEE & DO

Alta has a limited number of accommodations, although it makes a good base for offbeat excursions to the Lapp village of **Masi,** 44 miles from town on the main road to Finland. In the village, which has a Lapp school, the locals usually wear colorful costumes.

From the Lapp village, you can take a **riverboat excursion** on a long, flat-bottom boat with an outboard motor, driven by costumed Lapps. You have to negotiate the price, which will be based on your skills and the number in your party. The excursion usually lasts 4 hours.

Guests usually take a packed lunch from their hotel, then stop along the way—preferably in a secluded spot by the riverbank—for a picnic. While in northern Norway, try Lappbiff (a reindeer-meat sandwich) or *furstekake* (almond cake).

From Alta, it's possible to take a riverboat excursion along the Alta River up to the Alta Canyon at Sausto, the biggest canyon in northern Europe. It has been dammed. For details, get in touch with **Alta Riverboat Service** (tel. 78-43-33-78).

Take time to visit the rock carvings in **Hjemmeluft,** dating from 2,000 to 5,000 years ago and considered the largest area of prehistoric rock carvings in the north of Europe. The rock carvings lie 3 miles south of Alta's town center, adjacent to the premises of the **Alta Museum,** Altaveien 19 (tel. 78-43-63-77). Entrance to the museum allows you to view the rock carvings. The museum also contains exhibitions on the life of the Lapps, local flora and fauna, and geology. It is open May 22 through August 30 daily from 8am to 11pm. During the rest of the year, it is open Monday through Friday from 9am to 4pm and Friday and Saturday from noon to 5pm. Admission is 20 kroner ($3.50) for adults, 10 kroner ($1.70) for children.

WHERE TO STAY

INEXPENSIVE

PARK HOTEL ALTA, Rte. 6, N-9501 Alta. Tel. 78-43-62-11. Fax 78-43-63-80. 20 rms (all with bath). TV TEL

$ Rates (including breakfast): Winter, Sun–Thurs 695 kroner ($120.20) single; 790 kroner ($136.70) double. Winter, Fri–Sat 450 kroner ($77.90) single; 550 kroner ($95.20) double. Summer, 610 kroner ($105.50) single; 720 kroner ($124.60) double. AE, DC, MC, V. **Parking:** Free.

Built in 1987 and enlarged in 1992, this is a cozy alternative to the vastly larger and more expensive SAS Alta Hotel nearby. Just off the "North Cape Road," it offers modern, comfortable rooms. The hotel serves breakfast, but will also provide a simple evening meal, costing from 60 kroner to 100 kroner ($10.40 to $17.30) for a main dish.

SAS ALTA HOTEL, Rte. 6, N-9501 Alta. Tel. 78-43-50-00, or toll free 800/221-2350 in the U.S. Fax 78-43-58-25. 154 rms (all with bath). TV TEL

$ Rates (including breakfast): Winter, Sun–Thurs 1,035 kroner ($179.10) single; 1,230 kroner ($212.80) double. Winter Fri–Sat and summer, 525 kroner ($90.80) single, 675 kroner ($116.80) double. AE, DC, MC, V. **Parking:** Free.

A 10-minute walk from the harborfront, it is completely modern, with the largest number of drinking, dining, and dancing facilities. Bedrooms are well furnished and comfortable. The finest restaurant in town, Henrik's, has an interconnected dance bar, Pernille's. The Fritz Disco, in the basement of the hotel, is open on Wednesday, Friday, and Saturday night from 9pm to 1am charging a 40 kroner ($6.90) cover, with beer costing from 39 kroner ($6.70). The Café Eden is suitable for single-plate lunches, sandwiches, drinks, and coffee. The Alten Pizza Pub is also in the hotel.

WHERE TO DINE
MODERATE

HENRIK'S, in the SAS Alta Hotel, Rte. 6. Tel. 78-43-50-00.
   Cuisine: NORWEGIAN. **Reservations:** Recommended.
$ Prices: Appetizers 48–75 kroner ($8.30–$13); main dishes 125–210 kroner ($21.60–$36.30). AE, DC, MC, V.
   Open: Dinner Mon–Fri 5–11pm, Sat 1–11pm.

A 1-minute walk from the bus station, this is the finest restaurant in town, with a very modern, mostly pink decor. It has a smattering of big-city style in this remote northern outpost. Specialties include filet of reindeer, salmon, trout, and game dishes from northern Norway. Immediately adjacent is the Pernille Dance Bar.

---

6. HAMMERFEST

1,326 miles N of Oslo, 593 miles N of Bodø

GETTING THERE   By Bus   April to September, three buses a week arrive here on the 3½-hour trip from Alta. In the same season you can take a thrice-weekly bus from Oslo if you can sit for the 29 hours it takes.

By Coastal Steamer   A northbound steamer leaves daily from Harstad going to Kirkenes, with stopovers at Hammerfest.

By Car   A long trek—take the E6 north from Oslo until you reach the junction of Route 94 west. Hammerfest lies at the end of that route.

ESSENTIALS   The **Hammerfest Tourist Office,** Sjøgata (tel. 78-41-21-85), in the town center, is open Mon–Fri 8am–6pm and Sat–Sun 10am–3pm (June–Aug) and Mon–Fri 8am–3pm (Sept–May).

The Hammerfest area stretches from Måsøy, near the North Cape, to the municipality of Loppa in the south, embracing a wide area of geography, the most notable of which is the wild, rugged coasts ravaged by the Arctic Sea. The regional capital is Hammerfest, which many use as a center for exploring the North Cape.

Hammerfest is a major traffic hub for the area, and in summer there's a wide selection of regular excursions by boat and bus. The tourist office (see above) will have details of what's available at the time of your visit.

For an overview, take a zigzag walk up the 80-yard **Salen** "mountain" for a good view of the town. The old landmark on top of Salen was torn down during the war, but restored in 1984.

WHAT TO SEE & DO

This is the most northerly town in the world of any major size and a port of call for North Cape steamers. Destroyed in World War II by the retreating Germans, it has long since been rebuilt. Lapps from surrounding camps often come into town to shop. Count yourself lucky if they bring their reindeer with them.

The port is ice-free year-round, and shipping and exporting fish is a major industry. The sun doesn't set from May 17 to July 28. On the other hand, it doesn't rise from November 21 to January 23.

Why not take time to do as 70,000 others have done and join the **Royal and Ancient Polar Bear Society** here? Apply in person and get a membership while you're in Hammerfest. The club is filled with stuffed specimens of Arctic animals. It has a small museum devoted to the hunting heyday of Hammerfest, when eagles, Arctic foxes, and polar bears were trapped. It's in the basement of the Town Hall, Rådhuspladssen, and is open Monday through Friday from 8am to 6pm and on Saturday and Sunday from 10am to 3pm. Admission is free.

CRUISES TO THE NORTH CAPE

The first tour ships arrived in 1879, and they've been coming ever since. **FFR** (tel. 78-41-43-44) operates cruises from Hammerfest to the North Cape, including meals, bus ashore, and guide. The cost is 545 kroner ($94.30) per person round-trip; children 4 to 16 pay 300 kroner ($51.90). Children 3 and under go free. Tours run from June 8 to August 6 leaving Hammerfest Sunday through Thursday at 8:15pm and Friday and Saturday at 7pm, arriving at Honningsvåg (see Section 7, below) where a bus takes you the final lap of the journey. A stop is made at **Hjelmsøystauern,** one of northern Europe's largest bird sanctuaries. Buses return from the North Cape sometimes after midnight. Midnight is hardly the word—it's still daylight at departure time.

WHERE TO STAY
MODERATE

RICA HOTEL HAMMERFEST, Sørøygata 15, N-9601 Hammerfest. Tel. 78-41-13-33. Fax 78-41-13-11. 77 rms (67 with bath), 17 suites. TV TEL **Bus: 1, 2.**

$ Rates (including breakfast): Winter, Sun–Thurs 450 kroner ($77.90) single without bath, 950 kroner ($164.40) single with bath; 550 kroner ($95.20) double without bath, 1,125 kroner ($194.60) double with bath; from 1,800 kroner ($311.40) suite. Winter Fri–Sat and summer, 290 kroner ($50.20) single without bath, 525 kroner ($90.80) single with bath; 390 kroner ($67.50) double without bath, 625 kroner ($108.10) double with bath; from 725 kroner ($125.40) suite. AE, DC, MC, V. **Parking:** Free.

In the town center, opening directly onto the waterfront, this is the preferred place to stay in the area. Built in the mid-1970s on steeply sloping land, the hotel also has the best restaurant in Hammerfest. A member of a chain, it is the largest hotel in town and was completely redecorated in 1989. Bedrooms are modernized with a decor of Nordic-inspired pastels.

WHERE TO DINE
MODERATE

ODD'S MAT & VINHUS, Strandgata 24. Tel. 78-41-37-66.
Cuisine: NORTHERN NORWEGIAN. **Reservations:** Recommended.
$ Prices: Appetizers 35–60 kroner ($6.10–$10.40); main dishes 115–200 kroner ($19.90–$34.60). AE, DC, MC, V.

Open: Mon–Sat 11am–1am.

★ Since its opening in 1992, this consciously rustic restaurant has become famous thanks to a survey by a Trondheim radio station that voted it the best restaurant in Norway. It is adjacent to the town's largest pier, overlooking the harbor. Inside, every effort was made to simulate the wild splendor of Finnmark (North Norway), with the use of roughly textured wood, stone, and many yards of natural hemp knotted into ropes that form curtains. A kitchen, open to view from the dining room, provides touches of culinary theatricality.

Both the recipes and their ingredients are almost universally derived from northern Norway, with an emphasis on fish and game. Examples include filets of carp, partially dried in the sun, which are then boiled and served with mustard sauce and bacon fat. Other dishes include freshly killed grouse prepared "like beef" with a game-laced cream sauce. A popular appetizer is a filet of reindeer, served either raw and chopped, like a tartare, or smoked and thinly sliced, like a carpaccio.

RICA HOTEL RESTAURANT, in the Rica Hotel Hammerfest, Sørøygata 15. Tel. 78-41-13-33.
   Cuisine: NORWEGIAN. **Reservations:** Not required. **Bus:** 1, 2.
$ **Prices:** Appetizers 58–90 kroner ($10–$15.60); main dishes 149–215 kroner ($25.80–$37.20). AE, DC, MC, V.
   Open: Daily 11am–11pm.
This dining room in the cellar of the Rica Hotel Hammerfest (see "Where to Stay," above) opens directly onto the harborfront. Specialties are pepper steak and filet of reindeer. It also serves good-tasting fish dishes based on the day's catch from the fjord. After dinner, you can patronize the Rica Bar and Disco, also in the cellar of the hotel, which is open Sunday through Thursday from 5pm to 1am and on Friday and Saturday from 5pm to 3:30am. Admission is 50 kroner ($8.65), but only on Friday and Saturday night; other nights it's free. The minimum age is 20, and beer costs 39 kroner ($6.70) per half-liter.

---

7. HONNINGSVÅG

74 miles N of Lakselv, 111 miles NE of Alta, 81 miles NE of Hammerfest

GETTING THERE   By Bus   Buses arrive daily from Alta, Lakselv, Hammerfest, Kautokeino, Karasjok, and Kirkenes.

By Coastal Steamer   The *Hurtigruten* arrive daily, with northbound arrivals reaching Honningsvåg daily at 5:30pm, and southbound departures at 6:45am.

By Car   Take the E6 north to the junction with Route 95 north. That route leads to Honningsvåg with one ferry crossing.

ESSENTIALS   The **tourist office** in Nordkapphuset (tel. 78-47-28-94), can give you information on sightseeing boat trips, museums, walks, and deep-sea fishing. The **Honningsvåg Tourist Office** is open daily 8:30am–7pm (June–Aug) and Mon–Fri 8:30am–4pm (Sept–May).

SPECIAL EVENTS   The **North Cape Festival** is held for 1 week in the middle of June each year, with a wide display of local culture. During the festival, the **North Cape March** travels from Honningsvåg to the North Cape and back, a total of around 44 miles.

The world's northernmost village, the gateway to the North Cape, is a completely modern fishing harbor (only the chapel withstood the German destruction of 1944). It is some 50 miles nearer to the North Pole than Hammerfest, on the Alta-Hammerfest bus route.

Honningsvåg is on the southern side of the island of Magerøy, but is connected to the North Cape by a 22-mile-long road.

WHAT TO SEE & DO

NORDKAPPMUSEET, Nordkapphuset, Fergeveien 4. Tel. 78-47-28-33.
This museum has exhibits relating to the cultural history of the North Cape and fishery artifacts. The museum lies at the harbor and town center, a 3-minute walk from the coastal steamer and the SAS Hotel.
Admission: 15 kroner ($2.60) adults, 5 kroner (90¢) children.
Open: June 15–Aug 15, Mon–Sat 11am–3pm and 6–8pm; Sun 6–8pm; Aug 16–June 14, Mon–Fri 11am–3pm.

NORDKAPPHALLEN, Nordkapp. Tel. 78-47-23-33.
This visitors' center has a video presentation and museum exhibits. Downstairs you'll find a supervideograph and a cave with a panorama window facing the Arctic Ocean. On the way to the cave you'll see several scenes from the history of the North Cape. A monument honors the visit of King Oscar (ruler of Norway and Sweden) to the cape in 1873, and another monument honors the exiled "citizen king" of France, Louis Philippe of Orléans, who visited in 1855. There is also a monument marking the terminus of the "Midnight Sun Road."
Admission: 90 kroner ($15.60) adults, 30 kroner ($5.20) children.
Open: June–Aug, daily 9am–2am (it stays open so late because many people prefer to visit the cape at the peak period of the Midnight Sun); Sept and May, daily 9am–6pm. **Closed:** Oct–Apr.

A TRIP TO THE NORTH CAPE

The ✪ **North Cape** (Nordkapp) symbolizes the "top of Europe." (Actually, Knivskjellodden stretches about 1,500 yards farther north but is inaccessible.) In prehistoric times the North Cape Horn was a Sami place of sacrifice. Earlier, the name of the North Cape used to be Knyskanes, but in 1553 it was named "North Cape" by the English Lord Richard Chancellor, who was searching for a sea passage to China. The road to the North Cape is open to traffic from May 1 to October 20.
The first tour ships arrived in 1879. These anchored in Hornvika Bay, and the tourists had to climb 307 yards up to the plateau. After the road from Honningsvåg was opened in 1956, the flow of tourists turned into a flood. In summer four buses to the North Cape leave daily from the central marketplace at Honningsvåg, making a brief stop at the ferryboat terminal across from the Sifi Sommerhotell, then continuing to the visitors' center at the North Cape. The round-trip passage from any entry point along the route is 90 kroner ($15.60).
On the road to the cape is a Lapp encampment—a bit contrived perhaps, but visitors do get to go inside one of the tents, and they come away with an idea of how nomadic Lapps used to live.

WHERE TO STAY

MODERATE

ARCTIC BRYGGEN HOTEL, Vågen 1, N-9751 Honningsvåg. Tel. 78-47-28-88. Fax 78-47-27-24. 42 rms (all with bath), 3 suites. MINIBAR TV TEL
$ Rates (including breakfast): 650–850 kroner ($112.50–$147.10) single; 750–950 kroner ($129.80–$164.40) double; from 1,200 kroner ($207.60) suite. AE, DC, MC, V. **Parking:** Free.
Opened in 1990, the hotel is filled with facilities and accommodations for the fishing industry. In summer, some beds in the fishermen's cottages called *rorbuer* become available. The hotel itself offers well-furnished and comfortable bedrooms.
Dining/Entertainment: The hotel has a summer restaurant on the pier, seating 250 guests. It also has a pleasant bar, a Tavern/Pub, and a regular indoor restaurant. A dance bar, Tørrfeskloftet, is also available.
Services: Booking service for Arctic Adventures, boat rentals, water sports, laundry, babysitting.
Facilities: Sauna, Jacuzzi, a sauna lounge for 20 people, shops.

SAS HOTEL NORDKAPP, Nordkappgata 2-4, N-9750 Honningsvåg. Tel. 78-47-23-33, or toll free 800/221-2350 in the U.S. Fax 78-47-22-79. 174 rms (all with bath), 3 suites. TV TEL

$ Rates (including breakfast): Winter, Sun–Thurs 920 kroner ($159.20) single; 1,060 kroner ($183.40) double; from 1,370 kroner ($237) suite. Winter, Fri–Sat 445 kroner ($77) single; 590 kroner ($102.10) double; from 925 kroner ($102–$230) suite. Summer, 625 kroner ($108.10) single; 790 kroner ($136.70) double; from 925 kroner ($160) suite. AE, DC, MC, V. **Parking:** Free.

The world's northernmost hotel, 21 miles from the North Cape, is located in the downtown area near the quay. Early reservations are strongly advised. This five-story, white-fronted building has been enlarged and considerably upgraded since it was first established in 1956. Many bedrooms open onto views of the harbor. They are furnished with modern pieces and decorated in neutral tones. The Carolina restaurant is recommended separately (see "Where to Dine," below). The hotel also contains an unpretentious Bistro, open daily for lunch and dinner, serving meals less expensive than the Carolina's. The hotel's bar is open from 11am to 3am, and in the cellar is a disco, open nightly from 8pm to 1 or 2am. The disco is free except on Friday and Saturday when a 45 kroner ($7.80) admission is charged.

WHERE TO DINE
MODERATE

RESTAURANT CAROLINA, in the SAS Hotel Nordkapp, Nordkappgata 2-4. Tel. 78-47-23-33.
Cuisine: NORWEGIAN. **Reservations:** Recommended.
$ Prices: Appetizers 45–65 kroner ($7.80–$11.20); main dishes 125–210 kroner ($21.60–$36.30); summer buffet smörgåsbord 140 kroner ($24.20) per person. AE, DC, MC, V.
Open: Summer, daily noon–12:30am; winter, daily 7pm–12:30am.

In the cellar of the SAS Hotel Nordkapp (see "Where to Stay," above), this place is at its most elegant in winter (during the summer it is filled with tour groups). A la carte dinners in summer are served in the more informal Bistro, although the summer smörgåsbord is still presented in the Carolina. In the evening music begins at 8pm, and the place is very popular with locals. It is decorated with old-fashioned photographs of Honningsvåg. In summer its smörgåsbord is one of the most attended events in town.

---

8. VADSØ

275 miles NE of Alta, 255 miles E of Honningsvåg, 107 miles W of Kirkenes

GETTING THERE By Plane Wilderøe Airlines has daily flights to Kirkenes and Alta.

By Bus Vadsø and Kirkenes have a bus link—one to two buses daily on the 3½-hour trip. Buses also go between Vadsø and Vardø (see below)—one to three daily, taking 1½ hours.

By Coastal Steamer Northbound and southbound coastal steamers between Harstad and Kirkenes call daily at Vadsø.

By Car Continue along the E6 from the south of Norway until you reach the faraway junction with Route 98; then go east to Vadsø.

ESSENTIALS For information, **Vadsø Byutvikling,** Vadsø Kommune (tel. 78-95-38-80), in the town center, is open Mon–Sat 8am–9pm and Sun 10am–7pm (June–Aug) and Mon–Fri 9am–4pm (Sept–May).

Vadsø, the capital of Finnmark, is on the southern coast of the Varanger Peninsula, on the Varangerfjord. Vadsø used to be a Finnish-speaking town, and nearly half the population of Vadsø, it is estimated, have Finnish origins. Norway's largest herring-oil factory is here, but public administration is the largest employer of Vadsø's some 6,000 inhabitants.

WHAT TO SEE & DO

In spring, summer, and autumn, Vadsø offers unforgettable experiences for nature lovers, anglers, and birdwatchers. Ask at the tourist office (see above) about excursions and activities possible in the area. The only **birdrock** in Finnmark, at Ekkerøy, can be reached by car. It is a protected nature reserve but has trails for visitors. Deep-sea fishing can also be arranged at the SAS Vadsø Hotel (see "Where to Stay and Dine," below), as can excursions by boat on the Varangerfjord. One day's notice is necessary.

A guided sightseeing bus tour is arranged by **Lailas Gjestehus** (tel. 78-95-33-35). Tours go through the wilderness between Vardø and Hamningberg. Remnants from World War II can be seen.

The Vadsø area is also excellent for **hiking and skiing,** while numerous marked trails take you into the mountain plateau. You can also find small lakes and rivers where you can have a picnic (make arrangements with your hotel to have a lunch packed).

VADSØ MUSEUM, Hvistendahlsgata 31. Tel. 78-95-29-55.

The only remaining patrician buildings left in Finnmark, this museum includes the 19th-century Tuomainengården estate and Esbensengården estates. The museum also owns the airship mast to which Arctic explorer Roald Amundsen's *Norge* was moored in 1926. It was one of the few things to escape Nazi-set fires and Russian bombardments in World War II. This mast was also used on the famous North Pole expedition in 1928 of explorer Umberto Nobile.

Also part of the museum is Kjeldsen-bruket on Ekkerøy, a completely restored fish-processing complex with a quay that was built at the end of the 19th century.

Admission: 10 kroner ($1.70).

Open: Mon–Sat noon–5pm.

VADSØ KIRKE AND KONGENSTEINEN, Vadsø Kommune. Tel. 78-95-11-32.

Architect Magnus Paulsson called this church, built in 1958, an Arctic church. Outside the front door he placed two towers resembling two tall ice blocks to shelter people from the wind. The "king stone" from 1977 is placed right outside the church, bearing the signature of the late King Olav.

Admission: Free.

Open: June–Aug, daily 9am–2pm.

WHERE TO STAY & DINE

MODERATE

SAS VADSØ HOTEL, Oscars Gata 4, N-9800 Vadsø. Tel. 78-55-16-18, or toll free 800/221-2350 in the U.S. Fax 78-95-10-02. 57 rms (all with bath), 4 suites. TV TEL

$ Rates (including breakfast): Winter, Sun–Thurs 1,040 kroner ($179.90) single; 1,145 kroner ($198.10) double. Winter, Fri–Sat 500 kroner ($86.50) single; 650 kroner ($112.50) double. Summer, 450 kroner ($77.90) single; 650 kroner ($112.50) double. Year-round, from 1,395 kroner ($241.30) suite. AE, DC, MC, V. **Parking:** Free.

Rising atop a rolling hillside in the town center, near the airport, this long and stylish modern hotel offers comfortably furnished rooms, many recently renovated. The hotel also has the most drinking and dining establishments around. The upscale restaurant, Oscar's Mat & Vinhus, is the town's most famous eatery, serving both lunch and dinner. For those in a rush, there's always the Pizzeria. The hotel also has a nightclub and dancing bar, the Nobila Bar, and a disco, The Warehouse. The disco is open only on Wednesday, Friday, Saturday, and Sunday from 8pm to 1:30am. Entrance is free to hotel guests, but 40 kroner ($6.90) to others.

9. VARDØ

44 miles E of Vadsø, 151 miles W of Kirkenes

GETTING THERE By Plane Vardø's Svartnes Airport is 2 miles from the town center. Several daily arrivals and departures connect Vardø with Kirkenes and the fishing village of Båtsfjord.

By Bus One or two buses a day run between Kirkenes and Vadsø, taking 3½ hours. Vardø is connected by bus to Vadsø (see above)—one to three daily, taking 1½ hours.

By Coastal Steamer Vardø lies on the coastal-steamer route. Northbound boats arrive from Harstad and southbound boats arrive from Kirkenes.

By Car Take the E6 north from the south of Norway, turning east onto Route 98, going via Vadsø to Vardø. To reach the island town, you must take the 2-mile-long underwater tunnel that connects the town to the mainland, the first of its kind in Norway. Its deepest point is 96 yards below sea level.

ESSENTIALS For information, contact **Vardø Kommune,** Tiltakskonsulenten (tel. 78-98-71-71).

Vardø, founded in 1789, is the only town in Norway situated in the Arctic climate zone. On most July days you can see your breath. Norway's lowest mean average temperature and its greatest number of stormy days are recorded here. Vardø is also the easternmost town in the country and claims the easternmost point in Norway, the island of Hornøya. It has 3,200 inhabitants and an area of 363 square miles, and is often called the gate to the Barents Sea. Most people are in the fishing industry.

Ancient geographers called this part of the habitable world Ultima Thule. In the Middle Ages the area was also called the "empire of the devil." In 1564 a cardinal, considered a mathematical genius, estimated that 2,655,866,746,664 little devils came into the world through Ultima Thule.

The worst prosecution against witches in Norway took place in the Vardø area from 1621 to 1692, making it "the Salem of Norway." Eighty women were found guilty and burned to death here on trumped up charges of witchcraft. According to prosecution records of the time, the alleged witches were supposed to have had secret meetings with the devil on Demon Mountain.

WHAT TO SEE & DO

The **Vardøhus fortification** is the northernmost fortification in the world, built between 1734 and 1738. This was the third fortification erected in Vardø, the first dating from 1300 and the second from 1420. Guides are available to show you around the fortification from June 10 to August 31. Call 78-98-80-75 for information.

Vardøhus Museum, Pers Larssens Gate 32 (tel. 78-98-80-75), is housed in Lushaugen, and lies half a mile northeast of the town center, reached by taxi. Its main building dating from 1920, the museum has a *Kongestokken* where you'll find the signature of several kings. The museum also has artifacts of the area. From June through August the museum is open Monday through Wednesday from 9am to 3pm, Thursday and Friday from 9am to 6pm, and Saturday and Sunday from noon to 3pm. Off-season hours are Monday through Friday from 9am to 3pm (closed Saturday and Sunday). Admission is 15 kroner ($2.60) for adults and 5 kroner (90¢) for children.

At the **Vardø Post Office,** you can have your mail stamped, proving you have visited Norway's easternmost town. It's open Monday through Saturday from 9am to 3:30pm.

The little road that goes west from Vardø to the hamlet of **Hamningberg** has scenery that has been compared to a landscape on the moon.

WHERE TO STAY & DINE
INEXPENSIVE

HOTEL BARENTS, Keigate 8, N-9950 Vardø. Tel. 78-98-77-61. Fax 78-98-83-97. 42 rms (all with bath). TV TEL

$ Rates (including breakfast): Winter, Sun–Thurs 650 kroner ($112.50) single; 750 kroner ($129.80) double. Winter, Fri–Sat and summer, 400 kroner ($69.20) single; 600 kroner ($103.80) double. DC, MC, V. **Parking:** Free.

In the center of town, near the Vardøhus fortification and the steamer quay, this modern establishment is the best place in Vardø for rooms or food. Rooms are equipped for the handicapped. The pleasant, quiet dining room becomes a place for dinner dances on occasion. The hotel also has a bar, a lounge with an open fireplace, a sauna, a small gym, a solarium, and a disco.

---

10. KIRKENES

327 miles NE of Alta, 532 miles NE of Tromsø, 1,521 miles N of Oslo

GETTING THERE **By Plane** The Kirkenes Airport lies 9 miles from the town center. Several planes land daily from various parts of Norway, including Trondheim and Tromsø. Four flights a day come in from Oslo, taking 3 hours.

By Bus Buses from various parts of Finnmark arrive at Kirkenes. Buses are connected with routes to Oslo, Tromsø, Alta, and Hammerfest, even northern Finland. Tickets can be purchased on board, and it's not necessary to reserve the ticket in advance. The bus from Alta to Kirkenes takes 12 hours.

By Coastal Steamer Kirkenes is the end of the line for the coastal-steamer routes that begin in Bergen, with many stopovers along the way as outlined in previously previewed towns and cities.

By Car The E6 begins its long and tortuous run in Oslo, finally ending in Kirkenes near the Russian frontier.

ESSENTIALS The **Kirkenes Tourist Office** (tel. 78-99-25-44) is behind the Rica Hotel on Pasvikveien in a little wooden hut, lying off the E6.

This iron-ore-mining town is the end of the line for travelers in Norway, 170 miles north of the Arctic Circle. The Midnight Sun shines on Kirkenes from May 20 to July 25, but from November to January people live in darkness.

Kirkenes was bombed repeatedly during World War II—307 raids in all, until nearly the whole town was destroyed by 1944. During the infamous German retreat from Finnmark that year, surviving areas were razed by evacuating Nazis who didn't want to leave anything behind for the Russians.

Kirkenes lies in a section of eastern Finnmark called Sør-Varanger. It is the only Norwegian region with a common border with Russia—and 121 miles of it at that. Today's inhabitants of Kirkenes are descendants of Samic, Norwegian, Finnish, Russian, and other people.

Kirkenes opens onto the famous **Barents Sea,** where adventurers tried for centuries to trade furs, find the North Pole, or discover a passage to China. The enormous sea is named after a Dutchman, Willem Barents. After a shipwreck at Novaja Semlja in 1596, he had to spend the winter on the ice. It was his last expedition, and he died there. In the 18th century Russians from Arkhangelsk began sailing to Finnmark to trade with the Norwegians. This trading lasted until the Russian revolution of 1917.

It was not until 1878 that the Finnish-Swedish Arctic researcher Nordenskiøld succeeded in pushing forth through the North East Passage, looking for a northerly seaway to China. Later polar explorer Roald Amundsen followed this route with the ship *Maud*.

Large naval forces traveled through here in World War II, the ocean below becoming the graveyard of many soldiers on both sides of the conflict.

WHAT TO SEE & DO

The **Sør-Varanger Museum,** Strand, Pasvik (tel. 78-99-51-13), is decentralized and includes the Bygdetunet Bjorklund farm at Svanvik, Noatun at Vaffetem, and St. Georg's Chapel in Neiden. You can also see King Oskar's Chapel at Grense-Jakobselv, a stone church built in 1869, as well as the wooden Neiden Chapel at Neiden. The main building of the museum at Strand, Pasvik, is 25 miles from Kirkenes on Route 885. There is no public transportation available. The museum depicts the rich history of the area, its culture, its people, and its flora and fauna. Admission is 20 kroner ($3.50) for adults; free for children. Hours are June through August, Monday through Friday, from 9am to 2pm.

There's a **Monument to the Red Army,** a statue of a Russian soldier, erected in memory of the liberation of Finnmark by the Russians in 1944. There are also several memorials to Finnish and Norwegian soldiers killed in the war.

WHERE TO STAY

MODERATE

KIRKENES RICA HOTEL, Passvikveien 63, N-9900 Kirkenes. Tel. 78-99-14-91. Fax 78-99-13-56. 40 rms (all with bath), 2 suites. MINIBAR TV TEL

$ **Rates** (including breakfast): Winter, Sun–Thurs 975 kroner ($168.70) single; 1,080 kroner ($186.80) double; from 1,200 kroner ($207.60) suite. Winter, Fri–Sat 525 kroner ($90.80) single; 690 kroner ($119.40) double; from 920 kroner ($159.20) suite. Summer, 600 kroner ($103.80) single; 850 kroner ($147.10) double; from 1,000 kroner ($173) suite. AE, DC, MC, V. **Parking:** Free.

Located on top of a hill overlooking the town, half a mile from the quay, this hotel was built in 1956 and totally renovated after a fire in 1987. Its interior is colorful, with stained-glass accents and tapestries. Guests sometimes dance at night to the sounds of a combo. This licensed hotel also has a tennis and badminton court. Reindeer meat is a specialty of the Brasseriet.

RICA ARCTIC HOTEL, Kongensgata 1-3, N-9901 Kirkenes. Tel. 78-99-29-29. Fax 78-99-11-59. 80 rms (all with bath), 2 suites. MINIBAR TV TEL

$ **Rates** (including breakfast): Winter, Sun–Thurs 975 kroner ($168.70) single; 1,080 kroner ($186.80) double; from 1,280 kroner ($221.40) suite. Winter, Fri–Sat and summer, 600 kroner ($103.80) single; 850 kroner ($147.10) double; from 1,050 kroner ($181.70) suite. AE, DC, MC, V. **Parking:** Free.

This hotel, built in 1988, is the biggest and best in the area. Each bedroom is attractive and comfortable. The decor includes a winter-inspired color scheme. In the center of Kirkenes, the hotel's restaurant is considered the best in town (see "Where to Dine," below).

BUDGET

SOLLIA GJESTGIVERI, Storskog, N-9900 Kirkenes. Tel. 78-99-08-20. 9 rms (none with bath). **Bus:** Grense-Jakobselv from town center.

$ **Rates** (including breakfast): 300 kroner ($51.90) single; 450 kroner ($77.90) double. No credit cards. **Parking:** Free.

About 10 miles east of Kirkenes, just 66 feet from the Russian border, this guesthouse is modestly furnished, and most guests reach it by renting a car in Kirkenes and driving here (the Kirkenes Tourist Office will give you a map).

Reservations are needed, of course. The guesthouse is a white clapboard-sided structure originally constructed in 1935 as an orphanage, although it served briefly in World War II as a military hospital. Its family owners will prepare platters of food, costing 60 kroner ($10.40) at lunch and 100 kroner ($17.30) at dinner.

WHERE TO DINE

MODERATE

ARCTIC RESTAURANT, in the Rica Arctic Hotel, Kongensgata 1-3. Tel. 78-99-29-29.

Cuisine: NORWEGIAN. **Reservations:** Not required.
$ Prices: Appetizers 48–85 kroner ($8.30–$14.70); main dishes 158–210 kroner ($27.30–$36.30); daily platters 48–85 kroner ($8.30–$14.70). AE, DC, MC, V.
Open: Daily 7am–11pm.

Generally considered the best restaurant in Kirkenes, this dining room is on the lobby level of the Rica Arctic Hotel (see "Where to Stay," above) a 5-minute walk south of the bus station. The restaurant has a modern decor with dark colors. Daily platters are especially popular. Specialties include filet of reindeer and fresh Norwegian salmon.

GRILLSTUA, Dr. Wesselsgata 18. Tel. 78-99-12-87.

Cuisine: NORWEGIAN. **Reservations:** Not required.
$ Prices: Pizzas 72–85 kroner ($12.50–$14.70); main dishes 70–95 kroner ($12.10–$16.40). No credit cards.
Open: Daily 9am–10pm.

This is a simple café in a postwar building that once served as a makeshift movie theater. It's especially popular on weekends. Young people go here for pizzas, but hot food is also served. It's in the town center.

EASY EXCURSIONS

Some 75 miles south of the town is **Pasvik Valley,** known for its special flora and fauna. The trip takes you through the easternmost national park of Norway, where two different biological worlds, Asia and Europe, meet. The Pasvik River marks the boundary between Russia and Norway.

Along the way, you'll pass **Svanvik,** 25 miles from Kirkenes, where you can visit the beautiful Svanvik Chapel and see a government-owned experimental station.

ORGANIZED TOURS TO RUSSIA

In summer, a bus departs at 12:30pm to explore the Russian border and the **Sør-Varanger open-pit mines,** near Lake Bjørnevatn. The cost is 120 kroner ($20.80) for adults and 60 kroner ($10.40) for children. The trip takes 2 hours. Confirm the departure time and the point of embarkation with the tourist office (see above).

Kirkenes is only 4½ miles from the Russian frontier. ○ **Murmansk,** a large Russian seaport, the largest city in the world north of the Arctic Circle, is now open to visitors. In summer, a boat leaves Kirkenes daily at 8:30am, returning to Kirkenes at 12:30am. The boat trip is 4 hours one way, with a scheduled stopover in Murmansk of 7 hours. It is not necessary to have a visa, but the tour must be booked 14 days in advance. The cost is 1,000 kroner ($173). Reservations can be made in Kirkenes with **Soviet Reiser,** Storgaten 1 (tel. 78-99-19-81), or through the tourist office.

The journey in part is eerie, going at a speed of 43 m.p.h. You see Arctic nature, plus animals and birds up close through large panoramic windows. You are likely to be approached by a Russian warship for control as this is one of the most heavily militarized areas in the world. You can see the Severomorsk naval base, with several hundred submarines, cruisers, and battleships. Sightseeing in Murmansk ends, after all your souvenir buying, at a soldier monument. The soldier looks toward the northeast, overseeing the "valley of the dead" of World War II.

On the way back over the Barents Sea, the Midnight Sun lights the way, and you can have a Russian snack.

PART THREE

SWEDEN

CHAPTER 22

GETTING TO KNOW SWEDEN

Sweden is one of the most paradoxical nations on earth. An essentially conservative country, it is nonetheless a leader in social welfare, prison reform, and equal opportunity for women.

It has long had some of the highest wages and the highest standard of living in Europe, although, as part of the worldwide recession in the 1990s, it has faced trouble maintaining the value of its currency. It has also faced a post–World War II high in unemployment. There is definitely trouble in paradise, but, compared to most of the world, Sweden is better off than nearly all other nations.

The past and the future exist side by side in Sweden. In Stockholm and some of the cities along the west coast, you can enjoy stunning modern shopping complexes and up-to-date hotels. But a journey to Dalarna and Värmland or the historic walled city of Visby on the eastern coast transports you back to a more distant time.

Sweden was a poor backward nation at the dawn of the 20th century. Most of its citizens depended on farming for a living. But in one century it has transformed itself, becoming one of the examples of good living on the globe, a symbol of peace and prosperity.

The urbane and the untamed are said to live harmoniously in Sweden, where nearly everyone has room to live as they please. There are some 173,731 square miles for some 8.6 million residents.

Although Sweden has a long aristocratic history, it is a modern Western European democracy. It still has a king, who seems to be affectionately regarded by his people, but real power is in the hands of elected officials.

Within an hour's flying time of Stockholm, you can take in some of the climatic, cultural, and geographical variety of Sweden. That might include midsummer skiing on the northern snow fields, sunbathing on the tens of thousands of islands on both the east and west coasts, and thermal-spring bathing in the central forested plateau.

If you wander the Kungsleden (King's Trail), past Sarek, you will be exploring the last wilderness of Europe. Collecting summer berries in one of the forested national parks is another national pastime. In winter, dog sledding in Lapland is all the rage.

Three huge lakes, Vättern, Vänern, and Mälaren, attract thousands of summer visitors, but there are some 100,000 other smaller lakes. Swedes in their 700,000 boats, ranging from dinghies to ocean racers, love to "take to the waters."

Among the cities, Stockholm is the political capital, with a population of 1,435,000; Gothenburg, the car center with 704,000; and Malmö, the port of trade with 458,000.

Many visitors come to explore "the Kingdom of Crystal" in Småland province, where dozens of so-called glass huts, such as Orrefors and Kosta Boda, are tucked away in a landscape of lakes and forests.

DID YOU KNOW . . . ?

- Sweden, today's symbol of neutrality, was once a warmonger: It invaded Russia, conquered Britain, and grabbed Normandy.
- A survey showed that a large percentage of Americans think that Sweden is Switzerland.
- Half the couples living together in Sweden are unmarried.
- Sweden has added two words to international gastronomy: smörgåsbord and Absolut.
- The world's longest smörgåsbord was prepared in Sweden, stretching for 798 yards.
- James Joyce, F. Scott Fitzgerald, George Orwell, Marcel Proust, and Aldous Huxley *did not* win Sweden's Nobel Prize.
- Sweden is one of the five nations that established colonies in North America.

In the 18th century King Gustavus III built theaters, palaces, museums, and even founded the Swedish Academy, which awards the Nobel Prize for literature. Many of these buildings can still be visited. But in spite of the midsummer celebrations in Dalarna or the maypole dances on May 1, Sweden is no backward folkloric country.

Swedes are responsible for inventing much that has changed modern life, including the safety match, alternating current, the milk separator, the refrigerator, the vacuum cleaner, and the ball bearing, not to mention the zipper, which has led to all sorts of encounters between people all over the world.

1. GEOGRAPHY, HISTORY & POLITICS

GEOGRAPHY

Sweden is the fourth-largest nation in Europe—roughly the size of California—but it is sparsely inhabited. Forests cover more than half the land. From the manufacture of ball bearings to automatic beacons, Sweden is a heavily industrialized nation; less than 10% of the land is used for agriculture.

There is plenty of inland water, more than 100,000 lakes, including Vänern, the largest in Western Europe. The eastern half of the Scandinavian peninsula, Sweden shares more than 1,000 miles of frontier with Norway, but fewer than 350 with Finland.

Sweden is one of the countries on earth located farthest from the Equator. It extends from north to south at roughly the same latitude as Alaska or—in the Southern Hemisphere—the stretch of ocean between Cape Horn in South America and the Antarctic continent. In terms of area, it is similar to Spain or Iraq.

Ancient rock formations on both coasts created a huge number of bays and inlets. The northern coasts are still changing geologically, as new land areas continue to appear above the sea. Gotland and Öland, both in the Baltic, are the two biggest of Sweden's many islands.

Sweden is the largest country in Scandinavia, about twice the size of the United Kingdom. It has about 4% of the population of the United States, with a population density of 19 inhabitants per square kilometer. Nearly 80% of its people live in towns.

Sweden's seacoast is some 1,550 miles long. On the west it is bounded by the Kattegat and the Skagerrak, and on the east by the Gulf of Bothnia and the Baltic Sea. If all the inlets and islands were included, the coastline of Sweden would measure 4,650 miles.

Sweden is a long country, almost 992 miles from north to south. Much of it lies north of the Arctic Circle. The north, covered with ice and snow for some 8 months every year, is home to some 10,000 Lapps and approximately 50,000 Finns. Sweden's highest mountain, Kebnekaise, rising 6,946 feet, is in the far north. To reach the vast stretches of its land mass, Sweden maintains 7,440 miles of rail lines.

Its most important waterway is the Göta Canal, dating from the 19th century. It is 370 miles long, going from Gothenburg in the west to Stockholm in the east. Some

121 miles of canals were constructed to connect the various lakes and rivers that make up this waterway.

GÖTALAND   Götaland forms the southern part of Sweden, taking its name from the Goths of ancient times who some historians believe settled in this region, which is similar in climate and architecture to parts of northern Europe, especially Germany. This is the most populated part of Sweden, taking in eight provinces, including Östergötland, Småland (the kingdom of glass), Västergötland, Skåne (the châteaux district), Dalsland, Bohuslån, Halland, and Blekinge, plus the islands of Öland and Gotland. The Göta Canal cuts through this district. **Gothenburg** is the most important port in the west, and **Stockholm,** the capital, the chief port in the east. Other than Stockholm, **Skåne** is the most heavily visited tourist zone, often compared to the countryside of Denmark. Many seaside resorts are found on both the west and east coasts, including the islands of Öland and Gotland.

SVEALAND   Svealand is the name given the central region of Sweden, including the folkloric province of Dalarna (Dalecarlia in English) and Värmland (immortalized in the novels of Selma Lagerlöf). These are the districts most frequented by tourists. Other provinces include Västmanland, Uppland, Södermanland, and Nårke. Ancient Svealand is often called the cultural heart of Sweden. Along its eastern coast are found some 20,000 islands.

NORRLAND   Norrland is the north of Sweden, lying north of the 61st parallel and taking in about 50% of the land mass, although it is populated by only about 15% of Sweden's citizens, including Lapps and Finns. Norrland consists of 24 provinces, of which **Lapland** is the most visited by tourists. It is a land of thick forests, fast-flowing (and cold) rivers, and towering mountain peaks. Lapland consists not of forests, but tundra, the home of the Lapp reindeer herds. **Kiruna** is one of Norrland's most important cities, because of its iron-ore deposits. Many of the bodies of water of Norrland are frozen for months every year.

DATELINE	HISTORY
44 Sweden is first mentioned in a book, *Germania* by Tacitus.	The first mention of Sweden is found in *Germania,* by the Roman historian Tacitus (A.D. 77–117), who called the tribe Svear and described them as a "militant Germanic race." Later historians would describe them as "skiing hunters." The word *Sverige* (or the domain of the Svear) eventually became "Sweden."
829 Christianity introduced by St. Anskar.	The early Swedes were Vikings who carried on a thriving slave trade. St. Anskar was a Frankish missionary who introduced Christianity in 829, hoping it would tame the ravaging Viking spirit. But it took at least 2 centuries for paganism to die out. By the second half of the 11th century, Christianity had a foothold.
1248 Birger Jarl abolishes serfdom and founds Stockholm.	Olaf Skottkonung, a ruler in northern Sweden, spread Christianity after he was converted, but in time a civil war ensued. Under King Eric IX, who ruled until 1160, Christianity became firmly entrenched. He took a crusade to Finland and later became the patron saint of Sweden.
1319 Magnus VII of Norway unites Sweden with Norway.	Sweden's greatest medieval statesman was Birger Jarl, who ruled from 1248 to 1266, abolishing serfdom and founding Stockholm. His son, Magnus Ladulås, upon becoming king in 1275, gave great power to the Catholic church and founded a hereditary aristocracy.
1389 Margaret rules Sweden, Norway, and Denmark by the Union of Kalmar.	
1521 Gustavus Vasa founds the Vasa Dynasty.	**AN INTRA-NORDIC UNION** Magnus VII of Norway (1316–74) was only 3 years old when he was elected to the Swedish throne, but his election represented a recognition of the benefits of increased cooperation within the Nordic
1632 Gustavus II ensures the growth *(continues)*	

DATELINE

of Protestantism throughout Europe by winning the Battle of Lützen.

1648 Treaty of Westphalia grants Sweden the possessions of Stettin, Bremen, and West Pomerania.

1809 Napoléon names Jean Bernadotte as heir to the throne of Sweden.

1889 The Social Democratic party is formed.

1905 Sweden grants independence to Norway.

1909 Suffrage for men is granted.

1921 Suffrage for women and an 8-hour workday are granted.

1940 Sweden declares its neutrality in World War II.

1946 Sweden joins the United Nations.

1953 Dag Hammarskjöld becomes secretary-general of the United Nations.

1973 King Karl XVI Gustaf ascends the throne.

1986 Olof Palme, prime minister and leader of the Social Democrats, is assassinated.

1992 Sweden faces currency crisis.

World. Under his reign there developed a changing definition of Sweden's social classes. These included the aristocracy, the Catholic clergy (who owned more than 20% of the land), peasant farmers and laborers, and a commercial class of landowners, foresters, mineowners, and merchants. The fortunes and power of this last group were based on trade links with a well-organized handful of trading posts (the Hanseatic League) scattered within Germany and along the Baltic coastline. As trade increased, these cities (especially Visby on the island of Gotland) and their occupants thrived, and the power of the Hanseatic League grew.

The black death decimated the Swedes, beginning around 1350.

In 1389 the Swedish aristocracy, fearing the growing power of the Germans within the Hanseatic League, negotiated for an intra-Nordic union with Denmark and the remaining medieval fiefdoms in Norway and Finland. The birth process of this experimental union began in the Swedish city of Kalmar, which gave its name in 1397 to the brief but farsighted Kalmar Union. A leading figure in its development was the Danish Queen Margaretha, who was already Queen of Denmark and Norway when the Swedish aristocracy offered the throne to her in 1389. Despite its good intentions, the union collapsed after about 40 years, a result of a revolt by merchants, miners, and peasants in defense of Sweden's trade links with the Hanseatic League, coupled with power struggles between Danish and Swedish noblemen.

Although the union was considered a failure, one of its most lasting benefits was the establishment—partly as a compromise between differing political factions—of a *Riksdag* (government) with representatives from different towns and regions. It included some limited representation for the peasant classes.

Queen Margaretha's heir (her nephew, Eric of Pomerania; 1382–1459) was the crowned head of three countries (Norway, Denmark, and Sweden). He spent most of his reign fighting with the Hanseatic League. Deposed in 1439, he was replaced by Christopher of Bavaria, whose early death in 1448 led to a major conflict, and eventual dissolution of the Kalmar Union. The Danish King Christian II invaded Stockholm in 1520, massacred the leaders who opposed him, and established an unpopular reign with much civil disobedience, until the rise of the Vasa Dynasty threw the Danes out.

THE VASA DYNASTY In May of 1520 a Swedish nobleman, Gustavus Vasa, returned from captivity in Denmark and immediately began to organize the military ejection of the Danes from Sweden. In 1523 he captured Stockholm from its Danish rulers, won official recognition for Swedish independence, and was elected king of Sweden. In a power struggle with the Catholic church, he confiscated most church-held lands (vastly increasing the power of the state overnight) and established Lutheranism as the national religion. He commissioned a complete translation of the Bible and important works of the Protestant Reformation into Swedish, and violently repressed local uprisings in the Swedish provinces. He also established the right of succession for his offspring and ruled that his son, Eric XIV, would succeed him as king (which he did in 1543).

Although at first Eric was a wise ruler, his eventual undoing stemmed partly from the growing conflicts with Swedish noblemen and his eventual marriage to his unpopular mistress, Karin Mansdotter. (Previously, he had unsuccessfully solicited a marriage with the English queen, Elizabeth I.) Eric eventually went insane before being replaced by Johan III and then (after a brief interlude) by Karl IX.

The next 50 years were defined by Danish schemes to regain control of Sweden, and Swedish schemes to conquer Poland, Estonia, and the Baltic trade routes leading into Russia. A dynastic link to the royal families of Poland led to the enthronement of Sigismund (son of the Swedish King Johan III) in Warsaw. When his father died, Sigismund became simultaneously king of both Sweden and Poland. His Catholicism, however, led to his violent ejection from Sweden, which led in turn to the ascension of Karl (Charles) IX and a lasting enmity and a dangerous and expensive series of wars with Denmark, Russia, and its former ally, Poland.

Sweden was fighting even to survive in 1611, at the time of the ascension to power of Gustavus II Adolphus (1594–1632). Viewed today as a brilliant politician and military leader, he was one of the era's most stalwart Protestants in a bloodthirsty century where political alliances were often formed along religious lines. Organizing an army composed mainly of farmers and fieldhands, financed from income from the copper mines at Falun, he secured Sweden's safety, and with his armies penetrated as far south as Bavaria. He died in battle in 1632 near the city of Lützen, fighting against the Habsburg emperor's Catholic army.

When he died, his heir and only child, Christina (1626–89), was 6 years old. Actual power was held by the respected Swedish statesman Axel Oxenstierna, who continued the Thirty Years' War in Germany for another 16 years. Through military and political maneuvering, the war ended with the Treaty of Westphalia in 1648. Christina, never at home with warmongering anyway, and having converted against the advice of her counselors to an ardent faith in Catholicism, abdicated her throne in 1654 in favor of her cousin, Charles X Gustav (1622–60).

Ten years after his rise to power, Charles X (Karl) ejected the Danes from many of Sweden's southern provinces, establishing the borders of Sweden along lines that it has retained, more or less, to this day.

The long and fiscally traumatic reign of Charles XI (1655–97) followed. The endless series of wars with Denmark (and others with kingdoms in northern Germany) continued. Even more preoccupying was the growing power of the vastly wealthy Swedish nobles, who had amassed for themselves (usually through outright purchase from a cash-poor monarchy) an estimated 72% of Sweden's land. In a bitter and acrimonious process, Charles redistributed the land into approximately equal shares held by the monarchy, the nobles, and Sweden's independent farmers. The position of small landowners has remained secure in Sweden ever since, although power was funneled to an ever-increasing degree into the hands of an absolute monarch. With his new-found wealth, he greatly strengthened the Swedish military.

Charles XII (1682–1718) came to the throne at the age of 4, with his mother, the queen, ruling as his regent. Denmark, Poland, and Russia allied themselves against Sweden in the Great Northern War, which broke out in 1700. Charles invaded Russia but was defeated, and he was forced to escape to Turkey, where he remained as a prisoner for 4 years. In 1714 he returned to Sweden to continue fighting, but was killed in 1718. During his reign it can be said he presided over the collapse of the Swedish empire.

IMPRESSIONS

Sweden appeared to me the country in the world most proper to form the botanist and natural historian; every object seemed to remind me of the creation of things, of the first efforts of sportive nature.
—MARY WOLLSTONECRAFT, *LETTERS WRITTEN DURING A SHORT RESIDENCE IN SWEDEN*, 1796

Under Frederick I (1676–1751), Sweden regained some of its old strength. Real power was in the hands of the chancellor, Count Arvid Horn (1664–1742). He formed an alliance against Russia with England, Prussia, and France. The Hattar (Hats) and Mossorna (Caps) were the two opposing parties in the Riksdag of the day, and the Hats started a war with Russia in 1741. The conflict continued through the reign of the next king, Adolphus Frederick (1710–71). Although he initiated many reforms, encouraged the arts, and transformed the architectural landscape of Stockholm, Gustavus III (1746–92) revived the absolute power of the monarchy, perhaps in reaction against the changes brought on by the revolution in France. He was assassinated by a group of fanatic noblemen at a ball in the Opera.

THE 19TH CENTURY   Gustavus IV (1778–1837) followed on the throne. His hatred of Napoléon caused him to lead Sweden into the Third Coalition against France (1805–07). For his efforts, he lost Stralsund and Swedish Pomerania, and in 1808 Finland was lost in the wars against Russia and Denmark. In 1809 he was overthrown, following an uprising, and died in exile.

In 1808 a new constitution was written, giving an equal amount of power to the king and the Riksdag. Under these provisions, Charles XIII (1748–1818), the uncle of the deposed king, became the monarch.

Napoléon established his aide, Jean Bernadotte (1763–1844), as heir to the throne of Sweden. Bernadotte won a war with Denmark, forcing that country to cede Norway to Sweden. Upon the death of Charles, Bernadotte became king of Sweden and Norway, ruling as Charles XIV. During his reign Sweden began a policy of neutrality, and he established a royal line that is still on the throne today. He was followed by his son, Oscar I (1799–1859), who introduced many reforms, including freedom of worship and of the press.

The Industrial Revolution of the 19th century changed the face of Sweden. The Social Democratic party was launched in 1889, leading to a universal suffrage movement. All males were allowed to vote in 1909.

THE 20TH CENTURY   Norway declared its independence in 1905, and Sweden accepted the secession. Sweden followed a policy of neutrality in World War I, although much of the country was sympathetic to the German cause. Many Swedish volunteers enlisted in the White Army during the Russian Revolution of 1917.

In 1921 women gained the right to vote, and an 8-hour work day was granted. The Social Democratic party continued to grow in power, and after 1932 a welfare state was established.

Although Sweden offered weapons and volunteers to Finland in its Winter War against the Soviet Union in 1939, it declared its neutrality during World War II. It earned a long-lived resentment from its neighbor, Norway, whose cities were leveled by the Nazi troops who had been granted free passage across Swedish territories. Under heavy Allied threats against Sweden in 1943 and 1944, Nazi troop transports through the country were eventually halted. Throughout the war, Sweden accepted many impoverished and homeless refugees. The rescue attempts of Hungarian Jews led by Raoul Wallenberg have been recounted in books and films.

Sweden joined the United Nations in 1946, but refused to join NATO in 1949. Rather more disturbing was Sweden's decision to return to the Soviet Union many German and Baltic refugees who had battled against Russia in the war. They were presumably killed on Stalin's orders.

Dag Hammarskjöld, as secretary-general of the United Nations in 1953, did much to help Sweden regain the international respect that it had lost because of its wartime policies. He died in an air crash in 1961 toward the end of his second 5-year term.

Sweden continued to make reforms in the 1950s and '60s, launching a national health service.

Only 27 years old, King Karl XVI Gustaf became king of Sweden in 1973, following in the footsteps of his grandfather, Gustaf VI Adolf. The present king's father had died in an airplane crash when the king was still a child. In 1976 he married Silvia Sommerlath, who was born in Germany. King Karl XVI Gustaf and Queen Silvia have three children.

IMPRESSIONS

Sweden seems to me to be the most comfortable country in Europe—and the least cozy.
—KATHLEEN NOTT, *A CLEAN, WELL-LIGHTED PLACE*, 1961

The Social Democrats ruled until 1976, when they were toppled by a Center/Liberal/Moderate coalition. The Social Democrats returned in 1982, but lost their majority in 1985 and had to rely on Communist support to get bills passed.

The leader of their party since 1969, Olof Palme, was prime minister until his assassination outside a movie theater in Stockholm in February 1986. A pacifist, he was a staunch critic of the United States, especially during the Vietnam War. In spite of an arrest, the murder has not been satisfactorily resolved.

Ingvar Carlsson was elected prime minister following Palme's death.

Sweden faces the 1990s with troubling problems, including an austerity program and slow economic growth. Inflation is rising rapidly. The Social Democrats, the Green party, and the Swedish Communist party continue their struggle for control.

In 1992, its government—led by conservative prime minister Carl Bildt—faced a currency crisis that made headlines around the world. Sweden's ailing economy is forcing some cooperation between Bildt and the previously mentioned Carlsson, who preceded him as prime minister.

POLITICS

Sweden is a constitutional monarchy. Since the days of Queen Christina (which have been long remembered both in Sweden and in Hollywood) there has been a law saying that only men could occupy the throne. However, the constitutional law was changed when the firstborn child of Queen Silvia and King Karl XVI Gustaf was a girl. The heir to the throne is now Crown Princess Victoria. A prime minister heads a cabinet appointed by the king, and the cabinet is in turn responsible to the single-chamber Riksdag, the Swedish parliament.

2. FAMOUS SWEDES

Carl Michael Bellman (1740–95) Sweden's historically most popular composer as well as a major poet. Among famous works are *Fredmans Epistlar och Sanguar* (1790) and *Fredmans Sangar* (1791).

Ingmar Bergman (1918–   ) Sweden's greatest film director made his debut in 1938 as an amateur director at a theater in Stockholm. His first feature film, *Crisis,* was released in 1945, but it wasn't until the 1950s that he became world famous. He made such highly acclaimed films as *The Seventh Seal, Wild Strawberries,* and *Cries and Whispers,* all hailed as classics. In three decades he directed more than 40 films, each dealing with a universal theme such as human isolation.

Ingrid Bergman (1916–82) One of the world's finest stage and screen actresses predicted that in spite of her impressive achievements, her obituaries would carry the headline—"Star of *Casablanca* Dies." And so they did. An unknown, she left Sweden for Hollywood to make *Intermezzo,* followed by such great films as *Gaslight* (her first Oscar), *For Whom the Bell Tolls, Notorious,* and *Anastasia.* She embodied virtue in such films as *The Bells of St. Mary's* and *Joan of Arc,* which perhaps led to a massive outcry against her when she left her Swedish husband and child to marry the Italian film director, Rossellini. Sixteen years later, *Murder on the Orient Express* brought her her third and final Oscar.

Baron Jons Jakob Berzelius (1779–1848) A father of modern chemistry, Berzelius was named a member of the Royal Academy of Sciences in 1808, becoming secretary-for-life there in 1818. His many books on chemistry included

Theory of Chemical Proportions and Chemical Action of Electricity in 1844. He also created a system of chemical symbols and atomic weights of the elements.

Greta Garbo (1905–90) The screen goddess of *Anna Christie, Grand Hotel, Camille, Anna Karenina,* and *Ninotchka.* Born Greta Gustafsson in Stockholm. Among her early mentors was Mauritz Stiller, who directed her in the *Saga of Gösta Berling* (1922).

Dag Hammarskjöld (1905–61) In 1936, Dag Hammarskjöld became undersecretary in the Ministry of Finance and later president of the board controlling the Bank of Sweden. After serving as minister of state, he became secretary-general of the United Nations where he presided over bitter Cold War disputes. He was unanimously reelected for another 5 years in 1957. He met crisis after crisis, notably over the Suez Canal. His sending United Nations troops to the Belgian Congo was bitterly denounced by the Soviet Union, which demanded his resignation. He refused. He was posthumously awarded the Nobel Peace Prize.

John Hanson (1721–83) In 1781, when Maryland became the last of the 13 colonies to ratify the Articles of Confederation, the Continental Congress unanimously elected John Hanson the first president of the United States in a Congress assembled for a 12-month term—8 years before George Washington was elected. During his 1-year term (1781–82), he established the Departments of State, War, Navy, and Treasury, and set up a national judiciary, a national bank, and a post office. Virtually ignored or forgotten by most Americans, he is still remembered in Maryland on April 14, John Hanson Day.

Charles John (1763–1844) In 1810 Charles John was asked to become prince of Sweden. He allied with Russia, Great Britain, and Prussia to take Norway from Denmark and to fight Napoléon. The Danes were defeated in 1813 in the Battle of Leipzig, and Charles John took control of Norway.

Selma Lagerlöf (1858–1940) The towering woman writer of her country. Her works, including *The Saga of Gösta Berling* and *The Wonderful Adventures of Nils,* have been translated into 40 languages. In 1909 she won the Nobel Prize for literature, and in 1914 was made the first woman member of the Swedish Academy. At 75 she published her last collection of short stories and was at work on a novel when she died at her beloved Mårbacka, outside Karlstad (open to the public).

Jenny Lind (1820–87) "The Swedish nightingale," Jenny Lind was launched in opera in 1837. She appeared in France and England before her 2-year triumphant tour of the United States. Settling in England, she appeared in oratorios and concerts, eventually becoming a professor of music. Her last public appearance was at Düsseldorf, Germany, on January 20, 1870, singing an oratorio composed by her husband, Otto Goldschmidt.

Carolus Linnaeus (1707–78) Botanist responsible for developing the classification system for plants and animals used today.

Carl Milles (1875–1955) The most distinguished Swedish sculptor of the 20th century, he was greatly influenced by Rodin and sculpted in an impressionistic style, mainly in clay, wood, and stone. He worked in Sweden until 1930, but then lived in the United States where he became an American citizen and executed many notable commissions, including *Meeting of the Water* in St. Louis.

Alfred Nobel (1833–96) This 19th-century Swedish industrialist was the inventor of dynamite. He constructed and perfected detonators and amassed a great fortune, which he stipulated upon his death to go as prizes "to those who have conferred the greatest benefit on mankind."

Olof Palme (1927–86) A controversial leader, Palme was active in the so-called Socialist International, consisting of Social Democratic parties, and was particularly active in the Third World. His vehement attacks on the United States during the Vietnam War led to acrid exchanges with Washington.

Victor Sjöström (1879–1960) Actor and director whose early masterpieces included *Ingeborg Holm* and *Terje Viega.* He went to Hollywood to make several films, the best known of which is *The Scarlet Letter* (1926). Most filmgoers know him for his role in *Wild Strawberries* by Ingmar Bergman.

August Strindberg (1849–1912) Sweden's greatest playwright, Strindberg exerted a profound influence on international drama. He tried many professions before publishing his widely acclaimed novel *The Red Room,* written in 1879. Between stormy marriages, he wrote many plays, including *The Father* (1887) and *Miss Julie* (1888).

Emanuel Swedenborg   (1688–1772) Swedenborg, a scientist, philosopher, and theologian, influenced by Descartes, published many philsophical and pyschological works in the 1720s and 1730s, in which he saw the world as subject to mechanical laws. Concerned with the source and structure of matter, he concluded that the soul is material, as reported in his *Regnum Animale.* His theological insights had great influence on Dostoyevsky, Emerson, Balzac, Ezra Pound, and others; many congregations in the United States take Swedenborg's writings as their doctrinal basis. His *Journal of Dreams* is still widely read.

Anders Zorn   (1860–1920) A member of the association of artists founded in the 19th century. Famous works include *Midsummer Nights' Dance* and *Young Girls Bathing.* His works can be seen in Dalarna, Stockholm, and Chicago.

3. SPORTS & RECREATION

CYCLING   Much of Sweden is flat, lending itself to cycling tours. Places all over the country will rent bicycles, or sometimes country hotels will make them available, either free or for a small charge. Typical rentals cost 80 kronor ($14.40) a day. For more detailed information, write the **Swedish Cycling Association,** P.O. Box 6006, S-163 06 Spånga.

FISHING   In Stockholm, within view of the king's palace, you can cast a line for what are considered some of the finest salmon in the world. Ever since a decree issued in 1636 by Queen Christina, Swedes have the right to fish in waters adjoining the palace. From the north to the south of Sweden, fishing is an everyday affair. It is estimated that one of every three citizens is an angler.

But to fish elsewhere than Stockholm, you'll need a license, the cost of which varies from region to region. Local tourist offices in any district will advise. Pike, pike perch, eel, and perch are found in the heartland and the south of the country.

GOLF   After Scotland, Sweden may contain more golf addicts than any other country in Europe, with 283 courses. Unlike the Caribbean or other parts of the world, the courses are rarely crowded. Visitors are often granted local membership cards, and greens fees vary, depending on the club. Many golfers fly from Stockholm to Boden in the far north in the summer months to play by the light of the Midnight Sun. For information on courses, write **Svenska Golfförbundet,** P.O. Box 84, S-182 11, Danderyd (tel. 08/753-0265).

RAFTING   White-water rafting and river rafting are the two major forms of this sport. For white-water rafting you go in a fast river boat, the trip made all the more exciting by a series of rapids. Both short trips and adventures lasting a week are organized in Lapland with a safety-conscious guide. For details, write **Nordkallot Resor,** S-951 32 Luleå (tel. 0920/940-70).

River rafting is much tamer, as you gently go down a slow-moving river in Sweden's heartland. Many Swedes build their own log rafts. Adventurers sleep in tents and cook

---

IMPRESSIONS

The Swede is, surely, the human blackbird, with his copious, rich and liquid voice, in a language that reaches the extreme of voluptuous volubility.
—EDMUND GOSSE, 1911

If ever there was a Yankeer than Yankee, he's a Swede.
—HENRY ADAMS, 1901

their food over campfires, but they should bring along plenty of mosquito repellent in summer. For details about trips along the Klarälven River in Värmland, write to **Vildmark i Värmland AB,** Sundbergsvagen 13, P.O. Box 209, S-685 00 Torsby (tel. 0560/140-40).

RIDING   Sweden has many riding stables and riding schools. Ask about them at local tourist offices. One of the most popular excursions in the country is a pony trek through the region of Sweden's highest mountain, Knebnekaise.

SAILING & CANOEING   Canoes are for rent all over the country, from province to province, and details are available from local tourist offices. A day's rental costs about 75 kronor ($13.50). Often hotels situated near water-sports areas will rent you canoes. At places all over Sweden you can rent sailing boats as well. Again, most tourist offices have complete details.

SWIMMING   If you don't mind your waters a bit on the cool side, Sweden has one of the world's longest coastlines, plus some 100,000 lakes, in which you can take the plunge. The best bathing beaches are on the west coast. Both the islands of Öland and Gotland contain popular summer seaside resorts. Beaches in Sweden are open to the public in general, and nude bathing is allowed on certain designated beaches. However, topless bathing for women is everywhere. If a Swedish lake is suitable for swimming, it is always signposted.

WALKING & JOGGING   The almost-unlimited space of Sweden is ideal for either activity. Local tourist offices, depending on what part of Sweden you visit, generally will provide details and sometimes even free maps for the best trails or jogging paths. In Stockholm, hotel reception desks often tell you the best place to go jogging close to your hotel, as Stockholm has many "green lungs."

4. FOOD & DRINK

FOOD

The fame of the **smörgåsbord** is justly deserved. Utilizing a vast array of dishes—everything from Baltic herring to smoked reindeer—the smörgåsbord may either be eaten as hors d'oeuvres or as a meal in itself.

One cardinal rule of the smörgåsbord: Don't mix fish and meat dishes. It is customary to begin with *sill* (herring), prepared in many ways. Herring is usually followed by other treats from the sea (jellied eel, smoked fish, and raw pickled salmon); then diners proceed to the cold meat dishes, such as baked ham or liver paste, which are accompanied by vegetable salads. Hot dishes, often Swedish meatballs, come next, and are backed up by cheese and crackers—perhaps a fresh-fruit salad.

The smörgåsbord is not served as often in Sweden as many visitors seem to believe, as it requires time-consuming preparation. Many Swedish families reserve it for special occasions. In lieu of the 40-dish smörgåsbord, some restaurants have taken to serving a plate of *assietter* (hors d'oeuvres). One of the tricks for enjoying smörgåsbord is timing. It's best to go early, when fish dishes are fresh. Late arrivals may be more fashionable, but the food is often stale.

The average times for meals in Sweden are generally from 8 to 11am for the standard continental breakfast, noon to 2:30pm for lunch, and as early as 5:30pm for dinner to around 8 or 8:30pm (many restaurants in Stockholm are open to midnight—but don't count on this in the small villages).

A Swedish breakfast at your hotel may consist of cheese, ham, sausage, egg, bread, and perhaps filmjölk, a kind of sour-milk yogurt. **Smörgas,** the famous Swedish open-face sandwich, like the Danish smørrebrød and Norwegian smørbrød, is a slice of buttered bread with something on top. It is eaten for breakfast or anytime during the day, and you'll find it at varying prices, depending on what you order and where you order it.

Unless you decide to have smörgåsbord (never served in the evening) at lunch, you'll find that the Swedes do not go in for lavish spreads in the middle of the day. The usual luncheon order consists of one course, as you'll observe on menus especially in larger towns. Dinner menus are for complete meals, with appetizer, main course and its side dishes, and dessert included.

Generally Swedish chefs tend to be far more expert with **fish dishes** (freshwater pike and salmon are star choices) than with meat courses. The Swedes go stark raving mad at the sight of *kraftor* (crayfish), in season from mid-August to mid-September. This succulent, dill-flavored delicacy is eaten with the fingers, and much of the fun is the elaborate ritual surrounding its consumption.

A platter of thin **pancakes,** served with lingonberries (comparable to cranberries), is the traditional Thursday-night dinner in Sweden. It is often preceded by yellow split-pea soup seasoned with pork. It's good any night of the week—but somehow better on Thursday.

The Swedish cuisine used to be deficient in fresh vegetables and fruits, relying heavily on the tin can, but this is no longer true. Potatoes are the staff of life, but fresh salad bars long ago peppered the landscape, especially in the big cities.

The calorie-laden Swedish pastry—the mainstay of the konditori—is tempting and fatal to weight-watchers.

DRINKS

Kaffe (coffee) is the universal drink in Sweden, although tea (taken straight) and milk are also popular. The water is perfectly safe to drink all over Sweden. Those who want a reprieve from alcohol might find the fruit-flavored **Pommac** a good soft-drink beverage, but Coca-Cola is ubiquitous.

The state monopoly, Systembolaget, controls the sale of alcoholic beverages. Licensed restaurants may sell alcohol after noon only (1pm on Sunday).

Snaps or aquavit—served icy cold—is a superb Swedish drink, often used to accompany smörgåsbord. The run-of-the-mill Swedish **beer** (pilsner) has only a small amount of alcohol. All restaurants serve *lättol* (light beer) and *folköl,* a somewhat stronger brew. Swedish vodka, or **brännvin,** is made from corn and potatoes and flavored with different spices. All brännvin is served ice cold in schnapps glasses. Keep in mind that aquavit is much stronger than it looks, and Sweden has strictly enforced rules about drinking and driving. Most Swedes seem to drink their liquor straight; mixed drinks are uncommon. Either way, the drink prices are sky-high.

FROMMER'S SMART TRAVELER: RESTAURANTS

1. Look for the daily special—reasonable in price and prepared fresh that day.
2. Order fixed-price menus, especially at lunch. Often you can dine in expensive restaurants in Sweden by patronizing them at lunch and ordering the set menu.
3. Do as many Swedes do and have one or two open-face sandwiches for lunch.
4. Watch the booze—it can add greatly to the cost of any meal.
5. Go ethnic—the country has some great inexpensive foreign dining. Swedish restaurants tend to be expensive.
6. Best bet for a quick and inexpensive meal is a self-service cafeteria.
7. Fill up at the traditional Swedish breakfast buffets, so you'll need only a light lunch.

5. RECOMMENDED BOOKS, FILMS & RECORDINGS

BOOKS

HISTORY & MYTHOLOGY *The Early Vasas: A History of Sweden, 1523–1611,* by Michael Roberts (CUP), covers one of the most dramatic and action-filled eras in Sweden's long history.

Scandinavian Folk & Fairy Tales, edited by Claire Booss (Avenel), is an extraordinary collection filled with elves, dwarfs, trolls, goblins, and other spirits of the house and barnyard.

BIOGRAPHY *Swedes in North America (1638–1988),* by Sten Carlsson (Streiffert & Co.), traces the lives of some of the 2% of the North American population that have some sort of Swedish background—from Greta Garbo to Charles Lindbergh.

Alfred Nobel and the Nobel Prizes, by Nils K. Ståhle (Swedish Institute), traces the life of the 19th-century Swedish industrialist and creator of the coveted awards that bear his name.

Garbo: Her Story, by Antoni Gronowicz (Simon & Schuster), is a controversial, unauthorized memoir based on a long and intimate friendship, going behind the fabulous face, with many candid details of this most reluctant of movie legends.

LITERATURE & THEATER *A History of Swedish Literature,* by Ingemar Algulin (Swedish Institute), is the best overview on the subject—from the runic inscriptions of the Viking age up to modern fiction.

The Story of Gösta Berling, by Selma Lagerlöf (in various international editions), is the acclaimed work that Garbo filmed, originally published in 1891.

Three Plays: Father, Miss Julie, Easter, by August Strindberg (Penguin), provides an insight into the world of this strange Swedish genius who wrote a number of highly arresting dramas, of which these are some of the best known.

FILM *Ingmar Bergman: The Cinema as Mistress,* by Philip Mosley (Marion Boyars), is a critical study of Bergman's *oeuvre* dating from his earliest work as a writer/director in the late 1940s up to *Autumn Sonata.*

Swedish Cinema, from Ingeborg Holm to Fanny and Alexander, by Peter Cowie (Swedish Institute), covers the complete history of Swedish films, from the emergence of the silent era, to the rise of Ingmar Bergman, up to the most recent wave.

FILMS

The classics of Ingmar Bergman will perhaps be shown 100 years from now, including such works as *The Virgin Spring* (1959). *The Seventh Seal* opened new ground in the art of film upon its release in 1956. It concerned the fate of man in a world God has abandoned. *Wild Strawberries,* released in 1957, was viewed by some critics as his most formal and exquisite work. It dealt with a person's coming to self-knowledge by looking at the past. *Fanny and Alexander* (1982) won worldwide recognition for Bergman, doing well in the United States. Set in 1907, it pays tribute to the director's recollection of his childhood, growing up in Uppsala.

A major talent has emerged in Carl Gustaf Nykvist whose *The Women on the Roof* achieved recognition at Cannes. It is set in a Stockholm rooming house on the verge of World War I.

In 1992, *The Ox,* directed by Sven Nykvist, with English subtitles, was released in America. Nykvist is known for his role as Ingmar Bergman's cinematographer. He sets this Swedish tale of betrayal in a rural village in the 1860s, at the dawn of massive Swedish immigration to the United States. The great Liv Ullmann appears in a supporting role as Maria.

In 1992, *The Best Intentions,* directed by Bille August but written by Ingmar

Bergman, with English subtitles, was also released in America. This epic tells the Bergman family story before the arrival of little Ingmar.

RECORDINGS

BALLADS *Out in the Open* by Ulf Lundell (English lyrics by Roger Hinchliffe) continues the success of Lundell, who has achieved fame as both a novelist and a rock balladeer. His gravelly voice and lyrics evoke Bob Dylan. This song is often called "Sweden's second national anthem."

Fredman's Epistle No. 2 by Carl Michael Bellman (English lyrics by Paul Britten Austin) is a famed work by Sweden's most popular composer, who lived from 1740 to 1795 but is still widely performed today. It is said that Englishman Austin's command of "Bellmanese" is second to none.

Also available on records and cassette is *Fredman's Song No. 16* by Bellman, again with English lyrics by Austin. *Fredman's Epistle No. 45*, by Bellman, has English lyrics by Roger Hinchliffe.

Evert Taube (1890–1976) is honored in the re-release of *Calle Scheven's Waltz* (English lyrics by Helen Asbury and Roger Hinchliffe) as a "modern Bellman." Called a "living legend" in Sweden, Taube is still considered the most cosmopolitan of Scandinavian songwriters, even after his death. He often sings of the sea and the people who live there, as he does in this recording.

Swedish Ballads and Songs, performed by Håkan Hagegård with the Swedish Radio Symphony (Kjell Ingebretsen, conducting).

FOLK *The Lilac Years (Looking to America)* is a recently recorded Swedish traditional folk melody, with English lyrics by Kathy Green and Roger Hinchliffe. It tells of the mass immigration period to America in the mid-19th century.

CLASSICAL *Midsommarvaka,* performed by the New Philharmonic Orchestra, London (conducted by Paavo Berglund), is an orchestral work by 20th-century Swedish composer Hugo Alfven. Even more representative of his work (and conducted by him as well) is *Festspel Opus 25,* performed by the Royal Court Orchestra, Stockholm.

Pastoralsvit, Lyrisk fantasi for liten orkester, Opus 58, by Lars Erik Larsson, performed by the Stockholm Philharmonic Orchestra—lyrical and lighthearted music for small orchestras.

Drottningholmsmusiken/Sinfonia D Major, by Johan Helmich Roma, performed by the Drottningholm Chamber Orchestra. This recording gives a good idea of the small-scale orchestral performances popular among the Swedish aristocracy during the 18th century. This performance of the work of an 18th-century Swedish composer was recorded at Stockholm's perfectly preserved 18th-century Drottningholm Theater, near the king's private residence.

FOLK MUSIC/JAZZ/POPULAR *Greatest Hits,* by ABBA, Volumes I and II. Rock and disco music from ABBA, the most profitable and internationally famous Swedish group of the 1970s and 1980s.

Jazz pa svenska, with Jan Johansson, piano, and George Riedel, guitar. Highly danceable supper-club music of the kind popular with conservative middle-aged Swedes on a night on the town.

Svenskt Festspel (Swedish Highlights). The Swedish Radio Symphony Orchestra plays patriotic songs, including the Swedish national anthem, and symphonic renderings of songs dear to the patriotic hearts of most Swedes.

CHAPTER 23

PLANNING A TRIP TO SWEDEN

This chapter is devoted to the nitty-gritty of planning a trip to Sweden—costs, events, itineraries, and detailed practicalities like taxes, tipping, and emergencies. It should be read in conjunction with Chapter 1.

1. CURRENCY & COSTS

CURRENCY Sweden, too, has basic currency units of **kronor** and **öre,** but the Swedes spell kronor with an "o" instead of an "e" as in the kroner of Denmark and Norway. As of this writing, 1 krona is worth about U.S. $0.18 (about 5.8 kronor equal U.S. $1.) One krona is divided into 100 öre. Banknotes are issued in denominations of 10, 50, 100, 500, 1,000, and 10,000 kronor, and silver coins are issued in values of 10 and 50 öre, as well as 1, 3, and 5 kronor.

WHAT THINGS COST IN STOCKHOLM	U.S. $
Taxi from the airport to city center	54.00
Average taxi ride in the city center	12.00
T-bana from the train station to the suburbs	2.20
Local telephone call	.35
Double room at the Grand Hotel (deluxe)	394.20
Double room at the Eden Terrace (inexpensive)	196.20
Double room at the Domus Hotel (inexpensive)	121.50
Lunch for one at Eriks Bakfica (moderate)	15.30
Dinner for one, without wine, at Operakällaren (deluxe)	90.00
Dinner for one, without wine, at Prinsens (moderate)	30.00
Dinner for one, without wine, at Gröna Linjen (budget)	13.50
Pint of beer (draft pilsner) in a bar	7.50
Coca-Cola in a café	3.50
Cup of coffee in a café	2.90

	U.S.$
Roll of ASA 100 Kodacolor film, 36 exposures	10.50
Admission to Drottningholm Palace	4.50
Movie ticket	11.00
Budget theater ticket	12.60

WHAT THINGS COST IN KARLSTAD

	U.S. $
Taxi from the airport to the city center	10.50
Bus from the airport to the city center	3.00
Local telephone call	.35
Double room at the Stadshotellet (inexpensive)	198.00
Double room at the Gösta Berling (inexpensive)	153.00
Double room at the Grand (budget)	90.00
Lunch for one at Värdshuset Alstern (expensive)	24.30
Dinner for one, without wine, at Cafe Artist (moderate)	45.00
Dinner for one, without wine, at Plaza Vivaldi (moderate)	38.00
Dinner for one, without wine, at Skogen Terrassen (moderate)	33.30
Pint of beer (draft pilsner) in a pub	7.00
Coca-Cola in a restaurant	2.50
Cup of coffee	2.70
Roll of ASA 100 Kodacolor film, 24 exposures	9.50
Admission to Värmlands Museum	Free
Movie ticket	9.50
Budget theater ticket	12.00

2. WHEN TO GO — CLIMATE, HOLIDAYS & EVENTS

CLIMATE   Sweden's climate is hard to classify, since temperatures, aided by the Gulf Stream, vary considerably from the fields of Skåne to the wilderness of Lapland (the upper 10th of Sweden lies north of the Arctic Circle).

The country as a whole has many days of sun in summer, but it's not super-hot. July is the warmest month, with temperatures in both Stockholm and Gothenburg averaging around 64° Fahrenheit. February is the coldest, when the temperature in Stockholm averages around 26° Fahrenheit (Gothenburg is a few degrees warmer).

It's not always true that the farther north you go the cooler it becomes. During summer the northern parts of the country—from Halsingland to northern Lapland—may suddenly have the warmest weather and the bluest skies. Check the weather forecasts on television and in the newspapers, which are claimed by the Swedes to be 99% reliable.

THE KRONA & THE DOLLAR

At this writing, $1 = 5.8 Swedish kronor (or 1 Swedish krona = 18¢), and this was the rate of exchange used to calculate the dollar values given in the Sweden chapters (rounded to the nearest nickel). This rate fluctuates from time to time and may not be the same when you travel to Sweden. Therefore the following table should be used only as a rough guide:

Kronor	U.S.$	Kronor	U.S.$
.25	.05	125	22.50
.50	.09	150	27.00
1	.18	175	31.50
5	.90	200	36.00
10	1.80	225	40.50
15	2.70	250	45.00
20	3.60	300	54.00
25	4.50	350	63.00
30	5.40	400	72.00
40	7.20	450	81.00
50	9.00	500	90.00
60	10.80	600	108.00
70	12.60	700	126.00
80	14.40	800	144.00
90	16.20	900	162.00
100	18.00	1,000	180.00

Sweden's Average Daytime Temperatures (°F)

	Jan	Feb	Mar	Apr	May	June	July	Aug	Sept	Oct	Nov	Dec
Stockholm	27	26	31	40	50	59	64	62	54	45	37	32
Kalmar	36	34	31	40	53	60	63	60	55	44	33	33
Karesuando	6	5	12	23	39	54	59	51	44	31	9	5
Karlstad	33	30	28	37	53	63	62	59	54	41	29	26
Lund	38	36	34	43	57	63	64	61	57	47	37	37

A Note on the Midnight Sun: In summer the sun never fully sets in the northern part of the nation, and even in the south there is daylight as late as 11pm and the sun rises around 3am. Here are the best vantage points in Sweden and dates when you may see the thrilling spectacle of the Midnight Sun (all these locations are reached by public transportation): **Björkliden,** May 26 to July 19; **Abisko,** June 12 to July 4; **Kiruna,** May 31 to July 14; and **Gällivare,** June 2 to July 12.

Remember that although the sun may be shining brightly at midnight, it is not as strong as at midday. Bring along a warm jacket or sweater.

HOLIDAYS Sweden celebrates the following public holidays: January 1 (New Year's Day), January 6 (Epiphany), Good Friday, Easter Sunday, Easter Monday, May 1 (Labor Day), Ascension Day, Whitsunday, Whitmonday, Midsummer Day, All Saints' Day, and December 24, 25, and 26 (Christmas Eve, Christmas Day, and Boxing Day). Inquire at the tourist bureaus for the actual dates of most of these holidays, since some vary from year to year.

SWEDEN
CALENDAR OF EVENTS

In what follows dates are merely general indications of time. Always check with the tourist office before planning to attend an actual event.

APRIL

☐ **Walpurgis Night.** Celebrations with bonfires, songs, and speeches welcoming the advent of spring. Particularly lively celebrations among the students of Uppsala, Lund, Stockholm, Gothenburg, and Umeå. April 30.

JUNE

☐ **Midsummer.** Swedes celebrate Midsummer Eve (June 22) all over the country. Maypole dances to the sound of the fiddle and accordion are the rule of the day. Dalarna has the most traditional celebrations. June 22 and 23.

☐ **Music on Lake Siljan.** Nine days of concerts, courses, seminars, morning walks, homestead evenings, and special children's programs. June 30 to July 8.

JULY

✪ *FALUN FOLK MUSIC FESTIVAL* *International folk musicians' meeting, with concerts, seminars, lectures, exhibitions, and films on folk music. International folkloric groups perform.*
Where: Various venues in Falun. When: July 15–18. How: Contact Falun Folk Music Festival, S-791 71 Falun (tel. 023/19042).

☐ **John Ericsson/Sweden-America Festival.** Held in memory of one of Värmland's most famous sons, John Ericsson. The sea battle between the *Monitor* and *Merrimac* is reenacted on Daglosen Lake at Kyrkviken, Filipstad. July 29.

✪ *GOTLAND'S CHAMBER MUSIC FESTIVAL* *A major Swedish cultural event, this annual festival attracts world-class artists who perform in a medieval setting.*
Where: Visby, Gotland. When: July 27–Aug 10. How: Write the Tourist Office, Burmeisterska Huset, Strandgatan 9, S-621 58 Visby (Gotland).

AUGUST

☐ **Minnesota Day.** Swedish-American relations are celebrated at the Emigrants' Center, with speeches, music, singing, and dancing, climaxed by the election of the Swedish-American of the year. Utvandra Utvandrarnas Hus, Växjö (Småland).

STOCKHOLM
CALENDAR OF EVENTS

MAY

✪ *DROTTNINGHOLM COURT THEATER* *Some 28 opera and ballet performances presented in a unique 18th-century theater, with original decorative paintings and stage mechanisms.*
Where: Drottningholm Court Theater, Drottningholm. When: May

27–September 26. How: Call 08/660-82-55 or 660-82-82 for tickets. Take the underground to Brommaplan and a bus from there.

☐ **Round Gotland Race.** The biggest and most exciting open-water sailing race of the Scandinavian season starts and finishes at Sandhamn in the Stockholm archipelago. About 450 boats, mainly from the Nordic countries, take part. July 1.

☐ **Stockholm Festival.** Opera, concerts, ballet, theater, exhibitions, and other cultural events at various venues in Stockholm. August 18 to September 9.

☐ **Skansen Christmas Fair.** Sale of traditional handcraft articles, Christmas decorations, homemade candles, breads, and cakes. At Skansen open-air museum in Stockholm. December 2, 9, and 16.

✪ *NOBEL DAY   The king and members of the royal family attend the Nobel Prize ceremony for literature, physics, chemistry, medicine, physiology, and economics. The ceremony is followed by a banquet at City Hall.*
    Where: *Concert Hall, Stockholm.* ***When:*** *December 10.* ***How:*** *By invitation only.*

3. GETTING AROUND

BY PLANE

The airports of Gothenburg and Stockholm are the major gateways to Sweden. **Scandinavian Airlines System (SAS)** and the Swedish domestic airlines, **LIN (Linjeflyg)** maintain connections to 38 domestic airports, including Kiruna in Swedish Lapland; Visby, on the island of Gotland; Malmö, capital of the château country; Karlstad, center for Värmland; and Kalmar, a good base for exploring the glassworks district. From around June 1 to mid-July, flights depart from Stockholm north to Swedish Lapland and the Midnight Sun.

Air travel in Sweden is moderately priced because during the summer SAS and LIN offer **mini-fares,** charging a one-way price for a round-trip ticket! An accompanying spouse and children (ages 12 to 26) pay only 350 kronor ($63) to travel round-trip between Stockholm and any place in the country, regardless of distance, with one exception explained below. Children 2 to 12 pay 250 kronor ($45).

A minimum 2-night stay is required for these mini-fares, and you must depart and return between a Monday and a Friday. Always check with the airline or travel agency when buying your tickets about further restrictions.

The exception is between southern and northern Sweden (which includes Lapland, of course). For a change of aircraft in Stockholm and for nonstop travel between Gothenburg and Sundsvall, a surcharge of 150 kronor ($27) is assessed for each accompanying family member. Children under age 2 travel free.

Young people under 26 can take advantage of the SAS/LIN special **standby fares,** and senior citizens over 65 can apply for even more discounts, depending on their destination.

BY TRAIN

The Swedish word for train is *tåg,* and the national train system is Statens Järnvägar, the Swedish State Railways.

Swedish trains follow tight schedules. Trains leave Malmö/Helsingborg for Stockholm every hour throughout the day, Monday through Friday. The same applies to trains leaving Gothenburg for Stockholm. In fact, there are trains every hour, or every other hour, to most big Swedish towns.

On *expresståg* runs, seats must be reserved, at a cost of 15 kronor ($2.70) per person.

Discount tickets—called **"red departures"**—are available, and are linked with the purchase of a *Reslustkort* pass sold at all rail stations. This pass costs 250 kronor ($45) for adults, or 50 kronor ($9) for senior citizens. Children under 12 travel free if accompanied by an adult, and young people up to age 18 get a reduction without the card. Holders of the Reslustkort get 50% off on red departures, or only 25% off if they travel Tuesday through Thursday or on Saturday. The card is nontransferable but holders have the right to bring along one adult who is granted the same reductions.

BY BUS

Where the train stops its run, especially in parts of the north, a bus takes over, linking remote, off-the-beaten-path villages. Buses are usually equipped with toilets, adjustable seats, reading lights, and telephone. Fares depend on the distance traveled.

Weekend buses operated on Friday and Sunday by SWEBUS provide a cheap alternative to the train. A sample fare from Stockholm to Gothenburg, a bus route of 326 miles, is 215 kronor ($38.79) one-way. Reservations are necessary. In the Stockholm area, call 020/64-06-40.

BY CAR-FERRY

For a country with some 100,000 lakes and one of the world's largest coastlines, ferries play a surprisingly tiny part in the overall transportation network.

After the car-ferry crossings from northern Germany and Denmark, the most popular car-ferry route is from the mainland to the island of Gotland (capital: Visby), in the Baltic. Services are available from Oskarshamn and Nynäshamn. The famous "white boats" of the Waxholm Steamship Company also travel to many destinations in the Stockholm archipelago.

BY CAR

Despite its northerly latitudes, Sweden has an excellent network of roads and highways, particularly in the southern provinces and in the central lake district. Swedish Customs issues an insurance card for privately owned cars and motorcycles brought into the country, although if you've rented your car from any car-rental agency, this card will almost always be included among the rental documents at the time of your pickup. Current driver's licenses from Canada, Great Britain, New Zealand, Australia, and the United States are acceptable in Sweden.

RENTALS   All the major U.S.-based car rental firms are represented at locations throughout Sweden, both at airports and in downtown urban centers. Each of the companies' rates were aggressively competitive, although certain last-minute sales promotions will substantially alter the information contained within the paragraphs that follow. It is, therefore, to your advantage to phone around within 2 weeks or less of your anticipated departure from North America to avail yourself of the lowest available rates. Membership in AAA or similar auto clubs sometimes qualifies renters for moderate discounts.

At presstime, the prices of no-frills cars at **Hertz** (tel. toll free 800/654-3001 in North America) were lower than those at its competitors. A Ford Fiesta with manual transmission, if prepaid 14 days or more in advance of your departure from the U.S., cost $342 for a 1-week rental with unlimited mileage. This price, unlike prices at the competition, included the whopping 25% government tax, although a penalty of $50 was imposed for changes of any kind once the reservation had been made. Middle-bracket cars and luxury vehicles at Hertz were more expensive and less competitive in price than similar cars offered by the competition.

This price was hotly contested at **Budget** (tel. toll free 800/527-0700 in North America), which charged $351 for 1 week's rental, and $315 per week for rentals of 2 weeks or more, for a somewhat roomier Ford Fiesta with unlimited mileage. (In the case of Budget, however, the 25% government tax cost extra.) Many clients preferred to upgrade their choice of rental car to a solidly elegant Swedish-made Volvo 440 GL, priced at $458 plus tax for a week's rental with unlimited mileage. For families traveling together, Budget offered an Omega Caravan, styled like a North American station wagon with lots of room for luggage, for $575 plus tax per week, with unlimited mileage. These prices apply for rentals at Budget that were prepaid in North America 2 weeks prior to departure. No penalty was imposed for changes in pickup or dropoff dates. For clients who preferred to delay reserving their car until 2 days before the anticipated pickup, rates rose only about $10 to $15 extra per week from the rates quoted above. Dropoffs at any Budget office in Sweden (except Visby) were free, and dropoffs in Oslo and Copenhagen entailed a moderate extra charge of $50 and $100, respectively.

Avis (tel. toll free 800/331-2112 in North America) also offered a range of cars ranging from bare-bones minimalist to luxury. Their least expensive car, a Ford Fiesta or a Nissan Micra, rented for around $340 per week, plus 25% tax, with unlimited mileage. Avis's most expensive car, a Mercedes 230E with every imaginable amenity, rented for around $1,450 per week, plus tax, with unlimited mileage included.

A Word About Insurance: All three of the car-rental companies build a basic amount of automatic liability insurance into their rates. Despite that, most renters feel more comfortable after arranging additional insurance protecting them from fiscal liability in the event of theft or damage to the car. A collision damage waiver (CDW) is an optional insurance policy that can be purchased when you sign a rental agreement. For a fee of between $9 and $15 a day, depending on the value of the car, the rental agency agrees to eliminate all but a token amount of your financial responsibility for collision damage in case of an accident. If you don't have a CDW and you have an accident, you'll usually pay around $1,500 or more toward the cost of repairing the vehicle. Exact figures, penalties, and deductibles vary from company to company.

Some credit-card companies, usually including certain upmarket types of American Express and Diners Club cards, agree to reimburse card-users for the deductible in the event of an accident. Because of that, many renters have chosen to waive the cost of the extra CDW. However, although the credit-card issuers will usually (several weeks after the accident) reimburse the renter for the cost of damages, payments have sometimes been delayed with such coverage until after the completion of certain documents. Unless there's enough of a credit line associated with your particular credit card, some car renters involved in an accident will be required to pay sometimes large amounts of cash on the spot. Considering the unfamiliar terrain, if any doubt arises in your mind, even at the risk of "double coverage," it's usually a good idea to purchase the CDW, if only for the peace of mind it entails.

AUTOMOBILE CLUBS Motoring organizations in Sweden are the **Motormännens Riksförbund** (Swedish Automobile Association), Sturegatan 32, S-102 48 Stockholm (tel. 08/782-38-00), and the **Kunglen, Automobil Klubben (Royal Automobile Club),** Gyllenstiernsgatan 4, S-115 26 Stockholm (tel. 08/660-00-55).

GAS Nearly every village and certainly every town or city in Sweden has a filling station that sells "petrol" 24 hours a day. It's expensive. For a super-grade gasoline, you'll pay, as of this writing (but most definitely subject to change), about 6 to 7 kronor ($1.10 to $1.30) per liter, or about $4.10 to $4.75 per gallon. Gas is slightly cheaper in the self-service stations, but you'll need 10-krona ($1.80) or 100-krona ($18) notes to operate the pumps.

DRIVING RULES In Sweden, as in all of Scandinavia, traffic drives on the right. By law, you and your passengers must wear seat belts. During the day you are required to have your headlights on dim. Speed limits on standard roadways are 70 kilometers per hour (watch it, that's less than 45 m.p.h.), slowing to 50kmph (under 31 m.p.h.) in built-up areas, and 30kmph (about 18 m.p.h.) in school zones. On the motorways, the limits are 90kmph (56 m.p.h.) to 110kmph (68 m.p.h.), depending on the width of the roadway and the density of traffic.

Be warned: Sweden has very strict drunk-driving laws, with heavy fines levied if you violate them. You can be prosecuted after imbibing the equivalent of two cans of a strong beer.

MAPS   Ask for local road maps at local tourist offices, bookstores (for which you'll have to pay, of course), or at one of the Swedish automobile clubs (see above). The best commercial road maps, sold at most major bookstores in Sweden, are those published by **Hallweg.**

BREAKDOWNS   In case of a breakdown, call the police or the local branch of **Larmtjänst,** an outfit operated by Swedish insurance companies with a 24-hour phone line. Look in a local Swedish telephone directory for the number of the branch nearest your breakdown. The Swedish national emergency number (tel. 90-000) should be used only in case of a real emergency—that is, an accident or injury.

BY RV   Mobile homes can be rented in Sweden at widely varying prices, depending on the type of vehicle and the time of year. One outfit that specializes in this type of rental, and one which will provide complete information, is **Touring Cars Sweden AB,** Söderbyvägen 1C S-195 60 Arlanda (tel. 0760/22-015). The outlet lies about a 5-minute taxi ride from the Stockholm airport at Arlanda. Hours are Monday through Friday from 9am to noon and 1 to 4:30pm.

SUGGESTED ITINERARIES

IF YOU HAVE 1 WEEK

Day 1: Settle into Stockholm, the capital city.

Days 2 & 3: Explore Stockholm's attractions, including the raised royal flagship *Vasa.* One afternoon should be reserved for a boat trip through the archipelago and another for exploring Drottningholm Palace on the island of Lake Mälaren.

Day 4: Take a day-trip north to Sweden's oldest town, Sigtuna, on the shores of Lake Mälaren, and to the nearby 17th-century Skokloster Castle, which contains one of the most interesting baroque museums in Europe. Then it's on to the university city of Uppsala, and perhaps on to neighboring Gamla (Old) Uppsala to see Viking burial mounds.

Day 5: Begin a fast 4-day excursion through the most interesting folkloric provinces of Sweden, Dalarna and Värmland. Arrive first at the mining town of Falun to visit the Falun Copper Mine and the home of Carl Larsson, the famous Swedish painter. Spend the night here or in one of the smaller resort towns such as Tällberg, Rättvik, Mora, or Leksand.

Day 6: Visit the Lake Siljan towns just mentioned. This blue glacial lake, ringed by lush forests, is one of the most beautiful in Europe. Take a boat tour leaving from Rättvik. On its outskirts you can visit Gammelgården, an old farmstead, for a glimpse of the past and stay overnight again in one of the lakeside villages or towns.

Day 7: From Falun, Route 60 heads south to Karlstad. You'll pass through the heart of Selma Lagerlöf country (Sweden's most famous novelist). Have lunch at Filipstad, the birthplace of John Ericsson, who designed the U.S. Civil War iron-clad ship *Monitor.* Spend the night in Karlstad.

IF YOU HAVE 2 WEEKS

Days 1–7: Spend the first week as described above. But instead of cutting short your trip in Karlstad, extend it another week, using the following itinerary.

Day 8: Spend another night in Karlstad, exploring its own attractions, and branching out into the environs, including Rottneros Manor.

Day 9: In the morning, head south along the eastern shore of Lake Vänern. After lunch in charming lakeside Lidköping, head for Gothenburg, the second-largest city of Sweden.

Day 10: Explore Gothenburg and branch out on short trips to such attractions as Kungälv or Marstrand, a once-royal resort.

Days 11–13: Take the Göta Canal ride, a distance of 350 miles. This trip begins at Gothenburg and heads east to Stockholm. You'll go through 58 locks and capture the "essence" of Sweden along the way.

Day 14: Arrive in Stockholm and prepare for your return flight to North America.

IF YOU HAVE 3 WEEKS

Days 1–14: In addition to the 2-week itinerary outline above, those with extra time may want to explore Sweden's southern region.

Days 15 & 16: Head south from Stockholm to the largest island of Sweden, Gotland, whose capital is Visby. Spend the next day exploring the island's attractions.

Day 17: Return to the mainland and head south to the old city of Kalmar, where you can explore Kalmar Castle and other attractions.

Day 18: Visit the Glassworks District, centering at Växjö. Within less than an hour's drive of Växjö are several glassworks, including Orrefors and Boda, which offer guided tours. You can purchase "seconds" in their workshops.

Days 19–21: Explore Skåne, the southernmost corner of Sweden, often called the country's château district. Malmö, the third-largest city of Sweden, is an ideal base because of its many hotels and attractions. The university city of Lund, northeast of Malmö, is also a good bet, and Ystad is a favorite stop along the southern coastline. From Helsingborg, north of Malmö, you can cross into Denmark and see Hamlet's Castle.

FAST   SWEDEN

Business Hours   Banks are generally open Monday through Friday from 9:30am to 3pm. In some larger cities, banks extend their hours, usually on Thursday or Friday, until 5:30 or 6pm. Most **offices** are open Monday through Friday from 8:30 or 9am to 5pm (sometimes to 3 or 4pm in the summer); on Saturday, offices and factories are closed or open for only a half day. Most **stores and shops** are open Monday through Friday between 9:30am and 6pm, and on Saturday from 9:30am to somewhere between 1 and 4pm. Once a week, usually on Monday or Friday, some of the larger stores are open from 9:30am to 7pm (during July and August, to 6pm).

Camera and Film   Cameras (especially the famed Hasselblad), film, projectors, and enlarging equipment are very good values in Sweden. Practically all the world's brands are found here. Photographic shops give excellent service, often developing and printing in 1 day.

Currency   See "Currency and Costs," above.

Customs   The government allows you (unless you're under 15 years of age) to bring in—duty-free—400 cigarettes or 100 cigars. If you're over 20, you are also allowed 1 liter of liquor, 1 liter of wine, gifts totaling 600 kronor ($108), and what the Swedes call a "reasonable" amount of perfume. There's no limit on the amount of currency you can bring in, but you can't take more than 6,000 kronor ($1,080) with you when you leave.

Dentists   For emergency dental services, ask your hotel or host for the location of the nearest dentist. Nearly all dentists in Sweden speak English.

Doctors Hotel staffs can usually refer you to a local doctor, nearly all of whom speak English. If you need emergency treatment, your hotel should also be able to direct you to the nearest facility. In an accident or injury away from the hotel, call the nearest police station.

Driving Rules See "Getting Around" in this chapter.

Drug Laws There are severe penalties in Sweden for the possession, use, purchase, sale, or manufacturing of proscribed drugs. Penalties are often based on quantity, but all that can vary, of course. Possession of what is deemed a small amount of drugs, either hard or soft, can lead to a heavy fine and deportation. Possession of a "large" amount of drugs can elicit a prison term ranging from 3 months to 15 years, depending on the circumstances and the presiding judge.

Drugstores Called an *apotek* in Sweden, drugstores are generally open Monday through Friday from 9am to 6pm and on Saturday from 9am to 1pm. In bigger cities one drugstore in every neighborhood stays open until 7pm. All pharmacies have a list of names and addresses of these *nattapotek,* as they are called, in their windows.

Electricity In Sweden, the electricity is 220 volts AC. To operate North American hairdryers and other electrical appliances, you will need an electrical converter and plugs that fit the two-pin round continental electrical outlets that are standard in Sweden. Converters can be bought at hardware stores. Before using any American-made appliance, always ask at your hotel desk.

Embassies and Consulates The **U.S. Embassy** is in Stockholm at Strandvägen 101, S-114 56 Stockholm (tel. 08/783-53-00). The **British Embassy** is at Skarpögatan 6-8, S-115 27 Stockholm (tel. 08/667-01-40); the **Canadian Embassy,** at Tegelbacken 4, S-101 23 Stockholm (tel. 08/23-79-20). The **Australian Embassy** is at Sergels Torg 12, S-103 27 Stockholm (tel. 613-29-00), and **New Zealand** does not maintain an embassy in Sweden. New Zealanders can go to the Australian Embassy.

Emergencies Call **90-000** from anywhere in Sweden if you need an ambulance, the police, or the fire department (*brandlarm*).

Etiquette Swedes generally dress up if invited to a private party or someone's home, unless the host specifically states blue jeans or casual wear. Always bring a gift—chocolates or flowers. When meeting a man or woman in Sweden, extend your hand. It is also customary in this rainy country to remove your shoes when entering a private home.

Hitchhiking Although officially discouraged by the government, hitchhiking is not illegal in Sweden. The more presentably dressed you are, of course, the better your chances. There is always a certain risk involved. Drivers usually speak English. Because of weather conditions, hitchhiking is definitely not recommended in colder months, as you can get stranded in a wilderness somewhere when a driver lets you off.

Language The national language is Swedish, a Germanic tongue, and there are many regional dialects. Some minority groups speak Norwegian and Finnish. But none of this need be a problem for you. English is required in school and is commonly spoken, even in the hinterlands, especially among young people.

Liquor Laws Most restaurants, pubs, and bars in Sweden are licensed to serve liquor, wine, and beer. Some places are licensed only for wine and beer. Purchases of wine, liquor, and export beer are available only through the government-controlled monopoly, **Systembolaget.** Branch stores, spread throughout the country, are usually open Monday through Friday from 9am to 6pm. The minimum age for buying alcoholic beverages in Sweden is 20.

Mail **Post offices** in Sweden are usually open Monday through Friday from 9am to 6pm and on Saturday from 9am to 1pm. To mail a postcard to North America costs 5.50 kronor ($1). Letters weighing not more than 20 grams (7/10 oz.) cost the same. **Postboxes** are easily recognizable by the sign of a yellow post horn on a blue background. You can also buy stamps in most tobacco shops and stationers.

Maps Many tourist offices supply routine maps of their districts free, and you can also contact one of the Swedish automobile clubs (see Section 3, "Getting Around," in this chapter). Bookstores throughout Sweden also sell detailed maps of the country and of such major cities as Gothenburg and Stockholm. The most reliable country maps are published by **Hallweg.** The best and most detailed city maps are those issued by **Falk,** which have a particularly good and properly indexed map to Stockholm.

Newspapers and Magazines In big cities such as Stockholm or Gothenburg, English-language newspapers, including the latest editions of the *International Herald Tribune* or *USA Today,* are usually for sale. American newspapers are not commonly available, but in Stockholm and Gothenburg you can purchase such London newspapers as *The Times*.

Pets My advice is to leave them at home. Sweden places nearly all animals, including cats and dogs, in quarantine before they're allowed inside the country.

Police In an emergency, dial **90-000** anywhere in the country.

Radio and TV In summer, Radio Stockholm broadcasts a special program for English-speaking tourists, "T-T-T-Tourist Time," on 103.3 MHz from 6 to 7pm daily. Swedish radio transmits P1 on 92.4 MHz (FM band) and P2 on 96.2 MHz in the Stockholm area. P3 is transmitted on 103.3 MHz (102.9 MHz in southern Stockholm), a wavelength shared by Radio Stockholm and local programs. Radio Stockholm also has a channel of its own on 98.3 MHz, Community Radio for special-interest organizations, transmitted on 88 MHz in the city district.

Restrooms The word for toilet in Sweden is *toalett,* and public facilities are found in department stores, rail and air terminals, and subway (T-bana) stations. They are also found along some of the major streets, parks, and squares. DAMER is for women and HERRAR is for men. Sometimes the sign is abbreviated to D or H, and often the toilet is marked WC. Most toilets are free, although a few have attendants to offer towels and soap. In an emergency you can also use the toilets in most hotels and restaurants, although in theory you're supposed to be a client.

Safety Whenever you're traveling in an unfamiliar city or country, stay alert. Be aware of your immediate surroundings. Wear a moneybelt and carry your camera or purse carefully. This will minimize the possibility of your becoming a victim of crime. Every society has its criminals. It is your responsibility to be aware and alert even in the most heavily touristed areas.

Shoe Repairs Shoe-repair shops rarely do their work while you wait. In summer, especially in July, many shops close, but the larger stores in the center of Stockholm have their own repair departments. If all you want is a new heel, look for something called *klackbar* in the stores or shoe departments of the department stores. They repair while you wait.

Taxes Sweden imposes a "value-added tax," called **MOMS,** of 25% on most goods and services, which makes an already-expensive country even more expensive. Visitors from the U.S. and Canada can beat the tax, however, by shopping in stores with the yellow-and-blue TAX-FREE SHOPPING sign. There are more than 13,000 such stores in Sweden. For purchases in one of these stores totaling more than 200 kronor ($36), you are entitled to a refund. You pay the tax along with the purchase price, but get a tax-refund voucher before you leave the shop. You'll get your MOMS back, minus a small service charge, at your point of departure from the country (wherever you go through Customs). You can't use your purchase in Sweden, and it must be taken out of the country within 1 month. For tax-free shopping information in Sweden, phone 0410/19-560.

Telephone, Telex, and Fax Information on these facilities in Stockholm will be found in "Fast Facts: Stockholm" in Chapter 24. The same rules apply to calling from public phones elsewhere in the country. Avoid placing long-distance calls from your hotel, where the charge may be doubled or tripled when you get your final bill.

Time Sweden is on central European time, that is, Greenwich mean time + 1 hour or eastern standard time + 6 hours. The clocks are put forward 1 hour in summer.

Tipping **Hotels** include a 15% service charge in your bill. **Restaurants,** depending on their class, add 13% to 15% to your tab. **Taxi drivers** are entitled to 8% of the fare, and cloakroom attendants usually expect 4 to 6 kronor (70¢ to $1.10).

Water The water is safe to drink all over Sweden.

Yellow Pages Sweden has Yellow Pages, but unless you speak the language, finding a service you need may be difficult. Swedish words are quite different in most cases from the English. If you didn't speak Swedish, how would you know to look up the nearest liquor store under "Systembolaget"? Also, the Swedish alphabet is different from English, using symbols English doesn't, including Ö and Å. The word *Åbogatan* doesn't appear after *Abborrvägen,* but follows *Zornvägen.*

INTRODUCING STOCKHOLM

Stockholm (pop. 1.4 million) is built on 14 islands on Lake Mälaren, marking the beginning of an archipelago of 24,000 islands, skerries, and islets that stretches all the way to the Baltic Sea. A city of bridges and islands, towers and steeples, cobblestone squares and broad boulevards, Renaissance splendor and steel-and-glass skyscrapers, Stockholm also has access to nature only a few minutes away. You can even go fishing in downtown waterways, thanks to a long-ago decree from Queen Christina.

Although the city was founded more than 7 centuries ago, it did not become the official capital of Sweden until the mid-17th century. Today it is the capital of a modern welfare state. The medieval walls of the Old Town (Gamla Stan) no longer remain, but the winding streets do, as they were spared the ravages of World War II.

1. ORIENTATION

ARRIVING

BY PLANE You'll arrive at **Arlanda International Airport,** about 28 miles north of Stockholm on the E4 highway. A long covered walkway connects the international and domestic terminals. For information on international flights, phone 08/780-39-10; for domestic flights, 08/780-33-51.

A bus outside the terminal building goes to the Central Station, Vasagatan 6-14, about an 80-minute trip, for 40 kronor ($7.20). SAS has a limousine service from the airport, operated on a share-the-ride basis. It will take you from the limousine-service desk in the arrivals hall at Arlanda to central Stockholm for 280 kronor ($50.40). To arrange a return trip to the airport, call 08/15-12-10 well in advance of your flight.

A taxi to or from the airport is expensive, costing from 300 kronor ($54).

BY TRAIN Trains arrive at Stockholm's **Central Station** at Vasagatan 6-14 (tel. 08/22-50-60), where connections can be made to Stockholm's subway, the T-bana. Follow the sign marked TUNNELBANA.

Virtually every part of Sweden can be reached by rail from Stockholm's Centralstationen.

BY BUS Buses also arrive at the Centralstationen on Vasagatan, and from here you can catch the T-bana (subway) to your final Stockholm destination. For bus

WHAT'S SPECIAL ABOUT STOCKHOLM

Great Neighborhoods
- ☐ Gamla Stan, the Old Town, next to the Royal Palace, a warren of antique buildings and alleys dating from 1252.
- ☐ Skansen, the folklore center with more than 150 historic buildings, a summer rendezvous for Stockholm.

Monuments
- ☐ The Royal Palace, containing the Swedish crown jewels and the Royal Armory.
- ☐ Drottningholm Palace, home of the royal family, with one of the world's few surviving 18th-century theaters.

Parks/Gardens
- ☐ Millesgården, on Lidingö Island, the waterside residence of sculptor Carl Milles, containing his rich art collection.
- ☐ Djurgården (Deer Park), a former royal hunting ground; contains Skansen and the *Vasa*, but magnificent in its own right.

Events/Festivals
- ☐ The Nobel Prize awards in December. It's by invitation only, but you can attend speeches by the prize winners.
- ☐ Walpurgis Night, when Stockholm wakes up after a sleepy winter; bonfires in public places.

Ace Attractions
- ☐ *Vasa*, the world's oldest restored warship, which capsized on its maiden voyage in 1628.

Museums
- ☐ The Nordic Museum, on Djurgården, a repository of Swedish cultural life since the 16th century.
- ☐ National Museum of Art, the Swedish state collection of paintings and sculpture.

---

information or reservations, check with the bus system's ticket offices at the station. (tel. 23-71-90). Offices within the station designated SJ RESEBYRÅ sell both rail and bus tickets.

BY CAR   Getting into Stockholm by car is relatively easy because the major national expressway highway from the south, the E4, joins with the national express highway E3 coming in from the west, and leads right into the heart of the city. Stay on the highway until you see the turnoff for Central Stockholm or Sentrum.

Parking in Stockholm is extremely difficult unless your hotel has a garage. Call your hotel in advance and find out what the parking situation is. *Most hotels do not have parking.* However, if you're driving into the city, you can often park long enough to unload your luggage, where a member of the hotel staff will then direct you to the nearest parking garage.

BY FERRY   Large ships, including the **Silja Line,** Kungsgatan 2 (tel. 22-21-40), and the **Viking Line,** Stureplan 8 (tel. 44-07-65), arrive at specially constructed berths jutting seaward from a point near the junction of Södermalm and Gamla Stan. This neighborhood is known as Stadsgården, and the avenue which runs along the adjacent waterfront is known as Stadsgårdshamnen. The nearest metro stop is Slussen, a 3-minute walk from the Old Town. Holders of the Eurailpass can ride the Silja ferries to Helsinki and Turku free with their passes if valid.

Other ferries arrive from Gotland (whose capital is Visby), but these boats dock at Nynäshamn, to the south of Stockholm. Take a Nynäshamn-bound bus from the Central Station in Stockholm or the SL commuter train to reach the ferry terminal at Nynäshamn.

IMPRESSIONS

A Roman driver will stop his car to admire a beautiful girl. A Stockholm driver will stop his car to admire a beautiful salmon.
—ANONYMOUS

TOURIST INFORMATION

The **Tourist Center,** Sweden House, Hamngatan 27, off Kungsträdgården (Box 7542), S-103 93 Stockholm (tel. 08/789-20-00), is open mid-June to the end of August, Monday through Friday from 8:30am to 6pm and on Saturday and Sunday from 8am to 5pm; the remainder of the year, Monday through Friday from 9am to 5pm and on Saturday and Sunday from 9am to 2pm. Maps and other free material are available.

For more detailed information about study or cultural life, go to the **Swedish Institute Documentation Center,** upstairs. Librarians will show you the many pamphlets available on anything you want to know. The center's automatic answering service (tel. 08/22-18-40) details the day's events in English.

In summer daily from 8am to 9pm, you can obtain information at **Hotellcentralen** (tel. 24-08-90), at the Central Station. Another tourist service offered in Stockholm is the English-language news broadcast daily in summer from 6 to 7pm on 103.3 MHz.

CITY LAYOUT
MAIN STREETS & ARTERIES

On the island of Norrmalm north of the Old Town are Stockholm's major streets, such as **Kungsgatan** (the main shopping street), **Birger Jarlsgatan,** and **Strandvägen** (leading to the Djurgården). **Stureplan,** which lies at the junction of the major avenues named Kungsgatan and Birger Jarlsgatan, is considered the commercial hub of the city.

About 4 blocks east of the Stureplan rises **Hötorget City,** a landmark of modern urban planning, that includes five 18-story skyscrapers. Its main, traffic-free artery is the Sergelgatan, a 3-block shopper's promenade which eventually leads to the modern sculptures in the center of the Sergels Torg.

About 9 blocks south of the Stureplan, at **Gustav Adolfs Torg,** lie both the Royal Dramatic Theater and the Royal Opera House.

A block east of the flaming torches of the Opera House is the verdant north-to-south stretch of **Kungstradgården,** part avenue, part public park, which serves as a popular gathering place for students and a resting perch for shoppers.

Three blocks to the southeast, on a famous promontory whose seafront also contains the landmark Grand Hotel lies the National Museum.

Most newcomers to Stockholm arrive either at the SAS Airport Bus Terminal, the Central Station, or Stockholm's Central (Public) Bus Station. Each of these lie in the heart of the city, on the harborfront, about 7 blocks due west of the Opera House.

Kungsholmen, King's Island, lies across a narrow canal from the rest of the city, a short walk west of the Central Station. It is visited chiefly by those seeking a tour of Stockholm's elegant Stadshuset (City Hall).

South of the island that contains Gamla Stan (Old Town), separated from it by a narrow but much-navigated stretch of water, is **Södermalm,** the southern district of Stockholm. Quieter and calmer than its northern counterpart, it is an important residential center with a distinctive flavor of its own.

To the east of Gamla Stan, on a large and forested island completely surrounded by the complicated waterways of Stockholm, is **Djurgården** (Deer Park). Considered the rustically unpopulated summer pleasure ground of Stockholm, and also the site of many of its most popular attractions, it contains the open-air museums of Skansen, the *Vasa* man-of-war, Gröna Lund's Tivoli, the Waldemarsudde estate of the "painting prince" Eugen, and the Nordic Museum.

FINDING AN ADDRESS   All even numbers are on one side of the street, and all odd numbers on the opposite side. Buildings are listed in numerical order, but will often have an A, B, or C after the Arabic number.

NEIGHBORHOODS IN BRIEF

Any city spread across 14 major islands in an archipelago has many neighborhoods, but those that need concern the average visitor lie in Central Stockholm.
Gamla Stan [the Old Town]   This is the very "cradle" of Stockholm, lying at the entrance of Lake Mälaren on the Baltic. Its oldest city walls date from the 13th century. The Old Town, along with the *Vasa,* is the biggest attraction of Stockholm. It has only a few hotels, but dozens of restaurants. Its major shopping mall is Västerlånggatan, but many little artisan galleries and antiques stores abound on its small lanes. Its main square, and the heart of the ancient city, is Stortorget.
Norrmalm   North of Gamla Stan, this large island is the cultural and commercial heart of modern Stockholm. Once it was a city suburb, but now it virtually *is* the city. Your arrival will probably be at Norrmalm's Central Station on Vasagatan. Its major pedestrian shopping street is Drottninggatan, starting at the bridge to the Old Town.
The most famous park in Stockholm, Kungsträdgården (King's Garden), is also in Norrmalm. In summer, this park is the major rendezvous point in the city. Norrmalm also embraces the important squares of Sergels Torg and Hötorget, the latter a modern shopping complex.
Vasastan   As Norrmalm pushed ever northward, the new district of Vasastan was created. It is split by a trio of main arteries, including St. Eriksgatan, Sveavägen, and Odengatan. The area around St. Eriksplan is now called "the Off Broadway of Stockholm" because it has so many theater choices. Increasingly, this district is filled with fashionable restaurants and bars and has become a popular place to live for young Stockholmers on the rise in such fields as journalism, television, and advertising.
Kungsholmen   Once known as "Grey Friars Farm," today Kungsholmen (King's Island) is an island to the west of Gamla Stan containing the City Hall. Established by King Charles XI in the 17th century as a zone for industry and artisans, it has now been gentrified. Its major arteries include Fleminggatan. Along Norrmälarstrand, old Baltic cutters tie up to the banks. Stockholm's newspapers' headquarters are at Marieberg on the southwestern tip of the island.
Södermalm   South of Gamla Stan, Södermalm, where Greta Garbo was born, is the largest and most populated district of Stockholm. Once synonymous with poverty, today this working-class district is growing more fashionable, especially with artists, writers, and young people. If you don't come here to stay in one of the moderately priced hotels or to dine in one of its restaurants, you may want to take the Katarina elevator for a good view of Stockholm and its harbor.
Östermalm   In central Stockholm, east of the main artery, Birger Jarlsgatan, is Östermalm. In the Middle Ages the royal family used to keep their horses, and even armies, here. Today it is the site of the Army Museum. There are wide, straight streets, and also one of the city's biggest parks, Humlegården, dating from the 17th century.
Djurgården   To the east of Gamla Stan, the Old Town, is Djurgården (Deer Park), a lake-encircled forested island that is the summer pleasure ground of

---

IMPRESSIONS

It [Stockholm] is not a city at all. It is ridiculous of it to think of itself as a city. It is
simply a rather large village, set in the middle of some forests and some lakes.
You wonder what it thinks it is doing there, looking so important.
—INGMAR BERGMAN, IN AN INTERVIEW WITH JAMES BALDWIN, 1960

Stockholm. Here you can visit the open-air folk museums of Skansen, the *Vasa* man-of-war, Gröna Lund's Tivoli (Stockholm's own version of the Tivoli), the Waldemarsudde estate and gardens of the "painting prince" Eugen, and the Nordic Museum. The fastest way there is over the bridge at Strandvägen/Narvavägen.

MAPS

Free maps of Stockholm are available at the tourist office, but if you want to explore the narrow old streets of Gamla Stan, you will need a more detailed map. The best is published by **Falk,** a pocket-size map with a street index that can be opened and folded like a wallet. It is sold at most newsstands in central Stockholm and at major bookstores, including **Nya Akademibokhandeln,** Mäster Samuelsgatan 32 (tel. 21-15-90).

2. GETTING AROUND

BY PUBLIC TRANSPORTATION

You can travel throughout all of Stockholm county by bus, local train, the underground (T-bana), and trams, going from Singo in the north to Nynäshamn in the south. Routes are divided into zones, and one ticket is valid for all types of public transport in the same zone within 1 hour of when the ticket is stamped.

REGULAR FARES   The basic fare for public transport (which in Stockholm means either underground, tram/streetcar, or bus) is with tickets purchased from the person in the toll booth on the subway platform, not from a vending machine. Each ticket costs 6 kronor ($1.10), and to travel three stops requires one ticket. To travel within most of urban Stockholm, all the way to the borders of the inner city, requires only two tickets. The maximum ride, to the outermost suburbs, requires four tickets. You can transfer (or double back and return to your starting point) within 1 hour of your departure for free. Fares are doubled after midnight.

SPECIAL DISCOUNT TICKETS   Senior citizens and young people under 18 are granted almost 50% reductions on all Stockholm public transportation.

Your best transportation bet is to purchase a tourist season ticket. A 1-day card, costing 30 kronor ($5.40), is valid for 24 hours of unlimited travel by T-bana, bus, and commuter train within Stockholm. It also includes passage on the ferry to Djurgården. Most visitors will want the 3-day card for 105 kronor ($18.90), valid for 72 hours in both Stockholm and the county that surrounds it. The 3-day card is also valid for admission to Skansen, Kaknåstornet, and Gröna Lund. Children under 16 pay half price, and two children up to 7 years of age can travel free.

Tickets are offered at tourist-information offices, in subway stations, and at most news vendors.

The **Stockholmskortet (Stockholm Card)** is a personal discount card that allows unlimited free travel by bus, subway, and local trains throughout the city and county of Stockholm (except on airport buses). You can also take a free sightseeing tour with Turistlinjen, which allows you to get on and off as often as you want to, looking at the sights according to your own schedule. A free map and a guide booklet are given visitors who do not speak Swedish. These tours are available daily June to August; on Saturday and Sunday in April, May, and September to December; and on Sunday, January to March. The card also allows you to take a boat trip to the Royal Palace of Drottningholm for half price. Free admission to 50 attractions is included in the package.

You can purchase the card at several places in the city, including the Tourist Centre in the Sweden House, Hotellcentralen, the Central Station, the tourist-information desk in City Hall (in summer), the Kaknäs TV tower, SL-Center Sergels Torg (subway entrance level), and Pressbyrån newsstands. The cards are stamped with the date and time at the first point of usage. A 24-hour card costs 135 kronor ($24.30) for adults.

For a 48-hour card, the cost is 270 kronor ($48.60). For 3 days, it's 405 kronor ($72.90).

BY T-BANA [SUBWAY]   Before entering the subway, passengers tell the ticket seller the destination, then purchase tickets. Subway entrances are marked with a blue "T" on a white background. For information about schedules, routes, and fares, phone 600-10-00.

BY BUS   Where the subway leaves off, the bus begins. Therefore, if a subway connection doesn't conveniently cover a particular area of Stockholm, a bus will fill the need. The two systems have been coordinated to complement each other. Many visitors use a bus to reach Djurgården (although you can walk there), as the T-bana doesn't go there. For a list of bus routes, purchase the *SL Stockholmskartan,* which is sold at the tourist center at Sweden House, Hamngatan 27, off Kungsträdgården (tel. 789-20-00).

BY CAR

If you're driving around the Swedish capital, you will find several parking garages in the city center as well as on the outskirts. In general, you can park at marked spaces Monday through Friday from 8am to 6pm. Exceptions or rules for specific areas are posted at signs in the area. At Djurgården, parking is always prohibited, and from April to mid-September it's closed to traffic Friday through Sunday.

BY TAXI

Taxis are few in number and expensive—in fact, the most expensive in the world. A short ride can easily come to 75 kronor ($13.50). Those that display the sign LEDIG may be hailed, or you can order one by phone (tel. 15-00-00; 15-04-00 for advance booking), but it will cost 25 kronor ($4.50) extra. If you're near a cab rank, it will be cheaper to approach the first cab in the line and get in.

BY FERRY

Ferries from Skeppsbron in Gamla Stan (near the bridge to Södermalm) will take you to Djurgården if you don't want to go by bus or walk. They leave every 20 minutes Monday through Saturday, and about every 15 minutes on Sunday, from 9am to 6pm, charging 12 kronor ($2.20) for adults or 6 kronor ($1.10) for senior citizens and young people 7 to 18 years old.

BY BICYCLE

The best place to go cycling is on Djurgården. You can rent bicycles from **Skepp o Hoj,** Djurgårdsbron (tel. 660-57-57), for about 90 kronor ($16.20) per day. It is open daily from 9am to 9pm April through September.

FAST STOCKHOLM

American Express   American Express is at Birger Jarlsgatan 1 (tel. 14-39-81), open in July and August, Monday through Friday from 9am to 5pm and on Saturday from 10am to 1pm; September to June, Monday through Friday from 9am to 5pm.

Area Code   The telephone area code for Stockholm is **08.**

Babysitters   Stockholm hotels maintain lists of competent women who babysit. Nearly all of them speak English. There is no official agency; it's rather a "word of mouth" thing. The average rate for one child is 80 kronor ($14.40) per hour; for two or three children, the charge goes up to 100 kronor ($18) per hour.

Bookstores   For a good selection of English-language books, including maps and touring guides, try **Nya Akademibokhandeln,** Mäster Samuelsgatan 32 (tel.

21-15-90), open Monday through Friday from 9:30am to 6pm and on Saturday from 10am to 2pm.

Car Rentals See "Getting Around" in Chapter 23. In Stockholm, some of the big car-rental companies include **Avis,** Sveavägen 61 (tel. 34-99-10); **Hertz,** Vasagatan 24 (tel. 24-07-20); and **Europcar,** Birger Jarlsgatan 59 (tel. 23-10-70).

Currency Exchange There is a currency-exchange office, **Forex,** at the Central Station (tel. 11-67-34), open daily from 8am to 9pm. It's fully authorized by both the Bank of Sweden and the Swedish tourist authorities, gives some of the best exchange rates in town, and takes some of the lowest commissions for the cashing of traveler's checks. There's another branch, with less extended hours and no weekend hours, in the same building near the Arrivals Hall of the bus station.

Dentist Emergency dental treatment is offered at **Sct. Eriks Hospital,** Fleminggatan 22 (tel. 54-11-17), open daily from 8am to 7pm. Only urgent cases are dealt with after 7pm. After 9pm, consult the emergency dentist on duty (tel. 44-92-00).

Doctors If you need emergency medical care, check with **Medical Care Information** (tel. 44-92-00). There is also a private clinic, **Citvakuten,** at Hollåndargatan 3 (tel. 11-71-77).

Drugstores You'll find a pharmacy open 24 hours a day in Stockholm, **C.W. Scheele,** Klarabergsgatan 64 (tel. 24-82-80).

Embassies and Consulates The **U.S. Embassy** is as Strandvägen 101 (tel. 783-53-00); the **British Embassy,** at Skarpögatan 6-8 (tel. 667-01-40); the **Canadian Embassy,** at Tegelbacken 4 (tel. 23-79-20); and the **Australian Embassy** is at Sergels Torg 12 (tel. 613-29-00). **New Zealand** does not maintain an embassy in Sweden. New Zealanders should inquire at the Australian Embassy.

Emergencies Call **90-000** for the police, ambulance service, or the fire department. For car towing, call **Larmtjänst** (tel. 020/91-00-40).

Eyeglasses The **Nordiska Kompaniet,** Hamngatan 18-20 (tel. 762-80-00), one of the leading department stores of Stockholm, has a registered optician on duty at its ground-floor Service Center. The optician carries out sight tests, stocks a large selection of frames, and makes emergency repairs.

Hairdressers and Barbers Goran Peterson Hair Team, Regeringsgatan 15 (tel. 20-06-40), is one of Stockholm's most visible hairstyling centers. Located within a massive arcade near T-bana Centralen, it employs at least 10 hairstylists plus a mini-battalion of shampooers and other staff. A woman's haircut costs 310 kronor ($55.80), a woman's haircut and set costs 345 kronor ($62.10), and a man's haircut costs 280 kronor ($50.40).

Hospitals Call **Medical Care Information** at 44-92-00, and an English-speaking operator will inform you of the hospital closest to you.

Laundry and Dry Cleaning City Kemtvatt, Drottningsholmsvägen 9 (tel. 654-95-34), does dry cleaning and also laundry by the kilo for same-day delivery if it's delivered to them before 10am. Hours are Monday through Saturday from 7am to 6pm. Note that the old-fashioned system of coin-operated self-service laundries is outmoded in Sweden, and isn't very widespread anymore. The cost for laundry is 45 kronor ($8.10) per kilo (2.2 lb.) of wash. Clothes are neatly folded for you as part of the price.

Libraries The **Stockholms Stadsbibliotek,** Sveavägen 73 (tel. 23-66-00), is the biggest municipal library in Sweden, with 2.4 million books (many in English) and audiovisual aids. It also subscribes to 1,500 newspapers and periodicals (many in English). Hours are Monday through Thursday from 10am to 8:30pm, Friday from 10am to 6pm, and Saturday and Sunday from noon to 4pm.

Lost Property If you've lost something on the train, go to the Lost and Found Office in the Central Station, lower concourse (tel. 762-20-00). The police also have such an office at the police station at Tjårhovsgatan 21 (tel. 769-30-75). The Stockholm Transit Company (SL) keeps its recovered articles at the Rådmansgatan T-bana station (tel. 736-07-08), and Vaxholmsbolaget has one at Nybrokajen 2 (tel. 14-09-60, ext. 142).

Luggage Storage and Lockers Facilities are available at the Central Station on Vasagatan, lower concourse (tel. 762-25-50). Lockers can also be rented at the ferry stations at Värtan and Tegelvikshamnen, at the Viking Line's terminal, and at the Central Station.

Photographic Needs   Stockholm abounds with photo shops. One of the most centrally located is **Hasselblads Foto Video**, Sveavägen 71 (tel. 31-97-99).

Police   Call **90-000** in an emergency.

Post Office   The main post office is at Vasagatan 28-34 (tel. 781-20-00), open Monday through Friday from 8am to 8pm and on Saturday from 9am to 3pm. General delivery (post restante) pickups can be made here.

Radio and TV   The country has two TV channels and three national radio stations, plus a local station for Stockholm, broadcasting on 103.3 MHz (FM). Radio Stockholm broadcasts the news direct from the BBC, and in summer broadcasts a special program for English-speaking tourists, "T-T-T-Tourist Time," from 6 to 7pm daily. Many hotels are equipped to receive English-language TV programs broadcast from England, and many of the more expensive hotels have 24-hour CNN news broadcasts in English.

Religious Services   There are some 160 Lutheran churches in the Swedish capital. Protestant services are held at **St. Peter and St. Sigfrid Anglican Church**, Strandvägen 76 (tel. 663-82-48), and at the **United Christian Congregation**, Santa Clara Church, Kyrkogata 8 (tel. 723-30-29). A Roman Catholic cathedral, **Domkyrkan**, is at Folkungagatan 46 (tel. 40-00-82), and **Santa Eugenia Church** is at Kungsträdgårdsgatan 12 (tel. 10-00-70). Jewish worshipers can attend the **Great Synagogue** (Conservative), Wahrendorffsgatan 3A (tel. 23-51-50), or **Adas Jisroel** (Orthodox), St. Paulsgatan 13 (tel. 44-19-95).

Restrooms   Public facilities are found in the Central Station, all subway stations, and department stores, as well as along some of the major streets, parks, and squares. In an emergency you can also use the toilets in most hotels and restaurants, although in theory you're supposed to be a client.

Shoe Repair   In the basement of **Nordiska Kompaniet**, Hamngatan 18-20 (tel. 762-80-00), one of the leading department stores of Stockholm, there is a shoe-repair place which also repairs, if possible, broken luggage.

Taxis   See "Getting Around" in this chapter.

Telephone, Telex, and Fax   The **Telecenter**, open Monday through Saturday from 8am to midnight, is at Skeppsbron 2 (tel. 780-78-90), in the Old Town behind the Royal Palace. The office at the Central Station (tel. 10-64-39) is open Monday through Friday from 8am to 8pm and on Saturday from 9am to 10pm. For worldwide operator information, dial 24-28-00. Instructions in English are posted in public phone boxes, which you find on street corners. Pay phones are operated by two 1-krona (18¢) coins. You can send a telegram by phoning 00-21 anytime, or from offices bearing the sign TELE or TELEBUTIK, as well as from some post offices. To send a telex or fax, go to the Telecenter.

Transit Information   For information on all services, including buses and subways (Tunnelbana), even suburban trains (*pendeltåg*), call 23-60-00. Or else visit the **SL Center**, on the lower level of Sergels Torg. It provides information about transportation and also sells a map of the city's system, as well as tickets and special discount passes. Open in summer Monday through Thursday from 9am to 6pm, on Friday from 9am to 5:30pm, on Saturday from 9am to 4pm, and on Sunday from 10am to 3pm; the rest of the year, open only Monday through Friday.

3. NETWORKS & RESOURCES

FOR STUDENTS   Near Sweden House, at Sergels Torg in Stockholm, is the **Kulturhuset** (Culture House; tel. 700-01-00), a favorite gathering place for young people. You can sometimes enjoy live performances by local talent and international entertainers, view exhibitions (of art, craft and design, etc.), read books and newspapers in several languages, listen to records, watch TV, or eat at the snack bar.

Sweden has four major university centers—Stockholm, Gothenburg, Uppsala, and Lund, near Malmö—and each of these maintains a special **Student Reception Service** for visiting foreign students. Inquire about student accommodations, restaurants, a schedule of current events, discos, or whatever you need to know.

The student travel service, **SFS Resebyrå,** Kungsgatan 4 (tel. 23-45-15), books student flights and has information about low-cost youth fares on trains. It is open Monday through Friday from 10am to 5:30pm.

You can also visit the **Stockholms Universitets Studentkår** (Student Center), Universitetet (tel. 16-20-60), if you are in Stockholm between September and May (it's closed from June to August for summer vacation). The center is in the Allhuset, and is a beehive of activity, with a travel agent for students and places to dine, including the university restaurant, Lantis, where you can eat for about 40 kronor ($7.20). It is open Monday through Thursday from 11am to 6pm and on Friday from 11am to 2pm. T-bana: Universitetet.

FOR GAY MEN & LESBIANS Sweden is not as stridently liberal as Denmark, where gay marriages are accorded the same rights as heterosexual marriages, but it has enacted an antidiscrimination law and there are many gay and lesbian organizations operating in Stockholm that welcome visitors from abroad.

Foremost among these is the **RFSL** (Federation for Gay and Lesbian Rights), Sveavägen 57 (tel. 736-02-12), open Monday through Friday from 9am to 5pm. Established in 1950, its headquarters are located on the upper floors of the biggest gay nightlife center in Stockholm (see "Evening Entertainment" in Chapter 25). Meetings are held weekly—a Wednesday 3pm meeting for gay men over 60 and a twice-monthly meeting of "Golden Ladies" (yes, they use the English expression) for lesbians over 50, plus a Monday-night youth session for ages 18 to 21. They also operate a **Gay Switchboard** (tel. 24-74-65), staffed mostly with volunteers; call daily from 8 to 11pm for information. The center also runs the Rosa Rummet Bookstore, on the same premises, a nonprofit bookstore devoted to gay literature and information; open Monday through Friday from 6 to 7pm and on Saturday and Sunday from 3 to 8pm.

The RFSL distributes information on women's gay life, but a splinter group is known as **Lesbisk Nul** (Lesbians Now), Götgatan 83 (tel. 41-86-16), which also dispenses information about lesbian-related activites.

The city also has a **Stockholm Gay Radio,** broadcasting at 88 MHz (FM) on Tuesday and Sunday at 7:30pm. Call 736-02-16 for information. The broadcast is in Swedish, but at least you can enjoy the music.

FOR WOMEN Go to **Kvinnohuset,** Snickarbacken 10 (tel. 10-08-00), which is the major meeting place for feminists in Stockholm. Everybody speaks English, and foreign women are welcome. The women's center also operates a rape-crisis center.

FOR SENIORS Go to **Sweden House,** center of tourist information, Hamngatan 27, off Kungsträdgården (tel. 789-20-00), and ask about special discounts for senior citizens in Stockholm. These could take the form of reduced transportation costs or discount admission to museums and certain attractions.

4. ACCOMMODATIONS

Reservations are advised in summer just to be on the safe side. In most cases a service charge, ranging from 10% to 15% is added to the bill, plus the inevitable 25% MOMS (value-added tax).

Most of the medium-priced hotels are on the island of Norrmalm, north of the Old Town. Most of the least expensive lodgings are near the Central Station. There are comparably priced inexpensive accommodations within 10 to 20 minutes of the city, easily reached by subway, streetcar, or bus. I have a few selections in the Old Town, but these choices are limited and more expensive.

BOOKING SERVICES **Hotellcentralen,** Vasagatan (tel. 24-08-80), on the lower level of the Central Station, is the city's official housing bureau, and arranges accommodations in hotels, pensions (boardinghouses), hospices, and youth hostels— but not in private homes. There is a 20-krona ($3.60) service fee. It's open from May to the end of August, daily from 8am to 9pm; from September to the end of April, Monday through Friday from 8am to 5pm. Credit cards are accepted.

The least expensive way to live in Stockholm is in a private home. The best way to get booked into a private home is by going to the **Hotell Tjänst AB,** Vasagatan 15-17 (tel. 08/10-44-37 or 10-44-57). As you leave the Central Station, turn left on Vasagatan and proceed to this address, which is on the fourth floor of an elderly building. Here you will find Mr. Gustavsson and his staff. English is spoken. You'll be booked into a private room without breakfast for 220 kronor ($39.60) in a single or 330 kronor ($59.40) in a double, including the booking fee. From June 15 through August 15, this agency can also book you into Stockholm's major hotels at a big discount.

Mr. Gustavsson asks that you avail yourself of these bargains only upon your arrival in Stockholm. He is confident of booking you into a room, because of his long "secret" list of private addresses, and doesn't answer letters requesting reservations. Hotel Tjänst is open Monday through Friday from 9am to noon and 1 to 5pm. Advance booking is rarely accepted; however, if you should be arriving in Stockholm on a weekend when the office is closed, call or fax the office (fax is 08/21-37-16), and maybe Mr. Gustavsson will bend the rules.

A NOTE ON PRICES By the standards of many cities in the United States or Canada, hotels in Stockholm are very expensive indeed, even the so-called moderate ones.

It is hard to classify many Stockholm hotels into price brackets, because some moderately priced hotels, for example, might also have a few very expensive rooms. **Very Expensive** indicates hotels charging from 2,400 kronor ($432) for a double room, although some rooms in these hotels might be several hundred kronor cheaper than that. **Expensive** hotels, in general, ask about 1,550 to 2,200 kronor ($279 to $396) for a double room, while most **Moderate** hotels charge from 1,250 to 1,500 kronor ($225 to $270) for a double. **Inexpensive** hotels are in the 795 to 1,200 kronor ($143.10 to $216) price range. Under 700 kronor ($126) is **Budget.**

Before these high prices make you cancel your trip, read on. Dozens of hotels in Stockholm offer reduced rates on weekends all year and daily from June 18 to August 19. For further information, ask travel agencies or the tourist center (see above).

IN THE CENTER
VERY EXPENSIVE

SAS STRAND HOTEL, Nybrokajen 9, S-103 27 Stockholm. Tel. 08/678-70-00, or toll free 800/221-23-50 in the U.S. Fax 08/611-2436. 138 rms (all with bath), 18 suites. A/C MINIBAR TV TEL **T-bana:** Östermalmstorg.

$ **Rates** (including breakfast): July 1–Aug 15 and Fri–Sat year-round, 790 kronor ($142.20) single; 1,090 kronor ($196.20) double. Mon–Thurs the rest of the year, 1,550–2,600 kronor ($279–$468) single; 1,945–2,600 kronor ($350.10–$468) double. From 3,000 kronor ($540) suite. AE, DC, MC, V.

In the center of Stockholm, near the Royal Palace and Gamla Stan, this hotel stands on the waterfront. It dates from 1912, but in the early 1980s was completely renovated and modernized. It still has tradition, but is filled with modern services and amenities. Bedrooms are furnished in light pastels and contain such appliances as hairdryers and trouser presses. Part of the hotel, the Royal Club, has more facilities, better rooms, and many extras such as your own electronic safe and your own ice bucket. Even your bathrobe and slippers are laid out for you.

Dining/Entertainment: Strand's Piazza is a glass-roofed winter garden serving full meals, and the adjoining Strand's Bar is a popular meeting place. The specialty restaurant is Maritim, offering a buffet of fresh fish and shellfish. You can dance the night away in the hotel's disco.

Services: 24-hour room service, business service center, SAS airline check-in in lobby.

Facilities: Health club with swimming pool.

EXPENSIVE

BERNS' HOTEL, Näckströmsgatan 8, S-111 47 Stockholm. Tel. 08/614-07-00. Fax 08/611-51-75. 63 rms (all with bath), 3 suites. A/C MINIBAR TV TEL **T-bana:** Östermalmstorg.

$ **Rates** (including breakfast): 1,375–1,875 kronor ($247.50–$337.50) single; 1,575–2,075 kronor ($283.50–$373.50) double; from 2,800 kronor ($504) suite. AE, DC, MC, V.

One of the gems of Stockholm, this newly restored hotel, part of a drinking-and-dining complex recommended separately, is near Nybroplan. The hotel has been beautifully furnished, with well-designed and amenity-filled bedrooms that include a video and CD player in every room. Bathrooms are all in Italian marble. There is a wide variety of rooms, the most spectacular of which is the tower suite, with the famous Berns clock, a 19th-century clock tower over Stockholm's most famous nightclub, as one of its windows. This suite has its own special sauna. Guests sit out in summer enjoying the view from the hotel's roof terrace. Breakfast is taken in the Red Room, once the haunt of dramatist August Strindberg.

GRAND HOTEL, Södra Blaisieholmshamnen 8, S-103 27 Stockholm. Tel. 08/717-00-20. Fax 08/717-95-31. 321 rms (all with bath), 19 suites. MINIBAR TV TEL **Tram:** 10, 11. **Bus:** 46, 55, 62, 76. **T-bana:** Kungstädgården.

$ **Rates** (including breakfast): Fri–Sun and June 26–Aug 9, 750 kronor ($135) single; 1,110 kronor ($199.80) double. Mon–Thurs the rest of the year, 1,390 kronor ($250.20) single; 2,190 kronor ($394.20) double. Year-round, from 2,190 kronor ($394.20) suite. AE, DC, MC, V. **Parking:** 200 kronor ($36).

⭐ Opposite the Royal Palace, this hotel is grand in name and deed, the finest in Sweden. It has been the choice of everybody from Sarah Bernhardt to Nobel Prize winners, a bastion of elite hospitality. Built in 1874, it has been continuously renovated, but its old-world style has always been maintained. Bedrooms come in all shapes and sizes, but each is elegantly appointed with traditional styling. Some contain air conditioning. Pale-blue fabrics and light woods predominate. The bathrooms are decorated with Italian marble and tiles and have heated floors. The hotel's ballroom is an exact copy of the Hall of Mirrors of Louis XIV at Versailles.

Dining/Entertainment: The Grand Veranda specializes in traditional food served from a buffet, and the Franska Matsalen is the gourmet restaurant of the hotel. The CadierBar is one of the most sophisticated rendezvous spots in Stockholm.

Services: Shoeshine service, American Airlines check-in desk, valet parking, limousine service, 24-hour room service, business service center, same-day laundry and dry cleaning, ticket-securing concierge, house doctor.

Facilities: Beauty salon, sauna, hairstylist, drugstore, newsstand, florist, gift shop.

SAS ROYAL VIKING HOTEL, Vasagatan 1, S-101 23 Stockholm. Tel. 08/14-10-00, or toll free 800/221-2350 in the U.S. Fax 08/14-10-00. 336 rms (all with bath), 4 suites. A/C MINIBAR TV TEL **T-bana:** Central Station.

$ **Rates** (including breakfast): June 21–Aug 11 and Fri–Sat year-round, 850 kronor ($153) single; 990 kronor ($178.20) double. Sun–Thurs the rest of the year, 1,390–1,940 kronor ($250.20–$349.20) single; 1,590–2,140 kronor ($286.20–$385.20) double. From 4,000 kronor ($720) suite. AE, DC, MC, V. **Parking:** 200 kronor ($36).

Near the Central Station, this airline-affiliated hotel stands next door to the Stockholm World Trade Center. Its Royal Atrium, the heart of the hotel, with its soaring ceiling, offers big buffets meals in light, airy surroundings. The bedrooms are superbly equipped and furnished in light pastels, with stylized modern furniture and such amenities as hairdryers and trouser presses. Some rooms are duplex suites with their own bar, stereo system, video, sauna with bathrobe and slippers, Jacuzzi, and terrace. The Royal Club is the executive "hotel within the hotel," where you are spoiled with your own check-in, safe deposits, and lots of extras.

Dining/Entertainment: The Royal Atrium offers breakfast and lunch, and the Piano Lounge serves draft beer and exotic drinks. The Délice is a bistro, offering fresh vegetable dishes and country fare. The Royal Room is the hotel's specialty restaurant, its food prepared, when possible, with Swedish-grown produce. It offers French flair and excellent wines. Take the glass elevator to the ninth floor for the hotel's skybar, with a panoramic view of the Old Town.

Services: Complimentary refreshments, SAS EuroClass check-ins, express laundry, office away from home, room service.

Facilities: Viking pool club, with saunas, Jacuzzi, and a temperature-controlled pool with underwater music.

SERGEL PLAZA, Brunkebergstorg 9, S-103 27 Stockholm. Tel. 08/22-66-00, or toll free 800/THE-OMNI in the U.S. Fax 08/21-50-70. 406 rms (all with bath), 12 suites. A/C TV TEL **T-bana:** Central Station. **Bus:** 47, 52, 69.

$ Rates (including breakfast): Fri–Sat and June 19–Aug 16, 895 kronor ($161.10) single; 1,040 kronor ($187.20) double. Sun–Thurs 1,195 kronor ($215.10) single; 1,550–1,975 kronor ($279–$355.50) double. From 2,350 kronor ($423) suite. AE, DC, MC, V. **Parking:** 150 kronor ($27).

Originally designed as living quarters for members of the Swedish parliament in Stockholm, this hotel, built in 1984 at the entrance to Drottninggatan, the main shopping street, has been improved to such an extent that today it is one of the city's leading hotels. The elegant decor includes 18th-century artwork and antiques. It is a bastion of comfort and good taste, as reflected by the beautifully decorated bedrooms, each furnished with modern and traditional styling in light pastels and "Nordic sky" colors. The hotel has a special executive floor.

Dining/Entertainment: The Anna Rella, the gourmet restaurant, offers both Swedish and international specialties. There is also a lobby and piano bar.

Services: 24-hour room service, concierge, laundry, babysitting.

Facilities: Hair- and beauty-care facilities, saunas, solariums, Jacuzzis.

SHERATON STOCKHOLM & TOWERS, Tegelbacken 6, S-101 23 Stockholm. Tel. 08/14-16-00. Fax 08/21-70-26. 445 rms (all with bath), 15 suites. A/C MINIBAR TV TEL **T-bana:** Central Station.

$ Rates (including breakfast): June 19–Aug 16 and Fri–Sat year-round, 925 kronor ($166.50) single; 1,000 kronor ($180) double. Sun–Thurs 1,280–1,950 kronor ($230.40–$351) single; 1,480–2,150 kronor ($266.40–$387) double. From 3,250 kronor ($585) suite. AE, DC, MC, V. **Parking:** 170 kronor ($30.60).

Overlooking Gamla Stan, this hotel offers Stockholm's largest guest rooms, all of which have recently been renovated and are decorated in Scandinavian pastels. Seven rooms are equipped for the handicapped. The most luxurious accommodations are on the Towers floor.

Dining/Entertainment: The Sheraton Première Restaurant specializes in game, fish, meats, and fresh vegetables and fruits. Snacks or quick meals are served at Le Bistro. The hotel has a casino and the Lobby Lounge features live entertainment nightly. Die Ecke is a German Bierstube serving traditional Bavarian dishes.

Services: Laundry and valet service, secretarial assistance, same-day laundry and dry cleaning, 24-hour room service, wheelchairs upon request, physician on call.

Facilities: Sauna.

MODERATE

CASTLE HOTEL, Riddargatan 14, S-114 35 Stockholm. Tel. 08/679-57-00. Fax 08/611-20-22. 44 rms (all with bath), 4 suites. MINIBAR TV TEL **T-bana:** Östermalmstorg.

$ Rates (including breakfast): Early June–late Aug and Fri–Sun year-round, 600

STOCKHOLM ACCOMMODATIONS

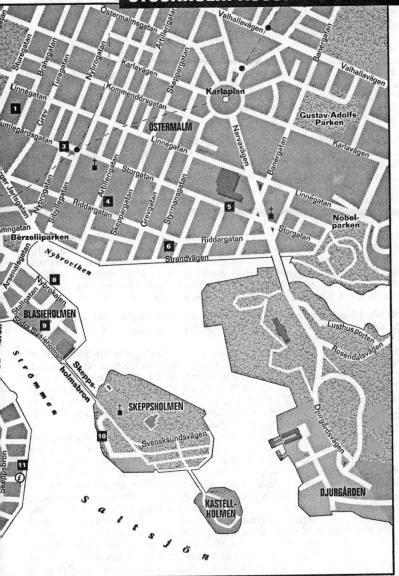

Subway — — — — Church ✝ Post Office ⊠ Information ⊙

Lord Nelson Hotel **14**
Mornington Hotel **3**
Sara Hotel Reisen **11**
SAS Royal Viking **18**
SAS Strand Hotel **8**
Sergel Plaza Hotel **17**

Sheraton Stockholm
  & Towers **16**
Stockholm Plaza **2**
Hotel Tegnérlunden **21**
Victory Hotel **13**
Wellington Hotel **5**

kronor ($108) single; 700 kronor ($126) double; from 800 kronor ($144) suite. Sun–Thurs the rest of the year, 990 kronor ($178.20) single; 1,300–1,500 kronor ($234–$270) double; from 1,600 kronor ($288) suite. AE, DC, MC, V.

A short walk east of the center in an expensive neighborhood, this house was originally built in 1920 as a private apartment house. In the late 1980s it was outfitted as a hotel. It has a gray marble floor in the lobby, and the bedrooms are decorated in Swedish colors of apple green and bitter blue, with gilded accents and art deco accessories to match the original construction of the building. You stock your own minibar, as they come empty. Several times a week, the hotel presents jazz evenings in a room that serves as a simple lunch-only restaurant, serving meals daily from 11am to 2pm.

ESPLANADE HOTEL, Strandvägen 7A, S-114 56 Stockholm. Tel. 08/ 663-07-40. Fax 08/662-59-92. 33 rms (29 with bath), 2 junior suites. TV TEL **T-bana:** Östermalmstorg. **Bus:** 47.

$ **Rates** (including breakfast): June 29–Aug 10 and Fri–Sat year-round, 550–650 kronor ($99–$117) single; 700–850 kronor ($126–$153) double; from 850 kronor ($153) suite. Mon–Thurs 1,175–1,275 kronor ($211.50–$229.50) single, 1,400–1,600 kronor ($252–$288) double; from 1,600 kronor ($288) suite. AE, DC, MC, V. **Closed:** Dec 25–Jan 2.

This informal hotel, next to the more expensive Diplomat, attracts diplomats from the nearby embassies and others who like its atmosphere. Originally constructed in 1910, it was transformed into a family-style hotel in 1954. Many rooms contain minibars, and each is furnished in an old-fashioned way. Four rooms have a water view, and the English lounge has a balcony with a view of the Djurgården. The junior suites cost as much as the most expensive doubles. Only breakfast is served.

KARELIA, Birger Jarlsgatan 35, S-111 45 Stockholm. Tel. 08/24-76- 60. Fax 08/24-15-11. 102 rms (all with bath), 9 suites. TV TEL **T-bana:** Östermalmstorg. **Bus:** 46.

$ **Rates** (including breakfast): Rooms, summer and Fri–Sun year-round, 490 kronor ($88.20) single, 700 kronor ($126) double, from 800 kronor ($144) suite; Mon–Thurs the rest of the year, 1,080 kronor ($194.40) single, 1,300 kronor ($234) double, from 1,500 kronor ($270) suite. Cabins, summer and Fri–Sun year-round, 375 kronor ($67.50) single, 525 kronor ($94.50) double; Mon–Thurs the rest of the year, 725 kronor ($130.50) single, 900 kronor ($162) double. AE, DC, MC, V. **Parking:** 130 kronor ($23.40). **Closed:** Dec 24–27.

(S) The Karelia is an elegant old-world hostelry on a busy commercial street, with an impressive turn-of-the-century facade and copper-capped tower. You'll enter under a large Romanesque arch and climb a decorative double staircase. The bedrooms are clean and well designed. The basement-level "cabins," as they're called, are bargains and immensely popular. They are small and have no windows, but are comfortable, well ventilated, and well maintained. Many Swedish and Finnish visitors request them for their good value. The hotel has a small-stakes casino, a swimming pool, and three saunas, which have been used by everybody from the king of Sweden to the late prime minister, Olof Palme. There are two restaurants: one enlivened by Finnish dancing nearly every night and the other serving Russian cuisine (see "Dining" in this chapter). Named after a province of Finland that was annexed by the Soviet Union after World War II, the hotel's bars and restaurants are a crowded and popular focal point for the Finnish community of Stockholm.

KUNG CARL, Birger Jarlsgatan 23, S-111 45 Stockholm. Tel. 08/611- 31-10. Fax 08/611-09-18. 87 rms (all with bath). MINIBAR TV TEL **T-bana:** Östermalmstorg.

$ **Rates** (including breakfast): June 16–Aug 6 and Fri–Sat year-round, 720 kronor ($129.60) single; 795 kronor ($143.10) double. Sun–Thurs the rest of the year, 850–1,195 kronor ($153–$215.10) single; 1,400 kronor ($252) double. AE, DC, MC, V. **Parking:** 150 kronor ($27).

The decor in this turn-of-the-century hostelry in the commercial center blends old-fashioned charm with examples of modern design. Some of the hallways, and many of the sitting areas, are richly detailed, with an occasional antique. The bedrooms are well furnished. The hotel was originally built in the 19th century as a shelter for women arriving from the countryside, and was run by a church. It was transformed into a conventional hotel in the 1870s, making it one of the longest continuously operated hotels in Stockholm.

MORNINGTON HOTEL, Nybrogatan 53, S-102 44 Stockholm. Tel. 08/ 663-12-40, or toll free 800/528-1234 in the U.S. Fax 08/662-21-79. 140 rms (all with bath), 1 suite. A/C TV TEL **T-bana:** Östermalmstorg. **Bus:** 49, 54, 62.

$ Rates (including breakfast): June 26–Aug 3 and Fri–Sat year-round, 700 kronor ($126) single; 850 kronor ($153) double. Sun–Thurs the rest of the year, 1,200 kronor ($216) single, 1,500 kronor ($270) double. Year-round, from 1,800 kronor ($324) suite. AE, DC, MC, V. **Parking:** 120 kronor ($21.60). **Closed:** Dec 23–Jan 2.

Proud of its image as an English-inspired hotel, this efficiently modern establishment has a concrete exterior brightened with rows of flowerboxes. It was built in 1956 and renovated several times since, most recently in 1989. Most rooms offer a stylish decor using exposed wood and color schemes of blue, yellow, and brown. The lobby contains a small rock garden and modern versions of Chesterfield armchairs. The hotel has no-smoking rooms and rooms for the disabled. It has a sauna and Turkish bath that are free to guests. Its Restaurant Eleonora serves both international and Swedish cuisine. The hotel also contains a Library Bar.

STOCKHOLM PLAZA, Birger Jarlsgatan 29, S-103 95 Stockholm. Tel. 08/14-51-20. Fax 08/10-34-92. 151 rms (all with bath), 8 suites. TV TEL **T-bana:** Hötorget, Östermalmstorg.

$ Rates (including breakfast): June 22–Aug 5 and Fri–Sat year-round, 500–700 kronor ($90–$126) single; 850 kronor ($153) double. Sun–Thurs the rest of the year, 1,095–1,295 kronor ($197.10–$233.10) single; 1,450 kronor ($261) double. From 1,850 kronor ($333) suite. AE, DC, MC, V. **Parking:** 135 kronor ($24.30).

Designed on a triangular-shaped lot that might remind some visitors of New York's Flatiron Building, this first-class hotel is a well-run and inviting choice in the city center. Bedrooms have light, fresh interiors, with many conveniences. Guests enjoy the food in the hotel's gourmet restaurant, the Plaza Grill, which serves both French and Swedish specialties. In the cellar, the hotel also operates one of the city's most popular nightspots, the Alexandra Charles, complete with caviar and champagne bar. King Karl Gustaf himself has been an honored guest here.

INEXPENSIVE

ADLON HOTEL, Vasagatan 42, S-111 20 Stockholm. Tel. 08/24-54-00. Fax 08/20-86-10. 69 rms (all with bath), 2 suites. TV TEL **T-bana:** Centralen.

$ Rates (including breakfast): June 18–Aug 9 and Fri–Sat year-round, 450–500 kronor ($81–$90) single; 650–700 kronor ($117–$126) double; from 850 kronor ($153) suite. Mon–Thurs the rest of the year, 750–940 kronor ($135–$169.20) single; 1,050–1,250 kronor ($189–$225) double; from 1,400 kronor ($252) suite. AE, DC, MC, V. **Parking:** 150 kronor ($27).

This 1890s building, only about 385 yards from the main train station and airport bus terminal, has gone through a total renovation on two of its floors. T-bana and bus stops are just outside. Bedrooms are equipped with radios, and the newly renovated units have hairdryers and controlled ventilation that eliminates tobacco smoke, among other amenities. There is 24-hour room service. A garage is 1 block away.

EDEN TERRACE HOTEL, Sturegatan 10, S-114 35 Stockholm. Tel. 08/22-31-60. Fax 08/660-80-67. 60 rms (all with bath), 6 suites. MINIBAR TV TEL **T-bana:** Östermalmstorg. **Bus:** 41, 46, 56.

$ Rates (including breakfast): June 19–Aug 8 and Fri–Sat year-round, 590–690 kronor ($106.20–$124.20) single; 790–890 kronor ($142.20–$160.20) double. Sun–Thurs the rest of the year, 990–1,190 kronor ($178.20–$214.20) single; 1,090–1,290 kronor ($196.20–$232.20) double. From 1,700 kronor ($306) suite. AE, DC, MC, V. **Parking:** 170 kronor ($30.60).

Located opposite the garden of the King's Library, in what looks like an office building, the Eden Terrace opened for the Stockholm Exhibition in 1930. It offers a large dining room and a rooftop terrace where guests enjoy drinks in the summer. The bedrooms are cozy and traditionally furnished, and come in many shapes and sizes. Also on the premises are a piano bar and a nightclub.

HOTEL CITY, Slöjdgatan 7 at Hötorget, S-111 81 Stockholm. Tel. 08/22-22-40. Fax 08/20-82-24. 300 rms (all with bath). TV TEL **T-bana:** Hötorget.

$ Rates (including breakfast): Mid-June to Aug 2 and off-season weekends, 680 kronor ($122.40) single; 800 kronor ($144) double. Off-season, weekdays 945 kronor ($170.10) single; 1,120 kronor ($201.60) double. AE, DC, MC, V.

Clean and functional, the City is run by the Salvation Army, which works hard to make this among the best hotels in its price bracket in Stockholm. It consists of two sections, one built as late as the 1980s. In a desirable location between two of Stockholm's biggest department stores, PUB and Åhléns, the hotel has small but comfortable bedrooms that have been elegantly redone using alluring combinations of mirror, hardwood trim, carpeting, and tilework. No alcohol is served in the restaurant off the lobby. Luxuriate in the hotel's sauna.

HOTEL TEGNÉRLUNDEN, Tegnérlunden 6, S-113 59 Stockholm. Tel. 08/34-97-80. Fax 08/32-78-18. 104 rms (84 with bath). TV TEL **Bus:** 47, 53 from Central Station.

$ Rates (including breakfast): June 18–Aug 16 and Fri–Sat year-round, 545 kronor ($98.10) single; 600 kronor ($108) double. Sun–Thurs rest of year, 900 kronor ($162) single; 1,000 kronor ($180) double. AE, DC, MC, V. **Parking:** 90 kronor ($16.20).

In a 19th-century building at the edge of a verdant city park, this hotel has a few public rooms and a lobby, but no restaurant or bar. The hotel's best feature is its tasteful rooms, each blissfully quiet, especially those opening onto the rear. Twenty rooms are particularly comfortable for families, because they consist of two adjoining bedrooms sharing a bathroom. The rooms with shared bath cost 75 kronor ($13.50) less than the rates given above. (This discount does not apply on weekends.) There's a sun terrace on one of the upper floors, a communal TV room, a sauna, and a nearby garage.

IN GAMLA STAN [OLD TOWN]

VERY EXPENSIVE

VICTORY HOTEL, Lilla Nygatan 3–5, S-111 28 Stockholm. Tel. 08/14-30-90. Fax 08/20-21-77. 44 rms (all with bath), 4 suites. A/C MINIBAR TV TEL **T-bana:** Gamla Stan. **Bus:** 48.

$ Rates (including breakfast): June 19–Aug 9 and Fri–Sat year-round, 950 kronor ($171) single; 1,400 kronor ($252) double. Sun–Thurs the rest of the year, 1,800–2,135 kronor ($324–$384.30) single; 2,400–2,600 kronor ($432–$468) double. From 3,650 kronor ($657) suite. AE, DC, MC, V.

A small but stylish hotel, the Victory opened in 1980 on the foundations of a 1382 fortified tower. In the 1700s the owners of the house buried under the basement floor a massive treasure of silver, which is housed today in the Stockholm Museum.

There's a shiny brass elevator, but if you take the stairs you'll see one of Sweden's biggest collections of 18th-century nautical needlepoints, many done by the sailors themselves during long sea voyages. The warm and inviting rooms, each named after a prominent sea captain, have a pleasing combination of exposed wood, carpeting, and antiques and 19th-century memorabilia.

Dining/Entertainment: The Restaurant Leijontornet specializes in fish, fowl, and game (see "Dining" in this chapter). A bistro, Leijontornet, named after the

18th-century family who lived in the building, serves Swedish home cooking in a cozy, informal atmosphere.

Services: Room service, same-day laundry and dry cleaning, a complete travel and concierge desk.

Facilities: Safe-deposit boxes, heated bathroom floors and towel racks, saunas.

EXPENSIVE

LADY HAMILTON HOTEL, Storkyrkobrinken 5, S-111 28 Stockholm. Tel. 08/23-46-80. Fax 08/11-11-48. 34 rms (all with bath). MINIBAR TV TEL **T-bana:** Gamla Stan. **Bus:** 48.

$ Rates (including breakfast): 795–1,900 kronor ($143.10–$342) single; 1,130–2,335 kronor ($203.40–$420.30) double. AE, DC, MC, V.

This hotel, consisting of a trio of interconnected buildings, stands on a quiet street in the Old Town, surrounded by antiques shops and restaurants—a very desirable location indeed. Dozens of antiques are scattered among the well-furnished bedrooms. You'll get a sense of the 1470 origins of this hotel when you use the luxurious sauna, which contains the stone-rimmed well that used to supply the house's water. Extra touches include 18th-century paintings, an ivory ship model probably made by French prisoners in the 1700s, and several carved figureheads from old sailing vessels. The ornate staircase wraps around a large model of a clipper ship suspended from the ceiling. The Friday and Saturday special rates apply only if there isn't a convention in town and only if you agree to stay both nights.

LORD NELSON HOTEL, Västerlånggatan 22, S-111 29 Stockholm. Tel. 08/23-23-90. Fax 08/10-10-89. 31 rms (all with bath). TV TEL **T-bana:** Gamla Stan. **Bus:** 48.

$ Rates (including breakfast): June 21–Aug 5 and Fri–Sat year-round, 715 kronor ($128.70) single; 990 kronor ($178.20) double. Sun–Thurs the rest of the year, 1,125–1,415 kronor ($202.50–$254.70) single; 1,450–1,840 kronor ($261–$331.20) double. AE, DC, MC, V.

In this gracefully designed glass and columned building, each floor is brightened by a full-length bay window filled with nautical memorabilia. Ships' helms, captains' chairs, military prints, navigational instruments, and a seaworthy reception desk crafted from teak and brass add to the decor's charm. The building dates from the late 16th century and was occupied by painter Ignatius Meuer from 1572 to 1589. Each comfortably efficient, although small, room is named after a type of ship and contains a private shower, not a tub. The hotel also has a sauna.

SARA HOTEL REISEN, Skeppsbron 12-14, S-111 30 Stockholm. Tel. 08/22-32-60, or toll free 800/223-5672 in the U.S. Fax 08/20-15-59. 114 rms (all with bath), 13 suites. MINIBAR TV TEL **Bus:** 43, 46, 55, 59, 76.

$ Rates (including breakfast): June 14–Aug 18 and Fri–Sat year-round, 730 kronor ($131.40) single; 980 kronor ($176.40) double. Sun–Thurs the rest of the year, 1,350–2,090 kronor ($243–$376.20) single; 1,740–2,140 kronor ($313.20–$385.20) double. From 3,900 kronor ($702) suite. AE, DC, MC, V. **Closed:** Dec 22–Jan 7.

In the Old Town of Stockholm, facing the water, this hotel lies just three alleyways from the Royal Palace. Dating from the 17th century, the three-building structure attractively combines the old and the new. A former coffeehouse that stood here was mentioned in the writings of national poet Carl Michael Bellman. Rooms are comfortably furnished in a stylish modern way, but inspired by traditional designs. Light florals and pastel colors are used.

Dining/Entertainment: The hotel's specialty restaurant, the Quarter Deck, serves a refined international and Scandinavian cuisine, and the Clipper Club specializes in grills. The Reisen also has the Library Bar and the Clipper Club Pianobar, with live entertainers Monday through Saturday.

Services: Laundry service, room service (7am to 11pm), guide services in summer, concierge.

Facilities: Indoor pool, sauna, Jacuzzis in some suites.

NORTH OF THE CENTER
INEXPENSIVE

DOMUS HOTEL, Körsbarsvägen 1, S-114 89 Stockholm. Tel. 08/16-01-95. Fax 08/16-62-24. 82 rms (all with bath). TV TEL **T-bana:** Tekniska Högskolan. **Tram:** 23, 24, 25.

$ Rates (including breakfast): Aug 2–17 and Fri–Sat year-round, 575 kronor ($103.50) single; 675 kronor ($121.50) double. Mon–Thurs the rest of the year, 800 kronor ($144) single; 900 kronor ($162) double. AE, DC, MC, V.

Just off a tree-lined boulevard, on a hillside with a good view, the Domus Hotel is within walking distance of the city air terminal and an open-air swimming pool. The hotel has a restaurant, Babylon, serving Swedish and international food, and there's an outdoor terrace. The hotel is just 5 minutes by subway from the Central Station. Its rooms are comfortable and well furnished to a good middle-class standard; 17 contain minibars. Services include babysitting, room service, and laundry service.

BUDGET

AF *CHAPMAN,* Västra Brobänken, Skeppsholmen, S-11 49 Stockholm. Tel. 08/679-50-15. Fax 08/611-71-55. 40 cabins (none with bath) containing 142 beds. **Bus:** 65.

$ Rates: 90 kronor ($16.20) per person for members, 125 kronor ($22.50) for nonmembers. Bed linen 30 kronor ($5.40) extra; breakfast 40 kronor ($7.20). MC, V. **Closed:** Dec 16–Apr 1.

Moored off Skeppsholmen, near the Museum of Modern Art, this authentic three-masted schooner has been converted into a youth hostel. Its staterooms have two, four, six, or eight beds. One section is reserved for men, another for women. Each section has showers and washrooms, but there are no single cabins or family rooms. Personal lockers are available. The gangplank goes up at 1am, with no exceptions, and a 5-day stay is maximum. Rooms are closed from 10am to 4pm. No cigarette smoking or alcohol is allowed. A summer café operates on the ship's deck. Breakfast, at an extra charge, is available in the self-service coffee bar and dining room. International Youth Hostel association cards can be obtained at the af *Chapman.*

5. DINING

Food is expensive in Stockholm, but those on a budget can stick to self-service cafeterias. At all restaurants other than cafeterias, a 12% to 15% service charge is added to the bill to cover tipping. Try ordering a *dagens ratt* (daily special).

One tip to save you a little inconvenience: Don't rush into a bar in Stockholm for your pick-me-up martini. "Bars" in Stockholm are self-service cafeterias, and the strongest drink that many of them offer is apple cider.

The category **Very Expensive** indicates restaurants where dinners generally cost $65 or more; **Expensive,** around $45 to $65, **Moderate,** around $25 to $45; and **Inexpensive,** anything under $25. Wine and beer can be lethal to your final bill, so proceed carefully.

IN THE CENTER
VERY EXPENSIVE

OPERAKÄLLAREN, Operahuset, Gustav Adolfs Torg. Tel. 676-58-00.
Cuisine: FRENCH/SWEDISH. **Reservations:** Essential. **T-bana:** Kungsträdgården.

FROMMER'S COOL FOR KIDS: HOTELS

Sheraton Stockholm (see p. 431). This well-run chain has always pampered children. Spacious rooms are comfortably shared with parents.

Hotel Tegnérlunden (see p. 436). Twenty big, airy rooms are ideal for families on a budget.

af Chapman (see p. 438). Although there are no family rooms, kids delight in staying in one of the staterooms (two to eight beds) aboard an authentic three-masted schooner.

$ Prices: Smörgåsbord 210 kronor ($37.80); fixed-price menu 500 kronor ($90) for 3 courses, 630 kronor ($113.40) for 7-course menu gastronomique; appetizers 110–240 kronor ($19.80–$43.20); main dishes 265–340 kronor ($47.70–$61.20). AE, DC, MC, V.

Open: Mon–Fri 11:30am–2pm and 5–11:30pm; Sat 11:30am–11:30pm; Sun 5–11:30pm.

Opposite the Royal Palace, this is the most famous and unashamedly luxurious restaurant in all of Sweden. Its elegant classic decor and style are reminiscent of a royal court banquet at the turn of the century. Its Paris equivalent would be Le Grand Véfour. Dress formally to enjoy its impeccable service and house specialties. Many come here for the elaborate smörgåsbord; others prefer the classic Swedish dishes or the modern French ones. A house specialty is the platter of northern delicacies, which includes everything from smoked eel to smoked reindeer along with Swedish red caviar. Salmon and game, including grouse from the northern forests, are both prepared in various ways.

PAUL & NORBERT, Strandvägen 9. Tel. 663-81-83.

Cuisine: CONTINENTAL. **Reservations:** Essential. **T-bana:** Östermalmstorg.

$ Prices: Appetizers 130–170 kronor ($23.40–$30.60); main dishes 220–300 kronor ($39.60–$54); 8-course *grand menu de frivolité* 870 kronor ($156.60). AE, DC, MC, V.

Open: Lunch Mon–Fri noon–3pm; dinner Mon–Fri 5:30–10:30pm. **Closed:** July and Dec 25.

Set within a patrician residence dating from 1873, adjacent to the Hotel Diplomat, this is considered one of the finest and most innovative restaurants in Stockholm. Seating only 30 diners, it has a vaguely art deco decor, a winter-inspired pastel color scheme, beamed ceilings, and dark paneling. Owners Paul Beck and Norbert Lang both worked in many of the top restaurants of Europe before opening this place. For appetizers, they prepare tantalizing tartares, including roe deer and salmon. It sounds banal, but their goose liver terrine is the finest in town. Their fish platter, worthy of three stars, combines grilled filets of turbot, salmon, sole, and saltwater crayfish, served on a "mirror" of three different sauces (champagne, lobster, and truffle), although you might prefer their breast of woodcock or marinated noisettes of moose with creamed morel sauce.

EXPENSIVE

GOURMET, Tegnérgatan 10. Tel. 673-58-14.

Cuisine: CONTINENTAL. **Reservations:** Recommended. **T-bana:** Rådmansgatan.

Å hlens City Restaurant 26

Bakfickan 5

Berns Salonger 10

Bizet 6

Cattelin Restaurant 17

Den Gyldene Freden 22

Djurgårdsbrunns Wårdhus 16

Erik's 23

Eriks Backfica 15

Fem Små Hus 21

Franska Matsalen 8

Gourmet 29

Grand Veranda 8

Gröna Linjen 3

Hötorgs Hallen Market 4

Karelia 28

STOCKHOLM DINING

Subway - - - **Church** ✚ **Post Office** ⊠ **Information** ⓘ

KB Restaurant ❹
Leijontornet ⑱
Lisa Elmquist ❶
Magnus Ladulås ⑳
Michel ㉛
Operakällaren ❼
Östermalms Hallen
  Market ❶

Paul & Norbert ⑬
Prinsens ⑪
Smörgåskringlan ⑭
Cafeteria Solliden
  (at Skansen) ㉔
Restaurant Solliden
  (at Skansen) ㉔
Stadshuskällaren ㉕

Stortorgskällaren ⑲
Sturehof ❷
Teatergrillen ⑫
Tennstopet ㉚
Tysta Mari ❶
Ulriksdals Wärdshus ㉛
Wedholms Fisk ❾

$ Prices: Appetizers 50–90 kronor ($9–$16.20); main dishes 140–198 kronor ($25.20–$35.60). Fixed-price lunch 79–189 kronor ($14.20–$34); fixed-price dinner 220–300 kronor ($39.60–$54). AE, DC, MC, V.
Open: Lunch Mon–Fri 11:30am–2pm, Sat–Sun noon–2pm; dinner daily 6–11pm. **Closed:** Dec 25.

This restaurant, cozily located in the cellar of a turn-of-the-century stone house, contains two dining rooms which are interconnected by a cocktail bar. One dining room is formally paneled in mahogany, the other in a more typical Swedish style, with bleached paneling, chandeliers, and birchwood tables. The kitchen specializes in a Swedish cuisine with continental overtones. You might begin with such classic dishes as smoked salmon with chanterelles, beef with red onions and a whitefish roe, or "archipelago soup," made with five different kinds of Baltic fish. For your main course you might select a lightly sautéed fried salmon on a ragoût of cucumber, fennel, and capers; venison with wild mushrooms from the woods; or filet of beef with potatoes. Desserts are delectable, including an old-fashioned rosehip cream, warm cloudberries with homemade vanilla ice cream, or a frozen soufflé flavored with Arctic raspberry liqueur.

MICHEL, Karlavägen 7. Tel. 662-22-62.
Cuisine: FRENCH. **Reservations:** Required. **T-bana:** Central Station. **Bus:** 54.
$ Prices: Appetizers 75–235 kronor ($13.50–$42.30); main dishes 275–345 kronor ($49.50–$62.10); fixed-price lunch 95–225 kronor ($17.10–$40.50); fixed-price dinner 265–300 kronor ($47.70–$54). AE, DC, MC, V.
Open: Lunch Mon–Fri 11am–2pm; dinner Mon–Sat 6–10:30pm. **Closed:** July.

This upmarket restaurant is set in a turn-of-the-century house and is decorated like the private living room of the Swedish *grande bourgeoisie*. Pink velvet curtains, white tablecloths, and fresh flowers make it even more inviting. The food is among the most elegantly prepared and served in all of Sweden. Try slightly grilled duck liver with fresh beetroot and a caramelized port wine sauce, or marinated salmon in puff pastry with crème fraîche flavored with Swedish caviar and red onions. The main specialty is a *délices de la mer*, a mixture of sole, salmon, turbot, and flounder served with a chablis sauce mixed with trout roe. The dessert extravaganza is a white-chocolate mousse built up into a miniature pagoda set on a "lake" of raspberry sauce.

WEDHOLMS FISK, Nybrokajen 17. Tel. 611-78-74.
Cuisine: SWEDISH/FRENCH. **Reservations:** Required. **T-bana:** Östermalmstorg.
$ Prices: Appetizers 60–165 kronor ($10.80–$29.70); main dishes 120–330 kronor ($21.60–$59.40); fixed-price lunch 130 kronor ($23.40); fixed-price dinner 285 kronor ($51.30). AE, DC, MC, V.
Open: Mon–Fri 11:30am–11pm; Sat 2–11pm. **Closed:** July 7–Aug 6.

This is one of the classic—and one of the best—restaurants of Stockholm. Housed in an old Swedish building whose decor has been stripped down to its rustic simplicity, it has no curtains at the windows and no carpets, but displays a collection of modern paintings by Swedish artists that is riveting. You might begin with marinated herring with garlic and bleak roe, or tartare of salmon with salmon roe. The chef has reason to be proud of such dishes as oysters with fresh spinach; sweet pickled herring with red onion, dill, and melted butter; or grilled filet of sole with a Dijon-flavored hollandaise. For dessert, try the homemade vanilla ice cream with cloudberries.

MODERATE

BERNS SALONGER, Näckströmsgatan 8. Tel. 674-07-20.
Cuisine: SWEDISH. **Reservations:** Recommended. **T-bana:** Östermalmstorg.
$ Prices: Appetizers 48–65 kronor ($8.60–$11.70); main dishes 98–155 kronor ($17.60–$27.90); 2-course fixed-price menu 245 kronor ($44.10). AE, DC, MC, V.
Open: Tues–Sun 7pm–3am.

Built in 1860, this "pleasure palace" was one of the most famous restaurants and nighttime venues of Stockholm. It was dramatically renovated in 1989 and is now one of the most atmospheric choices for dining in the capital, with a main hall adorned with galleries, mirrors, and wooden paneling, and lit by a trio of monumental chandeliers. The Nya Röda Rummet (New Red Room) upstairs is ideal for a drink. The real Red Room was frequented by August Strindberg, who described it in his novel of the same name. It's still there, plush furniture and all, and available for private parties. Each day a different Swedish specialty is featured, including fried filet of suckling pig with fresh asparagus. You might also try calves' liver with garlic and bacon, or grilled tournedos. A disco, open from midnight to 3am, is on the premises, charging a 50-krona ($9) entrance fee. Frequent shows are staged in an adjoining theater.

ERIKS BAKFICA, Fredrikhovsgatan 4. Tel. 660-15-99.

Cuisine: SWEDISH. **Reservations:** Recommended. **Bus:** 47.

$ Prices: Dinner platters 85–95 kronor ($15.30–$17.10); luncheon platters 85–95 kronor ($15.30–$17.10); appetizers 58–130 kronor ($10.40–$23.40); main dishes 92–210 kronor ($16.60–$37.80). AE, DC, MC, V.

Open: Mon–Fri 11:30am–11pm, Sat 1–11pm, Sun 3–11pm.

Although there are other restaurants in Stockholm bearing the name Erik's (see "In Gamla Stan," below), this one is relatively inexpensive and offers particularly good value. It features a handful of traditional Swedish dishes from the tradition of *husmanskost* (wholesome home cooking). The menu choices are the same in both. A favorite opener is toast Skagen, with shrimp, dill-flavored mayonnaise, spices, and bleak roe. There is also a daily choice of herring appetizers. Try the "archipelago stew," a ragoût of fish flavored with tomatoes and served with garlic mayonnaise. Marinated salmon is served with hollandaise sauce, and you might also try Erik's cheeseburger with a special secret sauce.

KARELIA, in the Hotell Karelia, Birger Jarlsgatan 35. Tel. 24-76-60.

Cuisine: FINNISH. **Reservations:** Not required. **T-bana:** Östermalmstorg.

$ Prices: Appetizers 52–78 kronor ($9.40–$14); main dishes 58–174 kronor ($10.40–$31.30). AE, DC, MC, V.

Open: Dinner only, Mon and Wed 5pm–1am, Tues and Thurs 6pm–1am, Fri–Sat 6pm–3am. **Closed:** Dec 24–26.

The city's leading Finnish restaurant lies on the second floor of a well-recommended, moderately priced hotel (see "Accommodations" in this chapter) in the center of the city. Begin with the classic Finnish salmon soup served with rye bread, or a wild-mushroom soup made with tiny mushrooms. For your main course, consider grilled filet of salmon stuffed with pike perch, a chef's specialty. For dessert, try cloudberries (from north of the Arctic Circle), served with a caramel sauce. There is live music and dancing 6 nights a week. There is a casino and cocktail bar in the restaurant.

PRINSENS, Mäster Samuelsgatan 4. Tel. 611-13-31.

Cuisine: SWEDISH. **Reservations:** Not accepted. **T-bana:** Östermalmstorg.

$ Prices: Appetizers 56–89 kronor ($10.10–$16); main dishes 89–163 kronor ($16–$29.30); fixed-price lunch 71 kronor ($12.80). AE, DC, MC, V.

Open: Mon–Thurs 11am–12:30am, Fri 11am–1:30am, Sat 1pm–1:30am, Sun 5–11:30pm.

A 2-minute walk from Stureplan, this is a favorite haunt of artists and has become increasingly popular with foreign travelers. It's been feeding people since 1897. Diners are seated on one of two levels, and in summer some tables are placed outside. The cuisine is fresh and flavorful, and includes such traditional Swedish dishes as veal patty with homemade lingonberry preserves, sautéed fjord salmon, and roulades of beef. For dessert, try the homemade vanilla ice cream. Basically, the menu lists Swedish food prepared in a conservative French style. Later in the evening, the restaurant takes on some of the qualities of a drinking club.

STUREHOF, Stureplan 2. Tel. 679-87-50.

Cuisine: SEAFOOD/SWEDISH. **Reservations:** Not required. **T-bana:** Hötorget.
$ Prices: Appetizers 45–103 kronor ($8.10–$18.50); main dishes 85–175 kronor ($15.30–$31.50). AE, DC, MC, V.
Open: Mon–Tues 11:30am–11pm, Wed–Sun 11:30am–midnight.

This seafood restaurant in the center of Stockholm was founded in 1897, and has a Scottish-style pub in front. Specialties include Swedish or Canadian lobsters and oysters, fried plaice, boiled salmon with hollandaise, and fresh shrimp. A daily menu of genuine Swedish *husmanskost* (home cooking) is a bargain. You might order the famous *sotare* (grilled small herring served with boiled potatoes).

TEATERGRILLEN, Nybrogatan 3. Tel. 611-70-44.
Cuisine: SWEDISH/FRENCH. **Reservations:** Recommended. **T-bana:** Östermalmstorg. **Bus:** 46.
$ Prices: Appetizers 78–185 kronor ($14–$33.30); main dishes 105–240 kronor ($18.90–$43.20). AE, DC, MC, V.
Open: Lunch Mon–Sat 11:30am–2:30pm; dinner Mon–Sat 5–11:30pm.
Closed: July–Aug 6.

For the theater buff, this restaurant decorated with theatrical memorabilia is near the Royal Dramatic Theater on Nybroplan, where Ingmar Bergman was once arrested on a tax investigation. Many typical Swedish dishes are offered at lunch, cooked grandmother's style, including fried herring with onion and potatoes, scrambled eggs with salmon, and pea soup with sausages. For dinner, try one of the roasts from the trolley, which are as good as Simpson's in the Strand in London. You can also order such elegant fare as snails braised in white wine with tarragon butter, and roe deer noisettes with a juniperberry sauce. Elaborate desserts include crêpes Suzette or an ice-cream tart with hot-chocolate sauce.

BUDGET

GRÖNA LINJEN, Mäster Samuelsgatan 10. Tel. 11-27-90.
Cuisine: VEGETARIAN. **Reservations:** Not required. **T-bana:** Östermalmstorg.
$ Prices: Buffet 75 kronor ($13.50). No credit cards.
Open: Mon–Fri 10:30am–8pm, Sat 11am–8pm.

Located in what appears to have been a very large private apartment, this self-service vegetarian place offers both raw and cooked selections. You help yourself from a large vegetarian buffet enjoying one of the best all-you-can-eat restaurant bargains of Stockholm. In the evening a fresh-fruit salad is added to the buffet, for which you pay an additional 10 kronor ($1.80).

IN GAMLA STAN [OLD TOWN]

VERY EXPENSIVE

ERIK'S, Österlånggatan 17. Tel. 23-85-00.
Cuisine: FRENCH. **Reservations:** Required. **T-bana:** Gamla Stan.
$ Prices: Appetizers 98–230 kronor ($17.60–$41.40); main dishes 193–378 kronor ($34.70–$68); luncheon plates 95 kronor ($17.10). AE, DC, MC, V.
Open: Mon–Fri 11:30am–11pm, Sat 1–11pm. **Closed:** July and Dec 25–Jan 1.

This restaurant occupying two floors of a building from the 1600s in the Old Town has a warmly autumnal color scheme and English country-house decor. Some food critics in Stockholm regard it as the best restaurant in the Old Town. Dishes include grilled scallops with a sauce of peppered ginger and deep-fried leeks, and grilled duck liver with a sauce of port wine and shallots, but the chef's specialty is duckling, served in two courses—first the breast in cider sauce, followed by the leg in a green-pepper sauce.

LEIJONTORNET, in the Victory Hotel, Lilla Nygatan 3-5. Tel. 14-23-55.
Cuisine: SWEDISH/INTERNATIONAL. **Reservations:** Required. **T-bana:** Gamla Stan.

$ Prices: Fixed-price dinner 420 kronor ($75.60); appetizers 100–185 kronor ($18–$33.30); main dishes 200–300 kronor ($36–$54). AE, DC, MC, V.
Open: Mon–Sat noon–midnight. **Closed:** July.

This is one of the Old Town's most stylish and fashionable restaurants, noted for its food and the quality of its service. From the small street-level bar where you can order a before-dinner drink, guests descend into the intimately lit cellar (the restaurant was built around a medieval defense tower). To reach this restaurant, you need to negotiate a labyrinth of brick passageways through the Victory Hotel.

You might begin with a lobster salad with saffron vinaigrette, poached oysters on a bed of cucumber with a sauternes sabayon, or wood pigeon pâté with marinated mushrooms. Main dishes include breast of wild duck with cèpes and duck liver, salmon and turbot in pastry with artichokes and a buttery mussel sauce, and médaillons of venison.

EXPENSIVE

DEN GYLDENE FREDEN, Österlånggatan 51. Tel. 24-97-60.

Cuisine: SWEDISH. **Reservations:** Recommended. **T-bana:** Gamla Stan.
$ Prices: Appetizers 75–130 kronor ($13.50–$23.40); main dishes 168–240 kronor ($30.20–$43.20). AE, DC, MC, V.
Open: Dinner only, Mon–Sat 6–11pm.

The "Golden Peace" was closed in 1985, but after a careful restoration, Stockholm's oldest tavern is back in business again. The building is owned by the Swedish Academy, and members are said to frequent the place on Thursday night when the traditional yellow pea soup is served. Inside, various cozy dining rooms are named for the Swedish historical figures who were patrons long ago. Today, artists, lawyers, and poets still patronize this establishment. You get traditional Swedish cookery here, especially fresh Baltic fish and game from the wilds of Sweden. Herring is a favorite appetizer. Specialty main courses include baked filet of turbot served with cèpes and guinea fowl sautéed with dried fruit and spruce twigs (yes, that's right).

FEM SMÅ HUS, Nygränd 10. Tel. 10-87-75.

Cuisine: SWEDISH/FRENCH. **Reservations:** Required. **T-bana:** Gamla Stan.
$ Prices: 3-course fixed-price dinner 350 kronor ($63); appetizers 68–128 kronor ($12.20–$23); main dishes 178–225 kronor ($32–$40.50). AE, DC, MC, V.
Open: Mon–Fri 11:30am–11:30pm, Sat–Sun 1–11:30pm.

This sophisticated and historic restaurant, whose cellars date from the 17th century, is furnished like the interior of a private castle, with European antiques and oil paintings.

FROMMER'S COOL FOR KIDS: RESTAURANTS

Räkan *(see p. 552).* Kids love this fish restaurant, especially the miniature battery-powered boat that delivers the shrimp.

The Skansen Dining Cluster *(see p. 447).* After a day spent watching the animals and enjoying the rides, kids like to patronize any of these places for their good, healthy food. **Stora Gungan** *(see p. 448)* features a rustic ambience and offers an interesting buffet as part of the meal.

Dining at the Produce Market *(see p. 448).* This place is as busy as a circus, but it's a lot of fun for parents with children to eat right in the center of all the activity. Small and big appetites are catered to at this food fair. **Tysta Mari** *(see p. 448)* features a wide variety of food, notably interesting seafood preparations, such as salmon pudding.

After being shown to a candlelit table somewhere in the nine rooms of the labyrinthine interior, you can order assorted herring, slices of fresh salmon in chablis, braised scallops with saffron sauce, terrine of duckling with goose liver and truffles, filet of beef with herb sauce, and sorbets with seasonal fruits and berries.

STORTORGSKÄLLAREN, Stortorget 7. Tel. 10-55-33.

Cuisine: SWEDISH. **Reservations:** Required. **T-bana:** Gamla Stan.

$ **Prices:** 3-course fixed-price dinner 165 kronor ($29.70); appetizers 70–98 kronor ($12.60–$17.60); main dishes 130–255 kronor ($23.40–$45.90). AE, DC, MC, V.

Open: May 1–Sept 5, daily noon–11:30pm; off-season, Mon–Fri 5–11:30pm, Sat–Sun noon–11:30pm.

Set beside a charming square opposite the Stock Exchange in the Old Town, this restaurant was created in the medieval wine cellars whose vaulted ceilings date from the 15th century. The old walls and chandeliers are combined with plush carpeting and subtle lighting to create a sophisticated effect. In summer, diners can choose an outdoor table with a view of the square.

The menu changes often here. You might begin with three kinds of herring or the house specialty, cured salmon and white bleak roe served with crème fraîche and onions. Typical dishes are likely to include filet of sole cooked several different ways, salmon stuffed with saffron, and marinated lamb.

MODERATE

CATTELIN RESTAURANT, Storkyrkobrinken 9. Tel. 20-18-18.

Cuisine: SEAFOOD. **Reservations:** Recommended. **T-bana:** Gamla Stan.

$ **Prices:** Appetizers 29–92 kronor ($5.20–$16.60); main dishes 59–185 kronor ($10.60–$33.30); fixed-price lunch 50 kronor ($9). AE, DC, MC, V.

Open: Mon–Fri 11:30am–11pm, Sat noon–11pm, Sun 1–10pm.

Opened in 1897, this fish restaurant in Gamla Stan serves some of the finest food in the Old Town. Look for the *plat du jour*, including, on my most recent visit, grilled filet Oscar. You might also try the broiled fresh salmon with hollandaise, always a delight.

MAGNUS LADULÅS, Österlånggatan 26. Tel. 21-19-57.

Cuisine: SWEDISH/INTERNATIONAL. **Reservations:** Recommended. **T-bana:** Gamla Stan.

$ **Prices:** 3-course fixed-price menus 160–300 kronor ($28.80–$54); appetizers 30–80 kronor ($5.40–$14.40); main dishes 80–180 kronor ($14.40–$32.40). AE, DC, MC, V.

Open: Mon–Fri 11:30am–11pm, Sat 4–11pm. **Closed:** Lunch in July.

This is a pleasant restaurant converted from a vaulted inner room of a 12th-century weaving factory. You can have a drink at the bar before your meal. A meal could include a mixed seafood plate with lobster sauce, fresh salmon from Lapland, or filet of beef in puff pastry with a deviled sauce. A specialty is steak cooked as you like it on a hot stone placed on your table.

AT KUNGSHOLMEN

MODERATE

STADSHUSKÄLLAREN, Stadshuset. Tel. 650-54-54.

Cuisine: SWEDISH/INTERNATIONAL. **Reservations:** Not required. **T-bana:** Rådhuset. **Bus:** 48, 62.

$ **Prices:** 3-course fixed-price dinner 195 kronor ($35.10); 2-course fixed-price lunch 175 kronor ($31.50); appetizers 65–95 kronor ($11.70–$17.10); main dishes 130–180 kronor ($23.40–$32.40). AE, DC, MC, V.

Open: Skänken, lunch only, Mon–Fri 11am–2pm; Stora Matsalen, Mon–Fri 11:30am–11:30pm, Sat 2–11:30pm.

Two dignified restaurants are located in the basement of the City Hall, near the harbor (the entranceway is recognizable by its beautiful carved wooden doorway). The chefs here also prepare the banquet for the annual Nobel Prize winners. They'll even arrange a banquet with a Nobel menu for you. The interior is divided into two sections, the Skänken, which serves only at lunchtime, and the Stora Matsalen. Meat dishes might include filet of elk or saddle of young reindeer. Fresh Swedish salmon is invariably featured as are fresh fish dishes.

AT DJURGÅRDEN & SÖDERMALM

MODERATE

DJURGÅRDSBRUNNS WÄRDSHUS, Djurgårdsbrunnsvägen 68. Tel. 667-90-95.
    Cuisine: SWEDISH. **Reservations:** Not required. **Bus:** 69.
$ **Prices:** Appetizers 25–65 kronor ($4.50–$11.70); main dishes 65–90 kronor ($11.70–$16.20); 1-course light lunch 59–64 kronor ($10.60–$11.50). AE, DC, MC, V.
    Open: Summer, daily 11am–8:30pm; winter, daily 11am–5pm.

    This inn in the Royal Deer Park dates from 1740 and caters to all tastes, whether in the elegant main dining room, the English-style pub, or the outdoor Pavilion, which includes a garden grill in summer. Enjoy an inexpensive, Swedish home-style lunch in the self-service café, or maybe have just a drink and snack in the pub. The restaurant serves grilled salmon with morel-butter sauce or noisettes of deer with fresh vegetables. *Frikadeller* (meatballs) and plates of roast beef are also featured. This place lies 2 miles east of Stockholm's center, a 10-minute ride on bus no. 69.

SPECIALTY DINING

DEPARTMENT-STORE DINING

With three restaurants and a bar, **Åhléns City,** Klarabergsgatan 50 (tel. 676-60-00), best known as one of Stockholm's largest department stores, is also a popular place to dine. Its street level contains the Plateau Restaurant, an apricot-hued very modern eatery with waitress service and platters of Swedish food. Light meals cost 100 to 150 kronor ($18 to $27); AE, DC, MC, V accepted.

On Level 2, a self-service cafeteria in a well-scrubbed and comfortable setting serves alcoholic drinks and wholesome, well-flavored platters and daily specials priced from 40 kronor ($7.20) each. Nearby, also on Level 2, the Caffino Bar offers coffee and drinks with or without alcohol. Irish coffee costs 40 kronor ($7.20).

Finally, a tearoom on Level 3 serves Danish open-faced sandwiches, pastries, and tea and coffee by the pot. Tea costs 11 kronor ($2) per cup, sandwiches cost around 45 kronor ($8.10) each.

SKANSEN DINING CLUSTER

Near the top of the Skansen compound, a Williamsburg-type park from 1891, **Cafeteria Solliden** (tel. 662-93-03) is actually a cluster of restaurants set in a sprawling building. This all-purpose dining emporium has an array of drinking, dancing, and dining facilities.

The least pretentious dining area is the ground-floor **cafeteria** featuring wood paneling, big windows, and budget prices. It serves open-face sandwiches and warm platters beginning at 45 kronor ($8.10). The ground-floor restaurant and an adjacent wood-sheathed pub are open all year. In summer hours are daily from 11:30am to 8pm, and off-season daily from 11:30am to 4pm.

Restaurant Solliden (tel. 662-93-03) is the best of the lot, offering both Swedish and French cooking. It serves a Swedish smörgåsbord at 210 kronor ($37.80) and a (Monday through Friday) tourist menu at 155 kronor ($27.90). You can also order à la carte, with main dishes priced from 148 to 205 kronor ($26.60 to $36.90). Reservations aren't necessary but are recommended. This upstairs dining room with ice-blue and crystal decor offers a panoramic view of Stockholm and attentive service. Main dishes include tournedos with morels and madeira sauce and roast breast of duck with cherry sauce. Open only May through September from noon to midnight.

Also in the Skansen compound, **Stora Gungan** (tel. 660-66-01) is located an escalator flight up from the main entranceway. It retains a 19th-century rustic ambience with wood-plank floors and rough-hewn tables. Traditional Swedish meals might include a salmon platter, selections from a herring buffet, and meatballs. Regardless of what you order, at least part of your meal will be self-served from a buffet near the bar. You can enjoy a beer on the front porch. It is open only from May through September, noon to 11pm.

To reach all these restaurants, take bus no. 44 or 47, or the Djurgården ferry lines.

LATE-NIGHT DINING
Moderate

BIZET, Gustav Adolfs Torg 20. Tel. 10-42-22.
  Cuisine: SWEDISH. **Reservations:** Recommended. **T-bana:** Kungsträdgården.
$ Prices: Fixed-price menus 220 kronor ($39.60); appetizers 52–98 kronor ($9.40–$17.60); main dishes 65–165 kronor ($11.70–$29.70). AE, DC, MC, V.
  Open: Mon–Sat 11:30am–3am, Sun 1pm–3am.

Charmingly located at the corner of this landmark square at the opera, this restaurant overlooks the Royal Palace. It has a rustic, old-fashioned charm, and satisfies a number of different tastes and pocketbooks. Dishes are likely to include such fare as veal liver with bacon and capers and filets of salmon trout poached in white wine and served with a butter sauce.

DINING AT THE PRODUCE MARKET
Inexpensive

LISA ELMQUIST, Östermalms Saluhall, Nybrogatan 31. Tel. 660-92-32.
  Cuisine: SEAFOOD. **Reservations:** Recommended. **T-bana:** Östermalmstorg.
$ Prices: Appetizers 50–95 kronor ($9–$17.10); main dishes 95–150 kronor ($17.10–$27). AE, DC, MC, V.
  Open: Mon 10am–6pm, Tues–Fri 9am–6pm, Sat 9am–3pm.

Under the soaring roof, and amid the food stalls of Stockholm's produce market (the Östermalms Saluhall), you'll find this likable café and oyster bar. Owned by one of the city's largest fish distributors, it serves a menu that varies according to the catch. Some clients come here to order a portion of shrimp with bread and butter for 75 to 100 kronor ($13.50 to $18). Typical dishes include fish soup, salmon cutlets, and sautéed filet of lemon sole. The establishment looks like a pleasant bistro under the tent at some country fair.

TYSTA MARI, Östermalms Saluhall, Nybrogatan 31. Tel. 662-60-36.
  Cuisine: SWEDISH. **Reservations:** Recommended. **T-bana:** Östermalmstorg.
$ Prices: Sandwiches 32–75 kronor ($5.80–$13.50); hot plates 65–90 kronor ($11.70–$16.20). MC, V.
  Open: Mon 10am–6pm; Tues–Fri 9am–6pm, Sat 9am–3pm.

You select what you want from a glass counter and eat it under a canopy set out in one corner of the bustling produce market. A meal might include a range of open-face sandwiches, lobster soup, and salmon pudding. Meals consist of platters of food that come with bread, butter, a salad, and either a light beer or coffee. Typical dishes include Swedish herring, fish soup, Italian pasta, and a shrimp or chef's salad.

HOTEL DINING
Very Expensive

FRANSKA MATSALEN [French Dining Room], in the Grand Hotel, Södra Blasieholmshamnen 8. Tel. 611-52-14.
Cuisine: FRENCH. **Reservations:** Required. **Tram:** 10, 11. **Bus:** 46, 55, 62, 76. **T-bana:** Kungsträdgården.
$ Prices: 5-course fixed-price menu 695 kronor ($125.10); appetizers 85–245 kronor ($15.30–$44.10); main dishes 175–345 kronor ($31.50–$62.10). AE, DC, MC, V.
Open: Dinner only, Mon–Sat 6–11pm. **Closed:** July.

⭐ Widely acclaimed as one of the greatest restaurants of Stockholm, this elegant restaurant is on the ground level of Stockholm's most deluxe hotel. The dining room is one of the most imperial in Sweden, featuring an ensemble of polished mahogany, ormolu, and gilt accents—all placed under a richly ornate plaster ceiling. Tables on the enclosed veranda have a view of the Royal Palace and the Old Town. Try such dishes as smoked breast of partridge with pears and celery, a mille-feuille of marinated salmon with coriander and shellfish, or filet of roebuck with savoy cabbage in cream. Dessert might be what the chef calls "variations of lemon" or deep-fried coconut and pistachio ice cream.

DINING WITH A VIEW
Moderate

GRAND VERANDA, in the Grand Hotel, Södra Blasieholmshamnen 8. Tel. 611-52-12.
Cuisine: SWEDISH. **Reservations:** Required. **Tram:** 10, 11. **Bus:** 46, 55, 62, 76. **T-bana:** Kungsträdgården.
$ Prices: Appetizers 60–110 kronor ($10.80–$19.80); main dishes 85–190 kronor ($15.30–$34.20); Swedish buffet 250–290 kronor ($45–$52.20). AE, DC, MC, V.
Open: Lunch daily 11am–3pm; dinner daily 6–9:30pm.

On the ground floor of Stockholm's most prestigious hotel, and fronted with enormous sheets of glass, this restaurant opens onto a stunning view of the harbor and the Royal Palace. The Veranda is famous for its daily buffets. These are occasionally upgraded to include a medley of shellfish that includes all the shrimp and lobster you want, costing 295 kronor ($53.10) at lunch and 410 kronor ($73.80) at dinner. Try such à la carte dishes as filet of reindeer marinated in red wine or braised wild duck and deep-fried root vegetables served with an apple cider sauce.

SMÖRGÅSBORD
Very Expensive

ULRIKSDALS WÄRDSHUS, Ulriksdals Royal Park, 171 71 Solna. Tel. 85-08-15.
Cuisine: SWEDISH. **Reservations:** Required. **Directions:** Take Sveavägen to Arlanda Airport (Exit E18), 3 miles north of Stockholm.
$ Prices: Smörgåsbord 275–450 kronor ($49.50–$81); appetizers 150–200 kronor ($27–$36); main dishes 285–295 kronor ($51.30–$53.10). AE, DC, MC, V.
Open: Mon–Fri 11:30am–10pm, Sat 12:30–10pm, Sun 12:30–6:30pm.
Closed: Dec 24–26.

⭐ This out-of-town establishment is said to serve the best smörgåsbord in Sweden. On the grounds of Ulriksdal's Royal Palace on Edviken Bay, you can dine in the all-glass Queen Silvia Pavilion opening onto gardens still owned by the king and queen. The smörgåsbord, featuring 86 delicacies (both shellfish and meat), is usually accompanied by beer or aquavit. Most people eat the smörgåsbord in five courses, beginning with herring (20 varieties), following first with salmon and then meat dishes, including *frikadeller* (meatballs) or perhaps reindeer, then a selection of cheese, and finally dessert. Some dishes are based on old farm-style recipes, including Jansson's temptation, which melds anchovies, heavy-cream potatoes, and onion.

A very Swedish experience. As the flag is lowered outside, diners stand and sing the national anthem.

LOCAL FAVORITES
Moderate

BAKFICKAN, Jakobs Torg 12. Tel. 24-27-00.
  Cuisine: SWEDISH. **Reservations:** Not accepted. **T-bana:** Kungsträdgården.
  $ Prices: Appetizers 53–67 kronor ($9.50–$12.10); main dishes 98–121 kronor ($17.60–$21.80). AE, DC, MC, V.
  Open: Summer, dinner only, Mon–Sat 5–11pm; off-season, Mon–Sat 11:30am–11:30pm.

Tucked away in the back of the Operakällaren, the "Back Pocket" is a chic place to eat for a moderate price. Its food is from the same kitchen as the very glamorous (and previously recommended) Operakällaren, but its prices are more bearable. Main dishes are likely to include salmon schnitzel, Backfickan's famous Lovbeef, and beef Ryberg (sliced thin tenderloin).

KB RESTAURANT, Smålandsgatan 7. Tel. 611-33-57.
  Cuisine: SWEDISH/CONTINENTAL. **Reservations:** Recommended. **T-bana:** Östermalmstorg.
  $ Prices: Fixed-price lunch 97 kronor ($17.50); fixed-price dinner 150 kronor ($27); appetizers 58–125 kronor ($10.40–$22.50); main dishes 115–250 kronor ($20.70–$45). AE, DC, MC, V.
  Open: Mon–Fri 11:30am–11:30pm, Sat 5–11:30pm. **Closed:** Mid-June to mid-Aug.

A traditional artists' hangout in the center of town, KB Restaurant features good Swedish cookery as well as continental dishes. Fish dishes are especially recommended. You might begin with salmon trout roe and Russian caviar, and follow with boiled turbot or lamb roast with stuffed zucchini in a thyme-flavored bouillon. Dishes are usually accompanied with aromatic, freshly baked sourdough bread. Desserts include sorbets with fresh fruits and berries and a lime soufflé with orange-flower honey. A *middag* costs from 97 kronor ($17.50). There is also a relaxed and informal bar.

TENNSTOPET [Pewter Tankard], Dalagatan 50. Tel. 32-25-18.
  Cuisine: SWEDISH. **Reservations:** Recommended. **T-bana:** Odenplan. **Bus:** 47.
  $ Prices: Appetizers 54–112 kronor ($9.70–$20.20); main dishes 71–175 kronor ($12.80–$31.50); 2-course fixed-price lunch 55 kronor ($9.90). AE, DC, MC, V.
  Open: Mon–Fri 11:30am–1am, Sat 2pm–1am, Sun 4pm–1am.

A well-known pub and restaurant, Tennstopet lies in the northern quarter of town, near Hotel Oden. It is the oldest pub in Sweden, set adjacent to a classical Swedish dining room. Main dishes might include a ragoût of fish and shellfish, salmon schnitzel, and plank steak. For lunch, you can have pork chops, vegetables, bread, butter, and coffee for 55 kronor ($9.90)—or just order a draft beer, toss some darts, and admire the setting. The place prides itself on serving genuine English pints. A pint of lager costs 42 kronor ($7.60).

PICNIC FARE & WHERE TO EAT IT

Fast-food eateries and fresh food markets abound in Stockholm, especially in the center of the city, around the Hötorget. There you can visit **Hötorgs Hallen,** a fresh food market where you can obtain the makings of an elegant picnic. Many Turkish food products are sold here by recently arrived immigrants, including stuffed pita bread.

For the most elegant fare of all, however, go to **Östermaims Hallen** at the corner of Humlegårdsgatan and Nybrogatan, east of the center. Here, stall after stall sells picnic fare, including fresh shrimp and precooked items that will be wrapped carefully for you.

Smörgåskringlan, Riddargatan 14 (tel. 611-82-80), in the center of town, 2 blocks from Stureplan, prepares a large choice of appetizing open-face sandwiches which they will wrap for you to take out. You can order velvety pâtés, cheese, ham, and shrimp. They also prepare tasty quiches. Open daily from 10am to 4pm. Closed in July.

With your picnic fixings in hand, head for **Skansen** or the wooded peninsula of **Djurgården.** If you like to picnic with lots of people around, go to **Kungsträdgården,** "the summer living room of Stockholm" in the center of town.

WHAT TO SEE & DO IN STOCKHOLM

Stockholm is loaded with things to do for people of all different ages no matter what time of year you visit. Everything from the *Vasa* Ship Museum to the changing of the guard at the Royal Palace to the Gröna Tivoli amusement park will keep your interest piqued. Even just window shopping for beautiful Swedish crafts can be an enjoyable way to spend an afternoon.

SUGGESTED ITINERARIES

IF YOU HAVE 1 DAY

Far too short, but take a ferry to Djurgården to visit the *Vasa* Ship Museum, Stockholm's most famous attraction, and to explore the open-air Skansen folk museum. In the afternoon, take "Walking Tour 1" of Gamla Stan (Old Town) (see below) and have dinner at one of its restaurants.

IF YOU HAVE 2 DAYS

Day 1: See "If You Have 1 Day," above.

Day 2: Get up early and visit the Kaknästornet television tower for a panoramic view of Stockholm, its many islands, and the archipelago. Go to the Museum of Nordic History for insight into 5 centuries of life in Sweden. After lunch, visit the Millesgården of Lidingö, the sculpture garden and former home of Carl Milles.

IF YOU HAVE 3 DAYS

Days 1 & 2: See "If You Have 2 Days," above.

Day 3: Spend the morning taking "Walking Tour 2" (see below). At noon (1pm on Sunday), return to Gamla Stan to see the changing of the guard at the Royal Palace. View this French-inspired building that has been the residence of Swedish kings for more than 700 years. In the afternoon, see the Nationalmuseum.

IF YOU HAVE 5 DAYS

Days 1–3: See "If You Have 3 Days," above.

Day 4: Take one of the many tours offered of the Stockholm archipelago. Return to Stockholm and spend the evening at the Gröna Tivoli amusement park on Djurgården.

Day 5: Visit Drottningholm Palace and its 18th-century theater. In the afternoon, explore the university of the city of Uppsala, north of Stockholm, easily reached by public transportation (see "Easy Excursions" in this chapter).

1. THE TOP ATTRACTIONS

Even the most hurried traveler will want to see the **changing of the Royal Guard.** In summer, you can watch the parade of the military guard daily, on Wednesday and Sunday in winter (on all other days you can see only the changing of the guard). The parade route on weekdays begins at Sergels Torg and proceeds along Hamngatan, Kungsträdgårdsgatan, Strömgatan, Gustav Adolfs Torg, Norrbro, Skeppsbron, and Slottsbacken. On Sunday the guard departs from the Army Museum, going along Riddargatan, Artillerigatan, Strandvägen, Hamngatan, Kungsträdgårdsgatan, Strömgatan, Gustav Adolfs Torg, Norrbro, Skeppsbron, and Slottsbacken. For information on the time of the march, ask at the Tourist Center in Sweden House. The actual changing of the guard takes place at noon Monday through Saturday (at 1pm on Sunday) in front of the Royal Palace in Gamla Stan.

KAKNÄSTORNET (Kaknäs Television Tower), Djurgårdsbrunnsvägen. Tel. 667-80-30.

The tallest artificial structure in Scandinavia is in the northern district of 'Djurgården, a radio and television tower that stands 508 feet high. Two elevators take visitors to an observation platform, where you can see everything from the cobblestone streets of the Gamla Stan to the city's new concrete-and-glass structures, and the archipelago beyond.

Admission: 12 kronor ($2.20) adults, 10 kronor ($1.80) children 7–15.
Open: Apr 15–Sept 15, daily 9am–midnight; off-season, daily 9am–6pm.
Closed: Dec 24–25. **Bus:** 69 from Nybroplan.

ROYAL FLAGSHIP *VASA,* Galärvarvet, Djurgården. Tel. 666-48-00.

⭐ This 17th-century man-of-war is the number one sightseeing attraction in Scandinavia—and for good reason. Housed in a museum specially constructed for it at Djurgården near Skansen, the *Vasa* is considered the world's oldest identified and complete ship.

In 1628, on its maiden voyage and in front of thousands of horrified onlookers, the Royal Flagship *Vasa* capsized and sank almost instantly to the bottom of Stockholm harbor. In a feat that was considered an engineering triumph, it was salvaged in 1961. On board were found more than 4,000 coins, carpenter's tools, sailor's pants (in a color known as Lübeck gray), fishbones, and other items of archeological interest. Perhaps best of all, 97% of the 700 original sculptures were found. Carefully restored and impregnated with preservatives, they are now back aboard the ship, which looks stunning now that it once again carries grotesque faces, lion masks, fish-shaped bodies, and other carvings, some still with the original paint and gilt.

A full-scale model of half of the *Vasa*'s upper gun deck has been rebuilt together with the admiral's cabin and the steering compartment. Several carved wooden figures represent the crew. By walking through the "gun deck" and the exhibition of original objects (including medical equipment, preserved clothes, and a backgammon board) the visitor can get a vision of everyday life on board.

Another exhibition tells the story of naval warfare in the *Vasa*'s (brief) heyday. A diorama shows a battle fought by the Swedish and Polish navies in 1627. The ships, sculpted in copper, are positioned on a large cupola. Inside the cupola, a film illustrates the horrors of war at sea.

Admission: 30 kronor ($5.40) adults, 10 kronor ($1.80) children.
Open: June–Aug, daily 9:30am–7pm; Sept–May, daily 10am–5pm. **Bus:** 44, 47,

STOCKHOLM ATTRACTIONS

Subway - - -   Church ✝   Post Office ⊠   Information ⊖

Skansen ❷
Stadshuset ⑬
Stadsmuseet ⑪
Stadsteatern ⑯
Strindbergsmuseet ⑱
Royal Flagship *Vasa* ❹

68, 69, 76. Ferry: From Slussen all year, from Nybroplan in summer only. **Closed:** Dec 24-26 and 31, Jan 1, May 1.

SKANSEN, Djurgården 49-51. Tel. 663-05-00.

Often called "Old Sweden in a Nutshell," this open-air museum is on Djurgården, near Gröna Lund's Tivoli. More than 150 dwellings from Lapland to Skåne, most from the 18th and 19th centuries, have been reassembled on some 75 acres of parkland.

The exhibits range from a windmill to a manor house to a complete town quarter. Browsers can explore the old workshops and see where the early book publishers, silversmiths, and druggists plied their trade. Many handcrafts for which Swedes later became noted (glassblowing, for example) are demonstrated here, along with such the traditional peasant crafts as weaving and churning. For a tour of the buildings, arrive no later than 4pm (2pm off-season). Chamber music recitals are given on Monday in July at the Skogaholm manor house. Folk dancing and open-air symphonic concerts are also featured. In summer, international stars perform at Skansen. Check the information office for these special events. There's much to do at night here (see "Evening Entertainment" in this chapter), and many places to eat.

Admission: 25 kronor ($4.50) adults; children under 15 free.
Open: Historic buildings, summer, daily 9am-10pm; winter, daily 9am-5pm.
Bus: 44 from Nybroplan. **Ferry:** From Slussen to Gröna Lund.

MILLESGÅRDEN, Carl Milles Väg 2, Lidingö. Tel. 731-50-60.

On the island of Lidingö, northeast of Stockholm, is Carl Milles's former villa and sculpture garden beside the sea, now a museum. Many of his best-known works are displayed here (some are copies), as are works of other artists. Milles (1875-1955), who relied heavily on mythological themes, was Sweden's most famous sculptor.

Admission: 30 kronor ($5.40) adults; children under 12 free.
Open: May, daily 10am-5pm; June to mid-Aug, daily 10am-7pm; Oct-Apr, Tues-Sun 11am-4pm. **Transportation:** Underground to Ropsten and from there bus to Torsviks torg or train to Torsvik. There is also a daily boat service from Nybroplan and Strömkajen to Millesgården from June to August.

STADSHUSET (Stockholm City Hall), Hantverkargatan 1. Tel. 785-94-99.

Built in what is called the National Romantic Style, the Stockholm City Hall or Stadshuset, on the island of Kungsholmen, is one of the finest examples of modern architecture in Europe. Designed by Ragnar Ostberg, it was completed in 1923. The red-brick structure is dominated by a lofty square tower 348 feet high, topped by three gilt crowns, the symbol of Sweden, and the national coat-of-arms. There are two courts: the open civic court and the interior covered court. The Blue Hall is used for banquets and other occasions, including the Nobel Prize banquet. About 18 million pieces of gold and colored mosaics made of special glass cover the walls, and the southern gallery contains murals by Prince Eugen, the painter prince. The 101 City Council members meet in the council chamber.

Guided tours of the City Hall are held daily at 10am and noon.
Admission: 20 kronor ($3.60) adults; children under 12 free.
Open: Tower, May-Sept, daily 10am-4:30pm; City Hall tours, daily year-round at 10am and noon. **T-bana:** Central Station. **Bus:** 48, 62.

KUNGLIGA SLOTTET (Royal Palace), Kungliga Husgerådskammaren. Tel. 789-85-00.

Kungliga Slottet is one of the few official residences of a European monarch that is open to the public. The king and his queen prefer to live and bring up their children at Drottningholm, although Kungliga Slottet remains the official address. Even the most hurried visitor may want to see the changing of the guard, Monday through Saturday at noon and on Sunday at 1pm. Built principally in the Italian baroque style between 1691 and 1754, the palace contains 608 rooms.

Visitors may walk through the Council Chamber where the king and his ministers meet several times a year. The **State Apartments,** with three magnificent baroque ceilings and fine tapestries, the **Bernadotte Apartment,** and the **Guest Apartment** are on view. They are beautifully furnished in Swedish rococo, Louis XVI, and Empire style.

In the cellar, the **Skattkammaren (Treasury)** (tel. 789-85-00) is worth a visit, exhibiting one of the most celebrated collections of crown jewels in Europe. You will see a dozen crowns, scepters, and orbs, along with stunningly beautiful pieces of antique jewelry. Nearly all visitors want to head for the **Royal Armory,** Slottsbacken 3 (tel. 666-44-75), also housed in the cellars of the palace. Kings used to ride in these elegant gilded coaches. You will also see coronation costumes from the 16th century, weapons, and armor. Guided tours are conducted Monday through Friday at 2pm (there is also a Sunday tour for adults at 3pm, and a special tour for children at 2pm).

Remains of the old Three Crowns Castle, built in 1187 and symbolizing the union of Sweden, Denmark, and Norway, can be viewed in the **Palace Museum.**

Gustav III's collection of sculpture from the days of the Roman Empire can be viewed in the **Antikmuseum (Museum of Antiquities)** (tel. 789-85-00).

Finally, the **Rikssalen (Hall of State)** (tel. 789-85-00), where the present king makes his "State of the Nation" addresses, is also open to the public.

Admission: Apartments, 30 kronor ($5.40) adults, 10 kronor ($1.80) children. Treasury, 25 kronor ($4.50) adults, 5 kronor (90¢) children. Royal Armory, 25 kronor ($4.50) adults, 10 kronor ($1.80) children. Palace Museum, 5 kronor (90¢) adults, 2 kronor (40¢) children. Museum of Antiquities, 5 kronor (90¢) adults, 2 kronor (40¢) children. Hall of State, 5 kronor (90¢) adults, 1 kronor (20¢) children.

Open: Apartments, May–Aug, Tues–Sat 10am–3pm; Sun noon–3pm; Sept–Apr, Tues–Sun noon–3pm. Treasury, May–Aug, Mon–Sat 10am–4pm; Sun noon–4pm; Sept–Apr, Mon–Sat 11am–3pm; Sun noon–4pm. Royal Armory, May–Aug, Mon–Fri 10am–4pm; Sat–Sun 11am–4pm; Sept–Apr, Tues–Fri 10am–4pm, Sat–Sun 11am–4pm. Palace Museum, June–Aug, daily noon–3pm (closed Sept–May). Hall of State, May–Oct daily noon–3pm (closed Nov–Apr). **T-bana:** Gamla Stan. **Bus:** 43, 46, 55, 59, 76.

RIDDARHOLM CHURCH, Riddarholmen. Tel. 789-85-00.

The second-oldest church in Stockholm is located on the tiny island of Riddarholmen, next to Gamla Stan. It was founded in the 13th century as a Franciscan monastery. Almost all the royal heads of state are entombed here, except for Christina, who is buried in Rome.

There are three principal royal chapels, including one—the Bernadotte wing—that belongs to the present ruling family. Queen Desideria, the first queen of the Bernadotte Dynasty, is buried here in a green marble sarcophagus.

Admission: Free.

Open: May 2–Aug, Mon–Sat 10am–3pm, Sun 1–3pm. **Closed:** Sept–May 1. **T-bana:** Gamla Stan. **Bus:** 48, 53.

NATIONALMUSEUM (National Museum of Art), Södra Blasieholmen. Tel. 666-42-50.

At the tip of a peninsula on Södra Blasieholmshamnen, a short walk from the Royal Opera House and the Grand Hotel, is the Swedish state's treasure house of paintings and sculpture, one of the oldest museums in the world. It celebrated its 200th anniversary in 1992. Its collections include a wide assortment of masterpieces by such artists as Rembrandt and Rubens (*Sacrifices to Venus*).

The first floor is devoted to applied arts (silverware, handcrafts, porcelain, Empire furnishings, and the like), but first-time visitors, if pushed for time, may want to head directly to the second floor.

Among the paintings from northern Europe is Lucas Cranach's most amusing *Venus and Cupid.* Also displayed is a rare collection of Russian icons, most of them—such as *St. George and the Dragon*—from the Moscow School of the mid-16th century.

On view is an exceptional number of excellent paintings by such masters as Perugino (*St. Sebastian*), Ribera (his oft-rendered *Martyrdom of Bartolomé*), El

FROMMER'S FAVORITE
STOCKHOLM EXPERIENCES

Ballooning Over Stockholm   In the early evening or early morning, pile into a wicker basket and ascend to a flight over Stockholm and the archipelago at 12 miles per hour. The pilot will head straight into a forest of old birch trees, only to pull free in a few seconds. Two hours of bird's-eye viewing ends in a champagne picnic and a diploma. Call Aventursresor (tel. 54-11-55) for reservations.

Experiencing Skansen   Butter churning or folk dancing, there's always something to excite and amuse people of all ages here. Wander at will through the world's oldest open-air museum, getting a preview of Swedish life in the long-ago countryside on some 75 acres of parkland.

Strolling Through Gamla Stan at Night   To walk the narrow cobblestoned alleys of the Old Town on foot at night, with special light effects, is like turning the clock and going back in time. It takes little imagination to envision what everyday life must have been like in this "city between the bridges."

Spending a Night on Barbara Hutton's Yacht   Even if you weren't around in the days of Cary Grant, and didn't get personally invited, you can either stay in Hutton's former cabin suite or dine at her former table, and if either of the above doesn't fit your budget, you can always go aboard the yacht *Mälardrottningen* for a beer.

Taking the Baths   Swedes, both men and women, are fond of roasting themselves on wooden platforms like chickens on a grill, then plunging into a shower of Arctic-chilled water. After this experience, bathers emerge lighthearted and lightheaded into the northern fresh air fortified for an evening of revelry.

Watching the Summer Dawn   In midsummer at 3am, you can get out of bed, as many Swedes do, and sit out on balconies to watch the eerie blue sky—pure, crystal, exquisite. Gradually it's bathed in peach as the early dawn of a too-short summer day approaches. Swedes don't like to miss a minute of their summer, even if they have to get up early to enjoy it.

Greco (*Peter and Paul*), Giovanni Bellini (*Portrait of Christ*), Lotto (*Portrait of a Man*), and Poussin (*Bacchus*). The gallery contains some outstanding Flemish works, notably Ruben's *Bacchanal at Andros* and *Worship of Venus,* and Jan Brueghel's *Jesus Preaching from the Boat.*

Perhaps the most important room in the entire gallery has one whole wall featuring the works of Rembrandt (*Portrait of an Old Man* and *Portrait of an Old Woman*), along with his *Kitchen Maid* (one of the more famous works in Stockholm). Here also is *The Oath of the Batavians.*

In yet another room is Watteau's *Lesson in Love,* and another salon is noted for its Venetian works by Guardi and Canaletto, as well as English portraits by Gainsborough and Reynolds.

Modern works include Manet's *Parisienne;* Degas's dancers; Rodin's nude male (*Copper Age*) and his bust of Victor Hugo; van Gogh's *Light Movements in Green;* landscapes by Cézanne, Gauguin, and Pissarro; paintings by Renoir, notably *La Grenouillère.*

Admission: 40 kronor ($7.20) adults; children 15 and under free.

Open: July–Aug, Tues–Wed and Fri–Sun 11am–5pm, Thurs 11am–9pm; Sept–

June, Tues and Thurs 10am–9pm, Wed and Fri–Sun 11am–5pm. **T-bana:** Kungsträdgården. **Bus:** 62, 65.

NORDISKA MUSEET [Nordic Museum], Djurgårdsvägen 6-16, Djurgården. Tel. 666-46-00.

On the island of Djurgården, this museum contains an impressive collection of implements, costumes, and furnishings of Swedish life from the 1500s to the present. The most outstanding museum of national life in Scandinavia houses more than a million objects. Highlights include dining tables, period costumes ranging from matching garters and ties for men to purple flowerpot hats from the 1890s. In the basement is an extensive exhibit of the tools of the Swedish fishing trade, plus relics from nomadic Lapps.

Admission: 30 kronor ($5.40) adults, 10 kronor ($1.80) children 7–15.

Open: June–Aug, Mon–Fri 10am–4pm, Sat–Sun noon–4pm; Sept–May, Tues–Wed and Fri 10am–4pm, Thurs 10am–8pm, Sat–Sun noon–5pm. **Bus:** 44, 47, 69.

DROTTNINGHOLM PALACE AND THEATER, Drottningholm. Tel. 759-03-10.

⭐ On an island in Lake Mälaren, **Drottningholm** (Queen's Island)—dubbed the Versailles of Sweden—lies about 7 miles from Stockholm and is easily reached by boat, escorted motorcoach tour, bus, and subway. Reflecting 18th-century French baroque trends, Drottningholm, with its courtly art, royal furnishings, and Gobelin tapestries, is surrounded by fountains and parks. The palace is inhabited by the royal family.

Nearby is the **Drottningholm Court Theater** (tel. 759-04-06), considered the best-preserved 18th-century theater in the world, with the original stage machinery and settings still in use. Performances are staged here each summer, between May and September (see "Evening Entertainment" in this chapter). There is also a museum that charts the development of the theater between the 1500s and 1700s.

The **Chinese Pavilion** (Kina Slott) (tel. 759-03-10) reflects Europe's fascination with the Far East at the turn of the century.

Nearby is a place for refreshments (Swedish waffles). Guided tours of the palace and theater are conducted every hour on the hour.

Admission: Palace, 25 kronor ($4.50) adults, 20 kronor ($3.60) children; Theater Museum, 22 kronor ($4) adults, 10 kronor ($1.80) children; Chinese Pavilion, 25 kronor ($4.50) adults, 20 kronor ($3.60) children.

Open: Palace, May–Aug, Mon–Sat 11am–4:30pm, Sun 11am–4:30pm; Sept, Mon–Fri 1–3:30pm. Theater, May–Aug, Mon–Sat 11:30am–4:30pm, Sun 12:30–4:30pm; Sept, daily 12:30–3pm. Chinese pavilion, Apr and Sept, daily 1–3:30pm; May–Aug, daily 11am–4:30pm. **Closed:** Oct–Mar. **T-bana:** Brommaplan; then transfer to the Mälärobus to Drottningholm. **Ferry:** From the dock near the Stadshuset.

2. MORE ATTRACTIONS

PRINS EUGENS WALDEMARSUDDE, Prins Eugens Väg 6. Tel. 662-18-33.

This once-royal residence of the "painting prince" functions today as an art gallery and a memorial to one of the most famous royal artists in recent history, Prince Eugen (1865–1947). The youngest of King Oscar II's four children (all of whom were sons), he was considered to have made innovative contributions to the techniques of Swedish landscape paintings, specializing in depictions of his favorite regions in central Sweden. Among his most visible works are the murals he painted on the inner walls of the Stadshuset.

Built between 1903 and 1904, and set directly on the water, the house is surrounded by a flower and sculpture garden. Eugen's private collection of paintings, which includes works by Edvard Munch, Carl Larsson, and Anders Zorn, is considered one of the most rewarding aspects of the entire residence. The house and its contents was willed to the Swedish government after the prince's death, and opened to the public for the first time in 1948.

The art gallery and the house that contains it are furnished as the prince left it. While at Waldemarsudde, see the Old Mill, built in the 1780s, and open only in the summer.

Admission: 30 kronor ($5.40) adults; children free.

Open: June–Aug, Tues–Sun 11am–5pm (also Tues and Thurs 7–9pm); Sept–May, Tues–Sun 11am–4pm. **Bus:** 47 to end of the line.

MODERNA MUSEET [Museum of Modern Art], Skeppsholmen. Tel. 666-42-50.

On the tiny island of Skeppsholmen, a short walk from af *Chapman*, this museum shows contemporary works by Swedish and international artists, including kinetic sculptures. Highlights include a small but good collection of cubist art by Picasso, Braque, and Léger, Matisse's *Apollo* découpage, the famous *Enigma of William Tell* by Salvador Dalí, and works by Brancusi, Max Ernst, Giacometti, and Arp, among others. There is as well a collection of pop art—from Rauschenberg's *Monogram*, via Oldenburg, to Andy Warhol. Among 1960s works by prominent New York artists are the 12-foot-high *Geometric Mouse* by Claes Oldenburg; *Fox Trot*, an early Warhol; and *Total Totality All*, a large sculpture by Louise Nevelson. Outdoors, in front of the museum, is *The Four Elements* by Alexander Calder, and behind and around the house a number of works by Nordic artists have been installed. Farther away, near the Skeppsholmen bridge, is *The Paradise*, a sculpture group by Niki de Saint Phalle and Jean Tinguely.

The museum's activities include a children's workshop, concerts, films, discussions, and theater. There is a bookshop with posters, cards, books, and reproductions, plus a restaurant with fresh salads and wine that you can enjoy outdoors in the garden.

Admission: 40 kronor ($7.20) adults, 20 kronor ($3.60) children under 16.

Open: Tues–Thurs 11am–9pm, Fri–Sun 11am–5pm. **Bus:** 65 from Vasagatan.

THIELSKA GALLERIET [Thiel Gallery], Sjötullsbacken 6-8, Djurgården. Tel. 662-58-84.

At the tip of Djurgården, this collection is one of Sweden's major art collections, surpassing, many feel, that of Waldemarsudde. The sculptures and canvases here were amassed by Thiel, a financier and banker who eventually went bankrupt. The collection was acquired by the Swedish state in 1924.

Some of the big names in Scandinavian art are here, including Norway's Edvard Munch and Sweden's Anders Zorn (see his nude, *In Dreams*). Gustav Fjaestad's furniture is also displayed. You'll also see a portrait of Nietzsche, whom Thiel greatly admired. Works by Manet, Rodin, and Toulouse-Lautrec, among others, round out the collection. Thiel is buried on the grounds beneath a statue of Rodin's *Shadow*.

Admission: 30 kronor ($5.40) adults; children under 12 free.

Open: Mon–Sat noon–4pm, Sun 1–4pm. **Bus:** 69.

STADSMUSEET [Stockholm City Museum], Peter Myndes Backe 6. Tel. 700-05-00.

At Slussen, beside the Katarina Elevator, is the Stadsmuseet. Its best-known exhibit is the rich Lohe treasure, but it also shows 17th-century trades and crafts and life in the industrial city of the late 19th century.

Admission: 15 kronor ($2.70) adults; children free.

Open: Mid-May to mid-Sept, Tues–Thurs 11am–7pm, Fri–Mon 11am–5pm; late Sept–early May, Tues–Thurs 11am–9pm, Fri–Mon 11am–5pm. **T-bana:** Slussen.

MUSEUM OF MEDIEVAL STOCKHOLM, Strömparterren, Norrbro. Tel. 700-05-00.

Built around archeological excavations, including parts of the old city wall dating back to 1530 (discovered in 1978–80), this museum traces the city's founding and development during the Middle Ages. The museum also contains the Riddarsholmship, leather goods, ceramics, and metal articles.

Admission: 25 kronor ($4.50) adults, 5 kronor (90¢) children.

Open: June–Aug, Tues–Thurs 11am–7pm, Fri–Sun 11am–5pm; Sept–May, Tues and Thurs–Sun 11am–5pm, Wed 11am–7pm. **Tram:** 43.

ÖSTASIATISKAMUSEET [Museum of Far Eastern Antiquities], Skeppsholmen. Tel. 666-42-50.

This small, intimate museum was opened in 1963 in an old building erected in 1699 and 1700 as stables for Karl XII's bodyguard. It's about a 7-minute walk from Karl XII Torg and very near the Museum of Modern Art. The permanent exhibition consists of archeological objects, fine arts, and handcrafts from China, Japan, Korea, and India. The collection is considered one of the finest and most important of its kind outside Asia. Among the outstanding displays are Chinese neolithic painted pottery, ritual bronze vessels, archaic jades, wood carvings, ivory, lacquerwork, enamelware, Chinese glass, Buddhist sculpture, Chinese painting and calligraphy, T'ang tomb pottery figurines, Sung classical stoneware such as celadon and temmoku, Ming blue-and-white wares, and Ch'ing porcelain made for both the Chinese and the European market.

Admission: 30 kronor ($5.40) adults; children under 16 free.

Open: Tues 11am–9pm, Wed–Sun noon–5pm. **Bus:** 46, 55, 62, 76 to Karl XII Torg. **T-bana:** Kungsträdgården.

THE SUBWAY ART OF STOCKHOLM

In 1950 two women came up with the idea of commissioning artists to decorate the subway stations of Stockholm. Some of the country's finest artists were asked to decorate the subway stations, and their work is now in some 100 stations, all the way from the center of Stockholm to the suburbs, a 173-mile-long art exhibition, "the longest and deepest art gallery in the world." Some 70 artists contributed their work.

3. COOL FOR KIDS

The open-air park, Skansen (see "The Top Attractions" in this chapter), on Djurgården, offers **Lill-Skansen,** the children's own "Little Skansen," containing lots of small animals. Children can also enjoy pony rides, a car track, and a miniature train. Lill-Skansen is open daily in summer from 10am to 4pm.

Kids can spend a day or several at Skansen and not get bored. Before going to Skansen, stop off at the **Vasa Museum,** which many youngsters find an epic adventure. The evening can be capped by a visit to **Gröna Lund's Tivoli** (see "Evening Entertainment" in this chapter), which is also on Djurgården.

Some other activities that will amuse children include the following:

STADSTEATERN, in the Kulturhuset, Sergels Torg. Tel. 700-04-00.

Although many of the performances at the Stadsteatern are designed for adult tastes, Saturday afternoons often relinquish the stage to performances for children. Schedules and venues change frequently, although time-tested favorites include both *Delfimen* and *Unga Klara* (Young Clara), both of which contain enough action, amusement, and fun to interest children in any language. Performances usually begin at 3pm on Saturday afternoons and last about an hour, short enough to keep most attention spans from wandering.

Admission: 50 kronor ($9) per person, adult or child.

Open: Various times (call the box office). **Closed:** Early June to mid-Aug.
T-bana: Central Station.

4. SPECIAL-INTEREST SIGHTSEEING

FOR THE LITERARY ENTHUSIAST

STRINDBERGSMUSEET (Strindberg Museum), Drottninggatan 85. Tel. 11-37-89.

This building popularly known as "The Blue Tower" is where August Strindberg, dramatist and novelist, spent the last 4 years of his life (1908–12). It contains a library, three rooms with his furnishings, and books, articles, and letters representing the last 20 years of his life. The library is a typical working author's library, with fiction and nonfiction works, including encyclopedias in Swedish, German, English, and French. Many of the volumes are full of pen and pencil markings—comments on the contents, heavily marked deletions of points he did not approve of, and underlinings indicating his diligent research into matters about which he wrote.

Of special interest to those familiar with Strindberg's plays is the fact that he furnished his rooms like stage sets from his plays, with color schemes as he visualized them. The dining room contains sculptures, casts of busts, and masks evoking for the writer people and events that were important to him. The museum also has a stage where Strindberg's plays are frequently presented.

Admission: 15 kronor ($2.70) adults; children free.
Open: Tues–Fri 10am–4pm (also Tues 6–8pm), Sat–Sun noon–4pm. **T-bana:** Rådmansgatan.

FOR THE ARCHITECTURE LOVER

In Stockholm, architects or those interested in the subject are captivated by the past, as reflected by such grand buildings as Drottningholm Palace and Riddarholm. But many of the expanding suburb "cities" of Stockholm are also worth seeing for their urban planning and architecture, which in Stockholm is considered among the most advanced in the world.

One of these model developments is **Farsta,** completed in 1960, although much altered since then. It lies 6 miles from the heart of Stockholm, and can be reached by the Farsta train departing from the Central Station, or by taking bus no. 18 to the end of the line. With its traffic-free shopping mall, its bright and airy modern apartment houses, its contemporary stores and restaurants, it makes for a good afternoon's tour.

Also pay a call at the:

ARKITEKTUR MUSEET (Museum of Architecture), Skeppsholmen. Tel. 679-75-10.

Near the modern art museum, this museum has exhibits on the architecture of Stockholm, extensive archives, and a shop with books on architecture, past and present. Special exhibitions are also staged here.

Admission: 20 kronor ($3.60) adults; children free.
Open: Tues 11am–9pm, Wed–Sun 11am–5pm. **Bus:** 65.

WALKING TOUR 1 — GAMLA STAN (OLD TOWN)

Start: Gustav Adolfs Torg.
Finish: Slussplan.
Time: 3 hours.
Best Time: Any day it's not raining.

WALKING TOUR — GAMLA STAN

N

0 [====] 100 m
     [====] 110 y

start here ☆ ❶ Gustav Adolfs Torg

Fredsgatan

Strömgatan

NORRBRO

❸

Riksplan ❷

Riksgatan

VASABRON

CENTRALBRON

NORRA JÄRNVÄGSBRON

SLOTTSKAJEN

SKEPPSBRON

Riddarhusgränd

Riddarhuskajen

Riddarholmes

Mynt-torget

MYNTGATAN

Högvaktsterrasen

❼

SLOTTSBACKEN

Ekensalen

❹ **Riddar-hustorget**

Storkyrko brinken

❽ ✝ Kållaregränd

Nygränd

❾

B. Jarls Torg

Wrangelska Backen

❻

Stortorget

Köpmangatan **Köpman-torget**

❿

Skott-gränd

⓫

Kindstugatan

Ferkens Gränd

Österlånggatan

Södra Riddars-holmshammen

❺

MUNKBRON

STORA NYGATAN

❶❹

Skomakargatan

Västerlånggatan

⓭

Lila Nygatan

Tyska Brinken

Mälar-torget

Kornhamns-torg

⓬

S. Bernickebr.

⓯ **Järn-torget**

Triewaldsgränd

MUNKBROLEDEN

Lake Mälaren

CENTRALBRON

Sluss-plan ⓰

finish here ☆

Karl Johans Torg

SKEPPSBRON

Church ✝

Railway ┼┼┼

Worst Time: Monday to Friday 8 to 9:30am and 5:30 to 7pm because of traffic.

Begin at:

1. **Gustav Adolfs Torg,** facing the Royal Palace, with the Royal Opera on your left. King Gustavus III, patron of the arts, was assassinated here at a masked ball in 1792.

   Walk across Norrbro Bridge heading toward the Royal Palace, passing on your right the:

2. **Swedish Parliament.** At Helgeandsholmen, the Parliament dates from 1897 when its foundation stone was laid. It can be visited only on guided tours. Along the bridge on your left are stairs leading to the:

3. **Medeltidsmuseet** (Museum of Medieval Stockholm), Strömparterren, with objects and settings from medieval Stockholm, including the Riddarholmship and parts of the old city wall.

REFUELING STOP One of the hidden cafés of Stockholm, **Café Strömparterren,** Helgeandsholmen (tel. 21-95-45), is also one of the most centrally located, lying next door to the Medeltidsmuseet. Many Stockholmers come here for a morning cup of coffee and a stunning view of the waterfront. Later they can fish for salmon—everybody can—right in front of the Royal Palace, a right that has existed since Queen Christina's day. In summer, tables are placed outside, and the interior of the café is built into the walls under Norrbro Bridge.

After leaving the museum, turn to the right and walk back to the bridge until you come to Slottskajen. Here, directly in front of the Royal Palace, make a right turn and head to Mynttorget, site of Kanslihuset, a government office building erected in the 1930s. The neoclassical columned facade remains from the Royal Mint of 1790.

Continue straight along Myntgatan until you reach Riddarhustorget. On your right is the:

4. **Riddarhuset,** the 17th-century House of Nobles, where the Swedish aristocracy met during the Parliament of the Four Estates (1665–68).

   Continue straight across Riddarholmsbron (the bridge) until you come to the little island of:

5. **Riddarholmen,** called "the island of the knights." It is closely linked to the Old Town and its chief landmark, which you'll see immediately, is Riddarholmskyrkan with its cast-iron spire. Founded as an abbey in the 13th century, it has been the burial place of Swedish kings for 4 centuries.

   Walk along the right side of the church until you reach Birger Jarls Torg. From there, take the 1-block-long Wrangelska Backen to the water. Then go left and walk along Södra Riddarholmshamnen until you come to a:

REFUELING STOP The *Mälardrottningen,* Riddarholmen (tel. 24-36-00), was the yacht of the mink-swathed Woolworth heiress Barbara Hutton, who owned this vessel, built in 1924—at the time, the largest power-driven pleasure craft in the world. It was originally called *Vanadis,* and was donated by Miss Hutton to the British navy in the early days of World War II. During her brief ownership, the heiress and her guests, including Cary Grant (the press called them "Cash and Cary"), along with a crew of 50, visited some of the world's most celebrated ports. Today it's a hotel and a restaurant. You can stop for drinks in the Captain's Bar.

After leaving the yacht, continue right along Södra Riddarholmshamnen. Veer left by the railroad tracks, climb steps, and go along Hebbes Trappor until you return to Riddarholmskyrkan. From here, cross over Riddarholmsbron and return to Riddarhustorget.

Cross Stora Nygatan and take the next right onto Storkyrkobrinken, passing the landmark Cattelin Restaurant on your right. Continue along this street, past the Lady Hamilton Hotel, turning right onto Trångsund, which leads to:

6. **Stortorget,** where you'll find park benches for resting. Meaning "Great Square" in English, this plaza was the site of the Stockholm Blood Bath of 1520 when King Christian II of Denmark beheaded 80 Swedish noblemen and displayed a "pyramid" of their heads in the square. The Börsen on this square is the Swedish Stock Exchange, a building dating from 1776. Every year the Swedish Academy meets here to elect the Nobel Prize winners in literature.

At the northeast corner of the square, take Källargränd north to view the entrance to the:

7. **Royal Palace,** opening onto Slottsbacken. The present palace dates mainly from 1760 after a previous one was destroyed by fire. The changing of the guard takes place here on this square, which is also the site of the:

8. **Storkyrkan,** on your right. This church was founded in the mid-1200s but it has been rebuilt many times since. It is the site for coronations and royal weddings. Kings are also christened here. The most celebrated piece of sculpture is *St. George and the Dragon,* a huge piece of artwork dating from 1489. The royal pews have been used for 3 centuries, and the altar, mainly in ebony and silver, is stunning, dating from 1652. This is still a functioning church, and you should visit when no services are being conducted. It's open Monday through Saturday from 9am to 7pm and on Sunday from 9am to 5:30pm; admission is free.

Continue right along Slottsbacken, either visiting the palace now or saving it for later. Go right as you reach Bollhusgränd, a cobblestone street of old houses leading to one of the most charming squares of the Old Town—

9. **Köpmantorget,** with its famous copy of the St. George and Dragon statue. From the square, take Köpmanbrinken, which runs for 1 block before turning into:

10. **Österlånggatan,** once the Old Town's harbor street, site of many restaurants and antiques shops. Continue along Österlånggatan, but take the first left under an arch, leading into:

11. **Stora Hoparegränd,** one of the darkest and narrowest of Gamla Stan streets. Some buildings along this dank street date from the mid-1600s. Walk down the alley toward the water, emerging at Skeppsbron. Turn right for 2 blocks until you reach Ferkens Gränd. Go right again up Ferkens Gränd, until you return to Österlånggatan. Go left on Österlånggatan until you come to Tullgränd. Take the street on your right, Prästgatan, named after the priests who lived on this street.

As you climb this street, note on your left:

12. **Mårten Trotzigs Gränd,** a street of steps that is the narrowest in Gamla Stan. Continue along Prästgatan, passing a playground on your right. Turn right onto Tyska Brinken until you come to the church:

13. **Tyska Kyrkan,** on your right. Since the beginning of the 17th century, this has been the German church of Stockholm. The church has a baroque interior and is exquisitely decorated.

After leaving the church, the street in front of you will be Skomakargatan. Head up this street until you come to Stortorget once again. From Stortorget, take a little street, Kakbrinken, at the southwest corner of the square, until you reach:

14. **Västerlånggatan,** where you should turn left. This pedestrian street is the main shopping artery of Gamla Stan, and the best place to purchase gifts and souvenirs of Sweden. The street leads to:

15. **Järntorget,** which used to be known as Korntorget when it was the center of the copper and iron trade in the 16th and 17th centuries. At times in its long history it has been the place of punishment for "wrongdoers." The most unusual statue in Stockholm stands here. The statue is of Evert Taube, the troubadour and Swedish national poet of the early 1900s. He is carrying a newspaper under his arm, his coat draped nonchalantly, his sunglasses pushed up high on his forehead.

From the square, take Järntorgsgatan to:

16. Slussplan and the water. Here you can catch a bus to return to the central city or you can board a ferry to Djurgården and its many museums.

WALKING TOUR 2 — ALONG THE HARBOR

Start: Stadshuset.
Finish: Museum of Modern Art.
Time: 3 hours.
Best Time: Any day it's not raining.
Worst Time: Monday to Friday 8 to 9:30am and 5:30 to 7pm because of traffic.

Start at the:

1. Stadshuset, Hantverkargatan 1, the town hall of Stockholm, on the island of Kungsholmen in the western part of the city. Kungsholmen has some of the loveliest and most varied waterfront walks in the city. It took 12 years, 8 million bricks, and 19 million gilded mosaic tiles to erect this town hall, which can be visited on a guided tour.

Go inside the courtyard on your own and admire the architecture. After exploring the building, exit and turn right, walking across Stadshusbron (Town Hall Bridge) to the island of Norrmalm. You'll see the Sheraton Hotel coming up on your left, and on your right is the Stadshuscafeet, where sightseeing boats depart on canal cruises in summer. Walk along past the boats and go under an underpass (watch out for fast-riding bicyclists).

Continue right along the canal until you reach Tegelbacken, a waterfront square. At the entrance to the Vasabron (bridge), cross the street and continue along Fredsgatan. Veer right at the intersection, hugging the canal. This will take you to Rosenbad, a little triangular park.

At the canal-bordering Strömgatan, the building on your right will be the:

2. Swedish Parliament, which can be visited on a guided tour. Upon your arrival at:

3. Gustav Adolfs Torg, you'll have a panoramic view of the Royal Palace across the canal and of the Royal Opera straight ahead. This is one of the most famous landmark squares of Stockholm, and perhaps the most scenically located.

Strömgatan resumes at the corner of the Opera House, site of the Operakällaren, for many years considered the finest restaurant in Stockholm. Continue along until you reach the southern tier of the:

4. Kungsträdgården, which is the summer living room of Stockholm. These royal gardens reach from Hamngatan in the north down to the waters. Established in the 1500s as a pleasure garden for the court, they are now open to all, with their cafés, open-air restaurants, and refreshment kiosks.

Continue along the waterfront, past Strömbron, a bridge leading to Gamla Stan, and emerge onto Södra Blasieholmshamnen, site of the:

5. Grand Hotel, at no. 8. For decades this has been the prestige address of Stockholm, attracting Nobel Prize winners and most visiting dignitaries and movie stars. On your right, any number of sightseeing boats depart in summer for tours of the Stockholm archipelago. From this vantage point, you'll have a good view of the Royal Palace and Gamla Stan.

Continue along this street until you reach (on your right) the:

6. National Museum, Södra Blasieholmen, which is the repository of the state's art treasures, everything from Renoir to Rembrandt.

Cross the Skeppsholmsbron (bridge) leading to the little island of:

7. Skeppsholmen, which has a number of attractions, including the modern art museum. After crossing the bridge, turn right along Västra Brobänken. On your right, you'll pass:

8. af Chapman, a "tall ship" with fully rigged masts that once sailed the seas under three different flags before going to permanent anchor here in 1949 as a

WALKING TOUR — ALONG THE HARBOR

N 0 ⌐ 200 m / 220 y

Djurgår

Djurgården

Djurgbron

Galärparken

Storgatan

Strandvägen

Riddargatan

Styrmansgatan

Grevgatan

Skeppargatan

Strandvägen

Riddargatan

Nybroviken

Berzelliparken

Hamngatan

Arsenalsgatan

Nybrokajen

Nybrogatan

Blasieholmsgatan

Södra Blasieholmsh.

Skepps-holmsbron

finish here

11

SKEPPSHOLMEN

Svensksundsvägen

Gröna Gången

9

KASTELLHOLMEN

10

7

8

Strömmen

Norrström

Kungsträdgårds gatan

M. Samuelsgatan

Hamngatan

Kungsträd-gården

Sergels Torg

4 Strömgatan

3 Gustav Adolfs Torg

Norrbro

Strömbron

Skeppsbron

2

Strömsborg

Slottskajen

Norr-ström

Stora Nygatan

Lilla Nygatan

Myntgatan

GAMLA STAN

Drottninggatan

Vattugatan

Herkulesgatan

Jakobsgatan

Fredsgatan

Klarabergsviadukten

Klarabergsgatan

Centralplan

Central Station

Vasagatan

Mäster Samuelsgatan

Vasabron

Centralbron

Centralbron

Kl. Mälarstrand

Klara Sjö

Norr-ström

Vasabron

Centralbron

Kungsbron

Riddarfjärden

Söder Mälarstrand

1 start here

Ragnar Östbergs Plan

① Stadshuset
② Swedish Parliament
③ Gustav Adolfs Torg

④ Kungsträdgården
⑤ Grand Hotel
⑥ National Museum

⑦ Skeppsholmen
⑧ af *Chapman*
⑨ Kastellholmen

⑩ Museum of Architecture
⑪ Museum of Modern Art

youth hostel. Turn left onto Flaggmansvägen. The sculptures you see on your left belong to the Museum of Modern Art. Continue along Holmamiralens Torg, passing the Nordiska Institute on your right. Cut right toward the water at Södra Brobänken. Take a right turn and cross the bridge leading to the mini-island of:

9. Kastellholmen, one of the most charming, but also the most undiscovered, in Stockholm. Head right along the water, going around Kastellholmskajen. Circle around and turn left at the end of Kastelleton. Walk back along Örlogsvägen, which runs through the center of the small island.

Cross the bridge, Kastellholmsbron, and return to the larger island of Skeppsholmen. This time go straight along Amiralsvägen, turning left onto Långaraden. Cut right and continue to walk along Långaraden, bypassing sculpture on your right. The first building on your left is the:

10. Museum of Architecture, which has slides and 500,000 architectural drawings and sketches from the last 100 years.

Bypass the museum and make a sharp right onto Svensksundsvägen. You'll approach the:

11. Museum of Modern Art, with a superb collection of both Swedish and international 20th-century art. It is also a venue for many temporary exhibitions of paintings, sculptures, and photographs.

REFUELING STOP   After such a long walk, the **Modern Art Museum Cafeteria,** Skeppsholmen, is an ideal luncheon-and-tea café. When the weather permits, you can load up a tray and take it out into the sculpture garden to an umbrella-shaded table. You can order a selection of salads, sandwiches, vegetable plates, and daily specials, washed down with wine or juices, and finished off with an espresso.

---

5. ORGANIZED TOURS

CITY TOURS   The quickest and most convenient way to see the highlights of Stockholm is to take one of the motorcoach tours that leave from Karl XII Torg, near the Kungsträdgården. **Stockholm Sightseeing,** Skeppsbron 22 (tel. 24-04-70), offers two "Grand City Tours," each lasting 2½ hours and costing 200 kronor ($36); half price for children. The first (10am daily) is highlighted by a visit to the Royal Palace and a trip through Gamla Stan (Old Town), with a stop at the cathedral. The second tour, leaving at 2pm, goes to the Vasa Museum and visits the city hall.

Other tours operated by Stockholm Sightseeing include a guided afternoon tour of Drottningholm Palace and the Royal Court Theater, costing 150 kronor ($27). (Although some visitors appreciate the guide for these two monuments, many others opt to visit these two sights on their own.)

Also, a 2-hour **canal tour** leaves from May to October nine times daily from Strömkajen, in front of the Grand Hotel, passing under the bridges of Stockholm, through locks and canals. It costs 95 kronor ($17.10).

Stockholm Sightseeing offers daily ✪ **tours of the archipelago** whose many islands preface the city's access to the Baltic Sea. They leave Strömkajen from May to October at 2pm, costing 60 kronor ($10.80) per person.

Tickets and reservations for all tours may be obtained at all authorized travel agencies and tourist information centers.

OLD TOWN STROLLS   Authorized guides lead 2-hour walking tours of the medieval lanes of Stockholm's Old Town. Called "Evening Walk in the Old Town," these walks are conducted from the end of May until mid-September, daily at

6:30pm, starting at the Obelisk on Palace Hill (Slottsbacken in Swedish). The fee is 30 kronor ($5.40) for adults (free for children under 16 who are accompanied by their parents). Reservations are not necessary.

In pricey Scandinavia, this tour is a remarkable bargain. Very often, the evening ends with a cup of coffee and some sandwiches in an Old Town café.

THE GÖTA CANAL TRIP The most important boat trip in summer—and one of Sweden's major attractions—is the 4-day ✪ **Göta Canal** ride, which travels 350 miles from Gothenburg (Göteborg) in the west to Stockholm in the east, or vice versa. The trip takes you through 58 locks (the highest more than 300 feet above sea level), and includes four or five stops, varying according to the direction. Day-trips and 5-day cruises with 11 to 15 stops are also offered.

The canal is a lovely waterway that passes the medieval Bohus Castle and goes through the narrow "Rock Canal" and into a lake district that includes Lake Vättern, the second-largest, and the most beautiful, lake in Sweden.

For information about booking tours, which should be done before you leave home, refer to "Package Tours/Cruises" in Chapter 1.

MOTORCOACH TOURS In summer the **Swedish State Railways**, St. Eriksgatan 113 (tel. 728-86-50), which also operates buses, arranges a number of motorcoach tours. A 2-day tour, for example, takes passengers from Stockholm to Copenhagen (or vice versa). The tour covers such areas as the glassworks district, the lake section, and the château country.

---

6. SPECIAL/FREE EVENTS

For major annual events, see the "Stockholm Calendar of Events" in Chapter 23. For other local events, *Stockholm This Week,* available at the tourist information center, is the best source for what's happening. Its "yellow pages" highlight everything from activities for children and auctions to special exhibitions, church music recitals, and other concerts. There's always a lot happening, regardless of the time of your visit.

On a summer night, head for the **Kungsträdgården,** the once-royal park in Norrmalm, adjacent to Sweden House. Concerts are presented here every evening— sometimes classical, often rock, even open-air theatrical performances. But perhaps best of all are the street musicians who entertain you, then pass around the hat. In winter an outdoor ice rink opens here.

In summer, the **Park Theater** performs in different open-air theaters throughout Stockholm. Thousands of people attend its productions, with a repertoire that is often classic. For information, call 661-79-45.

Thousand of international marathon runners participate in the **Stockholm Marathon,** which is usually in early June.

The June **Midsummer Celebration** is an excuse for the town to go wild. Special events are staged in the various parks, but the revelry doesn't need much organization as it has its own life.

During the last Friday and Saturday in June and the first weekend of July, **a Stockholm Jazz/Blues Festival** is presented. See *Stockholm This Week* for the venues.

In July and August, summer-night concerts—called **Sommarnättskonserterna**—are presented on the steps of the National Museum, Södra Blasieholmskajen (tel. 666-42-50).

Bellman Week, in mid-July, honors the national poet of Sweden, Carl Michael Bellman. Poetry and music are presented at Skansen.

In August, the Skansen open-air museum on Djurgården is the site of the **Augustimusiken** (August Music) presentation, with various folkloric and classical events. Admission to most of these events is covered by your park entrance ticket.

The finest sailing vessels in the Stockholm archipelago appear on **Sailboat Day,** the first weekend in September.

7. SPORTS/RECREATION

SPORTS

Soccer and **ice hockey** dominate spectator sports, and Stockholm offers world-class teams in both. Soccer is divided into a spring and fall season, and various stadiums host these matches. During the winter season (November through March) the top ice-hockey teams often appear at Globen, Johnneshov (tel. 600-34-00). **Basketball** is also played at this arena.

For schedules and ticket information, consult the tourist information office or pick up a copy of *Stockholm This Week,* which lists the times and places of the events.

One of the most popular sports, with gambling permitted, is trotting races, held at **Solvalla Stadium** (tel. 635-90-00 for information, directions, and ticket prices). Regular meets are held most of the year.

RECREATION

HORSEBACK RIDING, VIKING STYLE Iceland horses—gentle and small enough for children—can be ridden at the **Haninge Iceland Horse Center** at Hemfosa, 23 miles south of Stockholm, at a cost of 300 kronor ($54) per person for 2 days. Besides walking, galloping, trotting, and cantering, the horses also have another gait, the *tölt,* a kind of equine speedwalk that has no English translation. For more information, call 08/50-04-81-81.

SAUNA & SWIMMING There is a combination sauna, outdoor heated pool, and children's paddling pool, **Vilda Vanadis,** at Vanadislunden, near Sveavägen (tel. 30-12-11), within easy walking distance of the Oden Hotel. This is really an adventure park, with lots of different attractions. There's also a sauna and a restaurant. The entrance fee is 50 kronor ($9), but once inside, the attractions are free. It's open Monday through Friday from 6:30am to 6pm, and on Saturday and Sunday from 8am to 6pm.

If you want a more elegant sauna—one that has even attracted the king of Sweden—go to the **Hotell Karelia,** Birger Jarlsgatan 35 (tel. 24-76-60), which has strong Finnish connections. It costs 60 kronor ($10.80) if you're not a resident of the hotel. Open Monday through Friday from 3 to 10pm, and on Saturday from 3 to 8pm. Massages are also available.

TENNIS, SQUASH & WEIGHTLIFTING Besides tennis at the **Royal Tennis Hall,** Lidingövägen 75 (tel. 667-03-50 for bookings), you can also use weights and enjoy a sauna and solarium. The center has 15 indoor Plexipave courts, 4 outdoor clay courts, and also 8 squash courts.

8. SAVVY SHOPPING

THE SHOPPING SCENE

Stockholm is filled with shop after shop of dazzling merchandise—often at dazzling prices. In the land of super-taxes and super-welfare, Swedish craftspeople are noted—and well paid—for their skill and efficiency, as reflected in the high prices.

Bargain shoppers should proceed with caution. There are some good buys, but it takes a lot of searching. If you're a casual shopper, you may want to confine your purchases to handsome souvenirs and gifts.

Swedish glass, of course, is world famous. Swedish wooden items are outstanding, and many prefer Sweden's functional furniture in blond pine or birch. Other items to look for include playsuits for children, silver necklaces, reindeer gloves, stainless-steel utensils, handwoven neckties and skirts, sweaters and mittens in Nordic patterns, Swedish clogs, and colorful handcrafts from the provinces. The most famous souvenir to buy is the Dala horse from Dalarna.

TAXES & REFUNDS   The value-added tax in Sweden is called MOMS, and it is imposed on all products and services. When buying larger and more expensive items, you can avoids Moms if you spend over 200 kronor ($36). Just give the firm your name, address, and passport number and ask for a "Tax-Free Check." Leave the purchase sealed until you've left Sweden. The Customs official will want to see both the Tax-Free Check and your purchase. Cash refunds—minus a small commission— are granted on the spot. Hold onto your luggage until after you've received your refund, and then you can check your bag or carry the purchase on board if it's not too big. At the tourist information office (see above), you can pick up a pamphlet about tax-free shopping in Sweden.

SHOPPING STREETS & DISTRICTS   Everybody's favorite shopping area in Stockholm is **Gamia Stan** (Old Town). Site of the Royal Palace, it even attracts such shoppers as the queen. The main street for browsing is called **Västeriånggatan.** Many antiques stores are found here; don't expect low prices.

In summer, **Skansen** is an interesting area to explore for the craftpeople who display their wares here. Many gift shops are found here (some selling "Skansen glass") as well as individuals who display their wares on temporary stands.

In the **Sergels Torg** area, the main shopping street is **Hamngatan,** site of the famous shopping center Gallerian, at the corner of Hamngatan and Sergels Torg, and crossing the northern rim of Kungsträdgården at Sweden House. Big department stores, such as NK and Åhléns, are located nearby.

The **Kungsgatan** area is another major district for shopping, stretching from Hötorget to the intersection of Kungsgatan with Vasagatan. **Drottninggatan** is one long pedestrian mall, flanked with shops. Many side streets branching off from it are also filled with shops. Hötorget, home to PUB department store, is another major shopping district.

SHOPPING HOURS   Stockholm shops are open Monday through Friday from 9:30am to 6pm and on Saturday from 9:30am to somewhere between 1 and 4pm. Once a week, usually on Monday or Friday, some of the larger stores are open from 9:30am to 7pm (during July and August, to 6pm).

SHOPPING A TO Z

ART GALLERIES

ARONOWITSCH GALLERY, Sturegatan 24. Tel. 663-80-89.

One of the best-known galleries in Stockholm, this store was established in 1966. It is a showplace for nonobjective art, both Swedish and international. Some American artists are represented in the gallery's seasonal shows. It is closed from mid-June to mid-August. T-bana: Östermalmstorg.

STRANDGALLERIET, Strandvägen 5. Tel. 663-83-25.

This prestigious gallery accumulates only modern Swedish paintings, displayed in a single stark-white room near many embassies. It can always be counted on for having a startling array of modern art. Its owners keep up-to-date with changing trends in the art market. T-bana: Östermalmstorg.

AUCTIONS

AUKTIONSVERKET (The Stockholm Auction Chambers), Gallerian. Tel. 14-24-40.
The oldest auction company in the world, dating from 1674, this auction house is now centrally located in the Gallerian mall, just up Hamngatan from Sweden House. Auctions are held 5 days a week from 9am to "whenever," and you are allowed two viewings, on Friday and Saturday from 11am to 4pm. It is estimated that some 150,000 lots a year are auctioned off here with the pound of a gavel—everything from ceramics to Picasso. T-bana: Kungsträdgården.

BOOKS & MAPS

AKADEMIBOKHANDELN, Mäster Samuelsgatan 28. Tel. 21-15-90.
One of the best-stocked bookstores in Stockholm, and one of the most centrally located, this store carries a wide range of English-language books including many travel-related materials, especially maps. T-bana: Hötorget.

SVERIGE BOKHANDELN, Hamngatan 27. Tel. 789-23-01.
Whatever's available in English about Sweden can be found at this bookstore off Kungsträdgården, in Sweden House above the information center. It has many rare items for sale, including records of Swedish music. T-bana: Kungsträdgården.

CERAMICS

BLÅS & KNÅDA, Hörnsgatan 26. Tel. 642-77-67.
This store sells the best merchandise of a cooperative of 35 Swedish ceramic artists and glassmakers. Prices begin at 100 kronor ($18) for a single teacup, but rise to as much as 50,000 kronor ($9,000) for museum-quality pieces. T-bana: Slussen.

GUSTAVSBERG CERAMICS CENTER, Vardmö Island. Tel. 0766/356-50.
Bone china, stoneware dinner services, and other fine table and decorative ware are made at Gustavsberg Ceramics Center, on Varmdö Island, about 13 miles east of Stockholm. A museum at the center displays historic pieces such as Parian (a kind of plaster of paris or porcelain) statues based on the work of famous Danish sculptor Torvaldsen and other artists, hand-painted vases, Toby jugs, majolica, and willowware. There are also examples of Pyro, the first ovenware produced, of dinner services made for royalty, and sculptures by modern artists.
In summer, visitors to the center can watch potters at work and see artists hand-painting designs. You can even decorate a mug or plate yourself if you wish. There is also a shop at the center where you can purchase Gustavsberg ware, including seconds.
The ceramics center is open to the public Monday through Friday from 10am to 5pm, on Saturday from 10am to 3pm, and on Sunday from 11am to 3pm. Bus: 424, 440.

DEPARTMENT STORES

ÅHLENS CITY, Klarabergsgatan 50. Tel. 676-60-00.
In the center of Stockholm, this department store has a giftshop and a restaurant, and a food department that's famous. Also seek out the fine collection of home textiles and both Orrefors and Kosta crystal ware. The pewter with genuine Swedish ornaments makes a fine gift item. T-bana: Hötorget.

NORDISKA KOMPANIENT, Hamngatan 18. Tel. 762-80-00.
NK for short, this is the largest department store in Scandinavia. Most of the big names in Swedish glass are displayed at NK, including Orrefors (see the Nordic Light collection) and Kosta, the two most famous houses. Look also for Hackmanx stemware in original, unusual designs. Thousands of Swedish handcrafted items are found in the basement. Stainless steel, also a good buy in Sweden, is profusely displayed. T-bana: Kungsträdgården.

PUB, Hötorget 13. Tel. 791-60-00.

Greta Garbo got her start here in the millinery department. In general, the store offers less expensive merchandise than NK, but has many fine, high-quality items. There's a restaurant, too. T-bana: Hötorget.

FLEA MARKETS

SKÄRHOLMEN SHOPPING CENTER, Skärholmen. Tel. 710-00-60.

Much of the stuff at this huge market is junk but you might find some pleasing gift item discarded from an attic in Värmland. Try to go on Saturday or Sunday (the earlier the better) when the market is at its peak. Admission is 5 kronor (90¢) for adults, free for children. It's open Monday through Friday from 11am to 6pm, on Saturday from 9am to 3pm, and on Sunday from 10am to 3pm. T-bana: Line 13 to Skärholmen, a 20-minute ride.

FURS

SOPHIE ERICSONS, Mäster Samuelsgatan 45. Tel. 20-27-64.

One of the largest and finest fur outlets in Scandinavia, with a century-old reputation, this store sells leather items from both Scandinavia and Turkey, and fur coats from Scandinavia, Canada, and Germany. Most of the merchandise (fox, muskrat, raccoon, and many different kinds of mink) is for women, although a small selection for men includes garments made from coyote. T-bana: Östermalmstorg.

GEMS & MINERALS

GEOCITY, Tysta Marigången 5, Tegélbacken. Tel. 11-11-40.

Geocity offers exotic mineral crystals, jewelry, Scandinavian gems, Baltic amber, and lapidary equipment. Their staff includes two certified gemologists who will cut and set any gem you select, and do appraisals of jewelry you already own. Their inventory includes stones from Scandinavia and around the world, including Greenland, Madagascar, Siberia, and South America. T-bana: Hötorget.

GIFTS & SOUVENIRS

SLOTTSBODARNA (Royal Gift Shop), south wing of the Royal Palace, Slottsbanken. Tel. 789-86-30.

This unusual outlet sells products related to or copied from the collections within the Royal Palace. Items are re-created in silver, gold, brass, pewter, textiles, and glass. Every item is made in Sweden. T-bana: Gamla Stan.

GLASS & CRYSTAL

ROSENTHAL STUDIO-HAUS, Birger Jarlsgatan 6. Tel. 21-66-01.

This store has one of the biggest selections of modern crystal, porcelain, silverplate, and cookware in Stockholm. The staff will ship any item home for you. T-bana: Hötorget.

SVENSKT GLAS, Birger Jarlsgatan 8. Tel. 679-79-09.

Royal families patronize this establishment, but glass at every price level is featured. Orrefors and Kosta Boda glass are displayed here in stemware, candlesticks, flower-shaped bowls in full lead crystal, bar sets, vases, wineglasses, pitchers, and perfume bottles. A selection of beautiful crystal animals is sold here exclusively by Svenskt Glas. Worldwide shipping is available. T-bana: Östermalmstorg.

HANDCRAFTS & GIFTS

BRINKEN KONSTHANTVERK, Storkyrkobrinken 1. Tel. 11-59-54.

On the lower floor of a building near the Royal Palace in the Old Town, this mail-order business will send handcrafted brass, pewter, wrought-iron, or crystal anywhere in the world. About 95% of the articles sold are made in Scandinavia. T-bana: Gamla Stan.

DUKA, Kungsgatan 41. Tel. 20-60-41.

A large selection of crystal, porcelain, and gifts is available in this shop near the Konserthuset (Concert Hall). It offers tax-free shopping and shipping. T-bana: Hötorget.

GUNNARSSONS TRÅFIGURER, Drottninggatan 77. Tel. 21-67-17.

One of the city's most interesting collections of Swedish carved wooden figures includes such World War II figures as Winston Churchill and Franklin D. Roosevelt. All of the figures are carved by Urban Gunnarsson, a second-generation master carver. The figures also include a host of mythical and historical European personalities. Prices of the figures range from 250 kronor to 700 kronor ($45 to $126), although larger pieces, specially commissioned, cost up to 2,000 kronor ($360) each. Carvings are usually crafted from lindenwood or basswood. T-bana: Rådmansgatan.

KONSTHANTVERKARNA, Mäster Samuelsgaten 2. Tel. 611-96-60.

Created by a group of artisans, this store has an unusual selection of some of the best Swedish handcrafts, all of which have passed a strict jury test before they are offered for sale. Choose from glass, sculpture, ceramics, wall textiles, clothes, jewelry, silver, brass, and wood and leather work. Each item is handmade and original. Ask about the tax-free service. T-bana: Östermalmstorg.

SVENSK HEMSLOJD (Society for Swedish Handcrafts), Sveavägen 44. Tel. 23-21-15.

Svensk Hemslojd has a wide selection of glass, pottery, gifts, and wooden and metal handcrafts, the work of some of Sweden's best artisans. You'll also be shown a display of hand-woven carpets, upholstery fabrics, hand-painted materials, tapestries, lace, and embroidered items. You can also find beautiful yarns for weaving and embroidery. T-bana: Hötorget.

HOME FURNISHINGS

NORDISKA GALLERIET, Nybrogatan 11. Tel. 667-05-55.

This store features the finest in European furniture design, including the best from Scandinavian countries. Scattered over two floors are the latest designs in contemporary furniture. The store can arrange shipment. T-bana: Östermalmstorg.

SVENSKT TENN, Strandvägen 5. Tel. 670-16-00.

Along "embassy row," Swedish Pewter (its English name) has since 1924 been the most prominent store in Sweden for home furnishings. In spite of its name, pewter is no longer king and the shop now sells the best selection of home furnishings in Scandinavia—furniture, printed textiles, lamps, glassware, china, and gifts. The inventory is stylish and, although there aren't a lot of bargains, it's an excellent choice for insights into the newest trends in Scandinavia design. It's closed on Saturday in July. T-bana: Östermalmstorg.

HOUSEWARES

SVENSKT TENN, Strandvägen 5. Tel. 670-16-00.

For interior decoration and gifts, this is one of the most exclusive shops in Scandinavia (see above). For your convenience, they will pack, insure, and forward your purchases anywhere in the world. The showroom features furniture, lamps, textiles, cutlery, plated ware, crystal, china, and gifts, often in stunning, sophisticated designs. They carry an exclusive collection of Josef Frank's hand-printed designs on linen and cotton. Closed on Saturday in July. T-bana: Östermalmstorg.

MARKETS

ÖSTERMALMS SALUHALL, Nybrogatan 31.

One of the most colorful indoor markets anywhere in Scandinavia featuring cheese, meat, vegetable, and fish merchants who supply food for much of the area.

You may want a snack or a meal at one of the restaurants here (see "Dining" in Chapter 24). T-bana: Östermalmstorg.

PRINTS & LITHOGRAPHS

KONST-BIBIOFILEN, Västerlånggatan 6. Tel. 21-27-68.
One of the best collections of prints and lithographs, including limited editions, in Sweden. Closed Saturday and in July. T-bana: Gamla Stan.

SHOPPING MALLS

GALLERIAN ARCADE, Hamngatan 37. Tel. 796-93-40.
A short walk from Sweden House at Kungsträdgården, this modern two-story shopping complex is, to many, the best place in all of Sweden to go shopping. Merchandise in most of the stores is designed to appeal to local shoppers, not the tourist market, although in summer that changes a bit as more souvenir and gift items appear. T-bana: Kungsträdgården.

STUREGALLERIAN, Stureplan. Tel. 611-46-06.
In the center of Stockholm, this mall opened in 1989 and was immediately acclaimed as "Shopping Center of the Year in Europe" by the International Council of Shopping Centers. It has a dazzling array of merchandise, both foreign and domestic, in store after store. The merchandise changes with the season. Summer brings out more displays of souvenirs and gift items from Sweden. T-bana: Östermalmstorg.

TEXTILES

HANDARBETETS VÄNNER, Djurgårdsslatten 82-84. Tel. 667-10-26.
One of the oldest and most prestigious textile houses in Stockholm, with art weaving and embroidery items sold here as well. Closed during July. Bus: 47.

TEXTILGRUPPEN, Hornsgatan 6. Tel. 643-30-72.
This store was established in 1973 as a sales outlet for 44 of the best textile weavers in Sweden who weave in homes and workshops across the country. The outlet offers unique tapestries, prints, wall hangings, and unusual examples of what is called "fiber art," which are wall hangings. T-bana: Slussen.

TOYS

BULLERIBOCK, Sveavägen 104. Tel. 673-61-21.
You'll find a staggering selection of handmade and mass-produced wooden toys here, all made of natural materials. Many items were made in Sweden. T-bana: Rådmansgatan.

MJUKA DJUR, Hamngatan 11. Tel. 611-26-92.
This small one-room shop near Sweden House has one of the biggest selections in Scandinavia of stuffed animals—teddy bears, stuffed versions of cloth alligators, monkeys, whatever. The merchandise comes from all over the world—from New Zealand to Italy to Korea. T-bana: Kungsträdgården.

9. EVENING ENTERTAINMENT

Djurgården remains the favored spot for both indoor and outdoor spectacles on a summer evening. Although the more sophisticated may find it corny, it's the best bet in the early evening. Then you can make the jazz den and disco circuit—some of the clubs don't close until 3 or 4 in the morning.

THE ENTERTAINMENT SCENE

Pick up a copy of *Stockholm This Week*, distributed at the tourist information center (see above) at Sweden House to see what's on.

All the major opera, theater, and concert performances begin in autumn, except for special summer festival performances (see "Special/Free Events" in this chapter). Fortunately, most of the major opera and theatrical performances are funded by the state, which keeps the price of tickets reasonable.

CONCERT HALLS

BERWALDHALLEN (Berwald Concert Hall), Strandvägen 69. Tel. 784-18-00.

This hexagonal concert hall is the National Radio's big music studio. The Radio Symphonic Orchestra plays here, but other musical events are also held in the hall, such as lieder and chamber music recitals. The hall has excellent acoustics. The box office is open only for a very limited period, Monday through Friday from 12:30 to 2:30pm. T-bana: Karaplan.

Tickets: 65–130 kronor ($11.70–$23.40).

FILHARMONIKERNA I KONSERTHUSET (Concert Hall), Hötorget 8. Tel. 10-21-10.

Home of the Stockholm Philharmonic Orchestra, this is the principal place to hear classical music in Sweden. The Nobel Prizes are awarded here. Originally constructed in 1920, the building contains two concert halls—one, seating 1,600, better suited for major orchestras; the other, seating 450, suitable for chamber music groups. Besides local orchestras, the hall also features visiting ensembles, such as the Chicago Symphony Orchestra. Some series are entirely sold out in advance to subscription-ticket holders; others are less heavily attended and visitors can obtain seats. Sales begin 2 weeks before a concert and last up until the concert begins. Concerts are scheduled Tuesday through Thursday and on Saturday and Sunday, usually at 7:30pm. The box office is open Monday through Friday from 10am to 6pm and on Saturday from 10am to 1pm (closed in July). T-bana: Hötorget.

Tickets: 53–165 kronor ($9.50–$29.70).

OPERA & BALLET

DROTTNINGSHOLMS SLOTTSTEATER, Drottningholm. Tel. 660-82-25.

⭐ Founded by King Gustavus III in 1766, this theater, unique in the world, stands on an island in Lake Mälaren, 7 miles from Stockholm. It stages operas and ballets with full 18th-century regalia, complete with period costumes and wigs. Its machinery and some 30 or more complete theater sets are still intact and are in use today. The theater, a short walk from the royal residence, seats only 450 patrons, which makes tickets hard to get. Mozart is its perennial favorite. The season is May to September, and most performances begin at 8pm, lasting for 2½ to 4 hours. To order tickets in advance, phone the number above and give your American Express card number. (Only American Express is accepted.)

To get to the theater, take the subway to Brommaplan and transfer there to the bus marked MÄLARÖBUS. Or you can take the special bus departing 45 minutes before each performance from in front of the Grand Hotel, Södra Blasieholmshamnen 8.

Tickets: 45–400 kronor ($8.10–$72).

OPERAN (Opera House), Gustav Adolfs Torg. Tel. 20-35-15.

Founded by King Gustavus III, who was assassinated here at a masked ball, the Operan is the home of the Royal Swedish Opera and the Royal Swedish Ballet. The present building dates from the 1890s. Performances are traditionally given Monday through Saturday at 7:30pm (closed June 20 to August 20). The box office is open Monday through Friday from 11am to 7:30pm (closes at 6pm if no performance is scheduled) and on Saturday from 11am to 3pm. T-bana: Kungsträdgården.

Tickets: 50–230 kronor ($9–$41.40). Many tickets are discounted by 25% to 30% for seniors and students.

THEATER

The theater season begins in mid-August and lasts until mid-June.

KUNGLIGA DRAMATISKA TEATERN (Royal Dramatic Theater), Nybroplan. Tel. 667-06-80.

This is where Greta Garbo got her start (Ingmar Bergman used to be the director). The theater presents the latest experimental plays and the classics—but in Swedish only. Occasionally Shakespearean and other English-language plays are performed by visiting overseas troupes. Sometimes ballet performances are presented. The theater is open all year (with a slight slowdown in July), and performances are given Monday through Saturday at 7pm and on Sunday at 4pm. The box office is open Monday through Saturday from 10am to 7pm and on Sunday from noon to 4pm. Tram: 13, 14, 15.

Tickets: 70–135 kronor ($12.60–$24.30). Student discounts granted. Sun tickets reduced for seniors.

OSCARS 5D, Kungsgatan 63. Tel. 20-50-00.

Oscars is the flagship of Stockholm's musical entertainment world, the home of classic operetta and musical theater since the turn of the century. It is known for its extravagant staging of traditional operettas, and was among the first theaters in Europe to produce such hits as *A Chorus Line,* in Swedish. The box office is open Monday through Saturday from 9am to 5pm. T-bana: Hötorget.

Tickets: 350–500 kronor ($63–$90).

REGINA (The English Theatre), Drottninggatan 71A. Tel. 20-70-00.

The English Theatre is the only permanent English-language theater in Sweden. It also stages some productions in Swedish, although most of its repertoire is in English. Originally built in 1911 as a cinema, the building was converted for drama in 1960. The Regina Theater Company was established in 1980, and presents everything from Victorian thrillers to Dickensian Christmas musicals. Its London-style theater pub is unique in Sweden. Performances are given Tuesday through Saturday at 7:30pm. The box office is open Tuesday through Saturday from 10am to 5pm. American Express cardholders can reserve by phone. T-bana: Hötorget.

Tickets: 150–200 kronor ($27–$36).

LOCAL CULTURAL ENTERTAINMENTS

SKANSEN, Djurgården 49-51. Tel. 663-05-00.

This open-air museum also functions as an outdoor dancing pavilion. Costumed musicians play, and the dances range from folk to *vals.* Weather permitting, couples over the age of 30 flock here every night—except Monday and Tuesday.

Tired dancers can also stroll over to the Solliden Restaurant, where there's a large bandstand with weekend performances—mostly vaudeville, operatic, and symphonic concerts, plus the Skansen Folk Dancers. Beer costs 42 kronor ($7.60). Open Wednesday through Sunday from 8:30 to 11:30pm.

Admission: 25 kronor ($4.50).

AN AMUSEMENT PARK

GRÖNA LUNDS TIVOLI, Djurgården. Tel. 665-70-00.

Unlike its Copenhagen namesake, this is an amusement park—not a fantasyland. For those who like Coney Island–type amusements, it can be a nighttime adventure. One of the big thrills of Tivoli is to go up on the revolving tower for its after-dark view of Stockholm.

The park is open April 25 to June 5, Tuesday through Thursday from 6 to 11pm, on Friday from 6pm to midnight, on Saturday from 1pm to midnight, and on Sunday from 1 to 9pm; June 6 to July 27, Tuesday through Thursday from 1 to 11pm, on Friday and Saturday from 1pm to midnight, and on Sunday from 1 to 9pm; July 28 to August 16, Monday through Saturday from 1pm to midnight and on Sunday from 1 to 10pm; August 17 to September 6, Monday through Thursday from 6 to 11pm, on Friday from 6pm to midnight, on Saturday from 1pm to midnight, and on Sunday from 1 to 9pm. Closed mid-September to April 24. Bus: 44, 47. Ferry: Djurgården ferry from Nybroplan.

Admission: 30–40 kronor ($5.40–$7.20); children 7 and under free.

THE CLUB & MUSIC SCENE
NIGHTCLUBS/CABARET

CAFE OPERA, Operahuset, Karl's Torg. Tel. 676-58-07.
The café—Swedish beaux arts at its best—functions as a bistro, brasserie, and tearoom during the day and as one of the most crowded nightclubs in Stockholm in the evening. Visitors have the best chance of getting in around noon when a *dagens* lunch is offered for 99 kronor ($17.80). This establishment is not to be confused with the opera's main, and far more expensive, dining room, the Operakällaren, whose entrance is through a different door. Near the entrance to the café is a stairway leading to one of the Opera House's most beautiful corners, the clublike Operabären (Opera Bar), which is likely to be as crowded as the café. It is a monumental but historically charming place to have a drink; beer costs 51 kronor ($9.20). After 10pm, the place de-emphasizes the food service and devotes its energies to its role as a disco. Open Monday through Saturday from 11:30am to 3am and on Sunday from 12:30pm to 3am. At nighttime, long lines form outside of patrons trying to get inside. T-bana: Kungsträdgården.

Admission: 60 kronor ($10.80) after midnight.

DANCE CLUBS/DISCOS

THE DAILY NEWS/MELODY THEATER, Sverigehuset at Kungsträdgården. Tel. 21-56-55.
The most interesting part about this place is its bar area, which does a busy business every evening. There's also a restaurant on site, and a not-always-very-crowded disco (Backstage) in the cellar. The restaurant section serves meals in a separate street-level dining section where full dinners begin at 220 kronor ($39.60). Also available is a café on the upper floor. The complex was enlarged in 1989 when management transformed a run-down theater (The Melody) next door into a home for a revolving series of concerts. These concerts, which feature rock and jazz, are presented more or less randomly whenever an appropriate entertainer becomes available. You can order tickets by calling 20-11-21. T-bana: Kungsträdgården.

Admission: Downstairs disco, 50–60 kronor ($9–$10.80) after 11:30pm Sun–Thurs and after 10pm Fri–Sat; Melody Theater concerts, 100–150 kronor ($18–$27).

EMBASSY, Sturegatan 10. Tel. 61-60-07.
In this exclusive nightclub, supper club, and piano bar, most of the well-dressed guests are over 25. The restaurant has good food, service, and an attractive ambience, and the piano bar always has good entertainment. Dance music is frequently performed by live bands. Dinners cost from 225 kronor ($40.50); beer costs 51 kronor ($9.20). Open daily Tuesday through Saturday from 8pm to 3am. T-bana: Östermalmstorg.

Admission: Entrance free for men before 9pm and for women before 10pm. After those hours, entrance is 90 kronor ($16.20) per person.

NIGHTCLUB KOLINGEN, Kornhamnstorg 59. Tel. 10-07-22.
A cellar club connected to the Pub Engelen (see "Jazz Clubs," below). Disco music is played. You can dance, or dine at one of the restaurants. A large beer will set you back 50 kronor ($9). Open daily from 7pm to 3am; dancing begins at 11pm. T-bana: Gamla Stan.

Admission: 35–60 kronor ($6.30–$10.80).

ROCK CLUBS

HARD ROCK CAFE, Sveavägen 75. Tel. 16-03-50.
The Swedish branch of the chain is fun and gregarious. Sometimes an American, British, or Scandinavian rock 'n' roll band presents a live concert; otherwise it's a rock

blast on the sound track. Club sandwiches, hamburgers, T-bone steak, and barbecued spareribs are available. Beer costs 38 kronor ($6.80), meals begin at 175 kronor ($31.50). The café is open Sunday through Tuesday 11am to midnight, Wednesday through Saturday 11am to 2am. T-bana: Rådmansgatan.

Admission: Fri–Sat 50 kronor ($9); free otherwise.

JAZZ CLUBS

PUB ENGELEN, Kornhamnstorg 59B. Tel. 10-07-22.
Located in Gamla Stan, this bar has live performances, including jazz bands and singers, on Sunday from 9pm to midnight. The pub is connected to the Restaurant Engelen, which offers some of the best steaks in town. Meals cost from 200 kronor ($36); beer, 45 kronor ($8.10). Open daily from 4 to 11:30pm. T-bana: Gamla Stan.

STAMPEN, Stora Nygatan 5. Tel. 20-57-93.
This fun-loving pub attracts a crowd of jazz lovers in their 30s and 40s. Guests crowd in to enjoy live Dixieland, New Orleans, mainstream, and swing music from the 1920s, 1930s, and 1940s. From the high ceiling, a menagerie of stuffed animals and lots of old, whimsical antiques are suspended. Downstairs is a slightly less hysterical drinking bar, where a pint of beer costs 54 kronor ($9.70). Open Monday 8pm to midnight, Tuesday through Friday 8pm to 1am, and Saturday and Sunday 1 to 5pm and 8pm to 1am. T-bana: Gamla Stan.

Admission: 70–100 kronor ($12.60–$18).

STUREHOF, Stureplan 2. Tel. 679-87-50.
At this previously recommended pub and restaurant, live jazz, soul, and blues—some of the best in Stockholm, are performed 4 nights a week. It also makes a good place for drinking and dining. There's a quieter room one floor above street level, which is separated from the hubbub. Beer costs 45 kronor ($8.10). Performances are on Wednesday, Thursday, Friday, and Saturday nights, from 9pm until closing. The pub is open on Monday and Tuesday from 11:30am to 11pm and Wednesday through Sunday from 11:30am to midnight. T-bana: Östermalmstorg.

Admission: 40–50 kronor ($7.20–$9).

THE BAR SCENE

CADIER BAR, in the Grand Hotel, Södra Blasieholmshamnen 8. Tel. 22-10-20.
Named after the original builder of this deluxe hotel—one of the most famous in Europe—the bar enjoys a view of the harbor and the Royal Palace. It's one of the most sophisticated places for a rendezvous in Stockholm. You can also enjoy light meals—open-face sandwiches, smoked salmon, etc.—at any time of day in the extension overlooking the waterfront. Drinks run 95 to 200 kronor ($17.10 to $36); export beer, 50 kronor ($9). Open daily from noon to 2am, with a piano player performing Monday through Saturday from 6:30 to 7:30pm and 9:30pm to 1:30am. T-bana: Kungsträdgården.

VICTORIA, Kungsträdgården. Tel. 10-10-85.
This place, the most central café in Stockholm, gets crowded after 9pm, attracting a diverse crowd of patrons, including many gay people. Many people come here just to drink, but if you're hungry, you can have lunch or dinner in an inner section beyond the animated bar area. Meals begin at 160 kronor ($28.80), and might include reindeer or fried salmon trout with almonds. A bottle of lager will set you back 37 kronor ($6.70). Open Monday through Friday from 11:30am to 3am, Saturday from noon to 3am, and Sunday from 1pm to 3am. T-bana: Kungsträdgården.

GAY DRINKING & DINING

ALICE B./CAFÉ TIMMY/PRIDE DISCO, Sveavägen 57. Tel. 31-55-33.
These three interconnected establishments comprise the largest gay nightlife center in Sweden. Alice B. is an uncomplicated and likable restaurant that serves bistro-style food in a modern, half-Swedish, half-French ambience. Menu specialties include such

dishes as sole Waleska, lamb chops provençal, entrecôte Café de Paris, and such desserts as chocolate-mousse cake. Dinners begin at around 150 kronor ($27). You should make reservations for meals on Friday and Saturday nights. Alice B. is open on Monday, Tuesday, and Thursday from 6pm to midnight, and on Wednesday, Friday, and Saturday from 6pm to 1am.

The adjoining Café Timmy (tel. 736-02-14) is a pleasant spot from which to survey the scene, with its marble floors, skylight, and fountain. Sometimes live music is presented. A beer costs from around 48 kronor ($8.60). The café is open daily from 5pm to 3am.

The Pride Disco (tel. 31-55-53) is the largest, most popular, and oldest gay disco in Stockholm where, frankly, there isn't much competition for the title. The later you go here, the more crowded and animated it seems to get. Beer costs the same as at the Café Timmy. The disco is open nightly from 11pm to 3am. The first Friday of every month is lesbian night. T-bana: Rådmansgatan.

Admission: Disco, 70 kronor ($12.60) Fri–Sat; free other nights.

10. EASY EXCURSIONS

Some of Sweden's best-known attractions are clustered around Lake Mälaren—centuries-old villages and castles (Uppsala and Gripsholm) that revive the pomp and glory of the 16th-century Vasa Dynasty.

A very busy day can be spent exploring Sigtuna, Skokloster Castle, Uppsala, and Gamla Uppsala, staying overnight in Sigtuna or Uppsala where there are good hotels. Another easy day trip is to Gripsholm Castle in Mariefred or Tullgarn Palace.

A popular route is to take the boat from Klara Mälarstrand in Stockholm at 9:45am, going along the beautiful waterway, Mälaren, and the Fyris River to Sigtuna for a 2-hour stop before arriving at Uppsala at 5pm. There you can visit the magnificent cathedral and other interesting sights, dine, and return via train, a 45-minute trip. Trains run every hour until 11pm.

SIGTUNA

Founded at the beginning of the 11th century, Sigtuna, on the shores of Lake Mälaren, northwest of Stockholm, is Sweden's oldest town. Its **High Street (Stora Gatan),** with its low timbered buildings, is thought to be the oldest street in Sweden that still follows its original route. Traces of Sigtuna's Viking and early Christian heritage can be seen throughout the town.

It abounds in church ruins, mostly from the 12th century. Chief among them is **St. Per's,** Sweden's first cathedral. The 13th-century **Monastery of St. Maria** is open to the public daily. The well-preserved **Town Hall** dates from the 18th century.

Wander the narrow streets, and if you have time, visit the **Sigtuna Fornhem,** the archeological museum, where artifacts that were found in and around Sigtuna, dating back to the early medieval period, can be viewed.

Founded near the turn of the century, the **Sigtuna Foundation** is a Lutheran retreat and cultural center, often frequented by writers and one of the reasons for Sigtuna's resurgence. It is open to the public daily from 1 to 3pm.

Daily buses and trains connect Stockholm to Sigtuna and Uppsala. From Stockholm take a train to Märsta, then a bus for the 10-minute ride to Sigtuna. In summer boats run from Klara Strand in Stockholm and from Uppsala to Sigtuna.

WHERE TO STAY & DINE

Inexpensive

SIGTUNA FOUNDATION, Manfred Björkquists Allé 2-4, S-193 31 Sigtuna. Tel. 0760/51-610. Fax 0760/502-16. 52 rms (none with bath). **Bus:** 570, 575.

$ Rates (including full board): 600–750 kronor ($108–$135) for one, 800–1,200 kronor ($144–$216) for two. No credit cards. **Parking:** Free.

A stay within the solid early 20th-century walls of this massive building might provide one of your most memorable stopovers in Sweden. It was built as a center where various sociological and philosophical viewpoints could be aired, and as such, it's more a way of life than a hotel. Over the years, guest lecturers have included the Dalai Lama, an assortment of Indian gurus, and many of the leading theologians of postwar Europe. The establishment fulfills a threefold function as a conference center, a school, and a guesthouse. If you show up, there will be no proselytizing, although opportunities for the sharing of experiences might be frequent. There are secluded courtyards, lush rose and herb gardens, and fountains. Some of the bedrooms are streamlined and modern; others, comfortably old-fashioned. Management prefers visitors to phone or write in advance so that a room can be guaranteed. The foundation is less than a mile from the town center.

SIGTUNA STADSHOTELL, Stora Nygatan 3, S-193 00 Sigtuna. Tel. 0760/50-000. Fax 0760/515-87. 27 rms (all with bath). TV TEL **Bus:** 570, 575.

$ Rates (including breakfast): Sun–Thurs 740–840 kronor ($133.20–$151.20) single; 990 kronor ($178.20) double. Fri–Sat and June 23–July 12, 420 kronor ($75.60) single; 640 kronor ($115.20) double. MC, V. **Parking:** Free.

This Victorian-style hotel in the town center is a traditional choice, with the most comfortable accommodations in town. Rooms have an old-fashioned style, but are well kept, clean, and inviting. Full meals are served daily, with dinners going for 250 kronor ($45) à la carte. These might include Gorgonzola-flavored cream of morel soup, scallop of salmon with vermouth sauce, médaillons of reindeer with juniper berries, and braised snow grouse in cream sauce with apples and calvados—all topped off by warm cloudberry jam with strawberry ice cream. The restaurant is open from 11:30am to 10pm daily, with a fixed-price menu at 65 kronor ($11.70), offered Monday through Saturday from 11:30am to 3pm.

SKOKLOSTER CASTLE

Skokloster, Skokloster, S-198 00 Bålsta (tel. 018/38-60-77), is a splendid 17th-century castle and one of the most interesting baroque museums in Europe. It is located next to Lake Mälaren, 40 miles from Stockholm and 31 miles from Uppsala. With original interiors, the castle is noted for its rich collections of paintings, furniture, applied art, tapestries, arms, and books. Admission is 35 kronor ($6.30) for adults, 15 kronor ($2.70) for children, and it's open daily from May to September. You must view the castle on a guided tour, offered every hour from noon to 4pm.

The **Skokloster Motor Museum** (tel. 018/38-61-00) is on the palace grounds and contains the largest collection of vintage automobiles and motorcycles in the country. One of the most notable cars is a 1905 eight-horsepower De Dion Bouton. Unlike the castle, the museum is open all year. It costs 25 kronor ($4.50) for adults, 15 kronor ($2.70) for children. Open May to September, daily from 10am to 5pm; October to April, daily from 11am to 4pm.

Take bus no. 894 from Bålsta, which has a rail link to Stockholm.

UPPSALA

The major university city of Sweden, Uppsala, 42 miles northwest of Stockholm, is the most popular destination of day-trippers from Stockholm, and for good reason. Uppsala not only has a great university, but a celebrated 15th-century cathedral and a 16th-century castle. Even in the time of the Vikings, Uppsala was a religious center, the scene of animal and human sacrifices in honor of the old Norse gods and was once the center of royalty as well. Queen Christina occasionally held court here. The church is still the seat of the archbishop, and the first Swedish university was founded here in 1477.

The best time to be in Uppsala is on April 30, Walpurgis Eve, when academics celebrate the rebirth of spring with a torchlight parade and rollicking festivities lasting until dawn throughout the 13 student "nations" (residential halls).

The town is easily reached by train, in about 40 minutes from Stockholm's Central Station. Trains leave about every hour during the peak daylight hours. Boats from Stockholm to Uppsala (or vice versa) also stop at Skokloster and Sigtuna. For details, check with the tourist office in any of these towns. Some visitors prefer to stay in Uppsala and take the commuter train back to Stockholm at the end of the day. If you have a Eurailpass, you ride free.

The **Tourist Information Office** is at Fyris Torg 8 (tel. 27-48-00). It is open Monday through Friday from 10am to 6pm and Saturday from 10am to 2pm. From June 22 through August 14, hours are Monday through Friday from 10am to 6pm.

Bus no. 700 follows **"the tourist trail,"** in Uppsala, leaving from the Central Station daily from June 25 to August 19 at 11am and 1pm. It is equipped with a recorded commentary in English, describing the places of interest en route. Trip time is 2 hours.

WHAT TO SEE & DO

UPPSALA DOMKYRKA, Domkyrkoplan 5. Tel. 018/18-72-01.

⊛ The largest cathedral in Scandinavia, this twin-spired Gothic structure, nearly 400 feet tall, was founded in the 13th century. It was severely damaged in 1702 in a disastrous fire that swept over Uppsala, then was restored near the turn of this century. Among the regal figures buried in the crypt is Gustavus Vasa. The remains of St. Erik, patron saint of Sweden, are entombed in a silver shrine. Botanist Linnaeus and philosopher-theologian Swedenborg are also buried here. A small museum displays ecclesiastical relics of Uppsala.

Admission: Cathedral, free; museum, 10 kronor ($1.80) adults, 3 kronor (50¢) children.

Open: June–Aug, daily 8am–8pm; Sept–May, daily 8am–6pm. **Bus:** 1.

UPPSALA SLOTT, Nedre Slottsgatan. Tel. 018/14-48-10.

This 16th-century castle—founded by Gustavus Vasa in 1540—was the setting for one of the most memorable moments in Scandinavian history: the abdication of Queen Christina in 1654. It was badly damaged in the fire of 1702 and was partially restored in 1752 and 1816, but it never regained its original grandeur.

Admission: 35 kronor ($6.30) adults, 15 kronor ($2.70) children.

Open: Late June to mid-Aug, Mon–Fri 9am–7pm, Sat–Sun 10am–5pm; mid-Apr to late June and mid-Aug to Sept, Mon–Sat, 11am–3pm, Sat–Sun 11am–4pm. **Closed:** Oct to mid-Apr. **Directions:** Walk straight from the rail station along Bangårdsgatan and Slottsgränd.

LINNAEUS GARDEN AND MUSEUM, Svartbäcksgatan 27. Tel. 018/13-65-40.

The garden and former home of Swedish botanist Carolus Linneaus (sometimes known as Carl von Linné), who developed a classification system for the world's plants and flowers, is located on the spot where Uppsala University's first garden was laid out by Linnaeus, resembling a miniature baroque garden. Linneaus, who arranged the plants according to his so-called sexual classification system, left detailed sketches and descriptions of the garden, which have been faithfully followed.

Linnaeus was professor of medicine and botany at Uppsala University. His house has been restored to its original design and may be visited. A summer art gallery exhibits contemporary local artists.

Admission: 10 kronor ($1.80).

Open: Gardens, May–Sept, daily 9am–9pm; town house museum, Tues–Sun 1–4pm. **Closed:** Oct–Apr. **Directions:** Walk straight from the rail station to Kungsgatan, turn right, and walk for about 10 minutes to Svartbäcksgatan.

CAROLINA REDIVIVA (University Library), Drottninggatan. Tel. 018/18-39-00.

At the end of Drottninggatan is the Carolina Rediviva, with its more than three million volumes and 30,000 manuscripts, among them many rare works from the Middle Ages. But the one manuscript that draws the visitors is in the exhibition room of the library—the *Codex Argenteus* (Silver Bible), translated into the Old Gothic

language in the middle of the 4th century in about A.D. 525. It is the only book extant in the Old Gothic script. Also worth seeing is *Carta Marina,* the earliest map (1539), a fairly accurate map of Sweden and its neighboring countries.
Admission: Free.
Open: Exhibition room, June 16–Aug 15, Mon–Fri 9am–7:30pm, Sat 9am–5:30pm, Sun 1–3:30pm. **Closed:** Aug 16–June 15. **Bus:** 1.

An Excursion to Gamla Uppsala

About 15 centuries ago ✪ **Gamla Uppsala** was the capital of the Svea kingdom. In its midst was a sacrificial grove where both human and animal sacrifices were made. Viking burial mounds dating from the 6th century are believed to have contained the pyres of three kings.

Nearby, on the site of the old pagan temple, is a 12th-century parish church, once badly damaged by fire and never properly restored. Indeed, some people describe it as a stave church that has been turned into stone. Before Uppsala Cathedral was erected, Swedish kings were crowned here.

Across from the church is the **Stiftelsen Upplandsmuseet,** Sankt Eriksgränd 6 (tel. 10-22-90), an open-air museum with reassembled buildings, depicting peasant life in Uppland. It's open from mid-May until the end of August, daily from 9am to 5pm. Tours are conducted Monday through Friday at 1 and 2pm and on Saturday and Sunday every hour on the hour from noon to 4pm. Admission is free.

Gamla Uppsala, about 2 miles north of the commercial heart of Uppsala, is easily reached by bus no. 24, which leaves frequently from the Central Station.

WHERE TO STAY
Expensive

HOTEL UPLANDIA, Dragarbrunnsgatan 32, S-751 40 Uppsala. Tel. 018/10-21-60, or toll free 800/528-1234 in the U.S. 133 rms (all with bath). MINIBAR TV TEL **Bus:** 801.
$ Rates (including breakfast): Winter, Sun–Thurs 1,190–1,275 kronor ($214.20–$229.50) single; 1,500–1,605 kronor ($270–$288.90) double. Fri–Sat and June 29–Aug 2, 560 kronor ($100.80) single; 725 kronor ($130.50) double. AE, DC, MC, V.
The best hotel in town offers comfortably furnished bedrooms with such extras as a trouser press. A whirlpool and sauna are on the premises. On the lobby level is an elegant cocktail lounge, plus a spacious restaurant. Full meals, priced from 200 kronor ($36), are likely to include a mousse of shrimp and salmon, noisettes of veal, Alsatian sauerkraut, and a selection of all-vegetarian platters. Adjacent is the bus terminal.

SARA HOTEL GILLET, Dragarbrunnsgatan 23, S-751 42 Uppsala. Tel. 018/15-53-60. Fax 018/15-33-80. 169 rms (all with bath). A/C TV TEL **Bus:** 801.
$ Rates (including breakfast): Weekdays 1,200 kronor ($216) single; 1,600 kronor ($288) double. Weekends 620 kronor ($111.60) single; 920 kronor ($165.60) double. AE, DC, MC, V. **Parking:** 80 kronor ($14.40).
This attractively designed, first-class hotel contains well-furnished bedrooms, a breakfast room, a cozy cocktail bar and lounge, a swimming pool, and a sauna. The Seasons is a top-rated restaurant serving international dishes and Swedish country food. It's open on Monday and Tuesday from 11:30am to 11pm, Wednesday through Saturday from 11:30am to 1am, and on Sunday from 12:30 to 9pm.

Moderate

HOTEL LINNÉ, Skolgatan 45, S-75002 Uppsala. Tel. 018/10-20-00. Fax 018/11-75-97. 117 rms (all with bath), 6 suites. MINIBAR TV TEL
$ Rates (including breakfast): Sun–Thurs 1,075 kronor ($193.50) single; 1,440 kronor ($259.20) double; from 1,835 kronor ($330.30) suite. Fri–Sat 550 kronor ($99) single; 700 kronor ($126) double or suite. AE, DC, MC, V. **Parking:** Free.
This is one of the best-managed hotels in town. Rooms feature modern furniture and

plumbing, and each unit contains a refrigerator or minibar that you stock yourself. It's a good-value hotel, the only drawback being that the less expensive doubles are a bit cramped. The hotel has a bar and restaurant serving typically Scandinavian food. There is a sauna. The hotel is at the edge of the Linnaeus Garden.

Budget

DIAKONISTIFTELSEN SAMARITERHEMMET, Hamnesplanaden 16, S-751 25 Uppsala. Tel. 018/10-34-00. Fax 018/10-83-75. 42 rms (12 with bath). **Bus:** 14, 22, 54.

$ Rates (including breakfast): 330 kronor ($59.40) single without bath, 385 kronor ($69.30) single with bath; 495 kronor ($89.10) double without bath, 585 kronor ($105.30) double with bath. No credit cards. **Parking:** 30 kronor ($5.40).

One of the best bargains in town, this large guesthouse has spotlessly maintained rooms, and you are allowed to use a kitchenette with a refrigerator. It is run by a Christian charity. The house has a TV lounge. A wholesome and filling lunch is offered for just 50 kronor ($9).

WHERE TO DINE
Expensive

DOMTRAPPKÄLLAREN, Sankt Eriksgränd 15. Tel. 018/13-09-55.
Cuisine: SWEDISH. **Reservations:** Recommended. **Bus:** 1.
$ Prices: Appetizers 65–110 kronor ($11.70–$19.80); main dishes 155–210 kronor ($27.90–$37.80); fixed-price lunch 75–125 kronor ($13.50–$22.50); fixed-price dinner 235 kronor ($42.30).
Open: Lunch Mon–Fri 11am–2:30pm; dinner Mon–Sat 6–11pm. **Closed:** Dec 23–Jan 2.

There isn't another restaurant in Uppsala that can compete with this one for charm and atmosphere—it was built in the town center on the ruins of 12th-century cathedral buildings. The vaulted ceilings and copies of Jacobean paintings in the main dining room are complemented by the low-ceilinged, sun-flooded intimacy of the upper floors. If you request it, you can dine in a narrow room that imprisoned unruly students in the Middle Ages or in another that served as a classroom in the 17th century. The restaurant serves delectable salmon and reindeer and specializes in game. Salads are often exotic, including breast of pigeon with roasted nuts.

Moderate

RESTAURANT FLUSTRET, Svandammen. Tel. 018/13-01-14.
Cuisine: FRENCH. **Reservations:** Recommended. **Bus:** 24.
$ Prices: Fixed-price menus 150 kronor ($27); main dishes 100–150 kronor ($18–$27). AE, DC, MC, V.
Open: Lunch Mon–Fri 11am–2pm; dinner Mon–Sat 7pm–1am.

In a riverside setting near the castle, this recently constructed pavilion is an exact replica of its predecessor, a long-ago demolished Victorian building. Its spacious ground-floor dining room serves tasty meals, which might include lobster soup, salmon "boathouse style," veal steak Oscar, pheasant Véronique, and bananas flambé. A disco in the cellar is open from 9pm to 2am on Friday and Saturday nights only, charging from 90 kronor ($16.20) for admission.

RESTAURANT HALLEN, Saluhallen, Sankt Eriks Torg. Tel. 018/15-01-50.
Cuisine: SWEDISH/FRENCH. **Reservations:** Recommended. **Bus:** 1.
$ Prices: Appetizers 39–144 kronor ($7–$25.90); main dishes 79–169 kronor ($14.20–$30.40); fixed-price lunch 100 kronor ($18). AE, DC, MC, V.
Open: Lunch daily 11:30am–3pm; dinner daily 6–11pm.

A walk through the city food market will prepare your palate for the specialties served here up a flight of stairs. Specialties include halibut with chanterelles and a truffle dressing, fried filet of reindeer with Roquefort sauce, and grilled entrecôte with a red wine sauce. Dessert might be any of the tempting pastries.

EVENING ENTERTAINMENT

BAROWIAK TRÄDGÅRD & VERANDA, Svandammen. **Tel. 018/12-40-30.**

One of the most popular youth-oriented nightspots in Uppsala, presenting some kind of live music at least three times a week. Food is served, and beer costs 18 to 45 kronor ($3.20 to $8.10). Open Wednesday through Saturday from 6 to 9pm and on Sunday from 6pm to midnight. Bus: 24.

Admission: 100 kronor ($18) for live performances; otherwise free.

GRIPSHOLM CASTLE

On an island in Lake Mälaren, ✪ Gripsholm Castle (tel. 0159/101-94)—the fortress built by Gustavus Vasa in the late 1530s—is one of the best-preserved castles in Sweden, near Mariefred, an idyllic small town known for its vintage narrow-gauge railroad. The castle is 38 miles from Stockholm, easily reached by driving along the E3 south or taking the subway from central Stockholm to Liljeholmen, and boarding bus no. 40 which leaves every hour for Mariefred. In Stockholm, boats also leave mid-May to September at 10am from Stadshuset, the Klara Malarstrand Pier. The castle is a 5-minute walk from the center of Mariefred.

During the reign of the 18th-century actor-king Gustavus III a theater was built at Gripsholm, but the outstanding feature of the castle is its large collection of portrait paintings.

Even though Gripsholm was last occupied by royalty in 1864 (Charles XV), it is still considered a royal castle. It's open May to the end of August, daily from 10am to 4pm; in March, April, September, and October, Tuesday through Friday from 10am to 3pm and on Saturday and Sunday from noon to 3pm; November to February, only on Saturday and Sunday from noon to 3pm. Admission is 25 kronor ($4.50) for adults, 10 kronor ($1.80) for children.

WHERE TO STAY

Moderate

GRIPSHOLMS VÄRDHUS & HOTEL, Kyrkogatan 1, S-647 00 Mariefred. **Tel. 0159/130-20.** Fax 0159/109-47. 30 rms (all with bath), 15 suites. A/C MINIBAR TV TEL **Bus:** 40.

$ Rates (including breakfast): 950–1,250 kronor ($171–$225) single; 1,250–1,670 kronor ($225–$300.60) double; from 1,900 kronor ($342) suite. AE, DC, MC, V. **Parking:** Free.

✪ Originally built as an inn in 1609, making it among the oldest in Sweden, this building was restored and reopened in 1989, becoming the most stylish and charming hotel in the region. It's a few steps from the village church, in the center of Mariefred, a 10-minute walk from the castle. Each bedroom is individually decorated and furnished with a mixture of antiques and contemporary pieces. Walls and ceiling decors are painted in the old style. Amenities include such thoughtful extras as a bathrobe, hairdryer, and a bathroom with heated floors and towel racks.

Dining/Entertainment: The hotel has the best restaurant in the region (see "Where to Dine," below) as well as a pub for less formal meals. It keeps the same hours as the restaurant and serves platters of homemade Swedish cooking for 90 to 130 kronor ($16.20 to $23.40).

Services: Room service, massage, laundry.

Facilities: Solarium, recreation center, sauna, copper tub for ice baths, public bar.

WHERE TO DINE

Expensive

GRIPSHOLMS VÄRDHUS RESTAURANT, Kyrkogatan 1. **Tel. 0159/130-20.**

Cuisine: FRENCH/SWEDISH. **Reservations:** Recommended. **Bus:** 40.

$ Prices: Fixed-price lunch 265 kronor ($47.70); fixed-price dinner 365 kronor

($65.70); appetizers 78–135 kronor ($14–$24.30); main dishes 175–235 kronor ($31.50–$42.30). AE, DC, MC, V.

Open: Lunch Mon–Fri 11:30am–3pm; dinner Mon–Fri 6–10pm, Sat 1–11pm, Sun 1–6pm.

⭐ Traditional Swedish food and local game dishes are served along with an international cuisine at this elegantly appointed restaurant. The main dining room has an adjoining veranda opening onto Gripsholm Bay. Tastings can be arranged in the wine cellar. The menu changes according to the season, but is likely to include such dishes as mousse of wild grouse with port wine jelly and lingonberries, marinated salmon with a mild mustard sauce, or breast of wood pigeon braised in port (served with a sauce of wild berries and apple chutney).

TULLGARN PALACE

The royal castle of Tullgarn (tel. 0755/720-11), begun in 1719 in a panoramic setting on a bay of the Baltic Sea, was the favorite of Gustavus V (1858–1950), the great-grandfather of Sweden's present king. The well-kept interiors are from the late 19th century. Admission is 30 kronor ($5.40) for adults, 15 kronor ($2.70) for children. The palace is open to the public from May 15 to September 15. Guided tours leave the main entrance every hour from 11am to 4pm.

It lies 37 miles south of Stockholm. If you are driving, take the E4 south about 37 miles and follow the sign to the right directing you to Tullgarns Slott, near Vagnhärad. It's another quarter of a mile to the palace. Or take the Blue Train from the Central Station in Stockholm to Södertälje Södra, (about 20 minutes), and catch a bus to Trosa.

For lunch or dinner, the **Tullgarns Värdshus,** in Vagnhärad (tel. 0755/720-26), offers Swedish/French meals for 250 kronor ($45). It's open May 15 to September 15, Monday through Friday from noon to 2:30pm and 5 to 7pm and on Saturday and Sunday from noon to 7pm. Located in a wing of Tullgarn Palace, this inn offers three-course lunches or dinners. You can sample such dishes as salted salmon with creamed potatoes, an old Swedish specialty, or perhaps pâté of wild boar. You can also order breast of wild duck with a mousse of chicken liver or poached filet of salmon with a chive-flavored butter sauce.

You can also order a picnic lunch and eat in the royal park. Picnics of cold chicken or roast beef, with beer or coffee, in a take-away basket or a cup of coffee with a sandwich, can be ordered at the inn daily from 11am to 5pm. MC, V.

SANDHAMN & VAXÖN & THE ARCHIPELAGO OF STOCKHOLM

Stockholm is in what the Swedes call a garden of skerries, more than 24,000 islands (including some rocks jutting out of the water). The islands nearest to Stockholm have become part of the suburbs, thickly populated and connected to the mainland by car-ferries or bridges, but many are still wild and largely deserted, attracting those who can boat out to them for picnics and swimming. Summer homes dot some of the islands. July is the peak vacation month, when yachts crowd the waters.

You can see the islands by taking a boat trip from Stockholm harbor. For a stopover at one of the resorts, consider **Sandhamn,** where you will find shops, restaurants, and a hotel. The entire island takes about an hour to explore on foot. The beaches at the eastern tip are the best in the archipelago. **Vaxholm,** a bathing resort on the island of Vaxön, sometimes called "the gateway to the northern archipelago," with full tourist facilities also makes a good stopover. Many artists and writers have traditionally been drawn to Vaxholm, and some hold exhibitions during the summer when the population quadruples as tourists throng into town. The west harbor and the main sea route north are filled with pleasure craft.

Throughout the year (but much more frequently in summer), boats operated by several different companies depart from in front of the Grand Hotel at Södra

Blasieholmshamnen. Most of them are labeled Vaxholm, although boats often continue to Sandhamn after a stopover in Vaxholm. Be sure to ask before boarding.

The trip to Sandhamn takes 3 hours one-way and costs 65 kronor ($11.70), while going to Vaxholm takes only 35 minutes one-way and costs 25 kronor ($4.50). Vaxholm-bound boats depart every hour in summer and about five times a day in winter. For information, call the Vaxholm steamship company, **Vaxholmes Bolaget** (tel. 08/679-5830).

Buses to Vaxholm (nos. 670, 671, 672, and 673) often (but not always) go on to Sandhamn. They depart from the East Railway Station every 30 minutes beginning at 6am. The last bus from Vaxholm leaves at 1am. A one-way ticket costs 20 kronor ($3.60).

WHERE TO STAY

In Vaxholm: Inexpensive

VAXHOLM HOTEL, Hamngatan 2, S-185 00 Vaxholm. Tel. 0764/301-50. 32 rms (all with bath). TV TEL

$ **Rates:** Sun–Thurs (including breakfast), 900 kronor ($162) single; 1,150 kronor ($207) double. Fri–Sat (including half board), 725 kronor ($130.50) single; 1,250 kronor ($225) double. AE, DC, MC, V. **Parking:** Free. **Closed:** Dec 23–Jan 7.

Built in 1900, this stone-sided hotel, painted a bright yellow, is set directly at the pier where the ferryboats from Stockholm dock. It offers modern bedrooms. Its summer disco is open on Wednesday, Friday, and Saturday from 9pm to 2am, charging a cover of 60 kronor ($10.80). An informal pub, Kabyssen, is at street level. One floor above, with a view overlooking the water, is the Vaxholm Hotel Restaurant (see "Where to Dine," below).

In Sandhamn: Budget

HOTEL SANDHAMN, S-130 39 Sandhamn. Tel. 0766/530-03. 20 rms (none with bath).

$ **Rates** (including breakfast): 480–540 kronor ($86.40–$97.20) single; 640–690 kronor ($115.20–$124.20) double. AE, DC, MC, V. **Parking:** Free.

The hotel has been enlarged over the years, expanding from its original 1880 single-story core into the larger, several-story building you see today in the center, a 1-minute walk south of the ferryboat dock. Entire families used to come down from Stockholm to spend several weeks here in summer in the comfortably old-fashioned bedrooms. The hotel serves breakfast only on an outdoor terrace, but light snacks can be ordered later.

WHERE TO DINE

In Vaxholm: Moderate

VAXHOLM HOTEL RESTAURANT, Hamngatan 2. Tel. 0764/301-50.
Cuisine: SEAFOOD. **Reservations:** Required in summer.

$ **Prices:** Appetizers 65–100 kronor ($11.70–$18); main dishes 75–195 kronor ($13.50–$35.10). AE, DC, MC, V.

Open: Summer, Mon–Sat 11:30am–10:30pm, Sun noon–9pm; winter, daily 11:30am–9pm. **Closed:** Dec 23–Jan 7.

This restaurant, opening onto a view of the water directly at the pier where the ferryboats from Stockholm dock, is the best place to dine in Vaxholm. When queried, the chef said his specialties are "fish, fish, fish." The uncompromising house specialty is a platter of pan-fried Swedish herring served with mashed potatoes. It is also the best buy in the restaurant.

In Sandhamn: Moderate

SANDHAMN VÄRDSHUS, Sandhamn. Tel. 0766/530-31.

Cuisine: SWEDISH. **Reservations:** Not required.

$ **Prices:** Appetizers 48–90 kronor ($8.60–$16.20); main dishes 65–160 kronor ($11.70–$28.80). AE, DC, MC, V.

Open: Sun–Thurs noon–10pm, Fri–Sat noon–11pm.

The favorite restaurant of the island locals, established in 1672, opens onto a view of the moored boats on the harborfront. You can always get a good and reasonably priced meal here by selecting one of the fish dishes or the local choice, steak with red onions.

CHAPTER 26

DALARNA, VÄRMLAND & CENTRAL SWEDEN

Two provinces in the heart of Sweden's southern region represent the soul of this Scandinavian nation. In the province of Dalarna lies Lake Siljan, and in Värmland, farther south, is Lake Vänern, the third-largest inland sea in Europe.

Dalarna is the most traditional of all the provinces—replete with everything from maypole dancing and fiddlers' music, to folk costumes and handcrafts, including the Dala horse. Dalarna means valleys, and you'll sometimes see it referred to as Dalecarlia, the Anglicized form of the name.

Lake Siljan, maybe the most beautiful lake in Europe, is ringed with resort villages and towns. Leksand, Tällberg, and Rättvik attract visitors during summer with sports, folklore, and a week of music. In winter, people come here for skiing.

Karlstad, on the shores of Lake Vänern, makes an ideal stopover for exploring the province of Värmland. Lake Vänern is 87 miles long and 46 miles across at its widest point. Among its chief waterways are the Göta River and the Göta Canal. A smaller body of water, Lake Vättern, lies to the east of Vänern.

Anytime is ripe for a visit to Dalarna, but during midsummer, June 23 to June 26, the Dalecarlians celebrate the custom of maypole dancing. At that time they race through the forest gathering birch bows and nosegays of wildflowers with which they cover the maypole. Then the pole is raised and they dance around it—under the midsummer-lit sky—until dawn, a good old respectable pagan custom.

The quickest and easiest way to reach this province is by train from the Central Station in Stockholm, a 4½-hour trip. All the towns below have good rail connections with each other. Motorists from Oslo can stop over in Dalarna before venturing on to the Swedish capital. Similarly, visitors to Gothenburg can head north to both Värmland and Dalarna before seeing Stockholm. Our first stopover could also be a day's excursion from Stockholm.

SEEING DALARNA, VÄRMLAND & CENTRAL SWEDEN

GETTING THERE

By car is the best way, as you can see more of the scenery, including a drive along the road between Vadstena and Jönköping, which is spectacular as it winds along the eastern shore of Lake Vättern. If you want to see the area in a hurry, and are dependent on public transportation, you can fly to Mora and use it as a center for exploring Dalarna, or fly from Stockholm to Karlstad and use that city as a base for exploring the Värmland district. Both Karlstad and Mora also have good rail

WHAT'S SPECIAL ABOUT DALARNA, VÄRMLAND & CENTRAL SWEDEN

Great Towns/Villages

☐ Tällberg, the most genuine tourist village in Dalarna, overlooking Lake Siljan.

☐ Karlstad, capital of Värmland, lying at the point where the Klarälven River enters Lake Vänern.

☐ Vadstena, an important town from the Middle Ages with a beautiful Renaissance castle.

Castles

☐ Vadstena Castle, founded by Gustavus Vasa, king of Sweden in 1545, one of the most splendid of the Renaissance Vasa castles.

Artistic Shrines

☐ Carl Larsson-gården, at Sundborn, home of Sweden's famed watercolorist.

☐ Zornmuseet, Mora, home of Sweden's most famous painter, Anders Zorn.

☐ Vadstena Abbey Church, built between the mid-14th century and the 15th, launched by St. Bridget of Sweden and rich in medieval art.

Literary Shrines

☐ Mårbacka, the former home of Selma Lagerlöf, 1909 Nobel Prize winner, known for her *The Saga of Gösta Berling.*

☐ Rottneros Manor, the Ekeby in the saga of Lagerlöf, outside Sunne.

Special Events/Festivals

☐ Music at Lake Siljan, the first week of July, Sweden's biggest music festival; lots of fiddling.

☐ The 50-mile Vasa Race, a major ski event of Sweden in March at Mora in Upper Dalarna.

---

connections from Stockholm. Many visitors see a "nutshell" preview of central Sweden by taking the Göta Canal trip (see "Organized Tours" in Chapter 25).

A SUGGESTED ITINERARY

Day 1: From Stockholm, head to Leksand for your first night, the best "gateway" to Dalarna.

Day 2: Visit Tällberg and Rättvik en route to Mora for another night.

Day 3–4: From Mora, drive south along Route 234 to Karlstad. Spend the following day exploring sights in the environs, including the manors associated with Selma Lagerlöf.

Day 5: From Karlstad, head southwest along Route 45, cutting east again on Route 44 toward Lidköping. This takes you along the western shore of Lake Vänern. Connect with the E3 east, but turn south at the junction of Route 50 to Vadstena for an overnight stopover. From Vadstena, the nearby E4 express highway returns you to Stockholm, after you've traversed the historic "tourist trail" through central Sweden.

---

1. FALUN

303 miles NE of Gothenburg, 142 miles NW of Stockholm

GETTING THERE By Train Direct trains from Stockholm take 3 hours, and trains in the west from Gothenburg take 6 hours. Several trains run daily in both directions.

By Bus Buses from Stockholm service Falun once a day Friday through Sunday. For information in Stockholm, call **Varsatrafik** at 08/771-10-80. Buses from Gothenburg, although the distance is greater, arrive three times daily but make frequent stops along the way. These buses, run by **SWEBUS**, can be called in Gothenburg at 031/71-80-90.

By Car From Stockholm, take the E18 expressway northwest to the junction with Route 70. From there, continue to the junction with Route 60, where you head northeast.

ESSENTIALS For information, the **Tourist Office**, Stora Torget (tel. 023/83-314), is open Mon–Fri 9am–4pm and Sat 9am–1pm (June 15–Aug 15) and Mon–Fri 10am–3pm (Aug 16–June 14). The **telephone area code** for Falun is 023.

The old capital of Dalarna, Falun lies on both sides of the Falu River. This town is noted for its copper mines, the income from which supported many a Swedish king. Just 6½ miles northeast, you can visit the home of the famed Swedish painter Carl Larsson (1853–1919).

WHAT TO SEE & DO

You might go first to the market square, Stora Torget, and view the **Kristine Church,** a copper-roofed structure dating from the mid-17th century (the tower dates from 1865).
Falun is the site of one of the country's largest sports complexes, **Lugnet.** Here you can find Falun's famous ski jump and the largest sports hall in Scandinavia. Alpine skiers can enjoy the slopes at the Bjursberget ski resort, only 12½ miles from Falun.

FALUN COPPER MINE, Gruvplatsen. Tel. 158-25.

This copper mine, now in the town center, was the world's largest producer of copper during the 17th century, and supplied the raw material for the roof of Versailles. The mine tour begins with an elevator trip 180 feet below the surface. Guides take you through old chambers and winding passages dating from the Middle Ages. In one section of the mine you'll see a shaft divided by a timber wall more than 650 feet high, possibly the world's highest wooden structure.
Admission: 50 kroner ($9) adult, 20 kroner ($3.60) children under 18.
Open: May–Aug, daily 10am–4:30pm; Sept–Nov 15 and Mar–Apr, Sat–Sun 12:30–4:30pm. **Closed:** Nov 16–Feb.

CARL LARSSON-GÅRDEN, Carl Larssons Väg 12, Sundborn. Tel. 600-53.

A short 20-minute trip from Falun will take you to Sundborn, a small village whose main claim to fame is Lilla Hyttnas, Carl Larsson's home, now known as Carl Larsson-gården. Larsson became Sweden's most admired artist during his lifetime. Through his watercolors, this house has become known throughout Sweden. There are guided tours throughout the day, and English-language tours are sometimes available.
Public buses leave from the Falun bus station several times a day, dropping visitors in Sundborn, 5 minutes away from Carl Larsson-gården. Sundborn is a 4-hour train ride from Stockholm.
Admission: 45 kronor ($8.10) adults, 10 kronor ($1.80) children 7–15.
Open: May–Sept, Mon–Sat 10am–5pm, Sun and holidays 1–5pm. **Closed:** Oct–Apr. **Bus:** 64 from Falun.

WHERE TO STAY & DINE
MODERATE

SARA GRAND HOTEL, Trotzgatan 9–11, S-791 71 Falun. Tel. 023/187-00. Fax 023/141-43. 183 rms (all with shower), 1 suite. TV TEL **Bus:** 701, 704.

$ **Rates** (including breakfast): June 12–Aug 16 and Fri–Sat year round, 400–625 kronor ($72–$112.50) single; 550–625 kronor ($99–$112.50) double. Sun–Thurs the rest of the year, 920–1,195 kronor ($165.60–$215.10) single; 1,220–1,295 kronor ($219.60–$233.10) double. Year-round, from 2,280 kronor ($410.40) suite. AE, DC, MC, V. **Parking:** 65 kronor ($11.70).

This buff-colored hotel 100 yards south of the landmark Falun Church was built in the late 19th century, and a modern addition was constructed in 1974. The whole complex was renovated in the 1980s so that the bedrooms, featuring a tasteful modern or Chippendale-inspired decor, are among the best decorated in town. Ask about substantial summer reductions. About 23 bedrooms have a minibar. On the premises are a small indoor pool, a sauna, and a restaurant.

---

2. LEKSAND

166 miles NW of Stockholm, 322 miles NE of Gothenburg

GETTING THERE By Plane The nearest airport is **Dala-Airport,** in Börlange, 36 miles away, from which there is frequent bus and train service to Leksand. Car rentals are available at the airport.

By Train There is a direct line from Stockholm to Mora that stops in Leksand; travel time is 3½ hours. For reservations and information, call 0247/101-15.

By Bus Express buses run from Gothenburg to Gävle and Falun, stopping at Börlange, where bus and rail connections can be made to Leksand; total travel time is 8 hours. To reserve a ticket, call 0243/270-50.

By Boat One major boat, *Gustaf Wasa,* runs regularly on short tours and cruises, making one long trip from Mora to Leksand at 10am on Friday, going via Rättvik. One-way fare is 100 kronor ($18) per adult and 50 kronor ($9) for children. Tickets are sold on board. Call 010/52-32-92 for information and reservations.

By Car From Stockholm, take the E18 express highway northwest to the junction of Route 70, which continues northwest all the way to Leksand.

ESSENTIALS For more information, the **Leksands Turistbyrå,** Norsgatan (tel. 0247/803-00), is open Mon–Fri 9am–5pm and Sat 9am–1pm (mid-Aug–mid June) and Mon–Sat 9am–9pm and Sun noon–9pm (mid-June–mid-Aug). The **telephone area code** for Leksand is 0247.

SPECIAL EVENTS Sweden's biggest music festival, **Music at Lake Siljan,** takes place during the first week of July. It consists of some 100 concerts covering a wide range of music at venues in both Leksand and Rättvik. Much of it is folk music, "the meeting of the fiddlers." For information, write Music at Lake Siljan, Box 28, S-795 00 Rättvik (tel. 0248/102-90).

Leksands Noret, as it is called, is a doorway to Lake Siljan, and no less an authority than H. C. Andersen found the setting idyllic. Leksand—in its present form—dates back to around the turn of the century, when it was reconstructed after a fire had razed the settlement. But a settlement of some sort has been on this site since pagan times.

Many of the old traditions of the province still flourish here. Women still don traditional dress for church on Sunday and in June and July the long "church boats" from Viking times may cross the lake carrying parish residents to church. These same boats compete in a church-boat race on the first Sunday in July. Since World War II a miracle play, *The Road to Heaven,* has been presented in open-air performances, providing an insight into the customs and folklore of Dalarna. The play runs for 10 days at the end of July.

WHAT TO SEE & DO

The **parish church** with its onion-shaped dome was founded in the 13th century. Near the lakeside church is an open-air **museum** with several buildings dating from the 18th and 19th centuries. Examples of peasant art can be seen at the museum, where 18th- and 19th-century artists depict Christ and his Apostles in Dalarna dress. You can also visit a glassblowing factory and several handcraft shops. It is open mid-June to mid-August 11am to 6pm, Monday through Saturday, and noon to 6pm on Sunday. Admission is free.

Sports is a major pursuit in Leksand, and several tracks for walking and skiing start from here. Downhill skiing facilities are located at Karingberget and Asleden, less than 4 miles away. Other skiing facilities include electrically lit cross-country tracks. A sports center has a swimming pool, sauna, skating rink, and curling hall, and tennis and miniature golf are available when the weather is right for them.

Visitors who want to hook up with one of the **boat trips** around Lake Siljan or go on a tour of the province should stop at the tourist bureau for information.

WHERE TO STAY

During the summer, you might find it fun to rent a *stuga* (log cabin) with four beds for 250 kronor ($45) per night. The **Leksands Turistbyrå,** Box 52, S-793 01 Leksand (tel. 0247/803-00), will book you into one. You can also inquire about renting a room in a private home.

INEXPENSIVE

HOTEL KORSTÄPPAN, Hjörtnasvagen 33, S-793 00 Leksand. Tel. 0247/100-37. Fax 0247/141-78. 350 rms (all with bath). TV **Bus:** 58.

$ **Rates** (including breakfast): June 15–Aug 15, 350 kronor ($63) single; 500 kronor ($90) double. Aug 16–June 14, 565–655 kronor ($101.70–$117.90) single; 800–1,110 kronor ($144–$199.80) double. AE, DC, MC, V. **Parking:** Free.

This yellow building beside the lake, half a mile east of the railroad station, was originally constructed in 1906. The Blomgren family, the owners, live in one of the two annexes on the property; the other contains seven of the hotel's bedrooms. Each room is pleasantly old-fashioned, with serviceable furnishings. The owner's three sons take turns at cooking in the hotel restaurant, which is open daily from noon to 10:30pm. The house specialty is fresh fried herring served with mashed potatoes. At lunch a daily platter costs 95 kronor ($17.10), and at dinner a three-course fixed-price menu goes for 130 kronor ($23.40).

MOSKOGEN MOTEL, Insjövägen, 50 S-793 00 Leksand. Tel. 0247/146-00. Fax 0247/144-30. 52 rms (all with bath), 1 suite. TV TEL **Bus:** 58.

$ **Rates** (including breakfast): 500 kronor ($90) single; 800 kronor ($144) double; from 1,000 kronor ($180) suite. MC, V. **Parking:** Free.

Termed "a self-service holiday village," this motel of red-painted wood-sided huts makes a good base for excursions into the Lake Siljan environs. Bedrooms are well furnished and comfortable. Accommodations contain a tiny kitchen, TV, shower, toilet, and phone. A restaurant on the premises sells simple lunches and dinners. Facilities include a Jacuzzi, sauna, solarium, and gym room. The Moskogen is a mile west from the railway station.

WHERE TO DINE

MODERATE

BOSPOREN, Torget 1. Tel. 132-80.
   Cuisine: SWEDISH. **Reservations:** Not required.

$ Prices: Appetizers 45–65 kronor ($8.10–$11.70); main dishes 60–130 kronor ($10.80–$23.40); lunch specials 48–68 kronor ($8.60–$12.20). AE, DC, MC, V.
Open: Daily 11am–11pm.

This restaurant, 400 yards west of the railroad station, was given its Istanbul-derived name by its Turkish-born owners, who maintain longer and more reliable hours than any other place in town. In spite of the name, the good cuisine is traditionally Swedish. Dishes include many types of fresh fish, wienerschnitzel, and fish Waleska.

OLD CURTIS INN, Norsgatan 21. Tel. 105-70.
Cuisine: SWEDISH. **Reservations:** Not required.
$ Prices: Appetizers 49–55 kronor ($8.80–$9.90); main dishes 59–119 kronor ($10.60–$21.40). No credit cards.
Open: Tues 5–8pm, Wed–Thurs 5pm–midnight, Fri 3pm–1am, Sat noon–1am, Sun 1pm–midnight.

One floor above street level, this restaurant in the center, across the street from the town's only liquor store, is over its companion establishment, the town's most popular pub, where a large glass of Swedish beer costs 38 kronor ($6.80). The atmosphere is decidedly casual, and the fare is simple, including fish-and-chips, steak, and roast chicken. Thursday night is "taco night," and Wednesday is an all-the-food-you-can-eat night for 35 kronor ($6.30).

---

3. TÄLLBERG

8 miles N of Leksand, 174 miles NW of Stockholm, 322 miles NE of Gothenburg

GETTING THERE   By Train   Trains from Gothenburg require about 7 hours, with a change in Börlange. There are direct trains daily from Stockholm, but with many stopovers (trip time is 3½ hours). Trains also make the 10-minute run between Leksand and Tällberg.

By Bus   There is no direct bus service from Stockholm or Gothenburg. Bus passengers get off at either Leksand or Rättvik, where local bus connections can be made.

By Car   Take the E18 expressway northwest from Stockholm, then turn onto Route 70 toward Börlange and drive all the way to Tällberg, a 3-hour drive.

ESSENTIALS   For **information,** the Leksand Tourist Office handles queries (see above). The **telephone area code** for Tällberg is 0247.

This lakeside village, charmingly in tune with the spirit and tradition of Dalarna, is my favorite spot in the whole province, and the area of choice for nature lovers in both summer and winter. Skiing, curling, skating, and sleigh rides are popular sports, and swimming and boating lure summer visitors.

Tällberg's beauty was discovered after artists and other cultural celebrities built summer houses in the village. One of the artists created **Holens Gammelgård** (farmstead), which later became the center of the Dalarna folklore movement. The old farmhouse of **Ankarcrona** is now a summer museum, located at the highest point of Tällberg, with a superb view over Lake Siljan.

WHERE TO STAY & DINE

INEXPENSIVE

AKERBLADS I TÄLLBERG, S-793 03 Tällberg. Tel. 0247/508-00. Fax 0247/506-52. 63 rms (all with bath), 15 mini-suites. TV TEL

$ Rates (including breakfast): 640 kronor ($115.20) single; 920 kronor ($165.60) double; from 1,290 kronor ($232.20) mini-suite. AE, DC, MC, V. **Parking:** Free.
An old-fashioned family hotel since 1910, this establishment is 1¼ miles from Tällberg station at the crossroads leading down to Lake Siljan. The core of the house is still the wooden storehouse in the courtyard, but there has been much rebuilding over the years, including a recent addition of 15 mini-suites with complete baths and minibars. All rooms at the hotel are done in an attractive Dala style. A massage pool, sauna, solarium, and tennis court are some of the features. During the winter, sleigh rides are arranged and guests return to a log fire and hot mulled and spiced wine. Bicycles are also available for free. The hotel restaurant is known for its "grandmother's good cooking," buffets, and homemade bread. There is also a replica of an old pub where you can get a drink or a cheap pub lunch.

GREEN HOTEL, S-793 03 Tällberg. Tel. 0247/502-50. Fax 0247/501-30. 101 rms (all with bath). TEL
$ Rates (including full board): 690–2,000 kronor ($124.20–$360) single; 800–2,000 kronor ($144–$360) double. MC, V. **Parking:** Free.
This hotel, whose wide array of rooms ranges from budget to VIP, is located on a lawn sloping down toward the lake half a mile west of the railroad station. The staff wear regional costumes, and the lounge has a notable art collection. On the premises are five saunas and a swimming pool whose surface is covered every Saturday night with a glass top and converted to a dance floor. Open all year, the hotel offers an array of summer and winter sports. A few of the more luxurious bedrooms have their own fireplaces and private saunas, and some contain a TV. The hotel has a restaurant and bar.

BUDGET

LÅNGBERS, Toppen i Tällberg, S-793 03 Tällberg. Tel. 0247/502-90. Fax 0247/505-60. 55 rms (all with bath). TEL
$ Rates (including breakfast): 380 kronor ($68.40) single; 700 kronor ($126) double. AE, DC, MC, V. **Parking:** Free.
At 1,000 feet above sea level, on a hillside overlooking the town half a mile west of the railroad station, this hotel offers a fine view of Lake Siljan and its surroundings. Rooms are equally divided between the original hotel, built around 1930, and a newer annex erected in 1980 in basically the same architectural style. The buildings are set about 25 yards apart, and each has a view. The better and more charming rooms are the older ones because of their larger size, higher ceilings, and old-fashioned charm. The newer rooms are still very comfortable, furnished in a Nordic modern. There is a sauna on the premises, plus a restaurant offering fixed-priced lunches for 110 kronor ($19.80) and dinners for 280 kronor ($50.40).

SILJANSGÅRDEN, Sjögattu 36. S-793 70 Tällberg. Tel. 0247/500-40. Fax 0247/500-13. 28 rms (16 with bath), 10 cottages.
$ Rates (including breakfast): Summer rooms (no heat), 240 kronor ($43.20) single without bath; 400 kronor ($72) double without bath. Year-round rooms, 300–360 kronor ($54–$64.80) single with toilet (no shower); 460–520 kronor ($82.80–$93.60) double with toilet (no shower); 335–400 kronor ($60.30–$72) single with bath; 530–640 kronor ($95.40–$115.20) double with bath. Summer cottages, 270 kronor ($48.60) for two; 340 kronor ($61.20) for four. Sheet rental 50 kronor ($9) per person extra. Breakfast 45 kronor ($8.10) per person extra. DC, MC, V. **Parking:** Free.
Originally built in 1915, this charming, rustic, timber-sided hotel stands on 12 acres on the shores of the lake 1 mile west of the railroad station. On the grounds is a bathing beach, a tennis court, a rowboat, a mini-golf course, and a sauna. The hotel bedrooms are simply furnished but comfortable and, in addition, some rustic cottages are rented, suitable for up to four occupants, which make them a family favorite. A restaurant in the main building is licensed for beer and wine only, serving a one-course lunch for 75 kronor ($13.50) and a three-course dinner for 130 kronor ($23.40). In spite of the winter snows, the hotel is open all year, although the

cottages are available only in summer. Cottage renters bring their own sheets and sleeping bags, although sheets can be rented.

4. RÄTTVIK

13 miles SW of Leksand, 31 miles E of Mora, 171 miles NW of Stockholm

GETTING THERE By Train Three to five trains a day make the 30-minute run between Mora and Rättvik. Rättvik also has rail lines to Leksand; trip time is also 30 minutes.

By Bus Daily buses run between Mora and Rättvik and Leksand and Rättvik, taking 40 minutes.

By Car From Stockholm, take the E18 express highway northwest, reaching the junction with Route 70 where you should continue northwest all the way to Rättvik.

ESSENTIALS For information, the **Rättvik Tourist Office,** Torget (tel. 0248/109-10), is open Mon–Fri 9am–8pm and Sat and Sun 11am–8pm (summer) and Mon–Fri 9am–5pm and Sat noon–4pm (off-season). The **telephone area code** for Rättvik is 0248.

R ättvik is one of the most popular resorts bordering Lake Siljan, which has some of the best hotels in the district. In summer there are conducted tours around Lake Siljan from here. Culture and tradition are always associated with Rättvik—peasant costumes, folk dancing, Dalarna paintings, arts and crafts, "church boats," and fiddle music. There's an expression: "If you meet two men from Rättvik, three of them will be fiddlers." The old style of architecture is still alive, and you will find many timber houses. Carpenters and painters from Rättvik are known for their craftsmanship.

WHAT TO SEE & DO

For a view over the area, go to the top of the old wooden tower at **Vidablick** (tel. 100-13), about 3 miles out of town on the road to Falun.

One mile from the village is **Gammelgården** (tel. 114-45), an old Dalarna farmstead. It is open mid-June to mid-August, Monday through Saturday from 11am to 6pm and on Sunday from noon to 6pm. Guided tours are conducted at 1 and 2:30pm. Admission is 10 kronor ($1.80).

If you're interested in art, you can visit the artists' village at **Rättviks Hantverksby,** Gårdebyn (tel. 302-50), established by the Swedish artist Sören Erikson. Children can take a ride on a miniature train.

SCANDIC ACTIVE HOTEL, S-795 00 Rättvik. Tel. 0248/111-50. Fax 0248/111-77. 95 rms (all with bath), 1 suite. TV TEL **Bus:** 58, 70.
$ Rates (including breakfast): Midsummer and Fri–Sat year-round, 450 kronor ($81) single; 495 kronor ($89.10) double. Sun–Thurs the rest of the year, 820 kronor ($147.60) single, 1,003 kronor ($180.50) double. AE, DC, MC, V. **Parking:** Free.
Near the top of a hill overlooking Rättvik, a 10-minute walk north from the lake, this hotel is a 1988 stylish rebirth of a turn-of-the-century hotel that had fallen onto bad days. The only remaining part of the original is the Lerdalshöjden Restaurant, which retains the original walls and feeling of the old place (see "Where to Dine," below). Bedrooms are well furnished and maintained, and decorated with modern accessories and amenities. The hotel has a sauna with a view over the lake, plus an exercise room.

WHERE TO STAY
INEXPENSIVE

HOTEL GÄRDEBYGÅRDEN, 795 00 Rättvik. Tel. 0248/129-75. Fax 0248/10-257. 50 rms (26 with bath). **Bus:** 58, 70.

$ Rates (including breakfast): May–Sept, 350 kronor ($63) single without bath, 450 kronor ($81) single with bath; 500 kronor ($90) double without bath, 600 kronor ($108) double with bath. Oct–Apr, 390 kronor ($70.20) single without bath, 500 kronor ($90) single with bath; 700 kronor ($126) double without bath, 920 kronor ($165.60) double with bath. MC, V. **Parking:** Free.

This very good value hotel, located off Storgaten in the town center, was started in 1906 and is today owned by the Swedish Mission Church. A big breakfast is served every day—almost like a Swedish smörgåsbord—and almost every night there's some form of entertainment, often Dalarna fiddlers. Some nights are devoted to communal sing-alongs. Within a short walk of the lake, the hotel has expanded into a pair of outlying buildings. The bedrooms are comfortably and sedately furnished with conservative furniture. Some have a view of the lake. Cross-country ski trails and jogging paths are a short distance away.

WHERE TO DINE

MODERATE

LERDALSHÖJDEN, in the Scandic Active Hotel, Rättvik. Tel. 111-50.
   Cuisine: SWEDISH. **Reservations:** Recommended.
$ Prices: Appetizers 50–105 kronor ($9–$18.90); main dishes 100–190 kronor ($18–$34.20); fixed-price lunch 50 kronor ($9). AE, DC, MC, V.
   Open: Lunch Mon–Fri noon–2:30pm; dinner Mon–Fri 5:30–10pm, Sat–Sun 5:30–11pm.

Near the top of a hill overlooking Rättvik, a 10-minute walk north from the lake, this restaurant is the only original remaining section left from the 1988 remodeling of a turn-of-the-century hotel. It has long been a favorite with locals from the nearby lake district. They like its traditional Swedish home-style cookery, including fresh fish and beef dishes. Try, for example, steak tartare with bleak roe or fried ptarmigan with red currant sauce. In winter, the region's most popular dinner-dance is staged here most Saturday nights.

---

5. MORA

327 miles NE of Gothenburg, 204 miles NW of Stockholm

GETTING THERE **By Plane** Mora is connected by daily air service from Stockholm, taking 40 minutes. The airport lies about 4 miles from the center. Taxis meet arriving flights.

By Train There is direct service daily from Stockholm to Mora; trip time is 4 hours.

By Bus Certain weekend buses leave from Stockholm's Central Station on the 4¼-hour trip to Mora.

By Car Take the E18 express highway northeast from Stockholm until you connect with Route 70 heading northeast all the way to Mora.

By Boat The *Gustaf Wasa* cruises between Mora and Leksand. Departures from Leksand are in the afternoon. Departures from Mora are at 10am on Friday, costing 100 kronor ($18) one-way for adults and 50 kronor ($9) for children. Call 010/52-32-92 for information and reservations.

ESSENTIALS For information, the tourist bureau, **Mora Turistbyrå,** Angbåtskajen (tel. 0250/265-50), is open Mon–Sat 9am–8pm and Sun noon–9pm (summer) and Mon–Fri 9am–5pm and Sat noon–4pm (off-season). The **telephone area code** for Mora is 0250.

In Upper Dalarna, between Lake Orsa and Lake Siljan, the provincial town of Mora is our final stopover in the province. Summer travelers find this business and residential center a good base for exploring the district.

Mora was the village where Gustavus Vasa—after an initial unsuccessful attempt—finally rallied the peasants in Sweden's 16th-century war against Danish rule. In March of every year, this event is commemorated by a 50-mile Vasa Race, one of the major ski events.

WHAT TO SEE & DO

Mora has opened a **Santa complex,** inaugurated for the Christmas of 1984, featuring Santa's house and his factory. Visitors can meet "Santa," and see his favorite helpers making and gift-wrapping presents for children all over the world.

Mora was also the hometown of Anders Zorn (1860–1920), perhaps Sweden's most famous painter, and the town's three top sights are all associated with him. The first, **Lisselby,** is an area near the Zorn Museum made up of old houses that are now used as arts and crafts studios and boutiques. At **Balder-Lisselby,** a craft center, you can watch handcrafts being made Monday through Saturday between 9am and 6pm, except at lunchtime.

ZORNMUSEET (Zorn Museum), Vasagatan 36. Tel. 165-60.

This museum contains not only a wide collection of the artist's own works (among them, *Midnight*), but paintings from his private collection—including works by Prince Eugen and Carl Larsson, also of Dalarna. Major foreign artists (sculpture by Kai Nielsen of Denmark and etchings by Rembrandt) are also presented, along with rural art and handcrafts of Dalarna.

Admission: 15 kronor ($2.70) adults, 2 kronor (40¢) children.

Open: Summer, Mon–Sat 9am–5pm, Sun 11am–5pm; off-season, Mon–Sat 10am–5pm, Sun 1–5pm.

ZORNSGÅRDEN, Vasagatan 36. Tel. 165-60.

The artist's former home, adjoining the museum, has been left just as it was when Mrs. Zorn died in 1942. Its chief attraction, aside from the paintings displayed, is Zorn's personally designed Great Hall on the top floor.

Admission: 20 kronor ($3.60) adults, 2 kronor (40¢) children.

Open: Summer, Mon–Sat 10am–5pm, Sun 11am–5pm; off-season, Mon–Sat 12:30–5pm, Sun 1–5pm.

WHERE TO STAY

INEXPENSIVE

HOTEL MORAPARKEN, Parkvägen 1, S-792 00 Mora. Tel. 0250/178-00. Fax 0250/185-83. 75 rms (all with bath). TV TEL

$ Rates: Mid-June to Aug (including breakfast), 550 kronor ($99) single or double. Sept–early June, Sun–Thurs (including breakfast), 660 kronor ($118.80) single; 820 kronor ($147.60) double. Sept–June, Fri–Sat (including half board and a dance), 880 kronor ($158.40) per person. AE, DC, MC, V. **Parking:** Free.

With a wooden facade, this spacious, rambling hotel is beside the Österdal River in the vacation resort of Moraparken a quarter mile from Mora. Sports include swimming, sailing, tennis, mini-golf, and a wide array of winter sports. Rooms are comfortably modern. The hotel has a sauna, solarium, and outdoor swimming pool.

MORA HOTEL, Strandgatan 12, S-792 00 Mora. Tel. 0250/117-50. Fax 0250/189-81. 85 rms (all with bath), 55 mini-suites. MINIBAR TV TEL

$ Rates (including breakfast): Midsummer and Fri–Sat year-round, 505 kronor ($90.90) single; 675 kronor ($121.50) double; from 900 kronor ($162) mini-suite. Sun–Thurs in off-season, 550–925 kronor ($99–$166.50) single; 675–1,110 kronor ($122.75–$201.80) double; from 1,320 kronor ($237.60) mini-suite. AE, DC, MC, V. **Parking:** 70 kronor ($12.60).

A modern hotel, in the center of town across from the lakefront a minute's walk from the tourist bureau, the Mora Hotel has been renovated over the years to include sun terraces and glassed-in verandas. The interior is tasteful with bright colors. All accommodations have comfortable furniture, nonalcoholic minibars, and radios, as well as other amenities. On the premises is an indoor pool, along with several dining facilities. The best is the Terrassen, (see "Where to Dine," below). The hotel has a disco on Friday and Saturday charging a 65 kronor ($11.70) admission.

WHERE TO DINE

MODERATE

TERRASSEN, in the Mora Hotel, Strandgatan 12. Tel. 117-50.
   Cuisine: SWEDISH. **Reservations:** Recommended but not required.
$ Prices: Appetizers 60–85 kronor ($10.80–$15.30); main dishes 75–175 kronor ($13.50–$31.50). AE, DC, MC, V.
   Open: Lunch Mon–Sat 11:30am–3pm; dinner Mon–Sat 3–11pm.
This is one of the finest dining rooms in the area, and it's a good bet for a meal even if you aren't a guest of the Mora Hotel (see "Where to Stay," above). Fresh produce is used whenever possible, and fresh fish and Swedish beef dishes are a feature. You might begin with herring or enjoy a freshly made salad. Service is both polite and efficient.

NEARBY EXCURSIONS

NUSNÄS   In Nusnäs, about 6 miles southeast of Mora, are two places where you can watch the Dalarna horses being made. You are free to walk around the workshops watching the craftspeople at work, and the finished products can be purchased at shops on the premises. They also sell wooden shoes and other craft items. **Nils Olssons Hemslojd** is open Monday through Friday from 8am to 3pm, and **Grännas A. Olssons Hemslojd** can be visited from 8am to 4pm, also on weekdays. To find Nusnäs, take the main road east out of Mora, turning off to the right at Farnäs.

VÄRMLAND

Sometimes described as Sweden in miniature, Värmland is picturesque: mountains, rolling hill country, islands, and rivers. Värmland is also a province of festivals, music, art, literature, and handcrafts. Tourists can enjoy boating, fishing, skiing, hiking, folklore, and historic sights.

   Forests still cover a large part of Värmland, and the 170-mile-long Klarälven River carries logs to the industrial areas around Lake Vänern. In one of her most famous works, *The Saga of Gösta Berling,* Nobel Prize winner and native Swede Selma Lagerlöf lyrically described Värmland life in the early 19th century. Today the province remains much as she saw it.

6. KARLSTAD

154 miles NE of Gothenburg, 186 miles W of Stockholm

GETTING THERE   By Plane   Nine flights on Linjeflyg connect Stockholm and Karlstad daily, the "jump" taking 45 minutes.

By Train   Six trains a day run between Gothenburg and Karlstad, taking 3 hours; 10 trains a day arrive from Stockholm, taking 3 hours; and 3 trains a day from Oslo on the 3-hour trip.

By Bus   Three buses a day arrive from Gothenburg, taking 4 hours; four weekly from Stockholm, taking 4½ hours; and two weekly from Oslo, taking 4½ hours. Check locally for bus schedules, which change from month to month.

By Car From Stockholm, take the E18 west all the way, and from Gothenburg head north along the E6 expressway, turning northeast at the junction of Route 45, which runs all the way to Karlstad.

ESSENTIALS The **Karlstad Tourist Bureau,** Tingvallagatan 1D, S-651 84 Karlstad (tel. 054/19-59-02), is open Mon–Fri 9am–noon and Sat 9am–1pm (June 15–Aug 15) and Mon–Fri 10am–3pm and Sat 10am–noon (Aug 16–June 14). The **telephone area code** for Karlstad is 054.

The capital of Värmland, this port city is at the mouth of the Klarälven River. Karlstad has many attractions for visitors, plus many moderately priced restaurants and comfortable hotels. Because of its location, it has long been a center for administration, trade, and transport, and is a good starting point for many of the tourist routes of Värmland.

WHAT TO SEE & DO

A trading center called Thingwalla first stood on the site of the city, but in 1584, Duke Charles—later Sweden's King Charles IX—founded Karlstad. Here you can see Sweden's longest stone bridge, East Bridge, built in the 18th century. The oldest quarter, **Almen,** on Älvgatan, was saved from a disastrous fire in 1865 and can be visited, along with the old grammar school and the Bishop's House.

One of the best ways to acquire a quick orientation of Karlstad is to take a guided tour on a **Sola sightseeing boat,** leaving from the Residens Park (from the inner harbor at low water) at 1, 3, 5, and 7pm daily from mid-June to late August, with an additional 8:30pm trip in July, provided you reserve before 7pm (tel. 19-59-01). Passage costs 40 kronor ($7.20) for adults, 20 kronor ($3.60) for children.

VÄRMLANDS MUSEUM, Sandsgrundsudden. Tel. 11-14-19.

This museum traces the prehistory of the area and the culture of its residents. You can see collections of coins, textiles, arts, and crafts. The museum, in a park on the northern edge of town, is a 5-minute walk from the city center.

Admission: Free.

Open: June–Aug, Mon–Fri 11am–7pm, Sat–Sun noon–4pm; Sept–May, Tues and Thurs–Sun noon–4pm, Wed noon–8pm.

MARIEBERGSSKOGEN, Mariebergs Park. Tel. 15-92-00.

Mariebergsskogen is one of Sweden's top pleasure parks, with a fair, dancing, a theater, and an open-air museum, as well as an animal park and a restaurant. It's on the southern outskirts, a 15-minute walk south of the town center.

Admission: Free.

Open: Lillskogen children's zoo, daily 11am–6pm; fun fair, Mon–Fri 11am–6pm, Sat–Sun noon–6pm.

ALSTERS HERRGÅRD, on the E18 highway Tel. 83-40-81.

Alster Manor is maintained in the memory of Gustaf Fröding, one of Sweden's leading poets, who was born here in 1860. In one of the wings is a small exhibition on emigration from Värmland to America. There is a café on the premises, and you can stroll through the Fröding Grove. The manor is 5 miles east of Karlstad on the Stockholm road.

Admission: 15 kronor ($2.70) adults; children free.

Open: May–Aug, daily 11am–6pm. **Closed:** Sept–Apr. **Bus:** 15.

A NEARBY ATTRACTION

ALFRED NOBEL'S BJÖRKBORN, Karlskoga. Tel. 0586/818-94.

Some 30 miles east of Karlstad, near Karlskoga on Lake Möckeln, is the home of the manufacturer, inventor, and philanthropist who established the Nobel Prizes. You can visit the home (now a museum) and view the libraries, the study with Nobel's personal belongings, his bedroom, and the elegant salon. There is a café where you can enjoy drinks.

Admission: 20 kronor ($3.60) adults; children free.
Open: June–Aug, daily 1–5pm. **Closed:** Sept–May. **Directions:** Take the E18 east from Karlstad; turn off at the road sign for Björkborn.

WHERE TO STAY
INEXPENSIVE

GÖSTA BERLING, Drottninggatan 1, S-652 24 Karlstad. Tel. 054/15-01-90. Fax 054/15-48-26. 75 rms (all with bath). TV TEL
$ Rates (including breakfast): June 16–Aug 15 and Fri–Sat year-round, 375 kronor ($67.50) single; 475 kronor ($85.50) double. Sun–Thurs the rest of the year, 750–775 kronor ($135–$139.50) single; 850–900 kronor ($153–$162) double. AE, DC, MC, V. **Parking:** 65 kronor ($11.70).

Located at the beginning of the biggest shopping street in Karlstad, this relatively bland hotel has no real public rooms to speak of beyond a small lobby and unpretentious breakfast room. The heart and soul of the establishment are the comfortable, cozy, and plushly carpeted rooms, recently renovated. The hotel has a sauna.

PLAZA HOTEL KARLSTAD, Västra Torggatan 2, S-652 25 Karlstad. Tel. 054/10-02-00. Fax 054/10-02-24. 101 rms (all with bath), 2 suites. TV TEL
$ Rates: June 10–Aug 16 and Fri–Sat year-round, 495–595 kronor ($89.10–$107.10) single; 570–670 kronor ($102.60–$120.60) double; from 995 kronor ($179.10) suite. Sun–Thurs the rest of the year, 895–970 kronor ($161.10–$174.60) single; 980–1,100 kronor ($176.40–$198) double, from 2,100 kronor ($378) suite. AE, DC, MC, V. **Parking:** 20 kronor ($3.60).

This hotel in the town center, a minute's walk from the bus station, has been considerably upgraded and improved since it was built in 1984. Upstairs, each of the comfortable rooms contains built-in furniture. Rooms on the fourth and fifth floors are especially luxurious. If a guest asks for something extra, every effort is made to comply. The hotel has a garden and a greenhouse-style roof off the lobby containing the Plaza Garden-Restaurant, actually a brasserie in the French style. For information about its restaurant Plaza Vivaldi, one of the best in town, see "Where to Dine," below.

SARA HOTEL WINN, Norra Strandgatan 9–11, S-652 24 Karlstad. Tel. 054/10-22-50. Fax 054/11-12-65. 197 rms (all with bath), 2 suites. TV TEL
$ Rates (including breakfast): June 15–Aug 17 and Fri–Sat year-round, 440–650 kronor ($79.20–$117) single; 590–750 kronor ($106.20–$135) double. Sun–Thurs the rest of the year, 895–1,250 kronor ($161.10–$225) single or double. AE, DC, MC, V. **Parking:** 65 kronor ($11.70).

The most up-to-date and stylish hotel in town, in the center by the Klarälven, the Sara Hotel Winn has an alluring lobby-level piano bar and an in-house restaurant, the Café Artist (see "Where to Dine," below). Each of the bedrooms contains carpeting, video movies, radio, trouser press, and stylish brass-accented furniture. Some 28 rooms have a minibar. Laundry facilities and room service are available.

STADSHOTELLET, Kungsgatan 22, S-651 05 Karlstad. Tel. 054/11-52-20. Fax 054/18-82-11. 143 rms (all with bath). TV TEL
$ Rates (including breakfast): June 25–Aug 5 and Fri–Sat year-round, 550 kronor ($99) single; 610 kronor ($109.80) double. Sun–Thurs the rest of the year, 945–1,100 kronor ($170.10–$198) single; 1,100–1,500 kronor ($198–$270) double. AE, DC, MC, V. **Parking:** 65 kronor ($11.70).

One of the most impressive Stads hotels in all of Scandinavia, this hotel with its yellow-and-white imperial neobaroque facade was built as a guesthouse by the Swedish government in 1873. A treaty signed here in 1905 gave Norway its independence. Bedrooms range from sedately modern to the more old-fashioned, but all rooms were renovated in 1985. Twenty rooms contain minibars. Same-day laundry service is provided. The hotel is a 5-minute walk north from the rail station.

The gourmet restaurant Matsalon serves first-class food. The Cafeet Statt, open from 7am and continuing with lunch, afternoon beverages, and early or late dinner, offers dancing in the evening. You can dine amid elaborately carved turn-of-the-century walls beneath a ceiling embellished with sea serpents. On Friday and Saturday there is a 50 kronor ($9) cover charge. Also featured is the Olle Ferms Bar. Separate men's and women's saunas and solariums, and a garage and parking lot are provided.

BUDGET

GRAND HOTEL, Västra Torggatan, S-652 25 Karlstad. Tel. 054/11-52-40. Fax 054/11-79-57. 69 rms (all with bath), 1 suite. TV TEL
$ Rates (including breakfast): June 1–Aug 1 and Fri–Sat year-round, 400 kronor ($72) single; 550 kronor ($99) double; Sun–Thurs the rest of the year, 400–800 kronor ($72–$144) single; 500–1,200 kronor ($90–$216) double. Year-round, from 1,300 kronor ($234) suite. AE, DC, MC, V. **Parking:** 65 kronor ($11.70).
No longer the grandest hotel in town, it still has an old-fashioned charm. Dating from the late 19th century, it is the oldest hotel in Karlstad. It has a reddish brown semi-ornate facade and is located in the center of town 200 yards north of the railroad station. Each of the spacious high-ceilinged bedrooms has, among other amenities, a trouser press and radio. Meals are served in a dark-walled Victorian dining room.

WHERE TO DINE
EXPENSIVE

VÄRDSHUSET ALSTERN, Morgonvägen 4. Tel. 83-49-00.
Cuisine: FRENCH/SWEDISH. **Reservations:** Recommended.
$ Prices: Appetizers 50–120 kronor ($9–$21.60); main dishes 215–245 kronor ($38.70–$44.10); 1-course lunch 135 kronor ($24.30). AE, DC, MC, V.
Open: Lunch only, daily 1–7pm. **Closed:** Jan 1–7.
Two miles north of Karlstad near Route 63 on a hillside above Lake Alstern, this place makes a fine luncheon excursion. It occupies a 1920s Dutch-gabled building. Depending on the season, you can enjoy game specialties such as elk with hand-picked berries and wild mushrooms, along with nouvelle-inspired fish dishes, meats, and vegetables prepared just right.

MODERATE

CAFE ARTIST, in the Sara Hotel Winn, Norra Strandgatan 9–11. Tel. 10-22-50.
Cuisine: SWEDISH/FRENCH. **Reservations:** Recommended.
$ Prices: Appetizers 68–120 kronor ($12.20–$21.60); main dishes 148–250 kronor ($26.60–$45). AE, DC, MC, V.
Open: Mon–Fri 11:30am–midnight, Sat–Sun 6pm–midnight.
The hand-rubbed glow of its paneling and its 19th-century pinewood antiques make this one of the most interesting restaurants in town, occupying the ground floor of the Sara Hotel Winn (see "Where to Stay," above), 200 yards from the market square. The plush comfort of the Piano Bar is a good place for an apéritif. Dishes served in the main dining room include raw pickled salmon with herb sauce, filet of pork with calvados and cream, a collage of shellfish and fish from nearby lakes and seas, scampi in either a lobster sauce or with Pernod, filet of venison with green-pepper sauce and ginger, whisky-flambéed filet of beef with Gorgonzola sauce, and a dessert favorite of homemade vanilla ice cream with warm cloudberries.

PLAZA VIVALDI, in the Plaza Hotel Karlstad, Västra Torggatan 2. Tel. 10-02-00.
Cuisine: SWEDISH. **Reservations:** Recommended.
$ Prices: Appetizers 60–100 kronor ($10.80–$18); main dishes 145–210 kronor ($26.10–$37.80). AE, DC, MC, V.
Open: Lunch daily noon–2pm; dinner daily 6–11pm.
One of the best and most elegant restaurants in Karlstad is on the lobby level of the Plaza Hotel (see "Where to Stay," above). Its decor combines modern with antique

and traditional. Specialties of the chef are likely to include lime- and ginger-marinated salmon flavored with coriander, noisettes of reindeer with chanterelles, filet of veal in a creamy morel sauce, breast of pheasant with white wine sauce and grapes, and filet of monkfish.

SKOGEN TERRASSEN, Mariebergsskogen. Tel. 15-92-03.
  Cuisine: SWEDISH. **Reservations:** Recommended.
$ Prices: Smörgåsbord 185 kronor ($33.30). AE, MC, V.
  Open: Summer, Mon–Sat 11:30am–2pm; off-season, Mon–Sat 11am–6pm.
The allure here is the copious smörgåsbord buffet. You can eat either on a rustic terrace with a view of the spruces ringing the lake and the nearby amusement park, a 15-minute walk east of the center, or choose the veranda, or the spacious dining hall with its high wooden ceilings and antiques. You are presented with a lavish array of Swedish delicacies, including herring, shrimp, fish, salads, and meat, topped by a homemade dessert table.

---

7. SUNNE

236 miles W of Stockholm, 179 miles NE of Gothenburg

GETTING THERE   **By Train**   Four or five trains arrive daily on the 4½-hour trip from Stockholm, and from Gothenburg, another four or five trains a day, taking 3 hours 40 minutes. You always have to change trains in Kil, and sometimes in Hallsberg, depending on the train. From Oslo there are two trains a day, requiring a change in Kil; trip time is 3 to 4 hours.

By Bus   From Stockholm, it's too complicated with too many transfers—take the train. From Gothenburg, one bus a day arrives Monday through Friday on the 7¼-hour trip; transfer in Karlstad.

By Car   Drive north along Route 234 from Karlstad.

ESSENTIALS   For information, the **Sunne Turistbyrå,** Mejerigatan 2 (tel. 0565/135-30), is open Mon–Fri 9am–4pm and Sat 9am–1pm (June 15–Aug 15) and Mon–Fri 10am–3pm and Sat 10am–noon (Aug 16–June 14). The **telephone area code** for Sunne is 0565.

Lying on Lake Fryken, Sunne is the center for tourism in Fryksdalen (Fryken Valley). Known as the "Land of Legend," Fryksdalen is associated with the writings of Selma Lagerlöf. In fact, Sunne was the prototype for the village of Bro in *The Saga of Gösta Berling.* From Sunne, you can take boat trips on Lake Fryken, or play golf on a nine-hole course.

WHAT TO SEE & DO

SUNDSBERGS GÅRD, Ekebyvägen. Tel. 103-63.
  This museum shows three centuries of life in a Värmland manor house, from the kitchen to the drawing room. It's south of the town center, close to the landmark Hotel Selma Lagerlöf.
  Admission: 20 kronor ($3.60) adults; children free.
  Open: Mid-June to mid-Aug, Tues–Sun 1–6pm. **Closed:** Late Aug–early June.

ROTTNEROS MANOR, Rottneros. Tel. 602-95.
  The Ekeby in the saga of Selma Lagerlöf, Rottneros Manor, on the western shore of the lake, is one of Sweden's major attractions. You can only visit the park and sculpture garden, which has more than 100 pieces of sculpture, including works by Carl Milles. The foremost sculptors of each of the neighboring Scandinavian countries are also represented: Kai Nielsen of Denmark, Gustav Vigeland of Norway, and Waino Aaltonen of Finland. On the grounds is a cafeteria and a licensed restaurant.

Admission: 40 kronor ($7.20) adults, 15 kronor ($2.70) children.
Open: Mid-May to Aug, daily 9am–6pm. **Closed:** Sept to mid–May.

MÅRBACKA MINNESGÅRD, Mårbacka. Tel. 310-27.

⭐ On the other side of the water, 6 miles from Sunne and 36 miles north of Karlstad, Mårbacka is the former home of Selma Lagerlöf, who won the Nobel Prize for literature. The pillared building is kept much as she left it at the time of her death in 1940 (she was born here in 1858). The estate is filled with her furnishings and mementos. It was Lövdala in *The Saga of Gösta Berling*.

Admission: 35 kronor ($6.30) adults, 15 kronor ($2.70) children.
Open: May–Aug, daily 9am–6pm; Sept, Sat–Sun 10am–6pm.
Closed: Oct–Apr.

WHERE TO STAY & DINE

INEXPENSIVE

HOTEL SELMA LAGERLÖF, Ekebyvägen, S-686 00 Sunne. Tel. 0565/ 130-80. Fax 0565/123-66. 147 rms (all with bath), 3 suites. MINIBAR TV TEL
$ **Rates** (including breakfast): Midsummer, 250 kronor ($45) single; 295 kronor ($53.10) double; from 800 kronor ($144) suite. Sun–Thurs the rest of the year, 795 kronor ($143.10) single; 1,150 kronor ($207) double; from 1,550 kronor ($279) suite. Fri–Sat the rest of the year, 1,360 kronor ($244.80) suite. AE, DC, MC, V.
Parking: Free.

⭐ With its mansard roof and stately dimensions, it's difficult to believe that this hotel, one of the best in Sweden, was built only a few years ago in a consciously old-fashioned manor-house style. Its sweeping lawn overlooks Lake Fryken 5 minutes south from the center where the hotel has warm-weather sports facilities. Winter enthusiasts find easy access to the nearby Sunne Ski Center. Each room is comfortable and well decorated. An indoor pool, saunas, bars, and high-quality restaurants are on its premises.

Food is served from 11:30am to 2:30pm and 6 to 10pm Monday through Friday, on Saturday from noon to 3pm and 6 to 10pm and on Sunday from noon to 8pm.

---

8. FILIPSTAD

167 miles W of Stockholm, 192 miles NE of Gothenburg

GETTING THERE **By Train** It's not possible to go by train to Filipstad anymore. The nearest station is at Kristinehamn, from which you can make bus connections to Filipstad.

By Bus Daily connections are possible from Karlstad.

By Car Follow Route 61 via Arvika to Kil. Drive via Forshaga to Route 63 to Malkam and Filipstad.

ESSENTIALS The **Långban Information Center,** S-682 00 Filipstad (tel. 054/221-15), is open daily 9:30am–6pm (early June–end of Aug). The **telephone area code** for Filipstad is 054.

The tourist center for the Bergslag (mining) area of Värmland, Filipstad was founded in 1611. It is almost certain that iron ore was mined in this region even before the Black Death of the 14th century, and documentary evidence establishes it as being a thriving business in 1413. The main mine products were iron and manganese ore, but silver, copper, lead, and zinc ore were also found. Even gold has occasionally been unearthed.

Today the Filipstad Bergslag smelting houses have vanished and only two mines remain in operation, but visitors can see the old open mine shafts, ruins of ironworks, and grand manor houses where the ironmasters once lived. Other industries here include the making of Wasa Crispbread (knäckebröd) and tourism. Canoeing and hunting for minerals are favorite summer activities, while downhill and cross-country skiing lure winter visitors.

Filipstad's main claim to fame for Americans is that inventor John Ericsson (who was born in nearby Långbanshyttan) was brought back from his adopted home in the United States and buried here. When Ericsson immigrated to the United States, he was already a successful inventor, but gained further renown with his invention of the marine propeller. But it was for his warship *Monitor* that he earned a place in history. The ship he built fought the *Merrimac* of the Confederacy to a draw on May 9, 1862, saving the Union fleet and helping to win the Civil War at sea.

Other Ericsson successes include two heavy steel-drilled guns which he gave to the Swedish Navy, the steam fire engine, the hot-air engine or caloric engine, and improvements on steam boilers. Ericsson's brother was Baron Nils Ericsson, a noted construction engineer in Sweden.

Another well-known Filipstad figure is poet Nils Ferlin, whose realistic statue sits on a park bench in the center of town.

WHAT TO SEE & DO

On the peninsula of Lake Hyttsjon is **Tibergs Udde** (Tibergs Point), a beautiful nature reserve.

STORBROHYTTAN, Hembygdsgården, Munkeberg. Tel. 140-28.

Half a mile from the town center, this restored blast furnace and ironworks has been made into a mining museum with a wealth of mining artifacts.

Admission: 25 kronor ($4.50) adults, 15 kronor ($2.70) children.
Open: June 5–Aug 19, daily 10am–6pm. **Closed:** Aug 20–June 4.

LÅNGBANS GRUVBY, Hyttbacken. Tel. 221-81.

A visit to Filipstad wouldn't be complete without an excursion to this little settlement 12 miles northeast of town. The Långban mines were known in the 19th century for producing manganese, and during the last decades of activity they were primarily sources of dolomite. More than 300 different kinds of minerals have been found here. Långban today is a well-preserved mining village with mine holes, shaft towers, and Långban Manor.

Admission: 20 kronor ($3.60) adults, 10 kronor ($1.80) children.
Open: May 16–Aug, daily 10am–6pm. **Closed:** Sept–May 15. **Bus:** 401 from Filipstad.

WHERE TO STAY & DINE

INEXPENSIVE

HENNICKEHAMMARS HERRGÅRD, S-682 00 Filipstad. Tel. 054/125-65. Fax 054/11-717. 56 rms (all with bath). TV TEL

$ Rates (including breakfast): Summer, 475 kronor ($85.50) single; 550 kronor ($99) double. Off-season, 650–950 kronor ($117–$171) single; 1,000–1,600 kronor ($180–$288) double. AE, DC, MC, V. **Parking:** Free.

Built in 1725 as the home of a wealthy landowner, this hotel, with its elegant detailing and symmetrical facade, is a comfortable country spot loaded with personality and charm. On lawns close to the edge of Lake Hemtjarn, 2½ miles west of Filipstad, rooms here are either in one of several outbuildings or in the main manor house itself. Guests can swim in the lake, rent horses at a nearby riding school, play tennis, or enjoy golf at a course about 9 miles away. Each unit is stylishly comfortable, thanks to a renovation. The hotel restaurant is open daily from noon to 2pm and 6 to 8pm, charging 290 kronor ($52.20) for a fixed-price dinner. Many outside guests visit for the daily luncheon smörgåsbord at 200 kronor ($36).

9. GRÄNNA

174 miles SW of Stockholm, 143 miles E of Gothenburg

GETTING THERE   By Train   The town of Tranås, 25 miles from Gränna, is on the main rail route between Stockholm and Malmö. From there a bus connects with Gränna (see below).

By Bus   Gränna is connected by several buses a day from Tranås, the nearest rail link.

By Car   Take the E4 west from Stockholm.

ESSENTIALS   The **Tourist Information Bureau,** Torget (tel. 0390/110-10), in the town center, is open Mon–Fri 9am–4pm and Sat 9am–1pm (summer only). The **telephone area code** for Gränna is 0390.

An idyllic little town founded in 1652, Gränna was built on the slopes of Grännaberget (hill) in a series of steps leading down to a centuries-old church and village on Lake Vättern. A bus from Jönköping makes the 25-mile run to Gränna. Many wooden buildings have been preserved since the town's origin, and the original town plan is still followed.

WHAT TO SEE & DO

Grännaberget can be reached either by car from the road between Gränna and Tranås or by climbing the steps that are found in a couple of places in town up to the top. Here, you'll find a splendid view and a fine area for walking, plus a few buildings from the 17th century. If you're energetic, you can walk along a trail to **Skogstornet** (Forest Tower), from which the view of the area around Lake Vättern is breathtaking. The Gränna area is a rich repository of Iron Age weapons, tools, menhirs, and burial grounds, some 4,000 years old.

Gränna was the birthplace of the North Pole balloonist-explorer Salomon August Andrée, who made an ill-fated attempt in 1897 to cross the pole in the balloon *Ornen* (Eagle). The remains of the expedition were found in 1930 and may be seen in the **Andrée Museum,** Brahegatan 38 (tel. 110-15). Museigården, a part of the museum, houses exhibits illustrating the history of the area. The museum is open mid-May to late August, daily from 10am to 5pm; late August to mid-May, from noon to 4pm. Admission is 12 kronor ($2.20) for adults and 5 kronor (90¢) for children.

NEARBY VISINGSÖ ISLAND

A 20-minute ferry trip will take you from Gränna to the island Visingsö for 30 kronor ($5.40) round-trip. The distance is 4 miles across the water. Ferryboats leave every hour during the day in summer, and at the rate of eight per day in winter. Boats depart from the central harbor at Gränna. For information, call the harbormaster (tel. 110-25) or the ferryboat office (tel. 36-29-90). There is a tourist office (summer information) near the point where the ferryboat docks (tel. 410-93 for information).

The island can be traversed by car in 5 minutes, as it is long but very narrow. There are no road names or street numbers. In summer, some of the island residents meet arriving ferries with saddled horses for a 30-minute excursion past the architectural highlights of the island (see below). The cost is about 35 kronor ($6.30) per ride. There is no phone to call for information—it's all very casual. This has been an important site since humans first set foot here, some 6,000 years ago, and large gravefields from the Viking era indicate how busy this area once was. On the southern part of the island are the remains of Sweden's oldest secular building, **Näs Castle,** built around 1150. According to the Icelandic sagas, it had a large treasury and was an important target in the fighting between the eastern and western parts of southern Sweden in the Middle Ages. The castle burned down in 1319.

The remains of another castle, **Visingsborg**, are by the harbor. This was the seat of the Brahe family whose progenitor, Per Brahe, count of Visingsö, was a power in the Middle Ages in Sweden and Finland. Per Brahe also built the island's **parish church** in the 1680s, using the walls of the Stroja medieval church as the foundations. The tower and the door of the sacristy are from the old church, the door having old runic writing signifying that it was made in the 11th century. The church is baroque, unusual by Swedish standards. Also to be seen on Visingsö are herbaceous gardens in Count Brahe's reconstructed 17th-century garden.

Kumlaby Church, whose oldest parts date from the 12th century, has well-preserved 15th-century murals. Visitors can climb the tower to a small roof balcony where they have a panoramic view of the island.

WHERE TO STAY & DINE

MODERATE

SCANDIC HOTEL GYLLENE UTTERN, S-563 00 Gränna. Tel. 0390/108-00. Fax 0390/118-80. 53 rms (all with bath), 2 suites. TV TEL

$ Rates (including breakfast): 885–1,045 kronor ($159.30–$188.10) single; 1,025–1,360 kronor ($184.50–$244.80) double; from 1,500 kronor ($270) suite. AE, DC, MC, V. **Parking:** Free.

"The Golden Otter," its English name, is the honeymoon Shangri-la of Sweden, complete with a baroque wedding chapel in the basement. A step-gabled imitation castle (built in 1937), overlooking Lake Vättern a mile outside Gränna on the road to Stockholm, Gyllene Uttern offers the best in food and lodgings. The inn also offers 10 multilevel cottages and two annexes on its grounds. The main dining room, its deeply set windows with views of the lake, is highlighted by gilt-framed paintings, copies of great masters, medieval suits of armor, and a bas-relief fireplace. Food is served from noon to 10:15pm and fish from the lake is a specialty.

Although the dining room and public rooms are in the main building, it contains only nine accommodations; the rest of the rooms are spread across the grounds in the annexes or cottages that were constructed in the 1960s. Room prices are complicated, but guests in the cottages pay about 200 kronor ($36) less than occupants of the regular single and double rooms. On Friday and Saturday, rooms in the annex are discounted, but rooms in the main building are not. Because of the wide range of prices, when checking in always determine the type of accommodation and the price.

10. VADSTENA

159 miles SW of Stockholm, 161 miles NE of Gothenburg

GETTING THERE By Bus On Saturday and Sunday bus no. 855 departs from the Central Station in Stockholm. Bus no. 650 runs daily from Linköping.

By Car By far the best way to go. Take the E4 southwest from Stockholm; at the junction of Route 206, head northwest.

ESSENTIALS The tourist bureau, **Vadstena Turistbyrå,** is located at Rådhustorget, S-592 00 Vadstena (tel. 0143/151-25), is open Mon–Friday 10am–5pm and Sat 10am–3pm (May); Mon–Fri 10am–6pm and Sat 10am–1pm (June); Mon–Fri 10am–7pm and Sat and Sun 10am–1pm (July); Mon–Fri 10am–6pm and Sat 10am–1pm (Aug); Mon–Fri 10am–5pm (Sept); Mon–Fri 9am–1pm (Oct–Mar); and Mon–Fri 10am–4pm (April). The **telephone area code** for Vadstena is 0143.

The most important stopover on the Göta Canal trip is this medieval town full of narrow streets and old frame buildings on the eastern shores of Lake Vättern. It is known all over Sweden for its handmade lace—to see samples of this delicate product, walk along Stora Gatan, the main street.

WHAT TO SEE & DO

VADSTENA CASTLE, Slottsvägen. Tel. 151-24.

Founded by Gustavus Vasa, king of Sweden, in 1545, but not completed until 1620, this is one of the most splendid Renaissance Vasa castles, erected during a period of national expansion. It dominates the town from its moated position on the lake, just behind the old courthouse in the southern part of town. Vadstena was last inhabited by royalty in 1715, and was restored in the 19th century. Since 1899 the greater part of the castle has been used for provincial archives.

Admission: May–Sept, Mon–Fri, tours, 25 kronor ($4.50) adults, 10 kronor ($1.80) children.

Open: Hours are different yearly, check with the tourist office (see above).

KLOSTERKYRKAN (Abbey Church), Lasarettsgatan. Tel. 102-46.

Built between the mid-14th and the 15th century to specifications outlined by its founder, St. Birgitta (Bridget) of Sweden, this Gothic church is rich in medieval art. Parts of the abbey date from 1250. The abbey housed the nuns of St. Birgitta's order until their expulsion in 1595.

The New Monastery and Church, built in 1973, show the same traditional simplicity of style St. Birgitta prescribed for her order. The view through the huge windows is the only decoration in this otherwise stark church. The nuns, who returned to Sweden in 1963, will show the church and their guesthouse to interested visitors at times convenient to their own schedule. It's a 3-minute walk from Stora Torget.

Admission: Guided tours, 10 kronor ($1.80).

Open: May–Sept, daily 10am–5pm; June and Aug, daily 10am–6pm; July, daily 10am–7pm.

WHERE TO STAY & DINE

INEXPENSIVE

The tourist bureau, **Vadstena Turistbyrå,** at Rådhustorget, (tel. 151-25), dispenses information about private homes that accept paying guests. It's an excellent way to economize while experiencing life in a Vadstena home.

KUNGS STARBY HOTELL & RESTAURANG, Ödeshögsvägen, S-592 00 Vadstena. Tel. 0143/114-20. Fax 0143/102-63. 45 rms (all with bath). TV TEL **Bus:** 610 from Motala.

$ Rates (including breakfast): Fri–Sat 650 kronor ($117) single; 750 kronor ($135) double. Sun–Thurs 780 kronor ($140.40) single; 890 kronor ($160.20) double. AE, DC, MC, V. **Parking:** Free.

On the southern outskirts of the town, this licensed restaurant and inn was an old manor house. The hotel portion dates from 1984. As an estate, Starby dates back to the 13th century and was owned by the Vasa Dynasty. Bedrooms are furnished in bright modern designs with pastel colors and sleek functional styling. The inn is known for its buffets. Facilities include a swimming pool and a health club.

VADSTENA KLOSTERHOTELL, Klosterområdet, S-592 00 Vadstena. Tel. 0143/115-30. Fax 0143/136-48. 25 rms (all with bath). TV TEL

$ Rates (including breakfast): 660 kronor ($118.80) single; 790 kronor ($142.20) double. AE, DC, MC, V. **Parking:** Free.

This hotel is a former convent and royal summer castle dating from the 12th century. Completely modernized, it offers well-appointed rooms. You can see the nuns' refectory, adapted for a conference room, and the nuns' dormitory, its 59 cells opening onto the longest triple barrel vault (more than 190 feet long) in the north. On the lake, northeast of the castle, the hotel adjoins the historic abbey church. There are three lounges, all fresh and light. Breakfast is served in the 13th-century Kings' Hall.

CHAPTER 27

KALMAR & THE BALTIC ISLANDS

Kalmar, while a good base for exploring the district, is well worth exploration itself. It was here that the Agreement of Kalmar was signed in 1397, uniting Denmark, Norway, and Sweden in an ill-fated union. Across the water from Kalmar is the Baltic island of Öland, settled in prehistoric times.

Before journeying on to Kalmar or Öland, we'll hop over to Sweden's most popular tourist island, Gotland, nestled in the Baltic. In the forest-rich province of Småland, you'll find some of the most famous glass factories in the world, such as Orrefors.

SEEING KALMAR & THE BALTIC ISLANDS

GETTING THERE

Gotland, with Visby as its capital, is the summer playground of Stockholm, the beach life taking on a real *joie de vivre*. It can be reached on a 30-minute flight from Stockholm, and the airport is just 2 miles from the city. If you'd like to take a car or the train, the point of embarkation is Nynäshamn, south of Stockholm.

Kalmar, an interesting city in its own right, is the gateway to the glassworks district and an easy city to reach from Stockholm by plane, train, and bus. From Kalmar, a bridge leads to the island of Öland, best explored by private car because of inadequate bus transportation.

A SUGGESTED ITINERARY

Days 1 & 2: Fly or take the car-ferry to Visby. Spend 1 day exploring the town and another seeing the attractions on the island of Gotland.

Day 3: Go to see the historic city of Kalmar.

Day 4: Drive across the bridge and explore the island of Öland, which can be done while still based in Kalmar.

Day 5: You can still use Kalmar as a base, or check into a hotel in Växjö and explore the major factories of the glassworks district.

1. GOTLAND [VISBY]

136 miles S of Stockholm, 93 miles S of Nynäshamn, 55 miles E of the Swedish mainland

GETTING THERE By Plane Daily flights from Stockholm take 30 minutes. Bus service between Visby and the airport is 20 kronor ($3.60) each way.

By Train There is no rail service on Gotland.

By Bus & Car-Ferry From Stockholm, take a bus south to the port of Nynäshamn, a 1-hour ride. From there, take the car-ferry to Visby; it leaves at

☑ **WHAT'S SPECIAL ABOUT KALMAR & THE BALTIC ISLANDS**

Great Towns/Villages

☐ Visby, once a great medieval European city, capital of the island of Gotland, former Viking stronghold.

☐ Kalmar, one of Sweden's oldest towns, fortified in the 11th century as a stronghold against Denmark.

☐ Växjö, a former Iron Age trading station that's now the center for exploring Sweden's glassworks district.

Castles

☐ Kalmar Slott, once "the key to Sweden," a moated medieval fortress transformed into a Renaissance palace.

Ancient Monuments

☐ Eketorp Ring-Fort, on Öland, an excavated prehistoric fortified village.

☐ Dominican Monastery of St. Nicholas, from the early 13th century, now in ruins.

Ace Attractions

☐ Lummelunda Caves, north of Visby, with fossil remains, subterranean waters, and stalactite and stalagmite formations.

☐ The House of Emigrants, Växjö, which documents the 1.3 million Swedes who developed "America Fever" and emigrated.

Glassworks

☐ Orrefors Glasbruk, a famous name in Swedish glass, where you can watch glassblowers work.

☐ Kosta Boda Glassworks, founded in 1742, another big name in Swedish glass.

Special Events

☐ Medieval Week in Visby, in August, when the old Hanseatic city reverts to its "golden age."

---

midnight, taking about 5 hours. In summer there are also day connections. You can make reservations through your travel agent or directly with the ferry service for cabin and/or car space. It's wise to book deck space if you plan to go on a weekend. The ferry service is **Gotlandslinjen Bokningscentral** (tel. 08/23-61-70 in Stockholm).

By Car   Take Route 71 south to Nynäshamn and the car-ferry from there (see above).

ESSENTIALS   The tourist bureau, **Turistbyrån,** Östervåg 1 (tel. 21-47-60), is open Mon–Fri 9am–5pm (May–Aug). The **telephone area code** for Gotland is 0498.

SPECIAL EVENTS   For 8 days in August during **Medieval Week,** Visby becomes a Hanseatic town again. At the harbor, Strandgatan swarms with people in medieval dress, many of them tending market stalls. You meet the blacksmith, barber, cobbler, and trader. Musicians play the hurdy-gurdy, the fiddle, and the flute, while jesters play the fool. Toward nightfall a kingly procession comes into the square. The program has more than 100 such events during the festival, along with medieval mystery plays, masses, choral and instrumental music, tournaments, and displays of horses as well as archery competitions, fire-eaters, belly dancers, and walking tours of the medieval town.

In the middle of the Baltic sits the ancient home of the Goths, the island of Gotland, about 75 miles long and 35 miles wide. The Swedes go to Gotland for sunny holidays by the sea; North Americans are more interested in the old walled city of Visby. But an investment of a little extra time will reveal that Gotland, with its cliffs, odd rock formations, bathing beaches, and rolling countryside, is rich territory. Buses traverse the island, as do organized tours out of Visby.

At the end of the 12th century and during the 13th, the walled city of Visby rose to its zenith of power as the seat of the powerful Hanseatic merchants and as the trade center of northern Europe. Seventeen churches sprouted up during its heyday. Step-gabled houses were built of stone, and the townspeople lived in splendor. It was soon ransacked by the Danes, however, and the city subsequently declined. It has only recently become a tourist center, after it was recognized as a treasure house of medieval art, becoming the number one spot in all of Scandinavia for those seeking the charm of the Middle Ages.

WHAT TO SEE & DO

Visby is a town meant for walkers. It can easily be explored on foot, but you may want to take one of the three organized tours that are offered in season. Since so many of the sights, particularly the ruins of the 13th- and 14th-century churches, are better appreciated with some background, I recommend the tour.

The 2-hour combined bus and walking tour leaves daily from the 17th-century Lübeck merchant's house, **Burmeister,** Strandgatan 9. It operates from mid-June to mid-September, departing at 11am. The cost is 50 kronor ($9) for adults and 25 kronor ($4.50) for children, including entrance fees.

The tour takes guests to the old **Hanseatic harbor** (not the same harbor used today) and includes a walk through the beautiful **Botanical Gardens** (you'll know why Visby is called "the city of roses"), and passes two of the most famous towers in the old wall—the **Maiden's Tower** (a peasant girl was buried alive here for helping a Danish king) and the **Powder Tower** (the oldest fortification in Visby). Later the bus passes Gallow Hill, a medieval hanging station in use until the mid-19th century.

You'll have a chance to leave the bus and take a walk to the old ruins of the former **Dominican Monastery of St. Nicholas,** once part of a Dominican monastery. The church has a rose window cut from a single big stone—its diameter is more than 10 feet. Work began on the monastery in 1230 but it was destroyed by Lübeck forces in 1525.

Finally, the tour goes to the 13th-century Gothic and Romanesque **Cathedral of St. Mary.**

Another sightseeing recommendation—to be done on your own—is the **Gotlands Historical Museum,** Strandgatan 12-14 (tel. 24-70-10, opposite the Burmeister House on a medieval street noted for its step-gabled houses. The museum contains some of the most interesting artifacts discovered on Gotland, including carved stones dating back to A.D. 400, art from medieval and later periods, plus furniture and household items. It is open daily from 11am to 6pm, costing 20 kronor ($3.60) (children under 16 free).

A tour of the island—different every day—leaves from the tourist bureau. The price may be as low as 60 kronor ($10.80) or as high as 175 kronor ($31.50). But each day the tour visits the **Lummelunda Caves,** Lummelunds Bruk (tel. 27-30-50), with their stalactite and stagalmite formations, fossil remains, and subterranean waters. Visits on your own cost 30 kronor ($5.40) for adults, 20 kronor ($3.60) for children 5 to 15.

Lummelunda is a karst cave formed of limestone bedrock by a subterranean stream. The explored part of the stream cave stretches for 2.3 miles. But there is probably more to explore. A part of the cave with some of the biggest and most beautiful chambers is open to visitors.

The location is 8 miles north of Visby along Route 149. A bus departs from June 21 through August 16 from Österport Visby daily at 2pm. From May through June 13, hours are daily from 9am to 4pm; June 14 through June 27, daily 9am to 6pm; June 28 through August 2, daily 9am to 7pm; August 3 through 16, daily 9am to 6pm, and August 17 through September 13, daily 9am to 4pm.

ISLAND TOURS   Ask at the **Turistbyrån,** Östervåg 1 (tel. 21-47-60), about what island tours are featured during your visit. These tours are the best way to get a quick preview of Gotland.

Northern Gotland and **Fårö** are explored on one tour, costing 165 kronor ($29.70) for adults and 90 kronor ($16.20) for children. A coach runs to the ferry port of Fårösund, with a 10-minute trip over the strait followed by a tour around Fårö (Sheep Island) exploring dwarf forest and moor.

Returning to Gotland, the tour visits the open-air cultural history museum at **Bunge,** documenting the old peasant culture. That is followed by a tour of the **Blase limestone museum** in Fleringe, with two limekilns from the turn of the century that have been restored. Tours are conducted on Tuesday and Thursday in summer at 8:30am, ending at 5:30pm.

Another tour, on Wednesday from 9am to 5:30pm, costing 165 kronor ($29.70) for adults and 90 kronor ($16.20) for children, goes to the south point and the legendary "old man of **Hoburgen,**" a rock formation known as a chalk stack. The Iron Age village at **Gervide** is also explored, as are two farms from the 17th century. The journey goes along the west coast, with its windswept shoreline.

WHERE TO STAY

For all its attractions, Visby doesn't have enough hotels. Accommodations are packed in summer—so reserve in advance.

But if you haven't, head for the Accommodation Center of the tourist bureau (see above). The English-speaking personnel will arrange rooms in hotels or private homes in or near Visby. The average rate for an accommodation in a private home is 180 kronor ($32.40) per person per night or 320 kronor ($57.60) in a double. It's better to telephone for reservations from Stockholm.

MODERATE

VISBY HOTEL, Strandgatan 6, S-621 21 Visby. Tel. 0498/20-40-00. Fax 0498/21-13-20. 124 rms (all with bath), 10 suites. TV TEL MINIBAR

$ Rates (including breakfast): July 2–Aug 1 and Fri–Sun year-round, 500 kronor ($90) single; 900 kronor ($162) double, from 1,400 kronor ($252) suite. Mon–Thurs the rest of the year, 990 kronor ($178.20) single; 1,380 kronor ($248.40) double; from 1,880 kronor ($338.40) suites. AE, DC, MC, V. **Parking:** Free.

Since its radical restoration and upgrading in the early 1990s, this is now considered the best and most glamorous hotel on the island. Set close to the harborfront in the town center, its historic core includes medieval foundations and the solid stonework of a kind you'll see in other parts of Visby. Radiating outward from the core are newer additions which span several centuries. Newest of all is a facade added during the 1950s. On the premises are a restaurant, a bistro, two bars, and a conscientious staff. Room service is daily from 7am to 11pm, and saunas, massage, and babysitting service

---

IN THEIR FOOTSTEPS

Carolus Linnaeus (Carl von Linné) (1707–78) The great Swedish botanist compiled *Species Plantarum* (Plant Species) in 1753, which is a definitive catalog of plants. Nicknamed "the little botanist" at the age of 8, he began the modern system of botanical nomenclature.

• **Birthplace:** South Rashult, Sweden, on May 23, 1707.

• **Favorite Haunts:** Uppsala University, where he was given a chair of botany in 1742; Gotland and Öland, which he wrote of in his travels.

• **Residences:** Svartbäcksgatan 27, the Linnaeus Garden and Museum at Uppsala (open to the public). Here he received a "patent of Nobility" and the new name Carl von Linné.

• **Resting Place:** After suffering an apoplectic attack, he died on January 10, 1778, and was buried in Uppsala Cathedral.

are available. Bedrooms are conservatively elegant, in some cases containing reproductions of 18th-century furniture.

INEXPENSIVE

HOTEL S:T CLEMENS, Smedjegatan 3, S-621 55 Visby. Tel. 0498/27-95-75. Fax 0498/27-94-43. 50 rms (all with bath). TV TEL
$ Rates (including breakfast): 785 kronor ($141.30) single; 925 kronor ($166.50) double. Extra bed 165 kronor ($29.70). DC, MC, V. **Parking:** Free.
This 18th-century building in the town center has been successfully transformed into a well-run little hotel. It is decorated tastefully in a modern style, with light pastels used effectively. It's open all year, and the staff is helpful and efficient. Only breakfast is served. The hotel is equipped for handicapped guests. A sauna is provided.

HOTEL SOLHEM-PALISSAD, Solhemsgatan 3, S-621 46 Visby. Tel. 0498/27-90-70. Fax 0498/21-95-23. 112 rms (35 with bath), 3 suites. TEL
$ Rates (including breakfast): Summer, 370 kronor ($66.60) single without bath, 950 kronor ($171) single with bath; 570 kronor ($102.60) double without bath, 1,050 kronor ($189) double with bath. Off-season, 325 kronor ($58.50) single without bath, 820 kronor ($147.60) single with bath; 570 kronor ($102.60) double without bath, 950 kronor ($171) double with bath. Year-round, from 1,500 kronor ($270) suite. AE, DC, MC, V. **Parking:** Free.
On a hilly slope overlooking the harbor, just outside the wall, a 5-minute walk from the center, this is one of the best hotels in Visby. Rooms are clean and comfortable and furnished in a simple Nordic modern. Thirty-four of the rooms contain minibars and TVs. The hotel has a restaurant, a bar, and a sauna.

STRAND HOTEL, Strandgatan 34, S-621 02 Visby. Tel. 0498/21-26-00. Fax 0498/27-81-11. 120 rms (all with bath). TV TEL
$ Rates (including breakfast): 680-760 kronor ($122.40-$136.80) single; 800-1,000 kronor ($144-$180) double. Reductions of 25% Fri-Sat year-round and Aug 10-June 10. AE, DC, MC, V. **Parking:** Free.
One of the town's most inviting hotels, the Strand offers excellent bedrooms, furnished in a tasteful modern style. Many are for nonsmokers, and some are reserved for the handicapped. The hotel offers breakfast only, which is served in a modern courtyard. Facilities include a sauna and an indoor swimming pool.

WHERE TO DINE
MODERATE

BURMEISTER GÅRDEN, Strandgatan 6. Tel. 21-03-73.
  Cuisine: INTERNATIONAL. **Reservations:** Not required.
$ Prices: Appetizers 48-82 kronor ($8.60-$14.80); main dishes 110-165 kronor ($19.80-$29.70); pizzas 45 kronor ($8.10). AE, DC, MC, V.
  Open: Summer, restaurant and disco, daily noon-2am; off-season, nightclub only, Fri-Sat 10pm-2am.
This large restaurant in the town center offers dining indoors or under shady fruit trees in the garden of a 16th-century house originally built for the wealthiest citizen of Visby. From many of the tables, diners can look out on the surrounding medieval buildings. The well-prepared menu is Swedish, with choices of salmon, pork, and veal. A sizzling outdoor barbecue offers such dishes as Texas-size steaks and lamb chops. At night, pizza is the most popular item. After 10pm it becomes a disco, with no cover charge. In winter, Burmeister operates only as a nightclub, open on Friday and Saturday from 10pm to 2am. No cover is charged, but a large draft beer costs 39 kronor ($7).

GUTEKÄLLAREN, Stortorget 3. Tel. 21-00-43.
  Cuisine: SWEDISH. **Reservations:** Not required.
$ Prices: Appetizers 68-88 kronor ($12.20-$15.80); main dishes 82-195 kronor ($14.80-$35.10). AE, DC, MC, V.
  Open: Lunch Mon-Sat 11:30am-2pm; dinner Mon-Sat 6:30-10pm.

This restaurant and bar in the town center has been installed in one of the city's oldest buildings, a stone-sided inn dating back to the 11th century. It offers fresh fish and meat dishes, including some vegetarian specialties. You might begin with a fish soup made with lobster and shrimp, then follow with filet of sole Waleska or roast lamb chops. The dessert specialty in summer is a parfait made of local berries.

MUNKKÄLLAREN, Lilla Torggränd 2. Tel. 27-14-00.
  Cuisine: SWEDISH. **Reservations:** Required in summer.
$ **Prices:** Appetizers 60–82 kronor ($10.80–$14.80); main dishes 120–155 kronor ($21.60–$27.90). AE, DC, MC, V.
  Open: Mon–Tues 5pm–midnight, Wed–Sun 5pm–2am. **Closed:** Sun in off-season.

You'll recognize this place in the center of Visby by its brown wooden facade. The dining room is only a few steps from the street, and it is sheathed in white stone, parts of it dating from 1150. The restaurant, while not necessarily the most expensive in town, is considered one of the best. In summer, management opens the doors to another three of four pubs within the compound. Glasses of beer cost 39 kronor ($7). The main pub, Munken, offers platters of *husmanskost* (Swedish home cooking), including *frikadeller* (meatballs). In the restaurant you might begin with escargots in creamy garlic sauce or toast with Swedish caviar. Specialties include shellfish stew, salmon-stuffed sole with spinach and a saffron sauce, and venison in port wine sauce.

2. KALMAR

254 miles S of Stockholm, 211 miles E of Gothenburg

GETTING THERE By Plane Kalmar Airport receives daily flights, from Stockholm, taking 50 minutes.

By Train Seven trains a day make the 6½-hour run between Stockholm and Kalmar. Eight daily trains arrive from Malmö, taking 3 hours 40 minutes.

By Bus Three to seven buses a day come from Stockholm on the 7-hour trip. From Gothenburg, there is one bus on Friday and Saturday, taking 6 hours.

By Car From Stockholm, take the E66 south.

ESSENTIALS The Kalmar tourist office, **Turism i Kalmarbygåden,** is located at Larmagatan 6, S-391 20 Kalmar (tel. 0480/153-50), near the railway station, right in the town center. The office is open Mon–Fri 9am–9pm, Sat 9am–6pm, and Sun noon–7pm (summer) and Mon–Fri 10am–3pm and Sat 10am–noon (off-season). The **telephone area code** for Kalmar is 0480.

Today a thriving commercial center, this gateway city still retains many of its 17th-century buildings and sea captain's homes, clustered particularly around Stortorget. The first Swedish immigration to America, more than 3 centuries ago, originated from Kalmar, ending in Wilmington, Del.

WHAT TO SEE & DO

Kalmar boasts good **swimming** right in town, and a big **outdoor market** is held in front of the cathedral every Saturday from 8am to 3pm.
  The largest and oldest handcrafts shop in Sweden, **Hemslöjden,** Larmgatan 26 (tel. 209-01), invites browsers and shoppers, and it has an export department.

KALMAR SLOTT, Slottsvägen. Tel. 563-51.
  Founded in the 12th century, this strategically situated castle was once called the key to Sweden, and it's the principal sight in town. In the 16th century, under orders of King Gustavus Vasa and two of his sons, Erik XIV and Johan III, this moated medieval fortress was transformed into a Renaissance palace. Be sure to see the prison for women from the 18th and 19th centuries and the restored castle chapel. Tours are

conducted mid-June to mid-August, daily every hour. To get there, from the train station turn left on Tullbron.

Admission: 25 kronor ($4.50) adults, 15 kronor ($2.70) children 7–15.

Open: Apr, daily 1–3pm; May to mid-June and mid-Aug to Sept, Mon–Sat 10am–4pm, Sun 1–4pm; mid-June to mid-Aug, Mon–Sat 10am–6pm, Sun 1–5pm; Oct, daily 1–3pm; Nov–Mar, Sun 1–3pm. **Bus:** 1, 2, 7, 9.

DOMKYRKAN (Kalmar Cathedral), Stortorget. Tel. 283-50.

From the marketplace, you can wander over to Stortorget to visit the town's 17th-century cathedral.

Admission: Free.

Open: Mon–Sat 8am–6pm, Sun 8:30am–6pm. **Bus:** 1, 2, 7, 9.

KALMAR LANS MUSEUM (Kalmar County Museum), in Kalmar Slott on Slottsvägen and at Skeppsbrogatan 51. Tel. 563-00.

This county museum is partly housed in Kalmar Slott, where you can see royal furnishings, military artifacts, and maritime objects. The majority of the museum's exhibits, however, are in an old industrial house on the harbor. An interesting exhibit concerns the royal ship *Kronan*, which sank in the Baltic Sea off the island of Öland during a sea battle against the Danes in 1676 (only 42 of the 840 people on board survived). The museum is responsible for excavations at the wreck site, and the objects found by the marine archeologists—glass bottles, tin plates, nautical instruments, a seaman's chest, and many gold coins—are on display.

Admission: 25 kronor ($4.50) adults, 15 kronor ($2.70) children.

Open: June 15–Aug 15, Mon–Sat 10am–6pm, Sun 1–5pm; Aug 16–June 14, Tues–Fri 10am–4pm, Sat–Sun 1–4pm. **Bus:** 1, 2, 7, 9.

WHERE TO STAY

Kalmar offers an adequate range of accommodations, although many choose to stay on the island of Öland.

The Kalmar tourist office (see above) can help you rent rooms in private homes at 120 kronor ($21.60) for a single and from 150 kronor ($27) for a double, plus a booking fee starting at 30 kronor ($5.40).

MODERATE

HOTEL WITT, Södra Långgatan 42, S-391 22 Kalmar. Tel. 0480/152-50. Fax 0480/152-65. 112 rms (all with bath), 3 suites. TV TEL **Bus:** 1, 2, 7, 9.

$ Rates (including breakfast): Summer, 520 kronor ($93.60) single; 745 kronor ($134.10) double. Off-season, 975–1,175 kronor ($175.50–$211.50) single; 1,270–1,410 kronor ($228.60–$253.80) double. Year-round, from 1,930 kronor ($347.40) suite. AE, DC, MC, V. **Parking:** 85 kronor ($15.30).

In the town center, overlooking Kalmarsund, the Hotel Witt is the oldest in Kalmar, an inn on this site dating from the 17th century. The hotel rents comfortable and well-furnished bedrooms, all with radios, color TVs, and automatic alarm clocks. In the hotel restaurant there is dancing to live bands several times a week. An international cuisine is served. Facilities include a health club with sauna, solarium, indoor swimming pool, and massage. The hotel has a private airport coach and limousine service for guests.

KALMAR STADSHOTELL, Stortorget 14, S-392 32 Kalmar. Tel. 0480/151-80. Fax 0480/158-47. 140 rms (all with bath), 3 suites. MINIBAR TV TEL **Bus:** 1, 2, 7, 9.

$ Rates (including breakfast): June 26–Aug 3, 605–760 kronor ($108.90–$136.80) single; 790–970 kronor ($142.20–$174.60) double. The rest of the year, 975–1,360 kronor ($175.50–$244.80) single; kronor 1,270–1,570 ($228.60–$282.60) double. Year-round, from 1,800 kronor ($324) suite. AE, DC, MC, V. **Parking:** 85 kronor ($15.30).

Located on the main square in the heart of the city, this hotel was built in 1906. The recently renovated bedrooms feature hairdryers, radios, and trouser presses, among other amenities. Lunch, served in the cafeteria, costs from 85 kronor ($15.30). The hotel has four restaurants, a cocktail bar, a nightclub, a Jacuzzi, a sauna, and a solarium.

BUDGET

HOTEL VILLA ÄNGÖ, Baggensgatan 20, S-392 30 Kalmar. Tel. 0480/ 854-15. 9 rms (1 with bath). TEL

$ Rates: 300 kronor ($54) single without bath, 450 kronor ($81) single with bath; 400 kronor ($72) double without bath, 600 kronor ($108) double with bath. Breakfast 30 kronor ($5.40) extra. AE, MC, V. **Parking:** Free.

⑤ This stately Swedish house, almost like a manor house, is a good possibility for motorists who prefer a location 10 minutes east of the town center, near Ölandsbridge. Rooms are immaculately kept and come in many sizes. The one room with bath can be rented either as a single or double. Some of the more spacious rooms are ideal for families, accommodating three to five guests. Breakfast is the only meal served, although you can order sandwiches in the evenings. Facilities include a TV room, a sauna, a solarium, and billiards.

WHERE TO DINE
EXPENSIVE

WITTEN'S DANCE RESTAURANT, in the Hotel Witt, Södra Långgatan 42. Tel. 152-50.
   Cuisine: CONTINENTAL. **Reservations:** Recommended. **Bus:** 1, 2, 7, 9.
$ Prices: Appetizers 95–160 kronor ($17.10–$28.80); main dishes 152–255 kronor ($27.40–$45.90). AE, DC, MC, V. **Open:** Dinner only, Tues–Sat 7pm–2am.

The clientele tends to be 35 years of age or older, and the dance music is traditional. This is the best-known supper club in the area. The Saturday-night dinner-dance is the most popular nighttime venue in the area. Menu items include a symphony of seafood, with mussels, lobster, crab, and shrimp, or perhaps pepper steak and filet of breast of wild duck in a cream sauce. It's located on the lower level of the Hotel Witt (see "Where to Stay," above).

MODERATE

"BYTTAN" RESTAURANT, Slottsvägen 1. Tel. 100-85.
   Cuisine: SWEDISH. **Reservations:** Recommended in summer. **Bus:** 1, 2, 7, 9.
$ Prices: Appetizers 42–95 kronor ($7.60–$17.10); main dishes 65–195 kronor ($11.70–$35.10); lunch platters 55 kronor ($9.90). AE, DC, MC, V.
   Open: Summer, daily 11am–midnight; off-season, daily 11am–3pm.

In the City Park a 10-minute walk south of the town center near the base of the castle, this terraced pavilion, an institution for 50 years, overlooks the water and is one of the best spots for dining in Kalmar. Main courses range from omelets to filet of beef with red wine sauce and forest mushrooms. For an appetizer you can order everything from a bowl of freshly made soup to Swedish caviar. Guests may dine in the pavilion or in the vine-covered courtyard. The food is attractively prepared, and even if you don't come for a meal, the restaurant is a good place to have afternoon tea.

KALMAR HAMN KROG, Skeppsbrogatan 30. Tel. 110-20.
   Cuisine: INTERNATIONAL. **Reservations:** Required. **Bus:** 1, 2, 7, 9.
$ Prices: Appetizers 58–108 kronor ($10.40–$19.40); main dishes 125–228 kronor ($22.50–$41); fixed-price lunch 155 kronor ($27.90); fixed-price dinner 220 kronor ($39.60). AE, DC, MC, V.
   Open: Lunch daily 11:30am–2pm; dinner daily 6pm–midnight.

★ This restaurant, established in 1988, quickly became the most stylish and gastronomically sophisticated in Kalmar. It was built from scratch on an old pier where steamships used to deposit passengers from Öland. The interior is all blue and white. You might begin with a tomato-and-mozzarella salad or goose liver pâté, following with filet of roe deer with chanterelles, fresh baked lobster with two cold sauces, filet of saddle of lamb with cream sauce, or poached filet of sole with a saffron-flavored lime sauce. Wine from Austria, the United States, Italy, and France are featured.

MS CAPTAIN LINDSTRÖM, in the Hotel Witt, Södra Långgatan 42. Tel. 152-50.
Cuisine: SWEDISH. **Reservations:** Recommended.
$ Prices: Appetizers 42–85 kronor ($7.60–$15.30); main dishes 110–165 kronor ($19.80–$29.70); luncheon platters 55–68 kronor ($9.90–$12.20); 2-course business lunch 130 kronor ($23.40). AE, DC, MC, V.
Open: Lunch Mon–Tues and Thurs 11:30am–2pm; dinner Mon–Tues and Thurs 5pm–midnight, Wed and Fri–Sat 7pm–1am.

Within a 5-minute walk of the Kalmar waterfront, this restaurant on the lower level of the Hotel Witt (see "Where to Stay," above) offers good value and an appealing cuisine prepared with fresh ingredients. A dish invented in this dining room in the 19th century, a favorite of a regular client, Captain Lindström, was suggested to the chef. Today it is one of the most famous dishes of Sweden, beef Lindström, combining chopped beef with capers and pickled beetroot formed into a patty and fried. Many of the main courses are displayed raw for clients in glass-fronted cabinets. You indicate to the chef what you want and how you want it. You might, for example, prefer two small beef filets with your choice of sauces. For the price of a main course you have access to a help-yourself salad bar.

3. VÄXJÖ

67 miles W of Kalmar, 275 miles S of Stockholm

GETTING THERE   By Plane   Daily flights wing in from Stockholm to Växjö, taking 50 minutes.

By Train   Train connections are possible from Gothenburg, leaving at 8am daily and arriving in Växjö at 11:16am; from Malmö, leaving at 9am and arriving in Växjö at 11:16am; and from Stockholm, leaving at 10:06am and arriving in Växjö at 3:16pm.

By Bus   Bus connections are possible from Stockholm, leaving on Friday and Sunday (take SJ Buss) at 2pm and arriving in Växjö at 8:55pm.

By Car   From Stockholm, take the E4 south to Norrköping, then continue south along the E66 to Kalmar. At Kalmar, head west on Route 25.

ESSENTIALS   The **Växjö Tourist Information Office,** located at Kronobergsgatan 8 (tel. 0470/414-10), is open Mon–Fri 9am–4pm and Sat 9am–1pm (mid-June–mid-Aug) and Mon–Fri 10am–3pm and Sat 10am–noon (off-season). The **telephone area code** for Växjö is 0470.

Sweden's "Kingdom of Crystal" starts in Växjö, the central community for all of Småland. Some 16 factories here produce world-renowned Swedish glass. The name Växjö comes from *Vägsjön*, the "lake where the roads meet." Aside from glassworks, this 14th-century city is filled with lakes and forest, and traditional red-timbered cottages.

WHAT TO SEE & DO

In Växjö, there are numerous sports facilities, including one of Europe's most modern indoor swimming halls.

In summer, tours on Helgåsjön are arranged on the century-old steamer *Thor*. It costs 60 kronor ($10.80) for adults and 35 kronor ($6.30) for children under 12. For information on this and other activities, contact the tourist office (see above).

SMÅLANDS MUSEUM, Södra Järnvägsgatan 2. Tel. 451-45.

Sweden's oldest provincial museum, located near the rail station, will give you a better sense of the area as well as a look at the history of Swedish glass. You'll see tools and archives from the early days of this craft, with a special collection of more than 25,000 pieces. In a separate exhibit are displays of the finest artistic examples of Swedish glass produced over the centuries.

In other areas of the museum you can see one of Sweden's largest coin collections, art exhibits, religious objects, weapons, and a special room housing an ethnological collection. Forestry and agriculture exhibits are also included.

Admission: 20 kronor ($3.60) adults; children free.

Open: Mon–Fri 9am–4pm (also Wed 6–9pm), Sat 11am–3pm, Sun 1–5pm. **Bus:** 4.

SVENSKA EMIGRANTINSTITUTET MUSEIPARKEN (The House of Emigrants), Museiparken. Tel. 201-20.

This institution, founded in 1968, documents the 1.3 million Swedish people who left their homeland during the "American Fever" years, the 1850s to the 1920s, and moved to America. The house contains exhibits on emigrant history as well as archives and a research library. A permanent exhibition, the *Dream of America,* presents insights into the background and consequences of the emigration. Minnesota Day is a folk festival held the second Sunday in August each year, drawing thousands of Swedes and Swedish-Americans. The museum is near the Växjö railroad station.

Admission: 20 kronor ($3.60) adults, 5 kronor (90¢) children.

Open: Mon–Fri 9am–4pm, Sat 11am–3pm, Sun 1–5pm. **Bus:** 4.

VÄXJÖ CATHEDRAL, Linnégatan. Tel. 296-80.

Legend says that this cathedral stands on the spot where St. Sigfrid (Småland's missionary from York, England, in the 11th century) erected his little wooden church. The cathedral has copper-clad towers and a bright interior and its chimes are heard three times a day. Summer concerts are held in the cathedral on Thursday at 8pm.

Adjacent to the cathedral is **Linnéparken** (Linné Park), named for Carl von Linné (Carolus Linnaeus), the Swedish botanist who developed the scientific categories of plants. In the park an arboretum displays all 24 such categories of perennials. There are also other flower gardens throughout and a playground for children. The cathedral is in the town center, by Linnéparken.

Admission: Free.

Open: May–Sept, daily 8am–7pm; Oct–Apr, daily 8am–4pm. The museum in one of the turrets is open during summer, at times listed at the entrance. **Bus:** 4.

TELEBORG SLOTT, Teleborgatan. Tel. 410-00.

An impressive edifice in local granite, this castle was built in 1896 to 1900. It was the residence of Count Fredrik Bonde and lies in a public park a 5-minute bus ride from the town center. It can only be visited on a public guided tour in a group.

Admission: 20 kronor ($3.60).

Open: Bus departures are from the tourist office (see above), which will inform you of time and departure of group tours.

NEARBY ATTRACTIONS

Between Kalmar and Växjö, within an hour's drive, are several glassworks, including Orrefors, and Kosta Boda, where you can see the master glassblowers at work.

ORREFORS GLASBRUK, Rte. 31, S-380 40 Orrefors. Tel. 0481/340-00.

Orrefors, between Nybro and Lenhovda, 25 miles west of Kalmar, is one of the most famous names in Swedish glass. Guided tours are conducted Monday through Friday at fixed hours during the tourist season and on request during the rest of the year. The factory shuts down for annual vacations in July, but glassblowers demonstrate their work during this period. It is possible to purchase seconds (in most cases hardly distinguishable from perfect pieces), and gift shipments can be arranged. Tax-free shopping can also be arranged in the factory's shop.

Admission: Free.

Open: Museum and shop, Mon–Fri 9am–6pm, Sat 9am–3pm, Sun noon–4pm.

STRÖMBERGSHYTTAN, Hovmantorp. Tel. 0478/117-70.

This is part of the Orrefors group. You can watch glass being hand-painted. You can even have a go at painting some glass yourself and shop around in the factory outlet while you wait for your masterpiece to dry. It's 15 miles from Växjö, just after Lessebo on Route 25.

Admission: Free.
Open: Mon–Fri 8am–4pm.

KOSTA BODA GLASSWORKS, Hwy. 28. Tel. 0748/503-00.

Founded in 1742 and expanded since then, this is the main headquarters of the Kosta complex. Here you can see the Old Kosta Museum, with articles from the 18th and 19th centuries as well as exhibitions of contemporary glass. It's located between Eriksmala and the junction with Route 31, 12 miles east of Orrefors.

Admission: Free.
Open: Mon–Sat 9am–4pm. **Closed:** July, but one workshop remains open all summer.

KOSTA BODA GLASSWORKS, Storgatan, (Hwy. 25). Tel. 0481/240-00.

Boda Glassworks was founded in 1864, but long ago merged with Kosta. It is in an old work environment with a number of craft shops. It's 12 miles west of Nybro.

Admission: Free.
Open: Tourist shops and exhibition rooms, Mon–Fri 9am–6pm, Sat 9am–3pm, Sun noon–4pm; glassworks, Mon–Fri 10am–3pm. **Bus:** 218 from Lessebo, which has rail links to Växjö.

LESSEBO PAPERMILL, Hwy. 25. Tel. 0478/106-00.

In the heart of the glassworks district, the small town of Lessebo, on Route 25, 22 miles west of Orrefors, has as its great attraction the famous Lessebo Papermill, the world's oldest working producer of handmade paper. In existence since 1693, the mill is open to the public so you can watch as paper passes through the various stages, from cotton pulp to individual sheets that are pressed and hung to dry. There is a gift shop where you can purchase the handmade products, and tours are available in English.

Admission: Free.
Open: Tours, daily at 9:30 and 10:45am and 1 and 2:15pm.

WHERE TO STAY & DINE

MODERATE

HOTEL ROYAL CORNER, Liedbergsgatan 11, S-352 32 Växjö. Tel. 0470/100-00. Fax 0470/126-44. 165 rms (all with bath). TV TEL **Bus:** 4.

$ **Rates** (including breakfast): June 18–Aug 9 and Fri–Sat year-round, 550 kronor ($99) single; 700 kronor ($126) double. Sun–Thurs the rest of the year, 1,090–1,200 kronor ($196.20–$216) single; 1,300–1,400 kronor ($234–$252) double. AE, DC, MC, V. **Parking:** Free.

This first-class hotel in the town center offers spacious bedrooms with refrigerators and hairdryers. Well-prepared meals are served in the restaurant, or you might choose to have lighter meals in the café. A piano bar is a popular rendezvous. Guests are free to use the workout gym, with a swimming pool, whirlpool, solarium, and sauna.

SARA HOTEL STATT, Kungsgatan 6, S-351 04 Växjö. Tel. 0470/134-00. Fax 0470/44837. 130 rms (all with bath), 10 suites. TV TEL **Bus:** 4.

$ **Rates** (including breakfast): Summer (June 10 to mid-Aug) and weekends year-round, 500 kronor ($90) single; 680 kronor ($122.40) double. Off-season weekdays, 1,090 kronor ($196.20) single; 1,350 kronor ($243) double. Year-round, from 1,440 kronor ($259.20) suite. AE, DC, MC, V. **Parking:** Free.

This venerable old hostelry has, after several restorations, become a choice place to stay, successfully combining the old and the new. This landmark hotel, conveniently located in the center of town near the railroad station, has welcomed guests since 1840. The hotel's four restaurants serve excellent meals of Scandinavian, American, French, and Italian food. In summer, one of the restaurants serves outdoors. If you're looking for relaxation, try the Golden Grace and the Gyllene Oxen pub. The hotel also has a cocktail bar, a health club, sauna, and swimming pool, with a whirlpool bath and solarium.

INEXPENSIVE

SCANDIC HOTEL, Hejaregatan 19, S-352 46 Växjö. Tel. 0470/220-70. Fax 0470/256-78. 106 rms (all with bath). TV TEL **Bus:** 4.

$ **Rates** (including breakfast): Summer and Fri–Sat year-round, 475 kronor ($85.50) single; 530 kronor ($95.40) double. Sun–Thurs in off-season, 869 kronor ($156.40) single; 1,065 kronor ($191.70) double. AE, DC, MC, V. **Parking:** Free.

One of the best-value hotels in Växjö, built in 1979, the Scandic offers furnished bedrooms, including some large enough for families. Each room is the same size, fitted in bright shades of blue, green, or pink and yellow. There's a restaurant and a self-service cafeteria, along with a small indoor swimming pool and a sauna. The hotel lies 2 miles west of the center of town on the road going to the airport.

---

4. ÖLAND

25 miles E of Kalmar, 291 miles S of Stockholm

GETTING THERE   By Train   The island has no train service.

By Bus   Buses run from the Kalmar terminal to Borgholm on Öland in less than an hour; take no. 101 or 106.

By Car   From Kalmar, take the bridge over the sound, then turn left onto Route 136 to reach Borgholm.

ESSENTIALS   For information, the **Öland Tourist Association,** Box 115, S-387 00 Borgholm (tel. 0485/123-40), is open Mon–Fri 9am–4pm and Sat 9am–1pm (mid-June–mid-Aug) and Mon–Fri 10am–3pm and Sat 10am–noon (off-season). The **telephone area code** for Öland is 0485.

More Swedes emigrated from Öland to the United States during the 19th century than from any other province in Sweden. The Baltic island lost a quarter of its population. Many émigrés, however, returned to retire on this island.

Little wonder, considering how beautiful it is, with its sandy beaches, its treeless steppe (*Alvaret*) covered with wildflowers, its birdlife, and its profusion of windmills silhouetted against the summer sky.

Europe's longest bridge, nearly 4 miles long, connects Kalmar with Öland, a popular summer beach resort. The island is 87½ miles long and 10 miles wide. Beaches run along both coasts, and there is only one town, **Borgholm,** a quiet summer retreat. The royal summer residence is **Solliden.** To rent a summer house on the beach, get in touch with the **Öland Tourist Association** (see above).

WHAT TO SEE & DO

One of the more interesting attractions on Öland is **Eketorp Ring-Fort,** Degerhamn (tel. 0485/620-23) a prehistoric fortified village that has been excavated and reconstructed so that visitors can see how people lived in this area centuries ago. Eketorp is one of 15 known prehistoric forts on the island. Excavations have shown three phases of settlement here from A.D. 300 to 1300. Today a large selection of the massive wall that encircled this ring-fort has been reconstructed, along with Iron Age houses within the walls. You can see dwellings, cattle byres, and storehouses reconstructed using ancient crafts and materials, as well as species of livestock. Objects found in the excavations include simple tools, skillfully crafted jewelry, and weapons. The best of these finds are exhibited in a museum inside the fort wall. Unless you have a car, getting there is tricky, although four buses a day (no. 112) go there from the Mörbylånga bus station. Two buses make the run on Saturday and only one on Sunday. Check with the tourist office for bus timetables.

Eketorp can be visited from May to the first week in June, daily from 9am to 5pm daily, with guided tours weekdays at 2 and 4pm and on Saturday and Sunday at 10am, noon, and 2 and 4pm; from the first week in June to mid-August, daily from 9am to 6pm, with guided tours in English at 1pm, and other tours on the hour from 10am to 7pm; from mid-August to the end of the month, daily from 9am to 5pm, with tours at 10am, noon, and 2 and 4pm; during September, daily from 9am to 5pm, with guided tours on weekdays at 11am and 4pm and on Saturday and Sunday at 11am, 1pm, and 3pm. Admission is 30 kronor ($5.40) for adults, 5 kronor (90¢) for children 7 to 14.

WHERE TO STAY
MODERATE

STRAND HOTELL, Villagatan 4, S-387 36 Borgholm. Tel. 0485/888-88.
130 rms (all with bath). TV TEL **Bus:** 101.
$ Rates (including breakfast): 575–1,200 kronor ($103.50–$216) single; 995–1,400 kronor ($179.10–$252) double. AE, DC, MC, V. **Parking:** Free.

With a view over Kalmarsund, the Strand is right in the center of the island's entertainment. Some of its six restaurants and bars are open 24 hours a day in summer. Self-catering apartments are offered on a weekly basis. Twenty of the hotel bedrooms are privately owned and used as vacation homes by urbanites; these are rented to the public as regular hotel rooms when the residents aren't there. About half of the rooms contain a minibar. The hotel has a swimming pool, sauna, solarium, fitness room, restaurant, and tavern. Disco dancing is offered every night during the season. There are tennis courts and a marina in the hotel complex. The hotel also has its own yacht basin, which once won an award as the best privately owned yacht harbor in Sweden. It also has its own beach.

INEXPENSIVE

HALLTORPS GÄSTGIVERI, Högsrum, S-387 00 Borgholm. Tel. 0485/850-00. Fax 0485/850-01. 35 rms (all with bath). TV TEL
$ Rates (including breakfast): 700 kronor ($126) single; 950 kronor ($171) double. AE, DC, MC, V. **Parking:** Free.

This hotel, launched in 1975, is in one of the oldest manors of Öland, dating from the 17th century. A charming oasis, it is in a tranquil setting, 6 miles south of Borgholm, with a view across the Kalmarsund and the Halltorp Wood. Once it was a royal farming estate, and later a home for the elderly before it was transformed into an inn. Rooms are cozy and intimate, often with beamed ceilings; six of them have a lounge and loft. Laundry facilities and room service are provided.

The inn prides itself on its food, some of the best in the area. Ingredients are fresh, and the inn's home-spiced schnapps are flavored with herbs picked in nearby meadows. Lunch is 75 kronor ($13.50); a three-course menu of the week is 235 kronor ($42.30). There is an à la carte menu as well. Food is served May to September, daily from noon to midnight.

BUDGET

GUNTORPS HERRGÅRD, Guntorpsgatan, S-387 36 Borgholm. Tel. 0485/130-00. Fax 0485/133-19. 20 rms (all with bath). TV TEL
$ Rates (including breakfast): 595–635 kronor ($107.10–$114.30) single; 635–745 kronor ($114.30–$134.10) double. AE, DC, MC, V. **Parking:** Free.

This is a clean, comfortable place to stay, about half a mile from the town center. Built in 1919, with new wings added in 1986, it offers rooms in its main building and some kitchen units in an adjacent building. Fourteen of the rooms have a minibar. The hotel has a pleasant dining room, and a riding stable and beaches are nearby. It can arrange for babysitting and it also provides room and laundry service. It has even been known to help Swedish-American guests find their long-lost relatives. The hotel has a heated outdoor swimming pool.

WHERE TO DINE

EXPENSIVE

RESTAURANT BAKFICKAN, in the Hotel Borgholm, Trädgårdsgatan 15. Tel. 110-60.

Cuisine: SWEDISH/FRENCH. **Reservations:** Required in summer.

$ Prices: 3-course fixed-price dinner 250 kronor ($45); appetizers 50–110 kronor ($9–$19.80); main dishes 125–200 kronor ($22.50–$36). AE, DC, MC, V.

Open: Late-Apr to mid-Sept, daily 6pm–midnight. **Closed:** Off-season.

The best restaurant on the island, Bacfickan ("hip pocket" in English) takes pride in its fish, especially delectable Swedish salmon, and in its lamb dishes. If your table isn't ready, order an apéritif at the bar. Food items are well chosen and are based on market-fresh ingredients. The place becomes quite festive in summer, and deserves its widely acclaimed reputation. It's east of the main street, Storgatan.

CHAPTER 28

MALMÖ, HELSINGBORG & SKÅNE

In Sweden's southernmost corner, the province of Skåne offers varied scenery, large forests, and many waterways. The sea is always within easy reach, with ample, uncrowded beaches. Many of the larger towns discussed have a continental air, because of the nearness of Denmark and the rest of Europe.

Skåne's major urban cities are Malmö, Helsingborg, and the university and cathedral city of Lund, but many visit the little villages and undiscovered coastal towns in the summer months.

The topography of the area encapsulates almost every type of Nordic scenery, except fjords and snowcapped Lapp mountains. For decades, poets, authors, and painters have found it inspirational. On the tip of the Scandinavian peninsula was where Selma Lagerlöf's *The Wonderful Adventures of Nils* began. The story of the hero, who travels on the back of a wild goose, has been translated into all major languages.

The first settlers were deer hunters and fishermen who moved from the south of Europe as the ice melted. Over thousands of years their ancestors left many traces—from the Stone Age right to the Viking Age and the early beginnings of Christianity. There are no fewer than 300 small medieval parish churches in the province—all still in use. Castles and mansions, many founded 400 or 500 years ago, dot the landscape.

Once Skåne belonged to Denmark, but since 1658 it has firmly been part of the Swedish kingdom. The famous Swedish smörgåsbord is a Skåne tradition, and it is said that the most authentic smörgåsbords are served in the province. Skåne is known as the Swedish Riviera. For swimming and sunbathing, there are many beaches along its coast.

Skåne might be associated with the wild goose of young Nils, but actually this web-footed, flat-billed, and large-bodied bird is tame, never traveling far from home. That is, until November 10 when Scanians celebrate their almost sacred bird with a gargantuan dinner, enjoyed by all but the bird.

SEEING MALMÖ, HELSINGBORG & SKÅNE

GETTING THERE Skåne is easy to reach. You have a wide choice of flights, either to Malmö's Sturup Airport or to the Copenhagen airport from which there are frequent Hovercraft connections directly to the center of Malmö. Hovercraft also run between downtown Copenhagen and Malmö; and every 15 or 20 minutes—day or night—connections are possible by car-ferry from Helsingør, Denmark, to Helsingborg, Sweden.

If you're traveling by car, there are ferry routes from Denmark, Germany, and Poland.

WHAT'S SPECIAL ABOUT SKÅNE

Great Towns/Villages

☐ Malmö, Sweden's third-largest city and an important seaport.

☐ Lund, a great university city and the site of a major cathedral.

☐ Helsingborg, a major port with many attractions in its historic core and in the environs.

Castles

☐ Castle of Bösjokloster, site of a 1080 Benedictine convent, today filled with thousands of flowers and exotic shrubs.

☐ Christinehof Castle, on the Ystad-Kristianstad road, a fully furnished château with a wildlife sanctuary.

☐ Bäckaskog, the former country palace of King Charles XV, set in a 40-acre park.

Ancient Monuments

☐ Glimmingehus, between Ystad and Simrishamn, the best-preserved medieval keep in Scandinavia.

☐ The Kivik Tomb, one of the most remarkable monuments of the Bronze Age, discovered in 1748.

Churches

☐ The Cathedral of Lund, where romanesque architecture in Scandinavia reached its zenith.

☐ Dalby Church, outside Lund, an 11th-century former bishop's church, the oldest in Scandinavia.

A SUGGESTED ITINERARY

Day 1: Most arrivals are from Denmark, landing at Helsingborg, where a night's stopover is suggested to see the attractions of the town.

Day 2: Head south to Malmö for a day of sightseeing and stay the night.

Day 3: While still in Malmö, take the short train ride to Lund for a day's excursion to this old university town.

Day 4: Head for Ystad for the night and schedule a visit to the Castle of Bösjökloster, northeast of Lund. If time remains, visit Bäckaskog, the country palace of King Charles XV.

Day 5: From a base in Simrishamn, spend a day sightseeing in the area, visiting Backakra, the farm of Dag Hammarskjöld, and the Kivik Tomb, a prehistoric find.

---

1. BÅSTAD

125 miles S of Gothenburg, 65 miles N of Malmö

GETTING THERE   By Train   Båstad is accessible by train on the run from Gothenburg to Malmö. Trains run frequently throughout the day.

By Bus   Six buses a day run from Helsingborg to Båstad, taking 1 hour.

By Car   From Malmö, take the E6 north to the Båstad turnoff. Båstad lies 4 miles off the main road. From Gothenburg, head south on the E6.

ESSENTIALS   For tourist information, **Båstads Turistbyrå**, Köpmangatan 1 at Stortorget (tel. 0431/750-45), is open from mid-June to mid-August, hours are Mon–Fri 9am–4pm and Sat 9am–1pm (mid-June–mid-Aug) and Mon–Fri 10am–3pm and Sat 10am–noon (off-season). The **telephone area code** for Bastad is 0431.

Jutting out on a peninsula, surrounded by hills and a beautiful landscape, Båstad is the most fashionable international seaside resort in Sweden.

All the famous international tennis stars have played on the courts at Båstad. Swedish players of today have had much of their training here, inspired by the feats of Björn Borg. There are more than 50 courts in the district, in addition to the renowned Center Court. Tennis was played here as early as the 1880s, and became firmly established in the 1920s. King Gustaf V took part in these championships for 15 years from 1930 onward under the pseudonym of "Mr. G," and Ludvig Nobel guaranteed financial backing for international tournaments.

Golf has established itself almost as much as tennis, and the Bjäre peninsula offers a choice of five courses. In 1929 Nobel purchased land at Boarp for Båstad's first golf course. The bay provides opportunities for regattas and different kinds of boating. Windsurfing is popular, as is skin-diving. In summer, seabathing is also popular along the coast.

The Bjäre peninsula, a traditional farming area, is known for its early potatoes, which are in demand all over Sweden for the midsummer table with a selection of pickled herring.

WHAT TO SEE & DO

The scene of international tennis matches in summer, Båstad is also noted for one of the principal attractions of southern Sweden—the ✪ **Norrvikens Trädgårdar (Norrviken Gardens),** Kattvik, S-269 00 Båstad (tel. 710-10), 1½ miles west of the resort's center. Founded in 1906 by Rudolf Abelin, these gardens have been expanded and maintained according to his plans, embracing a number of styles. One garden is in Italian baroque style, with a pond framed with pyramid-shaped boxwood hedges and tall cypresses. A Renaissance Garden is reminiscent of the tapestry art of 15th-century Italy, with its boxwood patterns, and the flower garden, with bulb flowers competing with annuals. There are also a Japanese Garden, Oriental Terrace, Rhododendron Dell, a Romantic Garden, and a Water Garden.

At Villa Abelin, designed by the gardens' founder, wisteria climbs on the wall and is in bloom twice a year. The villa houses shops, exhibits, and information facilities. There is also a restaurant in the grounds.

The gardens may be viewed from May 1 until September 10, daily from 10am to 6pm. Admission is 45 kronor ($8.10) for adults, 25 kronor ($4.50) for children.

WHERE TO STAY & DINE
MODERATE

HOTEL RIVIERA, Rivieravägen, S-269 Båstad. Tel. 0431/708-70. Fax 0431/761-00. 50 rms (all with bath). TV TEL
$ **Rates** (including breakfast): 850 kronor ($153) single; 1,230 kronor ($221.40) double. MC, V. **Parking:** Free. **Closed:** Oct–Apr.

Often a favorite venue for conferences, this is one of the better hotels in the area, taking on somewhat festive air in summer. Located by the sea, half a mile from the railroad station and 2 miles east of the town center, it offers views from many of its modern bedrooms, as well as its 300-seat restaurant. Many guests sit out in the gardens or on the terrace, while others prefer to play on the tennis courts. There is a large, cozy bar, plus a summer café on a sun-filled loggia. The à la carte meals are excellent, a combination of Scandinavian and international food, and dinners with dancing to a live band are often presented in season.

INEXPENSIVE

GRAND HOTEL SKANSEN, Kyrkogatan 2, S-269 21 Båstad. Tel. 0431/720-50. Fax 0431/700-85. 52 rms (all with bath). TV TEL
$ **Rates** (including breakfast): 575 kronor ($103.50) single; 800 kronor ($144) double. AE, DC, MC, V. **Parking:** Free.

This former grain warehouse a few minutes' walk from the marina and beach has been transformed into a handsome and comfortable hotel. Its main building dates back to 1877, a beautiful old Swedish building listed as a cultural monument. The interior has a beamed roof, pillars, and views over the sea. Guests can relax on the terrace or have lunch or drinks at the little tables in the courtyard. Bedrooms, contained in five buildings constructed around tennis courts, have been decorated to a high standard. The hotel also has a nightclub, Grand Slam.

HOTEL-PENSION ENEHALL, Stationsterrassen 10, S-269 00 Båstad. **Tel. 0431/750-15.** Fax 0431/724-09. 60 rms (all with bath). TV TEL

$ Rates (including breakfast): 450–550 kronor ($81–$99) single; 650–750 kronor ($117–$135) double. Half board 450–550 kronor ($81–$99) per person. AE, DC, MC, V. **Parking:** Free.

On a slope of Hallandsåsen mountain only a few minutes' walk from the sea, this cozy, intimate place caters mainly to Swedish families, and some occasional Danes and Germans. There are many personal touches here and the rooms, although small, are adequately equipped. The food is tasty, the service polite and efficient.

---

2. HELSINGBORG

143 miles S of Gothenburg, 347 miles SW of Stockholm, 39 miles N of Malmö

GETTING THERE By Train Trains run hourly during the day between Helsingborg and Malmö, taking 50 minutes. Trains also arrive daily on the 7-hour trip from Stockholm.

By Bus Three buses a day run between Malmö and Helsingborg, but only Friday through Sunday; the trip takes 1 hour 10 minutes. Two daily buses leave Gothenburg for Helsingborg on Friday and again on Sunday, taking 3½ hours.

By Ferry Ferries from Helsingør, Denmark, leave the Danish harbor every 15 to 20 minutes, day or night; trip time is 25 minutes.

By Car From Malmö, head north on the E6; from Gothenburg, drive south on the E6.

ESSENTIALS The tourist bureau, **Turistföreningen i Helsingborg,** Rådhuset, Drottninggatan 7 (tel. 042/12-03-10), is open Mon–Fri 9am–7pm, Sat 9am–5pm, and Sun 3–6pm (June, Aug); Mon–Fri 9am–8pm, Sat 9am–7pm, and Sun 3–8pm (July); Mon–Fri 9am–5pm and Sat 9am–noon (Sept–May).

The **telephone area code** for Helsingborg is 042.

At the narrowest point of the Øresund (Öresund in Swedish), 3 miles across the water that separates Sweden and Denmark, is this industrial city and major port. Many people from Copenhagen who visit Kronborg Castle at Helsingør take a 25-minute ferry ride across the sound (leaving every 15 to 20 minutes) for a look at Sweden.

From Denmark, the round-trip fare for a car and up to five passengers is 405 kronor ($72.90). Pedestrians pay 32 kronor ($5.80) for a round-trip ticket. For information, call 49-21-12-55 in Helsingør, Denmark.

Of course, what they see isn't "Sweden," but a modern city with an ancient history. Helsingborg jointly controlled shipping along the sound with Helsingør in the Middle Ages. It is mentioned in the 10th-century *Nial-Saga,* and documents show that there was a town here in 1085. The city now has more than 100,000 inhabitants, with the second-busiest harbor in the country. It is the city that introduced pedestrian streets to Sweden, and it has long shore promenades along the sound.

Helsingborg (Hälsingborg) recently rebuilt large and vacant-looking sections of its inner city into one of the most innovative urban centers in Sweden. The centerpiece of these restorations lies beside the harbor, and includes an all-glass building, the

Knutpunkten, whose address is Järnvägsgatan. Contained within is the railroad, bus, and ferryboat terminals, an array of shops similar to a North American mall, and a heliport. Many visitors say that the railroad station, which is flooded with sunlight, is the cleanest, brightest, and most memorable they have ever seen. In addition, many dozens of trees and shrubs have transformed the center city into something like a verdant park, with trees between the lanes of traffic.

WHAT TO SEE & DO

Built in 1897, the **Town Hall (Rådhuset),** Drottninggatan 7 (tel. 10-50-00), has handsome stained-glass windows depicting scenes from the town's history. Two memorial stones outside were presented by the Danes and the Norwegians to the Swedes for their assistance during World War II. There is also a sculpture relief representing the arrival of Danish refugees.

In the main town square, the **Stortorget,** is a monument commemorating General Stenbock's victory at the Battle of Helsingborg in 1710 between Sweden and Denmark.

KÄRNAN, Kärngränden, off the Stortorget.

For a quick view of Helsingborg, go to the *terrassen* (terrace) of the Stortorget. An elevator leads from the terrassen in the central commercial zone, costing 2 kronor (40¢) per ride, up to the base of the 12th-century thick-walled medieval keep, the Kärnan. Many visitors, however, avoid the elevator, preferring instead to climb the flower-flanked and panoramic steps as part of their exploration of Helsingborg. Once inside the tower, an additional 147 steps remain before you're rewarded with that panoramic view. The tower, one of the most important medieval monuments in Sweden, represents the remains of Helsingborg Castle, torn down in the 17th century.
Admission: 10 kronor ($1.80).
Open: Daily 10am–8pm. **Bus:** 1, 6.

HELSINGBORGS MUSEUM, Södra Storgatan 31. Tel. 10-59-50.

Exploring this museum is like wandering in the city's attic. Anything the city didn't know what to do with they placed here: bottled fish, still life paintings, baby carriages, stuffed sharks, stuffed birds, antique dolls and clothing.
Admission: 15 kronor ($2.70) adults; children free. The same ticket admits you to Kärnan (see above); the Vikingbergs Konstmuseum (Vikingsberg Art Museum), on Vikingsgatan; and the Fredriksdal Open-Air Museum (see below).
Open: May–Aug, Mon–Sat 11am–6pm, Sun noon–6pm; Sept–Apr, Tues–Sat 11am–4pm, Sun noon–5:30pm. The Vikingsbergs Konstmuseum is open the same hours. **Bus:** 1, 6.

SOFIERO SLOTT, Sofierovägen. Tel. 14-52-59.

At this summer residence of the late King Gustav Adolf VI, the Helsingborgs Museum also maintains historical and art exhibitions. Built in 1864–65, the palace is a 5-minute drive north of Helsingborg in a large park. It has a café and restaurant, and there are also playhouses for children.
Admission: 20 kronor ($3.60) adults, 10 kronor ($1.80) children.
Open: May–June and Aug to mid-Sept, daily 10am–6pm; July, daily 10am–8pm.
Closed: Late Sept–Apr. **Bus:** 250, 252.

MARIAKYRKAN (Church of St. Mary), Södra Storgatan. Tel. 18-02-35.

A short walk east from the harbor at the intersection of Norra Storgatan, this church was built in the 13th century but substantially rebuilt in the 15th century. It is noted for its medieval altarpiece and its intricately carved Renaissance pulpit.
Admission: Free.
Open: Mon–Sat 8am–6pm, Sun 9am–6pm. **Bus:** 1, 6.

FREDRIKSDAL OPEN-AIR MUSEUM AND BOTANICAL GARDEN, Oscar Trapps Väg. Tel. 11-06-78.

This museum features farmhouses, a windmill, barns, even a malt drier that have been reassembled and the grounds of an 18th-century mansion donated to the Helsingborgs Museum. The botanical gardens contain chiefly the vegetation of Skåne.

Admission: Open-air park, free; mansion, 10 kronor ($1.80).
Open: Park, daily 10am–6pm; mansion, June–Sept, daily 10am–6pm. **Bus:** 202, 204, 232, 506, 520.

WHERE TO STAY
MODERATE

GRAND HOTEL, Stortorget 8-12, S-251 11 Helsingborg. Tel. 042/12-01-70. Fax 042/11-88-33. 130 rms (all with bath). MINIBAR TV TEL **Bus:** 1, 6.
$ Rates (including breakfast): Summer, 650 kronor ($117) single; 800 kronor ($144) double. Off-season, 1,050–1,125 kronor ($189–$202.50) single; 1,200–1,410 kronor ($216–$253.80) double. AE, DC, MC, V. **Parking:** 85 kronor ($15.30).

In the town center a 2-minute walk from the Rådhuset, this renovated but still comfortably old-fashioned 1920s establishment has retained its grand manner. Antiques, old paintings, numerous chandeliers, and bowls of fresh flowers are everywhere. The first-class bedrooms feature color TVs, video, hairdryers, and trouser presses, among other amenities. Use of the sauna and solarium are included in the prices. The Grand has an elegant dining room. From the hotel you can take a bus to Ängelholm Airport.

HOTEL MOLLBERG, Stortorget 18, S-251 10 Helsingborg. Tel. 042/12-02-70. Fax 042/14-96-18. 100 rms (all with bath). MINIBAR TV TEL **Bus:** 1, 6.
$ Rates (including breakfast): June 19–Aug 10 and Fri–Sat year-round, 475 kronor ($85.50) single; 700 kronor ($126) double. Sun–Thurs in off-season, 1,175 kronor ($211.50) single; 1,280 kronor ($230.40) double. AE, DC, MC, V. **Parking:** 85 kronor ($15.30).

Sweden's oldest continuously operating hotel and restaurant, the Mollberg dates back to the 14th century. Its elaborate wedding-cake exterior and high-ceilinged interior were most recently restored in 1986. Its first-class rooms all are equipped with color TVs, videos, trouser presses, and hairdryers, among other amenities. Use of the solarium and sauna are included in the rates. The Mollberg has a dining room, piano bar, and a cocktail lounge, decorated with dark paneling and opulent gilded-era accessories. The Café Mollberg is open Monday through Saturday from 11am to 11pm, offering a light cuisine and beverages.

RESO HOTEL HORISONT, Gustav Adolfs Gate 47, S-252 02 Helsingborg. Tel. 042/14-92-60. Fax 042/13-67-19. 170 rms (all with bath). TV TEL **Bus:** 1, 6.
$ Rates (including breakfast): June 17–Aug 19 and Fri–Sat year-round, 600 kronor ($108) single; 720 kronor ($129.60) double. Sun–Thurs in off-season, 995–1,185 kronor ($179.10–$213.30) single; 1,230 kronor ($221.40) double. AE, DC, MC, V. **Parking:** Free.

Set in a park at the edge of the commercial center of town, the angular and futuristic facade of this hotel was erected in 1985. It is considered the most alluring palace in town. The bedrooms are comfortably conservative, with plush upholstery and soundproof windows. On the premises is a warmly attractive piano bar lined with brick and touches of brass, and a high-ceilinged formal restaurant with potted palms. Relaxation facilities include a center with saunas, whirlpools, and solariums. The hotel is about a mile south of the ferryboat terminal.

INEXPENSIVE

HOTEL HELSINGBORG, Stortorget 20, S-252 23 Helsingborg. Tel. 042/12-09-45. Fax 042/11-54-61. 53 rms (all with bath), 3 suites. TV TEL **Bus:** 1, 6.
$ Rates (including breakfast): June 26–Aug 9 and Fri–Sat year-round, 495 kronor ($89.10) single; 590 kronor ($106.20) double; from 950 kronor ($171) suite. Sun–Thurs the rest of the year, 895 kronor ($161.10) single; 995 kronor ($179.10) double; from 1,300 kronor ($234) suite. AE, DC, MC, V.

Of the three hotels that lie along this grand avenue, this one is closest to the city's medieval tourist attraction, the Kärnan. It has a heroic neoclassical frieze and three copper-sheathed towers, and occupies four floors of what used to be a bank headquarters. Bedrooms are pleasantly modernized, and flooded with sunlight. The rooms retain a certain Jugendstil (art nouveau) look, with strong colors and many high-ceilinged decorative touches. All rooms were upgraded and renovated in the early 1990s. There's a lobby bar and a breakfast room. A sauna is on the premises, along with boutiques at street level.

MARINA PLAZA, Kungstorget 6. S-251 Helsingborg. Tel. 042/19-21-00, or toll free 800/528-1234 in the U.S. Fax 042/14-96-16. 177 rms (all with bath), 13 suites. TEL TV MINIBAR **Bus:** 41, 42, 43, 44.

$ Rates (including breakfast): May 15–Aug 15 and Fri–Sat, 650 kronor ($117) single or double. Mon–Thurs the rest of the year, 995 kronor ($179.10) single or double. Year-round, from 1,700 kronor ($306) suite. AE, DC, MC, V.

This is the most modern, most innovative, and most talked-about hotel in Helsingborg. Set adjacent to the city's transportation hub, the Knutpunkten, behind a light yellow facade studded with large glass windows, it contains an atrium-style lobby that overflows with trees, flowers, rock gardens, and fountains. A piano (often with an American-born pianist) provides evening entertainment near the lobby's popular bar. Bedrooms line the inner walls of the hotel's atrium and are outfitted, as the hotel's name would imply, with a color scheme of marine blue with nautical accessories. The hotel contains two restaurants, the upscale Hamnkrogen and the less formal Bistro Tabacen, as well as a disco, the Marina Nightclub. There's a health club, sauna, and solarium. The hotel is a member of the Best Western reservations system.

WHERE TO DINE
EXPENSIVE

ELINOR, Kullagatan 53. Tel. 12-23-30.
   Cuisine: SEAFOOD. **Reservations:** Required. **Bus:** 1, 6.
$ Prices: Fixed-price meals 240 kronor ($43.20) at dinner; 185 kronor ($33.30) at lunch; appetizers 55–140 kronor ($9.90–$25.20); main dishes 135–275 kronor ($24.30–$49.50). AE, DC, MC, V.
   Open: Lunch Mon–Sat noon–2:30pm; dinner Mon–Sat 6–11:30pm.

One of the best restaurants in town, Elinor is located on a pleasant pedestrian walkway in the town center, surrounded by boutiques and antiques shops. This is Helsingborg's answer to the sophisticated demands of nouvelle cuisine. There's a bar in back, along with a well-upholstered dining room.

The small but select menu changes frequently depending on seasonal ingredients and the chef's imagination. Dishes might include a ragoût of shrimp with chanterelles and combinations of crayfish, lobster, turbot, salmon, trout, and seasonal game.

MODERATE

ANNA KOCK, Järnvägsgatan 23. Tel. 18-13-00.
   Cuisine: SWEDISH. **Reservations:** Recommended at lunchtime, required at dinner. **Bus:** 3, 5, 7, 9, 12.
$ Prices: Lunch platters 45–50 kronor ($8.10–$9); 2-course fixed-price dinner 125 kronor ($22.50); appetizers 38–68 kronor ($6.80–$12.20); main dishes 89–154 kronor ($16–$27.70). AE, DC, MC, V.
   Open: Lunch Mon–Sat 11am–3pm; dinner Mon–Sat 5:30–11pm.

Decorated with the kind of antique knickknacks you might find in a Swedish farmstead, as well as a collection of modern Swedish watercolors, this cozy restaurant contains only 11 well-manicured tables. Opened in 1989, it was named after "Anna the Cook," a locally famous chef to the region's early 20th-century bourgeoisie and aunt of the present owners Claes and Sussan Andren. Menu items reflect the best of both modern and old-fashioned culinary techniques. Your meal might include Anna's pickled herring served with a Dutch blue cheese sauce, filet of reindeer on a bed of morels and lingonberry sauce, salmon with fresh herbs and a gravy of crayfish and cream, and a parfait laced with arctic berries. Lunches are simpler and less expensive than the carefully cultivated dinners which are the norm here.

RESTAURANT OSCAR, Sundstorget 7. Tel. 11-25-21.
   Cuisine: SEAFOOD. **Reservations:** Recommended. **Bus:** 3, 5, 7, 9, 12.
   $ Prices: Appetizers 45–130 kronor ($8.10–$23.40); main dishes 94–330 kronor ($16.90–$59.40); fixed-price lunch 62 kronor ($11.20); fixed-price dinner 98 kronor ($17.60). AE, DC, MC, V.
   Open: Lunch Mon–Fri 11:30am–2:30pm; dinner Mon–Sat 6–11pm.

For a really first-class meal, this is one of the best fish restaurants in town. Decorated in a tavern style, it overlooks a large parking lot near the ferryboats. The seafood is always fresh, whether it's included in the fish soup or served as grilled fish or bouillabaisse. Fresh vegetables and salads are also well prepared. Specialties include poached filet of sole with a chablis sauce and whitebait roe and crab filled with lemon sole and served with a saffron sauce, rice pilaf, and shrimp.

---

3. MALMÖ

177 miles S of Gothenburg, 384 miles SW of Stockholm

GETTING THERE   By Plane Malmö's airport is at Sturup, outside the city, which receives international flights from London, plus flights from cities within Sweden, including Gothenburg (50 minutes) and Stockholm (1 hour). However, its major international link with the world is Kastrup Airport at Copenhagen, to which Malmö is connected by Hovercraft service.

By Train The Stockholm-Copenhagen express train going via Helsingborg has a branch service through to Malmö. Service is frequent between Gothenburg and Malmö. From Helsingborg to Malmö, trains leave hourly on the 50-minute trip.

By Bus Two buses each on Friday and Sunday make the 4½-hour run from Gothenburg to Malmö. Buses from Helsingborg to Malmö run on Friday and Sunday, taking 1 hour 10 minutes.

By Hydrofoil Malmö and Copenhagen are linked by *Flygbåtana* (hydrofoil), with hourly service year-round daily from 5am to midnight, taking 45 minutes. Call 10-39-30 for information. Cost is 85 kronor ($15.30). Should the Øresund freeze over, service is suspended. SAS runs a Hovercraft from Kastrup Airport outside Copenhagen to Malmö from 8am to 8pm, taking 45 minutes.

ESSENTIALS The **Malmö Tourist Office,** Skeppsbron 2 (tel. 040/30-01-50), usually is open Mon–Fri 9am–5pm and Sat 9am–1pm. The **telephone area code** for Malmö is 040.

Sweden's third-largest city, a busy port across the Øresund sound from Copenhagen, is the capital of Skåne. A good base for exploring the ancient castles and manors nearby, it's an old city, dating from the 13th century.

From early days, Malmö prospered because of its location on a sheltered bay. In the 16th century when it was the second-largest city in Denmark, it vied with Copenhagen for economic and cultural leadership. Reminders of that age are Malmöhus Castle (see below), the Town Hall, and the Stortorget, plus several homes of rich burghers. Malmö has been a Swedish city since the end of a bloody war in 1658, when the Treaty of Roskilde incorporated the province of Skåne into Sweden.

WHAT TO SEE & DO

The **Malmökortet Card** entitles visitors to discounts and free admission to most of the city's attractions, free travel on Malmö's local buses, half-price fare on local trains, and substantial discounts on other excursions. A card good for 1 day (24 hours) costs

75 kronor ($13.50) for adults, half price for children. For 2 days, the price is 135 kronor ($24.30) for adults; half price for children; 3 days, 175 kronor ($31.50) for adults, half price for children. The Malmökortet is available at a number of outlets, including the Malmö Tourist Office (see above).

The Renaissance-era square surrounding the fountain on Stortorget is important architecturally, but the fountain itself is one of the most charming and imaginative in Scandinavia, including a nightingale, the symbol of Malmö. Built in 1964, it commemorates the most major dates in the city's history. Nearby is the 16th-century **Town Hall,** which still retains its look of Renaissance splendor. The **City Theater** at Fersens Väg, completed near the end of World War II, is considered one of the best equipped in Europe.

Four major attractions are under the direction of Malmö Museums, Box 406, S-210 24 Malmö (tel. 34-10-00). Heading the list is **Malmöhus Castle,** Malmöhusvägen founded in the 15th century by Eric of Pomerania and rebuilt by Christian III in the 16th century. Once a prison (the earl of Bothwell, third husband of Mary Queen of Scots, was incarcerated here from 1568 to 1573), the castle now houses the **City Museum,** the **Natural History Museum,** the **Aquarium,** and the **Art Museum.** The last contains a collection of old Scandinavian masters, especially those from southern Sweden, such as Carl Fredrik Hill (1849–1911), now considered one of Sweden's best landscape painters and a forerunner of European modernism. Most interesting is the large collection of Russian oil paintings from around 1900—the largest collection outside Russia. It also houses some modern art, and good samples of Swedish furniture and textiles. The lyrical sketches in the foyer are by Carl Larsson, one of the Sweden's best-known artists. West of Stortorget, the castle can be easily reached by foot.

Also in the group, across the street from the castle is **Kommendanthuset Malmöhusvägen,** a military museum and a piece of history in its own right, displaying military artifacts and equipment. **Tekniska Museet och Sjöfartsmuseet** (Museums of Technology and Shipping), Malmöhusvägen, is near the Kommendanthuset. Ancient means of communication are exhibited, as well as the submarine *U-3.* Technical history can be followed from the steam engine to the jet. The children's department even has a pirate ship, and in summer an old-fashioned tramway is in operation. **Vagnmuseet** (Carriage Museum), housed in the former military horse stable at Drottningtorget, displays carriages since the 18th century, coaches, and cycles.

A ticket costing 20 kronor ($3.60) for adults, 5 kronor (90¢) for children 15 and under, admits you to all sites mentioned above if visited on the same day. The museums are open Tuesday through Saturday from noon to 4pm and on Sunday from noon to 4:30pm.

Limhamn's Museum, Limhamnsvägen 102 (tel. 15-78-10), is an older soldier's cottage furnished like an ancient fisherman's home. It's open on Wednesday from 6 to 8pm and on Sunday from 1 to 4pm.

Malmö's S:t Petri (St. Peter's Church) (tel. 35-90-40) is another major sight, a copper-roofed brick church dating from the 14th century. Off Stortorget, it is noted for its Renaissance altar, baptismal font, and elegantly carved pulpit. It's open daily from 8am to 4pm.

One of the town centers for handcrafts is the painstakingly restored **Lilla Torg,** where half-timbered 16th-century houses surround cobblestones, fountains, and cafés. The Sparbanken Skåne, at one of the corners, is the most antique bank in town—some furnishings are at least 100 years old.

NEARBY ATTRACTIONS

Svaneholm, between Malmö and Ystad, was founded in 1530 as a fortress, and was later partially converted into an Italian-style palace. Today it houses a museum of paintings, furnishings, and tools dating primarily from the 18th and 19th centuries. The establishment is owned by the Svaneholm Castle Co-operative Society Ltd., and you can buy share certificates to help with the maintenance. For information, write Svaneholm Museum, 27400 Skurup (tel. 0411/400 12).

Admission to the castle is 15 kronor ($2.70) for adults, 5 kronor (90¢) for children. It's open March, April, and September to December, Wednesday through Sunday from 11am to 4pm; May to August, Tuesday through Sunday from 11am to 5pm; closed in January and February. Bus: no. 335 from Lund (see below).

WHERE TO STAY

EXPENSIVE

SHERATON MALMÖ HOTEL & TOWERS, Triangeln 2, S-200 10 Malmö. Tel. 040/74-000, or toll free 800/325-3535 in the U.S. Fax 040/23-20-20. 208 rms (all with bath), 14 suites. A/C MINIBAR TV TEL **Bus:** 12, 13, 14, 15.

$ **Rates** (including breakfast): June 19–Aug 6 and Fri–Sat the rest of the year, 630 kronor ($113.40) single; 730 kronor ($131.40) double; Sun–Thurs the rest of the year, 1,090–1,350 kronor ($196.20–$243) single; 1,800 kronor ($324) double. AE, DC, MC, V. **Parking:** 125 kronor ($22.50).

Malmö's first international luxury hotel lies in the city center, close to the Triangeln shopping center, the theater, the art hall, and the congress hall. It has a lobby bar in a glass-roofed garden, and a roof garden. The most expensive rooms are in the Sheraton Towers, three top floors with a separate check-in desk and its own lounge on the 20th floor. All bedrooms are tastefully and often luxuriously appointed, with many amenities.

Dining/Entertainment: "Upstairs" is the prestige restaurant of the hotel, with beautifully laid tables and attentive service. Meals are created from fresh products. International dishes are combined with Swedish home cooking and Scandinavian specialties. Piano entertainment is presented in the lobby. Adjacent is a casino offering roulette and blackjack.

Service: Room service, laundry and valet service, babysitting.

Facilities: World-class fitness center, parking area, sauna, solarium.

MODERATE

AB HOTEL KRAMER, Stortorget 7, S-201 21 Malmö. Tel. 040/701-20. Fax 040/23-09-37. 112 rms (all with bath). TV TEL **Bus:** 14, 17, 20.

$ **Rates** (including breakfast): Midsummer and Fri–Sat the rest of the year, 495 kronor ($89.10) single; 660 kronor ($118.80) double. Sun–Thurs the rest of the year, 1,090 kronor ($196.20) single; 1,320 kronor ($237.60) double. AE, DC, MC, V. **Parking:** 125 kronor ($22.50).

Set at the side of the town's main square, this châteaulike twin-towered building is one of the landmark hotels in town. Built in 1875, it was renovated at the height of the art deco era, and the rooms were redecorated in 1992. Rooms are among the most alluring in town, many designed like the largest staterooms of a 1930s ocean liner. You'll enjoy marble bathrooms, dark-grained paneling, curved walls, and beds where Mae West might have felt at home.

HOTEL NOBLE HOUSE, Gustav Adolfs Torg 47, S-211 39 Malmö. Tel. 040/10-15-00. Fax 040/11-68-37. 128 rms (all with bath), 4 suites. MINIBAR TV TEL **Bus:** 10, 11, 17, 20.

$ **Rates** (including breakfast): June 15–Aug 12 and Fri–Sat all year, 525 kronor ($94.50) single; 630 kronor ($113.40) double; 730 kronor ($131.40) suite. Sun–Thurs the rest of the year, 985 kronor ($177.30) single; 1,215 kronor ($218.70) double; 1,420 kronor ($255.60) suite. AE, DC, MC, V. **Parking:** 95 kronor ($17.10). **Closed:** Dec 22–26.

Named after the best-selling novel by James Clavell, this is one of the most modern and up-to-date hotels in town, and certainly the most glamorous. The comfortable pastel-colored rooms are decorated with copies of early 20th-century paintings. Because of the hotel's convenient location in the town center, its quietest rooms face the interior courtyard.

SAS ROYAL HOTEL, Östergatan 10, S-211 Malmö. Tel. 040/23-92-00, or
toll free 800/221-2350 in the U.S. Fax 040/11-28-40. 221 rms (all with bath), 4
suites. MINIBAR TV TEL **Bus:** 14, 17.
$ **Rates** (including breakfast): June 19–Aug 17 and Fri–Sat, 640 kronor ($115.20)
single; 730 kronor ($131.40) double; Sun–Thurs the rest of the year, 1,245–1,610
kronor ($224.10–$289.80) single; 1,340–1,725 kronor ($241.20–$310.50) double. Year-round, from 2,445 kronor ($440.10) suite. AE, DC, MC, V. **Parking:** 84
kronor ($15.10).

One of the best-equipped and run hotels in the south of Sweden, it is filled with
tastefully decorated rooms, each with elegant bathrooms and such amenities as video,
hairdryer, trouser press, and radio. Built in 1988, the hotel is seven floors high and was
designed to accommodate the disabled.

   Dining/Entertainment: An exceptionally good restaurant, Thott's serves an
elegant Scandinavian and continental cuisine in a half-timbered house from the
mid-16th century. For fast meals, try the cafeteria. There is also a bar.

   Services: Room service, babysitting, SAS EuroClass check-in on Hovercraft to
Copenhagen, express laundry, business service center.

   Facilities: Heated garage with direct access from the hotel, sauna.

SAVOY HOTEL, Norra Vallgatan 62, S-201 80 Malmö. Tel. 040/702-30.
Fax 040/97-85-51. 100 rms (all with bath), 8 suites. MINIBAR TV TEL **Bus:** 14, 17.
$ **Rates** (including breakfast): June 19–Aug 9 and Fri–Sat year-round, 550 kronor
($99) single; 700 kronor ($126) double. Sun–Thurs the rest of the year, 690–1,100
kronor ($124.20–$198) single; 1,100–1,300 kronor ($198–$234) double. AE,
DC, MC, V. **Parking:** 85 kronor ($15.30).

   This hotel has figured prominently in Malmö history; famous guests have
included Dag Hammarskjöld, Liv Ullmann, Alan Alda, and Johnny (Tarzan)
Weissmuller. Upstairs you'll find some of the most plushly decorated accommodations in Sweden. Each bedroom contains champagne-colored upholstery,
cabriole-legged or Chippendale-style furniture, and all the sophisticated extras of a
deluxe hotel. For a description of the hotel's cozy and intimate restaurant, Grillen, see
"Where to Dine," below.

INEXPENSIVE

HOTEL ANGLAIS, Stortorget 15, S-211 22 Malmö. Tel. 040/714-50. Fax
040/11-32-74. 82 rms (all with bath). TV TEL **Bus:** 14, 17.
$ **Rates** (including breakfast): June 19–Aug 9 and Fri–Sat year-round, 550 kronor
($99) single; 650 kronor ($117) double. Sun–Thurs in off-season, 850 kronor
($153) single; 1,000 kronor ($180) double. AE, DC, MC, V.

   This efficiently run 1912 hotel has few frills but plenty of comfort. Located on
the main square facing the town hall, it's one of the Salvation Army's best
old-world showcases. Rooms are cavernous enough to offer bed-sitting areas
and all is very clean. All units have showers or complete baths. The hotel has a
tearoom and a restaurant, open Monday through Friday from 6:30am to 5:30pm,
with two daily *dagens* menus priced from 52 kronor to 62 kronor ($9.40 to $11.20).

**SARA HOTEL WINN, Jörgen Kocksgatan 3, S-201 20 Malmö. Tel.
040/10-18-00.** Fax 040/11-44-33. 101 rms (all with bath). TV TEL **Bus:** 14, 17.
$ **Rates** (including breakfast): June 14–Aug 8 and Fri–Sat year-round, 500 kronor
($90) single; 680 kronor ($122.40) double. Sun–Thurs in off-season, 840–900
kronor ($151.20–$162) single; 1,100 kronor ($198) double. AE, DC, MC, V.
Parking: 85 kronor ($15.30).

The Sara Hotel Winn is a quiet and calm place to stay, despite its location in the heart
of Malmö, only a couple of minutes from the hydrofoils to Denmark and a short
distance from the railway station and airport buses. Bedrooms are large, with
comfortable chairs and beds and generously sized shower/bathrooms. Each has a
radio and automatic alarm clock, and 20 contain a minibar. The hotel has a sauna and
a recreation room.

WHERE TO DINE

Malmö has many restaurants, most in center city. **Salahallen,** near Lilla Torg, is an indoor food market with several small restaurants.

EXPENSIVE

KOCKSKA KROGEN, Franss Suellsgatan 3. Tel. 703-20.

Cuisine: SWEDISH/FRENCH. **Reservations:** Recommended. **Bus:** 14, 17.

$ Prices: Appetizers 73–120 kronor ($13.10–$21.60); main dishes 177–288 kronor ($31.90–$51.80); fixed-price lunch 56–120 kronor ($10.10–$21.60). AE, DC, MC, V.

Open: Mon–Fri 11:30am–midnight, Sat 6pm–midnight.

Kockska Krogen is named after a 16th-century Danish mayor who lived in the thick brick vaults of this building in the Old Town. To reach it, pass beneath an ornate fortified entrance used during the Renaissance as the city mint. Stop for a beer in the pub near the entrance or proceed into the labyrinth or plaster-covered vaults that make up the many dining rooms. Each of the well-prepared specialties is named after a legendary person important in the history of Malmö. You can order a concoction of Dover sole with lobster and chestnuts, flambéed beef filet, honey-fried breast of duck, followed by one of 10 succulent desserts, perhaps rum-raisin ice cream in flambéed crêpes.

MODERATE

CASA MIA, Södergatan 12. Tel. 23-05-00.

Cuisine: ITALIAN. **Reservations:** Recommended. **Bus:** 14, 17.

$ Prices: Appetizers 55–85 kronor ($9.90–$15.30); main dishes 110–185 kronor ($19.80–$33.30); fixed-price lunch 58 kronor ($10.40). AE, DC, MC, V.

Open: Mon–Fri 11am–midnight, Sat–Sun noon–midnight.

Suggestions of the gondola moorings of Venice ornament the front terrace of this Nordic version of a neighborhood trattoria. Troubadours stroll from table to crowded table singing Neapolitan ballads, and your waiter is likely to address you in Italian. You can begin with a steaming bowl of stracciatella alla romana or the fish soup of the house, then penne with shrimp, basil, cream, and tomatoes, or spaghetti with seafood. Later you can dig into saltimbocca alla romana, a portion of grilled scampi, escalope of veal stuffed with goose liver, or an array of grilled meats with aromatic herbs. There are 15 types of pizza on the menu and pastries are offered for dessert.

GRILLEN, in the Savoy Hotel, Norra Vallgatan 62. Tel. 702-30.

Cuisine: SWEDISH. **Reservations:** Recommended. **Bus:** 14, 17.

$ Prices: Appetizers 68–135 kronor ($12.20–$24.30); main dishes 115–290 kronor ($20.70–$52.20). AE, DC, MC, V.

Open: Mon–Fri 11:30am–midnight, Sat 5pm–midnight, Sun 1pm–midnight.

A cozy and intimate dining spot, Grillen has 17th-century Windsor chairs, touches of gleaming copper, and candlelight. Full dinners include an array of grilled specialties that you can watch being prepared. Your meal might include grilled salmon tartare with salmon roe, three kinds of pickled herring, smoked reindeer, filet of pork flambéed with tequila, chateaubriand with cognac and Gorgonzola, and a Swedish classic dish of ice-cellar salted salmon with creamed dill-flavored potatoes.

RÅDHUSKÄLLEREN, Kyrkogatan 6. Tel. 790-20.

Cuisine: SWEDISH. **Reservations:** Recommended. **Bus:** 14, 17.

$ Prices: Appetizers 48–105 kronor ($8.60–$18.90); main dishes 95–250 kronor ($17.10–$45); 1-course lunch 65 kronor ($11.70). AE, DC, MC, V.

Open: Mon–Sat 11:30am–11pm, Sun 1–6pm.

Even if your schedule doesn't allow you to dine here, you should at least drop in for a drink at the most atmospheric place in Malmö, the cellar of the Town Hall. Its severe exterior and labyrinth of underground vaults were built in 1546. Have a drink in the rustic pub or in the more formal crescent-shaped cocktail lounge before heading into the dark-vaulted dining room that for centuries stored gold, wine, furniture, and foodstuffs. Full à la carte meals include a changing array of daily specials and such staples as filet of sole Washington, stuffed sole, filet of veal, pepper steak, and roast duck.

RESTAURANT GOURMET, Låndbygatan 4. Tel. 12-08-35.
   Cuisine: SWEDISH/FRENCH. **Reservations:** Recommended. **Bus:** 14, 17.
$ **Prices:** Appetizers 65–85 kronor ($11.70–$15.30); main dishes 142–250 kronor ($25.60–$45); fixed-price 3-course dinner 320 kronor ($57.60); 1-course lunch 55 kronor ($9.90). AE, DC, MC, V.
   Open: Lunch Mon–Fri 11:30am–2:30pm; dinner Mon–Fri 5:30–11pm, Sat 1–11pm.

Near Lilla Torg, this elegant restaurant is in an 18th-century brick-vaulted cellar. To reach it, pass through a small garden where tables are placed in summer. The true elegance of the place comes out at night with the three-course fixed-price menu, and an à la carte selection costs about the same. Specialties include Canadian lobster, scallops poached with white wine and served with Swedish caviar, and filet of lemon sole stuffed with blue mussels and crab. The chef's special pride is his house duckling.

SAVVY SHOPPING

MATTSSONS PÄLS, Norra Vallgatan 98. Tel. 12-55-33.
   One of Sweden's leading furriers. Saga mink coats and jackets are the best buy, but Mattssons has a full range of fine furs at prices lower than in the United States. In the boutique are fur-lined poplins and accessories, all tax free for tourists. Bus: 92, 93, 94.

HANSA COMPANIET, Stora Nygatan 50. Tel. 770-00.
   At Malmö's largest department store, you'll find "A Very Special Swedish Shop," with glass, goods, handcrafts, and souvenirs of Sweden. Bus: 11, 19, 21.

SILVERBERGS MOBLER, Baltzarsgatan 31. Tel. 740-80.
   For glassware and crystal, this famous store competently and reliably ships its stunning collection of glassware, crystal, furniture, and gifts all over the world. Bus: 14, 17.

EVENING ENTERTAINMENT

Since Copenhagen is nearby, Malmö does not have much nightlife, but there are a few spots where you might find fun.

FOLKETS PARK (People's Park), Amiralsgatan 35. Tel. 709-90.
   From May to September, locals head for these sprawling amusement grounds and pleasure gardens, with dancing pavilions, vaudeville performances, open-air concerts, and restaurants. There is also a reptile center. Children will find a playhouse, plus a small zoo and a puppet theater. Bus: 32, 36, 37, 38 from Gustav Adolfs Torg. Open 3pm to midnight.
   Admission: Sat–Sun, 30 kronor ($5.40) adults, free for children under 12; Mon–Fri, free for all.

NIGHTCLUB ETAGE, Stortorget 6. Tel. 23-20-60.
   Probably the most innovative and creatively designed nightspot in the region, Etage is reached by climbing a circular staircase from an enclosed courtyard next to the main town square. There's a piano bar on the second floor, but the heart of the place is the third-floor restaurant, bar, and disco. There, amid a glittering decor of midnight-blue, black, and sparkling chrome, you'll find a futuristic-looking dance floor. The continental menu features a meal for 200 kronor ($36); drinks run 55 kronor ($9.90). Open Wednesday through Saturday from 8pm to 3am. Bus: 10.
   Admission: Disco, 80 kronor ($14.40) after 10pm, including first drink.

GOLDEN DAYS, Stora Nygatan 59. Tel. 785-85.
   English through and through, this place is decorated in the Ye Olde English Music Hall motif, with playbills on the walls and old records played continuously. You can get such main dishes as marinated salmon and stewed potatoes with dill, a special on Monday night. There's no dancing but there is entertainment nightly. A lunch costs

55 kronor to 75 kronor ($9.90 to $13.50). Beer costs 39 kronor ($7). Open Monday through Saturday from 11:30am to 1am and on Sunday from 1pm to 1am. Bus: 14, 17.

4. LUND

11 miles NE of Malmö, 187 miles S of Gothenburg,
374 miles SW of Stockholm

GETTING THERE   By Train   Trains run hourly from Malmö, a 15-minute ride.

By Bus   Hourly buses run from Malmö, taking 30 minutes.

By Car   From Gothenburg, head south along the E6; Malmö and Lund are linked by express highway (head in toward Route 15), a 20-minute drive.

ESSENTIALS   The tourist information office, **Lunds Turistbyrå**, at Kattesund 6, S-221 00 Lund (tel. 046/15-50-40), is open Mon–Fri 9am–6pm and Sat 9am–1pm (June); Mon–Fri 9am–6pm, Sat 9am–1pm, and Sun 11am–1pm (July, Aug); and Mon–Fri 9am–6pm (Sept–May).

The **telephone area code** for Lund is 046.

Lund was probably founded in 1020 by Canute the Great, ruler of the united kingdoms of England and Denmark, when this part of Sweden was a Danish possession. But the city really made its mark when its cathedral was consecrated in 1145. The city's 1,000-year anniversary was celebrated in 1990, since archeological excavations show that a stave church was built here in 990. Lund quickly became a center of religion, politics, culture, and commerce for all of Scandinavia.

The town has winding passageways, centuries-old buildings, and the richness of a university town—Lund University, founded in 1666, continues to play an active role in town life.

The most exciting time to be in Lund, as in Uppsala, is on Walpurgis Eve, April 30, when student revelries signal the advent of spring—but a visit to Lund at any time is a pleasure.

WHAT TO SEE & DO

DOMKYRKAN (Cathedral of Lund), Kyrkogatan. Tel. 35-87-00.

With this ancient cathedral, Romanesque architecture in Scandinavia reached its height, and the eastern exterior of the church is one of the finest expressions of Romanesque architecture in northern Europe. The sandstone interior has sculptural details similar to those in Lombardy and other parts of Italy in quality and character. There is also a crypt with a high altar dedicated in 1123, and intricately carved choir stalls from about 1375.

A partly reconstructed 14th-century **astronomical clock** not only tells the time and the date, but stages a splashy tournament from the Middle Ages—complete with clashing knights and the blare of trumpets. That's not all: The three Wise Men come out to pay homage to the Virgin and Child. To see all this, time your visit to the cathedral for when the clock strikes noon (1pm on Sunday) and 3pm.

Admission: Free.

Open: Mon–Fri 8am–6pm, Sun 9:30am–6pm. **Bus:** 1, 2, 3, 4, 5, 6, 7.

KULTUREN (Museum of Cultural History), Tegnérsplatsen. Tel. 15-04-80.

After leaving the cathedral, walk across the university grounds to Adelgatan, which the local citizens consider their most charming street. Here you'll find Kulturen, another open-air museum of Sweden—this one containing reassembled, sod-roofed farms and manor houses, a carriage museum, ceramics, peasant costumes, Viking artifacts, and old handcrafts, even a wooden church moved to this site from the glassworks district.

Admission: 25 kronor ($4.50) adults; children free.

Open: May–Sept, daily 11am–5pm; Oct–Apr, daily noon–4pm. **Bus:** 1, 2, 3, 4, 5, 6, 7.

HISTORISKA MUSEET, Kraftstorg 1. Tel. 10-79-40.

Founded in 1805, this is the second-largest museum of archeology in Sweden. Collections trace the development of the people of Skåne from antiquity to the Middle Ages. One of the skeletons found during an excavation is that of a young man, one of the oldest finds of a human body in northern Europe, dating around 7000 B.C. Most collections from the Bronze Age came from tombs. During excavations in eastern Skåne, a large gravefield was unearthed with jewelry and weapons which are on display. The medieval exhibition is dominated by church art.

Admission: 5 kronor (90¢) adults; children free.
Open: Tues–Fri 11am–1pm. **Bus:** 1, 2, 3, 4, 5, 6, 7.

DROTTEN MUSEET (Medieval Museum), Kattesund 6. Tel. 35-52-91.

During the excavations for an inner-city office building that was completed in 1986, workmen discovered the ruins of one of Sweden's earliest churches. A now-ruined Romanesque building that preceded the establishment of Lund itself by 100 years, it was built about a thousand years ago. Recognizing its remnants as historically and aesthetically valuable, civic leaders ordered the construction of a series of large windows in the new building, allowing pedestrians on the sidewalk outside to view the ruins from above. During limited hours (see below), visitors can actually walk among the ruins, viewing an exhibition of mannequins dressed in medieval garb in scenes of everyday life. Also on display are some of the skeletons unearthed from the excavation site.

Admission: 10 kronor ($1.80).
Open: For views from above, 24 hours a day; for closeup visits, Sat–Sun 10am–2pm. **Bus:** 1, 2, 3, 4, 5, 6, 7.

WHERE TO STAY

The tourist office (see above) can help you obtain housing in private homes for as little as 130 kronor ($23.40) per person. There is a booking fee of 40 kronor ($7.20).

MODERATE

GRAND HOTEL, Bantorget 1, S-221 04 Lund. Tel. 046/11-70-10. Fax 046/14-73-01. 83 rms (all with bath), 4 suites. MINIBAR TV TEL **Bus:** 1, 2, 3, 4, 5, 6, 7.

$ Rates (including breakfast): June 26–Aug 1 and Fri–Sat year-round, 500–600 kronor ($90–$108) single; 700 kronor ($126) double. Sun–Thurs the rest of the year, 920–1,290 kronor ($165.60–$232.20) single; 1,320–1,450 kronor ($237.60–$261) double. Year-round from 1,600 kronor ($288) suite. AE, DC, MC, V.

This château-style hotel, the most prestigious in town, overlooks the fountains and flowers of a city park. The marble lobby is grand. Upstairs, each room has an old-fashioned decor and a few modern touches including a radio. The rooms in the hotel's conical corner tower are the most desirable. The elegant restaurant offers fixed-price meals beginning at 165 kronor ($29.70).

HOTEL LUNDIA, Knut den stores gata 2, S-221 04 Lund. Tel. 046/12-41-40. Fax 046/14-19-95. 97 rms (all with bath), 2 suites. TV TEL **Bus:** 1, 2, 3, 4, 5, 6, 7.

$ Rates (including breakfast): July–Aug 4 and Fri–Sat all year, 710 kronor ($127.80) single; 830 kronor ($149.40) double. Sun–Thurs the rest of the year, 1,140–1,250 kronor ($205.20–$225) single; 1,350 kronor ($243) double. Year-round, from 1,795 kronor ($323.10) suite. AE, DC, MC, V. **Parking:** 65 kronor ($11.70). **Closed:** Dec 23–27.

Operated by the same management as the Grand Hotel (see above), this is perhaps the most pleasantly situated and most modern hotel in town. The interior has modern winding staircases, white marble sheathing, and big windows. Each bedroom has its own tile bath, clothes press, and refrigerator, and is designed with Scandinavian fabrics and unusual lithographs. Guests interested in a formal meal usually head for the dining room at the Grand, about a block away. Those interested in a less formal meal can patronize the in-house brasserie (see "Where to Dine," below). On the premises is a stylish nightclub.

INEXPENSIVE

HOTEL CONCORDIA, Stalbrogatan 1, S-222 24 Lund. Tel. 046/13-50-50. Fax 046/13-74-22. 49 rms (all with bath), 1 suite. TV TEL **Bus:** 1, 2, 3, 4, 5, 6, 7.

$ Rates (including breakfast): June 19–Aug 15 and Fri–Sat year-round, 595 kronor ($107.10) single; 640 kronor ($115.20) double. Sun–Thurs the rest of the year, 825 kronor ($148.50) single; 975 kronor ($175.50) double. Year-round, from 1,450 kronor ($261) suite. AE, DC, MC, V. **Parking:** 65 kronor ($11.70).

Next door to the brick house where August Strindberg lived in 1897, this charming ornate building was renovated a few years ago into a pleasant hotel. The modern rooms are sedate, and a few are reserved for nonsmokers. On the premises is a sauna. It's a 5-minute walk south of the rail station.

WHERE TO DINE
EXPENSIVE

PETRI PUMPA RESTAURANT, S:t Petri Kyrkogata 7. Tel. 13-55-15.
   Cuisine: SWEDISH/FRENCH. **Reservations:** Required. **Bus:** 1, 2, 3, 4, 5, 6, 7.
$ Prices: Appetizers 80–140 kronor ($14.40–$25.20); main dishes 160–240 kronor ($28.80–$43.20); fixed-price 3-course meals 265–360 kronor ($47.70–$64.80); 5-course *menu dégustation* 455 kronor ($81.90). AE, DC, MC, V.
   Open: Lunch Mon–Sat 11am–2:20pm; dinner Mon–Sat 6pm–midnight.

⭐ Generally acknowledged as the finest restaurant in Lund, this 45-seat restaurant is run by Swedish-born Thomas Dreying, who apprenticed briefly at several of the most glamorous restaurants in France (including Troisgros). Contained within a century-old, stone-fronted building in the historic heart of town, it's filled with exposed mahogany, marine-blue leather, and a changing exhibition of modern paintings provided by one of the leading art galleries in Sweden. Menu items change with the seasons, but combine some of the most innovative culinary techniques anywhere. Examples include grilled filet of brill with a beetroot and apple compote and horseradish; a fricassée of knuckle of veal with crayfish and savoy cabbage, and cutlets of venison with fried, cream-cooked brussels sprouts and chanterelles. Adjacent to the restaurant is the Petri Bar, which is recommended separately under "Evening Entertainment," below.

MODERATE

BRASSERIE LUNDIA, in the Hotel Lundia, Knut den stores gata 2. Tel. 12-41-40.
   Cuisine: SWEDISH. **Reservations:** Required on weekends only. **Bus:** 1, 2, 3, 4, 5, 6, 7.
$ Prices: Appetizers 32–55 kronor ($5.80–$9.90); main dishes 85–130 kronor ($15.30–$23.40); *dagens* menu 55 kronor ($9.90). AE, DC, MC, V.
   Open: Mon–Sat 11:30am–11:30pm.

Ⓢ One of the most popular cafeterias in town, and the only restaurant in Lund with its own in-house bakery. You'll find crisp salads, open-face sandwiches, and hot dishes as part of the full cafeteria meals. At night, the place becomes an à la carte restaurant with waitress service, serving brasserie steak tartare, fettuccine with salmon, tagliatelle bolognese, grilled filet mignon, grilled pork cutlet with pepper sauce, deep-fried Camembert, and seven kinds of alcohol-rich after-dinner coffees. It has a sophisticated decor with wood and russet-colored marble tables.

CARLSSONS TRADGÅRD, Märtenstorget 6. Tel. 13-81-20.
   Cuisine: SWEDISH. **Reservations:** Not required. **Bus:** 1, 2, 3, 4, 5, 6, 7.
$ Prices: Appetizers 38–62 kronor ($6.80–$11.20); main dishes 90–120 kronor
($16.20–$21.60). MC, V.
   Open: Mon–Thurs 11am–1am, Fri–Sat noon–2am, Sun noon–midnight.
A British pub-style place, Carlssons Tradgård is set back from the market square on a
cobblestone courtyard and built in the half-timbered style. The food is fairly good:
Try fried filet of beef with Gorgonzola, pepper steak, salmon and prawns, or
whisky-poached salmon. During the day it's strictly self-service, but in the evening
there is table service. The pub offers evening entertainment.

**GLORIA'S BAR AND RESTAURANT, S:t Petri Kyrkogata 9. Tel. 15-
19-80.**
   Cuisine: AMERICAN. **Reservations:** Recommended. **Bus:** 1, 2, 3, 4, 5, 6, 7.
$ Prices: Appetizers 39–89 kronor ($7–$16); main dishes 69–119 kronor
($12.40–$21.40). AE, DC, MC, V.
   Open: Mon 11:30am–midnight; Tues–Sat 11:30am–1am; Sun 11:30am–11pm.
The staggering success of this American-inspired sports and western bar would
gladden the heart of any U.S.-born ideologue. Contained within two floors of an
old-fashioned building in the historic heart of town, it offers a crowded and likable
bar on its street level, and an even larger bar upstairs. Scattered throughout the
premises are photographs and posters of American sports heroes, baseball and
football memorabilia, and artifacts from the Wild West. Draft beer costs 42 kronor
($7.60) for a foaming mug. Your appetites can be assuaged by copious portions of such
rib-stickers as hamburgers, steaks, hot-pepper chicken, blackened salmon, and an
array of dishes inspired by the Cajun cuisine of Louisiana. All of these will be served
to you by a staff clad, appropriately, in jeans, cowboy boots, and shirts emblazoned
with Gloria's logo. Live music is performed between 9:30pm and 1am Tuesday to
Thursday. Thursday night is a particular favorite because of its emphasis on rock and
roll.

GRIFO, Knut den stores gata 1. Tel. 12-52-50.
   Cuisine: INTERNATIONAL/STEAKS. **Reservations:** Recommended. **Bus:** 1,
2, 3, 4, 5, 6, 7.
$ Prices: Appetizers 32–55 kronor ($5.80–$9.90); main dishes 85–135 kronor
($15.30–$24.30). AE, DC, MC, V.
   Open: Mon–Sat noon–10pm.
A favorite with students, this modern tavern with outdoor summer tables is located
near the train station and opens onto a tree-shaded pedestrian mall. Meals are likely
to include beef steak, spaghetti, fried Camembert, fried scampi, beef Stroganoff, lamb
cutlet, and tournedos Rossini.

STAKET, Stora Södergatan 6. Tel. 11-93-67.
   Cuisine: SWEDISH. **Reservations:** Recommended. **Bus:** 1, 2, 3, 4, 5, 6, 7.
$ Prices: Appetizers 38–52 kronor ($6.80–$9.40); main dishes 83–135 kronor
($14.90–$24.30). AE, DC, MC, V.
   Open: Mon–Fri 11am–11pm, Sat–Sun noon–11pm.
An old tavern that serves good food in an unspoiled atmosphere, this 15th-century
cellar in a narrow, step-gabled, brick building is one of the city's finest restaurants. It
caters to hearty appetites, and dishes are likely to include fish soup, wienerschnitzel,
mussel salad, entrecôte, and tournedos flavored with cognac. Fondues are a specialty.

EVENING ENTERTAINMENT

In addition to the following, **Carlssons Tradgård** (see "Where to Dine," above)
offers nighttime entertainment in the pub.

LUNDIA NIGHTCAFÉ, Knut den stores gata 2. Tel. 12-41-40.
   In the cellar of the Hotel Lundia (see "Where to Stay," above), there is a
small-stakes casino (blackjack and roulette), two different bars, a dance floor, and a
modern cellar-style decor popular with students. Residents of the Hotel Lundia and

clients of the Brasserie Lundia enter free, but everyone else pays a cover charge. Draft beer costs 49 kronor ($8.80). It's open Wednesday through Saturday from 9pm to 2am. Bus: 1, 2, 3, 4, 5, 6, 7.

Admission: 65 kronor ($11.70); free for hotel guests.

PETRI BAR, S:t Petri Kyrkogata 7. Tel. 13-55-15.

Set adjacent to the previously recommended Petri Pumpa Restaurant, this beer and wine bar contains a zinc bar top and mahogany art deco accessories which were imported from a long-defunct Paris bistro from the 1920s. Established in 1984, it welcomes the art and academic worlds of Lund into its intimate and stylish interior. Wine comes in a wide array of vintages and sells for from 35 kronor ($6.30) per glass. Platters of such food items as steaks, French-inspired *choucroute,* and cheese plates sell for 60 to 135 kronor ($10.80 to $24.30) each. Live music is occasionally performed, but more frequently, the entertainment derives from the conversations of other members of the clientele. It's open Monday to Saturday 11am to midnight. Bus: 1, 2, 3, 4, 5, 6, 7.

EASY EXCURSIONS

From Lund, you may want to make a side trip to **Dalby Church,** (tel. 23-33-65), in Dalby, 8 miles east of Lund. This starkly beautiful stone built, and well-preserved 11th-century former bishop's church is the oldest in Scandinavia; be sure to visit its crypt. Open daily from 9am to 4pm. Several buses (no. 158 or 150) a day run between Lund center and Dalby.

About a 30-minute drive northeast of Lund (off Route 23) is the **Castle of Bosjökloster,** in Höör (tel. 0413/250-48), once a Benedictine convent founded around 1080. It was closed during the Reformation in the 16th century. The Great Courtyard is spectacular, with its thousands of flowers and exotic shrubs, terraces and a park with animals and birds. Indoors is the vaulted refectory and the Stone Hall where native arts and crafts, jewelry, and other Swedish goods are displayed. You can picnic on the grounds or enjoy a lunch at a simple restaurant in the garden, costing around 75 kronor ($13.50).

The park and gardens are open daily from 8am to 8pm; the restaurant and exhibition rooms are open May to October, daily from 9am to 6pm. Admission is 25 kronor ($4.50) for adults and 10 kronor ($1.80) for children. Don't miss the 1,000-year-old oak tree in the park. The castle lies 28 miles from Malmö and 18 miles from Lund. From Lund there is a rail link to Höör after that, take bus R02 to Bösjokloster lying on Route 23, 3 miles south of Höör.

---

5. YSTAD

34 miles E of Malmö, 28 miles W of Simrishamn

GETTING THERE By Train Monday through Friday, trains run roughly on the hour between Malmö and Ystad, taking 1 hour. On Saturday there are four daily trains, and on Sunday, six trains.

By Bus There are three daily buses Monday through Saturday from Malmö to Ystad taking 1 hour. On Saturday and Sunday, there is only one bus.

By Car From Malmö, take the E14 east.

ESSENTIALS The tourist bureau, **Ystads Turistbyrå,** S:t Knuts Torg, S-271 00 Ystad (tel. 0411/772-98), is located at the bus station in the same building as the art museum (Konstmuseum). It is open Mon–Fri 9am–7pm and Sat 9am–6pm (mid-June–mid-Aug) and Mon–Fri 9am–5pm (late Aug–early June). The **telephone area code** for Ystad is 0411.

Ystad makes a good base for exploring the castles and manors of Skåne. An important port during the Middle Ages, Ystad retains its ancient look, with about

300 half-timbered houses, mazes of narrow lanes—even a watchman who sounds the hours of the night in the tower of St. Mary's Church.

WHAT TO SEE & DO

For a glimpse of medieval Sweden, head for **Per Häisas Gård** in the town center, a courtyard encircled by brick-and-timbered houses.

Don't overlook **St. Mary's Church** at Stortorget, dating back to the early 1200s, noted for its white-and-gilt baroque interior. It's open mid-May to mid-September, daily from 9am to 6pm, charging no admission.

The **Town Hall**, also at Stortorget, was built on the site of a burned medieval municipal center. It still has the original vaulted cellar.

The **Museum of Modern Art** is on S:t Knuts Torg (tel. 77-285) in central Ystad, and includes a small military museum. Permanent exhibits feature mainly Scandian and Danish art from the last 100 years. The museum is open Monday through Friday from noon to 5pm and on Sunday from 1 to 5pm. In summer, it is also open on Saturday from 11am to 3pm. Admission is free. The Ystad Tourist Office is in the same building as the museum.

The **Charlotte Berlin Museum,** Dammgatan 23 (tel. 18-866), is right behind the Museum of Modern Art in central Ystad. The mid-19th-century house has been preserved in its original state and gives a good idea of late 19th-century bourgeois taste in interiors. Entrance is only 1 krona (20¢) for everybody. The museum is open only from June through August, daily from noon to 4pm.

The only museum in Sweden in a medieval monastic house is the **City Museum in the Grey Friars Monastery**, S:t Petr Kyrkoplan (tel. 77-286). Built in 1267, the building is a monument from the Danish era in the town of Ystad. Various antiquities in the museum trace the history of the area. The admission-free museum is open Monday through Friday from noon to 5pm and on Sunday from 1 to 5pm; in summer also on Saturday from 11am to 3pm.

NEARBY ATTRACTIONS

CHRISTINEHOF, Ystad-Kristianstad. Tel. 0417/261-10.

Built in the 18th century, this fully furnished château, northwest of Eljarod, is preserved essentially as it was when it was first built and features hunting museum exhibitions. The castle's sanctuary is full of wild boar and deer.

Admission: 20 kronor ($3.60) adults, 10 kronor ($1.80) children.

Open: May–June, Sat–Sun and holidays 11am–5pm; July to mid-Aug, Tues–Sun 11am–5pm; mid-Aug to Sept, Sat–Sun 11am–5pm. **Closed:** Oct–Apr.

BÄCKASKOG, Fjälkinge. Tel. 044/53-250.

Nine miles north of Kristianstad, this country palace of King Charles XV stands in a 40-acre park, managed by the Swedish Forest Service. The castle, a National Trust building, was originally a monastery founded in the early 13th century. The chapel dates from 1230 and the tower of the house of worship is from 1640. There's a lot to see at Bäckaskog, including a biblical garden, featuring trees, bushes, and herbs mentioned in the Bible or having some other religious connection. There is a restaurant, and some hotel rooms are available at the castle.

Exhibitions and sales of art and country furniture can be attended even when the castle is not open to visitors. Barn dances are held on Saturday during the summer. The palace can be reached by taxi from Kristianstad.

Admission: 20 kronor ($3.60) adults, 10 kronor ($1.80) children.

Open: Apr–Oct, daily 10am–5pm. **Closed:** Nov–Mar.

WHERE TO STAY

MODERATE

YSTADS SALTSJÖBAD, Saltsjöbadsvägen 6, S-271 39 Ystad. Tel.

0411/136-30. Fax 0411/118-35. 108 rms (all with bath), 1 suite. MINIBAR TV TEL
$ **Rates** (including breakfast): June 15–Aug 15 and Fri–Sat year-round, 550 kronor ($99) single; 785 kronor ($141.30) double. Sun–Thurs the rest of the year, 975 kronor ($175.50) single; 1,200 kronor ($216) double. AE, DC, MC, V. **Parking:** Free. **Closed:** Dec 23–Jan 6.

Beautifully located almost at the tip of Sweden near the sea, this hotel, opened in 1897, overlooks an expansive stretch of beach. The rooms are well furnished. The surrounding area offers excellent opportunities for sports and exercise, including tennis courts and an 18-hole golf course. The hotel also has an outdoor swimming pool with a water slide and a sauna. The hotel's Apotheket gourmet restaurant serves good international cuisine and features dancing several nights a week. There's a relaxing cocktail bar and two summer outdoor cafés.

INEXPENSIVE

HOTEL CONTINENTAL DU SUD, Hamngatan 13, S-271 22 Ystad. Tel. 0411/137-00. Fax 0411/125-70. 52 rms (all with bath). A/C MINIBAR TV TEL
$ **Rates** (including breakfast): June 21–Aug 4 and Fri–Sat all year, 525 kronor ($94.50) single; 650–850 kronor ($117–$153) double. Sun–Thurs the rest of the year, 625–975 kronor ($112.50–$175.50) single; 720–1,200 kronor ($129.60–$216) double. AE, DC, MC, V. **Parking:** Free.

In spite of modern appointments, this is one of Skåne's oldest hotels, dating from 1829. The hotel is attractively decorated. Bedrooms are furnished with tasteful Italian-inspired decor and a number of modern amenities. A restoration added a marble sheathing to the lobby and a glint of crystal chandeliers. The dining room is classically decorated, offering efficient and courteous service. The hotel owners take a personal interest in the welfare of their guests. It is located opposite the ferry terminal.

WHERE TO DINE

MODERATE

RÅDHUSKÄLLAREN YSTAD, Stortorget. Tel. 185-10.
Cuisine: SWEDISH. **Reservations:** Not required.
$ **Prices:** Appetizers 48–75 kronor ($8.60–$13.50); main dishes 90–165 kronor ($16.20–$29.70). AE, DC, MC, V.
Open: Mon–Sat 11:30am–11pm, Sun 1–10pm.

In a vaulted 16th-century stone cellar with small tables and a romantic candlelight atmosphere, this restaurant in the town center offers meals that include gratin of sole and beef filet stuffed with lobster. Lunch costs from 65 kronor ($11.70).

SANDSKOGENS VÄRDSHUS, Sandskogen. Tel. 147-60.
Cuisine: SWEDISH/HUNGARIAN. **Reservations:** Recommended.
$ **Prices:** Appetizers 42–68 kronor ($7.60–$12.20); main dishes 90–165 kronor ($16.20–$29.70). MC, V.
Open: Daily noon–10pm. **Closed:** Christmas–Mar.

A late 19th-century villa just outside Ystad a 5-minute ride east of the town center, this is a good place to get an excellent meal, and it's popular with local families. The service is polite, and English is spoken. A special Sunday lunch is offered for 150 kronor ($27), and a two-course lunch costs 140 kronor ($25.20).

---

6. SIMRISHAMN

391 miles S of Stockholm, 59 miles E of Malmö, 25 miles E of Ystad

GETTING THERE   By Train   Four trains a day (three on weekends) make the 45-minute trip between Malmö and Simrishamn.

By Bus   Nine buses a day arrive from Kristianstad (four a day on weekends), and 10

buses a day from Ystad (three on weekends). From Lund, there are eight daily buses. Tickets can be purchased on board the bus.

By Car From Ystad, take Route 10 northeast.

ESSENTIALS For information about hotels, boardinghouses, summer cottages, and apartments, check with the tourist bureau, **Simrishamns Kommun Turistbyrå,** Tullhusgatan 2, S-272 00 Simrishamn (tel. 0414/106-66). Hours are Mon–Fri 9am–4pm and Sat 9am–1pm (mid-June–mid-Aug) and Mon–Fri 10am–3pm and Sat 10am–noon (off-season). The **telephone area code** for Simrishamn is 0414.

One of the most idyllic towns along the Skåne coastline, Simrishamn features old half-timbered buildings, courtyards, and gardens. This seaport is the jumping-off point to the Danish island of Bornholm.

WHAT TO SEE & DO

Be sure to see the 12th-century, step-gabled **St. Nicholai Church** (open daily from 10am to 6pm), built of sandstone and containing a baroque altar. Ship models are suspended from the ceiling. A visit to the park, **Bergengrenska Trädgården,** off Stortorget, reveals one of the most charming aspects of the town.

NEARBY ATTRACTIONS

BACKAKRA, S-270 20 Loderup. Tel. 0411/260-10.

Located off the coastal road between Ystad and Simrishamn is the farm that Dag Hammarskjöld, the late United Nations secretary-general, purchased in 1957 and intended to make his home. Although he died in a plane crash before he could live there, the old farm has been restored according to his instructions. The rooms are filled with gifts to Mr. Hammarskjöld—everything from a Nepalese dagger to a lithograph by Picasso.

The site is 19 miles southwest of Simrishamn, and can be reached by the bus from Simrishamn marked Ystad. Likewise, a bus from Ystad, marked SIMRISHAMN, also goes by the site. Scheduling your return might be difficult because of infrequent service—check in advance.

Admission: 20 kronor ($3.60) adults, 10 kronor ($1.80) children.

Open: May 12–June 10 and Aug 20–Sept 16, Sat–Sun noon–5pm; June 11–Aug 19, daily noon–5pm. **Closed:** Sept 17–May 11.

GLIMMINGEHUS, Hammenhög. Tel. 320-39.

Located 6 miles southwest of Simrishamn, this bleak castle was built between 1499 and 1505. It is the best-preserved medieval keep in Scandinavia, but the somewhat Gothic, step-gabled building is unfurnished. Visitors can order snacks or afternoon tea at a café on the premises.

Admission: 15 kronor ($2.70) adults, 10 kronor ($1.80) children.

Open: Apr–Sept, Tues–Sun 9am–5pm. **Closed:** Oct–Mar.

KIVIK TOMB, Bredaror.

Discovered in 1748, this remarkable find is north of Simrishamn along the coast of Kivik. In a 1931 excavation, tomb furniture, bronze fragments, and some grave carvings were uncovered. Kivik has been recognized as one of the most amazing monuments of the Bronze Age. You can reach the site by car.

Admission: 5 kronor (90¢).

Open: May–Aug, daily 9am–5pm. **Closed:** Sept–Apr.

WHERE TO STAY & DINE

INEXPENSIVE

HOTEL KOCKSKA GÅRDEN, Storgatan 25, S-272 31 Simrishamn. Tel. 0414/117-55. Fax 0414/119-78. 18 rms (15 with bath). TV TEL

$ Rates (including breakfast): 460 kronor ($82.80) single without bath; 650 kronor ($117) single with bath; 560 kronor ($100.80) double without bath; 750 kronor ($135) double with bath. MC, V. **Parking:** Free.

Like an unspoiled black-and-white half-timbered coaching inn, this hotel is built around a large medieval courtyard in the town center. Its lounge combines the old and new, with a stone fireplace contrasting with balloon lamps. Bedrooms have been modernized, and the furnishings are up-to-date with tastefully coordinated colors. The only meal served is breakfast.

HOTEL SVEA, Strandvägen 3, S-270 00 Simrishamn. Tel. 0414/117-20. Fax 0414/14314. 61 rms (all with bath), 4 suites. TV TEL

$ Rates: Summer, 570 kronor ($102.60) single; 670 kronor ($120.60) double; from 790 kronor ($142.20) suite. Off-season, 820 kronor ($147.60) single; 900 kronor ($162) double; from 1,020 kronor ($183.60) suite. AE, DC, MC, V. **Parking:** Free.

Built in 1986, this waterfront hotel in the town center is the best in town. Many of its well-appointed and comfortably furnished bedrooms overlook the yacht harbor. Its lobby-level restaurant, the Svea, serves excellent food Monday through Saturday from 11am to 2pm and 3 to 10pm, and on Sunday from 11am to 5pm. Set with a view of the harbor, the restaurant makes a good luncheon stopover if you partake in the reasonably priced *dagens* menu, a one-course lunch for 65 kronor ($11.70).

GOTHENBURG

Called the gateway to northern Europe, Gothenburg (Göteborg in Swedish) is the country's chief port and second-largest city. Swedes say that Gothenburg is a friendlier town than Stockholm. Canals, parks, and flower gardens enhance its appeal.

The city has a large number of museums and the largest amusement park in northern Europe. It is a convenient center for excursions to the fishing villages and holiday resorts north of the city.

A walk down "The Avenue" is a Gothenburg tradition. This is Kungsportavenyn, called Avenyn (The Avenue) with its many outdoor cafés to watch the passing parade. Start at Parkgatan, at the foot of the Avenue. Gothenburg's pedestrian street is heated by underground pipes in the winter so that the snow melts quickly.

Gothenburg received its city charter from King Gustavus Adolphus II in 1621. The port contains a shipyard, Cityvarvet, and a manufacturer of platforms for oil rigs, Götaverken/Arendal. The city is also the home of the Volvo car manufacturer (the plant is about 15 minutes by car from the heart of the city), and of the Hasselblad space camera. Spanning the Göta River, Älvsborg Bridge (the longest suspension bridge in Sweden) is almost 3,000 feet long and built high enough to allow ocean liners to pass underneath.

SEEING GOTHENBURG

GETTING THERE

Gothenburg is one of the most easily reached ports in Scandinavia, with frequent flights from Copenhagen and Stockholm. It also maintains ferry links with Denmark and England. Train connections are good from all the major Swedish cities, including Helsingborg, Malmö, and Stockholm.

A SUGGESTED ITINERARY

Days 1 & 2: Gothenburg deserves at least this much of your attention, as it has a number of attractions and is, in summer at least, one of the most festive cities of Scandinavia.

Day 3: Take an excursion north to visit the sights and attractions at Kungälv and on the island of Marstrand.

WHAT'S SPECIAL ABOUT GOTHENBURG

Great Towns/Villages

☐ Gothenburg, the focal point of the west coast of Sweden, principal seaport of Scandinavia.

☐ Kungälv, a merchant town occupied since the 10th century, a fortress border town between Sweden and Norway.

☐ Marstrand, 16th-century herring center, now an island for summer fun.

Castles

☐ Bohus Fortress, at Kungälv, dating from the 14th century, which played a role in Nordic kingdom wars.

☐ Carlsten Fortress, built in 1658 by King Charles X Gustaf to protect the west-coast fleet, towers over the island of Marstrand.

Ace Attractions

☐ The Göteborg Maritime Center, with displays of ship models from Viking times to the present day; rich west-coast seafaring traditions live on here.

☐ Lisepark Park, the largest amusement park in Scandinavia and, in terms of visitors, the biggest tourist attraction of Sweden.

Special Events

☐ The international regatta days in July or August on the island of Marstrand.

1. ORIENTATION

ARRIVING

BY PLANE The premier airline of Scandinavia, **SAS** operates eight daily flights from Copenhagen to Gothenburg, most of them nonstop. Flights from the Danish capital are scheduled between 7:30am and 10:30pm. (Many Swedes living on the west coast of Sweden view Copenhagen as a more convenient airport for them than the one at Stockholm.) SAS also operates 10 to 15 daily flights between Stockholm and Gothenburg, departing from as early as 7:05am and continuing until early evening. There are no flights from Malmö to Gothenburg, although a Hovercraft crosses the sound from Malmö to Copenhagen where there are connecting flights to Gothenburg.

Arrivals are at **Landvetter Airport,** 16 miles east of Gothenburg. Airport buses run about every 20 minutes into the center. Catch the Flygbuss daily from 6am to 11:30pm; a one-way passage costs 50 kronor ($9). The bus takes 30 minutes to get to Drottningtorget.

BY TRAIN The Oslo-Copenhagen express train runs via Gothenburg and Helsingborg connecting two Scandinavian capitals. Trains run frequently on a north/south route between Gothenburg and Helsingborg/Malmö in the south. The most traveled rail route is between Gothenburg and Stockholm, with trains leaving hourly in both directions; trips take 4 hours 40 minutes.

Trains arrive at the **Central Station,** on one side of Drottningtorget. Inside the station is a currency-exchange bureau and an SJ office selling bus tickets for connections to the environs.

BY BUS Buses run from Gothenburg to Helsingborg/Malmö (and vice versa) on Friday and Sunday at the rate of two each day. Trip time from Gothenburg to

Helsingborg is 3½ hours; Gothenburg to Malmö, 4½ hours. On Friday, three daily buses connect Stockholm and Gothenburg, and two buses run on Sunday. Trip time is 7 to 8 hours. If you're going by public land transportation on other days of the week, including Saturday, take the train.

BY FERRY   **Stena Line** (tel. 42-09-40) has six crossings a day in summer from North Jutland. The ferries take about 3 hours to cross. For information about specific times of crossing (which vary seasonally), telephone 031/42-09-40. The vessels have excellent dining rooms.

In summer there is a daily ferry service between Harwich (England) and Gothenburg, taking 24 hours. During the rest of the year, service is curtailed to three times a week. From June to mid-August, there is also twice-weekly service from Newcastle upon Tyne (England) to Gothenburg, also taking 24 hours. This service is operated by **DFDS/Scandinavian Seaways** (tel. 031/675-06-00) for information. There is no railpass discount on the England-Sweden crossings.

BY CAR   From either Malmö or Helsingborg, the two major "gateways" to Sweden on the west coast, take the E6 north. Gothenburg is 173 miles north of Malmö and 141 miles north of Helsingborg. From Stockholm, take the E4 west to Jonköping and continue west the rest of the way via Borås to Gothenburg, a distance of 292 miles.

TOURIST INFORMATION

The **Gothenburg Tourist Office** is located at Kungsportsplatsen 2 (tel. 031/10-07-40). For tourist information, "What Is on Today," call **Miss Tourist** (tel. 031/11-74-50). At the tourist bureau, visitors to Gothenburg can apply to meet a local family ("of similar background and interests"). Sometimes it takes at least 2 days to arrange a visit, so make sure you'll be in Gothenburg that long. There is no charge for this service.

CITY LAYOUT

The layout of Gothenburg, with its network of streets separated by canals, is reminiscent of Amsterdam—not surprisingly, since it was designed by Dutch architects in the 17th century. And its wealth of parks and open spaces have given it a reputation as Sweden's greenest city.

Some of the old canals have now been filled in, but you can explore the major remaining waterway and the busy harbor—the most important in Sweden—by taking one of the city's famous Paddan sightseeing boats. *Paddan* is the Swedish word for "toad," and the allusion is to the squat shape of the boats which enables them to navigate under the many low bridges. A Paddan service takes you from the point of embarkation, Drottningtorget, near the main railroad station, direct to the Liseberg amusement park. The park is the most popular visitor attraction in the area, luring some three million visitors annually.

The best place to start sightseeing by foot is Kungsportsavenyn, called the **Avenyn,** a wide tree-lined boulevard with many sidewalk cafés. Avenyn leads to the **Götaplatsen,** a square whose centerpiece is a huge bronze fountain with a statue of the sea god Poseidon. The statue is by Carl Milles, and the square is the city's artistic and historical center.

The old and commercial section of the city lies on either side of the central canal. At the central canal is **Gustav Adolfs Torg,** dominated by a statue of Gustav himself. Facing the canal is the **Börshuset** (Stock Exchange building). On the western side is the **Rådhuset** (Town Hall), originally constructed in 1672. Around the corner, moving toward the river, the **Kronhuset,** off Kronhusgatan, is a 17th-century Dutch-designed building, the oldest in Gothenburg, from 1643.

Gothenburg is dominated by its **harbor,** which is best viewed from one of the Padden boats. The major attraction here is the **Maritime Center** (see below). The shipyards, whose spidery forms look like they were made from an erector set, are dominated by the IBM building and other industries. Part of the harbor is connected by an overhead walkway to the shopping mall of **Nordstan.**

2. GETTING AROUND

Visitors usually find that their exploration of Gothenburg becomes a lot cheaper if they buy a **Göteborgskortet** (Gothenburg Card). Available at hotels, newspaper kiosks, or at the city's tourist office, it provides free travel on local trams, buses, and ferryboats, free sightseeing tours, and either free or discounted admission to the city's major museums and sightseeing attractions, discounts at certain shops, and free parking in certain centrally located parking lots. It also allows one free taxi ride within Gothenburg's inner city, and a handful of extras which usually makes its purchase worthwhile. A ticket valid for 24 hours costs 100 kronor ($18) for adults, 50 kronor ($9) for children up to 18 years old; a ticket valid for 2 days costs 175 kronor ($31.50) for adults, 90 kronor ($16.20) for children; 3-day tickets cost 225 kronor ($40.50) for adults, 125 kronor ($22.50) for children.

For seniors, if you're planning to make excursions in the environs of Gothenburg, inquire at the Central Station before booking a train ticket. Sweden grants visitors 65 and older a 30% reduction on train tickets, good for both first- and second-class travel year-round, plus a further 30% reduction for travel other than on Friday and Sunday. This discount is good on all transportation operated by the Swedish State Railways.

BY PUBLIC TRANSPORTATION

BY TRAM A single tram ticket costs 13 kronor ($2.30); a 24-hour travel pass costs 30 kronor ($5.40). If you don't have an advance ticket, board the first car of the tram and buy one from the driver. One-way tram tickets are stamped by the driver who sells them to you. The second half of previously purchased round-trip tickets, however, must be stamped in the automatic machine as soon as one boards the tram.

BY TAXI Taxis are not as plentiful as you'd want them to be when you really need one. However, you can always find one by going to the Central Station. To call a taxi, dial 65-00-00. A taxi within the city limits now costs from 150 kronor to 170 kronor ($27 to $30.60). A 60 kronor ($10.80) reduction is a benefit of the Gothenburg Card.

BY CAR Because of parking problems, a car is not a practical means to tour Gothenburg. To compensate for its lack of parking, the city has good public transportation. A car is often needed to tour the environs, although there is public transportation to many sights. **Avis** (tel. 17-04-10) has a rental office at the Central Station and another at the airport (tel. 94-60-30). **Hertz** has an office at the center of town at Stampgatan 16 (tel. 94-62-10) and one at the airport (tel. 94-60-20). Compare rates and make sure you understand the insurance coverage before you sign the contact.

FAST GOTHENBURG

American Express This agency is represented by a private travel agency named **Ticket,** Öster Hamngatan 35 (tel. 13-70-12).

Area Code The telephone area code for Gothenburg is 031.

Bookstores The biggest and most central is **Akademi Bokhandeln,** Norra Hamngatan 32 (tel. 80-58-30).

Business Hours Shops are generally open Monday through Friday from 9am to 6pm, Saturday 9am to 1pm; **banks,** Monday through Friday from 9:30am to 3pm; **offices,** Monday through Friday from 9am to 5pm.

Currency Exchange Currency can be exchanged at **Forex,** in the Central Station (tel. 15-65-16). There is also a currency-exchange desk at Landvetter Airport, open daily from 8am to 8pm.

Dentists Call the referral agency **Akuttandkliniken** (tel. 80-31-40) daily from 8am to 9pm.

Doctors If it's not an emergency, your hotel can call a local doctor and arrange an appointment. If it is an emergency, go to **City Akuten,** Drottninggatan 45 (tel. 10-10-10).

Drugstores A 24-hour pharmacy is **Apoteket Vasen,** Götagatan 12, Nordstan (tel. 80-44-10).

Embassies and Consulates There is no U.S. consulate at Gothenburg; Americans must contact the embassy Stockholm, along with citizens of Australia, Ireland, and New Zealand. The **British Consulate** is at Norra Hamngatan 32 (tel. 80-07-78), and it's open Monday through Friday from 9:30am to 4pm.

Emergencies The number to call for nearly all emergencies (fire, police, medical) is **90-000.**

Eyeglasses Go to **Wasa Optik,** Vasaplatsen 7A (tel. 11-05-35).

Hairdressers and Barbers A good one is **Salong Noblesse,** Södra Larmgatan 6 (tel. 11-71-30).

Laundry and Dry Cleaning Laundries are hard to find. There's one at **Kärralund Camping,** Olbersgatan (tel. 25-27-61). For dry cleaning, go to **City Kem,** Drottninggatan 61 (tel. 11-22-22).

Libraries The main library is **Göteborgs Stadsbibliotek,** located at Götaplatsen (tel. 81-73-00), open Monday through Friday from 11am to 7pm and on Saturday and Sunday from 11am to 4pm.

Liquor Laws You must be 18 to drink. No alcohol can be served before noon (before 1pm on Sunday). Most pubs quit serving drinks at midnight, except special nightclubs with licenses to stay open until 2 or 3am. Liquor can be purchased at state-owned liquor shops, known as Systembolag.

Lost Property Go to the police station (see "Police," below).

Luggage Storage and Lockers It is possible to store luggage and rent lockers at the **Central Station** (tel. 80-50-00).

Photographic Needs An excellent store is **Arkadens Fotoshop** (Expert Photo Labs), Arkaden 9 (tel. 80-20-70).

Police The main police station is a **Polismyndigheten,** Skånegatan 5 (tel. 61-80-00).

Post Office The main post office is at **Posten Nordstan,** at the Nordstan Shopping Center (tel. 62-30-00), next to the railway station.

Radio and TV Gothenburg has Swedish-language TV broadcasts on TV1, TV2, TV3, and receives such foreign channels as Super Sky and BBC broadcasts from London. National radio stations include P1, P2, and P3; Radio Gothenburg broadcasts on 101.9 MHz (FM).

Religious Services The **Catholic church** is at Parkgatan 14 (tel. 11-92-65). The Swedish Reformed church has services at **Domkyrkan,** Kungsgatan. The **Gothenburg Synagogue** is at Östra Larmgatan 12 (tel. 88-12-15).

Shoe Repair Try **Service-Hörnan,** Postgatan 26-32 (tel. 15-58-08). Repairs are made while you wait.

Taxes Gothenburg imposes no special city taxes other than the value-added tax (MOMS), which is nationwide.

Taxis Call **Taxi Göteborg** at 65-00-00.

Telegrams, Telex, and Fax Go to **Telebutiken,** Hvitfeldtsplatsen 9 (tel. 90-200), open Monday through Friday from 9:30am to 6pm and Saturday from 10am to 2pm.

Transit Information For tram and bus information, call 80-12-35; for train information, call 75-75-75.

3. ACCOMMODATIONS

Reservations are important, but if you need a place to stay on the spur of the moment, you can try the **Gothenburg Tourist Office** at Kungsportsplatsen 2 (tel. 10-07-40), which lists the city's hotels and boardinghouses and reserves rooms in private homes. Reservations can be made in advance, by letter or phone. The tourist board charges a booking fee of 25 kronor ($4.50) in a hotel and 50 kronor ($9) in a private home. Single rooms in private homes start at 180 kronor ($32.40) and doubles begin at 260 kronor ($46.80). Breakfast is always extra.

The hotels listed as expensive actually become moderate in price on Friday and Saturday and during midsummer.

EXPENSIVE

SAS PARK AVENUE HOTEL, Kungsportsavenyn 36-38, S-400 16 Göteborg. Tel. 031/17-65-20, or toll free 800/221-2350 in the U.S. Fax 031/16-95-68. 320 rms (all with bath), 11 suites. MINIBAR TV TEL **Tram:** 1, 4, 5, 6. **Bus:** 40.

$ Rates (including breakfast): June 27–Aug 3 and Fri–Sat year-round, 710 kronor ($127.80) single; 850 kronor ($153) double. Sun–Thurs the rest of the year, 1,495 kronor ($269.10) single; 1,735 kronor ($312.30) double. Year-round, 2,500 kronor ($2,250) suite. AE, DC, MC, V. **Parking:** 125 kronor ($22.50).

Constructed in 1950 and renovated in 1985, this modern hotel, part of the prestigious SAS chain, stands on Gothenburg's major boulevard. Everyone from Henry Kissinger to the Beatles, from David Rockefeller to the Rolling Stones, has stayed here. The hotel has 10 floors, with attractively designed bedrooms. Those on the top enjoy excellent views of the city. Rooms contain a work desk, cable TV, hairdryer, and trouser press.

Dining/Entertainment: The Harlequin Restaurant and Music Bar has a charcoal grill, providing tender steaks, succulent grilled spareribs, giant hamburgers, and other fare such as fresh garden salads. The hotel's gourmet dining room, Belle Avenue, is one of the best known in Gothenburg, specializing in game or fresh fish from the Atlantic. The hotel's famous nightclub, Park Lane, is recommended separately (see "Evening Entertainment" in this chapter).

Services: SAS Airline check-in, "office-for-a-day," valet parking, house doctor, same-day laundry and dry cleaning, 24-hour room service.

Facilities: Garage, beauty salon, sauna, solarium, newsstand.

SHERATON GÖTEBORG HOTEL & TOWERS, Södra Hamngatan 59-65, S-401 24 Göteborg. Tel. 031/80-60-00, or toll free 800/325-3535 in the U.S. Fax 031/15-98-88. 300 rms (all with bath), 40 suites. A/C MINIBAR TV TEL **Tram:** 1, 2, 3, 4, 5, 6. **Bus:** 40.

$ Rates (including breakfast): June 27–Aug 16 and Fri–Sat year-round, 690 kronor ($124.20) single; 890 kronor ($160.20) double. Sun–Thurs the rest of the year, 1,360–1,590 kronor ($244.80–$286.20) single; 1,560–1,790 kronor ($280.80–$322.20) double. Year-round, from 2,500 kronor ($450) suite. DC, MC, V. **Parking:** 125 kronor ($22.50).

This unusual deluxe hotel was built around a large atrium, which seems like a tree-lined city square right inside the hotel. Opposite the rail station, it is one of the best-run and equipped hotels in Sweden. Rooms are large and luxuriously appointed (some suitable for the handicapped), and they're decorated in pastel shades. Opened in 1986, the hotel offers the finest bedrooms in town. Each room is stylishly decorated, with a high standard of comfort. The uppermost floor of the hotel is reserved for the Sheraton Towers, with the most exclusive accommodations. Guests who have stayed in the Royal Suite include everyone from Liza Minnelli to Michael Jackson, from Luciano Pavarotti to the royal family of Sweden.

Dining/Entertainment: In the atrium lobby are two restaurants: an international restaurant called Frascati, and a gourmet restaurant, Madeleine. There is also a piano bar and casino in the lobby. Finally, there's a nightclub, Mirage.

Services: 24-hour room service, laundry, babysitting.

Facilities: Health club, large swimming pool, Jacuzzi, saunas, solariums, indoor garage.

MODERATE

HOTEL EKOXEN, Norra Hamngatan 38, S-411 06 Göteborg. Tel. 031/ 80-50-80. Fax 031/15-33-70. 75 rms (all with bath). TV TEL **Tram:** 1, 4, 5, 6. **Bus:** 40.

$ Rates (including breakfast): June 29–Aug 5 and Fri–Sat year-round, 600 kronor ($108) single; 755 kronor ($135.90) double. Sun–Thurs the rest of the year, 1,195 kronor ($215.10) single or double. AE, DC, MC, V. **Parking:** 100 kronor ($18).

Ekoxen is an up-to-date and well-run hotel that often attracts business travelers, although summer visitors will gravitate to it as well. All rooms are individually designed and tastefully furnished. Amenities such as a trouser press are included. Most of the single bedrooms contain a studio-size bed. Included in the room price is a free sauna and Jacuzzi.

NOVOTEL GÖTEBORG, Klippan 1, S-414 51 Göteborg. Tel. 031/14-90-00, or toll free 800/221-4542 in the U.S. Fax 031/42-22-32. 150 rms (all with bath), 4 suites. A/C MINIBAR TV TEL **Tram:** 3. **Bus:** 91, 92. **Directions:** From Gothenburg, follow signs on the E3 to Frederikshavn, then the signs to Kiel; exit at Klippan, where signs direct you to the hotel.

$ Rates (including breakfast): June 19–Aug 9 and Fri–Sat year-round, 620 kronor ($111.60) single; 655 kronor ($117.90) double. Sun–Thurs the rest of the year, 955–990 kronor ($171.90–$178.20) single; 1,085–1,475 kronor ($171.90–$265.50) double. AE, DC, MC, V. **Parking:** Free.

This recently converted harborfront brewery 2½ miles west of the center is now a stylish hotel run by the French hotel conglomerate, Accor. Each plushly carpeted room has panoramic views of the industrial landscape. When it was completed in the 1980s, it was considered one of the most unusual restorations of a 19th-century building in Sweden. Within the hotel is a well-accessorized sauna. Laundry facilities are available. You can enjoy a drink at La Rochelle Bar, or order a full meal at Le Restaurant where the menu features both Gallic and Swedish specialties.

PANORAMA HOTEL, Eklandagatan 51-53, S-400 22 Göteborg. Tel. 031/81-08-80. Fax 031/81-42-37. 241 rms (all with bath), 2 suites. TV TEL **Tram:** 4, 5. **Bus:** 40, 51.

$ Rates (including breakfast): June 28–Aug 8 and Fri–Sat year-round, 480–580 kronor ($86.40–$104.40) single; 690–790 kronor ($124.20–$142.20) double. Sun–Thurs the rest of the year, 990–1,290 kronor ($178.20–$232.20) single; 1,240–1,390 kronor ($223.20–$250.20) double. Year-round, from 1,440 kronor ($259.20) suite. AE, DC, MC, V. **Parking:** Free. **Closed:** Dec 21–Jan 7.

Spacious and dramatic, the soaring tower of this hotel is a 10-minute walk from the center of town. It has a plant-filled lobby with a skylight, a piano bar, and a balcony-level restaurant. The bedrooms have stylish furnishings and soft lighting. On the premises is a whirlpool, along with a sauna and solarium.

INEXPENSIVE

HOTEL EGGERS, Drottningtorget, S-401 25 Göteborg. Tel. 031/80-60-70. Fax 031/15-42-43. 77 rms (all with bath), 2 suites. TV TEL **Tram:** 1, 2, 3, 4, 5, 6, 7, 8. **Bus:** 40.

$ Rates (including breakfast): June 15–Aug 15 and Fri–Sat all year, 390–490 kronor ($70.20–$88.20) single; 590–690 kronor ($106.20–$124.20) double; from

840 kronor ($151.20) suite. Sun–Thurs the rest of the year, 790–980 kronor ($142.20–$176.40) single; 910–1,090 kronor ($163.80–$196.20) double; from 1,295 kronor ($233.10) suite. AE, DC, MC, V. **Parking:** 70 kronor ($12.60).

⭐ The second-oldest hotel in Gothenburg was built in 1859, predating the Swedish use of the word to describe a building with rooms for travelers. Many emigrants to the New World spent their last night in the old country at the Hotel Eggers, and in World War II Germans and the Allies met here for secret negotiations. Today it is just as good or better than ever, with stained-glass windows, ornate staircases, and wood paneling. All rooms are individually furnished, and beautifully appointed, often with luxurious bathrooms. Room sizes vary. The gilt leather tapestry and polished mahogany evoke the 19th century in the hotel dining room.

HOTELL ROYAL, Drottninggatan 67, S-411 07 Göteborg. Tel. 031/80-61-00. Fax 031/15-62-46. 80 rms (all with bath), 1 suite. TV TEL **Tram:** 1, 2, 3, 4, 5, 6. **Bus:** 60.

$ **Rates** (including breakfast): June 15–Aug 15 and Fri–Sat year-round, 450–500 kronor ($81–$90) single; 600–750 kronor ($108–$135) double; from 1,050 kronor ($189) suite. Sun–Thurs the rest of the year, 650–800 kronor ($117–$144) single; 850–1,050 kronor ($153–$189) double; from 1,200 kronor ($216) suite. AE, DC, MC, V. **Parking:** 55 kronor ($9.90).

Founded in 1852, the oldest hotel in Gothenburg still in use, is next to the Sheraton Hotel about a quarter mile from the rail station (all major bus and tram lines pass by within a 2-block radius). It is decorated in a typical 19th-century style, with wrought-iron banisters and heavy cast-bronze lamps at the stairs. At the reception is a unique hand-painted glass ceiling. The hotel was carefully renovated in 1989. Rooms are individually designed and modernized. The breakfast buffet included in the price is generous. The hotel serves a light evening meal and sandwiches are always available.

RAMADA HOTELL, Gamla Tingstadsgatan 1, S-402 76 Göteborg. Tel. 031/22-24-20 or toll free 800/272-6232 in the U.S. Fax 031/51-21-00. 121 rms (all with bath). TEL **Bus:** 40, 45.

$ **Rates** (including breakfast): June 26–Aug 9 and Fri–Sat all year, 595 kronor ($107.10) single or double. Sun–Thurs the rest of the year, 840–1,025 kronor ($151.20–$184.50) single; 990–1,175 kronor ($178.20–$211.50) double. AE, DC, MC, V. **Parking:** Free.

This hotel, built in 1975, lies 2 miles from the ferry terminal and 17 miles from Landvetter Airport; it takes about 5 minutes by bus into the city center. This is a modern and well-run hotel, with large, tastefully decorated bedrooms in light pastels and many amenities. The lobby bar is a favorite meeting place, and the Restaurant Royal serves regional and continental specialties. Facilities include a swimming pool, hot sauna, and solarium.

4. DINING

VERY EXPENSIVE

RESTAURANG RÄKAN, Lorensbergsgatan 16. Tel. 16-98-39.
Cuisine: SEAFOOD. **Reservations:** Recommended. **Tram:** 1, 4, 5, 6. **Bus:** 40.

$ **Prices:** Appetizers 66–150 kronor ($11.90–$27); main dishes 225–410 kronor ($40.50–$73.80). AE, DC, MC, V.

One of the best seafood restaurants in Gothenburg, it naturally has a nautical decor with buoy lamps, wooden-plank tables typical of the Swedish west coast, and a shallow-bottomed re-creation of a Swedish lake. Your seafood platter will arrive on a battery-powered boat with you directing the controls. You can order various combinations of crayfish (in season), along with prawns, poached sole, mussels, lobster, oysters, filet of gray sole, and fresh crabs. A full wine list is available.

EXPENSIVE

THE PLACE, Archivgatan 7. Tel. 16-03-33.
   Cuisine: CONTINENTAL. **Reservations:** Required. **Tram:** 1, 4, 5, 6. **Bus:** 40.
$ **Prices:** Appetizers 85–175 kronor ($15.30–$31.50); main dishes 120–300 kronor ($21.60–$54); 3-course fixed-price menu 375 kronor ($67.50); 5-course fixed-price menu 595 kronor ($107.10). AE, DC, MC, V.
   Open: Dinner only, Mon–Sat 6pm–midnight. **Closed:** Dec 22–Jan 7.

This restaurant and brasserie is located outside the ground floor of a turn-of-the-century apartment building, dividing its floor space between a less formal bistro and a grand *luxe* gourmet restaurant. You enter a marble-floored reception area, then turn right for the bistro or go through glass doors to enter the restaurant. The restaurant is one of the most acclaimed in the city, although the bar is popular in its own right, as many people come here just to drink. Modern paintings decorate the walls. Food is likely to include such dishes as beef tartare à la Anton Wagner (with Russian caviar), smoked breast of pigeon with lukewarm salad and beetroot, suprême of chicken with goose liver wrapped in savoy cabbage and served with a lemon sauce, or warm fresh lobster with carrot tagliatelle and lobster sauce. Desserts are often spectacular, including fresh figs in baklava pastry with a cognac sauce.

RESTAURANT STALLGÅRDEN, Kyrkogatan 33. Tel. 13-03-16.
   Cuisine: SWEDISH. **Reservations:** Required. **Tram:** 1, 4, 5, 6. **Bus:** 40.
$ **Prices:** Appetizers 72–175 kronor ($13–$31.50); main dishes 152–235 kronor ($27.40–$42.30); 3-course lunch 185 kronor ($33.30). AE, DC, MC, V.
   Open: Mon–Fri 11:30am–10:30pm, Sat 1–10pm, Sun 1–9pm.
A table in this restaurant's enclosed courtyard is one of the most sought-after things in town. The black-and-white half-timbered walls were built in 1789 as a stable and dormitory, and the building has been declared a historic monument.

Enjoy an apéritif in the art deco–inspired cocktail lounge before dinner in one of the candlelit dining rooms. Dishes include curried lobster, veal steak, good terrines, baked hake, grilled scallops, lamb, broiled turbot with Norwegian lobster butter, saddle of reindeer with cloudberry-cream sauce, and a handful of vegetarian dishes.

SJÖMAGASINET, Klippans Kulturreservat. Tel. 24-65-10.
   Cuisine: SEAFOOD. **Reservations:** Required. **Tram:** 4. **Directions:** From the town center, head west on the E3, following signs to Frederikshavn and then to Kiel; exit at Klippan and then follow the signs for the Novotel.
$ **Prices:** Appetizers 72–175 kronor ($13–$31.50); main dishes 152–235 kronor ($27.40–$42.30). AE, DC, MC, V.
   Open: Lunch Mon–Fri 11:30am–2:30pm; dinner Mon–Fri 6–10:30pm, Sat 2–10:30pm, Sun 2–7pm.
By far the most interesting and intriguing restaurant in town, Sjömagasinet is located near the Novotel in the western suburb of Klippan, about 2½ miles from the center. You can have a drink in the cozy English colonial bar, or in the other bar in the eyrie, before dinner.

Very fresh seafood is served here: shrimp-stuffed crêpes with dill, shellfish with curry sauce, baked filet of beef and lobster, poached filets of sole with crayfish, and turbot béarnaise. Veal Oscar with asparagus, and deep-fried Camembert with cloudberry jam and a dessert soufflé flavored with Swedish punch are also available.

MODERATE

ATTA GLAS RESTAURANT, Göta Canal at Kungsportsbron. Tel. 13-60-15.
   Cuisine: SWEDISH. **Reservations:** Recommended. **Tram:** 1, 5, 6. **Bus:** 40, 60.

$ Prices: Appetizers 62–105 kronor ($11.20–$18.90); main dishes 65–182 kronor ($11.70–$32.80). AE, DC, MC, V.
Open: Mon–Thurs 11:30am–midnight, Fri–Sat 11:30am–1:30am, Sun 1–10pm.
This stationary old ship from the Sessan line serves good food with fast service in an elegant atmosphere. Each day fresh fish plates are offered, and the meat dishes, including the pepper steak, are also good. For an appetizer, you might try the fish soup or marinated salmon. Daily platters are offered, including, for example, filet of beef with a béarnaise sauce and potatoes. Fresh fish is always featured. The barge dates from 1937, but has spent most of its life wining and dining the residents of Gothenburg, as it never left the confines of the Göta Canal.

BRASSERIE LIPP, Kungsportsavenyn 8. Tel. 17-65-40.

Cuisine: SWEDISH/FRENCH. **Reservations:** Required. **Tram:** 1, 4, 5, 6. **Bus:** 40.
$ Prices: Appetizers 65–89 kronor ($11.70–$16); main dishes 98–198 kronor ($17.60–$35.60); daily platters 56 kronor ($10.10). AE, DC, MC, V.
Open: Lunch Mon–Sat 11:30am–2pm; dinner Mon–Sat 5–11pm.
On the main avenue of town, this brasserie is modeled after the legendary Left Bank bistro of Paris, with palate adjustments for Swedish tastes. Its food is a tantalizing combination of French and Swedish, as reflected by such dishes as escargots, sauerkraut or choucroute garnie (the most famous dish served at the Paris namesake), and pepper steak, along with many different kinds of fish, most of them caught in waters near Gothenburg. The salmon is delectable. The bar with a limited snack menu remains open until midnight on Monday, until 1am on Tuesday, and until 2am from Wednesday through Saturday.

LA GONDOLA, Kungsportsavenyn 4. Tel. 11-68-28.

Cuisine: ITALIAN. **Reservations:** Recommended. **Tram:** 1, 4, 5, 6. **Bus:** 38, 75.
$ Prices: Fixed-price menu 130 kronor ($23.40); appetizers 38–75 kronor ($6.80–$13.50); main dishes 65–189 kronor ($11.70–$34). AE, DC, MC, V.
Open: Mon–Thurs 4pm–midnight, Fri 4pm–1am, Sat noon–1am, Sun 1pm–midnight.
This restaurant evokes Venice with its striped poles, sidewalk awnings, and summer outdoor café. It does a lively pizza trade. The restaurant is said to have the best pizzas in town, costing from 60 kronor to 80 kronor ($10.80 to $14.40). It offers an elaborate menu as well, with many classic Italian dishes. The spaghetti Gondola is very good, and the saltimbocca ("jump in your mouth") alla romana is tasty. You might also try one of the grilled specialties, or fried scampi or plank steak. The minestrone is good and filling, and some velvet-smooth ice cream is served. There is a different lunch specialty every day, and an à la carte dinner is served daily.

LILLA LONDON, Avenyn/Vasagatan 41. Tel. 18-40-62.

Cuisine: SWEDISH/FRENCH. **Reservations:** Recommended. **Tram:** 1, 4, 5, 6. **Bus:** 40.
$ Prices: Appetizers 35–105 kronor ($6.30–$18.90); main dishes 95–220 kronor ($17.10–$39.60); daily lunch specials 55 kronor ($9.90). AE, DC, MC, V.
Open: Mon–Thurs 11:30am–1am, Fri–Sat 11:20am–2am, Sun 3pm–1am.
With a quiet publike atmosphere, the bar here is a local favorite. The restaurant, down a flight of steps, is dark and attractively designed, with illuminated paintings of clipper ships and nautical accents. Full meals might include grilled chicken with morels, beef and lamb filet in a mustard-flavored cream sauce, filet mignon, and broiled salmon with fresh asparagus. Light, less expensive meals are also available. The pub sells 10 different kinds of beer.

RESTAURANT TIDBLOMS, in the Hotel Tidbloms, Olskroksgatan 23. Tel. 19-20-70.

Cuisine: SWEDISH. **Reservations:** Recommended. **Tram:** 1, 4, 5, 6. **Bus:** 40.
$ Prices: Appetizers 52–65 kronor ($9.40–$11.70); main dishes 155–178 kronor ($27.90–$32); *dagens* menu 75 kronor ($13.50). AE, DC, MC, V.

Open: Lunch Mon–Fri 11am–2pm; dinner Mon–Fri 6–10pm, Sat 5–11:30pm. This restaurant will give you a taste of Sweden. The chef specializes in fresh fish and in season, game dishes. The reindeer steak here is excellent. The *dagens* menu comes with access to a particularly elaborate salad bar. The food is very fresh, tuned to the season and correctly assembled flavors. The decor is inspired by something you might find in southern Europe, vaguely Spanish or Italian.

VEGETARIAN

Inexpensive

SOLROSEN (Sunflower), Kapongargätan 4A. Tel. 11-66-97.
  Cuisine: VEGETARIAN. **Reservations:** Not required. **Tram:** 1, 3, 4.
  $ Prices: Soups 45 kronor ($8.10); main dishes 40–60 kronor ($7.20–$10.80). AE, DC, MC, V.
  Open: Mon–Sat 11am–11pm, Sun 2pm–6pm.
This is the best and most conscientious vegetarian restaurant in Gothenburg. Contained in the Haga district, in a low-rise neighborhood of 18th- and early 19th-century buildings, food is dispensed from a self-service counter, with an all-you-can eat salad bar free with any main dish. There's unlimited coffee and second helpings. Beer and wine are available.

LOCAL FAVORITE

Inexpensive

FROKEN OLSSONS CAFE, Östra Larmgatan 14. Tel. 13-81-93.
  Cuisine: SWEDISH. **Reservations:** Not required. **Tram:** 1, 4, 5, 6. **Bus:** 40.
  $ Prices: Coffee 18 kronor ($3.20); *dagens* menu 55 kronor ($9.90); hot pies with salad 54 kronor ($9.70); sandwiches 32–54 kronor ($5.80–$9.70). MC, V.
  Open: Mon 8am–7pm, Tues–Thurs 8am–10pm, Fri 8am–1am, Sat 10am–5pm and 9pm–4am.
Less than 2 blocks from the Avenyn, this traditional favorite with Gothenburgers is one of the preferred rendezvous spots of town. It is popular, crowded, and noisy at lunchtime. Even though it has a large interior, the scene overflows onto an outdoor terrace in summer. At night hot pies with a salad are featured, as is an array of baguette sandwiches containing such ingredients as shrimp or ham and cheese. They also serve a light beer, but no wine or liquor. Basically, it's light café dining, with homemade soups and such main courses as entrecôte.

A GAY RESTAURANT

Moderate

BACCHUS, Bellmansgatan 7-9. Tel. 13-20-43.
  Cuisine: SWEDISH/FRENCH. **Reservations:** Recommended. **Tram:** 1, 4, 5, 6. **Bus:** 40.
  $ Prices: 3-course dinner 190 kronor ($34.20); appetizers 45–58 kronor ($8.10–$10.40); main dishes 100–140 kronor ($18–$25.20); 2-course Sun special 110 kronor ($19.80). AE, DC, MC, V.
  Open: Fri–Mon 9pm–2am.
This, the leading gay bar, disco, and restaurant of Gothenburg, is in a building constructed some 120 years ago as a restaurant. The decor is pseudo-Italian with Mediterranean accents, and the disco and restaurant both share the street level. Specialties include smoked salmon with a mousseline sauce, coeur de filet provençal, giant shrimp, and a "melon surprise."

PICNIC FARE & WHERE TO EAT IT

Go to **Saluhallen,** Kungstorget, for the makings of an elegant picnic. Built in 1888, this is the colorful indoor market of Gothenburg. Shops sell meat, fruit, vegetables, and delicatessen products. Much of the food is already cooked and will be packaged for you to take out. The hall is open Monday through Thursday from 9am to 6pm, on Friday from 8am to 6pm, and on Saturday from 8am to 1pm. Take tram no. 1, 4, 5, or 6 to Kungsportsplatsen.

Take your picnic basket to any of Stockholm's major parks (see "Parks and Gardens" below). **Slottsskogen,** because of its size and secluded places, is the most ideal park for a picnic. It also has an outdoor café where you can purchase drinks and perhaps ice cream at the end of your picnic.

5. ATTRACTIONS

SUGGESTED ITINERARIES
IF YOU HAVE 1 DAY

Day 1: Have a cup of coffee at one of the cafés along the Avenyn in the center of Gothenburg; then take the classical *Padden* boat ride, traveling through the moat and canal out to the harbor and the giant docks. Return for a stroll along the Avenyn; then take one of the summertime vintage trams for a look at the part of the city ashore. Go to Liseberg amusement park in the evening.

IF YOU HAVE 2 DAYS

Day 1: See "If You Have 1 Day," above.

Day 2: Take a boat trip to Elfsborg Fortress, leaving from the Stenpiren in the Gothenburg harbor and continuing under the Älvsborg Bridge to Elfsborg. In the afternoon visit the Göteborgs Konstmuseum and the Botanical Gardens.

IF YOU HAVE 3 DAYS

Days 1 & 2: See "If You Have 2 Days," above.

Day 3: Get up early to take in the fish auction at the harbor (begins at 7am); then visit the Feskekörka (Fish Church) nearby. Take tram no. 6 to Guldhedens Vättentorn (water tower) for an overview of Gothenburg. Go to Götaplatsen to see the famed *Poseiden* fountain by Carl Milles. In the afternoon visit the Röhsska Museum of Arts and Crafts and stroll through the rose-filled Trädgårdsföreningen across from the Central Station.

IF YOU HAVE 5 DAYS

Days 1–3: See "If You Have 3 Days," above.

Day 4: Take an excursion to Marstrand and Kungälv, north of the city.

Day 5: Visit Nordstan, the biggest shopping center in Scandinavia. Spend the remaining part of the day exploring the southern archipelago, which you can do free with your Gothenburg Card (see "Getting Around" in this chapter). The MS *Styrsö* and the steamboat *Bohuslän* depart from Skeppsbron/Stenpiren on trips around the archipelago.

THE TOP ATTRACTIONS

For a quick orientation to Gothenburg, visit the **Guldhedens Vättentorn** (water tower), Syster Estrids Gata (tel. 82-00-09), 400 feet high. Take tram no. 9 from the center of the city, about a 10-minute ride. The elevator ride up the tower is free, and there's a cafeteria–snack bar on top. The tower is open Saturday through Thursday from noon to 8pm.

Early risers can take in the daily **fish auction** at the harbor, the largest fishing port in Scandinavia. The amusing auction begins at 7am sharp. You can also visit

Feskekörka (Fish Church), on Rosenlundsgatan, which is in the fish market. It's open Tuesday through Friday from 9am to 5pm and on Saturday from 9am to 1pm.

For a look at Gothenburg, the traditional starting point is the cultural center, **Götaplatsen,** with its **Poseidon Fountain,** the work of Carl Milles, Sweden's most important sculptor. The big triumvirate of buildings here is the **Concert Hall,** the municipally owned **theater,** and the **Göteborgs Konstmuseum.**

GÖTEBORGS KONSTMUSEUM, Götaplatsen. Tel. 61-29-77.

Götesborgs Konstmuseum is the leading art museum of Gothenburg, with a good collection of modern art, notably from French impressionists. Bonnard, Cézanne, van Gogh—even Picasso—are represented, along with sculptures by Milles and Rodin. The gallery is noted for its collection of the works of 19th- and 20th-century Scandinavian artists (Zorn and Larsson of Dalarna, Edvard Munch and Christian Krohg of Norway). Old masters are also represented, including Rembrandt and Rubens. The modern section includes work by Francis Bacon and Henry Moore.

Admission: 25 kronor ($4.50); children 16 or under free.

Open: Tues and Thurs–Fri 11am–6pm, Wed 11am–9pm, Sat–Sun 10am–5pm. **Tram:** 4, 5. **Bus:** 40.

RÖHSSKA MUSEUM OF ARTS AND CRAFTS, Vasagatan 37-39. Tel. 20-06-05.

This museum houses a large collection of European furnishings, china, glass, pottery, and Asian artifacts plus permanent and temporary exhibitions of modern handcraft and industrial design. Among the exhibits are books, silver, and Chinese and Japanese art. Lecture series and guided tours are part of the museum's program.

Admission: 25 kronor ($4.50); children under 16 free.

Open: May–Aug, Mon–Sat noon–4pm, Sun 11am–5pm; Sept–Apr, Tues and Thurs–Sat noon–4pm, Wed noon–4pm and 6–9pm, Sun 11am–5pm. **Tram:** 3, 4.

GÖTEBORG MARITIME CENTER, Lilla Bommen Quay. Tel. 10-10-35.

Located on the harbor, this museum is partly aboard the destroyer *Småland,* equipped with guns and torpedoes, and the *Fryken.* In authentic settings, you can see stockboats from the Stone Age, lightships, steamships, and tugboats, among other water craft. There are also opportunities to see Gothenburg either by one of the museum boats or by helicopter. There are cafés at the center and on the quay. Call for information on the boat or air trips and prices.

Admission: 35 kronor ($6.30) adults, 20 kronor ($3.60) children.

Open: Mar 31–June 28 and Aug 18–Nov 11, Sat–Sun 11am–5pm; June 29–Aug 17, daily 11am–5pm. **Closed:** Nov 12–Mar 30. **Tram:** 5 to Lilla Bommen.

MORE ATTRACTIONS

STADSBIBLIOTEK, Kungsportavenyn. Tel. 81-73-00.

Toward the end of the Avenyn is the public library, on the left at Götaplatsen. This is the main library of Gothenburg, the home of some 400,000 volumes in 40 languages—and a café. The library also contains a listening room with recorded music, as well as a reading room with more than 100 foreign daily newspapers. In one hall exhibitions continuously change.

Admission: Free.

Open: Mon–Thurs 11am–8pm, Fri 11am–6pm. **Tram:** 1, 4, 5, 6. **Bus:** 40.

LISEBERG PARK, Korsvägen. Tel. 40-01-00.

In terms of numbers of visitors, Liseberg Park is the number one tourist attraction in Sweden, and the largest amusement park in Scandinavia. For dining, nightlife, and entertainment in general, Gothenburgers head for this pleasure garden of fountains, pavilions, and flowers. The festively lit park comes alive with music, artists, dances, 21 rides, and open-air vaudeville shows on seven stages.

Admission: 40 kronor ($7.20) adults; children under 7 free.

Open: Mid-Apr to the end of Apr and Sept 1–23, Sat–Sun 10am–11pm; May–Aug, daily 10am–11pm. **Closed:** Late Sept to mid-Apr. **Tram:** 4, 5 from the city.

EAST INDIA HOUSE, Norra Hamngatan 12. Tel. 71-27-70.

This is a museum of archeology, ethnography, and history—all in the same house. In the archeological museum you'll find prehistoric artifacts excavated in western Sweden from the end of the Ice Age to the time of the Vikings. Walks to ancient sites in the region can be arranged every spring and autumn (tel. 61-25-80 for more information). In the ethnographical museum are collections from all over the world, with a particular emphasis on Latin America. Unique artifacts, including the more than 2,000-year-old Paracas textiles from Peru, are displayed. In the historical museum you'll find collections illustrating western Swedish culture and history.

Admission: 25 kronor ($4.50) adults; children 16 and under free.

Open: May–Aug, Mon–Sat noon–4pm, Sun 11am–5pm; Sept–Apr, Tues–Sat noon–4pm, Sun 11am–5pm (also Wed 6–9pm). **Tram:** 2, 3, 4, 7 to Lilla Torget.

COOL FOR KIDS

At **Liseberg amusement park** (see above), every day is children's day. The Liseberg Cirkus is a fun fair, and there are always comic characters to play with children. The pony merry-go-round, children's boats, and a fun-on-wheels merry-go-round are all free for tots.

Your children may like Scandinavia's most visited attraction so much they'll want to live there. That, too, is possible. From June 23 to August you can stay at the **Hotel Liseberg Heden** (tel. 031/20-02-80) at a special summer rate—a two-bedroom unit costs 285 kronor ($51.30) per person per night, including breakfast, admission to Liseberg for the whole family, and one ticket book (for the rides) per person. Call the hotel to work out arrangements for one of the family rooms.

Children delight in trips on the *Paddan* boats for a look at Gothenburg from the water (see "Organized Tours," below).

The **Natural History Museum,** Slottsskogen (tel. 14-56-09), contains stuffed animals from all over the world, including the only stuffed blue whale. Ecological displays are presented, along with an impressive collection of fauna from all over the world. In summer it is open daily, closing on Monday off-season. Weekday hours are from 9am to 4pm; on Saturday and Sunday, from 10am to 5pm. Admission is 25 kronor ($4.50) for adults; free for children 16 or under. Tram: 1, 2, 6. Bus: 51 to Linnéplatsen.

You can also visit a **Children's Zoo** at Slottsskogen from May to August (see "Parks and Gardens," below).

SPECIAL-INTEREST SIGHTSEEING

FOR THE ARCHITECTURE ENTHUSIAST

QUEEN CHRISTINA'S HUNTING LODGE, Ötterhallegatan 16. Tel. 13-34-26.

One of the oldest dwellings in Gothenburg, the hunting lodge was saved from demolition in 1971 by the Ötterhallen Historical Preservation Society and the Historical Museum. Today you can visit the 17th-century house for an inspection and enjoy coffee and waffles in its old-world atmosphere. Waffles cost from 22 kronor ($4).

Admission: Free.

Open: Daily 11am–4pm. **Tram:** 2, 3, 4, 7 to Lilla Torget.

PARKS & GARDENS

TRÄDGÅRDSFÖRENINGEN, Slussgatan, across from the Central Station.

On a fair day, another oasis in the city center is this park across the canal from the Central Station. In the center are a large rosarium containing some 10,000 roses of 4,000 different species and the Palm House, a large hothouse. Now and then there are various activities in the park, such as exhibitions, children's theater, and lunchtime music.

Admission: Park, free; Palm House, 10 kronor ($1.75) adults, 5 kronor (85¢) children.

Open: May–Aug, daily 7–7pm. **Closed:** Sept–Apr. **Tram:** 1, 4, 5, 6.

BOTANISKA TRÄDGÅRDEN, Carl Skottsbergsgata 22. Tel. 41-37-50.

In southern Gothenburg, the botanical garden, located opposite Slottsskogen Park, contains trees and shrubs from Asia, rock gardens, orchid plants, and greenhouses. The rhododendrons bloom in May and June.

Admission: Garden, free; greenhouses, 10 kronor ($1.80).

Open: Garden, daily 9am–sunset. Greenhouses, May–Aug, Mon–Fri 10am–6pm, Sat–Sun noon–6pm; Sept–Apr, Mon–Fri 10am–3pm, Sat–Sun noon–4pm. **Tram:** 1, 2, 7.

SLOTTSSKOGEN, near Linnéplatsen.

This is the largest park in Gothenburg, with some 274 acres. It was first laid out in 1874 in a naturally wooded area, and today contains beautiful walks, animal enclosures, a saltwater pool, bird ponds, and an aviary, as well as a children's zoo open May to August. A variety of events and entertainment is planned in the park in summer. There's an outdoor café at the zoo, plus restaurants at Villa Bel Park and Björngårdsvillan.

Admission: Free.

Open: Daily 24 hours. **Tram:** 1, 2 to Linnéplatsen.

ORGANIZED TOURS

A sightseeing boat trip along the canals and out into the harbor will show you the old parts of central Gothenburg from the canals, and take you under 20 bridges and out into the harbor. ❂ **Paddan Sightseeing Boats** (tel. 13-30-00) offer 55-minute tours May to September, daily from 10am to 4pm. They leave from the terminal at Kungsportsplatsen in the city center. Adults pay 55 kronor ($9.90); children 4 to 11, 37 kronor ($6.70); and families (two adults and two children), 155 kronor ($27.90).

The *Nya Elfsborg* is docked in the 17th-century fortress at the harbor's mouth. The boat takes you from Stenpiren on a 20-minute tour through the harbor to **Elfsborg Fortress.** The fortress was built in the 17th century to protect the Göta Älv estuary and the western entrance to Sweden during the 18th century. It still bears traces of hard-fought sea battles against the Danes. Carvings on the prison walls tell tales of threats and hopes of the 19th-century lifetime prisoners. A guide will be waiting for you at the cafeteria, museum, and souvenir shop. Departures are seven times a day from mid-May to the end of August. Adults pay 55 kronor ($9.90); children, 37 kronor ($6.70); and families, 155 kronor ($27.90). It is also possible to visit the fortress by public land transportation. Take tram no. 2, 3, 4 or 7, or bus no. 85 or 86 to Lilla Torget.

You can travel free in the southern archipelago with the Gothenburg Card (see Section 2, "Getting Around," in this chapter). MS *Styrsö* and the steamboat *Bohuslän* depart from Skeppsbron/Stenpiren on **trips around the Gothenburg archipelago** and Marstrand island. The MS *Poseidon* takes you for an evening cruise of the archipelago. For information about tours possible at the time of your visit, check with the tourist bureau (see Section 1, "Orientation," in this chapter) which provides excursion packages, brochures, tickets, and timetables.

If you'd like to participate in a guided **bus tour of Gothenburg,** go to the tourist office or call 10-07-40 for details. City tours are offered May to September daily, costing 70 kronor ($12.60) for adults and 35 kronor ($6.30) for children. Tours last 90 minutes.

6. SPECIAL/FREE EVENTS

Dates cited are subject to change from year to year. Check with the tourist board for exact dates.

Walpurgis Night, on April 30, is celebrated throughout Gothenburg, with bonfires, songs, and speeches in praise of the advent of spring.

The **Göteborg Music Festival,** June 24 to 30, is an international music festival for choirs, brass bands, big bands, and other groups. In one year alone, 30 brass bands, 10 choirs, and 10 big bands from eight nations participated. Much of the music is played on the streets and squares of the city. Exact locations are announced in the newspapers.

The **International Regatta Days** (check with the tourist office for annual dates) at Marstrand are the dream goal for the yachting set in July or August, depending on the year. Tall-masted yachts swarm the quayside and suntanned visitors stroll the waterfront, taking in all the nautical plush.

September is the time for the **International Consumer Goods Fairs** at Gothenburg, featuring "Household of Today" exhibits.

7. SAVVY SHOPPING

THE SHOPPING SCENE

Many Danes from Copenhagen to Helsingør come to Gothenburg just for the day to buy Swedish merchandise. You can too, but you should shop at stores bearing the yellow-and-blue TAX-FREE SHOPPING sign. These stores are scattered throughout Gothenburg. For purchases in one of these stores totaling more than 200 kronor ($36), you are entitled to a tax refund. You pay the tax along with the purchase price, but ask for a tax-refund voucher before leaving the shop. You will get the tax refunded, minus a small service charge, at your point of departure from the country when you clear Customs. You can't use such a purchase in Sweden, and it must be taken out of the country within 1 month of purchase.

MAJOR SHOPPING DISTRICTS   Nordstan, with its 150 shops and stores, restaurants, hotel, pâtisseries, coffee shops, banks, travel agencies, and the post office is the largest shopping mall in Scandinavia. Here you can find almost anything, ranging from exclusive clothing boutiques to outlets for the major confectionery chains to bookshops. There is also a tourist information center. Most shops here are open Monday through Friday from 9:30am to 7pm and on Saturday from 9:30am to 4pm.

Kungsgatan/Fredsgatan is Sweden's longest pedestrian mall, stretching 2 miles in length. The selection of shops is big and varied. Near these two streets you will also find a number of smaller shopping centers, including Arkaden, Citypassagen, and Kompassen.

At **Grönsakstorget/Kungstorget** little trolleys are put up daily with flowers, fruits, handcrafts, and jewelry, among other items. It's right in the city center, a throwback perhaps to the Middle Ages.

The often-mentioned **Avenyn,** with its many restaurants and cafés, also contain a number of stores selling merchandise of interest to the visitor.

Kronhusbodarna, Kronhusgatan, was originally a series of workshops of the Gothenburg Artillery. But now they contain shops in turn-of-the-century style, specializing in such crafts as goldsmithing, glassblowing, watchmaking, pottery making, and coppersmithing. It is open Monday through Friday from 11am to 4pm and on Saturday from 11am to 2pm. Tram: 1 or 7 to Brunnsparken.

SHOPPING A TO Z

DEPARTMENT STORES

BOHUSSLÖJDS, Kungsportsavenyn 25. Tel. 16-00-72.
This store has one of the best collections of Swedish handcrafts in Gothenburg. Amid a light-grained birchwood decor, you'll find wrought-iron chandeliers, carved wooden furniture, unusual wallpaper, fabric by the yard, and such other items as handwoven rugs, pine and birchwood bowls, and assorted knickknacks, ideal as gifts or souvenirs. Bus: 40.

C. J. JOSEPHSSONS GLAS & PORSLIN, Korsgatan 12 and Kyrkogatan 34. Tel. 17-56-15.

For Swedish glass, I recommend this store, which has been doing business since 1866 and has established an enviable reputation. The selection of Orrefors crystal and porcelain is stunning. Even more intriguing are the "ice blocks" of Vicke Lindstrand of Kosta Boda. The well-known designers Bertil Vallein and Goran Warff are represented with signed original pieces. There is a tourist tax-free shopping service plus full shipping service. The staff speaks English. Tram: 1, 2, 3, 4, 5, 7. Bus: 60.

NORDISKA KOMPANIET [NK], Östra Hamngatan 42. Tel. 17-33-00.

Most shoppers head first for this leading department store, recommended in Stockholm's "Savvy Shopping" in Chapter 25. The store's packing specialists take care to send your merchandise safely home. Typically Swedish and Scandinavian articles are offered—more than 200,000 items, ranging from Kosta "sculpture" crystal, Orrefors crystal in all types and shapes, Rorstrand high-fired earthenware and fine porcelain, stainless steel, pewter items, dolls in national costume, leather purses, Dalarna horses, Finnish carpeting, books about Sweden, Swedish records, and much, much more. Bus: 40.

HANDCRAFTS

Aside from some of the markets or streets already mentioned, the following establishments are centers for handcrafts as well:

KONSTHANTVERKSHUSET, Trädgårdsföreningen, Slussgatan 1. Tel. 15-13-80.

This handcrafts center is housed in the Botanical Garden's former seed store. It presents exhibition and sales of handcrafts from 40 different Swedish artists. It's open Tuesday through Friday from noon to 6pm and on Saturday and Sunday from 11am to 4pm. Tram: 1, 2, 3, 6, 7, 8 to Central Station.

LERVERK, Chalmersgatan 27. Tel. 18-22-66.

This is a permanent exhibition center for 30 potters and glass-making craftspeople. It is open Monday through Friday from 11am to 6pm, on Saturday from 11am to 4pm, and on Sunday from noon to 4pm. It is closed in July. Tram: 1, 4, 5, 6 to Valand.

8. EVENING ENTERTAINMENT

To the Gothenburger in summer, there is nothing more exciting than sitting out at a café along the Avenyn enjoying their short-lived summer. The townspeople are also fond of taking the whole family to the Liseberg amusement park (see "Attractions," above). Although clubs function in midsummer, they are not well patronized until cool weather sets in.

You must consult the newspapers or inquire at the tourist office for a listing of entertainment events staged at the time of your visit.

THE PERFORMING ARTS

THEATER

The Gothenburg Card (see "Getting Around" in this chapter) allows two tickets for the price of one. Call the theater in question or the tourist office for program information. Presentations are also announced in the newspapers.

FOLKTEATERN, Olof Palmes Plats, by Järntorget. Tel. 11-74-11.

This theater also stages productions of Swedish plays or foreign plays translated into Swedish. The season is from September to May, and performances are Tuesday through Friday at 7pm and on Saturday at 6pm. Tram: 1, 3, 4.

Tickets: 65–120 kronor ($11.70–$21.60).

STADSTEATERN, Götaplatsen. Tel. 81-99-60.

This is one of the major theaters of Gothenburg, but without exception the plays are performed in Swedish. Ibsen translated into Swedish might be a bit hard to take without a knowledge of the language, but a musical might be understandable. The season runs from September to May. Performances are usually Tuesday through Friday at 7pm, Saturday at 6pm, and Sunday at 3pm. Bus: 40.

Tickets: 115–130 kronor ($20.70–$23.40).

OPERA & BALLET

STORA TEATERN, Kungsparken. Tel. 13-13-00.

The opera season lasts from mid-August to June 1. If you're in Gothenburg during that period, by all means attend a performance at this 19th-century opera house where Eleonora Duse and Sarah Bernhardt appeared in front of the footlights. The theater presents not only operas, but operettas and ballets as well. Tram: 4, 5.

Tickets: 100–200 kronor ($18–$36).

CLASSICAL MUSIC

KONSERTHUSET, Götaplatsen. Tel. 16-70-00.

In the very center of Gothenburg, this is the major performance hall for classical music. In season, top world-class performers appear. The season is September to June. Bus: 40.

Tickets: 100–200 kronor ($18–$36), but could range lower or higher, depending on the performance.

THE CLUB & MUSIC SCENE

NIGHTCLUBS

GAMLE PORT, Östra Larmgatan 18. Tel. 11-07-02.

This restaurant, part of an evening entertainment complex, has a turn-of-the-century atmosphere. The oldest restaurant and nightclub in Gothenburg, this place is called a pleasure palace. One flight up is Gamle Port's nightclub, one of the leading ones in the city, and one flight below is an English pub you'd like to have a beer. And the three floors also contain a winter garden, piano bar, and casino. The restaurant is open daily from 11:30am to 11pm or midnight; dinners cost from 200 kronor ($36). The pub is open daily from 11am to 1am, and a beer will set you back 29 kronor ($5.20). The nightclub is open daily from 9pm to 3am; minimum age for entry is 23 for men, 21 for women. Bus: 40.

Admission: 80 kronor ($14.40) Sun–Thurs, 100 kronor ($18) Fri–Sat; free entry for anyone with the Gothenburg Card.

PARK LANE NIGHTCLUB, in the SAS Park Avenue Hotel, Kungs-portsavenyn 36-38. Tel. 17-65-20.

The leading nightclub along the west coast of Sweden, the dinner-dance room here has been known to feature international stars. In days gone by, they might have been Marlene Dietrich or Eartha Kitt or a name orchestra. The dance floor is usually well packed. The food—an international menu—consists of light supper platters. You can dine lightly, feeding on crab salad or toasted sandwiches. Beer costs 49 kronor ($8.80). The nightclub is open Tuesday through Saturday from 9pm to 2am. Tram 1, 4, 5, 6. Bus: 40.

Admission: 90 kronor ($16.20); hotel guests enter free.

MIRAGE NIGHTCLUB AND CASINO, in the Sheraton Göteborg Hotel & Towers, Södra Hamngatan 59-65. Tel. 15-88-65.

You can begin your evening early here in the Lobby Bar, which features piano entertainment every evening, before retiring to the casino to try your luck. At the adjoining Mirage, international flair and disco music are provided by the famous Juliana's of London. The nightclub has a professional sound-and-light installation, and has been known to hold as many as 250 patrons. It also offers a well-stocked record library, with a professional DJ. A beer will set you back 33 kronor ($5.90). The nightclub is open daily from 9pm to 2am. Tram: 1, 4, 5, 6. Bus: 40.

DANCE CLUBS

HEARTBREAK HOTEL, Östra Nordstan, Götagatan 14. Tel. 80-66-70.
This is a combination restaurant and disco, whose most vivacious night is Saturday. It's in a cellar in the middle of the shopping center a short walk from the Avenyn, and it turns to America for its decor inspiration. Minimum age is 20 for men or women. Meals start at 125 kronor ($22.50) and beer costs 29 to 48 kronor ($5.20 to $8.60). The disco is open Monday through Saturday from 9pm to 3am. Tram: 1, 4, 5, 6.

VALAND, Vasagatan 41. Tel. 18-30-93.
This combination restaurant and disco, one floor above street level in the center of town, is the biggest and most famous in Gothenburg. You enter to face a restaurant on your left and a large bar and dance floor on your right. There is also a small-stakes casino offering blackjack. Minimum age for entry is 25 for men, 22 for women. The restaurant is open Monday through Saturday from 7:30pm to 3am. For more memorable food, head for Lilla London, one floor below (see "Dining" in this chapter). Meals begin at 125 kronor ($22.50); a beer costs 47 kronor ($8.50). The disco, open daily from 7:30pm to 3am, becomes the most crowded after 9:30pm, the most fashionable after 11pm. Tram: 1, 4, 5, 6. Bus: 40.
    Admission: 80–100 kronor ($14.40–$18).

THE BAR SCENE

HUNTERS PUB, Östra Hamngatan 30-34. Tel. 15-00-45.
This time-tested pub and dance club opens onto Gustav Adolfs Torg in the center of the city. Music is featured in the evening, but most patrons come here just to drink; a beer costs 36 kronor ($6.50). Pizzas, costing 60 kronor to 80 kronor ($10.80 to $14.40), and some other Italian dishes are available. It's open daily from 11am to 2am. Tram: 1, 4, 5, 6. Bus: 40.

GAY GOTHENBURG

BACCHUS, Bellmansgatan 7-9. Tel. 13-20-43.
This is the leading gay bar and disco of Gothenburg, although it's also a restaurant (see "Dining," in this chapter). Technically, Swedes must have an annual membership card to patronize this establishment, but foreign visitors are allowed in for the price of the cover charge. The disco and restaurant both share the street level, and upstairs is a small room with an additional bar and a small-stakes casino and roulette table. The atmosphere is cruisy. Beer cost from 45 kronor ($8.10). It's open Friday through Monday from 9pm to 2am. Tram: 1, 4, 5, 6. Bus: 40.
    Admission: 80 kronor ($14.40) Fri–Sat and Mon, 25 kronor ($4.50) Sun.

9. NETWORKS & RESOURCES

FOR STUDENTS The **Kärralund Camping Site** is a great center for meeting and sharing a life with an international crowd of young people in summer. It's also a popular site with families.

Public showers are available at the **Nordstan Shopping Center** in Gothenburg, costing 15 kronor ($2.70), and luggage can be stored at the Central Station at the rate of 15 to 25 kronor ($2.70 to $4.50) per 24 hours.

Other centers for young people include a youth hostel, **Ostkupan (IYHF)** at Mejerigatan 2 (tel. 40-10-50), near Liseberg Park. Take tram no. 1, 3, or 6 to Redberg, then transfer by bus no. 62 to Gråddgatan. It is open June to August only.

FOR GAY MEN & LESBIANS The gay center in Gothenburg is **RFSL**, Esperantoplatsen 7 (tel. 11-61-51). The staff there will keep you informed of any gay-related activities happening in Gothenburg. They also operate the Hellman Café on the premises, which is open Monday, Tuesday, and Thursday from 7 to 11pm, Saturday from 11pm to 4am, and Sunday from 5 to 10pm. Also on the premises is Touch Restaurant, where dinners are served Wednesday, Friday, and Saturday from 9pm to 2am. Take tram no. 1, 3, or 4 to Järntorget.

The **Gay Radio Station** broadcasts locally on Sunday from 7:45 to 9pm and Monday from 7 to 7:30pm, but in Swedish only.

10. EASY EXCURSIONS

Several days could be spent exploring towns and fishing villages along the west coast north of Gothenburg, such as **Lysekil, Smögen,** and **Strömstad** near the Norwegian border. Bathers can lie on the rocks along this shore, lounging in the sun against a backdrop of yachts and fishing craft. There are several day-trips and evening cruises from Gothenburg to the archipelago. For tickets and information, consult the tourist office.

KUNGÄLV

If you're pressed for time, at least see Kungälv, 11 miles north of Gothenburg and reached by bus no. 301, 302, 303, or 330 from the Central Station. For information, contact **Kungälv Turistbyrå,** Fästningsholmen S-442 81 Kungälv (tel. 0303/120-35). The office is open in summer Monday through Saturday from 9am to 7pm and Sunday from noon to 4pm. Off-season hours are generally Monday through Friday from 9am to 4:30pm. Kungälv, known by the Vikings as Kongahälla, has 1,000-year-old traditions.

On the E6 highway lie the ruins of the 14th-century **Bohus Fortress,** Fästningsholmen (tel. 0303/156-62). This bastion played a leading role in the battles among Sweden, Norway, and Denmark to establish supremacy. Bohus Castle and Fortress (Bohus Fästning) was built by order of Norway's King Haakon V on Norwegian territory. It was later used as a prison, after it was ceded to Sweden in 1658. Climb the tower—"Father's Hat"—for a splendid view. Bohus is open May 1 to August 15, daily from 10am to 8pm, and August 16 to September 15, daily from noon to 6pm, charging 20 kronor ($3.60) for adults, 10 kronor ($1.80) for children 6 to 16. Take bus no. 301, 302, 303, or 330.

WHERE TO STAY & DINE
Inexpensive

HOTEL FARS HATT, Torget, S-442 00 Kungälv. Tel. 0303/109-70. Fax 0303/196-37. 130 rms (all with bath). MINIBAR TV TEL
$ Rates (including breakfast): June 28–Aug 15 and Fri–Sat year-round, 480 kronor ($86.40) single; 700 kronor ($126) double. Sun–Thurs the rest of the year, 890–920 kronor ($160.20–$165.60) single; 990–1,100 kronor ($178.20–$198) double. AE, DC, MC, V. **Parking:** Free.
Established in the 17th century in the town center, the site was used to refresh travelers with fish, game, and ale, and today the tradition continues. An outdoor swimming pool, lakeside pier, a sauna, a solarium, conference rooms, a nearby golf

course, jogging tracks, tennis courts, and airy dining rooms are some features. Bedrooms are well furnished, each modern and recently renovated, painted in pastels.

LÖKEBERGS KURSGÅRD PENSIONAT, Lökeberg, S-442 00 Kungälv. Tel. 030/271-90. Fax 0303/272-05. 102 rms (84 with bath). TV TEL **Bus:** 303, 312 from Kungälv.

$ Rates (including breakfast): June 15–Aug 25 and Fri–Sat year-round, 430 kronor ($77.40) single without bath, 500 kronor ($90) single with bath; 520 kronor ($93.60) double without bath, 680 kronor ($122.40) double with bath. Sun–Thurs the rest of the year, 470 kronor ($84.60) single without bath, 815 kronor ($146.70) single with bath; 615 kronor ($110.70) double without bath, 930 kronor ($167.40) double with bath. AE, DC, MC, V. **Parking:** Free.

Flat-roofed and modern, the cluster of buildings that make up this vacation hotel are on a meadow that slopes down to a lake 22 miles north of Gothenburg and 6 miles north of Kungälv. The public rooms are paneled with light-grained wood and on the premises is a modern restaurant, as well as a sauna. Each bedroom is furnished in a modern style and comfortably equipped. The decor is in light pastels or earth tones.

MARSTRAND

This once-royal resort, frequented by the former Swedish king, Oscar II, is on a secluded island. Its little shops, art galleries, and pleasant walks are reminiscent of Nantucket, Mass. Part of the fun of Marstrand is the trip to it.

To reach the island, motorists can head north along the E6 from Gothenburg exiting at the signs that indicate "Marstrand." These lead you to the village of Köön, where you'll park your car. From the wharf at Köön, ferryboats depart frequently for Marstrand. No cars are allowed either on the ferryboats or the island. Ferryboats depart at 20-minute intervals throughout the day over the short stretch of water.

A bus, the **Marstrand Express,** also departs from the Central Station in Gothenburg. The one-way fare is 55 kronor ($9.90). Departures are every 30 minutes in summer and every hour off-season. No reservations are necessary. The bus drops passengers off at the ferryboat landing at Tjuvkil.

Young people from Gothenburg and the surrounding district flock to Marstrand on weekends, filling up the clapboard-sided hotels. The resort, quiet all week, comes alive with the sounds of folksingers and the twang of guitars. But the big event on Marstrand's calendar is the **international regatta,** held annually—usually the first 2 weeks in July.

Don't miss the 17th-century **Carlsten Fortress,** S-440 30 Marstrand (tel. 0303/602-65), towering over the island. After a climb up the hill, pay a visit to the chapel, then walk through the secret tunnel to the fortress, charging an admission of 30 kronor ($5.40) for adults, 15 kronor ($2.70) for children. In 1658 King Charles X Gustaf arrived at Marstrand and decided that a fortress should be built to protect the Swedish west-coast fleet. The bastions around the lower castle courtyard were constructed from 1689 to 1705, and were completed during the first half of the 19th century.

WHERE TO STAY & DINE
Inexpensive

VILLA MARITIME, Hamngatan, S-440 30 Marstrand. Tel. 0303/610-25. Fax 0303/616-20. 70 apartments.

$ Rates: June 29–Aug 9, 865 kronor ($155.70) single; 965 kronor ($173.70) double. The rest of the year, 675 kronor ($121.50) single; 825 kronor ($148.50) double. MC, V.

Villa Maritime is next to the marina midway between the water and the stone fortress. Its red-tile roof, big windows, and glassed-in veranda are reminiscent of an updated Edwardian villa. The apartments, housing two, four, or six guests, are well furnished and color-coordinated, with sitting rooms, one or two bedrooms, and kitchens. Most of them also have private balconies. The villa has a gym, sauna, solarium, and laundry room. On the premises are a pleasant cocktail lounge and a dining room.

Youth Hostel

BÅTELLET, S-440 30 Marstrand. Tel. 0303/600-10. 20 4–5 bedded rms (no private baths).

$ Rates: 110 kronor ($19.80) per person. Breakfast 40 kronor ($7.20) extra. No credit cards.

This is a former bathing house in the town center that has been converted into a youth hostel with four to five beds per room. It attracts an international crowd. June through August are the busiest months. Breakfast is served only in season; at other times of the year, you can make your own in the communal kitchen. Guests make their own beds.

EVENING ENTERTAINMENT

OSKAR'S, Marstrand. Tel. 0303/615-54.

Set at street level in the town center, this is a combination restaurant and disco whose cozy interior is sheathed in wood. There's a large and convivial bar that is crowded in summer with gregarious Swedes. Music begins at 9:30pm for the dance floor. You can also order meals for 135 kronor ($24.30) and up, including sandwiches, pepper steak, veal steak, and hamburgers. Beer costs 46 kronor ($8.30). Oskar's is open daily from noon to 3am (closed September to April).

Admission: Disco, 80 kronor ($14.40).

TROLLHÄTTAN

Trollhättan is an important river town on the Göta Canal, with one of the largest power stations in Europe. The canal and lock area is an imposing sight set against a backdrop of rocks and islands. To see the river rush forth into the old riverbed is a dramatic experience you can enjoy at 2pm on Saturday and Sunday in May and June and on Wednesday and Sunday in July and August.

WHERE TO STAY & DINE

STRÖMBSBERGS TURISTSTATION, S-461 57 Trollhättan. Tel. 0520/129-60. Fax 0520/15600. 27 rms (all with bath), 19 dormitory beds. TV TEL

$ Rates: Hotel (including breakfast), midsummer and Fri–Sat year-round, 460 kronor ($82.80) single, 560 kronor ($100.80) double; Sun–Thurs in winter, 595 kronor ($107.10) single, 725 kronor ($130.50) double. Dormitory, 95 kronor ($17.10) per person members; 127 kronor ($22.90) nonmembers. Breakfast 50 kronor ($9) extra. AE, DC, MC, V. **Parking:** Free.

⑤ This establishment on a hill on the western bank of the Göta Canal, a 15-minute walk from the town's market square, has two different sections— the first with 19 beds divided among four dormitories, each room with hot and cold running water; showers are in the corridor. The dormitory is in the original wood-sided building from 1867. The modern annex, built in 1974 but renovated in 1990, lies a few steps away. Rooms here are modern and comfortably furnished. The hotel offers a small cafeteria and a restaurant all in one room. Lunches begin at 95 kronor ($17.10), with dinners priced at 130 kronor ($23.40).

CHAPTER 30

SWEDISH LAPLAND

Swedish Lapland—or Norrland, as the Swedes call it—is the last wilderness of Europe. This vast northern land of the Midnight Sun has crystal-blue lakes and majestic mountains, glaciers, water-falls, rushing rivers, and forests. Norrland covers roughly half of the area of Sweden, and one-quarter of the country lies north of the Arctic Circle.

The sun doesn't set for 6 weeks in June and July and the sky is illuminated with brilliant colors. In spring and autumn many visitors come here to see the northern lights.

Swedish Lapland is a paradise for hikers and campers—if you don't mind the mosquitoes in summer. You should get in touch with the **Svenska Turistföreningen (Swedish Touring Club)** before you go. This outfit maintains mountain hotels, and it has built bridges and marked hiking routes. It has even introduced regular boat services on some lakes.

There are hundreds of miles of marked hiking and skiing tracks. (March, April, and even May are recommended for skiing.) Some 90 mountain hotels or Lapp-type huts (called *fjällstugor* and *kåtor*) are offered, with beds and bedding, cooking utensils, and firewood. Huts can be used for 1 or 2 nights only. The club also sponsors mountain stations (*fjällstationer*).

You must be in good physical condition and have suitable equipment before setting out, as most of the area is uninhabited. Neophytes should join one of the hiking or conducted tours offered by the STF. For more details, contact the Swedish Touring Club, Drottninggatan 31-33, Box 25, S-101 20 Stockholm (tel. 08/790-31-00).

THE LAPPS (SAMI) IN SWEDEN The Lapps, or Sami, of whom 15,000 to 17,000 live in Sweden, have inhabited the country since ancient times. Some 2,500 still lead the nomadic life of their ancestors, herding reindeer in their multicolored costumes. The area of Lapp settlement (*Sapmi*) extends over the entire Scandinavian Arctic region and stretches along the mountain districts on both sides of the Swedish-Norwegian border down to the northernmost part of Dalarna.

Many Lapps maintain links to their ancient culture; others have completely assimilated.

The language of the Lapps belongs to the Finno-Ugric group. A large part of Lapp literature has been published in northern Sami, which is spoken by approximately 75% of Lapps. Like all arctic people, oral literature—not written—has played the most prominent role. Among Lapps, this oral tradition takes the form of *yoiking,* a sort of singing. Once governments tried to suppress this, but now yoiking is enjoying a renaissance. One of the classic works of Lapp literature is Johan Turi's *Tale of the Lapps,* first published in 1910.

Handcrafts play an important role in the Lapp economy. Several homecraft designers have developed new forms of decorative art, bringing about a revival in Lapp handcraft tradition.

Lapp is not a native term and is gradually being replaced by the indigenous

✓ WHAT'S SPECIAL ABOUT SWEDISH LAPLAND

Great Towns/Villages

☐ Kiruna, the most northerly town in Sweden, at the same latitude as central Greenland.

☐ Luleå, the gateway to Lapland, founded by Gustavus Adolphus in 1621.

☐ Kvikkjokk, one of the most beautiful resorts of Lapland, on the doorstep of the largest wilderness in Europe.

Ace Attractions

☐ The Midnight Sun, which can be viewed from many vantage points at midsummer.

☐ The Sami or Lapps, a mysterious arctic people with ancient traditions.

☐ The Kungsleden (Royal Trail), covering a distance of 210 miles—trail blazing through the last wilderness of Europe.

National Parks

☐ Sarek National Park, the largest wilderness area in Europe, filled with fascinating flora and fauna—for the adventurous only.

☐ Abisko National Park, called "ocean forest" by the Lapps, rich in flora, including orchids.

Museums

☐ Ajtte Museum at Jokkmokk, a rich repository of the culture of the Sami people.

Special Events/Festivals

☐ The great winter market of the Lapps at Jokkmokk, a tradition going back 400 years.

---

minority's own name for itself, *sábme,* or other dialect variations. Many members of the Sami community feel that the term "Lapp" has negative overtones. In English, a translation might be Saami or Sami. Sami seems to be the most favored English translation of Lapp, and the word is being introduced in English translations by local institutions and organizations.

SEEING SWEDISH LAPLAND

GETTING THERE

There are airports at Umeå, Luleå, Kiruna, and Gällivare. From Stockholm to Kiruna, flying time is 95 minutes, for example. You can take the train from Stockholm to Narvik in Norway, but before going to Norway, you can explore Swedish Lapland. There are three major rail junctions—Boden, Östersund, and Gällivare—from which rail traffic is funneled all over the rest of Lapland.

The express train *Nordpilen* takes 1 day and a night to travel from Stockholm to far north of the Arctic Circle. Once there you'll find mail-coach buses connecting the other villages and settlements.

A SUGGESTED ITINERARY

Day 1: Begin your exploration in the Luleå district.

Day 2: Transfer to Arvidsjaur for the night.

Day 3: Go to Jokkmokk for a day of exploration.

Day 4: Head west for an overnight stay at Kvikkjokk.

Day 5: Spend this day and night in the Gällivare region.

Day 6: Explore the district around Kiruna.

Day 7: Head for the wilderness, overnighting in either Abisko or Björkliden.

SOUTHERN LAPLAND

The best centers of southern Lapland are Luleå, Kittelfjall, and Tärnaby, previewed below. South of the Arctic Circle, Lapland is less forbidding. The mountains are easier to scale. If you hike to Rissjoen, you'll find one of the most attractive mountain lakes in Scandinavia.

1. LULEÅ

578 miles N of Stockholm, 213 miles SE of Kiruna

GETTING THERE By Plane There are 12 flights between Stockholm and Luleå each weekday (10 on Saturday and Sunday), taking 1 hour 15 minutes. There are 11 flights each weekday between Gothenburg and Luleå (7 on Saturday and Sunday), taking 2 hours 15 minutes. And 10 flights arrive weekdays from Malmö (6 on Saturday and Sunday) on the 3-hour trip.

By Train Six trains arrive daily on the 15-hour trip from Stockholm, 6 trains daily from Gothenburg, taking 19 hours, and 4 trains daily make the 22-hour run from Malmö. Trains from Stockholm to Kiruna deposit passengers bound for Luleå at the railway junction at Boden, 6 miles from Luleå. There they board one of three connecting trains a day going between Boden and Luleå. Train traffic from Gothenburg to Luleå also requires a transfer in Boden.

By Bus A bus runs between Stockholm and Luleå on Friday and Sunday, taking 14 hours. There is also bus service on Friday from Oslo, taking 17 hours.

By Car From Stockholm, take the E4 all the way. It's best to break up the trip with an overnight stopover.

ESSENTIALS For tourist information, go to the **Luleå Turistbyrå,** Rådstugatan 9 (tel. 0920/937-46). From mid-June through mid-August, hours are Monday through Friday from 9am to 4pm and Saturday from 9am to 1pm. Off-season hours are Monday through Friday from 10am to 3pm and Saturday from 10am to noon. The **telephone area code** for Luleå is 0920.

Often called the gateway to Lapland, Luleå is on the east coast of Sweden 70 miles south of the Arctic Circle. Founded by Gustavus Adolphus in 1621, this port city stands at the northern end of the Gulf of Bothnia. It is the biggest town in Norrbotten, and from its quay boats leave to visit some 300 offshore islets and skerries, known for their flora and fauna.

Luleå has a surprisingly mild climate—its average annual temperature is only 3° to 5° lower than Malmö's, on the southern tip of Sweden.

A port for shipping iron ore in summer, its harbor is frozen over until May. Fire has destroyed most of the Old Town. The location here of a state-owned ironworks has led to a dramatic growth in population.

The settlement has had an interesting history. Once it was ravaged by Russian Cossacks. Getting a city established this far north was laden with difficulties until development really took hold after 1940. Today, as the seat of the University of Luleå, the town has a population of 70,000 and is livelier when the students are there in winter, although most foreigners—other than businesspeople—see it only in summer.

WHAT TO SEE & DO

Gammelstad is 6 miles north of the city center. Gathered around its 15th-century church, the largest of its kind in Norrland, are 30 old houses and the largest "church village" in Sweden, consisting of more than 450 small church cottages. These cottages are still used today the way they used to be—that is, for overnight lodgings for faithful parishioners during important religious festivals.

Gammelstad Bay was part of a navigable channel into Luleå, but sailing ceased there when the city moved in 1649. Since then the bay has become shallow and is now a wetland area. In this area, just 3 miles north of the city center, ornithologists have counted 285 different species of birds during the spring migration. The area is classified as a nature reserve, but the public has access to it. Signposted tracks lead to the birdwatching tower and barbecue fireplaces.

The **Norrbottens Museum,** Storgatan 2 (tel. 203-55), close to the city center at Hermelin Park, presents a comprehensive look at Norrbotten's history over the centuries, showing how people lived in these northern regions in olden times. The museum possesses what is perhaps the most complete collection of Lapp artifacts. Admission is 20 kronor ($3.60) adults; free for children 16 or under. It is open Monday, Tuesday, Thursday, and Friday from 10am to 4pm; Wednesday from 10am to 8pm; and Saturday and Sunday from noon to 4pm. Bus: 1, 2, 4, 5, 8, 9.

WHERE TO STAY & DINE
MODERATE

SAS LULEÅ HOTEL, Storgatan 17, S-951 24 Luleå. Tel. 0920/940-00, or toll free 800/221-2350 in the U.S. Fax 0920/94-000. 198 rms (all with bath), 2 suites. TV TEL **Bus:** 1, 2, 4, 5, 8, 9.

$ Rates (including breakfast): Midsummer and Fri–Sat year-round, 490 kronor ($88.20) single; 690 kronor ($124.20) double. Sun–Thurs the rest of the year, 1,230 kronor ($221.40) single; 1,410 kronor ($253.80) double. Year-round, from 2,900 kronor ($522) suite. AE, DC, MC, V. **Parking:** 85 kronor ($15.30).

Redecorated in 1987, this hotel is located on the main street, less than 6 miles from the airport. Each bedroom contains a radio and trouser press, among other amenities; half of them offer minibars. The most expensive accommodations are in the Royal Club. For dining you can choose between the gourmet French restaurant Amphion, and the cozy Cook's Inn, with charcoal-grilled meat as a specialty. The Chapman Bar, connected to the Amphion, is a popular rendezvous spot, and the Cleo nightclub, open 4 nights a week, is known throughout northern Sweden. There is also a unique dining room called the Northbothnia Room, designed with a decor like that of a 19th-century coastal farm, with a rôtisserie and baker's oven built into the room. If you need to relax, there is the pool club, with an indoor swimming pool, gym, solarium, saunas, and billiards. Express laundry service is available.

STADSHOTELLET LULEÅ, Storgatan 15, S-951 31 Luleå. Tel. 0920/104-10. Fax 0920/670-92. 135 rms (all with bath), 3 suites. TV TEL **Bus:** 1, 2, 4, 5, 8, 9.

$ Rates (including breakfast): June 29–Aug 2 and Fri–Sat year-round, 790 kronor ($142.20) single; 990 kronor ($178.20) double. Sun–Thurs the rest of the year, 1,090–1,290 kronor ($196.20–$232.20) single; 1,490 kronor ($268.20) double. Year-round, 2,500 kronor ($450) suite. AE, DC, MC, V. **Parking:** 85 kronor ($15.30).

The oldest, grandest, and most traditional hotel in town is located in a stately and ornate brick-and-stone building in the center of town adjacent to the waterfront. Inside, the sedately modernized public area retains a few old-fashioned details from the original building. On the premises is a lounge with an open fireplace, a bar, and a restaurant. The bedrooms are comfortable and well furnished.

INEXPENSIVE

MAX HOTEL, Storgatan 59, S-951 31 Luleå. Tel. 0920/202-20. Fax 0920/947-90. 83 rms (all with bath). TV TEL **Bus:** 1, 2, 4, 5, 8, 9.

$ Rates: 775–975 kronor ($139.50–$175.50) single; 1,175 kronor ($211.50) double. Breakfast 20 kronor ($3.60) extra. AE, DC, MC, V. **Parking:** 45 kronor ($8.10).

If you're taking the bus from the airport, it will stop in front of the Max, on the main commercial street of town. Designed tastefully with clean lines and Nordic furniture, the hotel offers comfortable bedrooms. Free coffee, tea, and hot chocolate are offered day and night in the lobby. There's an in-house sauna and a very pleasant bistro.

2. TÄRNABY & HEMAVAN

223 miles NE of Umea, 273 miles N of Östersund, 626 miles N of Stockholm

GETTING THERE By Plane There is no airport. The nearest airport is at Umeå, in the east. Bus connections are possible from Umeå to Tärnaby.

By Train Two trains depart daily from Stockholm to the far northern rail junction of Storuman. Trains from Gothenburg headed for Storuman also are routed through Stockholm. From Storuman, it is necessary to go the rest of the way by bus.

By Bus From the rail junction at Storuman, there are three or four buses a day making the 78-mile run to Tärnaby. From the airport at Umeå, there are three or four buses a day going to Tärnaby, but it takes 5 hours.

By Car Take the E4 north to Stockholm, transferring onto Route E75 at the junction to Östersund. From there, take Route 88 north to Storuman, then head northwest on the E37 to Tärnaby.

ESSENTIALS For information, **Turistinformation,** in the town center (tel. 0954/104-50), is open Mon–Fri 9am–4pm and Sat 9am–1pm (mid-June–mid-Aug) and Mon–Fri 10am–3pm (off-season). The **telephone area code** for Tärnaby is 0954.

Tärnaby is considered the center of Sweden's most accessible alpine region, offering beautiful mountains and a chain of lakes. Hikers can strike out for Artfjället, Norra Storfjället, Mortsfjället, and Atoklinton, perhaps with hired guides. And Laxfjället, with its fine ski hills and gentle slopes, is nearby on the Blå Vägen (European Road 79).

Hemavan is the largest tourist resort in the area. Many paths lead toward Norra Storfjället. A delta formed by the River Ume is particularly rich in birdlife.

The greatest trail is the **Kungsleden** (Royal Trail), running from Hemavan to Abisko for a distance of 210 miles. This is considered one of the most fascinating trails in Europe. For more information, see "Abisko," in this chapter.

WHERE TO STAY & DINE

INEXPENSIVE

LAISALIDENS FJÄLLHOTELL, S-920 64 Tärnaby. Tel. 0954/210-63. Fax 0954/211-63. 18 rms (16 with bath). TV TEL **Bus:** Blåvägen bus from Umeå.
$ Rates (including half board): July 15–Aug 15, 590 kronor ($106.20) per person. MC, V. **Parking:** Free.

With windows opening onto views of the lakes, this traditionally decorated mountain hotel offers pleasant but undistinguished rooms that are kept immaculate. The hotel will arrange fishing trips as well as motorboat excursions to the nearby lakes. Built in 1953, the hotel was renovated in 1992. It lies 12½ miles west of Tärnaby, gloriously isolated. Individual clients are accepted only during their month-long opening in summer; the rest of the year, they are open only by prior arrangement to groups.

TÄRNABY FJÄLLHOTELL, Östra Strandvägen 16, S-920 64 Tärnaby. Tel. 0954/104-20. Fax 0954/106-27. 36 rms (all with bath). TEL **Bus:** Blåvägen bus from Umeå.
$ Rates (including breakfast): Summer, 520 kronor ($93.60) single; 625 kronor ($112.50) double. Off-season, 620 kronor ($111.60) single; 840 kronor ($151.20) double. AE, DC, MC, V. **Parking:** Free.

This is the larger of the two hotels in the town center. Its rooms are comfortably furnished and well maintained. The hotel offers a sauna, table tennis, a ski room, a "drying off" room, and several lounges. In addition to the regular bedrooms, the hotel rents 30 apartments, each with private bath, TV, and phone. However, these apartments—suitable for six to eight people—rent by the week, costing 4,500 to 6,800 kronor ($810 to $1,224).

3. AMMARNÄS

590 miles N of Stockholm

GETTING THERE   By Train   Take the train from Stockholm to Östersund, where you must change trains for a continuation of the northern route to Sorsele. From there, it's necessary to go to Ammarnäs by bus.

By Bus   From the south of Sweden, beginning at Stockholm, you should use the train as far as it runs. At Sorsele, buses meet arriving trains, and it's only a short run to Ammarnäs, depending on weather conditions.

By Car   Take the E4 north from Stockholm all the way to Umeå, where you connect with Route 363 heading toward the Norwegian frontier and going via Sorsele to Ammarnäs.

ESSENTIALS   The **telephone area code** for Ammarnäs is 0952.

A holiday paradise, Ammarnäs is in the Swedish highlands in the center of one of Europe's largest nature reserves, the Vindel Mountains. Leisure activities abound—you can fish, ski, or hike, depending on the time of year. The area is rich in varieties of birdlife.

WHAT TO SEE & DO

Local craftspeople specialize in the traditional handcrafts of the Sami, a seminomadic tribe of reindeer herders. If you visit here at the summer solstice, around June 21, you can take part in the **Sami Festival.** The best time to be here for an unforgettable experience, however, is in September, when you can watch the yearly **reindeer roundup.**

Don't miss seeing the **Potato Hill.** It's one of nature's mysteries—a place where tasty Mandel potatoes grow in abundance, often defying the laws of nature.

Ammarnäs has air taxis in summer and snow-scooter taxis in winter, to take you to the mountain and rivers. The village has such facilities as a filling station, post office, library, church, and store, and a skiing and leisure center at **Näsberget** (Näs mountain) nearby. Slalom skiing, ski lifts, and ski schools are all provided.

The famous **Kungsleden** (Royal Trail) hiking trail goes near here, leading down to Hemavan, visited above.

WHERE TO STAY & DINE

INEXPENSIVE

AMMARNÄSGÅRDEN HOTEL, S-902 75 Ammarnäs. Tel. 0952/600-03.
30 rms (none with bath).

$ Rates (including breakfast): 485–535 kronor ($87.30–$96.30) single; 720 kronor ($129.60) double. Full board 495–585 kronor ($89.10–$105.30) extra per person per day. No credit cards. **Closed:** Nov–late Dec.

In the licensed restaurant, you can sample freshly caught fish or reindeer. Once or twice a week there are dances in the Gobbakallar, a disco. A swimming pool, with a children's pool, and two saunas are on the premises. Rooms are furnished in a basic Swedish mountain-chalet style.

NORTHERN LAPLAND

This is true Lapp country, and if you have a limited amount of time, you will want to explore it instead of the southern sector. A wide range of centers, from Lapp settlements to mining towns to lakeside Arctic Circle resorts, are previewed below.

---

4. JOKKMOKK
740 miles N of Stockholm, 38 miles S of Gällivare

GETTING THERE   By Plane   The nearest airport is in Luleå, 123 miles away. From there you must take a bus.

By Train   There is one daily train from Stockholm to Jokkmokk, requiring a change of trains at Östersund.

By Bus   There is a single bus, which is deliberately timed to meet the plane's arrival, running daily from Luleå to Jokkmokk.

By Car   The E4 runs all the way from Stockholm north to Luleå, from which Route 97 then heads northwest to Jokkmokk.

ESSENTIALS   For information, the **Jokkmokk Turistbyrå,** at Porjusvägen 4 (tel. 0971/121-40), is open Mon–Fri 9am–4pm and Sat 9am–1pm (mid-June–mid-Aug) and Mon–Fri 10am–3pm (off-season). The **telephone area code** for Jokkmokk is 0971.

This community on the Luleå River, just north of the Arctic Circle, has been a Lapp trading and cultural center since the 17th century. With its population of 3,400 hearty souls, Jokkmokk (which means "bend in the river") is the largest population center in the *kommun.* Bus routes link Jokkmokk with the other villages in the area.

WHAT TO SEE & DO

The Lapps have an   ✪ **annual market** here in early February, when they sell their local handcrafts. Called the Great Winter Market, it's a tradition dating back 400 years. It is held on the first Thursday, Friday, and Saturday of each February, attracting some 30,000 buyers to the area. Actually people come to the market not so much to buy and sell, but more for the special experience of the place. If you're planning a subzero visit, you'll need to make hotel reservations a year in advance.

Salmon fishing is possible in the town's central lake, and locals jump in the river in summer to take a dip, but I suggest that you watch from the sidelines because of the temperature of the water. Jokkmokk is one of the coldest places in Sweden in winter, with temperatures plunging below −30°F for days at a time.

At the command of King Karl IX, the winter meeting place of the Jokkmokk Sami was chosen as the site of a market and church. The first church was built in 1607. Known as the **Lapp Church,** it was forced because of cold weather to have corpses interred in wall vaults until the spring thaw came and burial in the ground was possible.

You can visit a hill known as **Storknabben,** which has a café from which, given clear weather, the Midnight Sun is visible for around 20 days at midsummer.

Jokkmokk is the center of Sami culture in the area. Visit the local museum, ✪ **Ajtte Museum,** Kyrkogatan (tel. 170-70), in the center of town on the main street. This museum is the headquarters of Sami culture, and the many artifacts illustrate the lives of these once-nomadic people. It is one of the biggest museums of its type in the world, and wealthy in ethnographical detail. Entrance is 20 kronor ($3.60) adults; free for children 16 and under. The museum is open in summer Monday through Friday from 9am to 4pm, Saturday and Sunday noon to 4pm.

WHERE TO STAY & DINE
BUDGET

HOTELL GÄSTIS, Harrevägen 1, S-960 Jokkmokk. Tel. 0971/100-12. 20 rms (all with bath). TV TEL

$ Rates (including breakfast): 550 kronor ($99) single; 650 kronor ($117) double. AE, DC, MC, V. **Parking:** Free.

Dating from 1932, this hotel in the exact center of the town, about 200 yards from the rail station, is a landmark in the area. In some respects it has the qualities of a frontier-country hotel. Despite that, its restaurant has won many awards and offers well-prepared dishes, including what the Swedes call *husmanskost* (good home cooking), as well as continental dishes. In addition to this distinguished main restaurant, winner of several gastronomic awards, there is also a pizzeria and pub, Åkkjan. Entertainment and dancing are presented once a week. Run by the Åkerlund family, the hotel offers well-maintained bedrooms with modern furnishings. The sauna is free.

---

5. KVIKKJOKK

689 miles N of Stockholm, 60 miles W of Gällivare, 107 miles W of Luleå

GETTING THERE By Train Take the train to Jokkmokk (see Section 4, above), from which you must change to a bus to Kvikkjokk.

By Bus There are two buses a day running between Jokkmokk and Kvikkjokk, a distance of 74 miles. Unfortunately, the buses do not always connect with train arrivals from Stockholm.

By Car Take the E4 north from Stockholm to Luleå, then head northwest along Route 97 via Boden to Jokkmokk. From there, take Route 805 to the end of the line.

ESSENTIALS The **telephone area code** for Kvikkjokk is 0971.

One of the most beautiful resorts of Lapland, this mountain village is the gateway to **Sarek National Park,** the largest wilderness area in Europe, and one of the most representative of the highland regions. It's virtually inaccessible, almost entirely without tracks, huts, or bridges. Nevertheless, the most adventurous tackle it, as it contains fascinating flora and fauna.

The national park, between the Stora and Lilla Luleälv, covers a distance of 750 square miles. It contains some 100 glaciers along with 87 peaks rising more than 5,900 feet. Eight peaks tower more than 6,500 feet. The most visited valley, ✪ **Rapadel,** opens onto Lake Laidaure. In winter sled dogs pull people through this valley. The park contains remains of silver mines dating from the 17th century.

Sweden established this nature reserve in the wilderness in 1909 so that it could be preserved for future generations. Of course, to take a mountain walk through the entire park would take at least a week, and most visitors settle for a visit of only a day or two. The park should only be explored if accompanied by an experienced guide. Hotels in the area will put interested parties in touch with these guides.

Kvikkjokk, at the end of Route 805, is the starting or finishing point for many hikers using the **Kungsleden** (Royal Trail), already mentioned. One-day or 2-day outings can be made in various directions, as can an interesting boat trip accompanied by a local guide (inquire at the hotel recommended below). The boat explores a fascinating delta where the Tarra River and Karnajokk River meet. The area is also good for canoeing.

Kvikkjokk was a silver-ore center in the 17th century, and there are many historical relics from that period to be seen in the area today.

WHERE TO STAY
BUDGET

KVIKKJOKK FJÄLLSTATION, S-962 02 Kvikkjokk. Tel. 0971/210-22.
18 units (none with bath).
$ Rates: 400–500 kronor ($72–$90) double; 160 kronor ($28.80) per person triple or quad. Breakfast 55 kronor ($9.90) extra. No credit cards. **Parking:** Free.
Closed: Sept 14–June 12.

Run by the Swedish Touring Club, this mountain chalet offers views over the rivers, lakes, and peaks of Sarek National Park. Fishing and hiking trails fan out in all directions. Canoes can be rented, and a guide conducts half-day hikes. Furnishings are traditional—in all, a no-nonsense atmosphere. The establishment rents eight double rooms, eight single-bedded rooms, and two cabins, each containing four beds. On the premises is a sauna.

---

6. KIRUNA

818 miles N of Stockholm, 78 miles N of Gällivare

GETTING THERE By Plane Flights, which take 95 minutes, arrive from Stockholm daily.

By Train Two daily trains run between Gällivare (one of the major rail junctions from Stockholm) and Kiruna, taking 1½ hours. Two to three trains a day make the 16-hour trip from Stockholm to Gällivare.

By Bus There is daily bus service between Kiruna and Gällivare.

By Car Take the E4 north from Stockholm to the junction of Route 98, at which point you head northwest to Kiruna.

ESSENTIALS For information, the **Kiruna Turistbyrå,** Hjalmar Lundbomsvägen 42 (tel. 0980/188-80), is open Mon–Fri 9am–8pm and Sat and Sun 10am–6pm (mid-June–mid-Aug) and Mon–Fri 10am–4pm (off-season). The **telephone area code** for Kiruna is 0980.

Covering more than 3,000 square miles, Kiruna is the largest (in terms of geography) city in the world. This town has such extensive boundaries that it incorporates both Kebnekaise Mountain and Lake Torneträsk within its borders.

The most northerly town in Sweden, Kiruna lies at about the same latitude as Greenland. The Midnight Sun can be viewed from mid-May to mid-July.

WHAT TO SEE & DO

Kebnekaise Mountain, 50 miles away from the commercial center of town, rises 6,965 feet above sea level, the highest mountain in Sweden. Take a bus to **Aroksjokk** village, where you can get a motorboat to the Lapp village of **Nikkaluokta.** From here, it's 13 miles by foot, including a short boat trip, to Kebnekaise, where Lapp families can put you up overnight and arrange hikes or boating trips for you. The Swedish Touring Club has a mountain station at Kebnekaise, and the station guide there arranges mountaineering parties to the summit. It takes about 4 hours to reach the peak.

The town, which developed at the turn of the century, owes its location to the nearby deposits of the iron ore. **Guided tours of the mines** are offered in summer for 65 kronor ($11.70). Details and bookings are available at the tourist office (see above); children under 10 aren't permitted to go on the tour. The tours go through an underground network of tunnels and chambers. Tours are possible only in summer, Monday through Saturday at 10am, noon, 2pm, and 4pm; Sunday, at 2pm and 4pm.

Southeast of the railroad station, the tower of the **Rådhus** dominates Kiruna. It is open in summer, Monday through Saturday from 10am to 5pm and on Sunday from 11am to 5pm; in off-season, daily from 9am to 5pm. Inside there's an art collection and some Sami handcraft exhibitions.

A short walk up the road leads to the **Kiruna Kyrka,** which is open in summer daily from 10am to 6pm. This church was constructed like a stylized Sami hut, an origami design of rafters and wood beams. You can also visit the nearby **Hjalmar Lundbomsgården,** which is open June to August, daily from 10am to 8pm. Admission is free. This manor house contains displays of the town and some Sami artifacts.

The **Kiruna Samegård,** Brytaregatan 14, (tel. 170-29), is open mid-June to September, daily from 10am to 6pm, charging an admission of 10 kronor ($1.80) adults; free for children 16 or under. It contains an exhibition of Sami artifacts.

WHERE TO STAY & DINE

MODERATE

RESOHOTELL FERRUM, Lars Janssongatan 15, S-981 21 Kiruna. Tel. 0980/186-00. Fax 0980/145-05. 170 rms (all with bath). TV TEL
$ Rates (including breakfast): June 9–Aug 20 and Fri–Sat year-round, 595 kronor ($107.10) single; 910 kronor ($163.80) double. Sun–Thurs Aug 21–June 8, 1,090 kronor ($196.20) single; 1,325–1,350 kronor ($238.50–$243) double. AE, DC, MC, V. **Parking:** 50 kronor ($9).

This hotel, run by the Reso chain, is functional and uniform in design. It is one of your best bets for lodging and also for food in Kiruna, as it offers a good restaurant, plus a cocktail bar and casino. Bedrooms are modern and well furnished. Rooms for the allergic are available, and some accommodations are suitable for the handicapped. A garage is on the premises. The hotel also has a sauna.

INEXPENSIVE

HOTEL KEBNE, Konduktörsgatan 7, S-981 34 Kiruna. Tel. 0980/123-80. Fax 0980/821-11. 54 rms (all with bath). TV TEL
$ Rates (including breakfast): Fri–Sun 500 kronor ($90) single; 710 kronor ($127.80) double. Mon–Thurs 845 kronor ($152.10) single; 1,050 kronor ($189) double. AE, DC, MC, V. **Parking:** Free.

Next to the police station on the main road through Kiruna (the airport bus stop at its door), this hotel consists of two buildings, both of which were renovated in the 1980s. Bedrooms are modernized and comfortably furnished, and room service is available until 11pm. The hotel also operates one of the best restaurants in Kiruna, serving both Scandinavian and international food. Facilities include a sauna and a solarium.

7. KARESUANDO

114 miles NE of Kiruna, 967 miles N of Stockholm

GETTING THERE By Train Take the train from Stockholm via Boden to Kiruna. Three trains run daily. Some have transfers; others offer direct service. At Kiruna, continue on by bus.

By Bus There are several buses a day linking Kiruna, the nearest rail junction, with Karesuando.

By Car Head north from Stockholm along the E4, continuing north after Luleå along Route 392 and Route 400 until you reach Karesuando.

ESSENTIALS For information, the **Karesuando Turistbyrå** (tel. 0981/202-05), in the town center, is open Mon–Fri 9am–4pm and Sat 9am–1pm (mid-June–mid-Aug only). The **telephone area code** for Karesuando is 0981.

From Kiruna, a bus goes to the most atmospheric Lapp center at Karesuando, Sweden's most northerly village, near the Finnish border. This excursion, and certainly Karesuando, is decidedly offbeat.

Some adventurous motorists drive to Karesuando, 120 miles north of the Arctic Circle. For 7 midwinter weeks the sun disappears. To compensate, it never sets at all between May 26 and July 17.

Once at Karesuando, you can make car-ferry connections to Finland, where the road continues north through tundra regions to the most northerly part of Scandinavia. The Finnish tourist resort of Kilpisjärvi lies 72 miles northwest of Karesuando.

WHERE TO STAY

BUDGET

GRAPE HOTELL, Fack 34, S-980 16 Karesuando. Tel. 0981/200-22. Fax 0981/202-65. 39 rms (35 with bath). TV TEL

$ Rates (including breakfast): 355–375 kronor ($63.90–$67.50) single without bath, 395–420 kronor ($71.10–$75.60) single with bath; 455–475 kronor ($81.90–$85.50) double without bath, 495–530 kronor ($89.10–$95.40) double with bath. AE, DC, MC, V. **Parking:** Free.

This hotel was originally built in the 1930s by a German family. However, most of the present building dates from 1980s. It is owned today by a family from Israel. They offer comfortably furnished and well-kept bedrooms in this remote part of the world. The hotel has a sauna.

8. ABISKO

911 miles N of Stockholm

GETTING THERE **By Train** Go first to Kiruna (see Section 6, above). From there, take the bus.

By Bus Several buses service Abisko from Kiruna, with continuing service to Narvik.

By Car Take the E4 north from Stockholm, going northwest beyond Luleå onto Route 98, which runs to Kiruna and Abisko and beyond.

ESSENTIALS For **information,** make inquiries at the Turistbyrå at Kiruna (see above). The **telephone area code** for Abisko is 0980.

A resort north of the Artic Circle is a curiosity: Abisko, a resort on the southern shore of Lake Torneträsk, includes a scenic valley, a lake, and an island. A lift takes passengers to Mount Nuolja (Njulla). Nearby is the protected Abisko National Park, containing remarkable flora, including orchids.

WHAT TO SEE & DO

Abisko National Park, established in 1903, is situated around the Abiskojokk River, including its mouth where it flows into Lake Torneträsk. It is a typical alpine valley with a rich variety of flora and fauna whose highest mountain is Slåttatjåkka, 3,900 feet above sea level. There is also the mountain of

Njulla, rising 3,800 feet, which has a cable-transport line. The name Abisko is a Lapp word meaning "ocean forest." The park's proximity to the Atlantic gives it a maritime character, with milder winters and cooler summers than the more continentally influenced areas east of the Scandes or Caledonian mountains.

Another park in the area, **Vadvetjåkka National Park,** is smaller. Established in 1920, it lies northwest of Lake Torneträsk, with its northern limits set by the Norwegian frontier. It is comprised of mountain precipices and large tracts of bog and delta. It also has rich flora, along with impressive brook ravines. Its highest mountain is Vadvetjåkka, with a southern peak at 3,650 feet above sea level. Abisko is more easily accessible than Vadvetjåkka. Three sides of Vadvetjåkka Park are bounded by water which is difficult to wade through, and the fourth side is rough terrain with treacherously slippery slope bogs and steep precipices complete with rock slides. This park was once inhabited by settlers who eventually abandoned the land.

Abisko is one of the best centers for watching the **Midnight Sun,** visible from June 13 to July 4. It's also the start of the longest marked trail in the world, the Kungsleden. You'll also see a reconstruction of a Lapp encampment at the resort.

THE ROYAL TRAIL The ✪ **Kungsleden** (Royal Trail) runs from Abisko to Hemavan—about 210 miles. It's marked, of course, and mountain huts are spaced a day's hike apart if you can maintain the pace. Most of the stops are at what Swedes call *kåtors*. Here you cook your own food and clean up before leaving. At points the trail crosses lakes and rivers, where boats will be found for that purpose. The trail actually follows the old nomadic paths of the Lapps. Those with less time or energy will find the trail broken up into several smaller routings.

WHERE TO STAY & DINE
BUDGET

ABISKO TURISTSTATION, S-980 24 Abisko. Tel. 0980/400-00. Fax 0980/401-40. 109 rms, 52 cottages (none with bath).

$ **Rates:** 245–300 kronor ($44.10–$54) single, 410–510 kronor ($73.80–$91.80) double; with half board 330–480 kronor ($59.40–$86.40) per person. No credit cards. **Parking:** Free. **Closed:** Sept 30–Feb 22.

Owned by the Swedish Touring Club, this big, modern hotel about 500 yards from the bus station offers accommodations in the main building, the annex, and in bungalows. From the hotel you look out onto the lake and backdrop of mountains. The staff is helpful about providing information about excursions. Rooms are basic but comfortable, and some have exceptional views.

HOTEL GÄSTGÅRDEN, Abisko Östra, S-980 24 Abisko. Tel. 0980/401-00. Fax 0980/402-65. 45 rms (3 with bath).

$ **Rates:** 260 kronor ($46.80) single without bath, 340 kronor ($61.20) single with bath; 280 kronor ($50.40) double without bath, 350 kronor ($63) double with bath. No credit cards. **Parking:** Free.

This simple hotel 50 yards from the bus station is a welcome oasis in this part of the world. Twelve rooms are strictly self-catered. An additional 13 bedrooms, a shop, and a small restaurant are found in the main building, and others are in annexes. Boats and canoes are available for rent, and a small swimming pool is 50 yards from the hotel. You can ski, fish, take walks in the mountains, look at the Midnight Sun in summer or the northern lights in winter in a fantastically clean and natural atmosphere.

PART FOUR

FINLAND

CHAPTER 31

GETTING TO KNOW FINLAND

One of the world's northernmost countries, Finland is the last frontier of Western Europe. Lapland, which occupies nearly a third of its surface, is north of the Arctic Circle.

Technically Finland is not part of Scandinavia, but in spirit it is, as reflected in its modern architecture; its high standard of living; its avant-garde designs in textiles, furniture, and ceramics; and its advances in education (it claims almost 100% literacy).

Geographically remote (although easily accessible), Finland does not attract the visitors that Denmark, Norway, and Sweden do—and that's a shame, for Finland has much to offer the visitor in both summer and winter.

1. GEOGRAPHY, HISTORY & POLITICS

GEOGRAPHY

Suomi (its Finnish name) is one of the largest countries of Europe, stretching 718 miles in length, with a maximum breadth of 335 miles. It has a coastline of approximately 682 miles. It is also among the least populated countries of Europe, with some 4.9 million, for a population density of 15.7 inhabitants per square kilometer.

Finland shares its western border with Sweden, a land frontier of 363 miles, and with Norway, a border stretching 444 miles. But its longest frontier—a distance of 787 miles—is shared with Russia to the east.

Most of the country is lowland, its highest point being Halti, at 4,344 feet above sea level. Some 8% of the land is cultivated, while 65% is forested. Finland has more lakes than any other country, some 187,888 of them—10% of the country's surface is covered with water. The largest, Lake Saimaa, with its adjoining waters, is the fourth in size in Europe. However, many of the lakes are quite shallow, with an average depth of 24 feet.

In the south and west the country is bounded by the Gulf of Bothnia, the Gulf of Finland, and the Baltic Sea. Its largest archipelago is Saaristomeri, with some 17,000 islands and skerries. To the west is the large archipelago of the Åland Islands, between Sweden and Finland. Finnish rivers tend to be short; the longest river is the Kemijoki-Kitinen, stretching 342 miles.

THE REGIONS **Helsinki** and the south are the most industrialized sections of the country, with the densest concentration of population. Helsinki has been the capital

❓ DID YOU KNOW . . . ?

- Finland is a country of some 188,000 lakes and 180,000 islands.
- Finland was the first country to grant women the right to vote, in 1906.
- That vote was put to use: Today, one-quarter of the members of Finland's parliament are women.
- Two Finnish brothers hold the world's record for sitting on an anthill.
- The legendary bird of fairy tale and mythology—the whooper swan, *Cygnus musicus*—has been saved from extinction and once again nests in Finland.
- The world's northernmost film festival is held under the Midnight Sun of Lapland at Sodankylä.
- Finland has its own version of the tango, a far cry from Argentina's.
- Finland has launched news broadcasts in Latin.
- One of the most heavily forested regions on earth, Finland makes baseball bats out of fiberglass.
- Finland is the leading book-publishing country in the world—17.1 titles per 10,000 inhabitants.

of Finland since 1812. It is the center of the country's government, culture, and entertainment, standing at the crossroads between Eastern and Western Europe.

In the southwest, **Turku** is Finland's former capital, founded more than 750 years ago at the mouth of the Aura River. It is the country's southwestern gateway. Only 10 miles to its west is **Naantali,** a seaside summer resort of 18th-century wooden houses, brightly painted. West of Turku lie the **Åland Islands,** an archipelago that was long the subject of a bitter territorial dispute between Sweden and Finland.

One of the oldest towns in the south of Finland, **Porvoo** lies 31 miles east of Helsinki, a town of narrow cobblestone streets and wooden buildings that make it one of the most popular outings from the capital.

Finland's **lake region** would take months to explore, maybe a lifetime. Most of the country's 188,000 lakes lie in eastern and central Finland. Many of these lakes are interconnected, and in summer lake steamers cruise the waters around **Lappeenranta, Kuopio,** and **Savonlinna** in the lake district of Saimaa.

Lake Päijänne in central Finland connects two modern cities, **Jväsklylä** in the north and **Lahti** in the south. **Tampere,** Finland's second-largest city, 100 miles north of Helsinki, is part of the lake region. It is situated in the middle of the western lake district and is one of the main points of embarkation for lake cruises.

Nearly three-quarters of Finland is covered by forest, an exotic Lapp wilderness ideal for hiking, camping, white-water rafting, and canoeing. **Lapland** lures visitors from all over the world, and in June and July the sun never sets. Lapland is also reindeer country and the home of Santa Claus, whose workshop is there. The modern capital of Finnish Lapland is **Rovaniemi,** near the Arctic Circle at the confluence of the Kemijoki River and the Ounasjoki River.

DATELINE

- **100** Finland is inhabited by people from the southern Gulf of Finland and by Finno-Ugrians.
- **1155** Eric IX, king of Sweden, brings the crusades to Finland.
- **1581** John III of Sweden makes Finland a grand duchy.
- **1713–21** Russia invades and occupies Finland.

(continues)

HISTORY

Ten thousand years ago, as the ice sheets gradually melted, widely scattered Stone Age settlements developed among the lakes and forests of what is now Finland. The tribes who developed these communities were probably nomadic Lapps of Mongolian origin, although the mists of time have greatly obscured the exact nature of the communities.

With the arrival of new tribes of Finno-Ugric origin (starting in the 1st century A.D.) and other unrelated Germanic tribes from the southern edge of the Gulf of Finland, the original Lapps retreated farther and farther north. Today genetic research into the distribution of blood groups points to evidence that about two-thirds of the modern Finnish population is of Western (that is, European) origin. (Nonetheless, philologists stress the uniqueness of the Finnish language, Suomia, whose only close relative is Hungarian. Both tongues are members of the Finno-Ugric subdivision of the Uralic subfamily of the Ural-Altaic family, unrelated to the Indo-European family to which almost all Western European languages belong.)

The Viking incursions, for which written records begin in about A.D. 800, established cultural and trade routes as far east as Byzantium and Constantinople. Residents of the region now known as Finland early in their recorded history probably had multiple contacts with the Russian empire, and others with the maritime kingdoms of Estonia and Latvia. More important, they also established north-south trade links with the shores of the southern Baltic, to what is now Poland and the eastern regions of modern Germany. Many different cultures and bloodlines met and mingled in Finland, often with bloody wars between the various Finnish tribes, until the Swedes—fearing for the stability of their eastern neighbor—launched a series of attacks into territory within the old eastbound trade routes.

SWEDISH INTRUSIONS Eric IX, assisted by the English-born bishop of Uppsala, St. Henry, in A.D. 1155, launched a crusade for the political and religious conversion of the Finnish tribes. Their major opposition broke out in eastern Finland (Karelia) from the Novgorodians (at the time a powerful Russian kingdom) who were grabbing land and spreading the Russian Orthodox faith from the east. Their most famous battle occurred in 1240 at the River Neva, when Alexander Nevski, one of the most famous heroes of Russian literature, defeated the Swedes. Later, a treaty between the Swedes and the Novgorodians in 1323 divided Finland's easternmost province of Karelia between Novgorod and Sweden. Eastern Finland, from that moment on, became part of the Russian-Byzantine world, and although it shared a common language with its western brothers, would not be completely united to the rest of Finland again until a brief period early in the 20th century.

Meanwhile, with the largest section of Finland under Swedish rule, most of the population in the centuries to come enjoyed considerable autonomy, and (usually) mercantile prosperity, and the Swedish language became the medium of culture. Under Gustavus I, Helsinki became one of the Swedish Empire's most important trading bases in the Baltic. Lutheranism was introduced into Finland by Michael Agricola (1506–57) who, because of his translation into Finnish of the New Testament and his compilation of a Finnish grammar, is called "the father of Finnish literature."

King John III (1537–92) granted Finland the status of a grand duchy in 1581. Unfortunately, Finland became a battleground in the continuing wars with Russia, Sweden, Denmark, and Poland. The year 1671 established new boundaries, as Moscow was forced to yield certain lands in Karelia.

Finland entered the Thirty Years' War on Sweden's side, to which it was subjugated, its own language and culture suppressed in favor of Sweden's. The great famine of 1676 killed one-third of the population.

During the reign of Charles XII (1682–1718), Russia invaded and occupied Finland from 1713 to 1721. At the

DATELINE

- **1721** Sweden regains control of western Finland, but loses much Finnish territory in the east to Russia.
- **1809** Finland becomes a grand duchy of Russia under Czar Alexander I.
- **1821** The capital is moved from Turku to Helsinki.
- **1878** Under Alexander II, Finland gains its own conscript army, and Finnish replaces Swedish as the official language.
- **1905** Finns launch a national strike to oppose the oppressive policies of Nicholas II, who had revoked Finnish autonomy in 1899.
- **1906** Finland is allowed a single-chamber Diet with 200 elected deputies.
- **1917** Russia restores Finnish autonomy, as Finland declares its independence.
- **1918** Mannerheim succeeds in driving Russian forces from Finland.
- **1919** Finland establishes a constitution.
- **1920** Finland joins the League of Nations.
- **1939–40** The first Russo-Finnish War launched.
- **1941–44** Russo-Finnish Continuation War rages, with Finland allied to Germany.

(continues)

- **1955** Helsinki hosts the Olympic Games, as Finland pursues a policy of neutrality.
- **1956** Urho Kekkonen becomes president of Finland and presides over the long and tense Cold War era.
- **1982** Kekkonen resigns, as Mauno Koivisto is elected president.
- **1988** Koivisto reelected to a second 6-year term, as Communists decline in power.
- **1992** Finland celebrates its 75th anniversary of independence.

end of the war Sweden still ruled Finland, although some eastern territories, including southern Karelia, passed back to Russia. Russia gained new territories in another Swedish-Russian war, which raged from 1741 to 1743.

In 1808 Russia finally seized all of Finland at the peak of the Napoleonic Wars. Finland was granted the status of grand duchy under Czar Alexander I (1777–1825), and enjoyed broad autonomy throughout the 19th century, developing a democratic system relatively unimpeded by St. Petersburg.

LIFE UNDER THE RUSSIANS   Turku was the capital of Finland until 1821 when the czar moved it to Helsinki. In 1878 under Alexander II (1818–81) Finland gained its own independent conscript army, and the Finnish language was adopted as the official language, replacing Swedish.

Although Alexander III (1845–94) tried to follow a liberal policy regarding Finland, most of his advisors opposed him, preferring to keep Finland as a buffer zone between the then Russian capital of St. Petersburg and the rest of Europe. Alexander's conservative and reactionary son, Nicholas II (1868–1918), revoked Finnish autonomy in 1899 and began an intensive campaign of Russification. Russian became the official language in 1900, and in the following year the separate Finnish army was abolished. Mass arrests followed. Finns in 1905 called a national strike to protest these conditions, forcing Nicholas to ease some of his edicts. In 1906 Finland was allowed to have a unicameral parliament (the Diet) composed of 200 elected deputies, but it had little real power.

At the outbreak of World War I, Russia totally dominated Finland, and Finnish autonomy became a memory. The grand duchy status was removed and the country became a dominion of its more powerful neighbor to the east.

AN INDEPENDENT FINLAND   Finland was saved by the outbreak of the Russian Revolution and the collapse of czarist rule. The Russian provincial government restored Finnish autonomy on March 20, 1917. Nevertheless, Finns called a general strike, seeking total independence. A civil war followed, in which the leftist, pro-Russian Red Guard, supporting Russian troops in Finland, was opposed by the conservative-nationalist civil guard, the Whites.

On November 15, 1917, a proclamation placed control of the country's affairs in the hands of a Finnish government, and on December 6, President Svinhufvrud (1861–1944) declared the independence of Finland. Russia recognized Finnish independence on January 5, 1918, yet 40,000 Russian troops remained stationed in Finland supporting the Red Guard.

Baron Carl Gustaf Emil von Mannerheim (1867–1951) assumed control of the Whites and was determined to drive the Russians from Finland. With the help of a German expeditionary force, he managed to win the civil war, which ended on May 16, 1918. At the end of the war, Finland faced starvation.

Mannerheim was named regent of Finland on December 12, 1918, and in June of the following year a constitution was established, by which Finland became a republic. The new constitution called for the election of a president every 6 years. Mannerheim would wield supreme executive power, as did K. J. Stahlberg (1865–1952), the first president.

At Tartu in October of 1920, a peace treaty was signed between Russia and Finland. Russia got East Karelia. Finland joined the League of Nations on December 16, 1920, and in the following year the League ruled that Finland—not Sweden—was entitled to the Åland Islands.

The 1920s saw continuing struggles between the government and Finnish communists. In 1923 the Communist party was declared illegal, but it came back

IMPRESSIONS

A race of men very different in character and morals from the Swedes, namely the Finlanders; and as this race prevails among the inhabitants, a greater vivacity of spirit, a more irascible disposition, and a propensity to criminal actions begins to be manifested.
—E. D. CLARK, *TRAVELS IN VARIOUS COUNTRIES*, 1824

---

reincarnated as the Democratic League. During the 1930s many social and economic reforms were made.

WARS WITH RUSSIA A Soviet-Finnish nonagression pact was signed on January 12, 1932, but Russia continued to make demands upon Finland, including the annexation of the Hanko peninsula for use as a Soviet naval base. When Finland refused, Russian troops invaded on November 30, 1939.

The Winter War of 1939 and 1940 was one of the harshest ever fought in Finland, but the Finns, greatly outnumbered, resisted with bravery and courage. In March 1940 they accepted Russian terms, ceding territories in the north, the province of Viipuri, and the naval base at Hanko. The inhabitants of those districts left their homeland and moved within the new borders of Finland.

Resentment against the Russians led to a treaty with Germany. Hitler's request for transit rights across Finland was granted. Finland tried to remain neutral when the Nazis invaded Russia on June 22, 1941, but Russia bombed towns in southern Finland, and Mannerheim launched the Russo-Finnish Continuation War. Territories lost to the Russians were regained. But in 1944 Russia launched a big attack and Finland was forced to sue for peace. Russia regained the territory it had taken from Finland, and imposed severe war reparations. Matters were complicated since German troops stationed in northern Finland refused to withdraw. Thus Finland had to launch a war against the Nazis in Lapland in 1945.

Mannerheim was made president in 1944 but was forced to withdraw in 1946 because of ill health. In Paris in 1947 Finland and Russia signed an armistice.

MODERN FINLAND J. K. Paasikivi assumed the presidency of Finland in 1946, and concluded a mutual assistance treaty with the Soviet Union in 1948. In 1952 Helsinki became the site of the Olympic Games, focusing world attention on Finland, which in 1955 joined the United Nations.

In 1956 Urho Kekkonen became president of Finland, and he was to preside over the long Cold War era, resigning in 1982 because of ill health. During most of the Cold War Finland pursued a cliffhanging and neurosis-inducing policy of neutrality, earning for itself a reputation as a skillful diplomatic force. In 25 years in office he successfully walked the line between East and West, owing to his many-sided and dynamic personality. At the end of his regime, in the early 1980s, he saw the decline of the Communist party in Finland. In 1975 he had been host to the Conference on Security and Cooperation in Europe. He received the heads of state and the heads of government of 35 countries who signed the Helsinki Agreement in 1975.

Upon his resignation in 1982, Mauno Koivisto was elected president. Nearing the end of the long Cold War, Koivisto was reelected to a second 6-year term in 1988.

In 1992, Finland marked its 75th anniversary of independence, with architectural exhibitions, cultural programs, and folkloric festivals. The same year was also declared as Finnish Homecoming Year. A year-long program of events brought a lot of expatriate Finns back home for a look at their family roots.

IMPRESSIONS

*O to be in finland
now that russia's here.*
—E. E. CUMMINGS, FROM "O TO BE IN FINLAND," 1950

POLITICS

Under the amended 1919 constitution, the head of state of the Finnish republic is the president, elected to a 6-year term by a 300-member electoral college, which is selected by direct popular vote. The president plays a leading role in foreign policy and can influence legislation considerably. The 200 members of the unicameral parliament (the Eduskunta) are elected to 4-year terms by proportional representation. The chief executive body is the cabinet, headed by a prime minister, and responsible to parliament. Since World War II, most Finnish administrations have had to rely on coalitions between the major parties; today these are the leftish Social Democrats, the conservative National Coalition, and the Center Party, whose strongest support is in the rural north and east. Farthest to the left are the People's Democratic League and the Democratic Alternative (DEVA), neither with many seats in parliament.

Since 1988 the country has been divided into a dozen *lääni* or provinces, one of which, Åland, has enjoyed considerable autonomy since 1920.

2. FAMOUS FINNS

Alvar Aalto (1898–1976) Architect, furniture designer, and sculptor. Famous for his functionalist approach. He designed public buildings, apartment houses, factories, and whole communities such as Rovaniemi.

Wäinö Aaltonen (1894–1966) Sculptor. See the Aleksis Kivi monument in Railway Square in Helsinki and the statue of athlete Paavo Nurmi.

Erik Bryggman (1891–1955) Architect. Among his best works are the Åbo Akademi Library and the Turku's Cemetery Resurrection Chapel, the last example of the Finnish desire to integrate architecture and landscape.

Akseli Gallen-Kallela (1865–1931) Finland's most versatile artist, Gallen-Kallela painted portraits and landscapes in both watercolor and oil. His reputation rests mainly on his paintings, especially those based on the national epic, the *Kalevala*. He also designed furniture, textiles, and buildings. In the Finnish national romanticism movement, he remains a towering figure. His home, Tarvaspää, outside Helsinki, can be visited.

Urho Kekkonen (1900–86) Kekkonen was the longtime president of Finland (1956–82), presiding over some of the tensest years of the Cold War, as he walked a tightrope between East and West. For three decades he served in various cabinet posts and was once prime minister. Only 17 when Finland became independent, he fought to keep it that way.

Aleksis Kivi (1834–72) First great master of Finnish language. His *Seven Brothers* has been translated into 20 languages.

Mauno Henrik Koivisto (1923–   ) The president of the republic became a member of the cabinet in 1966 as minister of finance. Author of five books on economics and politics, he was elected president in 1982 and was reelected to a second term in 1988.

Eino Leino (1878–1926) Finland's most original lyric poet. His major work, *Helkavirsiä* (Songs of the Festival of Spring) was originally published in 1903 and 1916 in two different collections. In his work, he attempted to express the aspirations

IMPRESSIONS

From the beginning of your history onward, men and women of Finnish blood have played important roles in the development of our country. Their industry, stability, and resourcefulness have made them an important element in American nationality.
—FRANKLIN D. ROOSEVELT

and spirit of modern 20th-century people. Many of his poems were accompanied by the Finnish national instrument, the *kantele,* a kind of zither.

Elias Lönnrot   (1802–84) A philologist who collected Finland's ancient songs and legends and published them as the *Kalevala* (1835), the national epic.

Eliel Saarinen   (1873–1950) Architect who, with his partner, Lindgren, created buildings of bold sculptural masses with rough-hewn textures, including the National Museum and the railway station in Helsinki. In America he designed many of the performance halls at the Berkshire Music Center as well as the Sports Stadium at Yale.

Esa-Pekka Salonen   (1958–   ) This gifted young Finnish conductor is music director of the Los Angeles Philharmonic, a post he assumed in September 1992. One of the world's most sought after-artists, he became a guest conductor at the Finnish National Opera in the 1981–82 season and in the 1984–85 season he made his triumphant American debut. In 1985 he signed with CBS Masterworks to record Nielsen's Symphony No. 1 and Symphony No. 4 with the Swedish Radio Symphony Orchestra, as part of a complete Nielsen cycle.

Jean Sibelius   (1865–1957) Composer. Wrote music for violin and piano as well as chamber and orchestral music. His *Finlandia* (1900) conjures up the savage beauty of the Finnish countryside. Considered by his contemporaries to be one of the great composers of the time.

Mika Waltari   (1908–79) Achieved international fame with such novels as *The Egyptian* (1945), *The Adventurer* (1948), and *The Dark Angel* (1952).

3. SPORTS & RECREATION

THE SAUNA—A NATIONAL INSTITUTION   Regardless of where you've bathed, you really haven't been cleaned to the core until you've participated in the local ritual—a Finnish sauna. Whether for giving birth to babies or entertaining Russian ambassadors, the Finns regard the sauna as a national institution. It is estimated that there is one sauna in Finland for about every six citizens. The most authentic ones are log cabins beside a lake. Families and friends strip and head inside the chamber to take their places on slats. Later, someone throws water on heated rocks that give off hissing sounds. As is the custom, well-meaning friends pick up water-soaked birch boughs and switch the backs of fellow saunatics—great for the circulation, Finns claim. When the heat becomes unbearable—usually after 10 or 15 minutes for neophytes unaccustomed to 140° Fahrenheit temperatures—the bathers sprint out of the sauna and run to the icy-cold blue waters of a Finnish lake. In winter, rolling in the snow serves the same purpose.

Public saunas—contrary to popular foreign belief—are not mixed, and there are very few left. Attending a mixed sauna would invariably be a private affair, requiring an invitation. To be invited to a sauna by a Finn is the epitome of hospitality. To turn down the offer would be as gauche as burning the Stars and Stripes at an American Legion meeting.

Today in Finland, as in North America, most hotel saunas are heated by electricity. But unlike a Turkish bath, the air in a sauna is dry (until the water-on-the-rocks maneuver, anyway). Some saunas have attendants who soap, scrub, scour, and rinse you, but you can also go to a do-it-yourself one.

SKIING   Skiing conditions in Finland are among the best in the world. The season

IMPRESSIONS

Other composers offer their public a cocktail. I offer mine pure spring water.
—JEAN SIBELIUS, COMPOSER OF *FINLANDIA*

is long and the trails are good. The best skiing season in northern Finland is March to April, when there can be up to 16 hours of sunshine daily. But the early winter—*kaamos*, the season when the sun doesn't rise at all—has its own attractions for visitors after something different.

Finland is 620 miles long, so there are two extremities in the country. The south consists of gently rolling hills, with elevations not exceeding 3 feet, but the farther north one goes, the more deeply forested and mountainous the country becomes. The highest fells are in Lapland.

The slopes of Finnish ski resorts are known for the excellent condition in which they are kept. Skiing instruction—both cross country and downhill—is arranged at most resorts, and equipment can be rented on the spot.

Long-distance ski races are becoming increasingly popular, and the long trails, ranging from 25 to 55 miles, attract more and more participants from all over the world every year. As many as 15,000 skiers take part in the biggest event—the Finlandia Ski Race. A fair number of resorts organize guided ski treks. These take a few days, and overnight accommodation is arranged along in the trail in farmhouses or, in Lapland, in wilderness huts or shelters.

FISHING   In Finland there are more than 6,000 professional fishermen and about 1.5 million people fishing for recreation. For foreign visitors who fish for recreation, the usual fishing methods permitted are summer and winter angling, and fishing with lure and fly.

In Finland most fishing waters are privately owned, and cities and private companies also own fishing waters. The National Board of Forestry administers state fishing waters, mainly in northern and eastern Finland.

Foreign visitors must purchase a general fishing license if they intend to do recreational fishing in Finland (a separate license is needed for the Åland Islands). A general fishing license is obtainable from postal bank offices and post offices, costing 30 markkaa ($6.60) per person. The license is valid for 1 year.

GOLF   There are 71 golf clubs in Finland, the best courses being in Helsinki. These include Tali Manor, 4 miles from the center, and the Espoo Golf Course. Information about golf course and entry requirements and greens fees are available from the **Finnish Golf Union,** Radiokatu 20, SF-00240 Helsinki (tel. 90/144-284).

4. FOOD & DRINK

Many restaurants bring variety to their menus with typically Finnish dishes, particularly those that serve the Scandinavian smörgåsbord. There are restaurants to suit every purse and taste in Finland, and also an increasing number of ethnic restaurants in the bigger towns.

Breakfast is usually served between 7 and 10am, lunch between 11am and 2pm, and dinner any time from 4pm onward. Some restaurants in big cities stay open as late as 1am, and often nightclubs and discos—some of which serve food—are open until 3am.

Restaurants are called *ravintola* and many serve the smörgåsbord (called *voileipäpöytä* in Finnish). It includes a variety of fish and meat delicacies and hot dishes to choose from at a fixed price.

Inexpensive lunches are served at places called *kahvila* and *baari*. Baari is a place serving food and perhaps a mild beer, although coffee is the more usual drink consumed. All internationally known beverages are served throughout Finland in fully licensed restaurants and bars.

Potatoes, meat, fish, milk, butter, and rye bread are the mainstays of the Finnish diet. Soups are popular, especially pea soup and rich meat soups in which potatoes and vegetables are cooked together with chunks of beef.

FROMMER'S SMART TRAVELER:
RESTAURANTS

1. Look for the daily special, reasonable in price and prepared fresh that day.
2. Order fixed-price menus, especially at lunch. Often you can dine in expensive restaurants in Helsinki by patronizing them at lunch and ordering the set menu.
3. Do as many Finns do and make one or two open-face sandwiches for lunch.
4. Watch the booze—it can add greatly to the cost of any meal.
5. Eat at fast-food emporiums, shopping complexes, cafés, and self-service cafeterias. Food costs are sometimes one-third the price of more formal restaurants.
6. Fill up at the traditional Finnish breakfast buffets, so you'll need only a light lunch.

FOOD Every Finn looks forward to the crayfish season between July 20 and September, when some 225,000 pounds of this delicacy are caught in inland waters. Finns approach the eating of crayfish like an art, sucking out every morsel of flavor. After devouring half a dozen, they down a glass of schnapps. Called **rapu,** the crayfish is usually boiled in salt water and seasoned with dill. Of course, with all this slurping and shelling, you'll need a bib. Unless you're accustomed to schnapps, I suggest that you break with local custom and order a beer or glass of white wine instead.

The icy-cold waters of Finland produce some very fine fish, some of which are unknown elsewhere in the world. A cousin to the salmon, the 2-inch-long **muikku fritti** is found in inland waters of Finland. The fish is highly praised by gastronomes, and its roe is considered a delicacy. The most common fish, however, is **silakka** (Baltic herring), which is consumed in vast quantities. Rarely larger than sardines, the herring is not only pickled, but fried and grilled as well. Sometimes it's baked between layers of potato, the sauce made with milk, cheese, and egg. The fish is usually spiced with dill; in fact, dill seems to be the most popular herb in the country.

Finland has its own version of the Swedish smörgåsbord. It's called **voileipäpöytä,** which means "bread and butter table." That definition is too literal. Expect not only bread and butter, but an array of dishes, including many varieties of fish—such as pickled salt herring and fresh salted salmon—along with several cold meat dishes, including smoked reindeer.

Along with elk, bear, or reindeer tongue, Finns like the sharp taste of **puolukka,** a lingonberry. I hope you'll also have a chance to enjoy the Arctic cloudberry.

With an array of dishes, you can expect the two most popular salads of Finland: beet and cucumber. Bread is invariably served as well, including brown, white, black, and rye versions. The most typical is called **ruisleipä,** a dark, sour rye. Those open-face sandwiches, so familiar in all Scandinavian countries, are called **violeivat** here.

Fresh vegetables are plentiful in the summer, appearing less frequently during the long winter months. Boiled new potatoes are the most common vegetable and are served with sprays of fresh dill. Only in the most elegant places will you be served a

IMPRESSIONS

It is important to remember that in Finland the lavatory for men is called Miehille, *and for women* Naiselle. *For a gentleman to say* Viekää minut Naiselle *("Guide me to women") is to court disaster, and in any case the beds are very lumpy.*
—KARL BAEDEKER, 1914

convoluted morel known as "the black truffle of the north." It's the prize of all the mushrooms that grow in the vast forests of Finland.

Some Finnish hors d'oeuvres are especially good, especially **vorschmack.** Herring is ground finely, then mixed with garlic, onions, and lamb, which is then cooked in butter over a low flame for a long time, often several hours. This dish may have been introduced by Russian officers from St. Petersburg in the mid-19th century. The Russians have introduced a lot of dishes to Finland, and beef Stroganoff appears on many menus, especially in Helsinki. Borscht, a beet soup with sour cream, is another ubiquitous item.

One of the best-known regional specialties is from the province of Savo. **Kalakukko** is a mixture of a whitefish (known only in Finland) and pork baked in rye dough.

Another typical dish—this one from Karelia—is **karjalanpaisti,** a hotpot made with a combination of different meats. Another entry from Karelia is **karjalan piirakka,** oval-shaped rye pasties made with either rice or potatoes.

Boiled or broiled **pike perch** and **smoked whitefish** are some of my favorite Finnish dishes, and perhaps you'll like them too.

The Finns are hearty eaters, so portions are usually generous.

DRINK   The national drink of Finland is **milk** (sometimes curdled), and it can be drunk safely by North Americans. Similarly, water throughout Finland is safe to drink. Two famous Finnish liqueurs should be tasted: **lakka,** made from the saffron-colored wild cloudberry, and **mesimarja,** made from the Arctic brambleberry.

The Finns are heavy drinkers (**schnapps** is their favorite for an all-around tipple). A federal monopoly regulates the sale of alcohol, as Finland's well-intentioned attempt at prohibition didn't work out. But hard liquor, often imported, is expensive—and anyone on a budget had better stick to a domestic **beer** (Lahti is a good local brand).

5. RECOMMENDED BOOKS, FILMS & RECORDINGS

BOOKS

BIOGRAPHY   *Sibelius,* by Erik Tawaststjerna (Faber & Faber), is a splendid panoramic look at Finland's most renowned composer. Much of the research of this five-volume work was based on private papers made available by the composer's descendants. The title above is only the first volume published, covering the period from the composer's birth in 1865 up to 1904.

Axel, by Bo Carpelan (Manchester, England; Carcanet Press) is an easier read as it is a fictionalized but accurate portrait of the relationship of Sibelius with his patron, Axel Carpelan, great-uncle of the author. Carpelan had a tremendous influence on the life of Sibelius, even suggesting the name for his masterpiece *Finlandia.*

FICTION   *The Unknown Soldier,* by Väinö Linna (Panther). Presented on both stage and screen, this masterpiece depicts soldiers in the Winter War with Russia. Most portraits of that period portrayed Finnish soldiers as larger than life—"heroes in white"—but this was a more realistic "warts and all" depiction.

Kalevala (Harvard University Press). This is the greatest cultural masterpiece of the Finnish folkloric repertoire. It was gathered by Lönnrot, a regional doctor, and it is the embodiment of the oral traditions of ancient Finland and has been translated into many languages.

FILMS

Available on video cassette, *Ihmiselon ihanuus ja kurjuus* (The Glory and the Misery of Life) was a Grand Prix winner at the Festival of Nordic Cinema in Rouen in 1989. It was acclaimed as Matti Kassila's best film in years. The biggest name in Finnish cinema in the 1950s, Kassila returned to the screen with this adaptation of Sillanpää's autobiographical novel about a famous author coming to terms with his egoism.

The all-enduring Finnish cinema classic *The Unknown Soldier* is frequently revived and is available on cassette. Edwin Laine adapted the war novel of Väinö Linna, and it was first released in 1955, a powerful presentation of the intense physical experience of war. Its realistic setting is the Winter War of 1939–40 between Finland and Russia.

RECORDINGS

CLASSICAL A superb recording of Symphony No. 6, one of the less-performed works of Jean Sibelius, is on the RCA label, no. 60157. It contains the memorable *Scènes Historiques*, Suites 1 and 2, depicting various regional legends. The music is interpreted by Jukka-Pekka Saraste conducting the Finnish Radio Symphony Orchestra.

Ondine 730-2 was chosen as "record of the year" in 1989 by the Finnish Broadcasting Company. It is music so timeless that it can be performed any year. Timo Korhonen, a Finnish-born classical guitarist, interprets works by contemporary composers, including Koskelin, Donatini, and Ginastera. The record, incidentally, does not please all critics, as some found it "untraditional in sound."

Ondine 745-2 was called by one Finnish music critic "avant-garde classical music at its most hip and pleasurable best." Jarmo Sermila's "Contours," "Quatro Rilievi," "Love Charm Songs," and "A Prague Thoroughfare" are presented on this recording.

Finlandia 021 Oskar Merikanto: The Most Beautiful Song presents the music of Jorma Hynninen, the Finnish baritone and soloist who has appeared at the New York Metropolitan Opera. Hynninen, accompanied on this recording by pianist Ralf Gothoni, is the classic songwriter of Finland, and, as one critic put it, the sound is "appropriately nostalgic."

FOLK *The Old and the New Kantele,* SFLP 8578 (LP); SFMK 8578 (MC), introduces the national Finnish musical instrument, the kantele, in all the forms in which it has ever existed. Performing on the kantele in this recording are Martti Pokela, Eeva-Leenn Pokela-Sariola, and Matti Kontio, all experts. Folk music tunes for the kantele were gathered from all over Finland.

JAZZ *Downtown Dixie Tigers: 30th Anniversary Concert* (LP and MC) is the most famous traditional band in Finland, playing jazz. Their appearances in the country draw packed houses.

Pekka Poyry: Happy Peter (LP). This artist was the most talented alto sax and flute player in Finland until his death in 1980. This collection includes recordings made in the 1960s and 1970s, with leading Finnish bands.

CHAPTER 32

PLANNING A TRIP TO FINLAND

This chapter is devoted to the nitty-gritty of planning a trip to Finland—costs, events, itineraries, and detailed practicalities like taxes, tipping, and emergencies. It should be read in conjunction with Chapter 1.

1. CURRENCY & COSTS

CURRENCY The Finnish unit of currency is the mark—**markka** (plural markkaa) in Finnish—which is divided into 100 **pennia** (abbreviated "p"). At presstime, 1 Finnish markka is equal to about 22¢ in U.S. coinage. It takes about 4.5 markkaa to make $1 U.S. Coins are issued in denominations of 5p, 10p, 20p, and 50p, and 1 and 5 markkaa. Notes are issued in 5, 10, 50, 100, and 500 markkaa.

THE MARKKAA & THE DOLLAR

At presstime, $1 = 4.5 Finnish markkaa (or 1 markka = 22¢), and this was the rate of exchange used to calculate the dollar values given in the Finland chapters (rounded to the nearest nickel). This rate fluctuates from time to time and may not be the same by the time of your visit. Therefore, the following table should be used only as a guide:

Markkaa	U.S. $	Markkaa	U.S. $
.25	.05	125	27.50
.50	.11	150	33.00
1	.22	175	38.50
5	1.10	200	44.00
10	2.20	225	49.50
15	3.30	250	55.00
20	4.40	300	66.00
25	5.50	350	77.00
30	6.60	400	88.00
40	8.80	450	99.00
50	11.00	500	110.00
75	16.50	600	132.00
100	22.00	700	154.00

WHAT THINGS COST IN HELSINKI	**U.S. $**
Taxi from the airport to the city center	23.10
Single ticket on a tram or bus	1.80
Local telephone call	.45
Double room at the Hotel Hesperia (deluxe)	224.40
Double room at the Hotel Hospiz (moderate)	132.00
Double room at the Hotel Finn (inexpensive)	77.00
Lunch for one, without wine, at König (moderate)	25.00
Lunch for one, without wine, at Ostrobotnia (inexpensive)	7.50
Dinner for one, without wine, at Havis Amanda (expensive)	60.50
Dinner for one, without wine, at Kosmos (moderate)	25.00
Dinner for one, without wine, at Barbeque (inexpensive)	15.00
Pint of beer (draft pilsner) in a bar	5.50
Coca-Cola in a café	2.25
Cup of coffee in a café	3.00
Roll of ASA 100 color film, 36 exposures	6.60
Admission to Mannerheim Museum	4.40
Movie ticket	7.70
Theater ticket	8.80–35.20

WHAT THINGS COST IN TURKU	**U.S. $**
Taxi from the airport to the city center	15.40
Taxi within the city center	8.80
Local telephone call	.45
Double room at Hamburger Börs (moderate)	176.00
Double room at the Cumulus (moderate)	132.00
Double room at the Turun Keskushotelli (inexpensive)	81.40
Continental breakfast in a café	5.50–8.80
Lunch for one, without wine, at Brahenkellari (moderate)	15.00
Lunch for one, without wine, at Pinella (moderate)	7.90
Dinner for one, without wine, at Le Pirate (moderate)	30.00
Dinner for one, without wine, at Hansa Hotel (moderate)	32.00
Dinner for one, without wine, at Verso (budget)	7.50
Pint of beer (draft pilsner) in a pub	5.30
Coca-Cola at a café	2.25
Cup of coffee at a café	2.50
Roll of ASA color film, 36 exposures	5.50
Admission to City Historical Museum	3.30
Movie ticket	6.80
Theater ticket	9.90–13.20

2. WHEN TO GO — CLIMATE, HOLIDAYS & EVENTS

CLIMATE   The joke is that summer in Helsinki lasts from Tuesday through Thursday. In Lapland the **Midnight Sun** and the mosquitoes offer the visitor an unforgettable experience. The Midnight Sun is continuously above the horizon in the far north in Utsjoki from May 17 to July 28, in Ivalo from May 23 to July 22, in Sodankylä from May 30 to July 5, on the Arctic Circle and in Rovaniemi from June 6 to July 7, in Kuusamo from June 13 to July 1, and in Kemi from June 19 to June 25. There are almost 20 hours of daylight in Helsinki in the summer months.

Spring arrives in May, and the summers are short. July is the warmest month, with temperatures averaging around 59°F. The coldest months are January and February, when the Finnish climate has been compared to that of New England. The snow arrives in southern Finland in December, in northern Finland in October. It lasts until late April in Lapland.

Finland's Average Daytime Temperatures (°F)

	Jan	Feb	Mar	Apr	May	June	July	Aug	Sept	Oct	Nov	Dec
Helsinki	26	25	32	44	56	66	71	68	59	47	37	31
Turku	26	26	33	45	58	66	72	69	59	47	28	31
Tampere	24	24	32	44	57	66	72	68	58	45	36	29
Jyväskylä	21	21	31	43	56	66	71	67	55	42	33	26
Ivalo	17	17	26	27	47	60	67	62	50	37	28	21

HOLIDAYS   The following holidays are observed in Finland: January 1 (New Year's Day), Epiphany, Good Friday, Easter Monday, May 1 (Labor Day), Ascension Day, Whitmonday, Midsummer Eve, Midsummer Day (a Saturday), All Saints' Day, December 6 (Independence Day), and December 25–26 (Christmas and Boxing Days).

FINLAND CALENDAR OF EVENTS

Note: Dates given in this calendar can vary from year to year. Check with a Finnish Tourist Office.

FEBRUARY

☐ **Finlandia Ski Race,** Hämeenlinna-Lahti. Almost 50 miles of cross-country skiing, a mass event that is part of the Euroloppet and Worldloppet competitions. February 24–25.

MARCH

☐ **Tar Skiing Race,** Oulu. This cross-country ski race has been repeated every year without a break since first established more than a century ago. Following a course that stretches over 47 miles, with participation by hundreds of contestants, it is the oldest long-distance cross-country ski race in the world. March 11.

☐ **Ounasvaara Winter Games,** Rovaniemi. International skiing and ski-jumping events, including skiing World Cup finals. March 31 and April 1.

JUNE

☐ **Kuopio Dance and Music Festival,** Kuopio. International dancing event that takes a different theme every year, such as "Dance in the Mediterranean Countries." June 3–10.

☐ **Joensuu Song Festival,** Joensuu. An international event with concerts of symphonic and popular music, solo concerts, exhibitions, dance and theater performances. June 19–23.

○ *SAVONLINNA OPERA FESTIVAL One of Europe's most important and best-known music festivals it's part of a cultural tradition established in 1912. Dozens of performances are traditionally held in the island fortress of Olavinlinna Castle in July. The performers include artists of international repute from around the world, and in addition to the dozens of other offerings, at least one Finnish opera is presented.*

Where: Savonlinna. When: June 30 to July 29. How: For details and complete information, contact the Savonlinna Opera Festival, Olavinkatu 35, SF-57130 Savonlinna (tel. 957/514-700).

JULY

☐ **Pori Jazz Festival,** Pori. Big open-air concerts and jam sessions attract top jazz players from all over the world, including Finland's own big names. July 12–15.

AUGUST

☐ **Arctic Canoe Race,** Kilpisjärvi-Tornio. An international race for canoes and kayaks along a demanding route of 334 miles. August 4–11.

☐ **Turku Music Festival,** Turku. Programs stretch from the Renaissance and the baroque—played on the original instruments—to modern, light music. August 10–19.

NOVEMBER

☐ **All Saints Ice Regatta,** Rovaniemi. The opening of the world's ice sailing season. November 3–4.

HELSINKI CALENDAR OF EVENTS

FEBRUARY

☐ **Helsinki International Boat Show,** Helsinki. Boat show featuring the industry's latest models, developments, and sales pitches. Staged at the Fair Center. February 9–18.

APRIL

☐ **International Vermo Cup,** Helsinki-Vermo. One of the main trotting events in Finland. April 29.

MAY

☐ **Women's 10km,** Helsinki. A 6-mile-long running event for women. May 27.

JUNE

☐ **Finland Sports Festival,** Helsinki. An international sports event that draws athletes mainly from Scandinavia, but also from around the world. Some events are staged at Espoo and Vantaa. June 6–10.

AUGUST

✪ *HELSINKI FESTIVAL   A major music event of Scandinavia, the Helsinki Festival presents orchestral concerts by outstanding soloists and ensembles, chamber music and recitals, exhibitions, ballet, theater, and opera performances, along with jazz pop, and rock concerts.*
   __Where:__ Helsinki. __When:__ August 23 to September 9. __How:__ For complete information about the program or whatever, contact the Helsinki Festival, Unioninkatu 28, SF-00100 Helsinki (tel. 90/659-688).

NOVEMBER

☐ **Children's Festival,** Helsinki. Concerts, theater performances, and other events for children. Dates vary.

3. GETTING AROUND

BY PLANE

Finnair (tel. toll free 800/950-5000) offers the lowest domestic airfares in Europe and has one of the densest routings, covering towns and cities with about 100 inland flights daily.

It also offers an unlimited mileage **holiday ticket** that entitles a passenger to travel on all Finnair (also Karair and Finnaviation) domestic routes for a 15-day period. Total cost is around $300 (U.S.); those ages 12 to 23 pay $250 for the same ticket and conditions. This special ticket is sold through travel agents and major airlines in North America. The ticket can also be purchased in Finland, provided it is paid for in dollars and you can prove that you're not a permanent resident of Scandinavia. You can also purchase it in other Scandinavian countries with proof of non-Scandinavian residency. It cannot be transferred. This bargain gives North Americans a chance to see Lapland and the Finnish lake district and to travel north of the Arctic Circle. Regular flights to such points would cost far more.

BY TRAIN

Finland has its own **Finnrail Pass** for use on the country's elaborate network of railroads. The pass entitles a person to unlimited travel on all passenger trains of the Finnish State Railways. An 8-day ticket costs 705 markkaa ($155.10) in first class or 470 markkaa ($103.40) in second class; a 15-day costs 1,095 markkaa ($240.90) in first class and 730 markkaa ($160.60) in second class; and a 22-day costs 1,380 markkaa ($303.60) in first class and 920 markkaa ($202.40) in second class. Second-class trains in Finland are equivalent in quality to first-class trains in many countries. The Finnrail Pass should be purchased before you leave home.

As trains tend to be crowded, it's recommended that you reserve a seat in advance—in fact, seat reservations are obligatory on all express trains marked IC or EP on the timetable. The charge for seat reservations depends on the service level and the length of the journey, ranging from 12 markkaa to 70 markkaa ($2.65 to $15.40).

For more information, contact the **Finnish State Railways,** P.O. Box 488, Vilhonkatu 13, SF-00101 Helsinki (tel. 90/7071). In the United States, contact **Holiday Tours of America,** 425 Madison Ave., New York, NY 10017 (tel. 212/832-8989, or toll free 800/677-6454).

For other railway information, telephone 90/101-01-15 in Helsinki Monday through Saturday from 7am to 10pm, and Sunday from 9am to 6pm. Train tickets are sold at the main railway station in Helsinki Monday through Saturday from 6:30am to 10:10pm.

SENIOR CITIZEN DISCOUNTS   Visitors over age 65 may buy a special card for 50 markkaa ($11) at any railway station in Finland, which entitles the holder to a 30% discount. The card is not valid on Christmas Eve, Good Friday, Midsummer Eve, or 3 days before any of those holidays (a surcharge is added).

BY BUS

Finland has an extensive network of private bus companies. If you'd like to find out about bus travel, information is available at **Oy Matkahuolto,** Lauttasaarentie 8 (tel. 90/692-2088), in Helsinki Monday through Friday from 7:30am to 7pm, Saturday from 7:30am to 3:30pm, and Sunday from 9:30am to 5pm. Tickets can be purchased on board or at the bus station Monday through Friday from 7:30am to 7pm, and Saturday and Sunday from 7:30am to 6pm.

FOR SENIORS   **"65 Tickets"** are sold at bus stations, at travel agencies, and on buses to those who have a special 65 Card, available from Oy Matkahuolto (see above) to those 65 or over. The price of the card is 30 markkaa ($6.60), and it entitles the holder to a reduction for a ride of at least 80 kilometers (48 miles). A photograph and passport are necessary when the card is bought.

BY TAXI

Most public transportation stops in Finland after midnight, and a taxi (*taksi*) is used for getting around after that. If you're not near a taxi stand, cabs can be called. Look up *Taksiasemat* in the local yellow pages. Taxis are very expensive in Helsinki, but much cheaper in provincial towns. After a base charge of 14 markkaa ($3.10) or more you generally pay 6 markkaa ($1.30) per kilometer, although this can vary greatly from town to town. Surcharges are added on weekends and at night. If people share, of course, the cost is greatly reduced.

BY CAR

Because of the far-flung locations of Finland's attractions, and the relative infrequency of its trains and buses outside the cities, touring the country by car is the best way to savor its sights and charms. If you bring your own car into the country, you need to show proof of ownership and some insurance documentation, but if you rent a car in Finland, a valid U.S., Canadian, or other driver's license, plus the presentation of a cash deposit or major credit card and a passport, is the only paperwork you'll need.

Roads are surprisingly good, even in the north, but once you leave the main highways, roads can be confusing. Sometimes the road markings point to villages known only to local residents, and distances are sometimes vast. Because of this, a good map is essential. Spiked snow tires are required by highway authorities during winter. All car-rental companies will provide them during the appropriate seasons as standard equipment.

CAR RENTALS   Each of the three largest American car-rental companies are represented in Finland: **Avis** (tel. toll free 800/331-2112 in North America), **Budget** (tel. toll free 800/527-0700 in North America), and **Hertz** (tel. toll free 800/654-3001 in North America). Each company maintains 27 to 40 locations in Finland, usually in town centers or at airports, and sometimes in surprisingly obscure locations. For those who want to begin and end their Finnish odysseys in different cities, all three companies allow free dropoffs at other Finnish locations if a rental lasts for at least a week. Avis (but not Hertz or Budget) allowed dropoffs in other Scandinavian cities (such as Stockholm or Copenhagen) for a hefty surcharge of $580 and $890, respectively. In view of the costs of one-way rentals, most visitors opted instead for separate car rentals within each of the countries they visited.

Most companies will give you child seats, rooftop racks, and ski racks, sometimes free, and sometimes (depending on demand) for a nominal one-time fee of around $15 per item.

Charges for rentals of luxury cars with automatic transmissions (between $900 and $1,500 per week for the cheapest available models, depending on the company) were so high that most people quickly adapt to the manual transmissions that are considered standard equipment in Finland.

If you plan to do a lot of touring, you'll probably find that a weekly rental (which most companies define as between 5 and 7 days) with unlimited mileage is your most economical rental option. All three companies will offer a prepaid plan whose paperwork and advance payment must be completed 2 weeks prior to a renter's departure from home. (This lengthy advance payment is presumably to allow the necessary documents to reach you before you depart for Finland.) The only advantage of such a long prepayment is that it "locks in" a predesignated net rental price in dollars before you actually use the car. Unless the conversion ratios between the Finnish markka and the dollar fluctuate wildly in the interim, it might not be to your advantage to prepay so long in advance. Cancellation fees usually range from $50 to full forfeiture of your prepayment, depending on your timing and the policies of the rental company. Because of this, some experienced renters opt instead to confirm a reservation within 2 days of their actual pickup of the car, billing the payment in local currency to their credit card, and paying the bill in dollars several weeks later after they return home.

All three companies offered as their cheapest rental a manual transmission Ford Fiesta priced at $359 per week at Hertz, $412 per week at Budget, and $502 per week at Avis. Tax was an additional 22% of each of these rates, an add-on that can make an important difference in your final bill. To ease the shock a bit, all three companies quoted higher rates that included the tax as part of the net total.

A word about insurance: Additional insurance was available at each of the three companies in the form of a collision damage waiver (CDW), usually at rates beginning at around $13 extra per day. For this supplemental fee, the rental agency agrees to eliminate your financial responsibility in case of an accident. If you don't have a CDW and you have an accident, you'll usually pay for some or all of the damage to the car, sometimes even if it isn't your fault. Certain credit-card companies, including certain upscale divisions of American Express and Diners Club, agree to reimburse card users for their deductible in the event of an accident. Because of that, certain cardholders have chosen to waive the cost of the extra CDW. However, although the credit-card issuers will usually (several weeks after the accident) reimburse the renter for the cost of damages, payments have sometimes been delayed with such coverage until after the completion of certain documents. Unless there's enough of a credit line associated with your particular credit card, some car renters involved in an accident will be required to pay sometimes large amounts of cash on the spot. To avoid such misunderstandings, some car-rental companies usually offer their clients the option of automatically including the CDW as a part of the net total of the rental price, even though, in certain circumstances, it might result in "double coverage." In any event, it's always a good idea to ask questions about your insurance liabilities when initially reserving your car, as a means of avoiding insurance-related conflicts later on.

DRIVING RULES Finland observes right-hand traffic, and speed limits of 60, 80, 100, or 120kmph (about 35, 50, 60, and 75 m.p.h., respectively) are strictly enforced.

Many streets in Helsinki are one-way. It is illegal to drive a motor vehicle under the influence of alcohol, and the penalties for doing so are severe; the alcoholic content of one's blood may not exceed 0.5%.

FLY & DRIVE

Finnair, Avis, Budget, and **Hertz** offer tours combining flight and car rentals. Prices are in three different categories. When flying on the much-frequented "Blue Flights," the package price consists of a normal-tariff airfare and the car-rental rate. There are no discounts. When using the domestic less-traveled "Black Flights," a 25% discount on the normal airfare is offered in conjunction with the car rental. On even less frequented domestic "Red Flights," a 50% discount is granted on the airfare. Car-rental rates range from 460 to 990 markkaa ($101.20 to $217.80) a day (but prices will rise by the time of your visit). Rates include unlimited mileage, full insurance, tax, and car delivery to the airport.

All travel agents can make these arrangements, or you can call the **Finnair Tour Desk** in Helsinki at 90/818-7350. You can also request a copy of a "Finland Fly & Drive" brochure at Finnair offices around the world.

BY FERRY

Using ferries to cross the lakes of Finland often avoids the more circuitous road network. However, be warned that ferry prices tend to be high considering the mileage covered, and the progress is slow. But, to compensate, you get to see the Finnish lakeland. The routes are multifarious, and conditions and schedules change based on the season. Therefore, it's best to go to the local tourist office in the area in which you're visiting for information on schedules, fares, and connections. A sample fare, for the 11-hour ferry run between Lahti and Jyväskylä, is 280 markkaa ($61.60) for car and passengers.

SUGGESTED ITINERARIES

IF YOU HAVE 1 WEEK

Unlike the rest of Europe, in Finland it's not customary to drive around the country. Most people rely on trains and airplanes more frequently than they might in other places. However, I have outlined a week-long driving tour through Finland's "southern triangle." If you take the entire tour, the distance will be a total of 317 miles.

Days 1–3: The first day is spent flying to Helsinki and recovering from a transatlantic flight. Day 2 can be spent seeing the sights. The third day is devoted to exploring the nearby islands of the Baltic, such as Suomenlinna, or taking a steamer to Porvoo, the second-oldest town in Finland.

Day 4: Drive from Helsinki to Hämeenlinna, a distance of 61 miles. Take the E79 past forest-covered hills and meadows which eventually give way to open country dotted with lakes. About 20 miles south of Hämeenlinna you can visit Riihimaki, which has a Glass Museum (Suomen Lasimuseo) and a glass shop. By afternoon you'll be in Hämeenlinna. Finland's oldest inland town, founded in 1639, and the birthplace of Jean Sibelius. You can also explore a castle on the shores of Lake Vanajavesi. Hämeenlinna is the starting point of many Silver Line cruise boats which run to Tampere. However, those on a rushed schedule will want only to overnight in Hämeenlinna and continue our tour.

Day 5: Leave Hämeenlinna and drive along the E79 for 50 miles to Tampere. Folk dances and open-air concerts are performed in Hämeenpuisto Park in summer, and the city boasts one of the most famous summer theaters in the world. Many lake tours start from here. Spend the night in Tampere.

Day 6: Head for Turku on the west coast. Leaving Tampere, it's only 10 miles to

Nokia, famous for its rapids in the Nokia River. Continue southwest on Route 41 for 33 miles until you reach Vammala. The road continues to Huittinen, only 56 miles from Turku. Plan to spend the night in Turku, Finland's oldest city, taking in its many attractions.

Day 7: From Turku you may return straight to Helsinki on the E3. This 103-mile run may be broken by a stop at Salo, a lively town 33 miles from Turku. About 6 miles past Salo you can stop at the Muurla Glass Factory. Spend the night in Helsinki.

IF YOU HAVE 2 WEEKS

Days 1–7: Spend the first week as suggested in "If You Have 1 Week," above.

Day 8: Spend a full day in Helsinki getting to know the city better.

Day 9: After Helsinki, head northeast to Lappeenranta, one of Finland's most charming provincial towns, 137 miles from Helsinki and only 10 miles from the Russian border, for a full day of sightseeing in Finland's glorious lake district.

Day 10: After Lappeenranta, continue northeast to the historic city of Imatra, favored by the czars and site of the famous Imatra Rapids.

Days 11 & 12: From Lappeenranta, go to Savonlinna for 2 nights. On the first day explore the land attractions, and on the next tour by lake steamer.

Day 13: Go to Kuopio, in the north lake district, for a day of sightseeing.

Day 14: Journey to Joensuu, the major municipality of northern Karelia, for a day's sightseeing in this richly folkloric province, half of which Finland was forced to cede to the Soviet Union in World War II.

IF YOU HAVE 3 WEEKS

Days 1–14: See "If You Have 2 Weeks," above.

Days 15 & 16: Fly to Rovaniemi, capital of Lapland, for an exploration of the area at the Arctic Circle. On the second day, take a tour to the Arctic Circle and go shopping at Santa's Village, 5 miles north of Rovaniemi.

Day 17: Visit Ranua, 45 miles south of Rovaniemi, seeing its main attractions, the Ranua Wildlife Park. You can either overnight in Ranua or use Rovaniemi as your base.

Day 18: Visit the towns of Kemi and Tornio on the west coast of Finland, opening onto the Gulf of Bothnia. Tornio is only 5½ miles from Kemi.

Day 19: Go to Sodankylä, which many claim is the place where the real Lapland begins. Rovaniemi lies 81 miles to the south. Try your hand at "gold washing" in the environs.

Days 20 & 21: Fly to Ivalo and visit Inari. A good part of the day will be absorbed in making transportation to Ivalo, and the remaining time can be spent exploring the attractions of Inari, which is the name of a small village some 25 miles north of Ivalo but also the name of the largest county in Finland.

FAST FACTS: FINLAND

American Express This company is represented in Finland by **Area Travel,** Pohjoisesplanadi 2, Helsinki (tel. 185-51), open Monday to Friday from 9am to 5pm. Ask about possible affiliated travel agencies that might be tied in with American Express when you're visiting provincial towns. Sometimes there's an affiliate travel agency that can handle American Express clients.

Business Hours Most **banks** are open Monday through Friday from 9:15am to 4:15pm. You can also exchange money at the railway station in Helsinki Monday through Saturday from 8:30am to 8pm and on Sunday from 12:30 to 7pm, and at the airport daily from 6:30am to 11pm.

The hours for **stores and shops** can vary. Most are open Monday through Friday from 9am to 5pm and on Saturday from 9am to 2pm. Nearly everything is closed on Sunday. There are **R-kiosks,** selling confectionery, tobacco, toiletries, cosmetics, and souvenirs, all over Helsinki and in other towns, which are open Monday through Saturday from 8am to 9pm and on Sunday from either 9 or 10am until 9pm.

Camera and Film Most international brands of film are available in camera shops, but often at higher prices than in the U.S. It's better to bring in film duty free for your stay in Finland.

Cigarettes American and British brands are available in all Finnish cities and towns—but they're expensive. In Finland smokers buy their tobacco at one of the R-kiosks, which are all over the major towns.

Climate See "When to Go," above.

Crime See "Safety," below.

Currency See "Currency and Costs," above.

Customs All personal effects, including cameras and a reasonable amount of film, bedding, and other such personal articles are duty-free. Gifts to the value of 1,500 markkaa ($330) may be brought in duty-free. You can bring in 400 cigarettes or 1 pound of other manufactured tobacco. You can also bring in either 2 liters of beer, 1 liter of wine, and 1 liter of spirits or 2 liters of beer and 2 liters of wine. You need to be over 20 to bring in spirits and over 18 to bring in beer and wine. There are no restrictions on the amount of Finnish or foreign currency you can bring in, but you can only take it out if you can prove that you brought it in with you.

Driving Rules See "Getting Around," above, in this chapter.

Drug Laws Drug offenses are divided into two categories: normal drug offenses and aggravated drug offenses. Normal drug offenses include the possession of a small amount of marijuana carrying a maximum penalty of 2 years in prison and a minimum penalty of a fine for Finns and possible deportation for non-Finns. Aggravated drug offenses mean anything to do with ownership, sale, or dealing in drugs considered extremely dangerous, such as cocaine and heroin. This offense always carries a prison term ranging from 1 to 10 years. Penalties for smuggling across Finnish frontiers are even more severe.

Drugstores Medicines are sold at pharmacies (*apteekki* in Finnish). Chemists (*kemikaalipauppa* in Finnish) sell cosmetics only. Some pharmacies are open 24 hours, and all display notices in their windows giving the address of the nearest one on night duty.

Electricity Finland operates on 220 volts AC. Plugs are usually the continental size with rounded pins. Always ask at your hotel desk before plugging in any electrical appliance. Without the appropriate converter or adapter, you'll probably destroy the internal mechanics of your appliance and/or blow out one of the hotel's fuses and upset the management.

Embassies and Consulates The **U.S. Embassy** is at Itäinen Puistotie 14B, SF-00140 Helsinki (tel. 90/171-931); the **British Embassy** is at Itäinen Puistotie 17, SF-00140 Helsinki (tel. 90/661-293); and the **Canadian Embassy** is at Pohjoisesplanadi 25B, SF-00100 Helsinki (tel. 90/171-141). Travelers from Australia and New Zealand should contact the British Embassy.

If you're planning to visit Russia after Finland, and need information about visas, the **Russian Embassy** is at Tehtaankatu 1B, SF-00140 Helsinki (tel. 90/661-876). However, it's better to make all travel arrangements to Russia before you leave home.

Emergencies In Helsinki, dial **000** or **181-000** for medical services. All hospitals have doctors on duty around the clock.

Etiquette Both women and men shake hands when introduced. If invited for dinner, bring wine, flowers, or candy. In a sauna there is no loud joking or laughing. It's even considered impolite to whistle.

Gasoline See "Getting Around," above, in this chapter.

Hitchhiking   See "Getting Around," above, in this chapter.

Holidays   See "When to Go," above, in this chapter.

Language   The Finns speak a language that, from a point of view of grammar and linguistics, is radically different from Swedish and Danish. Finnish is as difficult to learn as Chinese, and a source of endless frustration to newcomers. More than 90% of Finland speaks Finnish, while the remaining citizens usually speak Swedish. Finland is officially a bilingual country, as you'll quickly see from maps and street signs in Helsinki, which usually list street names in both languages.

The use of English, however, is amazingly common throughout Finland, especially among young people. In all major hotels, restaurants, and nightclubs, English is spoken almost without exception. The best phrase book is the *Berlitz Finnish for Travellers,* with 1,200 phrases and 2,000 useful words, with pronunciation shown throughout.

Laundry   For listings of self-service laundries, see the individual city chapters.

Liquor Laws   Alcohol is retailed only from **Alko,** the state liquor-monopoly shops. These are open Monday through Thursday from 10am to 5pm, on Friday from 10am to 6pm, and on Saturday from 9am to 2pm; they're closed on Sunday and on May 1 and September 30. Drinks can also be purchased in hotels, restaurants, and nightclubs. Some establishments, incidentally, are licensed only for beer or for beer and wine. Only beer can be served from 9 to 11am. In Helsinki most licensed establishments stay open until midnight or 1am (until 11pm in some of the other cities).

A person age 20 can buy any kind of alcoholic drink from the Alko shops; those who are 18 and 19 years of age can purchase only the weaker alcoholic drinks containing less than 17% alcohol, such as wine and beer.

Mail   Airmail letters take about 7 to 10 days to reach North America, and surface letters—sent by boat—take 1 to 2 months. Parcels are weighed and registered at the **post office,** which may require you to make declaration on a preprinted form as to the value and contents of a package. Stamps are sold at post offices in all towns and cities, at most hotels, sometimes at news kiosks, and often by shopkeepers who provide service not for profit but for convenience. In Finland, **mailboxes** are painted bright yellow, and they have a trumpet embossed on them. Postal **rates** for airmail letters and postcards to North America are 3.40 markkaa (75¢) for letters and 2.90 markkaa (55¢) for postcards.

Maps   The following maps are published by the National Board of Survey: *Road Map of Finland* (GT 1:200,000), an accurate, detailed road and touring map, and *Motoring Road Map* (1:800,000), a new edition of the *Motoring Road Map of Finland,* appearing annually, and the only map with complete information on road surfacing. These maps are the most important ones, although the board also publishes numerous touring maps. They are for sale at major bookstores in Helsinki (see "Fast Facts: Helsinki" in Chapter 33) or may be obtained from the **Map Center of the National Board of Survey,** Karttakeskus Espa, Eteläesplanadi 4 (PB 209), 00131 Helsinki (tel. 90/154-3168).

Newspapers and Magazines   English-language newspapers, including the *International Herald Tribune,* are available at the larger bookstores, the railway station, and many kiosks in central Helsinki and other cities.

Pets   Live animals may be imported only with a permit from the Veterinary Department of the Ministry of Agriculture and Forestry. Dogs and cats, however, can be brought in provided they are accompanied by a certificate issued by a competent veterinary surgeon in the country of origin. The animal must have been vaccinated against rabies at least 30 days and not more than 12 months prior to importation. Travelers should remember that animals imported to Finland cannot be taken to Sweden or Norway without a quarantine period of 4 months in either country.

Police   Dial **112** in Helsinki. In smaller towns, ask the operator to connect you with the nearest police station.

Radio and TV   "Northern Report," a program in English, is broadcast at 558 kHz on the AM dial in Helsinki daily at 9:30am, 9:35pm, and at midnight. There's also a special Saturday-morning program from 10:30 to 11:30am. A news summary in English is given on the domestic FM networks 1 and 4 daily at 10:55pm. Radio

Finland international programs on 100.8 MHz (FM) in Helsinki are presented daily at 5:30, 7:35, 9:30, 11, and 11:30am, at 1:30, 2, 3, 4, 5:05, and 9:35pm, and at midnight, as well as on 94.0 MHz (FM) in Helsinki at 10:30pm. For information and a free publication, *Radio Finland,* about radio programs in foreign languages, telephone 90/401-3733 in Helsinki.

Restrooms Most public restrooms are located in terminals (air, bus, and rail). Hotels usually have very clean toilets, as do the better restaurants and clubs. Most toilets are designated by appropriate symbols to distinguish between facilities for men or women. Otherwise, *naisille* is for women and *miehille* is for men.

Safety Whenever you're traveling in an unfamiliar city or country, stay alert. Be aware of your immediate surroundings. Wear a moneybelt and don't sling your camera or purse over your shoulder; wear the strap diagonally across your body. Every society has its criminals. It's your responsibility to be aware and alert, even in the most heavily touristed areas.

Taxes A 22% sales tax is added to most retail purchases in Finland. However, anyone residing outside the country can shop tax-free in Finland, saving about 11% on purchases over 200 markkaa ($44). Look for the TAX-FREE FOR TOURISTS sticker which will guide you to shops participating in the program. Such shops will give the customer a check covering the tax, which can be cashed when leaving the country—even if the goods were bought on a credit card. The check and goods purchased must be presented at the point of departure from the country, and the amount of the check will be given to you. Tax-free purchases must be taken out of Finland, not used within the country. The refunds can be collected at airports, ferry ports, or highway border points.

Telephone, Telex, and Fax Finland has such a complicated system of telephone networks that it's best for you to inquire about making a call in the area where you're stopping. For information and number inquiries, phone 92020, and for price inquiries, 92023. Direct dialing is possible to most countries from Finland, and to order such a call, dial 92022.

To call to Finland from abroad, dial the international prefix, the country code to Finland, 358, the trunk code (without the prefix 9 otherwise given in the trunk code for in-Finland calls), and the number you are trying to reach.

It is customary in Finland to send faxes and the increasingly outmoded telex messages from your hotel. If your hotel is too small to own a fax, go to one of the larger hotels in whatever town you're staying in. Usually the staff will send a telex or fax for you—sometimes at cost, at other times for a small charge.

Time Finland has "summer time" from March 28 (3am) to September 26 (4am). In summer, it is 3 hours ahead of Greenwich mean time (GMT); in winter, 2 hours ahead of GMT. The time difference between U.S. eastern standard time and Finnish standard time is 7 hours. When it is midnight in New York, it is 7am in Finland. The time difference between eastern daylight time in the United States and Finnish daylight time is still 7 hours.

Tipping **Hotels and restaurants** add a service charge of 15%, and usually no further tipping is necessary. In restaurants, it's customary to leave just the small change. **Taxi drivers** do not expect a tip. However, it's proper to offer from 5 markkaa ($1.10) to **doormen,** and **bellhops** usually get 5 markkaa ($1.10) per bag. However, in most provincial hotels in Finland, you carry your own luggage to your room. At railway stations, porters usually get 5 markkaa ($1.10) per bag. Hairdressers and barbers don't expect to be tipped. **Coatcheck charges** are usually posted, and there is no need for further tipping unless you want to.

Water Water in Finland is generally safe to drink.

Yellow Pages Forget them! To a foreigner, the yellow pages in Finnish phone books are a disaster. You can't find anything unless you know the Finnish language. Better ask someone at your hotel the phone number or address of a service you are seeking.

INTRODUCING HELSINKI

Helsinki may stand at the doorway to Russia, but its cultural links are firmly in Scandinavia. It was originally founded in 1550 on orders of the Swedish king Gustavus Vasa, halfway between Stockholm and St. Petersburg, and is still known to the Swedes as Helsingfors.

Surrounded by water on three sides and fringed by islands, Helsinki grew up around a natural harbor overlooking the Gulf of Finland. A city of wide streets, squares, and parks, adorned with sculpture, Helsinki was one of the world's first planned municipalities, and is noted for its 19th-century neoclassical architecture. As it is relatively compact, most of the city can be reached on foot.

From the capital of an autonomous grand duchy of Russia, Helsinki was transformed in 1917, the year of the Russian Revolution, into the capital of the newly independent Finland. Today it is not only a center of government but the nation's intellectual capital, with a major university and many cultural and scientific institutions. Although also a business and industrial center (most major Finnish firms have their headquarters here), and the hub of Finland's air, rail, and road networks, Helsinki is relatively pollution free.

With a population of about half a million, Helsinki today is a city of urban sophistication—although locals still speak of it as "a big village." And its people are some of the most educated, best clothed, best fed, and best housed on earth.

1. ORIENTATION

ARRIVING

BY PLANE   Helsinki-Vantaa Airport (tel. 818-51) lies 12½ miles from the center of Helsinki, about a 30-minute bus ride. Buses to the airport leave from the Air Terminal at Asema-aukio 3 and the Hotel Inter-Continental in Helsinki, Mannerheimintie 46, two to four times an hour daily between 5:45am and 10:15pm; tickets cost 18 markkaa ($4). The coach also departs from the Hotel Ramada Presidentti, Eteläinen Rautatiekatu 4, hourly Monday through Friday from 6:05am to 8:20pm, Saturday from 8:20am to 5:20pm, and on Sunday from 10:55am to 7:20pm; a ticket costs 14 markkaa ($3.10). From Railway Square (Platform 26), bus no. 615 leaves one to three times an hour from 5:25am to 11:50pm, also costing 14 markkaa ($3.10). A taxi ride into the center costs 105 markkaa ($23.10). Instead a regular taxi, you can take a special yellow taxi at the airport terminal for only 50 markkaa ($11) per person. These can be ordered 24 hours a day, 7 days a week (call 2200-2500).

You must check in 20 minutes early for a domestic flight, 30 minutes for a

WHAT'S SPECIAL ABOUT HELSINKI

Monuments

☐ Suomenlinna Fortress, the "Gibraltar of the North," in the archipelago guarding the approach to Helsinki.

☐ Sibelius Monument, created by Eila Hiltunen to honor Finland's most famous composer.

Buildings

☐ The Finnish Parliament, a red granite structure from 1931, famous for its "gallery of nudes."

☐ The Cathedral, Senate Square, the 19th-century Evangelical-Lutheran cathedral designed by Engel and commissioned by the Russian czar.

Museums

☐ Mannerheim Museum, the former residence of Baron Mannerheim, considered the 20th century's military savior of Finland.

☐ National Museum of Finland, repository of many of the country's historical and artistic treasures.

Parks/Gardens

☐ Seurasaari Open-Air Park, set in a national park on an island, a miniature preview of Old Finland.

☐ Botanical Gardens of the University of Helsinki, filled with exotic plants, including palms and orchids.

Events/Festivals

☐ Helsinki Festival, highlight of the Finnish summer, attracting international artists for a 3-week-long program.

For the Kids

☐ The Helsinki Zoo, on Korkeasaari Island, with its collection of northern European animals, including wild forest reindeer.

☐ Linnanmäki, a fun fair run by the Children's Foundation of Finland.

European flight, 40 minutes for a flight to Russia, and 45 minutes for a flight to the United States.

BY TRAIN Helsinki Railway Station at Kaivokatu (tel. 65-94-11) has luggage storage lockers costing 10 markkaa ($2.20). The lost luggage department is open daily from 6:30am to 10:30pm.

BY BUS Helsinki Bus Station does not have a street address but it is located between Salomonkatu in the city center (tel. 97-00-40-00). Using Stockholm as your embarkation point for Finland, take a ferry to Turku on the west coast. At Turku, you can board one of 21 daily buses that make the 2½ hour run to Helsinki.

BY CAR Helsinki is connected by road to all Finnish cities. If you arrive in the west at the port of Turku on a car-ferry from Sweden, you can take the E3 express highway east to Helsinki.

BY FERRY Ferries arrive at Viking Line Terminal, Etelasatama (tel. 123-51) or at Silja Line Terminal on Laivasillankatu (tel. 180-44-55).

TOURIST INFORMATION

The **Helsinki City Tourist Office,** Pohjoisesplanadi 19, SF-00100 Helsinki (tel. 90/169-3757), is open May 16 to September 15, Monday through Friday from 8:30am to 6pm and on Saturday from 8:30am to 1pm; September 16 to May 15, on Monday from 8:30am to 4:30pm and Tuesday through Friday from 8:30am to 4pm.

The **Helsinki Tourist Association** is at Lönnrotinkatu 7 (tel. 90/645-225). For **recorded information** on what's happening in Helsinki, call 058.

CITY LAYOUT

MAIN ARTERIES & STREETS

Helsinki (Helsingfors in Swedish) is a peninsula city, skirted by islands and skerries. The main artery is the wide and handsome **Mannerheimintie,** named in honor of the former field marshal. East of Mannerheimintie, opening onto Kaivokatu, is the **Helsinki Railway Station.** Toward the harbor is **Senaatintori,** crowned by the landmark cathedral. This Senate Square, designed by Engel, also includes the government and university buildings.

Continuing east is a bridge crossing over a tiny island—**Katajanokka**—dominated by the Eastern Orthodox cathedral. Back across the bridge, sticking close to the harbor, past the President's Palace, is the most colorful square in Helsinki, the **Kauppatori (Market Square)** (see it early in the morning when it's the most animated). From the pier there, it's possible to catch boats for **Suomenlinna,** fortified islands that guard the sea lanes to Helsinki.

The great promenade street of Helsinki—**Esplanadi** (Esplanade)—begins west of the Market Square. Directly north of the esplanade and running parallel to it is **Aleksanterinkatu,** the principal shopping street.

FINDING AN ADDRESS

Street numbers always begin on the south side of streets running on a north-south axis, and on the eastern end of streets running east-west. All odd numbers are on one side of the street and all even numbers on the opposite side. In some cases, where a large building contains several establishments, there might be an A or B attached to the number.

NEIGHBORHOODS IN BRIEF

Helsinki divides roughly into distinct districts.

Downtown The monumental heartland stretches from **Senaatintori (Senate Square)** to **Esplanadi.** Senate Square is dominated by a Lutheran cathedral in its center, and Esplanadi itself is an avenue lined with trees. At one end of Esplanadi, the monumental **Mannerheimintie,** stretching for 3 miles, is the main road from the city center to the expanding suburbs. The section south of Esplanadi is one of the wealthiest in the capital, lined with embassies and elaborate houses, rising into **Kaivopuisto Park.**

Kruununhaka and Hakaniemi The district of **Kruununhaka** is one of the oldest. Helsinki was founded in 1550 at the mouth of the Vantaa River, but was resited in 1640 on the peninsula of Vironniemi in the place that is today known as Kruununhaka. This section, along with neighboring **Hakaniemi,** contain what buildings remain of Helsinki of the 17th century. The waters of Kaisaniemenlahti divide the districts of Hakaniemi and Kruununhaka.

The Islands Helsinki also contains several islands, some of which are known as "tourist islands," including **Korkeasaari,** site of the Helsinki Zoo. The main islands are linked by convenient ferries and water taxis.

Called "fortress of Finland" and the "Gibraltar of the North," **Suomenlinna** consists of five main islands, all interconnected, and is the site of many museums. You can spend a day here, exploring the old fortifications. **Seurasaari,** another island, contains a bathing beach and recreation area, and is also the site of a national park and the largest open-air museum in Finland.

Espoo In the environs, many workers in Helsinki treat Espoo as a bedroom suburb. Actually, since 1972, when it achieved its charter, it is the fourth-largest city of Finland, with a population of 150,000 people.

Tapiola Another "suburb city," Tapiola was founded in 1951, providing homes for some 16,000 residents. This "model city" greatly influenced housing developments around the world, with its wide variety of housing which ranges from multistory condo units to more luxurious one-family villas. The greatest Finnish architect, Alvar Aalto, was one of its planners.

MAPS

The best city map of Helsinki is called *Falk plan*. Containing a highly detailed and alphabetized street index, it can easily be carried in your pocket. *Falk plan* maps are sold at nearly all bookstores and many news kiosks in the central city, including the major bookstore of Helsinki, **Academic,** Keskuskatu 1 (tel. 121-41).

2. GETTING AROUND

Helsinki has an efficient transportation network, which includes buses, trams, subway (metro), ferries, and taxis.

BY PUBLIC TRANSPORTATION

DISCOUNT PASSES Visitors to Helsinki can purchase the **Helsinki Card,** offering unlimited travel on the city's public buses, trams, subway, and ferries, and a free guided sightseeing tour by bus (in summer daily, in off-season on Saturday), as well as free entry to about 40 museums and other sights in Helsinki. It also includes attractive hotel packages in several hotels in the capital. The Helsinki Card is available for 1-, 2-, or 3-day periods. The price of the card for adults is 75 markkaa ($16.50) for 1 day, 105 markkaa ($23.10) for 2 days, and 125 markkaa ($27.50) for 3 days. A card for children costs 45 markkaa ($9.90) for 1 day, 55 markkaa ($12.10) for 2 days, and 65 markkaa ($14.30) for 3 days. The cards can be bought at 35 sales points in the Helsinki area, including the Helsinki City Tourist Office, the Hotel Booking Center (see Section 1, "Helsinki Accommodations," in Chapter 34), travel agencies, and hotels. For further information, check with any Finnish Tourist Board, such as the one at 655 Third Ave., New York, NY 10017 (tel. 212/949-2333), or the Helsinki Tourist Association, Lönnrotinkatu 7 (tel. 645-225).

You can also purchase a **tourist ticket,** at 48 markkaa ($10.60) for adults and 24 markkaa ($5.30) for children, allowing unlimited travel on city transport lines within 24 hours. This ticket is sold in the City Transport Office, the city tourist office, and the hotel-booking center.

BY METRO/BUS/TRAIN The **City Transport Office** is at the Rautatientori metro station (tel. 472-2252), open Monday through Thursday from 10am to 5pm and Friday from 8am to 3pm. The transport system operates daily from 5:30am to 1:35am. A single ticket costs 8 markkaa ($1.80) for adults, 4 markkaa (90¢) for children. It's cheaper to purchase a multitrip ticket, allowing 10 individual journeys for 70 markkaa ($15.40) for adults, 25 markkaa ($5.50) for children. Transfers are allowed for single and multitrip tickets within 1 hour of the time stamped on the ticket.

BY FERRY Ferries depart from the end of Eteläesplanadi (no terminal) heading for the offshore islands of Suomenlinna and Korkeasaari (Zoo).

BY TAXI

There are a number of taxi stations around Helsinki, but cabs can also be hailed in the street or ordered by phone. A taxi is available if the yellow *taksi* dome is lit. Taxis are metered, and a basic fare costs 14 markkaa ($3.10) in Helsinki; an extra charge of 5 markkaa ($1.10) is imposed at night and on weekends from 2pm on Saturday until 6am on Monday. To arrange for a taxi a day in advance, call 1824.

Tipping has become fairly common, although taxi drivers do not expect it.

BY CAR

Driving around Helsinki by car is not recommended, because of limited parking. Either walk or take public transportation. However, touring the environs by car is ideal.

CAR RENTALS The major car-rental companies maintain offices in Helsinki. These include **Avis Rent a Car,** Fredrikinkatu 67 (tel. 441-114); **Budget Rent a Car,** Fredrikinkatu 61A (tel. 694-5300); and **Hertz,** Mannherheimintie 44 (tel. 446-910).

PARKING There are two parking garages in the center of Helsinki. They are **Forum-parkkihalli,** Mannerheimintie 20 (tel. 694-7500), and **City Paikoitus Oy,** Kaivokatu 8 (tel. 177-077). It's usually very difficult to find a place to park on the street.

BY BICYCLE

Bicycles can be rented at the **Youth Hostel Stadionin Maja,** Pohjoinen Stadionintie 3B, at the Olympic Stadium (tel. 496-071). The fee is 40 markkaa ($8.80) a day, plus a deposit of 100 markkaa ($22) or your passport.

FAST FACTS: HELSINKI

American Express The representative of American Express in Helsinki is **Area Travel,** Pohjoisesplanadi 2 (tel. 185-51). Hours are Monday through Friday from 9am to 5pm.

Area Code The telephone area code for Helsinki is 90.

Babysitters Every hotel in Finland has a list of employees, such as maids, who with advance notification will agree to babysit for your child. Most speak English. The rate in Helsinki is about 50 markkaa ($11) per hour (slightly less in provincial towns).

Bookstores The most famous bookstore in Finland—and the best stocked, with thousands of English titles—is **Academic Bookstore,** Keskuskatu 1 (tel. 121-41).

Business Hours Most **banks** are open Monday through Friday from 9:15am to 4:15pm. You can also exchange money at the railway station Monday through Saturday from 8:30am to 8pm and on Sunday from 12:30 to 7pm, and at the airport daily from 6:30am to 11pm.

Most **businesses and shops** are open Monday through Friday from 9am to 5pm and on Saturday from 9am to 2pm. Nearly everything is closed on Sunday. Many shops in the center of Helsinki are open until 8pm on certain nights, particularly on Monday and Friday. Shops in the Station Tunnel are generally open Monday through Saturday from 10am to 10pm and on Sunday from noon to 10pm.

There are **R-kiosk's,** selling confectionery, tobacco, toiletries, cosmetics, and souvenirs, all over Helsinki and in other towns, which are open Monday through Saturday from 8am to 9pm and on Sunday from 9 or 10am until 9pm.

Currency Exchange You can exchange dollars for markkaa at most banks and often in your hotel, if it's big enough. However, hotels are more for convenience as their exchange rates are not as favorable as the banks'. There is a currency-exchange kiosk at the Central Station, open daily from 11:30am to 6pm; after 4pm it imposes a 4 markkaa (90¢) surcharge.

Dentists There are English-speaking dentists on duty around the clock in Helsinki; call 736-166.

Doctors To summon a physician for **emergency calls,** call 112. For private medical service, contact the **Alekski Medical Station,** Mannerheimintie 8 (tel. 601-911 for an appointment); open Monday through Friday from 8am to 6pm. Most doctors speak English.

Drugstores Pharmacies dispensing medicines are known as *apteekki.* The **Yliopiston apteekki,** Mannerheimintie 96 (tel. 415-778), is open 24 hours daily, and service from 7am to midnight is available at Mannerheimintie 5 (tel. 179-092).

Embassies and Consulates The **United States Embassy** is at Itäinen Puistotie 14B (tel. 171-931); the **Canadian Embassy,** at Pohjoisesplanadi

25B (tel. 171-141); and the **British Embassy,** Itäinen Puistotie 17 (tel. 661-293). Citizens of **Australia** and **New Zealand** should go to the British Embassy.

Emergencies   Dial **112** or **181-000** for medical help, police, or a fire alarm. To call for an ambulance, dial **006.** An emergency hospital for foreigners is the **Helsinki University Central Hospital,** Meilahti Hospital (for both medical and surgical care), at Haart-maninkatur 4 (tel. 4711).

Eyeglasses   Finland offers dozens of high-quality opticians who can make new glasses in about a day. One well-recommended company is **Nissen,** Keskuskatu 3 (tel. 659-499), open Monday through Friday from 9am to 6pm and on Saturday from 9am to 2pm.

Gas Station   Open 24 hours a day is **Esso,** Pohjoinen Rautatiekatu 27 (tel. 440-611).

Hairdressers and Barbers   **Salon Tittihaapala,** Eerikinkatu 12 (tel. 611-110), is a large, modern, and hip hair emporium that cuts and styles hair for both sexes.

Hospitals   An emergency hospital for foreigners is the **Helsinki University Central Hospital,** Meilahti Hospital (for both medical and surgical care), at Haart-maninkatur 4 (tel. 4711).

Laundry and Dry Cleaning   Doing 1-day dry cleaning on the premises, **Lindström Ltd.** has shops in the City Passage (City-käytävä) opposite the railway station (tel. 657-251) in Helsinki and in the shopping center in Tapiola (tel. 463-633). At the laundry **Exprès Pikapesula,** Laivurinrinne 2 (tel. 639-524), clothes brought in early in the morning can be ready by the 5:30pm closing time.

Libraries   The **Helsinki City Library** has a main branch close to the Pasili Railway Station (the second most important rail station in town) at Rautatielaisenkatu 8 (tel. 159-7501). A more centrally located, but secondary, branch of the Helsinki Public Library is at Rikhardinkatu 3 (tel. 166-2820).

Liquor Laws   The legal age to consume beer and hard liquor in Helsinki is 18. Many nightclubs, however, with every legal right, admit only "well-dressed clients," who in some cases are 24 or older. Laws against drunken driving are rigidly enforced in Helsinki, much to the delight of taxi drivers who take home drunken club patrons.

Lost Property   The Lost Property Office is at Päijänteentie 12A (tel. 189-3180), open September to May, Monday through Friday from 8am to 4:15pm; June to August, Monday through Friday from 8am to 3:15pm.

Luggage Storage and Lockers   These facilities are found at the Central Station on Kaivokatu. The staff offers both a system of lockers with take-away keys and an employee-staffed area where you get a ticket for your luggage. The charge is 10 markkaa ($2.20) per bag. The service operates daily from 6am to 10:30pm.

Photographic Needs   One of the best-stocked camera stores in town— and the most centrally located—is **Helios,** Mannerheimintie 14 (tel. 680-1400), open Monday through Friday from 9am to 5pm and on Saturday from 9am to 2pm (closes at 1pm in summer). It takes only 1 hour to develop prints.

Police   In an emergency, dial 112. Otherwise, go to the **police headquarters** at Pieni Robertinkatu 1-3 (tel. 1891).

Post Office   For post office **information,** call 195-5117. The **main post office** in Helsinki is at Mannerheimintie 11, open Monday through Friday from 9am to 5pm. If you don't know your address in Helsinki, have your mail sent 00 100 *Poste Restante* (general delivery) in care of the main post office in Helsinki. At this Poste Restante, you can pick up mail (upon presentation of your passport) Monday through Saturday from 8am to 10pm and on Sunday from 11am to 10pm. You can purchase stamps at the railway station post office Monday through Friday from 7:15am to 8pm and on Saturday and Sunday from 10am to 8pm. Yellow stamp machines outside post offices function with 5-markkaa coins.

Radio and TV   **Radio Finland** broadcasts news in English every day on the national YLE-3 network at 9:55pm. The external service of the **Finnish Broadcasting Company** has daily programs in English which can be heard on 103.7 MHz (FM) Monday through Friday at 7:30, 9:30, 11, and 11:30am, and 1:50, 3, 4, 5, and 9:30pm, midnight, and 2am. **Radio One** features a BBC World Service News daily at noon (in winter, broadcasts are at 11am). Helsinki has two TV channels. Programs from abroad, such as those from the United States and Britain, are broadcast in their original languages, with Finnish subtitles.

Religious Services Lutheranism is the major religion of the population. Smaller groups—Catholics, Jews, Greek Orthodox—are also represented, and there is religious freedom for all. For Protestants, the Temppeliaukio Church, Lutherinkatu 3 (tel. 494-698), conducts an English-language service every Sunday at 2pm. **Roman Catholic** services are conducted at St. Henrik's Church, Puistokatu 1 (tel. 637-853). The **Anglican** church, Cathedral Chapel, Senate Square (tel. 563-4829), has services in English on Sunday at 10:30am. There's a **synagogue** at Malminkatu 26 (tel. 694-1302 for information).

Restrooms There's a centrally located public toilet at Sofiankatu 2. Otherwise, many locals use café toilets (it's polite to at least order a cup of coffee or a soft drink), or they make use of the facilities at transit terminals.

Shoe Repairs A centrally located shop providing this service is **Presidentin Suutari,** Olavinkatu 2 (tel. 694-3631), open Monday through Friday from 8am to 5:30pm and on Saturday from 9am to 2pm.

Taxes Helsinki, like the rest of Finland, imposes a value-added tax of 22% on goods and services.

Taxis See "Getting Around" in this chapter.

Telephones, Telegrams, Telex, and Fax For information and number inquiries, call 92-020 in Helsinki. If you're thinking about calling home (providing you're not calling collect) and want to know how much it'll cost, dial 92-023.

Automatic intercity (long-distance) calls can be made from call boxes, located throughout the city, that take 1 markkaa (20¢) and 5 markkaa ($1.10) coins; the routing numbers and rates are listed in the phone directory. Automatic calls to other countries can be made from these call boxes, or from the **Tele-Service** office, Mannerheimintie 11B. The Tele-Service office also handles other long-distance calls, telegrams, and telex; it is open daily from 7am to 11pm, but it offers 24-hour service by phone (tel. 021).

If you call from your hotel, the bill might be doubled or tripled.

For local calls inside the city limits of Helsinki, you do not need to dial 90.

It is customary to send faxes from hotels. If your hotel is too small to have a fax, go to one of the larger hotels and request that the staff there send a fax. You'll be billed not only for the fax, but perhaps a surcharge as well.

Transit Information The City Transport Office is at the Rautatientori metro station (tel. 472-2252). For railway information, call 010-115, and for information about city buses, trams, and metro, dial 010-111 or 765-966.

Weather Summers in Helsinki are often sunny, but temperatures rarely are so high as to be uncomfortable. (see "When to Go" in Chapter 32). The best weather is in July, which experiences the highest temperature, a comfortable 63°F on the average. Nights are greatly extended in midsummer in Helsinki when Lapland is bathed in the Midnight Sun. In winter, temperatures hover between 21° and 27°F, but it's not true that polar bears roam the streets.

3. NETWORKS & RESOURCES

FOR STUDENTS For travel arrangements, go to **Travela,** Mannerheimintie 5 (tel. 624-101), right near the train station. For students with proper IDs, it offers discount travel opportunities, and is familiar with making arrangements to tour not only Finland, but Russia and Eastern Europe as well. It's open Monday through Friday from 9am to 5pm.

The **Finnish Youth Hostel Association,** Yrjönkatu 38B (tel. 694-0377), south of the bus station, is another good source of information. It's especially helpful to young people planning to go hiking in Finland, including Lapland. The headquarters will provide information about all youth hostels in Finland. It's open Monday through Friday from 9am to 4pm.

Socially, the best place to meet fellow university students is **KY-Exit** (see "Evening Entertainment" in Chapter 35), which is owned and run by the Student Union of the Helsinki School of Economics.

Summer courses in Finnish for foreign university students are arranged by the Finnish Ministry of Education. Further information is available from the Council for Instruction of Finnish for Foreigners, Pohjoisranta 4A, 00170 Helsinki. A helpful booklet, "Courses in Finnish Language and Culture," is available from Finnish embassies and consulates, from university teachers of Finnish or Finno-Ugric languages abroad, or by writing to the Council for Instruction of Finnish for Foreigners (see above).

FOR GAY MEN & LESBIANS The gay scene for both men and women is dominated by a blanket organization called SETA, actually a loose confederation of "sexual minority groups." Each summer they stage Gay Pride Days, and foreign visitors are welcome to participate in these. Both men and women can find out what's happening in Helsinki by visiting the **SETA** headquarters at Mäkelänkatu 36A (tel. 769-642), open Tuesday from 10am to 2pm, Wednesday 10am to 6pm, Thursday 2 to 6pm, and Friday 10am to 2pm.

SETA sponsors a gay disco on Monday night, called "Triangle," at **Berlin,** Töölönkatu 3 (tel. 499-002), a club usually devoted to heavy rock or the latest "acid" sounds.

The major gay bar of Helsinki is **Gambrini** (see "Evening Entertainment" in Chapter 35). "Every other Saturday" at this club is reserved for women.

Many gay men and lesbians also patronize **Vanhan Kellari,** although this cellar is predominantly straight.

FOR WOMEN The headquarters of the **Finnish Feminists' Union** (Naisasialiitto Unioni) is at Bulevardi 11A (tel. 64-24-61), in the center of Helsinki. This is a friendly, helpful center, especially for women traveling alone in Helsinki. On the premises is **Naistenhuone,** a women's café and bookshop, open Monday through Friday from 4 to 9pm, Saturday from noon to 6pm, and Sunday from 2 to 6pm.

Women find Helsinki a safe destination, although the usual discreet precautions one follows anywhere should be observed here. Violent crimes such as rape against women are extremely rare. In such an unlikely emergency, women are advised to call the police at 112.

CHAPTER 34

HELSINKI ACCOMMODATIONS & DINING

1. HELSINKI ACCOMMODATIONS
- **FROMMER'S COOL FOR KIDS: HOTELS**
2. HELSINKI DINING
- **FROMMER'S COOL FOR KIDS: RESTAURANTS**

There's a big selection of accommodations and dining establishments in Helsinki. The trick is finding something that suits your budget. As is the rest of Scandinavia, Finland is not cheap. Your best bet with hotels is to plan in as far advance as possible and to take advantage of any discounts that might be offered. To make the most of dining in Finland, eat lunch at the more expensive places when prices will be greatly reduced and eat lightly or cheaply for dinner. Always watch the bar bill—drinking can make any meal expensive.

1. HELSINKI ACCOMMODATIONS

Hotels are classified as Very Expensive, Expensive, Moderate, and Inexpensive. Even a hotel classified as very expensive might offer a few moderately priced rooms, but these are usually booked quickly and hard to obtain for the average visitor. Price classifications, although there are exceptions, are 1,000 markkaa ($220) and up for a double room, **Very Expensive;** 830 to 990 markkaa ($182.60 to $217.80), **Expensive;** 510 to 830 markkaa ($112.20 to $217.80), **Moderate;** 300 to 510 markkaa ($66 to $112.20), **Inexpensive.** Midsummer and weekend discounts reduce these high charges substantially.

In Helsinki, peak rates are charged in winter, because most of the major hotels depend on winter business travelers—not summer tourists—to fill their rooms. The tourists still do not make up for the disappearing Finns who leave Helsinki for other summer pleasures.

A ROOM IN A HURRY The **Hotellikeskus** (Hotel Booking Center), Asema-aukio 3 (tel. 171-133), located in the heart of the city between the railroad station and the main post office, is open June 1 through August 30 Monday through Saturday from 9am to 7pm and Sunday from 10am to 6pm; from September through May, Monday through Friday, from 9am to 5pm. You state the price you are willing to pay, and the English-speaking attendant will phone a hotel and provide you with a map and instructions for reaching your lodgings. The secretary at the Hotellikeskus charges a booking fee of 10 markkaa ($2.20) for a single or double room. Ask for special "Helsinki Card" hotel rates, which do not have a booking fee (see "Getting Around" in Chapter 33).

IN THE CITY CENTER
VERY EXPENSIVE

All rooms in this category include private bath.

HOTEL HESPERIA, Mannerheimintie 50, SF-00260 Helsinki. Tel. 90/43-101. Fax 90/431-0995. 372 rms, 4 suites. A/C MINIBAR TV TEL **Tram:** 3B, 3T.

$ Rates: 780–880 markkaa ($171.60–$193.60) single; 1,020 markkaa ($224.40) double; from 1,800 markkaa ($396) suite. Breakfast 40 markkaa ($8.80) extra. AE, DC, MC, V. **Parking:** 80 markkaa ($17.60).

A leading Finland hotel, near Hesperia Park and the Finnair Terminal, the elegant Hesperia is a favorite of the business traveler. Built of Carrara marble, it has a color scheme of warm browns and light tints. Rooms are elegantly furnished, and the suites are named and decorated after Finland's other Nordic neighbors. The bedrooms have extra-wide beds and a number of amenities, such as trouser presses and radios. Each room contains a sofa.

Dining/Entertainment: The Fransmanni is a French-style restaurant, specializing in juicy steaks from a lava grill, and the Pub Fransmanni is open until 1am. The Lobby bar offers coffee, sandwiches, and salads. The hotel's specialty restaurant is the Russian Room, offering the late 19th-century cuisine of Imperial Russia. A nightclub features dancing to live music.

Services: Laundry, babysitting, room service, masseur.

Facilities: Four saunas, swimming pool, gym, barbershop, hairdresser, solarium, parking in hotel yard and a garage, gift shop, bank, travel agency.

INTER-CONTINENTAL, Mannerheimintie 46, SF-00260 Helsinki. Tel. 90/40-551, or toll free 800/327-0200 in the U.S. Fax 90/405-5255. 543 rms, 12 suites. **Tram:** 3B, 3T, 4, 7, 10.

$ Rates: 445–990 markkaa ($97.90–$217.80) single; 490–1,140 markkaa ($107.80–$250.80) double; from 2,000 markkaa ($440) suite. Breakfast included in higher-priced rooms; otherwise 45 markkaa ($9.90) per person extra. AE, DC, MC, V. **Parking:** 80 markkaa ($17.60).

Built in 1971 as one of the largest hotels in Finland, this is the northernmost European link in this famous chain. It's affiliated with another smaller Inter-Continental, also in Helsinki. Quality, comfort, and dependability are its motto. Behind a modern concrete facade and a small ornamental garden, it has a host of facilities and bedrooms. Within walking distance of the business center, it stands near the Finlandia Congress and Concert Hall. Bedrooms are tasteful and well furnished. The air terminal is in the same complex as the hotel.

Dining/Entertainment: The premier seafood restaurant of Helsinki, Galateia merits a separate recommendation (see "Helsinki Dining" in this chapter). The Brasserie is an all-day restaurant featuring local specialties. The Baltic Bar is a cozy rendezvous point.

Services: 24-hour room service, laundry and valet service, travel-service desks, masseur.

Facilities: Parking, beauty parlor, hairdresser, car-rental desk, Finnair check-in service, shopping gallery, three Finnish saunas, indoor swimming pool, no-smoking rooms.

PALACE, Eteläranta 10, SF-00130 Helsinki. Tel. 90/13-45-61. Fax 90/654-786. 50 rms, 15 suites. A/C MINIBAR TV TEL **Tram:** 3B. **Bus:** 16.

$ Rates (including breakfast): Aug–June, 820–1,360 markkaa ($180.40–$299.20) single; 970–1,650 markkaa ($213.40–$363) double. July, 360–1,360 markkaa ($79.20–$299.20) single; 500–1,650 markkaa ($110–$363) double. Year-round, from 2,400 markkaa ($528) suite. AE, DC, MC, V. **Parking:** 55 markkaa ($12.10).

A gem of a hotel overlooking the Presidential Palace, a few steps down from the Market Square, the Palace is a favorite among more discriminating travelers. It's part of a chain that includes some of the best restaurants in Helsinki, including the Havis Amanda for seafood and Alexander Nevski for Russian cuisine. The hotel

FINLAND

Helsinki

Academica Hotel **13**
Arctia Hotel Marski **8**
Hotel Dipoli **17**
Hotel Finn **7**
Hotel Hesperia **16**
Hotel Hospiz **4**
Inter-Continental **15**
Hotel Kalastajatorppa **18**
Hotel Klaus Kurki **9**
Martta Hotelli **11**
Hotel Olympia **2**
Palace **10**
Park Hotel Käpylä **1**
Ramada Presidentti Hotel **14**
Seurahuone-Socis **5**
Strand Inter-Continental **3**
Summerhotel
 Satakuntatalo **12**
Torni Hotel **6**

HELSINKI ACCOMMODATIONS

Aleksis Kivisgata
Lautatarhank
Sturenkatu
Helsinginkatu
Helsingegatan
Sörnässtrand väg
Agricolankatu
Castreninkatu
Porthanink
Hämeentie
Siltasaarenkatu
Kolmaslinja
Sörnäistenrantatie
Eläintar-banlahti
Säästöpank
Hakanranta
Pitkansillanranta
Siltavuoren-salmi
Kaisan-iemen-lahti
Kajsaniemenranta
Siltavuorenranta
Maurinkatu
Nora Kalan
Elisabetsgatan
Train Station
Unioninkatu
Snellmaninkatu
Mertullinkatu
Mariankatu
Pohjoisranta
Pohjoissatama
Kaisaniemenkatu
Fabianinkatu
Unionsgatan
Snellmansgatan
Kirkkokatu
Marjegatan
Hallituskatu
Aleksanterinkatu
Laivastokatu
Katajan
Luotsikatu
Pohjois esplanadi Nesplanaden
Kanavakatu
Kronbergsgatan
Kasarmikatu
Fabianinkatu
Kaserngatan
Eteläranta
Kanalgatan
Hogbergskatu
Eteläsatama
Bulevarden
Iso
Roobertinkatu
To Suomenlinna Fortress
&
Helsinki Zoo
Laivasillankatu
Valksaari
Jääkärinkatu
Tähtitornik Observgatan
Bergmansgatan
Vuorimiehenkatu
Luoto
Fabriksgatan
Ryssasaari
Tehtaankatu
Puistokatu
Iso Puistotie Stora Allén
Itäinen Puistotie Östra Allén
Ehrenströmintie
Puolimatkansaari
Pietarinkatu
Kaivopuisto
Juhani Ahontie
Havsgatan
Merisatamaranta
Ehrenströmintie

offers bedrooms overlooking the harbor. Rooms are decorated with an elegant but restrained taste, and the most expensive ones have balconies. For a five-star hotel it's small, but that ensures more personal service.

Dining/Entertainment: The specialty restaurant of this hotel, Palace Gourmet (see "Helsinki Dining" in this chapter), is considered the best in Finland, offering a stunning view from the 10th floor. The Ristorante La Vista is a second-floor restaurant, serving some of the best and freshest Italian food in the capital (see "Helsinki Dining" in this chapter). The American Bar enjoys an 11th-floor perch (see "Evening Entertainment" in Chapter 35). There is also a cafeteria on the second floor.

Services: Pressing and valet service, 4-hour laundry service, dry cleaning, 24-hour news service, 24-hour room service, complimentary 5 o'clock tea, telex and fax service.

Facilities: TV lounge with terrace, garage, three saunas on the 11th floor with open-air terrace and one heated with logs, safety deposit boxes, currency exchange, tour and car-rental desks, four guest elevators, barbershop.

SEURAHUONE-SOCIS, Kaivokatu 12, 00100 Helsinki. Tel. 90/170-441. Fax 90/664-170. 118 rms, 5 suites. A/C TV TEL **Tram:** 3T.

$ Rates: June 12–Aug 16 and Fri–Sat year-round, 370–445 markkaa ($81.40–$97.90) single; 480–550 markkaa ($105.60–$121) double. Sun–Thurs Aug 17–June 11, 680–990 markkaa ($149.60–$217.80) single; 890–1200 markkaa ($195.80–$264) double. Year-round, from 1,300 markkaa ($286) suite. Breakfast 40 markkaa ($8.80) extra. AE, DC, MC, V.

In the center of Helsinki, opposite the railway station, this hotel actually dates from 1833 and was moved to its present location in 1914. An old and traditional favorite, it's the nostalgic choice for many. Guests are housed either in the charming original building or in the modern wing. Rooms are either in a functional modern style or traditionally furnished. All are comfortable.

Dining/Entertainment: The art nouveau Café Socis is the traditional rendezvous point in the early hours of the morning in Helsinki, as it's open daily until 5am. The Socis Pub is open until 1am, and the Discothèque Rose dances until 2am. There is no major restaurant, although lunches are served in the café.

Services: Laundry service, car-rental service, sightseeing tickets available, room service 7am to 10pm.

Facilities: Two saunas.

STRAND INTER-CONTINENTAL, John Stenbergin Ranta 4, 00530 Helsinki. Tel. 90/39-351, or toll free 800/327-0200 in the U.S. Fax 90/393-255. 200 rms, 8 suites. **Tram:** 3T, 7.

$ Rates: Midsummer, 450 markkaa ($99) single; 500 markkaa ($110) double. Mid-Aug to mid-June, 920–990 markkaa ($202.40–$217.80) single; 1,070–1,140 markkaa ($235.40–$250.80) double. Year-round, from 2,100 markkaa ($462) suite. Breakfast 30 markkaa ($6.60) extra. AE, DC, MC, V. **Parking:** 80 markkaa ($17.60).

✪ Set at the edge of the water behind a bay-windowed facade of beige and brown brick, this is a great addition to Helsinki's hotels. Opened in 1988, it has the most dramatic atrium in the capital, festooned with plants and containing glass elevators rising to the top. The octagonal shape is repeated throughout the hotel's design. Rooms were designed by some of Finland's best talent, and decorated with local designs, including weaving and Finnish parquet floors. Marble from Lapland was used extensively. Half the well-furnished bedrooms open onto views of the harbor. Some bedrooms have facilities for the handicapped and others are for nonsmokers.

Dining/Entertainment: The Pamir Restaurant is one of the best fish and game restaurants in Helsinki (see "Helsinki Dining" in this chapter). Guests enjoy breakfast or late-night salad buffets in the Atrium Plaza Restaurant, or drinks in the Atrium Lounge and Bar.

Services: Key-card door lock, 24-hour room service, laundry and valet, tour and guest-relations desk.

Facilities: Four saunas, swimming pool, business center, movie channels, gift shop.

EXPENSIVE

All rooms in this category include private bath.

ARCTIA HOTEL MARSKI, Mannerheimintie 10, SF-00100 Helsinki. Tel. 90/68-061. Fax 90/642-377. 232 rms, 7 suites. MINIBAR TV TEL **Tram:** 3B, 3T, 6.

$ Rates: Midsummer, 470 markkaa ($103.40) single; 590 markkaa ($129.80) double. Mid-Aug to mid-June, 790–890 markkaa ($173.80–$195.80) single; 990 markkaa ($217.80) double. Year-round, from 1,800 markkaa ($396) suite. Breakfast 35 markkaa ($7.70) extra. AE, DC, MC, V. **Parking:** 80 markkaa ($17.60).

Although it looks like an office building from the outside, this is the finest hotel in the town center. The comfortable bedrooms are furnished with plush upholstery in warmly neutral colors, and every room has a hairdryer and trouser press, among other amenities.

Dining/Entertainment: Its breakfast buffet was voted the best in Helsinki. The basement-level Marskin Kellari is a favorite, serving reasonably priced meals in a tavern atmosphere. The Fizz Bar and Nightclub is recommended separately (see "Evening Entertainment" in Chapter 35).

Services: Laundry service, room service, message service.

Facilities: Warm garage, two saunas, no-smoking floor, 13 rooms for allergic persons.

HOTEL KLAUS KURKI, Bulevardi 2, SF-00120 Helsinki. Tel. 90/618-911. Fax 90/608-538. 135 rms, 2 suites. MINIBAR TV TEL **Tram:** 3B, 3T, 6.

$ Rates (including breakfast): 680 markkaa ($149.60) single; 840 markkaa ($184.80) double; from 1,200 markkaa ($264) suite. AE, DC, MC, V.

Opposite the Swedish Theater and a short walk from the Stockmann department store, this 1912 brick building was originally a lodging for hardware buyers. Constructed in the Romantic Jugend style, it was renovated in 1985 and turned into a stylish and up-to-date hotel with elegant public rooms. Bedrooms are comfortably and traditionally designed, with such extra amenities as hairdryers and radios.

Dining/Entertainment: Even if you don't stay at the hotel, don't overlook the Neo-Victorian cellar wine bar where exposed brick, ceiling beams, and ornate brass floor lamps offer an after-work rendezvous. There's also a richly paneled English bar, and a well-designed restaurant a few steps above the lobby.

Services: Same-day laundry service.

Facilities: Sauna with two lounges, two bedrooms for allergy sufferers.

RAMADA PRESIDENTTI HOTEL, Eteläinen Rautatiekatu 4, SF-00100 Helsinki. Tel. 90/69-11, or toll free 800/272-6232 in the U.S. A/C MINIBAR TV TEL 500 rms, 5 suites. **Tram:** 3B, 3T.

$ Rates (including breakfast): June 19–Aug 15, 295 markkaa ($64.90) single; 440 markkaa ($96.80) double. Aug 16–June 18, 840 markkaa ($184.80) single, 995 markkaa ($218.90) double. From 3,000 markkaa ($660) suite. AE, DC, MC, V.

Built in 1980 and recently renovated, this hotel stands in the commercial center of Helsinki, close to Finlandia Hall, Parliament House, and the railway station. Rated five stars, it's an imposing granite-and-copper structure with lots of drinking and dining facilities. Rooms are warm, comfortable, modern, and filled with such conveniences as hairdryers and trouser presses. Windows are triple glazed. Bus no. 614 departs from here directly to the airport.

Dining/Entertainment: The main restaurant, Four Seasons, the first carvery in Finland, features all you can eat carved from various joints of meat. The Evergreen Lounge is a piano bar, also serving light meals, and Le Club Pressa features international bands. Inexpensive lunches are served at the late-night Café Maria, and fresh-baked croissants direct from Paris are a feature in Café de Paris. The hotel also shelters Casino-Ray, the largest and most important casino in Finland.

Services: Room service (7am to midnight), laundry service.

Facilities: Swimming pool, three saunas.

TORNI HOTEL, Yrjönkatu 26, SF-00100 Helsinki. Tel. 90/131-131. Fax 90/131-1361. 147 rms, 8 suites. MINIBAR TV TEL **Tram:** 3, 4, 8.

$ Rates: June 21–Aug 11 and Fri–Sat year-round, 400 markkaa ($88) single; 500 markkaa ($110) double. Sun–Thurs Aug 12–June 20, 690 markkaa ($151.80) single; 880 markkaa ($193.60) double. Year-round, from 1,000 markkaa ($220) suite. Breakfast 35 markkaa ($7.70) extra. AE, DC, MC, V.

The Torni was the first "skyscraper" built in Helsinki, and many irate locals demanded that it be torn down. But instead it prospered, and became the number one choice for such visiting foreign stars as Josephine Baker and Zarah Leander, and a meeting place for such Finnish artists as composers Jean Sibelius and Mika Waltari. Even the illegal Communist party used to meet here. During the Winter War it had to use paper sheets, and in the postwar era it became the headquarters of the Soviet Control Commission. Once a meeting place of diplomats and spies in World War II, this refurbished 1931 hotel has an entrance lobby and paneled dining room that retain its old look, with recently renovated bedrooms that are comfortably contemporary. Each has big windows and carpeting.

Dining/Entertainment: There's an American Bar (named after the longtime resident American ambassador), plus another bar on the 13th floor, Atelier, opened in 1951 with changing art exhibits. The Irish pub, O'Malley's, is in the hotel, as is the foremost Spanish restaurant of Helsinki, Parilla Torni. The gourmet restaurant of the hotel is Ritarisali (Knight's Table).

Services: Room service, laundry service.

Facilities: Four saunas, summer terrace, rooms for nonsmokers.

MODERATE

HOTEL HOSPIZ, Vuorikatu 17, SF-00100 Helsinki. Tel. 90/170-481. Fax 90/626-880. 160 rms (145 with bath). TV TEL **Tram:** 3, 6.

$ Rates (including breakfast): 320 markkaa ($70.40) single without bath, 450 markkaa ($99) single with bath; 450 markkaa ($99) double without bath, 600 markkaa ($132) double with bath. AE, DC, MC, V.

A large and well-maintained establishment, this is owned and operated by the YMCA and accepts both men and women. It was built at the turn of the century with a newer wing added in 1950. The neighborhood is quiet, even though it's only a 4-minute walk from the main train station. Only a handful of the impressively clean and comfortable bedrooms don't have private baths, and the better rooms contain minibars. There's an inexpensive restaurant on the premises that serves a luncheon buffet for around 75 markkaa ($16.50) and a full dinner for 105 markkaa ($23.10).

MARTTA HOTELLI, Uudenmaankatu 24, SF-00120 Helsinki. Tel. 90/646-211. Fax 90/680-1266. 45 rms (all with shower). TV TEL **Tram:** 3T.

$ Rates (including breakfast): June 15–Aug 9 and Fri–Sat year-round, 300 markkaa ($66) single; 380–430 markkaa ($83.60–$94.60) double. Sun–Thurs the rest of the year, 410 markkaa ($90.20) single; 510–560 markkaa ($112.20–$123.20) double. AE, DC, MC, V. **Parking:** Free.

Half a mile north of main rail station, in a quiet residential part of town, this cozy little hotel is owned by a women's organization that was originally founded in 1899 as a radical feminist group committed to the educational advancement of Finland and at first suppressed by the czarist government. No longer radical, having achieved all their goals, they now run a home economics educational program. Their hotel was built in the late 1950s on land bequeathed by a wealthy donor. It is clean, comfortable, and inexpensive. Men and women are accepted. Bedrooms are in a streamlined Finnish design. The restaurant on the upper floor serves breakfast and lunch. At night, room service is available. Facilities include a sauna and a free covered parking area.

PARK HOTEL KÄPYLÄ, Pohjolankatu 38, 00600 Helsinki. Tel. 90/799-755. Fax 90/792-781. 40 rms (all with bath). MINIBAR TV TEL **Tram:** 1.

$ Rates (including breakfast): June 14–Aug 12 and Fri–Sat year-round, 330 markkaa ($72.60) single; 420 markkaa ($92.40) double. Sun–Thurs the rest of the year, 450 markkaa ($99.00) single; 580 markkaa ($127.60) double. AE, DC, MC, V. **Parking:** Free.

Rather undiscovered, known mainly to Finns, this hotel lies 3½ miles north of Helsinki's center, in a suburb (Käpylä) known for its wooden houses and old Finland charm, a favorite retreat of artists. The hotel was built in the 1950s, and completely renovated in 1990. Bedrooms are attractively decorated and are fully soundproof. A terrace and an inner courtyard are summer favorites, and there is also a well-stocked bar. Guests enjoy such recreational possibilities as a swimming pool and three saunas. The hotel has an excellent restaurant with many Finnish specialties.

INEXPENSIVE

HOTEL FINN, Kalevankatu 3B, SF-00100 Helsinki. Tel. 90/640-904. 28 rms (14 with shower). TV TEL **Tram:** 3, 4, 7, 10.

$ Rates: 250 markkaa ($55) single without shower, 290 markkaa ($63.80) single with shower; 300 markkaa ($66) double without shower, 350–380 markkaa ($77–$83.60) double with shower. Breakfast 30 markkaa ($6.60) extra. MC, V.

This is a clean and functional hotel, built shortly after World War II. It occupies the two uppermost floors (5 and 6) of a centrally located office building. It prides itself on being the cheapest hotel in Helsinki, and houses a scattering of tourists, dockworkers from northern and western Finland, and a handful of businessmen from the former Soviet Union. No meals other than breakfast are served, and there's no bar and no sauna. All toilets are shared facilities off the hallways.

NEAR THE OLYMPIC STADIUM

MODERATE

HOTEL OLYMPIA, Läntinen Brahenkatu 2, SF-00510 Helsinki. Tel. 90/750-801. Fax 90/750-801. 99 rms (all with bath). TV TEL **Tram:** 3B.

$ Rates (including breakfast): 480 markkaa ($105.60) single; 580 markkaa ($127.60) double. AE, DC, MC, V. **Parking:** Free.

Built in 1962, this hotel is more famous for its dining and drinking establishments than it is for its accommodations—although few overnight guests are disappointed with the comfortably modern units. It's near the Olympic Stadium of Helsinki, slightly more than a mile north from the central train station. The hotel has a famous Russian restaurant, Kazbek. Room service and laundry are available, as is a sauna; a swimming pool and tennis courts are at the stadium. The tennis courts and an outdoor pool freeze over in winter and become hockey rinks. A bowling alley is nearby.

WEST OF THE CENTER

EXPENSIVE

HOTEL KALASTAJATORPPA, Kalastajatorpantie 1, SF-00330 Helsinki. Tel. 90/45-811. Fax 90/458-1668. 235 rms (all with bath). A/C MINIBAR TV TEL **Tram:** 4.

$ Rates (including breakfast): 770 markkaa ($169.40) single; 890 markkaa ($195.80) double. AE, DC, MC, V. **Parking:** Free.

Translated from the Finnish, the tongue-twisting name of this hotel means "cottage of the fisherman." However, all that this place has in common with a cottage is its proximity to the water 2 miles northwest of the city center. Located on a ridge of land between two arms of the sea, this pair of marble- and granite-faced buildings were designed to meld as closely as possible with the surrounding landscape of birch and pines. The core of the hotel dates from 1937, and the newer sections contain some of the most modern convention facilities in Finland. Rooms are either in the main building or the hotel's seashore annex. On the premises is the state guesthouse where former president Ronald Reagan rested en route to Moscow.

The Round Room is a restaurant for dining and dancing, and the Fiskis Bar & Café is an informal place for light meals and drinks. The Red Room is a leading Helsinki nightclub (see "Evening Entertainment" in Chapter 35). The Terrace summer restaurant offers grills and opens onto a sea view. Laundry service, room service, and a message service are provided, and guided walks can be arranged. The hotel has a business center, hairdresser, gift shop, bank, a car-rental desk, and two heated parking garages. To keep you in shape there's a gym, five saunas (sometimes overheated guests dive directly into the sea), two indoor swimming pools, and a private beach.

SUMMER HOTELS

MODERATE

HOTEL DIPOLI, Jämeräntaival 1, SF-02150 Espoo. Tel. 90/435-811. Fax 90/464-674. 213 rms (all with shower), 2 suites. TEL **Bus:** 102 from Platform 52 at Helsinki Bus Station.

$ **Rates** (including breakfast): 595 markkaa ($130.90) single; 710 markkaa ($156.20) double; from 1,700 markkaa ($374) suite. AE, DC, MC, V. **Parking:** Free. **Closed:** Sept–May.

Six miles from downtown Helsinki, this student-run hotel is on the seashore surrounded by pine forests. The Dipoli offers about 600 beds in neat, college-dorm-type rooms at reasonable rates. There is a beer tavern, and two restaurants service the hotel—one outdoors. The hotel has a sauna and an indoor swimming pool. Room service is provided from 7am to 11pm daily.

INEXPENSIVE

ACADEMICA HOTEL, Hietaniemenkatu 14, SF-00100 Helsinki. Tel. 90/402-0206. 217 rms (115 with bath). TEL **Tram:** 3T from Central Station.

$ **Rates:** 195 markkaa ($42.90) single without bath, 245 markkaa ($53.90) single with bath; 240 markkaa ($52.80) double without bath, 320 markkaa ($70.40) double with bath. Breakfast 25 markkaa ($5.50) extra. AE, MC, V. **Parking:** Free. **Closed:** Sept–May.

This summer only hotel (renovated 1992), which becomes a student dormitory in winter, lies in the central area of Helsinki, only a short walk from the capital's most popular beach. It features a Finnish sauna, an indoor swimming pool, a self-service laundry, a solarium, a disco (Alibi), and an indoor tennis court. All the bedrooms are equipped with radios, kitchenettes, and refrigerators. There is a fully licensed restaurant, Perho, a short walk from the hotel.

SUMMERHOTEL SATAKUNTATALO, Lapinrinne 1A, SF-00180 Helsinki. Tel. 90/695-851. Fax 90/694-2226. 66 rms (none with bath). TEL **Bus:** 55, 65, 66 from the railway station.

$ **Rates** (including breakfast): 200 markkaa ($44) single; 290 markkaa ($63.80) double. AE, DC, MC, V. **Parking:** Free. **Closed:** Sept–May.

On a tiny street a short walk from the bus station, this hotel accepts tourists of all ages. There is only one shower on each floor, but there are two saunas and a laundry room with a washing machine. Also on the premises is a licensed restaurant where lunch or

---

ⓕ FROMMER'S COOL FOR KIDS: HOTELS

Martta Hotelli (see p. 618) Good, safe haven—comfortable rooms, moderate prices.

Hotel Olympia (see p. 619) Great for children because of its location near the Sports Stadium.

Academica Hotel (see above) A family favorite in summer with swimming pool and moderately priced restaurant.

dinner costs from 75 markkaa ($16.50); a self-service lunch costs from 25 to 50 markkaa ($5.50 to $11).

2. HELSINKI DINING

Food can be expensive in Helsinki, with many fat-cat tabs resembling, the war indemnity slapped on Finland by Russia. But don't retreat. Eating at the chain restaurants and at self-service cafeterias is one way to save some money. Hamburger houses, pizza parlors, and fast-food joints exist in profusion in central Helsinki if you're eating on the run.

In summer, if the weather's good, the residents of Helsinki often like to eat out at a summer dining room, preferably with a view of the water. Typical of such places is Walhalla (see recommendation below) on Kustaanmiekka Island, reached by boat.

Dress is informal, but not that informal. In first-class restaurants, men generally wear jacket and tie in the evening, whereas women wear casual dress or even a cocktail dress if the place is fairly luxurious.

If you're looking up a restaurant in the yellow pages the Finnish word for restaurant is *ravintola*. Tipping is not necessary, since a service charge will be added to your bill. However, in first-class and deluxe restaurants, it is the general policy to leave something extra, especially if service has been good.

Even though I've classified restaurants by price category, the cost of dining in a Helsinki restaurant depends in large part on what you order. Dishes that have to be imported always carry higher tabs. Yet on the same menu you'll find a number of reasonably priced Finnish dishes, such as Baltic herring and whitefish. In a restaurant rated **Very Expensive,** expect to spend $65 and up per person for dinner; **Expensive,** $50 to $65; and **Moderate,** $25 to $50. Anything under $25 is considered **Inexpensive.**

IN THE TOWN CENTER
VERY EXPENSIVE

PALACE GOURMET, in the Palace Hotel, Eteläranta 10. Tel. 134-561.
   Cuisine: FINNISH/FRENCH. **Reservations:** Required. **Tram:** 3B. **Bus:** 16.
$ Prices: Fixed-price meals 360 markkaa ($79.20) for a 4-course *menu finlandais,* 420 markkaa ($92.40) for a 6-course *menu dégustation,* 120–250 markkaa

---

IN THEIR FOOTSTEPS

Baron Carl Gustaf Emil von Mannerheim (1867–1951) The distinguished Finnish soldier and statesman, Mannerheim is virtually "the father of his country" to Finnish people. He fought in the Russo-Japanese War of 1904, became regent of Finland, and later, as field marshal, directed operations in the Winter War (1939–40) and the Continuation War (1941–44) against Russia. As president of the republic (1944–46), he presided over a peace treaty with Russia in which Finland had to surrender vast territories, including East Karelia.

   • **Birthplace:** Villnäs, near Turku, on June 4, 1867.
   • **Favorite Haunts:** Restaurant Savoy (still serving his favorite schnapps, Marskin Ryyppy) and König (where the marshal and his generals ate his favorite dish, vorschmack).
   • **Residences:** Kallionlinnantie 14, Helsinki, now a museum containing memorabilia of an illustrious career.
   • **Resting Place:** He died at Lausanne, Switzerland, on January 27, 1951, and is buried in Hietaniemi Cemetery in Helsinki.

($26.40–$55) for lunch; appetizers 70–200 markkaa ($15.40–$44); main dishes 130–180 markkaa ($28.60–$39.60). AE, DC, MC, V.
Open: Aug–June, Mon–Fri 11am–1am. **Closed:** July.

Offering exquisite cuisine since 1952, this place, on the 10th floor of the Palace Hotel (see "Helsinki Accommodations" in this chapter), is the most acclaimed restaurant in Helsinki. It offers excellent service and a unique ambience, with a stunning view of the harbor. It relies on the excellence of its cuisine and the beauty and fame of its decor to sell itself. The design hasn't been changed since Uiljo Rewell created it in 1952 (Rewell was the second most famous architect in Finland in the 1950s, competing with Aalto). It has wood paneling, a live pianist, large panoramic windows and—to a trained eye—the clue that its decor is among the finest examples of postwar Finnish design in the world. Its wine cellar is one of the best in the country, having won many awards. Fixed-price menus at lunch supplant à la carte meals. Even a two-course uncomplicated traditional lunch is featured. But, mainly, the restaurant is known for its superb à la carte dishes, including a timbale of Jerusalem artichokes with cold smoked salmon and roe of vendace, a soup of oxtail with beetroot, tongue of reindeer with cranberry sauce, and for dessert, a cake of Arctic brambleberries.

EXPENSIVE

ALEXANDER NEVSKI, Pohjoisesplanadi 17. Tel. 639-610.
Cuisine: RUSSIAN. **Reservations:** Required. **Tram:** 3T, 4.
$ Prices: Appetizers 39–98 markkaa ($8.60–$21.60); main dishes 69–155 markkaa ($15.20–$34.10); fixed-price lunch 80 markkaa ($17.60); fixed-price dinner 180–250 markkaa ($39.60–$55) dinner. AE, DC, MC, V.
Open: Aug–June, Mon–Fri 11am–1am, Sat noon–1am; July, dinner only, daily 6pm–1am.

At the southern corner of the Market Square, this is the finest Russian restaurant in Helsinki. Set in a 200-year-old building, the restaurant is named for the 12th-century Russian military hero. It has large beveled mirror panels in pastel frames, Lapland marble floors, stained-glass windows emblazoned with Romanov double-headed eagles and *faux-marbre* columns. The cuisine is a mixture of the best of the imperial tsarist cuisine with the best of Russian regional (peasant) dishes. A specialty is roast bear meat prepared in a clay pot. You might begin with Russian fish soup or a selection of appetizers called zakuska. Cabbage rolls arrive in a clay pot stuffed with filet strips of veal. The shashliks here are famous. The perfect apéritif is a mixture of Russian vodka with a Finnish liqueur made from brambleberries and raspberries, and for dessert you can sample iced berries with a caramel-fudge sauce.

HAVIS AMANDA, Unioninkatu 23. Tel. 666-882.
Cuisine: SEAFOOD. **Reservations:** Required. **Tram:** 1, 2, 3T, 4. **Bus:** 16.
$ Prices: Fixed-price meals 275 markkaa ($60.50) at dinner, 175 markkaa ($38.50) at lunch; appetizers 55–120 markkaa ($12.10–$26.40); main dishes 75–175 markkaa ($16.50–$38.50). AE, DC, MC, V.
Open: Lunch Mon–Sat 11am–2pm; dinner Mon–Sat 2pm–midnight. **Closed:** Lunch in July.

The finest seafood place in Helsinki, this cellar restaurant is decorated in a luxurious tavern style. In the peak of the summer you will see signs proclaiming that crayfish season has begun (it usually starts the last week of July). The crayfish is boiled Louisiana style and often is consumed with ice-cold beer. At any time of the year you can enjoy such good-tasting specialties, as fish soup of the house or assorted roes served as hors d'oeuvres, turbot braised in sour cream, and grilled salmon with those creamy morels. For dessert, it's most traditional to order Lapland cheese with cloudberry jam.

RESTAURANT SAVOY, Eteläesplanadi 14. Tel. 176-571.
Cuisine: FINNISH/INTERNATIONAL. **Reservations:** Required. **Tram:** 3B.
$ Prices: Appetizers 50–80 markkaa ($11–$17.60); main dishes 75–160 markkaa ($16.50–$35.20); fixed-price lunch 118 markkaa ($26). AE, DC, MC, V.

Open: Lunch Mon–Fri 11am–3pm; dinner Mon–Fri 3pm–1am.
In an office building near the harbor, this restaurant has a decor that represents the quintessence of Finnish modernism. In 1937 Finland's greatest architect, Alvar Aalto, designed every detail of the place, even the lighting fixtures. The restaurant, a national monument, has been kept almost exactly as he designed it. Its most famous customer was Finland's celebrated military hero, Marshal Mannerheim, who came here for his favorite schnapps, Marskin Ryyppy, made with vodka, aquavit, dry vermouth, and dry gin, stirred together and served icy cold. The food has changed with the times. Today you might begin with deer terrine with cranberry sauce or fish and seafood soup flavored with saffron. Fish dishes are likely to include poached filet of pike perch with crayfish and caviar sauce or filet of sautéed turbot with a red onion sauce. Among the meat selections are filet of reindeer and fried breast of duck.

MODERATE

BELLEVUE, Rahapajankatu 3. Tel. 179-560.
   Cuisine: RUSSIAN. **Reservations:** Required. **Tram:** 4.
$ Prices: Appetizers 35–72 markkaa ($7.70–$15.85); main dishes 70–148 markkaa ($15.40–$32.60); fixed-price lunch 110 markkaa ($24.20). AE, DC, MC, V.
   Open: Lunch Mon–Fri 11am–2pm; dinner Mon–Sat 5pm–midnight. **Closed:** July.
In the heart of Helsinki, next to the Uspenski Orthodox church, the Bellevue has since 1922 been an enduring favorite because of its good cuisine and moderate prices. You can dine in a long corridorlike main dining room or select one of the cozier and tinier side rooms. Herring, still served Russian style, is always a good beginning, or perhaps blinis and caviar. The chicken Kiev is a recommended main dish. For dessert, a flaming baba cake is carried through the main dining room, the presentation of which one longtime patron likened to "a wake for Czar Nicholas II." Real Russian wine is offered.

KÖNIG, Mikonkatutel 4. Tel. 171-271.
   Cuisine: SCANDINAVIAN. **Reservations:** Required. **Tram:** 3B, 3T.
$ Prices: Appetizers 28–52 markkaa ($6.20–$11.40); main dishes 45–105 markkaa ($9.90–$23.10). AE, DC, MC, V.
   Open: Daily 11am–midnight.
Established in 1892, this restaurant is perhaps the most traditional in Helsinki, lying in the cellars beneath one of the four largest banks of Finland, the SKOP bank. The great architect Saarinen redesigned the restaurant long after its founding into a precursor of the internationally modern style that later would sweep the world. Here, in what was at the time a private dining room, Marshal Mannerheim and his generals would gather for food and strategy talks during the darkest days of World War II. The place has hosted all of Finland's presidents and many of its greatest artists and composers, including Jean Sibelius. Dishes might include pike perch Waleska, smoked whitefish à

IN THEIR FOOTSTEPS

Jean Sibelius (1865–1957) Finland's greatest composer was often inspired by legend and national romanticism. His *Finlandia*, published in 1900, established his reputation, a tone poem conjuring up the wildness of the Finnish countryside. Awarded a life grant from the state, he produced seven symphonies, each filled with an emotional intensity. *Tapiola* was one of his great symphonic poems.

   • **Birthplace:** He was born at Hämeenlinna on December 8, 1865.
   • **Favorite Haunts:** König restaurant in Helsinki; Kappeli in Helsinki, where he had a favorite table.
   • **Residences:** Ainola, in Järvenpää, outside Helsinki.
   • **Resting Place:** Sibelius died on September 20, 1957, at Traeskaenda, near Helsinki, and was buried with his wife, Aino, on their property at Ainola.

FINLAND

Helsinki ⊛

Alexander Nevski **10**
Aurinkotuuli **22**
Barbeque **16**
Bellevue **11**
Café Brasserie Kappeli **9**
Carrols **6**
Elite **26**
Fanny's Restaurant **1**
Fazer Café **5**
Four Seasons Restaurant **24**
Galateia **28**
Havis Amanda **8**
König **7**
Kosmos Restaurant **19**
La Vista **14**
Mechelin **23**
Mestarikrouvi **27**
Mikado **20**
Ostrobotnia **25**
Palace Gourmet **14**
Pamir **2**
Pampan **4**
Parilla Torni **18**
Picnic Sandwich
  and Salad Bar **21**
Pizzeria Rivoli **17**
Ravintola Rivoli **17**
Restaurant Savoy **13**
Svenska Klubben **3**
Restaurant Walhalla **15**
Wellamo **12**

HELSINKI DINING

la König, blinis with seasonal roe, filet de boeuf à la patronne, and a seasonal variety of fish.

KOSMOS RESTAURANT, Kalevankatu 3. Tel. 647-255.

Cuisine: FINNISH. **Reservations:** Recommended. **Tram:** 3B, 3T. **Bus:** 15, 17.

$ Prices: Appetizers 49–74 markkaa ($10.80–$16.30); main dishes 42–108 markkaa ($9.20–$23.80); fixed-price lunch 78 markkaa ($17.20). AE, DC, MC, V.
Open: Mon–Fri 11:30am–midnight.

Near the center of Helsinki's main street, the Mannerheimintie, this restaurant is known throughout Finland as a gathering place for artists, writers, and television personalities. The decor is 1930s and simple, and the menu specialties include terrine of cold smoked rainbow trout with herb sauce, sweetbreads gourmet, stuffed mutton chops, and fried Baltic herring. Light meals, such as open tartare sandwiches, vorschmack with duchesse potatoes, and borscht, are also available. (Vorschmack is made with chopped mutton, herring, and anchovies, and it's served with baked potatoes, salted cucumbers, and beets.) In the summertime you can order "deep-fried" strawberries for dessert; pears drenched with a chocolate-cream sauce are also delicious. The special lunch is served until 3pm.

PARILLA TORNI, in the Hotel Torni, Yrjönkatu 26. Tel. 131-131.

Cuisine: SPANISH. **Reservations:** Recommended. **Tram:** 3, 4, 8.

$ Prices: Appetizers 39–74 markkaa ($8.60–$16.30); main dishes 74–140 markkaa ($16.30–$30.80). AE, DC, MC, V.
Open: Tues–Fri 11am–midnight, Sat 4pm–midnight, Sun noon–midnight.

Its decor is *faux espagnole,* and the stuffed bull's head and the crossed Spanish sabers against the roughly textured plaster evoke Iberian kitsch. In spite of that, the food is excellent and well prepared. The tascalike restaurant is on the street level of the famous Hotel Torni, once the rendezvous place of such artists as Jean Sibelius or the site of secret meetings of the illegal Communist party. Begin with smoked turkey and lentil soup; then follow with chicken and olives, perhaps grilled chicken with chocolate sauce, even herb-fried red snapper with garlic mayonnaise. The paella valenciana requires a minimum order of two. For dessert, you can settle for a typical flan (caramel custard) or order something more elaborate such as almond flambé bananas with cinnamon ice cream.

RAVINTOLA RIVOLI, Albertinkatu 38. Tel. 643-455.

Cuisine: FRENCH/FINNISH. **Reservations:** Recommended. **Tram:** 3B.

$ Prices: Appetizers 42–78 markkaa ($9.20–$17.20); main dishes 48–142 markkaa ($10.60–$31.20); fixed-price lunch 78 markkaa ($17.20). AE, DC, MC, V.
Open: Mon–Fri 11am–midnight, Sat 5pm–midnight.

The dining room is a florid and recently installed art nouveau fantasy set within a labyrinthine dining room, with upholstered banquettes. One of its subdivisions is named "Fish Rivoli," and from its separate menu you can order some of the finest seafood dishes in the city. In both dining rooms, you can enjoy such fare as filet of perch with herb butter and grilled salmon with mustard sauce. At lunchtime, special *husmanskost* cookery is offered, a reference to "grandmother's style," featuring such dishes as onion soup and grilled rainbow trout. The establishment also operates an adjoining pizzeria.

INEXPENSIVE

BARBEQUE, Annankatu 6. Tel. 680-1701.

Cuisine: BARBECUE. **Reservations:** Required for four or more. **Tram:** 3B.

$ Prices: Appetizers 16–35 markkaa ($3.50–$7.70); main dishes 42–85 markkaa ($9.20–$18.70); Mongolian barbecue buffet 65 markkaa ($14.30), subsequent servings 25 markkaa ($5.50). AE, DC, MC, V.
Open: Daily 11am–1pm.

A great dining bargain, this pick-and-choose format offers flavorful meals and a welcome culinary theatricality. A visit to the counter allows you to select your choice of fresh thinly sliced cuts of pork, beef, chicken, or reindeer, along with a garnish of fresh vegetables. You watch as the ingredients are sautéed into a stir-fry feast.

CAFE BRASSERIE KAPPELI, Eteläesplanadi 1. Tel. 179-242.

Cuisine: INTERNATIONAL. **Reservations:** Not accepted. **Tram:** 3B. **Bus:** 16.
$ Prices: Appetizers 27–46 markkaa ($5.90–$10.10); main dishes 38–75 markkaa ($8.40–$16.50). AE, DC, MC, V.
Open: Mon–Sat 8am–2am, Sun 9am–2am. **Closed:** Dec 24–25.

This famous restaurant and drinking complex is a Victorian Gothic fantasy set like an oversize gazebo in the middle of Esplanade Park, near the harborfront. Originally built in 1837 as a rendezvous for artists and "high-society gentlemen" (Sibelius had a favorite table), it was closed for many years until its restoration in 1976. You'll find a variety of different seating areas, even a cellar pub where pizza and pasta are served. In the oldest section, the café, most guests order sandwiches, pastries, or coffee. The centermost section is the main restaurant, Runeberg, where white linen tablecloths, increased elbow room, and formal service are the hallmarks. Main dishes, remarkably inexpensive by Finnish standards, include chateaubriand, pepper steak, entrecôte, fried salmon with red wine and pepper sauce, or whitefish.

OSTROBOTNIA, Dagmarinkatu 2. Tel. 408-602.

Cuisine: FINNISH. **Reservations:** Recommended. **Tram:** 4, 7, 10.
$ Prices: Appetizers 9.50–49.50 markkaa ($2.10–$10.90); main dishes 22.50–75.40 markkaa ($5–$16.60); fixed-price lunch 34–49 markkaa ($7.50–$10.80). AE, MC, V.
Open: Mon–Sat 11am–midnight.

Set in a residential neighborhood several blocks west of the Inter-Continental Hotel and the Finnair Bus Terminal, this restaurant prides itself on both its cuisine and its collection of 19th-century Finnish paintings lining the walls. There's a popular and interesting bar with an outdoor terrace which you'll see as you enter. You can enjoy such specialties as fresh fish, grilled noisettes of beef, sautéed reindeer, breast of chicken stuffed with sweetbreads, and wild berry pie. The chef is well known for his homemade Finnish bread, served with a homemade cheese pâté.

PAMPAN, Hallituskatu 15. Tel. 653-936.

Cuisine: FRENCH. **Reservations:** Recommended. **Tram:** 3T.
$ Prices: Appetizers 17–35 markkaa ($3.70–$7.70); main dishes 34–99 markkaa ($7.50–$21.80). AE, DC, MC, V.
Open: Lunch Mon–Sat 11am–2pm; dinner Mon–Sat 4pm–midnight.

Across from the Helsinki Hotel, this place looks a lot like a French bistro. It features an array of "light dishes," for those watching their waistlines. The kitchen always offers at least two different vegetarian main dishes. Specialties include fish soup à la Marseillaise, grilled salmon with stewed wild mushrooms and chateaubriand with butter sauce. Italian espresso is featured, along with several coffee drinks made from liqueur—one is café banana with rum from Martinique. In summer you can dine outside.

NORTH OF THE CENTER
MODERATE

FANNY'S RESTAURANT, in Fanny & Alexander's, Siltasaarenkatu 2. Tel. 753-2332.

Cuisine: FINNISH/CONTINENTAL. **Reservations:** Recommended. **Bus:** 17, 64, 72.
$ Prices: Appetizers 42–55 markkaa ($9.20–$12.10); main dishes 68–103 markkaa ($15–$22.70). AE, DC, MC, V.
Open: Mon–Fri 11am–midnight, Sat 6pm–1am.

A charming second-floor establishment owned by the Arctia hotel chain, Fanny's Restaurant stands across from the Strand Inter-Continental. In spite of its stark exterior, its interior is lushly Edwardian, filled with turn-of-the-century bric-a-brac. A dimly lit and intimate corner bar, with chintz-patterned wallpaper, palms, and fringed and beaded hanging lamps, lies near the restaurant's entrance. Full meals might include the house-style risotto, a casserole of flap mushrooms, sole stuffed with salmon mousse, or cheese raclette. See "Evening Entertainment" in Chapter 35 for Alexander's, a disco in the same building.

GALATEIA, in the Hotel Inter-Continental, Mannerheimintie 46. Tel. 40-551.
   Cuisine: SEAFOOD. **Reservations:** Required. **Tram:** 3B, 3T, 4, 7, 10.
$ **Prices:** Appetizers 45–80 markkaa ($9.90–$17.60); main dishes 82–145 markkaa ($18–$31.90). AE, DC, MC, V.
   Open: Dinner only, Mon–Fri 6:30–11pm.

⭐   The most elegant seafood restaurant in Helsinki, this establishment is on the ninth floor of a deluxe hotel, offering a panoramic view of the city. Only fresh fish (not frozen) flown in from Europe and the Caribbean is served. The favorite appetizers are two platters of cold marinated fish—"the catch from the Finnish archipelago," with salted salmon, marinated lamprey eels, marinated herring, and shrimp, and a cold Caribbean fish plate with marinated raw and cooked fish from the West Indies, including spiny Caribbean red snapper or perhaps even a reptile, alligator. Sashimi is available in many different variations. The least imaginative day is Monday when (because of delivery schedules) only Finnish fish is available. The most exotic catch appears Wednesday through Friday nights.

MESTARIKROUVI, Töölöntorinkatu 7. Tel. 496-386.
   Cuisine: FINNISH. **Reservations:** Required. **Tram:** 3B, 3T.
$ **Prices:** Appetizers 35–55 markkaa ($7.70–$12.10); main dishes 68–100 markkaa ($15–$22). AE, DC, MC, V.
   Open: Mon–Fri 11am–11:30pm, Sat–Sun noon–11:30pm.

Ⓢ   Although at first glance you'd think this was nothing more than a cozy neighborhood restaurant, the service and the Finnish specialties give it an added dimension. Sometimes the place, whose name in English means "tavern of champions," serves as a pleasant oasis for guests from the nearby Inter-Continental Hotel, but locals also appreciate the paneled bar, framed pictures, and homelike checked curtains. Finnish cuisine, such as elk filet with juniperberries and a selection of fish dishes, are featured. Try the cold smoked rainbow trout with mustard sauce.

SVENSKA KLUBBEN, Maurinkatu 6. Tel. 135-4896.
   Cuisine: FINNISH. **Reservations:** Required. **Bus:** 18.
$ **Prices:** Appetizers 40–90 markkaa ($8.80–$19.80); main dishes 100–140 markkaa ($22–$30.80); fixed-price lunch 100 markkaa ($22). AE, DC, MC, V.
   Open: Mon–Sat 11am–1am. **Closed:** July.

This place was originally conceived as a private club, and over the years its membership has included some of the city's most important businessmen, many of whom adorned its interior with their portraits and memorabilia. Today it accepts nonmembers into its dining rooms, and functions as both a private and a desirable public restaurant. Constructed in 1900 as a private home by a Finnish businessman for his Scottish-born wife, it has English Edwardian styling, from its 12-foot ceiling to the paneling used for decoration. The street level is open to the public, along with its adjoining pub, Patrick's. You can enjoy an apéritif in the bar, whose wintertime fireplace is charming. A fish-and-salad buffet is featured at lunch, although not considered a full meal—rather, a first course. The place is known for its game dishes, which the chef prepares without frills or fussy adornments, macho style. Wild duck with a cognac-flavored cream sauce is a great favorite.

INEXPENSIVE

MECHELIN, Mechelininkatu 7. Tel. 493-481.
   Cuisine: FINNISH/CONTINENTAL. **Reservations:** Not accepted. **Tram:** 8.
$ **Prices:** Appetizers 18–52 markkaa ($4–$11.40); main dishes 33–85 markkaa ($7.30–$18.70); fixed-price lunch platter (with salad and coffee); Finnish Sun buffet 80 markkaa ($17.60). AE, DC, MC, V.
   Open: Mon–Fri 11am–midnight, Sat–Sun noon–11pm.

FROMMER'S COOL FOR KIDS: RESTAURANTS

Carrols *(see below)* and **Pizzeria Rivoli** *(see p. 630)* If kids yearn for hamburgers, Carrols (several locations) can satisfy them. A wide variety of pizza and pasta is available at Pizzeria Rivoli.

Ravintola Rivoli *(see p. 626)* This excellent restaurant offers a special children's menu for 32 markkaa ($7), which might include a "fantasy pizza," a pasta, or a main dish with salad. Children yearn for the special dessert menu, including everything from lingonberry ice cream to blackcurrant pie.

Barbeque *(see p. 626)* Children delight in being taken here where they get to select their choice of meats for barbecuing: chicken, beef, pork, or reindeer ("No, I won't eat Prancer!"). It's one of the best family-dining values in Helsinki.

⑤ Lying half a mile east of the Central Station, this restaurant is run by a foundation called the Helsinki Culinary School, and is staffed by its trainees. All the cooking, however, is professionally supervised, and served efficiently and politely in attractive modern surroundings. Specialties include "Finnish pasta," with salmon and cold-smoked reindeer steak, and a vegetarian pasta made with tagliatelle, olives, and stewed mushrooms: The Sunday buffet is a real bargain.

ON KUSTAANMIEKKA ISLAND
MODERATE

RESTAURANT WALHALLA, Kustaanmiekka Island, Suomenlinna. Tel. 668-552.
  Cuisine: FINNISH. **Reservations:** Not required. **Bus:** Water bus to Walhalla.
$ **Prices:** Appetizers 50–75 markkaa ($11–$16.50); main dishes 115–145 markkaa ($25.30–$31.90); fixed-price lunch 100 markkaa ($22). AE, DC, MC, V.
  Open: May–Sept 15, lunch Mon–Sat noon–3pm; dinner Mon–Sat 7am–midnight, Sun noon–6pm. **Closed:** Sept 16–Apr.
You can only get to this restaurant by boat, as it's on the fortress island of Kustaanmiekka. Many claim that the trip is half the fun. This collection of sandblasted brick-and-granite vaults is right in the center of the Viapori fortress, so dining here is like eating in a living museum. Several eating places are on the premises, including a self-service restaurant, a panoramic terrace with waiter service, and a café. Traditional Finnish dishes, such as salmon soup, are served, followed by filet of reindeer and fried snow grouse. You can make your selections from the Delwing table, a Scandinavian buffet.

SPECIALTY DINING
LIGHT, CASUAL & FAST FOOD

CARROLS, Keskuskatu 3. Tel. 655-514.
  Cuisine: AMERICAN. **Reservations:** Not required. **Tram:** 3B, 3T.
$ **Prices:** Clubburger 22 markkaa ($4.80); french fries 9.50 markkaa ($2.10). No credit cards.
  Open: Mon–Thurs 10am–11pm, Fri–Sat 10am–midnight, Sun 11am–11pm.
Regardless of how good Finnish cuisine is, the craving for a hamburger can be satisfied by Carrols. The most central locations are near the railway station in City-käytävä (City Passage; tel. 611-632) and at Keskuskatu 3 (tel. 655-514). (The two restaurants are on different sides of the famed Stockmann department store.) Another location is at Mannerheimintie 19 (tel. 490-469).

Outside the center, Carrols has restaurants in Puotinharju, a suburb east of Helsinki (tel. 339-264), and in Tapiola district in the town of Espoo (tel. 462-508). In addition to the burgers, other fast food is also featured.

All branches are open the same hours.

PIZZERIA RIVOLI, Albertinkatu 38. Tel. 607-455.
 Cuisine: PIZZA/PASTA. **Reservations:** Not required. **Tram:** 6. **Bus:** 14.
$ **Prices:** Pizzas 28–53 markkaa ($6.20–$11.70); pastas 37–50 markkaa ($8.10–$11). AE, DC, MC, V.
 Open: Mon–Fri 10am–midnight, Sat noon–midnight, Sun 2–11pm.

Amid a pleasantly uncluttered decor evocative of southern Europe, you can enjoy some of the best pizzas in Helsinki. You have a choice of 20 different kinds of pies, or you can order one of the pasta dishes, a filling meal in itself. This is the least expensive of the restaurants run by Rivoli, which also operates a more expensive restaurant next door, specializing in a French/Finnish cuisine.

LOCAL FAVORITES
Moderate

ELITE, Eteläinen Hesperiankatu 22. Tel. 495-542.
 Cuisine: FRENCH. **Reservations:** Recommended. **Tram:** 3.
$ **Prices:** Appetizers 42–58 markkaa ($9.20–$12.80); main dishes 52–105 markkaa ($11.40–$23.10). AE, DC, MC, V.
 Open: Mon–Fri 11am–1am, Sat–Sun 1pm–1am.

A short walk west of Finlandia Hall, this pub-café was once the haunt of Helsinki artists. It now draws a wide range of clients. Established in 1938, it offers inexpensive food and good house wines. Begin with a soup or Baltic herring, perhaps a selection from the salad bar; then go on to such main courses as filet of beef with morels and smoked salmon, or a double filet of fried herring. In summer you can order drinks on the patio.

WELLAMO, Vyokatu 9. Tel. 663-139.
 Cuisine: FINNISH. **Reservations:** Not required. **Tram:** 4.
$ **Prices:** Appetizers 32–38 markkaa ($7–$8.40); main dishes 62–95 markkaa ($13.60–$20.90). AE, MC, V.
 Open: Tues–Fri 11am–11pm, Sat 4–11pm, Sun 1–8pm.

Not for everyone, this place is a local hangout with a bit of workaday charm. It's in a century-old house on the island of Katajanokka, abutting the northeastern edge of the south harbor. The classic Finnish meat patty, vorschmack, is a specialty, as is slightly salted marinated salmon. Lamb is prepared in many different ways, including roasted and served with either a garlic or mint sauce. Another specialty is balmaani, a Russian dish similar to Italian ravioli; the patty is stuffed with minced and seasoned lamb and served with a sour-cream sauce. Hearty regional soups precede most meals. The decor is warm, unpretentious, and cozy, and the service is overburdened, but hardworking.

HOTEL DINING
Expensive

FOUR SEASONS RESTAURANT, in the Ramada Presidentti Hotel, Eteläinen Rautatiekatu 4. Tel. 69-11.
 Cuisine: FINNISH. **Reservations:** Recommended. **Tram:** 3B, 3T.
$ **Prices:** Buffet 225 markkaa ($49.50) at dinner, 160 markkaa ($35.20) at lunch; appetizers 58–85 markkaa ($12.80–$18.70); main dishes 105–135 markkaa ($23.10–$29.70); menu finlandais 290 markkaa ($63.80); menu dégustation 340 markkaa ($74.80). AE, DC, MC, V.
 Open: Lunch Mon–Fri 11:30am–3pm; dinner Mon–Fri 6pm–midnight. **Closed:** Mid-June to mid-Aug.

Set on the third floor of one of Helsinki's most prominent hotels, this is a favorite luncheon stopover of Finnish president Mauno Koivisto, whose favorite dish is gutted and fried Baltic herring, silakka, prominently displayed on the buffet table. Designed in an elegant motif of dark paneling, big windows, and abstractly intriguing Finnish paintings, the restaurant features the most attractive spread of buffet foods in Helsinki. It is, in fact, the only carvery in Finland, and it's based on English models, but with a decidedly Baltic touch. Guests might begin with canapés of salmon tartare and follow with a second course from the self-service buffet table laden with fish, meats, salads, and vegetables. The same system, with such upgraded appetizers as braised lobster rolls with spinach or forest-mushrooms soup, is offered at night. There is also an à la carte menu, featuring such dishes as wild duckling with fresh lingonberries.

PAMIR, in the Strand Inter-Continental, John Stenbergin Ranta 4. Tel. 39-351.

Cuisine: GAME. **Reservations:** Recommended. **Tram:** 3T, 7.

$ Prices: Appetizers 70–110 markkaa ($15.40–$24.20); main dishes 90–170 markkaa ($19.80–$37.40). AE, DC, MC, V.

Open: Lunch Mon–Fri 11:30am–3pm; dinner Mon–Fri 6pm–midnight. **Closed:** Mid-June to mid-Aug.

Recently designed by one of Finland's top interior architects, this restaurant is sheathed in Karelian birch and upholstered in cool colors inspired by a Finnish stream. It contains rack upon refrigerated rack of fine European and American wines. Service is impeccable. Pamir is the premier game restaurant of Helsinki, although it also offers some of the best fish dishes as well. The menu changes with the season. For an appetizer, choices might include whitefish roe with blinis or tartare of smoked Baltic herring with endive. For a main course, a parade of dishes await you, including filet of hare in rosemary sauce, entrecôte of elk with pumpkin-ginger loaf, filet of turbot braised in sour cream, or braised pike perch with ginger sauce.

DINING WITH A VIEW
Moderate

LA VISTA, in the Palace Hotel, Eteläranta 10. Tel. 134-561.

Cuisine: ITALIAN. **Reservations:** Recommended. **Tram:** 3B. **Bus:** 16.

$ Prices: Fixed-price lunch 80–120 markkaa ($17.60–$26.40); appetizers 36–60 markkaa ($7.90–$13.20); pastas 39–59 markkaa ($8.60–$13); main dishes 50–150 markkaa ($11–$33). AE, DC, MC, V.

Open: Mon–Fri 11am–midnight, Sat 1pm–midnight, Sun 1–10pm.

This isn't the most expensive restaurant or the most prestigious in the harborfront Palace Hotel, but many visitors prefer it because of its market-fresh Italian food prepared with flair and served with a view overlooking the water. Many of the menu choices are displayed behind a glass counter, representing the best of an abundant Italian harvest of foodstuffs. The menu is changed four times a year, but typical choices are likely to begin with the hors d'oeuvres trolley or chicken risotto. Pasta offerings feature tagliatelle with smoked salmon, seafood, and cream and ravioli with Gorgonzola sauce. Main dishes are likely to feature noisettes of veal with ham and sage (the famous Roman saltimbocca) or filet of beef with rosemary and a red wine sauce.

LATE-NIGHT DINING
Inexpensive

MIKADO, Mannerheimintie 6. Tel. 607-463.

Cuisine: FINNISH/INTERNATIONAL. **Reservations:** Recommended. **Tram:** 4.

$ Prices: Appetizers 26–46 markkaa ($5.70–$10.10); main dishes 47–78 markkaa ($10.30–$17.20). DC, MC, V.

Open: Mon–Fri 11am–2am, Sat–Sun noon–2am.

Don't let the name fool you. This restaurant, next door to the Arctia Hotel Marski, isn't Japanese. The name was established by a former owner who was an opera lover. The food, some of which is international, is basically Finnish—so Finnish it even offers Marshal Mannerheim's favorite dish, vorschmack, a fried-meat patty served with baked potatoes, salted cucumbers, and beet root. As an appetizer, try a blini with seasonally changing fish roe, ranging from salmon roe to whitefish roe, and the most prized of all, vendace roe. You can also sample Finnish salmon soup with rye toast, fried Baltic herring with mashed potatoes, and chicken breast with garlic stuffing. Food orders are accepted to 1:30am, and this is the only high-quality restaurant in Helsinki where you can dine until the wee hours. The bar was chosen as the best singles venue in the capital by a local newspaper.

CAFES
Moderate

FAZER CAFE, Kluuvikatu 3. Tel. 666-597.
Cuisine: FINNISH. **Reservations:** Not required. **Tram:** 3, 4.
$ **Prices:** Appetizers 38–52 markkaa ($8.40–$11.40); main dishes 72–95 markkaa ($15.80–$20.90); lunch 45–55 markkaa ($9.90–$12.10). AE, DC, MC, V.
Open: Mon–Fri 11am–9pm, Sat 11am–6pm.

Fazer began as a pastry and chocolate shop in 1891, and today, many incarnations later, the pastries are still delicious, but the place is considerably more modern and the cuisine more comprehensive. There is a conservatively decorated dining room on the left as you enter, and lunches can include salmon soup, veal with morels, fried pork filet, and tournedos Rossini. The spacious café on the right, however, is the really popular section of this place. It contains a bistro-style, summery decor of ice-cream wagons, red-and-white tablecloths, framed artworks, a deli case loaded with salads and cakes, and dozens upon dozens of pastries and chocolates. You can also select from the racks of deli and *konditorei* shelves in another part of the store.

VEGETARIAN
Inexpensive

AURINKOTUULI, Lapinlahdenkatu 25. Tel. 694-2563.
Cuisine: VEGETARIAN. **Reservations:** Not required. **Bus:** 65A.
$ **Prices:** Soup 26 markkaa ($5.70); food platters 35–40 markkaa ($7.70–$8.80). MC, V.
Open: Mon–Fri 11am–6pm.

Everything here is self-service at this large vegetarian buffet. The price of your meal is based on if you take a small plate or a large plate to the buffet. Soups cost extra. This establishment is on the street level, with a simple decor, attracting budget-conscious young people.

PICNIC FARE & WHERE TO EAT IT

PICNIC SANDWICH AND SALAD BAR, Mannerheimintie 20. Tel. 607-713.
Cuisine: SANDWICHES. **Reservations:** Not required. **Tram:** 3B, 3T.
$ **Prices:** Sandwiches 18–28 markkaa ($4–$6.20); salads 32–35 markkaa ($7–$7.70). No credit cards.
Open: Mon–Fri 7:30am–9pm, Sat 10am–4pm.

From its cramped but immaculate premises on the main commercial thoroughfare of Helsinki, this little shop dispenses health-conscious fast-food-to-go items, many of which would be ideal for take-away picnics. On request (and at no extra cost), the plastic-wrapped take-away food will include plastic knives, forks, spoons, and disposable napkins.

With your little picnic basket, you can head for the national park on the island of Seurasaari, the most ideal spot in all of Helsinki for a family outing.

CHAPTER 35

WHAT TO SEE & DO IN HELSINKI

Helsinki is loaded with all types of things to do from exploring museums, to enjoying a Finnish sauna, to taking a summer cruise through the archipelago, or even just testing out a Finnish smörgåsbord. If your time is limited though, be sure not to miss the Mannerheim Museum, the home of Sibelius, the Seurasaari Open-Air Museum, or the Suomenlinna Fortress. For those with more time, and money to burn, Helsinki also offers a number of specialty shops. For an overview, stop in at Stockmann, Helsinki's largest department store.

SUGGESTED ITINERARIES

IF YOU HAVE 1 DAY

Day 1: Start the morning with a visit to Market Square, and, following in the footsteps of Lyndon Johnson, have coffee and a Karelian meat pie. The market opens at 7am. See the Presidential Palace and Uspenski Cathedral, and visit Senate Square and Eliel Saarinen's Railway Station. Before it's too late, call at the Stockmann department store or walk along Pohjoisesplanadi for a look at modern Finnish design in the store windows.

IF YOU HAVE 2 DAYS

Day 1: See "If You Have 1 Day," above.

Day 2: Visit the home of Baron Carl Gustaf Mannerheim, Finland's former field marshal and president, now a museum. Go to the Olympic Stadium to see the controversial statue of the famous runner Paavo Nurmi, and call on Finlandia Hall, Helsinki's main concert hall, designed by Alvar Aalto. Visit the National Museum and stroll through Sibelius Park, with its monument to the famous composer.

IF YOU HAVE 3 DAYS

Days 1 & 2: See "If You Have 2 Days," above.

Day 3: Visit some of the attractions in the archipelago, including the Seurasaari Open-Air Museum and Suomenlinna Fortress.

IF YOU HAVE 5 DAYS

Days 1–3: See "If You Have 3 Days," above.

Day 4: Head north on an excursion to visit the home of Jean Sibelius at Ainola in Järvenpää. Explore the nearby town of Hämeenlinna and see the birthplace of Sibelius.

Day 5: Take a 1-day excursion to Porvoo, the second-oldest town in Finland, 30 miles northeast of Helsinki.

1. THE TOP ATTRACTIONS

MANNERHEIM MUSEUM, Kallionlinnantie 14. Tel. 635-443.

This was the home of Baron Carl Gustaf Mannerheim, marshal of Finland and president of the republic from 1944 to 1946—a sort of George Washington in this country, considered one of the most effective military strategists of his era. Now a museum, the residence houses his collection of European furniture, Asian art, and personal items like uniforms, swords, decorations, gifts from admirers. The house remains the same as it was when he died in 1951.

Admission (including guided tour): 20 markkaa ($4.40) adults, 5 markkaa ($1.10) children over 12.

Open: Fri–Sat 11am–3pm, Sun 11am–4pm. **Tram:** 3B, 3T.

AINOLA, Ainolantie, in Järvenpää. Tel. 287-322.

Few countries seem as proud of a native composer as Finns are of Jean Sibelius, who lived here for more than half a century. He named the house after his wife, Aino (sister of artist Eero Järnefelt), and lived here from 1904 until he died in 1957; he and his wife are buried on the property. Considered avant-garde at the time of its construction, the house was designed by Lars Sonck, who also designed the summer residence of the president of Finland. The wooden interior of Ainola is lined with books and some surprisingly modern-looking furniture. Järvenpää is not quite 24 miles from Helsinki.

Admission: 15 markkaa ($3.30) adults, 5 markkaa ($1.10) children.

Open: May–Sept, Wed–Sun 11am–5pm. **Bus:** From Platform 1 of the Helsinki Bus Station, following the Helsinki-Hyryla-Järvenpää route, to a point where the road forks at a sign saying AINOLA, a 4-minute walk from the home. **Train:** Järvenpää station.

SEURASAARI OPEN-AIR MUSEUM, Seurasaari. Tel. 484-712.

Located on the island of Seurasaari, a national park, this museum is a cluster of about 100 authentically furnished buildings, including a 17th-century church and an 18th-century gentleman's manor. In addition, visitors can see an "aboriginal" sauna, which resembles a smokehouse. A restaurant operates in summer, and on some evenings from June to August there's folk dancing to the tunes of a fiddler.

Admission: 10 markkaa ($2.20) adults, 4 markkaa (90¢) children; 20 markkaa ($4.40) adults for folk dancing (free for children).

Open: May–Sept, daily 11am–5pm. **Bus:** 24 from Erottaja to the island; the 3-mile ride takes about 15 minutes.

GALLEN-KALLELA MUSEUM, Tarvaspää, Gallen-Kallelantie 27, in Espoo. Tel. 513-388.

Located on a wooded peninsula in a suburb of Helsinki, this museum is dedicated to the great Finnish artist Akseli Gallen-Kallela (1865–1931), who built the studio between 1911 and 1913, calling it his "castle in the air." A restless, fanciful personality, Gallen-Kallela today has a reputation based mainly on his paintings, especially those from the *Kalevala* (Land of Heroes). This Finnish national epic, first published in 1835, and often compared to Homer's *Iliad* and *Odyssey*, was illustrated by the artist. He wanted to illustrate all the cantos, but only managed a small part, which rank among masterpieces of Finnish art. The museum contains a large collection of his paintings, graphics, posters, and industrial design products. A café is beside the museum, in a wooden villa from the 1850s.

Admission: 25 markkaa ($5.50) adults, 10 markkaa ($2.20) children 7–16.

FROMMER'S FAVORITE
HELSINKI EXPERIENCES

Enjoying a Finnish Sauna Regardless of where you've bathed before, you haven't been cleaned to the core until you've participated in the local ritual—a Finnish sauna. Whether for giving birth to babies or entertaining Russian ambassadors, the saunatics of Helsinki regard the sauna with almost religious awe.

Hearing a Sibelius Concert To experience the work of Finland's greatest composer, Jean Sibelius, is a moving experience. This sensitive, vulnerable artist achieved a universal melodic language. In his lifetime, Sibelius and his music became the symbol of Finland, a nation striving for independence and recognition.

Partaking of a Finnish Smörgåsbord Feast on the harvest of the sea, Baltic herring in a tangy marinade, followed by lightly salted fish and roe, smoked and other cold fish dishes. Then smoked reindeer meat for a touch of Lapland (flavored with lingonberries), and for a finale, a selection of Finnish desserts, including fresh Arctic berries.

Cruising the Archipelago Since Helsinki is the capital of a country of 188,000 lakes, it, too, is best seen from the water. On a warm summer day, strike out on a cruise through the archipelago, passing innumerable little islands and navigating around peninsulas.

Open: May 15–Aug, Mon–Thurs 10am–8pm, Fri–Sun 10am–5pm; Sept–May 14, Tues–Sat 10am–4pm, Sun 10am–5pm. **Tram:** 4 to Munkkiniemi; then from Munkkiniemi, take bus 33 to Tarvo or walk about 1½ miles along the seaside (bus 33 runs Mon–Sat 9:20–11am and 1–3pm).

SUOMENLINNA FORTRESS

Known as the Gibraltar of the North, this 18th-century fortress (tel. 668-154) lies in the Baltic's archipelago on five interconnected islands guarding the maritime approaches to Helsinki. With their walks and gardens, cafés, restaurants, and old frame buildings, the islands make for one of the most interesting outings from Helsinki. Originally built in the mid-18th century when Finland was a part of Sweden, the fortress was named Sveaborg by the Swedes, and later became known by the Finns and Russians (who took it over in 1808) as Viapori. After Finland gained independence in 1917, it was given its present name, Suomenlinna, which means "the fortress of Finland." It served as a working part of the nation's defenses until 1973.

Today the main attraction is the part of the fortress sited on **Susisaari** and **Kustaanmiekka** islands, which are now joined together as one land body. Specifically, the sights include a small, well-preserved bastioned fort on Kustaanmiekka, with defense walls and tunnels, and another, larger, fortress on Susisaari, which includes a number of parks, squares, and gardens.

You can take a **ferry** from the Market Square to Suomenlinna year-round beginning at 6:20am daily. The boats run at intervals of about an hour, and the last one returns from the island at 1:45am. The round-trip ferry ride costs 15 markkaa ($3.30) for adults, 7 markkaa ($1.50) for children.

The island has no "streets," but individual attractions are signposted.

An **information kiosk** by Tykistolahti Bay is the starting point for **guided**

FINLAND

Helsinki

Botanical Gardens
Eduskuntatalo
 (Finnish Parliament) ⑨
Finlandia Hall ⑫
Helsinki City Museum ⑪
Helsinki Zoo ⑥
Kriegsmuseum ❶
Linnanmäki Amusement
 Park ⑮
Lutheran Cathedral
 (Tuomiokirkko) ④
Mannerheim Museum ❼
National Museum
 of Finland ⑩
National Theater ❸
Olympic Stadium ⑭
Temppeliaukio Church ❽
Sibelius Park
 & Monument ⑬
Suomenlinna
 Fortress ⑥
Svenska Teatern ❺

Taivallahti

Töölönlahti

Sibelius
Park ⑬

Pohjoinen Hesperiankatu
Eteläinen Hesperiankatu

Museokatu

Lapinlahti

Hietaniemenkatu

Arkadiankatu   Arkadiagatan

Hietanie-
menkatu

Pohj Rautatiekatu

Hietaniemi
Cemetery
Lapinlahdentie

Lapinlandenkatu

Malminkatu

Porkkalankatu   Porkalagatan

Itämerenkatu

Ruobolahti

Hietalahti

Saukonkatu

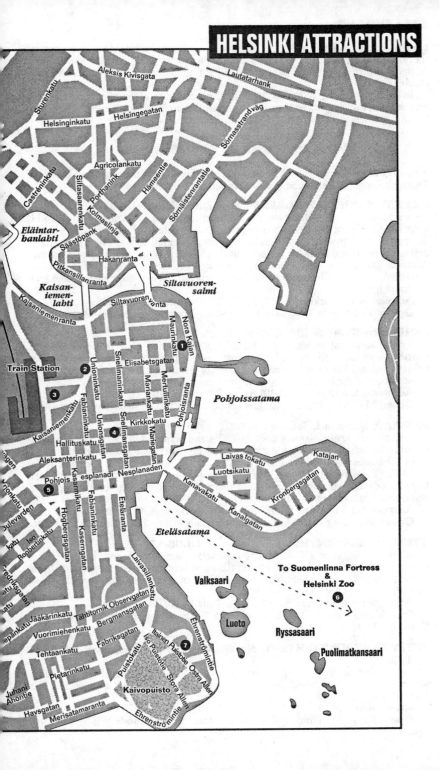

HELSINKI ATTRACTIONS

Eläintar-banlahti

Kaisan-niemen-lahti

Siltavuoren-salmi

Train Station

Pohjoissatama

Eteläsatama

To Suomenlinna Fortress
&
Helsinki Zoo

Valksaari

Luoto

Ryssasaari

Puolimatkansaari

Kaivopuisto

tours—offered in English—of the fortress; you can also buy maps and souvenirs at the kiosk. The tours are offered June through August, daily at 12:30pm and at 2:30pm, and they cost 15 markkaa ($3.30) for adults and 8 markkaa ($1.80) for children.

In addition to the following museums, other sights of Suomenlinna are the **Ryhmateatteri (summer theater)**, where plays are performed (in Finnish) at the Good Conscience Bastion (tel. 718-622 for information).

THE MUSEUMS OF SUOMENLINNA

A number of minor museums are found on either Susisaari or the connected island of Kustaanmiekka. These can be explored if you have the time.

COASTAL ARTILLERY MUSEUM, Kustaanmiekka. Tel. 161-5296.

In a vaulted 1776 powder room, this museum contains displays mainly from World Wars I and II. Opened in 1948, the museum is comprehensive, tracing the stages in the defense of Finnish shores from prehistoric times up until today. The weapons for defending the coastline today include missiles, motorized artillery, and turret guns. Also on display are equipment for directing fire, range-finders, and a marine surveillance camera. The newer technology is represented by close-range missiles and a laser range-finder.

Admission: 5 markkaa ($1.10) adults, 2.50 markkaa (60¢) children.
Open: Mid-May to Aug, daily 11am–5pm. **Closed:** Sept to mid-May.

EHRENSVÄRD MUSEUM, Susisaari. Tel. 668-154.

At this historical museum that includes a model ship collection and officers' quarters from the 18th century, there are also displays based on Suomenlinna's military history. The museum bears the name of Augustin Ehrensvärd, who directed construction of the fortress and whose tomb is on Susisaari.

Admission: 6 markkaa ($1.30) adults, 3 markkaa (70¢) children.
Open: May, daily 10am–4pm; June–Sept, daily 10am–5pm. **Closed:** Oct–Apr.

VESIKKO, Susisaari. Tel. 161-5295.

The submarine *Vesikko* was built in Turku and launched in 1933. Germany had ordered the submarine built for experimental purposes, but Finland bought it in 1936. The submarine fought actively during World War II, and it torpedoed the 4,100-ton Russian ship *Vyborg*. In the Paris peace treaty of 1947, Finland was forbidden to have submarines, and all of them except the *Vesikko* were scrapped. It was opened as a museum in 1973.

Admission: 5 markkaa ($1.10) adults, 2.5 markkaa (60¢) children.
Open: May, daily 10am–4pm; June–Sept, daily 10am–5pm. **Closed:** Oct–Apr.

ARMFELT MUSEUM, Kustaanmiekka. Tel. 668-131.

A reconstruction of a 19th-century upper-class home in a former barracks. The setting is ideal for its assemblage of porcelain and furniture, much of it dating from the 18th century. The objects exhibited were from a manor house owned by the Armfelts, a distinguished local family.

Admission: 6 markkaa ($1.30) adults, 3 markkaa (70¢) children.
Open: Mid-May to Aug, daily 11am–5:30pm; Sept, Sat–Sun 11am–5:30pm.
Closed: Oct to mid-May.

JETTY BARRACKS GALLERY, Nordic Arts Center, Susisaari. Tel. 668-143.

This gallery features changing exhibits of Finnish and Scandinavian art, some watercolors, others oil-based. Some of the painters were inspired by scenes in the archipelago.

Admission: Free.
Open: Early Apr to mid-Sept, Tues–Sun 11am–5pm. **Closed:** Mid-Sept to early Apr.

? DID YOU KNOW . . . ?

- Helsinki is famed for its architects, but it was a German, Carl Ludvig Engel, who designed the layout of the present inner city.
- Two brothers designed Temppeliauko Church out of a solid rock; it takes up most of a block, but from the street only the dome is visible.
- The Havis Amanda fountain, scandalized the city when it was placed in the Market Square in 1908, but now it's the symbol of Helsinki.
- The major boulevard, Esplanadi, was once a political dividing line—Finns walked on the south side and Swedes on the north.
- Wäinö Aaltonen caused an uproar in 1952 when his statue of Paavo Nurmi, the champion runner of the 1920s, was unveiled—he had depicted Nurmi fully nude.

2. MORE ATTRACTIONS

EDUSKUNTATALO [Finnish Parliament], Mannerheimintie 30. Tel. 4321.

A short distance from the post office, this building of red Finnish granite, built in 1931, shelters the 200 members of the one-chamber parliament, one quarter of whose members are women. The building is austere on the outside, but warms up considerably inside—especially in the gallery of nudes. Members meet in a domed cathedral, decorated with sculpture by Wäinö Aaltonen. The architect was J. S. Sirén, whose aim was to celebrate the new republic. He built it in a modernized neoclassic style that some critics found uncomfortably similar to that of Nazi Germany and oddly out of place in a democratic country like Finland. The parliament is open to visitors only when it is not in session.

Admission: Free.
Open: Summer, Mon–Fri at 2pm, Sat at 11am and noon, Sun at noon and 1pm. **Closed:** Winter. **Bus:** 69.

LUTHERAN CATHEDRAL, Senaatintori. Tel. 656-365.

Dominating the city's skyline on Senate Square is this green-domed, 19th-century Evangelical-Lutheran cathedral. It was designed by the German-born architect Carl Ludvig Engel when he was planning all the city's public buildings in the neoclassic style during the reconstruction of Helsinki (a fire had destroyed most of the town after the Russian czar annexed the country in the early 19th century). Considered one of the city's most visible symbols, it was built between 1830 and 1852.

Admission: Free.
Open: May–Sept, Mon–Sat 9am–7pm, Sun noon–7pm; Oct–Apr, Mon–Sat 9am–5pm, Sun noon–5pm. **Tram:** 1, 2, 3B, 3T.

OLYMPIC STADIUM [Olympiastadion], Paavo Nurmi tie 1. Tel. 440-363.

Helsinki was host to the Olympic Games in 1952, and leftover from its impressive sports stadium is a tower in which an elevator whisks passengers up for an exciting view of the city as well as the archipelago. The location is 1¼ miles from the center. The stadium was originally constructed in 1940, but those games were cancelled when war broke out. Outside the stadium is a statue by Wäinö Aaltonen of the great athlete Paavo Nurmi, "The Flying Finn." The runner is depicted in full stride and also completely nude, which caused a lot of controversy when it was unveiled in 1952.

Admission: 7 markkaa ($1.50) adults, 3 markkaa (70¢) children.
Open: Mon–Fri 9am–8pm, Sat–Sun 9am–6pm. **Tram:** 3B, 3T, 4, 10. **Closed:** During athletic competitions.

SIBELIUS MONUMENT, Sibelius Park, on Mechelininkatu.

This is a magnificent monument created by sculptor Eila Hiltunen in 1967 in honor of the celebrated Finnish composer Jean Sibelius (1865–1957). The monument is welded into a rhythmic whole out of hundreds of steel pipes.

Admission: Free.
Open: Daily 24 hours. **Bus:** 18 from railroad station, leaving every 10 minutes.

TEMPPELIAUKIO CHURCH, Lutherinkatu 3. Tel. 494-698.

Built into solid rock and consecrated in 1969, this church, called the "rock church," is about 2 blocks west of the National Museum in the Töölö residential district west of Mannerheimintie. Only the roof is visible from outside. Two brothers, Tuomo and Timo Suomalainen, were the architects. They selected a rocky outcrop rising some 40 feet above street level. Interior walls were blasted from bedrock. Because of its superb acoustics, the church is often used as a concert hall. English-language services are conducted every Sunday at 2pm. Tourists are welcome visitors.

Admission: Free.
Open: Mon–Sat 10am–8pm, Sun noon–2pm and 5–9pm. **Tram:** 3B, 3T.

HELSINKI CITY MUSEUM, at Villa Hakasalmi, Karamizininkatu 2. Tel. 16-93-444.

The history of Helsinki from its founding up to modern times is presented. A small-scale model of the town in the 1870s is on display, and there are exhibits of home decorations from the 18th and 19th centuries, glass, porcelain, and toys.

Admission: 10 markkaa ($2.20) adults, 5 markkaa ($1.10) children.
Open: Sun–Wed and Fri noon–4pm, Thurs noon–8pm. **Bus:** 69, 69A.

NATIONAL MUSEUM OF FINLAND, Mannerheimintie 34. Tel. 405-01.

Designed in the National Romantic style, this museum opened in 1916 and contains three major sections—prehistoric, historic, and ethnographic. Archeological finds on display reveal that from the earliest days of the Stone Age humans made their homes in Finland. Church art of the medieval and Lutheran periods, folk-culture artifacts, folk costumes and textiles, furniture, and an important coin collection are exhibited, and of particular interest are the Finno-Ugric collections.

Admission: 10 markkaa ($2.20) adults; 5 markkaa ($1.10) children.
Open: Mon and Wed–Sat 11am–3pm, Tues 11am–3pm and 6–9pm, Sun 11am–4pm. **Tram:** 4, 7A, 7B, 10.

HELSINKI ZOO, Korkeasaari Island. Tel. 199-81.

An interesting collection of northern European animals, including a herd of wild forest reindeer, wolverines, northern owl species, and a large number of other mammals and birds from Europe and Asia, can be found here. The Helsinki Card (see "Getting Around" in Chapter 33) covers admission to the zoo and includes free rides on the ferry and the water bus.

Admission: 26 markkaa ($5.70) adults, 12 markkaa ($2.60) children.
Open: May–Sept, daily 10am–8pm; Oct–Feb, daily 10am–4pm; Mar–Apr, daily 10am–6pm. **Ferry:** From Market Square. **Waterbus:** Leaves from Hakaniemenranta in front of Merihotelli. **Bus:** 16 (in winter).

KRIEGSMUSEUM [Military Museum], Maurinkatu 1. Tel. 161-6381.

Founded in 1929, this museum records, preserves, and displays material and traditions associated with the Finnish defense forces and with general military history. The museum possesses more than 60,000 items, only some of which can be displayed. Highlights include objects from the days of Swedish rule, as well as collections from the era between the two world wars. An exhibition of particularly gripping photographs from the war years 1939 to 1945 is displayed in the north corridor.

Admission: 5 markkaa ($1.10) adults; 2.50 markkaa (60¢) children.
Open: Sun–Fri 11am–3pm. **Bus:** 16, 18.

URHO KEKKONEN MUSEUM TAMMINIEMI, Seurasaarrentie 15. Tel. 480-684.

Urho Kekkonen, the Finnish president who held the longest term in office of any other, from 1956 until 1982, lived at Tamminiemi from the first year he took office until he died in 1986. Finns are especially fond of visiting this former seat of Scandinavian power, but foreign visitors will find it interesting too, as the house remains just as Kekkonen left it.

Admission: 10 markkaa ($2.20) adults, 5 markkaa ($1.10) children.

IMPRESSIONS

I became aware at once of the translucent, transparent, pure, elusive, clean, and clinical quality of Helsinki. I began to hate the almost paralyzing perfection of modern buildings, equipment, accommodation, accessories, service.
—JAMES KIRKUP, ONE MAN'S RUSSIA, 1968

Open: May 2–Sept 15, daily 11am–4pm; Sept 16–Apr 30, Mon–Sat 11am–3pm, Sun 11am–4pm. **Bus:** 24 from Erottaja.

PARKS & GARDENS

BOTANICAL GARDENS, University of Helsinki, Unioninkatu 44. Tel. 708-55.

These gardens, a 5-minute walk from the Central Station, feature a large collection of palms, orchids, cacti, and other exotic plants. Outdoors are shrubs and flowers, herbs, ornamentals, Finnish wildflowers, and indigenous trees and bushes.

Admission: Greenhouses, 10 markkaa ($2.20) adults, 5 markkaa ($1.10) children; gardens, free.

Open: Greenhouses, May–Aug, Sat–Wed noon–3pm; Sept–Apr, Sat–Sun noon–3pm. Gardens, daily 7am–9pm.

PIHLAJASAARI RECREATIONAL PARK. Tel. 630-065.

A popular attraction, this park is made up of two small neighboring islands filled with sandy beaches—it's a summer playground for the city. A restaurant and a café are in the park.

Admission: Free.

Open: Daily 24 hours. **Transportation:** Motorboat leaves from the end of Laivurinkatu daily at 9am, 9:30am, and then at hourly intervals until 8:30pm, May to mid-Oct, depending on weather.

SIBELIUS PARK, Mechelininkatu.

Called Sibeliuksen puisto in Finnish, this park was laid out to honor Jean Sibelius, Finland's most famous composer. The grounds are not particularly manicured, but are instead kept in a somewhat natural state. Old birch trees shade park benches and rocky outcrops divide the landscapes. The park was meant to evoke the rugged natural beauty of Finland itself, as inspired by Sibelius's work *Finlandia*. At one side of the park rises the monumental sculpture, Eila Hiltunen's monument to Sibelius, which was dedicated to the genius whose music was considered to give form to the soul of Finland. The monument was unveiled in 1967, a decade after the composer's death. It is said that it took 6 years to complete. Sibelius is depicted at the peak of his powers and his career.

Admission: Free.

Open: Daily 24 hours. **Tram:** 3B.

3. COOL FOR KIDS

There are a lot of activities of interest to children in Helsinki, not the least of which involves traveling on the **ferryboats and water buses** that link the city's various islands and attractions. The Helsinki Card (see "Getting Around" in Chapter 33) entitles them to free admittance or reduced rates at a number of the places visited elsewhere in this chapter. Among these, I have noted that children like the "Helsinki by the Sea" **boat tours** (see "Organized Tours"), the **Helsinki Zoo** (see "More Attractions"), the **Linnanmäki Amusement Park** (see "Evening Entertainment"), the **Pihlajasaari Recreational Park, Suomenlinna Fortress** and the model-ship collection in the Ehrensvärd Museum and the submarine *Vesikko* on

Susisaari Island (see "The Top Attractions"), the outdoor **Swimming Stadium** (see "Recreation"), and many other sights and excursions.

4. SPECIAL-INTEREST SIGHTSEEING

FOR THE ARCHITECTURE LOVER

Hvittrask, in Luoma, Kirrkkonummi (tel. 297-5779), the studio home of architects Eliel Saarinen, Armas Lindgren, and Herman Gesellius, was built of logs and natural stone and ranks among the most remarkable architectural creations of its time. The artistic unity of the house with its forest surroundings was considered a highly influential achievement. Today it is used as a center for exhibits of Finnish art and handcrafts. A first-rate restaurant, Hvittrask (tel. 297-6033) is open on Monday from noon to 8pm, Tuesday through Thursday from noon to 11pm, on Friday from noon to 8pm, and on Saturday and Sunday from noon to 8pm.

Admission is 10 markkaa ($2.20) for adults, 5 markkaa ($1.10) for children. It's open May to August, Monday through Friday from 10am to 7pm and on Saturday and Sunday from 11am to 6pm. To get there, take bus no. 166 from the central bus station, Platform 62, then walk about 1¼ miles. Or take the train to Luoma, then walk about 1¼ miles. By car, follow the Jorvas motorway about 12¼ miles, turn off at the Kivenlahti exit, drive 3 miles in the direction of Kauklahti, and then follow the Hvittrask signs.

Perhaps the most model of the model communities of Scandinavia is **Tapiola,** a self-contained city-within-a-city 6 miles west of Helsinki in the capital's neighbor, Espoo. This garden city, of the pre–World War II era, is filled with parks, splashing fountains, handsomely designed homes and apartments, shopping centers, play-grounds, schools, and churches. In the center of Tapiola is a large office building with a self-service cafeteria on top (a good choice for lunch). To get there, go to either stop no. 52 or 53 near the Central Station. From either these stops, take any bus marked Tapiola.

WALKING TOUR — DOWNTOWN HELSINKI

Start: Senate Square.
Finish: Helsinki Railway Station.
Time: Allow 3 hours, not including museum and shopping stops.
Best Times: Any day it's not raining.
Worst Times: Between 8 and 9:30am and 5 and 6:30pm, because of the heavy traffic.

The tour begins at:

1. **Senate Square,** at the base of the monument to Russian Czar Alexander II, erected in his honor shortly after the annexation of Finland. Helsinki's most historic and beautiful square was designed in the early 1800s at the height of the Russian Empire's fascination with the architectural glories of ancient Greece and Rome. The designer was Berlin-born Carl Ludwig Engel, who had created other public buildings in St. Petersburg. The:

2. **Lutheran Cathedral,** Senate Square, stands on the north side of the square. Capped with triplicate statues of saints, it has four small cupolas ringing its central dome.

As you face the cathedral, the Senate, capped by a low dome, and graced by six Corinthian columns, is on your right. Opposite the cathedral, on the south side of the square, stands the yellow ocher facade and Ionic columns of a house from 1762 which was redesigned by Engel.

Leaving the square, ascend the steeply inclined Unioninkatu, skirting the right-hand (western) edge of the square. The street was dedicated to the tsar in 1819 and, because of its difficult terrain, considered extremely expensive at the

WALKING TOUR —
DOWNTOWN HELSINKI

100 m
110 y

HELSINKI

Downtown

1 Senate Square
2 Lutheran Cathedral
3 Library of the University
   of Helsinki
4 Russian Orthodox Church
   of the Holy Trinity
5 Finnish State Archives
6 House of Scientific Studies
7 Bank of Finland
8 Official residence of the
   Lord Mayor of Helsinki
9 House of Nobility
10 Finnish War College
    and Military Museum
11 Burger's House
12 Kaisaniemi Park
13 National Theater
14 The Ateneum
15 Helsinki Railway Station

start
here

finish here

Church

time of its construction. The elegantly graceful building opposite the western facade of the cathedral is the:

3. **Library of the University of Helsinki.** Some critics consider this the most beautiful of the many buildings created by Engel. Admire its rhythmically repetitive Corinthian pilasters and columns before continuing uphill. At the northwestern corner of the cathedral's rear side rises the spire of the:

4. **Russian Orthodox Church of the Holy Trinity,** with an ocher-colored facade. Designed by Engel in 1827, it has an artfully skewed Orthodox double cross placed above its doorway.

After passing Kirkkokatu, turn right (east) onto Rauhankatu. The statue of the young girl, set onto a porphyry base near the corner, is named *Dawn* and the gray-fronted modern building serving as the statue's backdrop contains the printing presses and engravers' shops for banknotes issued by the Bank of Finland. Continue east on the same street, passing an ornately neoclassical building with a trio of wise women set on its pediment. This is the storage space for the:

5. **Finnish State Archives,** originally designed in 1890. As they grew, they were greatly expanded with annexes and underground vaults.

At the corner of Snellmaninkatu, turn right. The russet-fronted temple with four Corinthian columns and a single acanthus leaf at the pinnacle of its pediment is the:

6. **House of Scientific Studies,** erected in 1891. Just below its heraldic plaques is a heroic frieze cast in solid bronze, paying homage to the generosity of Czar Alexander II, who promised to retain the internal laws and religion of Finland after its 1809 annexation. For many years the frieze was the largest bronze casting in Finland. Across the Snellmaninkatu is a somber gray building set above a steep embankment—the central headquarters of the:

7. **Bank of Finland,** designed by a Russian-German architect, Bohnsted, in 1892. In front of the bank stands a statue of the Finnish statesman J. V. Snellman, the patriot whose life was devoted to placing Finnish legally on the same linguistic footing with Swedish. Snellman was also responsible for replacing Russian rubles with Finnish markkaa as the official currency of the country.

Continue to walk downhill along Snellmaninkatu, skirting the eastern edge of the cathedral's outbuildings. Shortly you'll reenter Senate Square. Proceed to the bottom of the square and turn left onto Aleksanterinkatu. At no. 14 on that street, behind a russet-colored 1823 facade, is the:

8. **Official residence of the Lord Mayor of Helsinki,** standing next door to the Theater Museum at Aleksanterinkatu 12.

Continue walking east along Aleksanterinkatu. In a short time you'll enter a small gate dotted with a handful of birch trees. Behind the trees rises the Neo-Venetian facade of the:

9. **House of Nobility,** completed in 1861 as a private club and the reunion hall of the Finnish and Russian aristocracy.

Walk along Aleksanterinkatu, crossing Marinakatu, and continue toward the harbor. Some of the buildings along here are among the oldest in Helsinki, dating from the 1760s. At the waterfront, turn left onto Meritullintori, skirting the edge of the harbor. A sweeping vista of the Russian Orthodox Uspenski Kathedralen (cathedral) comes into view.

At this point the street changes its name to Pohjoisranta, and continues to follow the harborfront. Continue along this street to the third intersection, Maneeskikatu, where the quay will widen into a formal park, ringed with art nouveau buildings, some of the finest in Helsinki. On the park's northwestern corner, behind a stately Edwardian facade is your:

REFUELING STOP Until just a few years ago, entrance to the prestigious social club, **Svenska Klubben,** at Maurinkatu 6, was strictly reserved only for members. Today, in more egalitarian times, its high-ceilinged dining room and Edwardian elegance are open to the public, many of whom revel in its enviable history. Originally built in 1900, it serves meals, coffee, and drinks to visitors.

After your refreshment, exit from the club's front door and, facing the park once again, notice on your left the red-brick Neo-Victorian mass of the:

10. **Finnish War College and Military Museum,** Liisankatu, originally constructed as a barracks in the 1880s. Turn left onto Liisankatu, heading west. Completed in 1813, the street honored the Russian Czarina Elisabeth (Liisa is the Finnish version of Elisabeth).

Take the second right, turning uphill onto Meritullinkatu. Cross (but don't turn onto) Kulmakatu. At this point, Meritullinkatu transforms itself into a pedestrians-only walkway for residents of the surrounding apartment buildings. At the dead end, turn left and negotiate a narrow, elevated sidewalk high above the street running below (Kristianinkatu). One block later, cross (but don't turn onto) Kulmakatu. A few paces later, at Kristininkatu 12, you'll see the simple stone foundation and ocher-colored clapboards of the:

11. **Burger's House,** Helsinki's oldest remaining wooden house, dating from the early 1800s and now housing a minor museum.

A few steps later, Kristianinkatu dead-ends at a pedestrians-only sidewalk, Oikokatu. Go right (downhill), descending two narrow flights of concrete stairs heading toward the lake. At the bottom, you emerge onto a busy avenue, Siltavuorenranta; turn left and notice the stylish bulk of the Hotel Strand Inter-Continental rising across the water. Walk along the curving embankment for a while, coming to the tramway and car traffic hub of Unioninkatu, which you should cross. You'll then enter:

12. **Kaisaniemi Park** ("The Company Keeping Park"), beloved by residents of Helsinki. Until the 1830s this tract of waterfront land was only a marshy bogland until it was drained and opened as Helsinki's first park. The park contains the Botanical Gardens of the University of Helsinki, which date from 1833.

Walk through the park, flanking the water on your right, and then follow the natural left-bending southward curve of the park's main path. Don't cross any of the railway tracks. After exiting from the park, your path will become Lantinen Teatterikuja, in a neighborhood of art nouveau apartment buildings. Follow the street for a block through the theatrical headquarters of Finland. On your left stands the:

13. **National Theater,** vaguely reminiscent of the opera house in Vienna. Note the decorative sculptures on its facade, especially the representation of bears. The theater was designed by the architect Tarjanne, in 1902. Across the square, immediately opposite the National Theater, is:

14. **The Ateneum,** designed by Hoijer and completed in 1887. Its interior contains the best art museum in Finland (still closed for restoration in 1992). The western side of the square (to your right as you face the Ateneum) is one of the most famous public buildings in Europe, the:

15. **Helsinki Railway Station,** designed by Eliel Saarinen in 1916. The sculptures are evocative of the monumental works of Pharaonaic Egypt. It has been copied endlessly ever since by avant-garde set designers of plays and films, including *Batman.*

At the end of this tour you will have walked 2 miles.

5. ORGANIZED TOURS

CITY TOURS   A city tour lasting 1½ hours is offered by **Suomen Turistianto Oy,** at Mannerheimintie 97 (tel. 588-5166); it departs at 11am and 1pm and costs 50 markkaa ($50.20) for adults and 20 markkaa ($4.40) for children 12 or under. The tour takes in the most important city sights, including the Sibelius Monument. Tickets can be purchased on the bus 15 minutes before departure.

For an **orientation sightseeing trip** without a guide, catch tram no. 3T which takes you by 35 major buildings and monuments of the city. The 45-minute trip is conducted only in summer. Tram no. 3T may be boarded in front of the railway station or at the Market Square Monday through Saturday from 6am to 1am and on Sunday from 7:30am to 1am. It leaves regularly every 5 to 15 minutes costing 8 markkaa ($1.80) for adults, 4 markkaa (90¢) for children 12 or under.

HARBOR TOUR Try to schedule your time to take the **Helsinki by the Sea,** a guided boat tour from the South Harbor, around the islands of Suomenlinna, Kulosaari, and Seurasaari. The tour operates from June to August, daily at 11am, noon, and 1, 2, 3, and 4pm, taking 1½ hours. Departures are from Market Square. **Royal Line,** Jokipolku 2 (tel. 358-228), operates the tour. It costs 50 markkaa ($11) for adults; children pay 25 markkaa ($5.50).

6. SPECIAL/FREE EVENTS

The **Helsinki Festival** is a highlight of the Finnish summer and a prelude to the capital city's generous autumn arts program. Attracting international artists, the festival is held at the end of August and the beginning of September. The nearly 3-week-long program offers concerts, opera, ballet, theater, films, exhibitions, jazz, and pop music. The main stage is the Finlandia Hall, Helsinki's concert and convention center opened in 1971. The Helsinki Festival, a member of the European Association of Music Festivals, is preceded by the **Helsinki Summer Concerts** in July. Further details may be obtained from Helsinki Festival, Unioninkatu 28, SF-00100 Helsinki (tel. 90/659-688). The hotel situation is rather difficult in Helsinki during the festival season, so travelers should make their reservations well in advance.

A free event popular with all visitors—is the **changing of the guard** at the Main Guard Post, behind the President's Palace every day at 1pm. It doesn't match the changing of the guard at Buckingham Palace, but it's a well-attended and much-photographed event, nevertheless.

7. RECREATION

Major sports events take place at the **Olympic Stadium,** Paavo Nurmi tie 1 (tel. 440-363), with its 236-foot tower which was designed by Yrjö Lindegren and Toivo Jäntti. In front is a nude statue of gold-medal runner Paavo Nurmi, called "The Flying Finn." In summer, soccer games between Finland and other countries of Europe are scheduled. *Helsinki This Week* publishes a program of events taking place at the stadium at the time of your visit. Tram: 3T.

HORSEBACK RIDING There are some strictly private riding stables close to Helsinki, but most of these clubs require references and membership. The best bet for riding devotees lies 37 miles west of Helsinki in the town of Vihti. **Vihdinratsastuskeskus,** Pääkslahti, SF-03400 Vihti (tel. 90/224-4676), is a privately owned stable enjoying a good reputation with the Finnish Equestrian Foundation. At the stable you can rent one of about a dozen horses costing from 100 markkaa ($22) per hour. You can ride a covered rink or—weather permitting—go for a trail ride through the surrounding forests. Telephone in advance for more details and reservations.

JOGGING To keep fit, Finns are just as fond of jogging as Americans or Canadians. The best paths are close to **Olympic Stadium** (see above) and in **Kaivopuisto Park** in the southern part of Helsinki. There are also some good jogging trails around

Hesperia Park, which is the most convenient if you're staying at a hotel in the city center.

SAUNAS & SWIMMING POOLS   Most of the hotels recommended have public saunas, which guests rent individually or with others to share the expense. If your hotel doesn't have a sauna, go to the outdoor **Swimming Stadium,** Hammarskjöldintie (tel. 402-9383), which is open only July through September, daily from 9am to 8pm. The charge is 10 markkaa ($2.20) for adults and 2 markkaa (40¢) for children.

Another sauna more centrally located is in the cellar level of the **Ramada Presidentti Hotel,** Eteläinen Rautatiekatu 4 (tel. 69-11). Nonresidents at Ramada can rent the entire sauna—suitable for a group of friends—for 1½ hours at a cost of 100 markkaa ($22), plus a 35 markkaa ($7.70) charge for each participant.

Far more interesting would be to go 5 miles north of Helsinki to a point on the windswept, often fog-bound Gulf of Finland. There you can visit the ✪ **Suomen Sauna Seura (Finnish Sauna Association),** at the end of Vaskenimemetie in the district of Vaskiniemi Lauttasaari (tel. 678-677), which, though it's technically a private club, welcomes foreign visitors. Established in 1937, it is the oldest (and perhaps only) sauna society in Finland. The society maintains four saunas, each of them authentically wood-burning, and each requiring a 5- to 6-hour warmup daily. Two of the four saunas are old-fashioned "smoke saunas." A wharf is built into the gulf for swimming. In winter, a hole is chopped into the ice to allow year-round bathing. No one wears bathing suits at this ritual. The association is open for men on Tuesday, Wednesday, and Friday from 2 to 8pm for men, and on Saturday from noon to 6pm. On Thursday, it is reserved for women and open from 1 to 8pm. It is closed Sunday and Monday, and the month of July. Entrance for nonmembers is 65 markkaa ($11.70). To reach it from the Svenska Teatern off Mannerheimintie, take bus no. 20.

For year-round swimming, try **Keskusta Pool,** Yrjönkatu 21 (tel. 60-981), in the city center near the Forum Shopping Complex. It divides its time among men and women; usually men swim in the morning and women in the afternoon, but call for the schedule before going. The cost for a swim, a sauna, and a towel is 20 markkaa ($4.40). Tram: 3B.

TENNIS   The best bet for playing tennis in Helsinki is to travel 6 miles west of the center to the Pitäjämäki district. There the **Tali SportsCenter,** Kutonokuja 3, Pitäjämäki (tel. 556-271), welcomes foreign visitors. The center maintains 10 indoor tennis courts and 6 outdoor courts. In winter, 5 of the 6 outdoor courts are covered with a plastic "bubble." A reserved court ranges from 50 to 90 markkaa ($11 to $19.80) per hour. You can rent a tennis racquet for 10 markkaa ($2.20) and buy tennis balls once you're there. Take bus no. 14 or 39 from the center of the city. It's open daily from 6am to 10:30pm, but call first to see if courts are free before going there.

8. SAVVY SHOPPING

Finland has taken a bold, creative lead in the highly competitive world of interior design. Search out ceramics and glassware (Arabia is famous), handwoven articles, hand-carved wood, jaunty fashions, and rugs.

Textiles and jewelry also bear the distinctive stamp of Finland, and toy stores brim with educational toys for each stage of a child's development. Among souvenirs, the range includes decorations made from reindeer skin, costume dolls, baskets, and pungently unusual berry liqueurs made from the yellow cloudberry, the cranberry, and the Arctic brambleberry. Of course, you'll find all your sauna needs here as well.

THE SHOPPING SCENE

Most stores are open Monday through Friday from 9am to 5pm and on Saturday from 9am to 2pm. Sometimes stores stay open until 4pm on Saturday, especially in the summer months.

SHOPPING AREAS The most important shopping neighborhoods are in the center of the city. These include **Esplanadi,** for those seeking the finest of Finnish design (but at high prices). Even if you don't buy anything, it's a delightful street for promenading in summer. Airline offices, banks, and travel agencies share the street with shops filled with the best of Finnish crafts, as well as a number of art galleries.

Esplanadi leads from the commercial heart of town all the way to the waterfront. At the bottom of the street, bordering the water, is **Market Square (Kauppatori),** a fresh open-air market open Monday through Saturday. In summer, peddlers set up trolleys and tables to display their wares. Most of the items for sale are produce (some of them ideal for picnic makings), but some souvenir and gift items also appear.

The other main shopping section is called simply **Central,** beginning at Esplanadi and stretching to the famous Helsinki Railway Station. Many of the big names in Finnish shopping are here, none more notable than the Stockmann department store. Many shopping complexes are also in this district, including Forum. One of the main streets for shopping in the district is **Aleksanterinkatu,** running parallel to Esplanadi, stretching from the harborfront to Mannerheimintie.

Other shopping streets, all in the center, include **Iso Roobertinkatu** and **Bulevardi,** lying off Esplanadi. Bulevardi, starting at the Klaus Kurki Hotel, winds its way to the water.

Nearly all stores arrange shipment of large purchases.

RECOVERING TAX Tax-free shopping is available at stores which display FINLAND TAX-FREE SHOPPING signs in their windows. This tax-free shopping is available to all visitors who reside outside the Nordic countries. The purchase tax on articles bought in these shops is refunded to you when you leave Finland. The tax-free minimum purchase is 200 markkaa ($44).

Most main department stores and shops will send your purchases directly to your home address. That way you avoid having to file a claim at Customs. If you take the merchandise with you, ask for a check for the tax amount. This check can be cashed at the airport or harbor from which you depart. The savings works out at about 11% and applies to both cash and credit-card purchases. However, should you use the goods before leaving Finland, you will forfeit the tax refund. Most international credit cards, such as American Express or VISA, are accepted at major shops, but always ask beforehand.

If you have any questions about the tax-free shopping scheme, contact **Finland Tax-Free Shopping,** Yrjönkatu 29C (tel. 693-2433).

A PREVIEW OF FINNISH DESIGN Before you begin to shop, you might want to have an overview of Finnish design in this century. Go to the **Museum of Applied Crafts,** Korkeavuorenkatu 23 (tel. 174-455), which is open Tuesday through Friday from 11am to 5pm and Saturday and Sunday 11am to 4pm. It charges 20 markkaa ($4.40) for adults, 5 markkaa ($1.10) for children. In what used to be a schoolhouse, the museum has on permanent display the best of Finnish design in wood, textiles, ceramics, glass, and other materials.

SHOPPING A TO Z
ART GALLERIES

BRONDA GALLERY, Töölönkatu 36. Tel. 40-78-27.
This is a well-established gallery, the finest in Helsinki, with an always-interesting range of paintings for sale. Sculpture is also exhibited, but rarely. Paintings come from different countries. Sometimes one country, such as Spain, is highlighted as part of a temporary exhibition. Tram: 3B.

BOOKS

ACADEMIC BOOKSTORE, Keskuskatu 1. Tel. 121-41.
Sprawling over two floors crammed with books in many different languages, this store, from the number of titles in stock, is the largest bookstore in Europe. It offers many English-language books, along with a number of travel aids. It

also carries the finest stationery department in Finland and sells greeting cards as well as high-quality gift and hobby articles. If you're here on a Friday, you can attend a literary get-together which assembles writers and members of the reading public, held in the store. All of Finland's major authors and leading politicians, as well as many foreign writers, including Kurt Vonnegut and the Norwegian actress Liv Ullmann, have attended these meetings. The building, with large skylit windows and Carrara marble slabs, was designed by Aalto. Tram: 3B.

DEPARTMENT STORES

STOCKMANN, Aleksanterinkatu 52. Tel. 176-181.

Helsinki's largest department store is also Finland's finest and oldest. Its main entrance is on Aleksanterinkatu, with other entrances on Keskuskatu and Mannerheimintie. Stockmann has a little bit of everything, the most diversified sampling of Finnish and imported merchandise of any store—the glassware, stoneware, ceramics, lamps, furniture, furs, contemporary jewelry, clothes and textiles, handmade candles, reindeer hides—everything. Purchases made through the store's Export Service grant you a full and immediate 16% deduction, and you don't have to carry your purchases home yourself. It maintains small shops at the airport, the Hotel Kalastajatorppa, and the Hotel Inter-Continental. In 1981 it also opened a store in Tapiola at Länsituulentie 5. Tram: 3B.

FASHION

ANNIKKI KARVINEN, Pohjoisesplanadi 33. Tel. 633-837.

Ms. Karvinen became famous for elevating *poppana,* Finnish cotton, into the stellar peaks of fashion. All poppana fabrics are handwoven, and she has adapted the same style to velvet, silk, and wool for more formal and more expensive fashion. She designs jackets for both indoors and outdoors. In addition, her outlet offers a number of household items for sale, including tablecloths and bedspreads. Tram: 3B.

LENA REWELL TEXTILE SHOP, Yrjönkatu 14B. Tel. 649-070.

Each of the richly textured woolens in this shop was designed by one of Finland's best-known textile designers. Since 1960 Lena Rewell's softly colored coats, hats, scarves, gloves, and sweaters have been exported throughout Europe and America. Two of her most popular items are the handwoven mohair blankets and wraparound stoles. You must call before going and arrange an appointment, at which time you will be shown around her studio. Tram: 3B.

MARIMEKKO, Pohjoisesplanadi 31. Tel. 177-944.

Ever since Jacqueline Kennedy in the early 1960s was photographed in Marimekko clothing, the name has been a familiar one to Americans. Meaning "Mary's frock," Marimekko offers large-scale prints in vivid colors splashed against the gray Finnish landscape of winter. The company was founded in 1951 by Armi Ratia, and now includes a collection of unusually textured fabrics sold by the yard for decorating homes and offices. Equally important are the knitted sportswear, place mats, and many other goods that are sold here, including Marimekko's famous knitted T-shirts and dresses. The inventory of shirts and colors changes with the season. Tram: 3B.

PENTIK, Pohjoisesplanadi 27. Tel. 625-558.

This outlet sells clothes, usually for women, made of leather and suede products from Finland. Other garments, especially the silks and cottons, come from Italy. They offer a few items of clothing, including some jackets, for men, but their main specialty is catering to style-conscious women. Tram: 3B, 3T, 4. Bus: 18.

FURNITURE

ARTEK, Keskuskatu 3. Tel. 177-533.

Established in 1935, Artek offers furniture based on designs of the late, great architect Alvar Aalto. His first models were avant-garde pieces designed in the late '20s and early '30s. Today they are considered classics, representing the best of their era. Aalto's works include the Paimio chair, with a laminated birch frame and his famous three-legged birch stool. Seats of the latter are often traditionally covered in black leather, but you can also get them in veneered ash. Designs by his wife, Aino, are also for sale, including pressed-glass tumblers and pitchers she made in the Bolgeblick pattern for the Karhula glassworks in 1932. In addition to furnishings, the store sells lamps, ceramics, glassware, tableware, and textiles. Tram: 3B.

SOKEAIN MYYMALA, Annankatu 16. Tel. 604-893.

The work of blind people, this is an impressive collection of unusual and well-designed furniture in rattan. The furnishings have style and flair, and are suited to both indoor and outdoor living. Tram: 3B.

GLASS, PORCELAIN & CERAMICS

ARABIA, Pohjoisesplanadi 25. Tel. 170-055.

This shop gathers together under one roof the products of some of the world's most prestigious manufacturers of household porcelain and art ceramics. Most of the products are made by Arabia, although some glass and art glass by Nuutajarvi is also offered. Located in the center of Helsinki's most prestigious shopping district, it inventories first-rate household goods designed by Finland's leading designers. The multilingual staff can arrange for any of your purchases to be mailed overseas.

Arabia was established in a suburb of Helsinki (Arabia) in 1873. Today its ceramic factories are among the most modern in the world. Arabia's artists create their own works of art, sometimes in highly collectible limited editions.

Although most visitors purchase their goods at the company's main store (see above), Arabia maintains a small museum and a spacious discount sales area at its factory in the environs of Helsinki at Hämeentie 135 (tel. 39-391). Take tram no. 6 to the end of the line to reach it. Here, discontinued styles as well as slightly imperfect seconds are sold—always at a serious reduction off the regular prices. Tram: 3B.

I-SHOP, Pohjoisesplanadi 27A. Tel. 663-305.

i-Shop is the local representative of a glassworks that has been in business for a century. The factory is Iittala, founded in 1881. In 1936 it produced, for example, Alvar Aalto's famed Savoy vase, which has now become the company's signature. You can purchase reproductions of the vase in four colors, including cobalt blue or opal white, in many different sizes. In 1981 Iittala merged with the equally famous Nuutajarvi glassworks, which was founded in 1793. i-Shop also carries that firm's best offerings.

Aalto's organic vases are classic standards within the repertoires of Finnish design, but this retail outlet also keeps abreast of changing styles and fashions, occasionally introducing the works of new designers. Many shoppers prefer the Kolibri series of unadorned wineglasses by Timo Sarpaneva. If you have the time, you can ask the shop to direct you to their factory outside town. There you can often find slightly flawed "seconds" at about 30% off the regular retail price. You can also go on a guided tour of the factory, although it's a good idea to arrange the details with the shop before you go. Tram: 3B.

HANDCRAFTS

AARIKKA, Pohjoisesplanadi 27. Tel. 652-277.

One of Finland's best selections of wooden toys for children is found here. Many different and unusual household utensils, each fashioned from wood, are also sold. The shop also sells gifts made in Finland, along with a selection of jewelry. Tram: 3B.

ARTISAANI, Unioninkatu 28. Tel. 665-225.

Near the Market Square, Artisaani is a cooperative of artisans who sell their own arts and crafts fresh from their country workshops. Ceramic sculptures, pottery, glassware, gold, silver, and bronze jewelry, leather goods, printed fabrics, and other textiles are displayed. Tram: 3B.

KALEVALA KORU [LAHJAVAKKA], Unioninkatu 25. Tel. 171-520.

Although this store is best known for its collection of jewelry, it sells a fine collection of handcrafts and gifts as well. Its most visible offering is knitwear, which usually comes in both traditional and modern designs. In inventory are knit dresses, coats, pullovers, caps, and mittens for both men and women. Designs from Lapland are usually dyed in subtle colors with naturally produced vegetable and mineral dyes, while the traditional garments from the folkloric regions of Finland's farmland are usually accented with more colorful stripes and patterns. Also for sale are a collection of handmade ceramic ornaments (usually designed to be hung from the top of a window), wood carvings, rugs, and unusual textiles sold by the yard. Tram: 3B.

RYIJYPALAVELU, Kasarmikatu 34, Esplanadi. Tel. 660-615.

A well-stocked second-floor shop specializing in Finnish weavings, called *ryas*, it is operated as a charitable foundation by the Women's Organization of the Disabled War Veteran's Association, as an assistance program for the many veterans disabled in Finland's wars. The traditional and modern Finnish rugs can be bought ready-woven for about $800 to $1,500, or you can buy them as kits to produce the same rugs at home. The kits cost about a third as much as the finished products. Tram: 3B.

SUOMEN KÄSITYÖN YSTÄVÄT [Friends of Finnish Handcraft], Tamminiementie 3. Tel. 482-010.

Suomen Käsityön Ystävät was founded in 1879 to maintain and develop the traditions of Finnish handcrafts. The center of activity is in an old villa about 3 miles from the city center. Here you can see a permanent exhibition of museum-quality *ryijy* tapestries. Textiles, table linens, towels, and gift items, such as shawls and embroidered work, including early 20th-century Jugendstil patterns, can be purchased here. Export service is available. Bus: 24 from the Swedish Theater at Erottaja, the terminus.

JEWELRY

GALERIE BJÖRN WECKSTRÖM, Unioninkatu 30. Tel. 655-529.

Specializing in Lapponia jewelry, as well as in sculpture and glass, this store has won Grand Prix prizes in international jewelry competitions. Björn Weckström has earned a reputation for making shapes inspired by nature, and the jewelry sold here has been called miniature sculpture. The glass collection of bowls, bottles, and dishes sometimes comes in lovely, mysterious colors whose exact ingredients remain a secret of the manufacturer. Tram: 3B, 3T.

KALEVALA KORU, Unioninkatu 25. Tel. 171-520.

Founded in 1937, this store is owned by the Association of Kalevala Women in Finland, whose aim is to preserve the best cultural traditions of a long-ago Finland. They accomplish this through educational programs and through sales of the most authentic reproductions of traditional designs and styles they can find. (See "Handcrafts," above, for some of their offerings.) The name of their organization is derived from the *Kalevala*, the Finnish national epic.

The store sells both traditional and modern jewelry in bronze, silver, and gold. Many of these pieces are based on originals uncovered in archeological excavations that date from the 10th and 11th centuries. Each is produced by some of Finland's foremost artisans. Copies of Lapp jewelry are also sold. The store works in close cooperation with the Finnish National Museum. Tram: 3B.

MUSIC

DIGELIUS MUSIC, Laivurinrinne 2. Tel. 666-375.

Offering a complete selection of both Finnish jazz and Finnish folk music, this shop is not the biggest music store in Helsinki, but it has one of the most knowledgeable and helpful English-speaking staffs. They are familiar with their stock, and are well informed about Finland's musical history. Tram: 3B.

FUGA, Unioninkatu 28. Tel. 631-181.

One of the best record stores in Helsinki, it has a good collection of classical records from all over Europe, as well as folk music recordings and a smattering of jazz. One of the two Nuotio brothers will advise. Tram: 3B.

SAUNA

SAUNA SOPPI-SHOP, Aleksan-terinkatu 28. Tel. 634-733.
Two Finnish women established this shop in 1974 because they believe in the therapeutic and emotional benefits of sauna rituals. Everything they sell is functionally important to the sauna. They offer buckets, ladles, thermometers, linen seat covers, washing mitts, door labels saying SAUNA, loincloths, and even a sauna-related "visitors' book." This is perhaps the most complete selection of sauna-related articles in the world. Tram: 3B.

SCULPTURE

SCULPTOR, Yrjönkatu 11. Tel. 646-903.
The organization that maintains this store, the Association of Finnish Sculptors, was originally established in 1910. Today it's the oldest association of artists in Finland, comprising 200 carefully screened members. This gallery exhibits only works by members, each of whom is Finnish. Only the work of living artists, or the work of artists deceased in the past 2 years, is exhibited. Sculptures are crafted from wood, bronze, stone, plastic, aluminum, steel, or ceramics. The range is from small medallions to monumental pieces. Tram: 3B.

SHOPPING COMPLEXES

FORUM SHOPPING COMPLEX, Mannerheimintie 20.
Stretching for 1 block, Forum shelters 120 shops, restaurants, and service enterprises—making it the number one shopping center in Finland. An atrium rises seven stories high. You'll find a wide array of merchandise for sale here—art, gold, jewelry, food, decorating items, clothing, yarns, leather, records, glasses, rugs, watches, and sporting goods, to cite only some of the items. Shops are open Monday through Friday from 9am to 8pm and on Saturday from 9am to 5pm. Cafés and restaurants are also open on Sunday to 5pm. Tram: 3B, 3T, 7A, 7B.

SPECIALTY SHOPS

KISELESS BAZAAR HALL, Aleksanterinkatu 22-28.
This recently renovated shopping quarter in the old center of Helsinki, located between the cathedral and Market Square, contains a group of small, specialized shops selling lots of unique gifts. The complex has another entrance on Unioninkatu and Sofiankatu and is open Monday through Friday from 10am to 6pm, on Saturday from 10am to 3pm, and on Sunday from noon to 4pm. Tram: 3B.

ITÄKESKUS SHOPPING COMPLEX, Itäkeskus. Tel. 343-1551.
Helsinki's newest complex of shops and restaurants opened in 1992 in a residential suburb. Located within a 15-minute subway ride east of Helsinki's center, it contains many of the attributes of an American shopping mall loaded with Scandinavian and Finnish merchandise. You'll find at least 60 shops, plus about 20 different kiosks and food stalls to allay your hunger pangs. Metro: Itäkeskus.

STAMPS

SUOMEN POSTIMERKKEILY OY, Ludviginkatu 5. Tel. 642-501.
This shop's owner, Ilppo Ylismaa, is considered Finland's leading authority on his country's postage stamps. His shop stocks and specializes in Finnish stamps "from the beginning"—in this case, from 1856. Those first stamps were issued with a portrait of

the Russian czar. This shop, established in 1943 during the darkest days of World War II, is the headquarters for many stamp auctions and sales. Tram: 3B.

YARD GOODS

VERHO SELLGREN, Frederikinkatu 33. Tel. 645-979.
This outlet sells an attractive assortment of yard goods for interior designs, most of it for curtains and upholstery. Most fabrics are woven—not always by hand—in Finland and are sold by the meter. Tram: 3B.

9. EVENING ENTERTAINMENT

Nightlife is not the reason to visit Suomi, although there are the usual restaurants with "nightclubs," but which people in other parts of the world call discos or dance clubs. Friday and Saturday nights are impossibly overcrowded, and if you're going out at all, you should show up early at a club—or risk not getting in. The older crowd sticks mainly to bars in the more popular hotels, such as the Strand Inter-Continental.

Theater is confined almost exclusively to the Finnish or Swedish languages. However, music is universal, and the Helsinki cultural landscape is always rich in music, either winter or summer. The major orchestral or concert performances take place in Finlandia Hall (see below). Operas at the Finnish National Opera are sung in their original languages.

The main agency for concert and opera tickets is **Musiikki-Fazer,** Aleksanterinkatu (tel. 560-11). Another agency for tickets to the opera, concerts, theater, and cinema is **Lippupalvelu,** Mannerheimintie 5 (tel. 97-00-47-00), in the Forum Shopping Complex.

Your best source of information—virtually your only source other than Finnish newspapers—is a little magazine called *Helsinki This Week,* distributed free at most hotels and at the tourist office. It has complete listings, not only of cultural events, but virtually anything that's happening in the Finnish capital—from the Baltic herring market to body-building contests.

THE PERFORMING ARTS

THEATER

SUOMEN KANSALLISTEATTERI [Finnish National Theater], Läntinen Teatterikuja 1B. Tel. 1733-1331.
The Finnish National Theater enjoys international fame, but its performances are all in Finnish. The theater itself, considered one of the architectural gems of 19th-century Helsinki, was established in 1872 and stages about 10 premieres a year. Tram: 3B.
Tickets: 40–75 markkaa ($8.80–$16.50).

SVENSKA TEATERN [Swedish Theater], Norra Esplanaden 2. Tel. 171-244.

THE MAJOR PERFORMANCE/CONCERT HALLS

Finnish National Opera, Bulevardi 23-27 (tel. 129-255).
Finlandia Hall, Karamzininkatu 4 (tel. 40-241).
Suomen Kansallisteatteri (Finnish National Theater), Läntinen Teatterikuja 1B (tel. 1733-1331).
Svenska Teatern (Swedish Theater), Norra Esplanaden 2 (tel. 171-244).

You might want to visit the horseshoe-shaped Swedish Theater if you speak Swedish. It has been presenting plays since 1866. The theater is in the absolute center of Helsinki, opposite the Stockmann department store. The theater is closed from June until August 1, resuming performances at the beginning of September. The box office is open on Monday from 10am to 6pm, Tuesday through Friday from 10am to 7pm, and on Saturday from noon to 7pm. The theater is closed on Sunday. Tram: 3B.

Tickets: 80–90 markkaa ($17.60–$19.80).

OPERA & BALLET

FINNISH NATIONAL OPERA, Bulevardi 23-27. Tel. 129-255.

The ballet and opera presentations of the Finnish National Opera enjoy international fame. Operas are sung in their original languages and, of course, the language of ballet is universal. The original Finnish National Opera was built in the 1870s as a Russian garrison theater. Sometimes during the autumn of 1993, the opera house will move to its new home on Mannerheimintie and change its phone number. The box office is open Monday through Friday from 10:30am to 5pm and on Saturday from 10am to 1pm; it also opens 1½ hours before opera performances begin. The opera and ballet season in Finland runs from August to May. Tram: 3B.

Tickets: 45–160 markkaa ($9.90–$35.20).

CLASSICAL MUSIC & CONCERTS

HELSINGIN KAUPUNGINORKESTERI [Helsinki Philharmonic Orchestra], Finlandia Hall, Karamzininkatu 4. Tel. 40-241.

The oldest symphony orchestra in the Scandinavian countries performs from September to May in the gracefully modern Finlandia Hall, designed by Alvar Aalto of white Carrara marble. Located a short walk north of the town center, it's considered the musical nerve center of Finland. Its box office opens 1 hour before the beginnings of concerts. For information and reservations, call Lippupalvelu (tel. 643-043). Concerts begin at 7:30pm. Tram: 3B.

Tickets: 45–75 markkaa ($9.90–$16.50).

LOCAL CULTURAL ENTERTAINMENTS

See Section 6, "Special/Free Events," in this chapter, for information on the **Helsinki Summer Concerts,** held in July, and the **Helsinki Festival,** held during the late summer.

THE CLUB & MUSIC SCENE
NIGHTCLUBS/CABARET

FIZZ BAR & NIGHTCLUB, in the Arctia Hotel Marski, Mannerheimintie 10. Tel. 68-061.

This club attracts some of the capital's most stylish visitors and residents. Decorated in exotic hardwood paneling from floor to ceiling, it has a stand-up bar and a collection of plushly comfortable high-backed chairs. The entrance is on the street level of the Arctia Hotel Marski (see "Helsinki Accommodations" in Chapter 34). Beer costs 22 markkaa ($4.80). The club is open daily from 8pm to 3am. Tram: 3B, 3T, 6.

Admission: 35 markkaa ($7.70) Mon–Sat, free Sun; free to hotel guests.

NIGHTCLUB PRESSA, in the Ramada Hotel Presidentti, Eteläinen Rautatiekatu 4. Tel. 69-11.

Deep in the cellars of one of Helsinki's biggest hotels (see "Helsinki Accommodations" in Chapter 34), this club offers a large and crowded bar and welcomes hundreds of nonresidents to its dramatically shadowy interior. From a raised stage at one end of the dance floor a rotating series of musical groups performs eminently danceable music. They might be from anywhere, often the Philippines or the United States. Many guests wear jacket and tie, and there's a small-stakes casino in the club. Beer costs 24 markkaa ($5.30). It's open daily from 9pm to 2:30am. Tram: 3B.

Admission: 30–60 markkaa ($6.60–$13.20); free for hotel residents Sun–Thurs.

THE OLD BAKER'S, Mannerheimintie 12. Tel. 605-607.

In many ways, the Old Baker's offers Helsinki's most complete nightclub entertainment. The upper floor contains a restaurant, two bars, a small-stakes casino, a disco, and lots of space for milling around with the energetic crowd. The Scottish-red-and-black carpeted Restaurant Sakkipilli, Kalevankatu 2, is in the pub's complex. Dinner is served in one of three or four different rooms, some of them more intimately secluded than others, and is available either à la carte or by ordering a fixed-price dinner costing 170 to 250 markkaa ($37.40 to $55). Menu specialties include fish salad, Teno River salmon, consommé of smoked meat, many beef dishes, several kinds of fresh fish, and potatoes prepared seven different ways. Although the place caters to a crowd aged roughly between 25 and 35, no blue jeans are permitted. A beer will set you back 18.50 to 26 markkaa ($4.10 to $5.70). The club is open Monday through Saturday from 11am to 1am. Tram: 3B.

Admission: Free Mon–Thurs, 30 markkaa ($6.60) Fri–Sat.

THE RED ROOM, in the Hotel Kalastajatorppa, Kalastajatorpantie 1. Tel. 488-011.

On the outskirts of Helsinki, the Red Room is among the most frequented nightclubs in town. Everything about the place—everything, that is, except the clients—is red, making a dramatic visual impact. It's customary for men to wear a jacket and tie. Many of the guests are staying at the hotel, but a lot of young professional people from Helsinki are also attracted to the place. Beer costs 20 markkaa ($4), and it's open Tuesday through Saturday from 9pm to 3am. Tram: 4 to its terminus.

Admission: Free Tues–Thurs, 50 markkaa ($11) Fri–Sat.

ROCK

BERLIN, Töölönkatu 3. Tel. 499-002.

The leading heavy-metal and acid-rock club in all of Finland, Berlin is off Mannerheimintie, near Finlandia Hall, three floors above street level in a 19th-century building. Monday is gay night, Wednesday is reggae night, Thursday is heavy metal, and Friday is "black beat" or soul music. On Saturday the house plays just about any kind of music it wants to, and on Sunday night the venue is "whatever we think we can get away with," a staff member claims. Enter into an all-black decor. A beer will set you back 24 markkaa ($5.30). Berlin is open Wednesday through Monday from 8pm to 1am. Tram: 3B.

Admission: 20–30 markkaa ($4.40–$6.60).

RIVERBOAT MUSIC BAR, Ruoholahdenkatu 4. Tel. 694-5118.

Although it's decorated like one of those Mississippi steamboats from the grand old days, here you can drink, chatter, and listen to recorded music of the greatest names of rock 'n' roll or new wave. Lunch is served from 10am to 2pm for a reasonable 36 to 52 markkaa ($7.90 to $11.45); a light dinner begins at 85 markkaa ($18.70) and a beer costs 22 markkaa ($4.80). It's open Monday through Friday from 10am to 1am, Saturday from noon to 1am, and Sunday from noon to midnight. Tram: 3B.

Admission: Free.

DANCE CLUBS/DISCOS

ALEXANDER'S DISCO, in Fanny & Alexander's, Siltasaarenkatu 2. Tel. 753-2332.

Fanny and Alexander's is a two-in-one dining-and-drinking complex that is a popular nighttime venue in the city, especially among young people (see "Helsinki Dining" in Chapter 34). The disco section is two flights above street level. It has a good sound-and-light system, and the DJ plays all the latest recordings from Britain, the

United States, and the Continent. A beer costs 18.50 markkaa ($4.10). It's open Monday through Saturday from 7pm to 1:30am. Bus: 17, 64, 72.

Admission: Free Mon–Thurs, 35 markkaa ($7.70) Fri–Sat.

ARKADIA, Frederikinkatu 48. Tel. 694-0151.

At presstime, this was one of the newest discos in town, barely proven as an enduring factor on Helsinki's nightlife scene, but much talked about nonetheless. Contained within an older building near the time-tested KY-Exit (see below), it contains two levels of music, drinking, and dancing, and a youthful allure of university students. The minimum age for entrance is 18. A large beer costs 24 markkaa ($5.30). It's open Tuesday to Saturday from 8:30pm to 2am. Tram: 3B.

Admission: 25 markkaa ($5.50) Sun and Tues–Thurs; 45 markkaa ($9.90) Fri–Sat.

COME BACK, Eerikinkatu 14. Tel. 680-6295.

Near the Forum Shopping Complex, off Mannerheimintie in the city center, this music bar prides itself on its computer-controlled sound system which penetrates into every nook and cranny of this two-level watering hole. All kinds of people come here, especially office workers after a long day. Happy hour, with heavily discounted drinks, is Monday through Friday from 4 to 8pm and all day on Saturday. The upstairs is more animated than the street level. Beer costs 23 markkaa ($5.10). The place is open daily 2pm to 2am. Tram: 3B.

Admission: Free.

HELSINKI CLUB, in the Sokos Hotel Helsinki, Hallituskatu 12. Tel. 171-401.

The Helsinki Club is one of the most sophisticated discos in town. Although the establishment is inside the Sokos Hotel Helsinki most guests enter through a separate sidewalk entrance. Inside there's a circular series of glass or mirrored bars, a collection of small tables, a dance floor with a centerpiece of potted palms, and lots of peach-colored and black glass. The sound here is designed so that you're able to engage in conversation. The minimum age is 23, but many patrons are a few years older than that. Drinks cost 32 markkaa ($7); beer 22 markkaa ($4.80). It's open daily from 8pm to 2am. Tram: 3T, 4.

Admission: Free Sun–Tues, 22 markkaa ($4.80) Wed–Thurs, 35 markkaa ($7.70) Fri–Sat; free for hotel guests.

KY-EXIT, Phojoinen Rautatiekatu 21. Tel. 407-238.

Lying 500 yards west of the Helsinki Railway Station, this place is owned by the Student Union of the Helsinki School of Economics. There has been some kind of social club here since the place was built in the 1940s, and today it's a disco with three levels and a different drinking area on each floor. The quietest is the Rock Dog Bar at street level, but the top floor is the one with the panoramic balcony opening onto a view of the dance floor. Management requests that clients wear clothing "other than jeans." Every night offers a different type of music. Beer runs 16 to 18 markkaa ($3.50 to $4). It's open daily from 8pm to 2am. Tram: 3B.

Admission: 18 markkaa ($4) Sun–Thurs, 40 markkaa ($8.80) Fri–Sat.

THE BAR SCENE
PUBS

O'MALLEY'S PUB, in the Torni Hotel, Yrjönkatu 26. Tel. 131-131.

This is a cramped, convivial, and gregarious pub, which evokes Ireland in spite of its Finnish doorman and Finnish clientele. Bar snacks are served, but as the evening progresses, drinking and more drinking—and lots of animated conversation—rule the night. Beer costs 22 markkaa ($4.80). O'Malley's is open Monday through Saturday from 9am to 1am and Sunday from noon to midnight. Tram: 3B.

PATRICK'S PUB, Liisenkatu 2. Tel. 135-1070.

This pub, next door to Svenska Klubben (see "Helsinki Dining" in Chapter 34), was named for the son of a Finnish businessman and a Scottish woman who moved to

England in 1935 and later worked hard for the war effort. The pub, which has never acquiesced to the dictates of fashion, is authentically English, and offers a flavorful fixed-price lunch for 40 markkaa ($8.80), which includes a platter of whatever food is available that day, along with salad, bread, and coffee. Of course, many Helsinki residents consider it their favorite "local" for dropping in for a drink. Beer costs from 22 markkaa ($4.80). It's open Monday through Saturday from 11am to 1am. Bus: 18.

RICHARD'S PUB, Rikhardinkatu 4. Tel. 179-281.
    Established in 1968, this is the oldest English-inspired pub in Helsinki, and is immensely popular. It's an old-fashioned-looking establishment, with high ceilings and red velvet wall coverings. In the spacious dining room you can enjoy such dishes as entrecôte Richard, Caucasian shashlik, fish and chips, Russian herring, and salmon sandwiches; main dishes run 40 to 80 markkaa ($8.80 to $17.60). Many people, however, come here just to drink, either at table or at the stand-up bar; beer costs 18.50 to 24 markkaa ($4.10 to $5.30). Richard's is open Monday through Friday from 9am to 11:45pm and Saturday and Sunday from 10am to 11:45pm. Tram: 3, 6, 10.

WINE BARS

BEER & WINE CELLAR, in the Hotel Klaus Kurki, Bulevardi 2. Tel. 618-911.
    To reach this wine bar, pass through the lobby of the Hotel Klaus Kurki (see "Helsinki Accommodations" in Chapter 34). In a cozy cellar you'll find a large bar and a warren of semiprivate banquettes. You can buy wine by the glass, for about 15 markkaa ($3.30), or by the bottle, from as far away as California, Spain, France, and Italy. The wine cellar, which has a woodsy Victorian-style decor, also offers food. The bill of fare includes such items as Finnish salmon soup, hamburgers Weinkeller style, entrecôte in butter sauce, and for dessert, fresh-fruit profiteroles stuffed with blueberries and raspberries. Main dishes cost 42 to 95 markkaa ($9.20 to $20.90). It's open Monday through Saturday from 11am to 12:30am and Sunday from noon to 12:30am. Tram: 3B, 3T, 6.

THE BARS

AMERICAN BAR, in the Palace Hotel, Eteläranta 10. Tel. 134-561.
    It has been suggested that if Betty Grable and Marilyn Monroe were trying to find *How to Marry a Millionaire* today, they would show up at this lofty retreat. Now a fashionable bar in a fashionable hotel, this 11th-floor room actually dates from the 1960s when it was originally designed as a men's toilet. Those memories are all but forgotten today in this charming little bar with glowing paneling and nautical accessories. In summer, tables are placed on an outdoor terrace overlooking the harbor. Special cocktails include Singapore Slings. Drinks costs 33 markkaa ($7.30); beer runs 22 markkaa ($4.80). The bar is open Monday through Friday from 11am to 1am. Tram: 3B. Bus: 16.

ATELIER BAR, in the Hotel Torni, Yrjönkatu 26. Tel. 131-131.
    Its tables are cramped, and the eagle's-nest position it occupies requires the ascent of an impossibly narrow iron staircase. On the uppermost floor of the famous old Hotel Torni (see "Helsinki Accommodations" in Chapter 34), site of many well-documented episodes of espionage during World War II, this is one of the most famous bars of Helsinki, yet many foreign visitors never find it. It welcomes some of the artists and writers of Helsinki, who don't seem to mind the lack of elbow room. Walls are decorated with original paintings, some of them by regular patrons. Take the elevator as far up as it will go and then navigate the rest of the way on foot. Drinks cost 33 markkaa ($7.30), and beer runs 22 to 33 markkaa ($4.80 to $7.30). It's open daily from 3pm to midnight. Tram: 3, 4, 8.

KÖNIG BAR, Mikonkatutel 4. Tel. 171-271.
    Visiting diplomats and the haute bourgeoisie are attracted to this landmark restaurant and bar (see "Helsinki Dining" in Chapter 34). Established in 1892, it has a bar designed by Saarinen, one of Finland's greatest architects. The bar is paneled with

wood and sheathed in a carefully restored leather wallpaper. Portraits of the most famous clients of the 1930s hang on the walls (a kind of historical gallery of Finland's famous) and the food is relatively inexpensive, considering the poshness of the place. It's possible, however, to come here just to drink, although a bar menu contains such items as club sandwiches and salads. Sandwiches cost 32 markkaa ($7) and salads run 26 to 36 markkaa ($5.70 to $7.90). Drinks go for 24 markkaa ($5.30); beer, 16.50 markkaa ($3.60). It is open Monday to Friday from 11am to 3pm, Saturday noon to 3am, and Sunday 4pm to 3am. Tram: 3B, 3T.

THE LOBBY BAR, in the Hotel Klaus Kurki, Bulevardi 2. Tel. 618-911.

On the street level of the Hotel Klaus Kurki (see "Helsinki Accommodations" in Chapter 34), this fashionable bar is vividly scarlet, with formal architectural detailings and a hanging collection of 19th-century engravings. Find yourself a cubbyhole within the labyrinth of seating arrangements, and perhaps order yourself the bartender's special, a "Finnish Marguerita" (Finnish vodka, Cointreau, and lemon juice). Drinks cost from 27 markkaa ($5.90). The bar is open Monday through Saturday from 11am to 12:30am and Sunday from noon to 12:30am. Tram: 3B, 3T, 6.

MORE ENTERTAINMENT

AN AMUSEMENT PARK

LINNANMÄKI AMUSEMENT PARK, Linnanmäki. Tel. 750-391.

Linnanmäki, 2 miles north of Helsinki, is a fun fair of splashing fountains, merry-go-rounds, Ferris wheels, restaurants, cafés, theaters, and discos. Founded in 1950 by the Children's Foundation to raise funds to care for the thousands of war orphans, Linnanmäki continues today to raise money to aid a new generation of children. The amusement park has a total of 25 different rides, including Europe's highest "big dipper," a fun house, and a railway for kids.

Admission: 10 markkaa ($2.20) adults, 5 markkaa ($1.10) children.

Open: June–Aug, Tues–Fri 4–10pm, Sat–Sun 1–9 or 10pm. **Closed:** Sept–May. **Tram:** 3B, 3T.

MOVIES

There are about 50 cinemas in Helsinki. Films are shown in their original language, with Finnish and Swedish subtitles. Showings are usually daily at 6pm and 9pm. Details of what's on and exact times of showings are given in the daily newspapers and a weekly publication available at the City Tourist Office.

Generally, the most interesting cinema is **Nordia,** Yrjönkatu 36 (tel. 131-19-250), which has three screens. It usually offers a fine program, screening both new "art" films as well as golden oldies and cult favorites.

GAMBLING CASINOS

In addition to the listing below, there are also small-stakes casinos in the **Old Baker's,** Mannerheimintie 12 (tel. 605-607), and the **Fizz Bar & Nightclub,** in the Arctia Hotel Marski, Mannerheimintie 10 (tel. 68-061), both discussed above.

CASINO RAY, Ramada Presidentti Hotel, Eteläinen Rautatiekatu 4. Tel. 694-2900.

Other than a handful of betting parlors that operate on cruise ships in offshore waters, this is the only large-stakes casino in Finland. Contained adjacent to the second-floor restaurant (The Four Seasons) of one of Helsinki's largest hotels, it allows maximum bets of 500 markkaa ($110) in blackjack, and roulette, and slightly less in some of the nearly 100 slot machines that fill the establishment's glittering interior. Croupiers, male and female, wear blue uniforms. Non-Finns have to show a passport at the entrance, and pay a first-time registration fee of 10 markkaa ($2.20) for a membership card that is valid for 4 years. This casino is not to be confused with the small-stakes casino in the Presidentti's Pressa nightclub, where the maximum allowable bet is 10 markkaa ($2.20). Tram: 3B.

Open: Roulette and blackjack, daily noon–4am; slot machines, daily 2pm–4am.

GAY NIGHTLIFE

GAMBRINI, Iso Roobertinkatu 3-5. Tel. 644-391.
It has only been in the last few years that gay people in Finland began to be allowed to congregate in public enclaves, and Gambrini is the result of that changing sociology. Today it's the premier gay bar of Finland. There's disco dancing in a small room to the side, but most of the guests gather near the leather/Levi's bar. Women's nights are staged every other Saturday. The entire staff speaks English. Beer costs from 20 to 25 markkaa ($4.40 to $5.50). Gambrini is open daily from 6pm to 2am. Tram: 3B, 3T, 10.
   Admission: Free Sun–Thurs, 30 markkaa ($6.60) Fri–Sat.

10. EASY EXCURSIONS

PORVOO [BORGÅ]

⭐ This colorful little town, 30 miles northeast of Helsinki, gives visitors a look at what a small town in this area was like a century or so ago; it's the second-oldest town in Finland. Simply strolling the Old Quarter with its narrow winding streets is a fun way to spend an afternoon.
   Founded as a Swedish town in 1346 at the mouth of a river, Porvoo was already an important trading center in the Middle Ages, and even before the town was given its charter, the Swedes had a wooden fortress on a hill that helped to control river and sea trade for several centuries. After Sweden finally relinquished Finland to the Russians, Porvoo was the scene of the first Finnish Diet in the early 19th century, when Czar Alexander I made the little country a grand duchy.
   Many of the citizens of Porvoo still consider themselves Swedes, and almost half the town's residents speak Swedish and cling to the old Swedish name of this town, Borgå.
   The town's most important industry today is the publishing firm of Werner Söderström, established in 1853, one of the largest in Scandinavia.

GETTING THERE

The most interesting way to come to Porvoo is by MS *J. L. Runeberg,* which sails in summer from the Market Square in Helsinki on Wednesday, Friday, Saturday, and Sunday. A one-way ticket costs 90 markkaa ($19.80) for adults, 35 markkaa ($7.70) for children. For bookings and inquiries, contact the **Ageba Travel Agency,** Olympia Terminal (tel. 90/944-625).
   The **Porvoo Tourist Office** is at Rauhankatu 20, SF-06100 Porvoo (tel. 915/170-145). Hours are Monday through Friday from 8am to 4pm and Saturday from 10am to 2pm.

WHAT TO SEE & DO

If you come to Porvoo via boat, you will get a good view of the old merchants' houses and warehouses along the water—most from the 18th century.

CATHEDRAL OF PORVOO, Kirkkotori. Tel. 915/189-1250.
   The oldest part of the present granite building dates either from the late 13th century or the early 14th century. The church has since been plundered or even burned down several times. It became a cathedral in 1723 when the episcopal see was moved from Viipuri to Porvoo. The church was once attended by Czar Alexander I of Russia.
   Admission: Free.
   Open: May–Sept, Mon–Fri 10am–6pm, Sat 10am–2pm, Sun 2–5pm; Oct–Apr, Tues–Sat 10am–2pm, Sun 2–4pm.

PORVOO MUSEUM, Valikatu 11. Tel. 915/580-589.

This museum's collections are housed in two buildings, the **Historical Museum** in the Old Town Hall and the art collection in the **Edelfelt-Vallgren Museum,** originally a merchant's house. The stone buildings stand on the Museum Square (also known as the Old Town Hall Square) of the Old Town, and both buildings contain artifacts from the 1700s that survived the big fires in 1760 and the 1800s. The art museum also has collections of Finnish art nouveau furniture and ceramics.

Admission: 10 markkaa ($2.20) adults; children under 16 free.

Open: May–Aug, daily 11am–4pm; Sept–Apr, Wed–Sun noon–4pm.

JOHN LUDVIG RUNEBERG HOUSE, Aleksanterinkatu 3. Tel. 915/581-330.

Porvoo is particularly proud of its association with the Finnish national poet John Ludvig Runeberg, who spent the last 25 years of his life here. His home is now a museum. Works of the poet's son, sculptor Walter Runeberg, can be seen here, including an interesting statue of his father. John Ludvig Runeberg's tomb is also in Porvoo, in the old cemetery west of the river.

Admission: 15 markkaa ($3.30) adults, 7.50 markkaa ($1.70) children 5–15.

Open: May–Aug, Mon–Sat 9:30am–4pm, Sun 10:30am–5pm; Sept–Apr, Mon–Sat 11am–3pm, Sun noon–4pm.

WHERE TO DINE
Moderate

WANHA LAAMANNI, Vuorikatu 17. Tel. 915/130-455.
Cuisine: FINNISH. **Reservations:** Recommended.

$ Prices: Appetizers 50–150 markkaa ($11–$33); main dishes 72–160 markkaa ($15.80–$35.20); fixed-price lunch 85 markkaa ($18.70) Mon–Thurs, 135 markkaa ($29.70) Sat–Sun. AE, DC, MC, V.

Open: Summer, daily 11am–midnight; off-season, Mon–Sat 11am–11pm, Sun noon–8pm.

Originally constructed as a private house near the medieval cathedral, not quite in the center, this late Gustavian-style restaurant whose name translates as "The Old Judge's Chambers," has an 18th-century decor. The chef turns out many Finnish specialties, such as smoked whitefish with creamed spinach or roasted filet of reindeer with game sauce.

HYVINKÄÄ

This young town, which was granted its charter as recently as 1960, has long been linked to Finland's railway network and is visited today chiefly because of its National Railway Museum (see below). Located 35 miles north of Helsinki, Hyvinkää can be reached by "H train," which leaves twice an hour from Helsinki, and by car, which takes an hour on Route 3. Buses labeled Hyvinkää also run here from the Helsinki bus station.

This rapidly growing industrial and commercial center is set in a part of Finland with beautiful scenery. Visitors can walk through **Hyvinkää Sveitsi,** the "Switzerland" of Hyvinkää a park within walking distance of the center of town, which has marked and lit walking paths and skiing tracks of various lengths. It also has a jogging track and ski slopes and jumps.

Hyvinkää's connection with the railway dates from 1862, when the link was added between Hämeenlinna and Helsinki. This railway culture is preserved in the **National Railway Museum,** in the center of town, at Hyvinkäänkatu 9 (tel. 914/18-351). The museum is housed in the original railway buildings dating from the 1870s. Exhibits include the oldest steam engine preserved in Finland, *Passi,* from 1868; Finland's oldest rail car, a Fiat from 1914; and a model railway, the largest of its kind in the country. But my favorite exhibit is a three-coach imperial train dating from the 1870s. Built for the Czar of Russia, the imperial coach train originally consisted of five coaches; the coaches of the Czar and Czarina, a saloon, a dining room, and a kitchen coach. The railway museum was founded in 1898 in Helsinki but was transferred to Hyvinkää in 1974. It is open May to August, Tuesday through Sunday from 11am to

4pm (in July, also on Monday); September to April, Tuesday through Friday from noon to 3pm and Saturday and Sunday from noon to 4pm. Admission is 15 markkaa ($3.30) for adults and 5 markkaa ($1.10) for children.

HÄMEENLINNA

Finland's oldest town, located 61 miles north of Helsinki, Hämeenlinna (Tavastehus in Swedish) was founded in 1639. It is one of the starting points for cruises on the Silver Line vessels (*Suomen Hopealinja*), which run to Tampere or along the scenic route to the ridge of Kangasala. Hämeenlinna is also the starting point for a series of 1-day cruises, the most popular of which goes to the Aulanko Tourist Center and to sculptor Emil Wikström's studio museum, Visavuori. If you go on one of these cruises, your car can be driven by the car-pilot service to await your arrival.

The **Hämeenlinna City Tourist Information Office,** Palokunnankatu 11 (tel. 917/142-388), is open from June 1 through August 30, Monday through Friday from 9am to 6pm. Off-season hours are Monday through Friday from 9am to 5pm.

WHAT TO SEE & DO

The large park at **Aulanko,** about 2½ miles from the center of Hämeenlinna, is one of the best-known tourist centers of Finland. Here you'll find a hotel (see below), a panoramic tower, tennis courts, a golf course, and a bathing beach.

SIBELIUKSEN SYNTYMÄKOTI, Hallituskatu 11. Tel. 917/25-698.

The great composer Jean Sibelius was born at Hämeenlinna on December 8, 1865, in this wooden house. It stands in the center of town, about 50 yards from the marketplace. The museum is also the setting for small chamber concerts and sells tapes of Sibelius's music.

Admission: 5 markkaa ($1.10) adults, 3 markkaa (70¢) children over 6 years and students.

Open: May–Aug, daily 10am–4pm; Sept–Apr, daily noon–4pm.

HÄME CASTLE, Kustaa III Katu 6. Tel. 917/675-6820.

Häme Castle dominates the town. Construction here has been going on for 700 years. The oldest sections date from the 1260s and are known as the fortified camp, including a square gray-stone wall with defensive towers at three corners. Once the residence of mighty nobles, the castle later became a strictly supervised outpost of the Swedish Crown. As the years went by, it served as both a granary and a prison. It now houses changing exhibits, and there is a café and restaurant on the grounds.

Admission: 14 markkaa ($3.10) adults, 7 markkaa ($1.50) children.

Open: May–Aug, daily 10am–6pm; Sept–Apr, daily 10am–4pm. **Bus:** 5, 12 from the marketplace.

WHERE TO STAY
Moderate

HOTEL CUMULUS, Raatihuoneenkatu 16-18, SF-13230 Aulanko. Tel. 917/52-881. Fax 917/528-8299. 100 rms (all with bath). MINIBAR TV TEL
$ Rates (including breakfast): Aug–June, 425 markkaa ($93.50) single; 570 markkaa ($125.40) double. July, 270 markkaa ($59.40) single; 390 markkaa ($85.80) double. AE, DC, MC, V. **Parking:** Free.
Located next to the main commercial street of town, within walking distance of Kauppatori (Market Square), this modern concrete-and-glass hotel has comfortable bedrooms and three attractive restaurants: Mama Leone, Prince Albert, and Tiffany. Two saunas are on the premises, plus a swimming pool. It's possible to book a no-smoking room, but you must specifically request it when making your reservations. Children under 14 are accommodated free with existing beds; otherwise, an extra bed costs 100 markkaa ($22) a day. The breakfast is huge.

RANTASIPI AULANKO, SF-13230 Aulanko. Tel. 917/588-01. Fax 917/21-922. 250 rms (all with bath). MINIBAR TV TEL

$ Rates (including breakfast): 590 markkaa ($129.80) single; 760 markkaa ($167.20) double. AE, DC, MC, V. **Parking:** Free. **Closed:** Dec 19–Jan 7.

Its name is instantly recognizable throughout Finland because of its location in one of the country's best-known nature preserves. It sits at the edge of Vanajavesi Lake near a sweep of open grassland surrounded by forested hillsides. Each room has an open-air balcony. On weekends through the year the dining room is likely to be overflowing. On the premises are tennis courts, a golf course, a labyrinth of walking paths, three saunas, a lakeside bathing beach, an indoor pool, riding stables, and a masseuse. In winter, cross-country skiing is a popular activity here. The hotel, a venue for important congresses, lies at the end of a series of prominent signs in Aulanko Park, 3 miles north of the rail station at Hämeenlinna.

WHERE TO DINE
Moderate

VALENTINO'S, Sibeliuksenkatu 3. Tel. 533-777.
Cuisine: FINNISH. **Reservations:** Recommended.
$ Prices: Appetizers 32–48 markkaa ($7–$10.60); main dishes 65–98 markkaa ($14.30–$21.60). AE, DC, MC, V.
Open: Dinner only, Mon–Sat 7pm–2am.

This is not only considered the best restaurant in town, but also the leading entertainment complex, offering not only a restaurant, but two different bars and the town's most popular disco. Specialties include pepper steak, salmon with a cream-and-mushroom sauce, and filet of reindeer with juniperberries. Service is polite and efficient. Dancing to disco music begins Mon–Sat at 9pm, with beer costing 22 markkaa ($4.80); admission to the disco ranges from 25 markkaa ($5.50) for recorded music to 40 markkaa ($8.80) for live music.

KOTKA

Lying 83 miles east of Helsinki at Kotka, ✪**Langinkoski** (tel. 952/210-50) was the imperial fishing lodge of the Russian czar's family, the summer retreat for Alexander III from 1889 to 1894. A log house, it stands on the River Kymi, and provides an insight into how the Romanovs lived long before the family met violent deaths in the Russian Revolution. Near the Langinkoski Rapids for which it is named, the lodge is open May to September, daily from 10am to 7pm, charging an admission of 8 markkaa ($1.80).

Information is available from the **Kotka Tourist Office,** Keskuskatu 17 (tel. 952/274-424). Hours are June through August, Monday through Friday from 9am to 4pm, Saturday 10am to 2pm. Off-season hours are Monday through Friday from 9am to 4pm. Kotka is a 2-hour drive from Helsinki if you have a car. Otherwise Kotka-bound buses depart frequently from the bus station in Helsinki. For example, if you take the 9:30am bus from Helsinki, you arrive at Kotka at 11:40am. Once there, you must take a 10-minute taxi ride to the czar's former lodge. Otherwise, take bus no. 20.

The mysterious Anastasia used to run wild along the turbulent rapids. Her girlish "A" can still be seen in the guestbook. The czar choose a spot in Finland's premier salmon-fishing area to build the lodge.

The lodge was constructed in 1889 on property consisting of half a dozen small islands interconnected by bridges. Its deliberately unpretentious architecture was in the Finnish style of hand-hewn pine logs, far removed from the grandeur of the family's 900-room palace outside St. Petersburg.

The czarina often prepared the family meals herself, and the copper pots she used can still be seen. Alexander III died in 1894, and the lodge held little appeal for his more formal son, Nicholas II, last of the Romanovs.

Ask at any Finnish Tourist Board, such as the one at 655 Third Ave., New York, NY 10017 (tel. 212/949-2333), about dates of theatrical performances in July of *One Day in the Life of the Czar.* Tour packages are sold for overnight stays in the area.

CHAPTER 36

TURKU & THE ÅLAND ISLANDS

Almost as interesting as Helsinki itself, Finland's former capital, Turku, is an ancient town with close links to Sweden. Swedes affectionately call it Åbo, and perhaps regret its loss. It is a town with proud traditions, and was the former center of the spiritual, secular, and commercial life of Finland before the capital was moved by the Russians to Helsinki.

Turku is Finland's oldest town. Records don't indicate the exact date, but it's estimated that Turku was founded around 1229.

In the Middle Ages, trade and seafaring were the main means of livelihood for the people of Turku. A university was founded in 1640, adding to its prestige. Tragedy struck on September 4, 1827, when Turku suffered the biggest fire ever to ravage a Scandinavian town. Following the fire, the Academy of Turku, the first university in Finland, was transferred to Helsinki. But following the independence of Finland, a Swedish-language university, Åbo Akademi, was founded, and Turku regained some of its lost prestige.

Turku, a city of 160,000 inhabitants, makes the ideal gateway for visiting the Åland Islands, an archipelago in the Baltic midway between Sweden and Finland. Many Swedes use the Ålands as a summer playground.

The islands are relatively autonomous, with 23,000 inhabitants, who have their own parliament and government, their own flag and culture, even their own postage stamps.

During the time of its world-famous shipowner Gustaf Erikson, Åland was able to boast the biggest fleet of sailing ships in the world. Its traditions as a maritime "nation" are ancient.

SEEING TURKU & THE ÅLAND ISLANDS

GETTING THERE

Turku is often used as a gateway to Finland, and it has rail and air links with Helsinki, and air and sea links to Stockholm. From Turku, you can go by boat to Mariehamn, capital of the Åland Islands, or you can fly there directly, often from Stockholm, but with more frequent flights from Helsinki.

A SUGGESTED ITINERARY

Days 1 & 2: Allow this amount of time to get to Turku and see the city's attractions.

Day 3: Take excursions to Naantali and Rauma.

Days 4 & 5: Settle into Mariehamn and spend any time left over exploring some of the attractions of the archipelago.

WHAT'S SPECIAL ABOUT
TURKU & THE ÅLAND ISLANDS

Great Towns/Villages

- ☐ Turku, the oldest town in Finland, its former capital.
- ☐ Naantali, 12 miles north of Turku, an excellent example of a Finnish town of the Middle Ages.
- ☐ Rauma, 60 miles north of Turku, third-oldest town in Finland.
- ☐ Mariehamn, the capital of the Åland Islands archipelago—a favorite with the summer yachting crowd.

Cathedrals

- ☐ Turku Cathedral, dating from the 13th century, one of the most important medieval monuments of Finland.

Museums

- ☐ City Historical Museum, Turku, housed in Finland's largest medieval castle from the 13th century.

- ☐ Wäinö Aaltosen Museum, Turku, containing many of the paintings and sculptures of one of Finland's greatest artists.
- ☐ Åland Maritime Museum, superb collections from the great sailing-ship era of the Åland Islands.

Special Events/Festivals

- ☐ Turku Music Festival in August, music from the Renaissance and baroque eras played on the original instruments.
- ☐ Åland Music Festival in July, offering various kinds of music, from jazz to blues to heavy metal.

1. TURKU

102 miles W of Helsinki, 96 miles S of Tampere

GETTING THERE By Plane Turku Airport is 4 miles from the center of town. It receives international flights from Stockholm as well as domestic connections, mainly from Helsinki, from within Finland. For information about flights to Turku, call 921/513-600 in Turku or 90/89-881 in Helsinki.

By Train Trains make the 2¼-hour run from Helsinki and Turku (and vice versa) at the rate of seven daily. Six trains a day leave in each direction between Turku and Tampere, taking 2½ hours.

By Bus Twenty buses make the 2½-hour run back and forth between Helsinki and Turku daily, and 16 buses travel each way between Turku and Tampere, taking 3 hours.

By Car From Helsinki, head west along the E3 all the way. From Tampere, go southwest on the E80 all the way.

By Ferry Two ferries a day depart from Stockholm's harbor heading for Turku, taking 12 hours for the trip. There is a connection between Stockholm and Turku every morning and every evening. For information, call the **Silja Line** in Turku at 921/652-233.

ESSENTIALS For information, the **City Tourist Office,** Käsityöläiskatu **3,** SF-20100 Turku (tel. 921/336-366), is open Mon–Fri 8am–4pm (June–Aug) and Mon–Fri 8:30am–4pm (Sept–May).

A **Turku Tourist Ticket** entitles you to unlimited travel on the city's buses within a 24-hour period. It costs 20 markkaa ($4.40) and can be purchased at the City Tourist Office.

The **telephone area code** for Turku is 921.

On the western coast, at the confluence of three rivers, the seaport of Turku (Åbo in Swedish) is the oldest city in Finland and was once the most important city in the country; it was both an ecclesiastical center and a trade center. In addition to the cathedral, the city acquired a citadel in the late 13th century—thereby achieving a position of power by the standards of the Middle Ages. Turku's cultural and financial power was solidified when the king of Sweden, who then controlled Finland, made Turku the seat of government directed by his representative.

In the 17th century an academy was established in Turku, and in 1808 Russia conquered Finland and moved its capital to Helsinki, which was closer to St. Petersburg and theoretically easier to administer. In 1827 a fire demolished much of Turku's old wooden city.

But Turku bounced back, developing into not only an important port and industrial city, but also a university town, with both a Swedish and a Finnish Academy. It was rebuilt by Carl Ludvig Engel, who designed Helsinki, with stone and brick buildings, a grid plan, and wide streets.

The legendary long-distance runner, Paavo Nurmi (1897-1973), known as "The Flying Finn," was the most famous son of Turku. He won a total of nine gold and three silver medals in three different Olympics.

WHAT TO SEE & DO

CITY HISTORICAL MUSEUM, Turun linna. Tel. 620-111.

Finland's largest medieval castle was constructed in the 13th century, but its main building was renovated after World War II. The outer castle houses the City Historical Museum whose collections include 17th- to 19th-century furniture, porcelain, tapestries, silver, pewter, glass, local history, ethnography, and costumes. Refreshments and light snacks are offered in the self-service cafeteria in the outer castle.

Admission: 15 markkaa ($3.30) adults, 7 markkaa ($1.50) children.

Open: Apr 16–Sept 15, daily 10am–6pm; Sept 16–Apr 15, Tues–Sun 10am–3pm. **Bus:** 1.

TURKU CATHEDRAL, Cathedral Square. Tel. 510-651.

⭐ The foundation of this brick cathedral also dates back to the 13th century, but it represents the architectural styles of many centuries. One of the most important medieval monuments in Finland, the cathedral, regarded as a national shrine, contains the tombs of many famous Scandinavians, including bishops, military heroes, and one queen, Karin Månsdotter, the wife of Erik XIV of Sweden. The cathedral museum houses a collection of relics and liturgical artifacts dating from the Middle Ages.

Admission: Cathedral, free; museum, 5 markkaa ($1.10) adults, 2 markkaa (40¢) children.

Open: Cathedral museum, Apr 16–Sept 15, Mon–Fri 10am–6pm, Sat 10am–3pm, Sun after mass–4:30pm; Sept 16–Apr 15, Mon–Sat 10am–3pm, Sun after mass–3pm. **Bus:** 25.

LUOSTARINMÄKI HANDCRAFTS MUSEUM, on Luostarinmäki (Cloister Hill). Tel. 620-350.

The outdoor compound housing this handcraft museum is a collection of little 18th-century cottages on a hillside, about a 5-minute walk from the city center, south of Vartiovuori hill near the Open-Air Theater. This is the only part of Turku that escaped the fire of 1827, and the 18 original structures now make up the working museum. You can watch a potter, goldsmith, bookbinder, and makers of wigs, gloves, and combs as they ply their trades. Displays of Finnish arts and crafts of all types can be seen.

Admission: 15 markkaa ($3.30) adults, 7 markkaa ($1.50) children.

Open: Apr 15–Sept 15, daily 10am–6pm; Sept 16–Apr 14, Tues–Sun 10am–3pm. **Bus:** 3.

SIBELIUS MUSEUM, Bishopsgatan 17. Tel. 654-494.

Although Finland's beloved composer neither lived nor worked in Turku, there is a fine collection of Sibeliana here, along with collections of instruments. Music lovers can sit in a small concert hall and listen to the works of the master every day or at concerts held on Wednesday evenings in spring and summer at 7:30pm. The Wednesday concerts sell out early so stop by in the morning to buy your ticket.

Admission: Museum, 15 markkaa ($3.30), 5 markkaa ($1.10) children; concerts, 50 markkaa ($11) adults, 30 markkaa ($6.60) children.
Open: Tues–Sun 11am–3pm. **Bus:** 25.

TURUN TAIDEMUSEO, in Puolalapuisto Park, Aurakatu 26. Tel. 330-954.

The Finnish art collection of the Turku Art Society, from the beginning of the 19th century to the present, is the second-largest and most important collection in Finland. Artworks from other Nordic countries and international graphics are also exhibited. The museum is near the Market Square.

Admission: 15 markkaa ($3.30) adults, 10 markkaa ($2.20) children.
Open: Mon–Wed and Fri–Sat 10am–4pm, Thurs 10am–4pm and 6–8pm, Sun 10am–6pm. **Bus:** 3.

WÄINÖ AALTOSEN MUSEUM, Itäinen Rantakatu 38. Tel. 355-690.

One of the best-known Finnish artists, Wäinö Aaltosen began his career on Hirvensalo, the big island owned by the city. The museum on the eastern bank of the Aurajoki River contains many of Aaltosen's own paintings and sculptures, as well as a permanent collection of contemporary Finnish pictures, sculptures, and other artwork. Changing short-term exhibitions are also featured.

Admission: 7 markkaa ($1.50) adults, 4 markkaa (90¢) children under 12.
Open: Tues–Sun 11am–7pm. **Bus:** 7, 15, 17 from the Market Square.

MARITIME MUSEUM/ASTRONOMICAL COLLECTION, at Vartiovuori. Tel. 337-140.

Local maritime history and the astronomical collections of academician Yrjö Väisälä are the subject of this museum in an observatory built for the Academy of Turku in 1819. It's near the Open-Air Theater southeast of Hämeenkatu.

Together with the City Historical Museum, the Handcraft Museum, Qwensel House and the Pharmacy Museum, and the Biological Museum, the maritime and astronomical museum is a part of the Turku Provincial Museum, Kalastajankatu 4 (tel. 303-300).

Admission: 7 markkaa ($1.50) adults, 3 markkaa (70¢) children.
Open: May–Sept, daily 10am–6pm; Oct–Apr, daily 10am–3pm. **Bus:** 3.

MARKET HALL, Eerikinkatu 16 and Linnankatu 15. Tel. 314-912.

A visit to Turku's cobblestone Market Square and the market hall, southeast of the train station, is the best way to experience the rhythms of the city at no cost. At the market hall, stalls in long corridors are filled with fresh vegetables, the best of Finnish cheeses, meat, fish, bread, cakes, health foods, and souvenirs. There's a café and a bank handy if you want to sip coffee or change traveler's checks. Other stalls in the Market Square offer lingonberries, cloudberries, salmon, and other typical Scandinavian foods.

Admission: Free.
Open: Open-air markets, mid-May to mid-Sept, Mon–Fri 8am–1pm and 4–8pm, Sat 8am–1pm; mid-Sept to mid-May, Mon–Sat 8am–1pm. Covered market hall, Mon–Fri 8am–5pm, Sat 8am–1pm. **Bus:** 3.

ORGANIZED TOURS

Year-round, a 2-hour **guided bus tour** (in English) leaves daily at 8:30am; it includes a visit to the cathedral. Tickets cost 70 markkaa ($15.40) for adults and 30 markkaa ($6.60) for children. A bus leaves from the harbor, then branches out to individual hotels to pick up tour participants. Tickets can be booked at the City Tourist Office (see above).

IMPRESSIONS

Turku is a wretched capital of a barbarous province.
—SIR N. W. WRAXALL, IN *A TOUR ROUND THE BALTIC*, 1775

Boat tours to the Turku archipelago depart from near the Auransilta bridge and from the Martinsilta bridge, and are offered daily from June 1 to August 31. For information about islands and sights in the archipelago, see "Excursions from Turku," below. Check with the City Tourist Office (see above) for available tours.

WHERE TO STAY

EXPENSIVE

ARCTIA MARINA PALACE, Linnankatu 32, SF-20100 Turku. Tel. 921/651-211. Fax 921/516-750. 183 rms (all with bath), 2 suites. MINIBAR TV TEL **Bus:** 1, 13.

$ Rates (including breakfast): 750 markkaa ($165) single; 900 markkaa ($198) double; from 1,500 markkaa ($330) suite. AE, DC, MC, V. **Parking:** 52 markkaa ($11.40).

An international hotel of a high standard, the Marina Palace, in the center of Turku by the Aurajoki River, is a modern chain-run hotel offering much comfort and good facilities. Its bedrooms are generally spacious, inviting, and comfortable, containing a number of amenities such as trouser press and hairdryer. The room price always includes a good breakfast, a sauna, and a dip in the hotel's indoor pool.

Dining/Entertainment: The eighth-floor Riverside Gourmet Restaurant opens onto a panoramic view of the city. Other dining and entertainment choices include the Dancing Marina Restaurant; the Calamare, a restaurant specializing in seafood; and a summer restaurant, Sunmarina. The Pub Nelson is a popular drinking spot.

Services: Room service, babysitting, laundry.

Facilities: Four saunas, swimming pool, solarium, sauna bar.

MODERATE

CUMULUS HOTEL, Eerikinkatu 28, SF-20100 Turku. Tel. 921/638-211. Fax 921/638-2299. 200 rms (all with bath). MINIBAR TV TEL **Bus:** 1, 13.

$ Rates (including breakfast): June 21–July, 270 markkaa ($59.40) single; 390 markkaa ($85.80) double. Aug–June 20, 455 markkaa ($100.10) single; 600 markkaa ($132) double. AE, DC, MC, V. **Parking:** 40 markkaa ($8.80).

Near Town Hall, 3 blocks from Market Square and 1 block from the main post office, this is one of the most modern hotels in the commercial center of town and caters to Scandinavian businesspeople. The bedrooms are tastefully contemporary, and some are equipped for the disabled or the allergic. The single rooms overlook a central courtyard, and doubles have views of the city. The Kirjava Satama Restaurant, adjacent to the reception area, serves well-prepared food in an ambience of abbreviated lattices and ornamental palms. There's an outdoor terrace lined with geraniums for summer drinks, plus a Harry's Bar. Room service and laundry facilities are offered, and four saunas, a swimming pool, a children's playroom, and a solarium are available to guests.

HAMBURGER BÖRS, Kauppiaskatu 6, SF-20100 Turku. Tel. 921/637-381. Fax 921/311-010. 186 rms (all with bath), 3 suites. MINIBAR TV TEL **Bus:** 1, 13.

$ Rates (including breakfast): June 16–Aug 15, 450 markkaa ($99) single or double. Off-season, 600 markkaa ($132) single; 800 markkaa ($176) double. Year-round, from 950 markkaa ($209) suite. AE, DC, MC, V. **Parking:** 40 markkaa ($8.80).

⭐ The leading hotel of Turku, this five-star choice near Kauppatori, the Market Square, in the city center, has long been a favorite with discriminating visitors. Guests enjoy the maximum luxury and comfort that Turku offers, from a morning sauna and swim to a breakfast buffet, with food and drink services all through the day, ending with a nightcap in the hotel's nightclub. Bedrooms are furnished in a traditional but modern styling, each with a number of amenities such as trouser press and satellite programs on TV.

Dining/Entertainment: In the lobby, the Café de Paris is a French-style café, ideal for snacks or drinks, and Le Bar also has a French ambience. The Brasserie Valtin offers both modern and traditional French cuisine, and is named for the founder of the hotel, Wallina Valtin. YläBörs on the second floor is a first-class gourmet restaurant, offering elaborate Finnish buffets. Hearty food and beer are served in the Hamburger Hof, and the most popular nightclub in town is the Börs Club, attracting artists from all over Europe.

Services: Room service, babysitting, laundry.
Facilities: Finnish sauna, swimming pool.

HANSA HOTEL, Kristinegatan 9, SF-20100 Turku. Tel. 921/167-000. Fax 921/617-722. 65 rms (all with bath), 1 suite. A/C MINIBAR TV TEL **Bus:** 1, 13.

$ Rates (including breakfast): Fri–Sun and June 15–Aug 3, 290 markkaa ($63.80) single; 360 markkaa ($79.20) double; 1,200 markkaa ($264) suite. Mon–Thurs the rest of the year, 390 markkaa ($85.80) single; 530 markkaa ($116.60) double; from 1,300 markkaa ($286) suite. AE, DC, MC, V. **Parking:** 30 markkaa ($6.60).

Ⓢ Built on the third and fourth floors of the Hansa Shopping Center, the major shopping center of Turku, this small hotel is one of the finest in western Finland. Bedrooms are tastefully designed and furnished, sometimes with pastel colors, and the atmosphere in each is homelike and inviting. The hotel has an attractive lobby bar and an excellent restaurant whose specialties include reindeer and salmon.

HOTEL JULIA, Eerikinkatu 4, SF-20110 Turku. Tel. 921/651-311. Fax 921/511-750. 118 rms (all with bath). MINIBAR TV TEL **Bus:** 1, 13.

$ Rates (including breakfast): June 15–Aug 15 and Fri–Sat year-round, 290 markkaa ($63.80) single; 380 markkaa ($83.60) double. Sun–Thurs Aug 16–June 14, 495 markkaa ($108.90) single; 660 markkaa ($145.20) double. AE, DC, MC, V. **Parking:** 45 markkaa ($9.90).

An attractive hotel in the center of town near the Market Square, the Julia has comfortably furnished bedrooms, with 36 of them reserved for nonsmokers. In addition to parquet floors and crisp colors, each room has a trouser press, hairdryer, and hair curler. The hotel's French-style restaurant offers good food, and the Hunter's Pub offers music; room service is available. In addition, there's a modern shopping center, banks, a cinema, a car-rental firm, a Finnair office, a sauna department with two saunas for 5 people and one for 20 plus an attractive sauna bar, a lounge with a fireplace, and a roof terrace.

PARK HOTEL, Rauhankatu 1, SF-2001 Turku. Tel. 921/519-666. Fax 921/617-750. 20 rms (all with bath), 1 suite. A/C MINIBAR TV TEL **Bus:** 1, 13.

$ Rates (including breakfast): June 15–Aug 15, 340–600 markkaa ($74.80–$132) single; 440–800 markkaa ($96.80–$176) double. Aug 16–June 14, 450–600 markkaa ($99–$132) single; 550–800 markkaa ($121–$176) double. Year-round, 900–1,300 markkaa ($198–$286) suite. AE, DC, MC, V. **Parking:** Free.

⭐Ⓢ This charming small hotel in the center near the station and Puolalaparken, originally a private home in 1904, has been skillfully converted into a well-run private hotel under the supervision of the dynamic Eva Dziedzic. Bedrooms are furnished in great taste, using subtle pastels for the most part, and every room is made homelike and comfortable. Bathrooms are tiled and well maintained, and each room is different. A dining room and bar are available for guests, and the hotel has a sauna.

INEXPENSIVE

ARCTIA HOTELL AURA, Humalistonkatu 7, SF-20100 Turku. Tel. 921/651-111. Fax 921/336-699. 159 rms (all with bath), 7 suites. A/C MINIBAR TV TEL **Bus:** 1, 13.

$ Rates (including breakfast); June 15–Aug 15 and Fri–Sat year-round, 270 markkaa ($59.40) single; 320 markkaa ($70.40) double. Sun–Thurs, Aug 16–June 14, 270 markkaa ($59.40) single; 400 markkaa ($88) double. AE, DC, MC, V. **Parking:** Free.

Recently taken over by the Arctia chain, this hotel—formerly the Ritz—has been a tradition in Turku since 1928. Set in the center of town near the train station, it was radically but tastefully renovated in 1989, and today is a comfortable and restful hotel. Some rooms were specifically designated for nonsmokers and persons with allergies. No meals other than breakfast are served here, although the hotel houses (via a separate entrance) a pub recently renamed The Farmer's Inn. The hotel also manages (but does not own) Turku's most popular disco, Time Out, housed in a former movie palace designed by Alvar Aalto (see "Evening Entertainment," below). Babysitting, laundry facilities, translation and guide services, and a sauna are also offered.

HOTEL KANTRI, Yliopistonkatu 29A, SF-20100 Turku. Tel. 921/320-921. Fax 921/518-870. 94 rms (all with bath). A/C TV TEL **Bus:** 1, 13.

$ Rates (including breakfast): Fri–Sat year-round and midsummer, 200 markkaa ($44) single; 250 markkaa ($55) double. Sun–Thurs the rest of the year, 290 markkaa ($63.80) single; 350 markkaa ($77) double. AE, DC, MC, V. **Parking:** 40 markkaa ($8.80).

Located near the Market Square, 50 yards from the station, on the most important commercial street in town, Hotel Kantri is one of the best hotels in the inexpensive range. It was built in the 1930s, but radically upgraded in 1985. Each room is smallish but stylishly furnished, clean, and comfortable. All but 10 rooms contain a minibar. The hotel's restaurant, Papukaija (Parrot), has a good reputation, and there is also a busy pub. Guests are invited to use the hotel's sauna at no additional charge.

TURUN KESKUSHOTELLI, Yliopistonkatu 12A, SF-20100 Turku. Tel. 921/337-333. Fax 921/337-333. 62 rms (all with bath). TV TEL **Bus:** 1, 13.

$ Rates (including breakfast and morning sauna): June 22–July 29 and Fri–Sat year-round, 210 markkaa ($46.20) single; 280 markkaa ($61.60) double. Sun–Thurs the rest of the year, 315 markkaa ($69.30) single; 370 markkaa ($81.40) double. AE, DC, MC, V.

The interior of this modern hotel makes full use of such Finnish materials as marble and birch. Established in 1974, and renovated in 1987, it is built around a graceful inner courtyard and lies in the heart of the city near the bus station. Extra facilities in the bedrooms include trouser presses and hairdryers. Some of the rooms are studios—one part bedroom, one part living room. A free morning sauna is included in the rates. Many restaurants are nearby.

SUMMER HOTELS

Inexpensive

DOMUS ABOENSIS, Piispankatu 10, SF-20500 Turku. Tel. 921/329-470. 76 rms (all with bath). TEL **Bus:** 25.

$ Rates (including breakfast): 210 markkaa ($46.20) single; 270 markkaa ($59.40) double. MC, V. **Closed:** Sept–May.

Owned and operated by the Åbo Academy, this is the best and most centrally located of the student hotels in Turku; it's near the cathedral. Many bedrooms are decorated like Mondrian paintings, with large rectangular blocks of color. There's a cafeteria.

SUMMERHOTEL IKITUURI, Pispalantie 7, SF-20510 Turku. Tel. 921/376-111. 144 rms (all with bath). TEL **Bus:** 50.

$ Rates (including breakfast): 320–455 markkaa ($70.40–$100.10) single; 380–

580 markkaa ($83.60–$127.60) double. AE, DC, MC, V. **Parking:** Free. **Closed:** Sept–May.

About 1½ miles from the Market Square, this hotel offers a swimming pool, games, bicycles, saunas, a gym, and a solarium. In a separate building you'll find a disco and pub. Meals are served in the hotel's restaurant until 12:30am. Rooms are furnished modestly in a college-dormitory style.

WHERE TO DINE
MODERATE

BRAHENKELLARI, Puolalankatu 1. Tel. 325-400.
Cuisine: FINNISH. **Reservations:** Recommended. **Bus:** 1.
$ Prices: Appetizers 30–45 markkaa ($6.60–$9.90); main dishes 40–100 markkaa ($8.80–$22). AE, DC, MC, V.
Open: Mon–Sat 11am–1am, Sun noon–10pm.

Turku's best-known wine restaurant is set within the thick stone walls of a century-old cellar. Diners can enjoy not only the atmosphere but also some of the best dishes—both meat and fish—in town. The service is polite and attentive.

LE PIRATE, Boren Puisto. Tel. 511-443.
Cuisine: FRENCH. **Reservations:** Not required. **Bus:** 1, 13.
$ Prices: Appetizers 32–65 markkaa ($7–$14.30); main dishes 60–125 markkaa ($13.20–$27.50); lunchtime platters 35 markkaa ($7.70). AE, DC, MC, V.
Open: June–Aug, daily 11am–midnight; off-season, Mon–Fri 11am–midnight, Sat 3pm–midnight.

Originally launched in 1907, this broad-beamed and stocky steamboat carried tar and timber through the inland waterways of eastern Finland. Today, though it's permanently moored in the river in the town center, you can enjoy café snacks and drinks on its upper deck, where the polite waiters speak English, or you can head for the restaurant below deck, which is warmly decorated in a nautical style. The French-inspired meals include half a dozen snails, scallops sautéed in snail-flavored butter, scampi flambé, fish of the day, hors d'oeuvres maison, fish terrine made with crayfish, and tempting desserts.

RESTAURANT PINELLA, Porthaninpuisto. Tel. 517-557.
Cuisine: ITALIAN. **Reservations:** Not required. **Bus:** 1, 13.
$ Prices: Appetizers 38–42 markkaa ($8.40–$9.20); main dishes 72–98 markkaa ($15.80–$21.60); lunch 36 markkaa ($7.90). AE, DC, MC, V.
Open: Restaurant, daily 11am–midnight; Pub Jajazzo, daily 4pm–midnight.

Located on the banks of the Jokiranta River between a city park and two of the busiest bridges in town, this restaurant has been a focal point for artists and philosophers since it was established by an Italian immigrant in 1848. It is the second-oldest restaurant in Finland. The entrance to Pub Jajazzo, where snacks are served, is beneath a neoclassical arcade facing the river. The main dining area, Puu-Pinella (Wooden Pinella), faces the park, and you can dine on the veranda leading into it. You can select from a Finnish buffet or order such specialties as veal in aspic, several preparations of herring, Miss Emmy's meatballs (named after the owner who made herself famous cooking here from 1936 to 1946), and an array of pizzas. Fresh fish is also served.

SAMPALINNA, Sampalinna Park. Tel. 311-165.
Cuisine: FINNISH. **Reservations:** Recommended. **Bus:** 1, 13.
$ Prices: Appetizers 32–48 markkaa ($7–$10.60); main dishes 62–88 markkaa ($13.60–$19.40). MC, V.
Open: Sun–Thurs 11am–1am, Fri–Sat 11am–2am.

Every taxi driver in town knows about this richly ornate Victorian building, which still retains its original complicated gingerbread from a century ago. It's near the river in the center of Turku, near the Myuysilta bridge. An outdoor café terrace ringed with trees near a bandshell features recorded jazz during the summer; nightly dance music begins here at 8pm. The food includes beef à la Sampalinna with Roquefort cheese and a red wine sauce, roast mutton with garlic-flavored potatoes, morel soup, salmon soup with rye bread, sizzling beefsteak on a plank, vegetarian platters, and a summer dessert of fresh cloudberries with a brandy-flavored cream sauce. Late at night you can order Scandinavian hash.

SEAPORT MATKUSTAJASATAMA, Matkustajasatama. Tel. 535-013.
   Cuisine: FINNISH/FRENCH. **Reservations:** Not required. **Bus:** 1.
$ **Prices:** Fixed-price menu 95 markkaa ($20.90); appetizers 62–120 markkaa ($13.60–$26.40); main dishes 55–105 markkaa ($12.10–$23.10). AE, DC, MC, V.
   Open: Daily 9am–2am.
A few steps from the harbor, this former warehouse contains the biggest dance floor in Turku, with dance band music beginning at 8pm nightly. Full meals might include platters of herring, pepper steak, reindeer chops in cream sauce, chili con carne, shrimp salad, Finnish salmon soup, or fresh fish dishes. There is also a cozy nautical-style bar.

BUDGET

RESTAURANT VERSO, Linnankatu 3. Tel. 510-956.
   Cuisine: VEGETARIAN. **Reservations:** Not required. **Bus:** 1, 13.
$ **Prices:** Fixed-price menus 34–44 markkaa ($7.50–$9.70). AE, MC, V.
   Open: Sept–May, Mon–Fri 11am–5pm, Sat 11am–4pm; June–Aug, Mon–Fri 11am–5pm.
   The only vegetarian restaurant in town, this is located in an art nouveau villa near the Italian consulate and the Town Hall. The high-ceilinged second-floor dining rooms have roughly textured tables in a consciously simple decor. You order the vegetarian specialties at a cafeteria counter. The restaurant steers away from eggs, fish, and (obviously) meat, and no smoking is permitted inside.

SHOPPING

AARIKKA, Yliopistonkatu 27. Tel. 313-562.
   Everything sold in this imaginative and well-stocked shop was made and designed in Finland. It's one of the best addresses in town for buying imaginative children's toys, wooden jewelry, and a full menagerie of carved wooden animals in several sizes.

MARIMEKKO, Hansa/Thalia, Aurakatu 10. Tel. 514-333.
   This shop represents the world-famous Marimekko design and offers clothes for men, women, and children, including dresses, blouses, and shirts of printed cotton. It is in the big Hansa Shopping Center, which has 117 shops selling clothes, furs, leather, shoes, jewelry, books, records, cameras, furniture, and giftware. You can take a break from your shopping spree in one of Hansa's cafés and restaurants, and under the same roof are banks with currency-exchange and other services.

PENTIK, Yliopistonkatu 25. Tel. 335-005.
   Carefully arranged within this shop's many carved armoires are some of the most beautiful ceramic table settings in town, all in a vivid range of northern colors. The shop also sells smooth-sanded wooden cups from Lapland and representations of Arctic birds in polychrome-covered wood.

STOCKMANN DEPARTMENT STORE, Yliopistonkatu 22. Tel. 337-344.
   At the "Harrods of Turku," you can find Finnish and international fashions, textiles, jewelry, and cosmetics. Finnish goods, such as Arabia pottery and china, Marimekko fabrics, and Iittala crystal are also sold, and Stockmann will ship your purchases home for you. When you need a break from shopping, you can have coffee and cake in the Stockmann cafeteria.

SYLVI SALONENOY, Yliopistonkatu 25. Tel. 334-100.
   This shop features hand-sewn screens, linen towels, and tablecloths, and many other kinds of handcrafts. Poppana cotton from Karelia province and *ryijy* rugs in bold designs are available here; the rug selection is reputedly the largest in the country.

The store also offers both decorative and everyday handmade articles from natural materials.

EVENING ENTERTAINMENT

TIME OUT, Humalistonkatu 7. Tel. 921/651-111.

Contained in a former movie palace, this is the most exciting and popular disco in Turku. Managed by Arctia Hotell Aura, it features flashing lights, recently released international dance music, a youngish clientele, and an elegant architectural framework designed by Alvar Aalto. A large beer costs 25 markkaa ($5.50). It's open Wednesday and Thursday 8pm to 4am, Friday and Saturday 9pm to 4am. Bus: 1, 13.
Admission: 15 markkaa ($3.30) Wed–Thurs, 35 markkaa ($7.70) Fri–Sat.

EXCURSIONS FROM TURKU

RUISSALO

This little island, 6 miles from Turku, has a number of elegant summer villas built during Ruissalo's heyday as a fashionable resort early in the 19th century. Today the island is owned by the city of Turku and is a national park. Finland's largest oak woods and a sandy beach make this a popular spot for walking, sunning, and swimming. At the busy marina, you can rent a boat for the day or book passage for a sailboat excursion among the islands.

NAANTALI

The people of this town resisted change so successfully in the 17th century that today Naantali remains a fine example of a medieval Finnish town. Naantali, 12 miles north of Turku, takes its name from a convent and monastery of St. Birgitta, called "the Valley of Grace," which moved to the coast in 1443. The convent was rich, and the little town prospered until the Reformation brought an end to the religious house.

Today you can stroll through little narrow lanes, called "cat tails," from medieval days, lined with wooden houses still on their original sites. In medieval times each house had its own name on a plaque over the door. Some of these plaques have survived, and the houses are known by their original names. The present buildings of the Old Town date from the late 18th and early 19th centuries.

After the Reformation, Naantali declined until the town became a popular health resort after a spa was established in 1863. The town enjoyed its heyday around the turn of the century. It was particularly popular with the Russians, who considered it a better health resort than St. Petersburg. This tradition has been revived recently and a new spa hotel has opened at Lalevanniemi.

The **Musiikkijuhlat,** an international music festival, is held at Naantali in June, and the main concerts are heard in the 15th-century Convent Church, with vesper hymns sung at 8pm. The **Tourist Office of Naantali** is located at Kaivotori 2, SF-21000 Naantali (tel. 921/850-850). Hours are daily from June until August 16 from 10am to 6pm. Off-season hours are Monday through Friday from 8am to 4pm.

Getting There

The easiest way to get to Naantali is to take a bus from Turku; buses run every 15 minutes and the trip takes 25 minutes. Car-ferries take passengers between Naantali and Kapellskär (Sweden), with two departures a day; the voyage takes 10 hours.

What to See and Do

The convent was demolished, but you can still see the **Convent Church,** completed in 1462 and renovated a number of times, including the addition of a tower in 1797. Exhibits in the church's collection include relics from the former convent, such as the crown worn by nuns when they took their vows and a Gothic tabernacle for the Reserved Sacrament. The church is open from May to the middle of August, daily from noon to 7pm; from the middle of August through April, daily from noon to 3pm.

At the **Naantali Museum,** Katinhanta 1 (tel. 921/755-321), you can visit three old wooden houses with outbuildings in the heart of the Old Town. Admission is 5 markkaa (90¢) for adults, 3 markkaa (70¢) for children. The museum is open June through August, daily noon to 6pm. The remainder of the year it can be seen by prior arrangement.

Kulturanta, a massive granite house on Luonnomaa Island, across the bay from the Convent Church, is the summer home of the president of the Finnish Republic. Visitors aren't allowed inside the house, but you can see the rose garden, which has more than 3,500 rosebushes. Admission is free, and the garden is open May to September, daily from 6 to 8pm.

Where to Stay and Dine: Moderate

NAANTALIN KLYPYLÄ SPA, SF-21100 Naantali. Tel. 921/857-711. Fax 921/857-790. 206 rms (all with bath). A/C TV TEL

$ Rates (including breakfast): 685 markkaa ($150.70) single; 720 markkaa ($158.40) double. AE, DC, MC, V. **Parking:** Free.

This spa, built in 1984, accommodates both holiday visitors and people seeking rehabilitation. Bedrooms are furnished in a simple but comfortable modern style. Some have balconies, and there are specially equipped rooms for the disabled. The hotel has two fully licensed restaurants, a cafeteria, and an open-air restaurant operating in summer, plus two public lounges. Vegetarian and special diets are available. Spa facilities include a Finnish sauna, Turkish bath, hot-water Roman pool with Jacuzzi, general swimming pool, and water and brush massage. Special courses are offered to cure stress, muscular maladies, insomnia, obesity, and tiredness. Beauty and fitness courses are also available.

RAUMA

At a harbor on the Gulf of Bothnia 60 miles north of Turku, the town of Rauma is the third oldest in Finland. The town was already a center of trade when it was chartered in 1442. Only ruins remain of the first house of worship, the Church of the Holy Trinity, but a Franciscan monastery was also constructed here—before 1449—and its Church of the Holy Cross has survived.

What to See and Do

The most prominent structure is the **Town Hall,** which was built in 1776 and houses the **Rauma Museum,** Kauppakatu 13. The museum features demonstrations of lace-making on Sunday from 2 to 5pm, and contains a permanent exhibition of artifacts related to navigation, bobbin lace-making, and other old professions. Admission to the museum is 5 markkaa ($1.10) for adults, 3 markkaa (70¢) for children. It's open May 15 to August 15, daily from 10am to 6pm.

The network of narrow streets and the building plots date from the 16th and 17th centuries, although most buildings are from the 18th and 19th centuries. **Kirsti House,** a lace-maker's home from the 18th century, is open May 15 to August 15, daily from 10am to 6pm; and **Marela House,** a shipowner's home and a well-preserved example of the affluence brought to Rauma by the maritime trade, is open May 15 to August 15, daily from 10am to 6pm.

Held at the end of July each year, **Rauma Lace Week** is a festive occasion, with exhibitions of folk art, folk-music concerts, and feasting on authentic local Finnish dishes. The highlight of the event is, of course, the making of lace. Demonstrations are given and various examples of the lace of Rauma are exhibited. For information on the festival, contact the **Rauma Tourist Office** at Valtakatu 2, SF-26100 Rauma (tel. 938/344-551). Hours are Monday through Friday from 9am to 4:30pm. The location is in the center of town near the bus station.

Where to Stay and Dine: Moderate

CUMULUS RAUMA, Aittakarintaku 9, SF-26100 Rauma. Tel. 938/37-821. Fax 938/378-2299. 104 rms (all with bath). MINIBAR TV TEL

$ Rates (including breakfast): June 12–Aug 16 and Fri–Sat all year, 270 markkaa ($59.40) single; 390 markkaa ($85.80) double. Sun–Thurs the rest of the year, 425

markkaa ($93.50) single; 570 markkaa ($125.40) double. AE, DC, MC, V. **Parking:** Free.

This hotel, south of Laivuripolku, has comfortable accommodations, two saunas, two restaurants, a bar, a swimming pool, and a large parking area with an ingenious plug-in method of keeping a car engine warm during a frosty night. The hotel's restaurants are open daily from 10am to 1am.

2. THE ÅLAND ISLANDS

The Ålands, off the west coast of Finland, between Turku and Stockholm, form an archipelago of 6,500 islands, islets, and skerries. The land mass is made up of 510 square miles, with 500 miles of roads. Yet it is the water that you remember—the sea stretches in all directions. Most of the islands are not inhabited, and there are only some 23,000 residents throughout the archipelago, but an estimated one million tourists visit the Ålands each year.

Åland comes from a word in the Old Norse language that meant "water island," and the English word "island" is also derived from the same word. The archipelago was settled some 5,000 years ago by seal hunters; large burial cairns can still be seen. In the Viking Age the lands became the most densely populated part of Scandinavia.

From medieval times until 1809 Åland was part of Sweden, but in that year Sweden lost both Åland and Finland to Russia. After the fall of the czar in 1917, Åland petitioned the king of Sweden to be allowed to rejoin his country, but Finland objected. The matter was settled by the League of Nations in 1921, which granted Finland sovereignty over the chain but protected Swedish culture and left Swedish as the official language. Today the residents of Åland are still more Swedish than Finnish, but technically Åland (pronounced *oh*-lant) still belongs to Finland. However, the Finnish government has given the people much autonomy, including the right to fly their own flag and, since 1982, to issue their own stamps—which are highly prized by collectors. Also, the young men of the islands are exempt from serving in the Finnish armed forces.

GETTING AROUND

Most of the inhabited islands are connected by a series of bridges, causeways, and ferry services. Except for the MS *Kumlinge,* fares are not charged on the local car-ferries unless you travel the complete route from end to end. "Road ferries" are always free, as they are intended as a road extension between the islands.

The largest island, 30 miles long, is called **"mainland,"** and about 90% of the population lives here. The island has dark coniferous woodland, much farmland and pastureland, fishing ports, and rocky fjords. The mainland is also known for its old fortresses and 11 medieval churches—the oldest built from the 12th to the 15th centuries. The reddish-brown and gray masonry of this outstanding collection of ecclesiastical architecture has given them the appellation "speckled hens," and a car or bicycle tour can easily include a visit to all of them.

The second-largest settlement, **Eckerö,** is the westernmost municipality in Finland. It was once a station on the mail route between Sweden and Imperial Russia.

Other major island targets include **Kumlinge,** which has a 15th-century church and is served by a ferry line from Långnäs; the crossing takes 2 hours.

Vårdö: This is the closest settlement to the Åland mainland, only 5 minutes away. The lush part of the island is in the south.

Brändö: The ferryboat from Långnäs (the same one that serves Kumlinge) also goes to this island—a municipality of some 1,000 islands. The largest of these are connected by causeways and bridges.

Föglö: Some 600 residents live on these clusters of islands, some of which are linked by bridges and causeways. Föglö, the largest of the island municipalities, is about 30 minutes from the Åland mainland.

Sottunga: From Långnäs, there is a 1½-hour ferry trip to Sottunga. Once there, you'll find only 150 residents in what is considered the smallest municipality in the Ålands.

Kökar: A rather bleak landscape. The remains of a 2,500-year-old Bronze Age community have been found at Karlby. Kokar is reached on a 2½-hour ferry crossing from Långnäs.

MARIEHAMN

The capital of the Ålands, Mariehamn is the only real town in the archipelago and has a population of 10,000. Founded in 1861, Mariehamn was named after the empress of Russia, Marie Alexandrova, wife of Alexander II. It lies on an isthmus with harbor facilities, and thousands of linden trees line its streets. The people here have always looked to the sea for their livelihood—that is, before the days of tourism.

The town is small, so no buses are required to get from one place to the other. However, there is a bus that runs from the harbor to the center of town, a distance of 2 miles.

The **Tourist Information Office** is located at Storagatan 18, SF-22100 Mariehamn (tel. 928/16-575). Hours are daily 9am to 6pm from June through August. Off-season hours are Monday through Saturday from 10am to 4pm. The **telephone area code** for the Åland Islands is 928.

GETTING THERE

The **airport** at Mariehamn is 2 miles outside the center of town. There are two round-trip flights daily from Stockholm, and four or five daily from Turku. Each flight takes about 20 minutes.

There is **bus service** in summer from both Helsinki and Turku, traveling via the interisland ferries.

The Viking Line runs **seagoing ferries** from Stockholm to Turku, with a stop en route at Mariehamn, and the Silja Line also makes the 6½-hour run from Stockholm to Mariehamn. There is usually one ship per day on each line. For prices, tickets, and information, contact the Viking Line at Stureplan 8 in Stockholm (tel. 08/222-480), or the Silja Line on the Stureplan in Stockholm (tel. 08/222-140 in Stockholm, 921/652-244 in Turku).

WHAT TO SEE & DO

Because Mariehamn is the administrative and economic center of Åland, the **Åland Self-Government House** is here. Also inside the town limits is **Tullarns äng Park,** a nature reserve open to visitors.

In Town

ÅLANDS MUSEUM, Öhbergsvägen. Tel. 28-25000.

At the eastern harbor between the Town Hall and parliament, this museum traces the history of the island beginning with the early settlers 5,000 years ago.

Admission: 7 markkaa ($1.50) adults, 4 markkaa (90¢) children.

Open: Summer, Wed–Mon 10am–4pm, Tues 10am–8pm; Sept–May, Wed–Sun 11am–4pm, Tues 11am–8pm.

ÅLAND MARITIME MUSEUM, Storagatan. Tel. 531-421.

This museum has a superb collection of exhibits from the great sailing-ship era of Åland.

Nearby is the four-masted barque **Pommern.** Built in Glasgow in 1903, it's a 310-foot clipper ship that participated in the Great Grain Race to Australia in the 1930s. Here you can see what life was like on board one of the windjammers.

Admission: Museum, 10 markkaa ($2.20) adults, 5 markkaa ($1.10) children; *Pommern,* 10 markkaa ($2.20) adults, 5 markkaa ($1.10) children under 12.

Open: Museum, May–Aug, daily 10am–5pm; Sept–Apr, daily 10am–4pm.

Pommern, mid-Apr to June and mid-Aug to Oct 20, daily 9am–7pm (closed July to mid-Aug and Oct 21 to mid-Apr).

Around the Island

There are also many nearby places worth a trek, including the **Ramsholmen Nature Reserve** and the region around the Lemstrom Canal. You can also take a drive out to **Ytternäs** and along the road across Nato to Jarso. Another inviting spot, on the other side of Slemmern Bay, southeast of Mariehamn, is **Chapel Bay,** which has its Lembote Chapel on a hilltop, the ruin of a medieval seafarers' chapel.

The **Jomala Church,** one of the most interesting churches, is 4 miles north of Mariehamn; part of it is from the 12th century, and it still contains 13th-century murals. About 8 miles southeast is the 13th-century **Lemland Church,** which has a triumphal cross and Madonna from the 14th century and a reredos from the 15th century.

At **Bomarsund,** 22 miles northeast of Mariehamn, you can see the ruins of a fortress built by Imperial Russia. Also of interest, the 13th-century **Kastelholm Ruins,** 6 miles from Bomarsund, are from when the Swedes constructed a fortress to mark their sovereignty over the islands.

WHERE TO STAY

Inexpensive

ESPLANAD HOTEL, Storagatan 5, SF-22100 Mariehamn. Tel. 928/16-444. Fax 928/17-363. 28 rms (all with bath). TV TEL

$ Rates (including breakfast): Summer, 225–310 markkaa ($49.50–$68.20) single; 320–420 markkaa ($70.40–$92.40) double. Off-season, 215–280 markkaa ($47.30–$61.60) single; 300–380 markkaa ($66–$83.60) double. AE, DC, MC, V. **Parking:** Free.

The limited number of bedrooms in the Esplanad, a comfortable and intimate hotel in the center of town, ensures a personalized touch. A lighthearted restaurant, La Cave, in the basement, features vegetarian platters and Finnish specialties.

HOTEL ADLON, Hamngatan 7, SF-22100 Mariehamn. Tel. 928/15-300. Fax 928/15-077. 52 rms (all with bath), 2 suites. A/C MINIBAR TV TEL

$ Rates (including breakfast): 240–440 markkaa ($52.80–$96.80) single; 350–550 markkaa ($77–$121) double; from 1,100 markkaa ($242) suite. AE, DC, MC, V. **Parking:** Free.

One of the most popular hotels in town, opened in 1973, this hotel has an ideal location—next to the western harbor where all the ferries and cruise ships berth. The restaurant is known for its good plain Scandinavian food and à la carte dishes. Rooms are comfortably and attractively furnished.

HOTEL ARKIPELAG, Strandgatan 31, SF-22100 Mariehamn. Tel. 928/28-24-020. Fax 928/28-24-384. 86 rms (all with bath). A/C MINIBAR TV TEL

$ Rates (including breakfast): 650 markkaa ($143) single; 825 markkaa ($181.50) double. Discounts June 21–Aug 4, 340 markkaa ($74.80) single; 420 markkaa ($92.40) double. AE, DC, MC, V. **Parking:** Free.

⭐ This leading hotel in town is located between the commercial center and the marina. The rooms are well furnished and well maintained. Most of them open onto a view of the yachts in the harbor. The huge restaurant, Arkipelag, is open Monday through Friday from 10am to 2am, on Saturday from 11am to 2am and on Sunday from 11am to 1am. There's also a pleasant bar. Facilities include two saunas with indoor and outdoor swimming pools, and a small-stakes casino.

HOTEL CIKADA, Hamngatan 1, SF-22100 Mariehamn. Tel. 928/16-333. Fax 928/17-363. 84 rms (all with bath). A/C TV TEL

$ Rates (including breakfast): Summer, 275–385 markkaa ($60.50–$84.70) single; 380–510 markkaa ($83.60–$112.20) double. Off-season, 230–360 markkaa ($50.60–$79.20) single; 270–480 markkaa ($59.40–$105.60) double. AE, DC, MC, V. **Parking:** Free.

A cluster of trees helps conceal this hotel, about 300 yards from the boat terminal, from the industrial sections of the nearby harbor. Each comfortable bedroom has its own narrow loggia. There are three different saunas for unwinding, plus a warm-weather drink-and-snack service on the outdoor terrace. The hotel's restaurant is open daily from 10am to 10pm.

PARK ÅLANDIA HOTEL, Norra Esplanadgatan 3, SF-22100 Mariehamn.
   Tel. 928/14-130. Fax 928/17-130. 79 rms (all with bath). TV TEL
$ Rates (including breakfast): 450 markkaa ($99) single; 600 markkaa ($132) double. AE, DC, MC, V. **Parking:** Free.
Each of the accommodations in this hotel 1 mile from the ferry harbor contains big windows and comfortable modern furniture. Both its in-house bar, Brittany, open from 11am to 2am, and its comfortable restaurant, open daily from 11am to midnight, extend onto the flag-draped boulevard. Facilities include a sauna and a swimming pool. Room service and laundry facilities are available.

WHERE TO DINE
Moderate

RESTAURANT NAUTICAL, Hamngatan 2. Tel. 11-931.
   Cuisine: FRENCH/FINNISH. **Reservations:** Required.
$ Prices: Fixed-price lunch 38–88 markkaa ($8.40–$19.40); appetizers 38–82 markkaa ($8.40–$18); main dishes 80–148 markkaa ($17.60–$32.60). AE, DC, MC, V.
   Open: Mon–Sat 10am–1am.
This pleasant restaurant has the look of a ship about to steam out to sea. It's in the same building as the Åland Maritime Museum, at the western harbor overlooking the museum ship *Pommern,* and as you'd expect, fresh seafood is one of the kitchen's specialties, including herring and fresh shellfish, with occasional lobster. Local ingredients are used whenever possible. As an appetizer, you might begin with slightly salted salmon with horseradish sauce or perch pâté with a spinach-and-scampi sauce. For a main dish, try the fried filet of perch stuffed with salmon in a fish-roe sauce or chateaubriand flavored with garlic. At least one vegetarian main dish always appears on the menu.

CHAPTER 37

THE LAKE REGION

Saimaa, an extensive lake district in eastern Finland, has thousands of islands and straits and lots of blue water. It's a land of sunshine, small villages, holiday centers, and pleasant people, wrapped in the peace and quiet of the wilderness.

From Lappeenranta, the center of Finnish lake tourism, you can book cruises lasting 2 hours or 2 days in the southern part of Lake Saimaa, or you can take a cruise to the Saimaa Canal and see the Russian border. In this region, you can swim in clean, clear water, fish with a seine, eat your catch cooked on a campfire, sail, windsurf, paddle a boat, dance, and enjoy saunas.

Tampere, Finland's second-largest city, is also set in a geographic area of myriad lakes. Tampere is a center for culture, tourism, and commerce, and its surrounding Pirkanmaa region is known for its vast waterways and forests.

Jyväskylä is often called the "capital" of central Finland. The hometown of Alvar Aalto, the great architect, Jyväskylä is the setting for the Thousand Lakes rally, a major boat competition in August.

Lahti, a busy commercial center, is also a sports center, site of many world skiing championships. It's a good base for exploring Lake Päijänne.

SEEING THE LAKE REGION
GETTING THERE

You can drive around the lake district, although the ideal way to go is by lake steamer, using Savonlinna as a gateway. For a preview of the lakes, the most popular steamer routes are the Kuopio-Savonlinna-Kuopio run, taking 12 hours, or the Savonlinna-Lappeenranta-Savonlinna run, taking 9 hours. But much shorter tours are also possible.

You can fly to many of the major "gateways," such as Tampere, Savonlinna, Jyväskylä, or Mikkeli. Trains and buses also service all the tourist centers we recommend, with daily departures from Helsinki. The entire area, in fact, can be explored by bus. You can take an express bus to a main center, then explore the remotest corners by bus.

A SUGGESTED ITINERARY

Day 1: Leave Helsinki and overnight in Lappeenranta.

Day 2: Drive or take public transportation to Imatra in the northeast for another day's sightseeing; spend the night.

Days 3 & 4: Transfer to Savonlinna and spend 2 nights exploring not only its own attractions but those in the environs. Allow a day for traveling on the lakes.

Day 5: Head west cross country for an overnight stay in Jyväskylä.

WHAT'S SPECIAL ABOUT THE LAKE REGION

Great Towns/Villages

- ☐ Savonlinna, in the middle of the Saimaa lake system, site of the famous opera festival in summer.
- ☐ Tampere, Finland's "second city," a leading industrial town and filled with attractions.
- ☐ Lappeenranta, the southerly port-of-call of the boats on Lake Saimaa and one of the best centers for exploring the eastern province of Karelia.

Museums

- ☐ Alvar Aalto Museum, Jyväskylä, honoring Finland's greatest architect in a town filled with buildings he designed.
- ☐ Old Kuopio Museum, in Kuopio, taking up a city block and offering a look back at the Finland of yesteryear.

Ancient Monuments

- ☐ Linnoitus, the fortress of Lappeenranta, defensive fortification begun by the Swedes as protection against Russian invasions.
- ☐ Olavinlinna Castle, at Savonlinna, a medieval fortress from 1475.

Ace Attractions

- ☐ Imatra Rapids, at Imatra, a mighty torrent that even drew the tourist interest of Catherine the Great.

Special Events/Festivals

- ☐ The Jyväskylä Arts Festival, oldest regular art festival in Finland.
- ☐ Savonlinna Opera Festival, in July, the major opera festival of Scandinavia.

Day 6: Go to Tampere in the southwest for a day of sightseeing and spend the night. Tampere is a good point to head back to Helsinki and your next destination.

1. TAMPERE

107 miles N of Helsinki, 96 miles NE of Turku

GETTING THERE **By Plane** Tampere-Pirkkala airport, 9 miles from the city center, has air links with some towns in Finland. But Tampere's air link to the world is via Helsinki, from which there are frequent flights.

By Train There are trains almost every hour making the 2¼-hour trip to and from Helsinki. Seven trains a day also connect Tampere with Turku, taking 2¼ hours.

By Bus Five buses a day, taking 2 hours, run back and forth between Helsinki and Tampere, and five buses a day, taking 2½ hours, link Tampere with Turku.

By Boat From June 4 to August 11, boats run between Tampere and Hämeenlinna in the south. This makes an interesting tour, as Hämeenlinna was the birthplace of Jean Sibelius. The one-way fare is 182 markkaa ($40).

By Car Both Helsinki and Turku are a 2-hour drive from Tampere. From Helsinki, take Route 3 north, and from Turku head northeast on Route 41.

ESSENTIALS The **City Tourist Office,** Verkatehtaankatu 2 (P.O. Box 87), SF-33211 Tampere (tel. 931/126-652), helps arrange for guides, sightseeing tours, and maps, and provides miscellaneous information. The office is open Mon–Fri 8:30am–8pm, Sat 8:30am–6pm, and Sun 11:30am–6pm (June–Aug) and Mon–Fri 8:30am–5pm (Sept–May). The **telephone area code** for Tampere is 931.

SPECIAL EVENTS Beginning in 1975 the **Tampere International Choir Festival** has taken place every other year. Dates in 1993 are June 2–6.

The **Tampere International Theater Festival** since 1969 has been Finland's only festival of professional theater, taking place in 1993 during August 10–15.

The **Tampere Jazz Happening,** considered Finland's best modern jazz festival, is set for November 5–7 in 1993.

Located on a narrow isthmus between two lakes, Lake Näsijärvi and Lake Pyhäjärvi, Tampere is Finland's second-largest city (pop. 170,000) and is primarily an industrial center; however, it remains one of the cleanest, brightest cities in Scandinavia and is filled with parks, water, museums, art galleries, theaters, and statues including some works by Wäinö Aaltosen. One statue he sculpted depicted a tax collector in the nude.

A vibrant young city with a university life, Tampere is host to one of Scandinavia's major attractions: the outdoor theater on Pyynikki with a revolving auditorium. Tampere's Swedish name is Tammerfors.

WHAT TO SEE & DO
ORGANIZED TOURS

From June 1 to August 31, a daily guided tour of the city leaves at 2pm from in front of the City Tourist Office, Verkatehtaankatu 2 (tel. 126-652), costing 25 markkaa ($5.50) for adults, 10 markkaa ($2.20) for children 7 to 16. The trip lasts 90 minutes, and the commentary is given in English.

From June 3 to August 15, Tampere is the meeting point of two popular lake cruisers, Finnish *Silverline* and *Poets' Way,* both of which have good restaurants. Route descriptions are available from Laivayhtioiden Tilauskeskus (Boatlines Booking Center), Verkatehtaankatu 2 (tel. 124-803).

THE SÄRKÄNNIEMI LEISURE CENTER

About a mile from the center of Tampere is the 25-acre Särkänniemi Leisure Center at Särkänniemi (tel. 248-81111). A joint ticket, the Särkänniemi-passport, includes entrance to the Dolphinarium and any five of the following: observations tower, Aquarium, Planetarium, Children's Zoo, amusement park, and Sara Hildén Art Museum. The passport, valid from the end of April to September 4, costs 70 markkaa ($15.40) for adults and 50 markkaa ($11) for children 12 or under. You can get to Särkänniemi by city bus no. 4 or 16.

NÄSINNEULA, in the Särkänniemi Leisure Center.
Towering over the grounds is the 560-foot-tall Näsinneula, the tallest observation tower in Finland, with a café, a revolving restaurant, and an open observation platform.
Admission: 12 markkaa ($2.60) adults, 6 markkaa ($1.30) children 12 or under; free with the Särkänniemi-passport.
Open: Daily 10am–8pm.

AQUARIUM, in the Särkänniemi Leisure Center.
The Aquarium has on display 2,000 specimens representing nearly 200 different species. It also has a seal pool with feeding times at 11am and 4pm.
Admission: 20 markkaa ($4.40) adults, 10 markkaa ($2.20) children 12 or under; free with the Särkänniemi-passport.
Open: May 28–Aug 9, daily 10am–8pm; off-season, Mon–Fri 10am–4pm, Sat–Sun 10am–5pm.

PLANETARIUM, in the Särkänniemi Leisure Center.
Here you can lean back in an armchair and follow the movements of the firmament, accompanied by expert commentary (in English and Finnish). This is very much a lecture-tour format rather than one that encourages random visits. Lectures and tours begin every 45 minutes.
Admission: 30 markkaa ($6.60) adults, 15 markkaa ($3.30) children 12 or under; free with the Särkänniemi-passport.

Open: May–Aug daily 10:45am–7pm; off-season, Mon–Fri noon–3pm, Sat–Sun noon–4pm.

FUNFAIR, in the Särkänniemi Leisure Center.
In summer only, the Funfair provides such entertainment as Ferris wheels and merry-go-rounds. Once inside, each ride costs an additional fee. Most visitors, once they pay the entrance fee and go inside, also pay a flat fee of 70 markkaa ($15.40) for adults and 45 markkaa ($9.90) for children, entitling them to unlimited access to all rides.
Admission: 10 markkaa ($2.20) adults, 5 markkaa ($1.10) children.
Open: Apr 30 to mid-May and Aug 15–31, Sat–Sun noon–8pm; mid-May to Aug 14, daily noon–8pm. **Closed:** Sept–Apr 29.

CHILDREN'S ZOO, in the Särkänniemi Leisure Center.
Just west of the Näsinneula observation tower, the Children's Zoo provides a common playground for children and domestic animals. Pony rides and rides in donkey-pulled carriages are available.
Admission: 20 markkaa ($4.40) adults, 10 markkaa ($2.20) children 12 or under; free with the Särkänniemi-passport.
Open: May 12–Aug 15, daily 10am–7pm. **Closed:** Aug 16–May 11.

DOLPHINARIUM, in the Särkänniemi Leisure Center.
At this Dolphinarium, the only one in Finland, are five dolphins giving five performances daily.
Admission: 30 markkaa ($6.60) adults, 15 markkaa ($3.30) children 12 or under; free with the Särkänniemi-passport.
Open: May 30–Sept 2, performances daily at 11:30am and 1, 2:30, 4, and 5:30pm. **Closed:** Sept 3–May 29.

SARA HILDÉN ART MUSEUM, in the Särkänniemi Leisure Center.
At the foot of the Näsinneula observation tower, this museum presents changing exhibitions of modern art. The Sara Hildén Foundation was founded in 1962 by Sara Hildén, who donated her works of art. Since then the collection has been greatly expanded, concentrating mainly on postwar art, including sculpture by Henry Moore and a painting by Francis Bacon. The museum is in beautiful lakeside surroundings, and some of the sculpture is displayed on the shores of Lake Näsijärvi, next to the museum.
Admission: 10 markkaa ($2.20) adults, 3 markkaa (70¢) students and children 7–16; free with the Särkänniemi-passport.
Open: Daily 11am–6pm.

MUSEUMS

TAMPERE ART MUSEUM [District Art Museum of Pirkanmaa], Puutarhakatu 34. Tel. 121-244.
Collections here include paintings, sculpture, drawings, graphics, regional art since the early 19th century, and the Tampere art collection. The museum also has changing art exhibits.
Admission: 10 markkaa ($2.20) adults, 3 markkaa (70¢) children 16 or under.
Open: June–Aug, daily 10am–6pm; Sept–May, Tues–Sun 10am–6pm.

MOOMINVALLEY MUSEUM, Hämeenpuisto 20. Tel. 121-244.
One of Finland's most charming museums is also one of its most frequently visited. The museum holds about a thousand india-ink drawings, and features more than 40 dioramas depicting the fictional characters created in the 1940s and 50s by Finland's beloved author of children's books, Tove Jansson.
Admission: 10 markkaa ($2.20) adults; 3 markkaa (70¢) children 3–16.
Open: Mon–Fri 9am–5pm, Sat–Sun 10am–6pm. **Bus:** 16, 25.

LENIN MUSEUM, Hämeenpuisto 25. Tel. 127-313.
Material dealing with the Russian Revolution and Lenin's connection with Finland is presented here.

Admission: 10 markkaa ($2.20) adults, 3 markkaa (70¢) children 12 or under.
Open: Tues–Sat 11am–3pm, Sun 11am–4pm. **Bus:** 16, 25.

WHERE TO STAY

The higher prices quoted below are high-season tariffs, which means winter rates. In summer, which is considered the low season, prices are reduced as on weekends. Nearly every hotel in Tampere has a sauna.

MODERATE

ARCTIA HOTEL ROSENDAHL, Pyynikintie 13, SF-33200 Tampere. Tel. 931/244-1111. Fax 931/233-375. 213 rms (all with bath). TV TEL **Bus:** 12.

$ Rates (including breakfast): July and weekends year-round, 360 markkaa ($79.20) single; 460 markkaa ($101.20) double. Sun–Thurs Aug–June, 600 markkaa ($132) single; 760 markkaa ($167.20) double. AE, DC, MC, V. **Parking:** Free.

Located about 1½ miles from the center of town, this hotel has a dramatic design enhanced by its position in a quiet forest at the edge of Lake Pyhäjärvi. The hotel was built in 1977 in a softly angled design of mirrored walls, polished stone, and lacquered ceilings—it's one of the most avant-garde hotels in the region. The elegant bedrooms are quiet, each with a trouser press, among other amenities. Most of them offer minibars. The Silver Line ships stop at the hotel's pier, and there's a lakeside bathing beach. The world-famous outdoor theater, Pyynikki, is nearby.

Dining/Entertainment: Many travelers stop for a meal in one of the hotel's several sun-flooded restaurants. The hotel also has a pub, a small-stakes casino, and a many-tiered basement-level nightclub (Joselin's) where live bands provide dance music.

Services: Massage, room service, laundry, babysitting.

Facilities: Tennis courts, miles of cross-country ski and hiking trails, swimming pool, children's pool, squash, mini-golf, golf simulator, six saunas, solarium.

GRAND HOTEL TAMMER, Satakunnankatu 13, SF-33100 Tampere. Tel. 931/228-111. Fax 931/230-757. 90 rms (all with bath). MINIBAR TV TEL **Bus:** 1, 2, 3.

$ Rates (including breakfast): June 16–Aug 4 and Fri–Sat year-round, 400 markkaa ($88) single or double. Sun–Thurs the rest of the year, 460 markkaa ($101.20) single; 620 markkaa ($136.40) double. AE, DC, MC, V. **Parking:** 50 markkaa ($11).

When this hotel was built (between rolling hills near a city park), by the well-known Finnish architect Bertal Strommer in 1929, it was considered the most glamorous hotel in town. Today its old-fashioned glamour offers the best perspective in town for an insight into Finnish art deco. To enter the dimly lit reception area, you pass beneath a five-story archway that soars to the roofline. The high-ceilinged, well-scrubbed bedrooms are comfortably furnished and have radios and trouser presses. Don't overlook the outdoor terrace, which offers pleasant views of the water.

Dining/Entertainment: The high-ceilinged dining room with Renaissance details serves buffet lunches for 110 markkaa ($24.20). At night both Finnish and international food is served. The hotel's nightclub, Club Grandy, is open daily from 8pm to 3am.

Services: Laundry service, room service, babysitting.
Facilities: Garage, swimming pool, car-rental desk.

HOTEL CUMULUS, Koskikatu 5, SF-33100 Tampere. Tel. 931/242-4111. Fax 931/2424-399. 230 rms (all with bath). A/C MINIBAR TV TEL **Bus:** 1, 2, 3.

$ Rates (including breakfast): July and Fri–Sat year-round, 270 markkaa ($59.40) single; 390 markkaa ($85.80) double. Sun–Thurs the rest of the year, 455 markkaa ($100.10) single; 600 markkaa ($132) double. AE, DC, MC, V. **Parking:** 50 markkaa ($11).

The popularity of its wining and dining facilities, plus its dramatic exterior, make this one of the most exciting hotels in town. Built in 1979, it sits at the edge of the graceful Koskipuisto Park near the river in the center of town, and the Finnair City Bus Terminal is immediately adjacent to the hotel. Each of the bedrooms is stylishly decorated with contemporary furniture. The Mona Lisa Wine Bar and the Tiffany Bar are on the lobby level. Room service is offered, and two saunas, a swimming pool, garage, children's playroom, fitness room, and solarium are available. For a less expensive Hotel Cumulus, see below.

HOTEL ILVES, Hatanpäänvaltatie 1, SF-33100 Tampere. Tel. 931/121-212. Fax 931/132-565. 336 rms (all with bath). A/C MINIBAR TV TEL **Bus:** 1, 2, 3.

$ Rates (including breakfast): June 12–Aug 2 and Fri–Sun year-round, 500 markkaa ($110) single or double. Mon–Thurs Aug 3–June 11, 560 markkaa ($123.20) single; 800 markkaa ($176) double. AE, DC, MC, V. **Parking:** 50 markkaa ($11).

Architecturally the most dramatic hotel in town (built in 1986), the Ilves contains bedrooms handsomely outfitted with modern Finnish furniture, textiles, and climate control.

Dining/Entertainment: Four different restaurants are on the premises (the Fransmanni Restaurant is recommended separately; see "Where to Dine," below). In the morning, a popular and airy café and lobby bar doubles as a busy breakfast room. A nightclub and disco have a glittering ambience.

Services: Room service, laundry, babysitting.

Facilities: Hairdresser, three saunas, sauna bar, swimming pool.

HOTEL TAMPERE, Hämeenkatu 1, SF-33100 Tampere. Tel. 931/2446-111. Fax 931/221-910. 250 rms (all with bath). TV TEL **Bus:** 1, 2, 3.

$ Rates (including breakfast): June 21–Aug 4 and Fri–Sat year-round, 290 markkaa ($63.80) single; 380 markkaa ($83.60) double. Sun–Thurs the rest of the year, 455 markkaa ($100.10) single; 600 markkaa ($132) double. AE, DC, MC, V.

A long-enduring traditional favorite opposite the railway station, Tampere offers clean and comfortable accommodations in a wide variety of styles. The newest rooms overlook a glass-capped atrium whose fountains and plants lend natural accents to the boutiques and cafés. There is a series of bars, cafeterias, and restaurants on the premises, including Restaurant Emma. Six saunas, an indoor swimming pool, fitness gymnasium, and solarium are available.

INEXPENSIVE

HOTEL CUMULUS, Hämeenpuisto 47, SF-33200 Tampere. Tel. 931/242-4242. Fax 931/242-4299. 184 rms (all with bath). TV TEL MINIBAR **Bus:** 1, 2, 3.

$ Rates (including breakfast): Fri–Sat year-round and June 15–July 30, 310 markkaa ($68.20) single; 360 markkaa ($79.20) double. Sun–Thurs the rest of the year, 390 markkaa ($85.80) single; 440 markkaa ($96.80) double. AE, DC, MC, V.

One of the newer hotels in town, this Cumulus features pastel-tone bedrooms that are clean, warm, and comfortable. It prides itself on being less expensive than its affiliated hotel, Tampere's second Cumulus (see above). On premises are a bar, the international restaurant Bastille, and a sauna.

HOTELLI VICTORIA, Itsenäisyydenkatu 1, SF-33100 Tampere. Tel. 931/2425-111. Fax 931/242-5100. 100 rms (all with bath). TV TEL **Bus:** 1, 2, 3.

$ Rates (including breakfast): June 15–Aug 3 and Fri–Sat year-round, 250 markkaa ($55) single; 360 markkaa ($79.20) double. Sun–Thurs the rest of the year, 390 markkaa ($85.80) single; 490 markkaa ($107.80) double. AE, DC, MC, V. **Parking:** 40 markkaa ($8.80).

On the outskirts of the main commercial center behind a forecourt clustered with fruit trees, this hotel contains one of the most likable bars and informal restaurants in town, the Tunneli, where exposed brick and 19th-century mannequins create an ambience you'd expect to find near Piccadilly Circus in

London. Most bedrooms contain a color scheme of pink or blue and lots of exposed wood. There's a sauna and an indoor swimming pool.

BUDGET

DOMUS, Pellervonkatu 9, SF-33540 Tampere. Tel. 931/133-222. Fax 931/225-409. 137 rms (83 with bath). **Bus:** 25.

$ Rates: 170 markkaa ($37.40) single without bath, 240 markkaa ($52.80) single with bath; 220 markkaa ($48.40) double without bath, 280 markkaa ($61.60) double with bath. Breakfast 30 markkaa ($6.60) extra. MC, V. **Parking:** Free. **Closed:** Sept–May.

⑤ One of Finland's finest student-run hotels, this is a compound of modern buildings with grassy courtyards located in the Kaleva district less than a mile from the center. The compact bedrooms are decorated in Finnish-modern style and have wall-to-wall desks, birch armchairs, wall shelves, built-in wardrobes, sofa beds, and brightly colored fabrics. Each room also has a small refrigerator and stove. The sauna and swimming pool can be used free in the morning. On the premises is the Fun Pub Rocky.

WHERE TO DINE
MODERATE

FINLAYSONIN PALATSI, Kuninkaankatu 1. Tel. 125-905.
Cuisine: FINNISH/INTERNATIONAL. **Reservations:** Recommended. **Bus:** 1, 2, 3.
$ Prices: Appetizers 30–40 markkaa ($6.60–$8.80); main dishes 60–95 markkaa ($13.20–$20.90); fixed-price menu 100 markkaa ($22). AE, DC, MC, V.
Open: Daily 11am–1am.
A palace built in 1899, this is an elegant eating place with a number of dining rooms and cozy private rooms. On the first floor are the Winter Garden, the Palace Hall, the Venetian Hall, and Alexander's Private Room. In summer, an outdoor restaurant is open in the park surrounding the palace. The chef concentrates on using local products wherever possible. The fish dishes, such as salmon and whitefish, are outstanding.

FRANSMANNI RESTAURANT, in the Hotel Ilves, Hatanpäänvaltatie 1. Tel. 121-213.
Cuisine: INTERNATIONAL. **Reservations:** Recommended. **Bus:** 1, 2, 3.
$ Prices: Appetizers 25–73 markkaa ($5.50–$16.10); main dishes 65–125 markkaa ($14.30–$27.50). AE, DC, MC, V.
Open: Daily 11am–1pm.
To reach this restaurant, you have to cross through the lobby of the Hotel Ilves (see above). The restaurant is elegantly decorated in a regional style, with a fireplace and a beamed ceiling. Specialties come from "the fishermen's net" or a steak grilled to your specifications. Lamb is a special dish.

RESTAURANT NÄSINNEULA, Särkänniemi. Tel. 124-697.
Cuisine: FINNISH. **Reservations:** Recommended. **Bus:** 4, 16.
$ Prices: Appetizers 28–55 markkaa ($6.20–$12.10); main dishes 65–125 markkaa ($14.30–$27.50). AE, DC, MC, V.
Open: Mon–Sat 11am–midnight, Sun 10am–8pm.
Near the city's recreational headquarters, Särkänniemi, this revolving circular restaurant has a panoramic view of two lakes, acres of heavily forested woodland, and an amusement park. You take a high-speed elevator to reach the restaurant. Full meals include salmon soup, morel-cream soup, pepper steak, noisettes of veal, chicken with fruit, smoked reindeer salad, sea trout braised with cream, and for two diners, a combination of flank steak and braised salmon.

RUSTHOLLI, Rusthollinkatu 16, Aitolahti. Tel. 620-111.
Cuisine: FINNISH. **Reservations:** Recommended. **Directions:** Best to drive, since it is 5 miles from the center toward Aitolahti.

$ Prices: Appetizers 30–55 markkaa ($6.60–$12.10); main dishes 62–98 markkaa ($13.60–$21.60). AE, DC, MC, V.
Open: Daily 9am–1am.

A fun restaurant near the lake, this has been an unmatched eating place for more than 30 years. Not only can you dine in the midst of nature, but you can also swim and then have a sauna before dinner. Specialties include fresh salmon, whitefish, Baltic herring, and reindeer.

TIILIHOLVI, Kauppakatu 10. Tel. 121-220.

Cuisine: INTERNATIONAL. **Reservations:** Essential for dinner. **Bus:** 1, 2, 3.
$ Prices: Appetizers 36–45 markkaa ($7.90–$9.90); main dishes 42–120 markkaa ($9.20–$26.40); fixed-price lunch 60 markkaa ($13.20). AE, DC, MC, V.
Open: Mon–Fri 11am–midnight, Sat noon–midnight, Sun noon–7pm.

In the center of Tampere in an intimate atmosphere of red-brick walls, wooden tables, and candlelight, this restaurant features the specialties of the Finnish cuisine and good charcoal-grilled dishes. Much of the food is influenced by France. The chef respects the natural taste of his produce. Specialties include morel soup à la Lapone, roast sea trout with black sesame seeds, and snow grouse à la Paris, and for dessert, cardamom ice cream. At a wine cellar, a new part of the restaurant, light meals are offered for 42 markkaa ($9.20).

SHOPPING

KEHRASÄÄRI BOUTIQUE CENTER, Kehrasäari Square. Tel. 28-080.

More than 40 boutiques here sell the best of Finnish art, handcrafts, glasswork, children's toys, ceramics, and an array of woven textiles in alluring shades of earth and sky. Even if you don't make a purchase, you might order a drink in the courtyard café.

PIRKANMAAN KOTITYÖ OY, Hatapään Valtapie. Tel. 503-400.

This well-stocked shop is owned and managed by a quasi-governmental association for the promotion of the region's handcrafts. You'll find a changing exhibition and sale of handcrafted textiles, toys, and knitware. Many crafts are inspired by Finnish design.

EVENING ENTERTAINMENT

PYYNIKKI SUMMER THEATER, Postilokero 246. Tel. 126-792 for reservations.

About a mile from the center of Tampere, this is the first outdoor theater in the world built with a revolving auditorium, and it seats 800. The plays are in Finnish, and a free synopsis of the action is outlined in English; but for most of these action-packed plays you don't need to know the subtleties of dialogue. Reserving tickets in advance is imperative. Summer plays are presented from mid-June to mid-August, Tuesday through Sunday at 7pm; two performances are given on Wednesday, Saturday, and Sunday, the late one at 10pm. Bus: 12.

Tickets: 100 markkaa ($22) adults, 70 markkaa ($15.40) children 12 or under.

---

2. LAHTI

64 miles N of Helsinki, 78 miles E of Tampere

GETTING THERE   By Train   Direct trains run several times daily between Helsinki and Lahti, taking 1½ hours.

By Bus   From the Helsinki bus station, Lahti-bound buses leave almost every hour, taking 1½ hours.

By Car   From Helsinki, take the E4 express highway north for 64 miles.

ESSENTIALS   For information, the **Lahti City Tourist and Congress Bu-**

reau, Torikatu 3B (tel. 918/818-2580), is open Mon–Fri 8am–7pm and Sat–Sun 10am–2pm (June–Aug) and Mon–Fri 8am–4pm (Sept–May). The **telephone area code** for Lahti is 918.

Best known for its winter sports attractions, Lahti has been called "the most American city" in Finland because it is industrial and modern. Founded in 1905, this former market crossroads lies in the center of southern Finland at the junction of major traffic routes. On the southern shore of Lake Vesijärvi, it was built between the two ridges of Salpausselka and marks the beginning of some of the most scenic lake districts of Finland. Lahti is considered the "gateway to central Finland." It lies at the southern end of one of the country's largest lake systems.

WHAT TO SEE & DO

With a population of 100,000, the seventh-largest city of Finland, Lahti has a rich cultural life, as reflected by its recurring festivals ranging from poetry marathons to organ-player festivals. But, as mentioned before, it is mainly known as a winter sports center. Skiers follow ridges formed during the Ice Age. Its **Ski Stadium,** said to be the best in the world, was host to the 1989 World Ski Championships. Even if you're a summer visitor you can visit the stadium, where from the top of the highest ski jump there are beautiful views over the forest and Lake Päijänne and Lake Vesijärvi. Near the bottom of the ski jumps is a swimming pool. The sightseeing platform at nearly 300 feet is open June through July, Monday through Friday from 11am to 6pm and Saturday and Sunday from 10am to 5pm. Admission is 10 markkaa ($2.20) for adults, 5 markkaa ($1.10) for children.

Even though Lahti is a modern city, it has some notable buildings, including the **City Hall,** Harjukatu (tel. 814-11), which was designed by Eliel Saarinen and completed in 1912, although restored in 1985. (Saarinen is best known for his design of the Helsinki Railway Station.) Alvar Aalto designed the parish church of Lahti, the **Church of the Cross,** Kirkkokatu 4 (tel. 891-290), which was completed in 1978 in the city center near the marketplace. Services, sometimes in English, are held on Sunday at 10am. One of the most visited places is the **Mukkula Tourist Center** on the shores of Lake Vesijärvi (tel. 305-553), 3 miles north of the city center. It was under the ancient oaks in the park that writers and people who specialized in reciting verses met in years gone by. Facilities range from a romantic manor hotel to a camping ground. Open year-round, daily from 10am to 5pm, the center has tennis courts, miniature golf, rowboats, bicycles, and surfboards for rent.

You can also visit the 30-mile-long **Saimaa Canal,** dating from the mid-1850s, which connects Lake Saimaa to the Gulf of Finland through Russia. The Finnish territory can be visited on a cruise. For details about these and other matters, contact the City Tourist Office (see above).

WHERE TO STAY

MODERATE

ASCOT HOTEL, Rauhankatu 14, SF-15110 Lahti. Tel. 918/897-11. Fax 918/897-1224. 232 rms (all with bath). MINIBAR TV TEL

$ Rates (including breakfast): June 14–Aug 6, 400 markkaa ($88) single or double. Aug 7–June 13, 480 markkaa ($105.60) single; 650 markkaa ($143) double. AE, DC, MC, V. **Parking:** 30 markkaa ($6.60).

Close to the bus station and the marketplace in the center of town, and not far from the sports center, this hotel features bedrooms with cozy, homelike decor in soft pastel hues. The hotel has seven different restaurants and drinking establishments (see below). Laundry facilities, babysitting, and room service are offered, and six saunas, a swimming pool, gym, and solarium are available.

LAHDEN SEURAHUONE, Aleksanterinkatu 14, SF-15110 Lahti. Tel. 918/577-11. Fax 918/577-3130. 120 rms (all with bath), 1 suite. MINIBAR TV TEL

$ Rates (including breakfast): June 12–Aug 16 and Fri–Sat year-round, 290 markkaa ($63.80) single; 380 markkaa ($83.60) double; from 380 markkaa ($83.60) suite. Sun–Thurs the rest of the year, 575 markkaa ($126.50) single; 680 markkaa ($149.60) double; from 750 markkaa ($165) suite. AE, DC, MC, V. **Parking:** 40 markkaa ($8.80).

⭐ Located on a central, tree-lined street near Tori, the marketplace, this hotel has comfortable, well-designed rooms. Special rooms are available for guests suffering from allergies and for nonsmokers. There are also two saunas and a swimming pool. Among the hotel's many distinguished guests have been Carl XVI Gustav of Sweden, Crown Prince Harald of Norway, Khrushchev, Bulganin, and Marshal Mannerheim. The hotel offers five restaurants and drinking establishments (see below).

WHERE TO DINE

IN THE ASCOT HOTEL The Ascot Hotel, Rauhankatu 14 (tel. 897-11), has a total of seven places to eat and drink. This is also the best place to go for evening entertainment. The **Café Bistro** is inspired by a farmhouse in Provence, offering herb-flavored French meals in a cozy atmosphere of wood floors, sofas, and an open fire. Wine is sold by the glass. The dining action overflows onto the Bistro Terrace in summer. The **Café Catalina Ristorante** is strictly Italian, with red-striped awnings, tile roofs, an open kitchen, and a salad trolley set up on the "square." Pizzas and pastas are the main fare here, although you can also order such main-dish specialties as steak. Finish off with an espresso after having the house ice cream. The festive **Emmanuel** is the number one dance spot in town, with a big bar, and the **Bar Cabaña** is an ideal place for an exotic cocktail. In summer you can dine at the **Terrazza** under a giant parasol, and later check out the action in either the **Pub Nelson,** with its dark-paneled walls and long bar, or in **Music Bar Wendy's,** where the music is nonstop.

Food service is daily from 11am to 1pm, and meals cost 95 to 250 markkaa ($20.90 to $55), depending on what you order. These restaurants lie close to the town marketplace in the center.

IN THE LAHDEN SEURAHUONE HOTEL The Lahden Seurahuone Hotel, Aleksanterinkatu 14 (tel. 577-11), offers a choice of five places to eat, each different. The **Marco Polo,** a rendezvous point for younger people, is a good place for snacks and drinks in early evening. For an à la carte meal of Finnish and international specialties, try **Hämesali** or **Eden,** the latter specializing in spicy peppered delicacies. The **Amoroso** nightclub is a major place in Lahti for evening entertainment. In summer, the **Pihatto** outdoor restaurant serves drinks and light meals.

Wednesday night is grand buffet night at the hotel. Meals range in price from 85 to 225 markkaa ($18.70 to $49.50), depending on what you order. Food service is daily from 11am–1pm.

---

3. JYVÄSKYLÄ

106 miles N of Lahti, 168 miles N of Helsinki

GETTING THERE **By Plane** Finnair flies nonstop between Helsinki and Jyväskylä. Frequency of flights depends on the time of year, usually taking 80 minutes. The airport is 10 miles north of Jyväskylä in Tikkakoski. Buses connect with arriving planes and takes passengers to the city center.

By Train Jyväskylä lies on the rail route from Tampere, from which connections can be made to Helsinki. Seven trains a day run back and forth between the two cities, taking 1¾ hours.

By Bus From Helsinki 10 buses daily go all the way to Jyväskylä, going via Lahti and Jämsä. You can, for example, take an 8am bus from Helsinki, arriving in Jyväskylä at 1:05pm. From Turku there are five daily buses, and from Tampere, six to eight buses.

By Car From Helsinki, head north to Lahti on the E4. Pass through the city and continue on the E4 via Jämsä to Jyväskylä.

By Boat In summer, you can tour Lake Päijänne, the longest and deepest lake in Finland. The big white ships sailing the lake—SS *Suomi,* MS *Suometar,* and MS *Suomen Neito*—begin their journey in Jyväskylä, Lahti, or Heinola. You can step on board at one of the intermediate landing stages on any day of the week. Pick up a cruise schedule from the tourist office (see below), or purchase a ticket at any travel agent. For more details, contact **Päijänne Risteilyt,** Pellonpää, SF-40820 Haapaniemi (tel. 941/618-885).

ESSENTIALS The **City Tourist Office,** at Vapaudenkatu 38 (tel. 941/624-903), is open Mon–Fri, 8am–6pm and Sat–Sun 10am–6pm (June–Aug) and Mon–Fri 8am–5pm (Sept–May). The **telephone area code** for Jyväskylä is 941.

SPECIAL EVENTS The **Jyväskylä Arts Festival** in June is the oldest regular art festival in Finland, offering a wide variety of exhibitions, cultural events, and seminars on sociology, politics, economics, and the arts. For more information, you can call 615-624 if you'd like to attend. Dates vary from year to year.

────────────

In 1834, Czar Nicholas II of Russia founded Jyväskylä on the site of an ancient marketplace at the northern end of Lake Päijänne, and today it's one of the most popular tourist cities of Finland. An old university city, it has long been a cultural center, with activities reaching their peak at the annual Jyväskylä Arts Festival in summer. The first Finnish-language secondary school in the country was founded here, and Jyväskylä today remains "a town of schools."

WHAT TO SEE & DO

ALVAR AALTO MUSEUM, Alvar Aalton Katu 7. Tel. 624-809.

Jyväskylä was the town where the famed Finnish architect Alvar Aalto started his career. He designed the modern buildings of the university and the City Theater, and his other works can be studied here in another building he designed. The museum has a permanent collection of Aalto memorabilia, including the architect's central design concepts and buildings. The design collection contains some 900 objects, such as classic Aalto furniture from the 1920s.

Admission: 10 markkaa ($2.20) adults; children free.
Open: Tues–Sun noon–6pm.

FINNISH HANDCRAFT MUSEUM, Seminaarinkatu 32. Tel. 624-946.

Established in 1982, this institution functions as a national museum of handcrafts. The collection includes both domestic and foreign handcrafts, and most of it dates from 1910 to 1930. In addition to the permanent displays illustrating various artisanal skills, short-term exhibitions of handcrafts are also staged here.

Admission: 10 markkaa ($2.20) adults; children free.
Open: Tues–Sun noon–7pm.

KESKI-SUOMEN ILMAILUMUSEO (Air Museum of Central Finland), Kuikantie 1, Tikkakoski. Tel. 752-125.

Near the E4 express highway about 12 miles north of Jyväskylä, this museum has many aircraft-related displays from World War I to the present, including planes, engines, signals, some 400 scale models, dioramas, uniforms, and a pictorial review of aviation history in Finland.

Admission: 20 markkaa ($4.40) adults, 10 markkaa ($2.20) children.
Open: June–Aug 20, daily 10am–8pm; Aug 21–May, daily noon–7pm. **Bus:** 22 leaving hourly from the Jyväskylä bus station.

VIHERLANDIA, Kuokkalanti 6. Tel. 261-255.

This is the largest garden center in the country. Here you can wander through large areas containing a massive variety of exotic plants. You can also visit special exhibitions and have snacks and drinks at the Café Eden.

Admission: Free.

Open: May–Aug, Mon–Fri 9am–8pm, Sat 9am–6pm, Sun 10am–6pm; Sept–Apr, Mon–Fri 9am–8pm, Sat 9am–4pm, Sun 11am–6pm.

VESILINNA WATER TOWER, Harju Ridge. Tel. 626-701.

This tower is the most prominent landmark in town. A series of 143 stone steps built in 1925 lead up the ridge to the summit where the tower is located. The observation terrace of the tower offers a panoramic view of the city and the lakes beyond. On the ridge is a jogging track and summer theater.

Admission: 5 markkaa ($1.10) adults, 3 markkaa (70¢) children.

Open: June–Aug 15, daily 10am–8pm; Aug 16–31, daily 10am–6pm. **Closed:** Sept–May.

WHERE TO STAY
MODERATE

ALEXANDRA, Hannikaisenkatu 35, SF-40100 Jyväskylä. Tel. 651-211.
Fax 941/651-200. 132 rms (all with bath). MINIBAR TV TEL

$ Rates (including breakfast): July and Fri–Sat year-round, 300 markkaa ($66) single; 400 markkaa ($88) double. Sun–Thurs the rest of the year, 490 markkaa ($107.80) single; 700 markkaa ($154) double. AE, DC, MC, V. **Parking:** 40 markkaa ($8.80).

A first-class hotel in the heart of town, Alexandra has elegant rooms featuring modern amenities. The Alexandra Restaurant is open Monday through Saturday from 10am to midnight and on Sunday from 10am to 10pm. Facilities include a special sauna section with sauna bar, whirlpool baths, solarium, and Acu-massage.

CUMULUS JYVÄSKYLÄ, Väinönkatu, SF-40100 Jyväskylä. Tel. 941/653-211. Fax 941/653-299. 203 rms (all with bath). MINIBAR TV TEL

$ Rates (including breakfast): July and Fri–Sat year-round, 270 markkaa ($59.40) single; 390 markkaa ($85.80) double. Sun–Thurs the rest of the year, 455 markkaa ($100.10); 600 markkaa ($132) double. AE, DC, MC, V.

This Cumulus is in the center of town a block from the rail station. The hotel, built in 1976 and added onto in 1983, has comfortable bedrooms. A café and a pleasant restaurant, which serves from 10am to 2am, are on the premises. Facilities include two saunas and a swimming pool.

RANTASIPI LAAJAVOURI, Laajavuori, SF-40101 Jyväskylä. Tel. 941/628-211. Fax 941/628-500. 200 rms (all with bath). MINIBAR TV TEL

$ Rates (including breakfast): June 22–July and Fri–Sat year-round, 300 markkaa ($66) single; 400 markkaa ($88) double. Sun–Thurs the rest of the year, 525 markkaa ($115.50) single; 680 markkaa ($149.60) double. AE, DC, MC, V. **Parking:** Free.

Located in a spruce forest 2½ miles from the town center, this hotel is near a lake, which is visible through many of its large windows. The comfortable bedrooms have stylishly modern Finnish furniture.

Dining/Entertainment: The Salitintti restaurant is known throughout the region. You can dine on pork in an aquavit-flavored fruit sauce, reindeer tongue with morels, or several different preparations of fresh salmon before heading into the hotel's nightclub. Dining facilities are open on Monday from 7am to 1am, Tuesday through Saturday from 7am to 3am, and on Sunday from 7am to midnight. The hotel also has a nightclub, sauna, and swimming pool.

SUMMER HOTEL

SUMMER HOTEL RENTUKKA, Tationiekantie 9, SF-40740 Jyväskylä. Tel. 941/607-211. Fax 941/251-174. 140 rms (all with bath). **Bus:** 25.

$ Rates (including breakfast): 220 markkaa ($48.40) single; 300 markkaa ($66) double. MC, V. **Parking:** Free. **Closed:** Sept–Apr.

Ⓢ Nine minutes by foot from the main downtown square, this hotel is in a university housing complex of apartments and dormitories. There is a good restaurant in the hotel, charging moderate prices by Finnish standards, where nightly dancing is offered. The bedrooms contain contemporary blond-wood student furnishings, and there are complete cooking facilities (bring your own utensils) and refrigerators.

---

4. LAPPEENRANTA

138 miles NE of Helsinki, 10 miles W of the Russian border

GETTING THERE **By Plane** In summer 30-minute flights between Helsinki and Lappeenranta operate 12 times a week (twice a day Monday through Friday and once a day on weekends). In off-season, four flights a day operate Monday through Friday.

By Train Seven trains a day run between Helsinki and Lappeenranta, taking 4 hours. There are also good train connections to the neighboring towns of Imatra, Savonlinna, and Mikkeli.

By Bus Five to seven express buses a day make the 4-hour run between Helsinki and Lappeenranta. Buses also run every hour between Lappeenranta and Imatra, taking 30 minutes to 1 hour, depending on the bus.

By Car Take the E4 north from Helsinki to Lahti, where you connect with Route 12 east until you reach the junction of Route 6 for the final approach to Lappeenranta.

ESSENTIALS The summer-only **Lappeenranta Maitkailu Oy,** Matkailu-toimisto (tel. 953/560-860), will provide you with information, arrange guides, and help you with sightseeing tours. Hours are Monday to Friday 8am to 6pm (to 8pm June 22 through July), Saturday 9am to 1pm (to 3pm June 22 through July), and Sunday 10am to 3pm (June 22 through July only). The **telephone area code** for Lappeenranta is 953.

This historic town, a border town between two different cultures, was founded in 1649 by Queen Christina of Sweden. It was fortified first by the Swedes who governed Finland as a province, then by the Russians. Lappeenranta has assumed increasing importance since World War II, following the loss of large parts of Karelia. For more than a century and a half the town has been a spa, and today Lappeenranta is one of the most important summer resort and excursion centers in eastern Finland. A bright, modern town, it nestles at the southern edge of the large Lake Saimaa.

WHAT TO SEE & DO
IN THE FORTRESS

Linnoitus, the fortress of Lappeenranta, on Kristiinankatu, was begun by the Swedes and continued by the Russians as a link in their chain of defenses. The entire chain fell into disuse after the Peace of Turku in 1812, when the part of the country known as Old Finland, including Lappeenranta, was reunited with other Finnish territory. The fortress was turned over to the town in 1835 and the defenses slowly deteriorated, but restoration has been ongoing since 1976. There are potteries and other handcraft shops in the fortress area.

The following three attractions—the Orthodox Church, the South Karelian Museum, and the Cavalry Museum—are all located within the fortress precincts.

The old **Orthodox Church** was completed in 1785, but only the high and narrow nave belong to the original building. One of the most valuable icons here is the *Communion of the Holy,* which is more than 200 years old. The Orthodox Church of Finland owes allegiance to the Ecumenical Patriarch of Constantinople.

The **Etela-Karjalan Museo (South Karelian Museum)** (tel. 518-514) is located at the northern end of the fortress in the 19th-century military storehouse. Museum displays include a model of the former Finnish town of Viipuri (Vyborg). The textile department of this museum is worth looking at, as there are examples of traditional Karelian clothing here. An **art museum** is now established in the soldiers barracks next to the Orthodox Church.

Admission to both museums is 15 markkaa ($3.30) for adults or children. However, by buying one ticket you can visit three museums, including the Cavalry Museum, described below. The two museums are open in summer, Monday through Friday from 10am to 6pm and on Saturday and Sunday from 11am to 5pm; off-season, Tuesday, Wednesday, and Friday through Sunday from 11am to 5pm, on Thursday from 11am to 8pm.

The **Cavalry Museum** (tel. 518-515) is in the oldest building in Lappeenranta, the former guardhouse of Linnoitus by the town gates, built in 1772. The history of the Finnish cavalry from the *hakkapeliitat* (the cavalry in the 1618–48 war) until modern times is depicted through uniforms, guns, and objects related to horse care. The museum is open in summer, Monday through Friday from 10am to 6pm and Saturday and Sunday from 11am to 5pm; off-season, Tuesday, Wednesday, and Friday through Sunday from 11am to 5pm, Thursday from 11am to 8pm.

AROUND TOWN

As noted, Lappeenranta is a lake town, the heart of Lake Saimaa and the eastern lake district. Both passenger ships and private boats sail from the harbor of Lappeenranta to the lake and down the Saimaa Canal to the Gulf of Finland. For a good view of the town, the lake, and the surrounding islands, take the elevator to the top of the pillar-supported **Vesitorni Observation Tower,** Pohjolankatu (tel. 451-2275) open in June and July, daily from 10am to 8pm; in May and August, daily from 11am to 6pm. Admission is 8 markkaa ($1.80) for adults, 4 markkaa (90¢) for children.

This is also a cultural town, with **summer concerts** held in the parks and **summer theater** on the fortified walls. Cavalrymen dressed in traditional skeleton tunics and red trousers, the uniform worn in 1922, ride in the fortress and harbor area in summer. **Guard parades and evening tattoos** are held several times during the summer months.

The **Marketplace** (see it in the morning), in the center of town, is the place to meet the local Karelian people and eat boat-shaped Karelian pies.

Near the Sports Stadium, the **Laura Korpikaivo-Tamminen's Museum for Textile Handicrafts,** Kantokatu 1 (tel. 518-509), has a collection of 2,000 handmade objects, including wall hangings, tablecloths, woven designs, and lace. Admission costs 10 markkaa ($2.20), and it's open Tuesday through Sunday from 11am to 5pm.

A VISIT TO RUSSIA

A popular side trip from Lappeenranta is a visit to Russia; write to the tourist office (above) for information. From May to September, the MS *Carelia* carries 300 passengers on day-trips to Vyborg, the old capital of Karelia before Finland was forced to cede it to the Soviet Union in World War II. The 1-day trip can be made by passengers from all countries having diplomatic relations with Russia, and no visa is required. Reservations and identification must be cleared with the **Matka-Lappee Travel Agency,** Valtakatu 46, SF-53100 Lappeenranta (tel. 953/53-430), at least 2 weeks before you wish to travel. The 1-day journeys include lunch and a sightseeing tour. A day cruise to Vyborg does not include a sightseeing tour, but it does permit 2½ hours of free time looking around before the boat returns to Lappeenranta. The boat departs every day in summer at 8am, and returns the same day at 10pm. Cost ranges from 100 to 190 markkaa ($22 to $41.80), depending on the time of the summer (mid-July is more expensive than early June). If you go by boat but return by bus, you'll save 2 hours off the total travel time.

The same tour can be extended to 2 days, with one overnight included. The price for that is around 500 markkaa ($110) per person, double occupancy. A city tour is included in that price.

WHERE TO STAY
MODERATE

HOTEL CUMULUS, Valtakatu 31, SF-53100 Lappeenranta. Tel. 953/ 5781. Fax 953/578-299. 95 rms (all with bath). MINIBAR TV TEL

$ Rates (including breakfast): June 19–Aug 2 and Fri–Sat year-round, 270 markkaa ($59.40) single; 390 markkaa ($85.80) double. Aug 3–June 18, 430 markkaa ($94.60) single; 570 markkaa ($125.40) double. AE, DC, MC, V. **Parking:** Free.

⑤ In the heart of the city on the main shopping street near the City Theater, this hotel, opened in 1982, has units for those with allergies. Bedrooms are modern, comfortable, and attractively furnished.

Dining/Entertainment: Three hotel dining and drinking establishments—one called Hullu Hanhi or "Crazy Goose," the Ferrari Pub, and the Tiffany Pub—are the most popular in town. There is a fitness room, two saunas, and a swimming pool.

HOTEL LAPPEE, Brahenkatu 1, SF-53100 Lappeenranta. Tel. 953/ 5861. Fax 953/53-295. 206 rms (all with bath), 2 suites. TV TEL

$ Rates (including breakfast): June 15–Aug 7 and Fri–Sat year-round, 400 markkaa ($88) single or double. Sun–Thurs the rest of the year, 480 markkaa ($105.60) single; 580 markkaa ($127.60) double. Year-round, 650–950 markkaa ($143–$209) suite. AE, DC, MC, V. **Parking:** Free.

This three-story white hotel, next to the Town Hall, features comfortable bedrooms with wheat-colored Finnish textiles and built-in birchwood furniture. From the windows of the chrome and red-velvet bar, you can see the sculpture and well-maintained buildings, which give Lappeenranta much of its charm.

On premises are five restaurants, a popular nightclub, a swimming pool, and five saunas.

INEXPENSIVE

GRAND HOTEL PATRIA, Kauppakatu 21, SF-53920 Lappeenranta. Tel. 953/5751. Fax 953/12-441. 131 rms (all with bath), 4 suites. A/C TV TEL MINIBAR

$ Rates (including breakfast): Fri–Sat year-round and June 15–Aug 15, 290 markkaa ($63.80) single or double; 340 markkaa ($74.80) suite. Sun–Thurs the rest of the year, 400 markkaa ($88) single or double, 450 markkaa ($99) suite. AE, DC, MC, V.

During the mid-1980s, the uncomfortable, circa 1896 Grand Hotel Patria was demolished. In its place rose a newer and ultramodern version bearing the same name. Opened in 1991, it is now generally acknowledged as the finest hotel in town. It's a concrete-and-glass structure with a soaring all-glass tower rising from its center. Within its walls are the Restaurant Fenex, the supper club Nectar, a lobby bar, two saunas, and a health club. Bedrooms each contain a balcony, and are decorated in soft tones of brown and russet. Each suite contains a private sauna.

KARELIA PARK, Korpraalinaktu 1, SF-53810 Lappeenranta. Tel. 953/ 5521. Fax 953/28-454. 90 rms (all with bath). TEL **Bus:** 26.

$ Rates (including breakfast): 200 markkaa ($44) single; 250 markkaa ($55) double. MC, V. **Parking:** Free. **Closed:** Sept–May.

⑤ A mile west of the town center near Lake Saimaa, this hotel has modern, well-equipped rooms. The restaurant is decorated with Finnish dragon symbols. Finnish regional cooking is served. The hotel has two saunas. Good swimming beaches and walking paths are in the neighborhood.

WHERE TO DINE
MODERATE

KASINO, Ainonkatu 10. Tel. 453-0200.
Cuisine: FINNISH. **Reservations:** Recommended.

$ Prices: Appetizers 45–50 markkaa ($9.90–$11); main dishes 85–105 markkaa ($18.70–$23.10). AE, DC, MC, V.
Open: May–Sept, Mon–Sat 11am–2am. **Closed:** Oct–Apr.
While wining and dining here, you can enjoy a splendid view of Lake Saimaa. Kasino has an excellent menu of fish and meat dishes—salmon done different ways, whitefish, Baltic herring, pork, veal, and prime beef. Lunches are offered, and there is occasional dancing to a live orchestra.

KIPPURASARVI, Rantatie in Lemi. Tel. 46-470.
Cuisine: FINNISH. **Reservations:** Required.
$ Prices: Appetizers 32–55 markkaa ($7–$12.10); main dishes 68–90 markkaa ($15–$19.80). MC, V.
Open: Daily 11am–8pm.
About 15 miles north of Lappeenranta, this restaurant specializes in traditional meals and is famous for its *sara,* a mutton dish baked in a wooden trough, served with potatoes, homemade *rieska* (rye) bread, and home brew. Kippurasarvi has four different sections, plus a terrace in summer.

RANTAPUISTO, Kipparintaku 7. Tel. 415-6756.
Cuisine: FINNISH. **Reservations:** Recommended.
$ Prices: Appetizers 28–48 markkaa ($6.20–$10.60); main dishes 68–90 markkaa ($15–$19.80). MC, V.
Open: Mon–Fri 8:30am–11pm, Sat–Sun 11am–11pm.
Furnished in Russian style, this is a cozy wine tavern and dining room is in the town center in the harbor area. Many visitors patronize it only at lunch for its good food at moderate prices, but it's cozier and more festive in the evening. The chef gives you the best of Finnish cuisine. Begin with Baltic herring or try the Finnish salmon or reindeer.

TASSOS, Valtakatu 41. Tel. 451-2965.
Cuisine: GREEK. **Reservations:** Usually not required.
$ Prices: Appetizers 22–55 markkaa ($4.80–$12.10); main dishes 53–105 mark-kaa ($11.70–$23.10). AE, DC, MC, V.
Open: Daily 11am–1am.
One of the few Greek restaurants outside Helsinki, this tavern lies half a mile north of the rail station, 600 yards from the harborfront. Its chef offers dishes from various regions of Greece. Locals come here for an evening of fun. All the lamb and kebab dishes are featured, along with Greek salads and wine.

INEXPENSIVE

VIVA ZAPATA, Kaupakatu 41. Tel. 453-2625.
Cuisine: MEXICAN/CHINESE. **Reservations:** Not required.
$ Prices: Appetizers 12–22 markkaa ($2.60–$4.80); main dishes 25–70 markkaa ($5.50–$15.40). V.
Open: Tues–Sun 11am–1am.
Culinary combinations here might be considered iconoclastic by even the most jaded of palates. Mostly outfitted in bare plank panels with a Tex-Mex decor, Viva Zapata also contains an out-of-the-way corner that's a red-and-black re-creation of an Oriental decor, where Chinese food is served. The establishment's Pancho Villa bar does a busy business, especially in frothy margaritas. Menu specialties include chicken with cashews in oyster sauce, beef in spicy orange sauce, and stir-fried rice with pork, as well as tacos, burritos, enchiladas, and refried beans. Note: You can mix and match any of these items for an unusual gastronomic experience.

A NEARBY CAFÉ

MAJURSKA, Kristinankatu 1. Tel. 453-0554.
Cuisine: FINNISH. **Reservations:** Recommended.
$ Prices: Cakes 16 markkaa ($3.50). No credit cards.
Open: Summer, daily 10am–8pm; off-season, daily 10am–5pm.
The most famous café in Lappeenranta, Majurska is located at the fortress 500 yards

from the town center, and is known for its homemade cakes made from different berries, which are considered to be the best in town. You might also try their tempting onion pie, which many visitors prefer as a light lunch. An adjacent shop has many interesting Finnish items, including wool blankets and animal skins. The decor is in the style of the late 1800s.

5. IMATRA

159 miles NE of Helsinki, 22 miles E of Lappeenranta

GETTING THERE   By Plane   You can fly from Helsinki to Lappeenranta in 30 minutes, then take a bus to Imatra.

By Train   There is frequent service daily between Helsinki and Imatra, taking 3 hours.

By Bus   Imatra has good bus links with Helsinki, taking 3½ hours, and with many neighboring cities, including Savonlinna and Lappeenranta (call 954/23-555 for schedules, which change seasonally).

By Car   Head east from Helsinki toward the Russian frontier all the way to Imatra.

ESSENTIALS   The **Imatra Tourist Office,** Kiikekeskus Mansikkapailkki SF-55120 Imatra (tel. 201-2500), is open Mon–Fri 9am–5pm (June–Aug) and Mon–Fri 8am–4pm (Sept–May). The **telephone area code** for Imatra is 954.

Already an attraction in the days of the Russian czars, Imatra is today a lively industrial and tourist city. Cooperation between Finland and Russia strongly influences Imatra's economy; this city is, after all, on Finland's southeastern edge and shares a 12-mile border with Russia.

WHAT TO SEE & DO

The ○ **Imatra Rapids,** a mighty torrent rushing through a cleft in the rock cut by the Vuoksi River, became Finland's most celebrated tourist attraction in the 18th century when Catherine the Great ruled Russia and came to see them. The fall of the rapids, one of the most forceful in Europe, is 75 feet, stretching almost 1,000 feet. They are surrounded by the Crown Park, established by Czar Nicholas I, which contains a handsome art nouveau building, Valtionhotelli (see below). The largest hydraulic power station in Finland stands on the river. The rapids were harnessed at Imatrankoski, the power being used for a hydroelectric plant, but they are released as a tourist attraction daily in summer.

Besides the rapids, the **Church of the Three Crosses,** Temppelikatu 1 (tel. 47-31-236), designed by Alvar Aalto, is worth seeing; it was the architect's first "multipurpose church." The **Industrial Workers House Museum,** Imatra Ritikanrant (tel. 681-6712), shows how living conditions have changed for Finnish workers since the turn of the century. It is open June and July, Tuesday through Sunday, from 10am to 6pm. In May and August, hours are Saturday and Sunday only, 10am to 6pm. The museum is closed for the rest of the year. Admission is 5 markkaa ($1.10) for adults, 2 markkaa (40¢) for children.

An area called **Niskalampi** was originally built in the 1890s as a cluster of wood-sided working-class houses lying 2½ miles north of Imatra. In 1986, these buildings were restored as part of a Finnish symposium on architecture. Today, privately owned and occupied, they are upscale residences known for their charm and historic distinction. The major street running through the hamlet is Saimaantie. To reach Niskalampi, take bus no. 7 from Imatra's center.

The **Karelian Farmhouse Open-Air Museum,** in the Pässiniemi section (tel. 681-6711), takes you back to a 19th-century South Karelian farm setting and comprises 11 different buildings. The museum is open in June and July, Tuesday through Sunday, from 10am to 6pm. In May and August, hours are Saturday and Sunday only, 10am to 6pm. The museum is closed the rest of the year. Admission is 5 markkaa ($1.10) for adults, 2 markkaa (40¢) for children.

Imatra's beautiful natural surroundings provide excellent opportunities for sports and recreation in both summer and winter. The **Imatra Leisure Center** at Ukonniemi on Lake Saimaa offers a wide range of activities all year. An 18-hole golf course of international standard is in a lovely setting in the meadows and woodland on the shores of Lake Immalanjärvi; it has a clubhouse and a winter practice course, and equipment can be rented.

Imatra's **summer markets** offer special South Karelian delights, and you'll also find interesting items for souvenirs and gifts in the city's cottage-industry shops.

WHERE TO STAY

MODERATE

IMATRAN KYLPYLÄ [Imatra Spa Hotel], Vapaa-Aikakeskus, SF-55420 Imatra. Tel. 954/2051. Fax 954/205-339. 94 rms (all with bath). MINIBAR TV TEL

$ **Rates** (including breakfast): 425 markkaa ($93.50) single; 580 markkaa ($127.60) double. AE, DC, MC, V. **Parking:** Free.

On a forested piece of lakeside land 3½ miles west of the town center, this hostelry is considered the most modern and health-conscious hotel in eastern Finland. Owned by one of Finland's largest industrial conglomerates, it exists for the pursuit of relaxation and better health. Most clients stay here for a week or more, enjoying the array of hydrotherapy, physical therapy, and beauty treatments. Each of the bedrooms is furnished in a comfortable style and has a refrigerator. On the premises is a small library, reading room, and a free washing machine for use by guests.

IMATRAN VALTIONHOTELLI [Imatra State Hotel], Torkkelinkatu 2, SF-55100 Imatra. Tel. 954/605-111. Fax 954/605-120. 150 rms (all with bath). TV TEL

$ **Rates** (including breakfast): Congress section, 460 markkaa ($101.20) single; 560 markkaa ($123.20) double. Castle section, 550 markkaa ($121) single; 720 markkaa ($158.40) double. AE, DC, MC, V. **Parking:** Free.

One of the most unusual hotels in Scandinavia, standing on parklike grounds in the city center, this hostelry was built in 1903 as a vacation hideaway for the grandest titles of the Russian Empire and was designed in semifortified art nouveau grandeur, complete with a series of conical towers and romantically ornate carvings. In 1988 it was almost completely rebuilt, and today the castlelike hotel has bedrooms that are undeniably stylish, each with a color scheme that decorators re-created from faded photographs, carpeting woven by a Dutch factory to the original abstract patterns, and all the modern electronic conveniences. Additional bedrooms were added in a glass-and-steel annex, the Congress Hotel, which features saunas and a greenhouse-style bar. A total of 96 rooms in the Congress section have a minibar.

INEXPENSIVE

HOTEL MARTINA, Lappeentie 3, SF-55100 Imatra. Tel. 954/63-555. Fax 054/65-902. 68 rms (all with bath). MINIBAR TV TEL

$ **Rates** (including breakfast): Sept–May, 300 markkaa ($66) single; 400 markkaa ($88) double. June–Aug, 200 markkaa ($44) single; 300 markkaa ($66) double. AE, DC, MC, V. **Parking:** Free.

Originally built in 1937, and fronted with blocks of local stone, this hotel was completely renovated into a more modern format in 1990. Set in the center of town, some of its rear windows overlook the raging current of the famous river. Bedrooms are soothingly outfitted in tones of subdued pink and white. On the premises are two restaurants, Valentino's and Martina's, and a boisterous pub, Rock House.

WHERE TO DINE
MODERATE

CASTLE ROOM, in the Imatran Valtionhotelli, Torkkelinkatu 2. Tel. 605-111.
   Cuisine: INTERNATIONAL. **Reservations:** Recommended.
$ **Prices:** Appetizers 46–68 markkaa ($10.10–$15); main dishes 89–110 markkaa ($19.60–$24.20). AE, DC, MC, V.
   Open: Lunch Mon–Fri 11am–2pm, Sat–Sun noon–3pm; dinner daily 6–10pm.
A turn-of-the-century dining room, this place has walls stenciled with art nouveau impressions of Karelian designs and Gothic-inspired arches. The menu here might include several preparations of salmon, a three-pepper beefsteak, noisettes of veal with bacon, and roast chicken with kiwi-and-apple stuffing.

KEISARISALI, in the Imatran Valtionhotelli, Torkkelinkatu 2. Tel. 605-111.
   Cuisine: RUSSIAN. **Reservations:** Required.
$ **Prices:** Appetizers 45–85 markkaa ($9.90–$18.70); main dishes 88–125 markkaa ($19.40–$27.50). AE, DC, MC, V.
   Open: Dinner only, daily 6–10pm.
Steeped in the Russian style, this downtown restaurant occupies the ground-floor premises that were once reserved for the exclusive use of the Russian czar. Smaller and more intimate than the hotel dining room next door, it has as its centerpiece a large 1987 impressionist painting of the nearby rapids and also features a stenciled ceiling and antique chairs. Full meals might include shashlik of chicken (inspired by a late 19th-century recipe), chicken cutlet Kiev, fried whitefish, and Russian-style poached salmon.

INEXPENSIVE

BUTTENHOFF CAFÉ-RESTAURANT, Lappeentie 4. Tel. 613-16.
   Cuisine: INTERNATIONAL. **Reservations:** Recommended.
$ **Prices:** Appetizers 28–48 markkaa ($6.20–$10.60); main dishes 48–85 markkaa ($10.60–$18.70). No credit cards.
   Open: Mon–Tues 8:30am–11:30pm, Wed–Thurs 8:30am–10:30pm, Fri 8:30am–1am, Sat 9am–11:30pm, Sun 11:30am–7:30pm.
In the center of town one floor above street level, this restaurant is decorated in traditional Karelian style. It's a cozy place to have lunch, and the menu offers such dishes as borscht made according to grandmother's own recipe, reindeer pot roast, specialties from the Russian kitchen—including chicken Kiev—and such international fare as tournedos with morels or pepper steak. The kitchen also turns out pizzas and a number of Karelian dishes. Certain nights are devoted to Russian food, others to French cuisine.

KARJALAN PORTTI (Gate of Karelia), Asematie 1, Rauha. Tel. 288-80.
   Cuisine: KARELIAN. **Reservations:** Recommended.
$ **Prices:** Appetizers 12–28 markkaa ($2.60–$6.20); main dishes 35–65 markkaa ($7.70–$14.30). MC, V.
   Open: Summer, daily 10am–8pm. **Closed:** Off-season.
Its country Victorian gingerbread and paneled walls re-create the elaborate and ornate carpentry that once helped make Karelia so famous. The restaurant is in the village of Rauha, about 2½ miles southwest of Imatra, and combines an antiques store (the only one around) with a pleasant restaurant. In winter it offers a Karelian buffet lavishly set out on trestle tables. Main dishes are likely to include filet

of roast reindeer with juniperberries, Karelian steak in a pot, and pepper steak, plus an array of sandwiches and daily platters.

6. SAVONLINNA

209 miles N of Helsinki, 143 miles N of Lappeenranta

GETTING THERE   By Plane   Two to four Finnair flights travel here daily from Helsinki, taking 50 minutes.

By Train   Trains run daily between Helsinki and Savonlinna, taking 5 hours.

By Bus   Daily buses connect Helsinki with Savonlinna. If you leave Helsinki on the 11:30am bus, arrival time in Savonlinna is 5pm.

By Car   From Helsinki, take the E4 to Lahti, then connect with Route 5 northeast. Take Route 5 to the junction of Route 14 going east to Savonlinna.

ESSENTIALS   The **Savonlinna Tourist Service,** at Puistokatu 1, SF-57100 Savonlinna (tel. 957/13-492), is open daily 8am–6pm (June 1–22, Aug 3–31), daily 8am–10pm (June 23–Aug 2), and Mon–Fri 9am–4pm (Sept–May). In summer, a second office is open on the Marketplace daily 8am–10pm. The **telephone area code** for Savonlinna is 957.

SPECIAL EVENTS   The ✪ **Savonlinna Opera Festival,** traditionally held in July in Olavinlinna Castle, is an important international event. For information, contact the Savonlinna Opera Festival Office, Olavinkatu 35, SF-57130 Savonlinna (tel. 957/514-700). Tickets range from 230 to 600 markkaa ($50.60 to $132).

Founded in 1639, Savonlinna is the oldest town in eastern Finland. Its major attraction, the castle of Olavinlinna (see below), dates back to 1475, built to protect what was then the eastern border of Sweden. The town slowly grew up on the islands around the castle.

The area around the town, forming part of the Saimaa waterway, has more lakes than any other area in Finland. Because of its strategic location, Savonlinna has been the scene of many battles. In fact, it belonged to Russia for 70 years until Savonlinna was returned to the Grand Duchy of Finland in 1812. In its heyday, wealthy families from St. Petersburg used Savonlinna as a holiday and health resort.

The old spa familiar to czarist Russia burned in 1964, and only a few czarist villas and the Wahna Kasino summer restaurant were spared. However, the Kylpylä Hotelli Casino, Kasinonsaari (see below), attracts spa enthusiasts to the area.

WHAT TO SEE & DO

The **Olavinlinna Castle** (Castle of St. Olof) (tel. 57-21-164), a three-towered medieval fortress founded in 1475, is the major attraction. It's on a small island in the middle of Kyronsalmi Straits and is reached by a rotating bridge. Some medieval features remain in the castle rooms. There have been several stages in the construction of Olavinlinna, one undertaken at the end of the 18th century, when the Russians replaced a badly damaged tower with a massive three-story structure called the Thick Bastion. Admission is 14 markkaa ($3.10) for adults, 7 markkaa ($1.50) for children. The castle is open June to August 21, daily 10am–5pm; the rest of the year, daily 10am–3pm. A summer opera festival is held here (see above). Bus: 1, 2, 3, 4.

Suruton Villa, previously the summer residence of Aino Ackte, Mika Waltari, and Eino Leino, is in Savonlinna on Kasinonsaari island. Since its restoration, an exhibition presenting the history of the opera festivals is displayed here.

Other sites include the **SS *Salama* museum ship,** built in Vyborg in 1874; it's the only steam schooner in Finland—perhaps in the world. The ship is docked in Riihisaari and is open June through August, Tuesday through Sunday from 11am to 5pm. Adults pay 10 markkaa ($2.20) for admission; children, 6 markkaa ($1.30).

The **Marketplace** in Savonlinna is one of the most interesting in Scandinavia and is the town's focal point in summer. As in Venice, sightseeing in Savonlinna is done by boat. Many around-the-town **cruises** depart from the harbor every day. In addition to the local tours, there are cruises to Punkaharju, Puumala, Rantasalmi, Kuopio, Mikkeli, and Lappeenranta.

Retretti, in Punkaharju (tel. 314-253), is an art center opened in 1982 in a grotto about 14 miles south of Savonlinna. It includes a concert hall, and during the opera festival in Savonlinna, chamber-music concerts are presented here. The major attraction is an exhibition of sculptures displayed on various levels of the cave with extraordinary lighting effects. It can be reached by boat from the Marketplace in Savonlinna; the trip costs 40 markkaa ($8.80) for adults, 20 markkaa ($4.40) for children 12 or under. It can also be reached by bus from the Savonlinna bus station, a round-trip costing 20 markkaa ($4.40). Entrance to the art center costs 60 markkaa ($13.20) for adults, 25 markkaa ($5.50) for children 7 to 16. It's open from May 22 to August 29, daily 10am to 7pm, and in July daily 10am until 8pm.

WHERE TO STAY

MODERATE

KYLPYLÄ HOTELLI CASINO, Kasinonsaari, SF-57101 Savonlinna. Tel. 957/57-500. Fax 957/125-24. 79 rms (all with bath). MINIBAR TV TEL **Bus:** 1, 2, 3, 4.

$ Rates (including breakfast): 500 markkaa ($110) single; 590–690 markkaa ($129.80–$151.80) double. AE, DC, MC, V. **Parking:** Free.

Accessible by walking across a bridge from the central railway station or driving just over half a mile, the hotel has a first-class restaurant and modern facilities including baths, clay treatment, massage, a swimming pool, and saunas. Bedrooms are well maintained and comfortably furnished, each with a balcony. The "islands of the Casino" form a quiet, relaxing natural park—yet they're right in the center of Savonlinna.

SUMMER HOTELS

PUNKAHAARJUN VALTIONHOTELLI, SF-58450 Punkaharju. Tel. 957/311-761. Fax 957/311-784. 28 rms (15 with bath), 15 cottages. TV TEL

$ Rates (including breakfast): 380 markkaa ($83.60) single without bath, 405–530 markkaa ($89.10–$116.60) single with bath; 465 markkaa ($102.30) double without bath, 555–615 markkaa ($122.10–$135.30) double with bath. MC, V. **Parking:** Free. **Closed:** Sept–Apr.

This hotel, surrounded by parkland, evolved from a forester's house erected on the top of Punkaharju ridge 17 miles from Savonlinna in 1845 by order of Czar Nicholas I, and the building became the center of Finland's first tourist business. In addition to the 28 rooms, there are 15 cottages rented in summer. Bedrooms are furnished in a comfortably old-fashioned way. The hotel has a restaurant and summer dining on the sun terrace where Finnish specialties are served. Sports facilities are on the premises. There are warm coves with sandy beaches.

SUMMERHOTEL MALAKIAS, Pihlajavedenkuja 6, SF-57170 Savonlinna. Tel. 957/23-283. Fax 957/12-524. 220 rms (all with bath). TEL

$ Rates (including breakfast): 200–260 markkaa ($44–$57.20) single; 270–320 markkaa ($59.40–$70.40) double. AE, DC, MC, V. **Parking:** Free. **Closed:** Mid-Aug to May.

On Route 14 a mile outside town, this hotel is perfectly suitable for a Finnish holiday. The rooms are comfortably furnished and contain small kitchenettes. The hotel has a breakfast room, and guests often take their meals at the far more luxurious Spa Hotel Casino, which is run by the same management.

SUMMERHOTEL VUORILINNA, Kasinonsaari, SF-57130 Savonlinna. Tel. 957/504-94. Fax 957/125-24. 215 rms (all with bath). TV TEL **Bus:** 1, 2, 3, 4.

$ Rates (including breakfast): 230–350 markkaa ($50.60–$77) single; 300–400 markkaa ($66–$88) double. AE, DC, MC, V. **Parking:** Free. **Closed:** Sept–May.

In the courtyard square of the Spa Hotel Casino, you can stay right on Casino Island, within walking distance over a footbridge to the center of town, enjoying all the facilities of the larger hotel. All the simply furnished units are equipped with shower, kitchenette, and wall-to-wall carpeting. There is no elevator. The Wahna Kasino, next to the hotel, is a favored rendezvous on a summer evening. The island is in the midst of beautiful lakeland scenery.

WHERE TO DINE
MODERATE

RESTAURANT SHIP *HOPEASALMI*, Kauppatori. Tel. 21-701 in summer, 21-092 in off-season.
   Cuisine: FINNISH. **Reservations:** Recommended. **Bus:** 1, 2, 3, 4.
$ Prices: Appetizers 24–35 markkaa ($5.30–$7.70); main dishes 72–125 markkaa ($15.80–$27.50). AE, MC, V.
   Open: Summer, daily 9am–1 or 2am; off-season, Fri–Sat 5pm–1am.
In front of the Marketplace, this restaurant complex consists of a wharfside terrace for summertime drinks and dining, and a pierbound passenger steamer originally built in 1903 and now permanently in dock. There is also a smaller boat for food service, which in 1927 was built as a lake-district cargo ship. The house specialty is a small Lake Saimaa freshwater fish, called *muikka*. Several are fried and served on the same plate with a green sauce and small new boiled potatoes. The fish soup is a good beginning, and you can also order pepper steak and filet of reindeer.

WAHNA KASINO, Kylpyläitoksentie Kasinonsaari. Tel. 22-572.
   Cuisine: FINNISH. **Reservations:** Recommended. **Bus:** 1, 2, 3, 4.
$ Prices: Appetizers 38–52 markkaa ($8.40–$11.40); main dishes 58–108 markkaa ($12.80–$23.80). DC.
   Open: Late May–late Aug, Tues–Sat 8pm–1:30am.
Adjacent to the spa hotel, the Kylpylä Hotelli Casino (see "Where to Stay," above), 220 yards from the railroad station, this is the preferred spot for dining. The pink-clapboard Wahna preserves the old atmosphere so beloved by vacationing members of the Russian imperial court. Meals are likely to include "gentleman's hash," fried rainbow trout, and salad of cold smoked salmon. Guests can dance to live band music.

MAJAKKA [The Lighthouse], Satanakatu 11. Tel. 21-456.
   Cuisine: SEAFOOD/FINNISH. **Reservations:** Not required. **Bus:** 1, 2, 3, 4.
$ Prices: Appetizers 20–30 markkaa ($4.40–$6.60); main dishes 45–100 markkaa ($9.90–$22). AE, DC, MC, V.
   Open: Daily 11am–midnight.
Located in the town center, this cozy restaurant and bar offers dishes like fried wendace, deep-fried tiny fish from the Baltic, served with mashed potatoes and vegetables, and beefsteak Majakka. The restaurant's building shelters about a dozen stores as well.

SNELLMAN'S, Olavinkatu 31. Tel. 273-104.
   Cuisine: FINNISH. **Reservations:** Required in summer. **Bus:** 1, 2, 3, 4.
$ Prices: Appetizers 18–42 markkaa ($4–$9.20); main dishes 35–102 markkaa ($7.70–$22.40); fixed-price lunch 55 markkaa ($12.10). AE, DC, MC, V.
   Open: Daily 11am–10pm.
Lying only 100 yards east of the Marketplace, this restaurant is in a century-old building. One of its features is its three-course lunch, which includes generous helpings from a fish and salad buffet, plus a main dish and a "cocktail" of smoked reindeer, fried rainbow trout, roast pepper steak, spicy shashlik with rice, and noisettes of veal with slightly salted salmon. Many of the loyal patrons come here for the roast lamb with a sour-cream sauce. Adjacent is the English-style Pub Nelson.

EXCURSIONS

At least 10 different lake steamers use Savolinna's harbor as a midsummer base. Throughout the day, beginning around 9am until sometimes late in the midnight twilight, about one boat per hour will depart for sightseeing cruises. Cruise rates vary with the itinerary, but range from 30 to 40 markkaa ($6.60 to $8.80) for adults, and from 10 to 20 markkaa ($2.20 to $4.40) for children. The tourist office (see above) will supply schedules and details.

There is regular boat traffic to **Punkaharju** by the SS *Heindvesi* and local cruises in Punkaharju on the MS *Princess* every day. At Punkaharju you can take a bus for local sightseeing, which includes a visit to a summer art exhibit, a look at a typical holiday village, and a leisurely lunch at a restaurant in the holiday village or at Valtionhotelli, an old and historic hotel.

At Punkaharju, 15½ miles southeast of Savonlinna, Lake Puruvesi is divided by a long Ice Age ridge stretching for 4½ miles and forming a causeway between the Puruvesi and Pihlajavesi lakes. This "thread" has been turned into a national park, one of the most famous and photographed beauty spots of Finland. You can also reach Punkaharju by bus or by train, but the preferred method is by boat.

Kerimäki, 14½ miles northeast of Savonlinna and connected by frequent bus service, has the biggest wooden church in the world. Built more than a century ago and large enough to accommodate 3,300 parishioners, the admission-free church is open May to September, Monday through Friday from 9am to 8pm, Saturday from 9am to 6pm, and Sunday from 11am to 8pm. To climb the adjacent bell tower, adults pay 5 markkaa ($1.10); children 12 or under, 2 markkaa (40¢).

In addition, by boat you can visit the **Hytermä nature reserve and museum islands,** where you'll see a large folkloric collection. Nearby is **Putkinotko,** the setting for Joel Lehtonen's novel of the same name. A little museum, with mementos of the author, is open June 19 to June 25, Tuesday through Sunday; daily from June 26 to August 6, daily; and August 7 to 19, Tuesday through Sunday. When it's open, visiting hours are always noon to 6pm, and admission is 5 markkaa ($1.10) for adults, 3 markkaa (70¢) for children.

If you want to spend a leisurely day on a boat while viewing the beautiful archipelago, take a cruise to Kuopio on the MS *Puijo* or MS *Kuopio.*

---

7. JOENSUU

273 miles NE of Helsinki, 84 miles E of Kuopio

GETTING THERE **By Plane** Joensuu has air links with Helsinki and any number of small towns in Finland. Flight frequency depends on the time of year. You can take an 11am plane from Helsinki and be in Joensuu 45 minutes later. The airport lies 7 miles outside Joensuu.

By Train Seven trains a day run between Helsinki and Lappeenranta, with continuing service to Joensuu.

By Bus Buses run north to Joensuu via Lappeenranta, and there are also bus connections through Savonlinna in the west. A 9:30am bus leaving Lappeenranta will arrive in Joensuu by 1:30pm.

By Car Take Route 6 all the way from Helsinki, going via Lappeenranta.

ESSENTIALS The **North Karelian Tourist Office,** at Koskikatu 1 (tel. 973/167-5300), is open Mon–Fri 9am–6pm and Sat 9am–2pm (June 15–Aug 15) and Mon 8am–5pm and Tues–Fri 9am–4pm (Aug 16–June 14).

The **telephone area code** for Joensuu is 973.

Joensuu, founded in the mid-19th century at the mouth of the Pieliskjoki River, is the major municipality of northern Karelia. A busy little city with a population of 47,000, it's the administrative and commercial center of the district. It is also a university town and has a flourishing local cultural life.

WHAT TO SEE & DO

The **Town Hall,** at Rantakatu 4, was designed in 1914 by Eliel Saarinen, who was the architect responsible for the famous railway station in Helsinki. Nearby at Rantakatu 2 you may want to purchase local handcrafts, for which the district is so well known. These include handwoven linen cloth, hand-knitted goods, shoes or knapsacks of birch bark, and soft leather slippers, among other items.

Both the Karelian and Orthodox traditions are still cherished, in rural areas. For a glimpse of that life, you can visit **Pohjois-Karjalan Museo,** Siltakato 1 (tel. 167-5384), on the island of Ilosaari in Karjalanto. The museum displays memorabilia from northern Karelia, including textiles, crafts, and folk art. It is open on Tuesday, Thursday, and Friday from noon to 4pm, Wednesday from noon to 8pm, Saturday from 10am to 4pm, and Sunday from 10am to 6pm. Depending on the exhibitions, adults pay an admission ranging from 5 to 15 markkaa ($1.10 to $3.30); and children, 3 to 10 markkaa (70¢ to $2.20). A restaurant on the premises serves traditional food and drink Tuesday through Friday from noon to 4pm (to 8pm on Wednesday), Saturday from 10am to 4pm, and Sunday from 10am to 6pm.

The surrounding area still carries out many of the traditions of the Orthodox church, and several religious processions, known as *praasniekka,* occur in summer.

On the western shore of Lake Pielinen, on which you can take boat excursions in summer, the **Koli Hills** rise to 1,070 feet, the highest point in northern Karelia. They are about 40 miles due north of the city and offer some of the most dramatic lake and river views in Finland.

If you're driving, you can continue north to **Nurmes,** which lies on an inlet of the northern part of Lake Pielinen. Here the chief attraction is the **Bomba Karelian Village** at Ritoniemi, which is a log manor house, beautifully decorated in a regional style. Accommodations are provided in holiday cottages, and Karelian food is served.

You can explore the eastern side of the lake going through **Lieksa,** where you can visit the **Pielinen Outdoor Museum,** Pappilantie 2 (tel. 204-90), which has 60 buildings containing authentic Karelian furnishings. Located along Route 73 less than a mile from the town center of Lieksa, the museum is open mid-May to mid-August, daily from 9am to 6pm; mid-August to mid-September, daily from 10am to 6pm; and mid-September to mid-May, Tuesday through Friday from 10am to 3pm and on Saturday and Sunday from 11am to 3pm. Admission is 10 markkaa ($2.20) for adults and 2 markkaa (40¢) for children 12 and under. Some 16 miles from the town on the eastern border, the **Ruunaa wilderness rapids** thunder down. At **Ilomantsi** village, 45 miles east of Joensuu, is an authentic center of Karelian culture, with a viewing platform at the top of the Ilomantsi water tower.

In this once war-torn area of eastern Finland, especially in **Petkeljarvi National Park,** you'll find many reminders of lost wars with the Russians, including trenches, machine-gun nests, and graveyards of fallen soldiers.

WHERE TO STAY

INEXPENSIVE

SOKOS HOTEL JOENSUU VAAKUNA, Torikatu 20, SF-80100 Joensuu. Tel. 973/27-311. Fax 973/27-323. 68 rms (all with bath). TV TEL

$ Rates (including breakfast): June 15–Aug 1 and Fri–Sat year-round, 350 markkaa ($77) single or double. Sun–Thurs the rest of the year, 400 markkaa ($88) single or double. AE, DC, MC, V. **Parking:** Free.

Its proximity to the town's Market Square makes this hotel's pleasant pub and dance restaurant popular with commercial travelers. In three upper stories are the rooms, including seven for nonsmokers, furnished comfortably and attractively in a modern style. In the hotel's restaurant you can have dinner Monday through Friday from 4 to

8pm for 85 markkaa ($18.70), and Saturday and Sunday from 6 to 8pm for 65 markkaa ($14.30).

SOKOS HOTEL KIMMEL, Itäranta 1, SF-80100 Joensuu. Tel. 973/1771.
Fax 973/177-2112. 230 rms (all with bath), 3 suites. MINIBAR TV TEL
$ Rates (including breakfast): June–Aug and Fri–Sat year-round, 395 markkaa ($86.90) single or double. Sun–Thurs the rest of the year, 490 markkaa ($107.80) single or double. Year-round, from 800 markkaa ($176) suite. AE, DC, MC, V.
Parking: Free.

Located on a peninsula of flat land in the town center, this modern hotel serves as a social centers. Bedrooms are cozily and efficiently furnished with Finnish textiles and built-in birchwood furniture. The hotel has an illuminated swimming pool and a sauna with an adjacent snack bar. Fransmanni restaurant features tasty food, and Moritz nightclub has a DJ.

WHERE TO DINE

MODERATE

TEATTERI-RAVINTOLA, Rantakatu 4. Tel. 293-06.
Cuisine: FINNISH. **Reservations:** Recommended.
$ Prices: Appetizers 45–55 markkaa ($9.90–$12.10); main dishes 58–105 markkaa ($12.80–$23.10); 4-course lunch 55 markkaa ($12.10). AE, MC, V.
Open: Daily 11am–1am.

This charming restaurant, like a Ratskeller, is in the basement of the Town Hall. The fixed-price lunch includes access to the salad table. At night, you can enjoy such dishes as fried pike perch flavored with herbs, sautéed salmon with caper sauce, and filet of beef.

---

8. KUOPIO

244 miles NE of Helsinki, 89 miles NE of Jyväskylä

GETTING THERE **By Plane** Frequent 35-minute flights connect Helsinki with Kuopio. The airport lies 11 miles from the center.

By Train Frequent trains make the 5-hour run between Helsinki and Kuopio, and six trains a day go between Kuopio and Jyväskylä, taking 3¾ hours. Five trains a day take 1¾ hours to run between Mikkeli and Kuopio.

By Bus Daily buses make the 5-hour run between Kuopio and Helsinki, and three buses a day run from Jyväskylä to Kuopio, taking 2¼ hours.

By Car From Helsinki, head north on the E4 to Lahti, which will join the E80 at Jämsä. From there, continue northeast along the E80 until you reach Kuopio.

By Steamer Traveling by steamer takes 12 hours from Savonlinna. Kuopio is the northernmost point served by the Saimaa lake steamers.

ESSENTIALS The **City Tourist Office,** at Haapaniemenkatu 17 (tel. 971/182-584), is open Mon–Fri 8am–6pm and Sat 8am–2pm (June 4–Aug 19) and Mon–Fri 9:30am–4pm (Aug 20–June 3). The **telephone area code** for Kuopio is 971.

The tourist capital of the eastern lake district of central Finland, Kuopio is the cultural and economic center of Savo province and is located in one of Finland's most beautiful areas. Visitors flock to this old lakeside garrison town in summer to take cruises on the Saimaa steamers, some of which are rather antiquated. Overlooking beautiful Lake Kallavesi, the town is a good starting point for excursions to Savonlinna. There is daily service on a Saimaa steamer, and the trip takes about 12 hours.

WHAT TO SEE & DO

Dominating Kuopio is the 770-foot **Puijo Hill,** a wooded area about 1½ miles northwest of the town. In summer it is reached by a good road, and in winter it's covered with ski trails. At the top of this hill is a tower and a restaurant, both discussed below.

The town center is the lively **Market Square,** called Kauppatori in Finnish, which contains fruit and vegetable displays. The **town hall** here dates from 1882. If you're visiting in summer, you can explore the narrow peninsula of **Vainolanniemi,** which has a bathing beach, a summer restaurant, and playgrounds.

PUIJON TORNI, at the top of Puijo Hill. Tel. 114-841.

This tower (1963), with a revolving restaurant (see "Where to Dine," below), is at the site of the international Puijo Winter Games, (1 mile north of the city), a wooded hillside that's a major summer and winter recreational area. The tower offers two panoramic viewing platforms, with a revolving floor moving at 360° per hour.

Admission: 15 markkaa ($3.30) adults, 5 markkaa ($1.10) children; free if you dine at the restaurant.

Open: June–Aug, daily 8am–11pm, May and Sept, daily 10am–6pm; Oct–Apr, Sat–Sun 10am–6pm. **Bus:** 3, 5.

ORTHODOX CHURCH MUSEUM, Karjalankatu 1. Tel. 118-818.

In the southeastern sector of town, this church has collections from old Karelian churches and monasteries, unique in the West. It is considered a major cultural statement. Its rich and beautiful exhibits mirror the history of the Orthodox church and include collections from such ancient monasteries as Valamo, Konevista, and Petsamo.

Admission: 10 markkaa ($2.20) adults, 4 markkaa (90¢) children 12 or under.

Open: May–Aug, Tues–Sun 10am–4pm; Sept–Apr, Mon–Fri 10am–2pm, Sat–Sun noon–5pm. **Bus:** 7.

KUOPION KORTTELIMUSEO [Old Kuopio Museum], Kirkkakatu 22. Tel. 182-625.

✪ Occupying an entire block of the town in the town center 200 yards south of Kuopio Church, this museum contains a representative section of the town's old, low wooden buildings, some on their original sites and others moved here and restored. The museum shows how people lived in Kuopio from the late 18th century to the 1930s, with residences, warehouses, an old hall of assizes, and other buildings. Guided tours are offered.

Admission: Free.

Open: Mid-May to mid-Sept, Tues and Thurs–Sun 10am–5pm, Wed 10am–7pm; mid-Sept to mid-May, Tues–Sun 10am–3pm. **Bus:** 7.

WHERE TO STAY

MODERATE

ARCTIA HOTEL KUOPIO, Satamakatu 1, SF-70100 Kuopio. Tel. 971/195-111. Fax 971/195-170. 141 rms (all with bath), 4 suites. A/C MINIBAR TV TEL **Bus:** 7.

$ **Rates** (including breakfast): June–July and Fri–Sat year-round, 325 markkaa ($71.50) single; 390 markkaa ($85.80) double; from 900 markkaa ($198) suite. Sun–Thurs the rest of the year, 520–580 markkaa ($114.40–$127.60) single; 690–700 markkaa ($151.80–$154) double; from 1,300 markkaa ($286) suite. AE, DC, MC, V. **Parking:** Free. **Closed:** Dec 22–26.

This stylish hotel is set on manicured lawns at the edge of a lake near the city center. The bedrooms are attractively furnished and decorated; the most desirable ones have windows opening onto the lake. The terrace overlooks the lake and is lit by torches at night. The hotel has a gourmet restaurant, the Messmarja, plus a nightclub, Moonriver. There are three saunas, an indoor swimming pool, a solarium, and a massage room.

HOTEL CUMULUS, Puijonkatu 32, SF-70100 Kuopio. Tel. 971/154-111. Fax 971/154-299. 143 rms (all with bath). MINIBAR TV TEL **Bus:** 7.

$ Rates (including breakfast): June 19–Aug 2 and Fri–Sat year-round, 270 markkaa ($59.40) single; 390 markkaa ($85.80) double. Sun–Thurs the rest of the year, 425 markkaa ($93.50) single; 570 markkaa ($125.40) double. AE, DC, MC, V. **Parking:** 35 markkaa ($7.70).

A handsome modern building in the town center, this chain-run hotel has a concrete facade, metallic windows, and a terrazzo-floored lobby. Bedrooms are well furnished and comfortable. The hotel has three restaurants, three saunas, a swimming pool, and a sauna bar. Its traditional Citybar is one of the most frequented in town.

HOTEL ISO-VALKEINEN, Päiväranta, SF-70420 Kuopio. Tel. 971/341-444. Fax 971/341-344. 100 rms (all with bath). TV TEL

$ Rates (including breakfast): June 9–Aug 13, 325 markkaa ($71.50) single; 400 markkaa ($88) double. Aug 14–June 8, 460 markkaa ($101.20) single; 570 markkaa ($125.40) double. AE, MC, V. **Parking:** Free.

At the edge of a lake 3 miles north of town along Route 5, this hotel overlooks an unspoiled natural setting. Motorists can park near their bedrooms. The staff can recommend walking trails. Bedrooms are furnished in a modern, functional style. There are two restaurants and a bar. Facilities include three saunas and a swimming pool.

SOKOS HOTEL PUIJONSARVI, Minna Canthinkatu 16, SF-70100 Kuopio. Tel. 971/170-111. Fax 971/170-117. 231 rms (all with bath), 5 suites. MINIBAR TV TEL **Bus:** 7.

$ Rates (including breakfast): June 12–Aug 9 and Fri–Sat year-round, 400 markkaa ($88) single or double; from 700 markkaa ($154) suite. Sun–Thurs the rest of the year, 430–480 markkaa ($94.60–$105.60) single; 550–600 markkaa ($121–$132) double; from 1,300 markkaa ($286) suite. AE, DC, MC, V. **Parking:** 50 markkaa ($11).

This centrally located brick hotel with bay windows is above a row of shops built into its street level. Furnishings are in an attractive modern style. The hotel has two restaurants, one with cabaret shows, and a lobby-level bar with its own summer outdoor terrace. Four saunas, a Turkish bath, and a Jacuzzi are on the premises.

INEXPENSIVE

SAVONIA, Sammakkolammentie 2, SF-70200 Puijo. Tel. 971/209-111. Fax 971/225-707. 50 rms (all with bath). MINIBAR TV TEL **Bus:** 3, 5.

$ Rates (including breakfast): 270 markkaa ($59.40) single; 330 markkaa ($72.60) double. Summerhotel Savonia (June 1–Aug 8), 200 markkaa ($44) single; 240 markkaa ($52.80) double. AE, DC, MC, V. **Parking:** Free. **Closed:** Dec 15–Jan 7 and Mar 28–Apr 2.

S A student-run red-brick and concrete hotel near Puijo Tower a mile north of the center, this hotel offers one of the best bargains around. The rooms are furnished in a modern, functional style. In addition to the 50 rooms listed above, an additional 26 rooms are offered in a nearby annex, Summerhotel Savonia. The hotel also operates a fine restaurant run by students who are learning the hotel trade; for dinner, expect to pay around 95 markkaa ($20.90).

SPORTHOTEL PUIJO, Puijon Torni, SF-70330 Puijo. Tel. 971/261-4841. Fax 971/123-735. 20 rms (18 with bath). TV TEL **Bus:** 3, 5.

$ Rates (including breakfast and sauna): 250 markkaa ($55) single without bath, 300 markkaa ($66) single with bath; 300 markkaa ($66) double without bath, 400 markkaa ($88) double with bath. AE, DC, MC, V. **Parking:** Free. **Closed:** Dec 23–24.

Located adjacent to Puijon Torni, a mile north of town, this hotel mainly functions as a winter ski hotel. The bedrooms have simple birch furnishings. The hotel has three saunas and a rustic restaurant.

WHERE TO DINE
MODERATE

MUSTA LAMMAS, Satamakatu 4. Tel. 123-494.
   Cuisine: SEAFOOD/CONTINENTAL. **Reservations:** Recommended. **Bus:** 7.
$ **Prices:** Appetizers 45–80 markkaa ($9.90–$17.60); main dishes 88–120 markkaa ($19.40–$26.40). AE, DC, MC, V.
   Open: Mon–Fri 11am–midnight, Sat 2pm–midnight.
In a windowless cellar that was formerly a brewery, this is the gourmet restaurant of the city. The menu is not extensive, but is well chosen, and whenever possible, fresh ingredients are used—including fish from the lakes of eastern Finland. Try whitefish in foil, lobster cardinal, or paupiettes of sole in lobster sauce.

INEXPENSIVE

PUIJON TORNI, in the Puijo Tower. Tel. 114-841.
   Cuisine: FINNISH. **Reservations:** Recommended. **Bus:** 3, 5.
$ **Prices:** Appetizers 30–57 markkaa ($6.60–$12.50); main dishes 45–95 markkaa ($9.90–$20.90); fixed-price menus 45 markkaa ($9.90), 65 markkaa ($14.30), 75 markkaa ($16.50), 85 markkaa ($18.70). AE, MC, V.
   Open: June–Aug, daily 11am–10pm. Off-season, lunch daily 11am–2pm, dinner daily 5–8pm.
If you want to enjoy good food and an excellent view from the highest tower in eastern Finland, come to this revolving restaurant in the Puijo Tower (see "What to See and Do," above). The restaurant makes one revolution per hour, and the panoramic view of the woodlands and lakeland scenery is extraordinary. The highest platform is almost 750 feet above Lake Kallavesi. Meals might include reindeer steak, rainbow trout, or fried flounder.

TAVERNA, Kauppakatu 40-42. Tel. 127-646.
   Cuisine: FINNISH. **Reservations:** Recommended. **Bus:** 3, 21.
$ **Prices:** Appetizers 35–48 markkaa ($7.70–$10.60); main dishes 42–120 markkaa ($9.20–$26.40). AE, DC, MC, V.
   Open: Mon–Sat 11am–7pm.
This restaurant is a block west of the marketplace. If available, request an order of *kalakukko*, a pie made from pork and a small whitefish native to Finland. Other main dishes include chateaubriand, coeur de filet à la maison, and grilled rainbow trout.

CHAPTER 38
FINNISH LAPLAND

Above the Arctic Circle, Lapland comprises one-third of Finland, the country's northernmost as well as its largest and most sparsely populated province. It is often called "The Last Wilderness in Europe," and you will experience a spacious land of unspoiled nature and scenic grandeur.

Lapland has four seasons, but the people sometimes talk about eight seasons a year. In the summer, the vegetation sprouts, flowers, and bears fruit all within 3 months, because the sun doesn't set for weeks on end. In Utsjoki, in the northernmost part of Lapland, starting in the middle of May, the sun does not set for nearly 70 days. If summer with its "Midnight Sun" is an extraordinary experience for the traveler, then so is the polar night, the twilight time of the year, when darkness is never really total, the sun glowing softly on the horizon.

The period of time in October and November, when there is no sun, is called *Kaamos*. Winter is the longest time of the year, but it includes the night light show of the northern lights. After the polar night come the dazzling spring snows, great for skiing until May when the sun gives twice as much light as it did in the dead of winter.

Lapland is a country of great forests, making their management and agriculture the most important sources of income. Finland's longest river, the Kemijoki, runs through the area, and its lower reaches are terraced with seven hydroelectric plants. Lapland also has Western Europe's largest artificial lakes—Lokka and Porttipahta.

Despite human intrusion, this is still a land of bears, wolves, eagles, and wolverines; however, the animal that symbolizes this land is the reindeer, and there are more than 300,000 here. The true natural wilderness has been preserved untouched in many nature reserves.

It is easy to travel to the far reaches of Lapland. Regular flights go to the province's capital, Rovaniemi, and beyond the Arctic Circle to Ivalo. By bus, one can travel comfortably to every corner of the province. Lapland also offers the traveler an array of events including the midsummer celebrations on Ounasvaara, Aavasaksa fells, and in Posio; the International Midnight Sun Film Festival in Sodankylä; the Goldpanning Competition in Tankavaara; the Whitefish Festival in Kukkolankoski; the Cloudberry Fair and Market in Ranua; Hetta's music festival; and the increasingly popular Arctic Canoe Race from Kilpisjärvi to Tornio.

ARCTIC ACCOMMODATIONS There is a great variety of hotels, summer hotels, motels, hostels, and cabins in Lapland, the cheapest being the youth hostels. There are 30 hostels in the province, with prices from 30 to 135 markkaa ($6.60 to $29.70) per night if you have an International Youth Hostel membership card. Otherwise the prices are 45 to 150 markkaa ($9.90 to $33) a night if you have your own sheets. You can also buy or rent sheets here. Many youth hostels have family rooms and even single rooms. For further information, contact the **Finnish Youth Hostel Association,** Yrjönkatu 38B, SF-00100 Helsinki (tel. 90/694-0377).

The summer hotels have higher standards, and the lodging houses (*matkustajakoti*) also have moderate prices—135 to 220 markkaa ($29.70 to $48.40) per person. There are many varieties of cabins, from high-level ones with their own saunas and kitchens to cheaper ones with just beds.

WHAT'S SPECIAL ABOUT FINNISH LAPLAND

Great Towns/Villages

☐ Rovaniemi, the capital of Lapland, a modern town designed by Alvar Aato, the great architect, in the wilderness.

☐ Sodankylä, where the Lapps say the *real* Lapland begins—the gateway to the majestic fell country.

☐ Kemi, the seaport on the Gulf of Bothnia, one of the oldest areas of habitation in Finland.

Ace Attractions

☐ The Arctic Road, one of the world's great engineering feats, stretching for 620 miles to the very edge of Europe.

☐ The 50-mile-long Lake Inarijärvi, in Inari country, containing more than 3,000 islands.

Cool for Kids

☐ Santa Claus Village at the Arctic Circle, outside Rovaniemi, where a child can meet Prancer.

☐ Ranua Wildlife Park, at Ranua, where you can introduce your kids to a large zoo of exotic Lappish animals.

Sporting Activities

☐ Panning for gold at Tankavaara Gold Village, 143 miles north of the Arctic Circle.

Special Events/Festivals

☐ The International Midnight Sun Film Festival in June at Sodankylä, with screenings of the latest films under the Midnight Sun.

Note that the Arctic hotels have high- and low-season prices; high season is March and April. Breakfast is normally included in the prices, and nearly all hotels and motels have saunas.

ARCTIC DINING   There is a wide range of restaurants too, from first class to small cozy coffee bars. From 11am to 1pm on weekdays, many restaurants offer solid lunches at low prices. Priced from 55 markkaa ($12.10), they are usually from a buffet that consists of salads, soups, and main courses, plus desserts. In the evening you can order from an à la carte list or ask for a fixed-price dinner. In the north, don't forget the "Lapland à la carte menu," which includes all the delicacies of the province, such as grouse, reindeer, salmon, and berries.

THE ARCTIC ROAD   North of the Arctic Circle, the Arctic Road lies as far north as the roadless tundras of Alaska, Greenland, and Siberia. The ✪ **Arctic Road,** however, provides easy access to the diverse scenery of the north.

As early as the 1930s, tourists from all over Europe traveled north in their cars, heading for Petsamo, the end point of the Arctic Road at that time. Today the Arctic Road is an adventure, stretching for more than 620 miles. It starts near the Arctic Circle at Rovaniemi and passes through central and northern Lapland, as it heads toward the Arctic Ocean and eastern Finnmark, on the very edge of Europe.

The views along the Arctic Road reveal the respect people have for their environment. Extensive areas have been protected and preserved for future generations to admire.

Modern transportation brings you to the start of your adventure. Rovaniemi, the point of departure, can be reached by car, train, or plane.

SEEING FINNISH LAPLAND

GETTING THERE

Since the whole of northern Finland is a vast wilderness, regular air flights are the fastest way to see the area. Many Americans settle for a quick Midnight Sun flight from Helsinki in midsummer, a fast overnight stay, and a return the next morning. But the region merits more attention than that. You can travel by train to Rovaniemi, and from there take one of the buses that spread like a fan across the region. Finnair flies as far north as Ivalo.

A SUGGESTED ITINERARY

Day 1: Drive north to Kemi for the night and explore this seaport opening onto the Gulf of Bothnia.

Days 2 & 3: Continue northeast to Rovaniemi where you can see the attractions of the area. The next day you can make journeys to the Arctic Circle and take a side trip to Ranua in the southeast.

Day 4: Continue north deep into the fell country for an overnight stopover in Sodankylä.

Days 5 & 6: Continue north for the final look at the "top of Finland." While still based in either Ivalo or Inari, spend your last day taking in the sights of the environs.

---

1. ROVANIEMI

518 miles N of Helsinki, 178 miles S of Ivalo

GETTING THERE By Plane There are frequent daily flights between Rovaniemi and Helsinki, taking 1 hour. The airport lies 5 miles north of the center of Rovaniemi.

By Train Four trains a day leave from Helsinki for Rovaniemi. If you take the 7am departure from Helsinki, arrival time in Rovaniemi is 5pm.

By Bus Rovaniemi is the bus terminal for the north of Finland. If you're in Helsinki, it's best to fly or take the train. But once you arrive in Rovaniemi, the bus becomes the all-important link for exploring Lapland. There are daily bus connections between Rovaniemi and Oulu, Kemijärvi, Kuusamo, Ranua, Kittilä, Sodankylä, Ivalo, Inari, and farther north—even all the way to the North Cape in Norway.

By Car The E4 goes all the way from Helsinki to Rovaniemi in the north.

ESSENTIALS The **City Tourist Office,** at Aallonkatu 1 (tel. 960/346-270), is open Mon–Fri 8am–6pm and Sat–Sun 9am–6pm (June–Aug) and Mon–Fri 8am–4pm (Sept–May). The **telephone area code** for Rovaniemi is 960.

When the Nazis began their infamous retreat from Lapland in 1944, they burned Rovaniemi, the gateway to Lapland and a prime rail and communications center, to the ground. But with characteristic Finnish *sisu* (suggesting courage and bravery against overwhelming odds) Rovaniemi bounced back, becoming a completely modern town, designed largely by Finland's greatest architect, Alvar Aalto, who created roads shaped like reindeer antlers.

Five miles south of the Arctic Circle, Rovaniemi is at the confluence of two great Finnish rivers, the Kemijoki and the Ounasjoki. This capital of Finnish Lapland goes back some 8,000 years, and the settlement at Rovaniemi was mentioned in documents in the 1400s. As a tourist and travel center, Rovaniemi has excellent road, rail, and air connections. Highway 4, which passes through the city, stretches from southern Finland to Inari in Lapland. You can drive to northern Norway on the Great Arctic Highway and to Kiruna, Sweden, and Narvik, Norway, by following the North Calotte Highway.

If you arrive by air, chances are you'll take a bus into Rovaniemi, although a reindeer-drawn *pulkka* would be a more colorful vehicle. Lumberjacks and an occasional Lapp may be seen, but they are not typical of the thousands of progressive Finns who inhabit Rovaniemi.

Regardless of the time of your arrival, you'll surely escape the heat. In July, the "hot" month, the temperature remains coolly under the 60° Fahrenheit mark; however, you won't escape the mosquitoes from the swampy wastelands.

WHAT TO SEE & DO

ROVANLEMEN KIRKKO, Kirkkotie 1. Tel. 313-781.

This church, the Evangelical Luthern parish church of Rovaniemi, was built in 1950 to replace the church destroyed during the war. Architect Bertel Liljequist designed it, and it stands on the same spot where three other churches were erected. The interior is quite beautiful, noted for its wall and ceiling decorations by Antti Salmenlinna, wood carvings by Gunnar Uotila, and the best yet, the altar fresco *Fountain of Life* by Lennart Segerstrale, which features everyday Lapp motifs.

Admission: Free.

Open: June to mid-Sept, daily 9am–8pm. **Closed:** Mid-Sept to May.

LAURI-TUOTTET OY, Pohjolankatu 25. Tel. 225-01.

This log cabin in the center of town is built in the typical architectural style of the Perapohjola region. Inside are workshops where craftspeople turn out both modern and traditional decorative articles, using such items as reindeer antlers or the gnarled roots of pussy willows as raw materials. In the café is a permanent sales exhibition, featuring curly birch products, wool and leather goods, jewelry, and Puukko knives.

Admission: Free.

Open: Mon–Fri 9am–6pm, Sat–Sun 10am–3pm.

LIBRARY HOUSE, Hallituskatu 9. Tel. 322-2463.

Library House, designed by Alvar Aalto, has a valuable Lapland collection. This is the earliest of a trio of civic buildings Aalto designed for the city in 1965.

Admission: Free.

Open: June to mid-Aug, Mon–Fri 11am–7pm, Sat 10am–4pm; mid-Aug to May, Mon–Fri 11am–8pm, Sat 10am–4pm.

LAPPIA HOUSE, Hallituskatu 11. Tel. 322-2497.

Also designed by Alvar Aalto, Lappia House is the theater, convention, and concert hall building of Rovaniemi. This is the second civic building designed by Aalto, dating from 1975.

Admission: Tours, free.

Open: Tours, June–Aug 15, Mon–Fri at 10am, 1pm, and 4pm.

LAPLAND PROVINCIAL MUSEUM, Pohjoisranta 4. Tel. 324-773.

This building, although not designed by Aalto, is still notable architecturally, having opened in 1992.

Set in the town center, it features exhibits related to the geology, climate, ethnography, history, and sociology of Lapland.

Admission: 30 markkaa ($6.60) adults, 10 markkaa ($2.20) for children under 12.

Open: May–Aug, Tues–Sun 10am–6pm; Sept–Apr, Tues–Sun noon–4pm.

KAUPUNTINTALO [Rovaniemi's Town Hall], Hallituskatu 7. Tel. 322-2288.

Opened in 1988, this is probably the most famous government building in north Finland because of its design by Alvar Aalto. Visitors are usually given a free 15-minute tour of the building by an employee.

Admission: Free.

Open: Mon–Fri 8am–4pm.

WHERE TO STAY

Rovaniemi has one of the finest selections of hotels in north Finland, although many tend to be expensive unless you book a summer discount or a weekend rate. Houses that take in paying guests are the best bargains. Ask at the tourist office (see above) for details. For the most part these are simple places sprinkled throughout the town—don't expect a private bath.

MODERATE

CITY HOTEL, Pekankatu 9, SF-96200 Rovaniemi. Tel. 960/314-501. Fax 960/311-304. 99 rms (all with bath). TV TEL
$ Rates (including breakfast and sauna): 430 markkaa ($94.60) single; 540 markkaa ($118.80) double. AE, MC, V. **Parking:** Free.

The management maintains a handful of wilderness cottages for rent outside the city limits, but the original section of this most serviceable hotel is in the center of Rovaniemi north of Ruokasenkatu. The hotel has a pair of saunas with a communal lounge with a fireplace, a ground-floor bar, and a restaurant. The tastefully modern, carpeted bedrooms feature in-house movies, recorded music, and built-in birchwood furniture. The hotel's Arctic Safaris offer a view of natural life north of the Arctic Circle.

RANTASIPI POHJANHOVI, Pohjanpuistikko 2, SF-96200 Rovaniemi. Tel. 960/33-711. Fax 960/313-997. 216 rms (all with bath). MINIBAR TV TEL
$ Rates (including breakfast): Fri–Sat, 495 markkaa ($108.90) single; 625 markkaa ($137.50) double. Sun–Thurs, 495 markkaa ($108.90) single; 625 markkaa ($137.50) double. AE, DC, MC, V. **Parking:** Free.

⭐ The oldest and most flamboyant hotel in town and the biggest in northern Scandinavia, this hostelry in the center off Koskenranta caters to European tourists. Originally built in 1936, it was reconstructed in 1947. From the sweeping windows of many of the sprawling public rooms, you can watch thousands of logs floating downriver to cutting mills. The bedrooms are comfortable and stylish, outfitted with shades of warm colors and well-chosen Finnish fabrics.

Dining/Entertainment: There is a well-frequented disco, a small-stakes casino, and a nightclub with live entertainment. Dance music usually accompanies meals in the large main restaurant. A second, more elegant restaurant, Valkoinen Peura, is recommended separately (see "Where to Dine," below).

Services: Room service, laundry, babysitting.

Facilities: Saunas, swimming pool with liquor service in an adjacent blue-tile alcove.

SKY HOTEL OUNASVAARA, Ounasvaara, SF-96400 Rovaniemi. Tel. 960/23-371. Fax 960/318-789. 69 rms (all with bath), 7 apartments. MINIBAR TV TEL
$ Rates (including breakfast): June–Aug, 385 markkaa ($84.70) single; 430 markkaa ($94.60) double. Sept–May, 470 markkaa ($103.40) single; 580 markkaa ($127.60) double. Year-round, from 750 markkaa ($165) apartment. AE, DC, MC, V. **Parking:** Free.

This hotel is devoted almost entirely to skiing and hiking. It is on a hilltop 1½ miles west of the town center amid more than 9 miles of illuminated cross-country ski trails and five downhill slopes with a chair lift and two T-bars. There's tobagganing down a stainless-steel chute from May to September. All but 20 of the comfortable rooms have their own saunas, and TVs with video movies and satellite reception. Apartments for two have their own kitchenettes and sauna.

SOKOS HOTEL VAAKUNA, Koskikatu 4, SF-96200 Rovaniemi. Tel. 960/ 33-22-11. Fax 960/33-22-199. 157 rms (all with bath). MINIBAR TV TEL
$ Rates (including breakfast): June 15–Aug 15, 480 markkaa ($105.60) single; 520 markkaa ($114.40) double. Aug 16–June 14, 560 markkaa ($123.20) single; 640 markkaa ($140.80) double. AE, DC, MC, V. **Parking:** Free.

This well-managed establishment, opened in 1992, rises five pink-toned floors above the town center. It contains a soaring lobby dotted with Finnish granite and verdant trees. Bedrooms are filled with discreetly flowered fabrics in pastel, spring-derived colors. On the premises is the nightclub Doris, two saunas, and a health club. The establishment's premier restaurant, the Fransmanni, is described separately in "Where to Dine," below.

INEXPENSIVE

HOTEL LAPPONIA, Koskikatu 23, SF-96200 Rovaniemi. Tel. 960/33-661. Fax 960/313-770. 167 rms (all with bath). MINIBAR TV TEL

$ Rates (including breakfast): Aug 15–June 15, 350 markkaa ($77) single; 390 markkaa ($85.80) double. June 16–Aug 14, 320 markkaa ($70.40) single; 350 markkaa ($77) double. MC, V. **Parking:** Free.

Opened in 1992 in the town center, the hotel is designed around a soaring five-story inner atrium, with a glass roof that floods the lobby with sunlight. The reception area contains a bar, and a winter garden whose rocks, ferns, fountains, and trees would be the envy of any greenhouse. On the premises are an à la carte restaurant (The A La Carte), and a disco, the Lapponia Nightclub, open every night from 10pm to 4am. Entrance is free for hotel guests. Bedrooms are comfortable, cozy, and outfitted in masculine colors of browns, grays, and blacks. Nine contain private saunas.

BUDGET

AMMATTIKOULUN KESÄHOTELLI, Kairatie 73-75, SF-96100 Rovaniemi. Tel. 960/192-651. 36 rms (all with bath).

$ Rates (including breakfast): 220 markkaa ($48.40) double. No credit cards. **Parking:** Free. **Closed:** Aug 8–June 15.

This establishment, 1½ miles west of the railroad station, becomes a summer hotel after students leave on vacation. Otherwise, it functions as a school. The bedrooms, all doubles, are simple but comfortable.

WHERE TO DINE

Most hotels offer an all-you-can-eat lunchtime buffet.

MODERATE

RESTAURANT FRANSMANNI, in the Sokos Hotel Vaakuna, Koskikatu 4. Tel. 33-22-11.
  Cuisine: INTERNATIONAL. **Reservations:** Recommended.
$ Prices: Appetizers 15–40 markkaa ($3.30–$8.80); main dishes 65–110 markkaa ($14.30–$24.20). AE, DC, MC, V.
  Open: Daily 11am–1am.

Set in a warm and elegantly rustic room on the lobby level of a previously recommended hotel, this restaurant offers an accommodating bar, a romantic and soothingly lit ambience, and food inspired by the cuisines of the world, including Lapland. Live trees soften the sightlines of this relaxed and comfortable eatery.

RESTAURANT OPPIPOIKA, in the Hotel Oppikpoika, Korkalonkatu 33. Tel. 20-321.
  Cuisine: LAPPISH. **Reservations:** Not required.
$ Prices: Appetizers 38–40 markkaa ($8.40–$8.80); main dishes 70–80 markkaa ($15.40–$17.60), fixed-price 3-course lunch 50 markkaa ($11); fixed-price 3-course dinner 65 markkaa ($14.30). AE, DC, MC, V.
  Open: Lunch daily noon–2pm; dinner daily 7–9:30pm.

One of Rovaniemi's best restaurants is for the most part staffed with students from the local hotel and restaurant training school. (The restaurant's name translates as "apprentice.") Devoted to the promotion within Finland of Lapp cuisine, the kitchens use fresh locally derived ingredients. In a modern dining room decorated in autumn tones, you can enjoy dishes like fried filets of salmon with warm roe sauce and Lapp potatoes and filets of reindeer studded with green peppercorns and fried.

RESTAURANT OUNASVAARA, in the Sky Hotel Ounasvaara, Ounasvaara. Tel. 23-371.
  Cuisine: LAPPISH. **Reservations:** Recommended.
$ Prices: Appetizers 43–54 markkaa ($9.50–$11.90); main dishes 68–150 markkaa ($15–$33). AE, DC, MC, V.

Open: Lunch daily 11am–4pm; dinner daily 4–10pm.
This restaurant is on the second floor of a previously recommended hotel (see "Where to Stay," above) and offers panoramic views. Its consciously simple furniture was designed as a foil for the grand vistas of lake and forest outside. Well known for its Lapp specialties, the establishment serves meals that include sautéed reindeer with red whortleberries, salmon soup, a herring tray, fried Camembert with cloudberry sauce, and several preparations of fresh trout and salmon. Dance music is featured 3 nights a week.

RESTAURANT VALKOINEN PEURA, in the Hotel Rantasipi Pohjanhovi, Pohjanpuistikko 2. Tel. 33-711.
   Cuisine: FINNISH. **Reservations:** Required.
$ **Prices:** Appetizers 45–55 markkaa ($9.90–$12.10); main dishes 72–140 markkaa ($15.80–$30.80). AE, DC, MC, V.
   Open: Daily 7pm–1am.
From the rooms with modern decor of marbleized ceilings and stained-glass windows imprinted with reindeer heads, you can watch thousands of logs floating down the nearby river. The menu features Finnish Lapland specialties including salmon from the River Teno, reindeer tongue braised in a red wine sauce, chateaubriand with a cream-and-morel sauce, grilled or sautéed rainbow trout, wild duck with cream sauce, and whitefish baked in foil.

SHOPPING

One popular item for sale up here is a certificate that proves a traveler has actually visited the Arctic Circle.

THE TRADING POST [SANTA'S VILLAGE], Arctic Circle, Hwy. 4. Tel. 620-96.
Five miles north of Rovaniemi right on the Arctic Circle (*Napapiiri*), this is one of the most unusual collections of boutiques in northern Europe. On the two floors of elegant shops, you'll find cloudberry jam, engraved horn-handled knives, birch and pinewood children's toys, beautifully detailed hand-knit sweaters, and the best of handwoven Finnish tablecloths and textiles. Also sold are pieces of regional jewelry fashioned from silver and a unique semiprecious form of feldspar called spectrolite (found only in parts of Russia, Canada, and Finland, it was first quarried in the 1950s).
   One store sells Saga mink coats for, the owner claims, less than half of what a similar coat would go for in a large city in North America, not counting Customs duty. Another boutique is in a log cabin, which was built in 6 days for the postwar visit of Eleanor Roosevelt to the devastated Rovaniemi. A few steps away, a family of reindeer grazes behind a wooden barricade.
   You can buy a certificate to prove that you've been north of the Arctic Circle, and if you mail your postcards from here, they'll receive a special Arctic Circle postmark. There's also an outdoor café for summertime Midnight Sun watching and a guestbook where, if you inscribe the names of your favorite small-fry, they'll receive a special Christmas postcard anywhere in the world "from Santa." In summer, the complex is open daily from 9am to 8pm; off-season, it is open daily from 9am to 5pm. Bus: 8.

MIESSI KY, Korkalonkatu 12. Tel. 362-410.
   You won't want to miss this store, which sells unusual silver pendants, cups, rings, and brooches that you won't find anywhere else. Many of the semipagan, quasi-regional designs are inspired by ancient objects excavated from Viking ruins. Don't miss the array of Lappish gemstones. One of them, spectrolite, is a semiprecious form of dark-hued feldspar whose iridescence is similar to that of an opal.

SAMPO CENTER, Koskikatu 17.
   Rovaniemi's newest cluster of shops occupies two floors of a modern building in

the town center. Most establishments are open Monday through Saturday from 9am to 6pm.

EXCURSIONS

If you don't have a car, the easiest way to travel to the **Arctic Circle** is to take a sightseeing bus that departs from near the City Tourist Office, Aallonkatu 1 (tel. 346-270), mid-June to mid-August at 3pm on Sunday. The tour lasts 3 hours and costs 50 markkaa ($11) for adults and 30 markkaa ($6.60) for children.

Although a private car allows you to travel away from Rovaniemi on explorations of the tundra, you won't be stranded in the center of town without one. Local bus no. 8 departs from Rovaniemi's railway station about once an hour every day of the year between 8:30am to 4pm in the off-season, and from 8:30am to 7pm in summer. One of its most important stops is at the previously recommended Santa's Village, a trip time of around 15 minutes. It also runs to the Arctic Circle. Transit costs 8.50 markkaa ($1.90) each way.

More intensive are the 2½ hour city tours offered twice a week in summertime by the tourist office. Departing from in front of the tourist office on Wednesday at 6pm and Sunday at 3pm, they include visits to the city's most important civic sights and some of its museums. Commentary is in English, with many insights into the flora, fauna, and sociology of the Lappish tundra. The cost is 30 markkaa ($6.60) for adults, and 10 markkaa ($2.20) for children.

2. RANUA

45 miles S of Rovaniemi, 56 miles S of the Arctic Circle

GETTING THERE   By Train   Go to Rovaniemi (see Section 1, above), then take the bus south to Ranua.

By Bus   Frequent buses run back and forth between Rovaniemi and Ranua, and there is also bus service from Helsinki.

By Car   Take Route 4 north to Rovaniemi (see Section 1, above), then go south to Ranua on Route 78.

ESSENTIALS   For **information,** ask at the Rovaniemi City Tourist Office (see Section 1, above). The **telephone area code** for Ranua is 960.

SPECIAL EVENTS   In August, Ranua holds the Cloudberry Fair and Market.

Ranua is a thriving county of agricultural and forest production and service industries, with many beautiful lakes and rivers, including the Simojoki River, stocked for salmon fishing.

WHAT TO SEE & DO

RANUA WILDLIFE PARK, Ranuan Eläinpuisto, Repoharju. Tel. 51-921.

This wildlife park is on Route 79, 2 miles north of the town center. It includes a zoo with large enclosures, public walkways, and viewing terraces. You can see polar bears, wolves, lynxes, wolverines, pine martens, stoats, wild forest reindeer, lemmings, voles, and many other animals native to the cold countries, as well as about 35 bird species. A geological exhibition features examples of the common minerals and rocks found in Finland. The park also offers horseback riding, mini-golf, a mini-car track, a nature trail, and a forest trail, plus a children's zoo with domestic animals for the youngsters to wander among.

Admission: 45 markkaa ($9.90) adults, 30 markkaa ($6.60) children 14 or under.
Open: May and Sept, daily 9am–6pm; June–Aug, daily 9am–8pm; Oct–Apr, daily 10am–4pm. **Closed:** Dec 24–26.

WHERE TO STAY
INEXPENSIVE

HOTEL ILVESLINNA, Keskustie 10, SF-97700 Ranua. Tel. 960/51-201.
Fax 960/51-284. 37 rms (all with bath).
$ Rates (including breakfast): 360 markkaa ($79.20) single; 420 markkaa ($92.40) double. AE, DC, MC, V. **Parking:** Free.
The greenery, comfortable furnishings, and good service make this hotel, built in 1986 on the main road from Rovaniemi to Kajaani, a pleasant place to stay. The bedrooms range from singles to units accommodating four people, and several were designed for individuals with allergies. Most, but not all, rooms contain TV, minibar, and phone. In the main restaurant, a ceiling of stars lends a touch of Christmas year-round. Finnish and Scandinavian specialties, along with some Lappish regional dishes, are served. There is also a Finnish beer house and a cocktail bar. In summer, drinks are served on the terraces, and food is also offered in a Lapp tent restaurant. An orchestra plays three times a week in the main restaurant. Facilities include tennis courts, a lakeside swimming beach, and transport rentals ranging from bicycles to canoes to snowmobiles.

3. KEMI

446 miles NW of Helsinki, 155 miles SW of Rovaniemi

GETTING THERE   By Plane   There are daily flights between Kemi and Helsinki. If you depart Helsinki daily on an 11:50am flight, you'll arrive in Kemi at 1:30pm.

By Train   From Oulu in the south, which has rail links to Helsinki, four trains a day pass through Kemi heading for Tornio on the border with Sweden. It takes 2 hours from Oulu to Kemi.

By Bus   From Helsinki you should fly or take the train. But from Oulu in the south, there are good bus connections to Kemi. There are also daily bus connections from Rovaniemi to Kemi.

By Car   From Helsinki, take the E4 northwest all the way; from Rovaniemi, head southwest on the E4.

ESSENTIALS   The **Kemi Tourist Office,** at Kauppakatu 22, SF-94100 Kemi (tel. 9698/199-466), is open Mon–Fri 8am–6pm and Sat 10am–6pm (June–Aug) and Mon–Fri 8am–5pm and Sat 9am–2pm (Sept–May). The **telephone area code** for Kemi is 9698.

The mouth of the Kemijoki River is one of the oldest areas of habitation in Finland. Merchants have come to the area since the 1300s because of the great stock of fish. Kemi, with a population of about 27,000, is the center of the province's wood-processing industry. Its two harbors function as Lapland's ports to the rest of the world through the Gulf of Bothnia.
In Kemi, the sea becomes trapped under a barrier of ice in winter more than a yard thick. Nevertheless, oceangoing ships continue to ply routes to Kemi's northern harbor. Shipping lanes are kept open with the help of special ice-breaking vessels.

WHAT TO SEE & DO

The finest view of Kemi is from the roof of the **city hall,** on town square, open daily from 8am to 6pm. Near here, Finland's largest river was blocked off in 1947 by the

Isohaara hydroelectric plant and the accumulation of floating logs above the power station toward the end of each summer is probably the most extensive in Europe.

KEMI ART MUSEUM, at the Cultural Center, Pohjoisrantakatu 9. Tel. 198-247.

This museum contains works by Finnish or Swedish-speaking Finnish artists who live mainly in the northern part of the country. Special exhibitions are staged. The museum is housed in an old fisherman's house, where you can see the original fish-smoking hut.

Admission: Free.

Open: Summer, Mon–Fri 10am–5pm, Sat–Sun 11am–5pm; off-season, Tues–Fri 10am–7pm, Sat 10am–5pm, Sun noon–7pm.

GEMSTONE GALLERY, Kauppakatu 29. Tel. 20-300.

This is one of the best gemstone museums in Europe and shows how the products of Lapland jade (serpentine) are made. You can also purchase Lapland jade products in the mineral shop at about 20% below normal prices.

Admission: 30 markkaa ($6.60) adults, 15 markkaa ($3.30) children 12 or under.

Open: Summer, daily 10am–8pm; off-season, daily 10am–6pm.

WHERE TO STAY
MODERATE

CUMULUS HOTEL, Hahtisaarenkatu 3, SF-94100 Kemi. Tel. 9698/22-831. Fax 9698/228-3299. 185 rms (all with bath). MINIBAR TV TEL

$ Rates (including breakfast): June 19–Aug 2, 270 markkaa ($59.40) single; 390 markkaa ($85.80) double. Aug 3–June 18, 455 markkaa ($100.10) single; 600 markkaa ($132) double. AE, DC, MC, V. **Parking:** Free.

This modern hotel near the Marketplace, built in 1982, is designed in the same compact format that has made the Cumulus chain well respected in Finland. The bedrooms are comfortable, each furnished in an attractive tasteful modern style. Some are suitable for nonsmokers and allergy sufferers. There are two restaurants, one with evening dance music. The hotel has three saunas, a swimming pool, and two squash courts.

INEXPENSIVE

HOTEL MERIHOVI, Kesuspuistokatu 6-8, SF-94100 Kemi. Tel. 9698/23-431. Fax 9698/16-316. 71 rms (all with bath). TV TEL

$ Rates (including breakfast): June–Aug and Fri–Sat year-round, 275 markkaa ($60.50) single; 330 markkaa ($72.60) double. Sun–Thurs the rest of the year, 380 markkaa ($83.60) single; 480 markkaa ($105.60) double. DC, MC, V. **Parking:** Free.

In the town center near a fountain, this hotel has comfortable rooms styled in a Finnish decor of exposed wood and tasteful colors. Nine bedrooms are fitted with private saunas, and special rooms are reserved for nonsmokers and allergy sufferers. Room with saunas carry a supplement of 50 markkaa ($11) to the rates quoted above. The main dining room serves salted salmon and Riimi beef with a forest-mushroom salad, "hidden" salmon (that is, a casserole of charcoal-broiled salmon with creamed morels), and workman's reindeer delicacy (reindeer filet stew with a bacon-and-game pepper sauce). Many locals patronize the long Ankkuri Bar on the ground floor. In summer there is an open-air restaurant and summer terrace on the sixth floor. Facilities include two saunas, a squash court, indoor and outdoor tennis courts, hydrotherapy, and a hairdresser.

WHERE TO DINE
MODERATE

KULTAKURA, Nahjurinkatu 6. Tel. 15-421.
Cuisine: FINNISH. **Reservations:** Not required.

$ Prices: Appetizers 28–48 markkaa ($6.20–$10.60); main dishes 52–135 markkaa ($11.40–$29.70). AE, MC, V.
Open: Sun–Fri 10am–midnight, Sat 10am–9pm.

This popular restaurant near the town hall shares its premises with a pub that keeps the same hours. It is a reasonably priced choice for Finnish and Lapp dishes. Plank steak cooked on a hot stove is a specialty, as is "butler's beefsteak," along with fresh Finnish salmon. Reindeer is prepared in several ways.

INEXPENSIVE

SAMAANI, Valtakatu 1. Tel. 15-192.
Cuisine: STEAKS. **Reservations:** Recommended.
$ Prices: Main dishes 55–87 markkaa ($12.10–$19.10). MC, V.
Open: Mon–Fri 10am–6pm, Sat–Sun 10am–9pm.

At this fully licensed restaurant on the main street you can enjoy a steak house allure, with lots of red (symbolizing blood) and wood paneling. Other than the salad bar, there are no appetizers, and the salad is included in the price of your main course. It is completely and exclusively a steak house for beef (not reindeer or elk).

---

4. SODANKYLÄ

81 miles NE of Rovaniemi, 598 miles N of Helsinki

GETTING THERE   By Plane   Fly to Rovaniemi, then take a connecting bus the rest of the way.

By Train   Go to Rovaniemi; then continue the journey to Sodankylä by bus.

By Bus   A 5:15pm bus leaving Rovaniemi will arrive in Sodankylä at 7:35pm.

By Car   Drive to Rovaniemi (see Section 1, above) and then continue along Route 4 all the way to Sodankylä.

ESSENTIALS   The **telephone area code** for Sodankylä is 9693.

SPECIAL EVENTS   Several events are listed below, under "What to See and Do."

Many say that the *real* Lapland begins at Sodanklyä, and that Rovaniemi is only the gateway. The fell country begins here, on Route 4 going north. In the south rises the Luosto fell, and in the north is the well-known Saariselka area with its grand fell district.

WHAT TO SEE & DO

The best sights are the **Tankavaara gold washings and museum** (see below) and the **Finnish and World Goldpanning Championships** in summer. The **wooden church,** built in 1689, is the oldest in Lapland. Porttikoski's **logging games** are an important summer event, as are the **International Midnight Sun Film Festival** in June and the **Jutajaiset-Lappish Folklore event.**

WHERE TO STAY & DINE

MODERATE

KANTAKIEVARI SODANKYLÄ, Unarintie 15, SF-9960 Sodankylä. Tel. 9693/21-926. Fax 9693/13-545. 53 rms (all with bath). MINIBAR TV TEL
$ Rates (Including breakfast): June–Aug and Fri–Sat year-round, 320–350 mark-

kaa ($70.40–$77) single or double. Sun–Thurs the rest the year, 390–410 markkaa ($85.80–$90.20) single; 520–550 markkaa ($114.40–$121) double. AE, DC, MC, V. **Parking:** Free.

This hotel is a focal point of the surrounding community, and you'll recognize its prominent red-brick facade in the center of the village. On the premises is a sauna, a children's playroom, a swimming pool, an air-rifle range, a lounge with fireplace, and table-tennis facilities. There's a warmly decorated tavern and a large restaurant, where you can order such dishes as whitefish rolls simmered in a dill-cream sauce or double reindeer chops with a morel sauce and mashed potatoes gratinée. Each comfortably modern bedroom has a radio and video movies. Furnishings are simple and functional. Special rooms are available for the allergic.

AN EXCURSION TO TANKAVAARA

About 62 miles from the village of Sodankylä and 143 miles from Rovaniemi and the Arctic Circle, near Route 4, to the north, is the **Tankavaara Gold Village** (tel. 9693/46-158), where you can try your luck at finding the precious metal. For 100 markkaa ($22), you can wash gold for a whole day, getting an introduction to gold panning and a pan for your own use; the price includes a place for a tent at the camping site. Or you can rent a cabin; they cost 190 to 240 markkaa ($41.80 to $52.80) and can accommodate two to four people; cabins with private baths cost 280 to 380 markkaa ($61.60 to $83.60). If you just want to try gold washing for a little while, you can take a course and get a pan for 30 markkaa ($6.60).

Tankavaara is also a gateway to a large nature park named for Pres. Urho Kekkonen, and the information center for the park is in this village.

The **Gold Museum** (tel. 9693/46-171) traces the history of gold prospecting in Finnish Lapland for more than a century—exhibits are both indoors and outdoors. Admission is 20 markkaa ($4.40) for adults, 5 markkaa ($1.10) for children, and it is open June to mid-August, daily from 9am to 6pm; mid-August through September, daily from 10am to 5pm; the rest of the year, daily from 10am to 4pm. See below for the Old Gold-Diggers Café in the Gold Village Complex.

WHERE TO DINE

Inexpensive

OLD GOLD-DIGGERS CAFE, in the Gold Village Complex. Tel. 9693/46-158.

   Cuisine: LAPPISH. **Reservations:** Not required.
$ **Prices:** Appetizers 15–50 markkaa ($3.30–$11); main dishes 60–100 markkaa ($13.20–$22). MC, V.
   Open: Daily 8:30am–9pm.

This café in the center of the complex has an award-winning kitchen. Try the "prospector's steak," which is served from a gold pan and includes a giant reindeer steak, pea stew, and mashed potatoes, plus salad.

---

5. INARI/IVALO

698 miles N of Helsinki, 180 miles N of Rovaniemi

GETTING THERE   By Plane   There are flights to Ivalo from many parts of Finland, including Joensuu, Jyväskylä, Kemi, Kuopio, and Lappeenranta. A 10:35am flight from Helsinki will arrive in Ivalo at 1:10pm.

By Train   Go to Rovaniemi (see above) and continue the rest of the way by bus.

By Bus   Three buses a day run between Rovaniemi and Ivalo, taking 5 hours. The village of Inari is also linked twice daily by bus to Rovaniemi, taking 6 hours.

By Car   Drive to Rovaniemi (see above), then continue along Route 4 all the way to Ivalo and Inari. Route 4 runs across Inari through its largest settlements to the Arctic

Ocean. There is a good road network from western Lapland, Kirkkoniemi, and Murmansk, Russia.

ESSENTIALS The **Tourist Information Office,** at Pisskuntie 5, SF-99800 Ivalo (tel. 9697/12-521), is open daily 8am–8pm (summer) and daily 8am–3pm (rest of year). The **telephone area code** for Ivalo and Inari is 9697.

Inari is Finland's largest county in area and its most remarkable feature is the 50-mile-long Lake Inarijärvi, containing more than 3,000 islands.

WHAT TO SEE & DO

IVALO/SAARISELKÄ The administrative center of the Inari area is the little town of Ivalo, which has daily connections with Helsinki. Some 6 miles north of Ivalo is a place along Route 4 where you can get a good view of the **scenery of Lake Inari,** with an **exhibition** depicting life in the area through the centuries. This and the scenic lookout are open from the beginning of June to mid-August from 8am to 1pm daily. For information, call the Hotel Riekonlinna at Saariselkä (see "Where to Stay and Dine," below) (tel. 9697/81-601).

The **Saariselkä resort area,** Finland's largest, has 11 downhill ski runs, six lifts, marked ski trails, 20 miles of lit ski track, and marked hiking routes with wilderness huts. Activities include skido (snowmobile) and reindeer safari, supper at a Lapp hut, and trips to Lapland's gold-panning area. Sights to see near the Saariselkä area are the **Ivalo River goldfields** with buildings and equipment (this was the site of Finland's first gold strike) and the heights of **Kaunispää,** where you can look out over the whole Saariselkä landscape and far into Russia.

INARI Inari is also the name of a small village some 25 miles north of Ivalo that opens onto the huge lake. In the village, you can take a water bus to the ancient sacrificial island of **Ukko.** Trips can be arranged at 2pm in June and August and at 10am, 2pm, and 6pm in July. A trip costs 55 markkaa ($12.10) per person and takes about 2 hours.

An outdoor **Lapp Museum** in the village features a herdsmen's settlement, a fishing colony, and exhibits of wild-animal snares and Lapp costumes. The museum is open June to September 20, daily from 9am to 4pm.

In Inari, you can also see original Lapland handcrafts at **Samekki** (tel. 9697/51-086), open June to the end of September, daily from 10am to 8pm; in winter, on Friday, Saturday, and Monday from 10am to 4pm.

Owned by a Lappish family, the **Inari Reindeer Farm,** 8½ miles from the village of Inari toward Kittilä, specializes in reindeer ranching and also raises racing reindeer, which have done well in the **Inari Reindeer King Races** held in March. On the farm, you can drive reindeer, help feed the herd, taste coffee made over the tepee's open fire, and learn about reindeer care and the Lapp culture. The farm is open all year and advance reservations are required (tel. 9697/56-512).

OTHER AREA ATTRACTIONS In the northern part of the country there are several interesting villages. For example, **Lemmenjoki** provides boat trips to the goldfields and **Sevettijärvi** is a place to study Lappish culture.

WHERE TO STAY & DINE
MODERATE

HOTEL RIEKONLINNA, SF-99830 Saariselkä. Tel. 9697/81-601. Fax 9697/81-602. 124 rms (all with bath). TV TEL
$ Rates (including breakfast): 545–680 markkaa ($119.90–$149.60) single; 680–860 markkaa ($149.60–$189.20) double. AE, DC, MC, V. **Parking:** Free.
In the town center, the Hotel Riekonlinna is a high-class conference and holiday hotel offering rooms with balconies, refrigerators, and drying cabinets for sportswear, among other amenities. Some rooms also have saunas. Special accommodations are available for families and persons suffering from allergies.

SAARISELÄN TUNTURIHOTELLIT, Saariseläntie 14, SF-99830
Saariselkä. **Tel. 9697/81-11.** Fax 9697/81-771. 91 rms (all with bath), 48
apartments. TV TEL **Bus:** From the Ivalo airport for 16 miles.
$ **Rates** (including breakfast): 400 markkaa ($88) single; 620 markkaa ($136.40)
double; 850 markkaa ($187) apartment. DC, MC, V. **Parking:** Free.
This hotel complex offers cozy accommodations; either singles or double in a cluster
of outbuildings; or a holiday cottage apartment with one to three rooms, a
well-equipped kitchen, an open fireplace, and a sauna. Most rooms contain a minibar.
Each unit is comfortably furnished in a modern, functional style. The hotel offers a
dance and dinner restaurant, a bar, and pub.

INEXPENSIVE

HOTEL IVALO, Ivalontie 34, SF-99801 Ivalo. **9697/21-911.** Fax 9697/21-
905. 94 rms (all with bath). TV TEL
$ **Rates** (including breakfast): 420 markkaa ($92.40) single; 490 markkaa ($107.80)
double. AE, DC, MC, V. **Parking:** Free.
This hotel in Ivalo center offers much modern comfort in a wilderness tract about 30
miles south of Inari. You can rent a boat for the nearby river and swim in the hotel's
pool after using a sauna. Bedrooms are furnished in a tasteful modern way. Meals are
noteworthy, especially the regional specialties, which include game soup made with
thin slices of snow grouse, reindeer meat, reindeer tongue, and smoked reindeer in a
clear broth (it's served with warm unleavened potato bread).

A. WEIGHTS & MEASURES

LENGTH

1 millimeter (mm)	=	0.04 inches (*or* less than ¹/₁₆ in.)
1 centimeter (cm)	=	0.39 inches (*or* just under ½ in.)
1 meter (m)	=	39 inches (*or* about 1.1 yards)
1 kilometer (km)	=	0.62 inches (*or* about ⅔ of a mile)

To convert kilometers to miles, multiply the number of kilometers by 0.62. Also use to convert speeds from kilometers per hour (kmph) to miles per hour (mph).
To convert miles to kilometers, multiply the number of miles by 1.61. Also use to convert speeds from mph to kmph.

CAPACITY

1 liter (l)	=	33.92 ounces	= 2.1 pints	= 1.06 quarts
	=	0.26 U.S. gallons		
1 Imperial gallon	=	1.2 U.S. gallons		

To convert liters to U.S. gallons, multiply the number of liters by 0.26.
To convert U.S. gallons to liters, multiply the number of gallons by 3.79.
To convert Imperial gallons to U.S. gallons, multiply Imperial gallons by 1.2.
To convert U.S. gallons to Imperial gallons, multiply U.S. gallons by 0.83.

WEIGHT

1 gram (g)	=	0.04 ounces (*or* about a paperclip's weight)
1 kilogram (kg)	=	35.2 ounces
	=	2.2 pounds
1 metric ton	=	2,205 pounds = 1.1 short ton

To convert kilograms to pounds, multiply the number of kilograms by 2.2.
To convert pounds to kilograms, multiply the number of pounds by 0.45.

TEMPERATURE

To convert degrees Celsius to degrees Fahrenheit, multiply °C by 9, divide by 5, then add 32 (example: 20°C × 9/5 + 32 = 68°F).
To convert degrees Fahrenheit to degrees Celsius, subtract 32 from °F, then multiply by 5, then divide by 9 (example: 85°F − 32 × 5/9 = 29.4°C).

B. SIZE CONVERSIONS

The following charts should help you to choose the correct clothing sizes in Europe. However, sizes can vary, so the best guide is simply to try things on.

WOMEN'S DRESSES, COATS & SKIRTS

American	4	6	8	10	11	12	13	14	15	16	18
Continental	36	38	38	40	40	42	42	44	44	46	48
British	8	10	11	12	13	14	15	16	17	18	20

WOMEN'S BLOUSES & SWEATERS

American	6	8	10	12	14	16
Continental	34	36	38	40	42	44
British	32	34	36	38	40	42

WOMEN'S SHOES

American	5	6	7	8	9	10
Continental	36	37	38	39	40	41
British	3½	4½	5½	6½	7½	8½

MEN'S SUITS

American	34	36	38	40	42	44	46	48
Continental	44	46	48	50	52	54	56	58
British	34	36	38	40	42	44	46	48

MEN'S SHIRTS

American	14½	15	15½	16	16½	17	17½	18
Continental	37	38	39	41	42	43	44	45
British	14½	15	15½	16	16½	17	17½	18

MEN'S SHOES

American	7	8	9	10	11	12	13
Continental	39½	41	42	43	44½	46	47
British	6	7	8	9	10	11	12

CHILDREN'S CLOTHING

American	3	4	5	6	6X
Continental	98	104	110	116	122
British	18	20	22	24	26

CHILDREN'S SHOES

American	8	9	10	11	12	13	1	2	3
Continental	24	25	27	28	29	30	32	33	34
British	7	8	9	10	11	12	13	1	2

INDEX

GENERAL INFORMATION

SWEDEN

FINLAND

DESTINATIONS

DENMARK

Note: Asterisk (*) indicates an Author's Favorite.

NORWAY

SWEDEN

FINLAND

Now Save Money on All Your Travels by Joining
FROMMER'S ™ TRAVEL BOOK CLUB
The World's Best Travel Guides at Membership Prices

FROMMER'S TRAVEL BOOK CLUB is your ticket to successful travel! Open up a world of travel information and simplify your travel planning when you join ranks with thousands of value-conscious travelers who are members of the FROMMER'S TRAVEL BOOK CLUB. Join today and you'll be entitled to all the privileges that come from belonging to the club that offers you travel guides for less to more than 100 destinations worldwide. Annual membership is only $25 (U.S.) or $35 (Canada and all foreign).

The Advantages of Membership

1. Your choice of three free FROMMER'S TRAVEL GUIDES. You can pick two from our FROMMER'S COUNTRY and REGIONAL GUIDES (listed under Comprehensive, $-A-Day, and Family) and one from our FROMMER'S CITY GUIDES (listed under City and City $-A-Day).
2. Your own subscription to **TRIPS & TRAVEL** quarterly newsletter.
3. You're entitled to a **30% discount** on your order of any additional books offered by FROMMER'S TRAVEL BOOK CLUB.
4. You're offered (at a small additional fee) our **Domestic Trip Routing Kits.**

Our quarterly newsletter **TRIPS & TRAVEL** offers practical information on the best buys in travel, the "hottest" vacation spots, the latest travel trends, world-class events and much, much more.

Our **Domestic Trip Routing Kits** are available for any North American destination. We'll send you a detailed map highlighting the best route to take to your destination—you can request direct or scenic routes.

Here's all you have to do to join:
Send in your membership fee of $25 ($35 Canada and foreign) with your name and address on the form below along with your selections as part of your membership package to **FROMMER'S TRAVEL BOOK CLUB, P.O. Box 473, Mt. Morris, IL 61054-0473**. Remember to check off 2 FROMMER'S COUNTRY and REGIONAL GUIDES and 1 FROMMER'S CITY GUIDE on the pages following.

If you would like to order additional books, please select the books you would like and send a check for the total amount (please add sales tax in the states noted below), plus $2 per book for shipping and handling ($3 per book for all foreign orders) to:

FROMMER'S TRAVEL BOOK CLUB
P.O. Box 473
Mt. Morris, IL 61054-0473
1-815-734-1104

[ ] **YES**. I want to take advantage of this opportunity to join FROMMER'S TRAVEL BOOK CLUB.
[ ] **My check is enclosed**. Dollar amount enclosed _____*
        (all payments in U.S. funds only)

Name_____
Address_____
City_____ State_____ Zip_____

To ensure that all orders are processed efficiently, please apply sales tax in the following areas: CA, CT, FL, IL, NJ, NY, TN, WA, and CANADA.

*With membership, shipping and handling will be paid by FROMMER'S TRAVEL BOOK CLUB for the three free books you select as part of your membership. Please add $2 per book for shipping and handling for any additional books purchased ($3 per book for all foreign orders).

Allow 4-6 weeks for delivery. Prices of books, membership fee, and publication dates are subject to change without notice.

Please Send Me the Books Checked Below

FROMMER'S COMPREHENSIVE GUIDES

(Guides listing facilities from budget to deluxe, with emphasis on the medium-priced)

	Retail Price	Code		Retail Price	Code
☐ Acapulco/Ixtapa/Taxco 1993–94	$15.00	C120	☐ Jamaica/Barbados 1993–94	$15.00	C105
☐ Alaska 1990–91	$15.00	C001	☐ Japan 1992–93	$19.00	C020
☐ Arizona 1993–94	$18.00	C101	☐ Morocco 1992–93	$18.00	C021
☐ Australia 1992–93	$18.00	C002	☐ Nepal 1992–93	$18.00	C038
☐ Austria 1993–94	$19.00	C119	☐ New England 1993	$17.00	C114
☐ Austria/Hungary 1991–92	$15.00	C003	☐ New Mexico 1993–94	$15.00	C117
☐ Belgium/Holland/ Luxembourg 1993–94	$18.00	C106	☐ New York State 1992–93	$19.00	C025
			☐ Northwest 1991–92	$17.00	C026
☐ Bermuda/Bahamas 1992–93	$17.00	C005	☐ Portugal 1992–93	$16.00	C027
			☐ Puerto Rico 1993–94	$15.00	C103
☐ Brazil, 3rd Edition	$20.00	C111	☐ Puerto Vallarta/Manzanillo/ Guadalajara 1992–93	$14.00	C028
☐ California 1993	$18.00	C112			
☐ Canada 1992–93	$18.00	C009	☐ Scandinavia 1993–94	$19.00	C118
☐ Caribbean 1993	$18.00	C102	☐ Scotland 1992–93	$16.00	C040
☐ Carolinas/Georgia 1992–93	$17.00	C034	☐ Skiing Europe 1989–90	$15.00	C030
☐ Colorado 1993–94	$16.00	C100	☐ South Pacific 1992–93	$20.00	C031
☐ Cruises 1993–94	$19.00	C107	☐ Spain 1993–94	$19.00	C115
☐ DE/MD/PA & NJ Shore 1992–93	$19.00	C012	☐ Switzerland/Liechtenstein 1992–93	$19.00	C032
☐ Egypt 1990–91	$15.00	C013	☐ Thailand 1992–93	$20.00	C033
☐ England 1993	$18.00	C109	☐ U.S.A. 1993–94	$19.00	C116
☐ Florida 1993	$18.00	C104	☐ Virgin Islands 1992–93	$13.00	C036
☐ France 1992–93	$20.00	C017	☐ Virginia 1992–93	$14.00	C037
☐ Germany 1993	$19.00	C108	☐ Yucatán 1993–94	$18.00	C110
☐ Italy 1993	$19.00	C113			

FROMMER'S $-A-DAY GUIDES

(Guides to low-cost tourist accommodations and facilities)

	Retail Price	Code		Retail Price	Code
☐ Australia on $45 1993–94	$18.00	D102	☐ Mexico on $50 1993	$19.00	D105
☐ Costa Rica/Guatemala/ Belize on $35 1993–94	$17.00	D108	☐ New York on $70 1992–93	$16.00	D016
			☐ New Zealand on $45 1993–94	$18.00	D103
☐ Eastern Europe on $25 1991–92	$17.00	D005	☐ Scotland/Wales on $50 1992–93	$18.00	D019
☐ England on $60 1993	$18.00	D107			
☐ Europe on $45 1993	$19.00	D106	☐ South America on $40 1993–94	$19.00	D109
☐ Greece on $45 1993–94	$19.00	D100			
☐ Hawaii on $75 1993	$19.00	D104	☐ Turkey on $40 1992–93	$22.00	D023
☐ India on $40 1992–93	$20.00	D010	☐ Washington, D.C. on $40 1992–93	$17.00	D024
☐ Ireland on $40 1992–93	$17.00	D011			
☐ Israel on $45 1993–94	$18.00	D101			

FROMMER'S CITY $-A-DAY GUIDES

(Pocket-size guides with an emphasis on low-cost tourist accommodations and facilities)

	Retail Price	Code		Retail Price	Code
☐ Berlin on $40 1992–93	$12.00	D002	☐ Madrid on $50 1992–93	$13.00	D014
☐ Copenhagen on $50 1992–93	$12.00	D003	☐ Paris on $45 1992–93	$12.00	D018
			☐ Stockholm on $50 1992–93	$13.00	D022
☐ London on $45 1992–93	$12.00	D013			

FROMMER'S TOURING GUIDES

(Color-illustrated guides that include walking tours,
cultural and historic sights, and practical information)

	Retail Price	Code		Retail Price	Code
☐ Amsterdam	$11.00	T001	☐ New York	$11.00	T008
☐ Barcelona	$14.00	T015	☐ Rome	$11.00	T010
☐ Brazil	$11.00	T003	☐ Scotland	$10.00	T011
☐ Florence	$ 9.00	T005	☐ Sicily	$15.00	T017
☐ Hong Kong/Singapore/ Macau	$11.00	T006	☐ Thailand	$13.00	T012
			☐ Tokyo	$15.00	T016
☐ Kenya	$14.00	T018	☐ Venice	$ 9.00	T014
☐ London	$13.00	T007			

FROMMER'S FAMILY GUIDES

	Retail Price	Code		Retail Price	Code
☐ California with Kids	$17.00	F001	☐ San Francisco with Kids	$17.00	F004
☐ Los Angeles with Kids	$17.00	F002	☐ Washington, D.C. with Kids	$17.00	F005
☐ New York City with Kids	$18.00	F003			

FROMMER'S CITY GUIDES

(Pocket-size guides to sightseeing and tourist accommodations
and facilities in all price ranges)

	Retail Price	Code		Retail Price	Code
☐ Amsterdam 1993–94	$13.00	S110	☐ Miami 1993–94	$13.00	S118
☐ Athens, 9th Edition	$13.00	S114	☐ Minneapolis/St. Paul, 3rd Edition	$13.00	S119
☐ Atlanta 1993–94	$13.00	S112			
☐ Atlantic City/Cape May 1991–92	$ 9.00	S004	☐ Montréal/Québec City 1993–94	$13.00	S125
☐ Bangkok 1992–93	$13.00	S005	☐ New Orleans 1993–94	$13.00	S103
☐ Barcelona/Majorca/ Minorca/Ibiza 1993–94	$13.00	S115	☐ New York 1993	$13.00	S120
			☐ Orlando 1993	$13.00	S101
☐ Berlin 1993–94	$13.00	S116	☐ Paris 1993–94	$13.00	S109
☐ Boston 1993–94	$13.00	S117	☐ Philadelphia 1993–94	$13.00	S113
☐ Cancún/Cozumel/Yucatán 1991–92	$ 9.00	S010	☐ Rio 1991–92	$ 9.00	S029
			☐ Rome 1993–94	$13.00	S111
☐ Chicago 1993–94	$13.00	S122	☐ Salt Lake City 1991–92	$ 9.00	S031
☐ Denver/Boulder/Colorado Springs 1990–91	$ 8.00	S012	☐ San Diego 1993–94	$13.00	S107
			☐ San Francisco 1993	$13.00	S104
☐ Dublin 1993–94	$13.00	S128	☐ Santa Fe/Taos/Albuquerque 1993–94	$13.00	S108
☐ Hawaii 1992	$12.00	S014			
☐ Hong Kong 1992–93	$12.00	S015	☐ Seattle/Portland 1992–93	$12.00	S035
☐ Honolulu/Oahu 1993	$13.00	S106	☐ St. Louis/Kansas City 1993–94	$13.00	S127
☐ Las Vegas 1993–94	$13.00	S121			
☐ Lisbon/Madrid/Costa del Sol 1991–92	$ 9.00	S017	☐ Sydney 1993–94	$13.00	S129
			☐ Tampa/St. Petersburg 1993–94	$13.00	S105
☐ London 1993	$13.00	S100			
☐ Los Angeles 1993–94	$13.00	S123	☐ Tokyo 1992–93	$13.00	S039
☐ Madrid/Costa del Sol 1993–94	$13.00	S124	☐ Toronto 1993–94	$13.00	S126
			☐ Vancouver/Victoria 1990–91	$ 8.00	S041
☐ Mexico City/Acapulco 1991–92	$ 9.00	S020	☐ Washington, D.C. 1993	$13.00	S102

Other Titles Available at Membership Prices

SPECIAL EDITIONS

	Retail Price	Code		Retail Price	Code
☐ Bed & Breakfast North America	$15.00	P002	☐ Where to Stay U.S.A.	$14.00	P015
☐ Caribbean Hideaways	$16.00	P005			
☐ Marilyn Wood's Wonderful Weekends (within a 250-mile radius of NYC)	$12.00	P017			

GAULT MILLAU'S "BEST OF" GUIDES
(The only guides that distinguish the truly superlative
from the merely overrated)

	Retail Price	Code		Retail Price	Code
☐ Chicago	$16.00	G002	☐ New England	$16.00	G010
☐ Florida	$17.00	G003	☐ New Orleans	$17.00	G011
☐ France	$17.00	G004	☐ New York	$17.00	G012
☐ Germany	$18.00	G018	☐ Paris	$17.00	G013
☐ Hawaii	$17.00	G006	☐ San Francisco	$17.00	G014
☐ Hong Kong	$17.00	G007	☐ Thailand	$18.00	G019
☐ London	$17.00	G009	☐ Toronto	$17.00	G020
☐ Los Angeles	$17.00	G005	☐ Washington, D.C.	$17.00	G017

THE REAL GUIDES
(Opinionated, politically aware guides for youthful budget-minded travelers)

	Retail Price	Code		Retail Price	Code
☐ Able to Travel	$20.00	R112	☐ Kenya	$12.95	R015
☐ Amsterdam	$13.00	R100	☐ Mexico	$11.95	R016
☐ Barcelona	$13.00	R101	☐ Morocco	$14.00	R017
☐ Belgium/Holland/Luxembourg	$16.00	R031	☐ Nepal	$14.00	R018
			☐ New York	$13.00	R019
☐ Berlin	$11.95	R002	☐ Paris	$13.00	R020
☐ Brazil	$13.95	R003	☐ Peru	$12.95	R021
☐ California & the West Coast	$17.00	R121	☐ Poland	$13.95	R022
☐ Canada	$15.00	R103	☐ Portugal	$15.00	R023
☐ Czechoslovakia	$14.00	R005	☐ Prague	$15.00	R113
☐ Egypt	$19.00	R105	☐ San Francisco & the Bay Area	$11.95	R024
☐ Europe	$18.00	R122			
☐ Florida	$14.00	R006	☐ Scandinavia	$14.95	R025
☐ France	$18.00	R106	☐ Spain	$16.00	R026
☐ Germany	$18.00	R107	☐ Thailand	$17.00	R119
☐ Greece	$18.00	R108	☐ Tunisia	$17.00	R115
☐ Guatemala/Belize	$14.00	R010	☐ Turkey	$13.95	R027
☐ Hong Kong/Macau	$11.95	R011	☐ U.S.A.	$18.00	R117
☐ Hungary	$14.00	R118	☐ Venice	$11.95	R028
☐ Ireland	$17.00	R120	☐ Women Travel	$12.95	R029
☐ Italy	$13.95	R014	☐ Yugoslavia	$12.95	R030